Contemporary
Literary Criticism

Guide to Gale Literary Criticism Series

When you need to review criticism of literary works, these are the Gale series to use:

If the author's death date is:	You should turn to:
After Dec. 31, 1959 (or author is still living)	**CONTEMPORARY LITERARY CRITICISM** for example: Jorge Luis Borges, Anthony Burgess, William Faulkner, Mary Gordon, Ernest Hemingway, Iris Murdoch
1900 through 1959	**TWENTIETH-CENTURY LITERARY CRITICISM** for example: Willa Cather, F. Scott Fitzgerald, Henry James, Mark Twain, Virginia Woolf
1800 through 1899	**NINETEENTH-CENTURY LITERATURE CRITICISM** for example: Fedor Dostoevski, Nathaniel Hawthorne, George Sand, William Wordsworth
1400 through 1799	**LITERATURE CRITICISM FROM 1400 TO 1800 (excluding Shakespeare)** for example: Anne Bradstreet, Daniel Defoe, Alexander Pope, François Rabelais, Jonathan Swift, Phillis Wheatley **SHAKESPEAREAN CRITICISM** Shakespeare's plays and poetry
Antiquity through 1399	**CLASSICAL AND MEDIEVAL LITERATURE CRITICISM** for example: Dante, Homer, Plato, Sophocles, Vergil, the Beowulf Poet

---

Gale also publishes related criticism series:

CHILDREN'S LITERATURE REVIEW

This series covers authors of all eras who have written for the preschool through high school audience.

SHORT STORY CRITICISM

This series covers the major short fiction writers of all nationalities and periods of literary history.

POETRY CRITICISM

This series covers poets of all nationalities, movements, and periods of literary history.

Volume 63

Contemporary Literary Criticism

Excerpts from Criticism of the
Works of Today's Novelists, Poets,
Playwrights, Short Story Writers, Scriptwriters,
and Other Creative Writers

Roger Matuz
EDITOR

Cathy Falk
Mary K. Gillis
Sean R. Pollock
David Segal
ASSOCIATE EDITORS

 **Gale Research Inc.** • *DETROIT* • *LONDON*

STAFF

Roger Matuz, *Editor*

Cathy Falk, Mary K. Gillis, David Kmenta, Sean R. Pollock, David Segal,
Bridget Travers, Robyn V. Young, *Associate Editors*

Jennifer Brostrom, Susan M. Peters, Susanne Skubik, Janet M. Witalec, *Assistant Editors*

Jeanne A. Gough, *Production & Permissions Manager*
Linda M. Pugliese, *Production Supervisor*
Maureen A. Puhl, Jennifer VanSickle, *Editorial Associates*
Donna Craft, Paul Lewon, Lorna Mabunda, Camille P. Robinson, *Editorial Assistants*

Victoria B. Cariappa, *Research Manager*
H. Nelson Fields, Judy L. Gale, Maureen Richards, *Editorial Associates*
Paula Cutcher–Jackson, Robin Lupa, Mary Beth McElmeel,
Tamara C. Nott, *Editorial Assistants*

Sandra C. Davis, *Permissions Supervisor (Text)*
Josephine M. Keene, Denise M. Singleton, Kimberly F. Smilay, *Permissions Associates*
Maria L. Franklin, Michele Lonoconus, Shalice Shah,
Rebecca A. Stanko, *Permissions Assistants*

Patricia A. Seefelt, *Permissions Supervisor (Pictures)*
Margaret A. Chamberlain, *Permissions Associate*
Pamela A. Hayes, *Permissions Assistant*

Mary Beth Trimper, *Production Manager*
Shanna G. Philpott, *External Production Associate*

Art Chartow, *Art Director*
C. J. Jonik, *Keyliner*

Contents

Preface   vii

Acknowledgments   xi

Authors Forthcoming in *CLC*   xvii

Preface

Named "one of the twenty-five most distinguished reference titles published during the past twenty-five years" by *Reference Quarterly,* the *Contemporary Literary Criticism (CLC)* series provides readers with critical commentary and general information on more than 2,000 authors now living or who died after December 31, 1959. Previous to the publication of the first volume of *CLC* in 1973, there was no ongoing digest monitoring scholarly and popular sources of critical opinion and explication of modern literature. *CLC,* therefore, has fulfilled an essential need, particularly since the complexity and variety of contemporary literature makes the function of criticism especially important to today's reader.

Scope of the Series

CLC presents significant passages from published criticism of works by creative writers. Since many of the authors covered by *CLC* inspire continual critical commentary, writers are often represented in more than one volume. There is, of course, no duplication of reprinted criticism.

Authors are selected for inclusion for a variety of reasons, among them the publication or dramatic production of a critically acclaimed new work, the reception of a major literary award, revival of interest in past writings, or the adaptation of a literary work to film or television.

The present volume of *CLC* includes August Wilson, whose 1990 play *The Piano Lesson* won the Tony Award, the Pulitzer Prize, and the New York Drama Critics Circle Award; Stephen Hawking, the English cosmologist who authored *A Brief History of Time,* a surprise international best-seller; Christy Brown, an Irish poet and novelist whose autobiography, *My Left Foot,* was recently adapted into an acclaimed film; and Nobel Laureates Saul Bellow and Boris Pasternak.

Perhaps most importantly, works that frequently appear on the syllabuses of high school and college literature courses are represented by individual entries in *CLC.* Joseph Heller's *Catch-22* and Tom Stoppard's *Rosencrantz and Guildenstern are Dead* are examples of works of this stature appearing in *CLC,* Volume 63.

Attention is also given to several other groups of writers—authors of considerable public interest—about whose work criticism is often difficult to locate. These include mystery and science fiction writers, literary and social critics, foreign writers, and authors who represent particular ethnic groups within the United States.

Format of the Book

Altogether there are about 500 individual excerpts in each volume—with approximately seventeen excerpts per author—taken from hundreds of book review periodicals, general magazines, scholarly journals, monographs, and books. Entries include critical evaluations spanning from the beginning of an author's career to the most current commentary. Interviews, feature articles, and other published writings that offer insight into the author's works are also presented. Students, teachers, librarians, and researchers will find that the generous excerpts and supplementary material in *CLC* provides them with vital information needed to write a term paper, analyze a poem, or lead a book discussion group. In addition, complete bibliographical citations note the original source and all of the information necessary for a term paper footnote or bibliography.

A *CLC* author entry consists of the following elements:

- The **author heading** cites the form under which the author has most commonly published, followed by birth date, and death date when applicable. Uncertainty as to a birth or death date is indicated by a question mark.

- A **portrait** of the author is included when available.

- A brief **biographical and critical introduction** to the author and his or her work precedes the excerpted criticism. The first line of the introduction provides the author's full name, pseudonyms (if applicable), nationality, and a listing of genres in which the author has written. Since *CLC* is not intended to be a definitive biographical source, *cross-references* have been included to direct readers to these useful sources published by Gale Research: *Short Story Criticism* and *Children's*

Literature Review, which provide excerpts of criticism on the works of short story writers and authors of books for young people, respectively; *Contemporary Authors,* which includes detailed biographical and bibliographical sketches of nearly 97,000 authors; *Something about the Author,* which contains heavily illustrated biographical sketches of writers and illustrators who create books for children and young adults; *Dictionary of Literary Biography,* which provides original evaluations and detailed biographies of authors important to literary history; and *Contemporary Authors Autobiography Series* and *Something about the Author Autobiography Series,* which offer autobiographical essays by prominent writers for adults and those of interest to young readers, respectively. Previous volumes of *CLC* in which the author has been featured are also listed in the introduction.

• A list of **principal works,** arranged chronologically and, if applicable, divided into genre categories, notes the most important works by the author.

• The **excerpted criticism** represents various kinds of critical writing, ranging in form from the brief review to the scholarly exegesis. Essays are selected by the editors to reflect the spectrum of opinion about a specific work or about an author's literary career in general. The excerpts are presented chronologically, adding a useful perspective to the entry. All titles by the author featured in the entry are printed in boldface type, which enables the reader to easily identify the works being discussed. Publication information (such as publisher names and book prices) and parenthetical numerical references (such as footnotes or page and line references to specific editions of a work) have been deleted at the editor's discretion to provide smoother reading of the text.

• A complete **bibliographical citation** designed to help the user find the original essay or book follows each excerpt.

• A **further reading** section appears at the end of entries on authors who have generated a significant amount of criticism other than the pieces reprinted in *CLC.* In some cases, it includes references to material for which the editors could not obtain reprint rights.

Other Features

• A list of **Authors Forthcoming in *CLC*** previews the authors to be researched for future volumes.

• An **Acknowledgments** section lists the copyright holders who have granted permission to reprint material in this volume of *CLC.* It does not, however, list every book or periodical reprinted or consulted during the preparation of the volume.

• A **Cumulative Author Index** lists all the authors who have appeared in *CLC, Twentieth-Century Literary Criticism, Nineteenth-Century Literature Criticism, Literature Criticism from 1400 to 1800, Classical and Medieval Literature Criticism,* and *Short Story Criticism,* with cross-references to these Gale series: *Children's Literature Review, Contemporary Authors, Contemporary Authors Autobiography Series, Contemporary Authors Bibliographical Series, Dictionary of Literary Biography, Something about the Author, Something about the Author Autobiography Series, Yesterday's Authors of Books for Children,* and *Authors & Artists for Young Adults.* Readers will welcome this cumulated author index as a useful tool for locating an author within the various series. The index, which lists birth and death dates when available, will be particularly valuable for those authors who are identified with a certain period but whose death date causes them to be placed in another, or for those authors whose careers span two periods. For example, Ernest Hemingway is found in *CLC,* yet a writer often associated with him, F. Scott Fitzgerald, is found in *Twentieth-Century Literary Criticism.*

• A **Cumulative Nationality Index** alphabetically lists all authors featured in *CLC* by nationality, followed by numbers corresponding to the volumes in which they appear.

• A **Title Index** alphabetically lists all titles reviewed in the current volume of *CLC.* Listings are followed by the author's name and the corresponding page numbers where the titles are discussed. English translations of foreign titles and variations of titles are cross-referenced to the title under which a work was originally published. Titles of novels, novellas, dramas, films, record albums, and poetry, short story, and essay collections are printed in italics, while all individual poems, short stories, essays, and songs are printed in roman type within quotation marks; when published separately (e.g., T.S. Eliot's poem *The Waste Land*), the title will also be printed in italics.

• In response to numerous suggestions from librarians, Gale has also produced a **special paperbound edition** of the *CLC* title index. This annual cumulation, which alphabetically lists all titles reviewed in the series, is available to all customers and will be published with the first volume of *CLC* issued in each calendar year. Additional copies of the index are available upon request.

Librarians and patrons will welcome this separate index: it saves shelf space, is easy to use, and is disposable upon receipt of the following year's cumulation.

A Note to the Reader

When writing papers, students who quote directly from any volume in the Literary Criticism Series may use the following general forms to footnote reprinted criticism. The first example pertains to material drawn from periodicals, the second to material reprinted from books:

[1]Anne Tyler, "Manic Monologue," *The New Republic* 200 (April 17, 1989), 44-6; excerpted and reprinted in *Contemporary Literary Criticism,* Vol. 58, ed. Roger Matuz (Detroit: Gale Research, 1990), p. 325.

[2]Patrick Reilly, *The Literature of Guilt: From 'Gulliver' to Golding* (University of Iowa Press, 1988); excerpted and reprinted in *Contemporary Literary Criticism,* Vol. 58, ed. Roger Matuz (Detroit: Gale Research, 1990), pp. 206-12.

Suggestions Are Welcome

The editors welcome the comments and suggestions of readers to expand the coverage and enhance the usefulness of the series.

ACKNOWLEDGMENTS

The editors wish to thank the copyright holders of the excerpted criticism included in this volume, the permissions managers of many book and magazine publishing companies for assisting us in securing reprint rights, and Anthony Bogucki for assistance with copyright research. We are also grateful to the staffs of the Detroit Public Library, the Library of Congress, the University of Detroit Library, Wayne State University Purdy/Kresge Library Complex, and the University of Michigan Libraries for making their resources available to us. Following is a list of the copyright holders who have granted us permission to reprint material in theis volume of *CLC*. Every effort has been made to trace copyright, but if omissions have been made, please let us know.

COPYRIGHTED EXCERPTS IN *CLC,* VOLUME 63, WERE REPRINTED FROM THE FOLLOWING PERIODICALS:

COPYRIGHTED EXCERPTS IN *CLC,* VOLUME 63, WERE REPRINTED FROM THE FOLLOWING BOOKS:

Authors Forthcoming in *CLC*

To Be Included in Volume 64

Anna Akhmatova (Russian poet and translator)—Banned from publishing in the Soviet Union virtually her entire career, Akhmatova is nonetheless considered one of the premier Russian poets of the twentieth century. This entry will feature criticism on Akhmatova from the 1980s, when much of her previously unpublished or untranslated works appeared in various English-language collections.

E. M. Cioran (Rumanian-born philosopher and essayist)—Cioran is considered a formidable successor to the nihilistic tradition of thought espoused by Friedrich Nietzsche. In his philosophical essays, Cioran employs irony and elegant, aphoristic prose to explore such themes as alienation, absurdity, history, God, and death.

Jules Feiffer (American cartoonist, playwright, and novelist)—Feiffer brings to his plays and fiction the rueful scrutiny of middle-class idealism that characterizes his widely-syndicated cartoons. In his plays, Feiffer blends farce and satire with black humor to examine the psychological and social conditions of modern life. The entry will include criticism on his most recent play, *Elliot Loves.*

Ken Kesey (American novelist and short story writer)—Kesey is considered a transitional figure linking the Beat generation of the 1950s with the counterculture movement of the 1960s. This entry will focus on his experimental novel *One Flew over the Cuckoo's Nest,* an important work of contemporary American literature.

Hanif Kureishi (English playwright, screenwriter, and novelist)—Kureishi gained international recognition with the screenplays *My Beautiful Laundrette* and *Sammy and Rosie Get Laid,* which examine racial and class conflict in present-day London. His first novel, *The Buddha of Suburbia,* is a semiautobiographical account of a British Pakistani coming of age in the 1960s.

Philip Larkin (English poet and critic)—Among England's most popular and respected post-World War II poets, Larkin wrote witty, self-deprecating verse addressing such topics as love, loneliness, the passage of time, and contemporary life. The entry will focus on the posthumously published *Collected Poems,* which contains his best-known verse as well as many previously unpublished works.

Peter Matthiessen (American novelist, nonfiction writer, and short story writer)—Matthiessen is a naturalist who writes with compassion and conviction about vanishing cultures, oppressed peoples, and exotic wildlife and locales. His recent works include *On the River Styx and Other Stories* and *Killing Mr. Watson.*

Vladimir Nabokov (Russian-born American novelist, poet, and essayist)—Recognized as one of the greatest literary stylists of the twentieth century, Nabokov investigated the illusory nature of reality in his fiction. By emphasizing stylistic considerations over social and political issues, Nabokov championed the primacy of wit and imagination. The entry will focus on his notorious novel *Lolita,* which satirizes American culture and values.

Tom Robbins (American novelist and short story writer)—Robbins is acclaimed for his wildly playful, metafictional novels that advocate nonconformist behavior to overcome the absurdity of existence. This entry will include criticism on his latest novel, *Skinny Legs and All.*

Tobias Wolff (American short story writer and novelist)—A prize-winning author, Wolff has garnered praise for his stark portraits of ordinary lives. Although he depicts characters of diverse ages and backgrounds, Wolff is perhaps best known for his early stories about Vietnam veterans. This entry will provide an overview of Wolff's career, including his most recent work, *This Boy's Life.*

To Be Included in Volume 65: Yearbook 1990

A. S. Byatt (English novelist and critic)—Considered an important voice in contemporary literature, Byatt won the 1990 Booker Prize for her recent novel, *Possession: A Romance*. A Victorian-styled novel set in the present day, *Possession* merges intellectual and sensual elements to examine love and romance.

E. L. Doctorow (American novelist and short story writer)—This entry will focus upon his recent novel, *Billy Bathgate,* winner of both the National Book Critics Circle Award and the PEN/Faulkner Award. Set in and around New York City, *Billy Bathgate* portrays post-Prohibition gangsterism from a young boy's perspective.

Robert Ferrigno (American novelist)—Ferrigno's first novel, *The Horse Latitudes,* is a contemporary crime thriller set in southern California.

Oscar Hijuelos (American novelist and short story writer)—Hijuelos frequently examines Cuban identity and the difficulties of Cuban assimilation in the United States. In his Pulitzer Prize-winning novel *The Mambo Kings Play Songs of Love,* Hijuelos chronicles the isolation and disillusionment of two Cuban immigrants who pursue the American dream of success.

Charles Johnson (American novelist and short story writer)—Johnson has consistently garnered critical acclaim for his imaginative and erudite fiction. In his novel *Middle Passage,* for which he received the National Book Award for fiction, the story of a freed slave who accidentally boards a slave ship bound for Africa serves as a parable for black experience in the United States.

Seth Morgan (American novelist)—Morgan gained attention for his exuberant comic narrative style. His first novel, *Homeboy,* is a quest-for-identity story set largely in San Francisco that details the narrator's experiences with drugs, prostitutes, and crime.

Edna O'Brien (Irish novelist and short story writer)—O'Brien often portrays women victimized by male domination, a judgmental society, and their own hunger for love. This entry will discuss *Lantern Slides,* a collection of short stories about human pathos and loneliness.

Octavio Paz (Mexican poet and nonfiction writer)—Recipient of the Nobel Prize in Literature for 1990, Paz has enjoyed a distinguished reputation as an inventive poet and nonfiction writer. His talent in the latter category is evidenced by *The Labyrinth of Solitude,* a sociocultural analysis of Mexican history, mythology, and social values.

Recent Trends in African-American Literary Aesthetics—This entry will include essays in which American critics and theorists discuss the nature of current African-American literary criticism, focusing on the works of such authors as Henry Louis Gates, Jr.

Charles Simic (Yugoslavian-born American poet and translator)—Simic is regarded as one of the most progressive and imaginative voices in American poetry. *The World Doesn't End,* for which Simic received the 1990 Pulitzer Prize, is a collection of dreamlike prose poems.

Ann Beattie

1947-

American short story writer, novelist, children's writer, and critic.

Beattie's fiction concerns members of the post-World War II, "baby boom" generation, whose passivity and inability to comprehend themselves or others trap them in dissatisfactory life situations. Beattie employs a prose style composed of flat, declarative sentences and detached observations, paralleling the listlessness of her characters. Her protagonists are typically well-educated people who experience a sense of loss as they attempt to reconcile the idealistic convictions of their youth with their present lifestyles. Refusing to resolve the dilemmas developed in her fiction, Beattie rarely explores the inner motivations of her characters. She focuses instead on their external environment, providing idiosyncratic and telling details, including frequent references to consumer goods and popular songs. While some critics object to her characters' lack of psychological and historical backgrounds, Beattie has been praised for the photographic accuracy of her descriptions, and most agree that her stories realistically reflect the disjointed and haphazard nature of contemporary life.

Beattie's first three volumes of short fiction focus on characters lacking permanent emotional ties who experience pervasive, vague despair and incomprehension regarding the direction of their lives. *Distortions,* her first collection of stories, features characters more affected by the consequences of experimenting with drugs and sexual freedom in the 1960s than with the political upheavals of that era. "Fancy Flights" includes a much-lauded depiction of a man high on marijuana. "Wally Whistles Dixie," also from this volume, concerns a thirty-year-old ballerina who marries someone half her age. *Distortions* gave Beattie a reputation for realistic depictions of passive people stranded in unfulfilling situations by their adventures in the feckless 1960s. *Secrets and Surprises* depicts similar characters in the increasingly conservative 1970s. Many of the characters in this collection are involved in relationships they cannot seem to leave, or remain saddened by the loss of a lover years after the end of the affair. *The Burning House,* Beattie's third volume of short stories, includes "Learning to Fall," in which a woman takes the son of her friend on a weekly outing to New York. They are accompanied by her lover, whom she can neither pledge herself to nor completely give up. The stark, crystalline quality of Beattie's prose coupled with an absence of commentary upon her characters' actions or inability to act is often considered unsettling.

Where You'll Find Me and Other Stories contains pieces in which the past helps illuminate, if not relieve, her characters' present dissatisfaction. Beattie depicts people at the onset of middle age who have never achieved the success or happiness they seemed destined for in their youth. Attempting to adjust to the death of their daughter, the couple in "In the White Night" possess a maturity lacking in most of Beattie's earlier characters. The most celebrated story in this collection, "Janus," concerns a woman's ob-

session with a bowl given her by a former lover. Critics note that, as in other Beattie stories, the determining factor in the protagonist's life is loss; thus, the beautiful bowl, perpetually empty, is symbolic of the woman herself. While generally highly praised, *Where You'll Find Me and Other Stories* was regarded by some as lacking the emotional and technical range of Beattie's earlier volumes. Others noted that while Beattie steadfastly refuses to judge her characters, her distinctive eliptical endings are somewhat less grim in this volume and offer the possibility of positive action in the future.

Beattie's novels utilize the same episodic style and concentration on short, intense moments of unenlightened feeling found in her short fiction. *Chilly Scenes of Winter* relies heavily on conversations between people in their late twenties whose nostalgia for the 1960s reveals their prolonged adolescence and bewildered approach to adulthood. In *Falling in Place,* Beattie focuses on a man's inability to choose between his family and his lover, a dilemma that is resolved when his son accidentally shoots his daughter. *Love Always* is a satire both of show business and the publishing industry. Beattie introduces nearly a dozen principal characters and relates the narrative from several viewpoints. While John Updike determined that:

"Unreality, insubstantiality, interchangeability . . . make up the novel's agenda, and are built disturbingly into its texture," other critics felt *Love Always* lacked the focus necessary to depict this situation effectively.

Beattie's highly acclaimed novel *Picturing Will* is divided into three sections, "Mother," "Father," and "Son;" interspersed throughout are italicized, first-person meditations on the relationship between parent and child. Will's natural father abandoned him and his mother, an ambitious photographer whose second marriage provides the boy with his only true parent. T. Coraghessan Boyle commented: "In *Picturing Will,* Ann Beattie has created a surprising, lyrical and deeply affecting work that is both radical in its movement and perfectly attuned to its telling."

(See also *CLC,* Vols. 8, 13, 18, 40; *Contemporary Authors,* Vols. 81-84; and *Dictionary of Literary Biography Yearbook: 1982.*)

PRINCIPAL WORKS

SHORT FICTION COLLECTIONS

Distortions   1976
Secrets and Surprises   1978
The Burning House   1982
Where You'll Find Me and Other Stories   1986

NOVELS

Chilly Scenes of Winter   1976
Falling in Place   1980
Love Always   1985
Picturing Will   1989

OTHER

Spectacles   (children's book)   1985
Alex Katz   (essays in art criticism)   1987

Joseph Epstein

A few years ago I spent three days as a visiting writer on the campus of a liberal-arts college. The campus may have been small, the college in the hills of Ohio, but the English department, whose paid guest I was, ran an absolutely up-to-date operation. Among its members were a black, a Jew, an Asian woman, a homosexual, a combat-booted feminist, and a young woman whose socio-political provenance I did not immediately make out. When I inquired about this woman of the young teacher who had been assigned as my guide, a man who had himself recently been denied tenure—and to be denied tenure at such an institution is always a splendid inducement to speak plainly about it—he replied, "Oh, you mean Ruthie. Ruthie is from the 60's." (p. 54)

In her early thirties, she was dark, chunky, and wore her hair in a Caucasian version of an Afro. She carried a backpack over a coat made out of the hide of some unidentifiable beast, a coat with string fringes and badly in need of a cleaning. She drove a Volkswagen bug, yellow, its back seat cluttered with books, Kleenex boxes, a large bottle of jug wine. Car and woman had a packed look, as if they might, without too great notice, take off for either coast. She was self-declared as a poet. She might have been a character in an Ann Beattie story, although I hadn't yet read Ann Beattie, and so could not have known this.

I first heard of Ann Beattie, in fact, at another gathering of Ann Beattie characters, this one rather more prosperous. It was at a dinner given by a couple who were then living together. She was a historian who had recently been appointed to the directorship of a newly established woman's program at a Midwestern university. He had an unfinished dissertation at Harvard and worked at intellectual odd jobs in and around the social sciences: a bit of teaching, a bit of consulting, a bit of time put in with public agencies. The other people there that evening, my wife and myself excepted, had been students in universities in the middle and late 60's and early 70's, a cause among them for some pride. A good deal of energy went into the preparation of the dinner, and a great deal of talk—about the bread, the wine, the pasta, the fish, the pastry—accompanied its digestion. Former hippies at least in spirit, these people took kindly to bourgeois habits while retaining adversary points of view; "the hippoisie" was the name they only half-jokingly gave to themselves. For a number of people there that evening, Ann Beattie was their writer, and to call them Ann Beattie characters would not, I suspect, have hurt their feelings.

I have now read Ann Beattie, her two novels and the three volumes of short stories that comprise her collected work to date. This is no small output for a writer of thirty-four. There are fifty of these stories. I believe I may have read some of them earlier when they first appeared in the *New Yorker.* I say "I believe" because I am not always certain. . . . [Ann Beattie's novels and stories] somehow do not stay with one; they seem to seem to slide off the page; one story melts into another, and the whole finally dissolves in the mind, like one of those small blue pills some of Ann Beattie's characters require to get through the day, a downer.

As I read through story after story of Miss Beattie's, I asked myself why these stories—stories written by a writer with a true command of prose style and a deadly eye for right details—were at once vaguely depressing and distinctly forgettable? I have, for example, been reading Miss Beattie's latest collection of stories, **The Burning House,** and turning back to the book's table of contents I notice that I cannot connect stories to titles. Was **"Afloat"** about the woman about to have a child with a man to whom she is not married? Is **"Playback"** about the young man who works for an advertising agency? Is **"Desire"** the story in which everyone gets stoned, or in which the woman's husband leaves her for another man? Beats me.

As for the depression, well, one is used to depression in modern fiction, which provides many laughs but very few smiles. One is used to it in traditional literature, too. *Anna Karenina* comes down with a bump. But however depressed that great book leaves you, you do feel you have got something for your sadness. The depression that comes with reading Ann Beattie is of a different order, and not just because she isn't Tolstoy. It is depression at reading about the sheer hopelessness of her characters' lives; from these lives, they learn nothing and neither do we.

Nor, by design, are we supposed to. In one of the stories in *The Burning House* it is said of a six-year-old girl: "She used to like stories to end with a moral, like fairy tales, but now she thinks that's kid's stuff."

Miss Beattie has a real subject, and a highly interesting one. Her subject is the fate of her own generation, the generation that was in college and graduate school in the late 60's and early 70's. (pp. 54-5)

About all of Ann Beattie's fiction there is something of an after-party atmosphere. Her stories begin after the 60's binge is done and gone. No mention is made of the Democratic convention of 1968, of the marches and protests, of any other of the momentous happenings of those years. In one of her stories a maimed Vietnam veteran appears, in another a woman's brother is mentioned as having been killed in Vietnam, and in yet another a veteran is said to be unable to stop talking about Vietnam. Yet Miss Beattie does not hammer away at Vietnam or speak of politics except obliquely, though a foul air of things gone wrong hovers about her characters and their world. Anxiety, disappointment, despair, these are the pollutants in the Beattie atmosphere, and both characters and readers are made to choke on them.

Already in *Distortions* (1976), her first book of stories, the general pattern of Ann Beattie's fiction is set. *Distortions* is very much a young writer's book, and hence rather more experimental than the more mature Ann Beattie's fiction will be. The book's opening story is about a marriage of dwarfs. An other story is done in short takes, rather like blackout sketches. "Wesley has gaps between his teeth," one such take begins; "Janie Regis' hair is all different colors," the next one picks up. Another experimental story is entitled **"It's Just Another Day in Big Bear City, California,"** a title which is almost a story in itself. But the less experimental Ann Beattie's stories are, the better. Taken by themselves, some of the straighter stories are quite impressive—**"Wolf Dreams,"** for example, written when Miss Beattie was only twenty-six. Nearly all the stories show a high degree of professional polish. The dialogue always feels right; the interior monologue, too, seems on target. The flat style, a Beattie trademark, is already in use in *Distortions,* as in this opening passage from a not very good story entitled **"Hale Hardy and the Amazing Animal Woman":**

> Hale Hardy went to college because he couldn't think of anything better to do, and he quit because he couldn't see any reason to stay. He lasted one and a half years. He did not exactly quit; he was thrown out. When that happened he went to visit his sister Mary, who was living with another girl, Paula, who was being supported by some dude. Hale didn't know the dude's name, or why he was supporting her, or why his sister was living there. He just went.

That passage reveals more than the style of Miss Beattie's fiction; it reveals the peculiar will-lessness of her characters. Passive agents, they do not act but are acted upon. "The important thing," one character in a story in *Distortions* advises another, "was to know when to give up." Here is a note Ann Beattie has held through all her books. The first story in *The Burning House* ends thus: "What Ruth had known all along: what will happen can't be stopped. Aim for grace."

Amazing grace. If grace is what Ann Beattie's characters aim for, very few achieve it. But then they don't aim very carefully. Not much in life interests them. Politics doesn't—though they are all convinced that America is hopeless—neither conventional politics nor emotional politics. "There aren't any answers," says a Beattie character. "That's what I've got against woman's liberation. Nothing personal." Although people have love affairs, once a couple moves in together, the end is in sight. Sex is no big deal. Miss Beattie rarely describes it. Detailed description tends to be reserved for getting stoned. Few relationships endure. Work is pointless. Things fall apart; the center, hell, in Ann Beattie's fiction not even the fringes seem to hold. (pp. 55-6)

Miss Beattie specializes in the inconclusive; inconclusiveness, in her fiction, is quite deliberate. It is part of her method. E. M. Forster once wrote that the king died and then the queen died is a story, but the king died and then the queen died of grief is a plot. Miss Beattie does not go in much for plot. Her work is, in some respects, anti-plot. In the story **"Greenwich Time"** in *The Burning House* a man is at the house of his former wife and her current husband; the house was one he once lived in with his wife. Now he is alone in it with his young son and the maid. His ex-wife and her husband are late—unusually late. Generally they are home long before now. It is worrisome. Yet why they are late, whether they will eventually arrive home safely, these are things we never learn. Instead, **"Greenwich Time"** ends with the maid telling the man that, though he may have been dispossessed from this house, she is still his friend. "Then they stood there, still and quiet, as if the walls of the room were mountains and their words might fly against them." That's it. End of story. Cut and print that (the *New Yorker* did, originally). (p. 56)

What her fiction strives to achieve is not development of character, accounts of motivation, or moral resolution—no, what she strives to achieve are states of feeling. This she often succeeds in doing. Thus in a story such as **"A Reasonable Man,"** from the collection *Secrets and Surprises,* she can show what a woman feels who is mismarried and on the edge of nervous breakdown—loneliness, frustration, anxiety, quiet terror—and you will feel it, too. Attempting to capture states of feeling, as opposed to doing so within the construction of careful plots, is of course a great aid to composition, which helps explain why Miss Beattie has been so prolific. What is less clear is why the states of feeling her stories reveal are always those connected with sadness and loss.

Another problem arises: the states of feeling Ann Beattie strives for, workable though they may be within the brief compass of a short story, are not sufficient to keep a longer work afloat. This is why her novels, in my view, sink. The first of them, *Chilly Scenes of Winter,* is about two young men, veterans of the 60's, who are now in their late twenties. One is a Phi Beta Kappa who hasn't the money to go to law school, so instead has to settle for a job selling men's jackets. The other has a government job that bores him stiff, a mother who goes in and out of mental hospitals, and a love for a woman with whom he had an affair but who is married to someone else and about whom he cannot stop thinking. The novel's title is also the title of a song by a group called the New Lost City Ramblers and Cousin Emmy.

The winter in question is that of 1974-75, the scene of such action as there is Washington, D. C. Very little sense of the city of Washington comes through. The characters are not described elaborately. What does come through, though, is that the characters in this novel are under a malaise. It is almost as if they had come back from a war, except they haven't. " 'The goddam 60's,' Charles says. 'How'd we end up like this.' " What, exactly, went wrong? A number of things, it turns out. The country, the United States, seems partly to blame: it provides no good work, it throws up characters like Richard Nixon, it is killing off its wildlife. Parents, partially, are to blame as well; at least most parents in Ann Beattie's fiction, as in *Chilly Scenes of Winter,* have troubles that they seem to pass on to their children: divorce, alcoholism, madness. The old dreams, from Norman Rockwell to the legend of Scott and Zelda Fitzgerald, are dried up and dead. Things are grim. "Unhappiness," said the young Henry James, "is a disease," and Ann Beattie's characters have caught it.

Perhaps I make this sound slightly grimmer than it is. Miss Beattie has a sly sense of humor. From time to time she will toss an interesting flake into her fiction, such as, in *Chilly Scenes of Winter,* the young woman who is making up her mind to be a lesbian, and who says of a friend in California: "She claimed she screwed Peter Fonda on the kitchen floor in an all-night health food restaurant, but I don't believe it." The novel's hero thinks perhaps he ought to move to California but then concludes that, at twenty-seven, "he is too old for the West Coast." The two principal characters in the book have longish exchanges—conversations are not quite what they are—about food, their pasts, their futures, that are Beckett-like in their comic hopelessness.

And yet a dark doleful cloud hangs over everything. At the close of *Chilly Scenes of Winter,* the married woman whom the hero of the novel loves, and about whom he ruminates at great boring length, leaves her husband and returns to our hero. "A story with a happy ending," he says. But that seems unlikely. Why mightn't she leave him again? Why mightn't he soon grow tired of her? Why not any of a thousand possibilities—in fiction that is so weightless, where events occur without cause and life has no lessons to teach, anything can happen. If Ann Beattie's fiction makes a single point it is this: the one thing you can depend on is that there is nothing you can depend on.

"It's selling you such a bill of goods to tell you that you should get married and have a family and be secure. Jesus! What your own family will do to you." So says a woman in *Falling in Place,* mother of three, whose husband, an advertising executive of forty, is having an affair with a young woman of the 60's generation currently resident in a small apartment along Columbus Avenue. *Falling In Place* is Ann Beattie's first novel about suburban, upper-middle-class family life, and that life—surprise, surprise—turns out to be hell. Not that the book is exclusively suburban. The cast of characters includes another assortment of 60's casualties. Among them are dropouts from Bard College; pilgrims from the West Coast; a drug dealer worried about Three Mile Island ("No way drugs explain why this is a bad world"); and a woman graduate student teaching high school in the summer who "was born the

year *Howl* came out, but she still felt sure that she was one of the people Ginsberg was talking about." In Miss Beattie's fiction there are, finally, two classes of people—those who came of age in the 60's and those who didn't, and those who did are better.

The interesting characters in *Falling in Place,* however, are the children. The advertising man and his wife have three: Mary, a fifteen-year-old who is mad for Peter Frampton and who responds to everything she doesn't care for—which covers a great deal—with the phrase, Suck-o; John Joel, her younger brother, detached, a compulsive eater, who spends a lot of time reading violent comics or perched in a tree in his yard; Brad, the baby, who lives with his grandmother. Their father wants to leave their mother, but cannot quite bring himself to do so. A friend at his advertising agency tells him, "The real killer was when you married the wrong person but had the right children." Mary and John Joel, it must be said, are not the right children. They loathe each other, and such denouement as the novel provides comes about when John Joel, quite by accident, shoots and wounds his sister.

This act forces the hand of their father, who can barely grasp what he feels to be the enormity of it, and who because of it determines to leave his wife at last. Only—and this seems to me a decisive only—he, the father, does not know that the shooting was an accident. He acts on incomplete knowledge, and Miss Beattie, in the course of the novel, sees no need to complete it for him. That characters get things wrong, that their vision of events is more than a little occluded, none of this seems to matter. The world, Ann Beattie seems to be saying, goes sourly on its way. Things fall in place.

I say the world goes sourly on its way, but some might argue that *Falling in Place* is a relatively sunny novel. The father of these children goes off with his lady-friend. His wife, without him, will have a better chance to pick up the pieces of her own shattered life. His children, being young, presumably will pull themselves together. Another couple in the novel—an Abbie Hoffman type minus the genius for publicity, and the graduate student born the year *Howl* was published—settle in after troublous days. Near the novel's close, a young man, a practicing magician, remarks: "It's a rotten world. No wonder people want answers. No wonder they want to have parties and get distracted. Sometimes something nice happens, though."

But not very often. How could it in a world seen through such dark glasses? As *Chilly Scenes of Winter* finishes off work, *Falling in Place* does the job on family. The surrounding culture provides no relief; there menace chiefly lurks. Join the magician in *Falling in Place* in his interior monologue: "He knew the real world was the Pentagon . . . and he was at least thankful that he was not involved in the real world." Cop a thought from the advertising man in the same novel: "It was true that someone could dress very conventionally and still be evil: Nixon with his jacket and tie walking on the beach, for example." (What would so many contemporary American novelists do without good old Dick Nixon still there to kick around?) Without work, without family, without support in the culture, what, really, is left for knowing people but such pleasure as can be taken on the run and the hope for some measure of personal salvation through awareness?

Awareness of what? Awareness, I believe Ann Beattie wants us to know, of what a dreadful crock life is. Philosophy resides in composition, and the method by which Miss Beattie creates her stories and novels tells much about their author's view of the world. There is, to begin with, the causelessness in her fiction. Her characters are seldom allowed to know why things happen as they do, and without such knowledge there cannot be any deliberate action. It is for this reason that almost every Ann Beattie character is so passive and, finally, so depressing. What, after all, can be more depressing than to be certain that one has no control whatsoever over one's destiny? Destiny, in the grand sense, simply does not exist in Miss Beattie's fiction. Her characters neither know about it nor seem to care about it. All that they do know is that they are living in the shade of a malaise; since this malaise is rather vague, so are the reasons for their unhappiness. Can it be, one sometimes wonders, that the reason they are so unhappy is that they do not feel happy enough—that they feel life has reneged on its promises?

What is more, as they grow older, it continues to do so. Certainly, Miss Beattie's fiction grows more and more cheerless. The first two stories in her latest collection, *The Burning House,* bring forth a brain-damaged child and a brain-damaged adult. The word cancer pops into the discussion fairly regularly. The intake of pills seems greater: yellow Valium, blue Valium, green Donnatal, reds. In one story a child is read to from the works of R. D. Laing, and in another a woman thinks, "Children seem older now." Many is the miscarriage and no fewer the abortions. Meanwhile, the 60's themselves begin to fade: Dennis Hopper—the usual prizes for readers who remember that name—puts in a cameo appearance in one story in *The Burning House,* and in another, set in Virginia, it is said that "Art Garfunkel used to have a place out there." People sit around and tell where they were when John F. Kennedy was shot. But I had better stop—this is beginning to get me down. (pp. 56-8)

Ann Beattie is a generation writer, and that is a severe limitation. Milan Kundera, in his novel *The Joke,* has one of his characters say: "The very thought of a generation mentality (the pride of the herd) has always repelled me." But a more severe limitation is that, while she knows a good deal about life's phenomena, she chooses to deny life's significance. In so doing, she ends by denying significance to her own work, for literature is finally about the significance and not the phenomena of life. At this point in her career, Ann Beattie is the chief purveyor of her own generation's leading clichés—the L. L. Bean of what passes for 60's existentialism. (p. 58)

> *Joseph Epstein, "Ann Beattie and the Hippoisie," in* Commentary, *Vol. 75, No. 3, March, 1983, pp. 54-8.*

Ann Beattie (Interview with Larry McCaffery and Sinda Gregory)

[Gregory]: *In your interview in the* New York Times Book Review, *you respond to the comment made by Joyce Maynard that you are primarily a chronicler of the 60s counterculture by saying, "It's certainly true that the people I write about are essentially my age, and so they were a certain age in the 60s and had certain common experiences and tend to listen to the same kind of music and get stoned and wear the same kind of clothes, but what I've always hoped for is that somebody will then start talking more about the meat and bones of what I'm writing about." The "meat and bones" that you refer to seems to me to involve the difficulties involved in people understanding each other—the difficulty of saying what we feel, of making ourselves clear, of having the courage or honesty to say what we mean. Would you agree that this issue of the breakdown of communication is one of the meat-and-bones areas you're referring to?*

[Beattie]: Yes, my fiction often has to do with that. A direct result of this breakdown of communication is the breakdown of relationships. I don't think the people in my stories are representative, by the way—that's really off the point of what you just asked me, but it's behind Maynard's comment, and behind what a lot of people have said about my work. I'd say that the people in my fiction reflect some of my own personal problems and concerns, perhaps to an exaggerated degree, but I don't mean them to be taken as representative of the culture. So that's part one of the answer. As to part two, what you're saying sounds perfectly insightful to me—I'd agree that these breakdowns *do* have a lot to do with my work—but even this, I think, tends to generalize a great deal. I mean if I were to ask you to be specific and cite to me what the common denominator is between two different stories of mine, I wonder what it would be?

[Gregory]: *I'd probably say that a lot of your stories that differ in many respects still seem to focus on relationships in the process of breaking down.*

Okay, I can see what you mean, but often the people in my stories are unstable in some way even before the relationship—their problems often predate the relationship we see, or there's no reason to think the breakdown is a *consequence* of the relationship itself.

[McCaffery]: *In quite a few of your stories you seem to imply that one of the reasons that people's relationships break down is because they can't express themselves. You don't always explain* why *they are unable to talk to each other, but often your stories have scenes with characters who are totally cut off from each other or who misunderstand each other.*

[Gregory]: *A good example of this is the scene in* **Falling in Place** *where the whole family is sitting around while John has taken them out for a Chinese dinner: at one time each one of them makes a gesture of generosity towards the others that is misconstrued and rejected, so they draw back; in that scene it seems impossible for anyone to express what they want to express.*

Yes, I'll have to agree that these kinds of scenes do appear in my work, in one form or another. But this is not something I'm doing deliberately. Personally, of course, I believe that many people have a lot of trouble communicating, but I'm afraid this sounds so banal that I hate to dwell on it because it's hardly something I originated. When I was working on that scene Sinda just mentioned, for instance, I was mainly thinking of the literary effects—the tension it creates—and not the general issue involved. I guess I feel that if you're mainly interested in showing people not communicating you ought to be at least as interesting as Harold Pinter.

[McCaffery]: *You know, what I really tend to notice in your fiction is not so much the issues you raise but the specific people you place into your stories. What interests you about your characters?*

I'm often interested in my characters because they can't break away from the situation they find themselves in. If they can't communicate to begin with, you'd think more of them would fly off than they do. Part of this interest is a reflection of my own experiences with people. I find it very hard to envy most of the couples I know. I can't imagine exchanging places with those that are together, even those that are happy, because it seems to me they have made so many compromises to be together. So I'm very interested in the fact that there are these personalities who have compromised in so many ways. On the other hand, there are so many people who are together because of all the obvious reasons: they don't want to be lonely or they are in the habit of being together, or this whole Beckettian thing—I can't stay and I can't go. This tug interests me more than the fact that they're not communicating—I want to find out why they're staying and not going.

[McCaffery]: *A lot of your characters are very self-conscious individuals—self-conscious about their roles, about the cliches they use to express themselves, about just about everything. Sinda and I notice this same sense of self-consciousness in ourselves and with the people we associate with—maybe it has to do with education or the kinds of people we have as friends—but we notice that this tends to intrude into relationships. It almost seems as if the more self-aware you become, this self-awareness gets in the way of spontaneity or whatever it is that is "natural" in relationships.*

Yes, I know just what you mean. This kind of intellectualizing or self-consciousness just allows you to hide from yourself forever. People can easily fall into the trap of thinking that to label something is to explain it.

[Gregory]: *It's the same thing with the irony your characters often seem to have—it's a kind of defense mechanism . . .*

Yeah, all these artifices assist in helping people delude themselves.

[Gregory]: *—even though these artifices and intellectualizing are supposedly, on the surface, helping people develop insights about their behavior and that of others.*

These insights aren't very profound, though. If you notice, usually in my stories one person is insightful and the other person isn't. They end up in a tug-of-war when it becomes inconsequential whether they're insightful or not. In a story like **"Colorado"** Robert knows what the score is with Penelope, but so what? And she understands why they've ended up in Vermont and her understanding doesn't matter. Charles Manson said there was a particular voice telling him to do something, and David Berkowitz said that it was a dog, Sam, up in the sky motivating him. Don't people always say that what motivates them is logical? What matters is that they're getting through life and they're unhappy and there's something missing. If I knew what it *was* that was missing, I'd write about it, I'd write for Hallmark cards. That would please a lot of my critics.

[McCaffery]: *Yeah, I've noticed that some critics have com-*

plained that your stories don't offer "solutions" or resolutions to your characters' problems. How do you respond to this idea—championed recently by John Gardner—that writers need to supply answers and not simply describe problems or situations?*

I don't expect answers of anyone other than a medical doctor, so no, it wouldn't occur to me that writers should have to supply answers. I certainly don't feel that it's the obligation of *any artist* to supply answers. (pp. 165-68)

[McCaffery]: *What seems to get you to sit down at the typewriter in the first place? Do you have a specific scene or character or sentence in mind?*

My stories always seem to begin with something very small. . . . If I were to say I usually begin with a character, that wouldn't mean that I would know the character's occupation or whether the character is happy or sad, or what the character's age was. I *would* know that the character is named "Joe," and, yes, sometimes the idea that the character's name is "Joe" has gotten me to the typewriter. More often it's really a physiological feeling that I should write something—this feeling doesn't always work out. Many times I'm wrong about it.

[McCaffery]: *What do you mean by a "physiological feeling"?*

I don't know how to talk about this without sounding like Yeats saying that the "Voices" were driving him into a room and dictating to him, but it's almost like that, almost that crazy to me. Something in me has built up and this is a compulsion to go and write something at the typewriter. And, yes, it's not totally amorphous, there is something in the back of my mind: it's a name, it's a sentence, it's a sense of remembering what it is like to be in the dead of winter and wanting to go to the beach in the summer, some vague notion like that. It's never more than that. I've never in my life sat down and said to myself, "Now I will write something about somebody to whom such-and-such will happen."

[Gregory]: *What you're saying is very interesting because I think most people assume that because your characters are so particularized and real-seeming that they must be based on people you've actually known. Does this happen very often?*

I probably shouldn't answer that because, given the nature of most of my characters, it wouldn't be much to my advantage to admit it if I did. It's interesting to me, though, that there have been some instances when I thought I've come very close to capturing the essence of somebody even though I've made some little change in their clothing or in the location of the story. These changes are made subconsciously, it's not something I do deliberately, but these changes are always enough to throw people off. That's what interesting to me—I don't think someone has ever said to me, "Hey, that's me," and been right.

[McCaffery]: *That's never happened?*

Not even when *I* thought it was most obvious. On the other hand in places where a character I've created has nothing to do with anyone I know, people have insisted that a particular line is something they've said. I had a sentence in a story called **"Like Glass"** and I was showing it to a friend; the woman who's narrating the story says of her husband that when he talked about his dreams his dreams were never full of the usual things like symbols but were summaries of things that had happened. And the friend of mine who was reading the story stopped and said to me, "This isn't true of my dreams!" So there you have it.

[Gregory]: *You said somewhere that when you began* **Falling in Place** *that you had no idea of where it was heading, that you only knew you wanted it to be about children.*

That wasn't quite true. I knew the beginning of the first sentence: "John Joel was high up in a tree . . . " and *then* it occurred to me that if somebody was up high in a tree, it would probably be a child, and if it were a child it was likely that there would have to be a family surrounding him. So then with that as an idea I proceeded to write the novel. I had seven weeks to go with this deadline at Random House. I understand that in the real world people don't come after you with whips that say "Random House" on the handles, but it still makes me very nervous to have deadlines because I don't like to have deadlines—and I've organized my life so that I don't have deadlines very often. But in this case I had this deadline that was making me very nervous, and I looked out my window and there was this wonderful peach tree out there. That's what started *Falling in Place.*

[McCaffery]: *But despite being written in seven weeks under the pressures of these Random House whips,* **Falling in Place** *seems to me to have a much greater sense of structure or "plot" in the traditional sense than, say,* **Chilly Scenes**—*that is, it seems to be working towards that climax, the shooting of Mary by John Joel.*

I was so surprised when that shooting happened.

[McCaffery]: *How far in advance had you realized that this is where the book was heading?*

Never. I was totally amazed to find the gun in the kid's hands. But then I remembered there had been that odd box which belonged to Parker's grandfather.

[Gregory]: *So you hadn't* planted *that box there with the gun in it?*

No, in fact, after the shooting happened I thought, "Oh, my God, we're only three weeks into the book and here Mary is dead on the ground—what am I going to do to resurrect her?" So I resurrected her. Really, I was very upset when that shooting happened.

[McCaffery]: *But despite these kinds of surprises, wouldn't you agree that* **Falling in Place** *is a more "writerly novel" than* **Chilly Scenes of Winter**—*that it has a tighter structure and is governed by a more coherent set of images and metaphors?*

Sure. Remember *Falling in Place* was written several years after my first novel. I wrote *Chilly Scenes* in 1975, and it was all dialogue, basically; it was really more like a play than a novel. And that book was written in *three* weeks. I hope that I did know more about writing in the summer of 1979 than I did four years earlier. And, of course, things happen to you that also help create a focus for your work. I was living in Redding, Connecticut when I wrote *Falling in Place,* and I had been living there about a year. While I was actually working on *Falling in Place*

I didn't really realize how much of Redding had gotten into my head. Actually I guess I had grown very hostile to Redding and was very upset by being there, so in a way it was almost a relief to write something like *Falling in Place* and sort of purge myself of these feelings. We had had more than a year of very bad times and total isolation living in this wealthy commuter community that had nothing to do with us. And I was watching the people at the market and it was like when you're sick and have a fever and everything seems in sharper focus. I went around with that kind of fever for about a year, and then I had this deadline, so I wrote *Falling in Place.* I don't think that it follows that this is the way I always work—if you put me in Alaska for a year I'm not sure I'd write about igloos—but it did happen that way in Redding, Connecticut. There was so much more I had subconsciously stored away that I wanted to get out than there had been about anywhere else I've lived before.

[Gregory]: *I have a question about the structure of* **Falling in Place.**

Yeah, what *is* the structure of that book? I've been wondering about that myself.

[Gregory]: *Why did you have every other chapter take the form of those brief, italicized sections?*

You want to know the truth about those chapters? I started out that novel by writing chapters—I would write a chapter a day. But after I wrote the first chapter—it was the opening chapter that's there now—I realized that I had forgotten to put any background information in it, so I made notes to myself of what I had to go back and include in the first chapter. The second day I wrote a chapter and then thought, "Here's what I left out of this one." The third day I thought, "I wonder if anyone has ever written a whole book like this. I wonder if this isn't too artsy?" Then I thought, "Who cares?" Eventually I went back and made these lists a little more articulate and they became the italicized chapters. If I were teaching this book, I could imagine myself making any number of pretentious guesses about why the book is structured this way, but in point of fact the book is structured this way because I left in these notes and comments to myself. Another thing I should mention is that I'll do anything to trick myself into thinking that I'm not writing a novel—it's easier if I just think in terms of chapter one, chapter two, chapter three—I can deal with that. So I thought of the italics at the end of Chapter One in *Falling in Place* as being a kind of coda. And of course the chapters in that book don't all function in the same way: some of them repeat what you already know, some of them tell you what you know is an absolute lie, some of them tell you what to anticipate later on. I think Random House was a little baffled and wondered, "What do we call these?"

[McCaffery]: *One of the things I like about your fiction is precisely the thing that some critics seem most troubled with—that is, your work often seems to recreate a sense of modern life's* aimlessness, *its lack of coherency and resolution. Is this a conscious strategy on your part—a desire to suggest life's formlessness, that life isn't shaped like most well-made stories and novels suggest—or does this sense emerge mainly as a function of your writing habits? In other words, does this "aimlessness" result from your view of the world or mainly from the fact that you don't know where your works are headed?*

There are at least two honest answers to that question. One is to repeat what I've said before that I've never known beforehand what I'm setting out to write, so that even when I write the ending to a piece it's only at *that point* that I know how it ends. I do agree how you characterize my endings—the sense of them is "aimless," but the language used to create this sense isn't. I imagine, though, that subconsciously this is aesthetically what I believe in . . .

[McCaffery]: *You mean that you can't wrap things up neatly with a nice climax and denouement?*

Not the people and situations that I'm writing about. I don't hate books in which this happens; in fact, I rather admire them. One of my favorite books is non-fiction, *Blood and Money* by Thomas Thompson. The last page is so apocalyptic and satisfying. If I could do anything like that—see things with such an overview—I would wrap things up neatly. But it's not the way my mind works; it would seem inappropriate to what I've done, and I've never been able to over-haul a story. In fact, stories often get thrown away in the last paragraph, even the last sentence, because I don't know how it can end. It seems to me most honest personally to write something that still implies further complexity. I'm not writing confessionally. If I want to do that I can write my grandmother and say, "The day began here and it ended here." It wouldn't occur to me that this approach would be pleasurable or meaningful in a story.

[Gregory]: *You've mentioned how* **Falling in Place** *started. Do you recall what the opening image was in* **Chilly Scenes of Winter?**

No, not really. All I remember about that is that I had an idea in mind about the friendship between two men, Charles and Sam. I wrote quite a bit of background about them, and I showed it to a good friend of mine who handed it back to me and there was only a little shard of paper left—the remains of page 51 with Charles saying, "Permettez-moi de vous presenter Sam McGuire." And everything about how Charles came to meet Sam, what town they lived in, everything else had been scissored away. And I thought, you're right, just jump in. So whatever had been my original intention as I began the book was gone. The book that now stands is what took over. My friend had done the perfect job of editing. When the book came out I was amused when reviewers would talk about "Beattie's amazing, stark beginning," when in fact my friend had actually taken the scissors to it. My friend J. D. O'Hara, to whom *Falling in Place* is dedicated and who teaches at the University of Connecticut, used to take the scissors to the ends of my stories. Maybe I'm just a victim of my friends' Freudian obsessions, but in both cases they were right. It was really O'Hara who, in literally taking the scissors to my pages, suggested that more elliptical endings to my stories might be advantageous.

[McCaffery]: *I've also noticed that you seem to almost be deliberately refusing to provide the kinds of background and psychological information that most writers do—you just put your characters in a situation and show the reader that* situation.

I don't think that my characters are what they are because of interesting psychological complexities. They're not clinical studies to me. That would be a mind that worked in a different way than mine works. It's like: I like *you*, but I don't care about your childhood; if we know each other for the next ten years I would no doubt be interested if you were to tell me about your childhood, but to think that having known you at some point in time would change my impression, help me in any way to uncover what I'm looking for in our personal relationship, isn't true for me. For whatever reasons, I just seem to react to what is right there in front of me. So that's usually the way I write. There is often background information—though I supply it late in the story.

[Gregory]: *Your prose style is one that most reviewers have called "deadpan" or "emotionless." Are you consciously aiming for a certain kind of effect in relying on this kind of style?*

I think that's the way people talk. I know I think that way—in short sentences. If I didn't describe things neutrally I would be editorializing, which is not at all what I mean to do. It may be that I have gone *too* far with my prose style in this direction. It's a very mannered style, really—or the effect of it is very mannered—but that effect is no more conscious on my part when I sit down at the typewriter than these other things we've been talking about. I write so fast that I couldn't possibly think about whether or not I'm putting compound or complex sentences into my prose, or whether I'm writing like a dope, or whatever. I mean, we're talking about writing a whole story in two or three hours.

[McCaffery]: *But from what you just said I take it that you are conscious about trying to eliminate an intrusive, editorializing narrator?*

Usually, but not always. There's a story of mine called **"Greenwich Time,"** which was in the *New Yorker;* it doesn't exactly have editorializing but it does have what is purple prose for me. So I won't say I never change my prose style or point of view. I don't think you would even recognize that **"Greenwich Time"** is by me, except maybe in terms of the characters—it's full of analogies, it's constructed like a prism, the language is extremely deliberate and insistent; it's ostensibly seen through the main character's eyes, but the author is so completely and obviously *there* that you couldn't possibly remove her.

[Gregory]: *Is this kind of different approach something you've been doing more of recently in your stories, or is it just an isolated incident?*

It's something I realize more that I can do now. But it certainly would be so damn hard for me to do it all the time that I avoid it. And, of course, the most important thing is that this different approach seemed appropriate for *that story,* whereas it wouldn't be in others.

[Gregory]: *When you say that you write the way you do because it's "too hard" to write in other ways, what do you mean?*

I don't think I have an overall view of things to express.

[Gregory]: *So you focus on trying to observe small things . . .*

Not so much small *things* as small *moments*. I wish that writing these stories would suddenly lead me to some revelation that could help me as well as existing as art, as well as pleasing others. But don't think I've ever written anything that's allowed me to put pieces together; or maybe I have a psychological problem that makes me resist putting pieces together, that's the flip side of it. But one or the other is true. (pp. 169-75)

[McCaffery]: *In your story* "A Reasonable Man" *one of your characters points to all the books lining his walls and then wonders whether or not any of them were written by happy people. Has writing made* you *happy, or does it tend to aggravate things, open up wounds, the way it apparently did for Sylvia Plath?*

Writing doesn't open up wounds for me; during the writing of them it has made me happy. There have been a couple of times, only three I can think of, where I have finished a story—and remember that when I start to write something I don't know what it is I'm going to write—and have gotten to the end of it and thought, "I really wish I had never had to put these pieces together." These were **"The Burning House,"** a story in *Vogue* called **"Playback,"** and a story that will be out in the *New Yorker* in a few months called **"Desire."**

[Gregory]: *Why did you regret finishing these?*

Each of these made me realize that I had kept at bay and deliberately misinterpreted painful truths. But it is worth the price of discovering what you don't want to know because you can also have the sheer pleasure of writing something absurd like **"It's Just Another Day at Big Bear City, California,"** and deciding to have spacemen take pornographic pictures. I mean, that's *fun* and I basically write because I think it's fun. There are a few things I wish I never had written only because I wish I hadn't found out the things I found out.

[McCaffery]: *So at least occasionally you feel that the process of writing allows you to discover things about yourself.*

Yes, but always only in retrospect. I don't ever sit down thinking that. I just *do it,* the way I get my groceries. (pp. 176-77)

Larry McCaffery and Sinda Gregory, "A Conversation with Ann Beattie," in The Literary Review, Fairleigh Dickinson University, *Vol. 27, No. 2, Winter, 1984, pp. 165-77.*

Carolyn Porter

It is fashionable these days, especially perhaps on the West Coast, to express a superior disdain for Beattie. Of the several people to whom I mentioned that I was writing this essay, not one expressed admiration for her work. They disliked her perspective, her style, her characters, or what they seemed collectively to regard as her snobbery. I confess to having shared this attitude, if in a milder version; I did not like the world she portrayed, but I could never manage to stop reading her. Rereading the five volumes of hers that have been published, I find that every one of these denigrators, myself included, could figure as a character in one of her books. Such an ironic tribute may mean nothing, or it may mean that Beattie has caught us out,

revealed us in a light that is not merely unflattering, but disturbing—much as an old photograph of a group of friends can, in retrospect, disturb us by uncannily exposing the concealed facts, such as who loved whom, who was deceiving or being deceived by whom, even who was doomed.

The analogy with photography is apt in more ways than one, but it is most obviously apt for what the photograph leaves out—*why* X is deceiving Y, for example, or *why* Z is doomed. Beattie's recent stories are beginning to address the why, but in her first collection, **Distortions,** the characters and their relations are exposed without being explained. In effect, the hidden is revealed but not redeemed from what Henry James called life's "splendid waste." Indeed, it is often the waste itself that is portrayed. A reader may complain that the picture lacks depth, but it remains disturbing. Further, if Beattie's techniques worked initially to represent the surfaces of a world perceived as surface, as I think they did, they have now begun to serve as a ground on which to build a more complex narrative.

A more formidable complaint is that such pictures lack breadth. Needless to say, the colleagues to whom I have referred as possible characters in Beattie's stories all come from and inhabit the same social stratum on which Beattie focuses her lens—the white, upper middle class. Here James's example is congruent, and one of his critical principles is apt: the author must be granted her subject. What does not figure in Beattie's fictive world would, and does, fill many people's lives—poverty, say, or hunger, or discrimination, to mention only the bluntest abstractions for all that remains unrepresented. James's point, of course, was to insist upon measuring a writer's worth, not by her subject, but by what she does with it. On the face of it a conservative principle, this rule applies as well from a certain time-honored perspective of the left. That is, if, as [influential social theorist George] Lukacs argued, the artist's subject and perspective are dictated by her historical period and class, and if, as Sartre insisted, an individual's project is to make something of what time and place have made her, then a writer's subject is circumscribed by socially and historically determined conditions, and the great writer is the one whose art makes the most of those conditions by representing them accurately. There are some problems with this line of reasoning, of course, not least of which is that it minimizes the question of an author's choice of subject. But this is not a troublesome issue for the kind of leftist to whom these remarks are addressed in order to remind him or her that the white upper middle-class world of Beattie's stories and novels is theoretically capable of displaying social truth. (pp. 10-11)

This said, we can proceed to the integrity of Beattie's art, specifically to the narrative techniques she has developed toward a contemporary novel of manners. I should emphasize *toward*, since Beattie's two novels, **Chilly Scenes of Winter** and **Falling in Place,** are not altogether successful as novels. In what follows, I will focus on her first short-story collection, **Distortions,** then on her more recent one, **The Burning House,** because in these works we can see Beattie's techniques take shape and develop. It is not only, however, that her techniques are more clearly visible in the stories, but also that they work more effectively in this short form, which leads me to concentrate on these volumes and to claim that they are superior to Beattie's novels. It remains to be seen whether Beattie can write a fully successful novel, but it is already clear that her mastery of the short story derives from the sensibility of a novelist of manners. Nor do I think such mastery worth any less than that of the novelist. The short-story collection in the modern era has roots in a tradition that goes back to *Dubliners* and *Winesburg, Ohio*, a tradition that has come to fulfill many of the same functions as the novel of manners. While none of Beattie's collections is unified around a town or a central character, each is focused—as the stereotype indicates—on certain social groups and on the present, the tense used by Beattie in almost all her stories and even in her first novel. Further, one of the social marks of the generation and the period she is primarily concerned with portraying is its mobility. These people's lives do not adhere to a city or town. Instead, they are attached to cars, plants, dogs—that is, not only to objects, but to transitory ones. In short, the narrative means of capturing the manners of contemporary life are not easy to come by, and the short-story collection may well have some advantages over the novel. It may also be meeting the demands of a reading public not only dwindling in size, but one becoming more responsive to synecdoche. That is, just as cartoons have been simplified, reduced from detailed visual plenitude to spare line drawings as we have become attuned to the comic strip, perhaps readers—at least readers of the *New Yorker*—have grown accustomed to an analogous economy of exposition in narration, an economy of which Beattie's stories are exemplary.

Having hovered over the affective fallacy, I now return to hover again over the mimetic one by claiming that Beattie's techniques, even while producing results that often seem highly artificial, are informed by a clean aim at the real, the here and now, and that those techniques, so far, have worked better at portraying contemporary life in her short stories than in her novels. The central reason for this is that Beattie's most marked talent is for eliminating discrete chunks of exposition, that laying out of background information which the short story must find a way of minimizing. One way of occulting exposition and at the same time exploiting the limits of the short story is to develop a symbolic context and meaning for the events being portrayed, as both Joyce and Anderson did. Beattie's solution is strikingly different. By using the present tense, she not only removes any temptation to lapse into straight exposition, forcing it to emerge either through a character's consciousness or through dialogue, but also limits the consciousness in question severely. At the same time, she refuses the rewards of the symbolic; that is, her narratives are supported, not by metaphor, but by metonymy. Not all this is necessarily apparent in any one story, but it becomes clear in the course of *Distortions* as a whole.

The simplest of Beattie's stories in this volume are those that are focused on a single character whose experience is represented in a series of frames, as in a cartoon strip. **"The Parking Lot,"** for example, follows an unnamed woman through a week in which she begins an affair. The affair itself is not represented, but the parking lot is. It serves not merely as visual background but as thematic center. The routine of her life is punctuated by her departure from the parking lot each day, the only time she seems to become conscious of herself or of her surroundings. The parking lot serves, not as symbol, but merely as link—virtually the only link in the woman's life. The story represents the cognitive dissonance endemic to the clerical worker's life, in which the cycle of work, exhaustion, eating, and sleeping repeats itself until "she finds herself in the parking lot, a whole day gone," wondering "what happened in the period between sitting at the dining table and now when she is walking across the parking lot?"

Despite the enlightened arrangement by which she and her husband work alternate years, her life is utterly conventional, as are her attitudes. She cannot see why other people's marriages fail, why they too cannot make arrangements. Despite the fact that she is treated with a sustained, if muted irony, this woman's story is curiously humorless. She would be an easy target for satire, if it were not for the pity her case evokes. By staying just inside the rim of her consciousness, the narrative voice never allows us the distance necessary for satire, but by clinging to that rim, the voice prohibits any view of a genuine interior and indeed suggests that there is no such interior. What is missing is any self-consciousness, any awareness of the dissatisfactions that lead her to start the affair.

Not all these stories are so humorless or so affectless, however. **"Wolf Dreams,"** like **"The Parking Lot,"** portrays a woman lost to herself, but its heroine, Cynthia, is painfully conscious of her own unhappiness, though just as painfully unable to understand it. Cynthia's life is a caricature of a story from *Bride* magazine. She marries Ewell W. G. Peterson at seventeen, then Lincoln Divine at twenty-nine, and is now planning to marry Charlie Pinehurst as soon as she loses twenty pounds and her hair has grown long enough for her to have curls falling to her shoulders on her wedding day. She has a recurring nightmare in which she is standing at the altar with Charlie in a wedding dress not quite long enough to hide the fact that she is standing on a scale. It may be no wonder to us that she finally rejects Charlie—and his rejection of her—but it remains a wonder to her.

While **"The Parking Lot"** is one monotonous series of days fused by a seamless present tense, **"Wolf Dreams"** almost produces a plot, a developing sequence of events ending in Cynthia's rejection by Charlie. (pp. 11-13)

"Marshall's Dog" is built out of segments arranged without apparent regard for chronology, plot sequence, or thematic development. The story opens with a segment describing Marshall's eighty-two-year-old mother. This is followed by a scene at Sam's cafe, where some teenage girls are being teased by a couple of boys. It turns out that one of them, Mary, is Marshall's niece. Marshall and his sister Edna live with their mother. Their brother, George, is Mary's father. George has had an affair with Beverly, a waitress in Sam's cafe. Marshall and Edna drive a snowmobile. Marshall's dog shows up occasionally at the cafe.

As these facts emerge, we get a peculiar family portrait, peculiar because of the way the portrait is composed. One segment is often linked to the next by the most arbitrary verbal association. At the end of one section, Mary's mother offers to drive Mary to school and "looks at the car through the frosty window." The next section opens, "It is cold in the house," but this is Marshall's house, and this segment deals with Marshall's mother. Or again, this segment ends with "the dog is barking. The soup is boiling over," a statement that seems, but actually is not, continuous with the opening line of the next segment, "What a mess." This "mess," it turns out, refers to the pizza smeared on Mary's shirt at Sam's cafe one summer when Mary is fifteen. Such metonymic associations serve not only to connect segments, but also to generate them. The opening segment, for example, begins:

> She was eighty-two when she died. She had the usual old-lady fears—Democratic Presidents, broken bones. When the spaghetti was snapped in half and dropped into the boiling water she heard the sound of her own bones cracking. She loved spaghetti. They had to eat so much spaghetti. She wouldn't eat the sauce. She had butter with her spaghetti. She used to knit for her son, Marshall. She loved her son, she knitted all the time. Once she knitted him a bathrobe and he broke out in a rash all over, an allergy to wool.

Even when metaphors appear, they refuse to function normally—that is, to create and develop symbolic meanings. Instead, they act as metonymy does in Roman Jakobson's theory, returning to the relations of contiguity which generate narrative movement. Here, "old-lady fears" lead to "broken bones." "Broken bones" are like "spaghetti . . . snapped in half," but rather than building on this metaphor, the narrator goes on to what accompanies the spaghetti—sauce or butter. Spaghetti is, again, like yarn. But no sooner is that similarity functioning than it collapses once more into metonymic roaming until it reaches its end in the memory of Marshall's rash.

In a sense, the whole of "Marshall's Dog" is generated by this metonymic association, as if Beattie simply picked up one thread and then another in a piece of fabric, pulling each until it would not give any more, but meanwhile gathering the cloth into a pattern that highlights its textures. The technique resembles smocking. Such a conceit, however, fails to capture what is most elusive and disturbing about Beattie's metonymic method here—its capacity to substitute for the closure of a conventional plot development, a closure that feels like the expiration of a breath or of a life. The story opens with an announcement of the old lady's death but ends with the death of Marshall's dog, which serves as the referent for the title. But these deaths do not stand in any resonant symbolic relation to each other. Rather, when Marshall's dog is run over in the snow, it is simply that all the metonymic lines have been played out. They do not meet on some symbolic note; there is no epiphany, either about dogs or death. They simply exhaust themselves. Such a technique has the curious effect of making the arbitrary seem real, or perhaps of revealing how arbitrary is the real.

If, however, this world is real in some sense, it remains off balance, leaving us hoping that we have missed something. The title of the story underscores this quality. Marshall's dog is given pride of place even though its death evokes no great pathos. Unlike some of Beattie's dogs, it is genuinely peripheral to the lives of the characters. The dog is not there, throughout, and at the end it is not there for good. Perhaps, after all, it is the missing center, what is not there, that throws the metonymic engine into gear. (pp.14-16)

Whether comic or somber, these early stories produce a vision of a world in a state of lack. Henry James would have called Beattie's a scenic method, and would have been right up to the point at which he would have despaired at the lack of a center. But it is that lack of a center which distinguishes Beattie's narrative method. Beginning with a set of characters in situation and bringing them into focus only gradually—and then obliquely—Beattie exposes and develops them as if they were a piece of film. This is both the virtue and the defect of her early work, and it is signaled, I think, by the title she gave her first collection. For ***Distortions*** refers not only to the distorted forms of human life portrayed in the stories, but also to the distortion implicit in her method of representation. Beattie's various means of telling-it-slant tell a certain truth, perhaps, but a limited one.

As I have indicated, the most significant advantage of Beattie's method is the remarkable economy that it facilitates. Exposition is always deftly woven into narration. Sometimes this technique leaves the reader in doubt about the relations that the narration develops. **"Victor Blue,"** for instance, obscures the gender of the narrative voice, destablizing the reader's perspective for much of the story. Here, the lack of discrete exposition is exploited to provoke sudden, retrospective enlightenment; the narrator is not, we discover, a sister or companion to Ms. Edway, but is *Mr.* Edway. More often, however, the exposition spun out along with the narration has no such dramatic function, but serves rather to represent characters as fused with their contexts—geographical, familial, social—from the outset. While the result is striking in its capacity to encompass character and background in one narrative motion, the price paid for such economy is high. Characters so fused to their contexts cannot stand out from them, much less alter them. This sense of characters fused to a frame, of course, is most marked in such stories as **"The Parking Lot,"** but even in **"Marshall's Dog"** or **"Big Bear"** it is less the development of characters than the deft manipulation of the frames by which the illusion of motion and change is created. The metonymic associations expand the frame, elaborating a larger picture, but the characters remain fixed within it.

It would be possible to argue, of course, that such limits are built into the genre of the short story itself, the art of which is that of revelation rather than of complex development. But the advance marked by ***The Burning House*** suggests that Beattie is more than capable of expanding these limits. (I pass over ***Secrets and Surprises,*** Beattie's intervening and transitional volume of stories, for the sake of economy.) The same techniques we have seen her use in ***Distortions*** are recognizable in ***The Burning House***—story construction by segment, simultaneous narration and exposition, reliance on metonymy and the present tense—but here they produce a far more resonant result.

The economy mastered in ***Distortions,*** for example, is now put to more ambitious uses. In **"Learning to Fall,"** Beattie tells one story, at the same time using it to tell another. One story is Ruth's. Ruth is the mother of Andrew, an eight-year-old who has suffered slight brain damage and facial paralysis as a result of a mangled forceps delivery. Andrew's father left Ruth six months before Andrew was born. Ruth teaches at a community college, where she earns hardly any money. Once or twice a month, her lover, Brandon, comes to spend the day with her. "Like many people," Brandon envies Ruth. "He would like to be her, but he does not want to take her on. Or Andrew." When Brandon visits Ruth, Andrew goes to the city with Ruth's friend, who tells the story and whose own story eventually emerges in the course of her narration. She is married to one man, Arthur, and in love with another, Ray. Although she has broken up with Ray, she meets him in the city when she takes Andrew there. Indeed, it was when she quit being Ray's lover that she began taking Andrew to the city. By the third page her story begins to creep out around the edges of Ruth's and eventually encircles it. In effect, one narrative serves as exposition for the other, and then they change places, Ruth's story providing context for the narrator's.

By the end of the day in New York, where events form the actual narrative line, the unnamed narrator has given up trying to resist loving Ray. Taking her cue from Ruth, whose dance instructor has been teaching her to fall and is her model of valor in the face of an unjust fate, the narrator recognizes "what Ruth has known all along: what will happen can't be stopped. Aim for grace." Here the associations by which the story unfolds are far more controlled than those in *Distortions*. One source of control is Beattie's use of a first-person narrator, a choice she makes far more often in *The Burning House* than in *Distortions*. As a consequence, what the narrator sees and does is circumscribed and guided by her own preoccupations. Further, while they seem to unroll metonymically as before, the associations turn out to be partially metaphorical, to build a loose structure of meaning. The pool of blue water at the bottom of the Guggenheim is related to Hall's Pond, where Ruth swam the day before Andrew was born; it is related in terms made explicit by the narrator when she hears herself admonishing Andrew not to drop pennies into the pool from the walkway because he might hurt somebody. Realizing the irony of protecting others from a child himself mangled at birth by an impatient doctor, she feels guilty, a feeling later made specific by her recognition that she has been using Andrew as an excuse to meet Ray. Meanwhile, Hall's Pond, introduced in the preceding segment in a scene remembered merely because it preceded Andrew's birth, has begun to function as the basis for a set of images in which birth, pain, pools, and drowning prefigure the narrator's own fears of letting go, losing control. Consequently, when the story lands on the line "Aim for grace," its almost onomatopoeic resonance derives from a whole train of moments of which this line is the echo and the culmination.

If such a reading seems strained, it is—at least in the sense that such images are never allowed by Beattie to sit around festering with symbolic meaning in the way such a reading might imply. The story unfolds with an easy grace, moving from one scene to the next until the day's end, and it does so by means of the techniques that I have described— apparently random associations recorded in the present tense, incorporating exposition seamlessly along the way. What is new here is that when the reader reaches the end, something has changed. The narrator has reached a turning point toward which the story has been driving all along. She has learned to fall, a phrase whose verbal origin may seem arbitrary, but whose meaning is enriched by its appropriateness to Ruth's entire life.

Beattie's stories now end, then, with more than arbitrary closes because their associations are no longer purely arbi-

trary. And whether it is cause or effect of Beattie's technical control in *The Burning House,* her characters have also changed. They are more likable, and their relationships with each other are stronger, whether for good or bad. The women, particularly, move out of their frames and come alive, whether with love and envy, as in **"Playback,"** or with lonely terror, as in **"Waiting."** There is the same sense of something lost, something missing, but Beattie is now zeroing in on it, sometimes even naming it. In the title story, **"The Burning House,"** a woman wonders why, though she has "known everybody in the house for years," she knows them "all less and less" as time goes by, and then she finds out. "Your whole life you've made one mistake," her husband tells her at the end, "you've surrounded yourself with men." He continues: "Let me tell you something. All men—if they're crazy, like Tucker, if they're gay as the Queen of the May, like Reddy Fox, even if they're just six years old—I'm going to tell you something about them. Men think they're Spider-Man and Buck Rogers and Superman. You know what we all feel inside that you don't feel? That we're going to the stars." A comic epiphany, this, but with a punch, since it accounts perfectly for the behavior of every man in the story. (pp. 18-21)

In *Distortions,* Beattie was spinning a net of words with which to catch life in motion almost at random. Her means were often extravagant, and extravagantly displayed, as in **"Big Bear City"** or in other stories such as **"Wally Whistles Dixie,"** a parody of J. D. Salinger. In *The Burning House,* no such display is made of the artist's artistry, and there is nothing random about her aim. Yet the techniques developed in *Distortions* clearly served as necessary apprentice work for the lucid perfection of many of the stories in *The Burning House.* **"Winter: 1978,"** the most ambitious story in the volume and arguably the finest piece of work Beattie has done so far, presupposes stories such as **"Marshall's Dog"** but leaves them far behind in its mastery of a similar subject—a group of people whose relations are captured in an emotional nexus in time.

The advance marked by **"Winter: 1978"** seems partly the result of a technique of juxtaposition. Just as in **"Learning to Fall"** two narrative planes operate in relation to each other and in **"Running Dreams"** the past suddenly stands over against the present, in **"Winter: 1978"** two settings, California and Connecticut, serve to enforce the story's move from a hollowed-out now to a then that proves almost as empty. Like many of the characters in *The Burning House,* Nick and Benton in **"Winter: 1978"** are the now successful members of the baby-boom generation. Benton's art sells well in L. A., through the agency of one Allen Tompkins, whose library in Beverly Hills is "illuminated by lamps with bases in the shape of upright fish that supported huge Plexiglass conch shell globes in their mouths." Nick has made money in the record industry and spends his time making sure that such bands as "Barometric Pressure" are provided with chicken tacos. Both Nick and Benton come from wealthy families, but their own successes are personal, although accidental. Benton's work was discovered by Tompkins one night in the framing shop where Benton worked. Nick's entrance into the record industry is the result of his getting a job in exchange for making a dope connection with the former supplier of a philosophy professor's daughter.

"Winter: 1978" portrays these characters as they confront death, specifically the death of Benton's younger brother, Wesley, and generally the death of their youth. The story is constructed, as usual, out of segments, but because the past tense is used, the segments are ordered almost conventionally. They depict events that proceed chronologically in a single sequence, beginning in Los Angeles, where Nick lives and where Benton has come with his girl friend, Olivia, to sell his latest pictures to Tompkins, and ending in Connecticut, where Wesley has drowned and has been buried before Benton could be reached. That Nick should accompany Benton and Olivia back to Connecticut almost as if he were along for the ride is made entirely plausible by the portrait of life in L. A. with which the story opens. Once in Connecticut, however, Nick serves as a center of consciousness, sufficiently out of the picture to see it whole, yet sufficiently involved by his own common history with Wesley and Benton to take it personally.

For Nick, the East is home. As soon as he is headed there, he remembers "what Thanksgiving used to be like, and the good feeling he got as a child when the holidays came and it snowed." He wishes for snow throughout his visit. In a passage that echoes Nick Carraway's famous description of his Midwest, Nick drives past "houses that stood close to the road. There was nothing in California that corresponded to the lights burning in big old New England houses at night." Nick's sentimental longing for the New England winters of his youth, is undercut by the scene he confronts in Connecticut. Wesley's mother, Ena, presides over a parody of the "big old New England houses" of Nick's memories. She has assembled the fragments of her family at Wesley's house as a "tribute to Wesley—no matter that in the six months he'd lived there he never invited the family to his house." She relentlessly invokes a rural New England tradition, ordering wood, for instance, from Hanley Paulson whom she seems to regard as a trusted servant of the gentry. It is not Paulson, however, who shows up with the wood, but his son, who steals all Wesley's pumpkins. The entire scene at Wesley's house testifies to the gap between Nick's sentimental image of New England and the reality of a world all too reminiscent of California. Uncle Cal, for example, has recently moved to East Hampton and hired a vegetarian decorator named Morris, "who paints the walls the color of carrots and turnips."

Similarly, Nick's romantic memories of his own youth are undercut once his discrete images come unraveled. A snowy Christmas scene turns into a revelation of family disorder when Nick recalls his father's drunken impersonation of William Tell. The image of a large red stocking his uncle had hung for him during another Christmas turns into another scene of conflict between his uncle and his father. The only images that resist such disintegration are those Wesley saw and photographed.

Wesley's photographs—of wind chimes hanging on a broomstick in a graveyard, of a "tombstone with a larger-than-life dog stretched on top," of Nick's hands folded on top of the *New York Times*—provide the only clues to a puzzle that no one save Nick is really concerned to solve: who Wesley was. Recalling Wesley's photographs becomes for Nick a means of mourning, although primarily a mourning for the loss of his own youth. Looking at his hands, Nick realizes that "what Wesley had seen about

them had never come true." Wesley himself remains an enigma whose death is appropriately imagined in the form of a photograph of two bright orange life vests floating beside a boat in water "gray and deep," a photograph Nick captions "Lake Champlain: 1978." Such captions suggest why these images retain their force. As Nick remarks, "Photographer gets a shot of a dwarf running out of a burning hotel and it's labeled 'New York: 1968'". The caption refuses to refer to the people or events photographed. It refers only to when and where the photographer was when he took the picture. This, the caption suggests, is what he saw at that time and in that place. No comment. No explanation. Even to inquire how the effect of a picture was achieved is a vain endeavor. When Nick asks Wesley how he got the "softness" in the picture of his hands, Wesley replies, "I developed it in acufine."

Such photographs resemble Beattie's earlier stories in their insistence on simply portraying a scene without comment or interpretation. What and where take such precedence over why as almost to annihilate it. But here, such photographic images serve a larger narrative interest. "Lake Champlain: 1978" cannot be explicated. It cannot be read as a symbolic construct. But because it is situated within a narrative about time and loss, it can function not merely as an image, but as an experience of time and loss, as it manifestly does for Nick: "He had to catch his breath when the image formed. He was as shocked as if he had been there when they recovered the body." The imagined photograph becomes an event in the story, specifically the event of Wesley's death as witnessed by Nick, and the story, in turn, becomes **"Winter: 1978"** because it recounts an equally resonant moment. On the one hand, Nick's images of New England unravel, as Connecticut and the past are exposed as the same world as California and the present, a world in which parents try to get rid of their children only to pretend to themselves later that they always cared. But his is not merely the ironic loss of something that never existed, for on the other hand, he experiences a real loss, one described perfectly in Benton's closing speech to his son, Jason: "Benton told him this fact of evolution: that one day dinosaurs shook off their scales and sucked in their breath until they became much smaller. This caused the dinosaurs' brains to pop through their skulls. The brains were called antlers, and the dinosaurs deer. That was why deer had such sad eyes, Benton told Jason—because they were once something else." The cryptic copyright notice in *The Burning House,* "Irony & Pity, Inc.," is ironic in its self-reflectiveness, but it speaks as well to Beattie's larger capacity for pity.

If, as I have argued, Beattie's narrative method works by a metonymic unraveling, a movement from one detail to the next, her advances in *The Burning House* derive from a new focus on and control of that method. Her more frequent use of the first person, her willingness to let metaphors grow from and give resonance to the train of associations on which her stories ride, her use of the past tense— all these are marks of an author still experimenting, but with tools now refined and proven. The distance she has crossed could also be measured by comparing *Chilly Scenes of Winter* with *Falling in Place,* but her second novel fails, in my judgment, to live up to the promise of **"Winter: 1978."** It remains to be seen whether Beattie's techniques can be made to work for the novel, but they have already made something new of the short story, enabling it to cut into contemporary life where it hurts. (pp. 21-5)

Carolyn Porter, "Ann Beattie: The Art of the Missing," in Contemporary American Women Writers: Narrative Strategies, *edited by Catherine Rainwater and William J. Scheick, The University Press of Kentucky, 1985, pp. 9-25.*

Michiko Kakutani

"The middle of the target was this blue star," says a character in one of Ann Beattie's new stories [collected in *Where You'll Find Me*]. "I was such a great shot that I was trying to win by shooting out the star, and the guy finally said to me, 'Man, you're trying to blast that star away. What you do is shoot *around* it, and the star falls out.'"

For readers of her previous novels and short stories, the foregoing could serve as a succinct description of Ms. Beattie's narrative method—a method that works through omission and understatement, irony and indirection. There tends to be little authorial comment in her fiction— few attempts to interpret behavior or conversations and almost no effort at all to situate her characters within some larger frame of reference, moral or historical. Instead, things simply happen—someone drifts out of one relationship and into another or moves from one house to the next.

In Ms. Beattie's finest work, this method has resulted in widely imitated narratives that mirror in their very structure the fragmented, fragmentary nature of their characters' lives, narratives that capture the strobe-light effect of contemporary life through their pointillist detail and fractured observation. Unfortunately, it's also a technique with decided limitations—the author's deadpan delivery can devolve into a pose of anomic detachment that's as irritating (and ultimately as ineffectual) as her characters' relentless passivity; and her gift for external description can be used to avoid looking at more elusive emotions. We may end up knowing what her people listen to on the radio, what they keep on their end tables and what they say to their dogs—all without having the faintest idea of who they really are.

Certainly *Where You'll Find Me*—Ms. Beattie's fourth volume of stories—includes several tales that suffer from such weaknesses. **"Snow"** is a mannered prose poem about lost love that reads like a random collection of notebook jottings. **"The Big Outside World"** becomes a labored attempt to draw some sort of analogy between an upsetting incident—some street people ambush a package of clothes meant as a Goodwill donation—and an anxious woman's state of mind. And **"Coney Island"** seems like a formulaic exercise in the depiction of our inability to connect: we're told that the two-old pals sitting around the kitchen table both have problems—one has a wife in the hospital, the other is thinking about an old love affair—but a sense of their personalities and friendship is telegraphed by only the broadest, most obvious details. . . .

Happily, many of the stories in this volume are more substantial—more sympathetic toward their characters as well as denser and most satisfying as fictions. Ms. Beattie's

people—the battered emotional casualties of the 1960's and the hip survivors of the Me Generation—are teetering now on the margins of middle age, and the aging process has made them somewhat less careless about their lives. . . .

A sense of sadness hangs over many of these characters— in part, it's a nostalgic yearning for their receding youth ("We'll put on some Fifties music and play high school," says one); and in part, an apprehension of the terrible precariousness of life. Memories of a summer in Vermont prompt a man to re-examine the emotional losses he's incurred (**"Summer People"**); and a desultory chat in the kitchen jars a housekeeper and her now grown charges into a mood of melancholy recollection. The heroine of **"In the White Night"** remembers the time their Christmas tree caught fire and their little girl, Sharon, tried to rush toward the flames; and she also remembers the night in the hospital when they learned that Sharon had leukemia.

Whereas many of Ms. Beattie's earlier stories tended to take a random, almost improvisatory shape, several of the ones in *Where You'll Find Me* evince a pointed interest in sustained narrative form. **"Janus"**—which portrays a woman's obsession with a bowl given to her by a former lover—becomes a highly crafted, almost surreal meditation on the intrusion of time past into time present and on the perils of everyday life. And **"Spiritus"** grows from a stream-of-consciousness riff into a portrait of a man torn between his devotion to his wife and his passion for another woman.

As ever, the stories in this volume attest to Ms. Beattie's gift for weird analogies, her ability to grab cheap, glittering bits of dialogue out of the air. What's new about these stories is their intermittent lyricism, combined with a shift of voice that signals a willingness on the part of the author to risk subjectivity. A man is transfixed at the moment his car crashes by a glimpse of an old friend going trick-or-treating with her children—dressed, absurdly enough, as a skeleton. And a woman whose daughter has recently died imagines as she drifts off to sleep beside her husband that "in the white night world outside, their daughter might be drifting past like an angel." With such passages, Ms. Beattie's cameralike accuracy with detail gives way to something a little more personal and poetic, and the result is stories that have the capacity to move as well as persuade us.

Michiko Kakutani, in a review of "Where You'll Find Me and Other Stories," in The New York Times, *October 1, 1986, p. C23.*

Thomas R. Edwards

Though most of the stories in Ann Beattie's new collection, *Where You'll Find Me,* are pretty terse, one of them, called **"Janus,"** is sufficiently open and worked out to give convenient access to the materials from which they all are made. In **"Janus,"** Andrea, a successful suburban real-estate agent of a certain age, uses a glazed bowl of her own to provide a special touch of elegance to the houses she shows for sale. It is "both subtle and noticeable—a paradox of a bowl," and Andrea is sure that it brings her professional luck. . . .

She sometimes dreams about it coming "into sharp focus,"

she imagines a "deeper connection" between it and herself, her use of it becomes more deliberate, possessive, anxious about damage. It emerges that it was a gift from her lover, who later left her because she would not give up her "two-faced" life and commit herself to him alone. The story ends with her continuing in her undemonstrative but acceptable marriage, often looking at the bowl, "still and safe, unilluminated," an image of feeling made esthetic and thus endurable: "In its way, it was perfect: the world cut in half, deep and smoothly empty. Near the rim, even in dim light, the eye moved toward one small flash of blue, a vanishing point on the horizon."

If the story is perhaps a little diagrammatic, this ending is fine, especially since Andrea is not allowed fully to recognize how aptly the bowl reflects her own condition. And her condition, with due allowance for individual circumstances, is essentially that of most of the women, and some of the men, in these stories. The recurrent motive is loss, and diminished replacement. Divorce, the loss of lovers and friends and expected futures, childlessness or the death of children, departures from former homes—Ms. Beattie's people suffer emotional and moral disconnection in a world that has yet been rather generous to them in material ways. They live comfortably enough in New York, the suburbs, the country; they work at business, finance, editing, modeling, writing, the law; they have been to college and sometimes graduate school, and now, as they approach 40, they miss what they remember as the innocence and intimacy of student community, "all those people" (as one character wistfully reflects) "who took themselves so seriously that everything they felt was a fact."

The belief that feelings are facts is what has been lost, or safely displaced onto objects like Andrea's lucky bowl. Estranged from their own emotional centers, these people experience their lives as revisable hypotheses, stories, sources of metaphors that they can never quite accept as literal connections between people or things. And yet they are not free—people, places and objects, present or remembered, continue to ask for the directness of response that can't now be given. "People and things never really got left behind," one character discovers after a humiliating attempt to give her old clothes to Goodwill, and the imperishability of relations that can no longer be enjoyed or used is the painful figure in the carpet.

Ms. Beattie is a pre-eminent writer of her generation, and it's easy enough to think it a second "lost generation," but simply to call hers post-Vietnam fiction or whatever is a crude and deceptive historicizing at best. . . .

Ms. Beattie contemplates life through the sensibilities of educated, upper-middle-class people born soon enough to have been marked and directed by the 1960's and 70's but also late enough not to have suffered the sharpest personal consequences of those times. They are drawn to the country but are not counterculturalists (nor indeed anything else—no articulate political or social passions stir in them at all). If they occasionally smoke a little pot, they seem in no danger of involvement with any worse substance. Traditional work and its rewards do not deeply engage them, but they have no trouble amassing money and property. Their marriages and relationships often fail, but whose don't these days? On the analogy of "yuppies" they might be called "nummies"—not-so-young urban mal-

contents—but it's greatly to Ms. Beattie's credit that she concerns herself not with the supposed public sources of their numbness but with the insight it provides into the desires of people thwarted by their immediate culture, as human desires so commonly are.

A few of the stories in *Where You'll Find Me* pursue economy to the point of inconclusiveness, but most of them have the sensitive elegance one hopes for from this remarkably gifted writer. The cultivation of brevity, however, makes it hard to read as a book—only two of the stories run to more than 11 pages, and a kind of vertigo sets in as one struggles to adjust to rapid changes of characters, settings and issues.

Ms. Beattie's earlier story collections—*Distortions* (1976), *Secrets and Surprises* (1978) and *The Burning House* (1982)—were considerably more ample in scale and mood. I assume that she has been trying to pare things down, to minimize explanatory and connective matters, to distill significance into moments of speech, gesture, image. If so, a purer art is achieved at some cost. Those earlier stories that are longer are sometimes rough and wasteful, but they are full of energy, exuberance and daring, what I can only call *life*. So too is Ms. Beattie's most recent novel, *Love Always* (1985), whose impressive gravity of outlook has plenty of room for a large, outrageous comic inventiveness that many of the earlier stories also draw on. But there are few laughs or even smiles to be had in *Where You'll Find Me,* and few venturings beyond a rather buttoned-down obliquity and economy of means that make even more evident how narrow Ms. Beattie's social theater now is.

> *Thomas R. Edwards, "A Glazed Bowl of One's Own," in* The New York Times Book Review, *October 12, 1986, p. 10.*

Jonathan Penner

Most of [the stories in *Where You'll Find Me*], like the works of a painter's blue or green "period," have a family resemblance. Hanging in a row, they seem familiar as you side-step by, and what you recall in the cab home is partly a prototype.

That essential story begins with a vivid, briefly mysterious line of dialogue ("Don't think about a cow," or "My feeling is that for whatever reason you duck your head and slam on the brakes, it's *mad* to act like that in the Holland tunnel"). Within the first paragraph several people are named, the warp of a social web. You start calculating who is whose what and what to whom.

You transit representative passages in the lives of clever people, who are pursuing guiltless but disappointing love affairs and live between complacency and despair. Background (especially an ex- or absent lover) predominates over foreground: nothing now, nothing new, can prick or please like memory.

The story loosely assembles observations and meditations, often delivered in dialogue of inspired accuracy. There is charming portraiture—"Sometimes I think I'm falling in love with Coop. He's always on top of things. He can get people off the phone in less than a minute"—and detail of maddening pointlessness, such as the biographical minutiae of characters who never appear.

In the closing lines, examination becomes compulsively microscopic, leaving a sense of exhaustion or disconnection. Not even a ripple reveals the story's intended final effect, its emotional meaning, as the author somehow steps out of the tub without disturbing the water.

This essential Ann Beattie story takes human nature seriously. People are understood to be complex. The author is not cynical, never bored with us. And yet the events of the story are not caused by its people, but rather happen to them, drastically reducing the role of character. The women and men have personalities, not characters.

Something begins to seem wrong. No line is badly written, no detail dimly observed. If the plot is perhaps slight—two people discussing old love affairs, or an unnamed narrator preparing breakfast for an unnamed spouse—a story need not reside in a plot. Still, it needs to reside somewhere. And though its absence, like God's, is hard to conceive or demonstrate, one reads and rereads these stories with a growing sense of emptiness beneath a crowded surface.

The stories have little organic necessity, few working parts. Their internal order is not systemic but serial. Accurate observation follows accurate observation without regard to literary value, to whether the story is *using* it. . . .

The 15 stories include two that depart from Beattie's usual manner. In **"Janus,"** a woman falls in love with a bowl. She becomes obsessed with it, as no Beattie character ever becomes with a human lover. Normally an associative writer, continually thinking of something else we ought to know, Beattie treats this weird romance with an unaccustomed exclusivity. The beloved bowl becomes a psychoanalytical symbol, odd as an archaeopteryx in Beattie's post-Freudian world.

The other surprising story, **"Snow,"** is the collection's only dramatic monologue, a reminiscence of a long-dead love affair, declaimed by the woman to the absent man. This story is also the most adventurous in its diction. Usually Beattie's language seems deliberately ordinary, avoiding clumsiness and evading beauty with equal care. But the narrator of **"Snow,"** speaking in the privacy of her mind, risks a lyricism that would embarrass the hip citizens of the other stories. She tells the man that their love affair was "as hopeless as giving a child a matched cup and saucer." . . .

[These] stories tell the truth. What they don't do, won't do, is try to make any sense of that truth. And this refusal will disappoint readers who want everything from fiction—to see how we live, but more—to learn when we matter, and to feel why.

Jonathan Penner, "Ann Beattie: The Surface of Things," in Book World—The Washington Post, *October 19, 1986, p. 7.*

Carol des Lauriers Cieri

First published by *The New Yorker,* included in an annual collection of best short stories, and now in [*Where You'll Find Me*], **"Janus"** is considered one of the best stories Ann Beattie has written. It is the story of a real-estate agent's attachment to a strangely beautiful bowl. The woman begins to place it, successfully, in homes she wants to sell. Given to her by a lover she spurned, it becomes to her a symbol that "she was always too slow to learn what she really loved." I think **"Janus"** is one of the weaker, certainly the most belabored, of the stories in *Where You'll Find Me.* It lacks the quicksilver dash that marks the best of Beattie—as if she had been browbeaten by her editor into finishing every last thought, to draw out every last inference.

That belabored quality separates **"Janus"** from the other stories in this collection. There is a wildness to the rest of them, an odd just-rightness in the way the stories turn, as if she took the lid off and let go. She says she starts with a visual image and then, "Something comes in and takes over." What happens is magical and exhilarating. Beattie writes so well that the strains of sadness in these stories are not burdensome. There are grace notes of weary sweetness, even lyricism. And best of all, there are recognizable virtues, like loyalty, fortitude, and patience.

This can be seen in the first story of the collection, **"In the White Night."**

A long-married couple returns home from a dinner party. Vernon falls asleep on the sofa with his wife's jacket over his head. Carol doesn't want to wake him by curling up with him, but she doesn't want to go to bed alone. So she stretches out on the floor next to the couch and pulls his camel's-hair coat over her for warmth. "Ready to sleep in this peculiar double-decker fashion, in the largest, coldest room of all," Carol asks the inevitable, "What would anyone think?"

She thinks of the hard times she and Vernon have had since their daughter, Sharon, died. Carol resolves that "anyone who was a friend would understand exactly. In time, both of them had learned to stop passing judgment on how they coped with the inevitable sadness that set in, always unexpectedly, but so real it was met with the instant acceptance one gave to a snowfall. In the white night world outside, their daughter might be drifting past like an angel, and she would see this tableau, for the second that she hovered, as a necessary small adjustment."

In a recently published interview, Beattie said she was fascinated by "reflective people in a mess." But for all the messes they get into, few of her characters are reflective.

These stories depend so much on the apt detail, the careful phrasing, and not paragraphs of explanation and analysis. Much has been written about this, as if Beattie were using a yuppie code of brand names to tell her stories.

Actually, something far more powerful is at work. She has gathered material with a rapt and affectionate eye, and she has refined it as only a very fine writer can. . . .

If there is a fault in Ann Beattie's new book, it is this: Her stories hardly seem to be stories. It is moments that she catches and catches so beautifully: the sudden lightness of a car as it goes into a skid, the "Tide-scented steam" outside a laundry, the couple sleeping in "double-decker fashion" on a snowy night. They can be moving moments because we feel them as the characters feel them, and we are drawn in. But they are fragments, nonetheless.

To Beattie and, it seems, to her readers, this is not a fault at all. It is closer to how we are, to what we feel and remember. As a woman tells the story of a failed affair in the story, **"Snow,"** Beattie writes, "Who expects small things to survive when even the largest get lost? People forget years and remember moments. Seconds and symbols are left to sum things up." This Beattie does admirably.

Carol des Lauriers Cieri, "Short Stories that Catch Moments Seen with an Affectionate Eye," in The Christian Science Monitor, *November 10, 1986, p. 30.*

Mark Silk

" 'Don't think about a cow,' Matt Brinkley said. 'Don't think about a river, don't think about a car, don't think about snow. . . . ' "

So begins [*Where You'll Find Me*], and a fitting beginning it is. For a dozen years now, Beattie has been the mistress of what might be called the tale of impaired consciousness, through which the characters move in a cloud of unknowing, not thinking about, hardly sensible of, what ails them. Non cogito, ergo what?

What ails Vernon and Carol, the middle-aged couple Matt Brinkley is talking to in **"In the White Night,"** is the death of their daughter from leukemia years before. But something new is going on here. Vernon may try hard to think "positively," but he is "never impervious to real pain." Carol is feeling the pain, and she knows whence it comes. After the two have driven home through a thickly falling snow, they lie down in the living room, he on the sofa, she on the floor below. "In the white night world outside, their daughter might be drifting past like an angel, and she would see this tableau, for the second that she hovered, as a necessary small adjustment." Have the inhabitants of Beattieland finally grown up, become aware of themselves, figured out how to cope with the feelings? If so, they've come a long way.

Consider Michael—unemployed, separated from his wife and small daughter, and stoned on hash—in the following passage from **"Fancy Flights,"** one of the first stories Beattie published in the *New Yorker* (in 1974), reprinted in her first collection, ***Distortions.***

> He turns the record off and then is depressed that there is no music playing. He looks over the records, trying to decide. It is hard to decide. He lights his pipe again. Finally, he decides—not on a record but on what to eat: Chunky Pecans. He has no Chunky Pecans, but he can just walk down the road to the store and buy some. He counts his change: eighty cents, including the dime he found in Prudence's underwear drawer. He can buy five Chunky Pecans for that. He feels better when he realizes he can have the Chunky Pecans and he relaxes, lighting his pipe. All his clothes are dirty, so he has begun wearing things that Richard left behind. Today he has on a black shirt that is too tight for him, with a rhinestone-studded peacock on the front. He looks at his sparkling chest and dozes off. When he awakens, he decides to go look for Silas. He sprays deodorant under his arms without taking off the shirt and walks outside, carrying his pipe. A big mistake. If the police stopped to question him and found him with that. . . . He goes back to the

house, puts the pipe on the table, and goes out again.

A more exquisite rendering of drugged-out inanition can scarcely be imagined, and it is as if cannabis had extended its influence over all the stories in the collection: *distortions* indeed, and not in the benign sense of dopey bliss. There is the slovenly woman in **"Downhill"** who is so disoriented that she cannot keep track of how long her husband has been gone, and imagines she is spending her birthday alone. There is the college dropout in **"Hale Hardy and the Amazing Animal Woman"** for whom getting to the Grand Canyon becomes an *idée fixe* (comparable to those munchies for the Chunky Pecans). . . .

Did Beattie mean to condemn these numbed-out lives? Certainly she did no moralizing, and her carefully wrought endings always quivered enigmatically, as if to say, you're not going to catch me making any judgments. (p. 22)

From the fag end of "the sixties," Beattie proceeded in her second collection, ***Secrets and Surprises,*** into that cultural Thermidor known as the Me Decade. The characters give the impression not so much of being stoned as of having washed up on shore—human flotsam miserable about where the tide has deposited them but powerless to move.

"Weekend," a hair-raising story about a philandering, alcoholic professor turned down for tenure, concludes with the female protagonist, the long-suffering woman with whom he lives, leaning her head on his shoulder, "as if he could protect her from the awful things he has wished into being." Nick, in **"A Vintage Thunderbird,"** is a monument to fecklessness—the kind of person who gets mugged in public, who expects his telephone calls to end with people hanging up on him. He remains obsessed with his old girlfriend Karen, and the talisman of his obsession is the Thunderbird convertible she bought when they were in love. In the end it turns out that she, who had appeared to be merely tolerating him out of pity, is no more able to get on with her life than he is with his. The car, however, has been sold, and the best they can do is to think of how to get it back.

If ***Secrets and Surprises*** was filled with longing for relationships that have fallen apart, Beattie's next collection, ***The Burning House,*** seemed to abandon all hope. The title story ends with the husband taking his wife's hand. " 'I'm looking down on all of this from space,' he whispers. 'I'm already gone.' " At the end of **"Afloat,"** the first-person narrator is overwhelmed by "the desire, for one brief minute, simply to get off the earth." The key story may be **"Learning to Fall,"** about an outing to New York City taken by a nameless first-person narrator and the mildly retarded son of her friend Ruth. The boy, Andrew, "likes to do things in private. You can see the disappointment on his face that other people are in the world." Like many another Beattie character, the narrator is in a similar condition. She can't stop herself from calling her sometime lover Ray, but sounds "disappointed, far away" when he says hello. When he shows up she won't take his hand, so he puts it around her shoulder: "No hand-swinging like children—the proper gentleman and the lady out for a stroll. What Ruth has known all along: what will happen can't be stopped. Aim for grace." Grace? The theological resonance is hard to miss. In a predestinarian world where what will be will be, how *can* one aim for such a thing?

That is the question to which Beattie, in [*Where You'll Find Me*], seems to be seeking an affirmative answer. Where else to go but up? In **"Snow,"** a woman looks back fondly on a love affair; longing has softened into nostalgia. **"Skeletons"** ends with one of those hapless Beattie males thinking back to a woman who had been his ideal. In **"Times,"** a woman manages to recapture her childhood love of Christmas at her parents' house. **"Heaven on a Summer Night"** recalls an elderly housekeeper's "life she loved so much." The timeless present of *Distortions* has now given way to the discovery of a usable past. But it is not only the past which holds moments of grace.

In **"Lofty,"** a woman climbs a tree and gazes down at the place where she had lived with her former lover, then descends and—with no hint of ambivalence—throws her arms around her husband. In **"Coney Island,"** a man musters the strength to see his former girlfriend. "Ches," he asks his drinking buddy, "Have you ever been in love?" The "objective" situations of these characters have not changed; there are still the broken marriages, the lost relationships that Beattie's readers have come to expect of her. What is missing is the resignation and despair. At the end of **"High School,"** one friend says to another, "Come on— you can't quit on me now." In **"Spiritus"** and **"Where You'll Find Me,"** flirtations offer the promise that somewhere love is possible, if only over the rainbow.

The results are decidedly uneven. **"Cards,"** a slight account of a pick-up at a fashionable restaurant, is barely a cut above women's magazine fiction. **"Janus,"** an *"idée fixe"* story about a woman's attachment to the ceramic bowl given to her by a former lover, is dull and unconvincing. And the writing at times displays an unaccustomed sloppiness—wasted words, an excessive reliance on abstractions, inept images. "She went to sleep with no more interest in her surroundings than she would have had in an anonymous motel room." The sentence is deflated by that "anonymous." "She was right; parks of any real size rarely had a discernible shape any more." *Any more?*

The broader problem is, in a sense, existential. In her earlier bleakness, Beattie had a way of twisting a knife in the guts of her stories; a grim finality was almost always achieved. But putting across a happier or more open-ended message is trickier business, and she still seems to be struggling to figure out how to manage it. In one case, however, she unquestionably succeeds.

"Summer People" may or may not refer to Hemingway's posthumously published "Nick Adams" story of the same name. Besides sharing a title, both use images of a seal, and both are about Sex and the Man. The Hemingway story recounts how Adams, the young would-be writer, and his beloved Kate make love for the first time (at her insistence) on a blanket in the Michigan woods. Beattie's tale is more complicated. Tom and Jo are vacationing in Vermont with his son by his first marriage. Where Nick is bursting with his limitless future, Tom is disquieted—by an odd stranger who wants to buy his property, by Jo's continual hunger for sex. He can't "imagine caring for anyone more than he cared for her," but is he still in love? If only an author would step in and tell him "what would happen, if he had to try, another time, to love somebody."

The story ends with a pool attendant whistling as he makes "an adjustment to the white metal pole that would hold an umbrella the next day." Just so. Beattie's new world is one where the necessary small adjustments are starting to be made. (pp. 22-3)

Mark Silk, "The Beattietudes," in Boston Review, *Vol. XI, No. 6, December, 1986, pp. 22-3.*

Susan Jaret McKinstry

The act of speaking is an act of choosing speech over silence, deciding where to begin and end. . . . Beattie's female speakers are telling stories with value, self-assertion, and closure. But they puzzle readers because they tell two stories at once: the open story of the objective, detailed present is juxtaposed with a closed story of the subjective past, a story the speaker tries hard not to tell. In the space between these two narratives lies the point of the story.

Seymour Chatman makes a useful distinction between the closed and open narrative, which he calls the resolved plot and the revealed plot:

> In the traditional narrative of resolution, there is a sense of problem solving . . . of a kind of ratiocinative or emotional teleology . . . "What will happen?" is the basic question. In the modern plot of revelation, however, the emphasis is elsewhere, the function of the discourse not to answer that question or even pose it. . . . It is not that events are resolved (happily or tragically) but rather that a state of affairs is revealed.

Unlike Chatman, Beattie does not distinguish between the two plots, but juxtaposes them. Trying to avoid telling the closed story, Beattie's speakers create unintentional resolution as they tell stories of undesired revelation. This narrative reluctance results in a disembodied, objective voice whose analytical language and photographic descriptions—often using free indirect speech rather than a more traditional first or third-person perspective—emphasize the disparity between the emotional past and the seemingly objective present, between the closed story and the open story. In **"Waiting,"** for example, the narrator talks about her husband's leaving in terms of things, not emotions: "He forgot: his big battery lantern and his can opener. He remembered: his tent, the cooler filled with ice, . . . a camera, a suitcase, a fiddle, and a banjo." The narrator herself is omitted from either list. (pp. 111-12)

Carolyn Heilbrun comments that "women, like children, have told stories in which the details are more important than the plot, in which their own action is not possible, not imagined." For Beattie's speakers, action seems impossible because the story has already ended; the details allow the narrator to objectify the present and disguise her emotional response to the past. For example, **"Like Glass"** suspends the narrative present by beginning with a description of an old family photograph of a father, baby and dog that puzzles the narrator because the baby is "gazing into the distance." When her husband explains the picture to her, she says, "I was amazed that I had made a mystery of something that had such a simple answer. It is a picture of a baby looking at its mother." But her original interpretation, based on what is missing in the photograph, reflects the complex juxtaposition of closed and open stories. What is absent may reveal what is present: "The collie is dead. The man with a pompadour . . . was alive, the last time I heard. The baby grew up and became my husband, and now is no longer married to me." Her narrative is motivated by the desire to reopen the past by describing two events—glass broken in celebration and glass broken in anger—and thus link "two things that are similar, although they have nothing in common" in order to create a happy ending. "The point is that broken glass is broken glass" she tells her daughter, but her narrative connects these past events and the present failure of her marriage as resolution and revelation meet. "One mistake and glass shatters," the narrator warns. And the story ends with the question, "What do you do with a shard of sorrow?" What the narrator's dual stories have in common is loss: focusing on details rather than on closure—"What's new with me? My divorce is final"—the narrator still tells us, through the resolved tales she tells her daughter and the revealed tale she tells us, that broken glass is more than broken glass.

Margaret Atwood claims that "these stories are not of suspense but of suspension" [see excerpt in *CLC*, Vol. 40]. I think this effect is caused by the double narrative that juxtaposes open and closed story, revealed and resolved plot. Beattie's stories use images of physical suspension, like characters ascending in glass elevators in **"The Cinderella Waltz,"** treading water in **"Afloat"** in "the desire, for one brief minute, simply to get off the earth," and "looking down . . . from space" in **"The Burning House."** In **"Downhill,"** a story from her first collection [*Distortions*], Beattie's narrator describes this suspension: "As he leads he tilts me back, and suddenly I can't feel the weight of his arms anymore. My body is very heavy and my neck stretches farther and farther back until my body seems to stretch out of the room, passing painlessly through the floor into blackness." This narrative disembodiment is physical, emotional and verbal, creating a subtle interpretive suspension. In **"Gravity,"** the narrator thinks of astronauts and feels "the lightness of a person who isn't being kept in place by gravity, but my weightlessness has been from sadness and fear." Atwood compares a Beattie narrator to a "climber seizing the next rung on the ladder without having any idea of where he's going or wants to go," and in one Beattie story a professor ridicules a student's interpretation by asking her if she would "also climb a ladder using the spaces between rungs" (**"Sunshine and Shadow"**).

In their desire to speak themselves into silence, Beattie's narrators try to erase their individuality by comparisons and doublings. They always fail. "People often mistake us for sisters," brags the narrator in **"Playback,"** but her story is really about their differences: "Simple, fortune-cookie fact: someone loved Holly more than anyone had ever loved me" and "that went a long way toward explaining why we looked so much alike, yet she was more beautiful." In **"Afloat,"** the narrator explains to her stepdaughter "that there should be solidarity between women, but that when you look for a common bond you're really looking for a common denominator, and you can't do that with women." Even so, she claims that "our common denominator is that none of us was married in a church and all of us worried about the results of the blood test we had before we could get a marriage license." "Most of these

things have to do with love, in some odd way" admits the narrator in **"Running Dreams,"** and in these stories love (and its failure) inevitably reinforces individuality rather than commonality.

In Beattie's world of multiple divorce and infidelity, these speakers dream of conventional romance and its happy ending to disguise the failure of love in their individual stories. Repeatedly, Beattie's speakers seek "erotic texts," in Nancy K. Miller's phrase, in which "the heroine" will not just triumph "in some *conventionally* positive way but . . . will transcend the perils of plot with a self-exalting dignity" and marry the man she loves. Repeatedly, Beattie's women fail to find such endings. As Claudine Hermann notes, "If women did not generally experience the love they desire as a repeated impossibility, they would dream about it less. They would dream of other, perhaps more interesting things. . . . Woman's 'daydreaming' is a function of a world in which nothing comes true on her terms." Miller comments that "the daydream, then, is both the stuff of fairy tales ('Someday my prince will come') and their rewriting ('Someday my prince will come, but we will not live happily ever after')." Beattie's narrators dream of the happy ending even as they speak its sad revision in their own lives. They seek fairytales, but "Was my persistence willfulness, or belief in magic?" asks the narrator in **"The Cinderella Waltz."** "Who could really believe that there was some way to find protection in this world—or someone who could offer it?" asks the bereaved mother in **"In the White Night."** "What happened happened at random, and one horrible thing hardly precluded the possibility of others happening next." And the narrator of **"Learning to Fall"** ends her story with a sort of moral: "What will happen can't be stopped. Aim for grace."

Beattie's story **"In the White Night"** ends with this grace. Although the story employs the narrative doubling I have described, it is unusual in Beattie's works because there is a reconciliation between the open and closed stories. Recalling her dead daughter's camera, the central character Carol thinks, "There were two images when you looked through the finder, and you had to make the adjustment yourself so that one superimposed itself upon the other and the figure suddenly leaped into clarity." This struggle to juxtapose separate images describes the technique of the story itself. Trying not "to bring up a sore subject," the story focuses on mundane details as Carol and Vernon return from a party at Matt and Gaye Brinkley's house, yet the resolved story that is revealed is the death of Carol and Vernon's daughter Sharon. Such closure is unchangeable. Yet endings—as a sort of narrative death—become the focus of the story, which includes three resolved anecdotes: Vernon's illness, the death of their dog, "the time when the Christmas tree caught fire, . . . and Vernon pushed her away just in time," and even "the moment when Sharon died . . . (Carol had backed up against the door, for some reason)." Carol's desire to remove herself from Sharon's death fails in both past and present, and the story re-embodies both grieving mother and dead daughter. The narrative juxtaposes that closed story with an open present in a connotative metonymy of desire: "one signified acts as the signifier of another signified not actually named" as the narrative present signifies the unspeakable past.

This linguistic and temporal elision makes absence present. "Don't think about an apple," says Matt to his departing guests, and Carol responds: "Why had Matt conjured up the image of an apple? Now she saw an apple where there was no apple, suspended in midair, transforming the scene in front of her into a silly surrealist painting." The signifier "apple" becomes a disembodied signified, linking word and object, absence and presence. The story follows this pattern throughout, as Carol and Vernon focus on precisely what they are trying to avoid: the past presence that has become present absence, the death of their daughter. The story signifies a transcendence of closure: just as the apple became image, Sharon has become a verbal ghost haunting the text.

Like Beattie's other speakers, Carol tries to refuse the closure of the past through narrative disembodiment. She has to "blink herself into focus" after crying for her daughter Sharon, and she and her husband Vernon try to superimpose the two families to erase the difference between them, closure of death. "Vernon said, quite sincerely, that Matt and Gaye were their alter egos, who absorbed and enacted crises, saving the two of them from having to experience such chaos;" Carol thinks that the husbands "looked like two children," and the daughters "had sat side by side, or kneecap to kneecap, and whispered that way when they were children—a privacy so rushed that it obliterated anything else." Yet the mother, "remembering that scene now, could not think of what passed between Sharon and Becky without thinking of sexual intimacy;" her attempted evasion does not distance Carol from the story, but instead reinforces her loss as the sexuality that created Sharon is displaced onto a past scene and thus effectively disembodied.

Carol's narrative desire to regain the past and thus her daughter recognizes the transformative power of language. As Carol and Vernon drive home through the snowstorm, in the light of a streetlamp "there seemed for a second to be some logic to all the swirling snow. If time itself could only freeze, the snowflakes could become the lacy filigree of a valentine." Through metonymic transformations, the physical world evokes the emotional, the dangerous snow becomes beautiful, transparent lace, and emotion and language meet in a *love letter*. The narrative itself becomes a sort of love letter as Carol's perspective illuminates the double narrative by such transformations.

Carol is faced with three alternatives when Vernon falls asleep on the couch: "The sofa was too narrow to curl up with him. She didn't want to wake him. Neither did she want to go to bed alone." Since nothing is just right, the heroine must make her own ending. Lying down on the floor next to the couch, she wonders: "What would anyone think? She knew the answer to that question, of course"—that their physical positions would be interpreted as drunkenness. But she understands that even common events tell tales, that the everyday is no protection from painful stories: "Such odd things happened. Very few days were like the ones before." "In time," the grief for Sharon and the love for Vernon have both become part of "the inevitable sadness that set in, always unexpectedly but so real that it was met with the instant acceptance one gave to a snowfall." Thus absence meets presence. Like the superimposed images in Sharon's camera, the story focuses. In accepting the story of death that she is really telling, Carol tells herself exactly the ending that she needs to hear: "In the white night world outside, their daughter might be drifting past like an angel, and she would see this tableau, for the second that she hovered, as a necessary small adjustment."

Beattie's narratives surprise us because they demand the sort of double vision I have been describing, and it is no small adjustment. Anatole Broyard claims in *The New York Times* that Beattie causes "the shock of unrecognition": after reading Beattie's stories he admits that "I felt like a psychiatrist at the end of a hard day. I would like to run out and hug the first stodgy person I can find. I am beginning to feel like an alarmed ecologist of personality." But like any good analyst, like any careful reader, we must listen to the tale not being told in order to understand Beattie's narrative acts. Fortunately for readers, Beattie's speakers do not choose silence. (pp. 113-17)

> *Susan Jaret McKinstry, "The Speaking Silence of Ann Beattie's Voice," in* Studies in Short Fiction, *Vol. 24, No. 2, Spring, 1987, pp. 111-17.*

Gene Lyons

Though somewhat shorter than any of her previous novels, *Picturing Will* took Beattie three long and difficult years to write, leaving her both "exhausted and totally fixated. This novel was the single hardest thing I've ever worked on." At one time or another, fifteen chapters were removed and replaced—or were not replaced at all. Major characters and themes also came and went several times. There were one or two occasions, Beattie admits, when she thought about giving up and going on to something else. "You can work on something too long," she acknowledges, "until it gets so subtle it doesn't exist."

But what kept her going was the intense hold the characters and theme had on her imagination. Though the novel is anything but autobiographical—*Picturing Will* tells of the tangled and fragile love between a parent and a child, while Beattie herself has chosen to remain childless—she acknowledges that it contains more of her personal view of the world than any of her previous books. Indeed, much of the material cut from successive versions of the story consisted of long, nineteenth-century-style narrative preambles and didactic harangues. "The book started as a series of objective, essaylike ruminations about childhood," Beattie says.

> But I was finally unwilling to go on the record. I think twenty years ago I might have been that stupid. Now I think that telling readers that something is the case—that this is absolutely how life works—is as presumptuous as cornering them at a cocktail party and boring them to death talking about plastics. I'm that skeptical now. I lack the audacity to write a book that instructs anybody about anything.

In form, *Picturing Will* resembles a series of chronologically arranged snapshots in a family album. A broken family, that is, making the significance of certain details early in the story significant only in light of later events. Divided into three sections simply entitled "Mother," "Father," and "Child," the novel begins with the same deceptively simple, seemingly offhand narrative style that has led many of Beattie's critics—not to mention, one suspects, a lot of ordinary readers—to identify the author with her characters.

Mother's name is Jody. Apart from the fact that her ex-husband Wayne left her one bright summer morning before she and baby Will had opened their eyes for the day, that is pretty much all we know of her at first. Jody's last name, maiden name, city or state of origin, educational history, religious background—in short, all of the defining details that realistic novelists use to place their characters in the world—remain simply unstated. While Beattie's refusal to supply these kinds of homely details can be irritating, it also lends an air of intensity to those things we *do* know. Jody, we are told, married Wayne almost blindly:

> Without knowing much about him—without even knowing, until they applied for a marriage license, that he had been married before, without ever pausing to consider how strange it was that he had no friends and that his own brother was mystified that he had been asked to attend the wedding, without any knowledge beyond what she saw in his eyes and what she felt when she touched his body—she was willing to leave behind worried friends, argue with and finally stop speaking to her parents, and view her own ambition with skepticism.

Following her husband's desertion, Jody ends up in a "small Southern town she had driven to almost randomly, and she had gone from being a clerk in a camera store to working as a much-in-demand wedding photographer." She has an unhappily married friend whose son Wag (short for Wagoner) is little Will's best buddy. They play in the sandbox with their GI Joes while their mothers, neither of whom knows what to do about her own life, take turns solving each other's problems. Jody thinks Mary Vickers should leave her drunken insurance agent husband, while Mary cannot imagine why on earth Jody hesitates to marry her lover Mel, move to Manhattan, and begin a glamorous career as a serious photographer. Mel has the connections she needs to get started. Mary herself would go in a minute.

What Beattie offers readers, in short, is a situation out of a hundred "women's" novels stripped to bare bone: a man incapable of feeling and a plucky heroine making her way, living by her wits, and seeking True Love. But as readers get to know Jody a bit better, a series of small-scale moral shocks begin to accumulate—none definitive, but subtle enough to establish an odd foreboding. Take, for example, Jody's habit of mailing off to Wayne at odd intervals manila envelopes containing bits and pieces of her and her son's lives; pharmacy receipts, notes from Will's teacher, parking tickets, offers to purchase time shares in Florida condos, that kind of thing. Once or twice, sure. But Jody keeps it up for years. "This is what the careful kisses of years ago . . . had become: a lick along a line of glue, and a flap folded and pressured in place with the strength of one person strangling another."

Similarly, Jody understands that she can keep putting Mel off on the question of marriage so long as she keeps putting out.

> That was . . . part of the trick: to get as close physically as the other person wanted. To jump into the tub when they were showering, pull cold cham-

pagne from under the bed, announce on the way to dinner with another couple that you were not wearing underwear. If you came through physically, men would give you a lot of time to decide whether you would marry them, because some part of them would foolishly think that you had already chosen.

It's a shrewd discovery all right, albeit a cold-hearted one. But who will pay the consequences of Jody's having made it? Expect no editorials from Beattie. At least implicitly, her manner seems to suggest, readers who don't feel a chill wouldn't benefit from the sermon anyway. And the sorrowful truth in Beattie's fictive world is that there seem to be an irreducible number of people who can't and won't feel it—and never will. In her own generation as in every other since the beginning of time, it's not a sociological truth, it's a human one.

By the time Jody leaps out of her car on Halloween night to begin snapping photographs of her costumed friends as they examine the carcass of a deer that the horrified Mary has accidentally run down with her car, it begins to look as if poor Wayne may have gotten out just in time. Maybe Jody can conquer the Manhattan art world after all; she's certainly ruthless enough.

But where does this leave little Will? In alternating chapters throughout the novel, an unidentified voice gives expression to every parent's darkest fears. The message of every self-help book on child rearing, every talk-show psychologist, every pediatrician

> is always to change doubt to certainty and *proceed*. . . . Check the baby-sitter's references. Lock the cabinet that contains the cleaning products below the sink. Regular visits to the doctor. Two security blankets, so one can be washed. . . . Do everything right, all the time, and the child will prosper. It's as simple as that, except for fate, luck, heredity, chance, the astrological sign under which he was born, his order of birth, his first encounter with evil, the girl who jilts him in spite of his excellent qualities, the war that is being fought when he is a young man, the drugs he may try once or too many times. . . .

Except, that is, for life.

In "Father," a couple of years have passed. Readers learn that Jody, now consigned to the background, has indeed married Mel and gone to New York. Her brilliant photographs of Mary Vickers's highway accident earned her a prominent spot in Lord Haverford's trendy art gallery and helped launch a brilliant career. Left to the care of his stepfather Mel and "Have-abud"—as his mother's "manic mentor" is known to all—Will is on his way to visit Wayne in Florida. Also to see, the little boy secretly hopes more than anything, his "blood brother" Wag, who lives nearby. Along for the ride is an older boy named Spencer—the curiously androgynous offspring of an earlier discovery of Haveabud's. And an oddly disorienting, finally terrifying ride it turns out to be.

Where the novel's first section was subtly subversive of its characters, "Father" turns savagely so. The doting, seemingly unsuspecting Mel and his trusting charge are two innocents turned loose in a world of moral monsters: the energetic Haveabud, a charming con man spouting art cant he doesn't understand and hardly pretends to believe; not to mention Wayne himself, a self-pitying whiner on the lookout for an easy score or a cheap thrill, but just handsome and glib enough to keep fooling women like his doting wife Corky. With a child of their own, Corky imagines, Wayne would settle down to be a devoted father. She means to be kind to Will, Corky does. To show Wayne what a wonderful mother she could be. But Wayne's got other things on his mind, and dramatic events intervene before she gets the chance.

But no plot summary can do justice to the disquieting reverberations that *Picturing Will* sets going in the reader's mind. The adjective *haunting*—though normally used by reviewers to describe melodramatic fiction that is anything but—comes to mind as the only one that applies to Ann Beattie's work at its best. The novel's final chapter, a kind of coda narrated by Will himself some twenty years after the disastrous trip to Florida, comes as a startling counterpoint to all that has gone before. Nothing seems to have worked out exactly as the reader, and certainly the characters, might have expected or wished. As in life, fate and justice fail to coincide. Yet in another sense the prayers of the anonymous parental voice in the alternating chapters, now identified, have been answered: Will has not only survived his childhood, although not all of the other characters have survived with him, but has forgiven and continued to love those who inflicted it upon him. (pp. 106, 108, 110)

Talking with Beattie, it's easy to get the impression that in addition to her intrinsic fascination with her story, she wrote *Picturing Will* almost to confound those critics who persist in seeing her as a spokeswoman for her generation—a label she abhors. The novel has nothing to do with the sixties generation's coming of age, the hypocrisy of the counterculture, or any of the trendy topics her previous books have been assumed to be about. It is a novel about love and betrayal, holding and letting go, art and obsession, loving and letting go, folly and pity, willpower and fate.

Above all, *Picturing Will* makes vivid the powerlessness and vulnerability of children against the obsessions of the adults in their lives. So does she mean to suggest that artists like her and her husband, painter Lincoln Perry, ought to avoid having children of their own? "I think," Beattie says carefully, "that the pairing of one's occupation and preoccupation can be dangerous. I think the stakes are very high when that is the case. There are great disadvantages to children." She pauses. "But once again, I was unwilling to go on the record. If I'd come to any succinct conclusions about that, I guess I'd have written an essay."

Beattie trusts her readers to understand things like that, even when professional critics do not. Her experience has been that they do. (p. 110)

> *Gene Lyons, in a review of "Picturing Will,"*
> *in* Vogue, *Vol. 180, No. 1, January, 1990, pp.*
> *106, 108, 110.*

T. Coraghessan Boyle

Ann Beattie is a master of indirection. Her stories are propelled not so much by event as by the accumulation of the details that build a life as surely as the tumble and drift of sediment builds shale or sandstone. Pay attention to the small things, she tells us. All the rest will fall in place. In

the novels, the technique does not always work with the grace that illuminates the stories, but here, in her fourth novel and eighth work of fiction, it positively shines. *Picturing Will* is her best novel since *Chilly Scenes of Winter* in 1976, and its depth and movement are a revelation.

The eponymous Will, a 5-year-old abandoned by his father, is at the center of the novel, which is an extended meditation on generation, parenthood and the way in which individual lives are shaped by experience. Will's mother, Jody, is a photographer with higher aspirations compelled to earn a living by documenting weddings and other small-town social gatherings. The irony of her position is not lost on her, and she transforms the seemingly routine moments of the nuptial ceremony with a unique and wistful vision—a vision that will eventually make her the darling of the New York gallery scene. In fact, Jody reflects a good deal on art and photography, and one of the book's many joys is the insight into the creative process Ms. Beattie allows us through the eyes of her heroine. (p. 1)

To picture Will is to capture the world around him, the world of his mother, of his father, of his stepfather-to-be, and of all the characters who crowd his life and the lives of the supporting cast. This is the strategy of the novel, which focuses on Will's crucial sixth year, a year in which his mother is surprised by fame and he loses one father only to gain another. Ms. Beattie gives us multiple points of view in order to help us picture Will, and she divides the book into three sections—"Mother," "Father," "Child"—as a way of examining each of these interlocking relationships. The first two sections are of nearly equal length; the last is a six-page coda in which Will, 20 years older and a father himself, takes his place in the hierarchy of generations.

The first section is Jody's. We see her some four years after she has been deserted by Will's father, Wayne, as she struggles to raise Will and make a career for herself in Charlottesville, Va. She is aided and abetted by Mel, the sort of fairy-tale prince who inhabits so much of Ann Beattie's fiction. Like Frank, the herb-growing lawyer of her story **"Where You'll Find Me,"** or Noel, the sweet hippie of **"Vermont,"** Mel is nurturing and supportive, if not particularly exciting: "Mel was nobody's fool and came close to being ideal. He was a more patient lover than Wayne and found Will's laughter contagious. He loved her and had let it be known that he was very sad that she had not yet chosen to marry him and move to New York." Through Mel, Jody is able to establish an equilibrium that will enable her work to blossom—and further, it is through Mel's connections in the art world that she first meets Haveabud, the starmaker who will back her first show in New York.

If Mel seems somewhat bland in the opening pages, it is perhaps by design, the author's way of masking his true importance in the scheme of Will's life. For to picture Will is to allow for surprise, and Ms. Beattie purposely keeps the reader off balance by shifting focus and constantly rearranging the pieces of the puzzle. The moment of transcendence, the moment when the pieces cohere, reveals Mel as the heart and soul of the book.

There is a trick here, and it works beautifully. Interwoven with the narrative is a series of unascribed italicized sections that speak directly to the reader in the intimate way of a diary or monologue. The language is inspired, rhapsodic and true, and the voice speaks to us of the connection between parent and child, of the child's needs and fears and the parent's responsibilities. We assume that these are Jody's thoughts, but in the book's climactic pages, when Wayne has finally and irrevocably absolved himself of any interest in Will, we discover that we have been reading Mel's journal all along, that it is Mel who has been the truest parent, the wisest and most loving. In the end, he leaves the journal for Will, that he might profit from its advice.

The second section, "Father," seems at first to belong to Wayne, the most vividly realized character in the book, but in fact it points to the ultimate triumph of Mel. It is the story of Will's journey to Florida, accompanied by Mel, Haveabud and Haveabud's 7-year-old ward, for a visit with his father. Again, through the use of multiple points of view, Ms. Beattie gives us a portrait of Wayne in composite, and we come to see just how selfish, violent and self-deluding he is, and how little he cares for Will. When Will arrives, his father is not there to greet him—Wayne is preoccupied with thoughts of a fling he is having with a young woman tourist and leaves Will to his third wife, Corky, who becomes, for a brief period, yet another of Will's trial parents. And as Will prepares to leave, prematurely, Wayne is absent again—this time at the behest of the local police. Will peers out the window to see his father handcuffed and led away, out of his life for good. Then he returns to Jody, now living in New York. And to Mel. (pp. 1, 33)

The final section, "Child," turns the screw one more time. Not only do we discover that Mel has been the rock of Will's life, we begin to understand that Jody has largely abrogated responsibility for him. She has sacrificed Will to her career—and this is in no way more powerfully revealed than when she refuses to hear a negative word spoken against Haveabud, who, in one of the book's more arresting moments, exposes the young Will to a disturbing homoerotic scene. Now, 20 years later, Wayne has vanished from Will's life, and Jody has grown increasingly distant. But Mel is there, always there, and in the final chapter he gives Will his journal, passing the torch to the next generation. It is a beautiful, affirmative moment: the traditional nuclear family may have disintegrated, but we learn to live perhaps with a different and no less meaningful notion of what family is. How do you raise a child? How do you protect him from the hurts of the world? How do you finally compose the picture of him? . . .

In *Picturing Will,* Ann Beattie has created a surprising, lyrical and deeply affecting work that is both radical in its movement and perfectly attuned to its telling. Her style has never been better suited to a longer work, and she writes out of a wisdom and maturity that are timeless. But look to the details, the small things. They are everything here. (p. 33)

> *T. Coraghessan Boyle, "Who is the Truest Parent?" in* The New York Times Book Review, *January 7, 1990, pp. 1, 33.*

Otto Friedrich

Ann Beattie first became celebrated 15 years ago as the young chronicler of what has been called the Woodstock generation, the Aquarius generation and even the Beattie generation. Vaguely disaffected and disconnected people drifted in and out of other people's cars and beds, looking for something but not sure what, then finding something else but not sure why. And all this was reported in a coolly detached and often witty style, which made bizarre events seem perfectly natural.

[In *Picturing Will,* these] unhappy people are now entering middle age, as is Beattie, 42, and they seem to have learned virtually nothing about anything. Wayne, who "had always been *about* to create a life for himself," earns a living of sorts by rewiring lamps. He leaves no note when he walks out on his wife Jody and their son Will. Jody drives "almost randomly" to some unnamed Southern town, gets a job as a clerk in a camera store, then becomes a successful wedding photographer. New characters keep appearing for a scene or two, then disappearing, as though this were not Beattie's fourth novel but her fifth book of short stories.

The only really likable characters are the son Will, his best friend Wag and another youth named Spencer, who is obsessed with the disappearance of the dinosaurs. "In the boy's bedroom were hundreds of dinosaur models . . . An inflated Rhamphorhynchus dangled from the ceiling fixture. ('It means "prow beak," ' Spencer said.)" Spencer is showing his dinosaurs to a hungry-eyed art-gallery owner named Haveabud, who, in a truly sinister scene watched by Will, seduces him during a trip to Florida. There is quite a bit of sex in Beattieland, most of it adulterous and joyless.

Like one of those ominously quiet sequences in a Hitchcock film, Beattie's low-key style tends to create the tension of expectation. For example: "Corky pushed the door open and turned and looked at Wayne, sitting on the step, holding a Schlitz. It was the last drink he would have before his life changed." But all that happens is that Wayne gets arrested on a false charge of possessing cocaine. We never do find out what became of him except, in an epilogue, that he is now living in Mexico City. . . .

Beattie once told an interviewer, "I've never written anything that I knew the ending of . . . I wonder if there *are* novelists who feel they know how to write novels. I wonder if this knowledge exists."

It is possible that she was just being disingenuous, but it is also possible that the drawbacks to improvisation are somewhat greater than she realizes.

> *Otto Friedrich, "Beattieland," in* Time, *New York, Vol. 135, No. 4, January 22, 1990, p. 68.*

FURTHER READING

Gerlach, John. "Through 'The Octascope': A View of Ann

Beattie." *Studies in Short Fiction* 17, No. 4 (Fall 1980): 489-94.

    Analyses the short story "The Octascope" as representative of Beattie's fictional style and content.

Murphy, Christina. *Ann Beattie.* Boston: G. K. Hall, 1986, 138p.

    Only full-length critical overview of Beattie's work.

Opperman, Harry and Christina Murphy. "Ann Beattie (1947-): A Checklist." *Bulletin of Bibliography* 44, No. 2 (June 1987): 111-18.

    Lists both primary and secondary materials.

Saul Bellow

1915-

Canadian-born American novelist, short story writer, dramatist, essayist, lecturer, editor, and translator.

The recipient of the 1976 Nobel Prize in Literature, Bellow is among the most celebrated authors of the twentieth century. He addresses the question of what it is to be human in an increasingly impersonal and mechanistic world. Writing in a humorous, anecdotal style that combines exalted meditation and modern vernacular, Bellow often depicts introspective individuals who suffer a conflict between Old World and New World values while trying to understand their personal anxieties and aspirations. In a period when many writers insist on the impossibility of human communication or heroism, Bellow has been commended for his humanistic celebration of sensitive individuals. While critical debate surrounds most features of Bellow's works, particularly his intentional redundancy and constrained plots, he has received three National Book Awards and a Pulitzer Prize, and is widely regarded as among the most original stylists of the twentieth-century. According to Irving Howe, he has evolved "the first major new style in American prose fiction since those of Hemingway and Faulkner."

In their many books and essays on Bellow's works, critics often concentrate on two aspects of Bellow's fiction: his skillfully crafted protagonists, who collectively exemplify the "Bellow hero," and his expansive prose style. Bellow's typical protagonist, who is generally a male, urbanite Jewish intellectual, was described by the Nobel Committee as a man "who keeps trying to find a foothold during his wanderings in our tottering world, one who can never relinquish his faith that the value of life depends on its dignity, not its success." In developing his characters Bellow emphasizes dialogue and interior monologue, and his prose style features sudden flashes of wit and philosophical epigrams. As his protagonists speak to themselves and to others, the reader is drawn into their struggles with self and society. Bellow's earliest novels, *Dangling Man* and *The Victim,* are written in a disciplined, realistic style that he later rejected as constraining. In *Dangling Man,* a young man named Joseph anticipates being drafted into the United States Army. When his induction is delayed by bureaucratic ineptitude, Joseph attempts to decide how to structure his life. When he is finally inducted, he is relieved from the oppressive responsibility of choosing his own future. *The Victim* focuses on Ava Leventhal, an editor who attends a job interview arranged for him by an acquaintance, Kirby Allbee. When he insults the interviewer, Allbee loses his job and becomes increasingly unbalanced, demanding that Levanthal make restitution.

During the 1950s, Bellow developed a lively prose style that could accomodate comic misadventures and philosophical digression, and began to write picaresque narratives that employ larger-than-life protagonists and various rhetorical elements. *The Adventures of Augie March,* for example, features an extroverted, exuberant character who believes that a "man's character is his fate." Disre-

garding his brother's materialistic values, Augie undertakes a personal odyssey and becomes involved in a variety of illegal ventures before learning to channel his energies toward positive ends. Bellow returned to his early formal style in his novella *Seize the Day,* a highly successful work that focuses on Tommy Wilhelm, a middle-aged man who aspired to become rich and famous but who has failed in both business and human relationships. By coming to terms with his fear of mortality, however—a prominent theme in Bellow's fiction—Wilhelm gains a better understanding of himself and an appreciation of others. In his next novel, *Henderson the Rain King,* Bellow diverges from his usual subject matter to focus on an arrogant Anglo-Saxon millionaire who travels to Africa to confront his anomie and fear of death, a trip which some critics interpret as a journey into his subconscious. Seeking transcendance by asserting his superiority over the natives, Henderson learns to surrender his excessive egoism in order to experience love.

With *Herzog,* Bellow successfully fused the formal realism of his early works with the vitality of his picaresque novels of the 1950s. Like the typical Bellow hero, Herzog is an animated but tormented Jewish intellectual who has difficulty maintaining human relationships, especially with women. In response to his wife's decision to divorce him for his best friend, Herzog retreats from what he views as the corrupting influence of the urban environment. Although he initially becomes absorbed in pointless intellectual exercises, such as mentally composing letters to his wife and friend in which he justifies himself and denies any personal responsibility, Herzog is finally able to remain responsive to himself and to the world. *Herzog,* which garnered Bellow a wide popular and scholarly readership, won praise for its exploration of various Western intellectual traditions and for its evocation of poignant events and colorful minor characters.

Mr. Sammler's Planet has often been identified as Bellow's most pessimistic novel due to its protagonist's melancholy musings on the passing of Western culture. Mr. Sammler, an old man who has experienced the promises and horrors of twentieth-century life, offers an extensive critique of modern values and speculates on the future after being confronted by a pickpocket he has observed on a bus. Although many critics disagreed as to whether Mr. Sammler succeeds as a perceptive commentator on contemporary existence, the character is often regarded as one of Bellow's most fully realized protagonists. *Humboldt's Gift,* for which Bellow received the Pulitzer Prize, centers on the conflict between materialistic values and the claims of art and high culture. The protagonist, Charles Citrine, is a successful writer who questions the worth of artistic values in modern American society after enduring exhaustive encounters with divorce lawyers, criminals, artists, and other representative figures of contemporary urban life. He also recalls his friendship with the flamboyant artist Humboldt Fleischer, a composite of several American writers who despaired in their inability to reconcile their artistic ideals with the indifference and materialism of American society. Citrine finally concludes that he can maintain artistic order by dealing with the complexities of life through ironic comic detachment. Many critics have contended that Citrine's beliefs reflect those of Bellow himself and that Humboldt is modeled on Bellow's friend, poet Delmore Schwartz.

In *The Dean's December,* Bellow more directly attacks negative social forces that challenge human dignity. Set in depressed areas of Chicago and Bucharest, Romania, this novel focuses on Albert Corde, a respected journalist who returns to academic life to revive his love of high culture. In the course of the book, Corde admonishes politicians, liberal intellectuals, journalists, and bureaucrats in both democratic and communist nations for failing to maintain humanistic values. Critics often disagree as to whether the novel's many autobiographical elements are as skillfully employed as in Bellow's previous fiction. *More Die of Heartbreak,* set in a midwestern city reminiscent of Chicago, focuses on Benn Crader, a contemplative botanist engaged to the wealthy daughter of an avaricious surgeon who seeks to use Benn to undermine Benn's Uncle Vilitzer, a corrupt political boss. The novel is related by Benn's nephew, Kenneth Trachtenberg, a professor of Russian literature who draws parallels between the Russian revolution and the present state of America while ruminating on his own failed love relationships. Fearful of the possibility that "more die of heartbreak than of radiation," Benn finally deserts his bride-to-be. Although some critics found the novel overlong, disingenuous, or misogynistic, others concurred with Terrence Rafferty: "[Bel-

low] has always been a smart, likable trickster, even when, as in this new novel, he seems to take forever working his little surprises free of his sleeve. For better or worse, that's how he is."

Bellow has also written several works of short fiction. In the pieces collected in *Mosby's Memoirs and Other Stories* and *Him with His Foot in His Mouth and Other Stories,* Bellow depicts sensitive ordinary people and intellectuals who struggle to maintain personal dignity and to reaffirm humanistic faith. Bellow's novella *A Theft* focuses on Clara Velde, a woman raised in a strict religious area of Indiana who has risen to become "the czarina of fashion writing" in the publishing industry of New York City. Intelligent yet vulnerable, Clara lives with her fourth husband while maintaining a relationship with Ithiel Regler, an erratic companion who once bought her an emerald ring as a symbol of their love. When Clara's ring is stolen, she finds her stability shattered. Most critics found the novella's development hasty and Clara's ultimate self-fulfillment willed rather than inherently realized. However, John Banville commented: "[A Theft] has the coherence and tension of a furled flower. It is packed with colour and wit, and a fervent gaiety." The unnamed narrator of a second novella, *The Bellarosa Connection,* is a Russian Jew whose belief in the importance of memory in defining identity led him to found the Mnemosyne Institute of Philadelphia, where executives and politicians are trained in the art of total recall. The narrator relates the story of a Jewish man named Harry Fonstein, who was rescued from Hitler's Nazi regime during World War II by the "Bellarosa Society," a front for an entertainer named Billy Rose who wished to remain anonymous. Years later, Harry's wife attempts to blackmail Billy into seeing her dispirited husband and to acknowledge his responsibility for her husband's present life.

(See also *CLC,* Vols. 1, 2, 3, 6, 8, 10, 13, 15, 25, 33, 34; *Contemporary Authors,* Vols. 5-8, rev. ed.; *Contemporary Authors Bibliographical Series,* Vol. 1; *Dictionary of Literary Biography,* Vols. 2, 28; *Dictionary of Literary Biography Yearbook: 1982; Dictionary of Literary Biography Documentary Series,* Vol. 3.; and *Concise Dictionary of American Literary Biography: The New Consciousness, 1941-1968.*)

PRINCIPAL WORKS

Novels

Dangling Man 1944
The Victim 1947
The Adventures of Augie March 1953
Henderson the Rain King 1959
Herzog 1964
The Last Analysis 1965
Mr. Sammler's Planet 1970
Humboldt's Gift 1975
The Dean's December 1982
More Die of Heartbreak 1987

Short fiction Collections

Mosby's Memoirs and Other Stories 1968
Him with His Foot in His Mouth and Other Stories 1984
The Bellarosa Connection (novella) 1989

A Theft (novella) 1989

PLAYS

The Last Analysis 1964
*Under the Weather 1966; also produced as *The Bellow
     Plays,* 1966

OTHER

**Seize the Day 1956
Great Jewish Short Stories [editor] 1963
Recent American Fiction: A Lecture 1963
*Like You're Nobody: The Letters of Louis Gallo to Bellow,
     1961-1962, Plus Oedipus-Schmoedipus, The Story
     That Started It All* 1966
The Portable Bellow 1974
Nobel Lecture 1976
To Jerusalem and Back: A Personal Account (memoirs)
     1976

*Includes the one-act plays *Out from Under, A Wen,* and *Orange
Soufflé.*

**Contains two short stories, a novella, and a one-act play, *The
Wrecker.*

Terrence Rafferty

Saul Bellow's new novel, **More Die of Heartbreak,** about
the affectionate bond between an unworldly Midwestern
botanist and his equally abstracted nephew, might have
been conceived as a test of our family feeling for the author
himself. It's like an impossibly long letter from a relative
to whom not very much has happened in the years since
we last heard from him. Both the familiarity and the un-
eventfulness are a relief—no change, no catastrophes—
and we're pleased enough to accept the trade-off of being
a little bored. The first third of **More Die of Heartbreak**
is restless, eccentric, and discursive in Bellow's usual way,
and really phenomenally dull. The book picks up speed
when, after a hundred pages of chatty exposition, the plot
kicks in at last, but to get us even that far Bellow needs
to call on every bit of the good will he has built up over
the last forty years. We listen for echoes of the voice we
know intimately, and hear them everywhere, in a lighter
tone, like whispered, jokey asides overheard at a party.
The dawdling, anecdotal style tells us that nothing new or
especially serious (by Bellow standards) is going on here.
This is **Herzog** without real despair; a tiny moon of **Mr.
Sammler's Planet**; **Humboldt's Gift** in a Cracker Jack box.
In one of Bellow's recent stories, an elderly intellectual
gives a talk on Marx's "Eighteenth Brumaire of Louis Bo-
naparte," the great essay that begins with the thesis that
all the major events and characters of history occur twice,
first as tragedy and then as farce; **More Die of Heartbreak** demonstrates, probably consciously, that novelists'
themes can obey the same law.

The action—such as it is—of **More Die of Heartbreak**
takes place in a nameless Midwestern city that is explicitly
not Chicago, though it shares at least a couple of key features with Bellow's home city: a major university and rampant civic corruption. This is Bellow's ironic version of the
never-never lands of Shakespeare's late philosophical
comedies—an island of professors and crooks dead center
in the vast American nowhere, a windy city of the mind.
His narrator, a young Russian-literature scholar named
Kenneth Trachtenberg, blows punishing gusts of theory,
history (global and personal), and physical detail at us,
pausing only occasionally to catch his breath and apolo-
gize for his inability to edit himself. Even his apologies
turn into mini-dissertations:

> If you venture to think in America, you also feel an
> obligation to provide a historical sketch to go with
> it, to authenticate or legitimize your thoughts. So
> it's one moment of flashing insight and then a quar-
> ter of an hour of pedantry and tiresome elabora-
> tion—academic gabble. . . . One has to feel sorry
> for people in such an explanatory bind. Or else (a
> better alternative) one can develop an eye for the
> comical side of this.

One of Bellow's previous narrators put it more bluntly:
"As usual, I gave more information than my questioner
had any use for, using every occasion to transmit my sense
of life. My father before me also did this. Such a habit can
be irritating." The chummy self-consciousness of these
passages shouldn't deceive us: in Bellow's recent work,
such sheepish digressions are often the clearest statements
of his themes. By far the best way to read **More Die of
Heartbreak** is as a comedy of overelaboration: America
imagined as an exhausting freewheeling seminar, *A Night
at the University* with a pedantic Groucho presiding.

That's the idea, anyway—not an entirely fresh one for Bellow. He has always been interested in how American artists and intellectuals tie themselves up, has always mar-
velled at the ingenuity with which they put the mind-
forged cuffs on themselves. The unfortunate professor
Moses Herzog, deranged by his betrayal at the hands of
his wife and his best friend [in **Herzog**], deals with his pain
by cranking his highly developed mental machinery into
overdrive: he spends his days in a fury of pointless intellection, composing (in his head) elaborate self-justifying letters, which function less as a means of problem-solving
than as a kind of mild anesthesia. (Ideas are his endor-
phins.) The poet Von Humboldt Fleisher wastes his life in
scheming for recognition and security [in **Humboldt's
Gift**], cajoling American society for the stature he feels is
due him, and dies paranoid and destitute. His chronicler,
Charles Citrine, a lesser writer who has lucked into some
comfort and success, winds up taking refuge from small-
time hoodlums, savage divorce courts, and guilt about
Humboldt's end by holing up in a crummy Spanish *pen-
sión* and immersing himself in the cracker-barrel mysticism of Rudolf Steiner. . . . In Bellow's America, artists
and intellectuals just can't win; in a sense, they don't even
belong in the game. The comedy, for Bellow, is how his
characters' high-powered cerebral equipment, designed to
transcend the imposing machine of American business
and law, gets tangled up in the works anyway—how
brains developed for lofty philosophical detachment struggle to reverse their hard-won evolution, to recover the simple animal cunning needed to disengage themselves from
the culture's traps. The pure products of America may, as
William Carlos Williams wrote, go crazy, but in Bellow's
fiction the impure products—those who, by virtue of their
immigrant ancestry or their education in the exalted tradi-

tions of European culture (or both), try to live in the New World with Old World values—go crazier.

More Die of Heartbreak takes this notion about as far as it can go. Both Kenneth, an American who was born and brought up in Paris but came to the United States because it's "where the action is," and his uncle, Benn Crader, who zips around the globe attending botanical conferences, are helpless American innocents in the guise of citizens of the world. They're most comfortable up where the air is thin: their lengthy talks have the unreal, immobilized quality of conversations between passengers in an airplane cruising high above the clouds. And their verbosity is inexhaustible. As if to emphasize that these are men of reflection, not action, Bellow has constructed his novel so that almost nothing is presented to us directly: most of the book's crucial events take place off-page, and are reported in the course of conversations between Kenneth and his uncle or in the form of Kenneth's philosophical recaps. It's as antidramatic as characters reciting their lines from garbage cans in a Beckett play (Benn and Ken would make fine names for a Beckett couple), and Bellow's characters, clever and voluble as they are, never manage to move from their appointed spots—perhaps because, as Kenneth remarks with his usual self-importance, "the quality people are always knee-deep in the garbage of 'personal life.'" Since his picaresques of the fifties—the lumbering *Adventures of Augie March* and the nimbler, more exuberant *Henderson the Rain King*—Bellow has turned his attention to characters who seem more sedentary with every book. His fiction in the last three decades traces the decline of the brash assurance that informed Augie March's opening statement: "I am an American, Chicago born—Chicago, that somber city—and go at things as I have taught myself, free-style, and will make the record in my own way." Kenneth and Benn, a pair of jabbering, irresolute dreamers from a city that never existed, look like the end of the line.

Bellow has certainly developed his eye for the comical side of his characters' various binds—rather a cold eye, it appears at first. The garbage of Benn's personal life—his disastrous late marriage to young, ambitious Matilda Layamon, whose *haut bourgeois* family manipulates him like a puppet—buries him completely. He's a helpless schlemiel, no match for the forces determined to make him act against his gentle nature. (The Layamons want him to threaten a lawsuit against his own uncle, Harold Vilitzer—a crooked old machine boss, now dying and politically embattled, who gypped Benn's family out of their fair share of the city's most valuable piece of real estate.) Benn has the kinds of problems that Bellow's heroes often have, but his spirit seems smaller, his resources more limited; he's the purest victim Bellow has created since *Seize the Day*'s Tommy Wilhelm, thirty years ago, and Wilhelm had the advantage of a noble, eloquent third-person narration to give weight and dignity to his trials. Here the story is told by ridiculous Kenneth, a man in his mid-thirties who lives in a college-dorm room and imagines himself and his mild uncle as great world-historical minds, agents of a "desperately needed human turning point." It's impossible to take anything he says very seriously—at least until near the end, when, after unloading a particularly grandiose set of *pensées* about Eros in America, he admits,

Of course, we all have these thoughts today instead

of prayers. And we think these thoughts are serious and we take pride in our ability to think, to elaborate ideas, so we go round and round in consciousness like this. However, they don't get us anywhere; our speculations are like a stationary bicycle. . . . These proliferating thoughts have more affinity to insomnia than to mental progress. Oscillations of the mental substance is what they are, everincreasing jitters.

The amazing thing about *More Die of Heartbreak* is that Bellow is willing to put before us this twitching mind, in full spasm, purely for its own sake. (Though Kenneth's ruminations often serve as formidable weapons against the reader's insomnia, that's probably not what they're meant to do.)

Bellow tries our patience with these heads-in-the-clouds characters, dares us to find them mere buffoons—and then dares us to transcend our irritation and honor the good in them, too. Kenneth, that intellectual wind machine, blows more smoke than a music-video director, but, when it clears, something solid remains in view: the strong natural kinship of the uncle and the nephew. The depth of their attachment catches us off guard; this isn't the sort of relationship that's often celebrated in literature, so we read most of the novel expecting a bitter falling-out or, at least, a revelation of dark ulterior motives. Early on, Kenneth warns, "I grant you the difficulty of making a case for enduring human bonds. Everybody fears being suckered through the affections, although cynical people still adopt a lip-service attitude towards them." Instead of using this statement in the usual cunning literary way, as a setup for Kenneth's disillusionment, Bellow fools us by playing it straight: he tries, amid all the farce complications and philosophical bluster, to make the difficult case for the simpler feelings.

The emergence of these basic (in Bellow's terms, European) values of familial love from such a dense, compulsively detailed (i.e., American) verbal texture is the novel's most striking effect. And there's a nice irony in the way Benn and Kenneth finally make their escape from the predatory Layamons: it's their emotional, not their intellectual, capital that earns their passage out. But does Bellow have to put *all* their academic baggage on display, just for the comic effect of watching them jettison it when they're forced to run for their lives? It's like those little ironic flourishes that thrillers and adventure movies favor: the gold dust scatters in the wind, the suitcase full of stolen money pops open at the airport, and speech gives way to the laughter of nature or fate. The schemers in these movies never do wind up with the loot; the scholars in *More Die of Heartbreak* leave all their painstakingly assembled intellectual possessions piled high on the runway when they take flight, in their different ways, from their unmanageable lives; and Bellow, for all his intelligence and audacity, doesn't quite get away with the job he's planned here, either. He outsmarts himself. He's put so much energy and ingenuity into the diversionary action that when he finally gets his hands on the prize it's anticlimactic: it looks tiny, a little unreal, maybe not worth the feverish intricacy of the effort.

More Die of Heartbreak dies, at last, from overkill. Its quirky characters and its family themes belong with the short stories and novellas of Bellow's 1984 collection, *Him with His Foot in His Mouth,* where the small, intimate emotional truths that Bellow is searching for these days don't have to struggle so hard to assert themselves. For what he's after, a quick strike like the thirty-two-page classic **"A Silver Dish"** is more effective. That story, about a middle-aged Chicago businessman remembering his father's theft of an ornate dish from the living room of a very rich and proper Swedish woman, says as much about Europe and America as anything Bellow has written, and as much about the nature of "enduring human bonds." Its hero eulogizes his father like this: "You could never pin down that self-willed man. When he was ready to make his move, he made it—always on his own terms. And always, always, something up his sleeve. That was how he was." It's a eulogy, in a way, for Augie March's free-style, for the impure, lawless energy of this country's finest confidence men and artists. It expresses, too, the qualities of Saul Bellow that have claimed our affection over the years: his deviousness and transparency, his powerful will and emotional delicacy, his Old World values and New World irreverence. He has always been a smart, likable trickster, even when, as in this new novel, he seems to take forever working his little surprises free of his sleeve. For better or worse, that's how he is. (pp. 89-91)

Terrence Rafferty, "Hearts and Minds," in *The New Yorker, Vol. LXIII, No. 22, July 20, 1987, pp. 89-91.*

Leon Wieseltier

Nobody seems to have noticed that Saul Bellow's new novel really is Saul Bellow's new novel. There is something in [**More Die of Heartbreak**] for which Bellow's previous books have not quite prepared us. That something is Benno Crader, the novel's hero. Crader will be experienced by most readers and writers of American fiction as an embarrassment: he lives metaphysically. Not intellectually; metaphysically. Kenneth Trachtenberg, on the other hand, lives intellectually. He is Crader's nephew, and the narrator of Crader's ordeal in America. Trachtenberg is not new; he is another of Bellow's pathologically reflective men, the latest incarnation of Bellow's impatience with the failure of ideas to perfect life.

The critical fact about **More Die of Heartbreak**—its argument, really—is the difference between Benno Crader and Kenneth Trachtenberg. It is a difference that Terrence Rafferty, in an uncomprehending review in the *New Yorker* [see excerpt above], fails to remark upon. "These heads-in-the-clouds characters," he calls Crader and Trachtenberg, "a pair of jabbering, irresolute dreamers." It is true that neither of them is a man of affairs, what Trachtenberg calls "full-blooded men," and also that both of them are academics. (It is true, too, that Bellow's book is too much talk and too little action; the traditionalist has come to confuse discourse with narrative almost as completely as the *nouveaux* he loves to hate.)

But Trachtenberg is a literary historian and Crader is a botanist. Trachtenberg is the voluble votary of art and politics, a common idolater of history. Crader is stiller, more concentrated, more universal, a fundamental man. He studies plants not as a professor, but as a man consecrated to the search for a higher significance. Trachtenberg is a mind. Crader is a soul. But Rafferty (who writes of "the cracker-barrel mysticism of Rudolph Steiner") thinks that

Crader's "spirit seems smaller, his resources more limited" than Bellow's other heroes. The poverty of urbanity is plain again.

If Crader is "smaller," may the good Lord shrink us all. Trachtenberg marvels at what he calls his uncle's "magics." "I approach my uncle," he begins, "with the thought that what everybody today requires is a fresh mode of experience." A fine late-20th-century thought. Unlike Trachtenberg, however, Crader "was not worried about a fresh mode of experience because he always interpreted experience for himself." Crader is a "Citizen of Eternity." His science is a technique of spirituality. Empirical observation spills over into poetic intuition; the visible conducts to the invisible. Crader is not another grant grabber and conference creeper. There is Romanticism in his laboratory.

The leap of Bellow's novel consists partly in the enchantment of its hero. Crader is a Goethean figure. In 1790 Goethe published *The Metamorphosis of Plants;* the object of his investigations was the *Urpflänze,* the inner form that animates the phenomena beneath his gaze. "To recognize living forms as such, to see in context their visible and tangible parts, to perceive them as manifestations of something within, and then to master them in their wholeness through a concrete vision": these were Goethe's aims as a scientist. Or as he put it elsewhere, "to liberate the phenomena once and for all from the gloom of the empirico-mechanico-dogmatic torture chamber." This is Crader's spirit (and the "cracker-barrel" spirit of Steiner) exactly. Crader is a hero of consciousness, but not the *Partisan Review* kind. He has made it past history to life.

Crader's achievement is a wonder to his nephew, not least because of the success of his resistance to his surroundings. His serenity, after all, and his personal acquaintance with the patterns and the forces of organic life have been achieved smack in the middle of that great empirico-mechanico-dogmatic torture chamber that is the modern American city—in this instance, in a boisterous, corrupt, power-soaked, frantically hungry, Chicago-like city in the Midwest. The plot of **More Die of Heartbreak** is simply (perhaps a little too simply) the undoing of the mystic by the city.

Crader finds himself tricked into marriage by the father of his betrothed. Crafty Dr. Layamon has correctly concluded that Crader is in a position to recover vast sums of money from his own uncle, the political boss Harold Vilitzer, who stung Crader's family in a real estate swindle many years ago. But it is not only Crader's innocence that the perfidious Layamons play upon. It is to their advantage, too, that Crader is in need of love. The empyrean that Crader inhabits does not include the experience of women. He is sexually without confidence and without judgment. And he is lonely. For the lesser but cleverer people around him, Crader is an easy hit. Gimpel the botanist.

The helplessness of the other-worldly before the this-worldly is Bellow's theme. His reverence for Crader is a little at odds with the robustness with which he describes Crader's humiliation. He displays his characteristic delight in the details of ordinary depredations and unexceptional defilements, his proud understanding of the way the world works. Here is the old Bellow, straddling streets and books, head in the clouds *and* feet on the ground, a fiend of irony. But this Bellow could not have imagined Crader. Crader is the creation of a man who wants to turn his back, who has concluded that the way the world works is often the way the soul fails.

Bellow has never precisely sided with reality. He has insisted only that it is foolish not to understand reality, and that intellectuals are therefore the most regular of fools. His new novel seems premised, however, upon the conviction that reality contaminates, that the understanding of it may be a form of complicity with it, that there may be a spiritual price to pay for the closeness required for comprehension. The author of *Herzog* was content to be smart. The author of *More Die of Heartbreak* is not. The character of Crader represents more than the mere criticism of criticism.

If Bellow is more than Trachtenberg, though, he is less than Crader. His novel is inflamed by the possibility of extrication, but it narrates the near-impossibility of extrication. Crader is successfully duped, and barely gets away. This is a work of spleen. It gives a soul, and then gives it away. For a hundred pages or so, Crader is pictured in all his purity; and then he is left to the lions. Trachtenberg tells the tale of Crader's obstacles, of the conditions of his life that capture his vision and begin to lay him low. Finally the novel is an inventory of impediments to spiritual life.

The first of the impediments is America. Though Bellow's novel is brimming with American energies and American excesses, it is, in a sense, spiritually anti-American. America is presented as a disperser of the spirit, a commotion of deceits and distractions, a shallow, crowded, broken-down, tawdry shrine to money and power. Again, there is Bellow's admiration for the very fierceness of America's faults, for the great thrill of the American secular. "The U.S.A. is where the action is," Trachtenberg announces; and Bellow is almost vain about his alertness to the "action." But this time the "action" fills Bellow with contempt, because he is measuring its consequences not upon a false inner life, but upon a true one.

Of course Bellow is right: this is an essentially profane and profaning society. (The development of its religions is the proof.) Yet Bellow does not seem quite aware that he has produced a vivacious indictment of America. Instead he misplaces his anger. His book is sprinkled, for example, with an unworthy scorn for what he calls "the Third World." It is saddening to see Bellow become a party to the fashionable neo-colonialist rant. How exactly do the troubles of "the Third World" (there is no such place, except in the demonological schemes of frightened Western intellectuals) interfere with an American's search for meaning? What trips Crader up are the political and social practices of the United States. The inadequacy is native. Indeed, if Bellow wishes to measure societies by the support they provide for metaphysical exertion, he will have to concede that there are regions of "the Third World" in which a sublime being like Crader will be more at home than in Crader's country.

Then there is the intellectual impediment. In his foreword to Allan Bloom's *The Closing of the American Mind,* Bellow records his complaint about the American intellectual

in a way that bears directly upon his new novel. Writing of *Herzog,* he observes that it

was meant to be a comic novel: a Ph.D. from a good American university falls apart when his wife leaves him for another man. . . . What is he to do in this moment of crisis, pull Aristotle or Spinoza from the shelf and storm through the pages looking for consolation and advice? The stricken man, as he tries to put himself together again, interpret his experience, make sense of life, becomes clearly aware of the preposterousness of such an effort. . . . I meant the novel to show how little strength "higher education" had to offer a troubled man. In the end he is aware that he has *no* education in the conduct of life.

Crader's nephew may as well be Herzog's son: Trachtenberg, too, is a man lousy with culture who is regularly bested by the mess of human intimacy. "There are times," Bellow writes, "when I enjoy making fun of the educated American." *More Die of Heartbreak* is another of those times. (pp. 36-7)

Looking back on *Herzog,* however, Bellow notes that

there is one point at which, assisted by his comic sense, he is able to hold fast. In the greatest confusion there is still an open channel to the soul. It may be difficult to find because by midlife it is overgrown, and some of the wildest thickets surrounding it grow out of what we describe as our education. But the channel is always there, and it is our business to keep it open, to have access to the deepest part of ourselves—to that part of us which is conscious of a higher consciousness, by means of which we make final judgments and put everything together. The independence of this consciousness, which has the strength to be immune to the noise of history and the distractions of our immediate surroundings, is what the life struggle is all about. The soul has to find and hold its ground against hostile forces, sometimes embodied in ideas which frequently deny its very existence, and which indeed often seem to be trying to annul it altogether.

These wise and beautiful sentences capture the objective of Bellow's book perfectly. This time his comedy of thinkers is mounted not in the name of the mind, but in the name of the soul. This time the distinction that matters is not between true culture and false culture, but between culture and nature; not between true positions and false positions, but between positions and essences. Bellow has discerned the far-reaching difference between intellectual life and contemplative life. And also that there are significant elements of a modern intellectual's education that must be unlearned, if a beginning is to be made. The adjective "restless" may not be the highest compliment we can pay to the noun "mind." Of course, science is Crader's good fortune; his "magics" might have been harder to come by in the wastes of critical discourse.

There is still another impediment to the American Contemplative in Bellow's account. Generally, it is what he refers to violently as "the garbage of 'personal life.'" "The private life is almost always a banquet of sores with a garnish of trivialities or downright trash." Specifically, it is women. *More Die of Heartbreak* is unrelenting in its disgust for women, who are portrayed as if their reason for being is the frustration of the better selves of men. Matilda, Treckie, Caroline, Della: they are all curses in makeup, utterly ridiculous figures, plotting predators, exploiters of desire. (There is also one Dita, with whom Trachtenberg finds respite, who is exempt from the great excoriation; but she is also exempt from sexual interest.) At one point Bellow's horror of women is promoted into a theory of history: "The East has the ordeal of privation, the West has the ordeal of desire"—sort of a cross between Strindberg and Solzhenitsyn.

More Die of Heartbreak is a sorry tale of male self-pity. (The title itself is rather shocking in its unBellovian bathos.) Once again a man has mistaken the sexual incompetence of men for the sexual competence of women. Crader and Trachtenberg are both erotically hapless; and the excellence of their intellect is adduced as a kind of proof that their failure in love cannot be their own fault. The roughness of Bellow's attitude mars the nobility of his purpose.

It is probably the case that the contemplative life is not possible without some leaving of the world. But the world must be left in peace. If it is left in rancor, it is not left at all. You cannot leave something that you continue to hate. Your hatred merely reproduces the relationship. Bellow's predicament seems to be that he has been given the gift of contemplation, but not the gift of calm. Instead, he seems shackled by rage, diminished by resentment. He is a prisoner of his wounds, with an eye on the promised land.

At the end of the novel, at the very end, Crader does get away. He saves himself, he "rises from the ashes," by rashly setting out for Antarctica, where he will study lichens and live in night and in ice. He will recover his morphological armor. He will abandon affect to save his soul. Crader's flight to Antarctica, the land of light covered in darkness, is moving; the link between inner beauty and outer barrenness is a feature of real renunciation.

But Crader's flight is also striking for its artificiality. It is virtually a flight from the novel itself. The ending does not "work," for the hundreds of pages of disappointment and disillusion that precede Crader's redemption have taught that it cannot happen. It is, in the strict sense, unaccountable. When it does happen, we have reached not only the limits of credibility, but in a way the limits of the form as well. Transcendence cannot be a part of a plot, since it marks the end of plot itself. Thus we hear nothing of Crader in Antarctica, just as we heard nothing of Crader in his laboratory, studying his specimens, saving the appearances. Crader is discussed, but he is not shown. For Crader is, in his laboratory, a creature of certainty, and it may be that the novel was not designed for certainty. "The novel is the epic of a world that has been abandoned by God," wrote Lukács.

If not as a man, then certainly as a novelist, Bellow seems trapped. He is fixed upon final truths, but he commands a form that does not tolerate salvation. (Compare the last chapter of *Crime and Punishment* with the rest of the novel; you will pine for the contradictions.) The novel can point, but it cannot follow. And the temptation to surrender skepticism anyway must be hard to resist, particularly for a writer who has raised skepticism into art. Bellow is resisting. (pp. 37-8)

Leon Wieseltier, "Soul and Form," in The New Republic, *Vol. 197, No. 9, August 31, 1987, pp. 36-8.*

Craig Raine

[In his earliest novels], *The Victim* and *Dangling Man,* Bellow is paying his dues to Modernism, serving his time. 'Ironic tales of empty lives', they are crafted, careful and slightly comatose—except for one page of *Dangling Man* in which Bellow stumbles on what is to be his subject. That is, autobiography, the long clear packed morning of life, evoked in street-wise, high-minded, headlong prose. The hero is cleaning his wife's shoes:

> it was doing something I had done as a child. In Montreal, on such afternoons as this, I often asked permission to spread a paper on the sitting-room floor and shine all the shoes in the house, including Aunt Dina's with their long tongues and scores of eyelets. When I thrust my arm into one of her shoes it reached well above the elbow and I could feel the brush against my arm through the soft leather.

When Bellow reaches 'their long tongues', the prose suddenly stirs and Joseph is taken back to St Dominique Street and a series of memories whose vividness is their only justification, ending with: 'two quarrelling drunkards, one of whom walked away bleeding, drops falling from his head like the first slow drops of a heavy rain in summer, a crooked line of drops left on the pavement as he walked'. Cleaning shoes: for any admirer of Bellow, this moment links directly with the end of *Herzog,* where the style is less constrained, more ejaculatory and excitable:

> Moses could remember a time when Willie, too, had been demonstrative, passionate, explosive, given to bursts of rage, flinging objects to the ground. Just a moment—what was it, now, that he had thrown down? A brush! That was it! The broad old Russian shoe brush. Will slammed it to the floor so hard the veneer backing fell off, and beneath were the stitches, ancient waxed thread, maybe even sinew.

This little miracle of particularity, and many others like it, is what we read Bellow for. As Herzog puts it, 'he sometimes imagined he was an industry that manufactured personal history.' This personal history is the placenta which has nourished so many of Bellow's novels, keeping up an endless supply of rich details. Nothing is too small for him to notice. In *Humboldt's Gift,* it might be a clothesline, 'old and dark grey': 'It had burst open and was giving up its white pith.' Or it might be a locker room, where 'hair pieces like Skye terriers waited for their masters'; or a courtroom, where a lawyer called Cannibal Pinsker has 'a large yellow cravat that lay on his shirt like a cheese omelette'; or an old man's trouser fly, three feet long. As a writer, Bellow sees. He sees the bare toes of Pierre Thaxter 'pressed together like Smyrna figs'. But what he *has* seen, in the past, is, if anything, more vivid: at the Division Street Turkish baths, everything remains as it was, and Franush

> crawls up like a red salamander with a stick to tip the latch of the furnace, which is too hot to touch, and then on all fours, with testicles swinging on a long sinew and the clean anus staring out, he backs away groping for the bucket. He pitches in the water and the boulders flash and sizzle.

Bellow is not one of those purely imaginative writers like Golding or Ian McEwan who invent copiously and logically from first premises. You cannot imagine him wondering what it is like to be an ape married to a young woman writer who is having trouble with her second novel after the success of the first. Or wondering what might transpire if a group of boys was placed on an island without adult supervision. Bellow uses experience, his own life. And so has gone a stage beyond Solotaroff. No surprise, then, to see *The Adventures of Augie March* cited as a key text in 'Silence, Exile and Cunning'—cited because it embraced American experience instead of taking up an alienated posture. Something in Solotaroff's analysis makes this seem like a tactic, almost a lucky break, a trend that he, Solotaroff, didn't spot early enough. Certainly, unlike Solotaroff, virtually everything of Bellow's life in its formative years suddenly gets into his writing with *The Adventures of Augie March.* There and in the best subsequent fiction, Bellow's writing is earthed in the American city. St Dominique Street, Napoleon Street, Jefferson Street— Bellow gives his imaginative source several different names, but it is always the street where he lives: 'here was a wider range of feelings than he had ever again been able to find . . . What was wrong with Napoleon Street? thought Herzog. All he ever wanted was there.'

With this subject comes a distinctively American voice, capable of using a slang word like 'slugger' as well as 'fancy' words like 'tergiversate'. But the Ivy League intonation was always there in Bellow. The slang arrives with *Augie March,* and although the full title acknowledges Twain's *The Adventures of Huckleberry Finn,* it is a reasonable supposition that Salinger's *The Catcher in the Rye* gave Bellow the example he needed of a fluent and formidable vernacular. Certainly, it is difficult to read a sentence like 'But I enjoyed Caroline's company, I have to admit' without being reminded of Salinger even now. And to say that this is merely American is to miss the point. Before Salinger, it was American, but it was not American literature.

In *Herzog,* there is a heart-stopping description of Valentine Gersbach losing his leg in a childhood accident:

> 'Seven years old, in Saratoga Springs, running after the balloon man; he blew his little *fifel.* When I took that short cut through the freight yards, crawling under the cars. Lucky the brakeman found me as soon as the wheel took off my leg. Wrapped me in his coat and rushed me to the hospital. When I came to, my nose was bleeding. Alone in the room . . . I leaned over,' Gersbach went on, as if relating a miracle. 'A drop of blood fell on the floor, and as it splashed I saw a little mouse under the bed who seemed to be staring at the splash. It backed away, it moved its tail and whiskers. And the room was just full of bright sunlight . . . It was a little world underneath the bed. Then I realised that my leg was gone.

This brilliantly haphazard, grammatically spontaneous narrative, by the man who has stolen Herzog's wife, receives this accolade from Herzog: 'each man has his own batch of poems.' And these poems of experience are repeated, recited by everyone, again and again: 'there were stories about himself, too, that Moses had told a hundred times, so he couldn't complain of Gersbach's repetitiveness.' This weakness is a trait which Madeleine, his wife, satirises: 'Yes, I know, your darling mother wore flour sacks.' And his mistress, Ramona, is familiar with Gers-

bach's leg-action: 'As you told me. Like a gondolier.' As Herzog, so Bellow. The novels have their share of repetition. Augie and Herzog both remember having their hair washed with a bar of Castile soap—by a mother who made sheets out of Ceresota sacks. In *Dangling Man,* 'I warmed myself at a salamander flaming in an oil drum near a newsstand.' In *Augie March,* 'down the cold alleys flames tore from the salamander cans of people selling chestnuts.' In *Augie March,* his girlfriend's father wears 'a white drill suit and a helmet with a nipple at the top'. In *Henderson the Rain King,* Henderson has a 'helmet with its nipple at the top'. (pp. 3, 5)

In fact, though they are quite numerous, these repetitions can usually be discounted because Bellow's memory-hoard is so fecund. There is always plenty that is new, like 'the long hard rays of tendons' on the backs of Mrs Renling's hands, or Gorman the gangster putting away his gun: 'he was reaching inside his sleeve with a lifted shoulder, almost like a woman pulling up an inside strap.' Likewise the drawbacks of Bellow's fast-talking prose, which, though generally effective, can sometimes produce redundancies worthy of a freak show: 'Wilhelm let out a long, hard breath and raised the brows of his round and somewhat circular eyes.' Yet, set beside Bellow's wonderful dialogue, glittering with redundancy and anacoluthon, does the odd failure matter? Isn't it a necessary risk which can produce this: 'I know about suffering—we're on the same identical network'; or 'Daisy didn't married yet?' Yes, we say, yes.

And then again, we say no. The new novel, *More Die of Heartbreak,* is ruined by repetitions and echoes of earlier work, since there is scarcely any redeeming specificity to compensate, nor any form to speak of. It is a dismally thin performance. The characters are the merest tokens: Benn Crader is an Arnoldian representative of pure culture, a natural contemplative, whose botanical interests are pure rather than applied science; his fate is to be mangled in the machinery of modern sexual desire. In physical terms, he has a humped back like a wing-case and eyes that look like the mathematical symbol for infinity. Well, they would, wouldn't they? The central ideas are laughable and garnished with reading which, in other Bellow novels, might generate strenuous discussion, but here amounts to little more than perfunctory citations from a Russian literature binge. Kenneth Trachtenberg, the narrator, teaches Russian literature—hence the garland of dusty immortelles he hangs on his cousin, Fishl: 'he was flavoured with essences belonging to that period of Rosanov, Meyerhold, the late Chekhov, Mandelstam and Bely.' With as little potential meaning, you might say that someone now was flavoured with the essences belonging to, for example, Peter Ackroyd, Anita Brookner, William Boyd, Anthony Burgess and Peter Hall. This is typical, alas.

First repetition: Kenneth has left Paris, even though his father has promised to introduce him to the 'agent who had forced Tsvetaeva's husband to work for the GPU'. Kenneth prefers the Midwest because 'that's where the action is now—the real modern action.' In *The Dean's December,* Albert Corde had written 'a few pieces on the poetess Tsvetaeva as she was remembered by the Russian colony in Paris. How her husband, whom she loved deeply, became a member of the GPU and was forced to take part in killings'. Corde, too, left Paris for the Midwest because 'America is where the real action is.' Kenneth, however, has an additional motive: he wants to remain in close contact with his uncle, Benn Crader, the world-class botanist, who wishes to remarry—or, in the Swedenborgian lingo of the novel, desires an exchange of souls in love. This, of course, involves sexual needs and, in that sphere, Crader has to compete in a world where women have a composite ideal of the male:

> candid women will tell you, I'd like some of this and some of that—a little Muhammad Ali for straight sex, some Kissinger for savvy, Cary Grant for looks, Jack Nicholson for entertainment, plus André Malraux or some Jew for brains. Commonest fantasy there is.

So common, in fact, that it has already been given an outing in *Mr Sammler's Planet:*

> He fetched back, for example, a statement by Angela Gruner, blurted out after several drinks when she was laughing, gay, and evidently feeling free (to the point of brutality) with old Uncle Sammler. 'A Jew brain, a black cock, a Nordic beauty,' she had said, 'is what a woman wants.' Putting together the ideal man.

Of course, in these trying times, there are external considerations, too. Aids, for instance, though that is 'an elaborate terrifying organic figure' (apparently) for some inner spiritual malaise. In the same way, lead poisoning in *The Dean's December* 'stands for something else that we all sense'. As for sex, it is, for most people, a cure for all problems: 'they turn to sex as the analgesic.' In *The Dean's December,* Corde's sister makes 'an aspirin marriage'. All the same, at first it seems possible that Crader will make it work with his much younger, beautiful bride, Matilda Layamon. After all, perhaps Crader's insight into plants can be transferred to human beings:

> he was wrapped in nature. The whole vegetable kingdom was his garment—his robe, his coat—and that to me meant fundamental liberty from low-grade human meanness, it meant universality. Still, Uncle's garment was incomplete. It didn't quite button.

Neither did the garment of Von Humboldt Fleisher in *Humboldt's Gift* and look what happened to him—heart failure in a flophouse. 'Humboldt wanted to drape the world in radiance, but he didn't have enough material. His attempt ended at the belly. Below hung the shaggy nudity we know so well.' Shaggy nudity is a feature of *More Die of Heartbreak,* where we learn that 'this literalness, from a sexual standpoint, is lethal. When it becomes a matter of limbs, members and organs, Eros faces annihilation.' Not a lot has changed, in that case, from *The Dean's December:* there 'the horror is in the literalness—the genital literalness of the delusion. That's what gives the curse its finality. The literalness of bodies and their members—outsides without insides.' 'Insides', in both novels, means the soul, rather than viscera. Maybe Crader can escape literalness, since he is 'an outstanding "noticer" (there is such a type).' The parenthesis can be confirmed by anyone who has read *The Dean's December* because there Corde is just such a type: 'He looked out, noticing. What a man he was for noticing! Continually attentive to his surroundings.' Either character, given this faculty, might have noticed that Bellow's use of Baron Hulot, from *Cousine*

Bette, had already been used as an instance of indestructible desire in *The Dean's December* and *Humboldt's Gift.* Or that Forster's aphorism 'How do I know what I think till I see what I say?' had already appeared (uncredited) in *Humboldt's Gift,* admittedly in a different form: 'Still, I don't seem to know what I think till I see what I say.' An outstanding noticer might have noticed, too, that Dita Schwartz's 'hive of bandages', following her facial surgery, is a repeat from *Augie March,* where a brawler appears in court wearing 'a bloody beehive of bandages, totter-headed'.

Dita Schwartz, incidentally, shows how inattentive and incompetent Bellow has become in this novel: she is twice mentioned by name before she is properly introduced. On page 113, Kenneth's mother refers enigmatically to 'a young woman named Dita Schwartz', who is 'evidently glad to listen' to Kenneth for the sake of her education. On page 121, Crader refers to 'your friend Dita Schwartz'. But it isn't until page 173 that the reader is given any data to go with this name. Her role in the novel is to be the ideal woman, with the drawback of a poor complexion. In every way except the physical, she is perfect for Kenneth. She admires his Russian name-dropping and, as only a course student can, she audits him. He, however, is still infatuated with Treckie, the mother of his daughter, but not his wife. Kenneth is considerate and she prefers to be brutalised in bed and, as a result, has shins which are bruised like the markings on peacock feathers. As Herzog remarks, 'nothing can be done about the sexual preferences of women. That's ancient wisdom. Nor of men.' Kenneth is fixated by Treckie's body which is that of a child-woman.

Crader, on the other hand, has married a woman, who, though beautiful, doesn't suit him. Matilda's shoulders are too wide and her breasts are too far apart. Lest these seem trivial considerations, little imperfections that a mature personality might come to love, Bellow is forced to draft in the Swedenborgian system of correspondences. If everything is a sign, these imperfections presumably show that Matilda, for all her beauty, is too like her father—is, in point of fact, a bloke. How else can one explain her father's revelation that, when she was born, it was difficult to tell what sex she was? Crader is in no doubt: physically, she's a woman. But, we are meant to infer, only venture beyond the literal and she's a bloke, for Crader much like Norman Bates masquerading as his mother in *Psycho,* a film which Crader finds worryingly pertinent.

By now you may have some notion of how wacky *More Die of Heartbreak* is. Common sense seems to have deserted Bellow utterly. A strip show in Kyoto provokes Kenneth to reflect, as the women dilate themselves manually: 'Miss Osaka and Miss Nara put it in front of you, as literal as it was possible to be, and the more literal it was, the more mystery there seemed to be in it . . . All these botanists, engineers, inventors of miraculous visual instruments from electron microsopes to equipment that sent back pictures of the moons of Saturn, cared for nothing but these slow openings.' Bellow's conclusion seems to be that the precious life of the mind is ultimately in thrall to an orifice. Which is another version of Kenneth's belief that 'the quality people are always knee-deep in the garbage of "personal life."' Now this nexus of assertions is comic. I don't myself find it surprising that engineers, botanists, inventors of electron microscopes, or (for that matter) winners of the Nobel Prize for Literature, should take a look if a woman chooses to open her vagina for them. Bellow appears to have an exaggerated idea of the dignity of his own mind.

The central theme of the novel is equally nutty in its presentation. It is that more die of heartbreak than are killed by radiation. In the East, there are prison sentences, camps, mental and physical abuse; in Africa, there is famine; in the West, there is heartbreak. Bellow allows his characters to ironise the dichotomy, but it is clear that the purpose of the novel is ultimately to endorse it. Thus, Kenneth's mother, working with refugees in Somalia, herself a refugee from her husband's philandering, parodies the position by setting her husband against the work-camp at Kolyma: 'suddenly Dad was paraded in front of us with all his chicks in various stages of undress. *That* was an ordeal!' The truth is that suffering is manifold and it is very stupid to make meaningless comparisons. Why say more die of heartbreak than of radiation when there are no statistics for either? Unless, of course, you want to trail your coat, or take off into the unprovable—the latter being an area of which Bellow has always been over-fond. Sometimes the famous resonance just sounds hollow, and it can be irritating when he pretends to be the last believer in the soul.

One of the worst features of *More Die of Heartbreak* is its gabbiness, which is not unrelated to the rhetorical sauce he ladles out so generously. There is built into the novel a kind of negative commentary of asides and reminders which supply reasons why no one should bother to read it: 'I will remember that I am not here to lecture on history but to relate the strange turns in the life of my uncle Benn'; 'so it's one moment of flashing insight and then a quarter of an hour of pedantry and tiresome elaboration'; 'but let me not be sidetracked again'; 'excuse the language; I'm in a hurry and I can't stop to pick and choose among the available terms.' This digressive garrulity, this formlessness, one might argue, is of no importance in Bellow because his work has always repudiated form. In a *Paris Review* interview, he said:

> I could not, with such an instrument as I developed in the first two books, express a variety of things I knew intimately. Those books, though useful, did not give me a form in which I felt comfortable. A writer should be able to express himself easily, naturally, copiously in a form which frees his mind, his energies. Why should he hobble himself with formalities? With a borrowed sensibility? With the desire to be correct?

In *Augie March*, Bellow's greatest novel, form is accordingly dismissed on the first page. The narrator declares for spontaneity: he will 'go at things as I have taught myself, free-style, and will make the record in my own way: first to knock, first admitted.' And yet, in the midst of Dickensian detail ('loud-breathing and wind-breaking', Winnie the dog 'lay near the old lady's stool on a cushion embroidered with a Berber aiming a rifle at a lion'), there is a formal polarity to which everything refers. On the one hand, there is the wised-up pragmatic-realist stance of Grandma Lausch, which is responsible for the disposing of the retarded Georgie into a home: 'And now he realised that we would leave him and he began to do with his soul, that is, to let out his moan, worse for us than tears, though many

grades below the pitch of weeping. Then Mama slumped down and gave in utterly. It was when she had the bristles of his special head between her hands and was kissing him that she began to cry.' On the other hand, there are the impracticalities of pure feeling, of idealism, which at first are embodied by brother Simon, on whom '*Tom Brown's Schooldays* for many years had an influence we were not in a position to afford.' Even the eagle in Mexico conforms to the pattern—by turning out, after all, to be less than one hundred per cent ruthless; 'well, it was hard to take from wild nature, that there should be humanity mixed with it.' Augie himself is poised between the two poles, though there is no doubt that his final destination will be in the camp of those with feelings.

In *Humboldt's Gift,* the polarity around which the novel is organised is 'rot or burn.' Humboldt, Cantabile, are the obvious exemplars of frenetic activity to which Citrine is attracted, but Citrine's brother, Ulick, an ostensible digression, is also part of the pattern:

> You know what I found the other day? The deed to the family burial plots in Waldheim. There are two graves left. You wouldn't want to buy mine, would you? I'm not going to lie around. I'm having myself cremated. I need action. I'd rather go into the atmosphere. Look for me in the weather reports.

Here, Bellow has literalised Humboldt's philosophy of life:

> if life is not intoxicating, it's nothing. Here it's burn or rot. The USA is a romantic country. If you want to be sober, Charlie, it's only because you're a maverick and you'll try anything.

At the centre of *Humboldt's Gift* is a long exposition of, in effect, Lambert Strether's advice to Little Bilham in *The Ambassadors* ('Live as much as you can, young man. It's a mistake not to'):

> Or as William James put it, human beings really lived when they lived at the top of their energies. Something like the *Wille zur Macht*. Suppose then you began with the proposition that boredom was a kind of pain caused by unused powers, the pain of wasted possibilities or talents, and was accompanied by expectations of the optimum utilisation of capacities.

As you might by now expect, in *More Die of Heartbreak,* this last idea is brought out of retirement. The sexually hyper-active Rudi Trachtenberg, we are told, 'is responding to a talent, and a talent will cause your death if you try to hide it.' Notice how the idea is now overstated, how a possibly flashing insight has become a merely flashy insight.

This is a haunted novel. The dim ghosts of better books are everywhere. For Picasso, the ultimate failure was not to copy others, but to copy himself. *More Die of Heartbreak* is pure Parnassian. At its end, Crader, his marriage in ruins, flees to the frozen wastes of the symbolic Arctic, and it is *The Dean's December* which can supply the most lucid gloss on his behaviour: 'these badgering perplexities, intricacies of equilibrium, sick hopes, riddling evils, sadistic calculations—you might do worse than to return to that strict zero-blue and simple ice.' (pp. 5-6)

In one important particular, Bellow hasn't copied himself. His real territory—Napoleon Street, for short—has been pushed out of the picture. When Benn Crader, like any Bellow protagonist, wants to reminisce about his youth on Jefferson Street (now replaced by the Ecliptic Circle Electronic Tower), he is discouraged by his bride: 'she doesn't care for that far-away-and-long-ago stuff'; 'she doesn't care for your imaginative background music.' There is a great deal of intuition of souls in this book, which perhaps provides one with an excuse for looking at *More Die of Heartbreak* in the same way oneself. Superficially, the novel exactly fits Citrine's description of 'the insignificant Picasso sculpture with its struts and its sheet metal, no wings, no victory, only a token, a reminder, only the *idea* of a work of art'. This latest effort is without a soul, mainly because it is all about the soul, the soul and ideas. Real life is somewhere else—as it must be for Bellow after the elevation of the Nobel Prize. Unconsciously, he has dramatised his predicament in Uncle Benn Crader, who stands in his rich duplex, feeling uncomfortable, miles above Jefferson Street, listening to the moans of the sycamores far below. Only Uncle Harold Vilitzer comes alive—not smoking, but mashing up twenty cigars a day, still tough in temperament, but physically as hollow as a wicker basket. 'Only the pacemaker unit under his shirt had any weight.' Not that Vilitzer compares with Lollie Fewter, a minor character in *Augie March* on whom the young Bellow lavished his brimming gifts: 'young Lollie Fewter who was fresh up from the coal fields, that girl with her green eyes from which she didn't try to keep the hotness, and her freckled bust presented to the gathering of men she came among with her waxing rags and the soft shake of her gait'. The whole of *More Die of Heartbreak* isn't worth that one hectic, ungrammatical, accurate sentence, utterly unforced in its plenitude. (p. 6)

Craig Raine, "Soul Bellow," in London Review of Books, *Vol. 9, No. 20, November 12, 1987, pp. 3, 5-6.*

John Banville

At the very start of [*A Theft*] the author blazons the name of his heroine—Clara Velde—like a declaration of intent. Bellow always opens bravely, plunging his readers into the midst of things, and if the bravery sometimes strikes us as mere bravado (as for example, with Augie March's 'I am an American . . . '), the headlong stride of the style, its weight and energy, sweep us forward unresisting. Here, however, the clarion call of Ms Velde's name gives pause. It is very American, yet it is not quite contemporary. We seem to hear in it an echo of an earlier New York scene, of the jewelled and grandly brocaded America of the late 19th century. In short, the reigning spirit here might be that of Henry James.

This is a surprise. It is a long time, forty years or so, since Saul Bellow abandoned the Flaubertian tradition and decided to break out, to let rip ('I am an American . . . '). The result was an extraordinary gain in vigour. What other novelist in our time has produced work to equal in sheer strength such books as *The Adventures of Augie March,* or *Herzog,* or (his masterpiece, for my money) *Humboldt's Gift?* In art, of course, every gain entails a loss: in cutting the 'European' link in favour of being an *echt* American, Bellow risked surrendering to formlessness. His novels tend to go at full tilt, like a man in a heavy overcoat thrashing hip-deep through water, until they run out of energy and just stop, winded, and sometimes far from shore.

A Theft, however, has the coherence and tension of a furled flower. It is packed with colour and wit, and a fervent gaiety. The tendentiousness and hectoring tones of some of his later fiction are absent, as are the faintly crackpot obsessions. It is less a moral than an ethical tale (how should one live?), and comes down firmly, as Bellow always does, on the side of lived life and, that rarest of all things these days, common decency.

The story is organised, with craft and much craftiness, in a binary series. Situations and predicaments repeat themselves over time with small but telling variations; this system is never merely mechanical, but is managed with lightness and grace. The constant throughout the action is a Jamesian 'little thing', an emerald engagement ring which is bought and presented, lost, found, stolen and returned; like the golden bowl or the spoils of Poynton, it increases steadily in significance, turning from a trinket into a talisman 'involved with Clara's very grip on existence'. She has 'come to base her stability entirely' on the ring—though she does also refer to it dismissively as 'this love-toy emerald, personal sentimentality'.

Clara is big, blonde, large-headed, 'a raw-boned American woman . . . from the sticks', the daughter of Indiana farm people and small-town store-owners, brought up on the Bible and old-time religion; it is one of the book's sly jokes that this famously 'Jewish' novelist should take as his protagonist a corn-fed shiksa from the Bible Belt. She has more familiar Bellovian marks, however: she has 'studied Greek at Bloomington and Elizabethan-Jacobean literature at Wellesley'; she has tried suicide once and is to try it again; by the age of 40 she had set up a thriving journalistic agency specialising in high fashion, and later sold it to an international publishing company and is now one of the company's high-powered executives, the 'tsarina of fashion writing'. She has three children, and is on her fourth unsatisfactory husband.

Perhaps it will seem paradoxical to say that Clara is a wonderfully compelling character who is not wholly convincing (this is not unusual, I find, in Saul Bellow's books). She is, it would seem, just too many things, a kind of portmanteau into which Bellow, impatient as ever, has bundled assorted bits and pieces of his latest preoccupations. And although she is recognisably female, there is something about her bigness, her driveness, that seems to warrant a hormone-test. At times she is suspiciously like one of Bellow's male heroes in drag.

The fourth husband is Wilder Velde, a political speechwriter and fixer, 'big and handsome, indolent, defiantly incompetent', who spends most of his days sitting about in their Park Avenue apartment reading thrillers. . . . Clara's real, only and continuing love, however, is for Ithiel 'Teddy' Regler, the man who bought her the engagement ring twenty years ago, but whom she did not marry.

Teddy Regler is the most immediately interesting character in the novella. He is a Henry Kissinger type, but handsomer, and certainly more attractive than the shuttle diplomatist ever showed himself to be. Bellow has always been fascinated by the great world of politics and money. While other writers—Gore Vidal, let's say—look on this world with a mixture of envy and disgust, it is obvious that Bellow loves to get up close to the sources of power and feel the glow on his face and see the sparks fly. If he is part social philosopher who knows his Vico and his Max Weber, there is another, ineradicable part of him that that is for ever the fast-talking, street-wise Chicagoan still with the smell of the stockyards in his nostrils. Regler (Clara describes him as 'somewhere between a Spanish grandee and a Mennonite') is one of Bellow's international men, the geopolitical fireman that the author himself, one suspects, half wishes he had been. . . .

It is the figure of Teddy Regler which lifts the story into the realm of the 'international tale'. He descends into these pages out of the rarefied strata of first-class travel, still trailing a whiff of the brandy-and-leather air of grand hotels and the well-appointed houses of the great and powerful. He has had his troubles (a terrible wife has stripped him of his possessions, leaving him only a bare marriage-bed), but he is still the rock of good sense and sympathetic advice onto which Clara flings herself when the sea of troubles threatens to engulf her: 'The more hidden his activities, the better she felt about him. Power, danger, secrecy made him even sexier. No loose talk. A woman could feel safe with a man like Ithiel.'

The current difficulties that Clara brings to him for his expert consideration have arisen from the matter of her Austrian au pair girl, Gina Wegman. Gina comes from a highly respectable background—her father is a banker—and she is very good with children, especially Lucy, the eldest, 'a stout little girl needing help': yet from the start Clara recognises in her a young woman eager for experience—and where better to find that than in New York, or Gogmagogsville, as Bible-reared Clara calls the place. And sure enough, Gina quickly takes up with a ghetto boy, a Haitian of great good looks and dubious morals. Clara warns her of the dangers of such a liaison, yet cannot help but recall that once, angry at Teddy Regler, she herself acquired a young lover, a French-speaker too, but this one from France, who was anything but a model companion for a good Midwestern girl; and there is another boy, from farther back, who every year still sends her a Christmas card, from his cell in Attica.

As we expect, and as Clara expects, Gina's young man steals the emerald engagement ring. Even here, however, Clara's indignation is tempered by the knowledge that in such matters she is herself not entirely lily-white. At this point the layers of moral ambiguity built into the book are worthy of the Master himself. First of all, the jeweller from whom the ring was purchased undervalued the emerald, as Clara discovers when she comes to insure it; it is not Clara's fault, of course, that the jeweller made a mistake, but, on the other hand, she does nothing to right the balance. Then she misplaces the ring and claims the $15,000 insurance money, but a year later, when the ring turns up again, she does not inform the insurance company, and keeps the money. Here the irony of the singular in the title *A Theft* becomes apparent.

Gina, confronted with her boyfriend's crime, leaves the apartment and disappears. Clara, on Teddy Regler's advice, hires a private detective to track her down—not for the purpose of visiting retribution on her, but because

Clara has grown fond of the girl, and worries for her safety. The private eye discovers that Gina has moved in with her Haitian. While Clara is trying to make contact with her, the ring mysteriously reappears in Clara's bedroom: how did it get there, past all that expensive security equipment? The answer is a surprise (a twist in the tail!), one which lifts Gina, and Clara, and Clara's children, onto a higher plane of interest, and intensifies them as characters wrestling with life's commonplace yet immensely subtle moral dilemmas.

A Theft is not perfect; it does not have the seamless, enamelled finish that James would have given to it. Although there is less loose writing here than in many of the full-length novels, an occasional idiosyncrasy leaves one blinking. Yet Bellow is such a strong, such a lively writer that what in others would be carelessness can seem carefree in him. Even at their most knockabout, his novels make wonderful talk, provide wonderful lines: a tough old lawyer is 'like Santa Claus with an empty sack who comes down your chimney to steal everything in the house'; or this, passed on from Alexander Zinoviev commenting on glasnost and the crushing of the dissidents: 'After you've gotten rid of your enemies, you're ready to abolish capital punishment.' As always with Bellow, the people here have a tangible presence, a thereness; one feels they existed before the book began, and that they will go on after it ends. This verisimilitude is not exactly fashionable today, but Bellow has a healthy contempt for fashions—*haute couture* in fiction is not for him.

This is a 'late' work, and there is a touch of autumn in it: the leaves tremble and glow, and a porcelain-blue sky shows through the branches, but the going is deceptive underfoot, and there is a distinct chill in the air. 'These people'—Haitians and other ghetto-dwellers—came up from the tropical slums to outsmart New York, and with all the rules crumbling here as elsewhere, so that nobody could any longer be clear in his mind about anything, they could do it—who is speaking here, one wonders uneasily: is it just the 'hereditary peasant' in Clara, or is it Saul Bellow the social observer turning bitter?

Clara, no doubt about it, is a tough American who will brook no nonsense from a world that is half silly and half savage. Even her most generous impulses have a pearl of harshness at their core. She attempts to bring Gina and Teddy Regler together, partly out of a desire to rescue the past and fulfil the promise that she and Teddy missed, but also because her Sino-American confidante, Laura Wong (shades of Fanny Assingham and her numerous avatars), has set her own sights on Teddy. It all ends in tears, but they are different from the ones poor Tommy Wilhelm could not contain at the close of a previous novella, *Seize the day* (1956). Wilhelm weeps for the sadness and brevity of life, Clara for something altogether different; and her tears seem a celebration.

        John Banville, "International Tale," in London Review of Books, *Vol. 11, No. 7, March 30, 1989, p. 21.*

Robert Towers

When I think of the women in Saul Bellow's novels, a vivid composite figure flashes before my eye. She is likely to be big-boned, full-breasted, with gorgeous legs and an extravagant mane of hair. Something of a bimbo or dame, she is an avid consumer who loves clothes and wears sexy underwear. Lively in bed, she has an ebullient personality and loves to have a good time everywhere. She is also greedy and aggressive and may have an even greedier mother or aunt egging her on. Woe betide the divorced husband whom she ruthlessly takes to the cleaners! Thea, who hunts with eagles, perfumed Ramona in her black lace underthings and three-inch spike heels, Angela, Shula, Denise, who knows how to handle divorce judges, Renata, with the rapacious Señora in tow—they streak through the novels, bemusing Sammler and bowling over Augie and Herzog and Charlie Citrine. But we experience them only through men—we must always take the men's word for what these disturbing creatures are like. The novelty of *A Theft*—a novella which Bellow has published as a paperback original—is that a woman with some of the qualities of Bellow's earlier women is now the central character.

She is Clara Velde, a four-times married fashion executive who lives with Wilder Velde, her current husband (who has "stud power" but is otherwise unsatisfactory), three children, and an Austrian *au pair* girl in a Park Avenue apartment. Like the others, Clara has plenty of physical presence:

> Really, everything about her was conspicuous, not only the size and shape of her head. She must have decided long ago that for the likes of her there could be no cover-up; she couldn't divert energy into disguises. So there she was, a rawboned American woman. She had very good legs—who knows what you would have seen if pioneer women had worn shorter skirts.

It will not escape the reader that this description too comes to us by way of a masculine—not to say sexist—eye for women, but Bellow evidently makes an effort to enter Clara's mind—or at least her voice—and to place her at the center of events.

The other voice in the novella is that of Ithiel (Teddy) Regler, an adviser to presidents and other powerful people, a man who knows the "big picture," who appears on TV shows with Dobrynin and helps the Italian police track down terrorists—a man who, in Clara's opinion, "could be the Gibbon or Tacitus of the American Empire." . . . Unfortunately, Ithiel has a low taste in women—"overdressed sexpots, gaudy and dizzy, 'ground-dragging titzers,' on whom a man like Ithiel should never have squandered his substance"—and has never acceded to Clara's plea to marry her. He did however once buy her an emerald engagement ring, which she has treasured ever since. It is the disappearance of this ring from Clara's bedside table that provides *A Theft* with its minimal plot, which involves, among others, the *au pair* girl and Clara's difficult daughter Lucy.

What charm this somewhat undernourished little book possesses lies in its language. Both Clara and Ithiel are loquacious, speaking (and thinking) in the racy, colloquial, highly colored urban idiom that so many of Bellow's characters use, whatever their imputed background or class. (Clara, for instance, comes from a small-town, Bible-reading Indiana family—but never for a moment sounds like it.) Here, for instance, is Ithiel on the subject of psy-choanalysis when Clara asks him how he "interprets" her loss of the ring.

> "I don't," said Ithiel. "It's a pretty bad idea to wring what happens to get every drop of meaning out of it. The way people twist their emotional laundry is not to be believed. *I* don't feel you wronged me by losing that ring. You say it was insured?"
>
> "Damn right."
>
> "Then file a claim. . . . "
>
> "I'm really torn up about it," said Clara.
>
> "That's your tenth-century soul. Much your doctor can do about that!"
>
> "He helps, in some respects."
>
> "Those guys!" said Ithiel. "If a millipede came into the office, he'd leave with an infinitesimal crutch for each leg."

But such verbal exuberance is not enough to make *A Theft* seem more than skimpy to those who enjoy, as I do, the abundance offered by a novel like *Mr. Sammler's Planet* or *Humboldt's Gift.* Instead of a realized work of fiction, *A Theft* suggests only the armature for an uncompleted and much weightier work based upon the relationship of Clara and Ithiel. The resolution of the ring's theft seems perfunctory and without much consequence for either of the leading characters. Many of Bellow's shorter stories have been more substantial. It was, after all, the dense representation of felt life within a restricted space that endeared the "blessed *nouvelle*" to James and Turgenev. There is no density—or compressed energy—here. Bellow has taken no particular advantage of the form. Underplotted and slackly rendered, *A Theft* may provide a mildly pleasant read for admirers of Bellow, but it serves mainly as a reminder of how much more we have come to expect from this writer. (pp. 51-2)

> *Robert Towers, "Mystery Women," in* The New York Review of Books, *Vol. XXXVI, No. 7, April 27, 1989, pp. 50-2.*

John Updike

A novella of scarcely a hundred pages, [*A Theft*] is a curious work in several respects, not least the manner of its publication—in quality paperback, forgoing the hardcover profits that even a minor offering by our preëminent fiction writer would blamelessly generate. Bellow, at this point in his career, has sat atop the American literary heap longer than anyone else since William Dean Howells; it has been over thirty-five years since the publication of *The Adventures of Augie March* established him as our most exuberant and melodious postwar novelist, and as the most viable combination of redskin and paleface in our specialized, academized postwar era. Street-smart and book-smart with an equal intensity, he has displayed, in a salty, rapid, and amazingly expressive idiom, heroes grappling with and being thrown by the great ideas of Western man. Until *A Theft*, he had not presented a woman as an autonomous seeker rather than as a paradise sought; his women have tended to be powerfully tangible and distressingly audible apparitions warping his heroes' already cluttered intellectual horizons. This venture into the female soul has made both the redskin and the paleface jumpy, the idiom becoming gruff and the great ideas sinking into a peculiar form of celebrity-consciousness. (p. 113)

[Clara Velde] has had, we are told, quite a life—four husbands and three daughters by the age of forty, and a meteoric career in journalism that has left her high and rich: "In the boardroom she was referred to by some as 'a good corporate person,' by others as 'the czarina of fashion writing.' " Who is confiding all this, with such aggressive breathlessness? A curious tone has been adopted, a gossipy tone, as if fictional characters were a subdivision of the rich and famous. These certainly keep fast company—for instance, Clara's third husband, Spontini, "Spontini the oil tycoon, a close friend of the billionaire leftist and terrorist Giangiacomo F., who blew himself up in the seventies." F. for Feltrinelli, in case you missed the news that day.

The celebrity parade doesn't begin to roll, however, until we meet Clara's true love, who bears the name, fit for an angel, of Ithiel Regler. "Ithiel Regler stood much higher with Clara than any of the husbands. 'On a scale of ten,' she liked to say to Laura, 'he *was* ten.' " He never got around to marrying her, we presume, partly because there's nothing, as the Princess of Cleves perceived long ago, like marriage to spoil a perfect love, and partly because he was too busy chasing around in his curious profession of free-lance big shot, "a wunderkind in nuclear strategy," based in Washington but treasured and telegenic wherever he goes. "People of great power set a high value on his smarts. Well, you only had to look at the size and the evenness of his dark eyes." . . . To Clara, at least, there appears no limit to Ithiel's abilities. She reflects, while doting upon him in a Washington restaurant:

> Why, Ithiel could be the Gibbon or the Tacitus of the American Empire. . . . If he wanted, he could do with Nixon, Johnson, Kennedy or Kissinger, with the Shah or de Gaulle, what Keynes had done with the Allies at Versailles. World figures had found Ithiel worth their while. Sometimes he let slip a comment or a judgment: "Neither the Russians nor the Americans can manage the world. Not capable of organizing the future." When she came into her own, Clara thought, she'd set up a fund for him so he could write his views.

If Ithiel's brilliance fails to flash out in the judgment above, and Clara's adoration boggles belief, we are persuaded beyond doubt that Bellow's fascination with the seriocomic world of international power has not abandoned him in the years since he wrote *Herzog.*

Plot: The alleged countrywoman once upon a time induced the alleged wunderkind, at the height of their romance, to buy her an engagement ring, an emerald "conspicuously clear, color perfect, top of its class." The engagement founders, but the sentimentally priceless ring remains in her care, is stolen once, recovered (though she doesn't give the insurance money back), and then stolen again—by, Clara thinks, the sexy, slinky Haitian boyfriend of her solidly bourgeois but not unsexy au pair from Vienna, Gina Wegman, for whom she has strong motherly feelings. This is Bellow's first fictional visit since *Mr. Sammler's Planet* to New York City, which *A Theft* calls "Gogmagogsville"; it is bracing to share his updated view of how the decline of the West is locally proceeding. Clara surprises a party Gina is giving for her new friends: "The room was more like a car of the West Side subway. Lots of muscle on the boys, as if they did aerobics." But Gottschalk, the "minimal sleaze" private detective whom Clara hires, sums up the Haitian boyfriend as "Casual criminal. Not enough muscle for street crime." He does do one plainly wicked thing, though: while petting on the sofa with Gina, he puts his combat boots up on Clara's silk pillows.

The simple story is told in a purposefully dishevelled way, much of it by means of Clara's confidences to an ill-defined Manhattan neighbor, Laura Wang. We are often reminded of Ithiel's rather abstract wonderfulness and of Clara's loyalty, which she shares with her creator, to a theological perspective but learn almost nothing about Wilder, her present husband and the father of her three girls, or about her job, which seems all glamour and no performance. The book is jumpy and skimpy, and feels like a set of signals to someone offstage. The clearest thing about Clara is her sparkling view of Ithiel; the murkiest, her maternal feeling toward Gina.

For all this, *A Theft* holds a gallant intention and a great gift. Who but Bellow can swoop in with a coinage like "Clara found Ithiel in a state of sick dignity" or unashamedly physicalize an emotion in such a trope as "She felt as if the life had been vacuumed out of her"? . . . The brain fever that races through a Bellow narrative can always catch fire into poetry, a poetry present in the otherworldly names he bestows—Odo Fenger, Etta Wolfenstein, Wilder Velde, Bobby Steinsalz. Marginal characters can suddenly flare into an arresting vividness: Clara, visiting her psychiatrist, Dr. Gladstone, notes his "samurai beard, the bared teeth it framed, the big fashionable specs," and while visiting Ithiel's lawyer, Steinsalz, she "could not help but look at the lawyer's lap, where because he was obese his sex organ was outlined by the pressure of his fat." The pressure of an overflowing sense of life keeps Bellow adding touches to his central characters, too—filling them in, or refreshing old touches. In a taxi to her last conversation in the narrative, Clara leans "her long neck backward to relieve it of the weight of her head and control the wildness of her mind." Her big head weighs on her; we are still learning about her, she is still being created, she is unfinished, in process, and perhaps that is the point. "Won't the dynamic ever let you go?" she asks herself. Evidently not, if her lover is to be believed when he tells her, "Well, people have to be done with disorder, finally, and by the time they're done they're also finished." (pp. 113-14)

> *John Updike, "Nice Tries," in* The New Yorker, *Vol. LXV, No. 11, May 1, 1989, pp. 111-14.*

Rick Marin

[Publishing *A Theft*] *only* in paperback edition seems a move either of sublime crankiness or craftiness on Saul Bellow's part. As the story goes, Bellow's agent shopped the Nobel Laureate's 25,000-plus words around to a select few of the better magazines and was told, No thank you, too long. Would the NL care to have another go with the blue pencil? The NL would not. Nuts to the *New Yorker*—

surely one of the unnamed mags—and its ilk. Bellow would publish *A Theft* without them and uncut, as "A Novella By. . . . " in paperback. Like Jay McInerney! And behold: the book becomes not just a publishing event, which any new work by Saul Bellow already is, but a Media Event, essential "Life" news for *USA Today.* Cranky *and* crafty, it's the old master's way of telling the world he still has a few tricks up his sleeve.

Though it's been received with polite enthusiasm, all the blurbable ink on *A Theft* still reads like a tribute to what might have been. In 109 pages of his elegant, supremely confident prose, Bellow packs a wallop of possibility. *Herzog, Mr. Sammler's Planet, Humboldt's Gift:* all reasons to seek out the author's latest fictional pronunciamento, whatever its form, and read on. But breezing through *A Theft* is so fast and fluid a business that it leaves the devoted reader in a state of constant, breathless expectation. When does the great writer's long story, his short novel, start to get great? The short answer is never. The long answer: it's worth the trip anyway.

The heroine is Clara Velde. Meet her on page one, beginning, as Bellow suggests, with "what was conspicuous about her":

> . . . short, blond hair, fashionably cut, growing upon a head unusually big. In a person of an inert character a head of such a size might have seemed a deformity; in Clara, because she had so much personal force, it came across as ruggedly handsome. She needed that head; a mind like hers demanded space. She was big-boned; her shoulders were not broad but high. Her blue eyes, exceptionally large, grew prominent when she brooded. The nose was small—ancestrally a North Sea nose. The mouth was very good, but stretched extremely wide when she grinned, when she wept. Her forehead was powerful.

She needed that head. Big head, big-boned, shoulders not broad but high, eyes *exceptionally* large. . . . Sound familiar? Glance at the authorial mug-shot on the back cover. The nose isn't North Sea (maybe North Side) but the mouth is very good, stretching, as it does, extremely wide when "grinned." And such a head! Among contemporary American novelists this one still reigns king of what D. H. Lawrence called "head culture." Has Bellow conjured a female after his own image, from a prime cut of his own rib? Not exactly. But Clara is a woman after his own heart, more substantial than the erotic playthings he's plunked in the beds and bathtubs of dozens of male alter egos over the years. Powerful and rich in her middle age, the "czarina of fashion writing" is formidably outsize. She doesn't purr, she roars. She is woman, trumpets *A Theft.* Yet for all that, she never seems quite real.

And that's the problem. Bellow spends a great deal of time inventing Clara, preparing her and us for The Theft—her four husbands, digressions up the family tree, the days when she used to cook dinner naked but for a pair of clogs, and so on—to the point where you wish he *had* gone at it again with the blue pencil. "Anybody who had it in mind to get around her was in for lots of bad news." When this vicariously gossipy tone isn't just right—Bellow enjoying a colloquial stroll up Fifth Avenue—it becomes society-column, banal "bad news."

The thievery in question doesn't occur until near the half-

way mark, a playful dalliance. The pilfered *object* is an emerald ring, a sentimental memento *cum* "fairy-tale object" symbolic of Clara's first and last true love, Ithiel "Teddy" Regler. Readers disconcerted to find a woman the center of Bellow's fictional attention can take ample solace in Ithiel's robust, manly company. An inspired, global brain who Clara boasts "thinks no more of going to Iran than I do about Coney Island," Regler is a major *macher,* a backstage adviser to international potentates ("The Shah likes to talk to him") and a constantly talking head, on and off MacNeil/Lehrer. If this weren't the pre-Ayatollah 1970s he'd be opining on "Nightline."

When on stage, Ithiel takes over, like a strong character actor supporting weak leads. He rails, Clara swoons. *"Tell!"* she begs. And he does, inveighing against psychiatry ("keeps you infantile"), child abuse ("normal punishment in my time"), and even—Bellow taking a slightly anachronistic shot here—glasnost. "They strangled the opposition, and now they're pretending to be *it.*" Regler is a regular font for Bellow's bile. Not that Clara doesn't have her splenetic moments too. . . . New York City she dubs "Gogmagogsville."

But Bellow's most daring rhetorical parry is his casting of the *au pair*'s Haitian boyfriend as the ring thief. He's "French-speaking, dark-skinned, very good looking, arrogant like," according to Clara's Hispanic cleaning lady. Sidney Poitier? Not if Bellow can help it: "These people came up from the tropical slums to outsmart New York, and with all the rules crumbling here as elsewhere, so that nobody could any longer be clear in his mind about anything, they could do it." The cocky boy with his combat boots up on Clara's silk pillows is a direct descendant of the giant Negro pickpocket who exposed himself to old man Sammler back in 1969.

Gog and Magog—last of the giants. A quarter century after Herzog's feverish memos to posterity, Bellow still sees the walls tumbling down around Civilization, with the jungle (and its lawless barbarians) creeping inexorably in. It's Bellow the polemical reactionary, the stubborn counterrevolutionary, who's most alive in *A Theft.* He too rails, with Clara and Ithiel, against indiscriminate sex, the criminal breed, Communism. Bellow the humanist, the intimate sage of heart and mind, doesn't keep up. The characters never seem equal to their eloquence, even by Bellovian standards. Much of Clara's story is told in the presence of her confessor, an inscrutable Oriental named Laura Wong. As a fictional device their one-sided "conversations" are functional, but never quite credible. Self-knowledge and a clearer grasp of what she calls "the Human Pair" come to Clara when she finally dismounts the proverbial couch. (All this from the former Reichian turned shrink-basher.) Her concluding sentiments are typically high-ceilinged Bellow, but the architecture is too puny to hold them.

A Theft isn't a triumph of nuance or portraiture, like some of the stories in *Him With His Foot in His Mouth.* It's the skeleton for a novel. Clara is less a character than Bellow's idea for one: "his failed concept," to borrow a phrase from the book. Ithiel—a name plucked from Old Testament obscurity (meaning "God with me") and a resonant echo of Milton's warrior-angel Ithuriel—is a seer, one who takes in "the big, *big* picture." Clara insists he's the man to write the "wrap-up of wrap-ups" for the twentieth century, a

"Gibbon or Tacitus of the American Empire." Such was Saul Bellow's promise; a writer of big books, not little ones. *A mind like hers demanded space.* His too, his too. (pp. 47-8)

Rick Marin, in a review of "A Theft," in The American Spectator, *Vol. 22, No. 7, July, 1989, pp. 47-8.*

Christopher Lehmann-Haupt

The subject of memory pervades Saul Bellow's intriguing but ultimately elusive new novella, **The Bellarosa Connection,** which is the second short work of fiction, after **The Theft,** that the 1976 Nobel laureate in literature has brought out as a paperback original this year.

Memory is the specialty of the novella's nameless narrator, a Russian Jew from New Jersey who owes his "worldly success" to having founded the Mnemosyne Institute of Philadelphia and there trained executives, politicians and members of the defense establishment in the art of remembering.

And memory is what prompts his narrative, which is largely the story of a refugee couple named Fonstein whom the narrator's father once introduced to him. "I was at the bar of paternal judgment again, charged with American puerility," he writes. "When would I shape up, at last! At the age of 32, I still behaved like a 12-year-old, hanging out in Greenwich Village." His father "hoped it would straighten me out to hear what people had suffered in Europe, in the real world."

What Harry Fonstein had suffered, predictably enough, was persecution by the Nazis. At a crucial point, he had been rescued from an Italian jail and shipped to Ellis Island by what he at first understood to be something called the Bellarosa Society but later discovered to be none other than the show-biz impresario Billy Rose.

Yet what impresses the narrator most about Fonstein is his hugely fat and serious wife, Sorella, and how she has figured in her husband's history. Having saved Fonstein, Billy Rose wouldn't meet him; he wanted nothing more to do with the man. But Fonstein, long since made wealthy by the invention of a new thermostat, still feels incomplete. Sorella digs up dirt on Billy Rose and tries to blackmail him into meeting her husband for just 15 minutes. In Jerusalem's King David Hotel, where Rose is staying while he plants a sculpture garden for Israelis to remember him by, Sorella corners him and plays her card.

These improbable events are knitted together and made credible by Mr. Bellow's familiar idiomatic voice, philosophizing, cracking wise and putting its inimitable spin on the world. . . .

Still, for all his keenness of memory, the narrator of **The Bellarosa Connection** ends up forgetting the most essential thing. Sorella Fonstein, who turns out to be "well up on the subject" of Jewish history, draws her own conclusions from her encounter with Billy Rose:

> The Jews could survive everything that Europe threw at them. I mean the lucky remnant. But now comes the next test—America. Can they hold their ground, or will the U.S.A. be too much for them?

Shortly after she asks the narrator this question, he stops seeing the Fonsteins.

> Maybe the power of memory was to blame. Remembering them so well, did I need actually to see them? To keep them in a mental suspension was enough. They were a part of the permanent cast of characters, in absentia permanently. There wasn't a thing for them to do.

But then one night in his rich old age, he has a dream of being defeated by a man wearing boots.

> Despair was not principally what I felt, nor fear of death. What made the dream terrible was my complete conviction of error. . . . I was being shown—and I was aware of this in sleep—that I had made a mistake, a lifelong mistake: something wrong, false, now fully manifest.

He muses on:

> It wasn't death that had scared me, it was disclosure: I wasn't what I thought I was. I really didn't understand merciless brutality. . . . I had discovered for how long I had shielded myself from unbearable imaginations—no, not imaginations, but recognitions—of murder, of relish in torture, of the ground bass of brutality, without which no human music ever is performed.

Now I believe what Mr. Bellow is saying here is that the narrator has failed the test of America that Sorella Fonstein foresaw—that the United States has been too much for him in the same way that it was too much for Billy Rose. Both of them, precisely by cutting themselves off from the Fonsteins, have made themselves a part of the Bellarosa Connection.

True, such an interpretation is more an idea than a feeling or intuition; it seems a willed construct on Mr. Bellow's part, not something a reader grasps with his heart. But the final irony appears to be nothing more than that this memory master has forgotten Jerusalem. And if, contrary to the Psalmist's wish, his right hand has not exactly forgotten her cunning nor his tongue cleaved to the roof of his mouth, still, all he can do, as he concludes his narrative, is "record everything I could remember of the Bellarosa Connection, and set it all down with a Mnemosyne flourish."

Christopher Lehmann-Haupt, "On the Forgetfulness of a Memory Expert," in The New York Times, *September 28, 1989, p. C22.*

William H. Pritchard

Saul Bellow's new novel [**The Bellarosa Connection**] is a tall (but very short) tale narrated in the first person by a nameless figure, the founder of the Mnemosyne Institute, a Philadelphia memory-training ground for "executives, politicians, and members of the defense establishment." Now retired, the institute in the hands of his son, he would like to *"forget* about remembering"—but that is not so easy to do. . . .

As a writer in his 70's, Saul Bellow has determined not to retire, and during the past two years he has published first a long novel, **More Die of Heartbreak,** then two short ones, **A Theft** and the book at hand. None of these works is notable for its plot; indeed, they lead one to recall Dr. Johnson's remark about the novelist Samuel Richardson—that if you read him for the plot, you would hang yourself. Mr. Bellow's most carefully developed plot is that of *The Victim,* written over 40 years ago, after which he became steadily less interested in the matter. One reads him instead—more precisely, one listens to him—for the line of talk he so ingeniously generates. In his recent books especially, nothing much happens except (it is an important exception) within the idiom and cadence, the flashes and twists of a voice intent on giving its distinctive note to things.

"The Bellarosa Connection" of this novel's title is a name misheard, since it really refers to an underground operation supposed to have been run by the American theatrical impresario Billy Rose with the object of helping European Jews escape from Italy during World War II. One of these refugees, Harry Fonstein, flees to the United States through the help of what he takes to be something called the "Bellarosa" connection; he later learns the name of his true benefactor, yet his persistent efforts to express his gratitude to Billy Rose are met only with rebuffs. Eventually, Fonstein's wife, Sorella, confronts Rose in his suite at Jerusalem's King David Hotel, threatening to publish a damaging account of him by one of his old employees unless he grants Fonstein a 15-minute interview.

These unlikely, even preposterous, events are brought to imaginative life through the narrator's memory (as a younger man he knew the Fonsteins) and are told in the accents of an individual voice, such accents as may be heard in the following sentences about the manner in which Billy Rose took charge of the rescue operation:

> No, it was Billy acting alone on a spurt of feeling for his fellow Jews and squaring himself to outwit Hitler and Himmler and cheat them of their victims. On another day he'd set his heart on a baked potato, a hot dog, a cruise around Manhattan on the Circle Line. . . . Billy was as spattered as a Jackson Pollock painting, and among the main trickles was his Jewishness, with other streaks flowing toward secrecy—streaks of sexual weakness, sexual humiliation. At the same time, he had to have his name in the paper. As someone said, he had a buglike tropism for publicity. Yet his rescue operation in Europe remained secret.

It is an idiom that can accommodate tropism and a baked potato, Jackson Pollock and Himmler; first heard in *The Adventures of Augie March,* it reached full expression in *Herzog.*

If, in Robert Frost's phrase, we become "ear-readers" rather than merely eye-readers of Saul Bellow's prose, the rewards are great—as when the narrator, whose father is convinced that Jews should be "strong but compact" rather than "unnecessarily large," confesses to having broken the mold:

> My length was superfluous, I had too much chest and shoulders, big hands, a wide mouth, a band of black mustache, too much voice, excessive hair; the shirts that covered my trunk had too many red and gray stripes, idiotically flashy. Fools ought to come in smaller sizes. A big son was a threat, a parricide.

This is vintage Bellow, fluent and racy in its presentation of excess, right down to the too many stripes of those "idi-

otically flashy" shirts. The result is a vivid, ludicrous image of this "big son."

Mr. Bellow's previous book, *A Theft,* was a traditional third-person narrative with a relatively faceless storyteller who refrained from imposing an individual slant on characters and events. This made for a somewhat flat or muted effect, not one for which Mr. Bellow is usually noted. By contrast, the new book is more expressively daring and has a lot more fun with its style: "Fonstein said that with Italians, when they had secrets to keep, tiny muscles came out in the face that nobody otherwise saw." Those tiny muscles are like the ones that come out in Mr. Bellow's prose when it is more than usually energetic. "A first-class man subsists on the matter he destroys, just as the stars do," says the narrator about Fonstein, one of those people whose "aim is to convert weaknesses and secrets into burnable energy." The novel is filled with such metaphors for its own secret operation.

In fact it is Fonstein's wife, Sorella, who increasingly absorbs the narrator's attention, especially as she attempts to bend Billy Rose to her will. Our man of memory dwells extensively and obsessively on Sorella's bulk, her "expansion" from the figure he had first met years ago in New Jersey: "She made you look twice at a doorway. When she came to it, she filled the space like a freighter in a canal lock." In one of his fanciful extravagances, he speculates that "maybe Sorella was trying to incorporate in fatty tissue some portion of what he [Fonstein] had lost—members of his family." This, of course, goes too far, but it has been Mr. Bellow's mark as a writer to go too far, even to this outrageous parenthesis about Sorella: "All I can say is that it (whatever it was at bottom) was established with some class or style." At bottom, indeed.

More than once the narrator apologizes for "needlessly digressing," but "digression" is of the essence in a novelist whose specialty is a line of talk. One of the most pleasurable moments in *The Bellarosa Connection* occurs when the founder of the Mnemosyne Institute suddenly can't remember the name of the Swanee River, celebrated in song. Momentarily he is shattered—"Not everyone, needless to say, would take such a lapsus so to heart. A bridge was broken: I could not cross the——River." A few minutes later, behind the wheel of his car, the connection is reestablished, "and I began to shout 'Swanee—Swanee—Swanee,' punching the steering wheel." Although this moment is thematically linked to the premise out of which the novel is written—that memory is life and its lapsing a foretaste of death—the only live connection it bears to the Fonstein-Rose story is as another example of Mr. Bellow's inventiveness, his ability to make memory interesting by the improvisations of a speaking voice. And though the Holocaust and its aftermath—the Jew from Europe assimilating and changing in America—are central to the novel, we don't come away with something we might call Mr. Bellow's "point" or "idea." As the narrator puts it, wisely I think, "No idea is more than an imaginary potency, a mushroom cloud (destroying nothing, making nothing) rising from blinding consciousness."

That consciousness has always been Saul Bellow's essential subject, and near the end of this book the narrator's mind becomes more strange—self-accusatory, uncertain of its own powers and virtue, lapsing like the lost bridge to the Swanee River. Compared to the eloquent rhetoric with which Mr. Bellow's masterpiece, *Seize the Day,* concluded, the end of *The Bellarosa Connection* is abrupt, matter-of-fact, almost offbeat. It is a conclusion, perhaps, in which nothing is concluded (whereas in *Seize the Day* everything is concluded), but it is appropriate to the overall pitch and voice of this cannily resourceful entertainment.

> *William H. Pritchard, "Blackmailing Billy Rose," in* The New York Times Book Review, *October 1, 1989, p. 11.*

Garry Wills

One of the many ways Alfred Hitchcock improved John Buchan's novel for his movie *The Thirty-Nine Steps* was the introduction of "Mr. Memory." Hitchcock had recalled such a virtuoso of memorization from a vaudeville act, and he turned that performer's odd skill into a means by which complex defense formulae could be transmitted to England's enemies. But Mr. Memory's gift becomes a tragic blessing, like Cassandra's compulsion to prophesy. Asked to recite the "classified" formulae, even on a vaudeville stage, he must prove his retentiveness. Only a bullet fired by his foreign employer stops him at the movie's climax. Mr. Memory's achievement was his undoing because his flow of information was automatic, recallable on cue; rendered up, as it had been committed to his memory, without regard to content. He was as replayable as a machine, and he died by the hypertrophy of one function.

The narrator in Saul Bellow's new book [*The Bellarosa Connection*] is an updated Mr. Memory, someone who not only has a knack for memorizing but can teach it to others—especially to "members of the defense establishment" (just to make the debt to Hitchcock clear). This man has founded the Mnemosyne Institute, which apparently does for memorizing what Evelyn Wood claimed to do for reading, with an emphasis on rapidity, retention, and indifference toward the material being processed. The Mnemosyne business has brought its founder millions of dollars and a large empty house in Philadelphia, where he lives alone after his wife's death and his son's marriage. He regrets that remembering is a line of work from which he cannot retire. Part of his method has been "to learn to make your mind a blank," but the mind will not stay blank. The only way to control unsummoned memories is by marshaling again entire chains of deliberate memories, automatically linked to the "themes" that were his mnemonic device for acquiring them in the first place. Thus when he starts one train of recollection, he must run through it by a necessity of his mind—the mind formed by exploiting his initial gift.

The memory chain that begins (and must therefore end) Bellow's novel deals with his cousin and contemporary named Fonstein. Details about Fonstein have been stored in the birthday-card and Passover-greeting file—things one remembers to remember, even if one does nothing further about them. "But that's what the Passover phenomenon is now—it never comes to pass." The narrator had resented Fonstein when they first met. As a pampered American boy, the future Philadelphia millionaire felt guilty when his father brought home a cripple who had escaped from Italy's Fascists and was already successful in America. "Surviving-Fonstein, with all the furies of Europe at his back, made me look bad."

Fonstein's wife, Sorella, was also someone to be avoided. Her encyclopedic knowledge of the persecutions in Europe oppressed the narrator, who did not want to remember so much painful detail (and cannot, of course, forget it once Sorella has reeled it off). Though he cannot forget, he will not examine: "First those people murdered you, then they forced you to brood on their crimes." If he must have memories, they will be of facts detached from meaning. What *could* a holocaust mean anyway? "Stars are nuclear furnaces too. Such things are utterly beyond me, a pointless exercise."

But Sorella is a force as well as a purveyor of facts. She is fat on a superhuman scale. "She made you look twice at a doorway." Bellow has always found something funny yet demonic about fat. The victim of life's bad magics in *Seize the Day* (1956) goes finally broke by investing in the lard market. Character after character stoops to a destiny loaded in to his fleshy upper back. One person in **"Cousins"** (1984) has a face so puffy that it is all one "edema of deadly secrets." Sorella, however, enters a new dimension of the obese, putting a strain on the imagination even while one looks at her. She has "gestures that only a two-hundred-pound woman can produce, because her delicacy rests on the mad overflow of her behind."

The dramatic highpoint of the book, placed at its center, is the confrontation between this huge woman and the tiny American showman, Billy Rose of Broadway, the man whose Mafia connections allowed Fonstein and other Jews to slip out of Italy into boats heading for America. This underground activity was called "The Bellarosa Connection." Fonstein, as he grows up, thinks the clue to his own American identity will be found in the secret grace disguised under Billy Rose's outer vulgarity. But Rose refuses to see the product of his dark favor, repulsing every approach through an intermediary, and snubbing Fonstein when he approaches him in public. So Fonstein retires into proud reticence, the self-containment he had learned while crossing the ocean with refugees who had too many stories to tell, tales they had better not begin because it would be difficult to end or control the flow of things remembered. Fonstein's own resigned attitude leaves Sorella and the narrator to wonder at tawdry Billy's evasion of the consequences of what may have been his one series of good acts. "Too Jewish a moment," the narrator suggests of Billy facing Fonstein.

But that is a moment that *must* happen, Sorella has determined. With her fierce intelligence, she collects from Rose's secretary a damning file of his less creditable secrets, hoping to confront him with such "whitemail" and force him into an act of virtue. Her chance comes in Israel. She is visiting there; the narrator is present on Mnemosyne business; and Rose has brought over Isamu Noguchi to lay out his sculpture garden at the museum. It is not fair for a reviewer to say what happens when Sorella meets Billy, except that Sorella calls it "a one-hundred-percent American event." But one can say that the narrator should have taken the opportunity to look at Sorella's dossier on Rose. This is the central document of the story, the equivalent of Hitchcock's "thirty-nine steps" of defense information, something a memory expert could have stored up for those hoping to explain the puzzle of Fonstein's involvement with America. But this "Mr. Memory" prefers, as usual, not to burden himself with avoidable memories.

There is a falling off in the story's pace after the scene in Israel, but there is clearly meant to be. The narrator loses track of the Fonsteins. He is called about a Fonstein relative needing help in Israel, tries to reach Sorella and her husband, finds they are dead, learns of their son's American life, and is left trying to work out his memories of them without fresh information from Sorella. He had avoided the Fonsteins earlier because they put a strain on his method, which is to render items of information disjunct from any emotions that might gum up the operations of his memory. Besides, his rich Philadelphia wife did not consider the grotesque Sorella worthy, not a proper visitor to the house whose emptiness now mocks the narrator with its memorizable items of choice furniture. . . . As he looks back on this sequence of memories, the narrator finds person after person not good enough for one situation, or too good for another. Experiences are too Jewish to be indulged, or too American to be taken seriously. Even an energy like Sorella's becomes an embarrassment, something that can only be expended in nonfunctional cleverness, in a diplomacy as ingenious as it is futile.

The narrator is a fine comic invention because he is almost entirely ignorant of his own absurdity. He likes to talk of memory as the source of life, the key to identity; but he can merely observe, not explain, the fact that his institute catches on in Japan and Korea but not in Israel. Saint Augustine describes memory in Book X of his *Confessions* as cavernous but luminous, its chambers resonating from liquid pools and distant recesses. The Mnemosyne Man's memory looks more like a switchboard with most of the lines unplugged. . . .

"Mr. Mnemosyne" is not simply a loser, like the hero of *Seize the Day.* But neither, thank God, is he one of Bellow's Herzog-bores, one of those Big Thinkers he neglected to equip with big thoughts, the Chicago Spenglers railing at gangsters and the blacks. The discipline of shorter forms has often been good for Bellow (though not in his last novella, *A Theft*). And his irony is at its finest when, as in the short story collection *Mosby's Memoirs* (1968), the consciousness being explored does not get the point of its own story. This new tale's demon rememberer is bombarded by unwanted and unusable information, forced to register what he has no resource for affecting. Even the disjointures, personal and generational, between Americans and Israelis—starting with the freakish benefactions and neglect by Billy Rose—are not a political allegory so much as a sardonic reflection on the fact that ours is called the era of "modern communications." All the narrator can do is look in dogged hope back to the conundrum of Sorella's vividness breaking all conceivable bounds. As he nears his own grave, he keeps thinking of the woman who made one look twice at the size of doors.

Garry Wills, "Mr. Memory," in The New York Review of Books, *Vol. XXXVI, No. 15, October 12, 1989, p. 34.*

John Leonard

It's nice of Saul Bellow to publish his novellas in cheap paperbacks—sort of Regular American of him, populist and democratic. I just wish they had more bite. **The Bellarosa Connection** improves on **A Theft,** his previous paperback original. It's feistier, full of headlong motion, slapdash dazzle. But it stops so suddenly, as if worried about the great theme around the next curve, that we collide. There's reader whiplash. We have barely got acquainted with Harry Fonstein, a European Jew rescued from Hitler by the Broadway impresario Billy Rose; and Fonstein's American wife Sorella, who wants Rose to acknowledge his personal responsibility for Fonstein's implausible survival. We want to hear more from our nameless narrator about the meaning of it all. But this narrator—a man made wealthy by teaching memory tricks to politicians, business executives and members of the defense establishment; an American Jew perhaps too much asimilated—chooses to forget. Forgetting, we are told, is the sleep of consciousness, a kind of death. But what exactly is he choosing *not* to remember? The Americanization of the Jews? The end of innocence in the Nazi death camps? Jerusalem itself? We don't really know the narrator well enough to decide, and Bellow, from whom we expect a flourish, turns off like a radio.

Until then, on this radio, there's been snap, crackle and pop. The problem here isn't ideas; Bellow's full of them. They're promiscuous, even disdainful: "the canned sauerkraut of Spengler's Prussian socialism," complained Herzog years ago; "the cant and rant of the pipsqueaks about inauthenticity and forlorness." And the problem isn't language, either. His art, as always, is brilliant, twitchy talk: mandarin and colloquial; long ironies and low laughs; Talmudic mutter and gangster slang; Melville, Huck Finn, Rudolf Steiner, Lenny Bruce. . . . And who else but Bellow would see "the slapstick side" of death camps, the Dada and Surrealism? "Prisoners were sent naked into a swamp and had to croak and hop like frogs. Freezing slave laborers lined up on parade in front of the gallows and a prison band played Viennese light opera waltzes."

The problem, instead, is character. Fonstein is too indistinct to care about. About Sorella we know mainly that she's fat: "She made you look twice at a doorway. When she came to it, she filled the space like a freighter in a canal lock." But why does she have to be—why not tall, skinny, blond or bald?—except that, invariably, there is something grotesque, something physically threatening, a pair of *Psycho* shoulders, about women in Bellow's fiction? When our narrator chooses to forget, is it because he's American, or rich, or childless, or divorced—or an adviser to military types? Why, anyway, did Israel reject his bag of memory tricks? None of this really adds up. Cynthia Ozick's recently published *The Shawl* is just as much about memory, and even shorter than **The Bellarosa Connection** and yet it breaks the heart . . . because it has one. (pp. 652-53)

John Leonard, in a review of "The Bellarosa Connection," in The Nation, *New York, Vol. 249, No. 18, November 27, 1989, pp. 652-53.*

FURTHER READING

[*Listed below are some of the critical works published on Bellow during the 1980s.*]

Aharoni, Ada. "Women in Saul Bellow's Novels." In *Studies in American Jewish Literature,* edited by Daniel Walden, pp. 99-112. Albany: State University of New York Press, 1983.

In opposition to those critics who consider Bellow's portrayals of women unconvincing or sexist, Aharoni asserts that Bellow is commenting upon society's attitudes toward women and that he "has given us a vast and rich gallery of convincing and vivid women of all kinds."

Braham, Jeanne. *A Sort of Columbus: The American Voyages of Saul Bellow's Fiction.* Athens: The University of Georgia Press, 1984, 151 p.

General study relating Bellow's exploration of the nature of humanity's freedom and the quest of modern individuals for communal values to the American literary tradition.

Bruckner, D. J. R. "A Candid Talk with Saul Bellow." *The New York Times Magazine* (15 April 1984): 52, 54, 56, 60, 62.

Article combining observation with Bellow's comments on such topics as Chicago, politics, literature, and stories in *Him with His Foot in His Mouth.*

Christhilf, Mark. "Saul Bellow and the American Intellectual Community." *Modern Age* 28, No. 1 (Winter 1984): 55-67.

Examines Bellow's critique of intellectual attitudes in his various novels.

Cronin, Gloria L., and Goldman, L. H., eds. *Saul Bellow in the 1980s: A Collection of Critical Essays.* East Lansing: Michigan State University Press, 1989, 328 p.

Contains original and reprinted essays on both general and specialized topics by such contributors as Daniel Fuchs, Ellen Pifer, and Matthew C. Roudané.

Cronin, Gloria L., and Hall, Blaine H. *Saul Bellow: An Annotated Bibliography, Second Edition.* New York: Garland Publishing, Inc., 1987, 312 p.

Includes a chronology of Bellow's career, a primary bibliography, and a checklist of articles and books on the author up to 1986.

Eiland, Howard. "Bellow's Crankiness." *Chicago Review* 32, No. 4 (Spring 1981): 92-107.

Asserts that Bellow's disagreeability functions as an eccentric comment on modern times and expresses "a profound ambivalence: an allegiance divided between claims of conscience and spontaneity."

Fuchs, Daniel. "Bellow and Freud." *Studies in the Literary Imagination* XVII, No. 2 (Fall 1984): 59-80.

Compares Bellow's debt to and rejection of Freudian psychoanalytic notions.

———. *Saul Bellow: Vision and Revision.* Durham, N. C.: Duke University Press, 1984, 345 p.

Attempts "to define the writer's literary and cultural mileus" and in separate chapters examines each of Bellow's major works, beginning with *The Adventures of Augie March* and concluding with *The Dean's December,* "from the point of view of how it was composed."

Goldman, L. H. *Saul Bellow's Moral Vision: A Critical Study of the Jewish Experience.* New York: Irvington Publishers, Inc., 1983, 269 p.

General analysis of Bellow's major works through *Humboldt's Gift* in which Goldman asserts that the author's writings "epitomize the moral vision that is an integral part of the Jewish outlook."

———. "The Holocaust in the Novels of Saul Bellow." *Modern Language Studies* XVI, No. 1 (Winter 1986): 71-80.

Insists that Bellow's novels "present a concerted attack on Nazism and on those ideas which gave rise to the phenomenon of Nazism."

Gullette, Margaret Morganroth. "Saul Bellow: Inward and Upward, Past Distraction." In her *Safe at Last in the Middle Years: The Invention of the Midlife Progress Novel,* pp. 120-45. Berkeley: University of California Press, 1988.

Analyzes the themes of midlife crisis and renewal in Bellow's novels from *The Adventures of Augie March* onward.

Hassan, Ihab. "Saul Bellow." *The Antioch Review* 40, No. 3 (Summer 1982): 266-73.

Favorable assessment of Bellow's contribution to contemporary literature.

Hollahan, Eugene. " 'Crisis' in Bellow's Novels: Some Data and a Conjecture." *Studies in the Novel* 15, No. 3 (Fall 1983): 249-64.

Contends that Bellow may make frequent use of the word *crisis* "to induce certain perspectives on the characters and events in his books, thereby in part coping with the technical demands of writing a novel."

Kiernan, Robert F. *Saul Bellow.* New York: Continuum, 1989, 270 p.

Detailed biographical and critical study of Bellow's life and works through *More Die of Heartbreak.*

McCadden, Joseph F. *The Flight from Women in the Fiction of Saul Bellow.* Lanham, Md.: University Press of America, 1980, 291 p.

Explores relationships between the sexes and characterizations in the author's works "in order to illuminate the psychological drama that constitutes an important element in Bellow's art."

Melbourne, Lucy L. "The Unreliable Diarist: Saul Bellow's *Dangling Man.*" In her *Double Heart: Explicit and Implicit Texts in Bellow, Camus and Kafka,* pp. 37-140. New York: Peter Lang, 1986.

Detailed examination of Bellow's first novel based upon a phenomenonological approach to first-person narrative.

Nagel, James. "Saul Bellow and the University as Villain." In *The American Writer and the University,* edited by Ben Siegel, pp. 114-35. Newark: University of Delaware Press, 1989, 195 p.

Explores Bellow's attacks on university intellectuals and critics, the literary scene, and academic magazines.

Newman, Judie. "Saul Bellow's Sixth Sense: The Sense of History." *The Canadian Review of American Studies* 13, No. 1 (Spring 1982): 39-51.

In response to prevailing views that Bellow's fiction expresses a universalized urge toward transcendance rather than a particularized sense of history, Newman argues "that the historical content of his work does enter the novels functionally, organizing their structure."

Pifer, Ellen. "If the Shoe Fits: Bellow and Recent Critics." *Texas Studies in Literature and Language* 29, No. 4 (Winter 1987): 442-57.

Addresses Bellow's reluctance to accept critical labels and the concomitant need for such categories.

Rodrigues, Eusabio L. *Quest for the Human: An Exploration of Saul Bellow's Fiction.* Lewisburg, Pa.: Bucknell University Press, 1981, 287 p.

Analyzes Bellow's exploration of "fundamental questions about human existence and action in our day."

————. "Beyond All Philosophies: The Dynamic Vision of Saul Bellow." *Studies in the Literary Imagination* XVII, No. 2 (Fall 1984): 97-110.

Explores the shift in Bellow's fiction away from reliance upon established Western orthodoxies and toward personal intuition and insight.

Ryan, Steven T. "The Soul's Husband: Money in *Humboldt's Gift.*" *Genre* XIII, No. 1 (Spring 1980): 111-21.

Affirms the primacy of the soul over the pursuit of wealth in Bellow's novel.

Schechner, Mark. "Down in the Mouth with Saul Bellow." In his *After the Revolution: Studies in the Contemporary Jewish American Imagination,* pp. 121-58. Bloomington: Indiana University Press, 1987.

Overview of Bellow's major works through *The Dean's December* emphasizing the variousness of his fiction.

Scheffler, Judith. "Two-Dimensional Dynamo: The Female Character in Saul Bellow's Novels." *Wascana Review* 16, No. 2 (Fall 1981): 3-19.

Contends that Bellow's abstraction of women as minor or two-dimensional characters subordinate to his main character "offers wide-ranging implications about the protagonists' development and Bellow's characterization in general."

Christy Brown

1932-1981

Irish novelist, poet, and autobiographer.

Perhaps best known in the United States for the 1989 film adaptation of his 1954 autobiography, *My Left Foot,* Brown was more famous in Great Britain for several novels and volumes of poetry published between 1970 and his death from asphyxiation in 1981. Brown was born into an impoverished Irish family in Dublin, the tenth of twenty-two children. Crippled from birth by cerebral palsy, Brown was diagnosed by doctors as mentally impaired and was believed incapable of movement or communication until his family discovered that at the age of five he could grasp objects using his left foot. *My Left Foot,* which Brown wrote on a typewriter using his toes, recounts his relatively normal childhood, during which his brothers took him along with them during their sojourns in Dublin by means of a boxcart; his unhappy adolescence and subsequent immersion in painting, reading, and writing; and his release from seclusion as a patient of Dr. Robert Collins, a Dublin specialist who elicited some improvement in Brown's movement and speech using an innovative treatment for cerebral palsy. Brown's autobiography was praised for its lack of resentfulness and candid, rich descriptions. Carol Stewart commented: [*My Left Foot*] is not a book only for those directly concerned with cerebral palsy. We can all learn from the writer's refusal to be shut in by self-pity and bitterness over his limitations."

Brown achieved literary fame with his first novel, *Down All the Days.* Written fifteen years after *My Left Foot,* this book echoes his own autobiography in its story of an unnamed crippled man with the use of only his left foot. As part of a large family living in near poverty, the narrator observes but rarely participates in the activities of those around him, and focuses particularly upon his drunken, abusive father and caring but exhausted mother. After suffering from feelings of guilt and persecution as an adolescent, the protagonist seeks refuge in writing. Although faulted as verbose, episodic, and derivative of the works of James Joyce and Sean O'Casey, the novel became a best-seller and garnered praise for its revealing observation of characters and situations. Robert Ostermann called *Down All the Days* "an unforgettable literary experience," and Maurice Capitanchik commented: "[By writing this novel], Christy Brown shows himself to be a great man. Never again will we be able complacently to assume a deformed child to be a deficient human being."

Brown's second novel, *A Shadow on Summer,* focuses on Riley McCombe, a crippled Irish writer with one successful novel. McCombe leaves his homeland at his publisher's request to tour New York City while "working on a novel about New England as seen through Irish eyes, not always smiling." While traveling, McCombe becomes involved in two unsuccessful love affairs and seeks escape in writing and alcohol. Although many critics faulted the novel's prose style as static and overwritten, many praised Brown's delineation of pompous and spurious social types. Brown also received mixed notices for *Wild Grow the Lil-*

ies: An Antic Novel, a picturesque narrative in which a cynical Dublin journalist, who is by his own admission infatuated with words, aspires to write "a chronicle of Dublin writ large" while visiting the city's brothels and bars. *A Promising Career* is a posthumously published novel set amidst the popular music scene in Great Britain. This work contrasts the stormy marriage of a musical duo with the moral decline of their agent, who neglects his dying wife in favor of dissolute sexual relationships.

In addition to his novels, Brown also completed several volumes of poetry. *Come Softly to My Wake: The Poems of Christy Brown,* a collection of love poems written in prose form, achieved commercial success but lesser critical attention than his novels. Although this volume was faulted by critics as discursive, unfocused, or overly derivative of the works of James Joyce and Dylan Thomas, Brown garnered praise for the frankness and accessibility of his verse. Brown also published two ensuing volumes of verse, *Background Music* and *Of Snails and Skylarks.* Robert Greacen commented of Brown's posthumously published *Collected Poems:* "His work, though not outstanding in a purely literary sense, scores highly for humanity and sincerity. . . . Despite his disadvantages, he obviously loved being alive and enjoyed people. . . .

These poems, for all their technical shortcomings, stand as a monument to a remarkable and brave man."

(See also *Contemporary Authors,* Vol. 105 and *Dictionary of Literary Biography,* Vol. 14.)

PRINCIPAL WORKS

AUTOBIOGRAPHY

My Left Foot 1954; also published as *The Childhood Story of Christy Brown,* 1972

NOVELS

Down All the Days 1970
A Shadow on Summer 1974
Wild Grow the Lilies: An Antic Novel 1976
A Promising Career 1982

POETRY

Come Softly to My Wake: The Poems of Christy Brown 1971
Background Music 1973
Of Snails and Skylarks 1977
Collected Poems 1982

The New Statesman & Nation

[Mr. Christy Brown] suffers from a form of brain injury at birth which resulted in helplessness, writhing movements and the inability to speak. The writing of [*My Left Foot*] is a proof of not only his own efforts but his mother's energy and belief in him. Though she bore 22 children in a small house in Dublin, and 13 of them survived, she yet made time to teach this middle son whom doctors had given up as mentally defective. Suddenly finding that he could use his left foot for grasping, painting and writing, Mr. Brown in his unhappy adolescence took refuge in the only kind of self-expression left to him. Earlier his brothers and sisters had taken him so much for granted that he had hardly realised that anything was wrong. This book tells simply, with some humour, of family life. It includes a trip to Lourdes, which brought spiritual exaltation but not physical improvement. It ends hopefully, for the author was drawn from his solitude by Dr. Robert Collins, who was trying in Dublin a new treatment for cerebral palsy.

One would expect the life of such a boy to have distinctive experiences, a spiritual growth different from the average. In fact Mr. Brown sees the world of his family and friends very much as a normal boy would, except that he had more time to give to the arts. In his teens he did begin to feel different, watching his brothers and sisters growing to maturity, work and marriage while he himself remained static. He had the feeling too of being imprisoned in his body without an outlet. Rather drily he describes how he contemplated suicide. But in general he is so much like other young men that the reader tends to forget his disabilities and so to give him less honour than he deserves. Here and there he shows traces of pride in achievement but nowhere of self-pity.

A review of "My Left Foot," in The New Statesman & Nation, *Vol. XLVIII, No. 1234, October 30, 1954, p. 558.*

The Times Literary Supplement

Mr. Christy Brown was born in Dublin in 1932, the son of a bricklayer. There were nine children before him and twelve after; of these twenty-two births only thirteen survived and one of them was an invalid. Although his mother became aware when he was only four months old that something was wrong, no action was taken until after his first birthday. The doctors diagnosed mental defect: "Don't look to this boy as you would to the others." At five he could not even mumble and was convulsed with "wild, stiff, snake-like movements." He owed his final release from these disabilities to the resourcefulness and patience of his mother. It was she who spent hours in persuading him to practise after the impulse came to him to use his left foot. He saw his sister writing sums on a slate with a piece of yellow chalk. "I wanted desperately to do what my sister was doing. . . . Then—without thinking or knowing exactly what I was doing, I reached out and took the stick of chalk out of my sister's hand—*with my left foot.*" To a child who had never picked up anything in his life before, or used any limb in any way, it was the crucial moment of his life. Under his mother's tuition he learned to paint as well as to write letters and words, always with his left foot. In later years when he attended a clinic, the use of it was discouraged until he had obtained the use of other limbs.

He tells how he began to write his autobiography [*My Left Foot*], using long words and imitating Dickens, and how Dr. Robert Collis, who has written a preface and epilogue to the book, talked to him about the art of writing. He is obviously very imitative, and this is his salvation from the cerebral palsy from which he suffers. If he had the full use of his limbs, and above all of speech, he would probably have no desire to write. As it is he tells his story simply and well, with no more naivety than Dr. Collis, who says, " . . . coming as I do from a strangely literary family."

The most attractive part is the author's account of his early childhood before he became conscious of his condition. His brothers took him about with them in an old gocar and the episode of the hungry children and the fruit trees—"Seventh—thou shalt not steal!" says the conscientious but inaccurate brother—shows promise that the writer might achieve something real with stories of Dublin life. Why the boys, having stolen the fruit, yet could not eat it must be discovered by the reader. Everyone will wish Mr. Brown well and hope that his book will bring him in enough to buy the electric typewriter. It is a story of tremendous effort and achievement.

"Fight Against Odds," in The Times Literary Supplement, *No. 2766, February 4, 1955, p. 75.*

Carol Stewart

The son of a Dublin bricklayer, Christy Brown was born in 1932 with an injury to his brain which so damaged his power of movement that, till he was eighteen, he could not even sit normally, nor use his hands nor articulate words. . . .

[*My Left Foot*] is his autobiography. In it he describes, simply and vividly, how he fought for the means to express himself and contribute to his world: how he learnt to write with his foot; the passion with which he began painting when he was nine and first became fully aware of his position; . . . how he began to write stories and to educate himself by reading and, finally, how he went at the age of eighteen to the clinic for treatment of cerebral palsy started by Dr. Robert Collis (who contributes a foreword and medical epilogue to his book), where he learnt to sit and stand normally, walk a little and speak so that strangers can understand him. It is the story of fantastic courage, the courage of Christy Brown himself and of his mother who first refused, against all the evidence, to believe that he was mentally defective and then, with twelve other children to look after, had the strength and faith to urge him continually forwards. It is not a book only for those directly concerned with cerebral palsy. We can all learn from the writer's refusal to be shut in by self-pity and bitterness over his limitations.

> *Carol Stewart, in a review of "My Left Foot,"* in The Spectator, *Vol. 194, No. 6608, February 18, 1955, p. 201.*

Nancy Nickerson

As a handicapped person myself, I am of the belief that no book on the subject of physical disability can stand alone on its shock value as a horror tale, or alone on its sentimental appeal as an "uplift" story, or alone as a psychological wallowing. I believe that any book which has been graced with covers should stand primarily as a work of art, of valid literary achievement. A handicapped person is in a prime position to be an artist, since he has already been put off by fate on the island of which Anne Morrow Lindbergh writes in *Gift from the Sea.*

Certainly Christy Brown, the author of *My Left Foot,* lives on a human island as isolated as can be imagined and perhaps it has been his confinement on his island of contemplation which makes his book [worthy of] literary distinction. Until the age of five he had no understandable means of communication with another human being. Spastic with cerebral palsy, the tenth child in the family of a Dublin bricklayer, he was loved and accepted, but isolated.

Then suddenly one day he broke from behind his wall. With the toes of his left foot he grabbed a piece of chalk from his [sister] and as his family watched in awe he copied off the letter A on the chalk board. With his new-found power of control over a single portion of his body—his left foot—he learned to write and became an inveterate painter. He joined his brothers' rollicking life from his little go-car. But when he was eleven the wall closed in again; his go-car broke down and he was left alone in the garden. "I looked down at my hands," he writes, "twisting and twisting."

In sharp, incisive little pictures whole segments of the author's experience are crystallized—his first self-conscious examination of himself in a mirror, the visit of the neigh-borhood flirt, the pilgrimage to Lourdes, the wedding of his beloved amanuensis. And in the keenness of the feelings he evokes we find how deeply we have lived his life with him.

This ability of Christy Brown to make the reader live his story may be due to the doctor-author to whom Christy turned desperately for help at the age of seventeen. Already the boy who lived in his room in lonely subjectivity had taught himself the difficult techniques of orderly prose construction. Now the doctor taught him to avoid "clichés and purple patches." His hardest task, however, was to wean Christy away from nineteenth-century wordiness which was the natural result of the fact that Dickens's novels were the only books which had ever come his way, and as a result the picture of the clinic for cerebral palsy children writhing on the floor is pure Dickensian imagery, and, to me, the least telling portion of the book. But the miracle of Christy Brown's story is that against the drab and uncreative background of his existence, painting, music, and especially writing, richly fed his extraordinary personality. "If I could not know the joy of dancing," he writes, "I could know the ecstasy of creating." And he has. (p. 17)

> *Nancy Nickerson, "Alone on an Island," in* The Saturday Review, *New York, Vol. XXXVIII, No. 34, August 20, 1955, pp. 17, 33.*

Maurice Capitanchik

Christy Brown's novel [*Down All the Days*] is a lyrical, fictionalised account of a life almost too painful for the rest of us to contemplate. . . . The difficulty in understanding spastics is, apparently, to know whether the sufferer is an intelligent being or a human vegetable. As Christy Brown wrote an autobiography at the age of twenty-one, despite never having been to school, there has been no doubt for many years that he is the former. Now, at thirty-seven, he has produced a book which, although over-written and over-worked, has rich descriptive quality, vivid fantasy, is devoid of self-pity, and, for reasons only partly to do with Mr. Brown's physical condition, must be one of the saddest books ever written.

This is a story with a double theme: the tragic waste of life through brutalising ignorance as well as spasticity. Taken by his tough brothers to see a nude peep-show, the crippled hero hates them for arousing his sense of shame, reminding him of the time he saw his sister's naked body:

> . . . his whole body suddenly flaming and a loud roaring in his temples, he saw her pale breasts appear over the dark satin cupolas . . . the lace pattern of the curtains swaying on her flesh, the nipples dark as berries in the snow; it was beauty and perfection and terror . . .

These feelings merely harm his relationships. A girl deliberately provokes him sexually to see if he reacts 'like the rest'; while she does so, her younger brother drowns. The violent, drunken father, taking out every frustration on his exhausted wife and frightened children, causes the elder boys to join the army and the eldest girl to run away. The most amazing aspect of this work is the way the crippled youth, seeing and understanding more than the others, although never able to use his aggression-laden sexuality, realises the tragic implications of instinct and has compassion for what it does to 'normal' people. In a slightly maudlin but impressive chapter, the father, near to death, realises the futility of his life, for which he blames no one: 'he saw finally his own utter weakness.' The author never condemns helplessness, his indignation is reserved for its abusers: the doctor who doesn't explain why he fondles the cripple's genitals, the nurses who laugh at his erection. If there is a villain, it is, by implication, the Catholic church, which turns men towards destruction by condemning their desires.

This novel has a curious affinity with the work of the American author, Thomas Wolfe. There is a similar predilection for the rhetoric of frenzy, words such as 'glittering', 'teeming', 'marvelling', and a similar ability to portray characters alive in every physical detail, especially the obscene-tongued widow Red Magso, with her 'coarse moist mouth opening wide on a tremendous trumpet-wail of infuriated protest', but both are more controlled and less erudite than in Wolfe. Physically, Wolfe was the opposite to Christy Brown; huge, athletic and a wanderer, yet the source of his intensity, a narrow, claustrophobic upbringing, bound him emotionally perhaps even more. The implication of this, like the implication of Mr. Brown's writing, is that the true cripple is the psychological cripple—freedom is of the mind.

This is not a great novel, it is too close to the root of experience, and the echoes of Joyce and O'Casey ring too loud. But by writing it, Christy Brown shows himself to be a great man. Never again will we be able complacently to assume a deformed child to be a deficient human being. (p. 652)

Maurice Capitanchik, "Saddest Story," in The Spectator, *Vol. 224, No. 7403, May 16, 1970, pp. 652-53.*

The Times Literary Supplement

Christy Brown's Dublin slums, in this remarkable autobiographical novel [*Down All the Days*], are larger than life, dens of roistering blasphemy and fornication. But he has astutely avoided retrospective falsification simply by moving sideways from the child's vision into a highly effective adult fantasy—while still preserving the child's faculties of observation. It is not a *faux naïf* position but a standpoint which enables him to blend the data of the child's imagination with a mature adult view of it. His is a conscious and intelligent art.

The unnamed hero of *Down All the Days,* like Mr. Brown himself, has been severely disabled from birth. When the book opens he is being lifted by his brother out of the boxcar in which he is wheeled about, to watch the risqué peepshow in a penny machine. The sight stirs in him the first sense of dawning adolescence. Intuition of sexual feelings illuminates the slum world around him, a world in which his mother has borne seemingly countless children to a drunken father, his brothers are experimenting with the local teenage piece, his sister runs away from her father's beatings to marry in London. From the position of an observer who can rarely, if ever, participate, he builds up a highly personal episodic picture of Dublin living two decades ago.

Mr. Brown's debts to various chroniclers of Dublin's poverty, seediness and earthy glory are clear, but the final distinctive character of the novel is altogether his own. The stricter kind of realism is abandoned in favour of a vein of fantasy which raises his main characters—Mother and Father—to an almost epic level, archetypal representatives of Dublin's despair and defiance. Sometimes the invention becomes indulgent, as in the frequent dreamsequences of sexual terror or persecution. At certain points the style and the situations are too facilely romantic and anecdotal. But at his best, Mr. Brown writes with a breadth of understanding and resourcefulness that make him already one of the most discerning and lively observers of Irish life.

"Dublin Archetypes," in The Times Literary Supplement, *No. 3561, May 28, 1970, p. 577.*

John Bowen

[*Down All the Days*] is an account of life in a large working-class family in Dublin. Its characters include a mother who is all patient endurance; a father who is all drunken violence; two loosely differentiated elder brothers; a proud and plucky elder sister who runs away to London, gets married, and begins to settle into the same life her mother has known; and a mass of younger children. The whole is seen from the point of view of the one cripple among them, who is dragged about in a boxcart in order to be part of the events he describes.

In a perfect world, the publishers of *Down All the Days* might have offered it to us simply as a book, to be judged, relished or rejected on its own merits. But the world of publishers is not perfect, and writers are often more marketable than the books they write. What we are offered, therefore, is a work that may claim the freedom of a novel and the authenticity of autobiography. Always present in the reader's mind will be the knowledge of the painful and difficult conditions under which it was composed.

It may most easily be accepted, I think, neither as a novel nor autobiography, but as a series of prose poems, highly variable in quality, written on a linked theme. It lacks the narrative structure of a novel. There are episodes of action, but they do not lead to or follow from each other. For example, when the father secretly keeps £35 of union subscriptions in a pocket of a suit, the mother pawns it on the day he is to render his accounts. We do not know he has acquired this responsibility. Nor do we know what happens when he explains the loss of the money—or even if he tries to get it back. We have the scene, and that is all.

Nor can I think of any way to accept the prose itself except as a kind of poetry. It has virtues. Mr. Brown has a comic sense that is not exercised frequently enough. He has energy. He delights in describing drunkenness, violence, dirt and death. If, after *Portnoy's Complaint,* masturbation is still fashionable in American literary circles, his book should find a large public, for there is a deal of that. The prose is all images. Some are vivid and reverberative, as when the child, in one of his many dreams, sees a rat eat its way from the inside of his father's head—and this just after Mr. Brown has shifted his viewpoint suddenly, and shown the father to us from his own side, no longer a drunken ogre, but a tired and despairing man on the edge of death.

The prose has virtues, and grave defects. That ingenuous, damaging devil of a blurb-writer tells us—in Mr. Brown's presence—that "when it comes to the use of the English language, most of us are cripples." This is simply not true. The author's prose is poetic, but it is often very bad. Nouns are sunk beneath the weight of the adjectives he piles on them. Verbs are dragged down by adverbs. Often the adjectives consist of hyphenated nouns. Often they are meaningless. Alliteration abounds.

Even if one reads the book as a collection of prose poems—that is, a little at a time—there are too many images for imagery's sake. Consider this:

> The houses stood like squat, disgruntled cocker-spaniels along the snow-mantled streets.

At first reading, the simile is attractive: the houses are like a row of dogs, lining the street. But visualize a cocker-spaniel—domed head, long ears (most unlike the eaves of a town house), long nose, large eyes, curly coat. Then visualize a row of houses, in or out of snow. Ask "Why are the dogs disgruntled?" Would they look less like houses if they weren't happy or even patient? Compare the image with Dickens's in *Hard Times* of factory machinery as "melancholy-mad elephants."

It doesn't compare. Images in any language should have a purpose. When everything is like something, nothing is like anything. *Down All the Days* is said to be the first volume of a trilogy. In the second installment, I hope Mr. Brown will allow some of his houses to look like houses. (pp. 4, 20)

> *John Bowen, in a review of "Down All the Days," in* The New York Times Book Review, *June 14, 1970, pp. 4, 20.*

Robert Ostermann

As their prose and poetry clearly demonstrate, the Irish have a distinct way with misfortune and suffering: They tame these things, in effect, by giving them house room. . . . Irish literature's testimony is that only a fool would expect life to be any different, that joy and suffering jostle each other in a crowd of experiences. They are simply some of the facts of life.

These thoughts are a valuable prelude to considering a remarkable novel, *Down All the Days,* by a 37-year-old Irishman named Christy Brown. It's the story of life in a Dublin slum, as observed and experienced by a youth so severely crippled and deformed that he must be hauled around in a wagon by his brothers or carried on their shoulders.

The boy's family endures enough hardship and misery for 10 households. The father is often drunk and regularly brutal; he believes children are better if reared with a leather belt and wives are best if beaten before being taken to bed. The mother makes her annual trip to the maternity hospital, sews patches on the patches of her children's clothes, and watches the poverty accrue in her family like interest on a childhood investment of despair.

But through all its scenes of coarseness and brutality, of wasted lives and bleached hopes, *Down All the Days* throbs with defiant vitality. Life is not summed up by the oppressions it endures, the author asserts, and he raises a whirlwind of mesmerizing words to affirm that the ultimate victor is the human individual.

Let one brief passage stand for those that crowd the pages of this novel. It occurs when the crippled boy is trying to hold in his memory one of the brief moments of tenderness he has witnessed between father and mother:

> Nothing of peace or charm lasted longer than it took his beating heart to feel it, and he was back once more in the walled garden of his thoughts, chasing the shadows of such moments, listening always rapt and intent for the wings of his ambiguous angel, the touch of felicitous fingers upon his brow that turned always and abruptly to a vicious cheek-stinging slap dashing the tears from his eyes.
>
> Awkward as an animal, and more immediately mute, he was learning to grow and live without being blinded by the stars.

Christy Brown has every right to his triumphant affirmative. For in its broad lines, Christy Brown's novel is Christy Brown's life. . . .

Down All the Days was typed out letter by letter with the little toe of Christy Brown's left foot over a span of 15 years.

It is impossible to detach one's reaction to this book from the unique circumstances of its creation. The very fact that it exists at all gives *Down All the Days* an unassailable value; it would be worth attention if it had no literary merit, which is far from the truth. Further, some of its features that cry out for comment are inescapably connected to its origins.

For example, the book lacks the vivid particularity of scene and place that is typical of Irish fiction backwards and forwards from Joyce. The streets, buildings, churches, and rooms are amorphous, generalized; they could be anywhere. But place is the last thing you would expect to count for much in Christy Brown's life. What is sure and precise, exposed like a heart laid bare for surgery, is the agony of the crippled youth who absorbs the life of every person around him, liberating himself in the re-creation of those lives. This agony, moreover, is not something that Mr. Brown has set down as if at arm's length; it clearly informed the composition of the book, and it thereby pervades every sentence, every phrase—twisting out 10 words where 3 would do, heaping up adjectives that hide instead of reveal meaning, sometimes overpowering the senses with erotic frustration. It makes *Down All the Days* an unforgettable literary experience.

> *Robert Ostermann, "Agony Pervades Every Sentence in the Story of a Crippled Life," in* The National Observer, *June 29, 1970, p. 19.*

William Beauchamp

> O Matt me darling man! . . . I hope you're with God in heaven tonight, but I know in me heart it's down in the quare place you are with a red-hot

poker up your arse and you screaming for mercy
and finding none.

The speaker, Red Magso—widow, toper, sexagenarian,
wielder of the biggest damn tits in the whole of Dublin—
incorporates all that is salty and good in [*Down All the
Days,* the] first novel by Christy Brown, a brawling,
mirthful, poetic, but often boring book even though cas-
cades of images and metaphors body forth the "blooming,
buzzing confusion of life" in a working-class Dublin family in the late Thirties.

Much of the phantasmagoria—mostly juxtaposed blocks
of episodes and description, with little plot—filters
through a modified "central intelligence": the crippled, ef-
faced adolescent son. His awakening to a lust for life,
through the first simmerings of sex, provides the book's
leitmotiv, as well as an occasion for wordy, self-indulgent,
lyrical sin.

Christy Brown is superb at dramatization and Irish dialogue, but tiresome in description (landscape, cityscape,
soulscape), stream of consciousness, hallucinations,
dreams. At worst he lapses into second-rate Celtic super-
glut:

> Slowly the cars ground to a halt and disgorged their
> passengers, swarming in their black-garbed grief
> and importance over the glistening pavements and
> standing in gabbling clusters waiting for the in-
> cense-swinging priest to come out from his snug lit-
> tle white–walled house next to the ivy-covered
> chapel to lead the wind-raw way to the grave, gap-
> ing like a jagged wound under the wailing sky. . . .

The author conjures up scenes of marvelous tenderness,
pathos, farce: a mindless wrangle over a nationalist hero
that ends in the flinging of cabbage and potatoes; a boyish
debate over the shaving habits of a certain broad-hipped
girl of fourteen; the incredible wake of Red Magso's
daughter, a boisterous mash of litanies, booze, and fornication.

Bawdy humor and colorful language abound, and at moments Mr. Brown achieves poetry: "Another bird para-
chuted softly down, folded its wings, and cuddled in a
brown dream in the folds of the infant's cherubic neck."
(Even here, though, doesn't one itch to blue-pencil "cherubic"?)

Nevertheless, Christy Brown has produced a sensuous, exuberant, noteworthy book. Too bad he didn't slash the
fancy stuff by half. If he should do so in his second novel,
it could be a real literary event.

> *William Beauchamp, in a review of "Down All
> the Days," in* Saturday Review, *Vol. LIII, No.
> 31, August 1, 1970, p. 28.*

Paul Kameen

Christy Brown is thirty-eight. [*Come Softly to My Wake:
The Poems of Christy Brown*] is his first book of poetry
(though he has achieved a great deal of prominence as a
novelist). He has yet to learn that one clear word is more
impressive than a vague stanza, and that a tight short
poem is better than a cluttered long one.

Poems which contain much that could be of value are
scarred with weaknesses:

> I pensively sipped my drink
> staring out at the unseen lawn.
>
>   . . .
>
> I stared at a pair of faded pink slippers
> imagined the toes in them
> most ordinary and naked
> and savagely devoured my drink. . . .

There is potential in Brown's unique vision of the world.
The achievement, though, is badly flawed by verbal imprecision and excess. "I want," Brown says, "to be recognized
more than anything else as a poet." That he may well accomplish; but he seems indecisive concerning the adjective
which will inevitably modify his title.

> *Paul Kameen, in a review of "Come Softly to
> My Wake: The Poems of Christy Brown," in*
> Best Sellers, *Vol. 31, No. 20, January 15,
> 1972, p. 459.*

John Mellors

[Reading *A Shadow on Summer*], you get a nasty shock
from the disorder of Christy Brown's 'highly charged battery of instant hysterical response'. The trouble with hysterical responses is that while, no doubt, they relieve the
writer, they place a heavy burden on the reader. And it is
not just a question of which you happen to prefer, sense
or sensibility, the sober or the sensational. When an author just wants to get to his typewriter and 'pound upon
it with as much passion and frenzy as a love-crazed man
might pummel the flesh of the woman he loved', the result
is inevitably careless, inaccurate and irritating. For example, Brown describes a fat man sleeping on a beach: 'pudgy
fingers entwined upon an Everest of a belly'. Everest?
What belly ever looked like a Himalayan mountain peak?

A Shadow on Summer is the story of Riley McCombe, a
crippled Irish writer who has been invited to America by
his publisher, partly to be fêted for the best-seller he has
written, partly to be encouraged to write an even better
second novel. Two women fall in love with him, but he is
in thrall to his typewriter, obsessed with words: they 'poured
from him, random and raging, roaring and ranting, swallowing up page upon page'. This kind of writing works
when it is used to describe Riley's drunkenness and his impressions on a whirlwind tour of New York, but the con-
gruity of style with subject is only intermittent. One of
Riley's women keeps urging him to tone down his prose:
'The talent you have needs constant care, constant prun-
ing, it cannot be allowed to be choked in a proliferating
wilderness of language.' The author must, then, be alive
to his own faults. (p. 157)

> *John Mellors, "Law and Disorder," in* The
> Listener, *Vol. 92, No. 2366, August 1, 1974,
> pp. 156-57.*

Valentine Cunningham

Christy Brown's first novel [*Down All the Days*] was just

another of those genial Irish fictions contentedly becalmed on oceans of booze and words.

A Shadow on Summer has the good sense to cool it verbally, if only a bit. Indeed it's all about the novelist Riley McCombe—crippled, Irish, in the middle of an American fêting for his successful first novel, and not exactly unakin to his author—having coolness urged upon him in the fiction he's currently about. 'Words. Oh, Riley, when are you going to get away from words?' his hostess and constant critic wants to know. Well, he does manage a break or two from the typewriter, slotting in the odd hour between the sheets with a lissom girl photographer, and putting back a few drinks at the parties his American publisher is always arranging. After all, he needs the material since, as he informs one of the authors who are constantly being pressed on his attention, he's 'working on a novel about New England as seen through Irish eyes, not always smiling'. And our novelist's eye and ear for recording pomposities, bores and pseudery are agreeably acute. But if words alone are uncertain good they're mighty attractive, and Riley is continually drawn back to his not quite intolerable wrestle with them. Though the novel gets at times too coy about Riley's authorship problems ('I am a pygmy Narcissus,' he wails, not expecting to be believed, 'endlessly gawking at himself in a golden pond of whiskey—boring, boring'), and is frequently too gushing about Riley's triumphs, its sharpest insights concern the necessary privateness and privations of creativity. At its best, and worst, Christy Brown's prose is static, given lengthily to pursuing and explicating the sensations of each slow moment: very much the product of living at the edge of immobility. It's a marvelously apt medium for rendering the feelings of a hero who is also marooned on crutches or stuck at a table, familiar most of all with the stench of his own armpits and the race of his own thoughts.

Valentine Cunningham, "Unsmiling," in New Statesman, *Vol. 88, No. 2263, August 2, 1974, p. 163.*

Anatole Broyard

I don't find writers who are "drunk with words" any more interesting than ordinary drunks. I'll show you why, with a sentence from *A Shadow on Summer,* by Christy Brown:

> And children, always the children, glorifying the day, making a hymn of it, splashing in the listing surf, taking the great harm out of the world, laughing as only children can in the rare ecstasy of their time, making sand castles, destroying them, building new ones, racing joyously to meet the ceaseless waves, crying in their freedom, squaring up to each other, causing sweet chaos in the sand, their very rowdiness lending an odd peace to the bay, water glistening down their small articulate limbs, happy and victorious, playing with life and sure of winning.

I think Mr. Brown has crammed almost as many unwarranted generalizations into that sentence as it will hold. If this were the only sentence of its kind in *A Shadow on Summer,* I would not make an issue of it, but they were almost all like that.

Though they are long and full of qualifying refinements, giving the illusion of carrying a thought to its apotheosis,

these lines are static, beginning and ending with a stale preciosity. Their litany-like rhythms are as gratuitous and mechanical as the music you hear piped into elevators. The author is not trying to make us feel what he describes: he is trying to impress us with his description of it. His "eloquence" is not urgent, but complaisant.

Such as it is, Mr. Brown's style is the inevitable instrument for his characters. I have never seen a book so entrenched in clichés. Riley McCombe, the hero, is a young Irish writer who, after bringing out one brilliant novel, is having difficulty with his second. His British publisher suggests that he needs to "get away" and proposes to send him to Connecticut to recollect his emotions in tranquility. His friends, Laurie and Don Emerson, will be glad to put Riley up. Riley accepts, and soon he is anxiously listening to Laurie criticize his work. It is worthy and obscure, she says, true to her Emerson New England heritage of clarity, honesty and economy. " 'That's the only way I can write—the only way for me,' he broke in quickly, having the sudden sick feeling that she misunderstood what he was so laboriously so heart-achingly trying to say."

Soon Riley's heart is aching not only for his work, but for Laurie as well. He thrusts aside the unworthy emotion. "Suddenly he wanted to get back to his typewriter, converse with it, to pound upon it with as much passion and frenzy as a love-crazed man might pummel the flesh of the woman he loved, seeking an answer or an ending to his existence." He would do better, judging by that sentence, to seek a grammar book first.

Enter Abbie—lost, wistful, gamine-like, wanting only to be with Riley, to share silently in his struggle, to sit and look out with him at the waning moon after his frenzy at the typewriter has subsided. Riley is a cripple who wears braces on his legs: for this reason, in spite of his passionate nature, he is a virgin. Abbie doesn't know: she seduces him. But alas, he cannot give himself. He is monogamously married to his muse. He is only a spectator, a ghost at the banquet of being. "I must hold onto myself at all costs," he tells Abbie,

> I must not try to escape through other people, through their love, kindness, understanding—call it what you will. God knows I don't wish to be alone, to remain forever on the outside, but in the end I would rather be trapped within myself than to lose myself in others.

There is more, and worse, to come. Mr. Brown's conception of a writer reminds me of those people who think of Vincent Van Gogh as a madman who cut off his ear and gave it to a prostitute because he was too pure to give her anything else. It is unfortunate that the author of *A Shadow on Summer* is an almost total spastic . . . but I don't see how the badness of his second novel can be blamed on that. Any man who can learn to type with his left foot can learn to write better than he has here.

Anatole Broyard, "A Libel on Writers," in The New York Times, *February 3, 1975, p. 23.*

Peter La Salle

Christy Brown's first novel, *Down All the Days,* was a lyrical recreation of life in the Dublin backstreets, and it sold well on both sides of the Atlantic. . . .

In this second novel, an Irish novelist, Riley McCombe, comes to suburban Connecticut to wrestle through finishing a second novel after the enormous success of his first. There are three painful love affairs for McCombe: one with his typewriter, a second with his host's straight wife and a third with a hip Greenwich Village photographer. The plot evolves out of the interaction of the three.

McCombe is crippled himself, and, obviously, much of this is autobiographical. I should say here that I interviewed Brown in his native Ireland in 1970. He flatly told me that his method is Wolfean—i.e., he wants to fictionalize his own life story—the scenes, the emotions—in powerful writing that will make that story worth reading. *A Shadow on Summer* demonstrates again that Brown is a master word-wielder. He can write resonant passages of piled participles and striking images that are moving in themselves.

The trouble is that there is that same tendency to get carried away with words as there is in Thomas Wolfe—or James Agee, or Jack Kerouac or even Norman Mailer, for that matter. The reader sometimes finds himself buried under a cascade of prose, and it all begins to look like mere showing off. The saving grace here, though, is that McCombe candidly admits that overwriting is a fault in his work. Made aware of McCombe's shortcoming, the reader tends to forgive Brown, whom McCombe represents, and keep reading. The tolerance pays off when the resonance does sound again.

A larger problem is that those two important women characters often don't seem believable, and the book's essential conflicts naturally depend on their convincingness. Both repeatedly turn cute, and they like to deliver stilted speeches instead of just talk. *A Shadow on Summer* simply is not a novel on a part with Brown's first. But again, it is worth reading because encountering Brown's way with words, when that way works, is a rare experience indeed.

> *Peter LaSalle, in a review of "A Shadow on Summer," in* America, *Vol. 132, No. 11, March 22, 1975, p. 217.*

Valentine Cunningham

'Words alone are certain good': there have never been any prizes for spotting that an Irishman thought that, and in his first two novels Christy Brown, like many another marathon Irish talker, proceeded as though producing fictions that merely produce engulfing spates of blarneyfield eloquence were self-justifying enough. This time around, though, he's found from somewhere the good sense to chivvy himself for the practice. At least, in *Wild Grow the Lilies* the central character, a Dublin journalist called Luke Sheridan (occasion of lots of knowing quips about Richard Brinsley and Le Fanu, that one), is from time to time chided for excessive wordiness. 'Don't you ever give your jaws a rest?' inquires a whore (or *brasser* or *mot* or *rossie:* this novel stretches your stock of low vocables if nothing else) of whom he's fond. The novel Sheridan is also about—'a chronicle of Dublin writ large'—will, accuses 'Countess Sonny', a sexy piece mixed up in an obscure high-life crime Sheridan's paper has him investigat-

ing, be a 'verbose hobgoblin'. Naturally Luke isn't exactly mute in his own defence but, creditably, the author has evidently realised that his own indubitably energetic recipe for the muscle-boundedly verbal novel might just fail to be a continually unalloyed delight to one and all. Nonetheless, delight there is in Mr. Brown's filthy-minded pun-palace, with its *stultifera navis* of grotesques (more Bosch than bosh, but only just) zestily afloat on the polluted sea of blackest Irish humour.

> *Valentine Cunningham, "Pincers," in* New Statesman, *Vol. 91, No. 2352, April 16, 1976, p. 514.*

Victoria Glendinning

Wild Grow the Lilies, lively, fluent, and derivative, will probably be every bit as successful as [Christy Brown's earlier novel], *Down All the Days.* Subtitled "An Antic Novel," it traces the mollockings of a Dublin journalist, first cousin in literary terms, need one say, to Buck Mulligan and the Ginger Man. There is a brothel in the city and a sexy German lady out in Howth . . . , a deadline to meet and a running joke about Oscar Wilde and Golden Miller which is peculiarly funny. It is a grossly entertaining novel which would be a terrible bore if it did not move so fast. Never before in my experience has so much alcohol been consumed between hard covers. Christy Brown indulges in all the basic male fantasies and celebrates them unself–consciously. It's the only way.

> *Victoria Glendinning, "Alienation Effects," in* The Times Literary Supplement, *No. 3866, April 16, 1976, p. 455.*

Duncan Fallowell

Christy Brown has written another hectic book, *Wild Grow The Lilies,* passion, skittles and farce, in short as bilious an example of gas-meter literature as any flushed down the corridors of publishing this year. Set in Dublin it characterizes the efforts of a newspaper reporter to write the Great Irish Novel, an object clearly intended to resemble this one, while trying simultaneously to reclaim his mistress. A big job, stuffed with blarney and blasphemy and long confrontations in dialogue, its riotous glee might put one in mind of *Tom Jones* were the writing not like something running headlong after Brendan Behan. (p. 21)

> *Duncan Fallowell, "In the Soup," in* The Spectator, *Vol. 236, No. 7712, April 17, 1976, pp. 20-1.*

Robert Ostermann

Christy Brown, you will remember, is the Dubliner [who] . . . , with his left foot tapped out a novel called *Down All the Days.* It was in every way an astonishing achievement, for it poured out in a verbal flood the coming to physical, imaginative, and intellectual life of a Dublin slum child born into the same crippling prison as its author.

Days could have been, but was not, the end of the literary line for Christy Brown. Several volumes of poetry followed, uncomfortably self-conscious, more poetic ore than refined metal. And now, *Wild Grow the Lilies,* a novel, which stands about as far as can be from *Down All the Days.*

For one thing, it immediately adopts the picaresque mode—honored as far back as Cervantes—with one Luke Sheridan tilting at Irish windmills in Dublin's bars, brothels, and mansions. Luke is a journalist, hard-drinking, cynical, profligate, with a pedantic manner of speech, like Dr. Sam Johnson gone soft-headed and windy. He can't, for example, say anything so simple as that the paper employing him is rotten and ought to be blown up. Instead, "I always thought it could do with some gelignite attached to its somewhat pallid tabs."

Sheridan, in short, is a bore. True, Brown is saying his picaresque hero represents why the Irish don't get anywhere. The Ireland he portrays is little more than a mouthful of adjectives and a few precious active verbs stalled knee-deep in conversation. Here is no Stephen Dedalus of Joyce's intellectually picaresque *Portrait of the Artist as a Young Man,* setting forth to "forge . . . the uncreated conscience of my race." Only words.

But—and this is troubling—the fault is not Sheridan's. It's Brown's, who has barely stayed the flood of words so fitting for *Days,* and can't resist muffling every sentence in *Lilies* with five adjectives where one would do. Sure, it's reminiscent of Joyce, but a Joyce too intoxicated to measure his effects. And Luke inevitably recalls Dedalus, for tucked away somewhere in this dreary bed-sitter is the start of a novel that will tell "all" about contemporary Ireland. Is *Lilies* that novel? Is Brown actually afflicted with his character's logorrhea? Neither is clear.

At any rate one is certain the novel Luke Sheridan is writing will never be completed, just as nothing will ever come of his love for Rosie, Madame Lala's favorite prostitute, or of the aborted murder Luke was supposed to cover or of the faint pure longings of Babysoft, the exquisite whore who loves her work, or of the taximan Ranter's stubborn fortitude in a life composed of too many children and a lockstep marriage.

Alas, alas, it's no longer the Dublin of Yeats and Joyce. And that may be the worst, and the best, that can be said of *Wild Grow the Lilies.*

> Robert Ostermann, " 'Wild Grows the Lilies'. . . And, Alas, Even Wilder Grows the Verbiage," in The National Observer, September 25, 1976, p. 21.

Françoise Borel

Who was not struck and puzzled by Christy Brown's novel, *Down All the Days* when it first appeared in the glow of 'red-hot whiskey' and flaring imagination? It was a strange novel that seemed to have no centre and no boundaries, a collection of scenes and sights, descriptive patches, little one act plays, streams of poetic expressionism; another chronicle of Dublin's wonders and monstrosities. We are confronted with a violent world, that is alive with the echo of harsh voices and with the endless reflections of images caught in bits of broken glass, a world of rumour and vision.

And yet, from the start, the reader is pulled up short by the over-powering presence of the ever present 'He'. The narrator depicts things through the eyes of a cripple watching from his boxcar, forgotten and alone. From that mental viewpoint, the author and 'He', in connivance, are busy sifting facts with ruthless amazement, letting people in with clear-sighted geniality, and curtly refusing to yield to sentimentality. (p. 287)

Animal instinct and shameless Rabelaisian verve pervade every page with bawdy gusto. All the scenes and pictures testify to a fantastic vitality and furious appetite for life. 'He' has an ear for the genuine brand of Irish talk, for strong worded dialogue, pithy terms, full-bodied jokes, for the unexpected impact of any kind of verbal inventiveness. So from his remote vantage-point, through filtered rumours of the wild life abroad, arises a pattern of clamorous pictures connected by an obsessive awareness of violence, elemental tenderness, dark and colorful peering into the microcosm around.

But it is hard to face facts too bluntly, and Christy Brown measured the difficulty; the artist's insight gathered a mythical group of protagonists—the archetypal unit of Father, Mother, and Child, or rather Children. The model is repeated throughout the book with obstinate simplicity: first of all, inside the family, Father, Mother, 'He' and his brothers and sisters.

Father is the bully, the drunk, dealing blows, a crazed and fantastic tyrant, capable at times of tenderness, as he recalls past memories of the time when his wife was young. Mother—a little too much of an angel perhaps—perpetually gives birth to the last one in the room upstairs, terrified and loving. The swarming children join numberless crowds of other children for play and mischief, learning what they want to know of human nature, sex and life through direct observation. 'He', a mere 'voyeur' bound to devour with staring eyes scenes he should have been spared, becomes an object of sexual discovery for the girls.

And the three character drama of family life with a cast of Father, Mother, Offspring is going to be acted again at a precocious age by Lil, the helpless elder sister, who marries in defiance of her father and soon gets pregnant; she has a child which, within a very short time, falls victim to the unsanitary condition of the slum, where she lives; her affectionate husband is already partial to the pint.

Then comes the truculent counterpart to the pattern, Red Magso and her next of kin. The memory of the amorous feats of her late husband does not prevent her from being conscious of her still desirable body:

> 'Amn't I in me prime, woman?' she said, slapping herself on the chest, thrusting out her large bosom that swelled out in the blouse like the full-blown sails of a schooner. 'Take a look at *them!*' she cried proudly; 'you won't buy the likes of *them* in Woolworth's!'

Her weakness for the bottle helps her to forget the worst: her widowhood and the death of her consumptive daughter. At the girl's wake neighbors, friends, and family celebrate the sadness of death and the triumph of vital forces in drunken bouts and desperate orgies.

Most scenes are not really individual scenes, but rather basic models interminably duplicated, rendered in the frequentative mood, with obsessive reiteration, while, behind the scenes, the effect of 'distancing' is produced by the combined use of 'He' and the remote past tense. A few striking episodes are thrown into unique relief by the intrusion of the present tense or the punctual simple past tense. The interplay of person and tense, the intricate chronology of events and revelation give *Down All the Days* a contrasted rhythm of developing narrative, fluid retrospect and broken flashes of imaginative vision freed from the shackles of time. The underlying time pattern emphasizes the startling abruptness and the hallucinatory quality of the novel.

From the first line to the last the author remains 'He', without a name; although we notice that "his" father's surname is Mr. Brown, this clue is not sufficient to make us consider the book as an autobiography.

Christy Brown never claimed that his book was an autobiography, and we must not identify him with the 'He' of the novel. Nevertheless, the relationship between author, narrator, protagonist and reader is far from simple. The distance created by the use of the anonymous 'He' is partly abolished by devices implying the first person singular commitment. References to 'Father' and 'Mother' are heavy with the underlying connotations of possessives like 'my' or 'our'; their deletion suggests the dialectics of distance and closeness that exist throughout the novel.

Conscious of the danger of excessive personal implication, the author refuses to yield to the temptation of self-assertion and self-pity. This was a Promethean task for one whose awareness of life and of the complexities of events could only be expressed by ability to break through his walled-in self. He had to teach himself a language, which was, at first, bound to be inadequate and tentative, and inadequate to his deepest turmoil.

He preferred to give the reality of his desire, frustration, and urge for life, the symbolic scope of impersonal dream and fictitious imagery, by making *Down All the Days* the tumultuous metaphor of the daily fever and weariness of life he encountered in the slums.

That direct crudeness of facts is never wholly present in his autobiography, *My Left Foot,* which lacks the cogency of the novel. This personal narrative is a 'proper' autobiography in the technical sense of the term: author, narrator, and protagonist are one and the same person, referred to as 'I', and 'Christy Brown' in dialogue parts, and the reader is clearly made to accept the convention of authentic self-revelation.

Its factual accuracy cannot be questioned; it tells us the life story of a cripple and is essentially an autobiography of youth. The really tragic dimension is what is left untold, for it states facts plainly so that it is hard to fathom the depth of the child's torment or to sense a more adult grasp of recollections, present questioning or reinterpretation. (pp. 288-90)

[Since] Christy Brown had not been trained or schooled properly, his life-story could not have the dimension of self-evaluation and appraisal inherent in good autobiographies. He lacked adequate means of expression. Self-evaluation seems to be more present in his novel, though subject to rhetorical exaggeration and visionary distortion, than in his autobiography. The 'truth' of an autobi-ography cannot exist independently of the truthfulness of vision arising from the backward look that tries to take in a man's view of himself. *My Left Foot,* however, remains an invaluable document illustrating the first efforts of a man to express himself:

> It would not be true to say that I am no longer lonely, now that I have reached out to thousands of people and communicated to them all the fears, frustrations and hopes which for so long lay bottled up inside me. I have made myself articulate and understood to people in many parts of the world, and this is something we all wish to do whether we are crippled or not. It is a common need to make ourselves understood by others, for none of us can live entirely alone or by our own devices. Yet like everyone else I am acutely conscious sometimes of my own isolation even in the midst of people, and I often give up hope of ever being able to really communicate with them. It is not only the sort of isolation that every writer or artist must experience in the creative mood if he is to create anything at all. It is like a black cloud sweeping down on me unexpectedly, cutting me off from others, a sort of deaf-muteness.

It was through this attempt at formulating the circumstances of his life and its inarticulate aspirations in his first novel that Christy Brown felt free to launch out into a new venture in which he vindicated his right to be considered as a startlingly original writer. The potentialities of his talent were released in the rhapsody of *Down All the Days* that left many readers breathless.

The process through which Christy Brown gained command over his material and possessed himself of a common inheritance enables him to achieve a brutal perfection that unites a dialogue that is full of direct richness with cataracts of dreams and images. This adjectival itch reaches alarming proportions in the second novel *A Shadow on Summer.* Such an inflation of modifiers cannot but hide a multitude of sins. And the brand of adjective proves too often outmoded and unnecessarily erudite or pedantic, we come across gardens 'redolent of memories' and a dog which 'wisely returned to the canine limbo from whence it had been disturbed'. More generally speaking, many turns and terms smell of the lamp, which implies that the novelist tends to consider style as an envelope rather than the constitutive web and woof of his work.

In this second novel, the vein of imitation is much more loquacious for it is not held in check by poignant creative tension. Long winded similes and breathless approximations with inadequate suggestive power make us regret that stream of consciousness techniques should ever have been discovered:

> He looked back, seeing the intricate maze of imprints the car tyres had made in the sand, and thought wryly how these markings resembled the twists and turns of his own life leading now to this strange moment carved out of some dear improbable nowhere, awakening in him all the old inklings and tinklings of the immense wonder and inconquerable mystery of even the most mundane mortal existence . . .

Even in tenser moments, the writer gives vent to a repetitive garrulity that can only dilute the violence of the impression aimed at. . . . (pp. 291-92)

Frequently, the plain statement of facts, whose flatness hasn't even the linear acuity of good drawing, cannot sustain the attention of the reader who feels deprived of any sense of scope in objects or human beings:

> Laurie drove the car into the garage and helped him negotiate the steps that led from there into the huge kitchen with its shelves stacked with cookery books, condiments, spices, gleaming utensils dangling from silver hooks, ladles, gargantuan pots and pans, walnut presses, glittering sink and oven, the innumerable paraphernalia of a kitchen at once modern and charmingly antique, festooned with bright odd drawings and posters extolling the virtues of various seaside resorts . . .

Why did Christy Brown tackle the hazardous theme of a writer's delivery of his work in a land of exile, through the care of a mothering mother of a midwife, Laurie, a literary bore, tediously faithful to a husband, who is the only one to win our sympathy? If there was to be a real competition, Abbie shouldn't have had much more of the enticing siren in her to be worth the contest.

The only way to deal with this pathetic quadrangular plot would have been the mock-heroic register; at times, there are indications that it could have been the case, but on the whole, we are only confronted with a disappointing American T.V. serial.

Why did Christy Brown come to write *A Shadow on Summer* which seems to be an example of escapism in all directions? Having transcended the world of direct experience in *Down All the Days,* its doom and suffering, to project its image at a symbolical level of expression, he had to cope with the world of literary production, literary fame, publicity, and bear the brunt of many artificial allurements. It was courageous of him to accept the challenge and assume the contradiction. But the dissolving powers were legion.

The personal situation of the crippled writer is also present, though rather watered down, in *A Shadow on Summer.* The author in the book is clear-sighted enough about the threat of failure he senses at the core of his attempts, but the author-narrator drowns the flashes of disquieting intuition with too much gushing sentimentality.

Yet the gleams of visionary intensity have not absolutely vanished, but they are few and far between, and liable to be erased by some flat anticlimax. The author's being is still at stake, he is 'without identity', his self has very improbable contours; he shrinks before 'the grand myth of clinical impartiality'. His frustration, not discernible from his appetite for sex, is translated into pseudo Lawrence approximations, reinforced by ill-digested Freudianism.

But we have not left the world of *Down All the Days.* The same images prey on the writer's mind, put him in bodily fear, the cold sweat running along the limbs against the damp sheets. The question is still that of 'the guts and the cowardice'. If one attempts to formulate a judgement in the name of a common hunger, which is rarely serene, one might venture to say that, at a dangerous crossroads, a writer is expected to face ultimate ruthlessness rather than the flowery path. (pp. 292-93)

> *Françoise Borel, "' I Am Without a Name':*
> *The Fiction of Christy Brown," in* The Irish

Novel in Our Time, *edited by Patrick Rafroidi and Maurice Harmon, Publications de l'Universite de Lille III, 1976, pp. 287-95.*

Alan Young

Christy Brown is deservedly well-known for his novels and for an autobiography, *My Left Foot.* His verse, like his prose, is masculine, direct, unsophisticated and, above all, "a good read". Like many other novelist-poets he picks words up more easily than he is willing to discard them. Consequently, *Of Snails and Skylarks,* his third volume of verse, contains much that is merely prosaic and wordbound. Christy Brown knows that genuine lyric inspiration comes to him rarely, and it is for such honesty as well as for his compassionate involvement with the ordinary events of ordinary lives that we want to read him. His verse muse is, as he calls it himself, *"A Blunt Instrument"*:

> A thing of remorseless gluttony
> of immense invincible vacuity
> is my muse.
>
> Yet it sang once in a rare moment
> a small pure indomitable sound
> escaping from twisted strings
> and somehow after that
> I could almost love the grotesque creature
> as one can sometimes come to love the misbegotten.

> *Alan Young, "From Power to Passion," in* The Times Literary Supplement, *No. 3972, May 19, 1978, p. 550.*

Frank Tuohy

Christy Brown, who first came to general notice with the publication of *Down All the Days,* died a year ago. His last novel, *A Promising Career,* is the first of his books to be set outside his native Ireland and it deals, though at some remove, with the world of pop singers in Britain.

The career in question is that of a young singer, Janice, and perhaps also of her talented song-writer husband, Art, who accompanies her singing on the guitar. The ups and downs of their marriage are contrasted with the general moral decline of their agent, Simon Sandford, a rich man with peculiar tastes, who neglects his dying wife and goes in for sado-masochistic relationships—first with a black South African girl and later with the family *au pair,* a Wagnerian German lady who finally takes him over and fulfills his fantasies.

Christy Brown's early writing triumphed over devastating physical disability and an impoverished background. He was fortunate only in that the moral traditions of Catholic Dublin provided him with twenty-two siblings who helped him to survive. In addition, as a native Irishman, he had the ability to translate into coherent and rhythmic prose some of the untiringly fluent speech—that sense of talking your way into life—which was part of the surrounding scene. His later separation from this source was perhaps inevitable, but the abandonment of whatever experience, even indirect, that it gave him proves in the event to have been disastrously mistaken.

Nowadays aspiring writers often show competence coupled with an impression of complete falsity, which is quite different from the lapses into cliché or melodrama which on occasion afflicted even the most distinguished writers of the past. Long scenes are presented in which nothing comes to life, in which zombie-like characters exchange unnaturally informative dialogue. The influence comes from television. Throughout *A Promising Career,* it is pervasive, in spite of the impressively elaborate surface of the prose. Only romantic fiction of the Cartland-Mills & Boon type works by imprecision: other popular writers get their effects by knowingness—hence the "researched" novel with its flaunted expertise. But *A Promising Career* offers no information about contracts or recording sessions. Everything is vague, with the possible exception of the sexual encounters.

Pornographic fiction seems to demand parody, and a number of humorous writers have taken shots at it. I wanted to believe that this was what was happening here, but the stylistic connections with the rest of the novel forbid such an interpretation. The prose style goes over the top early on, and it remains there.

What we have, then, is a literary curiosity, one which is the result of a talent moving blindly in the wrong direction—a world, in short, that can only do damage to the reputation created by Christy Brown's earlier books. The Irish literary tradition is a fairly strong one, but the antecedents of *A Promising Career* are not to be found there. I was reminded, however, of another figure, indubitably Irish but too often forgotten. Perhaps the works of Mrs. Amanda Ros, the post-mistress of Larne, author of *Irene Iddesleigh* and *Poems of Puncture,* should be revived as a warning for every new literary generation.

> *Frank Tuohy, "Vox-Pop," in* The Times Literary Supplement, *No. 4141, August 13, 1982, p. 888.*

Robert Greacen

The poetry of Christy Brown (1932-81) [included in his *Collected Poems*], is immediately accessible: autobiographical, frankly emotional, occasionally sardonic and somewhat overwritten in the manner of Sean O'Casey. His work, though not outstanding in a purely literary sense, scores highly for humanity and sincerity. Indeed, Christy Brown's life and work represent a triumph of individual will over the cerebral palsy he suffered from birth and the deprivations of an upbringing in a slum district of Dublin. Despite his disadvantages, he obviously loved being alive and enjoyed people. As he puts it in **"Terminal Thoughts"**: 'Friend, you are more than welcome to death; / it is something I can well do without.' These poems, for all their technical shortcomings, stand as a monument to a remarkable and brave man.

> *Robert Greacen, in a review of "Collected Poems," in* British Book News, *December, 1982, p. 763.*

Joseph Parisi

Accessible and always engaging, [the pieces in *Collected Poems*] reveal Brown's more-than-generous Irish literary gifts. Blessed with a keen eye and knowing heart, he speaks with a human voice to the paradoxes and mysteries of life, in lines suffused with wonder, vivid images, and witty wordplay. What he "failed to do" or could not experience firsthand, he "dreamed of most fervently," and, he notes, "most illogically I continue to sing / Of love, the only lovely thing."

> *Joseph Parisi, in a review of "Collected Poems," in* Booklist, *Vol. 79, No. 16, April 15, 1983, p. 1071.*

FURTHER READING

Rudley, Stephen H., and Lynes, C. L., "Unforgettable Christy Brown." *Reader's Digest* 120, No. 722 (June 1982): 71-7. Biographical overview of Brown's life and career written less than a year after his death.

Albert Camus

1913-1960

Algerian-born French novelist, essayist, playwright, short story writer, and journalist.

Camus is widely considered among the most important literary figures of the twentieth century. In his varied career he consistently and passionately explored his major theme: the belief that people can attain happiness in an apparently meaningless world. Throughout his work, Camus defended the dignity and goodness of the individual and asserted that through purposeful action one can overcome nihilism. Camus posited that to resolve the conflict between life in an "absurd universe" and the human desire for rationality—as he demonstrated most clearly in his essay *Le mythe de Sisyphe* (*The Myth of Sisyphus*)—one must recognize that life is "absurd," that is, irrational and meaningless, and then transcend that absurdity. Although this worldview has prompted many commentators to label Camus an existentialist, he rejected that classification. Respected for his style as well as his ideas, Camus is praised as a fierce moralist who expressed an unwavering faith in humankind. He was awarded the Nobel Prize for literature in 1957.

Camus was born into poverty and finished school by earning scholarships and working part-time jobs. Camus never knew his father, who died in 1914 while fighting in World War I, and his mother was an illiterate who rarely spoke or showed affection for her child. Despite the lack of intellectual stimulation at home, Camus excelled at school. At the Lycée d'Algiers Camus studied philosophy, but contracted tuberculosis before entering the university, which prevented him from pursuing a career as an academician. The disease also forced Camus to face the prospect of mortality, a theme which appears in much of his early work. Instead of teaching, Camus became a journalist, editing the resistance newspaper *Combat* and immersing himself in the Algerian intellectual scene. His interest in the theater was already evident, for during this period he helped to found the theater group Théater du Travail, adapted works for the stage, and collaborated on an original play. Camus's first two books, *L'envers et l'endroit,* translated as *The Wrong Side and the Right Side,* and *Noces,* translated as *Nuptials,* are collections of lyrical essays written in the mid-1930s that detail his early life of poverty and his travels through Europe. During this time Camus wrote his first novel, *La mort heureuse* (*A Happy Death*). This posthumously published work, though less stylistically developed than his later novels, touches on the themes of absurdity and self-realization that recur throughout Camus's writings. During World War II he moved to Paris, where, with Jean-Paul Sartre, he became a major intellectual leader of the French Resistance opposing the German occupation of France.

In both *The Myth of Sisyphus* and *L'étranger* (*The Stranger*), Camus develops his concept of absurdism. Camus presented the story of Sisyphus, a figure from Greek mythology who was fated to push a rock up a hill only to see it repeatedly roll back down, as a metaphor for the human

condition. For Camus, life, like Sisyphus's task, is senseless, but awareness of this absurdity can help humankind to surmount this condition. Meursault, the protagonist of *The Stranger,* shoots an Arab for no apparent reason, but is convicted not so much for killing the man as for refusing to conform to society's expectations, as illustrated by his emotionless response to his mother's death. Because he seems indifferent to everything except the most basic sensations of life, Meursault is alienated from the society that wants him to show contrition more expressively. Approaching his execution, Meursault accepts life as an imperfect end in itself and resolves to die happily and with dignity. He finds consolation in resigning himself to what Camus calls the "benign indifference of the universe."

Camus's following novel, *La peste* (*The Plague*), deals with the theme of revolt. Complementing his concept of the absurd, Camus believed in the necessity of each person to "revolt" against the common fate of humanity by seeking personal freedom. Dr. Rieux, the protagonist of *The Plague,* narrates the story of several men in the plague-ridden Algerian city of Oran. Throughout the novel, Camus parallels the conflicting philosophies of Rieux and Father Paneloux over how to deal with the plague: Rieux, a compassionate humanist who repudiates conventional religion, maintains that human action can best combat the disease; Paneloux, a Jesuit priest who views the plague as God's retribution on the sinful people of Oran, holds that only through faith and divine intervention can the city be salvaged. Ultimately, the characters overcome their differences and unite to defeat the plague, at least temporarily, through scientific means. Many critics have interpreted *The Plague* as an allegory of the German occupation of France during World War II. Camus's emphasis on individual revolt also pervades the long essay *L'homme révolté* (*The Rebel*), which exemplifies his dictum "I revolt, therefore we are." Examining the nature and history of revolution, Camus theorizes that each individual must revolt against injustice by refusing to be part of it. Camus opposed mass revolutions because he believed they become nihilistic and their participants accept murder and oppression as necessary means to an end.

Camus's belief in the supremacy of the individual lies at the heart of one of the most publicized events in modern literature—his break with his long-time compatriot Jean-Paul Sartre. These two leading figures of the postwar French intellectual scene had similar literary philosophies but their political differences led to a quarrel in the early 1950s that ended their friendship as well as their working relationship. Sartre saw the Soviet purges and labor camps of the 1940s as a stage in the Marxian dialectic process that would eventually produce a just society. Camus, however, could not condone what he perceived to be the Communist state's disregard for human rights. Played out in the Paris and the international press, the debate was conceded by intellectuals to Sartre. This affair disheartened Camus and his subsequent fall into public scorn affected him over the remainder of his career.

In the following years Camus suffered from depression and writer's block. His reputation was further damaged when he took a neutral position on the issue of Arab uprisings in his native Algiers. Both the French government and Arabs denounced him, and the furor extracted an additional toll on his mental health. His next novel, *La chute* (*The Fall*), is a long, enigmatic monologue of a formerly self-satisfied lawyer who suffers from guilt and relentlessly confesses his sins in order to judge others and induce them to confess as well. Some commentators detected a new tone in this work and suggested that Camus had submitted to nihilism by asserting that every person shares the guilt for a violent and corrupt world. Many argued, however, that Camus's essential love and respect for humanity is a major element of *The Fall* and viewed his wish for a common confession as an attempt to reaffirm human solidarity.

Although Camus maintained a lifelong passion for the theater, his plays generally garnered mixed critical reaction. Of his four original dramas, *Caligula* is often considered his most significant. This work recounts the search of the young eponymous Roman emperor for absolute individual freedom. The death of his sister, who is also his lover, shocks him into an awareness of life's absurdity, and as a result he orders and participates in random rapes, murders, and humiliations that alienate him from others. Most scholars view *Caligula* as a parable warning that individual liberty must affirm, not destroy, the bonds of humanity. *Le malentendu* (*The Misunderstanding*), the story of a man's murder by his sister and mother, is often considered Camus's attempt at a modern tragedy in the classical Greek style. *L'etat de siège* (*The State of Siege*) has been variously perceived as a satiric attack on totalitarianism and an allegory demonstrating the value of courageous human action. A plague that ravages a town and terrorizes its citizens is stopped only when one character sacrifices his life for the woman he loves. Scholars who view this play as an attack on ruthless governments believe it reflects Camus's experience of living under the Nazi occupation of France. *Les justes* (*The Just Assassins*) portrays a revolutionary who refuses to throw a bomb because his intended victim is accompanied by a young nephew and niece. This work further emphasizes Camus's strong sense of humanity: he reasons that the end does not justify the means if the cost is human lives. Most critics agree that Camus's overriding concern with intellectual and philosophical issues makes his dramas overly formal and lifeless, also contending that his characters function too often as mere representatives of specific ideologies. While Camus is admired as a director and innovator and his scripts are generally well regarded, critical consensus deems his plays inferior to his fiction.

When Camus published his first collection of short stories, *L'exil et le royaume* (*Exile and the Kingdom*), many critics detected a new vitality and optimism in his prose. The energy of the stories, each written in a different style, led many scholars to suggest that Camus had regained direction in his career and established himself as a master of short fiction. In ensuing years Camus worked around political quarrels, family troubles, and poor health to begin work on a new novel, *Le premier homme*. He worked diligently and with great hope, but before the text was completed, he died in an automobile accident.

Despite marked fluctuations in Camus's popularity—his rise to literary fame in the 1940s occurred as rapidly as his fall from popular appeal in the years preceding his death—his literary significance remains largely undisputed. His work has elicited an enormous amount of scholarly attention and he continues to be the subject of much serious study. A defender of political liberty and personal freedom, Camus endures not only as an important contributor to contemporary literature, but also as a figure of hope and possibility.

(See also *CLC*, Vols. 1, 2, 4, 9, 11, 14, 32; *Contemporary Authors*, Vols. 89-92; and *Dictionary of Literary Biography*, Vol. 72.)

PRINCIPAL WORKS

NOVELS

L'étranger   1942
   [*The Stranger,*   1946;   published in Great Britain as
      The Outsider]
La peste   1947
   [*The Plague,*   1948]
La chute   1956
   [*The Fall,*   1956]
La mort heureuse   1971
   [*A Happy Death,*   1972]

ESSAY COLLECTIONS

*L'envers et l'endroit   1937

Noces 1939
Le mythe de Sisyphe 1942
  [*The Myth of Sisyphus and Other Essays,* 1955]
L'homme révolté 1951
  [*The Rebel,* 1953]
L'eté 1954
Resistance, Rebellion and Death 1961

PLAYS

Le malentendu 1944
  [*The Misunderstanding*]
Caligula 1945
L'etat de siege 1948
  [*The State of Siege*]
Les justes 1949
  [*The Just Assassins*]
Caligula and Three Other Plays 1958; comprises *Caligula, Le malentendu, L'etat de siège,* and *Les justes*
Les possédés 1959
  [*The Possessed,* 1960]

SHORT FICTION COLLECTION

L'exil et le royaume 1957
  [*Exile and the Kingdom,* 1958]

*These collections were incorporated in *Lyrical and Critical Essays,* 1968.

R. Barton Palmer

I would like to propose here that, in one sense, [*The Stranger* and *The Myth of Sisyphus* are] commentaries on one another. It is that both are concerned with the epistemology of the human condition, with the changes that occur in man's perception of himself, his life, and his world as the individual process of existence runs its course. While *The Myth* presents Camus's development of absurdism as a *raisonnement,* that is, as a line of argument, the novel dramatizes Meursault's journey toward the epiphany which, on the eve of his execution, enables him to see clearly for the first time.

The Myth offers a sudden insight into a life whose only order is mechanical and artificial. This order is imposed by man himself on an experience otherwise gratuitous. To see through it is to begin to live thoughtfully. . . . The essay develops at some length the consequences of this newly conscious existence. One begins, Camus believes, by understanding the world's indifference and also the human desire for reason. If the terms of this dialectic are violated by neither the leap of faith nor by suicide, then man lives in the absurd, that is, in truth. And if he so persists, he is rewarded by a sense of freedom, by the impulse to revolt, by the life force of passion.

For absurd man, then, life has three stages. The theatricality of a daily routine ends with the realization that conventional wisdoms are invalidated by existence's ultimate meaninglessness. The feeling of absurdity which follows responds to the misproportion between the demands of consciousness for order and a confronting reality that offers none. But this misproportion, Camus argues, should not cause despair, but rather liberate man to enjoy the life given him unasked: " . . . completely turned toward death (taken here as the most obvious absurdity), the absurd man feels released from everything outside that passionate attention crystallizing in him." Absurdity thus frees man to grasp the whole of his life as a process completed in itself, since it lies outside any notion of universal justice. Camus in this way derives a new meaning from the familiar irony of *nascentes morimur.* For death, though not in any Christian sense, releases man to live.

The Myth goes on, of course, to explore some patterns of living which exploit most successfully an existence whose value is itself. Camus's concern here for an ethic of quantity finds no substantial reflection in *The Stranger.* Nor does Meursault resemble the conqueror, Don Juan, or the artist, those absurd types to whom the essay pays so much attention. But the epistemology of absurdism developed therein, a process of awareness undoubtedly parallel to Camus's personal experience, gives the novel its peculiar structure.

For all its superficial clarity, the first section of *The Stranger* puzzles and confuses. The events narrated are clear enough, but, presented with a first person narrative, we wonder why and when the narrator is telling his story. The use of present and *passé composé* verbs suggests a diary, but diary style is otherwise absent. The convention of first person narrative generally includes some information about the speaker, his purpose in writing, and the audience he addresses, even when, as in *Notes from Underground,* such indications deny the attempt to communicate itself. In *The Stranger* we are certain about what has happened, but uncertain about why we have been so informed. Why begin with the receipt of the telegram? Why end with the murder of the Arab? Here is a succession of events that lack what Aristotle calls *mythos,* the plot that imparts causality to experience's raw data. What Camus here presents is in fact a slice of the daily routine, devoid of intention and plot as it must be, a procession of events linked only by chronology. Event succeeds event, perception replaces perception, without any values by which the process may be interpreted.

Thus reproducing the daily routine's automatism has posed two insoluble technical problems for Camus. These are connected with the process of verbalization itself. First, the narrator, as Fitch has labored to show, must be placed in the present, looking back at this sequence of events. This *tranche* of experience, of course, has significance only because of what happened at the trial, where Meursault is convicted more for his mother's death in the asylum than for the Arab's on the beach. The narrator's viewpoint presupposes reflection and analysis. But Part I represents Meursault's apprehension of life *before* he is forced to assign it value and meaning. Second, by translating Meursault's consciousness (preconsciousness?) into language, Camus alters its character. Speech is an act of will, but the Meursault of Part I is someone without the will to speak. Finally, of course, the slicing of Meursault's experience, giving it a beginning and an end, confers a value on those events that destroys their significance as they were lived, without thought about a future that would judge and order them.

At this stage Meursault is hardly a stranger to society. He follows accepted forms, like work and ritual, as closely as he can. He accepts relationships with others. He takes some joy in what life has to offer. He is, as he maintains before the trial, just like everybody else. But Meursault is at this time a stranger in one important sense. Like others, he is a stranger to his own existence. He is more an instrument than an actor. He feels but does not reflect. The daily routine, after all, does not demand otherwise. Much that happens is all the same to him. He shows no capacity for emotion. In this humble acquiescence to what we consider everyday living, Meursault is like most of us. The examined life may well be the only life worth living, but the world seldom calls upon us to penetrate the opacity of our own experience.

Meursault, however, is elected to penetrate that experience by a bizarre and ultimately inexplicable series of events. Why does he pull the trigger? And why then does he fire four more shots into the Arab's lifeless form? The novel offers an unsatisfactory answer to the first of these questions (it is that the sun itself made Meursault fire) and no answer to the second. But these are valid questions only if the hero's portrait is ethically motivated, if he is to be seen as the champion of truth. Camus's disregard for these issues suggests otherwise. The murder figures simply as the given event that permits Meursault to understand himself and the human condition. The process of justice, as Champigny points out, reduces to absurdity the theatricality of society, which attempts to impose the *mythos* of causality on what happens. And so the events of Part I become the elements of a plot. We know there is no connection between Meursault's behavior at his mother's funeral and his shooting of the Arab. But the prosecution's attempt to establish one betrays the very human need for a *mythos,* for a connection between character and motive and between motive and action. Upon the unorder of Part I is imposed a misorder that the reader and Meursault as well must reject. Camus thus makes us feel the difference between the world as experienced and the world as men would conceive it. Meursault is jerked from his automatism as he is faced with a human order that is no more than a fatuous theatricality. He begins to live in the absurd. As in *The Myth,* however, it is death that finally liberates him to live.

For Meursault the trial and its consequences reveal death as the central fact of the human condition. Meursault in this way finds his sentence not an exile from human society, but the key to understanding his full involvement in the life of his fellow condemned. Appropriately, it is in prison that Meursault becomes the narrator of his own experience as he feels the need, served by words, of understanding what has happened and also the desire to communicate that understanding to others. He has the right now to speak, for he has become once again like everyone else. He is the representative of a human race sentenced without real cause to die. As he sees it, death orders life, conferring on all actions a perfect equivalence and on disparate destinies the same finale. But he does not despair. In *The Myth* Camus explains his rejection of solutions like the Christian to human life: "they relieve me of the weight of my own life, and yet I must carry it alone." At the end of the novel Meursault grasps the perfected destiny that is his. He discovers what he calls "the benign indifference of the universe," that is the cosmic meaninglessness which enables man to live his life as his own. Like Aeschylus's Cassandra, he recognizes the inevitability of his destiny

and opens himself freely to it. Unlike Cassandra, however, he finds in that inevitability a happiness that overcomes all feelings of loss. In the shadow of death, he feels the urge to live, even if life at this point means only the memory of what has been lived. *The Stranger* and *The Myth* both propose a world without meaning in which death ends existence. Both works, the novel perhaps more dramatically, reject suicide as a solution to the dilemma posed by meaninglessness and mortality. Essay and novel trace instead a process of awareness that culminates in a paradoxical truth: that only in the shadow of annihilation can man discover his freedom, his passion, and, most of all, the grandeur of self-possession. (pp. 123-25)

R. Barton Palmer, " 'The Myth of Sisyphus' and 'The Stranger': Two Portraits of the Young Camus," in The International Fiction Review, *Vol. 7, No. 2, Summer, 1980, pp. 123-25.*

Stephen Miller

At the time of his death, Camus's reputation was certainly inflated, as he himself would have been the first to admit. He claimed to dislike his public persona and complained in an interview a year before his death about those who praised his honesty, conscience, and humanity—"you know, all the modern mouthwashes." He was also dissatisfied with his own work, and said in 1958 that "I still live with the idea that my work has not even begun." Yet the air went out of his reputation even faster than might have been expected. By 1966, H. Stuart Hughes was uttering a commonplace when he said in *The Obstructed Path* that Camus's prose "was already beginning to sound dated." At the end of the decade, a shadow hung over his work; though he still had fervent admirers, the consensus among *bien-pensant* intellectuals was negative: Camus was an uneven novelist and a muddled thinker.

Behind this verdict lay a political judgment: Camus had squandered whatever talents he had in becoming, as Conor Cruise O'Brien argued in 1970, an obsessed cold warrior as well as, indirectly, an apologist for colonialism. These objections were offered more in sorrow than in anger. Camus's choice, O'Brien said, "wrong as we may think it politically, issued out of the depths of his whole life history." David Caute, too, attributed Camus's literary and political confusions to his ancestry and upbringing. Thus, the conqueror of Paris was himself vanquished in the end by followers of that quintessential Parisian intellectual, Jean-Paul Sartre, who detested Camus's politics.

But if, ten years after his death, Camus's reputation was under a cloud, now, twenty years later, the cloud is beginning to lift because of the profound change in French intellectual life wrought by the revelations of Aleksandr Solzhenitsyn. With the reigning Marxist orthodoxy under serious challenge for the first time in thirty years, Camus is once again being taken seriously. . . . Perhaps the time has come for a new look at Camus's work and for an attempt to reassess his achievement in the light of the last two decades. (p. 53)

By 1941, when he was twenty-eight, the first phase of Camus's work was completed. It includes *Caligula,* a play;

the extended essay, _The Myth of Sisyphus;_ and, of course, the novel, _The Stranger,_ indisputably Camus's most popular work. _The Stranger_ is an uneven novel—marred, I think, by the shift in tone between its two parts. Part I is full of luminous detail about the daily life of an easygoing and laconic young man dedicated to the joys of physical life, attractive both in his desire to lead an uncomplicated life and to be true to his feelings. Suddenly in Part II, this same easygoing youth, having committed a gratuitous murder, is transformed into a profoundly cryptic individual who stubbornly refuses to save his life by uttering conventional pieties. Camus later explained the actions of Meursault, the protagonist, by saying he "is animated by a passion that is deep because stubborn, a passion for the absolute and the truth." But the Meursault of Part I has no trace of such heroic severity, and, in fact, casually tells a lie to help a passing acquaintance out of a jam. Thus the novel seems disconnected, and also peculiarly dismissive—though this is seldom remarked upon—of the murder itself.

Why has it been so popular? O'Brien is probably right in his view that "the main secret of its appeal lies in its combination of a real and infectious joy of living, with a view of society which appears to be, and is not, uncompromisingly harsh." The novel celebrates life as absurd—that is to say, as having no intrinsic meaning. The only "meaning" to existence is the sensual enjoyment to be derived from it. If this sounds superficial, there is also a tragic dimension, insofar as death hangs over us continually. Camus said in his _Notebooks_ at the time he was writing _The Stranger:_ "No one who lives in the sunlight makes a failure of his life." So the novel exhorts us to live in the sunlight, and to revolt against those who invoke sentimental pieties in order to make sense out of human existence. The novel is popular with young readers because they are especially apt to resent the pieties of their elders, and also, no doubt, because these rather shallow propositions sound philosophically "deep." Yet in effect, the novel merely tells us in a roundabout way that by invoking the magic word, Absurd, we can tell everyone to go to hell and run off to the beach—a notion which is obviously quite exhilarating, and makes life very simple indeed.

The Myth of Sisyphus, which Camus started soon after he finished _The Stranger,_ is a theoretical exposition of these same ideas: the universe may be devoid of meaning, but the recognition of this meaninglessness is inspiring. Man can then "decide to accept such a universe and draw from it his strength, his refusal to hope, and the unyielding evidence of a life without consolation." But whereas _The Stranger_ has some fine moments of novelistic detail—especially the opening scenes, when Meursault attends his mother's funeral—_The Myth of Sisyphus_ is tedious in its neo-Nietzschean banalities and murky observations which sometimes sound like a Woody Allen parody ("For everything begins with consciousness, and nothing is worth anything except through it"). In any case, by the time Camus finished _The Myth of Sisyphus_ he was ready to jettison the notion of the Absurd, for the German occupation of Paris had suddenly given life meaning. Camus soon came to realize that the Absurd has nothing to teach us about how to conduct ourselves in the face of real danger—the Nazis, for example—and his _Notebooks_ make it clear that by 1942 he had abandoned the notion. Ten years later he admitted that "this word 'Absurd' has had an un-

happy history and I confess that now it rather annoys me."

The main work of Camus's second phase was _The Plague,_ which he began in 1941 and worked on intermittently for the next five years—his time taken up with work in the Resistance and editorial chores at _Combat._ In this phase, Camus was preoccupied with the problem of action in the face of overwhelming odds, action that necessarily required the cultivation of trust among men who had every reason to distrust each other. The Nazis dispatched members of the Resistance summarily, so that a man's life was held in the balance not only by a small circle of friends but also by many others in the Resistance whom he might not even know—men who might betray their compatriots on any number of grounds, torture being the most obvious. One of Camus's most moving essays is the introduction he wrote to the _Poésies Posthumes_ of René Leynaud, a friend in the Resistance who had been caught by the Nazis and executed. _The Plague,_ a novel that is in many ways about the problem of fraternity, has as a central scene the moment when Rieux and Tarrou go for a swim "for friendship's sake." The swim over, the narrator remarks that "they dressed and started back. Neither had said a word, but they were conscious of being perfectly at one, and the memory of this night would be cherished by them both."

There is, though, something wooden about this fraternal moment, as there is about the entire novel. O'Brien calls _The Plague_ "a great allegorical sermon," but the allegory is both too obvious and not obvious enough. The novel is an allegory of France under the Occupation, but it is not clear how a city in the throes of plague can stand for a country controlled by a foreign army. Or, to put it another way: French conduct during the war years raises questions that cannot be dealt with through this metaphor, among other things because infectious organisms behave in a uniform way, whereas the soldiers and administrators of an occupying army do not. As one critic has said, _The Plague_ "is neither deeply rooted in the real stuff of life nor in the poetical matter of myth." The novel is inert, its characters little more than walking editorials in favor of courage, common decency, fraternity, and so forth. Camus himself was unhappy with it, calling it a "tract," and writing in his _Notebooks:_ "Plague. In my whole life, never such a feeling of failure. I am not even sure of reaching the end." In any case, by 1946, when he raised these doubts, his mind was elsewhere. A new problem was preoccupying him, the problem of liberty. He had already begun notes for a book he would not finish until five years later: _The Rebel._ (pp. 54-5)

The tension between liberty (or freedom) and justice is the subject of _The Rebel._ At first, Camus had believed that the two could be reconciled, but as the Resistance years receded into the past, he became aware that many people he had been close to and to whom he still remained attached were fervent in their desire for social justice but less inclined to defend freedom. They were driven by a concern for the collective rather than for what Camus called "individual fates," and were therefore very susceptible to Maurice Merleau-Ponty's argument, in _Humanism and Terror_ (1947), that Stalinist violence, though not to be condoned, should be regarded as a passing phase in a society moving in the direction of social justice. In other words, since the Soviet Union was marching toward social justice, it would be wrong to dwell on the fate of particular individuals who were being mistreated, even killed, along the way. Doing so could only serve to undermine a progressive regime, and indirectly to aid reactionary ones. In the late 40's, it should be noted, Merleau-Ponty, as managing editor of Sartre's *Les Temps Modernes,* was an influential figure, and this line of reasoning became the standard justification on the French Left for suppressing anti-Stalinist criticism. (p. 55)

Camus himself wrote for Sartre's magazine and moved in the same circles as those intellectuals inclined to think well of the Soviet Union. Friendship between Sartre and Camus was still possible, for Sartre's position had not yet hardened, and he had even publicly criticized Stalin's forced-labor camps, for which he was attacked by the French Communists. By 1950, however, after the Korean war broke out, Sartre called the United States the greatest obstacle in the way of "the salvation of mankind," and decided to submit, as an act of self-discipline, to total acceptance of the Soviet viewpoint, though he would still insist at times that he was not a Marxist.

But though Sartre and Camus were political adversaries in the early 1950's, it is a mistake to assume that their positions were antithetical—that if Sartre embraced Marxism-Leninism and defended the Soviet Union, then Camus must have embraced capitalism and defended the United States. In fact, Camus had nothing good to say about capitalism and clearly disliked the United States. His basic sympathies were with the non-Communist Left, especially the Spanish syndicalists and anarchists, among whom he had many friends, but his politics were always inconsistent: though he considered himself a socialist, he also harbored strong anarchist tendencies and tended to distrust all governments.

In one thing, however, he remained constant: he was a passionate defender of liberty, and in 1950 he saw that the greatest danger to liberty came not from the Right but from the Left. In two plays written in the late 1940's— *State of Siege* and *The Just Assassins*—Camus had touched upon the totalitarian mentality often concealed behind what in his *Notebooks* he called a "mania for virtue," but *The Rebel* constitutes his most fully developed attack on those who dream of a society based on absolute justice.

The Rebel is Camus's most ambitious book, and it suffers from its ambitiousness. Attempting to provide a complete anatomy of rebellion in all its aspects, *The Rebel* zooms all over the landscape of European intellectual history, with Camus in the role of tour guide, making sweeping generalizations about entire historical epochs and coming in the end to the lame conclusion that the ultimate good is a sense of limits—a view supposedly characteristic of that "Mediterranean mind" of which Meagher is so enamored. Despite such mystifications, however, there does exist at the core of the book a well-argued essay against the notion that the sins of Russian Communism should be excused because the Soviet Union is on the right historical track. Camus goes even further, arguing that Russian Communism and German fascism have much in common—both despise "bourgeois" democracy, for one thing—but that Russian Communism is even more dangerous to the world since "the German revolution had no hope of a future" while Russian Communism, by contrast,

"openly aspires to world empire. That is its strength, its deliberate significance, and its importance in our history."

Camus, it should be stressed, is not arguing here that the idea of social justice should be dismissed altogether, but that the notion of absolute justice advanced by Marxist-Leninists is a formula for tyranny. Two sentences sum up the book: "Absolute freedom mocks at justice. Absolute justice denies freedom."

In the complicated politics of the early 1950's, Camus's book was well received by parts of the French intelligentsia and condemned by other parts. (pp. 55-6)

In 1952 Sartre also had the difficult task of assigning a reviewer for Camus's book. Despite political differences, the two were still on reasonably good terms and Sartre had, in fact, published a chapter of *The Rebel* in his magazine. Nevertheless, the review that finally appeared in *Les Temps Modernes* by Francis Jeanson, one of Sartre's fervent disciples, was scathing; Jeanson accused Camus of accomplishing an "objectively" reactionary task by attacking Marxism-Leninism, and to prove it he cited the favorable reviews Camus had received not only in the bourgeois press but also in a right-wing journal that was an organ of *Action française*. Stung by the review, Camus replied in a long letter that appeared in the August 1952 issue, along with a response from Sartre himself, commenting both on the particular charges made in Camus's letter and on Camus's politics in general.

Thus, the famous break between Camus and Sartre, which was an event not only in France but in the world press as well. (p. 56)

The last eight years of Camus's life, following the break with Sartre, may be said to constitute a fourth and final phase of his career: he was embittered by the break and haunted by the war in Algeria, but despite long periods of depression, he did work through to a freer prose that is less stilted and pompous than his earlier writing. In several short essays and stories, he is more concise and witty than ever before, and his last and best novel, *The Fall,* successfully combines the earlier lyricism with a new and mordant irony. (p. 57)

The Fall is a bleak novel, yet a curiously exhilarating one. Laced with witty observations about the perversities of human conduct, it is very much in the French *moraliste* tradition, a descendant of Montaigne's *Essays,* La Rochefoucauld's *Maxims,* and Diderot's novella, *Rameau's Nephew*. The narrator, Jean-Baptiste Clamence, is a fascinating character, a self-proclaimed "empty prophet for shabby times" who subtly and ingeniously confesses his own moral failings in order to avoid being judged by others. "The more I accuse myself," he says to his silent companion, "the more I have a right to judge you. Even better, I provoke you into judging yourself, and this relieves me of that much of the burden."

Some critics have regarded Clamence as a self-portrait, an attempt by Camus to exorcise the burden of his supposed "sainthood"; others see it as a portrait of Sartre, the man who continually proclaimed his own guilt over belonging to the bourgeoisie. But whoever sat for it, this portrait of a twisted hero of our times, who perverts notions of Christian guilt in order to maintain his own sense of self-esteem and to dominate others, is Camus's masterpiece. It is also a fascinating, extended gloss on Lionel Trilling's observation that "the life of competition for spiritual status is not without its own peculiar sordidness and absurdity."

But in the end, Camus's literary achievement is secondary to his importance as a political intellectual. (pp. 57-8)

In summing up Camus's importance, it is almost enough to say simply that he never joined those "progressive" French intellectuals on their shepherded journeys around the Soviet Union. Camus was not an original philosopher, and it would be foolish to make great claims for the profundity of his work. But he was a perceptive political journalist who was one of the first French intellectuals to recognize that the central debate was not between capitalism and Communism but between liberty and tyranny. And he was one of the first also to question the notion that poor people do not care about freedom. As he said in a seminal essay, "Bread and Freedom": "The oppressed want to be liberated not only from their hunger but also from their masters, since they are well aware that they will be effectively freed of hunger only when they hold their masters, all their masters, at bay."

Camus was instrumental in rallying intellectual opinion to the defense of democratic liberties at a time when many Western intellectuals were reluctant to believe anything ill of the Soviet Union. To paraphrase Orwell, he was a man who struggled constantly to see what was in front of his nose—to see what many Western intellectuals tried, and still try, desperately not to see. (p. 58)

Stephen Miller, "The Posthumous Victory of Albert Camus," in Commentary, *Vol. 70, No. 5, November, 1980, pp. 53-8.*

Donald Palumbo

Camus and Sartre agree that the idea of God's absence condemns man to his sense of alienation, and the profound alienation suffered by their protagonists is presented as both an indication and a consequence of that absence. This alienation reveals itself in a number of ways: the failure of father-son relationships, alienation-from-the-self, social and sexual alienation, and a sense of separation from nature, the past, and the present. Of these manifestations, the failure of father-son relationships is that which most clearly symbolizes, as well as indicates and precipitates, man's isolation from God. Alienation-from-the-self, which partially results from man's abandonment of the idea of God, is also closely related to the failure of father-son relationships, and these are the two types of alienation that stem most immediately from the crisis of faith.

Several of Sartre's and Camus' characters reveal a consciousness of the general connection between alienation and the abandonment of God. In Sartre's *The Devil and the Good Lord* Goetz laments, "I killed God because He divided me from mankind, and now I see that His death has isolated me even more surely." In Camus' **The Possessed,** Shatov tells Stavrogin, "You can't love anyone because you are a man without roots and without faith." And in rejecting Zeus to embrace his freedom, Orestes discovers in Sartre's *The Flies* that in severing relations with God one cuts oneself off from both men and the world. He complains to Zeus, after he rebels against Him, "Yesterday, when I was with Electra, I felt at one with Nature, this Nature of your making. . . . Suddenly, out of the blue, freedom crashed down on me and swept me off my feet. Nature sprang back, my youth went with the wind, and I knew myself alone, utterly alone in the midst of this well-meaning little universe of yours." Although he formed a bond of blood between himself and the people of Argos in killing Aegisthus, Orestes must exile himself from the city if he is to relieve them of their remorse and defy Zeus; he can remain as King only if he accepts Zeus' will, accepts God, and maintains the status quo.

Those characters who most completely reject God are not only those who are most aware of their alienation but are also those who most often exhibit symptoms of alienation, for the alienation between man, his fellows, and the world is the sign as well as the consequence of man's isolation from God. Although man's alienation—in all of its aspects taken together—indicates his divorce from God, this divorce is most clearly and appropriately symbolized in the nature of father-son relationships. The father, like a king or tsar, is a secular emblem of God, particularly to a child, over whom the father's power, like God's, is seemingly absolute. In the works of Sartre and Camus (and in those of other modern existentialist writers) the feeling that one has been abandoned by the father often parallels the feeling of having been abandoned by God, while indifference to or rejection of the father is likewise mirrored in a character's indifference to or rejection of the idea of God. Even on a literal level Orestes rebels against Zeus in killing Aegisthus, his step-father and the king; but he also symbolically abolishes God in thus avenging his father's death, for the king (who rules by divine right and assumes the figurative role of father to his people) is, even more than a biological or legal father, an earthly representation of the divinity. And, although there are many cases where such information is withheld, not one of Sartre's or Camus' protagonists in *Nausea, The Flies, The Devil and the Good Lord, The Condemned of Altona,* **The Stranger, The Plague,** or **The Possessed** is portrayed as having a successful relationship with his father, just as few (and none of those whose parental relationships are revealed to us) believe in the possibility of communion with God.

Many central characters feel that they have been abandoned or betrayed by their fathers, and it might well be that it is in half-conscious, symbolic revenge that these characters later dismiss the idea of God or even rebel against Him. (pp. 12-13)

Camus' Jean Tarrou, an avowed athiest, rediscovers in **The Plague** that "it is in the thick of calamity that one gets hardened to the truth—in other words, to [God's] silence." And Tarrou is disillusioned in his father, who must supervise the execution of criminals in his capacity of prosecuting attorney, when, as a child, he goes to court and hears him demand the death penalty for an offender. Nearly a year later Tarrou leaves home on the eve of a prospective execution, rejecting his father as he will later reject that God whom he feels condemns all men to death. Ever since his disillusionment, as [Maurice] Friedman notes, "Tarrou's chief aim in life has been to side with the 'victims' rather than 'executioners,'" and he thus fights, not only against the plague, but also on the losing side in the Spanish Civil War, i.e., against God and the king.

Peter Verkhovensky and all in his circle of nihilistic revolutionaries [in **The Possessed**] are unbelievers, as is

Stavrogin, who would be a Christian if he could believe but who argues "to make a jugged hare, you need a hare. To believe in God, you need a God." Peter's hatred of and rebellion against the tsar parallels his hatred of and rebellion against God, and his attitude towards both is mirrored in his attitude towards his father, Stepan. Peter feels his father had abandoned him early in life and complains, "I wasn't weaned yet when you shipped me off to Berlin by the post. Like a parcel." When they meet after twenty years' separation, Peter breaks free of his father's embraces and insists that he be left alone. Cruelly proclaiming that he never reads Stepan's letters through, Peter nevertheless betrays his father's confidences by maliciously revealing their delicate contents in public. He calls Stepan a "parasite," claims that Varvara Petrovna is "keeping" him, and boasts to his face of having laughed at his love letters to her. When the father, infuriated by this abuse, rhetorically asks, "Are you or aren't you my son, Monster?" Peter mockingly replies, "You must know better than I. To be sure, fathers are inclined to have illusions about such things."

In Camus' **The Stranger,** Meursault, when pressed, reveals his complete lack of faith to an absolutely incredulous magistrate and, later, to a chiding prison chaplain. He reports, "I said I saw no point in troubling my head about the matter; whether I believed or didn't was, to my mind, a question of so little importance." Earlier, in thinking of his father, Meursault recalls, "I never set eyes on him. Perhaps the only things I really knew about him were what mother had told me." He, like Peter, had been abandoned in his infancy. Significantly, the prosecutor concludes his case against Meursault by telling the jury, "I am convinced . . . that you will not find I am exaggerating the case against the prisoner when I say that he is also guilty of the murder to be tried tomorrow in this court," which is "that most odious of crimes, the murder of a father by his son." Meursault has long since slain God, to whom he is as indifferent as he is to the memory of his father, in his heart; while it is logically and practically absurd, the prosecutor's summation, as [Phillip H.] Rhein notes, reveals this aspect of his trial's symbolic meaning.

The failure of the father-son relationship combines with the initial sense of God's absence to contribute to yet another mode of alienation, alienation-from-the-self. Friedman argues that "the father is the first and often the most lasting image of man for the son. It not infrequently happens, however, that the father is not really present for the son, either because he is dead or absent or inattentive, or because he is in no sense a father, or because he is too weak or despicable for a son to be able to emulate him." In those cases where the father is a physical, even a perversely dominant presence, however, the son inevitably receives from him a share of his personality; and the son is estranged from and rejects a part of himself to the extent that he is estranged from and rejects the father. Also, "the inner division which results from the alienation between fathers and sons is as much a commentary on the absence of a modern image of man as on the breakdown of the specific father-son relationship. At the heart of this breakdown, in fact, is the inability of the father to give his son a direction-giving image of meaningful and authentic human existence." To a large extent, man's image of his ideal self and his anthropomorphic image of God coincide. The rejection of this image of God inevitably erodes the

concomitant image of man, and the father cannot provide his son with a direction-giving image of man because, having also abandoned his idea of God, as in Herr Gerlach's case, he has no coherent image of man himself. Finally, the frequency with which certain characters are depicted in non-human terms in Camus' and Sartre's works both indicates that their authors associate the realization of God's non-existence with this erosion of the image of man and further suggests alienation-from-the-self, from a character's "human" nature. (pp. 14-15)

Other characters created by Camus and Sartre also exhibit unmistakable signs of alienation-from-self. Although this division cannot always be attributed to their relationship with their fathers, it always parallels their atheism; and it is in one other case clearly a product of father-son conflict. (p. 15)

Camus (no doubt inspired by the characterization of Roquentin [protagonist of Sartre's novel *Nausea*] p. 17) also recognizes the presence of the inhuman in man, seeing it both in man's trivial actions and in the core of his being. He writes,

> Men, too, secrete the inhuman. At certain moments of lucidity, the mechanical aspect of their gestures, their meaningless pantomime makes silly everything that surrounds them. A man is talking on the telephone behind a glass partition; you cannot hear him, but you see his incomprehensible dumb show; you wonder why he is alive. This discomfort in the face of man's own inhumanity, this incalculable tumble before the image of what we are, this "nausea," as a writer of today calls it, is also the absurd. Likewise the stranger who at certain seconds comes to meet us in a mirror, the familiar and yet alarming brother we encounter in our own photographs is also the absurd.

Since his inherent inhumanity reveals the divergence between man as a reality and man as a concept invented by men, Camus sees the absurd, which often prompts or is recognized through a character's loss of faith, both in it and in the alienation-from-self that it suggests.

Camus argues further that man can see himself as being human only through social relationships, that "in simple words, man is not recognized—and does not recognize himself—as a man as long as he limits himself to subsisting like an animal. He must be acknowledged by other men. All consciousness is, basically, the desire to be recognized and proclaimed as such by other consciousnesses. It is others who beget us. Only in association do we receive a human value, as distinct from an animal value." That certain characters see themselves in non-human terms is, then, symptomatic of their extensive social alienation, of which father-son ruptures is the beginning, as well as of their alienation-from-self. (pp. 16-17)

> *Donald Palumbo, "The Crisis of Faith, Father-Son Ruptures, and Alienation-from-the-Self: Their Interconnection in the Works of Sartre and Camus," in* The CEA Critic, *Vol. 44, No. 3, March, 1982, pp. 12-17.*

Patrick McCarthy

La Peste seems such a traditional novel. A plague strikes

the North African town of Oran. First the rats come above ground to die and then the people fall ill and cannot be cured. The authorities are helpless and the population despairs. A group of men band together to combat the plague: Rieux, the doctor who can limit the plague's ravages but can no longer heal, the mysterious Tarrou, who has crusaded against the death penalty, the journalist Rambert, who at first tries to escape but then realizes he must stay, Paneloux, the Jesuit for whom the plague is a trial of his faith, and Grand, the minor civil servant who spends his evenings writing the first sentence of a novel. The group sets up special hospitals and vaccinates people until the plague disappears as suddenly as it has come. Paneloux and Tarrou have died while Rieux is left to tell the story.

Camus stressed that *La Peste* was to be a more positive book than *L'Etranger.* Rieux and his friends demonstrate the moral values of courage and fraternity which do not defeat the plague but which bear witness against it. *La Peste* was read as a parable about the Occupation and Rieux's band was perceived as a group of resistants who are fighting against the overwhelming power of the Nazis. Yet one doubts whether these more positive values represent Camus's main achievement. The outstanding feature of *La Peste* is the way this seemingly simple tale is told and the way in which the narrative technique breaks with traditional novel-writing.

A quotation from Daniel Defoe stands at the head of the book but Defoe's narrators are omniscient; they tell their tales like men who are sure they dominate the world. *La Peste,* however, is recounted by a narrator who flaunts the limits of his understanding. Camus is continuing down the path he had traced in *L'Etranger.* Meursault had tried to understand his life and to communicate its meaning to us. He did not succeed but at least there was an "I" in the novel. In *La Peste* the story-teller remains anonymous. Not until the end does he identify himself as Rieux; for most of the novel he is a disembodied voice. He too tries to interpret what is happening but the plague defies his attempt to understand and hence dominate it. The opening lines set the tone: "The strange events which make up the subject of this chronicle, took place in 194-, in Oran. They were untoward and somewhat out of the ordinary, at least in most people's opinion. At first sight Oran is in point of fact an ordinary town, nothing more than a French perfecture on the Algerian coast."

The precision of time and place is banished by phrases like "in most people's opinion." These simple facts are not necessarily true; they depend for their veracity on other unnamed narrators. Nothing is real, Camus is telling us, unless it can be stated by a human intelligence; yet the narrator's intelligence enables him only to speculate without affirming. As if trained in Cartesian logic he draws general conclusions from the specific traits of Oran. But his "therefores" are soon entangled with "buts," while his long paragraphs are composed of statements, developments and contradictions.

Whereas Meursault had relied on his own impressions, this narrator is a dutiful historian who parades his documents and witnesses. But this is a subterfuge because he does not trust them: "he proposes to use them as he thinks fit and to cite them whenever he pleases. He also proposes." The only real witness is a narrator who does not

finish his sentences and about whom the reader knows nothing.

The inadequacy of the narration cannot be stated until it has been resolved. Then Camus writes of the bond between Rieux and his mother: "a love is never strong enough to find its own expression so he and his mother would always love each other in silence." Writing should be a confession; instead it circles around its subject. Free indirect speech—the hallmark of *L'Etranger*—recurs in *La Peste* because it weakens the emotional veracity of the confession. In important moments such as Rambert's decision to stay in Oran, Camus allows his characters to speak directly. Rambert states that he will join with the others to fight against the plague; this is an affirmation of human courage. But such moments are rare because the narration must remain remote.

The theme of storytelling lies at the heart of *La Peste* which abounds in discussions of language and in narrators. First come the official storytellers like the town government and the newspapers. The government hides reality behind bureaucratic jargon while newspapers console; they keep forecasting that the plague will soon end. Men in authority make bold, ridiculous pronouncements. . . . (pp. 107-09)

Each of the main characters—Rambert, Paneloux, Grand and Tarrou as well as Rieux—acts as a storyteller and each is a part of the greater anonymous narration. Rambert poses an intriguing problem. A professional journalist, he is the man who should write about the plague. Yet he does not because Camus feels that journalism is a particularly inadequate form of language.

Paneloux, who is an expert on Saint Augustine, delivers two sermons. The first affirms that the plague is a punishment sent by God and that the people of Oran must repent and do penance. This is a traditional piece of rhetoric and Camus uses another storyteller to mock it: Tarrou says that he is waiting for silence to replace bombast. The second sermon affirms that the plague is not sent by God; it is part of an evil which is present in the universe and which the Christian must confront. This sermon is filtered through the scepticism of Rieux who is sitting in the church. He notes that it is heretical but that its very doubts contain some truth. Paneloux's language is more restrained than in his first sermon, while Rieux's language is even more tentative. The second sermon contains some truth because it depicts evil as a painful riddle.

The difficulty which these storytellers encounter when they start to tell their tales is personified in the figure of Grand. His one-line novel is both an expression of Camus's fear that he will be unable to write and an illustration of the uncertainty of language. Grand puzzles over such words as "promise" and "right"; they have a life of their own and they do not convey what he thinks they should. Grand is a frustrated Cartesian who would like to make general statements, but when he makes them, they come out as platitudes. (p. 109)

Grand has another aim which is to express fully what he feels. He has been married to a woman called Jeanne whom he still loves. So he wants to write her a love-letter that will make her realize what she means to him. Once more writing should be a confession but Grand cannot find the words to express his love so he sets about his novel instead. One might see in this a parable about absurd art. Language cannot seize human experience directly or totally; it must offer partial insights by "saying less." Grand's inability to go beyond the first sentence is a parody of the anonymous narrator's inability to explain the plague.

Tarrou's diary is the best example of "saying less" and it contains some of the finest writing in *La Peste*. "Tarrou's chronicle seems to stem," says the anonymous narrator, "from a quest for insignificance . . . he sets out to be the historian of things which have no history." Camus had thought of composing an anthology of insignificance but Tarrou's journal is a substitute for it. Convinced that the world does not make sense, Tarrou describes objects and conversations detached from their context and indicating only the absence of coherence. This seems like Meursault but it is not. Meursault hoped to understand Algiers, whereas Tarrou knows there is nothing to understand in Oran. He asks questions to which he does not expect answers and he spends a page describing the bronze lions on the main square. Irony and brevity are the keys to his art which must surely have appealed to Francis Ponge.

Yet there is a trap in Tarrou's lucidity. Since he knows everything he could become an omniscient narrator, which would contradict everything he knows. In order to preserve the incomplete nature of Tarrou's art Camus presents it via his anonymous narrator who does not understand Tarrou's aim and puzzles over his sentences. He wonders why Tarrou describes the bronze lions; they have no historical or allegorical quality and are just ridiculous objects. Such incomprehension prevents Tarrou's cult of insignificance from becoming an explanation of the world.

As *La Peste* goes on, a tension arises within the narration. In yet another discussion about language the medical authorities shrink from using the term "plague." "It doesn't matter whether you call it plague or growth fever," argues Rieux, "what matters is that you prevent it from killing half of Oran." Language cannot be used propositionally but it can be a weapon. It can combat the plague even if it cannot explain it. So the anonymous narrator turns out, unsurprisingly, to be the plague's chief enemy, Dr. Rieux. If stated at the outset this would have robbed the novel of its remote character; Rieux had to remain anonymous in order to depict the plague as an entity outside man's understanding. But he now states that he has "deliberately sided with the victims" and that he is "speaking for everyone."

The gradual change in the point of view is accompanied by a change in the themes. Camus spells out the values which enable men to battle against their condition. The key theme is indifference which is Rieux's special trait. In order to make his rounds and to isolate the people who are infected he has to repress the pity and sympathy which he feels for them. The doctor-patient relationship turns into inadequacy and hatred; the patients hate Rieux because he cannot cure them. But he must ignore this hatred and get on with his work. He feels that he is growing less and less human and that he is as "abstract" as the plague.

Camus is, characteristically, showing how a destructive force may be creative. The indifference which Rieux feels is a kind of courage which is shared by the men around him. The common bond of courage creates the second value of fraternity. Camus's moral thinking has never been

more austere and heroic. Rieux, Tarrou and the others are an aristocracy who sacrifice their personal happiness in order to fight the plague.

The flaw in this moral thinking was pointed out by Sartre and by Roland Barthes. Camus had asserted the need to act but he had not treated the more difficult problems of which action one chooses, how one is changed by it and what influence it will have. Although the plague was nonhuman, it was supposed to be an image of the Occupation. But the Occupation was far from nonhuman and it involved agonizing choices. Tarrou illustrates this weakness when he links his stand against the plague with his rejection of violence. Sharing Camus's views on the death penalty and on left-wing tyranny, Tarrou affirms that he will not kill. So he can combat the plague but he could have combatted the Germans only if one assumes, as Camus did in '43, that the Resistance had its hands clean. Even if one sets aside the problem of the parallels with the Occupation the flaw in *La Peste* remains. Any political or social action would sully the purity in which Tarrou—like Camus— believes.

So the aristocrats of *La Peste* are frozen in their heroic posture. They defy the plague rather as Sisyphus defied his rock and their values are religious rather than practical. This is less a union of men who have very different characters and backgrounds than a communion of indifferent saints whose asceticism has dissolved all character. Tarrou, who broods ironically on sanctity, is writing yet another chapter in Camus's dialogue with his own religious temperament.

Yet these men are not saints, as Camus's Dominican friend, Bruckberger, pointed out. Examining Paneloux's death Bruckberger writes that the Jesuit confronts an absent God in static silence; he does not rail against Him, love Him or live with Him. Grace, love and prayer are all absent from *La Peste*. Bruckberger's criticism complements Barthes's: neither the religious notion of grace nor the human virtue of practicality is present in Camus's moral thinking.

The present-day reader may take yet a different view and he may feel that Rieux and Tarrou are exaggeratedly heroic. Indeed Camus's moral thinking is at its best when it depicts the inadequacy of heroism. The dying Tarrou is not content with courage so he turns to Rieux's mother in an appeal for love. Rieux himself is desperately lonely when he walks through liberated Oran at the end of the novel. He and Tarrou are the most masculine of men—tough, ascetic and proud. Yet *La Peste* echoes with the absence of what have traditionally been the values of women: tenderness and warmth. This is far more convincing than the philosophically dubious, uselessly saintly heroism.

The need to present these moral values brings about the gradual change in the narration. At the outset Rieux is a character like Tarrou or Grand and he knows no more than they. Then he begins to show a greater understanding of his friends and of himself. He traces the growth of his indifference and he watches Rambert's hesitations. Meanwhile the anonymous narrator strikes a lyrical note in [a] description of Oran. . . . (pp. 109-12)

As the novel goes on the two tendencies—Rieux's awareness and the anonymous narrator's lyricism—increase until they fuse into the discovery that Rieux is the narrator. This makes the novel more conventional because Rieux almost becomes a traditional, omniscient storyteller. Camus tries to prevent this by reverting to the earlier, fragmentary manner but even Tarrou's diary has changed. From being whimsical and insignificant it has become a treatise about insignificance. Camus is grappling with a real problem: there is a thin line between depicting men who show courage in the face of the unknowable and affirming that the world is unknowable so men must show courage. Once one tilts towards the second position then omniscient narrators and traditional novels reenter by the back door. Camus's language grows more rhetorical and his antitheses—"man's poor and awesome love"—grow heavier.

Yet the incomplete quality of the narration persists to the end. The last entries in Tarrou's journal are puzzling reflections on Rieux's mother and they open a new and mysterious theme of Tarrou's mother. The closing pages of the novel are written in the same remote style as the opening pages. There are celebrations, reunions and dancing; they take place according to some new order which is as undefinable as the old.

Despite the presence within the narration of a moralist, *La Peste* does not really make the world more human or more penetrable than *L'Etranger* did. Anonymity and amputation remain the watchwords of Camus's art. He tried to offer a viewpoint which would be positive because collective but the pages where it dominates are conventional, whereas the remote narrator who puzzles over Grand and Tarrou is a superb and thoroughly modern achievement. However, most of Camus's contemporaries did not interpret *La Peste* in this way. Camus, the tragic writer who depicted an alien universe, gave way to Camus, the apostle of brotherhood. This view of his writing, which he himself fostered, helped to shape his life over the next years. (pp. 112-13)

> *Patrick McCarthy, "The Plague," in* Albert Camus, *edited by Harold Bloom, Chelsea House Publishers, 1982, pp. 107-13.*

Robert L. Duncan

Martin Luther and Albert Camus would seem to have little in common, the one a believing Bible scholar and ardent Christian theologian, the other a skeptic and critic of Christianity whose use of the Bible was largely ironic. The Camus of his first novels (*The Stranger; The Plague*) does have little in common with Luther, for in these novels Camus presents a nonrational universe in which there are no moral absolutes and man is a victim of "the absurd," a view not at all consonant with Luther's conception of man as a sinner responsible before God for his sin. Camus, in fact, once wrote that he did not know the meaning of the word "sin." But in his third novel, *The Fall* (1956), "no longer not even 'knowing the meaning of the word "sin," '" Camus set out to explore the whole problem of moral responsibility in Christian terminology." In this novel Camus questions the existence of human perversity, the same question probed by Luther in his commentary on Paul's Epistle to the Romans as well as elsewhere in his voluminous writings. Camus, however, unlike Luther, does not offer Christian answers to these questions, but

both identify egocentrism as the central feature of human evil. (p. 47)

In the protagonist of *The Fall*, Jean-Baptiste Clamence, Camus presents his version of *homo incurvatus in se* ["man curved in upon himself"]. Camus, like Luther, makes extensive use of traditional Biblical language and imagery. But, unlike Luther, he juxtaposes these with the plight of guilty twentieth-century man in such a mocking fashion that the dominant tone of *The Fall* is painfully ironic, an irony resulting from the sharp contrast between the largely negative but intrinsically hopeful Biblical view of human nature mirrored in the traditional meaning of this language and imagery, and the wholly negative and hopeless view of man in the novel.

The Fall is comprised of the monologue of Clamence, who ostensibly is confessing to his hypocritical behavior while he was a Parisian lawyer. Living in Amsterdam, he now frequents the *Mexico City* bar where he button-holes customers in order to make his confession. *The Fall* is one such confession to a single unidentified listener extending intermittently over a period of five days.

Clamence's apparent motive at the outset is to reveal his *former* duplicity. Thus he relates to his listener how he as a trial lawyer sought to give the impression of altruism in his defense of the underdogs of society and of the blind. He was proud of these activities, but he was also proud of his athletic prowess and his sexual appetite. As the result of his failure to save a suicidal young woman who apparently flung herself into the Seine River, he was stricken, as by a revelation, when he began to hear peals of mysterious laughter that, he concluded, mocked his pretense of compassion for the suffering and needy. He had done it all for show. In fact, he realizes, he is a virtuosic hypocrite.

Thus *The Fall* at first appears to be the confession of a man who has been crushed by the discovery of his hypocrisy. But as Clamence continues to "confess" it becomes evident that he has a motive other than the desire to relieve himself of his burden of guilt: he seeks to implicate his auditor and, through him, all human beings, in his personal guilt. No one is innocent, he contends, "whereas we can state with certainty the guilt of all. Every man testifies to the crime of all the others—that is my faith and my hope." The hopelessness of the human condition is underscored by Clamence's contention that it is not God but men who, without a divine law, judge one another as guilty. This is the worst judgment of all because it offers man no possibility of reestablishment "in an order he believes in."

At this point Clamence has already peeled away two layers of self: the first, that provided by the façade of honor and magnanimity while he served himself by serving the law; the second, the layer that gave the impression that he was seeking only to unburden his own conscience through his confession when in fact he was leading up to an indictment of all mankind. He now proceeds to peel away yet another layer of self to reveal that his entire confession has insidiously aimed at gaining an advantage over his confessor by means of the device of the "judge-penitent," a term he deliberately delays explaining until the last day of his "confession."

Expounding his role as judge-penitent, Clamence admits that his words, poured out over a five-day period, "have the purpose obviously of silencing the laughter, of avoiding judgment personally." His method for avoiding this judgment is "to begin by extending the condemnation to all, without distinction." His goal in "getting everyone involved," he admits, is "in order to have the right to sit calmly on the outside." To accomplish this, he developed a technique of condemning himself that evoked a confession from his listeners, thereby anticipating and precluding their judgment of him. To become a judge, he reasons, one must first become a penitent. Thus the role of judge-penitent is a stratagem contrived by Clamence to gain an advantage over others, all of whom are, like himself, under judgment—the judgment of men, not of God. He proffers his confession of duplicity and egocentrism, ironically, to elevate himself above his confessor, who, like himself and all men, is also hypocritical and egocentric. Thus Clamence wins the battle of the egos by being the first to admit that he is egocentric. He confesses his egocentricity to gain egocentric advantage. "I, I, I *is* [emphasis mine] the refrain of my whole life," he admits early in his confession. The present tense implies that his egoistic "refrain" is continuous—his discovery and confession of his duplicity have not "silenced" it. Near the end of his confession, he makes the devastating admission: "I haven't changed my way of life; I continue to love myself and to make use of others." Clamence remains the egocentric who is so curved in on himself that he relates to people only as he can use them.

Although he has confessed his hypocrisy, he has not renounced it—in fact, he has accommodated himself to it: "I have accepted duplicity," he admits. Instead of being upset about it, he adds, "On the contrary, I have settled into it and found there the comfort I was looking for throughout life." Sara Toenes points out that Clamence "never expresses the anguish of self-digust . . . the reader waits in vain for any sentiment of remorse." Clamence's reaction to his discoveries "is never more than a vague discomfort. His efforts are directed not toward repentance but toward conserving the remains of his pride."

Throughout his confession, Clamence's top priority is to do as he pleases without regard for others: "The essential is being able to permit oneself everything, even if, from time to time, one has to profess vociferously one's own infamy. I permit myself everything again and without the laughter this time." Toenes remarks that Clamence's "desire for public exposure is not self-inflicted punishment, but a new source of self-satisfaction. . . . He has accepted his guilt, even exploited it in an attempt to build a new universe for his Satanic pride." She concludes, "Clamence has made of public confession the only condition which must be fulfilled in order to soar once again on the heights of self-satisfaction."

For Clamence, therefore, confession and the role of judge-penitent are devices he employs so that he can continue to gratify his ego as before, but without the mysterious laughter that first made him aware of his hypocrisy. He has travelled full circle, from egocentric duplicity to self-discovery, from self-discovery to confession of duplicity, from confession of duplicity to egocentric duplicity; or more accurately, he has remained *homo incurvatus in se* throughout the entire experience. He is yet the egocentric who lives entirely for self. Confession of his "crimes" has led to no renunciation of his "infamy" but is a technique designed to enable him to avoid judgment, "make use of

others," and "begin again lighter in heart." His "repentance," rather than being soul-shaking and life-changing, is "charming." Unlike Dante the pilgrim, whose journey into self leads to purgation and redemption through God's grace, this modern Dante has penetrated the depths of his own duplicity only to "accept" and find "comfort" in it. Above all, Clamence seeks to gratify self, to "permit himself everything." One is reminded of Dostoevsky's declaration, "If God does not exist, all things are permitted." God does not exist in Clamence's world; thus everything is permitted for the ego aggrandizement of this modern *homo incurvatus in se.*

Clamence's role as judge-penitent has thus freed him to do what he pleases and to dominate and judge others: "since finding my solution, I yield to everything. . . . I dominate at last, but forever. *Once more* [emphasis mine] I have found a height to which I am the only one to climb and from which I can judge everybody." The words "once more" underscore the consistency of his determination to elevate himself above others, whatever the role he plays. He must be above others, must be the "only one" to dominate them. As Toenes states, "his life is dedicated to a search for heights, not heights of morality, but heights of pride. Having reached these desired heights of self-satisfaction, he basks in his own glory, profoundly content with his own existence."

At times Clamence describes his addiction to the role of judge-penitent in such grandiose terms that one is reminded of Dostoevsky's "man-god." Felix S. A. Rysten points out, "With Clamence we find the confirmation of Camus' thesis in *The Rebel* that a man who no longer believes in God feels the need to become a godhead because he cannot and dares not live with the limitations of being merely man." Speaking of the "technique" he practices on the denizens of *Mexico City,* Clamence says, "I couldn't do without it or deny myself those moments when one of them collapses, with the help of alcohol, and beats his breast." Elatedly, he continues, "Then I grow taller, *tres cher,* I grow taller, I breathe freely, I am on the mountain, the plain stretches before my eyes. How intoxicating to feel like God the Father and to hand out definitive testimonials of bad character and habits." As Rysten says, "Clamence is caught in the universe of his own ego, which he has filled with his own image." His description of himself as Almighty God at the Last Judgment becomes even more explicit:

> I sit enthroned among my bad angels at the summit of the Dutch heaven and I watch ascending toward me, as they issue from the fogs and the water, the multitude of the Last Judgment. They rise slowly; I already see the first of them arriving. On his bewildered face, half hidden by his hand, I read the melancholy of the common condition and the despair of not being able to escape it. And as for me, I pity without absolving, I understand without forgiving, and above all, I feel at last that I am being adored.

Clamence speaks ironically, of course, but it would be a mistake to blunt the egomaniacal thrust of this passage by calling it irony alone. Certainly, Clamence does not literally believe himself to be God. But *homo incurvatus,* as Luther stressed, uses all things, even the Biblical God, for self-aggrandizement. Clamence, unlike Luther, does not believe in God, but he uses "God-talk" copiously to describe his aspirations to be a man-god. And though this man-god "pities" and "understands," he, unlike Luther's God, does not "absolve" or "forgive," but instead seeks personal exaltation. In fact, rather than being God, he is an inverted Miltonic Satan who, having emerged from the exploration of the Dantesque Hell of his own ego, now "sits enthroned among [his] bad angels" to judge without grace those who are drawn into the web of his insidious "confession."

This "Satan," however, is not without spiritual perception. Following his egomaniacal outburst, he experiences a moment of exaltation in which he "soars over this whole continent which is under my sway without knowing it," but then quickly slips into a mood of depression and expresses a longing for innocence and a new beginning: "Oh, sun, beaches, and the islands in the path of the trade winds, youth whose memory drives one to despair." In this moment of clarity he admits that his "solution is not the ideal." But, he reasons, "when you don't like your own life, when you know that you must change lives, you don't have any choice, do you?" Then he asks the crucial question: "What can one do to become another? Impossible." Why is it impossible? Because, he says, "One would have to cease being anyone, forget oneself for someone else, at least once." Precisely, Luther would respond. "But how?" is Clamence's question, as he forlornly concludes, "we have lost track of the light, the mornings, the holy innocence of those who forgive themselves." *Homo incurvatus in se,* Luther contended, cannot set himself free from his bondage to self; he must rest upon God's gracious forgiveness and strength. In this way he can learn to forgive himself. Modern *homo incurvatus,* however, no longer has any divine basis for the self-forgiveness that produces a sense of "holy innocence." Paradoxically, therefore, Clamence's ego-exalting pride is combined with an unforgiving self-hatred that does not permit self-forgiveness, "that hatred for which," according to the Catholic novelist Georges Bernanos, "there is not pardon."

Thus, despite his pride, his desire for "the heights," his egocentrism, Clamence longs for innocence; he wants to begin again, to become another person, to be born anew, in Johannine terms (John 3:1-5). But he lacks the conviction and the capacity for a new beginning—he cannot "forget himself for someone else." And, unlike Luther, he cannot believe in a God who in Christ has demonstrated his willingness to grant a fresh start; thus he cannot forgive himself and begin again. Clamence, in fact, ironically dismisses the idea of salvation through the redemptive death of Christ, the salvation that Luther offers as the only escape from human incurvedness: Christ "died without knowing," Clamence asserts, and "left us alone. People naturally tried to get some help from his death. After all, it was a stroke of genius to tell us: 'You're not a very pretty sight, that's certain! Well, we won't go into the details! We'll just liquidate it all at once, on the cross!' "

Clamence's rejection of divine grace is further illustrated by his cynical observations on the snow that begins to fall on the last day of his confession: "there will be purity, even if fleeting, before tomorrow's mud." The snowflakes remind him of the doves whose failure to descend he has noted frequently, a contrasting allusion to the descent of the Holy Spirit as a dove on the head of Jesus at his baptism, symbolizing the invasion of the world by God's grace. "They finally make up their minds to come down, the little dears," he remarks without conviction. "What an invasion!" he exclaims, and continues, "Let's hope they are bringing good news." The heavy irony of this passage is underscored by the remarks that follow: "Everyone will be saved, eh?—and not only the elect. Possessions and hardships will be shared and you, for example, from today on you will sleep every night on the ground for me," a cynical reference to his earlier anecdote about a man who slept on the floor because he did not wish to experience comfort that his imprisoned friend did not enjoy. Not only does this passage illustrate Clamence's cynical attitude toward the idea of divine grace, but it also epitomizes the manner in which he manipulates Biblical images and allusions, frequently employing the language of faith and alluding to Biblical events, but in such an ironic fashion that the Biblical message mocks rather than inspires.

He really does not believe that the doves will come down, but it is significant that the ironic reference to the possibility occurs in conjunction with his forlorn dismissal of recovered innocence and the hope of "salvation." In this oblique manner Clamence recognizes that restored innocence and the salvation that bears fruit in commitment to others are dependent on a divine invasion of the human sphere, a theological perspective that is at the heart of Luther's interpretation of the Gospel in his commentary on Romans. Clamence's mocking tone in his remarks on the possibility of sacrificial sharing reveals his belief that *homo incurvatus* is incapable of this. Luther would agree that such self-giving is impossible—apart from divine grace. But the difference lies in Luther's conviction that in Christ the "doves" have "come down," and that saving grace has thus become a reality through the Gospel. Clamence does not believe in such grace; he consequently concludes his dove homily with a mocking allusion to two epiphanies in the story of Elijah the prophet, his contest with the prophets of Baal on Mt. Carmel (1 Kings 18:20-39) and his translation into heaven by a chariot and horses of fire (2 Kings 2:9-12). . . . (pp. 50-8)

Clamence's very "altruism" as a Parisian lawyer is a parody on divine grace, God's "altruism," in that it is wholly egocentric. In the Christian story God's grace is revealed through self-giving (John 3:16), not self seeking. It pursues the good of others rather than merely its own good (Philippians 2:3-8). Unlike Clamence's "altruism," it is not showy and theatrical but humble and self-effacing, for there was nothing attractive about death on a Roman cross. Clamence also rejects grace in his ironic portrayal of himself as "God the Father" judging mankind but "without absolving" or "forgiving. Clamence, therefore, both in his explicit comments and in his self-absorbed "altruism" and ironic apotheosis denies the possibility of authentic grace, human and divine. He is a twentieth-century incarnation of Luther's *homo incurvatus in se,* equipped with the symbols of Luther's Biblical faith, but hopelessly entrapped in a self-conscious egocentricism that admits no entrance to Luther's redemptive grace.

Late in his confession Clamence admits that "authors of confessions write especially to avoid confessing, to tell nothing of what they know. When they claim to get to the painful admissions you have to watch out, for they are about to dress the corpse." He adds significantly, "Believe me, I know what I'm talking about." The corpse metaphor is further developed when he speaks of his room as a "clean and polished . . . coffin." Clamence's confession of the unreliability of confessions provides the ultimate glimpse into the abyss of his ego. The credibility of his entire confession is undermined by this admission. Only one certainty remains: that he seeks his egoistic advantage, even though it is a matter of "dressing the corpse." And since Clamence has ruled out help from beyond, one can only conclude that this modern *homo incurvatus* is forever buried in the coffin of his own ego.

Luther's conception of man as "curved in" on himself provides a useful theological perspective for analyzing the character of Clamence in Camus' *The Fall.* Luther uses the term in the sense that man in all things seeks only himself, that beneath every layer of the self which is peeled away there lies yet another layer of the self. In Luther's view this is not a hopeless condition because the realization of it can impel one to turn to and lean upon the grace of God for redemption from self. *The Fall,* though not by Camus' design, may be read as a modern exposition of Luther's doctrine of human "curvedness," but without Luther's trust in saving grace. Thus the character of Clamence gives bleak twentieth-century embodiment to a sixteenth-century theological conception of the nature of man.

Clamence, the master role-player, is ostensibly engaged in stripping away the egocentric pretenses that he has employed at various stages of his life; however, as each role is confessed, another egocentric role is revealed, so that contemplating his character is like looking into an infinite series of opposed mirrors. It finally becomes apparent that Clamence is even using his confession as a means of ego exaltation, and one is led to conclude that were he to go on confessing forever the final truth about him would yet remain unrevealed.

Indeed, the only final truth about Clamence is that he is "curved in" on himself, that he is hopelessly enmeshed in his own egocentrism. Thus his every word and action is turned to the inflation and gratification of his own ego. And since Camus's epigraph to the English translation of *The Fall* implies that Clamence "is the aggregate of the vices of our whole generation in their fullest expression," one concludes that Clamence is his image for modern man. Thus Camus, in one of the most devastating analyses of twentieth-century man in modern literature, explicates, though unwittingly, Luther's sixteenth-century view of the perversity of the human heart, but without Luther's remedy of divine grace. (pp. 59-61)

> *Robert L. Duncan, "Homo Incurvatus in Se: Luther and Camus on Human Nature," in* The Centennial Review, *Vol. XXVII, No. 1, Winter, 1983, pp. 47-61.*

John M. Dunaway

Albert Camus and Simone Weil were contemporaries in the world of French thought and letters. They both were given the rigorous training of philosophy teachers (under the tutelage of two famous master teachers, Jean Grenier and Alain) and they wrote similar philosophical analyses of the human condition, but they were too vitally concerned with the grim realities of human suffering to remain on the level of intellectual abstraction. Instead, they both engaged themselves in active struggle for the cause of justice: Camus most notably in the publication of the clandestine newspaper *Combat* and Weil as a laborer and trade union activist. Both had first-hand experience of poverty and debasement: Camus because he rose from such humble origins and Weil because she humbled herself to share the lot of those whom she wished to liberate. Their writings are focused largely on the same problems of human experience, and their sources appear remarkably similar.

We know that Camus was convinced that Weil's writings were immensely important. He devoted much time and effort to the posthumous publication of several of her works in the Gallimard collection *Espoir,* of which he was editor, and in his preface to the original edition of *L'Enracinement* (The Need for Roots, 1949) he called her "the only great mind of our time." Robert Cohen has suggested that Weil's *Waiting for God* may have had an important influence on Beckett's *Waiting for Godot.* Did Weil's work have a similar influence on certain of the later writings of Camus? Let us begin this investigation by examining the prophetic visions of the human condition in Camus and Weil and their common sources, and then we shall close with some speculative conclusions on how closely we may associate their philosophies.

Meursault in *L'Etranger* (**The Stranger,** 1942) is estranged from his society in that he refuses to lie. He is a martyr to the constraints of an untruthful, unjust world. Camus says Meursault is in love with the sun because it represents perfect justice and truth. It also represents the direct, honest experience of the cosmos (the kingdom of this world) that he calls "la pensée du midi" (the thought of the south) in the conclusion to *L'Homme révolté* (**The Rebel,** 1951). Dr. Rieux in *La Peste* (**The Plague,** 1947) is similarly cast into a state of estrangement by the irrational, unrelenting menace of the plague. The horrible disease is one of those imposing metaphors—like the sun and the sea—which always make of Camus's fiction a mythic world and of his plots a recurrent ritual enactment of destiny. It may represent not only mortality and destruction but the incomprehensible absurdity of fate. Rieux, like D'Arrast in **"La Pierre qui pousse"** ("The Growing Stone") is a mythic hero in a Messianic sense because they both struggle to achieve the salvation of a people. Daru of **"L'Hôte"** ("The Guest") and Janine of **"La Femme Adultère"** ("The Adulterous Woman") are perhaps most painfully aware of the nature of their estrangement, and they make good-faith efforts to reintegrate themselves into the kingdom of man.

The title of the collection in which Camus published these three stories is *L'Exil et le royaume* or *Exile and the Kingdom* (1957). It expresses a metaphorical polarity that applies not only to the five stories of the collection but to all of Camus's fiction, and it corresponds closely to Weil's analysis of the crisis in modern culture as it appears in *L'Enracinement.* The "kingdom," as I have already hinted, refers to what Camus calls the kingdom of this world, or the kingdom of man. The goal of Camus's protagonist is always to be at one with the cosmos, in harmony with his universe. This goal is usually portrayed in terms of harmony with the natural world that surrounds him, but it ultimately and ideally would include as well his reintegration into a redeemed social order. To readers of

L'Enracinement this description of life within the king-dom will sound strikingly similar to Weil's notion of rootedness, the "real, active, and natural participation in the existence of a collectivity" that cannot take place in isolation from the land.

"Exile," on the other hand, is somewhat more ambiguous. The estrangement that it symbolizes can be a positive, ben-eficial state, both for Camus and for Weil. Meursault is a stranger or outsider, a pariah, because he refuses to con-form to the expectations of his society. He is condemned by the court not so much because he shoots the Arab but because he cannot conjure up enough grief to cry at his mother's funeral. When his attorney asks him in prison whether he loved his mother, he replies that he liked her well enough, but that "all healthy people have more or less wished the death of those they love". The lawyer, quite naturally, is highly disturbed by such brutal honesty and makes him promise not to say such things in court. Thus, the estranged Meursault exposes the sham and pretense of his society. Just as Simone Weil so often spoke of the ne-cessity to refuse the false security of the social group—or the Great Beast, as she sometimes called it—just as she fled the dangerous comfort offered by pronouncing the word "we," so Camus in the same sense offers in Meur-sault a picture of adamant fidelity to truth in opposition to a collectivity. And let us not forget that the first of the vital needs of the soul listed by Weil in *L'Enracinement* is the need for truth.

On the negative end of the spectrum, exile is the painful separation from one's sociocultural and spiritual nourish-ment and from the land. The fundamental difference be-tween good and bad forms of exile, of course, is that the good forms described above are voluntary, while the bad are imposed from without. Meursault is literally and forci-bly exiled by his imprisonment. So is Daru's guest, whom he tries to free. Janine is exiled by her position in a dehu-manized, deracinated industrial society that has been transplanted to an inhospitable land. D'Arrast feels a sim-ilar estrangement from the poor, primitive Brazilian vil-lage people in whom he senses an enviable harmony with the world. The inhabitants of Oran are threatened with ab-solute estrangement and uprootedness by the arbitrary and ominous pestilence that Rieux fights. The Weilian pic-ture of exile is "déracinement" (uprootedness), which can take the form of military conquest, genocide, slavery, po-litical oppression, religious persecution, or deportation, to cite only its most violent forms. It includes the dehuman-ization of the urban technological culture and the erosion of meaningful work possibilities in rural areas. In other words, uprootedness is being cut off from any of the needs of the soul that Weil sees as vital nourishment for human life. Camus's fictional protagonists are in exile, deracinat-ed, severed from God, from the land, from their fellow men. Hence the absurdity of their existences.

All five of Camus's characters that I have chosen are con-fronted, to some degree or other, with the problem of colo-nialism, an issue about which Simone Weil was deeply concerned. (pp. 35-7)

Many readers have found it somewhat puzzling that the mystical exaltation of Meursault in *L'Etranger* is found precisely in the moments of his rejection by the world. When his appeal is refused, he resigns himself to his death and even begins to see in it his justification. Then at the

end of the book, as he envisions his approaching execu-tion, he opens himself for the first time to the "tender in-difference of the world". . . . Meursault's execution most probably would not be solemn; he imagines that "one is killed discreetly, with a little shame and a lot of preci-sion," and he wishes for the crowd to greet him at the scaf-fold with "cries of hatred." However, one might see in his attitude toward the execution a dim presage of the reinte-gration into society that Weil calls for. And the "tender indifference of the world" to which Meursault opens him-self sounds very much like Weil's descriptions of the Stoic love of the beauty of the world order which welcomes good and evil alike—pleasure and suffering—as expres-sions of the divine, impersonal justice of Stoic necessity.

Simone Weil's lifelong philosophical inquiries led her to many sources, but the one most important source of all her thought was the ancient Greeks. Albert Camus was intro-duced by Jean Grenier to Greek philosophy and literature and he, too, became fascinated with it for the rest of his life. His thesis was on Plotinus and Augustine. He some-times explained the basic difference in his philosophy and Sartre's by saying that Sartre had been nourished by Ger-man literature while he had been brought up on the Greeks. Plato was more important for him that Kant or Hegel, whereas Sartre would have preferred the Germans. This Mediterranean orientation in Camus's thought, which recalls the "pensée du Midi" of *L'Homme révolté,* is closely akin to Weil's. I am also reminded parentheti-cally of Valéry's "Cimetière marin," where the central image of the noonday sun, "Midi le juste," calls up meditations on equilibrium—a key concept for both Camus and Weil—and many classical Greek allusions. In fact, the re-integration into the kingdom of man that Meursault's exe-cution represents for him can also be termed a restoration of the equilibrium of the sun which he had destroyed when he shot the Arab—"I understood," he says after firing, "that I had destroyed the equilibrium of the daylight, the exceptional silence of a beach where I had been happy."

One could pursue the similarities in the role of Greek trag-edy for Weil and Camus, their interest in Greek myths (Is not Sisyphus a hero of the Stoic ethic so admired by Weil?), their fundamentally Greek notions of destiny, ne-cessity, and justice. One might also take note of the fact that both of these thinkers used the Bible extensively as a philosophical source, and they both approached the Scriptures originally as unbelievers, but with the open atti-tude of honest seekers devoted to the cause of truth. (pp. 39-40)

If Camus's religious thought was taking on an increasingly Christian flavor at the end of his career, as several critics have suggested, Simone Weil's writings may have counted for something in such a development. Most of the evi-dence, however, suggests that while he was intrigued with the degree of similarity in their sociopolitical thought, the profound differences in their fundamental visions of God and the divine ordering of the universe may have prevent-ed Camus from being significantly influenced by Weil.

Dr. Rieux's words to Tarrou are an apt illustration of Camus's theological orientation. "Since it is death that rules the order of the world, perhaps God prefers that we not believe in Him and struggle with all our might against death, without lifting our eyes toward the heaven where He remains silent." Here is a man who desperately hungers for a God of absolute justice, one who would not allow the innocent to suffer. Since the affliction symbolized by the plague is permitted by God, the Camusian hero (whether Rieux or Sisyphus) sees no alternative but to turn from Him and create his own meaning, his own value.

Simone Weil could never be accused of insensitivity to human suffering. However, her perspective on affliction could scarcely be more diametrically opposed to Camus's. In fact, her view of the subject is not very far from that of Father Paneloux, whom Camus portrays rather ironically in *La Peste* as typical of what he no doubt considered to be the misguided Christian concept of suffering. Paneloux, preaching on the significance of the plague, invites the inhabitants of Oran to look for "that exquisite glimmer of eternity that lies beneath all suffering. It is a glow that lights the twilight path to deliverance. It manifests the divine will that unfailingly transforms evil into good." Weil certainly shared Camus's agonizing over the suffering of the innocent in this world, but she believed that man's response should be different. Meursault is more in agreement with her in his tranquil acceptance of the "tender indifference of the world." For Weil, it is this very indifference in the world order that is the mark of God. He allows the rain to fall on the just and the unjust alike, for His justice transcends our ability to comprehend it. The humble but lucid acceptance of the world order that characterizes Weil's Christian Stoicism is an "attente de Dieu," a waiting on God and His revelation of the true kingdom. Although Weil, like Rieux, is painfully aware of the silence of God, she seeks evidence of His character in the beauty of the world order, and she repeatedly recalls God's promise that He does not give a stone to those who ask Him for bread—a promise that is crucial for the exiled pilgrim of attentive waiting.

The balance sheet on the question of literary and philosophical influences is usually a matter of speculation, and the case of Weil and Camus is no exception. It is obvious, for example, that the similarities we have noticed between certain aspects of *L'Etranger* and Weil's ideas on criminal justice and rootedness are not a question of influence, since Camus wrote his first great novel before encountering Weil's writings. While *L'Homme révolté* may owe something to *L'Enracinement,* the basic polarities of exile and kingdom and of estrangement and rootedness in these two thinkers can best be attributed to commonality of interests and sources. It is certainly safe to say, at the very least, that Camus and Weil brought to bear on the crisis of culture in the twentieth century two prophetic voices schooled among the same tutors and full of the same profound compassion for a world exiled from the kingdom of rootedness. (pp. 40-2)

> *John M. Dunaway, "Estrangement and the Need for Roots: Prophetic Visions of the Human Condition in Albert Camus and Simone Weil," in* Religion and Literature, *Vol. 17, No. 2, Summer, 1985, pp. 35-42.*

Elwyn F. Sterling

Nearly forty years after publication of *La Peste,* there is a broad critical consensus on the significance of the central metaphor. Jacqueline Lévi-Valensi perhaps summarizes it best in asserting that, beyond a fictional representation of the Second World War and the occupation of France, it is ["the mortal condition of man which is represented in *The Plague* . . . Oran is nothing more than an image of our earth and of our absurd world, and . . . Rieux and his friends are incarnations of human attitudes before the calamity which is inherent in our condition."] Critics have quite naturally focused their attention on the positions taken by various characters towards the murderous and inescapable presence of the plague in the city of men. As a result, the attitudes of the principal characters—Rieux, Tarrou, Paneloux, Rambert, and Grand—have been analyzed in considerable depth. The attitudes of secondary characters have, however, received far less attention and, among them, Cottard's has received amazingly short shrift. . . . Even Donald Haggis, in a book devoted entirely to *La Peste,* speaks little of Camus' black marketeer beyond summing up the common critical view. Cottard, he states, in concurrence with Rieux, has ["affinities with the plague"]; he is a "man who . . . has become a victim of fear and despair. Cottard's attitude . . . is the very antithesis of 'revolt.' . . . Camus suggests his activity springs . . . not so much from a deliberate evil intention to take advantage of others, as from a moral abdication that is the consequence of his inner despair." This seems to be a fair, if cursory, statement of Cottard's motives but it leaves a question unanswered: what is Cottard's function within the thematic structure of the chronicle? It would appear, at least from the point of view of the author, that this function extends beyond the presentation of a personal "quirk" of nihilism (Lazère). ["It is fitting," states Rieux, "for this chronicle to end on him who had an unfeeling, that is to say, solitary heart."] Because Rieux's account is presented from a retrospective point of view, Cottard's final appearance would seem to be no less important to the sense of the novel than, say, the scene which presents the death of Philippe Othon, a scene which introduces in microcosm one of the fundamental themes of the book. To obtain a just reading of the book, then, it is necessary to examine the following question: why is it right and fitting that *La Peste* should end with the episode of Cottard's madness?

It is useful at this point to reexamine Cottard's role prior to the *dénouement.* The reader first encounters Cottard after his failed attempt at suicide. Significantly, Cottard has twice signaled before this attempt to Grand—one of those "rare" men ["who always have the courage of their good feelings"]—if not his intention, at least his need for dialogue and understanding. But Grand, although the most unself-consciously solidary and sympathetic rebel of *La Peste,* is absorbed in his own esthetic endeavors and personal problems. He has consequently failed to discern the appeal for help. Henceforth Cottard, subject to police prosecution for a crime committed and known only to himself, liable to a sentence of forced labor or prison, if he is lucky, if not ready to re-begin his attempt to find a way out of his anguish in suicide, finds the random threat of death from the plague less menacing than the certain threat of separation from his "habits" and human associations, a separation which would cast him into a situation of alienation. Thus if he consequently proves willing to consent to the random suffering and death of others as a means of finding a temporary respite from his own torment, as both he and many critics have noted, his consent does not reflect evil intentionality as does, for example, that of Caligula in Camus' play. Indeed, there are things to "admire" in him as well as to "despise." He regularly sends money to a needy sister. Tarrou has asked Cottard not to try to spread the plague's deadly virus and he makes no overt attempt to do so. If his words are implicitly murderous—and they are not more so than those of Paneloux—his conduct, confined to the importation of contraband and the profitable provision of means of escaping the threat of the plague to people like Rambert, provides relief in a somewhat backhanded and perverse way to human suffering. Certainly this conduct is ultimately less deadly than Tarrou's invitation to join the "sanitary squads" or Rieux's condemnations of those infected by the malady to hospital: such confinement, as he well knows, constitutes a probable death sentence.

Can one argue that Cottard's refusal to revolt against the plague reinforces in some small way its fatal virulence? Not really, for none of its victims is lost or saved as a direct result of human efforts. Viewed sentimentally those efforts are emotionally satisfying but viewed objectively they are without demonstrable negative or positive results. Doubtless this is the underlying sense of the pathetic scene where a symbol of innocence, *le fils* Othon, assumes the posture of a "crucifié grotesque" in a long and painful revolt against his destiny. Insufficiently noted, perhaps, is the fact that neither the scientific intervention of Castel's serum and Rieux's medical knowledge, nor Paneloux's prayer, nor Rieux's attempt to sustain the child through emotional solidarity, nor the child's protest itself prove to be of the slightest efficacy. As Camus had already put it in *Noces,* before the deadly mathematics which govern our condition, ["the mind is nothing, nor even the heart"]. But this was, of course, in the author's view, one of the fundamental themes of *La Peste:* ["The underlying equivalence of variant points of view in the face of . . . the absurd . . . "]. Logically, in the harsh light of equivalence, Cottard can be objectively guilty of nothing. The notion of equivalence precludes not only the efficacy of human effort before the random but finally unavoidable imposition of the death sentence; it also simultaneously excludes the possibility of innocence or guilt. Objectively, everything is permitted after all. There is, in fact, a certain stubborn honesty revealed in Cottard's refusal to conceal from others his motives and his insistence on stating his truth and living accordingly, an honesty which recalls Meursault's refusal to say more than he feels. But it is precisely this sentimental error that Tarrou—the agnostic "savior" of souls on this earth—and Rieux—the "savior" of bodies—find unacceptable. It is this crime of a heart unfeeling for the suffering of others which Tarrou can understand but finds himself emotionally obliged to pardon; it is also this crime that prevents Rieux from speaking for the little black marketeer as he does for the other Oranais. These post-absurdist protagonists, who know the truth, find it affectively unacceptable, as it was for Camus. ["The truth is unacceptable even for him who finds it"] (*Carnets II*). And so, if Cottard tells them nothing which they do not already know when he declares ["my notion is that you will not achieve anything"], he is more precocious when he tells them a truth which they do not wish to know: ["the only way of getting people together is to send them the plague"]. But Cottard has good reason to be more perspicacious. If Tarrou has suffered intellectually and emotionally from man's inhumanity to man and Rieux has found unbearable the suffering imposed by the

human lot, Cottard suffers from the concrete persecution of his fellow men for what he deems to be a purely human "error". Nevertheless, it is precisely this human error, together with that of an unfeeling heart which results from unwanted imprisonment in the depths of his own anguish, that requires *understanding* (. . . —if one is not to prove oneself, at best a passive, if not an active propagator of the plague). Here is to be found, perhaps, the key to Cottard's role within the thematic structure of *La Peste* and it is within this context that the final episode of the chronicle should be examined.

As the plague's strength weakens, Cottard—it will be recalled from Tarrou's notes—is subject to an ever-increasing anxiety, his hope now reduced to either a resurgence of the malady's virulence or the question of whether or not the mortal sickness will have "changed anything" in the city, whether or not ["everything will start over as before, that is to say, as if nothing has happened"]. Tarrou's response to the question is ironically ambiguous: clearly the city's inhabitants will want to act as if nothing has changed and, consequently, [". . . nothing in a sense will be changed, but . . . in another sense, even with the necessary will . . . the plague will leave traces, at least in people's hearts"]. Contrary to Cottard's hopes, the plague will not recover its strength and he will not have the opportunity to "start over" from "zero" with a clean slate. Men, at least in the form of the collectivity, have learned nothing from their ordeal. This was, from the author's perspective, one of the thematic conclusions of the chronicle: [" . . . *The Plague* demonstrates that the absurd *teaches nothing*"] (*Carnets II*). So much then for the not infrequent critical charge that Camus while asserting the "need to act," avoided the "more difficult problems of which action one chooses, how one is changed by it and what influence it will have" ([Patrick] McCarthy). Camus did not believe that men are changed as a result of their common revolt against catastrophe: [" . . . the solidarity of combat is a futile thing; it is the individual sentiments which triumph"] (*Carnets II*). To learn this is in itself an important step forward: ["It is the definitive progress"] (*Carnets II*). Rieux would not disagree: ["The old man was right," he concludes, "men were always the same"]. Not surprisingly, then, at the very moment that Cottard is expressing his hopes, two representatives of the collectivity, two policemen, step from the darkness in pursuit of him. Collective solidarity against human suffering begins to revert to the imposition of solitary pain, as Cottard had foreseen. Feeling cornered, Cottard—like Caligula after the death of Drusilla—flees into the night. (pp. 177-81)

It has been stated that Rieux remains uninfected by the plague and that in a more general sense, *La Peste* fails to put the human conscience to the test of moral ambiguity. But in Rieux's case, at least, the seeds of torment have been sown. As he makes his way towards Cottard's home, he is pursued by the memory of Cottard and ["the dull thud of fists which were bruising the latter's face. Perhaps it was harder to think of a guilty man than of a dead man"]. Certainly Rieux's musing is ambiguous: after all who is guilty? Cottard, who has openly consented to the plague? The policeman who has brutalized a helpless victim? Rieux, who has implicitly consented to the infliction of gratuitous pain by virtue of his failure to protest, and by his subsequent denial of "understanding" and "sympathy" to the sufferer? If Rieux, or any other fictional character has a future, he will probably continue to mull over the question and eventually discover that the plague has indeed left "traces" in his heart and that there is in him too something to condemn. Will he then find that he still possesses that naive "light" of "holy innocence" which will permit him to forgive himself? Or will he, like Clamence, find himself incapable of self-pardon and seek relief from torment by becoming an apostle of universal guilt? The answers to these questions must, of course, remain purely speculative but they do suggest why the narrator of *La Peste* ambiguously declares it fitting that the chronicle end ["on him who had an unfeeling, that is to say, solitary heart"].

At one point in the evolution of the manuscript of *La Peste,* Cottard agrees to participate in the "sanitary squads" on the grounds that, for the first time in his life, he finds himself to be ["exactly like the others"] (**"Notes et Variantes"**). Why, then, did Camus transform his role from one of revolt to consent and deny him an opportunity for redemption? The first reasons that spring to mind are not sufficient to explain the transformation. It is not simply because Camus disapproved of black marketeers or passive collaborators. The minor character, Gonzalès, falls into that category and he not only enters the "sanitary squads" but is treated sympathetically by the narrator. And the transformation of the role is not primarily the result of an attempt to make the chronicle more realistic through the presentation of at least one character who does not instinctively revolt against the suffering implicit within the human condition or the explicit pain which men inflict upon each other. Rather the transformation would seem destined to underline the exceptional character of human solidarity during times of extraordinary stress and the moral ambiguity implicit in human behavior in ordinary circumstances. The exemplary punishment of Cottard, together with his role in the story, has little importance for its own sake. Instead, it serves as a vehicle for summing up and bringing together the ultimate themes of *La Peste.* It also serves as a balance point which reestablishes an equilibrium between an essentially optimistic view of human reaction to a clearly defined menace to the general welfare and a no less pessimistic view—ignored by most readers, as McCarthy indicates—of human indifference to the suffering of others in the absence of a clear and present danger. Contrary to conventional wisdom, it underscores the "moral ambiguity" of human answers to the questions posed by either life or men. Finally, it serves to point to the future evolution of Camus' thought and fiction. Like all men, Rieux and Grand prove to have ["the ethics which they find sympathetic or antipathetic"] (*Essais*). Their reaction suggests that there indeed exists a human nature which does not change, a notion with which Camus will deal in *L'Homme révolté* (*Essais*). As for the fiction, it suggests that, if there are more things in men to "admire" than to "despise," one must ultimately come to grips with what is despicable within one's nature as Clamence must do in *La Chute.* (pp. 182-83)

Elwyn F. Sterling, "Albert Camus' 'La Peste': Cottard's Act of Madness," in College Literature, *Vol. XIII, No. 2, Spring, 1986, pp. 177-85.*

Louise K. Horowitz

That Albert Camus systematically excluded—one is tempted to say eradicated—both women and the colonial Arab population of North Africa from his work is a literary fact. Yet, traditionally, to call attention to that fact is to make a political statement, and, in particular, to risk being branded as the very type of left-wing intellectual ostensibly abhorred by Camus. Even those Western critics who pinpoint the racial foundation of Camus's fiction ultimately retreat into apologetic statements for having revealed the all too obvious. Thus, Renée Quinn, in an article entitled "Le theme racial dans *L'Etranger,*" signals a retreat at the end of that study: "Sans prétendre, bien entendu, épuiser la signification de *L'Etranger* par cette interprétation on peut penser qu'elle lui apporte une dimension supplémentaire."

For one decade (not surprisingly the 1960s), analysis of Camus's work in a political light did occur. In January, 1961, *France-Observateur* published two comments—one by Henri Kréa, the other by Pierre Nora—which emphasized the racial underpinnings of *L'Etranger.* Both these studies focused on Camus's own racial insecurities and fears, on the concealed anxieties of the white lower class of Algeria, which, according to Kréa, Camus never psychologically left. In 1969, Renée Quinn's study appeared, leaning on the *France-Observateur* assessments, yet unwilling or unable to assume wholly the potent, if disturbing, revelations. Finally, in 1970, Conor Cruise O'Brien published his study of Camus, exposing dramatically the racial core of Camus's fiction, but this volume has ostensibly failed to convince many Western critics. The proceedings from a major conference on Camus, for example, held at the University of Florida in 1980, include no analyses specifically along these lines. Clearly, Camus's own voice has eclipsed those of his detractors, and we have modeled our criticism of *L'Etranger* on what the author himself stated in the 1955 school edition. "le seul Christ que nous méritions," etc. Why this should be the case is not entirely clear. We don't read Corneille's plays according to his own belated *Examens,* except insofar as to point out certain silences therein. It would appear that a generation of critics has adopted Camus's voice, for it offers a comforting, if unconscious, parallel with their own experience. My intent here is to continue and expand the evaluations of the above mentioned critics, reading the text of Camus (but *not* Camus!) in the light of racial and sexual motivations, which together form one discourse of repression, however "silent" it may be.

That there are critics who have seen the "heart of darkness" and retreated from it, is obvious from the work of Brian Fitch and Philip Thody. As the citation from Renée Quinn's article confirms, however, one need not abandon racial and sexual motives in favor of the "sun" (as Fitch does to explain Meursault's murder of the Arab), to seek a pull-back from uncomfortable revelations gleaned not by interpretation, not by exegesis, but merely by contemplating the plot, the story line. Thus, the critic proposes that the racial cast apparent in Camus's writing is only one aspect, supplementary to the more fundamental "human" concerns that writing purportedly conveys. But one errs in this conclusion, for the so-called human predicament involved, that which has allowed multifold readers to refer to Meursault as a "brother," is ultimately highly restrictive, its "universality" limited to the Occidental male, perhaps to the adolescent fantasies of that reader, and the sociological explanation which Fitch himself calls for in his effort to grasp the popularity of Camus in the United States, is possibly to be found here. The question is not whether a condition of solitude and alienation has implications for the whole of the human race: that, at least, is a cherished Western belief. And alienation *per se* need not be gender typed. At issue here, however, is whether Camus's formulation of the Absurd is not, contrary to popular thought, rooted in a very particular experience, whose roots are at once misogynist (if not homoerotic) and racial.

The intention of Camus in depicting certain situations, and thus the question of the author's identification with his characters, is nigh impossible to resolve. To conclude in favor of authorial identification with the protagonists (indeed, even to suspect it) leads to queasy moral problems for the readership. Perhaps that is why so many critics focus on the more abstract writing which proliferates in these works, on the metaphysical, rather than the physical domain. The "radical" critic, on the other hand, either Western or Arab or feminist, will focus precisely on the physical dimension—in the case of Meursault, on his curious indifference to various brutalities—and accuse Camus of complicity, subconscious or conscious, in allowing the book's second half to move away from that reality. Whereas the majority of readers will see the failure to refer to the Arab's murder in the novel's second half as the result of Meursault's "solar" conditioning, which thus absolves him of premeditated intent to kill, other readers will come to see in such silence Camus's own (one that foreshadows no doubt the ambivalent positions he assumed concerning the Algerian revolution), a silence that is thereby a sort of hegemony-in-narrative. The sleight of hand accorded the murder of the Arab throughout the second half is seen as Camus's own dismissal of the murder and preceding violence. Thus, we remain polarized, asked either not to condemn this writing as racially and sexually exploitative (for in this view such issues are secondary to the major "humanistic" ones), or to believe that Camus was a saboteur, presenting in *La Peste,* for example, a sanitized colonial fiction at the expense of a troubled and troubling colonial reality.

The fact of the matter is that one need not evade or condemn. The eradication of women and Arabs from Camus's work can neither be denied, nor explained away ("it was the sun"), nor seen as a colonial lapsus. Camus has placed in his work men who reflect a collective attitude or mentality of sexual and racial fear and ill concealed desire for degradation. He himself calls attention to these issues, often in the early pages of his works, and only subsequently allows us to dismiss them, thereby encouraging our participation—but without our being made aware of it—in the exploitative situation at hand. That the "human" dimension—be it fear of death, solitude, alienation from the social unit—comes to dominate in the discussion of these works is only a reflection of how such discourse inevitably detracts from other textual realities. *Caligula* is perhaps the most obvious example of how fear of the female is submerged in favor of abstract discussion concerning death and the limits of human happiness. The incestuous experience with Drusilla (reflecting the traditional patriarchal sexual assumptions inherent to such an act), the bloody

moon-female figure conveted by Caligula as a sign of the Impossible, yet ultimately rejected in favor of a pure auto-erotic experience ("Vivre, c'est le contraire d'aimer"), the toe-nail polishing episodes, the ballet dancer episode replete with tutu, the Venus episode, all point to a figure less concerned with abstract absolutes than with vaguely delineated, adolescent fears of the female (except, of course, when sexual acts may occur "en famille," the sister a clear stand-in for the mother, with Caesonia functioning as another double of the matriarchal figure). Claude Treil has observed that for Caligula, "amour-mort équivaut à sexualité-chasteté." Fears of establishing a clear male identity lead to fantasies of pure solitude unspoiled by the bitter odors of lovemaking, and lead also to transvestism. The earliest versions of the play, from the late 1930s, more sharply depict these preoccupations, and the female-fearing, even homosexual theme is there readily apparent (although I believe it is visible in the later version as well).

For Meursault, . . . violence is sexually conditioned, and here is doubled by racial motivation. The semi-abusive relationship with his mother, which culminates, as psychologically oriented critics have seen, in the beach attack on the Arab is linked to the murder additionally by the brutality against "la Mauresque." In the episode involving Raymond's prostitute, the double roots of racial and sexual violence find a voice. (The term "Mauresque," moreover, is not so much here a slight to the Arab world, as Quinn and O'Brien and others have suggested, a mildly derogatory term, but, in my opinion, is a linguistic mask for the Occidental reader, for whom the term would have precisely the opposite connotation than it would for an Arab, i.e., an almost Baudelairian, exotic overtone, which dilutes the racial prejudice inherent to the word.) In this light, justifying Meursault's "innocence" can occur only if the reader, too, experiences a diminished sense of guilt regarding the manifest brutalities of the novel, just as Meursault does, just as the court does, condemning him for matricide and patricide. (These are implied here, perhaps, as elsewhere in Camus's works, although I am sure with his conscious intent, given that such symbolism is scarcely subtle. In fact, however, it is not a mother or father who is killed here, but an Arab stranger.)

In *La Peste,* the banishing of both women and Arabs from the text contrasts strongly with the statements in the book's early pages, where the poor relationships between men and women are discussed and condemned, and the deplorable living conditions of the Arab population are discussed prominently by Rambert and Rieux, never, however, to be brought up again. The effective elimination of women and Arabs should become essential to the novel, given the arrival of the prominently punishing plague, and following the preliminary revelations of acute social disharmony. And in a way, that is what occurs, but only subliminally, for such discord is never mentioned again directly. Exploitation as an apparent theme is textually banished, just as it is repressed by readers for whom such concerns are layered over by a bonding of Occidental brotherhood. The signs are prominent, laid forth in the book's early pages, yet they are consumed by a textual apparatus which parallels a pre-existing reader willingness, subconscious no doubt, to dismiss. The apparent silence on racial and sexual issues in the remainder of *La Peste* is thus the sole commentary on the indictments posed in the early pages, just as in *L'Etranger,* the silences of the book's second half point the way to grasping the nature of Meursault's acts.

Ultimately, in Camus, pronouncements of a highly universal nature result from highly *specific* experiences. Male protagonists are subject to disquieting reactions linked to sexual and racial antipathy and fear, which then give rise to ostensibly general conclusions on the condition of all mankind. Brian Fitch has said that to focus on the murder of the Arab, or on the brutal victimization of the Arab prostitute, is to offer "une explication partielle," by which, despite disclaimers, he means "partiale" as well. My contention is that the discovery of the Absurd, as it is conveyed in the works under consideration here, is a restrictive experience, whose universality exists solely in the minds of those able and willing to participate in the unspoken, but nonetheless screamingly apparent premises of the works. Nothing need be at work other than collective conditioning, so visible in Meursault himself, but this is sufficiently damning. The physical basis for the cherished metaphysical discussion is so polarized as to exclude all be Occidental males, reflecting both real and fantasized power structures, the very ones which Jean Genet exposed in his theater.

In an absorbing and perceptive article, Anthony Rizzuto has claimed "progress" on the part of Camus, gleaned from study of his later works, notably *L'Exil et le Royaume* and *La Chute*. Attempting to shore up Camus's reputation in a consciousness-raised era, Rizzuto reveals what he believes is an increasing self-awareness on Camus's part which leads him to select a female protagonist in **"La Femme adultère,"** and to focus on guilt over the woman's suicidal plunge—as symbolic of Clamence's generalized guilt for his exploitation of women—in *La Chute*. *La Chute* is complex, but I think the blatantly ironic tone goes a long way toward diminishing the idea of new-found understanding. The concealed "secrets" of the earlier works suddenly surface in *La Chute* to become revealed "secrets." But Clamence's bitterly sardonic voice negates these revelations, which Camus dangles tantalizingly before us, refusing them, however, their grave implications. The mood of *La Chute* is summarized in Clamence's regret concerning the black slave trade: "On ne cachait pas son jeu en ce temps-là." Revealed, the secret, which is nostalgia for permissible and sanctioned domination (if not oppression), is nonetheless never canceled. In **"La Femme adultère,"** Janine is searching primarily for male desire and approval—be it from her husband, from the French soldier whose earliest contact is via the oral experience of a lozenge offered and accepted (but who then fails to notice her later on), or the solitary Arab figure before whom she and her husband tremble, or all the Arabs who figure as a shadowy mass throughout the tale. Sexual status and reflection remain intact, freed from the brutalities of the earlier works, but nonetheless constant. For Rizzuto, the claim to sex and therefore to life inherent to this tale demonstrates a "new" Camus who had discovered the limitations of self-love and male bonding, the latter a plural reflection of the former. Whereas it is true that the life force is given a standing in "La Femme adultère" which it was denied in *Caligula,* the stereotyping of such desire severely curtails the claim for heightened awareness. In fact **"La Femme adultère"** may clarify better than any other work the powerful sexual and racial myths of Camus's earlier fiction. If he selected a female protagonist,

it was to avoid the homosexual thrust which would otherwise color the tale. The Arabs in **"La Femme adultère"** are an erotic mass, so powerfully attractive that for once they have the same value as the French officer, the very symbol of the colonial power structure. The sexualizing of the Arab is a prominent factor in Camus's writing: he banishes the Arab and the woman together, brutalizes them, rapes them, or executes them, for each stands as a disruptor to the narcissistic stance of Western man, alone or in groups. The erotic potential of women in Camus's writings, and of Arabs, conforms perfectly to the myths of Western male society: female and native sexuality seen as primitive, intense, destabilizing, destructive, a double cause for "fall." These are, I believe, the myths at work in Faulkner, too, and herein lies Camus's fascination with the American writer.

Of course, it takes no great perception to realize that women and Arabs fare poorly in *L'Etranger,* or that the Oran described in the early part of *La Peste* bares little resemblance to the colonial reality of the 1940s. We are, however, made to believe that the myth and symbols created here can be sustained only by the abstractions generated by this reality. Since *La Peste* is ostensibly a parable of war, of World War II, and hence a European novel, it is acceptable that the Arab population be banished, and that the entire colonial system cease to function textually. But why, then, situate the book in Algeria? Since *L'Etranger* is a parable on modern man's isolation from the social unit, it is fitting that Meursault's "innocence" be maintained. Yet, for it to be not only maintained, but accepted, the Arab and female victims must be seen not as victims, but as inevitable and necessary losers in a bitter social struggle. Stephen D. Ross, in his book, *Literature and Philosophy: An analysis of the philosophical novel,* ponders how so many readers have confronted *L'Etranger* without reacting *morally* to the murder of the Arab. In this regard, there are other troubling aspects to Meursault's character. His willingness to participate in brutal acts (for one cannot forget the easy accommodation he makes to Raymond's requests) is not the only questionable sign. Rather, his rejection of the whole feminine world, his assumptions concerning that world (Raymond is, after all, a pimp; Meursault disparages marriage and more than that, women's emotional values, and says so explicitly as he returns to the beach for the second and fatal encounter), are also central to his character. Such behavior testifies to a mentality that is misogynist in the extreme, just as his racial fears, unspoken but paramount in the text, convey the colonial insecurity which was particularly strong in Algeria during and following the worldwide Depression.

Critics and readers have bypassed these central points to focus on the moralistic considerations which come prominently into play in the novel's second half. Indeed, the brotherhood our society has been ready to confer on Meursault can only confirm that his "liberation" was one deeply shared by large segments of the Western world. Camus offers his readers two texts, and it is the second, the metaphysical voice, which allows the other to be canceled and repressed, a remarkable fact given the all too evident "signs" of discord which the author himself displays in his fiction.

Persisting in seeing Camus as the expressor of modern liberal, human values denies the narcissistic and both sexually and racially polarized sides of his protagonists. In eliminating in the second part of *L'Etranger,* any reference to Meursault's sexual and racial violence, in failing throughout the novel to give introspective voice to the very fears which by necessity are hidden in these acts, Camus textually parallels the ongoing reader reaction, it too prepared, at least subconsciously, to focus on the encompassing "humanistic" text, prepared to repress the fears lying underneath the claims of the individual spirit. This metaphysical text becomes the means for Meursault, and for Camus's readers, to deny (without even having to deny) the subliminal currents flowing underneath. That the discovery of the Absurd should reveal itself, ultimately, as partial is perhaps a saddening experience; it cannot be denied, however, once there is recognition that the Absurd, in this body of literature, functions as yet one more discourse of repression. (pp. 58-9)

> *Louise K. Horowitz, "Of Women and Arabs: Sexual and Racial Polarization in Camus," in* Modern Language Studies, *Vol. 17, No. 3, Summer, 1987, pp. 54-61.*

George J. Makari

The central act and central scotoma of [*The Stranger*] is Meursault's murder of the Arab. This act led Edmund Wilson to declare the work inexplicable. Camus' biographer [Patrick McCarthy] called the portrayal of this event "the most puzzling pages Camus ever wrote." Why does Meursault kill? Why the Arab? Why does he fire four shots into a body already made lifeless by a first round?

In terse bits of prose Meursault introduces himself to the reader:

> Mother died today. Or, maybe, yesterday: I can't be sure. The telegram from the home says: 'Your Mother Passed Away Funeral Tomorrow. Deep Sympathy' which leaves the matter doubtful; it could have been yesterday.

The narrator's logic scurries away from the emotionally charged content of the telegram, and fixes instead on a temporal detail. Meursault does not seem concerned with his Mother's death. Instead he simply would like to establish the date of her demise. Furthermore the narrator is not content with alluding to this temporal detail once; he repeats himself. Like Leonardo Da Vinci's remembrance of his recently deceased father, this passage reveals the narrator's defenses—displacement and repetition—fully mobilized to deny the expression of an unconscious conflict.

Amidst these defensive maneuvers Meursault's reaction to his Mother's death defies easy understanding. The narrator expresses no remorse, and no dejection. He is not wholly within the process of either mourning or melancholic depression. His unprovoked negative affirmations ("It's not my fault, you know") concerning his Mother's funeral reveal a sense of guilt more consistent with the narcissistic injury incurred in melancholia. But this similarity is a bit forced. What astonishes the reader and Meursault's community is not his sense of guilt, but his indifference.

In a 1915 paper "Instincts and their Vicissitudes," Freud explores the relationship of indifference to love and hate:

> Originally . . . the ego is cathected with instincts and is to some extent capable of satisfying them on itself. We call this narcissism . . . At this time the external world is not cathected with interest . . . and is indifferent for purposes of satisfaction . . . the ego loves itself and is indifferent to the external world.
>
> (pp. 359-60)

Is Meursault trapped in an emotional prison of narcissistic love/object indifference? His relationship with his lover, Marie, supports this contention. Meursault coolly informs Marie that marrying her would mean no more or less to him than marrying any other woman. Marie "murmurs something about my being a 'queer fellow'. 'And I dare say that's why I love you' she adds. 'But maybe that's why one day I'll come to hate you'." For Marie the condition of loving or hating is somewhat dependent on her Other, the beloved. The narrator however conceives of Marie not as a willful subject but merely as a replaceable object. In jail the narrator wonders if Marie has died during his imprisonment. He thinks "her memory would mean nothing to me. I couldn't feel interest in a dead girl." With regard to Marie, Meursault has located himself in the narcissistic world of object inconstancy.

Is Meursault's indifference to his mother's death similar? Meursault's small talk at the funeral, his lack of interest in seeing the body, his seeming lack of regret or sentimental remembrance all seem to suggest a cold indifference towards his Mother. After sending his Mother to a nursing home, Meursault remembers: "during her first few weeks she used to cry a good deal . . . After a month or two she'd have cried if she'd been told to leave the home." Meursault's Mother quickly accustoms herself to the loss of her son; she too seems to be narcissistically indifferent to the object of her desire. In addition, the narrator recalls "When we lived together Mother was always watching me, but we hardly ever talked." "For years she never had a word to say to me . . . " This image of a silent scrutinizing mother hints at the frustration Meursault may have experienced in childhood. A mute unempathetic environment the narrator seems to imply, led him to his own strategic retreat from the unrewarding world of externally directed desire.

But when Meursault returns home from the funeral he thinks:

> It suited us well enough when Mother was with me, but now that I was by myself it was too large and I'd moved the dining table into my bedroom. That was the only room I used . . . the rest of the flat was never used, so I didn't trouble to look after it.

Here Meursault symbolically reveals his sense of loss, and his emotional engagement with his Mother. Meursault has withdrawn from the communal rooms, and set up a self-sufficient world in the bedroom of his Self. And yet the memory and longing for the time when the apartment was not "too large", too empty, remains. Meursault's indifference to the external world is betrayed as a defense.

What desire then, is this defense intended to conceal? Let us examine Meursault's "indifference" to Raymond, for in this relationship the narrator's desires are less veiled.

While Meursault stresses his uncaring acquiescence to Raymond's will in forging the letter and falsely testifying at the police station, here indifference is clearly a defense. It would be anomalous for a man buried in narcissism to endanger his world "just because." True indifference would bow out when confronted by the danger of another's battles. Meursault pens a letter luring Raymond's "unfaithful" woman to her punishment, perhaps as he would have liked to respond to the telegraph his Mother "sent" revealing her total abandonment of him. The narrator's identification with Raymond's punishment of the unfaithful woman, his voyeuristic fascination with the actual violence, and his willingness to defend Raymond before the police, all hint at the fulfillment of some passive intent that lies underneath his stoicism.

How does intent turn passive? Freud argues that the reversal of a desire from activity to passivity is manifested most often in two polarities; sadism-masochism and scopophilia exhibitionism. It is my contention that these two polarities are precisely the unconscious determinants beneath Meursault's indifference towards his Mother's death.

Meursault's involvement in sado-masochism is hinted at by his mingling of sympathy and affection with violence. Upon feeling the urge to kiss Marie, the narrator informs us "it was just then that the row started in Raymond's room." Meursault's associations to the figure of Salamano also point toward sado-masochistic desires. As the narrator listens to Salamano's dog wailing from its tortures, his tone becomes lyrical: "through the sleep-bound house the little plaintive sound rose slowly like a flower growing out of silence and darkness." This image of a painful but beautiful shattering of silence is perhaps an association the youthful Meursault first developed in masochistically seeking the only kind of concern (i.e. punishment) he could garner from his otherwise stoic Mother. Meursault's retreat into narcissistic indifference would then not be a reaction to ambivalence or lack of empathy, but would represent part of a sado-masochistic constellation.

When the broken hearted Salamano weeps because his brutal escapades with his dog have been ended by the poor brute's escape, Meursault reinforces the idea that his Mother is an object of his sado-masochistic fantasies. Upon hearing the old man's miserable sobbing, the narrator observes: "For some reason, I don't know why, I began thinking of Mother."

I have attempted to suggest that Meursault employs the defense of object indifference to mask sado-masochistic desires. With this hypothesis in mind, I shall turn to the central puzzle: why does Meursault murder the Arab? Even more centrally and more perplexingly why does Meursault "indifferently" fire four shots into the inert body of his lifeless victim?

Meursault, Raymond and Masson meet two Arabs on the beach, one of whom Raymond asserts is the brother of the woman he recently beat. Raymond and Masson march up to the Arabs. Then Meursault reports "the native lowering his head", to which the narrator adds the fanciful simile "as if to butt him (Raymond) in the chest." Lowering or bowing the head is not an aggressive, threatening posture: it is not the way one person customarily attacks another. Even the "exotic" label "Arab" cannot veil this fact. Meursault has projected his violent urges onto the Arab

who is then "justifiably" flogged till he reveals a knife and cuts Raymond.

Afterwards with vengeance in mind, Raymond insists on returning to the beach by himself. Nonetheless, with indifference as his only stated motive. Meursault follows. Again Meursault's indifference is unmasked as a defense against unconscious inner agendas. Here Meursault defies his friend's will in order to re-encounter the Arabs and the scene of violence.

The two pied-noirs find the Arabs by the boulders:

> They looked harmless enough, as if they didn't bear any malice and neither made a move when we approached . . . For a while nobody moved; it was all sunlight and silence except for the tinkle of the stream and those three little lonely sounds . . . Raymond put his hand to his revolver pocket but still the Arabs didn't move.

The Arabs sitting peacefully and impassively by the stream, seem to be in a trance. The threat of death does not alter their impassivity. In a startling change of character, Meursault expresses tenderness and empathy towards these Arabs. He unexpectedly dissuades Raymond from killing them and disarms his friend just before the "natives" disappear.

Raymond is relieved by the peaceful routing of the Arabs, but Meursault has only been further aroused by this second encounter. He pauses at the steps of the bungalow. Disgusted by the thought of "making myself amiable to the women," he turns around and heads "toward the boulders." "To stay or make a move—it came to much the same," Meursault remarks as he heads straight back to the scene of violence. The reader cannot share Meursault's bewilderment at once again finding an Arab there.

Leaving the "strain and effort" behind, Meursault heads for the Arabs, for in this pied-noir's imagination the Arab holds a symbolic significance. The Arab is the idealization of Meursault's defense of object indifference. Unlike the crying women in the bungalow, the Arab he heads toward is at peace; passively experiencing fates and fortunes, indifferent to death, and without the anxiety of desire. The Arab sits calmly near the stream playing the same three notes on his flute over and over; he has killed off the inner passions that threaten Meursault. Earlier Meursault had observed:

> I saw some Arabs lounging . . .They were staring at us silently, in the special way that these people have—as if we were blocks of stone . . . I . . . looked back. They were exactly as before gazing in the same vague way at the spot where we had been.

Because Meursault has projected his own defense of affective impassivity onto the Arabs, his own deviance from indifference in disarming Raymond and saving the Arabs from death becomes clear. Meursault has generated the only tenderness a narcissist can, tenderness for his own Ego-Ideal.

Meursault's desire for the impassive Arab, and the narrator's participation in Freud's other polarity, scopophilia-exhibitionism, begins to become manifest at the boulders. Meursault's pleasure in viewing the Arab's body exhibited under the sun is revealed in the erotically charged language. The Arab is:

lying on his back, his hands behind his head, his face shaded by the rock while the sun beat on the rest of his body. One could see his dungarees steaming in the heat.

While the Arab's body is exposed in the glaring light, his face and eyes are eclipsed by shadow. The scopophillic pleasure of seeing without being seen allows Meursault to focus freely on the Arab's pants. Meursault steps toward the prone Arab, to get out of the sun, and join the Arab in the shade's relief. Meursault steps forward again saying "I knew it was a fool thing to do," and the Arab draws a knife. The sun catches the blade, blinding Meursault and throwing him into a frenzy.

The lounging Arab, impassive to Meursault's gaze, impassive to the sun and death, totally will-less, has astonishingly expressed will. But is Meursault truly astonished? Suddenly the reader must wonder about Meursault's intent in seeking out the "indifferent Arab". We recall the acts of violence that needed to be banished to create such a myth. We recall that Meursault's first fanciful projection ("butting") revealed his unconscious belief in the Arab's threat. We recall the state of arousal that the first two dangerous encounters threw the narrator into, and how these moments of violence threatened to topple his stoic pose. Meursault's defense of indifference has masked his unconscious intention to engage himself in a situation that will be violent.

The Arab draws his knife and becomes castrating and humiliating. Indifference disappears as Meursault falls swiftly into a struggle for mastery. The narrator's language shifts from tautly controlled sentences to an effusive gush. He imagines his eyes gouged out, and is "blinded" by a "veil of brine and tears." When the Arab pulls his knife. Meursault's scopophillic pleasure is shattered. Meursault is transformed from the subject to the object of voyeurism. Now he is passively exhibited under the killing eye of the Arab, just as he once was scrutinized by his Mother. In these moments Meursault feels bombarded by colors and heat signifying his regression into primary process ([Charles] Brenner). Meursault's defense of indifference is prempted and his sadistic rage is finally vented. He pulls out Raymond's pistol and fires the murderous first bullet through the Arab.

The symbolic significance of Meursault's return to the beach can now be further clarified. Before Meursault returns to the beach, he says he is emigrating from the women, leaving behind "the glare, the sight of women in tears, the strain and the effort." Later on the beach with the sun beating down upon him, Meursault remarks "it was the same sort of heat as at my Mother's funeral." Meursault is symbolically re-enacting the funeral march, fleeing not only Mrs. Masson's tears but also the women mourning at his Mother's funeral. Meursault feels inner "strain" in "making himself amenable" to these mourners for he is filled with rage towards the mother who has in death recapitulated her symbolic abandonment of her son in life. It is this sadistic rage that is now barely masked by his crumbling defense of indifference. He leaves the mourners behind and heads through the sun and heat to the cool, deathly shade of the boulders to vent his rage at his indifferent Mother. Consciously Meursault has merely sought access to the peace of complete narcissistic indifference symbolized by the Arab; a guilt-free world where his

own defense would reign supreme. But unconsciously the narrator hates and seeks revenge against this "indifferent" world. Previous violent encounters with the Arabs have shown the narrator that the impassive object approached too closely will turn violent, and rage will be allowed expression.

Restored to his senses/defenses, Meursault recalls the first shot with the phrase: "the trigger gave . . . " He immediately denies any active intention, and ascribes the first shot to some unknown power, some "it" within him. This first bullet fired in rage "began it all" and "shattered the balance of the day." But then standing over the inert body after calming and collecting himself, Meursault strangely fires four more shots into the dead Arab.

These four shots are Meursault's central symptom, containing both his desire and its defense. Firstly, these shots are a defensive attempt to regain the hegemony of narcissistic indifference. In this compulsion to repeat, Meursault defuses the power of his uncontrollable rage, and regains mastery over his impulses. He seeks to repair the narcissistic injury of losing conscious control by deluding himself into believing indifference guided him; that "one might fire or not fire and it would come to absolutely the same thing." But Meursault knows that those last four shots will make a crucial difference. His pretense of consciously willing these four shots is not only a defense against his rage, but also serves another psychic agenda: self-punishment.

Later, under the magistrate's questioning, Meursault acknowledges "there was only one point in my confession that badly needed clearing up—the fact that I'd waited before firing a second time. All the rest was, so to speak, in order." It is those four shots, and not the commonplace murder of a "native" that will force the colonial community to question Meursault's "psychology" and punish him. Those last four shots fired impassively subvert the colonial community's fantasies of motive, and irrevocably make Meursault an outsider, a loner, a psychopathic killer. Meursault understands this. After the murder Meursault predicts the fulfillment of his masochistic wishes. And he knows that it is the last four shots, not the simple murder of an Arab, which insure his punishment. After firing the pistol five times, the narrator speaks a most revealing sentence that is obscured by Stuart Gilbert's English translation. Gilbert's translation reads: "And each successive shot was another loud fateful rap on the door of my undoing." But the original French reads: "Et c'etait comme quatre coups brefs que je frappais sur la porte du malheur." Meursault omits the actual murdering shot and writes of the last four shots as being the "raps on the door of my misery."

The murder, Meursault observes, "breaks the silence". The repressed active desires of sadism and scopophilia have finally been voiced. With the expression of his rage, and his release from constant diligent repression, Meursault achieves some insight into his desires and his defenses: "I could truthfully say I'd been quite fond of Mother—but really that didn't mean much. All normal people . . . had more or less desired the death of those they loved at some time or another." After listening to the prosecutor re-write his own narrative shorn of alibis and defenses, Meursault acknowledges it "all seemed quite plausible."

But Meursault knows one of the prosecutor's accusations to be false. Meursault's last four shots are not intended to "make a good job" of the killing. They are shots which as the narrator says, make no mark on the dead man. These four seemingly meaningless shots are symbolically intended for their firer. Meursault has mastered the Other by murder and now masochistically decrees his own punishment. He has viewed and now will be exhibited.

In jail, Meursault's passive desires of masochism and exhibitionism are fulfilled. Under the watchful eye of guards and the questions of the examining magistrate, his attempt to extort concern succeeds, but it is the concern of his executioners. Meursault has re-created the bonds of his childhood: he has returned to the silent unempathetic scrutiny of a Mother who only shows attention in punishment. Revealingly Meursault desires his lawyer's "sympathy", not his "making a better job of my defense." Meursault finds happiness in the realm of sympathetic punishment; while being interrogated he feels "one of the family."

In the final passages of *The Stranger,* Meursault relates an "epiphany" that is intended to convey the wisdom his reflections in jail have unfolded before him. Like his mythological Arab, Meursault relates his acceptance of the "benign indifference of the universe." But the reader recognizes this as Meursault's old defense reasserting itself over his violent impulses. His attempt to withdraw from the world outside into narcissistic indifference finally and pathetically fails. *The Stranger* ends with Meursault's pitiful fantasy of passively engaging others in the only way he can, in masochistic exhibitionism:

> For me to feel less lonely, all that remained to hope was that on the day of my execution there should be a huge crowd of spectators and that they should greet me with howls of execration.

> (pp. 361-69)

I have sought to show how the last four shots are Meursault's symptom marking his defense of indifference and his sado-masochism, but they are also colonialism's symptom. The simple murder of an Arab will not bring about Meursault's punishment because of racism in colonial Algeria. Meursault's masochistic desire can only be fulfilled by his odd firing of extra bullets into his lifeless victim. Furthermore Meursault's final fantasy of his own execution reflects his own desires for masochistic union and exhibitionism, and his colonial society's pathology. For who are those people in that huge crowd, howling with execration, but the embodiment of every colonialist's fear: the "natives" shattering the projection of desireless indifference and violently turning against their masters in revolution?

In 1957 during the Algerian revolt, Camus received the Nobel Prize for Literature. At that time the author was asked why he hadn't spoken out against the widespread torture of Arabs in Algeria. Camus replied that if you asked him to choose between his mother and justice, he would always choose his mother (Geha). It is that investment of love in an unjust object which defines the pathos of both Camus/Meursault's relationship to his mother, as well as the colonialist's relationship to "his" country. (pp. 373-74)

George J. Makari, "The Last Four Shots: Problems of Intention and Camus' 'The Stranger'," in American Imago, *Vol. 45, No. 4, Winter, 1988, pp. 359-74.*

Dorothy Bryson

Few texts have been as nicely picked over as *L'Étranger.* And yet, although it might seem that only the most refinedly rarefied of its aspects now remain to be exploited, there is still something important to be said about its most obvious character as a literary statement about moral values—something crucial to the defence of Camus's disputed good name as a man lucidly and sincerely committed to the cause of humanity.

Like Philip Thody's article of 1979 [see excerpt in *CLC,* Vol. 14], Isabelle Ansel's study of *L'Étranger* published in 1981 represents a reformulation (while at the same time a considerable enrichment, with the wealth of original insights it contains) of Conor Cruise O'Brien's notorious contention of yore (itself an elaboration on kindred ideas put forward a decade before by Pierre Nora and Henri Kréa) that Camus effectively colludes in a racist indifference in his hero Meursault to the fate of the Arab victims in the text. For Dr. O'Brien, Meursault's innocence is contrived at the expense of the very human status of the man he kills and this bespeaks the quintessential colonialist contempt in Camus for the subject people; for Mme Ansel, eleven years on, ["The colonial problem constitutes a blind spot in Camus's work and thought"] and he cannot perceive a positive will in his own protagonist, the product nonetheless of his authorial psyche, to liquidate the Arab on the beach. *Même cause,* then (insuperable *pied noir* conditioning), *même* disturbing *effet.* It is time this calumny was definitively disposed of.

Variously deceived (O'Brien) by Camus's dominant narrative strategy, over-influenced (Thody) by remarks he made about the text and misled (Ansel) by the evidence she detects in it of a thoroughly colonial Camusian subconscious, these critics fail to discern the existence of a counter-plot in *L'Étranger* that is the very refutation of their arguments and the precise point of imbrication of the absurdist phase of Camus's writing and that of Revolt. Right in perceiving Meursault's lack of concern for Sintès's mistress as the ugly root of the more conspicuous evil of the killing on the beach, they are quite wrong in their contention that Camus, like his character, turns a deaf ear to the woman's screams or is in any way indifferent authorially to Meursault's function as *bourreau* [agent of suffering or death]: the text itself disproves this.

The overt rhetorical thrust of *L'Étranger* is provided by the theme of guilt, whose ironic development describes a chiasmic pattern whereby initially non-specific guilt in Meursault in the eyes of the reader (a guilt acknowledged by himself) is transformed into the necessary innocence of Absurd Man even as a contrary change is being effected in terms of the bourgeois society of the text, with the presumed innocence of an unremarkable, hard-working life, in Part I, being exchanged, in Part II, for judicial and wider moral guilt. The primary aspect of this process, however, on which the other (and the perception of society's own guilt) depends, is the relationship between Meursault and the reader, and a crucial function attaches here to the spuriously naïve parataxis constituting the unique narrative particularity of the text. Indispensable to the creation of the scandal that is Meursault, vis-à-vis the reader, at the beginning of *L'Étranger,* this elimination of the vocabulary of causality from the process of narration forms the specific basis, in Part II of the novel, for the transferred scandal of Meursault's judgement: where, for Meursault himself (and his intimate, the reader), the events of Part I were related only by their chronology, his judges restore casual connections on the essentialist level of malign motivation. For them, there has to be a plot.

And a plot there indeed is, in *L'Étranger*—or, rather, there are two of them. Camus's very explosion, paradoxical in its utter want of *éclat,* of the conventionally-integrated narrative, his provocative choice of "story" as the vehicle for literature, constitutes an anti-plot in the same way as his hero is an anti-hero, and to the same very limited extent. The sustained "story" of *L'Étranger,* which seems to indict the orthodox practice of narration by association with the "literature" that philosophical orthodoxy of a patently untenable order inspires in Meursault's judges, is reestablished as *intrigue* at the end of the novel, when causality (and hence literary convention) is reinstated retrospectively: Meursault has not explained or integrated his experience because (*because*) he lives, and has known himself to live, in a world that is irrational, a world finally incapable of explanation. Camus dismantles "plot" in *L'Étranger* in order the better to reconstitute it—underlining, indeed, its status in textual teleology by plotting at the same time the definitive ensnarement of the reader, in whom an intellectual assent procured by the revelation of Meursault's absurdist reasons should complete the process whereby initial detachment from the character is replaced by sympathy and self-identification.

More important, however, in the light of the Camus-as-closet-racist thesis of the heirs of Nora and Kréa, the thus disingenuously paratactic first level of *L'Etranger* conceals a less deviously orthodox *intrigue,* a sub-plot constructed not with or through Meursault, but rather against him. And this conventionally-integrated and entirely authorial authorially-arranged hidden corollary to the experimentally exploded narrative reflecting the consciousness of the character himself presents the history of an authentic guilt in Meursault that mitigates more than a little the scandal of his judgement by the court. The "story" of Meursault's innocence (which is exactly that) conceals a plot by Camus to condemn him.

As has repeatedly been observed, the first cause of the sentence passed on Meursault in Chapter 4 of Part II of *L'Étranger* is his collaboration with Raymond Sintès in Chapter 3 of Part I. Without Sintès, it is obvious, there would have been no killing on the beach: no letter would have been written to the Arab woman, no insult would have been sustained by her brother, no gun would have been to hand to shoot with. More than that, however, the involvement with Sintès has its prolongation in Part II, where the psychological replacement of Meursault by Sintès matches the replacement of his supposed crime of murder by that of moral matricide and its displacement from the beach outside Algiers to the graveside at Marengo. The last witness to be called in II,3, Sintès is Judas to Meursault's Christ: immediate and unsolicited, his assertion of Meursault's innocence becomes the blackest of stigmas by (anti) virtue of Sintès's own character as

"moral monster"; as Sintès's "friend", Meursault is of the same vicious ilk as he. In II,4, the prosecutor presents the revised version of the death of the Arab, which Meursault has planned in collusion with Sintès, perfecting the assimilation of unlike to unlike in his last words to the jury: harking back to his earlier definition of Sintès, he contends that "rien que de monstrueux" ["nothing but monstrous"] is to be read in Meursault's face. In the event, Meursault knows precisely that fate which at the start of his trial he had recognised as being "trop grave" ["too grave"]: being judged as someone he is not—as Raymond Sintès.

The literally vital importance of causality is thus asserted in *L'Étranger* on the level of authorial organisation that subtends the merely juxtapository narrative identified with Meursault the character. Of necessity, the progressive experience of reading throws the emphasis on the seemingly scandalous outcome of Meursault's connection with Sintès; but the corollary to this outcome, all the more strongly implied for the implacably rigorous nature of the concatenation of factors preparing it, is the conferment of a special significance, in retrospect, upon the fulcrum of fate (of fatality, indeed) for Meursault—the writing of the letter on Sintès's behalf that sets in train the process of his destruction. And disengaged with hindsight from its contextual gangue in Part I, the episode of the letter is defined, not only as the root of personal evil for Meursault, the real point where "tout a commencé"; but as constituting also the very paradigmatic instance of the primary act of interpersonal abuse as Camus was later to define and deplore this in *L'Homme Révolté.* In writing the letter for Sintès, Meursault crosses the moral boundary between the legitimate exercise of individual, individualistic freedom and the illegitimate infringement of another's rights. In doing so, he presents the perfect, concise illustration, in mid-absurdism, supposedly, for Camus, of the "intolerable intrusion" that inspires the movement of Revolt—as also, indeed, of the effortlessly exponential spread of human evil described by Tarrou in *La Peste:* Sintès's mistress returns not only to humiliation but to brutality—and with the consequences we know both for her brother and for Meursault himself.

When Chapter 3 of Part I of *L'Étranger* is considered with the attentiveness that Camus's remorseless chain of cause and effect suggests to be appropriate, it is evident that he is at pains, the letter having been written, to establish the intimate connection between it and the killing on the beach and its consequences, between *le mal* [evil] and *le malheur* [misfortune]: it is on leaving Sintès at the end of I,3, his temples throbbing as in I,6, that Meursault has his premonitory intimation of the "souffle obscur" of II,5 and the whine from Salamano's dog signals the disaster Meursault instinctively tries to stave off. More than this, however, it is also apparent that Camus seeks, in the passage preceding the writing of the letter, to establish the moral distinction to be made between the covert and overt determinants of Meursault's fate. For unlike the pulling of the trigger in I,6, relegated emphatically (*pace* Ansel) to the volitionless level of physical reflex, the act of writing in I,3 is presented as utterly deliberate and meticulously prepared. (pp. 272-75)

Meursault himself never accepts his own failure of humanity. The sybilline moral ("Il ne faut jamais jouer" ["You should never gamble act a part"]) he draws from the story of the Czech he ponders in prison no more than confesses the awareness he had, at the moment of writing the letter for Sintès, of its possible consequences for himself. The term "deserved" must certainly apply to himself as much as to the Czech ("De toute façon, je trouvais que le voyageur l'avait un peu mérité" ["In any case, I thought that the traveller had rather deserved what he got"]), but it implies, in context, the neutral mechanics of cause and effect, rather than the moral responsibility it inherently tends to suggest—something like "he asked for it". It is only, however, the existence of such a real, if unavowed, moral responsibility on Meursault's part for the harm done to the Arab woman, a moral sense identified by Camus as all-important while suppressed by the character in favour of his own immediate comfort and freedom, that explains Camus's plot against his hero, his bringing him to book in such implacable fashion.

In making death the price Meursault pays for the letter, Camus gives (as it were) the lie to Kréa, Nora, O'Brien and all those who, after them, reproach him with racism. Far from being helplessly and haplessly involved, in *L'Étranger,* in ethical self-contradiction, Camus displays on the contrary both absolute moral self-consistency and an aesthetic control that is evidence of total lucidity. In identifying Meursault's absurdist practice as flawed by excess, he makes of the character the more discreet sibling of the manifestly monstrous Caligula (a "moral monster", then, indeed); on the ethico-aesthetic level, his judgement of his hero provides the fundamental, founding ambiguity of a text famed for the plurality of readings it allows; while the relentless process whereby, from I,3 to II,4, cause leads to baleful effect and Meursault's real crime is visited upon him, reproduces *en abyme* the symmetrical composition of *L'Étranger* overall.

Far from being (as Camus himself misleadingly suggested) a moral "degré zéro", *L'Étranger,* while on its first level, certainly, proclaiming the inalienable, pagan innocence of Absurd Man, at the same time argues, in contradictory counterpoint to this, the need—the need we ignore only at our gravest peril—to observe the dictates of common, of our common, humanity. Camus's supposed "martyr de la vérité" ["martyr for the truth"] is "le seul christ que nous méritions" ["the only christ we deserve"] not, surely, because he is without sin (what then would account for that bitter "deserve"?), but precisely because (as Camus can never have known better than in 1955, with *La Chute* on his mind) he is as morally tarnished as the next one. (pp. 275-76)

> *Dorothy Bryson, "Plot and Counter-plot in L'Étranger," in* Forum for Modern Language Studies, *Vol. XXIV, No. 3, July, 1988, pp. 272-79.*

Patrick Reilly

Only eight years separate [*Nineteen Eighty-Four* and *The Fall*], but the propinquity goes far deeper than a matter of mere chronology, for both exhibit all the marks of a parallel disillusionment and dread in the face of the same disaster. There are, indeed, a number of persuasive parallels between Orwell and Camus. Both won fame as heroes of truth, sworn to an uncompromising honesty which scorned to found the Just City upon a lie, however pious

or well-intentioned; both were extolled as atheistic saints whose purity of thought was redemptive in a world dominated by one-eyed ideologues and party *apparatchiks*. Yet at the same time some found only confusion, even double-think, in these alleged truth-tellers and sceptically rejected the celebrated integrity as a mask for reactionary views; others, less censorious, nevertheless maintained that both men, in their refusal to make an unreserved commitment to the revolutionary cause, were, however inadvertently, supporting an unjust status quo. Both in their admirers and in their detractors, in the reasons advanced for praise and censure alike, the parallelism persists.

One obvious link is that each was primarily a moralist who unremittingly subjected the world of politics to a keen ethical scrutiny, unprepared to make exemption in favour of extremism or terrorism. Camus's fall from intellectual favour in the sixties recalls the opposition to Orwell a decade earlier and it is indisputable that a decisive factor in fuelling these antipathies was the emphatically unselective moral stance of both writers. When Orwell proclaimed a willingness to attack Stalin as the litmus test of moral courage for those on the left, when Camus in his Nobel Prize speech declared that he had always condemned the use of terror, each was affirming the primacy of ethics over ideology. (p. 114)

Camus's 'defection' was the more offensive because he had seemed so securely on the revolutionary side. His career and reputation were linked to a defiance of right-wing tyranny. Andrei Sinyavsky once said that he owed his vocation to the KGB. Camus might equally have thanked the Nazis, for, in imposing upon Europe a reign of terror, they gave *The Myth of Sisyphus* and *The Plague* a far greater vogue than they might otherwise have enjoyed. At the end of the war, Camus's revolutionary fervour seemed as fierce as ever. He vehemently opposed Mauriac's plea for leniency, a national amnesty, in the uncompromising accents of a modern Saint-Just: 'Who would dare speak here of pardon?' He sided with his future foe, Sartre, in demanding death for collaborators; what else should the guilty expect, now that the long-tormented virtuous ones had finally triumphed? By 1946, however, sickened by the 'virtuous' terror of post-liberation France, he had crossed over to Mauriac and was pleading that there should be *'ni Victimes ni Bourreaux',* neither victims nor executioners. In the less passionate atmosphere of post-war Britain Orwell attacked those on the left who wanted to take revenge upon their defeated enemies—even the Fascist Mosley should not be kicked when down.

The parallels multiply the more we read. The claims of honesty are pressed to the point of discomfort and even pain. When Clamence, speaking for his creator, permits us to have slaves if we must, but only on condition that we stop calling them free men, it echoes Orwell's denunciation of doublethink: no attacking the British Empire while sharing in its dividends or advocating pacifism behind the shield of the Royal Navy or espousing egalitarianism while sending one's children to public schools. Reform yourself before you reform the world—it is the demand most calculated to enrage the dedicated revolutionary. Yet another point of resemblance is their common detestation of Stalin and what his cult implied. Orwell identified power-worship as the salient iniquity of our times and linked it, astonishingly in view of his own undeviating atheism, to the fact of religious decline—the atheist intellectual, prostrating himself before Stalin, is indulging an upmarket form of the same emotions as the slum boy idolising Al Capone. Clamence utters the same provocative accusation when he remarks that every intelligent man dreams of being a gangster and makes the same scandalous tie-up between atheism and modern servitude: 'one must choose a master, God being out of fashion'. Behind these criticisms is the indignation of inflexible moralists sickened at the ease with which so many modern intellectuals put their gifts at the service of tyrants. Orwell and Camus would have no part in this *trahison des clercs* [breach of trust].

Most pertinent of all to the present argument is the intriguing affinity between their last books, extending to the sense of anger and betrayal that they provoked in so many of their readers. The outrage is certainly intelligible at what so many could only interpret as a sell-out, for, undeniably, these texts were gleefully seized upon and lauded for their insight by people whom the authors had spent their lives opposing. In *Nineteen Eighty-Four* the crystal spirit is as irreprievably shattered as Winston's paperweight, the last man in Europe is crushed and the only prospect for humanity is a boot in the face for ever. It is a strangely dispiriting message to come from a man whose whole life had been a crusade for the underdog, for the book condemns man to be an underdog for all time. But the shock of betrayal was even greater for the readers of *The Fall.* Orwell had always been something of a desponder; a melancholy, even a lugubriousness, is detectible from *Burmese Days* on, and he was, after all, a dying man when he wrote his pessimistic masterpiece—those scandalised could always placate themselves by attributing the despair to a terminal illness; the book reflected the sad condition of its author's lungs rather than the world either as it is or might conceivably be.

No such refuge offered itself with Camus. That *The Fall* is a surprising book is proved by the fact that everyone was suprised by it, and with full justification. The very title was an affront, offensive from anyone, outrageous from the man who, even in a century of death, had achieved fame as the singer of happiness. Meursault is happy even in the death-cell; the closing sentence of *The Myth of Sisyphus* commands us how to feel as we watch the absurd hero grapple yet again with his unmasterable, unleavable rock: 'one must imagine Sisyphus happy'. Camus once told an interviewer that 'when I come to look for what is fundamental in myself, I find a taste for happiness', and in his early book of essays, *Noces,* he declared that 'happiness itself is a duty'. The fact is that up to the writing of *The Fall,* happiness is, for Camus, inseparable from innocence and innocence is the datum from which his analysis of the human condition begins. He had always regarded innocence as the supreme good, had established his reputation as the apologist of man—like prelapsarian Clamence, Camus, too, is a defence lawyer. Man, he insists, is not guilty, whatever reactionaries say. Even in the earlier works, the phase of the stranger, dealing with the conflict between the *isolato* and his absurd surroundings, there is no condemnation of the criminal. Despite killing the Arab, Meursault is presented as an innocent man whose conviction indicts his society, not himself. Whether the stranger was viewed in contemporary, historical or mythological garb, as Meursault, Caligula or Sisyphus,

whether he shot an Arab, terrorised a state or offended Zeus, Camus insisted on seeing him as victim, insulted by the absurdity of existence and determined to deny the agreed mendacities within which his fellows sheltered from the inane sky.

The next phase, the phase of heroic brotherhood, enhanced even more Camus's claim to be humanity's champion. In *The Plague* he moves from solipsism to solidarity as men band together to defy evil in all its manifestations: disease and occupation, guilt and superstition, rats and judges, Nazis and Jesuits. How account for the somersault from this celebration of heroism to a book like *The Fall?* 'What we learn in a time of pestilence: that there are more things to admire in men than to despise'—so asserts Dr Rieux in *The Plague.* Clamence tells us the opposite: there is nothing but malice and nastiness in the human soul and the only basis for a perverse solidarity is the fellowship of the fallen and the community of the corrupt. Having discovered his own debasement, Clamence now slakes his Everest complex, his need to look down on other men, by gloatingly convicting others of the guilt that festers in his own soul. For the truth is that everyone is guilty, and guilty beyond all hope of recovery. This is the message of the new Baptist crying in the Dutch wilderness, but promising, instead of salvation, attaint and humiliation. Most monstrous of all, Camus seems to collude with the misanthrope in his hellish project to ensnare other men; the text will not permit us simply to dismiss him as a madman—Clamence is horribly right because things are horribly wrong, and if it is easy to dislike him, it is painfully difficult to deny the truth of what he says, a loathsome truth but no easier to evade on that account. 'We felt, alas, that by telling his story, Michel had made his action more legitimate. Our not having known at what point to condemn it in the course of his long explanation seemed almost to make us his accomplices. We felt, as it were, involved.' The reluctant complicity experienced by the friends of Gide's Immoralist is intensified to agony point by a reading of *The Fall.* Michel defies us to condemn him, but Clamence condemns himself as a means of incriminating us; the Immoralist's story simply secures an acquittal where Clamence's touches a nerve.

Of course, as with Gulliver and Winston Smith, discrimination is essential, for we must not carry identification too far, joining Gulliver in the stable or Winston in gin-soaked despair or Clamence in venomous spite; but neither are we to detach ourselves too cheaply from their compromising company, thanking complacently whatever God we believe in that we are not like other men. The problem common to all of these texts is precisely this: at what baffling point in the narration can we break the relationship without incurring the charge of Pharisaism? If the problem is difficult to the point of being insoluble, this is surely because the writers have cunningly contrived it so: we are trapped and it will take all our intelligence and integrity to break free. Simply asserting one's superiority is too glib, denying the relevance of these lives to our own is mere evasion—that is the way, not to freedom, but to deeper entanglement.

The 'hero' of *The Fall* is an especially awkward adversary, for he is the supreme exponent of a dishonest honesty in his consummate strategy of the *juge-pénitent*—self-accusation as a device for incriminating others, ultimate trick in the repertoire of the malign polemicist. 'I meant no harm by it, believe me', he apologises, but the phoney politeness only makes him an even more dangerous predator. It is much more difficult to resist someone who invites you to confess your sins, having just handsomely confessed his own, than to send packing a self-righteous bully like Alceste who claims a purity that everyone else lacks. Clamence is a much trickier opponent, for he leaves you with two equally unattractive options: to confess your guilt, accepting, with Winston Smith, that you *are* a bag of filth, or to join the Duchess of Buckingham in affronted proclamation of your Pharisaical blamelessness.

Beneath the surface candour is the malicious entrapment of Baudelaire (*o hypocrite lecteur, mon semblable, mon frère!*), the treacherous courtesy of Gulliver's appeal to the 'gentle reader'. 'The portrait I hold out to my contemporaries becomes a mirror'; as David with Nathan, we have been lulled into believing that the shameful deeds are another's when they are really our own; thou art the man. It is our own tale we have unwittingly listened to and Clamence has been patiently preparing throughout for that climactic moment when he can launch his devastating demand: 'Then tell me, please, what happened to you one night on the quays of the Seine and how you managed never to risk your life.'

We can, if we wish, dismiss Clamence, as some have dismissed Gulliver and Winston Smith, as a mistaken or perverted man whose aberrations are his own regrettable concern. Sympathy for a poor, afflicted soul aside, why should it trouble us if he has got himself hopelessly entangled in pointless, neurotic guilt? Why should it touch us if Gulliver has lost his wits among the horses or if Winston has behaved shamefully in Room 101 or if Clamence has had bad luck on bridges? And yet there is that accusatory epigraph adopted from Lermontov for the sole purpose of making us confess kinship: 'Some were dreadfully insulted, and quite seriously, to have held up as a model such an immoral character as *A Hero of Our Time* . . . *A Hero of Our Time,* gentlemen, is in fact a portrait but not of an individual; it is the aggregate of the vices of our whole generation in their fullest expression.' Could anything be plainer? We may continue to feel insulted but not to assume that we do so with Camus's approval. Like it or not, it is unarguable that Camus accosts us in the same mood as Hamlet does his mother:

> Come, come, and sit you down; you shall not budge.
> You go not till I set you up a glass
> Where you may see the inmost part of you.

To take refuge in indignation or to pronounce the speaker mad because we resent the message is scarcely what Camus or Shakespeare desires.

Yet, however undeniable, this leaves us with the problem still to solve. Why should Camus of all men have written a book about guilt and condemnation, providing us with one of the most searing presentations of the dark epiphany in our times? 'At the heart of my work there is an invincible sun', he had once declared, but his sun is now totally shrouded in the murky mists of a Dutch city. So startling is the paradox that some readers are tempted to treat the whole work as pure satire, a joke at its misanthropic narrator's expense with Camus inviting us to join him in deriding the purveyors of gloom and guilt. It *must* be a joke,

since the views it expresses cannot be reconciled with its author's previous opinions—Clamence's pessimistic appraisal of man is precisely what Camus does *not* want his readers to adopt. But apart from the fact that this marks the surrender of criticism to biography, it undermines the seriousness of the book's intent. We are challenged to show where Clamence is wrong, not to assume he is—it is discrimination that is demanded, not this easy evasion of judgment. Camus's best novel must be engaged in an altogether different way. 'The idea that comes most naturally to man, as if from his very nature, is the idea of his innocence.' Niebuhr is puzzled as to how men can continue to cherish this idea while acting as they do, but, whatever we believe, in the century of Hiroshima, Auschwitz and the Gulag, it is no laughing matter and we can be sure that **The Fall** was not written to make us laugh. Its target is not guilt but bogus innocence; it denounces the self-righteous, the Pharisees, those who insist that innocence exists and that they have the monopoly. It is the delusion of innocence that must be destroyed; no one is to go on cossetting the myth of his own blamelessness, for the sinner is man, not capitalist man nor colonialist man nor western man nor any other conceivable subset, and the Pharisee lives in every band of the political spectrum. No wonder **The Fall** infuriated so many of those who read it.

To say that the book derides nineteenth-century doctrines of innocence based upon Rousseau will not explain the outrage it provoked. Certainly, Rousseau is implicitly rejected. As in Hugo's *Les Miserables* everything hinges on one dramatic moment: Clamence is as irrevocably lost in that fatal lapse on the bridge as Valjean is redeemed in that instant when the saintly bishop treats him like a brother. In **The Fall** the descendant of Hugo's saint receives a very different return for his charity; the disembowelled pacifist at once casts an ironic light upon the bishop's facile success in redeeming the brutalised convict and exposes the nineteenth-century dream of salvation for the sentimental nonsense it is. But exposing Rousseauistic sentimentalism hardly accounts for the scandal of Camus's last book.

Complexity comes from the difficulty of identifying the target, for the target is chameleon, altering disconcertingly as we aim. There is general agreement that it is an acute analysis of Pharisaism, but dispute as to who the Pharisee is. Clamence has been identified as Camus himself, the novel interpreted as a personal *mea culpa,* an exercise in self-chastisement. Despite his assertion in another context that 'a character is never the writer who created him', there is ample internal evidence that Clamence is to a considerable degree modelled upon his creator. The epigraph from Lermontov indicates as much: 'others shrewdly noticed that the author had portrayed himself'. Camus was presumably reacting against his own cult in embarrassed rejection of the excessive adulation paid to him as the godless saint, the one just man. No one could have lived up to such overblown tribute, but to his enemies Camus appeared to be both pretentious and self-righteous, and Sartre rapidly became the leader of those who told him so. Clamence is above all a debunker and derider (*diabolos*), a modern Thersites railing against all virtue as a racket, and it is hard not to detect in all this an element of self-ridicule. Camus joins his detractors in baring his feet of clay. If Clamence is not wholly Camus, neither is he just a separate creation; he is a fusion of autobiography and art, evidence of Camus's unease at his beatification by over-enthusiastic admirers.

Hence the book's confessional form, its pervasive Christian imagery, its obsession with guilt and insistence that the admission of one's own sins is the first step in any progress towards truth—Camus acts as devil's advocate towards the cause of his own virtue. But, as deviously as his own 'hero', Camus turns his confession into an attack upon his attackers; the novel moves in contradictory directions at the same time, is simultaneously self-criticism and self-defence. In *A Modest Proposal* Swift denounces the satirist, i.e. himself, in order the more effectively to denounce his enemies: landlords, English government, Irish people. Camus, similarly, admits his faults but only so that he can retaliate the more devastatingly upon his critics— 'but just think of your life, *mon cher compatriote!*' The latter is undoubtedly Sartre—Sartre, who recognised only the sins of other men, especially Americans, while denying his own failings and those of his Russian allies. Sartre was not loath to proclaim his own innocence; Camus invites us to consider who the real Pharisee is. Pilloried for posing as the righteous man, told to climb down from his moral pedestal, Camus does so in the guise of Clamence, but immediately converts the portrait into a mirror to incriminate his critics.

But if the book were no more than a personal vendetta, it would not be the masterpiece it is. Clamence transcends Sartre to become representative of the elitist intellectual in the tradition of Dostoevsky's Grand Inquisitor, justifying slavery in the name of realism. The new theme announced in Camus's work by *The Rebel* and *The Fall* is the increasing violation of the rights of the individual by society and a fear that political realism could so easily be used to justify tyranny. Camus refused Sartre's assurance that the only threat came from the right: 'Over the dead body of innocence the judges swarm . . . those of Christ and those of the Anti-Christ, who are the same anyway, reconciled in the little-ease.' (pp. 115-22)

The chorus of disapproval that greeted *The Fall* will not surprise us, once we recognise that, not Rousseau's, but another doctrine of innocence provoked Camus's attack: the twentieth-century innocence of the revolutionary ideology, dividing the world into elect and reprobate, and indemnifying the former for every act whereby they sought to cleanse the world of their enemies. Camus finally wrote against innocence because he feared what the belief in innocence was being used to legitimise in our own time. The terrible paradox is that innocence had become an instrument of murder. If it is God who is under attack in *The Plague,* it is man in *The Fall.* No wonder Sartre felt threatened, for it was his doctrine of innocence that was being arraigned. The sense of injury experienced by Bolingbroke confronting *Gulliver's Travels* has its parallel in the resentment of the revolutionary ideologues as they looked into Camus's mirror to find the face of guilt staring back. (pp. 122-23)

'After prolonged research on myself, I brought out the basic duplicity of the human being': it is, as Clamence says, his key discovery. Sartre deplored such morbid introspection as a blind alley, a styptic to revolutionary action, and offered instead an infallible creed as the cure for this stultifying psychology. From Saint-Just to Lenin the revolutionary encouraged a flight from the dubieties of self into

the certainties of inquisition and the search for a salvation beyond individuality. In *The Rebel* Camus summarises the apocalyptic-terrorist process as killing God to build a church. Kolakowski argues that politics in our time is a pursuit of the old religious questions in new guise, and Camus is so urgent an interpreter of contemporary history because of his intuition that twentieth-century politics has increasingly become the pursuit of religion by other means. Thus the individual who devotes himself to overthrowing a wicked society, a kingdom of darkness, is absolved from all guilt in the means he employs to achieve that blessed consummation. History is a grateful deity to her servants; those willing, better still, eager, to dirty their hands in this service are not merely exonerated but beatified as the saints of the revolutionary hagiography. For all their differences, the ideologues from 1792 to 1917 dreamed the same dream of a new dispensation that would license the faithful to commit virtuous murder; history, as beneficiary of the violence, could be trusted to pardon the perpetrators. That Camus took a very different view is plain if we contrast his play *Les Justes* with Sartre's play *Les Mains sales.* Kaliayev and Dora believe that there are limits imposed by basic humanity upon revolutionary action; it is the chill Stepan who says that there are no limits, since the revolution justifies everything. Hoederer, Sartre's hero, likewise insists that everything is permitted and is prepared to do anything that will advance the cause, for the end justifies the means. *Les Justes* is Camus's answer to Sartre, and in *The Rebel* and *The Fall* he attacked the whole moral infrastructure upon which the doctrine of revolutionary innocence was based.

But the quarrel with Sartre and the recoil from a murderous innocence carried Camus beyond the confines of an historical period, however crucial, to a reflection upon the essential meaning of the human being; *The Fall* is as timeless as *Gulliver's Travels,* for each transcends the purely historical conditions that produced them. The more we learn about Whigs, Tories and freethinkers, about Cold War and Parisian literary politics, the better for us, but this kind of knowledge, valuable though it be, is finally irrelevant to the enduring significance of these texts. It is a matter of permanent truth rather than of transient political excitement. (pp. 123-24)

It is . . . in *The Fall* that we find the perfect dramatisation of Freud's thesis. The misanthrope's story demonstrates how an excessively high valuation of human nature must end in disillusion, how pride goes before a fall. The major divergence is that there is not, as in Freud, calm acceptance of the depressing truth. Men are not as good as they think they are: Freud's insight is a simple scientific statement with no hint of reproach, no summons to penance or self-contempt; the sensible scientist has no quarrel with truth. Clamence, however, is, like his creator Camus, a moralist and when he discovers that he is not as good as he thought, the shock is traumatic. How can he live with this shameful self? Freud's war criminals have the blessed ability to forget and return; Clamence, psychologically speaking, can never go home again.

'Ah, this dear old planet! All is clear now. We know ourselves; we now know of what we are capable.' This emphasis upon a specific historical moment is revealing, indicating as it does the mental landscape of Europe after the end of the Second World War and the full revelation of its abominations. But, as with Freud, a particular historical catastrophe becomes a lense for seeing the abiding truths of human nature, for understanding man as he was, is and always will be. The bitterness is inseparable from a sense of betrayal: man is a fraud, virtue an illusion, exorbitant expectations jar with reality and turn into despair. The Grand Inquisitor rebukes Christ for thinking too highly of men and Freud levels the same charge against his contemporaries in 1915. Clamence likewise discovers that his cherished goodness is a bogus thing, easily produced when the cost is small and the gratification great, but evaporating when the test is real and the price painful. Anyone can be a hero when there is no danger, as Sartre's Garcin in *Huis Clos* so tormentedly realises.

'I am malicious because I am miserable.' Frankenstein's Creature can teach us why Clamence turns so vindictively upon virtue, innocence and happiness—it is because the shock of his own corruption reveals that there are illicit ways of being happy, bogus ways of being good and spurious ways of being innocent. We scan in vain the pages of Camus's earlier novels for such perceptions. The book opens with Clamence as polite predator, poised in the seedy Amsterdam bar to pounce upon the first unwary prey that comes along. It is, we soon learn, a familiar routine and even from the start, courtesy notwithstanding, flashes of malevolence appear. But the story he tells is chronological and it begins when he was a happy, self-satisfied man, working in Paris as an admired and much sought-after defence lawyer whose life is one long, delightful indulgence in virtuous deeds and altruistic enterprises. He enjoys being good: he defends the poor without payment, consoles widows, befriends orphans, goes about eagle-eyed to help beggars and blind men. The account that he gives of his life before the catastrophe entitles us to link him with pre-Houyhnhnmland Gulliver, two happy, genial men complacently at ease in their social roles. True, Gulliver is a respectable family man, a husband and father, while Clamence has a string of complaisant mistresses, but, given the change in sexual mores, this, far from being cause for reprehension, merely enhances his sense of accomplishment and provokes envy in his admiring contemporaries—the brilliant lawyer and zealous philanthropist are complemented by the polished lover; we could not have a better instance of man as all-rounder. Gulliver and Clamence are men perfectly adapted to their environments, untroubled men with no shadow of a cloud on their social horizons. Gulliver lives contentedly in England but Clamence, ostensibly in Paris, is really resident in Eden: 'I took pleasure in my own life and in my own excellence.' Adam before the fall undoubtedly felt the same.

With a bit of luck Gulliver and Clamence might have gone to their graves blissfully undisturbed, loving their fellowmen so easily because they love themselves so much. But Gulliver goes on his fourth voyage and Clamence walks home over the bridge and catastrophe occurs. Can we seriously regret this or lament that they did not stay the obtuse, complacent men they were? Would it have been better for Gulliver to continue jingoistically blind to the faults and follies of his dear native land or for Clamence to have gone on hugging the myth of his own goodness? Isn't their very honesty, their initial wholeness of self, a limitation which they do well to abandon, and if each becomes *une âme déchirée* ['a tormented soul'] (as Rousseau described

himself) isn't this very disintegration the paradoxical proof of their ascent to a higher level of self-awareness? Surely we must agree that it is good that they stopped being the men they were, even if we still have grave doubts about the men they become. Such doubts will result not from the discoveries they make but from what they make of the discoveries. After the incident on the bridge, Clamence can no longer maintain, at least in their old form, the twin beliefs that have made him happy: that he is good and that he is superior. Yet neither can he complain that no warning of the test to come was given, that he was taken unawares by the challenge for which he was so unfairly ill-prepared. Already, some years before the cry from the river, he had been shaken by a mysterious, untraceable laugh on another Seine bridge, and deep within he senses uneasily that the laugh is on him.

But why should anyone presume to laugh at so triumphant a man, half Cerdan, half de Gaulle? The encounter with the motorcyclist, from which he emerges feeling so foolish and humiliated, might have supplied the clue had not self-love worked to prevent the lesson being learned. But after the second bridge incident (no wonder he shuns bridges in Amsterdam) the truth is inescapable and he is forced to review his whole life in the light of this epiphany: 'my dream had not stood up to facts'. He is a fake, a mere play-actor; all of his 'good' deeds were performances, for the sake of the public's applause and his own self-esteem. He recalls how he used to tip his hat to the blind men he escorted across busy streets—who else was that intended for but the admiring audience? Beneath this sham is the true self, vicious and nasty. Every memory, once treasured as proof of his worth, now torments him as proof of his worthlessness; the significance of the perplexing laugh now dawns on him—it is the universe deriding the gross counterfeit. Like Gulliver schooled by the Houyhnhnms to despise what he had once prized, so Clamence retrospectively appraises his life and finds that what used to be lustrous is now leprous. La Rochefoucauld is right: there may be 'virtuous' actions but never 'virtuous' motives. The very word 'justice' infuriates Clamence; he dreams of tripping up blind men, wrecking invalid cars, slapping children, he orders the restaurant manager to drive away the beggar who is making him feel uncomfortable as he eats his meal. It is a transformation as total as Gulliver's. The latter learns that he is a Yahoo, Clamence that he is a Pharisee. What does a Pharisee do when he see through the fraud of his own virtue? He lies in wait for his brethren to trap them into confessing their own sins.

To ask why Clamence doesn't repent and try to become a better man is to miss the point of this pessimistic book. Why doesn't Rastignac, having gazed into the corruption of Paris, retire to a cave in the country? Because he hasn't changed, he still wants Paris and what it stands for, he means to conquer the city, not forsake it. The self as a bondage, as Pascal says—*le moi est haïssable* ['the ego is detestable']—and in Clamence we see egoism so ineradicable that it survives unabashed the worst disgrace and the deepest infamy. 'I, I, I is the refrain of my whole life': the very form of the narrative, the monopolistic monologue that denies the auditor's right to respond, supports stylistically this psychological fact. As much as Winston Smith, Clamence is impotent before the claims of self-transcendence. Bernanos, counselling against self-hatred, tells us that grace means forgetting oneself, but it's easier said than done. Even in the safety of the Chestnut Tree Café, the smell of rats, recalling the moment of his shameful survival, mingles with the smell of Winston's gin. Clamence claims that there is nothing extraordinary in his story: every man is a shabby Narcissus. Both men are stuck with their sordid selves forever, though Clamence still characteristically strives, in the greatest of literary *tu quoques,* to make even this discovery a source of superiority, while Winston, by contrast, is as drained as O'Brien promised to make him.

Only externally for Clamence do things change; essentially he remains the same. True, the erstwhile 'good' man has now become actively malicious, almost as if Winston had joined the Thought Police, but this is simply a new strategy to achieve the same old end. The need to dominate is strong as ever; when he discovers his own ignominy, this drive simply takes a more devious, underground route for its gratification. Herostratus sought fame through infamy: better to be known for burning the temple of Diana than accept nonentity—to be the centre of attention is all, the reason for it is secondary. There is a hint of Herostratus in Clamence: if he can no longer be the Thespian of virtue, he will be the impresario of vice. Given that 'society is entirely made up of assumed personalities', that all the world's a stage, the only thing that matters is to grab a leading role. Even in such intimate transactions as death and love, grief and orgasm, man puts on a show. Everything stems from vanity and affectation. La Rochefoucauld observes that 'perfect valour consists in doing without witnesses what one would be capable of doing before the world at large', though nowhere in the *Maxims* does he suggest that such valour really exists. *The Fall* is even more pessimistic in insisting that the imposture needs no other audience than the self; his own applause persuades Clamence that he is a good man; he is his own deluded, deluding spectator. Unfortunately, this is not enough to guarantee the performance. On a bridge crammed with spectators, he *might* have dived into the water; with nobody to impress, he thinks of the risk and hurries away from the scene because it isn't one. The failure is decisive; henceforth impersonation is impossible.

The Fall marks a partial return to the moral outlook of the religion which Camus had long since repudiated. At its Augustinian extreme, Christianity pronounced virtue impossible; man was a sink of iniquity whose only hope was to be granted a grace he could never merit. In its more moderate form, it still regarded virtue as extremely difficult, for within man Satan's fifth columnist was firmly entrenched—every victory for good was sorely won in an unceasing psychomachia which split the self into two warring factions. On such a view there is something distinctly worrying about the easy way the prelapsarian Clamence zestfully notches up his triumphs for goodness. The sharp contrast between himself and his 'very Christian friend' towards the beggar is instructive. The friend has to subjugate the old Adam in forcing himself to be charitable towards the beggar; Clamence exults when he sees a beggar approaching and he scans the ground for blind men as avidly as a trickster for fools. This passion for liberality is akin to a miser's for gold or a lecher's for women, and La Rochefoucauld teaches us how to assess such benevolence: 'What is called generosity is the more often just the vanity of giving, which we like more than what we give.' Such virtue is really self-indulgence, for the hurt which is the

proof of true goodness is ominously absent. The way to heaven is hard; it is the primrose path that leads to the everlasting bonfire.

In the eighteenth century Shaftesbury, anxious to refute the black legend of Augustinian-Hobbesian man, proposed instead as his ideal good man one who finds pleasure in the happiness of others and who strives to promote and extend that happiness. Fielding's Mr Allworthy is the clearest fictional representation of this ideal, but Gide's criticism of Fielding shows how the Shaftesburian model conflicts with other views of the moral life. Gide faults Fielding for his inability to conceive a saint, i.e. someone who has to battle with himself to be good, overcoming the enemy within who is far more difficult to circumvent than all the external hindrances added together. Allworthy has no enemy within; at worst, he makes mistakes, errors of judgment, going wrong as a man does when he fails to solve a quadratic equation—he *wants* the right answer but fails to see it. But this is not the manner in which Macbeth goes astray. *Video meliora proboque, deteriora sequor:* here is the key to Macbeth's anguish—the corrupt will and not the defective intelligence. Macbeth is a divided man, Allworthy (as his name implies) is a unity.

So too is the unfallen Clamence: 'I enjoyed my own nature to the fullest and we all know that therein lies happiness . . . few creatures were more natural than I. I was altogether in harmony with life.' To live in harmony with oneself and nature is to be resident in Eden; to have no sense of self-division is the privilege of prelapsarian man, to live without consciousness of defect is to inhabit a mental landscape far removed from that of Ovid or St Paul: the good that I would do I do not, and the evil that I would not do I do. The fall occurs when a sense of unity gives way to a realisation that the self is double, that Janus is the presiding deity of man's nature. At the moment of crisis Clamence discovers that he is not one but two: 'I told myself that I had to be quick and I felt an irresistible weakness steal over me.' It is the first intimation of this 'essential discovery', the revelation of 'the basic duplicity of the human being' which finally dawns on him 'after prolonged research on myself'. Henceforth, oxymoron is, for Clamence, the figure under which man reveals himself: Christian landowner, adulterous humanist, *juge-pénitent.* Contemplating the various trade-signs of the old merchants in the streets of Amsterdam, Clamence proposes the sign for the house of man himself—a charming Janus, a double face—and supplies the appropriate motto: 'Don't rely on it.' The disciple of Shaftesbury has deserted to Augustine.

With this realisation of division and duplicity comes the loss of harmony and the exit from Eden. 'Indeed, wasn't that Eden . . . no intermediary between life and me?' Unfallen man needs no intermediary, for not until accusation does one need to brief defence counsel. The peculiar torment of the story Clamence tells is that he starts out needing no redeemer and ends up unable to find one: 'there is no lamb and no innocence any longer'. Salvation is a fiction but the need is more clamant than ever. Clamence has fallen out of Eden into duplicity; the joy of stretching freely, the delicious liberty of the unconfined limbs, is lost and Clamence is condemned forever to living in the little-ease. His one recourse is to ensure that nobody else continues to enjoy his old innocence of movement: 'I have accepted duplicity instead of being upset by it. On the contrary, I have settled into it and found there the comfort I was looking for throughout life.' Since we are in hell, let's make the best of it.

Man is trapped inescapably in the little-ease, the finely appropriate home for one who begins his story, in hubristic abandon, by declaring that he 'felt like a king's son, or a burning bush'. Clamence's dream is an even more blasphemous aspiration than Gatsby's and it is fitting that he should be undone in a manner that would have been approved by ancient and Christian moralist alike. He has just enjoyed an excellent day: a blind man helped, a reduced sentence secured, a grateful client's homage, a brilliant improvisation among friends on the sins of other men, a hard-hearted governing class, hypocritical leaders. Walking alone afterwards on the bridge, he feels in harmony with himself and the world: 'I dominated the island. I felt rising within me a vast feeling of power and—I don't know how to express it—of completion, which cheered my heart.' The ancient Greeks would have identified this as hubris; it is thus that Oedipus strides onto the stage, resolved to detect the sinner, who is, of course, some other man, for how could it be himself? With such an attitude nemesis is a certainty; so conceited a man cannot avoid being exposed as polluted. Nor can the alert Christian fail to recall Christ's fulminations against the Pharisees, those smug servants of God, all show without, whited sepulchres within. It is this moment of arrogance that is punctured by the unaccountable laugh which is the beginning of a radical unsettlement.

Yet *The Fall* cannot be called Christian, since the essential element of salvation is absent. It is yet another point of resemblance to *Nineteen Eighty-Four,* for both texts deal with the ubiquity of guilt and the unavailability of pardon. Winston and Clamence can neither shrive themselves nor find absolution. Guilt becomes exasperated before the vacancy of heaven, man is left facing the unavailing stare of his fellows. The psychoanalyst's craft is futile, for to become innocent it is not enough to accuse oneself; advertising one's infamies does not in itself bring relief and may well intensify the sense of self-contempt. Winston and Julia admit betrayal but in the dull despair that they would do it all over again. Clamence is left 'strangely aching' by his failure to dive but does not know where to find the healing balm. La Rochefoucauld puts the problem in a form pleasing to the humanist exasperated by fairy-tales of divine deliverance: 'When you cannot find your peace in yourself it is useless to look for it elsewhere.' How mistaken, as Feuerbach explains, to look to the sky for the help that is really within. Hence the scandal of *The Fall,* exhibiting the problem of the anguished atheist, finding absolution nowhere and solace only in multiplying, like a malevolent leper, the number of fellow-sufferers.

In spiteful mockery Clamence tells of the man who slept on the floor in sympathy with his imprisoned friend, but knows no one who could emulate such self-sacrifice: 'Who, *cher* Monsieur, will sleep on the floor for us? Look, I'd like to be and I shall be. Yes, we shall all be capable of it one day and that will be salvation.' It echoes Swift and Orwell—the Swift who despised *rationis capax* as yet another shift of devious man, a promise to be good in the future made all the more worthless by the resolve to go on being shamelessly Yahoo in the present. We detect in Clamence's words the same cracked and jeering note, the yellow note that the broken Winston hears in the mocking music at the café: heroic self-sacrifice is an illusion; we look after ourselves, whatever the cost. Clamence's vow of future heroism is as idle as the promises of O'Neill's derelicts in *The Iceman Cometh,* and he knows it—hence the aggressive derision of his tone.

Guilt is forever: there is no do-it-yourself absolution kit, no amnesiac return to the old life with the shameful deeds forgotten. On his recuperative sea-trip Clamence is shocked to see a body far out on the waves. It turns out to be a piece of flotsam, but he now knows that his sin will haunt him forever. He is at the same time too honest to take comfort in the lie that a second chance is all he needs; if by some miracle the bridge should come again, the result would be exactly the same. The coward who redeems himself is a Hollywood cliché; the penitent thief, whether in the gospel or Victor Hugo, is a sop to sentimentalism. Clamence knows that the future is simply a repetition of the past and he knows how he has acted in the past: 'I drank the water of a dying comrade'—and did so, moreover, fortified by the good old utilitarian argument that only by saving himself could he be of any service to those depending on him. Clearly, some people are more important than others and so have a greater right to survive; join this conviction of superiority to a raging thirst and it easily becomes nonsensical to waste the precious water upon an inferior man who is, in any case, dying. It was in a very different spirit that Sir Philip Sidney gave *his* water to the wounded soldier or that Captain Oates walked into the storm. But these instances of self-transcendence belong to an order concept of man which in the age of the dark epiphany seems either inconceivable or so unrepresentative as to be no norm for everyday life or ordinary men.

Winston Smith is still seared with sterile guilt over the chocolate snatched from his dying baby sister many years before—dying comrades and sisters have no chance against thirst and hunger, and in Winston's case the boy is father to the man; the childhood act of self-preservation is a rehearsal for the betrayal in Room 101. The book implies that it is our shame, too, that we will all cave in when put to the test, interposing our own Julias between us and the horror. Clamence similarly ends his story by making it ours, inviting us vindictively to tell him, in turn, how *we* managed never to risk our lives. In each case the trap for the reader is cunningly sprung: we refuse Winston and Clamence absolution, but who are we to refuse it? Like Claudius, we, too, are 'guilty creatures, sitting at a play', and entrapment is as much the aim of Camus and Orwell as it is of Hamlet.

What distinguishes the works of the dark epiphany from Freud is the very different reactions which their discoveries evoke. Freud seems altogether too casually permissive in describing the easy return from atrocity to civilisation. To reply that this is, in fact, what really happens is not much help, for this tranquil resumption of the old, interrupted life is more outrageous than the outrages themselves: after such knowledge, what forgiveness? Gulliver, Marlow, Aschenbach, Smith and Clamence are much more serious in their awareness that everything is altered, that their journeys to the interior have taken them forever from the old lives, and here, at least, they surely have their creators' support: why write books which leave us where we started out?

Clamence begins his story with the quiet assertion that 'we are at the heart of things here'. 'Here' is Amsterdam, a Dutch hell, dismal and rainswept, where the doves alight on no heads, for the Paraclete is forever absent, and where the predator lurks—'that's where I wait for them'—to lead his victim ever deeper into the damned circles until escape is impossible: 'Now I shall wait for you to write to me or to come back. For you will come back, I am sure!' This journey is in the opposite direction from that described by Dante; no one emerges from this inferno to look once more upon the stars. Nevertheless, the text forbids us to repudiate even this place in favour of the bland mendacities of Paris. Paris, with its false innocence and deluded happiness, is behind us forever; too many truths, however hideous, stand between us and renewed residence in the city of lies.

It is an appropriately Swiftian conclusion to a Swiftian book. 'Admit, however, that today you feel less pleased with yourself than you felt five days ago?' Or, as in the *Travels,* four voyages ago. To vex the world was precisely Swift's vocation; his satire, like **The Fall,** is a critique of happiness and virtue, an attempt to revoke unearned content and to instil guilt where a conviction of innocence had been. When, near the end, Clamence brutally tots things up and tells us that we are all incorrigible evil-doers, 'just like that. Just as flatly', we recall Gulliver's similar list of depravities and similarly insulting conclusion: 'this is all according to the due course of things'. Both men will permit no appeal against the undeniable evidence of our daily lives: 'That's the way man is, *cher* Monsieur.' When Clamence extols the perverted genius that invented the little-ease and the spitting-cell, he echoes Gulliver praising the invention of gunpowder or deliberately omitting all mention of the refined debaucheries unknown to the Yahoos of Houyhnhnmland but cultivated by their European brethren.

We approach the final paradox of these two writers. The little-ease is undoubtedly a diabolic invention, yet Swift and Camus alike scheme to catch their readers in its literary equivalent, for their texts are traps which we serenely enter only to find our comfort cancelled and our exit barred. **The Fall** leads us to the little-ease and leaves us there. Clamence declares it to be our abiding home and recommends us to reconcile ourselves to it. The text implicitly challenges us to prove him wrong, but this means breaking the prison, not pretending that it isn't there. Hugo's escape route is too facile, Sartre's too frightful. The greatness of **The Fall** is that it shows just how immensely difficult escape will be. (pp. 128-37)

> *Patrick Reilly, " 'The Fall': Living in the Little-Ease," in his* The Literature of Guilt: From 'Gulliver' to Golding, *Macmillan Press Ltd., 1988, pp. 114-137.*

FURTHER READING

Anderson, Kirsteen H. R. "Justification and Happiness in Camus's *La Mort Heureuse.*" *Forum for Modern Language Studies* XX, No. 3 (July 1984): 228-46.

Notes how Camus's conception of justice and individual happiness was influenced by the thought of Plotinus and Augustine, especially as evidenced in his first novel.

Bloom, Harold, ed. *Albert Camus.* New York: Chelsea House Publishers, 1989, 195 p.

Collection of critical essays on many aspects of Camus's work. Includes pieces by Paul de Man, Patrick McCarthy, and Donald Lazere.

Cohn, Robert Greer. "The True Camus." *The French Review* 60, No. 1 (October 1986): 30-8.

Favorable overview of the author's life and career in which Cohn concludes that Camus was "beyond all intellectual fashions and ideological factions, the finest, most authentic voice of his age."

Ellison, David R. "Camus and the Rhetoric of Dizziness: *La Chute.*" *Contemporary Literature* XXIV, No. 3 (Fall 1983): 322-48.

Contends that the uncharacteristically complex narrative style of *La chute* renders indeterminate the moral of the novel.

Fitch, Brian T. *The Narcissistic Text: A Reading of Camus's Fiction.* Toronto: University of Toronto Press, 1982, 125 p.

Focuses upon the self-consciousness of Camus's writing and uses this quality to identify the author as a precursor of the French new novelists.

Gifford, P. "Socarates in Amsterdam: The Uses of Irony in 'La Chute'." *Modern Language Review* 73, No. 3 (July 1978): 499-512.

Examines the multidimensional functions of irony in *La chute.*

Goldstein, Richard. "Visitation Rites: The Elusive Tradition of Plague Lit." *VLS,* No. 59 (October 1987): 6-9.

Survey of plague literature that notes similarities between Camus's *The Plague* and Daniel Defoe's *A Journal of the Plague Year.* Goldstein observes that in both novels pestilence ironically unites the societies it afflicts.

Greene, Robert W. "Fluency, Muteness and Commitment in Camus's *La Peste.*" *French Studies* XXXIV, No. 4 (October 1980): 423-33.

Praises *La peste* as Camus's "most convincing effort in socio-cultural criticism" and "a brilliant amalgam of theory of literature and imaginative literature long before such combinations were as widely attempted as they are today."

Greenfeld, Anne. "Camus's Caligula, Ubu and the Surrealist Rebel." *Romance Notes* XXVI, No. 2 (Winter 1985): 83-9.

Argues that Camus based the rebellious protagonist of his play *Caligula* on Père Ubu, the central character of Alfred Jarry's drama *Ubu roi.*

Hopkins, Patricia. "Camus's Failed Savior: *Le Malentendu.*" *Rocky Mountain Review* 39, No. 4 (1985): 251-56.

Discusses the "situational, thematic, and verbal ironies" manifested in this play, which result from Camus's theme of the inept redeemer.

Lambert, Richard T. "Albert Camus and the Paradoxes of Expressing a Relativism." *THOUGHT* 56, No. 221 (June 1981): 185-98.

Explores the role of relaivism in Camus's thought, particularly as expressed in his book of philosophical essays, *The Myth of Sisyphus.*

Little, J. P. "Albert Camus, Simone Weil, and Modern Tragedy." *French Studies* XXXI, No. 1 (January 1977): 42-51.
   Notes the influence of the French religious thinker Weil on Camus's plays.

Manly, William M. "Journey to Consciousness: The Symbolic Pattern of Camus's *L'Etranger. PMLA* LXXIX, No. 3 (June 1964): 321-28.
   Attempts to demonstrate that "Meursault's adventure [is] a parable of mental awakening or consciousness which corresponds to the adventure of the mind in *Le Mythe de Sisyphe.*"

McCarthy, Patrick. *Albert Camus: The Stranger.* Cambridge: Cambridge University Press, 1988, 109 p.
   Concise, lucid book-length study of *The Stranger* that places the novel in the context of French-Algerian history and culture.

Merton, Thomas. "The Stranger: Poverty of an Antihero." In *The Literary Essays of Thomas Merton,* edited by Patrick Hart, pp. 292-301. New York: New Directions, 1985.
   Contends that Meursault's spiritual poverty "is the product of a social system which needs people to be as he is and therefore manufactures them in quantity—and condemns them for being what they are."

Nagy, Moses M. "The Theatre of Camus: A Stage for Destiny." *Claudel Studies* IX, No. 1 (1982): 17-25.
   Explores the reasons for Camus's passion for the theater.

Ohayon, Stephen. "Camus' 'The Stranger': The Sun-Metaphor and Patricidal Conflict." *American Imago* 40, No. 2 (Summer 1983): 189-205.
   Argues that Meursault acts as a fictional surrogate for Camus, through which he expresses his repressed aggression, which stems from the author's quest for the father he never knew.

Porter, Laurence M. "From Chronicle to Novel: Artistic Elaboration in Camus's *La Peste.*" *Modern Fiction Studies* 28, No. 4 (Winter 1982-1983): 589-96.
   Analyzes the significance of Camus's decision to write *La peste* in chronicle form.

Saint-Amour, David. "Underground with Meursault: Myth and Archetype in Camus's *L'Etranger.*" *International Fiction Review* 4, No. 2 (July 1977): 110-18.

Finds parallels to the myths of Oedipus and Orestes in Camus's novel.

Slade, Carole. "*La Chute* and Lord Jim." *Romance Notes* XXIV, No. 2 (Winter 1983): 95-9.
   Compares and contrasts the protagonists of *La chute* and Joseph Conrad's *Lord Jim,* focusing on their failure to help others during crises.

Sprintzen, David. *Camus: A Critical Examination.* Philadelphia: Temple University Press, 1988, 310 p.
   Analysis of Camus's entire *oeuvre,* focusing on his concepts of revolt, dialogue, and community.

Thody, Philip. *Albert Camus.* London: Macmillan, 1989, 125 p.
   Biographical and critical study. Includes bibliography.

Weitz, Morris. "The Coinage of Man: 'King Lear' and Camus's 'L'Etranger'." *Modern Language Review* 66, No. 1 (January 1971): 31-9.
   Argues that the Shakespeare play and the Camus novel both present human life as ultimately meaningless.

Zepp, Evelyn H. "The Generic Ambiguity of Albert Camus's *La Chute.*" *French Forum* 7, No. 3 (September 1982): 252-60.
   Explores the ways in which narrative genre affects reader response to the text of this novel, concluding: "*La Chute* . . . has gone beyond the limitations of form and structure of any one genre to create a generic ambiguity, might we even say a genre of ambiguity, which is its own statement about the nature of man and his language."

———. "The Popular-Ritual Structural Pattern of Albert Camus' *La Chute.*" *Modern Language Studies* XIII, No. 1 (Winter 1983): 15-21.
   Claims that the grotesque tradition, contrary to critical consensus, "is highly relevant to Camus' fictional works, and especially to *La Chute.*"

———. "Self and Other: Identity as Dialogical Confrontation in *La Chute.*" *Perspectives on Contemporary Literature* 12 (1985): 51-6.
   Analyzes the relationship of self and other in the character of Clamence, asserting that the traditional division between these aspects of personality does not occur in this figure.

Terry Eagleton

1943-

(Full name Terence Francis Eagleton) English critic, essayist, novelist, editor, and playwright.

Considered England's foremost Marxist literary critic, Eagleton often examines the role of Marxism in understanding ideologies as they are expressed in literature. Marxist literary theory emphasizes the relationships of historical, political, and social conditions in works of literature; in his criticism, Eagleton attempts to create an authentic "science of the text," which he believes can transcend the theoretical misconceptions of other critical approaches. A controversial figure who is sometimes faulted for shifting aesthetic criteria, Eagleton is nonetheless praised for clarifying obscure critical theories for novices while advancing stimulating arguments for specialists.

Eagleton's first book, *The New Left Church,* reflects his involvement with a group of liberal Catholics associated with the British journal *Slant* whose passion for social justice inspired them to combine Marxism and Catholicism. The essays in *The New Left Church,* which blend literary criticism, Catholic theology and liturgy, and Marxist political analysis, display the eclecticism that characterizes Eagleton's subsequent work. Bernard Bergonzi commented: "From the beginning [Eagleton] has been a fast, volatile thinker who leaps rapidly from idea to idea, or position to position, without any indication of difficulty or of the obdurate way in which the world resists one's mental processes." *The Body as Language: Outline of a "New Left" Theology* is a religious and philosophical work that advocates a coalition between revolutionary socialism and Christianity to overcome alienation fostered by capitalism. This volume marked the end of any discussion of Christian doctrine and the Catholic church in Eagleton's criticism.

Eagleton's first traditional work of criticism, *Shakespeare and Society: Critical Studies in Shakespearean Drama,* investigates the conflict between individualism and social responsibility in the late plays of Shakespeare. In his next volume of criticism, *Exiles and Emigrés: Studies in Modern Literature,* Eagleton addresses why, in his estimation, most important twentieth-century literature has been written by such non-Englishmen as Joseph Conrad, Henry James, T. S. Eliot, and James Joyce. Eagleton attributes this presumed superiority to the inability of English authors to envision "society as a totality." *Myths of Power: A Marxist Study of the Brontës* analyzes the impact of the emerging English industrial class of manufacturers on the aristocracy as developed in the work of the Brontë sisters.

In *Marxism and Literary Criticism,* a volume comprising four essays on major elements of Marxist criticism, Eagleton posits the concept of author as producer rather than creator and discusses the correlations between literature and history, form and content, and the writer and social commitment. In *Criticism and Ideology: A Study in Marxist Literary Theory,* a highly abstract work often faulted for excessive use of jargon, Eagleton argues for the privi-

leged neutrality of Marxism, which he believes is the only methodology to escape the taint of ideological bias that accompanies humanist, empirical, and aesthetic approaches. Eagleton asserts that the task of criticism is to expose the ideological forces that constitute a text. *Criticism and Ideology,* however, provoked anger from both leftist and conservative critics, and Eagleton later renounced much of the content of this work.

Walter Benjamin; or, Towards a Revolutionary Criticism evidenced Eagleton's adoption of a less dogmatic and more personal style of writing and exhibited his first interest in feminist criticism. In this book, Eagleton proposes that Benjamin has been underestimated by the critical establishment and was as revolutionary a critic as Bertolt Brecht and Mikhail Bakhtin. Eagleton's next work, *The Rape of Clarissa: Writing, Sexuality, and Class Struggle in Samuel Richardson,* utilizes Marxism, psychoanalysis, and feminist argument to interpret Richardson's eighteenth-century novel, *Clarissa. Literary Theory: An Introduction* is both a survey and denunciation of such major literary theories as structuralism, semiotics, and phenomenology in which Eagleton reaches the disputable conclusion that literary theory—as well as literature—is an illusion. Rather than relying exclusively on the study of literature, Eagleton suggests that students would benefit from the more comprehensive discipline of rhetoric as practiced from antiquity until the eighteenth century. Eagleton maintains that varied cultural discourse devoting equal treatment to all media would lead to the eradication of elitist distinctions between literature and nonliterature. Wallace Jackson remarked: "[Eagleton] de-mythologizes the high-cultural pretensions of literary study in the university, recognizes that in fact such study underwrites the practices of state capitalism, and effectively nullifies whatever radical power literature may have as an instrument of social criticism and social change." *The Function of Criticism: From "The Spectator" to Post-Structuralism* is a polemical history of the critical establishment from the turn of the eighteenth century to the present. *The Ideology of the Aesthetic,* considered Eagleton's most substantial and complex work, endeavors to show how society's aesthetic conceptualizations influence and are influenced by its social and economic conditions.

Eagleton's only novel to date, *Saints and Scholars,* is a satirical exploration of the beginnings of modern European thought. Set in Ireland in 1916, the story humorously imagines that Irish revolutionary James Connolly escaped execution for his role in the Easter Rising and met the philosophers Ludwig Wittgenstein and Bertrand Russell, as well as Nikolai Bakhtin, the brother of Marxist literary critic Mikhail, and Leopold Bloom, fictional hero of James Joyce's *Ulysses.* In the process, Eagleton details how religious, political, and economic forces affected society in the first quarter of the twentieth century.

(See also *Contemporary Authors,* Vols. 57-60 and *Contemporary Authors New Revision Series,* Vols. 7, 23.)

PRINCIPAL WORKS

CRITICISM

Shakespeare and Society: Critical Studies in Shakespearean Drama 1967
Exiles and Emigrés: Studies in Modern Literature 1970
Myths of Power: A Marxist Study of the Brontës 1975
Marxism and Literary Criticism 1976
Criticism and Ideology: A Study in Marxist Literary Theory 1976
Walter Benjamin; or, Towards a Revolutionary Criticism 1981
The Rape of Clarissa: Writing, Sexuality and Class Struggle in Samuel Richardson 1982
Literary Theory: An Introduction 1983
The Function of Criticism: From "The Spectator" to Post-Structuralism 1984
The Ideology of the Aesthetic 1990

OTHER

The New Left Church (essays) 1966
The Body as Language: Outline of a "New Left" Theology (nonfiction) 1970
Against the Grain: Selected Essays, 1975-1985 1986
Saints and Scholars (novel) 1987
Saint Oscar (play) 1989

The Times Literary Supplement

Mr. Eagleton's starting point [in *Exiles and Emigrés: Studies in Modern Literature*] is the notion, first outlined in Raymond Williams's *The Long Revolution,* that while the great nineteenth-century novels showed individual characters and their society interacting in a creative tension, most twentieth-century novels present individuals in isolation, with their society either invisible or reduced to a remote backcloth. As a descriptive account of some important differences between two kinds of novel, this has much to recommend it; but it comes dangerously close to a myth of catastrophe, one more account of the unique fall from grace that the twentieth-century literary consciousness is so addicted to. And it is precisely this aspect of Mr. Williams's original distinction that Mr. Eagleton seizes on and enlarges for his own ends; for him, not only the realistic novelists, but the great Romantic poets also, had the capacity, now lost, to see their society as a whole and to grasp in a total act of apprehension all the vital forces at work in it. Mr. Eagleton calls this process "totalization", a bit of neo-Marxist terminology which he uses often, and with never-failing relish, finding it equally in Blake and Wordsworth, Dickens and George Eliot.

Having established this stage of his argument, at least to his own satisfaction, he then attaches to it a further myth of catastrophe, derived from Mr. Perry Anderson's essay, "Components of the National Culture". This attempts to explain the undoubtedly curious fact that, as Mr. Eagleton says, "With the exception of D. H. Lawrence, the heights of modern English literature have been dominated by foreigners and émigrés: Conrad, James, Eliot, Pound, Yeats, Joyce." And Lawrence, as a working-class Englishman, was no less alien to the hegemonic national culture than the other outsiders who made up the modern movement. This abdication by the traditional literary culture is seen as reflecting a deep-seated crisis and loss of nerve in English society during the early twentieth century; the Strange Death of Liberal England, in fact, followed by the First World War.

Mr. Eagleton's sweeping explanations have an attractive assurance about them, however brashly they are offered. . . .

Having set up his conceptual apparatus, Mr. Eagleton proceeds to search for evidence of the prevailing crisis in a variety of modern and post-modern authors. His way of proceeding is less like literary criticism, which should be a tentative, patient exploration, than like a series of briskly delivered demonstration lectures, or even a form of minor surgery. Mr. Eagleton knows exactly what he wants to find, and he has no difficulty in finding it. One after the other the inert bodies in front of him are opened up, and after a moment of deft probing the fatal evidence of contradiction or ambivalence or ambiguity is removed and triumphantly exhibited, and then he is on to the next. . . .

In his first chapter he remarks that *Under Western Eyes* raises what he sees as the central question of his book: "the problem of a kind of novel which can neither fully accept, nor fully escape, the conventions and habits of its own culture". On any common-sense view this would be true of any novel ever written that had claims to literary originality. But common sense is not Mr. Eagleton's forte (he would probably invoke Gramsci's dictum that it is a ruling-class concept), and he is vehemently against anything that smacks of "the human condition", or any suggestion that man is never likely to be fully at home in the world, however humane the society. He would, no doubt, utterly reject the obvious conclusion that the contradiction and ambivalence that he sees as evidence of particular cultural malaise are at the heart of all literature, and indeed part of the very fibre of human existence. Mr. Eagleton shares with his master, Raymond Williams, a horror of the onto-logical: they are both inclined to press the panic button at the very suggestion that "myth" is a perennial part of human experience, since they see it as an alarming escape from historicity. Yet a more mature Marxist thinker than either of them, Ernst Fischer, shows in his *Art against Ideology* that there is no necessary contradiction between myth and Marxism. And for that matter Mr. Eagleton might consider the significance of those contemporary de-bates in Eastern Europe about the possibility that alien-ation might persist even in a socialist society.

Like Raymond Williams again, he is an instinctively nos-talgic writer; he is at his best where he is on warmly famil-iar ground, like the first part of *Sons and Lovers,* which he discusses with real if predictable enthusiasm. But he is sniffily dismissive about *Women in Love:* "What is shown is the despairing vacuity of a particular group of bored middle-class intellectuals, hopelessly alienated from the concrete social realities they analyse at such length." One needn't accept F. R. Leavis's valuation of the novel to find this absurdly simplistic and formulaic; even in Marxist terms there are far more interesting things to be said, as has been illustrated in a recent essay by John Goode. Marxist criticism is, at its best, valuable for its illumina-tion of the relations between literature and society, even for those who do not accept its premises. Mr. Eagleton's book comes nowhere near to doing this: it merely offers, as he himself might put it, an unresolved conflict between dogmatic aplomb and uncertain shallowness. (p. 1219)

> *"From Totalization to Catastrophe," in* The Times Literary Supplement, *No. 3582, Octo-ber 23, 1970, p. 1219.*

J. R. Harvey

The writing [in *Criticism and Ideology*] sometimes has the clarity of his shorter book [*Marxism and Literary Criti-cism*] (which, in broader argument, can look harshly dia-grammatic), but is often made inaccessible by the theoreti-cian's vocational density, where meaning periodically im-plodes in black holes of jammed abbreviation. . . . But he is emphatic that there are great masterpieces and most books are not such, and certainly he is aware of the com-plexities. Though (unlike [Raymond] Williams) he is ex-plicitly a determinist, he recognizes that the determination works in so indirect and complicated a way that it would be ridiculous to seek a simple correspondence between lit-erary values and political. He is severe on theoreticians who concede value to a poem only in proportion as the 'general ideology' is there mimed, negotiated or coded.

In extending the determinism to art, he differs from (say) Marx, Lenin or Trotsky, who recognized a realm of 'aes-thetic values' independent of ideology. But logic is surely on his side, for if Marxism (he usually says Materialism) *is* a general philosophy, it is hard to see how literature can

both be outside it and matter. He proposes a literary sci-ence which, analysing in all their complexity the determi-nants of a literary work, would establish the work's value, so emancipating criticism from subjective infirmity. The problem with the science is that to analyse *all* the com-plexity is to postpone full understanding to a time none of us will live to see. And again it really is a question whether the science ever could provide an irrefutable relative ap-praisal of, say, Baudelaire, Mark Twain and Chaucer, without the determinants becoming either too numerous to be counted, or uselessly inclusive and vague. Eagleton's position is complicated further by his (necessary) allow-ance that determination can work both ways, since some-times ideas in books change the means of production. A *mutual* determinism calls into question the priority of any determinant, and so might deprive the science of a recog-nizable Marxist character, and of bite. The underlying problem is the word 'determine' (on which Williams, in *Keywords,* is helpful): its meaning can—and in the present theory it does—vary conveniently between setting wide limits to what may happen, and bringing about specific events.

To meet difficulties, Eagleton multiplies categories; and yet they are not enough, while also the problem of keeping so broad a theory single proves insuperable. In practice one finds (if one undertakes the arduous unravelling) that the theory operates two distinct principles of value. On the front line and in attack, a heavy neo-Brechtian emphasis is placed on 'contradiction': the novel or play is valued be-cause it lays bare, in its own fractures and distortions, the contradictions within the outlook that has produced it. But not all works are so divided, and elsewhere (less obtru-sively) the theory rests literary value on the complexity of the non-literary values invoked by the writer. In these un-derpinning and defensive positions, the theory looks like a Materialist transposition of Leavis's criterion of 'com-plexity'.

I take it that the difference between 'complexity' and 'con-tradiction' is that 'complexity' involves unity; and the dis-crepancy in the theory shows up when, on some occasions, Eagleton allows for unity with no depreciatory suggestion, while on others 'disunity', along with 'fissuring' and 'split-ting', are acclaimed as though they were direct indices of value. He allows that there is a degree of disunity, fissur-ing and splitting which is collapse and artistic failure, but has no means from within his logic of determining where that point comes—except presumably by some literary equivalent of catastrophe theory. The product of 'com-plexity' and 'contradiction' is then a theory, offered as the foundation of a science, which is broadly able to distin-guish important authors from negligible ones, but has no means of verifying fine valuations, and has large areas where, even for crucial modernist works (such as *Finne-gan's Wake*), it is incapable of decision. (pp. 59-61)

[For] Eagleton value is, militantly, value in theory: to be determined at a fit scientific remove from the text, in ac-cordance with his extraordinary inaugural axiom, 'the function of criticism is to refuse the spontaneous presence of the work.'

This refusal is accompanied by an extreme wariness (at least) with regard to experience itself; and this complicates Eagleton's discussion of the genre to which Materialist theory is otherwise best adapted—the novel. There, the refusal shows above all in the generalized depreciation of 're- alism'. The drive against realism, strong in 1910, is strong- er now: it has acquired a life of its own, and become a gen- eral phenomenon. As a result, a particular description of Dickens has come to describe the ideal of fiction: attention is devoted to the non-realistic techniques he combines in his long novels, the novels themselves being 'decentred to- talities' corresponding to the decentred totality of Victori- an high-industrial society. There are different realisms, but it is a curious development of Materialist criticism to dissolve in 'decentred totality' a creation like Peggotty— the nurse in *David Copperfield*—in whom maternity, in its ancient class dis-location, is realized as and with a *force* of Nature in an unforgettable live individual. (p. 63)

As represented by Eagleton, current Marxist theory is im- mensely more sophisticated than that of Marx, and yet is only marginally more helpful with (for instance) Dickens. Dickens never was the great Realist he used to be repre- sented as being, but since criticism has now gone so far to the other extreme that he seems not to have a real bone in his body, it should be said that the description of the novels as both 'non-realistic' and 'decentred' is the oppo- site of the truth. The novels do have centres, and they are 'real' people—pursued, in the case of David Copperfield and Pip, with unrelaxing, and severe, psychological real- ism. What is true of the novels as wholes is true also of the large 'corporate structures' which (as Eagleton notes) help to make them wholes: at the centre of the Chancery fog and mystification in *Bleak House* there is not a void or a caricature, but the person of the Lord Chancellor, whose brief appearance, ungowned in his chambers, with his cool tactful affability, is a triumph of proto-Tolstoyan realism. In *Little Dorrit*, the psychological realism is covertly in control even of apparently stereotypical characters on the periphery, like Bar and Physician.

But in any case it is a clear fact of literary history that whether characters begin as 'real people', allegories, or hy- postases of ideology, when a significant drama is followed through to the crisis, the art at the same time thickens with palpable accuracies of 'realism', and organizes itself with extraordinary economies and audacities of styliza- tion.

I have emphasized my objections because Eagleton's book is decidely 'not innocent' of the cuckooism of new literary sciences. One drive in it is absolutely consistent through- out, and that is the drive to establish that all aspects of lit- erature and literary value can only validly be described in ideological terms. That drive shows most clearly in delib- erate shock-statements that are, however, quite seriously meant:

> The phrase 'George Eliot' signifies nothing more than the insertion of certain specific ideological de- terminations—Evangelical Christianity, rural or- ganicism, incipient feminism, petty-bourgeois mor- alism—into a hegemonic ideological formation which is partly supported, partly embarrassed by their presence.

He is referring to the woman, not the work, but one quan- tity here excluded from the woman is thus necessarily ex- cluded from her writing, where it is a 'literary value' that the phrase 'George Eliot' signifies. That quantity is a radi- ating wise humanity in excess of observable historical de- terminants and not assimilable to a specific 'humanism'.

It is a quantity which, let observation with intensive view survey literary theory from Cambridge to Paris, is ade- quately allowed for nowhere and by no one. The evasion is part of the current ideological situation in which reduc- tive (but talismanic) categorization cooperates with the necessary epidemic anti-realism in legalizing the mind's escape from experience. (pp. 64-5)

> *J. R. Harvey, "Criticism, Ideology, Raymond Williams and Terry Eagleton," in* The Cam- bridge Quarterly, *Vol. VIII, No. 1, 1978, pp. 56-65.*

Walter Kendrick

[The] glut of technical terminologies makes literary theory impenetrable to the general reader. To fill the gap, a num- ber of guides and handbooks have appeared, by far the best of which is Terry Eagleton's *Literary Theory: An In- troduction.* Published last year in England and now here, this concise and lucid volume offers a satisfying survey of all the major theories, from structuralism in the 1960's to deconstruction today, that have made academic criticism both intriguing and off-putting to the outsider. And there's a surprising sting in its tail.

Mr. Eagleton's first aim is "to provide a reasonably com- prehensive account of modern literary theory for those with little or no previous knowledge of the subject." He succeeds admirably; but *Literary Theory* also argues "a particular *case*," and it is this case, gradually emerging as the book proceeds and stated point-blank at the end, that makes Mr. Eagleton's book more than a mere vade mecum. The case is simply that literary theory, like the lit- erature it studies, is "an illusion."

> It is an illusion first in the sense that literary theory . . . is really no more than a branch of social ideologies, utterly without any unity or identity which would adequately distinguish it from philos- ophy, linguistics, psychology, cultural and social thought; and secondly in the sense that the one hope it has of distinguishing itself—clinging to an object named literature—is misplaced. We must conclude, then, that this book is less an introduc- tion than an obituary, and that we have ended by burying the object we sought to unearth.

It might seem perverse for a writer to make himself as fa- miliar with a field as Mr. Eagleton clearly is with literary theory just to junk it. But *Literary Theory* is far from a purely negative book. Its positive intention is to place today's literary theories in a double context—of the other ways of treating literature that have preceded them and of the political world in which all literary theories, wit- tingly or not, have participated. He is able to show that contemporary theories, though they rattle sabers, in fact merely continue a tradition of self-protective collaboration with the status quo. This has characterized the Anglo- American academic establishment from the time of Mat- thew Arnold a century ago through T. S. Eliot in the 20's and 30's, F. R. Leavis in the 40's and the New Criticism in the 50's. In political terms, nothing whatever distin- guishes today's rabid semiotician from his grandfather, the Arnoldian appreciator. All have preached the isolation of "literature" from social and political life; all have therefore done their best to reinforce the prevailing ideology of their times.

This would, perhaps, be no great sin if literary critics acknowledged it. Matthew Arnold was fairly frank about his allegiance to the Philistines, but in the last century critics have consistently mystified their position by appealing to something called literature, which supposedly dwells beyond ideology and can be studied in a pure state. No such realm exists, as Mr. Eagleton handily demonstrates; the honorific label "literature" is attached to certain written works for historically determined ideological reasons. "English," for example, did not become an academic discipline until the late 19th century, when the influx of the petite bourgeoisie and women into British universities made it expedient to replace the old classical curriculum with something more accessible and relevant, yet imbued with a proper high seriousness. Born as an ad hoc response, "English" has gone on ever since protecting the illusion of its independent existence.

"Literature," then, is an ideological term, all the more so because it pretends not to be. And professors of literature are ideologues, whether they call themselves deconstructionists or Arnoldians. The admission of this fact would abolish literature and literary theory, but it would neither depopulate our campuses nor reduce us all to card-carrying members of some party or other. *Literary Theory* concludes with a sketch of "political criticism," by which Mr. Eagleton means a general social critique reminiscent of the program of the Frankfurt School. Literature would still be studied but as a mode of rhetoric, the ancient science that embraces all forms of persuasive discourse from polemical pamphlets to *Paradise Lost.* Professors of rhetoric would be Marxists or feminists or Republicans as pleased them, but their ideological stance would be clear and their engagement in the real world assured.

Literary Theory is intended mainly for nonacademic readers, but academics will be unable to ignore it. Mr. Eagleton's expositions render even the most jargon-ridden of contemporary theories accessible to the ordinary educated person, and the questions posed by *Literary Theory* will have to be answered, either by the theoreticians themselves or by those who validate them by accepting their authority. For myself, a professor of literature, *Literary Theory* came as a shock, though eventually a reassuring one. It announces the death of my discipline, but it suggests that an illusory field of study can be subsumed in an enterprise of genuine value and more than illusory significance. (pp. 9, 17)

> Walter Kendrick, "Criticism as Ideology," in
> The New York Times Book Review, *September 4, 1983, pp. 9, 17.*

Denis Donoghue

Literary Theory: An Introduction purports to provide "a reasonably comprehensive account of modern literary theory for those with little or no previous knowledge of the topic." Comprehensive? Only if it doesn't matter that the diverse theories of Valéry, Virginia Woolf, T. E. Hulme, Maurice Blanchot, Umberto Eco, and Wayne Booth are ignored. But Eagleton's sentence is misleading in a more serious way: the aim of the book, which is disclosed only at the end, is to get rid of literary theory. It follows that the undergraduates for whom the book is intended are released from the chore of reading the theorists in question.

The book starts out as if it were an ordinary guide to modern literary theory. But the first chapter is a dismissive and inaccurate account of Eliot, Leavis, the work of *Scrutiny*—"the essentially petty-bourgeois character of *Scrutiny*," as Eagleton referred to it in **Criticism and Ideology**—I. A. Richards, and the American New Critics. We hear yet again the libel that these critics were indifferent to historical considerations, and paid attention to "the words on the page" rather than to "the contexts which produced and surround them"—as if Allen Tate hadn't written *The Fathers* and the essay on Emily Dickinson; or L. C. Knights *Drama and Society in the Age of Jonson,* or John Crowe Ransom *God without Thunder.* Or as if the formula of attending to "the words on the page" could account for Eliot's essays on Pascal, Baudelaire, and James, the force of their intelligence and care, the telling power of Eliot's moral, biographical, and historical reference.

The second chapter deals with phenomenology, hermeneutics, and reception theory. The main sources of these errors, according to Eagleton, are Husserl and Heidegger. Phenomenology is predicated upon the idea of "a meaningless solitary utterance untainted by the external world." In this spirit Husserl was responsible for the Geneva school (Georges Poulet, Jean Starobinski, Emil Staiger, and others) and eventually for E. D. Hirsch, Jr. This part of the chapter is unfair. Those who have read Starobinski's book on Rousseau, for instance, will appreciate how rich its acknowledgment of the external world is. It is a deliberate injustice, too, to dispose of fundamental interests, as Eagleton does, by tracing a rough-and-ready line from Heidegger ("the Olympian heights of Heidegger's ponderously esoteric prose") to Hans-Georg Gadamer, who is allegedly guilty of "projecting on to the world at large a viewpoint for which 'art' means chiefly the classical monuments of the high German tradition."

"Reception theory," which assumes that the meaning of the text is not a quality of the text itself but the reader's experience in realizing it, is examined through the work of Hans Robert Jauss, Wolfgang Iser, Roman Ingarden, and Stanley Fish. But Eagleton finds in it only the same old sin. (p. 43)

The third chapter deals with structuralism and semiotics, dismissing both. Structuralism was merely

> yet one more form of philosophical idealism . . .
> hair-raisingly unhistorical: the laws of the mind it
> claimed to isolate—parallelisms, oppositions, in-
> versions and the rest—moved at a level of generali-
> ty quite remote from the concrete differences of
> human history.

The point is not well taken. It is not news that structuralism concerned itself with the synchronic rather than the diachronic aspects of a text; or that, as a result, the text seems more deeply becalmed than it would appear if genetic considerations, changing social forces, and historical process were recognized. But you can study a skeleton without constantly meditating on how it came to be what it is. In any case, this is an old charge against structuralism; Eagleton has nothing new to say about it. (p. 44)

The same chapter deals with semiotics (C. S. Peirce and Yury Lotman) and speech act theory (J. L. Austin), but it brushes them aside to make space for Bakhtin's *Marxism and the Philosophy of Language* (1927), which is claimed to have "laid the foundation for a materialist theory of consciousness itself." But Eagleton doesn't go into the implications of Bakhtin's distinction between the "monological" novel, which holds its several voices within a single objective world governed by the novelist's unified consciousness, and the "dialogical" novel—Dostoevsky is Bakhtin's example—in which the unity of a given event is qualified by the plurality of equal consciousnesses and their several worlds. Eagleton's account of Bakhtin is useful, as far as it goes; but it's not at all as informative or far-reaching as Julia Kristeva's in her *Semiotike* (1969).

Post-structuralism arrives, not a moment too soon, in the next chapter; but Eagleton won't be appeased. He looks at Roland Barthes's later books, paraphrases Derrida's *Of Grammatology,* adverts to Paul de Man, but his heart isn't in the work; he thinks deconstruction merely a gun with blank ammunition. "Literature for the deconstructionists testifies to the impossibility of language's ever doing more than talk about its own failure, like some barroom bore." Derrida's work has been "grossly unhistorical, politically evasive and in practice oblivious to language as 'discourse.'" It is neither my business nor my pleasure to speak for deconstruction, but I'm sure it is a more formidable thing than Eagleton's version suggests, even if in the long run one decides that it belongs not to philosophy but to rhetoric, as a nuance of irony.

Eagleton's next chapter, on psychoanalysis, is a more spirited performance: at least in Freud he has someone he can take seriously as the source of his own occasional essays in psychoanalytical criticism, in *The Rape of Clarissa* and other books. The chapter paraphrases the most available arguments of Freud, Jacques Lacan, Harold Bloom, and Norman Holland. Freud is paraphrased on the Oedipus complex, dreams, parapraxis, and the unconscious; Lacan on language and the unconscious, and the "mirror stage" of a child's development; Holland on the ego and social life; Bloom on his attempts "to rewrite literary history in terms of the Oedipus complex."

Kenneth Burke gets half a sentence: he "eclectically blends Freud, Marx and linguistics to produce his own suggestive view of the literary work as a form of symbolic action." Julia Kristeva is mentioned, but Eagleton isn't sure whether her work is acceptably feminist or not. Since women play the role in Eagleton's work that the proletariat played in early Marxism, feminist critics have to be strictly orthodox.

And then, in a conclusion, Eagleton says what he has apparently wanted to say from the start, that most of the theories and theorists he has been obliged to discuss are not worth discussing, they are merely secretions of bourgeois liberalism, sunk in "the ephemeral pieties of twentieth-century liberalism" which he mocked in *The Rape of Clarissa.* Specifically: modern literary theories are politically corrupt. "The great majority of the literary theories outlined in this book have strengthened rather than challenged the assumptions of the power-system." They have conspired with "a political system which subordinates the sociality of human life to solitary individual enterprise." "The story of modern literary theory [is] . . . a flight from

real history . . . into a seemingly endless range of alternatives: the poem itself, the organic society, eternal verities, the imagination, the structure of the human mind, myth, language and so on." Such criticism has no right to exist. That being so, "if literary theory presses its own implications too far, then it has argued itself out of existence. This, I would suggest, is the best possible thing for it to do."

The weakest part of Eagleton's argument is where he thinks it is strongest. History, sometimes asserted as "real history," is for Eagleton that which cannot be doubted or deconstructed. History puts a stop to the "play of signifiers." "The 'truth' of the text," he declares in *Criticism and Ideology,* "is not an essence but a practice—the practice of its relation to ideology, and in terms of that to history." He doesn't say what history is, or how it proves invulnerable to the irony he so relentlessly directs against other ultimate categories: Being, logos, origin. (pp. 44-5)

So what is criticism supposed to do, short of doing the honorable thing? Eagleton's clearest program is in his book on Benjamin [*Walter Benjamin; or, Towards a Revolutionary Criticism*]:

> Let us briefly imagine what shape a "revolutionary literary criticism" would assume. It would dismantle the ruling concepts of "literature," reinserting "literary" texts into the whole field of cultural practices. It would strive to relate such "cultural" practices to other forms of social activity, and to transform the cultural apparatuses themselves. It would articulate its "cultural" analyses with a consistent political intervention. It would deconstruct the received hierarchies of "literature" and transvaluate received judgments and assumptions; engage with the language and "unconscious" of literary texts, to reveal their role in the ideological construction of the subject; and mobilize such texts, if necessary by hermeneutic "violence," in a struggle to transform those subjects within a wider political context.

What this curriculum amounts to, in *Literary Theory,* is: a rhetorical analysis of discursive practices. Works of literature would get into the syllabus, but without any special privilege. You would start by deciding what you wanted to do, presumably what "political interpretation" you wanted to make; then look for the material that would best help you to do it. The material might include *Paradise Lost,* "The MacNeil-Lehrer Report," *MAD* magazine, and whatever else your sense of the task required. It is not clear what Eagleton hopes to achieve from these analyses, since he evidently agrees with Barthes that "the real is not representable." How, then, is Eagleton to get from discourse to the irreducibly real, if language, as he says in *The Rape of Clarissa,* is "a ceaselessly digressive supplement which . . . will never succeed in nailing down the real"? As for method: "Any method or theory which will contribute to the strategic goal of human emancipation, the production of 'better people' through the socialist transformation of society, is acceptable." Strangely, Eagleton finds a good word to say about liberal humanism at last: while it "has dwindled to the impotent conscience of bourgeois society, gentle, sensitive and ineffectual," it can still teach rhetoric something about the "humanly transformative" power of discourse. So perhaps his curriculum isn't as daunting as it has seemed: it may not bother his colleagues, the Fellows of Wadham College, Oxford, at all.

But the odd thing about Eagleton's curriculum is that he describes it as novel. Isn't the rhetorical analysis of discursive practices what Barthes spent most of his life doing? Isn't Foucault's entire work such an analysis? Kenneth Burke has been engaged, for more than fifty years, in the rhetorical analysis of discursive practices, according to his maxim of "using all there is to use." I. A. Richards's work is rhetorical analysis of discourse. If more routine work is in question, I have for some years been reading essays that fulfill Eagleton's curricular requirements—though I can't vouch for the purity of their socialism—in such magazines as *Signs, Poetics Today, Studies in Romanticism, Critical Inquiry, Glyph, Raritan, The Quarterly Journal of Speech,* and *Social Text.* Eagleton refers to "the reinvention of rhetoric that I have proposed." The proposal is redundant, I'm afraid, and the claim embarrassing. Rhetoric, reinvented many years ago, for example by Kenneth Burke, is an industry coast to coast. Rhetorical analysis probably accounts for most of our current activity in the humanities. How useful to have a negative guide to it and then go right on with it. It is precisely because of the prevalence of rhetorical analysis in our universities and colleges—and because of the hospitality a bourgeois liberal society extends to its opponents—that Eagleton can anticipate the success of his book. (p. 45)

> *Denis Donoghue, "A Guide to Revolution," in* The New York Review of Books, *Vol. XXX, No. 19, December 8, 1983, pp. 43-5.*

Walter Kendrick

[In] *Literary Theory,* Terry Eagleton gave us concise, brilliant outlines of structuralism, semiotics, deconstruction, and the other faddish methodologies that have been ruffling the calm of academic literary criticism for the past decade. *Literary Theory* remains the best handbook to those arcane ics and isms, both for academy members and for any civilians who, having heard the distant roar of professorial cannons, might wonder what the skirmishing's about. But Eagleton wasn't content with summaries: he also submitted the whole theoretical enterprise to a damning critique that seemed to render it sterile and promise its speedy demise.

His argument was simple and, to my mind at least, irrefutable. No matter how loudly it rattles its sabers, literary theory remains housed within the academic establishment and focused on an elusive entity called "literature"; the result is that its potentially disruptive implications are neutralized and transformed into props of the status quo. Eagleton's brief but trenchant historical survey showed how the academic study of literature was developed in the late 19th century as a means of absorbing and taming the women and lower-class men who for the first time were gaining access to a college education. By isolating "literature" from real life, enclosing it in classrooms, and entrusting its transmission to certified authorities, the established order insured that no dangerous ideas would get spawned in those new students' heads.

The process continues unabated; in England and America, it has succeeded in co-opting even the most radical theories, adapting them handily to an academic function which has hardly changed since the days of Matthew Arnold. What irked Eagleton most in *Literary Theory,* however, wasn't so much the built-in conservatism of Academe as its resolute blindness. Today's avant-garde academic theorists can wax pretty feisty when the status of the signifier is in question, but all their disputes are impotent because they fail to take into account the social and political arrangements that make it possible to argue about signifiers in the first place. God did not create literary critics; they evolved historically, in response to changing cultural conditions that invented their job and told them how to do it. Neglecting (or refusing) to investigate their own heritage, even the extremest literary theorists run in tracks laid down a century ago.

Provocative as it was on these issues, *Literary Theory* only sketched them in; now, in *The Function of Criticism,* Eagleton has provided a sort of supplement to the earlier book, tracing the history of English literary criticism from its earliest recognizable appearance around the turn of the 18th century to its present institutionalized form. The undertaking is vast and would have been interminable if Eagleton had approached it in the old-fashioned scholarly manner that requires the doing of justice to nuances. He is very much a "theorist" himself, however, so he's able to tear through the whole business in 115 pages, nuances be damned. *The Function of Criticism* is driven by a fierce personal enthusiasm that sometimes degenerates into breathless haste; it can be read at one sitting and might have been written that way, occasionally at the cost of readability. But no old-fashioned scholar could have told this story, and the time is overdue for its telling.

Eagleton echoes the title of Matthew Arnold's over-anthologized 1864 essay "The Function of Criticism at the Present Time," a landmark in the development of the critic as a cultural type. Arnold's ghostly chains clank mightily throughout *The Function of Criticism,* though Arnold himself gets fair, even sympathetic treatment. Arnold was the first academic literary critic in anything like the modern sense: he stood at a point of transition from the hackwork and dilettantism of prior generations to the self-justifying alienation of the future. He was also the first—his successors should have followed him more closely in this—to reflect upon the value of criticism and the nature of the critic.

The Function of Criticism takes off from an imaginary Arnoldian moment, "in which a critic, sitting down to begin a study of some theme or author, is suddenly arrested by a set of disturbing questions. What is the *point* of such a study? Who is it intended to reach, influence, impress? What functions are ascribed to such a critical act by society as a whole?" Late in the book, these questions get restated: "It is hard to believe that, in a nuclear age, the publication of yet another study of Robert Herrick is justifiable. Should criticism, then, be allowed to wither away, or can some more productive role be discovered for it?" It's doubtful that would-be Herrickists ever become so reflective; for them, the necessity is to do a study of *something,* to get it published by some academic press whose editors also avoid certain questions, to achieve tenure, promotion, prestige, or whatever institutional benefit such an act might yield. The machine works, and lives as well as egos are funded by it, so it's hardly a surprise that no one in Academe (the only place where such transactions matter) poses Eagleton's Wittgensteinian query, "What is going on?" or its ruder translation, "What the hell is all this?" (p. 6)

The last pages of *The Function of Criticism* contain some new remarks on the genesis and prospects of literary theory, most intriguingly Eagleton's tracing of the theory boom back to the student turmoil of the '60s. For all their technocratic vocabulary, theorists, like flower children, assume a stoned attitude toward the world; in their wide-eyed naiveté (rhetorical, of course, not real), they insist upon the "mysterious, perhaps even comic arbitrariness" of what everyone else takes for granted. As it comes up to the present, however, *The Function of Criticism* falls apart into scattered observations, often striking in themselves but without the sharp polemical focus that holds the rest of the book together.

This is understandable, since it's always more difficult to get a coherent overview of the present than of the distant past. At the very end, though, Eagleton seems to renege on his whole project: having proven incontrovertibly that the current conditions under which criticism must operate preclude its exercising any significant influence on society at large, he suddenly shifts into a hopeful mood. His last chapter is given over to a nervous, pushy eulogy of his model and mentor Raymond Williams, the "single most important critic of post-war Britain," who apparently offers Eagleton an image of what the critic might aspire to in a post-critical world. *The Function of Criticism* concludes with a call to arms: "Modern criticism was born of a struggle against the absolutist state; unless its future is now defined as a struggle against the bourgeois state, it might have no future at all."

The "might" is feeble, and the call is more like a squeak; a critic himself after all, Eagleton is unable to consign criticism to the dust heap. Instead, he takes refuge in a knee-jerk Marxism that's already been rendered futile by the argument leading up to it. If you skim the last chapter, however—and try to ignore the willed self-blindness it reveals—*The Function of Criticism* makes a powerful case and raises uncomfortable, necessary questions. (p. 7)

> Walter Kendrick, "God Didn't Invent Literary Critics and Other Tenure-Inhibiting Remarks," in VLS, No. 37, March, 1985, p. 6-7.

Charles Sugnet

Literary Theory: An Introduction may not be anyone's idea of an appetizing title, but this is a remarkable and important book. Under cover of writing a primer on current literary criticism, British Marxist critic Terry Eagleton dissolves his own field of inquiry by arguing that there is no such thing as "literature," and therefore no "literary theory." Written in an accessible and energetic style, the book has already sold over 20,000 copies in North America alone, an exceptional sale for a book on such an arcane topic. . . .

Eagleton begins by arguing that the creation of a special class of writing called "literature" is a relatively recent historical formation. This new invention, together with the corresponding creation of an academic elite to regulate it, has benefitted the ruling class tremendously, according to Eagleton. By taking writing out of the historical context of its production, by insulating the aesthetic from the po-

litical, and by deflecting linguistic talent away from rebellious cultural analyses, "literature" has helped pacify an otherwise unruly territory.

An early chapter, titled "The Rise of English," is full of wonderful quotes from Victorians like George Gordon, Professor of English Literature at Oxford, whose inaugural address observed that "England is sick, and . . . English literature must save it. The Churches having failed . . . and social remedies being slow, English literature must save our souls and heal the State." Matthew Arnold, the Victorian poet and school inspector who wrote *Culture and Anarchy,* also believed the State needed literature. His work makes it clear that he thought the proper sort of education could keep the lower classes from behaving uncontrollably, and Eagleton evokes Arnold's era with nice irony: "Since literature, as we know, deals in universal human values rather than in such historical trivia as civil wars, the oppression of women, or the dispossession of the English peasantry, it could serve to place in cosmic perspective the petty demands of working people for decent living conditions. . . . It would communicate to them the moral riches of bourgeois civilization [and] impress on them a reverence for middle-class achievements."

Starting from that era, Eagleton treats the various theories that have made a mark on literary study, including New Criticism; the German school (phenomenology, hermeneutics, reception theory); semiotics; structuralism and deconstruction; and psychoanalysis. Each theory gets a polemical summary and critique based on Marxist principles. The common complaints are that literary theory has been ahistorical, and that it has been a veiled form of ideology, one which refuses to acknowledge its own status as ideology. The early sections dealing with T. S. Eliot and F. R. Leavis are wonderfully pungent. Psychoanalysis gets a long and sympathetically critical treatment because, according to Eagleton, "what Freud produces, indeed, is nothing less than a materialist theory of the making of the human subject."

The book's style is blunt, colloquial, and witty, with occasional outright laughs, rare enough in literary theory. Deconstructionists, says Eagleton, can only talk endlessly about the failure of language, "like some barroom bore." Needling Eliot's doctrine of the dissociation of sensibility, he observes that after the seventeenth century, "thinking was no longer like smelling." . . .

He argues that there are insoluble theoretical problems in demarcating "Literature" off from the rest of writing. Does he then suggest that the literature teachers disband and leave their offices to the engineers or the economists? Not exactly. He suggests instead that literary studies be dissolved into a wider field, which he would be happy to call "cultural studies," or analysis of "discursive practices" (after French historian Michel Foucault), or even old-fashioned "rhetoric." This new field of study would be free to analyze Milton's blank verse, but would be equally free to examine the way women are presented in advertising or the rhetorical techniques used in government reports. *Moby Dick*, the Muppets, John Dryden, and Jean-Luc Godard would all be fit objects for study.

These ideas are not all new. Some of Eagleton's critique of other theories has been anticipated by Fredric Jameson's Marxist attack on structuralism in *The Prison-House of Language,* for example, or by Frank Lentricchia's *After the New Criticism.* And at least since Roland Barthes published his series of *Mythologies* (brief newspaper analyses of everything from soap boxes to movie stars) the field of inquiry open to literary critics has been widening. Eagleton's book does what a good introduction should do—it synthesizes tendencies already in the air and makes them widely accessible in clear prose. (p. 5)

Literary Theory has, to begin with, the usual lure of summaries, the promise of a painless (and illusory) sense of mastery over difficult material. Who could resist the chance to understand post-structuralism by reading only 23 easy pages? And Eagleton's lucid style is easy, a feature which accounts for the books' usefulness as a school text, and thus for some of its high sales.

A book that treats these subjects so briefly (post-structuralism in 23 pages, phenomenology, hermeneutics, and reception theory in 37 pages) and in such a tone is bound to draw objections for failing to do justice to one theory or another. Thus, Denis Donoghue, writing in the *New York Review of Books* [see excerpt above] called Eagleton's first chapter "a dismissive and inaccurate account of Eliot, Leavis, [and] the work of *Scrutiny.*" David Van Leer, in *American Quarterly* conceded the difficulty of writing brief summaries, but said: "Even so, the dismissal of Heidegger—more for his politics than for his philosophy—will strike some readers as cavalier and uninformed."

Even when such objections are true, they seem beside the point. Eagleton may not mean to be uninformed, but he certainly intends to be provocative, and maybe even cavalier. I doubt very much that Eagleton wanted to "do justice" to the various theories competing under critical pluralism. It is Eagleton's strongly held point of view that gives the book its value, and makes it in fact a better introduction than a more "neutral" description of the various theories would be. A beginning reader of *Literary Theory* will see more clearly what is at stake in the choice of a literary theory, and will therefore understand more clearly what makes each of the theories distinctive.

Even in an avowedly Marxist book, this ease and enjoyability may be a sign of conservatism. As David Van Leer put it in *American Quarterly* " . . . the wise-cracking tone that Eagleton takes is, however indecorous, philosophically conservative, requiring a largely stable base to play off." Janet Montefiore, in *New Left Review,* adds the observation that while Eagleton proposes doing away with the canon of English literature, his book achieves its wide intelligibility partly by taking many of its examples from canonical authors like Shakespeare, George Herbert, the Brontës, and D. H. Lawrence.

The book can also be used as a club against "theory" and against what Walter Kendrick (*New York Times Book Review*) [see excerpt above] called "French invasions." Eagleton doesn't just summarize all those theories, he dismisses them, frankly calling his book an "obituary" for theory. Viewed as the revenge of Anglo-American common sense over Continental gibberish, *Literary Theory* can be embraced even by conservatives like John Bayley, who praised Eagleton's "lively and useful guidebook" in the *Times Literary Supplement* for its critique of "the chic stalls of contemporary critical fashion." Even among critics who resist any serious social change (and that's most of the critics writing in English today), there is a feeling that criticism and theory have gotten too far from social reality. The new theories are hard to explain to the public and nearly impossible to teach to undergraduates, inspiring a great longing to be able to talk again about "the world" as ordinary people understand it. I think this longing accounts for a good deal of interest in Marxism right now—paradoxically, it offers conservatives a way back to social reality, and masks that retreat as a hip new theory, not just a backward-looking denial. Critics with a slight headache from the thin atmosphere of deconstruction or advanced psychoanalysis may welcome what Walter Kendrick called Eagleton's "engagement with the real world."

For nonradical critics to embrace this engagement, though, a certain discounting of Eagleton's Marxist commitment is first necessary. Thus Kendrick decides that Republicans will be as welcome as Marxists and feminists in Eagleton's rhetoric department, and Bayley reassures himself that Eagleton "is not wholly serious in peddling Shakespeare as the class enemy." *Literary Theory* plays beautifully into this need by omitting any extended positive account of Marxism. Eagleton endorses both Marxism and feminism, but wants to avoid what he calls the "category mistake" of including them with other theories. They are not alternative literary theories, but alternatives to literary theory, so they don't get a chapter of their own. Marxism is used as a fulcrum to pry other theories out of place, but is left (pleasantly for some readers) open and unspecified. Readers of Eagleton's earlier books will have a good idea of his position, but his earlier books are not selling 20,000 each!

The omission of a detailed description of Eagleton's own position also accounts for some of the more serious objections reviewers made to *Literary Theory.* Denis Donoghue faulted the exemption granted Eagleton's own method, citing particularly the use of the term "history," which he found uncritical. Richard King, in *Kenyon Review,* [see Further Reading list], gave this objection a more explicit and Jamesonian formulation: "He never engages the line of reasoning which would see Marxism, for all its practice of the hermeneutics of suspicion, as a master narrative, one which envisions some sort of historical closure." Van Leer added that Eagleton's account suggests his own position is somehow independent of the notions of authority he critiques, but does not show this.

The feminism Eagleton endorses so strongly is, if anything, even less fully expressed than the Marxism, and feminist readers also registered disappointment. Janet Montefiore liked *Literary Theory* for the most part, but objected to the account of feminism and questioned whether a male critic could base his methodology on an oppression he had never experienced. (pp. 5-6)

Richard King calls Eagleton's omission of a positive account of his position an "evasion." I don't want to go this far, or to impugn Eagleton's motives. He has written an interesting and provocative book. But I do think the lack of an account of Marxism and feminism makes the book more palatable to its wide audience. Many of them don't like Continental theory, but will be horrified when their department someday offers "Cultural Studies 101: Images of Women in Late Capitalist Advertising." (p. 6)

Charles Sugnet, "Academic Class: Theories of the World, Unite!" in The American Book Review, *Vol. 7, No. 4, May-June, 1985, pp. 5-6.*

Bernard Bergonzi

Terry Eagleton's position as our top Marxist critic and literary theorist remains unchallenged. But in 1983 he reached the age of forty and thus joined what Péguy called *le parti des hommes de quarante ans,* membership of which is likely to complicate one's ideological stance. . . . This seems a good occasion on which to look back over his intellectual career, which though limited in location—being entirely confined to Cambridge and Oxford—has been marked by rapid movements between the many mansions in the spacious house of Marxist criticism.

The title of Eagleton's first book. *The New Left Church* (1966), recalls that he grew up as a Lancashire Catholic, and that as a young man he was a leading member of a group of left-wing Catholics whose commitment to social justice led them to attempt a fusion of Marxism and Catholicism, and who disseminated their ideas in the journal *Slant.* What began as an attempt at intellectual and practical co-operation between Catholics and Marxists ended as virtual absorption by the latter; at least, several onetime members of the *Slant* group are no longer Catholics. *The New Left Church* ambitiously draws together literary criticism, Catholic theology and liturgy, and Marxist political analysis. It is a very 1960s book in its easy eclecticism, where all sorts of names are cheerfully thrown into the pot: Marx, Sartre, Heidegger, Wittgenstein, Leavis, Laing, Raymond Williams. But for all the political and philosophical name-chasing, Eagleton's frame of reference is clearly literary-critical, heavily indebted to Leavis and to Raymond Williams, who was his supervisor at Cambridge. *The New Left Church,* though an immature book, provides early examples of Eagleton's basic qualities of mind. From the beginning he has been a fast, volatile thinker who leaps rapidly from idea to idea, or position to to position, without any indication of difficulty or of the obdurate way in which the world resists one's mental processes. (pp. 188-89)

Eagleton's early Catholic education at the De La Salle College, Pendleton, was an important formative factor. *The New Left Church* is the work of an orthodox Catholic, though it is noticeable that Christ is referred to much more often than God, and that Eagleton seems to regard Christ as in some sense a metaphor for humanity. More interesting, though, is his constant recourse to the analogical thinking characteristic of scholastic philosophy and traditional Catholic apologetics. Throughout his career Eagleton has been ready to regard analogies and parallels as having actual logical force. *The New Left Church* is pervaded with them, of which one sweeping example can suffice: 'What happens to money under capitalism is what happens to language in a symbolist poem, and to the eucharist in a ceremony like benediction.' (What happens in all these cases is the process of reification.) It is common enough for French or Italian Marxist intellectuals to have had a Catholic education in youth. Eagleton offers the much rarer example of an Englishman who has followed the same path. He shows how the subtle scholastic distinc-

tions of Catholic theology can be adapted to Marxist dialectic. (p. 189)

Eagleton's first book of literary criticism proper was *Shakespeare and Society,* published in 1967. It is dedicated to Raymond Williams, whose influence is rather fulsomely acknowledged. . . . *Shakespeare and Society* is a systematic application to a group of Shakespeare's plays of the argument in Williams's earlier books about the need to overcome our habitual belief in a necessary opposition between 'individual' and 'society'. Eagleton's treatment is both moralistic and schematic; Martin Green has summed up his view of *Hamlet* as 'Hamlet exemplifies a life-pattern we should avoid' and has dryly observed that in his treatment of *Anthony and Cleopatra* Eagleton wants to turn Cleopatras into bigger and better Octavias. *Shakespeare and Society* remains Eagleton's least interesting book.

It was followed in 1970 by another book of literary criticism, *Exiles and Emigrés: Studies in Modern Literature,* and a short work of religious and philosophical speculation, *Body as Language.* The latter contains Eagleton's last overtly Catholic writing. It shows the same energetic eclecticism as *The New Left Church,* lining up Catholicism, Marxism and phenomenology, but is subtler and generally less brash than the earlier book. It was considerably influenced by Fr Herbert McCabe, a left-wing Dominican theologian associated with the *Slant* group. Eagleton takes his taste for instant analogies to great lengths, notably in the chapter called 'Priesthood and Leninism', where he proposes an appropriate role-model for the Catholic priesthood in the Leninist ideal of a group of trained and dedicated revolutionaries who live among the people, sharing the privations of their daily lives, whilst leading and inspiring them in a revolutionary struggle. The idea that the local parish priest ought to see himself as a kind of guerilla leader or underground activist fighting the bourgeois world is piquant enough, but it raises the question of how far Eagleton wants such analogies to turn into actual identities. His thought often seems at the mercy of his intellectual models. (p. 190)

Body as Language points to a growing tension between Eagleton's Catholicism and his Marxism, which is emphasized rather than concealed by his ready recourse to ingenious analogies. He freely restates Christian concepts in Marxist language, as when he says of theology, in a dense burst of Lukácsian jargon: 'Its aim is nothing less than to become, at every changing historical moment, the "totality of totalities": the definitive totalization of the varied meanings of human history.' At some point after 1970 Eagleton appears to have abandoned Catholicism, though he has never publicly repudiated it. One can assume, though, that whereas a Catholic could have written *Exiles and Emigrés* and even *Myths of Power* (1975), the whole temper of *Criticism and Ideology* (1976) is irreconcilable with any form of religious commitment.

Lukács's concern with totalities and totalization pervades *Exiles and Emigrés,* though Lukács is not in fact mentioned in the book; the acknowledged influences are, again, Raymond Williams, and Perry Anderson's well-known essay, 'Components of the national culture'. Anderson argued that in the first half of the twentieth century the commanding heights of English intellectual culture had been taken over by Continental emigres, usually Austrians or Poles of conservative ideological views, such as Malinowski, Popper, Wittgenstein, Namier and Gombrich. Eagleton adapts this approach to the literary situation: 'With the exception of D. H. Lawrence, the heights of modern English literature have been dominated by foreigners and emigres: Conrad, James, Eliot, Pound, Yeats, Joyce.' And Lawrence, as a working-class Englishman, was scarcely less alien to the displaced hegemonic circles of the national culture. Their abdication is seen to indicate a deep-seated crisis and loss of nerve in English society in the early twentieth century: the Strange Death of Liberal England, in fact, completed by the First World War. *Exiles and Emigrés* can be recommended to students of modern literature for its value as provocation rather than as insight or understanding. Indeed, to try to see what is wrong with the book, what it leaves out and what it distorts, would not be a bad way of sharpening one's sense of the period. Eagleton's readings of modern English authors are brashly reductive, directed in all cases to probing for some significant trace of contradiction or ambiguity or ambivalence, which is homologous with the contradictions permeating the culture at large. Thus, Virginia Woolf sometimes satirizes and sometimes endorses English upperclass values; in Waugh there is a struggle between a sense of morality and a sense of style; Orwell shows an unresolved conflict 'between an impulse to lonely and defiant moral gesture and a sense of the collective decency of drably normative life'; Greene's Catholic orthodoxy is denied by a humanism which is itself affected by Catholic attitudes. It did not need the vogue of Deconstructionist criticism to tell us that conflict and ambiguity are features of many literary works that we admire, but Eagleton takes them as signs of fatal weakness, both ideological and personal. Now and then he goes beyond conflict-detection to a mode of vulgar-Marxism, as when he says of *Women in Love,* 'What is shown is the despairing vacuity of a particular group of bored middle-class intellectuals, hopelessly alienated from the concrete social realities they analyse at such length.' One does not have to be a Leavis to find this an absurdly inadequate account of a major modernist text. (pp. 191-92)

[*Myths of Power: A Marxist Study of the Brontës*] is one of Eagleton's best achievements in straightforward literary criticism. It makes one ask how far 'Marxist' readings of literature are necessarily dependent on the Marxist metaphysic of dialectic and class struggle and historical materialism. In this book Eagleton places the Brontës in a concrete historical context, as a group located between the gentry and the emergent industrial class of the West Yorkshire manufacturers. I find his approach often illuminating, and a useful corrective to the romantic individualism that dominates criticism of the Brontës. Eagleton develops this distinction with a free use of analogies and polarities: the opposition between old gentry and new bourgeoisie is paralleled by a succession of other oppositions located in the Brontë texts: 'past / future', 'imagination / society', 'fantasy / realism'. Eagleton uses them to look for some underlying grammar: 'The fundamental structure of Charlotte's novels is a triadic one: it is determined by a complex play of power-relations between a protagonist, a "romantic-radical" and an aristocratic conservative.' The objections to this kind of analysis are familiar and are often made; that it is abstract and schematic and adds nothing to our appreciation of the unique literary work. To speak for myself I find the uncovering of such family resemblances more helpful than not, as opposed to the at-

omistic examination of one discrete text after another. But the only point I want to make now is that this is a critical debate which can be conducted without much overt or prolonged reference to ideology. To write the kind of criticism in *Myths of Power* one needs a good understanding of social history and a taste for analogies and homologies; one does not absolutely need to be a Marxist. Indeed, much of the criticism in this book is at bottom quite traditional, concerned with the interactions of character and theme, and the accent is as much Leavisite as Marxist. In so far as there is a conceptually Marxist element in *Myths of Power* it is derived from that heterodox Marxist, Lucien Goldmann. Eagleton takes from Goldmann the idea of 'categorial structure', which is described as 'a primary mediation between the novel and society, a crucial nexus between the fiction and history'. Goldmann's 'categorial structure' has many affinities with Raymond Williams's 'structure of feeling'. Eagleton points out that his 'admiration for Goldmann's work is laced with strong reservations'. However strong these reservations, there is no doubt that 'categorial structure' is a fundamental concept in *Myths of Power:* 'Text, author, ideology, social class, productive forces: these are the terms I shall seek to bring together, by the mediating concept of categorial structure.'

Marxism and Literary Criticism is a brief, lucid, dogmatic introduction, comprising four essays on major aspects of Marxist criticism, together with a fighting preface warning off academics who think that 'Marxist criticism' is just one more method to be ranged on the shelf alongside Freudian Criticism or myth criticism. (The vehemence with which Eagleton, who has spent his whole life as an academic, excoriates other academics is a notable feature of his writing). . . . *Marxism and Literary Criticism* exemplifies one of Eagleton's strongest qualities, his capacity for the clear exposition of complex ideas. Inevitably the summary implies the author's attitude of acceptance or rejection, and there is a good deal of rejection in this book, notably of Lukács and Goldmann, to whom Eagleton had been indebted in his preceding books of criticism. Eagleton's impatience with Lukács is now evident. Many of Lukacs's intellectual and personal positions are, of course, vulnerable to attack, whether from a Marxist or 'bourgeois' position, given the contradictions between the trimmer and the dedicated intellectual. In Eagleton's book Lukács is criticized for being more Hegelian than Marxist, and condemned for his conservative literary tastes and for his bourgeois ideas about the nature of the aesthetic. With Brecht set up as an opposing figure, Lukács is found wanting on many counts. Eagleton is even more severe about Goldmann; he is denounced for holding a concept of social consciousness that is more Hegelian than Marxist and thus seeing too direct and undialectical a relation between social consciousness and literary text. In saying this, Eagleton is implicitly rejecting the approach he had employed with some effectiveness in *Myths of Power.* (pp. 192-94)

There are favourable references in *Marxism and Literary Criticism* to Louis Althusser and Althusser's disciple, Pierre Macherey. In *Criticism and Ideology,* the much more substantial book published in the same year, Eagleton emerges as a committed Althusserian, give or take a few reservations. The Althusserian moment in English Marxism might be described as a storm in a doll's teacup, given the small number of people, even on the left, who knew anything about it. Yet for a few years in the seventies the impact of Althusser generated much bitter debate among Marxist intellectuals. . . . Although he has by now implicitly or explicitly repudiated much of [*Criticism and Ideology*] it remains the work which established his international reputation as that rare creature, an English Marxist intellectual. This role is one that Eagleton has consciously accepted for himself. (pp. 194-95)

The defiantly abstract and theoretical nature of *Criticism and Ideology* is apparent in its chapter headings: 'Mutations of critical ideology', 'Categories for a materialist criticism', 'Towards a science of the text', 'Ideology and literary form', 'Marxism and aesthetic value'. The rebarbative note is, no doubt, a deliberate affront to the qualities associated with traditional literary criticism: humanism, empiricism, aestheticism. At the same time, there is a faint hint of parody about the book, as if Eagleton were not so much producing a stern, 'scientific' Althusserian treatise as a very accomplished imitation of one. This is particularly evident in the second chapter, where he states: 'It is possible to set out in schematic form the major constituents of a Marxist theory of literature.' They prove to be six in number: General Mode of Production (GMP); Literary Mode of Production (LMP); General Ideology (GI); Authorial Ideology (AuI); Aesthetic Ideology (AI); Text. Having launched these symbols Eagleton proceeds to play Space Invaders with them for the remainder of the chapter: 'A double-articulation GMP/ GI-GI / AI / LMP is, for example, possible, whereby a GI category when transformed by AI into an ideological component of an LMP, may then enter onto conflict with the GMP social relations it exists to reproduce.' Once the game is under way, there is no reason why it should ever end. My difficulty is in telling just how serious Eagleton is in large parts of *Criticism and Ideology.* Assuming that he is indeed (or was at the time) wholly committed to the truth of what he writes, much of the book provides an extreme instance of his tendency, already evident in his early Catholic writings, to find in words, signs and concepts, not uncertain pointers to reality, but reality itself.

Not all of the book is so perversely expressed. In so far as there is an argument in it, coherently developed in words, it directs itself to the literary text as something placed midway between 'ideology' and 'science'. The critical enterprise is seen, following Macherey as tracing and opening up the gaps and absences in a text, so that it may symptomatically reveal the ideological forces which produced it and which it endeavours to conceal (in this kind of discourse texts not authors are the active elements). Eagleton does not wholly throw overboard his abilities as a literary critic, and the chapter called 'Ideology and literary form' contains a series of short essays on nineteenth and twentieth-century English writers. These symptomatic readings are uncompromising in method and terminology; yet Eagleton thows out sufficiently arresting or challenging remarks about his subjects to give one some new ideas about them. (pp. 195-97)

In 1976 Eagleton undertook the repudiation of various critics who had previously influenced him, such as Lukács and Goldmann. In *Criticism and Ideology* he devotes twenty pages to a polite but pained exposure of the errors and inadequacies of his former mentor Raymond Wil-liams, who had been a dominant presence in Eagleton's early books. The demolition begins with generous but ritual praise—Williams has produced 'the most suggestive and intricate body of socialist criticism in English history', for which there is no available English parallel, and which must be placed for comparative assessment alongside the work of Lukács, Benjamin or Goldmann (though in this phase of Eagleton's development invocation of Lukács or Goldmann seems back-handed praise). After this friendly opening gesture Eagleton warms to his task and demonstrates that Williams's work is marred by Romantic populism, idealist epistemology, organicist aesthetics and corporatist sociology. His development as a critic of the left has been gravely hampered by his theoretical thinness and intellectual provincialism. In his attachment to personal experience and the concrete empirical response he is still unhappily influenced by his Leavisite origins. Eagleton concludes by comparing Williams not only to Leavis but to Lukács; and this time the comparison is not meant to be honorific.

It is an understatement to say that *Criticism and Ideology* is a bold book. Unrelenting in its scorn of 'bourgeois' attitudes and beliefs, it is equally harsh about much of the cultural thinking of the left. It is not altogether surprising, therefore, that the severest treatment of the book that I have come across is not by a 'bourgeois' critic, but by another Marxist, Kiernan Ryan, in a review-article on Eagleton's three books of 1975-6 published in the West German Marxist review, *Gulliver.* Though critical of the book on the Brontës, Ryan finds much to admire in it; but he is strong in his condemnation of *Marxism and Literary Criticism* and *Criticism and Ideology.* Ryan gives Eagleton credit for having energetically provoked debate about Marxist approaches to literature, then adds, 'But insofar as his work has at the same time moved increasingly towards the kind of anti-humanism and theoretical elitism so characteristic of Althusserian intellectuals it must also be strongly criticized as the dehumanized literary history of a dehumanized Marxism.' Ryan, writing as a Marxist humanist, is scandalized by Eagleton's attacks on Lukács and Williams and what he regards as the Althusserian technologizing of intellectual discussion. He concludes his account of *Marxism and Literary Criticism* with these words:

> The fully dehumanized, technologist approach to literature to which this book implicitly points is realized all too successfully in the thoroughly alienated, elitist theoreticism of Eagleton's latest book, the arid and opaque *Criticism and Ideology.* Its main virtue is as a warning of the cold dead end to which the Althusserian road invariably leads; theory, declutching from any meaningful sense of praxis, spins on furiously but vainly in a self-generating void.

Writing as a 'bourgeois' critic, I find Ryan's eloquent denunciation very much to the point; 'arid and opaque' is a fair description of *Criticism and Ideology.* Ryan is particularly telling in his comments on Eagleton's compulsive use of the word 'ideology': 'continually invoked but never clearly enough defined to be very meaningful, the term begins to sweat blood from all the duty it has to do.' However much Eagleton has now moved on from the positions in *Criticism and Ideology* his use of that word still deserves Ryan's criticism. 'Ideology' is a valuable concept in intellectual discourse, and not only for Marxists. But it is inevitably complex and ambiguous, as many Marxists have realized.

In *Marxism and Literature* Raymond Williams grapples with the term in his thoughtful, characteristically dense fashion, and offers three different definitions: (1) a system of beliefs characteristic of a class or group; (2) a system of illusory beliefs—false ideas or false consciousness—which can be contrasted with true or scientific knowledge; (3) the general process of the production of ideas and meanings. Eagleton's loose but compulsive use of the term tends to be restricted to Williams's second sense, and at weak points in an argument he reaches for it with the automatized gesture of a heavy smoker lighting up one more cigarette. Eagleton evidently sees ideology, as Eliot said of Pound's hell, as being for other people. The privileged Althusserian critic is assumed to wear a kind of gas-mask to protect him from the prevailing cloud of ideological contamination; or, to switch the metaphor, he keeps within a magic circle where he is safe from harm. As Eagleton puts it, 'criticism must break with its ideological prehistory, situating itself outside the space of the text on the alternative terrain of scientific knowledge.' Ryan insists that the idea of such a safe terrain is illusory: 'the notion of a privileged "neutral" domain of scientific knowledge "beyond ideology" is a positivist fantasy.' The same passage from Eagleton has come under attack from a different quarter; Christopher Norris has shown how Eagleton is imprisoned by his visual and spatial metaphors.

Perhaps in response to such attacks, Eagleton decided within a few years that the Althusserian territory he had moved into in *Criticism and Ideology* was no longer tenable and must be evacuated. (pp. 197-99)

Eagleton's new bearings emerged in 1981, with *Walter Benjamin or Towards a Revolutionary Criticism,* which contains elements of a muffled retraction: 'the book marks a development from my *Criticism and Ideology* . . . which was less overtly political and more conventionally academic in style and form.' Certainly *Walter Benjamin* seems much more the work of a human being; after the computerized dogmatism of its predecessor, it is personal, self-reflective and dialectical (the last concept meaning that contradictory propositions can both be true if one wants them to). It is also a more directly political book, considerably influenced by feminism and in particular by the political model offered by feminist criticism. I do not feel competent to discuss the book's central argument, which is that Walter Benjamin, far from being the marginalized Marxist intellectual and aesthetician of customary 'bourgeois' accounts, in fact shows the way for a truly revolutionary criticism. In Eagleton's new phase Althusser and Macherey, though not totally dismissed, are less favourably regarded than Benjamin and Brecht and Bakhtin. The book also contains partial rehabilitations of critics who had been roughly handled by Eagleton in the intellectual purges of 1976. (p. 200)

In his next book, *The Rape of Clarissa,* Eagleton returned to more or less straightforward literary criticism. This is a generally excellent—and very readable—short study of Richardson, in which Marxism no longer holds the stage alone but is harnessed in a troika with psychoanalysis and feminism. Richardson is an author of both psychological and social-historical interest, being at the same time a kind

of proto-feminist and a master-printer who moved into literary production. Eagleton's book is full of incidental insights and provocations, but what it essentially does is to offer new arguments for an old (and valid) case: that *Clarissa* is a great novel. Like the book on the Brontës, *The Rape of Clarissa,* despite its sophistication, presents a traditional approach; the reading of Richardson is basically in terms of characters and author-psychology. In so far as Marxism now coexists with, or is diluted with, psychoanalysis the book might well be a source of suspicion to ideological hard-liners. Marxists' traditional opposition to Freudian ideas has always struck me as quite justified, given their premises. In so far as *The Rape of Clarissa* does make use of a Marxist frame of references, it raises, as did *Myths of Power,* the question of how far its critical insights actually depend on Marxist presuppositions. (p. 201)

Literary Theory: An Introduction . . . offers a remarkable combination of good and bad qualities. Like *The Rape of Clarissa* it is clearly and vigorously written, which is in itself a problemetical element; lucidity and ease of communication are regarded in some Marxist quarters as ideologically suspect, since they fit altogether too neatly and smoothly into the system of capitalist cultural dissemination. . . . At its best *Literary Theory* is an admirable example of *haute vulgarisation.* Eagleton, with his insatiable appetite for ideas, has read very widely in recent work in literary theory and shows an impressive capacity to summarize much abstruse and knotty material in a lucid, lively, sometimes slangy way.

The middle chapters of the book, 'Phenomenology, hermeneutics, reception theory', 'Structuralism and semiotics', 'Post-Structuralism', 'Psychoanalysis', can be recommended to the intelligent enquirer who wants to have some idea of the subjects of recent arguments and to know what, roughly, is now going on in literary studies. These chapters do not attempt to conceal their bias, and are full of coat-trailing remarks, jokes, and assorted raillery and jeers. On the whole, these things do not much disrupt a reasonably fair and straightforward exposition. In the opening and concluding sections of the book, however, Eagleton's tendentiousness becomes confused and misleading. The opening chapter, 'What is literature?' dwells at length on the problem of adequately defining literature. As a concept it is, of course, notoriously hard to pin down. Eagleton makes much of the fact that some kinds of writing—philsophy, historiography, religious discourse—can be treated as literature, even though they were written as something else. From this fact, and the indisputable further fact that all attempts at formal definition of literature are partial and inadequate, Eagleton tries to conclude that there is no such thing; or almost so. At the end of the Introduction he writes, 'What we have uncovered so far, then, is that literature does not exist in the sense that insects do.' Many things, it seems to me, do not exist 'in the sense that insects do', like love or justice or music or the labour theory of value or the Catholic Church. Yet we do not conclude that they do not exist. At the end of the book the insects have been dropped, and Eagleton writes, 'I began this book by arguing that literature does not exist.' Eagleton may have tried to argue that case, but he certainly hasn't established it. The real problems of defining literature are better met, I think, not by saying that there is no such thing, but by seeing it in terms of W. B. Gallie's discussion in *Philosophy and the Historical Understanding* of 'essentially contested concepts'. This approach might help one to cope with some perennial problems in literary debate, such as how far 'literature' is a wholly honorific term, as Leavisites would claim, or a wholly descriptive one as the Russian Formalists believed. Eagleton can only offer assertive obfuscation of this genuinely difficult question.

He puts up a stiff resistance to the idea of literature as specifically aesthetic discourse. This is partly, one imagines, a matter of individual psychology, but it is also a characteristic of the generation of neo-Marxists who have been affected by Althusserianism. . . . However much Eagleton has shifted from his Althusserian stance the approach to literature in **Literary Theory** is still symptomatic rather than aesthetic or affective. . . . To have no aesthetic sense, or to have had one and deliberately extirpated it for a political end, is clearly a misfortune. But strange things can happen to a consciousness which is convinced that the class struggle lies at the heart of reality. The impression one gets from Eagleton's copious writings is of a sensibility that engages exclusively with words and ideas. He is widely read not only in literature and criticism, but also in theology and philosophy and politics; he has not, however, betrayed any interest in painting or music, architecture or landscape.

The conceptually incoherent introduction to **Literary Theory** is followed by a chapter called 'The rise of English', which surveys the nineteenth-century events leading to the establishment of 'English' as a major academic subject. This consideration of origins is worth undertaking, since it can help one to understand the much-discussed present crisis in English studies. Eagleton looks at the many strands that went to make up 'English'. There was the need to find a humane study that was available to more readers than Latin and Greek literature, particularly to women and to the increasingly better educated working class. Another strand was the cultural nationalism that emphasized the English heritage, closely entwining literature and history, and which left its great linguistic monument in the *Oxford English Dictionary*. Added to these was the moralistic search for a substitute for traditional religion which found its goal in literature; in this aspect of the subject there is a clear continuity from Arnold to the 'Newbolt Report' on the teaching of English in 1921, and then on to Leavis and *Scrutiny*. Eagleton covers all this ground rapidly and lucidly and much of the chapter is usefully informative. His overarching assumption, that the whole process was a capitalist conspiracy to keep the lower classes in line, is unconvincing enough to be ignored. (pp. 202-04)

In the concluding chapter Eagleton argues, quite sensibly, for a revival of the ancient discipline of rhetoric, so that any piece of writing, indeed, any semiotic system, can be analysed in order to see how it works and to what end. The value of rhetorical understanding has always been one of the unacknowledged bases of 'English' (along with the aesthetic and the cultural-nationalist) and there is nothing very new in the idea that the skills involved in the close reading of a literary text might well be directed at other kinds of text. As it happens, departments of rhetoric are well established in leading American universities. Eagle-

ton makes good sense in what he advocates here, even if he is to some extent pushing at an open door.

Most of the chapter, though, is engaged in re-enacting and extending the confusions of the opening chapter: literature and literary theory don't really exist; nevertheless, for many purposes it is convenient to talk about them as if they do exist. Eagleton argues that the theories and approaches examined in the preceeding chapters are really political, whatever they present themselves as, and more often than not political in unacceptable ways. Eagleton's argument takes a predictable turn here: to say that a literary theory is 'really' political sounds as if one is attributing an essential quality to it, whereas a simple tautology applies, in that everything is political for those who have decided to see everything as political. Foucault is an underlying presence in this final chapter; Eagleton regards literary discourse, like all discourse, as fundamentally about power. But Foucault's idea of how power operates, in so far as I understand it, seems to me closer to Hobbes than to Marx; everyone is trying to exercise power over everyone else, all the time. . . . As the chapter unfolds Eagleton unveils an Althusserian argument: 'Departments of literature in higher education, then, are part of the ideological apparatus of the modern capitalist state.' Eagleton adds that this particular apparatus does not work very efficiently, since literary study can inculcate quite other values than those of the dominant society (one of the traditional defences of 'English' as a source of value). To this extent the capitalist state is spending a lot of money for no very sure return. There is also the consideration that graduates in English are not at all well placed for getting good jobs in the power-holding ranks of society and thus reinforcing the dominant ideology. But Eagleton tends to be at a loss when his ideas impinge on current social and political realities. Having looked forward to the prospect that departments of literature as we know them might cease to exist he acknowledges that such an eventuality might well be in line with current official thinking; so, 'it is necessary to add that the first political priority for those who have doubts about the ideological implications of such departmental organizations is to defend them unconditionally against government assaults.' Eagleton has got himself into a difficulty here, but it is an understandable one. The coincidence in time of doubts and debates about literary study with the Thatcherite combination of sado-monetarism and crass philistine populism may not be accidental; it may well be a sign of an underlying loss of nerve. Leavis, in his day, provided a powerful and compelling rationale for 'English', which is now pretty well exhausted; the fashionable derivatives from Formalism and structuralism offer an intense but narrow interest, directed at professionals rather than the broad readership envisaged in the early years of English as a discipline. Eagleton has focused on a real and urgent problem, though his own solution of a totally politicized criticism is not likely to appeal widely, either theoretically or practically.

For all his advocacy of the primacy of politics and his jeers at liberal-humanist compromises, Eagleton remains, deep down, a literary critic in a traditional mould, much influenced by the Leavisite atmosphere of Cambridge in the early 1960s. It shows in his language, as when he unfavourably compares what he calls the abstract democracy of the ballot box with 'specific, living and practical democracy'; it is interesting that this phrase slips in after much previous condemnation in Eagleton's writing of the empirical critic's opposition between the 'abstract' (bad) and the 'specific and living' (good); Eagleton treats this opposition as highly ideological and mystificatory, but it is still at the roots of his own thinking. Similarly, he has devoted much space and energy to attacking the 'organic' approach to literary texts, which finds ultimate value in unity and the reconciliation of opposites. If one regards the text as an analogue of society 'organic' readings will paper over the cracks which ought to reveal the naked class struggle. Nevertheless, Eagleton's own conception of a political criticism is inspired by a kind of moral organicism, which wants everything in society to relate to everything else, so that activities like reading literature can be directly connected to social struggles. It is, perhaps, a scandal, though not a new one, that some people should write poetry or read it or write about it or teach it, while other people are starving or homeless or in prison or undergoing torture. If one finds the scandal unbearable one can give up literature and devote oneself wholly to political activity or social reform; that is a possible and honourable course. But to insist on a quasi-organic yoking together of the cultural and the political is to distort both activities. Eagleton's likely rejoinder, that there is no difference between them, requires far more solid argument than he has ever found it necessary to produce. To say, as he has done on occasion, that everything is political, is to deny the term any differentiating force or real meaning: if everything is political then nothing is. In rejecting Eagleton's political organicism, I am included to take over his own Althusserian way of looking at texts and apply it to civilization itself, which is riven with gaps and fissures and contradictions, though they reveal not the ultimate fact of the class struggle, but the familiar spectacle of human villainy and folly. Eagleton quotes Walter Benjamin's famous dictim, 'There is no cultural document that is not at the same time a record of barbarism.' I am inclined to agree with this, assuming it is a proposition that asks to be agreed with; Auden expressed something similar in 'Museé des Beaux Arts'. But I cannot deduce any specific political programme from Benjamin's words, nor see them as a recommendation for tearing up cultural documents.

Leszek Kolakowski, who was toiling at the coal-face of Marxist thought when Eagleton was still absorbing Catholic apologetics at De La Salle College, has summarized the organicist appeal of Marxism: 'Marxism has been the greatest fantasy of our century. It was a dream offering the prospect of a society of perfect unity, in which all human aspirations would be fulfilled and all values reconciled.' In addition to this fantasy, Marxism offers a system of scholastic complexity and rigour, which also provides opportunities for the dialectical play of mind. Such a system is obviously attractive to a voracious intellectual like Eagleton, who was previously trained in an earlier scholastic system and who thinks readily in models and categories and analogies. Yet, within the framework of a broad Marxist allegiance, Eagleton's development has been mercurial, rapidly reactive, and impelled by a series of partial self-repudiations. At the same time, his own uncertainties and shifts of position have never prevented him from dismissing, confidently and aloofly, the liberal-humanist critics whom he sees as caught up in soft-headed woolliness and confusion, in contrast to the 'scientific' rigour of Marxist thought (this, again, is a variant of traditional Catholic rhetoric). I must declare an interest here, having myself

been thus categorized by Eagleton, and placed in the distinguished company of what he calls 'the Kermode/Lodge/Bergonzi/Bradbury establishment of liberal-empiricist aesthetics. . . .'

Eagleton has stayed with Marxism longer than many of the people who were drawn to it in the sixties. In France a whole generation of intellectuals has abandoned Marxist allegiance, and compared with twenty years ago Marxism seems to have run out of conviction, even though no Western intellectual can disregard its influence. . . . A proper scepticism about political claims has always seemed appropriate as an attitude for literary critics. How Eagleton will move on from this interesting historical and personal juncture is unpredictable. Despite himself, he has become a familiar English type, an Establishment radical; and, as I have suggested, his current combination of Marxism with psychoanalysis and feminism may lead him towards an intellectual eclecticism that he would once have found unacceptable. Eagleton is an important enough public figure, as critic and intellectual, to deserve discussion at some length; though how far his importance is symptomatic and how far it is intrinsic is a matter for very fine discrimination. (pp. 205-09)

Bernard Bergonzi, "The Terry Eagleton Story," in his The Myth of Modernism and Twentieth Century Literature, *The Harvester Press, Sussex, 1986, pp. 188-209.*

John Lucas

In an essay [in *Against the Grain: Selected Essays, 1975-1985*] called **"The Idealism of American Criticism"**, Terry Eagleton compares the state of literary theory in America and in England. His conclusion is that they manage these things far better in the United States. Raymond Williams was "only in his very early writing a 'literary critic' ", and if you leave him aside who, apart from Frank Kermode and George Steiner, can be set against "Ransom, Poulet, Krieger, Hirsch, de Man and Bloom (to give a mere handful of salient names)?" An English reader's first response to this is likely to be one of rueful agreement. The second will in all probability involve the search for an explanation. America is simply bigger and so has more of everything, including literary theory. Besides, it is easier for American academics to discover funding bodies who will give them the leisure and money they need if they are to write.

And at this point the reader may well be pulled up short. For of course what Eagleton is essentially talking about is literary theory as an academic pursuit. In other words, he tacitly accepts a particular kind of institutionalizing of such theory. This may seem unfair. After all, in the essay **"Liberality and Order: The Criticism of John Bayley,"** he attacks the double life of certain well-known members of English academies whose "racy iconoclasm" as literary journalists "contrasts tellingly with the bland caution of their scholarly productions". But then such academics aren't theorists: "Intellectual seriousness is reserved for the editing of texts; criticism functions as a little light relief from such sober enterprises." I do not suggest that Eagleton would prefer that the editing of texts should be light relief; but he certainly sees theory as a sober enterprise. It is this which leads him to promote academic literary theory at the expense of any other, this which is the justification for being an academic. And the narrowing of focus involved in this becomes apparent once you realize that he takes no account of, among others, Jack Lindsay, John Berger or Adrian Stokes, all of whom in the course of their working lives have advanced theoretical statements which are of considerably more value than those associated with the frequently modish names whose work is examined in *Against the Grain.*

Eagleton is one of a number of critics and theorists on the left who have necessarily drawn attention to improper or at least ideologically-based privileging of certain authors and texts. Yet his own procedure, while scrupulously critical of the authors he writes about, nevertheless privileges them because it takes for granted their ultimate worth. The first essay in this collection is on the work of **"Macherey and Marxist Literary Theory"**. But Macherey's theory of the text seems far less fruitful than Jack Lindsay's, as that is worked out in much of his writing. And one does not have to agree with Donald Davie's politics or his view of Pound to think that his *Ezra Pound: Poet as Sculptor,* which makes excellent use of some of Adrian Stokes's ideas, is more deeply suggestive about problems to do with modernism than is the work of Frederic Jameson, to which Eagleton devotes a good deal of space. Perhaps neither Lindsay nor Davie is theoretical enough for Eagleton, but it is difficult to see in what ways the abstractions of Macherey and Jameson are of much use in grappling with the nature and status of literary texts. Thus Eagleton's essay **"Capitalism, Modernism and Postmodernism"** takes its cue from a remark of Jameson's, and as a result gets into all kinds of difficulty. According to Jameson, "modernism was born at a stroke with mass commodity culture". Eagleton's argument, conducted it must be said with exemplary clarity, is that modernist works wish to "fend off" reduction to commodity status, but the very ways in which they strive to become unavailable or unassimilable make it possible for them to be turned into "commodity as fetish". Postmodernism is then the acceptance of this fetishism, and indeed postmodernist art actively conspires in accepting its "ephemeral function" as "this or that act of consumption".

An initial problem with this argument is that mass commodity culture begins well before modernism. What else was Ruskin writing about in *The Nature of Gothic* or Veblen characterizing as conspicuous consumption? Far from placing modernism securely within history, as Eagleton seems to think, Jameson's approach is nearly as vague and idealist as (say) Wellek's theory of Romanticism. So is Eagleton's, because it depends on an entirely abstract claim that modernist art is identifiable through its ironic withdrawal, its would-be refusal of its commodity status. At one point he becomes uneasy over this and, with Brecht in mind, says that there "is indeed a political modernism . . . but it is hardly characteristic of *the movement as a whole*". (My italics.) This begs the question of whether there is any such movement, rather than a number of works and authors which, as Alfred Kazin has recently suggested, have been given undue prominence. It is also decidedly odd. For who comprises this movement? Yeats? Eliot? Pound? Lawrence? Eagleton may not like their politics but to deny that they were often overtly political seems taking things too far. . . .

Eagleton has an excellent essay on **"Form, Ideology and The Secret Agent"** in which he identifies its self-contradictory character as arising from "the internal conflicts of the Conradian ideology—a form of 'metaphysical' conservatism equally hostile to petit-bourgeois myopia and revolutionary astigmatism". And that he doesn't think we should be neutral about this is clear from another essay, **"The Critic as Clown"**, where he remarks that "a nineteenth-century irrationalist current . . . emerges at its most disreputable in such writers as Conrad". Once you make this kind of distinction and you cannot securely hold on to Jameson's totalizing claim that we are all postmodernists now. (And again, of course, the uselessly vague nature of the claim makes it impossible to know what postmodernist works are like, and therefore which works we can argue are not postmodernist.)

As it happens, Eagleton sidesteps many of the problems he sets himself, partly out of genuine intellectual nimbleness, partly by not stopping for an answer, and partly because his way of writing makes it difficult to be sure where he actually stands on any particular issue or argument. In his spry tribute to William Empson, he remarks that " 'irony' is the device whereby the modern bourgeois critic can at once collude with and privately disown the ideological imperatives of the modern state". I do not know whether he would want those words to apply to himself, but there is something ironic about calling your collection *Against the Grain* and then characterizing your ideological opposite, John Bayley, as exercising power "in a literary world where others of his sensibility and 'social tone' are undoubtedly marginal". Marginal to what? (p. 731)

John Lucas, "Irony of Ironies," in The Times Literary Supplement, *No. 4344, July 4, 1986, p. 731.*

Geoff Dyer

Less than a month after the defeat of the Easter Rising in Dublin, James Connolly was executed in Kilmainham gaol on 12 May 1916. In Terry Eagleton's novel [*Saints and Scholars*], however, Connolly dodges the hail of bullets and escapes to a cottage on the West Coast of Ireland.

There he runs into Ludwig Wittgenstein who, in his relentless asceticism (he once said he could eat anything as long as it was always the same thing) remains at once one of the most unremittingly serious and inherently comic men of the century. With him in the cottage is his friend from Cambridge, Nikolai Bakhtin, brother of the famous Marxist aesthetician. In the middle of a developing three-way debate on language and revolution they are disturbed by the bewildered Leopold Bloom from *Ulysses* who then takes his place in this fortuitous meeting that history neglected to convene. Now all of this is reminiscent of Tom Stoppard's *Travesties,* of course. The important question is how well the idea works on paper as opposed to on stage.

At least part of Eagleton's considerable and deserved reputation has been built on a rare talent for provocative synopses of the complexities of critical theory. In his first work of fiction that skill is so pronounced as to have resulted in a new literary form that might be called the synoptic novel. Over half the book is taken up with epigramatic summaries of the historical forces which have converged on the characters. . . . Unfortunately much of the action of the novel feels . . . summarised rather than realised. Not only are the characters' actual words intercalated ingeniously and easily into the text (no complaints about that) but, true to the synoptic urge, much of what they say and do is mediated through the words of others: 'I can't go on, I'll go on,' reflects Connolly before the firing squad; two out of three of Bakhtin's mistresses turn out to be police informers. 'It seemed a reasonable percentage,' notes Eagleton. In both cases the nod, this time towards Beckett, is reflexive and pointless. You rarely feel that the characters are doing things so much as that they are being described doing them. (p. 28)

There is a lack, in other words, of traditional novelistic skills: the imbuing of characters with an independent and tactile existence, the palpable creation of an imagined reality and so on. Qualities like these inevitably recall the critical prerogatives of F. R. Leavis and John Bayley, both of whom Eagleton has taken so brilliantly to task elsewhere, but, simply on the level of technique, they seem to me indispensable to the work of the novelist.

Questions of technique lead inevitably to questions of form and the real difficulty with *Saints and Scholars* is that the internal dynamics of the book do not adequately insist that it should have achieved this form rather than some other; the material of the book doesn't demand the form it has taken. The passages on Vienna could as easily have found their way on to the small screen as commentary for a documentary on Karl Kraus and his world. As for the passage where Leopold Bloom explains that Molly has gone off with Stephen Dedalus . . . well, that kind of thing is better left for Oxford revues.

Having said all this, there is no other academic in Britain whose fiction I would have read so eagerly. Perhaps it is now historically impossible for major imaginative writing to be created from within the academy. (pp. 28-9)

> *Geoff Dyer, "Critical State," in* New States-man, *Vol. 114, No. 2945, September 4, 1987, pp. 28-9.*

Scott L. Malcomson

"If salvation lay anywhere it lay in the word, but the word had to be its own reality. . . . There was nothing behind it." Terry Eagleton places this despairing conclusion in the mind of James Connolly, Irish revolutionary, poet, and organizer, as he awaits arrest following the Easter Rising. It's an odd statement to find near the end of a lyrical novel [*Saints and Scholars*] devoted to the ideas behind words. Eagleton seems to say: Now that you've eaten the sacrament of my text, I can tell you it's nothing but a tasteless wafer. Such are the meager rewards of postmodern authorship.

The premise of *Saints and Scholars* is like a Cambridge version of the old civics class gambit: write 10 double-spaced pages on what would happen if Washington and Lincoln met at Plymouth Rock for a drink. Think of the crazy things they'd say! Eagleton puts Ludwig Wittgenstein and Nikolai Bakhtin (Mikhail's brother) in a remote cottage on the west coast of Ireland, then throws in Con-

nolly and, toward the end, Leopold Bloom. Bertrand Russell also has a cameo. That Terry Eagleton, what a lunatic!

Eagleton's characters do say crazy things. They even do crazy things. Wittgenstein declaims while lying on the carpet, Bloom tries to sleep in a garbage can. Amid these high jinks, the great ideas of the 20th century are considered and more or less demolished. Wittgenstein makes the philosophy-is-totalitarian-madness argument. Bakhtin is there to argue for the importance of the body, the indifference of history, and situationism generally. . . .

Saints and Scholars is a comic opera designed to lampoon modernism's miserable stasis. That's right, it's the death throes of Meaning. Like any postmodern text, *Saints and Scholars* is about modernism and history's fall from grace. We're talking about time and human destiny here, which can be summed up in three sentences (don't wait for the video): Society tottered along in the grip of medieval community until the Enlightenment, when people became individuals, time became linear, and ideas became competitive. Then, roughly after World War I, it emerged that any totality (Smith, Marx) would always be totalitarian. We've all been quivering pluralistically since then, fingering our guns, waiting for a sign from the People.

Eagleton's diagram of history is good for a few smug laughs. And, in fairness, the lilting style is often a pleasure. His critical prose has always been graceful; the language of his fiction can be exhilarating. . . .

The real interest of *Saints and Scholars,* however, lies not in its pretty language and familiar ideas, but in the sinister glimmers of meaning that remain on the floor after Eagleton's postmod vacuum cleaner has supposedly sucked them all away. It's as if the destruction of meaning has left a void that only prejudice can fill. When his own voice takes over from his characters', Eagleton holds onto class caricatures, racism, and female essence as lonely rafts in the indeterminate ocean. The *bas peuple* come in for some heavy slanging as primitives who cannot see beyond their mouths and their genitals. "In the cottages and tenements people cursed and promised, wept and copulated, living hand-to-mouth without absolutes. It was this, not mathematics, which was the ultimate beauty. There was nothing beneath it; it was what it was." This endearing grunt-and-snort lifestyle, of course, has its down side; the beasts just can't be moved to *do* anything. As Bakhtin says, "The people want carnival, not collective farms; they know the only lasting revolution is one of the flesh."

"The flesh," apart from romanticized prole sensuality, takes on two other forms: race and sex. Even accounting for a certain purple irony, Eagleton's descriptions of St. Petersburg and Ireland are poetic masterpieces of ethno-political stereotype. . . .

Women play only an incidental role in *Saints and Scholars* until its conclusion, when "the enigma of women" makes an appearance. The sensual Bakhtin wonders, "Where are these womenfolk, may I ask? There seems a curious absence of them in these environs." Indeed there does; but Bakhtin is a questionable ally, since what really worries him is not the absence of women but the absence in revolutionary politics of what he takes to be women's signal trait: frivolity. The passage continues. "Three male philosophers sitting around talking politics . . . I fear for your revolution, my dear sir; I fear it will never succeed because you've not yet learnt to be frivolous." Bring on the dancing girls!

Eagleton's eleventh-hour recollection of humanity's other half echoes a common malady these days: male postmod theoreticians mentioning at the end of despondent tomes that feminism is the only believable struggle anymore, and those gals are really on to something. (Eagleton's relationship to feminism within academia has been heavily criticized by Elaine Showalter and Gayatri Spivak, among others.) What do men want? To be saved by women, I suppose. Except that being rescued implies giving up power. So Eagleton's male saints and sinners give nothing up, preferring either to die immediately (Connolly) or to live a romance with death (Wittgenstein, Bakhtin), unsaved but not unpublished. (p. 56)

Scott L. Malcomson, "Where Eagleton Dares," in The Village Voice, Vol. XXXII, No. 40, October 6, 1987, p. 56.

Kathleen McCracken

Saints and Scholars is a comic-ironic tour de force, a satirical examination of the origins of modern European thought. Readers of Terry Eagleton's lucid literary criticism will be delighted to discover in this, his first work of fiction, an equally adroit control of language combined with a provocative dramatization of conflict in philosophical, political, religious and literary assumptions. The characters in the novel are animated as much by their bizarre idiosyncrasies as the varying ideologies they represent. Jettisoned from their respective historico-fictional niches, each takes part in a revised version of the aftermath of the Easter Rising.

The story begins at "ten minutes to six on the morning of 12 May 1916," when James Connolly's cell in Kilmainham is invaded by nine prison administrators: "It is surprising how many officials are needed for an execution." Connolly, however, is not executed. After a sardonic description of the preparatory proceedings worthy of Dean Swift, the narrator intervenes to rearrange the facts in a more "aesthetically pleasing manner":

> Seven bullets raced towards Connolly's chest, but they did not reach it, at least not here they didn't. Let us arrest those bullets in mid air, prise open a space in these close-packed events through which Jimmy may scamper, blast him out of the dreary continuum of history into a different place altogether.

This "different place" is a demythologized Ireland, "land of saints and scholars, martyrs and madmen," where the high ideals of the Irish Renaissance, the republican uprising and British imperialism are debunked through bristling parody and the cameo appearances of such figures as Yeats and Synge, Padraic Pearse and Jim Larkin, Lady Aberdeen and Lord Iveagh. It is into this subverted paradise (epitomized by the abandoned cottage) that the Viennese philosopher Ludwig Wittgenstein, accompanied by Nikolai Bakhtin, brother of the Russian critic Mikhail Bakhtin, wants to disappear. His goal is to wed manual and mental labor, a Marxist ideal of which he has but the vaguest concept how to actualize. While Connolly dodges the British army, managing only to reify himself into

"symbol," Wittgenstein, in his efforts to dissolve the absolute, arrives not on the "rough ground" of concrete, pragmatic discourse, but is returned to the "ice" and "bog" of metaphysical illusion.

Wittgenstein's frustrated desire to actualize his ideas in physical work is counterpointed by Connolly's single-minded action. Their intercourse is offset by Bakhtin's physical appetites and Bloom's commonsensical materialism. . . .

The narrative poses a series of "what if's," the solutions to which depend on a radical dislocation of historical and literary fact. A prefatory note states, "Wittgenstein did indeed live for a while in a cottage on the west coast of Ireland, although at a later time than suggested here." What if he had indeed managed to escape from the "prison-house" of metaphysics into the dissolute reality of ordinary language? What if Bloom's quest had not ended in a Dublin bedroom, outstripped by Molly's monologue? And what if James Connolly had not been executed? The novel appears, on one level, to challenge the doctrine of dialectical materialism, to place mind over matter, giving imagination full sway. But on a more fundamental plane it reinforces the inescapability of history, the relentless impingement of social, economic and political forces on all spheres of human activity. At least this is what the climactic argument between Wittgenstein and Connolly, who are not so much opponents as mirror images of their own desire for absolute purity, decides. . . .

While *Saints and Scholars* evokes real and imaginary figures to expose and evaluate a range of philosophical viewpoints, it also provides a detailed picture of how religious, political and economic pressures determined the societal dimensions of place during the first quarter of the 20th century. The turmoil and decadence of pre-revolutionary Russia and the hypocritical veneer of a cancerous Venetian culture are powerfully conjured, but the bitterest depiction is reserved for Dublin, a city "filled with living wreckage."

If Eagleton interprets modern history and thought from an essentially Marxist perspective, fictionalizing "the facts" in terms of potential responses to a network of external forces, he does not avoid "deconstructing" that same formula. His novel goes well beyond the strictures of a single ideology: Indeed, its central thrust includes not just the mutability of history and ideas, but the inherent mutiplicity of language itself. *Saints and Scholars* is more than a black comedy; it is also a skillfully-realized linguistic polemic. The narrative concludes with a concrete image of what Eagleton, in another context, has described as "that self-destructing moment . . . in which the impossible 'truth' of language is disclosed at the very point of its annihilation." The linguistic paradox is echoed in Wittgenstein's ultimate inability to bracket off the metaphysical from the material, and in the failure of Connolly's martyrdom to introduce full-scale revolutionary change. But it is most subtly rendered by the way in which the novel releases meaning. Returned to the firing squad, Connolly's final "transformation" is emblematic of that point where history and language move into "truthful" conjunction:

> As the rifles were raised he was already fading, dwindling, fragments of his body flaking away to leave only an image beneath. When the bullets

reached him he would disappear entirely into myth, his body nothing but a piece of language, the first cry of the new republic.

Saints and Scholars appeals as lively entertainment, judicious satire and stimulating argument. However one approaches it, Eagleton's novel is an indisputably good read.

Kathleen McCracken, "Judicious Satire, Stimulating Argument," in Irish Literary Supplement, *Vol. 7, No. 2, Fall, 1988, p. 17.*

David Simpson

Despite its title and its author's position as a distinguished literary critic at Oxford University, [*Saints and Sholars*] is not a "university novel." (p. 12)

Terry Eagleton does not want to give up on the possibility that the professorial class, at least in its most eminent incarnations, and despite the mythology of the cloister, might articulate some sort of relation to a wider world. *Saints and Scholars* raises questions about 1916, and questions about 1987. In the sphere of the historical, the figures Eagleton presents are not the squalid nonentities of the tribe, whose ambitions do not go beyond a senior lectureship and a crack at one of their colleagues' wives; they are Russell and Wittgenstein, the two most important philosophers of their time and place, and Nikolai Bakhtin, the brother of the famous Marxist literary critic. These men, adapted out of the ordinary world, rub shoulders with James Connolly, the Irish nationalist leader who was in fact executed shortly after the failure of the Easter Rising, but is here allowed to escape and hide out long enough to have some conversations with the professors, and with Leopold Bloom, the entirely fictional hero of *Ulysses* who is here made real by fiction. A crazy salad. And, since much of the debate within the novel concerns what is real or fictional about the world, and about Ireland, it is clear that Eagleton knows what he is doing.

In the context of 1987, then, we may read this novel as addressing the question of whether there is or might be a serious connection between the life of the mind and the life of action, between the fate of a discipline and that of a nation. Even if that connection be one of absolute contrast (which it is not), or brought about by the privileges of fantasy (which it is), the persistence of Eagleton's interest in the passages from the study to the street is hard to miss. This interest is quite proper to an active Marxist who had already found in the nonprofessionalized mind of Walter Benjamin the permission to "blast" the record "out of the continuum of history" in the service of impulses that are "political rather than academic" (preface to *Walter Benjamin or Towards a Revolutionary Criticism,* 1981). Fiction allows even more space for this tendency, and it works wonderfully. Humor, panache, and considerable intellectual brilliance never allow this novel to subside into the *Tendenzroman* dreaded by Engels and many others. Eagleton's one-liners are as good as Chandler's—"He washed up with a jovial air, like royalty driving a steam engine"—and the extended theoretical debates do not make us decide between what is funny and what is serious. The greatest language philosopher of his generation, with a professed admiration for ordinary speech, cannot get his English obscenities right, and constantly says "bollock"

for "bollocks" (cunning little joke, that one!). There are plenty of insider references for the professors, but at no point does the reader need to know the codes. The historical and classmarked structures of social life are brilliantly rendered as the fabric of character itself; in the extended descriptions of Wittgenstein's Vienna, Bakhtin's St. Petersburg, and everybody's Dublin, there are passages that stand comparison with Benjamin's account of Baudelaire's Paris. For much of the novel, one senses that it is Ireland—and especially the Ireland of Connolly's death cell—that provides the dimension of realism against which the fictionality of the rest of the writing can be measured. But one of the novel's leading questions is exactly about what this "Ireland" might be, outside of the languages of those who address it. The arguments between the protagonists are carried on with full awareness of the implications of life after Derrida, as well as after Wittgenstein, and it is Eagleton's achievement that despite the almost irresistible desire to *connect* that both his own political priorities and the conventions of the novel must have impressed upon him, he has here produced an exercise in disconnection. Or at least, an exercise in suspension of judgment. Neither philosophers nor men of action are immune to doubts and indecisions; no one has a sure knowledge of history until it has happened. But happen it does, in some ways rather than in others, sorting out by some process what in language is *only* language, and what comes to be the case. Connolly's death, at last allowed to happen at the end of the book, passes into a language that is "the first cry of the new republic." But Eagleton does not use the privilege of hindsight to tell us why or how, and in blasting apart the continuum of history he has left us with more questions than answers. This will surprise many readers, and may even surprise the author. But Marxist theory is ready for a dose of skepticism, and it has always been short on fun. Eagleton provides both, and his humor is never merely the material for an emergent cynicism. There are few laughs in Connolly's death cell, and only a mention of the fields of Flanders, in passing. Eagleton means us to notice that. The world, if it is all that is the case, is never all to any of us. But this too may be bollock. (pp. 12, 19)

David Simpson, "Life after Derrida," in The American Book Review, *Vol. 10, No. 5, November-December, 1988, pp. 12, 19.*

Sebastian Gardner

The Ideology of the Aesthetic is Terry Eagleton's most substantial work to date, and it represents a comprehensive engagement with the history of modern philosophical aesthetics. Marxists tend to fall into one of two temperamentally if not intellectually opposed groups: those for whom art and aesthetics are by and large a matter of indifference, and those who seem to regard the economic-political core of Marxist theory as complete, and for whom aesthetic questions are instead an object of central and passionate concern. Dr Eagleton belongs, firmly and obviously, in the second group. His ambition is to get to the heart of thought about aesthetic experience and unravel its connections with the political exterior: the project, as it is described in the introduction, is to demonstrate in intricate detail how aesthetic thought is implicated with, and in turn reacts on, the social and economic conditions of the society out of which it is formed. Eagleton, more than anyone else writing in this vein (with the arguable exception of Frederic Jameson), is aware of the blandness which tends to afflict claims of this sort, and takes care to distance himself from simple-minded reductionism and determinism. . . .

Despite the breadth, scholarly energy and philosophical competence of the book, there are problems. The key idea is that with the arrival of bourgeois society there evolves what one could call a structural homology between the idea of the artwork as a sort of autonomous subject, and the concept of the individual human being as similarly self-determining and isolable from its social context. Both are concepts of "free particulars", generated by the demands of the bourgeois mode of production. This thesis is worked out in the first five chapters with reference to eighteenth-century British aesthetics and German idealism.

There are difficulties in evaluating this idea, given that, in the form in which it is advanced, it appears to depend neither on historical evidence, nor on conceptual considerations; Eagleton looks down on those who are "enamoured of 'concrete illustration' " and means to "frustrate" the expectation that examples will be provided. The existence of such a relation, understood simply as an analogy, is nevertheless a perfectly intelligible proposition, and far from implausible. What would make it more persuasive, surely, would be some demonstration that consciousness of the alleged equation between person and artwork is actually alive in the artistic products and critical discourses of the historical period in question; consequently, like many of the conjectures in this book, the idea seems to be best understood—contrary to Eagleton's view of the independence of theory from criticism—as a suggestion for others engaged at a less elevated level to work on.

There is an underlying difficulty facing the ideological critique of philosophical thought when it is pursued without detailed substantiating reference to its historical context, and it suggests itself very early on. What exactly is involved in a structural homology, and in aesthetic theory's thereby being, as Eagleton puts it, "closely bound up with" the material process by which culture is produced? This could mean a number of different things, and for Eagleton's claims to have the significance he wants, it must mean something more than merely that the relation between aesthetic theory and political ideology allows for an abstract judgment of formal likeness. On the other hand, when we are told that the new bourgeois subject "is modelled on the aesthetic artefact", the claim looks too strong; surely aesthetic theory did not take the lead in forming bourgeois concepts of subjectivity. The nature of this relation is the crux of the matter, and it is unfortunate that Eagleton does not tell us in explicit terms what he envisages it as consisting in.

The kinds of ideological problems to which aesthetic theories are said to be direct responses are, of course, not themselves material problems. Sometimes, as with Schiller, this does not interfere with the claim that there is an important relation between the aesthetic and the ethical or political, since it lies sufficiently near the surface of the text. But where an ethical or political component is not part of an aesthetic theory's explicit content, and cannot be shown to be conceptually implied by it, ideological unmasking

has to proceed by seeing the theory as a response to a problem that it does not represent itself as recognizing. In order to be able to view aesthetic theory as (in one of its fundamental aspects) a totalitarian hegemonic instrument, Eagleton does not hesitate to supply such a problem: "how can any political order flourish which does not address itself to this most tangible area of the 'lived', of everything that belongs to a society's somatic, sensational life? How can 'experience' be allowed to fall outside a society's ruling concepts?" To which rhetorical questions the natural answer is: Very easily—what is there to make us think that political authority is importantly dependent on the success of a ruling class's current philosophical theory in conceptualizing perception and sensation? Other startling assertions seem to carry similar implications of an overvaluation of the immediate political role of philosophical ideas: "Nothing could be more disabling than a ruling rationality which can know nothing beyond its own concepts." Again, one wants to protest that more urgent worries must confront ruling classes than philosophical conceptualism.

One therefore has to suppose that the ideological dilemmas discerned by Eagleton are of a very loosely conceptual, perhaps even imaginary order; perhaps they concern the manner in which theory is experienced, rather than its content. This seems to be what is happening when we are told for example that the "bourgeois subject requires some Other to assure itself that its powers and properties are more than hallucinatory" (which is said to motivate Kant's transcendental deduction). But this creates new doubts and difficulties. Understood as quasi-imaginary or experiential, these sorts of ideological problem have no objective relation to real practical exigencies, and seem to hinge on an appreciation of what is effectively a metaphorical relation between political reality and aesthetic theory. Eagleton's diagnoses thus seem to presuppose something like the kind of thinking which Freud calls primary process, but unlike psychoanalytic interpretations, they are not tied down by any requirements of psychological explanation. Granted that ruling classes may seek to legitimate their authority through intellectual appropriation, why should we believe that they do so at this level, and what guarantee do we have, if critique is not answerable to "concrete illustration", that the alleged ideological dilemmas are not just engineered by the rhetorical manner in which Eagleton has characterized the theories? Where, furthermore, are we to think of them as being psychologically realized? Especially since the evidence seems in many instances to weigh against the attributions of ideological role. Kierkegaard's individualism is interpreted as "rampant individualism of bourgeois society" pressed "to an unacceptable extreme", and yet, as Eagleton tells us, Denmark was at that period a society of "monarchical absolutism", and Kierkegaard himself was "a full-blooded apologist for the forces of political reaction". Similarly, perhaps the best explanation for the "ideological paucity" which is said to afflict Kant's moral theory is that it is not after all ideologically motivated.

After the exposition of the artwork/bourgeois subject identification, this idea is effectively put to one side, and no other readily discernible single thesis takes its place to dominate the reading of aesthetic thought since Hegel. That the discussion from Hegel up to post-modernism goes its own way is in fact to the book's advantage, for it gains a different sort of interest, and displays virtues absent from the earlier treatments. Here Eagleton is closer to home, and comes to deal with figures in the contemporary literary-theoretical pantheon, often viewed as objects of criticism rather than allies. Several of the studies hit the mark exactly: the chapters on Schopenhauer and Heidegger are extremely acute. This amounts to something more like a history of philosophy, with particular reference to the aesthetic, of a Hegelian sort: what we have are imaginatively cast portraits of theories, rather than narrowly argumentative critiques, and loose tensions and incompatibilities rather than propositional inconsistencies. Eagleton's critical survey of contemporary Continental philosophy, and his diagnosis of post-modernism as "aesthetic imperialism", contain powerful insights. A spirit of commonsensical political concern, and a fierce and reliable moral sense seem to come to the fore, and the result is much more persuasive than the deconstructionism with which in the earlier chapters Eagleton often seems to want to associate his Marxism.

> *Sebastian Gardner, "Free Particulars Tied Down," in* The Times Literary Supplement, *No. 4539, March 30-April 5, 1990, p. 337.*

Roger Kimball

[In this essay], I wish to take the occasion of the publication of Terry Eagleton's new book, *The Ideology of the Aesthetic*—at 426 pages, two or three times as long as his many other books and clearly meant to be something of a *magnum opus*—to discuss the evolution and significance of his distinctive brand of Marxist criticism.

Born in 1943, Professor Eagleton was educated at Cambridge University, where he studied with the Marxist critic Raymond Williams and where he taught briefly before going to Wadham College, Oxford, in 1969. If we strip away the accretions of fashionable academic rhetoric—an increasingly prominent feature of his work since the mid-Seventies—we see the origins of Professor Eagleton's criticism in a compound of Williams's socialist organicism, F. R. Leavis's meticulously autocratic practical criticism, and left-wing, liberationist Catholicism. His early work, especially, was written under Williams's shadow. *Shakespeare and Society* (1967) is dedicated to Williams, "without whose friendship and influence this book would not have been written." In its main theme—the relation of the individual and society as it emerges in Shakespeare's late plays—it rehearses in smaller compass the kind of analysis Williams undertook in *Culture and Society* (1958). As is the case with Williams, Professor Eagleton apparently cannot write a work on any subject without an exhibition of his political *bona fides*. At the end of this book on Shakespeare, we are confronted with the suggestion that "spontaneous living is crippled by industrial capitalism," just as Williams concludes *Culture and Society* with a plea for the achievement of a socialist-based "common culture" because "we shall not survive without it."

Professor Eagleton subsequently learned that organic models of society are politically suspect and went out of his way to distance himself—respectfully, it must be said—from Williams. In *Criticism and Ideology: A Study in Marxist Literary Theory* (1976), he criticizes Williams for his "political gradualism" and "populism," even his

"humanism" and "idealism," while also praising his work as "one of the most significant sources from which a materialist aesthetics might be derived." What is remarkable, though, is not Professor Eagleton's criticism of his mentor but how much the very things he criticizes continue, despite protestations to the contrary, to inform his own work.

The same cannot be said for the influence of Leavis or of Catholicism. Indeed, religion in general persists in Professor Eagleton's work mostly in the form of certain rhetorical tics and occasional recourse to millenarian imagery. . . . By the mid-Seventies Professor Eagleton is arguing from the "'taken-for-granted' post-atheism of Marx." (Whether such a position differs significantly from the left-wing, activist Catholicism of his youth is a question we must leave to one side.)

The sobering influence of Leavis's practical criticism had approximately the same fate in Professor Eagleton's criticism as did religion: it is gradually forgotten as he moves away from being a mere literary critic to assume the fashionable mantle of Marxist "critical theorist." The main difference is that for the literary critic, literature—actual, specific works of literature—remains the chief focus of his endeavors, whereas for the critical theorist literature takes a back seat to quasi-philosophical speculations about epistemology, sex, society, politics: anything but literature. Individual literary works come into the picture, in so far as they do come into the picture, only as illustrations of the theory being advanced. In *Shakespeare and Society,* Professor Eagleton insists that his discussion of the relation between the individual and society "needs to be above all a work of practical criticism, where the general assertion can be sustained by actual reference." By 1976, he is complaining that "bourgeois criticism," content with its role as "handmaiden" to literature, does not stand up to "the inexhaustible godhead of the text itself." And by the time he comes to write *The Ideology of the Aesthetic,* he explicitly rejects the idea that "theory" should refer to particular works and boasts straightway that his study will not include "any examination of actual works of art."

At the center of Marxist thought is a vision of the world determined by economic imperatives: the economic "base" of society determines the cultural "superstructure" of politics, art, religion, and so on. Like most academic Marxists, Professor Eagleton knows that, put baldly, the doctrine of economic determinism is patently absurd. So he employs various gambits to soften or conceal the absurdity, without ever really denying the basic model of economic determinism. (pp. 18-20)

To appreciate the corrosive nature of Professor Eagleton's use of the notion of ideology, consider his explanation of how a Marxist might use the term to analyze *The Waste Land.* Predictably, the poem appears as a reflection of a "crisis" of bourgeois imperialism (everything bourgeois is always in crisis for the Marxist), but "as a poem, it does not of course *know itself* as a product of a particular ideological crisis, for if it did it would cease to exist. . . . In this sense *The Waste Land* is ideological: it shows a man making sense of his experience in ways that prohibit a true understanding of his society, ways that are consequently false." How, one might ask, does Professor Eagleton know they are false? What puts him in a position superior to poor T. S. Eliot, blinded as he was by ideology? Why, the magic key, of course: Marxist doctrine. Ideology may simply be "the ideas, values and feelings by which men experience their societies at various times," but the Marxist is in the uniquely happy position of being exempt from the blinders of ideology. As Professor Eagleton explains, "historical materialism"—that is, Marxism—"stands or falls by the claim that it is not only not an ideology, but that it contains a scientific theory of the genesis, structure and decline of ideologies."

Professor Eagleton expatiates further on the notion of ideology in *Literary Theory: An Introduction.* He spends his introductory chapter attempting to convince readers that the idea of literature is so indeterminate that, when you come right down to it, "literature" (the scare quotes are his) doesn't exist. What we have are the products of various "social ideologies." Perhaps you thought that George Eliot was the author of *Middlemarch.* No: according to Professor Eagleton,

> The phrase "George Eliot" signifies nothing more than the insertion of certain specific ideological determinations—Evangelical Christianity, rural organicism, incipient feminism, petty-bourgeois moralism—into a hegemonic ideological formation which is partly supported, partly embarrassed by their presence.

Similarly, he tells us that Henry James, like Joseph Conrad, "is . . . no more than a particular name for . . . an aspect of the crisis of nineteenth-century realism." The idea is to downgrade the notion of individual genius, as if George Eliot's personal contribution to the writing of *Middlemarch* were somehow accidental, the more important thing being the "specific ideological determinations" she embodied. The main point of all this is that nothing is what it seems; or, as Professor Eagleton puts it in *Criticism and Ideology,* "there is no 'immanent' value": everything in the realm of culture is determined by something outside culture—namely (catch that whiff of vulgarity?) the oppressive economic relations of capitalism.

In *Literary Theory,* Professor Eagleton argues that the *"point"* of studying literature "is not itself, in the end, a literary one." Now there is a sense in which "bourgeois criticism," as he likes to call it, would agree. And in this context it is worth noting that when we insist on the basic *autonomy* of art, we do not suggest that art exists in a vacuum, apart from any human values or concerns; we mean, rather, that art should not be pursued as a species of propaganda but as realm of experience that possesses its own criteria of validity. Finally, "in the end," the *"point"* of studying literature is "outside" literature, just as the point of reading—and understanding what is read—is outside the act of reading. This is what we mean when, for example, we say that studying literature is enriching, that it broadens our horizons, that it deepens our understanding.

Professor Eagleton scoffs at the "liberal humanist" idea that literature "makes you a better person" because such formulations are too vague, too idealistic, too "abstract" (this latter being a favorite Marxist criticism). What he wants is a program. But there are times when vagueness and abstractness are virtues. When Rilke ends his famous sonnet on the archaic bust of Apollo with the admonition *Du musst dein Leben ändern*—"You must change your life"—we are in fact as grateful for its vagueness as we are for its enspiriting challenge. We know perfectly well what the demand to change one's life means. Yet for Professor Eagleton, as for all professing Marxists, the experience of art is incomplete when it is "only" about beauty or "only" involves a moment of self-recognition. They want art to issue specific instructions: contemplating that antique fragment of sculpture we should realize that its message is "You must overthrow the ruling class" or at least "You must realize that the social order that gave birth to this sculpture was oppressive."

In the end, Professor Eagleton is in the uncomfortable position of being a literary critic who doesn't care much for literature except in so far as it is an instrument for social change. (pp. 20-1)

In many respects, *The Ideology of the Aesthetic* is a summary and update of Professor Eagleton's views on the relation between aesthetic experience and ideology. (In this sense, it might just as well have been titled *The Aesthetics of Ideology.*) But it is also something of an historical overview of philosophical thinking about aesthetics from the eighteenth century down to the present. Despite Professor Eagleton's disclaimer that he was not attempting to provide a history of aesthetics, that is largely what the book amounts to, and we can be sure that it will be adopted as such by many colleges and universities. It gives special emphasis to Marxist critics like Walter Benjamin and Theodor Adorno, and it includes provocative chapter titles like "Schiller and Hegemony" and "The Marxist Sublime"; but otherwise it provides a fairly predictable trip through the literature. Beginning with the work of Alexander Baumgarten—who coined the term "aesthetic" in 1750—Professor Eagleton takes fourteen chapters to rehearse the aesthetic theories of Burke, Shaftesbury, Kant, Schiller, Hegel, Nietzsche, Heidegger, and others. Mostly, the names are as familiar as the opinions Professor Eagleton expresses. Indeed, by the time one comes to "From the *Polis* to Post-modernism," the longest and most original chapter, one has the distinct impression of having just sat through Professor Eagleton's latest batch of homework assignments to himself.

As usual, the sheer bulk of the assignments is formidable. Professor Eagleton has read a great deal and has clearly devoted much effort to the book. Yet considered as an introduction to aesthetic theory, *The Ideology of the Aesthetic* is a dismal failure. For one thing, notwithstanding his prodigious reading, Professor Eagleton is often not up to the task of explaining the philosophy he discusses—largely, one suspects, because of his ideological commitments. For example, Baumgarten's aesthetic theory, growing out of the work of philosophers like Leibniz and Christian Wolff, was essentially an effort to supplement the rationalism of Cartesian thought by providing a fuller account of the "sensuous perfection" that was embodied in art. As logic was to the faculty of reason, so aesthetics was to the faculty of taste. But for Professor Eagleton, "the call for an aesthetics in eighteenth-century Germany is among other things a response to the problem of political absolutism." His discussion of Baumgarten's aesthetics transforms a philosophical innovation into a dramatic example of class warfare with reason cast as the tyrant and aesthetics as a kind of proletarian lackey. "Reason," he writes, "must find some way of penetrating the world of perception, but in doing so must not put at risk its own absolute power"—as if reason were a feudal lord oppressing the "serfs" of sensation.

Then, too, in his eagerness to uphold the universality of class warfare, Professor Eagleton often drastically misreads the philosophers he discusses. About Schopenhauer's extreme pessimism, for example, he writes that it is "a fact that throughout class history the fate of the great majority of men and women has been one of suffering and fruitless toil. . . . The dominant tale of history to date has indeed been one of carnage, misery and woe." But this is totally to misunderstand Schopenhauer, for whom suffering and woe were essential, irremediable aspects of existence, not the products of "class history." Sometimes, indeed, Professor Eagleton's explanations take on a positively surreal quality, especially when he ventures into modish literary theorizing. (p. 22)

To all this Professor Eagleton might reply that, first, he was not attempting to present a standard history of aesthetics and, second, that his real interest is in the way the aesthetic embodies the contradictions of the middle class under capitalism. This brings us to one of Professor Eagleton's central claims in *The Ideology of the Aesthetic,* namely, the whole idea of the aesthetic is based on or embodies a "contradiction." One must always be suspicious when a Marxist uses the term "contradiction," because it usually means that some aspect of reality is not conforming to his vision of things. . . .

Professor Eagleton holds that the aesthetic is "contradictory" because aesthetic experience gestures toward a freedom usually denied to man while at the same time it embodies the ideological imperatives of the ruling class. Hence the aesthetic is both "the ideal paradigm of material production" and "the very paradigm of the ideological"—indeed, he tells us that "aesthetic judgement is every bit as coercive as the most barbarous law" though "this is not the way it feels." Now, at least since the time of the Greeks, art has been held up as a source of great spiritual refreshment, so it is no surprise that Marxists, too, should single it out as a model for "unalienated labor." But why should we grant that the aesthetic is fundamentally ideological? If nothing in our experience suggests that it is—and nothing does—why should we cede art and aesthetic experience to Marxist theory?

The Ideology of the Aesthetic is a deeply confused work that tells us almost nothing about art or aesthetic experience. It is more revealing on the subject of ideology, but mostly an example of ideology in action, not as an explanation or analysis of the phenomenon. Yet it must be admitted that there is an unusually perceptive critic lurking in the interstices of this book. Professor Eagleton is not very good as an expositor of philosophy, and his ruling passions—to be politically correct and to be intellectually fashionable—regularly lead him into any number of silly statements.

But his last chapter, especially, shows him to be capable of trenchant and perceptive criticism. True, this chapter contains the usual quota of Marxist hooey. Yet it also contains a some perceptive criticism of a subject that is clearly dear to Professor Eagleton's heart: Marxist criticism. For one thing, Professor Eagleton makes what he rightly calls the "vital distinction" between liberal capitalistic society and totalitarian regimes: This in itself is a welcome change

from the typical academic Marxist tactic of pretending that the United States is a recapitulation of Hitler's Reich. But even more to the point, he even ventures to criticize several chic leftwing theories and their proponents. Thus he warns his fellow academics against the deconstructionist attack on the notion of truth, noting that it is not the case that "ambiguity, indeterminability, undecidability are always subversive strikes against an arrogantly monological certitude." You might think this could be taken for granted; but in the prevailing climate in the academy, to challenge the triumph of undecidability and ambiguity is to risk the charge of heresy.

Professor Eagleton also dares to characterize thinkers like Michael Foucault and Jacques Derrida as "libertarian pessimists," and to suggest that Foucault underestimated the Enlightenment's "vital civilising achievements." He makes similar observations about other left-wing academic saints, from Jürgen Habermas to the exalted Fredric Jameson. Perhaps it is this side of Professor Eagleton that the historian Maurice Cowling had in mind when he spoke of his "intellectual brutality." In any event, though it is rarely on view in his work, such critical independence is to be encouraged. (p. 23)

Roger Kimball, "The Contradictions of Terry Eagleton," in The New Criterion, *Vol. 9, No. 1, September, 1990, pp. 17-23.*

FURTHER READING

Alter, Robert. "The Decline and Fall of Literary Criticism." *Commentary* 77, No. 3 (March 1984): 50-6.

Laments the influence of progressive European literary theorists on contemporary criticism, citing Eagleton's popular *Literary Theory: An Introduction* as a primary indication of its decline.

Freadman, Richard, and Miller, S. R. "Three Views of Literary Theory." *Poetics* 17, Nos. 1 & 2 (April 1988): 9-24.

Analyzes the critical approaches of F. R. Leavis and Eagleton, viewing them as paradigms of two extreme methods of criticism: Leavis stressed close textual reading and moral values while Eagleton examines how various social, historical, and economic factors impinge upon a given text.

Kavanagh, James H., and Lewis, Thomas E. "Interview: Terry Eagleton." *Diacritics* 12, No. 1 (Spring 1982): 53-64.

Interview with Eagleton in which he discusses his Marxist approach to literary criticism and its relationship to the theories of such thinkers as Louis Althusser, Jacques Derrida, and Julia Kristeva.

King, Richard. "On Literary Theory." *The Kenyon Review,* n.s. VI, No. 4 (Fall 1984): 114-18.

Generally positive, in-depth review of *Literary Theory: An Introduction.*

Tess Gallagher

1943-

American poet, short story writer, and essayist.

Gallagher has garnered praise for composing verse considered both philosophically and emotionally profound. Her personal lyrics illuminate relations between family members, childhood and adulthood, and dreams and reality. Critics have praised the rhythmic qualities of Gallagher's free verse, deriving from her use of colloquial cadences that lend her poems the natural flow of conversation. In her short stories, Gallagher explores emotional crises in the lives of men and women in small towns in the American Northwest.

The oldest of five children, Gallagher was born into a working-class family in Port Angeles, Washington. She has taught literature and creative writing at universities throughout the United States. Gallagher lived and worked with celebrated short story writer Raymond Carver from 1979 until his death in 1988, and many commentators attribute Gallagher's late interest in writing prose fiction to Carver's influence. Gallagher continues to live and work in the Pacific Northwest, the setting for much of her work.

Instructions to the Double, Gallagher's first full-length and perhaps most celebrated publication, explores the type of guidance she received as a girl and young woman regarding her proper role in life and how these directions changed after she became an adult. Gallagher utilizes the traditional roles of caretaking and listening as means of observing others and of incorporating other sensibilities into what is otherwise personal poetry. The dominant image throughout this collection is the double, which appears in the form of family members and others who have greatly influenced the speaker, as well as in a plethora of reflecting entities, including mirrors, bodies of water, eyes, shadows, and photographs. The most lauded poems in *Instructions to the Double,* including "Two Stories," "Coming Home," and "Black Money," depict Gallagher's home and family through concrete imagery and mature insights.

Gallagher's next major collection, *Under Stars,* is divided into two sections. Inspired by her travels in Northern Ireland, the first section—"The Ireland Poems"—garnered praise for Gallagher's ability to discern and ponder the depths beneath a quickly realized cultural surface. In "Start Again Somewhere," the second section of *Under Stars,* Gallagher returns to exploring relations between people. "My Mother Remembers That She Was Beautiful" and "If Never Again" are especially praised for their compassionate yet humorous insights.

Willingly collects poems concerning the breakup of Gallagher's marriage and the death of her father, along with pieces that continue to expand the poet's range of subjects outside her personal life. "Each Bird Walking," a meditation on love in which a man tells of caring for his mother during her terminal illness, is one of Gallagher's most celebrated poems. The somber subject of this poem and those concerning the death of her father, are mediated by the gentle humor that commentators agree illumines the grief

that inspired the piece. While some reviewers find the persona inappropriately intrusive in pieces ostensibly about others, many critics praised the expansion of Gallagher's poetic range. Both *Willingly* and *Amplitude: New and Selected Poems* find Gallagher venturing into politics and public life. Vickie Karp commented: "People do volunteer work, go camping, or have affairs, for that matter, hoping to experience moments of rightness like the ones often encountered in Tess Gallagher's poetry. Deep in the waters of the work is a raging conviction for justice, to ascertain and assert everyone's real needs, hopes, and triumphs."

In such stories as "The Lover of Horses" and "Girls" from her first prose collection, *The Lover of Horses and Other Stories,* Gallagher explores long-term relationships. Her narrative style interweaves rhythmic and colorful phrasings of her small-town characters. Bette Pesetsky remarked: "What I tried to do in reading Ms. Gallagher's stories was to forget what a fine poet the author is. And the reward was to find an excellent writer of prose who savors the elegance of simplicity and whose stories resonate and linger."

(See also *CLC,* Vol. 18 and *Contemporary Authors,* Vol. 106.)

PRINCIPAL WORKS

POETRY

Instructions to the Double   1976
Under Stars   1978
Willingly   1984
Amplitude: New and Selected Poems   1987

SHORT FICTION

The Lover of Horses and Other Stories   1986

Emily Grosholz

Tess Gallagher's . . . *Willingly* contains a group of poems about her father's death. They testify to a tender and steadfast filial relationship and to a man who showed the ordinary courage of fathers, . . . that is, he went to work for thirty years even after he had forgotten why.

But Gallagher fails to transform her own memories into memorable poems because her formal means are insufficient. The strongest of these poems, **"Boat Ride"** and **"Black Silk,"** contain simple, poignant anecdotes which reveal their subject's moral strength.

> In a lull I get him to tell stories,
> the one where he's a coal miner in Ottumwa,
> Iowa, during the Depression and the boss
> tries to send the men into a mine where
> a shaft collapsed the day before, "You'll
> go down there or I'll run you out of
> this town," the boss says. "You don't
> have to run me. I'm not just leaving
> your town, I'm leaving your whole goddamned
> state!" my father says, and he turns
> and heads on foot out of the town, some
> of the miners with him, hitching from there
> to the next work in the next state.
>
>   **"Boat Ride"**

Despite the telling incident, this stanza does not justify its existence as poetry; it might better function as a paragraph in a prose memoir. For there is little verbal music, and the lineation is arbitrary. In fact, when Gallagher strives most for poetic effect, her verse becomes most awkward. Concluding an account of a dream of her father, she writes: "So does / a bird dismiss one tree for another / and carries each time the flight between / like a thing never done." Another poem, about paying homage, begins: "I was taking the little needed, not more, / so the earth could carry me, the way / a tree is able for many birds at once if / they are sure to leave and bear themselves lightly." The management of metaphor is confused, the aural patterning minimal and the grammar pointlessly nonstandard. (pp. 656-57)

> *Emily Grosholz, "Family Ties," in* The Hudson Review, *Vol. XXXVII, No. 4, Winter, 1984-1985, pp. 647-59.*

William Logan

Willingly or not, Tess Gallagher's . . . collection [entitled *Willingly*] repeats themes that characterized her earlier work—severed loves, minor events with major implications, consolation in the family drama. Whether recounting very movingly the death of her father or detailing the social awkwardness accompanying a dessert of crêpes flambeau, she finds in other lives the behavior that measures her own. Like so many other poets of her generation, a generation now reaching artistic maturity, she speaks relentlessly in what the reader is encouraged to construe as the voice of the poet at work. It is most engaging when it takes itself least seriously, as when it listens to itself listen on the telephone:

> Are they filming this? I mean you
> putting your mouth to the receiver
> personally. I'm doing it too, naturally,
> out here in my cabin on the bay. Lots
> of windows to let in water, weeds
> sitting around drying up in mason jars.
> All that woodsy romance.

Miss Gallagher's free verse, elegant by opportunity rather than commitment, borrows the rhythms of prose without becoming enslaved to them. **"Naturally"** leads quite naturally to nature, and in other poems she attends as carefully to what she is saying.

She attends as well to what others are saying—over half of her poems rely on direct quotation (" 'Today, today! / the light says' "—something's always talking in these poems). The poet's voice is to an extent complicated by such recourse to the words of others, though only rarely is another character allowed to speak a whole poem. The most afflicting and afflicted character is her father, and in a series of poems she reflects on his life and his death:

> What not to do for him
> was hardest, for the life left in us
> argued against his going
> like a moon banished in fullness, yet
> lingering far into morning.

The compulsive scenario of her poetry, as might be expected of a writer so attentive to surroundings, requires moments of physical connection, even with strangers. Something in the self is released when it touches the other (her first book was titled *Instructions to the Double*), and the tension of these connections is heightened when they are in danger of lapsing:

> Your silence is leaning toward judgment.
> Yesterday I bragged, writing to calm
> my paranoid friend, that I never assume
> the worst when my pals don't write. Now
> assuming the worst, I think what I must have
> done, or not done.

In the vacant possibilities of the unanswered letter and, more seriously and sadly, a man washing his sick mother, Miss Gallagher makes public what is private about loss, if a poem is public and not merely a private utterance we have the privilege of overhearing.

Increasingly her poems have become minor fictions, with beginnings, middles and ends. Her weaknesses are all too poetic: She adores ludicrously epic similes:

> I am in a state of mourning
> for your coat which traveled with us that while
> like a close relative concealing a fatal illness
> in a last visit

and is prey to displays of overeager emotion (in a rainstorm: "Until I'm looking up / to let my eyes take the bliss"—one would think it were raining manna). Who would have thought that so many poems of essentially similar properties could be written about the difficulties of love? These are, however, local difficulties in a collection often willed and rarely wild. Following the arc from confusion to certainty, it finds its first word in "Maybe" and its last in "home." (p. 13)

William Logan, "Poets Elegant, Familiar, Challenging," in The New York Times Book Review, *August 26, 1984, pp. 13-14.*

Kenneth Funsten

We all know people who talk best when they talk about themselves. For them, every subject revolves back to their own individualized and "unique" experiences. Tess Gallagher is such a poet. Evidently, there are many readers who can identify, because Gallagher is very popular. Her poems appear in popular magazines such as *Life, Ms.* and *Vanity Fair,* as well as in the largest subscriber-based poetry magazines such as *American Poetry Review*—where that most personalized of artifacts, your picture, appears next to your poems. My point isn't that Gallagher has in any way "sold out." The point is how accessible to popular taste Gallagher and her poems must be. There's evidently lots of what the "slicks" call "reader identification."

In *Willingly,* . . . Gallagher's obsession with herself as the center of a wheel does not always make bad poetry. A plaintive lyricist can be expected to have moments of nicely made poetic habit, such as:

If I take a lover for every tree, I
will not have again such an
opening as
when you flew from me.

Gallagher writes well of how a marriage broke up, how the wedding band slipped off his knuckle "like a vow / in reverse"; then she asks her ex-husband:

Did we meet again in daylight? Did stars
pause in their journeys? Were we
two black ships, flags black, black
our hope and blacker still
the way forward alone?

This commonplace metaphor of lovers as two ships meeting in the dark is more melodramatic than a soap opera with its foghorn bellows of "black . . . black, black . . . blacker." The reader is sold an answer to the poem's question with the slickness of Madison Avenue. Gallagher's "personality"—her obsessive "I"—is the packaging.

There are poems ostensibly about other people, other things, but they are always unified through the perspective of her fictive ego. This strategy of self-involvement that grips Gallagher is used without taste or measure, indeed, with obsession. The height of inappropriateness occurs in one of the book's last poems, **"Each Bird Walking,"** which tells of a man bathing his sick, aged mother, and "she helped him, moving / the little she could."

"Each Bird Walking" might have been a fine, unusual poem if left alone, but Gallagher chooses to add herself—

as the man's lover—into the poem and then slickly gives that self the same last words as the man's dying mother, "That's good, that's enough." Such a pat ending trivializes the poem's real subject—how we relate to dying parents. It has the no-substance appeal of an advertisement. Such an ending implies that the poet is *more* important than the ideas in the poem. We have come full circle from Bollingen.

Kenneth Funsten, in a review of "Willingly," in Los Angeles Times Book Review, *September 23, 1984, p. 10.*

Peter Stitt

For many years now the aim of most contemporary American poets has been to explore themselves—their feelings, their experiences, their family histories—in preference to exploring anything more objective. Poetry, it has been thought, is almost as good a way as psychoanalysis to achieve self-understanding. Moreover, because of the sincerity of this effort, and because many writers believe that formalism somehow breeds insincerity, much of our recent poetry has been written in the "plain style." But understanding traditional forms enough to use them well (as with using science, history, and philosophy; as with echoing Hopkins, Browning, Crane, and Frost) requires objective learning—in distinction both to employing the plain style and to talking about the self. One of the aims of most poetry is communication; why bother to write at all if you don't wish anyone to read? Discourse which centers too exclusively upon the self threatens to become private discourse.

Even so good a poet as Tess Gallagher sometimes illustrates the tendencies I am talking against. Her newest book, *Willingly,* is long enough to contain some poems one wishes had been either left out or written more objectively. For example, in **"I Save Your Coat, But You Lose It Later,"** the speaker and her friend are on their way to the planetarium, "heading for stars":

It was a coat worth keeping even with
you in no condition to keep track, your mind
important to things you were seeing out
the window. We had changed seats on the bus
so a little breeze could catch
our faces. The coat was back there in a spot
of sunlight, its leather smell
making a halo of invitation around it.

Since narrative is everything in this poem, I will summarize the rest of the story. When the two characters leave the bus, the coat is left behind, so the speaker runs to retrieve it: "We had a forty-year reunion right there / on the street, as if the coat / had met us again in its afterlife. We were / that glad, hugging it between us." They tour the planetarium, and then: "Some weeks later, you write your coat was / stolen after a long night of drinking and / music. . . . I am in a state of mourning / for your coat."

When the poem ends with the speaker saying, "I make too much of this, / your coat, which, stolen or lost, did not belong / to me, which I never wore," the reader tends to agree. In fact, it is the unpromising nature of the subject that probably causes the preciousness of the writing here—the "hugging" of the coat, its "halo of invitation," its "afterlife," the "mind" improbably "important to things you were seeing out / the window." This style does not deepen the poem; it only gussies it up. The problem seems to be that, while the experience was of considerable importance to the speaker, it has not been made important to the reader. The poet has relied on something inside, something only two readers could share, rather than on something outside that many could share. Such externalization could be achieved through subject matter, though in this case it would obviously have to come through style. But the style used here is simply not objective enough to overcome inadequacies of subject matter.

Happily, there are not many poems like this one in **Willingly.** Elsewhere, Gallagher shows herself to be a sophisticated stylist, able to use rhetorical devices as a poem demands. Two succeeding sentences in the poem **"Linoleum"** illustrate her command of the syntactical possibilities of the English language; I quote the second of them:

> I appreciate the Jains,
> their atonements for my neglect,
> though I understand it makes poor farmers
> of them, and good we all
> don't aspire to such purity so
> there's somebody heartless enough to
> plow the spuds.

The effect is one of irony; the complicated inversions and ellipses here implicitly question the purity of these dogooders, as does the surprising use of "spuds" at the end.

Something similar happens in one of Gallagher's best poems, **"Conversation with a Fireman from Brooklyn,"** which I quote in full:

> He offers, between planes,
> to buy me a drink. I've never talked
> to a fireman before, not one from Brooklyn
> anyway. Okay. Fine, I say. Somehow
> the subject is bound to come up, women
> firefighters, and since I'm
> a woman and he's a fireman, between
> the two of us, we know something
> about this subject. Already
> he's telling me he doesn't mind
> women firefighters, but what
> they look like
> *after* fighting a fire, well
> they lose all respect. He's sorry, but
> he looks at them
> covered with the cinders of someone's
> lost hope, and he feels disgust, he just
> wants to turn the hose on them, they
> are that sweaty and stinking, just like
> him, of course, but not the woman he
> wants, you get me? and to come to that—
> isn't it too bad, to be despised
> for what you do to prove yourself
> among men
> who want to love you, to love you,
> love you.

Gallagher skillfully and ironically mingles the narrative viewpoints of these characters. The speaker is present in the nice rhetorical gesture, "Okay. Fine, I say," and in the general moral attitude of the poem; she of course also has the last word. The fireman is present in such rhetorical gestures as "you get me?", but is most tellingly presented in the phrase "they lose all respect." The speaker and the poet realize the irony present in the grammatical error,

while the fireman does not. An excellent poem, and typical of Tess Gallagher at her best—and she is mostly at her best in this volume, which contains such other sterling performances as **"Painted Steps," "Skylights,"** and **"Devotion: That It Flow,"** to name but three. (pp. 628-30)

Peter Stitt, "Objective Subjectivities," in The Georgia Review, *Vol. XXXVIII, No. 3, Fall, 1984, pp. 628-38.*

Vickie Karp

[Tess Gallagher] provides a sort of portable stillness. Her poetry moves inch by inch, stopping all the time in order to allow an image or the lush cadence of a word to resonate. In **"Boat Ride,"** a poem from her most recent book, **Willingly,** she writes: "I stare into the water folding / along the bow, *gentian*—the blue with darkness / engraved into its name, so the sound petals open with mystery." Confronted with such mysteries, she is frank, ruminative, and receptive. Ideas make a knot that she ties and unties slowly. Sometimes the difficulty of the effort overwhelms and becomes the subject of a poem. "This knot could make you cry," she writes in **"Zero,"** (**Instructions to the Double**) "how it slips past itself, now a / bracelet, now a white stem / drawn in the serious air of your breath. / Letting itself down, the careful / ballerina closing the halo / of her partner's arms." She is devotedly alert to gestures, glances, and pauses, which for her are the gates between worlds of equal value—the seen and the unseen—as described in a love poem called **"The Calm":** ". . . If I knew where to find you / I would say goodbye / and have the hurtful ease of that, / but the gates are everywhere / and this calm—an imagined forgiveness, / the childhood before we meet again." (p. 408)

People do volunteer work, go camping, or have affairs, for that matter, hoping to experience moments of rightness like the ones often encountered in Tess Gallagher's poetry. Deep in the waters of the work is a raging conviction for justice, to ascertain and assert everyone's real needs, hopes, and triumphs. In **"My Mother Remembers That She Was Beautiful,"** Gallagher stirs up some of the privileges of the ordinary by manipulating reality:

> . . . She keeps her coat on, called into
> her childhood by such forgetting
> I am gone or yet
> to happen. She sees herself
> among the townspeople, the country glances
> slow with field and sky
> as she passes or waits
> with a brother in the hot animal smell
> of the auction stand: sunlight,
> straw hats, a dog's tail
> brushing her bare leg . . .

In **"Start Again Somewhere"** she mocks the standard consumer romance:

> . . . We've seen her type—the soft mouth
> and the set of the head like a dare.
> Who could resist?
> You only did well to catch yourself
> in time. Before your heart
> made a mess of it . . .

There is a movement in these poems—a search for the telling detail—which is not unlike that of a documentary if one substitutes imagery for visuals. As in a documentary, the largest statements are made through an accretion of personal testimony.

In an essay on poetry in translation, Gallagher wrote:

> I know that as a woman writer I had been unconsciously searching for a poet-heroine who was passionate, capable of supreme acts of the spirit; one who possessed intellect and personal dignity without disappearing over the horizon into the otherworldly. In my own poetic past I had Emily Dickinson who lived with her mother and father—Emily with her reclusive long-distance battles with God and a bodily death. I had Marianne Moore who lived with her mother and pirated from their conversations, and also those famed probings of the encyclopedia. In most recent times there has been a spectrum of man-haters, sexual and spiritual martyrs, suicides, placid say-no-evils, mild-mannered girl reporters, and faithful red riding hoods.

The poet-heroine she is looking for is, I think, the same person she often speaks to when she writes. This heroine encompasses the type of character one might call a traditional man—the sort who opens doors for others, picks up checks, says the hard things, makes his own way. It's unfortunate such an honor code has ever become confused with gender, but of course it has, and it is this exact confusion that overturns the focus of Gallagher's poetry and creates a surprising depth. She can be still, distilled, or she can simply freeze a motion so that you distill something from it yourself. The poet-heroine she speaks to and creates is made up of people she has loved deeply. The pace of the poetry is often their walk, the poetry's anguish their failings, and the poetry's victories their tribute. She writes, in **"Devotion: That It Flow; That There Be Concentration"**:

> Looking back to him from the train, I'll
> wave, though not too long—like a soul heading into
> the underworld—but more as one standing at
> the beginning of the beginning, a faint
> smile, or as with stage fright suffered inexplicably
> in an orchard.

If not for involvement with others, why stage fright? The failure she risks is diminishment through lack of resolve, by falling prey to distractions—the hazards of questing. Such battles often occur on her home ground of the Northwest. In poems such as **"The Woman Who Raised Goats"** she speaks of some of the false starts and wrong turns in finding her path: "My father worked on the docks. . . . My brothers succeeded him in this, but when I, / in that town's forsaken luster, offered myself, / the old men in the hiring hall creeled / back in their chairs . . . 'Saucy,' they said. 'She's saucy!' " She struggles for love— to find it, to shape it—in **"The Perfect Sky"** where she writes, "Cunningly, cunningly / she gives to those of her table / and they without apology / raise their bright forks. . . . Made calm / by some deeper neglect / her silhouette returns to the doorway." In **"Strategy,"** "I'll go; I'll say / forget that other, the one you took / to make the waiting shorter. / I'll say you didn't mean to / make a death of it like that. . . ." She battles for the honor of the worker, the family man / woman, the reliable provider in an unreliable world. From the title poem of **Under Stars**:

> In the yellowed light of a kitchen
> the millworker has finished his coffee,
> his wife has laid out the white slices of bread
> on the counter. Now while the bed they have left
> is still warm, I will think of you, you
> who are so far away
> you have caused me to look up at the stars.
>
> Tonight they have not moved
> from childhood, those games played after dark.
> Again I walk into the wet grass
> toward the starry voices. Again, I
> am the found one, intimate, returned
> by all I touch on the way.

In these shrewd stanzas, where the very solidity of the scene creates a wall between present and future, the reader and poet negotiate their relationship. How does anyone make his or her mark, it asks, in this marked-up world?

Her first book, **Instructions to The Double,** opens with an interesting biographical note:

> Tess Gallagher was born and raised between the Straits of Juan de Fuca and the Olympic Mountains in Northwestern Washington. She is the oldest of five children born to a father originally from Oklahoma and a mother from the Missouri Ozarks. The "woods" around the logging sites of her parents' small logging partnership were a memorable part of her childhood. Her father later became a longshoreman and bought a farm so as to teach his children "something not learned in books."

> Ms. Gallagher began working as a journalist at 16, and later attended the University of Washington where she studied with Theodore Roethke in the last class he taught. She later studied at the University of Iowa's Writers' Workshop, where she also made films. She has taught at St. Lawrence University and Kirkland College.

There is a rift between the two paragraphs. One can feel that the good student of the second paragraph is grateful to know the native daughter of the first and that the poet-heroine she seeks is the reconciliation between the two. The first paragraph is an American adventure story told with such economy and freshness it is in some ways already a poem. It has her voice. There is in it a fascination for region and heritage, a system of values I think I might accurately dub the American work ethic, and an earnestness that is seductive. There is pride in the naming of things: "Straits of Juan de Fuca"! One intuits that the poetic elements—selection, timing, order, detail, choice of range, tone, magnification—are clues which suggest to us not only who Tess Gallagher is but who she will be in the poetry. They tell us that when she talks about herself she is also not talking about herself but personifying a selection of impressions. Her father and mother are the patriarch and matriarch of these personifications:

> She was cleaning—there is always
> that to do—when she found,
> at the top of the closet, his old
> silk vest. She called me
> to look at it, unrolling it carefully
> like something live. . . .
>
> "Black Silk"

In the discrepancy between the two paragraphs is an instruction: *We're in this together,* says the second paragraph; *Just don't crush all the life out of the facts,* says the first. The instruction is repeated often in the work. In **"Devotion: That It Flow; That There Be Concentration,"** she begins, "My friend keeps kissing me goodbye, the kisses / landing, out of nervousness, on and about / the face. 'Leave the mistakes in' Ives told / his conductor, handing him the new score. . . ." The facts as they stand are what's important. They provide a place to begin. The first mission is to gather them up. In the title poem of *Instructions to the Double,* the double is the bait:

> So now it's your turn,
> little mother of silences, little
> father of half-belief. Take up
> this face, these daily rounds
> with a cabbage under each arm
> convincing the multitudes
> that a well-made-anything
> could save them. Take up
> most of all, these hands
> trained to an ornate piano
> in a house on the other side
> of the country.
>
> I'm staying here
> without music, without
> applause. I'm not going
> to wait up for you. Take
> your time. Take mine
> too. Get into some trouble
> I'll have to account for. . . .

Emotional signals often appear as the repetition in a line of a single word: "little mother of silences, little"; "without music, without." Trouble is irresistible because it is life itself. As an event, it takes the form of tough loves, displacements, fights for recognition, acceptance, and respect not only for oneself but for others and no one more than the independent-minded daughter or the hard, strong, rough father. Perhaps the most moving sequence of such poems is in a section of *Willingly* which concentrates on her father's life, death, and dying. Pride sweeps the work along. Pride is the strength of continuing. From **"Boat Ride"**:

> Being early on the water, like getting first
> to heaven and looking back through memory
> and longing at the town. Talking little, and
> with the low, tender part
> of our voices; not sentences but
> friendlier, as in nodding to one who already
> knows what you mean.
> Father in his rain-slicker—seaweed green over
> his coat, over blue work-shirt, over cream-
> colored thermal underwear that makes a white V
> at his neck. His mouth open so the breath
> doesn't know if it's coming or going—like any
> other wave without a shore. His mind
> in the no-thought of guiding the boat . . .

To talk about her father is to talk about the land. The long description of what he wears might be the description of the earth—green over blue over white. His life as a logger, longshoreman, farmer, fisherman anneal his every action to the land. So symbolized, he is the vehicle to and from her innermost world. It is an American landscape where pride, sometimes a hindrance to love, is essential to romance. The romance is spun out in the use of dialect, in dialect submerged until only its syncopated echo carries, and in the absolute fidelity of the poet's eye. Her percep-

tion of him is so large he changes her voice and rhythm from something smooth and trimmed to something rippled and hugely tender. "You can sing sweet / and get the song sung," she writes in the opening poem of this sequence about his death, "but to get to the third dimension / you have to sing it / rough, hurt the tune a little. Put / enough strength to it / that the notes slip. Then / something else happens. The song / gets large."

There is a movement outward in her latest book, *Willingly,* to distant places and distant dramas. In this attempt to reach across regions of time and space she is sometimes less successful. **"Stepping Outside"** is more a preparation for a poem than a sufficiently realized result. "Hearing of you," she writes to Akhmatova, "I never lost a brother though I have, never saw a husband to war, though I have, never kept with my father / the emptiness of his hand, my mother / the dying of her womb." In **"Eating Sparrows,"** a poem about China, there is a trumped-up concern about killing and eating one's meat—in this case the unlikely sparrow—that has an uneasy humor and does not compare with the complexity of **"Boat Ride,"** in which her father kills the dogfish tying up his fishing line. *Under Stars* contains a group of poems about Ireland in which her strengths are evident in poems that suggest her immediate experience of travelling such as **"Second Language,"** but other poems seem petulant, cursory. **"Woman Enough,"** for example, is a snapshot with a finger in the way of the lens. More successful, I think, is **"Second Language,"** an appealing idea to anyone who writes poetry. It draws some of its strength from the fact that the emotions of travel, of wandering alien landscapes until they give up their mystery and their people step out where you can see them, has had a long gestation period in this writer's heart:

> Outside, the night is glowing
> with earth and rain and you
> in the next room take up
> your first language.
> All day it has waited
> like a young girl in a field.
> Now she has stood up
> from the straw-flattened circle
> and you have taken her glance
> from the hills.

Here, language itself is a heroine, a culmination of conflicts and credos, practicalities and passions, a choreography of the mind. (pp. 415-21)

Vickie Karp, "Two Poets: Several Worlds Apiece," in Parnassus: Poetry in Review, *Vol. 12-13, No. 2, 1, 1985, p. 407-421.*

Elizabeth Alexander

Tess Gallagher's characters have comfortable, old-fashioned names like May, Ada, and Dotty. They make peach preserves, install their own storm windows, and fix plugged drains. This is a world of small towns and neighbors, a world where, in Gwendolyn Brooks' words, "it is our business to be bothered." But the day-to-day lives in *The Lover of Horses* are mined with small, extraordinary moments of epiphany and unsettling insight.

The Lover of Horses is the first volume of short stories from Tess Gallagher, who is best-known as a poet. If the fiction writer betrays her poetic side, it is with her strong, distinct voices that carry these stories instead of simple dramatization. Rather than employing purely objective third-person narration, Gallagher moves inside her protagonists' minds and lets them perceive and describe their own lives.

Yet these voices never veer from concrete impressions. In ["The Lover of Horses"], the narrator explores a streak of wildness in her family. This bent originates with her great-grandfather, who is either gypsy, drunk, or both, depending on who's describing: "Ever since my great-grandfather's outbreaks of gypsy-necessity, members of my family have been stolen by things—by mad ambitions, by musical instruments, by otherwise harmless pursuits from mushroom hunting to childbearing or, as was my father's case, by the more easily recognized and popular obsession with card playing." The difficult magic of family love, of heredity, of allegiance, permeates this book.

Gallagher freezes her character's lives at moments when something extraordinary seems to be occurring, publicly or privately. In **"Desperate Measures,"** a 17-year-old gofer-girl at a local paper and an off-beat photographer (who later robs a bank) go to take pictures of an 8-year-old's elaborate treehouse. Up among the branches, the young woman observes: "Before long, the day began to move into that intimate time which belongs to childhood, and to things we treasure and ultimately leave behind as having no currency in the unmysterious business of our daily lives." Gallagher's characters share the desire to nourish their imaginations and wrestle with intimacy. . . .

The closing story, **"Girls,"** is Ada's account of her efforts to make an elderly girlhood friend remember her. The two trade tales and thumb through snapshots, but Esther never does recognize her long-lost girlfriend Ada. Still, Ada washes Esther's hair and rubs her feet; Esther cooks Ada "wieners, and green beans fixed the way they'd had them back home." From Ada's perspective, the story concludes that "Somehow the kindness and intimacy they'd shared as girls had lived on in them. But Esther, no matter how much she might want to, couldn't remember Ada, and give it back to her, except as a stranger." True intimacy is hard-won in these stories, but the characters nonetheless concern themselves with each other's lives.

Gallagher favors winding, rhythmical sentences and lots of adjectives. She is good at gracefully incorporating her characters' colloquialisms into her narration; a limp handshake, for instance, "didn't have much squeeze to it." Each story is rich with these small specificities, and rather than forcing "folksiness," they simply tell us who's talking.

Gallagher's narrative progression is at moments awkward, jumping suddenly in time or lingering too long with plot offshoots. She also at times over-articulates the stories' moments of epiphany. These moments are usually found in a story's final paragraph. They become expected and merely underline what Gallagher has already shown with great subtlety.

But these distractions are minor. As with most of our lives, the day-to-day doings in *The Lover of Horses* are "unmysterious." Gallagher's eye is trained on the remarkable moments embedded in each life.

Elizabeth Alexander, "Extraordinary Epiphanies, Unsettling Insights," in Book World—The Washington Post, *September 14, 1986, p. 8.*

Bette Pesetsky

Here is another collection of short stories about small town American life, currently so popular a theme and overflowing with practitioners. Familiarity in the employ of a skilled writer is not to be scorned. The accomplishment of *The Lover of Horses,* the first collection of stories by the poet Tess Gallagher, is in the unique sensibility that extends our awareness of this territory. Ms. Gallagher writes her own small town. She is a chronicler of important moments in the circumscribed lives of her characters, echoing the past and forcing the pain of self-examination. Her sentences generously frame the inner life—and how gratifying not to be besieged by brand names in these stories, not to wander again through a K Mart.

The small town women whose lives control many of the stories are brilliantly particularized and do not saunter with a mere change of name from tale to tale. In **"Beneficiaries,"** one of my favorite stories here, childless Louise overhears her husband name as beneficiaries of a life insurance policy his children by his first marriage. She cannot bear knowing this, and—perhaps, as she says, to make things fair, or perhaps in retaliation—she names her brother's children as her beneficiaries. It has happened, cannot be undone, and the reader is moved through the texture of thick lives.

> What you imagined affected you: Louise could see that now. It did not stay in the mind. It got into the heart and into your words and changed the things you had hoped would give comfort. It stripped you bare, this imagining. It laid you in your grave and counted out your belongings and told you who would weep, who would go through your closets, taking what they needed. . . .

What shall we say the stories are about? Do they depict the frontiers of small town life? **"Turpentine"** is a portrait of secrets. In this story, Ginny and Tom Skoyles practice the modern mobile life—living a year or two in houses that Ginny repairs for resale while her husband designs computers for universities. Enter an Avon lady—transmogrified here into a bringer of psychic mysteries and sexual tensions. In **"Bad Company,"** Mrs. Herbert has chosen not to be buried near her husband—that she changes her mind and chooses to be buried at his side is a decision made too late.

In **"Recourse,"** one of Ms. Gallagher's finest stories, the author builds a complex and uneasy world where lives cross and recross. After years spent apart, Jewel Kirk and the narrator, Johnny, find themselves neighbors once again in their old hometown, the geography of their youth. Childhood sweethearts, spoiled marriages, betrayals—here, as elsewhere in this collection, the narrative directness and meticulous presentation of the banal details of life create a durable world. The characters of **"Recourse"** yearn to reach the American panacea for troubles—"There's nothing left now except California." Still, they fear to go.

I lay there with my mind empty awhile. Then I thought of the river, of leaving it behind, and I felt something that had nothing to do with California or anywhere else I might ever be. I was getting close to sleep, but I seemed to be moving through images of my young days on the Little Niangua River.

Some of the stories, while well written, are still too predictable in their conclusions—for example, **"The Wimp,"** where a husband cannot strike a blow against his bullying brother-in-law as his insulted wife desires; yet in the end the husband is not found wanting. "This peaceable good man I had meant to squander with blows against my brother," the wife concludes. In **"Desperate Measures"** we have a newspaper employee, a braggart-liar, who comes with his imagined past to work magic on the narrator. In **"A Pair of Glasses"** the allusions are too easy—a world made different through dime-store glasses.

What Ms. Gallagher is *not* is carried away often enough. We are sometimes too aware of the controlling intelligence behind the story. What we want sometimes is a greater emotional leap, a noisier epiphany. But even the less arresting stories here are richly layered. . . .

What I tried to do in reading Ms. Gallagher's stories was to forget what a fine poet the author is. And the reward was to find an excellent writer of prose who savors the elegance of simplicity and whose stories resonate and linger.

> *Bette Pesetsky, "Secrets and Surprises in a Durable World," in* The New York Times Book Review, *September 28, 1986, p. 9.*

Greg Johnson

The most distinctive feature of American short fiction in the 1980's is its variety. A contemporary writer of short stories is more likely to produce work that is idiosyncratic, wayward, richly individual—which is to say, more classically "American"—than at any other time in the recent past. The current, much-publicized renaissance of the short story may owe a great deal, in fact, to the absence of any dominant aesthetic program in the genre. If the cultural upheavals of the 1960's appeared to prescribe the radical experimentation of John Barth, Donald Barthelme, and their many imitators, and if the inward-turning disillusionment of the 1970's spawned the oblique, pareddown realism of Ann Beattie, Raymond Carver, and *their* many imitators, it would appear that this decade has produced no corresponding major trend except in the direction of an extreme and heartening diversity. The short story collections (many of them first books) which lately have been pouring from New York publishers and small presses alike, and which often receive the kind of enthusiastic promotion and advertising once reserved for novels, suggest a lessening allegiance to institutional kinds (*The New Yorker* story, the workshop story) and an increased willingness to range along a broad aesthetic spectrum, according to the writer's individual perspective. (p. 409)

Thanks to the resurgence of interest in the short story, the unwritten rule that a fiction writer must produce a novel before hoping to publish a book of stories no longer has currency: the reputations of such younger writters as Amy Hempel and Peter Cameron rest solely upon their work in the shorter form (as does Raymond Carver's, of course), while David Leavitt and Bobbie Ann Mason made their names via impressive first books of stories before venturing into the novel. Occasionally, though, the rush to publish talented writers has resulted in some very uneven collections, and this is the case with Tess Gallagher's *The Lover of Horses.* Already possessed of a substantial and well-deserved reputation as a poet, she may have won publication as a story writer more easily on that account; but while *The Lover of Horses* contains two or three remarkable stories, most of the book reads like apprentice work, promising but undistinguished both in content and style.

Gallagher's prose is determinedly spare, direct, and plain. If her models are writers like Hemingway and Carver, however, her everyday prose lacks the energy and careful nuance of the "stripped-down" style they so deliberately achieved. Many of Gallagher's stories read as if they were pounded out at the typewriter during a single morning; they have no distinctive voice, and their subject matter is mundane to the point of monotony. In **"A Pair of Glasses,"** for instance, a young girl is determined to participate in the adult world by wearing glasses, even though she doesn't need them. Eventually girl gets glasses. Then girl loses glasses. Finally, she "felt she had fallen into the company of people who hated eyeglasses. She didn't know why this was so." End of story. Evidently Gallagher is trying for a Chekhovian simplicity here, a touching parable of childhood, but the characters never come to life and the story stops rather than ends.

The collection does include a couple of impressive stories. In **"The Wimp,"** a woman becomes enraged when her husband avoids a confrontation with her hostile, abusive brother; in the course of the story, she must re-examine her stereotyped notion of relationships between the sexes, and the ending is both amusing and bittersweet. Even better is **"King Death,"** in which a couple deals with a potentially violent next-door neighbor called "The Mad Hatter" and a hobo called "King Death." The story is allegorical but never heavy-handed, and it makes a powerful statement about contemporary paranoia and isolation. Such stories would have made a fine start for a future, impressive collection by Gallagher; unfortunately she has published a first volume which, on the whole, lacks clarity and scrupulous attention to craft. (pp. 410-11)

> *Greg Johnson, "Short Fiction in the Eighties," in* The Georgia Review, *Vol. XLI, No. 2, Summer, 1987, pp. 409-14.*

Rhoda Carroll

Tess Gallagher's *Amplitude* establishes her as a stunning and original contemporary voice. This volume, which contains selections from *Instructions to the Double* (1976), *Under Stars* (1980) and *Willingly* (1984), as well as 26 new poems, has precisely the right title, so ably presenting the extent and range of Gallagher's poetry. Individually, the poems are meticulously crafted; as a collection, they demonstrate Gallagher's depth and virtuosity: the mix of the local and the surreal in **"Instructions to the Double"** ("Pine needles drift / onto my face and breasts / like the tiny hands / of watches"), the strengthening narrative line in **"Under Stars"** ("The dead / were unspectacular, scattered and inarticulate / preferring to be handled and stepped over, / though at times they seemed to argue /

among themselves, a continual racket about the beauty / of the universe or the piteousness of the human / voice, filling the ancient night / with their elaborate nostalgia"), and the ripening devotion of **"Willingly"** ("Some paint has dropped onto your shoulder / as though light concealed an unsuspected / weight. You think it has fallen through / you. You think you have agreed to this, / what has been done with your life, willingly"). These are all strong and delicate poems, resonant with wisdom and generosity and the vicissitudes of family life. It is hard to believe, in these cynical times, that such a voice could be convincing, but it is. Amply.

Rhoda Carroll, in a review of "Amplitude: New and Selected Poems," in Small Press, *Vol. 5, No. 4, April, 1988, p. 61.*

Marianne Boruch

In *Amplitude,* Tess Gallagher's . . . collection of new and selected poems, it is especially clear in the recent work that a . . . sea-change is at hand. Gallagher's poems have always been unique: witty and heartfelt, honed to absolute matters of friendship and family, open to an increasingly difficult complexity of nuance, often of cadence, a work, she reminds us again in the poem which served as the title poem of her first volume, clearly "a dangerous mission. You / could die out there. You / could live forever" (**"Instructions to a Double"**). All these qualities continue, still cut with personal relish in the new poems though some of the work approaches a different level of being. One hesitates to use the word *rhetorical,* a stance popularly kept distant in its armor, rigid with little single-celled needles. Less kneejerk, more gratefully certain, one could call this new edge a slippage into a world, a vision of the world wrought equally by mystery and purpose.

Many of the new poems do actively seek a way to know. The poet, for instance, takes on a whole generation's way of knowing in **"The Story of a Citizen,"** which begins in conversation, a rainy day, a coffee shop, an Alan, a Jerry, a whomever else, a you, of course the speaker, all fixing definition against *"our* era," a time to be "known for its blatant political / pornography: 'No contours, only oscillating / transitions . . .'" or against art where one witnesses the "elevation of a dead dog into / negotiable value. . . ." All this—given rain, given downpour into which the speaker departs—seeds profound melancholy, in turn seeding a rapid-fire, long-sentenced, at times dazzling fury, high oratory really, of personal, generational discovery. It is, in short, "the history of how I"—the speaker, the poet—"became a soldier . . . / . . . who / waits uneasily for orders, who despises / her superiors, who once was a mist of tenderness, / . . . who is apolitical which is / the tribe of the soldier . . . / who thinks, 'A short nap / in the snow would be exceedingly nice,' . . . / whose campaign is the Campaign Under Moonlight / " baying " . . . like a wolf / . . . the hotline / to the spirits of her ancestors. . . . " On and on, this . . . is litany *against,* shot through, indelibly stained and heightened by the "sacrificed, the bodies . . . of civilian saints . . . / though saint," she tells us, "is a word in poverty / when the memories of nations die with them. . . . "

Like [poet Philip] Levine, Gallagher is intent on recovery, personal, at times, national, in a style more and more nar-

rative. Her style begins to honor a greater discursive, abstract naming as well, by turns giddy, then urgent with clauses, heaping them up, letting them fall into a texture near music. In one of the strongest poems here, [**"Amplitude"**], Gallagher takes the best invention of these options, and weaves the personal thread—a Christmas day ride with her brother—into a philosophical reverie of time which links up quickly with larger issues of identity and change. It is, after all, a Mercedes that takes them now through the home town, "past the shack we were raised / in" where, in childhood, these same riders flung rocks at the "bumper-to-bumper Californians, dragging / their mobile homes and over- / sized boats" back. Then the inevitable hallucination, the poet blacking out years to pick up those children for a brief ride of "wordless awe" and putting them back again on the simple street where, at once, in habit, they "set to / with a slingshot" at the vanishing car. So "memory," Helen Vendler recalls Lowell saying at a reading, "is genius." And a slow fire, too, it rankles and burns, moving us to conclusions, some terrible, beyond memory. (p. 40)

Marianne Boruch, "Blessed Knock," in The American Poetry Review, *Vol. 17, No. 4, July-August, 1988, pp. 39-41.*

Margaret Randall

At times one senses a strangely bitter (or wistful?) resignation in the "being woman" of Gallagher's poems. Her opening [poem in *Amplitude: New and Selected Poems*], **"Kidnaper,"** seems to set the mood for much of the book: "He is lost. I believe him. It seems / he calls my name. I move / closer. He says it again, the name / of someone he loves. I step back pretending / not to hear. I suspect / the street he wants / does not exist, but I am glad to point / away from myself."

Certainly there are moments in this collection in which the poet's own craft changes the weight she displaces, pulls her to full height in lines such as these on which we enter **"Beginning to Say No"**: "BEGINNING TO SAY NO / is not to offer so much as a first, is / to walk away firmly, as though / you had settled something foolish, / is to wear a tarantula in your buttonhole / yet smile invitingly, unmindful / how your own blood grows toward the irreversible / bite. No, I will not / go with you. No, that is not / alright. I'm not your sweet-dish, your / home-cooking, good-looking daf- / fodil." The lines are perfectly broken. Craft and meaning are one.

What about Tess Gallagher's retrieval of memory? In **"Ritual of Memories,"** as in other poems, she does it through a male counterpart: "you came up / like a man pulling himself out of a river." And she tells him: "Remember, it was a country road / above the sea and I was passing / from the house of a friend. Look / into these eyes where we met. / I saw your mind go back through the years / searching for that day and finding it, / you washed my eyes / with the pure water / so that I vanished from that road / and you passed a lifetime / and I was not there."

Margaret Randall, "Speaking Out of Memory," in Belles Lettres: A Review of Books by Women, *Vol. 4, No. 1, Fall, 1988, p. 16.*

Nicci Gerrard

[In *The Lover of Horses,*] Tess Gallagher displays a solid and slightly cranky talent. She does not flash her gifts, she ruminates upon a lunatic world. Few of her stories develop any real narrative; instead they chew upon a theme, extracting all its juice and flavour. Amplification takes the place of plot, as a tiny event or a simple character gathers implications. Instead of a climax the narrator (often a solitary woman speaking from a lonely house in small town America, whose understatements conceal a wealth of pain) will sum up her tale's significance, emphasising how the smallest episode can trigger an emotional crisis.

So **"King Death"**, for instance, describes a suburban wife's reactions to the wino who curls in a heap of raw limbs and ragged clothes outside her well-cleaned windows. Nothing actually happens; the story's interest lies in the slow growth of the narrator's grudging and disquieting compassion. It is a description of a crucial internal moment with no impact on the outside world.

In the best of these stories, Tess Gallagher's undramatic intelligence works wonders with her static form. [**"The Lover of Horses"**], in which a girl tends her dying father as he plays his final game of poker, is a robust and patient examination of obsession; the prose develops by memory association, and its assurance nourishes the frail narrative. But in the less successful tales such linguistic confidence becomes ponderous, and melancholy tenderness sours into lugubrious pondering. And in spite of their very different subjects—a housewife developing a compulsive interest in a pale young Avon lady, a schoolgirl becoming obsessed with owning a pair of glasses, a couple arguing over who should be beneficiaries in their wills—there is too much similarity of tone in *The Lover of Horses.* A resigned bafflement at life's sly surprises dominates the collection, giving it a vigorous but unsurprising eccentricity.

Sometimes the pain of self-reflection gets waterlogged by repetition and Gallagher's sense of time and place, her controlled prose and her meticulous details, are dragged down into the slow-moving depths of her narrative. Usually, however, the stories in *The Lover of Horses* work by stealth. Their simplicity and undemonstrative poignancy linger in the memory.

Nicci Gerrard, "Life's Sly Surprises," in New Statesman & Society, *Vol. 2, No. 44, April 7, 1989, p. 42.*

Lex Runciman

A book such as *Amplitude*—one which combines old work with new—is both fish and fowl. Readers familiar with Tess Gallagher's work will almost certainly find their earlier favorites here, poems which consistently reward readers' attention. My own list would have to include **"The Coats," "Rhododendrons," "Instructions to the Double," "The Ritual of Memories," "Under Stars," "Woodcutting on Lost Mountain,"** and **"Reading Aloud,"** to name but half a dozen plus one. Readers new to Gallagher's work might consider these poems by way of introduction.

From another perspective, a volume of new and selected poems provides an opportunity for early conclusions about a writer's strengths, her development, and her most current poetic aims. Tess Gallagher's early poems show her as a poet of what one could loosely refer to as "the private life." Her early work embodies and confronts central questions of individual selfhood and of one's relationships inside the family. By speaking movingly and successfully about such private matters, Gallagher's poems become a significant voice, a significant force, in the interior lives of her readers.

In *Willingly* (the volume prior to this one) and certainly here in the new work, Gallagher clearly wants to write a more public, overtly political kind of poem. The difficulties here are formidable, and Gallagher has not entirely overcome them. Alas, in poems like **"That Kind of Thing,"** the lines go alarmingly slack. In fact, the verse paragraphs in that poem could easily be recast as prose.

But there are a variety of fresh, witty, compassionate, wise, and meditative poems here too. They constitute (to borrow from the opening of **"Bonfire"**), "The inflections of joy. The inflections of / suffering. And strangely / sometimes the mixing / of the two."

Lex Runciman, in a review of "Amplitude: New and Selected Poems," in Western American Literature, *Vol. XXIV, No. 1, May, 1989, p. 85.*

John Clute

At first glance, [the stories in *The Lover of Horses*] are quiet tales of small lives sunk into the backwaters of the continent, far from any dreams of heroism; anecdotes of men and women drowned too deep in the huge unreadable world to afford us histories. It is only as they end that Gallagher's stories reveal themselves. The final words of each story in the book—even including the strained exorbitance that terminates [**"The Lover of Horses"**], the weakest tale in the collection—transform mute lives into significance, recoup solitary existences into the mosaic of the whole. If the secret of writing a short story is knowing how to end it, then Gallagher is a master.

In her genius for control over closure, Gallagher resembles the late Raymond Carver, who shared with her the last years of his life; but she is a far more talkative writer than he is—at times almost to the point of slackness, so that the final moments of tales such as **"Recourse"** and **"The Wimp"** surprise the reader with a singular vividness, a sudden joy of understanding not often found in the work of her husband. The long circumstantial meanderings of **"Recourse"**, during which several characters meet and part over several decades, ends in a stunningly well-prepared image of the river that also flows through these lives, on its way to the sea; and at this moment the protagonist's planned removal to California takes on a signification that is both unexpected and fully earned. In **"The Wimp"**, narrated by the wife of an elderly and ineffectual man, the humiliations of a painful family quarrel with her violent brother threaten to corrode a sane marriage, until finally a drunken beggar blunders fortuitously into their lives to transform her sense of things. "I understood then that the dangers of manhood were all around us. And I felt I knew intimately what he was thinking and feeling, this peaceable good man I had meant to squander with blows against my brother." In the elegant density of these closing sentences, the protagonists of **"The Wimp"** are joined and bear witness to the larger world, the world of meaning and history our novels claim to inhabit as by right.

> John Clute, "Survivors' Stories," in The Times
> Literary Supplement, No. 4503, July 21-27,
> 1989, p. 803.

Linda Gregerson

Tess Gallagher's earliest instincts were those of a fabulist, and the contours of fable, or narrative-in-a-clearing, continue to inform her more recent poems, even those most conspicuously grounded in the clutter and wash of experience. From the beginning, she has made parables out of the dramatized self and its doubles (a kidnapper, a shadow, the nascent breasts that divide a girl from her brothers), and this dramatized self forges large-scale unities of method even as the poet moves from isolate and universalized paradigms to the increasingly explicit contexts of autobiography. The "I" is unremittingly present in [***Amplitude: New and Selected Poems***], set upon the stage of the poem as its chief poetic figure, embodying one portion of poetic consciousness ("I dance / like a woman led to a vault of spiders"; "I went to you in that future / you can't remember yet") and speaking another ("Time to rehabilitate your astonishment, I said / to myself and plunged on / into the known"; "I was suited more to an obedience / of windows. If anyone had asked, / I would have said, 'Windows are my prologue' "; "I think I said some survivals need / a forest. But it was only the sound / of knowing"). "The sound of knowing" is bread and butter to these poems, which prefer sensibility to sense. The "I" here, as even random excerpts would make clear, is treated very tenderly by the hand that writes; this "I" loves the drama of gesture and temperament and above all loves publicity.

Gallagher uses performative or dramatized means of assertion—phrases cast as the speeches of a shadow persona—as a kind of vatic license: she can play with the oracular and the histrionic while seeming to temper them with irony and afterthought. The playful capacities of estrangement are perhaps most apparent in the further reaches of Gallagher's diction: "Dear ones, in those days it was otherwise"; "Denial, O my Senators, / takes a random shape." Less playful and more worrisome tonally are the estrangements of syntax: " . . . he knew something he couldn't know / as only himself, something not to be told again / even by writing down the doing / of it"; "She was brought up manly for a woman / to dread the tender word." Part of the intention here seems to be a kind of new-forged contract between consciousness and language, perception frictionally and ingenuously reinventing the wheel of the sentence. But the record of consciousness thus produced too often seems to be straining after effect. (pp. 231-32)

The dramatized self in these poems bears the burden of moral consciousness, of course, mapping the cultural terrain by gestures of empathy (toward a Russian poet, toward celebrants at an Irish wedding) and repugnance (toward the agents of privilege and neo-colonialism in impoverished Brazil). The central moral fable of Gallagher's four books is the fable of class, and foothold here is precarious. The plot, quite common in American poetry during the last forty years, is one of escape from the working class to the writing class and the privileges of reflection. "Is that / what you do for a living?" asks a black porter of the poet on a train. "You're lucky." The poet's honorable response is to make of the poem "a morality," "a living" in more than the economic sense. Nevertheless, the luck that divides her from the lives of her parents and siblings while preserving that other life as poetic subject and the commonly-coded ground of poetic "authenticity" is luck with a cutting edge. Such luck tends, for one thing, to complicate virtue with virtue's spoils. When the poet whose motive and range of sympathies derive in part from early constraint writes a poem about visiting Brazil, she and her famous companion are guests of the lecture circuit; they stay at a luxury hotel. Carolyn Forché, in her strategic second book, tackled head-on this bifurcation of experience and the related circle of self-promotion. In a preemptive gesture of simultaneous boast and confession, Forché wrote, "If you read this poem, write to me. / I have been to Paris since we parted," this to a childhood friend who never got out, who lives with her broken husband in a trailer near Detroit. Gallagher means, I think, to explicate the same double bind, but her equipment is cruder. In [**"Amplitude"**], Gallagher drives with her brother through the mill town of their childhood in "Ray's Mercedes." Less willing than Forché to discredit the boast herself, Gallagher lets the boast discredit her.

The wages of self-consciousness are mixed. Much to the credit of ***Amplitude,*** its poems make of memory a dialectical movement, framed and double-framed by the mortal distance of gain and loss. The moving collection of poems to the poet's father, to her mother, to her brothers dead and alive, find in the heart's good chambers and in the filiations of domestic love plenty of room to accommodate mere contradiction (see, for instance, the genial tough-mindedness of **"Cougar Meat"**). The disciplined naysayings of **"Message for the Sinecurist"** and **"The Story of a Citizen"** lend counterpoint and sinew to the varied affirmations of **"Redwing,"** **"Small Garden Near a Field,"** **"Bonfire,"** and a host of other poems. And among the other attractions of this volume, there are poems—**"Black Silk"** from ***Willingly*** and **"His Shining Helmet: Its Horsehair Crest"** among the new poems—whose emotional and material economies are shapeliness itself. (pp. 232-33)

> Linda Gregerson, in a review of "Amplitude:
> New and Selected Poems," in Poetry, Vol.
> CLV, No. 3, December, 1989, pp. 231-33.

Bin Ramke

The great joy in reading Tess Gallagher's poetry comes from discovering that she can and will do anything with language. Consider, for instance, **"Time Lapse with Tulips,"** in which she shows us "a house with a harp / in the window"; the image is in itself worthy and wonderful. But in this poem the more serious issue has to do with lying and with art: "Whatever the picture says, it is wrong"; the issue also has to do with the effect of framing, making art which implicates a violence that is both life and art:

> . . . and that harp
> seen through a window suddenly so tempting
> you must rush into that closed room, you must
> tear your fingers across it.

Years after she wrote this, she wrote a poem called **"If Poetry Were Not a Morality,"** in which she said, while looking for the *simplicity* which some think poetry can offer: "If the heart could be that simple. / The photo / of Ghandi's last effects taped near / my typewriter." The speaker at this point thinks that she is speaking about, for instance, getting her own life down to "a few essentials," as Ghandi seemed to do. Later, she thinks of her grandfather:

> one of those chiefs who could never
>
> get enough horses. Who if he had two hundred
> wanted a hundred more and a hundred more . . .
>
>   . . . their horseness
> gleamed back at him like soundless music until
> he knew something he couldn't know
> as only himself, something not be told again
> even by writing down the doing
>
> of it. I meet him like that sometimes,
> wordless and perfect, with more horses than he
> can ride or trade or even know why
> he has.

"More horses than we need" comes to mean, in this poem, joy—even to the joy that can make a life that *will* end worthwhile. It seems that morality and joy are closely allied for this poet, for those horses are of a moral dimension, are a moral measure. The need to regret nothing has less to do with "doing good" than with recognizing the necessity of going beyond sufficiency. Which is to say, going into art.

"That Kind of Thing" is a poem from the "New Poems" section of [*Amplitude: New and Selected Poems*]. . . . The argument of the poem has to do with an Information Officer from the American Consulate of Salvador, Brazil, and it has to do with the curiosity and confusion of the American visitors—an American poet and a famous fiction writer. Eventually the Information Officer takes his leave, reminding his visitors to call on him for help: " 'that's what / I'm here for,' (in this hell hole, he / seemed to want to add)." But just before leaving the hotel room the Officer says he has read Ray's work, but finds it too depressing. "I have to live / with that kind of thing / down here all the time." The tag, "Bahia, Brazil, 1984" adds the last touch of authenticity, a further reassurance that what has been said is Truth, not merely Art.

In its apparent directness and obvious presentation of "just the facts, Ma'am," this poem achieves something which as in every good poem, goes beyond what the poet thought she was doing. There are hints here and there, in this as in all of Gallagher's work, of something bigger than what even the poet is able to deal with. In fact, it seems that the times when Gallagher fails are the times when she feels too much in control, too much aware of the line between "reality" ("I have to live / with that kind of thing") and "art" ("that harp / seen through the window"). In **"Devotion: That It Flow; That There Be Concentration"** she admits that:

> The mind flies out
>   into this unconcealing.

> Shadows
>   kissed.

The attempt to kiss the shadows sometimes tempts her into believing she knows the difference between the concealing and the unconcealing. But most of the time, as in this excellent long poem, the difference is unclear, and the poetry can happen, wild and willful and without redress. " 'Leave the mistakes in,' Ives told / his conductor, handing him the new score" quotes Gallagher. Of course she also said, earlier (in **"Zero"**), "Stupid tranquility, to be most sure / in the abstract." She was quite right then and remains quite right in her latest work, recognizing that the *sureness* of the abstractness is stupid tranquility. But she also recognizes the power in poetry-of-the-abstract as in poetry-of-the-specific, that "the careful / ballerina closing the halo / of her partner's arms" is lovely for our failure to see the partner, for his presence being purely abstract.

In fact, it is the abstract which allows Gallagher to write her poems, allows her to escape the pain of her own past and enter the greater pain of the present tense of art. Consider the dangerous domesticity of these titles: **"Kidnapper," "My Mother Remembers that She was Beautiful," "The Ritual of Memories," "I Save Your Coat, But You Lose It Later," "3 A.M. Kitchen: My Father Talking," "If Blood Were Not as Powerful as It Is."** The past of her own family, her heritage in all its difficult stubborn reality, gritty and lovable and hateful, she bears through all these poems. But she recognizes her burden as being greater than this specificity alone. She *is* a poet, and a good one, and the sometimes terrifying implication of her talent is that she abstracts even her own loves, her own people and places, and she doesn't know why; she only knows that the language will tell as surely as the blood. From **"Small Garden, Near a Field"** (surely a title as certain of its realisms and coziness as any), comes this amazingly credible beginning:

> While any two are talking, one,
> without glimpsing it, has already shed
> the confident smile of the living.

This happens to be my favorite of Tess Gallagher's most recent poems, but I cannot explain exactly why. I will suggest that in this poem, which is about her family (and which is also what some used to call "confessional"), the power of the poem is in the recognition of language and its curious abstractness: " . . . not enough beds so they sent you / into mine to be thralled sleepward with stories. / Language to you is still errand and magic." (pp. 7, 28)

I am reminded by this poem of, oddly enough, Maya Lin's design for the memorial to the Vietnam War dead. Lin is the daughter of a poet mother and a ceramicist father. The hardness of her father's art suggests the glossy, glassy mirroring surface for all the faces which come to look; and the text of that least abstract poem—the real poem of any war, the roll of names—is related to her mother's art of poetry. It is the combination of the hardness and abstractness that lets each of us who looks at the memorial see our own faces looking back, whether crying or merely curious. But it is the specific poetry of the name that brought us there to face the issue first.

Tess Gallagher's poetry is a similar sort of memorial. She names those people or issues or landscapes for us, which we think we love, so that we gather to look. But even beyond the poet's own knowledge, the hardness of the language, the edge of the abstract is sharp enough to draw blood, hard enough to reflect all our losses and longings; this is what keeps us enthralled. (p. 28)

Bin Ramke, "The Confident Smile of the Living," in The Bloomsbury Review, *Vol. 10, No. 1, January-February, 1990, pp. 7, 28.*

William Gibson

1948-

(Full name William Ford Gibson) American-born Canadian novelist, short story writer, and scriptwriter.

Gibson is a leading practitioner of "cyberpunk," a futuristic style of science fiction that combines the tough atmosphere and scatological language of crime fiction, imagery from the punk counter-culture movement, and technical developments of the 1980s. Like "New Wave" science fiction writers of the 1960s, who introduced such topics as sex and drugs to a traditionally conservative genre, Gibson updates conventional science fiction concerns to reflect contemporary trends. His first novel, *Neuromancer*, for which he received a Nebula Award, a Hugo Award, and a Philip K. Dick Memorial Award, established him as the most popular and seminal writer of cyberpunk. Mikal Gilmore commented: "Of the dozen or so authors working in the cyberpunk style, Gibson is clearly the movement's pick to click. With his swift, colorful dialogue and his flair for creating a believably gritty future, he has forged the most convincing blend of sci-fi and hard-boiled detective styles in American pulp history."

Neuromancer introduces the near-future world of "the Sprawl," a huge, urbanized area covering much of the United States. Gibson blends the ominous ambience of 1940s *film noir* with detailed depiction of poverty, pollution, and technical opulence in the manner of Ridley Scott's film, *Blade Runner.* Ruthless corporations control the world's economy and governments, hiring "mercs" (mercenaries) for kidnappings and assassinations and to steal information from other corporations. The underworld, which is controlled by equally amoral criminal and counterculture elements, employs specialists known as "cowboys." By linking their brains directly with computers, cowboys attempt to pirate data by breaking through the "cyberspace matrix," a subreality simulated by a sentient, globally-linked computer database. The protagonist of *Neuromancer* is Case, a cowboy whose previous employers deprived him of his semi-psychic ability to penetrate cyberspace for conspiring against them. With the aid of Molly who, like many of Gibson's characters, uses concealed cybernetic weapons, including surgically implanted razors beneath her fingernails, Case attempts to penetrate a global information grid and thwart a plot involving an enormous artificial intelligence. Although faulted for weak characters and an obfuscated plot, Gibson's novel, according to many critics, revitalized the science fiction genre. Pat Cadigan stated that the creation of cyberspace "may be Gibson's best, most original, and thus most enduring contribution to speculative fiction."

The setting and underlying premise of *Neuromancer* are developed in detail in *Burning Chrome,* a volume of Gibson's early short fiction that also includes pieces written in collaboration with fellow "cyberpunks" Bruce Sterling, John Shirley, and Michael Swanwick. Several of these pieces have been widely anthologized and are generally praised for their consistent craftsmanship and subtle portrayals of characters caught up in fantastic events. J. R.

Wytenbroek commented: "These stories show careful craftsmanship and a true literary edge. Gibson, like so many of his [science fiction] predecessors and colleagues, shines in the short story form. His characters seem human, vulnerable and three-dimensional." *Count Zero,* a continuation of *Neuromancer* set seven years after the events of the previous novel, revolves around Bobby Newmark, a novice cowboy who uses the name "Count Zero" as his handle. After entering the cyberspace matrix for the first time, Newmark is held captive by cultists who worship a form of artificial intelligence that has fragmented into various cybernetic beings. This plot converges with two other stories, one of which concerns a cybernetic specialist who helps a scientist's daughter evade mercenaries seeking software implanted in her body. Algis Budrys commented that despite the novel's complex subplots and themes, *Count Zero* is "ultimately a story about love, on a level of sophistication well beyond . . . what anyone in [the science fiction] field except Gene Wolfe and a very few others have attained. . . . It does not replicate or sequelize *Neuromancer,* it completes it."

In his novel *Mona Lisa Overdrive,* Gibson elaborates upon and answers technical questions raised in *Neuromancer* and *Count Zero.* In this work, characters may "die" into computers, where they may support or sabotage the outer world's reality. The book features multiple plots, including one involving a thirteen-year-old girl sent to London as protection from her wealthy father's business rivals. However, she conspires with a cybernetically altered woman to defeat his associates. Edward Bryant commented: "[Gibson] has crafted a cool, exciting, praiseworthy novel that brilliantly pyramids the successes of its predecessors. While other science fiction writers are still recapping every decade from the thirties up through the present, Gibson is already writing for the nineties and beyond."

(See also *CLC,* Vol. 39 and *Contemporary Authors,* Vol. 126.)

PRINCIPAL WORKS

NOVELS

Neuromancer   1984
Count Zero   1986
Mona Lisa Overdrive   1988

SHORT FICTION COLLECTION

Burning Chrome   1986

Howard Coleman

I think I'm safe in assuming that readers of this august publication know who William Gibson is and that his novel ***Neuromancer*** won the 1985 Hugo. That much said, I'll also hazard a guess that most of you realize that his most recent book, ***Burning Chrome,*** is neither a work of exotic metallurgy nor a manual for the disposition of antique car parts. What it is, is a collection of all of Gibson's short fiction published to date. More than that, ***Burning Chrome*** is also a Notable Event in SF.

It's notable because it contains the stories by which Gibson became the exemplar of "cyberpunk" SF, whether he wanted to be or not. . . . It's also notable because, on the basis of a few of these pieces, Gibson became an extremely "hot" writer. (To borrow from the spirit of the National Pastime, just before ***Neuromancer*** appeared, Gibson's Acclaim-to-Words-Published Ratio led the league.) Other writers notice all this, of course, and even now the wave of William Gibson-inspired SF breaks around us. Having Gibson's stories all here in one place will provide some interesting perspectives into this onrushing tide.

It will also provide some interesting perspectives into the stories themselves. For those of you who aren't fans, but just read the stuff, there is some pretty good SF in this book. . . .

Of the ten stories in ***Burning Chrome,*** seven are by Gibson alone, and three are collaborations, with John Shirley, Bruce Sterling and Michael Swanwick. (There's also a preface by Sterling.) Six of the Gibson solos and **"Dog-fight,"** written with Swanwick, are set in or around the near future world of ***Neuromancer*** and of Gibson's second novel, ***Count Zero.***

An interesting way to get there is through the other solo story, **"The Gernsback Continuum."** The Gernsback of the title, is, of course, our very own Hugo, patron saint of scientifiction and of that almost baroque faith in the infinite perfectability of human society through technology. The story's protagonist is afflicted with a condition which parodies our famous optimistic futurism: he actually sees the world of sleek space opera shapes and noble human specimens who lived in the pages of pulp magazines, and it terrifies him. To rid himself of this unwanted sense of wonder, he overdoses on reality, on the everyday catastrophe and havoc of life. Whatever it takes to meet the future, unreasoning belief that aircars and telescreens will cushion the shock is worse than no belief at all.

Stepping from the Gernsback to the Gibson continuum, to the world of Chiba City and the Sprawl, we enter the unforgiving, glitzy, high-tech world of ***Neuromancer*** and ***Count Zero.*** There has been no nuclear Armageddon (though hostile one-man parafoils have ghosted through the night skies above Kiev, and chemically enhanced pilots have engaged in hurtling combat above Central American jungles). Technology's progress has accelerated it into a projectile which has shattered the global village of our dreams into a million razor-edged shards. Society is a planet-wide cybernetic jungle ruled by corporations which seem to coexist with, or perhaps only to tolerate governments.

Some of Gibson's most memorable characters (see **"Johnny Mnemonic"** and **"Burning Chrome"**) are creatures of this jungle, roaming the neon-lit streets of the endless cities and the glowing electronic paths of cyberspace. Their lives are spent on the edge between lying low to avoid the attention of larger, meaner predators (there is always someone stronger) and getting enough of the action to survive, for now.

Even the technology which permits seeing through another's eyes, living inside another's skin, does not ease but intensifies isolation (**"Fragments of a Hologram Rose"**). We take a brief look at the rest of the Universe, in **"Hinterlands,"** only to find that it is so strange, so hostile, that human sanity is the price to pay for a ride on the cosmic tollway. Whatever cruelties human society holds, the answer to the question, "What's it like, Out There?" seems to be "You don't want to know."

But some still *do* want to know, to try, even in the face of certain failure. These stories are saved from being unrelenting recitations of hopelessness by characters who still take chances on the unaffordable luxuries of hope and dreams and love. Sometimes, as in **"The Winter Market,"** the hope takes the form of an absolute ambition to escape the realities of life for a cybernetic existence which may or may not be better, but is at least different. In **"Johnny Mnemonic,"** the ambition is simply to survive a business transaction which has gone very bad.

Love is a dangerous matter, for Gibson's characters. Shaped by the hostile isolation of their world, they commit the crime of trust only at great risk. In **"Burning Chrome," "The Winter Market,"** and **"Fragments of a Hologram Rose,"** the result is loneliness. In **"The New Rose Hotel,"** it is death. In any case, it seems that the tenuous link between Gibson's characters and their constantly endangered humanity is just this romantic notion, that love still counts, whatever the odds against it.

It's this quality that fails in **"Dog-fight,"** a story with all the props but none of the substance. The protagonist (I don't like that word, but Gibson does not write about heroes) earns no sympathy and very little identification on the reader's part. Perhaps because of what has been done to him before the story opens, he has ceased to have any recognizably important human qualities. The story (on this year's Hugo ballot) has been described, oddly, as a tragedy. It is not. There is nothing noble about the character or about his empty victory. We can't believe he has sacrificed to attain his goals, when he actually had nothing to give up to begin with. But the story "sounds" right: the relentless pace and the can't-put-it-down style triangulated somewhere between Harlan Ellison and Raymond Chandler are instantly recognizable. It will serve to set off the remaining works in this book and to supply us with a "Gibson-clone" story which is not quite right against which to compare the deluge of such we can expect.

The remaining pieces, **"Red Star, Winter Orbit,"** written with Bruce Sterling, and **"The Belonging Kind,"** with John Shirley, are good stories which are very different from the rest of the book. They lack the raw energy of Gibson's solo style but not the realism it relates. From a grim view of where space travel in particular and society in general might be in just a few years, **"Red Star"** develops a resolution that depends not on technology but on the people who use it. (p. 38)

> Howard Coleman, "Other Voices, Other Voices," in Science Fiction Review, No. 61, Winter, 1986, pp. 38-9.

Fernando Q. Gouvea

William Gibson's first short story collection [*Burning Chrome*] is an important book. Gibson, who won both the Nebula and the Hugo awards for his first novel, is one of those suddenly rising stars that appear every so often in SF; he has also become the most notable of a group of talented and imaginative new writers, the "cyberpunks." This book deserves **all** the attention it will receive, however, because most of the stories are very good.

Gibson's fiction is marked by a flashy and fast-paced style and by exhaustively imaginative and innovative settings, very different from the traditional SF vision. (One of the stories, **"The Gernsback Continuum,"** offers an ironic comment on that vision.) Only two of these stories occur in space, and even these are downbeat, describing the last days of a decaying Russian space station (**"Red Star, Winter Orbit"**), and experiences which drive people crazy (**"Hinterlands"**).

The most characteristic setting for Gibson's stories is "the Sprawl," the ultrahigh-tech, computerized world of *Neuromancer.* The heroes of these stories are the people who live on the underside of society: amoral swindlers and down-and-outs who struggle against the multinational corporations which seem to have almost total power. This collection's four "Sprawl" stories all share first-person narrative, amoral heroes, exposition via flashbacks, emotional intensity—and pessimism. They are stories of passion, of rare victories and of all-too-common defeats.

There are analogies between what Gibson (and the "cyberpunks") are doing and what Campbell's writers did in the forties: he is imagining a future that is consistent both internally and with present trends, and his heroes tend to be people who are in some sense competent in the ways of their world. The difference is that Gibson's vision is of and for our time, and that much greater care is taken to write effectively.

Gibson is still a developing writer, but this collection of mostly excellent stories manifests both his talent and his importance for the field. It will give great pleasure to the serious SF reader. (pp. 22-3)

> Fernando Q. Gouvea, "Flashy, Fast-Paced Collection," in Fantasy Review, Vol. 9, No. 4, April, 1986, pp. 22-3.

Colin Greenland

Gibson's first novel, **Neuromancer** (1984), an agreeably hectic caper, was honoured with the three major science fiction awards. It provided the same adrenalin verve and random pyrotechnics as contemporary SF cinema, managing at the same time to be intellectually substantial. Gibson acknowledges the influence not so much of Alfred Bester (whose *future noir* thrillers caused similar excitement thirty years ago) or Philip K. Dick, but of Robert Stone, Thomas Pynchon and early Len Deighton.

Count Zero shows a conscientious broadening of scope and modulation of tone without any loss of brio. Since feminism, and the efforts of writers such as Ursula K. Le Guin to humanize the genre, it has not been necessary for the characters of "tough guy" SF to be either tough or guys. Gibson here gives us, in alternating chapters, the separate but convergent stories of three very different denizens of his "sexy dystopia": Count Zero himself, alias Bobby Newmark, an aspiring but touchingly dim young computer-crook; Marley Krushkhova, a Paris art dealer whose career is in ruins after her attempt to sell a fake foisted on her by her unscrupulous lover; and Turner, a mercenary in industrial espionage, a tough guy (as his mononym indicates) whose latest assignment will lead him away from taciturn violence to reconciliation with his past and the values of domesticity and peace. Each is summarily overtaken by an enigma that requires dedicated pursuit and precipitates personal change, enabling Gibson to add degrees of emotional warmth and subtlety to his range of description.

The complexity of his plot sufficiently indicates the complexity of this world, whose thrones and dominions are not always to be found where one might look for them. All the power and all the money are ostensibly with the zaibatsus, supranational industries that demand tribal allegiance and function like huge predatorial organisms. "The blood of a zaibatsu", says a character in Gibson's short story **"New Rose Hotel"**, "is information, not people. The structure is independent of the individual lives that comprise it." Politics has mutated into economics, and that into cybernetics. It is an economy of information, and therefore of secrecy. Everything runs on credit, in both senses: the fiscal (cash is conventionally reserved for illicit transactions) and the fiducial (any system of knowledge rests upon a system of belief). The machinery of communications can be used to make people believe things. The fictions computers generate become real. In *Count Zero* as in *Neuromancer,* many computers require their operators to work in an illusory "cyberspace", a landscape of gleaming towers of data where security programs offer physical violence. Money is a consensual fiction, and holographic recording, psychoactive chemicals and cyborganic surgery are commonplace. Ambiguity is rife, reality elusive. . . . It is significant that the thief's methods and motives are indistinguishable from those of the corporations from whom he steals. Gibson notes: "Burgeoning technologies require outlaw zones." Moral certainty is concealed in the lurid shadows: genuine humanity is to seek. Down these mean streets a man must go.

> Colin Greenland, "Into Cyberspace," in The Times Literary Supplement, *No. 4342, June 20, 1986, p. 683.*

Andrew Andrews

The word "technopunk" is bandied about nowadays, since it is so fashionable to think of many of the newest stars of science fiction with guaranteed awe and respect, and because it's just a fad, "with-it" phrase. What does it mean? What is "techno?" What is "punk?"

Technopunk is supposedly a brand of "New Wave" attempts to set new trends in the SF field. (Where've we heard this before?) It supposedly singles out those computer-age authors fully indoctrinated into the vestibule of the age's axioms, idioms, jargon and beliefs. You are supposedly with it if you read technopunk.

Readers are tired of reading heavy-handed stories of Big Computers Plotting to Take Over the World. Let's be more sophisticated, folks: Let's make a huge computer so vast that it is sentient (call it the Cyberspace Matrix, a "synergistic," linked computer database that reaches through all of Earth) and introduce a computer "hacker" named Count Zero—sort of a cyberspace "cowboy" in the urban complex called Sprawl (covering every populated area from Boston to Houston), and what you have is cyberpunk. You have *Count Zero.*

Based loosely on his award-winning *Neuromancer, Count Zero* takes much of the same from the former—the ideas and concepts are gorged with imagination. Most people don't realize the matrix is sentient. Except for one Arizona child, the result of a secret experiment to link a normal human with the matrix. The child, the daughter of a megacorporate scientist, is not aware she has such capabilities—all this while her father is the target of a conspiracy to be abducted by a corporate mercenary soldier. These events entwine; the result is a mixed emotion. It is hodgepodge; spastic; incomprehensible in spots, somehow just *too much.* On one level it is noisy, brash; almost as if Gibson were at the same time trying for an effect and just pulling words from the sky. This novel is, for lack of a better word, a *trip.*

What makes this novel dark to the reader is that, as a reader, you must oftentimes sit back and analyze what is going on. Although a novelist should allow the character and plotting to flow unencumbered, like ice cream on a hot day, Gibson's work *demands* parenthetical statements to explain why some characters react so strangely. How has

this bizarre future come about? Why is the logic so flawed; and why are the ideas flashed out, indecipherable from context?

Sure, *Count Zero* can be judged a success from the concepts alone; it is experimental; it is challenging. But why is it so heavy with inexactness, and why is it so choppy? There is literally no flow in spots; it is almost as if the author were struggling to be original, and the work came up clumsy.

To some, *Count Zero* may be an original, eventful novel; to this reader, it has its moments, but for the most part, it is noisy, borderline hackwork. (In style and execution alone; if ideas and concepts are your thing, be my guest. I prefer a novel that is concise, with fleshy, human characters, and that has continuity, logical progression. I can't find those qualities here, sad to say.)

> Andrew Andrews, in a review of "Count Zero," in Science Fiction Review, *No. 59, Summer, 1986, p. 62.*

Algis Budrys

Hello, Bill.

A while ago—not too long ago—a slim, tall, very quiet Canadian named William Gibson published a short story called **"New Rose Hotel"** and a novel called *Neuromancer,* and a new school of writing SF was born. *Neuromancer,* as you must know by now, won the Philip K. Dick, Nebula and Hugo awards last year, to name just the top three of its various winnings. It also aborted SFs seemingly unstoppable trend toward interminably lengthy and classically romanticized works, and this burst of success also revealed the existence of several other writers—Bruce Sterling, John Shirley and Michael Swanwick, for three—whose work could be made to fit the "same" pattern, so that the "Cyberpunk" school could be named.

Now, once something has been named it must exist in fact, correct? Gardner Dozois named it, Norman Spinrad traces it back to Harlan Ellison—which makes sense if you stress the street-life aspect of the mode. . . . (pp. 66-7)

The mode, as it came to flower in *Neuromancer,* describes the blackly existential peregrinations of a street-wise hero, or someone whose *beau-ideal* is a street-wise hero, and whose preferred milieu is the data-terrain. Gibson calls these people "cowboys," though not all of them are male and not all of them continue to exist in the gross physical milieu. The latter is a near-contemporary Earth and some of its orbital stations; a heavily industrialized world dominated by Japanese electronics and a Eurasian biotechnology, and evidently so impressed with the Oriental *geist* that it lives crowded and scruffy even though there still ought to be quite a bit of room. It is not truly the future, in other words . . . it is today written large, just as Gernsback did it in his day.

Plugged into rigs that give them the advantage of being able to "see" schematic representations of the data-banks and -nets, the cowboys range over an electronic landscape that represents the world but is more real and elegant than it, doing this for a combination of hackerly kicks and of money; industrial espionage is a lucrative, if perilous, profession. Ipso facto, the cowboys are rustlers. Some, having been detected, captured and coerced by the forces of law and order, are pressed into service against their former comrades, or at least against that which gave them joy.

The prose format in which this mode is couched is, indeed, very reminiscent of Ellison in such stories as "Pretty Maggie Moneyeyes." But it is usually far more deadpan and less inclined to rub-in its message than, for instance, "Repent, Harlequin, Said the Ticktockman." What is most engaging about it, apparently, is its fluid use of techie jargon both actual and invented, and its non-stop display of fresh gadgets, such as "claw," an unlikely—but momentarily plausible—biomedical technique that substitutes an engineered millipede for surgical stitching or stapling.

Speed equals stability in this kind of writing as much as it does in riding a bicycle. "Claw," thought about, seems just a piece of flash, yet it is crowded at once offstage by the next gadget, and the reader, casting a last glance over his shoulder as it dwindles down the back-trail, thinks, "Well, if it wasn't that appurtenance to the surgical-procedures scene, it would have been another." The result is as satisfactory as it would be if it were truly quantifiable; it is not only flash, it is very much identified as flash, therefore off the main point, therefore can be specious without making the story specious.

"Claw" appears, incidentally, in *Count Zero,* which while not a direct sequel to *Neuromancer* is set in the same universe, and develops some of *Neuromancer's* premises rather fruitfully. There is, for instance, quite a bit of space devoted to industrial sabotage and terrorism, in which the object is to kidnap or kill corporate employees who can generate valuable data, such as new biotechniques. There is also the introduction of voodoo.

Voodoo. The pantheon of that religion serves in *Count Zero* to provide a rationale for the electronic and biological technology and to personify its forces.

There is also sculptural art that can be and is perceived by the computerized person of a very rich collector who is in fact being kept physically alive, if that is the term, in a proliferated support system. He can't actually see, smell, taste, hear or touch anything, but he can generate "realities" into which non-computerized persons can be sucked, and where he can meet them under special circumstances which Gibson makes entirely believable. Of course, Gibson makes the voodoo analogy work, too.

What this is—and it is, by the way ultimately a story about love, on a level of sophistication well beyond anything in *Neuromancer,* the stories in *Burning Chrome,* or what anyone in this field except Gene Wolfe and a very few others have attained—this story in which all the main characters are motivated by love or by abhorrence of it—is a work put together once, and once only, by a mind that creates directly from available materials within its storage. It does not replicate or sequelize *Neuromancer,* it completes it.

Hold that thought. Meanwhile, in *Burning Chrome,* we get seven Gibson short stories—I believe these are *the* Gibson canon, so rapidly has he moved up—an introduction by Bruce Sterling, and three collaborative stories; one each with Sterling, Shirley and Swanwick. (pp. 67-8)

All three of these gents are nice guys with talent, and with the ambition to deliver much good reading over the years. But with *Count Zero* it comes clear that when Dozois lumped them all in together [under the rubric "cyberpunk"] and gave them a common name, he put three (or more) oranges in with one apple, of which this field has as yet taken only its first bite.

[These writers have all completed] enormously satisfactory books *qua* book. I can't imagine a better entertainment value, whatever level of entertainment you seek in SF. Burt Sterling's manifesto of an introduction to *Burning Chrome,* for all its brave phrasings and its declarations of intent to sweep the old aside and get on with the perfectable new, is at one with that "Gernsback Continuum" of which Gibson speaks so non-punkishly and fondly in his eponymous short story [*"The Gernsback Continuum"*].

[B] Attendant paradox: they are going to look around one day soon, the cyberpunks, and discover that they have hared off into *here,* and William Gibson has wandered off *there,* and is holding a ball of string, a Zener-Blosser propelling pencil, a balloon, three cans of Dennison's hot chili, an axle from a Radio Flyer wagon and a GE steam iron with its pores clogged, and in the background, revving up to 15,000 rpm with all sixteen valves dancing like Cadmus's soldiers will be something unimaginable, until after Mr. Gibson has blinked, looked [at] it, and said: "Of course!" (p. 69)

Algis Budrys, in a review of "Count Zero" and "Burning Chrome," in The Magazine of Fantasy and Science Fiction, *Vol. 71, No. 2, August, 1986, pp. 66-9.*

Tom Easton

The hero of William Gibson's *Count Zero* uses the title as his handle. He is really Bobby Newmark, a slum youngster hung upon the image of Gibson's patent "cowboy," plugged-in rider of the cyberspace range, data thief, slick manipulator of electron flows and great gobs of cash. That makes him a sucker. His connection slips him a piece of software, assures him it will break the blackest of "ice" (data security), and points him at a nice, safe databank to crack. Poor sucker. Poor chump. Things are not what they seem! The target's ice grabs him and is in the process of burning out his brain when a mysterious, apparently female figure steps through the veils of cyberspace to save his ass. He runs, and soon after a bomb blows his apartment to pieces.

Meanwhile, "executive recruiter" Turner is mounting a mission. A top scientist, Mitchell, responsible for the marvel of biochips, wants to defect from Maas Biolabs and join Matsuda. Maas will use guns to stop his departure; Turner's job is to dodge, fight, and run, as necessary, to get Mitchell to safety. But things are not what they seem. Instead of Mitchell, it's his daughter, her brain loaded with biochips, who flies the ultralight to Turner's camp, and as she lands, someone blows the mission to blazes. Only Turner and the girl escape.

Meanwhile, disgraced art dealer Marly Krushkova is being hired by tycoon and art collector Josef Virek to track down the artist responsible for several "boxes," mounted montages of everyday items with a unique power. The trail leads her to Wigan Ludgate, a burned-out cowboy who is convinced that God resides in the world's computer net, and that God talks to him.

And here Gibson's plot lines intersect. Behind all the intrigue and action-adventure lie the independent artificial intelligences of the net. They hide from humans most of the time, but occasionally they emerge, sometimes posing as the gods of voodoo, sometimes as Wigan's God, sometimes as . . . I won't say. Gibson has knitted a masterful yarn, action-filled, suspenseful, thought-provoking. Read it, and enjoy. (pp. 179-80)

> *Tom Easton, in a review of "Count Zero," in* Analog Science Fiction/Science Fact, *Vol. CVI, No. 12, December, 1986, pp. 179-80.*

Mikal Gilmore

William Gibson never really expected things to tumble this way. Seated in his room at the Beverly Hills Hotel, the tall, studious-looking science-fiction author sips distractedly at a glass of whiskey and tells how, only a few hours before, he sold the film rights to his first novel, *Neuromancer*—a tense, harrowing tale of high-tech outlawry set in a not-so-distant, not-so-improbable future.

Gibson seems bemused that *Neuromancer*, which he calls the "anti-*Star Wars* of science fiction," has appealed to the film world. And yet Cabana Boys Productions, a brash, young Hollywood outfit, not only has paid the author $100,000 for the option to the novel but has assembled an impressive team of collaborators, including William Burroughs and Timothy Leary as creative consultants and Earl MacRauch (*Buckaroo Bonzai*) as screenwriter. The producers are also courting veteran Douglas Trumbull (*2001: A Space Odyssey, Blade Runner*) to create the special effects, Andy Summers to write the score and Peter Gabriel to play a leading role.

Still, Gibson smiles wryly when he contemplates his hard-edged characters' making it to the big screen—desperadoes like Case, a washed-up computer cowboy with an appetite for speed, and Molly, the coldblooded assassin in mirrored shades who sports surgically implanted razors beneath her fingernails. Gibson's dissolute, violent heroes, though unlikely for the science-fiction genre, are also frayed idealists, struggling to retain their humanity in a dangerous high-tech terrain. Some critics have detected the influence of novelist Robert Stone in the characterization of these outlaw adventurers, but Gibson cites another source: "I would say that the world of my stories probably has more in common with Lou Reed's world, his moral universe. It certainly doesn't have much in common with the world one finds in most mainstream American science fiction."

If anything, Gibson appears mystified—not just by his recent Hollywood success but by his work's having found acceptance among the sci-fi masses. "The thing is," he says, "I've never run into the kind of resistance I was anticipating, and that's left me totally confused. I thought I was on this literary kamikaze mission—that is, I thought my work was so disturbing it would be dismissed and ignored by all but a few people. But here I am"—he laughs gently—"holed up in Los Angeles having meetings with movie people, enjoying more credibility than I would have

expected in years, instead of at home, writing the twisted, killer fiction this medium needs to survive."

Actually, Gibson, who lives with his wife and two children in Vancouver, British Columbia, has little cause for guilt. At age thirty-nine, with only two novels and one short-story collection under his belt, he has already revitalized s.f. (as it's known to its practitioners) as no other single force has in nearly a generation. In fact, *Neuromancer*, with its crisscrossed images of moral decay and technological progress, pretty much upended the genre on its own, capturing the Nebula, Hugo and Philip K. Dick awards for 1984 in an unprecedented sweep. Equally important, the book also helped popularize a new movement known as cyberpunk, which, as its name implies, has drawn much of its nerve and imagery from the aesthetics of late-Seventies punk music.

Of the dozen or so authors working in the cyberpunk style, Gibson is clearly the movement's pick to click. With his swift, colorful dialogue and his flair for creating a believably gritty future, he has forged the most convincing blend of sci-fi and hard-boiled detective styles in American pulp history. In doing so, he has yanked science fiction down from its recent Arcadian heights and forced it to wander mean, futuristic streets, where flesh is cheap and dreams are lethal.

"There's no question: science fiction had been in a tailspin for years," says Bruce Sterling, author and self-described "core polemicist" of cyberpunk. "The genre just wasn't dealing realistically at all with germane modern concerns or even the currency of pop culture," adds Sterling, who, under the pseudonym Vincent Omniaveritas, edits the movement's controversial review-newsletter, *Cheap Truth*. "And then along came the cyberpunks: Eighties writers and rebel techies who are very much into pop culture. To paraphrase the Clash, we wanted to start a riot of our own. Then, after Gibson won those awards, it was suddenly possible."

Though it has been dismissed as all flash by the more staid s.f. establishment, cyberpunk is actually reinvigorating a debate older than science fiction itself: namely, the question of whether technology is a blessing or a curse. Unlike their predecessors, who took a more cynical view of man's machines, cyberpunks are saying that while technology is rampant and scary, it can also be redemptive. In some of the movement's most inventive works, such as Greg Bear's *Blood Music,* Bruce Sterling's *Schismatrix* and Rudy Rucker's *Software,* technology leads to both transcendence and negation of the human spirit, occasionally at the same time.

"The cyberpunks *do* get a kick out of the idea that the future is going to be complex and bizarre beyond belief," says Gradner Dozois, editor of *Isaac Asimov's Science Fiction Magazine* and an early advocate of the movement. "They're willing to admit that there are going to be enormous doses of future shock. As a result, they are probably the first movement in s.f. to have invented a vision of the future that could have grown out of our present, out of the Eighties that we know." Lewis Shiner, author of *Frontera,* one of the genre's more arresting books, puts it a bit more seductively: "The last generation of science-fiction writers was very much of the mind that machines and computers are killing us, whereas William Gibson is having sex with these machines."

Gibson, though, has his own view on the specter of technology and on his place in the cyberpunk movement. "I'm neither a technophiliac nor technophobiac," he says. "In fact, I take a good look at a machine before I let it into my house. I think what I'm writing about is the idea that technology has *already* changed us, and now we have to figure a way to stay sane within that change. If you were to put this in terms of mainstream fiction and present readers with a conventional book about modern post-industrial anxiety, many of them would just push it aside. But if you put it in the context of science fiction, maybe you can get them to sit still for what you have to say."

These are fairly unusual sentiments for a genre hero—even a cyberpunk—but then Gibson came to his current prominence in science fiction in a rather round-about fashion. "Growing up in an isolated Virginia town, I read all the science fiction I could get my hands on," he says, "but by the time I was sixteen I burned out on it. It just no longer seemed to cut it in terms of what was starting to happen in that Sixties world around me. I kept up with a few writers who seemed to be doing something worthwhile within the form, like J. G. Ballard, Philip K. Dick and Samuel Delany, but certainly, when I thought about writing, I didn't think about writing s.f. It seemed like such a goofy, unhip thing to do." Gibson led a typical Sixties existence for the next few years, drifting until he ended up in Canada. While studying as an English major at a Vancouver university, Gibson took a science-fiction course, thinking it would be an easy way to pad his credits. When he told his teacher that he didn't have time to write a term paper for the class, she shot back, "Okay-write a story instead."

"It was an agonizing thing," he recalls. "It took me about three months, and it was only thirteen pages long." A while later, at the prompting of a friend, writer John Shirley, Gibson wrote another story and submitted it to *Omni.* He hasn't received a rejection slip since.

A good part of what immediately set Gibson's prose apart from his contemporaries was the depth that he brought to his characterizations. In a field where the most inventive authors tend to favor ideas over character, Gibson often focuses on moral frailty, the one human deficiency that technology will never rectify. Indeed, in Gibson's best short fiction—such as **"New Rose Hotel," "Johnny Mnemonic," "Dogfight"** (co-written with Michael Swanwick) and **"Burning Chrome,"** the title story of his collection—the most indelible characters are those who gamble everything for their desires. "I tend to side with the ones who somehow manage to retain a degree of humanity," he says, "though sometimes I'm intrigued by the ones who don't. If they seem memorable, perhaps it's because most science fiction is still being written for people who don't want to face up to the myriad opportunities that human beings have for fucking up and betraying themselves in the world. Actually, in some ways, that may be my theme."

Gibson placed his characters in a hazardous milieu where multinational corporations have supplanted political systems and where computer networking has become complex, lucrative and deadly. In fact, the book's hidden antagonist is a sentient computer network that has learned

enough about humanity to become aspiring, artful and murderous. Among *Neuromancer's* cast of high-tech lowlifes, it is the computer cowboy Case, caught in the cross fire between human fear and computer avarice, who is the most memorable figure. At the story's outset, Case has been on the skids for some time, working as a two-bit contrabandist in the virulent underbelly of Japan's Chiba City. Abruptly, he comes across a chance to regain everything he ever lost—all he has to do is plug into a living computer matrix and ferret out some hot data. In part, admits Gibson, Case *is* derived from Robert Stone's writing. "That is to say he's a character who seems to know his way around some very edgy territory. But he also came from my having spent some time around computer hackers. They have this whole style of language, this kind of poetic deconstruction, which attracted me simply for the intensity with which they talked about their machines. I immediately heard in that a real echo of the teenagers I grew up with talking about cars. It was that same language of power and, in some way, of escape—the kind of thing Bruce Springsteen writes of so well. In fact, I was listening to *Darkness on the Edge of Town* a lot when I started *Neuromancer.* I was wondering if there couldn't be a mythology of computers that had something in common with Springsteen's mythology of cars."

Gibson's new novel, **Count Zero,** is billed as something of a sequel to *Neuromancer*—though with a new cast and a more colloquial prose style. As the book opens, seven years after the events of *Neuromancer,* a handful of seemingly unconnected characters—Turner, a transient American mercenary; Bobby, a New Jersey-born hacker fuckup; and Marly, a discredited Parisian art dealer—are all pursuing bad-news ambitions. In alternating chapters, each character gets pulled closer to a spreading cataclysm, until it seems they are all being drawn toward a common fate in the Sprawl, an urban complex that reaches from Boston to Houston.

"I was deep into this book, and parts of it were still a mystery to me," says Gibson. "There were a couple of rather dodgy days when I had to pull out brown wrapping paper and make flow charts—and it finally came to me. I saw who was doing what to whom and solved the mystery only minutes before I had to." He laughs shyly. "Anyway, I was going for something a little different with this book. *Neuromancer* was a bit hypermanic—simply from my terror at losing the reader's attention—and this time I aimed for a more deliberate pace. I also tried to draw the characters in considerable detail. People have children and dead parents in *Count Zero,* and that makes for different emotional territory."

At present, Gibson is at work on *Mona Lisa Overdrive*—a book he claims will clarify many of the mysterious implications of his first two novels. "I suppose that means I'm guilty of writing a trilogy, one of those all-too-common excesses that characterize modern-day science fiction. At the same time, I was puzzled by things that were implied in *Count Zero* and *Neuromancer,* yet never really resolved. It doesn't feel like the story's finished to me.

"Roughly speaking, *Mona Lisa Overdrive,* will have the same relation to *Count Zero* as *Count Zero* had to *Neuromancer.* That is, it will take place several years after the events of the previous book and will incorporate one or two of the same characters—such as Molly, in a somewhat different guise—but it won't be an exactly linear sequel. Actually, it's my hope that when I finish this, I will have three books that work independently of one another, that can be comprehended separately yet can also fit together."

The obvious question is whether a writer of Gibson's ability will stay in science fiction. There are rumors, after all, that cyberpunk may have already played its hand—that, in fact, it is currently being overrun by a crop of eager Gibson imitators.

"You know, on one level," says Gibson, "I'm hoping to see this kind of stuff pop up all over the place. It isn't that I want what I write to take over—I mean, *I'm* not even trying to write that way anymore—nor is it that I feel particularly evangelical about science fiction. It's just that if you're going to have a pop form, why not have it be vital? The bulk of the stuff being published in this genre is just not interesting.

"Still, one of the things that put me off writing science fiction in the first place was the thought that I might be trapped in it. I know I'll eventually try something else. Actually, I'd like to think that if I'm still writing in twenty years, everything else will have receded into the background, and I'll be writing about human relationships. Just like Lou Reed." (pp. 77-8, 107-08)

Mikal Gilmore, "The Rise of Cyberpunk," in Rolling Stone, *No. 488, December 4, 1986, pp. 77-8, 107-08.*

Edward Bryant

William Gibson demonstrates in *Mona Lisa Overdrive* that he has a lot of balls. A one-man Flying Karamazov Brothers, he shows us also that he can adroitly keep all those balls juggled in the air at the same time. It's a neat feat that should entrance the hundreds of thousands of readers who found themselves hypnotized by the supercharged prose and mirror-sharded surfaces of his earlier novels, *Neuromancer* (1984) and *Count Zero* (1986).

Gibson, presently enmeshed in such Hollywood projects as writing scripts for *Alien III* and *New Rose Hotel*, holds down an enviable spot in contemporary speculative fiction. Thus far he is *the* writer of and for the eighties. At this point in the instant literary history of the waning twentieth century, he has accumulated something of the sales track record and sizeable audience of the mainstream's McInerney, Ellis, Leavitt, and Janowitz (plus he can write rings around any of *that* crowd). All this while using the reflecting and refracting surfaces of a sometimes glitzy, often grungy, future to focus what he wants to say about human survival in an often inhuman universe. Gibson has brought more excitement, new readers, outside attention, controversy, and just plain much-needed energy to the SF field than any other new writer of the decade.

He's a tough act to follow, particularly for himself. So how does *Mona Lisa Overdrive* measure up? I'll give it a 90—it's got a great beat, and you can dance to it. *Mona Lisa Overdrive,* although open-ended in itself, serves as an independent, finely crafted, and reader-pleasing climax to the novelistic sequence begun with *Neuromancer* and continued through *Count Zero.*

All three novels take place in the now-familiar high-tech cyberspaced post-World War III world where the multinational corporations have expanded into orbit and pretty much run the world. Hired corporate mercs are far more dangerous than cops, and the gritty streetwise lives of the huge underclass are primarily affected by sex, drugs, and rock 'n' roll, or at least the author's projections of same.

Integral to the shared background of Gibson's three novels is the concept of the cyberspace matrix, effectively an electronically shared consensual hallucination. Cyberspace is the techno-metaphor through which computer cowboys perceive the enormously complex linkages of the global information system when they're plugged into their decks. It's a neat literary trick, a nice technological extrapolation, and a grand image, but it's not at all what the book is really about.

After *Neuromancer* burst on the scene in 1984, William Gibson was taken to task by some critics for apparently seeming more interested in style and plot than character. The new novel addresses that. Most of the first quarter of the book is devoted to the introduction of new characters, and the re-introduction of some old ones. Tough, tender Molly, for example, with her razor-edged nails and permanently implanted mirrorshades, is back. She's cleverly disguised, to be sure, but she's definitely on stage.

We meet Kumiko Tanaka, alienated young daughter of a mysterious Japanese power-broker; . . . Mona Lisa herself, a sort of futuristic Val-girl (in this case, the Ohio Valley) who has not the slightest idea what's going on in this plot in which she figures centrally, yet is a born survivor who persists first through luck, then, finally, prevails through a dawning perception of self. . . . Bobby Newmark, the eponymous character from *Count Zero,* is back—now an adult, and now a human vegetable on life support and plugged into the largest and most enigmatic chunk of software outside the cyberspace matrix. Also returned is the purveyor of gray and black market technology, the Finn, presently a ghost in the machine. Back too are the metaphorical Voudun gods, the manifestations of various artificial intelligences. And so on. The cast is enormous and bizarre, but unceasingly fascinating.

For the first half of the book, it is virtually impossible to keep track of which character is who, where individual allegiances truly lie, and essentially what's going on. The second half, fortunately, sorts everything out. We discover why it is that certain forces wish to kidnap Angie Mitchell and substitute the surgically modified Mona. We learn what Bobby Newmark is *really* up to in his pocket universe. We find out Sally/Molly's motives and the true nature of the helpful boy-chip, Colin. Ditto for the big-guy artificial intelligences, mysteriously maneuvering in both cyberspace and the physical universe.

Just as *Neuromancer* describes a fairly standard plot-structure hidden beneath the flash of designer surfaces (Dumas and other romantic adventure writers by way of Alfred Bester, crossbred with the hard-boiled *roman noir* of Chandler and Hammett), so *Mona Lisa Overdrive* betrays traditional roots. The novel has all the labyrinthine plot devices, multiple identities, hairbreadth escapes, hidden secrets, and dramatic revelations that any nineteenth-century reader could wish for. It also has a satisfying climax and conclusion in which everyone, for the most part, gets what he or she deserves. William Gibson manages to do all this with a kind of low-temperature eighties detachment that minimizes the melodrama by keeping most of the overt action offstage. This is a technique that should give readers plenty of opportunity for argument.

So do you have to be a hardcore hacker or dedicated programmer to enjoy such a novel as this? Absolutely not. Gibson, gifted student of semiotics, is nearly as innocent of technology as thee and me. But he can read the signposts. He has an abiding interest in the future of technology and what all that means to human lives. He possesses an instinctive gift for envisioning the prospective relationships of humans and machines. But he does all that through art. You'll find no wiring schematics here.

Gibson has come through again. He has crafted a cool, exciting, praiseworthy novel that brilliantly pyramids the successes of its predecessors. While other science fiction writers are still recapping every decade from the thirties up through the present, Gibson is already writing for the nineties and beyond. (pp. 12, 18)

Edward Bryant, "Signposts of the Future," in The Bloomsbury Review, *Vol. 8, No. 5, September-October, 1988, pp. 12, 18.*

Pat Cadigan

In *Mona Lisa Overdrive,* William Gibson rounds out the long, complicated story begun in *Neuromancer* and continued in *Count Zero.* Although *Mona Lisa Overdrive* can stand alone as a story, much of Gibson's terminology will be unclear without the background provided by the first two books—though perhaps only at first. The technology explosion, exemplified by the proliferation of the personal computer, has meant that many people are more conversant with Gibson's ideas than they were when *Neuromancer* first appeared in 1984.

Cyberspace, a concept that reappears in *Mona Lisa Overdrive,* may be Gibson's best, most original, and thus most enduring contribution to speculative fiction. In less than a decade since this idea's introduction in *Neuromancer,* other authors have already appropriated it in a big way. Cyberspace, a computer-simulated reality—Artificial Reality—is familiar enough, but Gibson's is an inspired variant, the answer to the question "What does information look like?" It's a question almost no one thought of asking, let alone answering.

Gibson's way of looking at things from new, unexpected angles might be enough to account for the magnitude of his appeal to science-fiction readers, especially the hard core who feel, rightly or not, that they've seen it all in print. But it's Gibson's characters that give his work a less pyrotechnic but, in the end, greater strength. He doesn't postulate a future populated with supermen and superwomen; each character is at the mercy of his or her surroundings, circumstances, appetites, hopes, fears, strengths, and weaknesses. Even the most knowing and hardened have a certain naiveté or vulnerability. Nobody really knows everything (nobody human, that is).

Against the backdrop of a familiar, polluted, rain-slicked world accessorized with alien high-tech gadgetry, the landscape of *Mona Lisa Overdrive* unfolds through alternating viewpoints that give the book the energy of skilful cinematic quick cuts. Some of the transitions from character to character are sharp—to the point of abruptness—but the story demands this sharpness, not just to create momentum but to reflect the turns each character's life takes. We are first introduced to 13-year-old Kumiko Yanaka, the daughter of a wealthy Japanese businessman, who is suddenly dispatched to London (for protection from her father's rivals) and finds herself in the custody of some rather dubious caretakers. Among them she meets the volatile Sally Shears, whose mirrored lenses meet her pale skin "with no sign of a seam" and who involves Kumiko in her intrigues as she plots against Mr. Yanaka's business associates. . . .

Waif-like Mona, a small-town girl caught up in the seamy side of Miami night-life, longs to escape her lot, dancing for men high on stim who attain sexual gratification in puppet parlours. Mona's dream of leaving is realized when her pimp arranges a deal with a man claiming to be a talent scout in need of "a sort of actress" and willing to pay big for her.

Angie Mitchell, a star athlete in the game of Sense/Net, retreats to Malibu after spending a short time in a detoxification clinic where doctors used chemical pliers to pry her addiction from receptor sites in her brain. As she walks along the beach, passing by "Frail-looking neon-embedded replicas of the Watts Towers lifted beside neo-Brutalist bunkers faced with bronze bas-reliefs," she is under constant surveillance—accompanied by an armed remote, a tiny helicopter that hovers silently and is programmed to avoid her line of sight. But she soon finds herself once again ridden by loa and voudou, godlike entities that inhabit cyberspace (that peculiar realm of pure information that she has always been able to access without hardware).

The book is the multi-sensory experience readers have come to expect from Gibson. It is simultaneously surreal and ultra-real, such as at the moment one character is distracted as she walks down a street of unlicensed food stalls:

> Somebody was playing a trumpet in the asphalt square that had been the parking lot, a rambling Cuban solo that bounced and distorted off the concrete walls, dying notes lost in the morning clatter of the market. A soapbox evangelist spread his arms high, a pale, fuzzy Jesus copying the gestures in the air above him. The projection rig was in the box he stood on, but he wore a battered nylon pack with two speakers sticking over each shoulder like blank chrome heads. The evangelist frowned up at Jesus and adjusted something on the belt at his waist. Jesus strobed, turned green, and vanished. Mona laughed. The man's eyes flashed God's wrath, a muscle working in his seamed cheek. Mona turned left, between rows of fruit vendors stacking oranges and grapefruits in pyramids on their battered carts.

One of Gibson's strengths is his ability to deliver fantastic images in familiar settings. If, as Gibson says, the street finds its own uses for things, then Gibson himself is science fiction's top street visionary.

Those readers who do decide to sample Gibson for the

first time with this novel will undoubtedly be impelled to seek out the other two books to fill out the fascinating details of the extended plotline and to taste more of cyberspace, ice, the Sprawl, and the rest of Gibson's original, highly textured vision of the future.

In a time when the trilogy seems an abused privilege and the word "sequel" means more of the same, Gibson has pulled it off. He has given us a future and a story that really is substantial enough for three books. Or more. Rather than tying everything up neatly, the ending of *Mona Lisa Overdrive* will stimulate new questions in the reader. Whether or not Gibson will choose to deal with those questions in some future book (word has it he won't) doesn't matter. Readers will be left not only wanting more but imagining what it might be.

That's called science fiction at the top of its form.

> *Pat Cadigan, "Accessing Gibson's Peculiar Realm of Cyberspace," in Quill and Quire, Vol. 54, No. 12, December, 1988, p. 20.*

Thomas M. Disch

Cyberpunk is the label under which some of the younger science fiction writers of the 1980's have been marketing their wares, and as neologisms go it represents a fair description of their product. Cyberpunk sci-fi, in its ideal form, is compounded of two elements: a re-envisioning of the consensual future in terms not of space travel and other feats of mega-engineering but of a plastic (that is, wholly malleable) mental landscape that derives from the new possibilities of computer graphics; and punk style, in clothes, hair, sexuality and the abuse of controlled substances. Like punk rock, and like most traditional rocket-and-blaster science fiction, Cyberpunk caters to the wish-fulfillment requirements of male teenagers, but this is a job that can be done with varying degrees of panache, and there is currently no more accomplished caterer than William Gibson. He is the undisputed champion of Cyberpunk.

Mona Lisa Overdrive might be considered the concluding volume of a trilogy (with *Count Zero* and *Neuromancer*), except that the book's last chapter so patently advertises a sequel. These days nothing short of the author's death can keep a commercially successful work of science fiction from being cloned into sequels as long as the product moves from the shelves. A sense of closure, and so of narrative architecture, is not among the pleasures a reader should expect from *Mona Lisa Overdrive.* What Mr. Gibson offers in its place is flash—quick, high-intensity glimpses that linger on the retina of the imagination, like the sets (but not the narrative) of the movie *Blade Runner,* which Mr. Gibson has acknowledged as an influence. The new novel has plenty of flash, as in the following short travelogue from the inhabited ruins of a future Florida, seen from the point of view of the teen-age hooker who is the novel's title character:

> About the only thing to like about Florida was drugs, which were easy to come by and cheap and mostly industrial strength. Sometimes she imagined the bleach smell [which pervades the beaches] was the smell of a million dope labs cooking some

unthinkable cocktail, all those molecules thrashing their kinky little tails, hot for destiny and the street.

> She turned off the Avenue and walked down a line of unlicensed food stalls. Her stomach started growling at the smell, but she didn't trust street food, not if she didn't have to, and there were licensed places in the mall that would take cash. . . .

Decoded, the impacted implications of this passage tell us that this is a world made nearly uninhabitable by industrial waste; a world under constant surveillance, in which almost all monetary transactions are controlled by computer; a world in which visual illusion is as cheap as canned sound is today. Mr. Gibson excels at piling up such implications to make a self-consistent, gritty-textured future junk heap of a world. In opposition to that world is the realm of cyberspace, into which humans who have been surgically adapted to interface with computers can go voyaging, as upon an ocean that is the confluence of all data bases, a Pac-Man universe of infinite complexity.

Mr. Gibson's first novel, *Neuromancer,* offered more dazzling vistas of cyberspace than those to be found in *Mona Lisa Overdrive,* but at the expense of requiring more developed reading skills than many sci-fi readers could bring to bear. *Mona Lisa Overdrive* seems to be written purposely to admit a larger readership to the marvels of cyberspace. While Case, the hero of *Neuromancer,* was a professional computer "cowboy," a Ulysses of cyberspace, the four main characters in *Mona Lisa Overdrive* are innocents and naïfs, who move through the novel with all the autonomy of passengers in a ride at Disneyland.

Only in retrospect, however, is *Mona Lisa Overdrive* a disappointment. Zing by zing, its 45 chapters provide a sufficiency of non-nutritive fun. As with *Neuromancer,* the plot is strictly from 1946, but knowingly so, like a Brian De Palma film noir. Indeed, the book virtually begs to be filmed: there is a climactic duel between police helicopters and customized robots; a juicy double role for the leading lady; lots of martial arts huggermugger performed by a leather-clad Wonder Woman; everything except a title song for Madonna or Cyndi Lauper to sing as the credits roll.

> *Thomas M. Disch, "Lost in Cyberspace," in The New York Times Book Review, December 11, 1988, p. 23.*

Istvan Csicery-Ronay

William Gibson is probably the most highly regarded young writer of U.S. SF. With the stories collected in *Burning Chrome* (1986) and his brilliant first novel, *Neuromancer* (1984), he has established himself as the leading exponent of the cyberpunk style, a fusion of hip technopop entertainments and elaborately detailed visions of a cyborgized, data-powered future. . . .

Mona Lisa Overdrive, Gibson's third and latest novel, continues the series of cyberspace novels begun in *Neuromancer* and continued in *Count Zero* (1986). What began in *Neuromancer* as a breakneck-paced thriller, involving a plot to unify the separated halves of a Super-Artificial Intelligence, became in the next novel an expansive cosmo-historical myth depicting the evolution of an entire parallel universe inhabited by artificial intelligences in the representation of the global information grid, the "consensual hallucination" of cyberspace. By the time of the action of *Mona Lisa Overdrive,* fourteen years after the action of the first novel and seven years after the second, the interface between the human social world and cyberspace has been drawn tight enough to allow human characters to die into cyberspace on a regular basis, and, from there, to infiltrate, plot against, or defend the physical world.

Gibson remains a virtuoso stylist, and he can turn his virtuosity on at will. But while in earlier works it was always on, one can almost hear the clicks in *Mona Lisa Overdrive.* Some parts in the novel are as clear and moving as anything Gibson has written before—but the whole is oddly off. Gibson's edge here is dull, and the clarity has gone with it. His prose has cooled, scattered among several different points of view and venues. So many things happen in so many parallel universes, incited by so many different beings of diverse hierarchies, that confusion reigns.

More surprising than the confusion, though, is the *tameness* of this book. Gibson has apparently fallen between two stools writing *Mona Lisa Overdrive.* He is trying to become a more versatile writer while remaining loyal to an unyielding SF setting. The characterizations are indeed emotionally richer than in his earlier works, but their richness does them no good—it separates them from the background of Pure Power; but it is that Pure Power that draws us most, in the end. The mythology, meanwhile, is, with each novel, leading Gibson into increasingly complicated enigmas that he is unable to resolve. Like Continuity, the new, book-writing Artificial Intelligence in the new novel, Gibson seems to be rewriting the same book again and over again, trying to get it right one more time, but always making new problems for himself. It may be time to let well enough alone and turn to other reaches of the Sprawl.

Mona Lisa Overdrive shows the problems faced by a serious and commercially successful young artist writing SF in the U.S., trying to write authentically without giving up the hip formulas that now characterize commercial SF. Writing in the belly of the technetronic Beast, where his art risks becoming an advertisement for an *Omni*-ized, slick futuristics, Gibson can't seem to give up the protection of the Beast completely; so, despite his wonderfully inventive imagination and scintillating style, he has nothing new to say about the new, which is all he claims to know.

Istvan Csicery-Ronay, "Cyberspace," in The American Book Review, *Vol. 10, No. 6, January-February, 1989, p. 7.*

Erik Davis

Gibson is the most celebrated cyberpunk, whose *Mona Lisa Overdrive* completes a loose trilogy that began in 1984 with the watershed, mega-award-winning *Neuromancer,* and continued with *Count Zero* in 1986. While no apologist for the cutthroat corporations that wield political power in his books, Gibson clearly revels in both the perverse gloss of late capitalist culture and the possibilities of its machines. Science is technology and technology is either corporate or loose on the street. His multinational

(Maas-Neotek, Hosaka, Ono-Sendai) are almost characters in his novels, capitalist nation-states loosed from geography, organizations so complex and dynamic they begin to resemble organic entities, evolving into ever more complex forms. (Time-Warner, anyone?) Governments are corporate puppets, and scientists are more crucial than military men. The plot of *Count Zero* concerns the failed defection of Chris Mitchell, a top biochip researcher, from Mass Biolabs to Hosaka, which results in a small nuclear explosion.

The labyrinthine, multi-charactered plot of *Mona Lisa Overdrive* revolves around Mitchell's daughter Angie, a megastar on the Sense/Net media network (the audience directly experiences the actors' sensations), whose dad grafted a biochip into her brain, enabling her to contact mysterious entities in the world's computer networks. The net she's caught involves corporate operatives, low-life street techies, wireheads addicted to data, sentient AI (artificial intelligence) programs, technological performance artists and the superwealthy cloned clan of the Tessier-Ashpools. Chapters are short, speedy and high-res, and following the various strands of the plot resembles watching four different TV programs by rapidly changing channels.

Even more than its two predecessors, *Mona Lisa Overdrive* relies not on plot but on style. Gibson cross-wires high-tech jargon, brand names, street slang and endless acronyms into a techno-pop semiotics that draws its *logos* from corporate logos. He squeezes a high-density poetry from words like "polycarbon," "matrix" and "chrome." Along with his networked narratives, Gibson's prose can generate what Jameson called the post-modern sublime, a rush born of the attempt to represent the impossible totality of the decentered global network of multi-national capital. By festishizing the logic of late capital, Gibson brings to the surface the beast that lurks behind the dense surreal surface of pop culture, simultaneously as meaningful and empty as a video screen.

Gibson's greatest conceptual coup, "cyberspace," is itself a screenlike construct devised to represent the global system of data and capital. Cyberspace is a "consensual hallucination" that represents all the world's data in a three-dimensional multicolored universe of grids and icons. Users project their minds into cyberspace through video game decks, floating around the green cubes of Mitsubishi Bank of America and the distant spiral galaxies of military systems, their data all protected by "ice":

> People jacked in so they could hustle. Put the trodes on and they were out there, all the data in the world stacked up like one big neon city, so you could cruise around and have a kind of grip on it, visually anyway, because if you didn't, it was too complicated, trying to find your way to a particular piece of data you needed."

Cyberspace points to the strange sense of space that computers produce, a nonspace that paradoxically reorganizes how humans perceive their own geographic standing. As Angie states, echoing Gertrude Stein, "There is no *there* there." Gibson's cyberspace puts the Chicago Board of Trade's Aurora system in a whole new light, because in its attempt to replicate the open-outcry system, Aurora simulates the trading pit and represents brokers as colored badges which can be "hit" with the PC's mouse.

Gibson is particularly adept at showing how new technologies always and necessarily create new conditions for subversion. A number of his main characters are "cowboys," console jocks who do dirty deeds in cyberspace. . . . But Gibson doesn't suggest many avenues of collective resistance in his world—his outsiders remain hustlers, solo entrepreneurs, anarchists. On the other hand, he may be indicating that the very conditions of resistance change within a radically computerized society, and that hacking, illegal or not, is always in some fundamental sense subversive. (pp. 636-38)

> Erik Davis, "A Cyberspace Odyssey," in The Nation, *New York, Vol. 248, No. 18, May 8, 1989, pp. 636-39.*

J. R. Wytenbroek

One of the hottest new authors to hit the science fiction scene in decades, agree most of the rave review-snippets printed page after page inside the covers of **Neuromancer** and **Count Zero,** is William Gibson. **Neuromancer** alone won the Hugo, Nebula and Philip K. Dick awards the year it was published. It is no mean feat to win the two most important science fiction awards for one book, and a first novel at that. Gibson is now completing the filmscript for the Hollywood movie version of **Neuromancer.** (pp. 162-63)

Gibson's presentation of this near-future world is as grim and harsh as any in the cyberpunk field. His world is full of unchecked corporate violence perpetuated by the handful of conglomerates which rule the world's economy, conglomerates which are in a continual race to outdo each other in the field of high technology, especially computer-based technology. Lives are advanced, ruined or even terminated according to their value to the monster conglomerates. Much of the rest of the world, it seems, is involved in mercenary shadow operations, hired by one conglomerate to work against another, either by stealing information through the "matrix," a huge, sub-reality created by networks of computerized data, or by stealing key personnel. Each major data field in the matrix is protected by "ice" which "cowboys" attempt to penetrate at the constant risk of brain-death.

Neuromancer (1984) is concerned primarily with theft through the matrix. Case is the protagonist, a cowboy who got caught stealing data from his employers and who had the "jacking" function of his brain removed by them as punishment. He is discovered in the seedy, cut-throat underworld of Chiba, a major Japanese centre on this urbanized planet, by Molly, a street mercenary hired by Armitage who has been hired by . . . ? They repair the damage done to Case's brain and set him to stealing data from some of the toughest data fields in the matrix. As the plot convolutes along, Case and Molly, now lovers-by-convenience, get curious as to who Armitage really is and whom he is employed by. Finally, after multiple attempts on their lives and minds, multiple gruesome murders committed by Molly or those out to stop Chase, and multiple shifts of venue, they find themselves in a tug of war between two overly talented, overly developed computers, owned by an incredibly wealthy, incestuous and self-murdering family. One of these computers hired Armitage to hire Case to bring it the necessary data to create a final

binding between it and its antagonistic counterpart, which will allow it to break the legal bounds of its intelligence and create a new artificial intelligence, completely autonomous and unique, the highest and greatest intelligence on the planet.

As far as I understand it, this is the basic plot-line of the novel. The plot, however, is loaded down with and obscured by layers of technical jargon. Since terms such as "cowboy," "jacking," "matrix" and "ice," the most important of dozens of such "futuristic" terms, are not explained at any point in the novel, readers must wade through them as they would through treacle, in search of a plot. Furthermore, because they are both alien and undefined, these terms set up no images to help the reader envision this grisly and highly unattractive future. The characters, if they wish to survive, must be as grisly as the world itself, and therefore evoke no sympathy and little interest. Molly seems to exist simply to slice up anyone who gets in her way, in the most gruesome way possible, while Case spends his time doing unexplained, unfathomable things in the matrix.

Count Zero (1986) is, on the whole, a much better written novel than **Neuromancer.** The plot-line is much easier to follow, although it revolves around three protagonists whose individual stories do not coincide until the last few chapters of the book. Most of the major characters are a little more interesting and a lot less blood-thirsty than Case and Molly. The protagonists have emotions, motivation and substance. Much of the jargon used is defined to some extent. The world itself remains as brutal as ever, but that brutality is relieved a little by the characters. As the story is largely concerned with a mercenary who deals with stealing people, an art connoisseur and a "hot dog" (a would-be or apprentice cowboy), much less time is spent in the matrix. **Count Zero** is a better-written, better-structured novel with a more coherent and interesting plotline, and more realistic and interesting characters than **Neuromancer.** Needless to say it won no awards and is not (yet) being considered by Hollywood.

The key to understanding much in both novels, however, lies in **Burning Chrome,** a volume of short stories which Gibson wrote between 1977 and 1985. The stories **"Johnny Mnemonic," "New Rose Hotel"** and **"Burning Chrome"** deal with the same world as the two novels, but explain that world and the jargon used much more clearly. Thus although this volume was published two years after **Neuromancer,** any reader wishing to save himself a lot of time and confusion should read **Burning Chrome** first. These stories show careful craftsmanship and a true literary edge. Gibson, like so many of his sf predecessors and colleagues, shines in the short story form. His characters seem human, vulnerable and three-dimensional. His plots are fascinating and well constructed. Gibson is a clever writer, but in the novels one can be so easily overwhelmed by the cleverness that one fails to notice the lack of substance. He shines in the short stories, yet the short stories show up the true hollowness of the novels. Catch-22.

One further minor criticism. Apparently, in the world of the future, Canada does not exist. Japan and the Eastern Seaboard of the U.S.A. are the centres of the new world. Turkey, L.A., Arizona, South American and outer space all sneak themselves into the novels in some minor way, but Canada does not exist. Perhaps Canada just did not make it in Gibson's nightmare world. Perhaps that is something to be grateful for. (pp. 163-64)

> *J. R. Wytenbroek, "Cyberpunk," in* Canadian Literature, *No. 121, Summer, 1989, pp. 162-64.*

FURTHER READING

McDonagh, Maitland. "Clive Barker and William Gibson: Future Shockers." *Film Comment* 26, No. 1 (January-February 1990): 60-3.
  Examines Gibson's recent venture into Hollywood scriptwriting, incorporating his comments on his screenplay *Aliens III* as well as on adaptations of his short stories "New Rose Hotel" and "Burning Chrome."

Stephen W. Hawking

1942-

(Full name Stephen William Hawking) English cosmologist, mathematician, and editor.

A leading theoretical physicist, Hawking has made significant contributions towards better understanding of gravity, black holes, time, and the origin of the universe. He has expanded upon the implications and principles of quantum physics and Albert Einstein's Theory of Relativity, generally regarded as the two most important advancements in the physical sciences during the twentieth century. Hawking endeavors to achieve a "unification of physics," consolidating diverse formulations that explain particular phenomena into a single, complete theory that would illuminate the history and nature of the cosmos. He discusses this quest as well as complex theories, concepts, and speculations on the physical universe in *A Brief History of Time: From the Big Bang to Black Holes,* a surprise international best–seller. Related in an engaging style accessible to non-specialists, the book reflects Hawking's belief that "the basic ideas about the origin and fate of the universe can be stated without mathematics in a form that people without a scientific education can understand."

While a graduate student at Cambridge University during the early 1960s, Hawking was diagnosed as suffering from amyotrophic lateral sclerosis (ALS), commonly known as "Lou Gehrig's Disease," which attacks and deteriorates the central nervous system and usually causes death within five years. Hawking's health stabilized, but the disease left him paralyzed, able to control only his hands. During the mid-1980s, Hawking lost his ability to speak after undergoing a tracheostomy following complications from pneumonia. He composes and communicates through a computer that allows him to choose words displayed on a screen and which is equipped with a voice synthesizer. Leon Jaroff observed: "While ALS has made Hawking a virtual prisoner in his own body, it has left his courage and humor intact, his intellect free to roam. And roam it does, from the infinitesimal to the infinite, from the subatomic realm to the far reaches of the universe. In the course of these mental expeditions, Hawking has conceived startling new theories about black holes and the tumultuous events that immediately followed the Big Bang from which the universe sprang."

Hawking first gained recognition for his Ph.D. thesis concerning black holes, on which he collaborated with Roger Penrose, a mathematician. Theoretically, a black hole occurs when a star exhausts its energy and collapses, creating an area of extremely powerful gravity from which light and matter cannot escape. Within a black hole is a point of infinite density, referred to as a singularity, where the laws of nature break down. Hawking and Penrose demonstrated the validity of black holes, which scientists had previously been reluctant to acknowledge because of lack of empirical evidence or mathematical proof. Hawking later suggested that some subatomic particles and radiation could escape from a black hole, summarized in his famous statement, "black holes ain't so black." These em-

missions are known as Hawking Radiation. *A Brief History of Time* relates these discoveries and their implications, offers a survey of historical and modern developments in physics, addresses various cosmological theories, and relates Hawking's quest for the unification of physics. Although some took issue with Hawking's assertion that "humanity's intellectual struggle to understand the universe" is nearly complete, *A Brief History of Time* was widely acclaimed as a clear, informative, and entertaining introduction to complex ideas that have significantly challenged traditional scientific and metaphysical views of the cosmos. Jeremy Bernstein stated: "The most original parts of Hawking's book consist of the descriptions of his own work. Since this has been of such great importance in modern cosmological theory, and since he describes it so lucidly, this gives the general reader an opportunity to learn some deep science directly from the scientist." He added: "Hawking has been for several years the Lucasian Professor of Mathematics at Cambridge. It is the professorship held by Isaac Newton and by the late P. A. M. Dirac, one of the founders of quantum theory. Hawking has been a worthy successor, and one wishes him many future years. He has a great deal to teach us."

(See also *Contemporary Authors,* Vol. 126.)

PRINCIPAL WORKS

The Large Scale Structure of Space–Time   1973 [with G.
    F. R. Ellis]
A Brief History of Time: From the Big Bang to Black Holes
    1988

Leon Jaroff

Darkness has fallen on Cambridge, England, and on a
damp and chilly evening King's Parade is filled with students and faculty. Then, down the crowded thoroughfare
comes the University of Cambridge's most distinctive vehicle, bearing its most distinguished citizen. In the motorized wheelchair, boyish face dimly illuminated by a glowing computer screen attached to the left armrest, is Stephen William Hawking, 46, one of the world's greatest
theoretical physicists. As he skillfully maneuvers through
the crowd, motorists slow down, some honking their
horns in greeting. People wave. "Hi, Stephen," they shout.

A huge smile lights up Hawking's bespectacled face, but
he cannot wave or shout back. Since his early 20s, he has
suffered from amyotrophic lateral sclerosis (ALS), or "Lou
Gehrig's disease," a progressive deterioration of the central nervous system that usually causes death within three
or four years. Hawking's illness has advanced more slowly, and now seems almost to have stabilized. Still, it has
robbed him of virtually all movement. He has no control
over most of his muscles, cannot dress or eat by himself
and needs round-the-clock nursing care.

A few years ago, Hawking's voice had deteriorated to a labored moan that only his family and a few associates could
understand; one of them always stood close by to interpret
his words. Then, in 1985, after Hawking nearly suffocated
during a bout with pneumonia, he was given a tracheostomy that enabled him to breathe through an opening in his
throat and a tube inserted into his trachea. The operation
saved his life but silenced his voice. Now he "speaks" only
by using the slight voluntary movement left in his hands
and fingers to operate his wheelchair's built-in computer
and voice synthesizer.

While ALS has made Hawking a virtual prisoner in his
own body, it has left his courage and humor intact, his intellect free to roam. And roam it does, from the infinitesimal to the infinite, from the subatomic realm to the far
reaches of the universe. In the course of these mental expeditions, Hawking has conceived startling new theories
about black holes and the tumultuous events that immediately followed the Big Bang from which the universe
sprang. More recently, he has unsettled both physicists
and theologians by suggesting that the universe has no
boundaries, was not created and will not be destroyed.

Most of Stephen Hawking's innovative thinking occurs at
Cambridge, where he is Lucasian professor of mathematics, a seat once occupied by Isaac Newton. (p. 58)

Hawking was born on Jan. 8, 1942—300 years to the day,
he often notes, after the death of Galileo—to parents who
were Oxford graduates. As a small boy, he was slow to
learn to read but liked to take things apart—a way of
"finding out how the world around me worked." But he
confesses that he was never very good at putting things
back together. When he was twelve, he recalls wryly, "one
of my friends bet another friend a bag of sweets that I
would never come to anything. I don't know if this bet was
ever settled and, if so, who won."

Enthralled by physics, Stephen concentrated in the subject
at Oxford's University College, but did not distinguish
himself. He partied, served as coxswain for the second-
string crew and studied only an hour or so a day. Moving
on to Cambridge for graduate work in relativity, he found
the going rough, partly because of some puzzling physical
problems; he stumbled frequently and seemed to be getting clumsy.

Doctors soon gave him the bad news: he had ALS, it would
only get worse, and there was no cure. Hawking was dev-
astated. Before long, he needed a cane to walk, was drinking heavily and ignoring his studies. "There didn't seem
to be much point in completing my Ph.D.," he says.

Then Hawking's luck turned. The progress of the disease
slowed, and Einsteinian space-time suddenly seemed less
formidable. But what really made the difference, he says,
"was that I got engaged to Jane," who was studying modern languages at Cambridge. "This gave me something to
live for." As he explains, "If we were to get married, I had
to get a job. And to get a job, I had to finish my Ph.D. I
started working hard for the first time in my life. To my
surprise, I found I liked it."

What particularly intrigued Stephen was singularities,
strange beasts predicted by general relativity. Einstein's
equations indicated that when a star several times larger
than the sun exhausts its nuclear fuel and collapses, its
matter crushes together at its center with such force that
it forms a singularity, an infinitely dense point with no dimensions and irresistible gravity. A voluminous region
surrounding the singularity becomes a "black hole," from
which—because of that immense gravity—nothing, not
even light, can escape.

Scientists years ago found compelling evidence that black
holes exist, but they were uncomfortable with singularities, because all scientific laws break down at these points.
Most physicists believed that in the real universe the object at the heart of a black hole would be small (but not
dimensionless) and extremely dense (but not infinitely so).
Enter Hawking. While still a graduate student, he and
Mathematician Roger Penrose developed new techniques
proving mathematically that if general relativity is correct
down to the smallest scale, singularities must exist. Hawking went on to demonstrate—again, if general relativity is
correct—that the entire universe must have sprung from
a singularity. As he wrote in his 1966 Ph.D. thesis, "There
is a singularity in our past."

Stephen later discerned several new characteristics of
black holes and demonstrated that the stupendous forces
of the Big Bang would have created mini-black holes, each
with a mass about that of a terrestrial mountain, but no
larger than the subatomic proton. Then, applying the
quantum theory (which accurately describes the random,
uncertain subatomic world) instead of general relativity
(which, it turns out, falters in that tiny realm), Hawking
was startled to find that the mini-black holes must emit

particles and radiation. Even more remarkable, the little holes would gradually evaporate and, 10 billion years or so after their creation, explode with the energy of millions of H-bombs.

Other physicists, long wedded to the notion that nothing can escape from a black hole, have generally come to accept that discovery. And the stuff emitted from little black holes (and big ones too, but far more slowly) is now called Hawking radiation. "In general relativity and early cosmology, Hawking is the hero," says Rocky Kolb, a physicist at Fermilab in Illinois. Caltech Physicist Kip Thorne agrees: "I would rank him, besides Einstein, as the best in our field." And what if a mini-black hole explosion is finally observed? "I would get the Nobel Prize," says Stephen, matter-of-factly.

Hawking's ability to perceive complex truths without doodling long equations on paper astounds his colleagues. "He has an ability to visualize four-dimensional geometry that is almost unique," says Werner Israel, a University of Alberta physicist who has collaborated with Hawking in relating mini-black holes to the new cosmic-string theories. Observes Kolb: "It's like Michael Jordan playing basketball. No one can tell Jordan what moves to make. It's intuition. It's feeling. Hawking has a remarkable amount of intuition."

Now, hoping to fulfill a career-long dream of seeing his books at airport newsstands, Stephen is putting the finishing touches on *A Brief History of Time*. . . . (pp. 58, 60)

Meanwhile, Hawking [is seeking] what Cambridge Astronomer Martin Rees calls the physicists' Holy Grail: a theory that will combine general relativity with the quantum theory. This requires "quantizing" gravity, the only one of nature's four basic forces that cannot yet be explained by the quantum theory.

In the course of that search, Hawking, who has no qualms about recanting his own work if he decides he was wrong, may have transcended his famous proof that singularities exist. With Physicist James Hartle, he has derived a quantum wave describing a self-contained universe that, like the earth's surface, has no edge or boundary. If that is the case, says Hawking, Einstein's general theory of relativity would have to be modified, and there would be no singularities. "The universe would not be created, not be destroyed; it would simply be," he concludes, adding provocatively, "What place, then, for a Creator?" (p. 60)

> *Leon Jaroff, "Roaming the Cosmos," in* Time, *New York, Vol. 131, No. 6, February 8, 1988, pp. 58-60.*

Marcia Bartusiak

The history of physics in the 20th century is a tale of two revolutions—general relativity and quantum mechanics. Both upheavals forced physicists to adopt new ways of thinking at each end of the distance scale. At the level of atoms and nuclear particles, quantum mechanics replaced surety with uncertainty. Researchers learned that events within that minuscule realm do not flow smoothly and gradually; rather, they change abruptly and discontinuously. Nature became a game of probability. At the same time, over the vast distances between stars and galaxies,

Einstein's theory of general relativity instructed us that gravity, the weakest of nature's forces, is best described as a geometric effect, a curvature or warp in space-time. In this view, the earth remains in orbit simply because it is caught in the indentation our massive sun makes in space.

The next triumph in physics will arrive when these two seemingly diverse provinces are connected. Stephen W. Hawking, who occupies the Lucasian chair of mathematics at Cambridge University in England (as Sir Isaac Newton did), has been attempting to accomplish just that. Early in his legendary career, Mr. Hawking realized that a full understanding of the universe's birth, as well as a determination of its end, will not be attained until the macrocosm is joined with the microcosm in one unifying theory.

As the title implies, *A Brief History of Time* is a succinct review of this challenging task, providing the reader with a jaunty overview of key cosmological ideas, past and present—including multidimensional space, the inflationary universe and the cosmic fates that may befall us. Special attention is paid to how nature's forces—gravity, electromagnetism and the strong and weak nuclear forces—are related to one another. Time takes center stage because it is a concept that has no meaning before our celestial genesis. Both space and time emerged at the instant of creation. (p. 10)

The American physicist John A. Wheeler once said that "physicists, like patients in a physician's office, only really believe they know what their problem is when it has been given a name." In 1968, Mr. Wheeler gave the black hole its name, initiating a public fascination that has scarcely abated. This bizarre celestial creature was the dark, gravitational abyss from which no light or matter could escape for all eternity, the result of a massive star collapsing to oblivion in its old age. And at the black hole's center resided a point of infinite density, called a singularity, where the known laws of physics completely broke down.

However, prompted by a discussion with two Soviet theorists, Mr. Hawking startled the astronomical community nearly 20 years ago when he announced that black holes "ain't so black." "One evening in November [1970], shortly after the birth of my daughter, Lucy," he recalls, "I started to think about black holes as I was getting into bed. My disability makes this rather a slow process, so I had plenty of time."

While largely written in the style of a scholarly lecture, *A Brief History of Time* lights up at such moments, when Mr. Hawking allows us a peek at his impish humor, inner motivations, theoretical goofs and scientific prejudices. Science buffs yearn for such personal admissions from scientist-authors working at the frontier. Only then can the scientific process, so often viewed as dry and pedantic, be rightfully perceived as a natural function of the human endeavor. Although this book was clearly not intended to be an autobiography, it is still disappointing that Mr. Hawking keeps such revelations to a minimum.

In applying the laws of quantum mechanics to the strange, warped space surrounding black holes, Mr. Hawking discovered that they are probably evaporating by slowly emitting radiation. These collapsed stars, then, are not so immortal. Given enough time, about a trillion trillion trillion trillion trillion trillion years, stellar black holes, along with their singularities, would actually disappear.

By the 1980's, Mr. Hawking extended his studies to the greatest singularity of them all—the primordial seed that evidence suggests wildly expanded some 15 billion years ago to produce the universe as we know it. Considering how quantum mechanics dramatically altered the physics of the black hole, Mr. Hawking tells us how present conceptions of the big bang might be equally affected.

In his preliminary figurings, Mr. Hawking surmises that the embryonic universe did not emerge from a singularity. Instead, he imagines a union of space and time that was finite yet boundless in the beginning, much the way the surface of a globe has no edges. Now expanding, this four-dimensional bubble is fated to contract innumerable eons from now. Current astronomical observations do not support Mr. Hawking's vision, as yet; not enough matter, either luminous or dark, has been found to close the universe back up. Indeed, the author admits that his idea is merely a theoretical proposal at this point, even an esthetic wish. "But if the universe is really completely self-contained, having no boundary or edge," he muses, "it would have neither beginning nor end: it would simply be. What place, then, for a creator?"

Some may feel uncomfortable at Mr. Hawking's mention of a creator, a theme that resonates throughout the book. The job of science, after all, is to explain the world around us without invoking divine interventions. Philosophically, though, his question is a valid one. If science should truly develop a "theory of everything," does the need for a Supreme Being vanish?

To help solve this conundrum, Mr. Hawking longs for the return of the philosopher-scientist, perhaps someone like Immanuel Kant, who in the 18th century hypothesized the existence of "island universes" beyond the Milky Way galaxy. Yet with astronomical discoveries and grand unifying theories increasing at an exponential rate and the mathematical language of physics becoming more and more arcane, nonspecialists are severely hampered in forging a synthesis. What is learned today changes tomorrow. "However, if we do discover a complete theory," Mr. Hawking writes, "it should in time be understandable in broad principle by everyone, not just a few scientists. Then we shall all, philosophers, scientists, and just ordinary people, be able to take part in the discussion of the question of why it is that we and the universe exist. If we find the answer to that, it would be the ultimate triumph of human reason—for then we would know the mind of God."

Through his cerebral journeys, Mr. Hawking is bravely taking some of the first, though tentative, steps toward quantizing the early universe, and he offers us a provocative glimpse of the work in progress. (pp. 10-11)

> Marcia Bartusiak, "What Place for a Creator?," in The New York Times Book Review, *April 3, 1988, pp. 10-11.*

Jeremy Bernstein

Near the beginning of *A Brief History of Time* Stephen Hawking's charming and lucid book on cosmology and astrophysics, there occurs a discussion of what are known as "the Hawking-Penrose singularity theorems." Penrose is the British mathematical physicist Roger Penrose, and

the singularity in question—of which more later—refers to conditions at the center of a black hole or at the instant of the Big Bang. The scientific exposition is interrupted by the following almost casual paragraph:

> At first sight, Penrose's result applied only to stars; it didn't have anything to say about the question of whether the entire universe had a big bang singularity in its past. [Some cosmologists write "Big Bang" and others write "big bang." Hawking is of the latter school, and I am of the former.] However, at the time that Penrose produced his theorem, I was a research student desperately looking for a problem with which to complete my Ph.D. thesis. Two years before, I had been diagnosed as suffering from ALS, commonly known as Lou Gehrig's disease, or motor neuron disease, and given to understand that I had only one or two more years to live. In these circumstances, there had not seemed much point in working on my Ph.D.—I did not expect to survive that long. Yet two years had gone by and I was not that much worse. In fact, things were going rather well for me and I had gotten engaged to a very nice girl, Jane Wilde. But in order to get married, I needed a job, and in order to get a job, I needed a Ph.D.

Hawking learned of his amyotrophic lateral sclerosis when he was barely in his twenties; he is now forty-six, and the progress of the disease has been relentless. He is permanently confined to a wheelchair, and retains the use only of three of his fingers. In 1985, he developed pneumonia and, to save his life, a tracheostomy was performed, which deprived him of the power to speak. Fortunately, computer-synthesized speech technology is now sufficiently advanced to enable him to use a finger-activated speech synthesizer, which is attached to his wheelchair. He notes in the acknowledgments section of his book, "This system has made all the difference: In fact I can communicate better now than before I lost my voice." The impression that Hawking makes on one in a scientific meeting, or when he lectures, is complicated. One would have to be less than human not to be appalled by the ravages of his illness. There seems to be no connection between the being one sees and the sunny brilliance of his papers—indeed, the sunny brilliance of this book.

In a sense, Hawking's *A Brief History of Time* is a complement to Steven Weinberg's seminal 1977 book, *The First Three Minutes*. Both books deal with the early universe and, to some extent, with the ultimate fate of the universe—its eschatology. But Weinberg was writing at a time when the study of cosmology was not taken entirely seriously by the full community of physicists and astrophysicists. His book, although it was written ostensibly for a popular audience, helped to change that. Weinberg, who won the Nobel Prize in Physics in 1979 for his work on the theory of elementary particles, had even then a reputation both as a creative scientist and as a hardheaded critic of scientific ideas. If *he* took cosmology seriously, one felt, then there must be something to it. (A parallel can be drawn between Weinberg's book and Erwin Schrödinger's *What Is Life?*, published in 1944. The fact that Schrödinger, one of the creators of the quantum theory, found deep intellectual content in certain questions of biology inspired many young people of the time to become biologists.) Weinberg focussed, no doubt deliberately, on the least speculative and least outré aspects of what can be a very speculative and outré scientific discipline. Most of his book deals with the theory of the formation, in the first three minutes, of the helium that makes up twenty-five per cent (by mass) of the visible universe. The fact that a quarter of the visible universe appears to be made up of helium—most of the rest is hydrogen—has, as it turns out, an explanation in terms of the nuclear reactions that took place as the universe was cooling off after the Big Bang. After the first three minutes, most of the helium we find in the universe had been formed. Weinberg also made a careful study of the development of modern cosmology, taking the trouble to read the original papers, and even to seek out their authors to learn the history behind those papers. He did not hesitate to use equations when necessary, and the appendices to his book could serve as the basis of an introductory course in the subject. Furthermore, there is a marked austerity in the philosophical outlook that animates the book. . . . (pp. 117-18)

In many ways, Hawking's book and philosophical outlook are mirror images of Weinberg's. In the first place, there is no need to persuade anyone that the book is serious science, since it has been written a decade later, when cosmology is one of the most fashionable of the scientific disciplines, attracting a vast community of elementary-particle physicists, astrophysicists, and even chemists and biologists. While Hawking does treat some of the bread-and-butter cosmological problems, such as helium formation, his real interest, both professionally and in the book, is in the deep fundamentals of the subject: What conditions actually prevail at the center of a black hole or were present at the instant of the Big Bang, and are these conditions describable in terms of the physics we know? In the second place, Hawking's treatment involves almost no formal mathematics. . . . Hawking's professional papers, too—those he has written alone—are full of ideas and relatively free of equations. They read more like prose than like mathematics. (I have often wondered if this was connected to the way he must have to work. Theoretical physicists are notorious scribblers; no piece of paper, from the back of an envelope to a placemat, is safe. A few physicists—Hans Bethe and John von Neumann, for example—have been prodigious mental computers, but most of them scratch and scribble. What does Hawking do? He has always worked with students and assistants, who—at least in recent years, one imagines—write down the equations for him. One supposes that he must therefore have been forced to do a great deal of mental computation and must also constantly have had to explain his ideas orally; he does not have the option of jotting things down on pieces of paper or on a blackboard.) Finally, Hawking's book is more benevolent than Weinberg's in its philosophical outlook. Hawking makes frequent and amiable references to God—somewhat the way Einstein used to do—but since he calls Him "him" one is not quite sure how to take this. (p. 118)

The most original parts of Hawking's book consist of the description of his own work. Since this has been of such great importance in modern cosmological theory, and since he describes it so lucidly, this gives the general reader an opportunity to learn some deep science directly from the source. Hawking's first important work in cosmology grew out of his Ph.D. thesis. Roger Penrose had noted in 1965 that whenever massive stars collapsed under the weight of their own gravitation to form the objects known

as black holes the result would necessarily be what mathematicians refer to as a "singularity." The singularity, in this case, would be a point in spacetime where the physical quantities describing a black hole—such as the gravitational field inside it—become literally infinite, as opposed to merely unimaginably large. This is a very important distinction. True infinities never, as far as we know, occur in nature, and if a theory predicts them it can be taken as an indication that the theory is "sick" or, at the very least, is being applied in a regime where it is not applicable. Here the theory at stake was Einstein's theory of general relativity and gravitation—the very theory that Robert Oppenheimer and his students had used in the late nineteen-thirties to show that what came to be called black holes might indeed exist. (The term was invented in 1969 by the physicist John Wheeler.) Penrose's result suggested a potential paradox in Einstein's theory when it was applied to regimes in which gravitation was very strong. Hawking made the fundamental observation—which became the basis of his Ph.D. thesis—that the Big Bang was like a black hole in reverse. A classical black hole—the qualification "classical" is necessitated by another of Hawking's fundamental discoveries, which he describes in a chapter entitled "Black Holes Ain't So Black"—simply swallows any matter or radiation that comes near it, whereas the Big Bang, instead of swallowing everything, emits everything. It is in some sense a black hole running backward in time. This was the insight that Hawking had in 1965 which, as he informs us, enabled him to get his Ph.D., so that he could get married. (The Hawkings, incidentally, now have three children.) But the discovery had more serious consequences for cosmology.

Black holes might or might not exist. The Big Bang, however, *must* exist if modern cosmology is to make any sense at all. Hence Hawking's result suggests that when Einstein's theory is applied to the beginning of the universe, it leads to a singularity—infinite temperatures, pressures, and gravitational fields—and therefore breaks down. By 1970, Hawking and Penrose had shown that this singularity was a feature of any model of the expanding universe which used Einstein's theory of general relativity and gravitation as its basis. The conclusion that Hawking, and many others, came to was that Einstein's theory must be incomplete. Certainly one thing missing from it was quantum mechanics. That Einstein left quantum mechanics out of his thinking about general relativity is hardly surprising, since he thought that quantum theory, with its uncertainties and probabilities, was only provisional and would eventually give way to some sort of classical theory—of which general relativity is the great paradigm. As Cocteau once remarked, "a true poet sings from his family tree." Einstein apart, it had been recognized by physicists since the nineteen-thirties that gravitation would have to be "quantized" but that the mathematics of this was almost hopelessly complex. (It still is.) Nonetheless, quantum mechanics is built on certain general principles, such as the Heisenberg uncertainty relations, that transcend mathematical complexities. Hawking realized in the early seventies that the Heisenberg relation between energy and time had remarkable implications for black holes; namely, that they "ain't so black."

In essence, the Heisenberg relation between energy and time states that no measurement that takes a finite as opposed to an infinite time to perform—that is, no actual measurement—can determine the energy of a system precisely. This carries all sorts of implications for physics. In particular, it implies that space can never be quite empty. An empty space would have no energy content, but this itself is a precise measurement; hence, such a statement would violate the Heisenberg relation. Space is alive with the spontaneous creation and annihilation of particles of matter and antimatter—for example, the electron and the positron. Under ordinary circumstances, we cannot detect these virtual—"virtual" because their existence violates the principle of the conservation of energy—particles directly, since they disappear back into the vacuum just rapidly enough not to violate the conservation-of-energy principle. (They do have indirect effects—in, for example, atomic physics.) But, Hawking argues in his book, if this process goes on at the surface of a black hole then the hole might grab either the electron or the positron and supply the negative energy needed to satisfy the principle. The remaining particle would be liberated, and the black hole, emitting particles, would appear to an observer to be glowing like an incandescent lump of coal. For arcane reasons involving entropy, the more a black hole radiated, the more it would shrink; the more it shrank, the hotter it would get; and the hotter it got, the more it would radiate. The whole process runs away with itself, and in the end, in Hawking's words, the black hole "would disappear completely in a tremendous final burst of emission, equivalent to the explosion of millions of H-bombs." Big black holes, of the kind produced when a massive star collapses, would take many billions of years to explode, but there might be, Hawking speculates, small black holes, which could explode in the present era. If this idea is right, these exploding black holes should be detectable as sudden bursts of radiation. The experimental problem is to distinguish these bursts from other sources of radiation. So far, there is no certain evidence for an exploding black hole, at least in this neck of the universe.

Making this kind of semi-phenomenological prediction, which, in a way, sidesteps the need for a fundamental quantum theory of gravitation, leaves most physicists, including Hawking, dissatisfied. For this reason, much has been made of recent attempts to develop a true quantum theory of gravitation by the use of "strings." The last part of Hawking's book is devoted to a description of this activity, and to raising some probing questions addressed to the practitioners involved in it, who sometimes claim that they have constructed, or are about to construct, the Theory of Everything—TOE, in the jargon. In pre-string elementary-particle theory, particles were thought of as points in space-time. A theory of point particles makes for all kinds of singularities, which, in the case of gravitation, become ineluctable. This problem led to the idea of replacing the point particles by tiny two-dimensional structures—loops of string—which would resemble points if one were not too close to them, but which might avoid the singular behavior of points. Miraculously, if this amalgam is conjoined to gravity, then in a small number of interesting cases the resulting theory is non-singular. This is what has led to the excitement over strings—an excitement that is somewhat tempered by the fact that these theories require at least ten dimensions (nine spatial and one temporal), while we exist in four. The practitioners claim that the extra dimensions in their theories are "curled up," so that they are unobservable, which puts the burden on these theories to explain how it happens that just four of the ten dimensions know enough not to curl up as well. Aside from this (and on this point Hawking is especially good), there is an entire philosophical Pandora's box that is opened when one talks about a Theory of Everything, and the practitioners not only leave this box unopened but seem blissfully unaware of it. Here is what Hawking has to say:

> Even if there is only one possible unified theory, it is just a set of rules and equations. What is it that breathes fire into the equations and makes a universe for them to describe? The usual approach of science of constructing a mathematical model cannot answer the questions of why there should be a universe for the model to describe. Why does the universe go to all the bother of existing? Is the unified theory so compelling that it brings about its own existence? Or does it need a creator, and, if so, does he have any other effect on the universe? And who created him?

One might object that these are not really scientific questions, but the statement that one has constructed the Theory of Everything is not science either. In science, one counts oneself fortunate if one succeeds in constructing the theory of something.

As much as I like Hawking's book, I would be remiss if I didn't point out an important way in which it might be improved. Hawking has a somewhat impressionistic view of the history of recent science. Very few active scientists—Weinberg is an exception, and that is one of the reasons his book is so good—actually take the trouble to read the papers of their early predecessors. A kind of folklore builds up which bears only a tangential relationship to reality, and when someone with the scientific prestige of Hawking repeats these legends it gives them credibility. This is not the place to indulge in historical exegesis, but one example may make the point. Furthermore, this example has—at least, in my view—the virtue of making the anecdote funnier than Hawking's rather garbled version of it. The anecdote has to do with the history of the discovery of the radiation left over from the Big Bang. The Big Bang produced light quanta of unimaginably high energy. In the fifteen billion years or so since that event, these quanta have cooled down to an average temperature of some three degrees above absolute zero. They have wavelengths of a few centimetres, which puts them in the microwave category, and in 1964 Arno A. Penzias and Robert W. Wilson, of the Bell Laboratories, accidentally found them while using a radio telescope connected to a microwave detector. There are about four hundred such light quanta in each cubic centimetre of the universe; their detection began the modern era in cosmology. But as early as 1948 George Gamow and his students Ralph Alpher and Robert Herman had predicted that such microwave radiation should exist and should have about the temperature that it has turned out to have. Their prediction was ignored, since, as I have noted, cosmology was not taken altogether seriously at the time. Gamow, who died in 1968, was an irrepressible, larger-than-life Russian eccentric, whose scientific genius was underrated during his lifetime. In any event, here is Hawking's version of the history:

> This picture of a hot early stage of the universe was first put forward by the scientist George Gamow in a famous paper written in 1948 with a student of

his, Ralph Alpher. Gamow had quite a sense of humor—he persuaded the nuclear scientist Hans Bethe to add his name to the paper to make the list of authors "Alpher, Bethe, Gamow," like the first three letters of the Greek alphabet, alpha, beta, gamma: particularly appropriate for a paper on the beginning of the universe! In this paper they made the remarkable prediction that radiation (in the form of photons) from the very hot early stages of the universe should still be around today, but with its temperature reduced to only a few degrees above absolute zero ($-273°$ C). It was this radiation that Penzias and Wilson found in 1965.

Now to the history. It is quite true that Alpher, Bethe, and Gamow published a paper—really a brief letter—in the *Physical Review* in 1948. It was entitled "The Origin of Chemical Elements," and nowhere in it is the microwave radiation mentioned. Rather, the paper concerned the general question of where the chemical elements comes from. At the time, Gamow thought that all the elements were manufactured in the first few minutes after the Big Bang. (This is not so, and within a few years he decided that the idea did not work.) Apart from the fact that the paper had nothing at all to do with the Big Bang radiation, to describe the events that led to the odd marriage of authors by saying that Gamow "persuaded the nuclear scientist Hans Bethe to add his name to the paper" is to miss the beauty of the story. When Gamow wrote the paper, he stuck Bethe's name between his own and Alpher's, being careful to keep things legitimate by adding "in absentia" after Bethe's name. The editor of the *Physical Review* must have smelled a rat, because he sent the paper to Bethe to referee. Bethe, who has always had a certain fondness for this kind of jape, checked the calculations to see if they followed from the assumptions, removed the words "in absentia" after his name, and recommended that the paper be published. The first prediction of the relic radiation from the Big Bang was actually published that same year, in a letter to the British journal *Nature,* by Alpher and Robert Herman, Gamow's other student. Hawking's retelling of this tale denies Alpher—and, more important, Herman—the proper credit for a major discovery in theoretical physics. (Gamow writes in one of his books that for several years he tried, unsuccessfully, to get Herman to change his name to "Delter." It is little wonder that Gamow's truly original contributions to both physics and biology were not taken as seriously as they might have been.)

Stephen Hawking has been for several years the Lucasian Professor of Mathematics at Cambridge. It is the professorship that was held by Isaac Newton and by the late P. A. M. Dirac, one of the founders of the quantum theory. Hawking has been a worthy successor, and one wishes him many future years. He has a great deal to teach us. (pp. 118-20)

> *Jeremy Bernstein, in a review of "A Brief History of Time," in* The New Yorker, *Vol. LXIV, No. 16, June 6, 1988, pp. 117-22.*

Jerry Adler

Like light from a collapsing star, exhausted by the struggle against gravity, the thoughts of Stephen Hawking reach us as if from a vast distance, a quantum at a time. Unable to speak, paralyzed by a progressive, incurable disease, the 46-year-old British physicist communicates with the world by a barely perceptible twitch of his fingers, generating one computer-synthesized word approximately every six seconds, consuming an entire day in composing a 10-page lecture. And the world awaits the words, for the same reason that astronomers search the heavens for the precious photons from remote galaxies, or that Newton spent his last years consumed by Biblical prophecy: Hawking is trying to read the mind of God.

He believes he is as close as man has ever come. (p. 56)

Hawking is one of a number of scientists searching for the magnificently named Grand Unification, a theory linking the two greatest intellectual achievements of the 20th century, relativity and quantum mechanics. The former deals with the large-scale structure of the universe, as determined essentially by gravity; the latter is concerned with the forces that operate at the atomic scale and below. Reconciling these two theories, a goal that eluded even Einstein, might hold the key to understanding how the universe came into being. A grand-unification theory would deserve not just a Nobel Prize but the last Nobel Prize; as Hawking puts it, "There would still be lots to do [in physics], but it would be like mountaineering after Everest."

Necessarily, Hawking pursues these questions on a purely cerebral level. But also by choice: he is a theoretical physicist, a discipline that in recent years has far outstripped the ability of scientists to make observations. In his book Hawking quotes a description applied to the great theoretical physicist Wolfgang Pauli, of whom it was said that "even his presence in the same town would make experiments go wrong." But, after all, experimenters deal in mere data; it would be a puny sort of God who let himself be seen in a radio telescope or trapped in a particle accelerator. Hawking prefers to stalk him on what he considers the higher plane of human intellect, armed only with the language he is confident they both speak, mathematics.

Hawking's most famous work has been on the nature of black holes. These are regions of extremely dense matter in which gravity is so strong that nothing, not even light, can escape. Astrophysicists believe a black hole might form when a burned-out star collapses. Surrounding a black hole is a surface known as the event horizon, a kind of trapdoor through which matter could pass in only one direction—inward—sealing off the hole from the rest of the universe. The existence of black holes was first posited in the 18th century (by a Cambridge don, Hawking notes smugly). They have been written about and studied and cited so often that it comes as a bit of a shock when Hawking observes that there is still no conclusive physical evidence that they exist. Hawking has a wager riding on the question with the physicist Kip Thorne at Caltech. Hawking bet *against* the existence of black holes; if he wins, much of his life's work will be wasted, but he will get a four-year subscription to Private Eye, a British satirical magazine. If black holes do exist, Thorne gets a year of Penthouse and, conceivably, Hawking gets the Nobel Prize.

In 1974, at a conference near Oxford, Hawking set out to show that it was possible for black holes to emit radiation. His calculations were based on the principle of quantum mechanics that at the subatomic level particles do not obey the same laws that we see in material objects around us. They lead a strange kind of contingent existence, in which their position and momentum are usually uncertain, subject to random fluctuations over infinitesimal fractions of a second. Particles can even be created out of empty space—with the proviso that they are created in pairs of "virtual particles" that must instantly collide and annihilate one another. What would happen if such a pair were to come into existence right at the event horizon? Hawking demonstrated that it was possible for one of the particles to be sucked into the black hole and the other to escape into space. This was such a revolutionary assertion that the chairman of the conference stood up to denounce it on the spot, but it has gained considerable acceptance since then, and the radiation that would result from this process has come to be called Hawking radiation. Of course, no one has ever found it in nature, either. The real significance of Hawking's paper was that it married quantum mechanics—the source of virtual particles—to relativity, the theory that predicts black holes. He had taken the first step on the road to a Grand Unification. (pp. 56-7)

For a successor to the mantle of Newton and Einstein, Hawking seems not to rate many perks. His office is a narrow, cluttered cubicle in the Department of Applied Mathematics and Theoretical Physics, which occupies a building as charmless and functional as its name. He spends his days there writing, seeing students or taking tea with them in the drab common room. He usually rolls up in his motorized wheelchair, which he steers with a joy stick on the half-mile ride from home in late morning, and works until around 7 in the evening. On a typical Friday last month, he began his day at the lunchtime meeting of a relativity seminar he leads. Two dozen students filled the room, sharing boxes of cookies and packages of luncheon meat, as Hawking wheeled quietly in and surveyed the scene.

His fingers twitched and the screen mounted on his wheelchair flickered. "Like old times," came a metallic voice from a speaker behind his seat.

Hawking's computers are cleverly designed for someone who can make only one movement. On the screen before him, the cursor flicks among letters of the alphabet, stopping at one when he squeezes his switch; this calls up a screen full of preprogrammed words beginning with the chosen letter. There are 2,600 such words, mingling the esoteric language of his field with the mundane nouns a man needs to get around in the world—thermal, theory, topology; thanks, Thursday, tea. The cursor scrolls down the lists until Hawking makes his choice, and the word is added to a sentence at the bottom of the screen, ready to be pronounced—or, in a formal interview, displayed on a desk monitor for precise note-taking. He can also spell out new words, which he does with no shortcuts or abbreviations. Anyone trying to finish his sentences for him feels the silent scorn of that imperturbably flicking finger. (p. 58)

[There] is a self-righteous streak in Hawking that some colleagues find nettlesome. In his book, he recounts discussing an unpublished theory of the Russian physicist Andrei Linde at a lecture in Philadelphia in 1981. Paul Steinhardt, a young assistant professor at the University of Pennsylvania, was in the audience and later published a paper, with Andreas Albrecht, proposing "something

very similar to Linde's idea . . . ," Hawking wrote. He added, "[Steinhardt] later told me he didn't remember me describing Linde's ideas . . . " The implications of a remark like this, from a world-famous scientist about a lesser-known colleague, can be devastating. Steinhardt—who says he had already corrected Hawking on the point—was disturbed enough when the story reappeared in the book to dig up a videotape of Hawking's lecture, which he says supports his assertion that Hawking never mentioned Linde's work. "Hawking is an outstanding physicist," said Steinhardt, now a full professor, "but he's not a god, he's a human being." Steinhardt sent the tape to Hawking, and—after *Newsweek* raised the question—Hawking announced, through his U.S. publisher, that the account will be expunged from future editions.

To be sure, Hawking wasn't seeking credit for himself but for his friend Linde. And, already living on borrowed time, he can perhaps be forgiven for his impatience in correcting what he sees as injustice. Has a similar attitude of impatience affected his scientific work? Penrose believes that Hawking's condition has forced him to work more creatively, to take imaginative leaps where someone with a less uncertain future might want to cogitate a little longer. Hawking himself dismisses that notion utterly. The only effect of ALS on his work he is willing to concede is that "I avoid problems with a lot of equations, because I cannot manage to do them in my head. But," he adds, "those are the most boring problems."

There is really only one interesting problem, which is the problem of everything. "My goal," Hawking has said, "is a complete understanding of the universe, why it is as it is and why it exists at all." And slowly, painfully, he has advanced on that goal. The journey has taken some surprising turns. Hawking, together with Penrose, was a leader in postulating a property of black holes known as singularities. As predicted by relativity, these are points at which matter is not merely tremendously dense but *infinitely* dense—the remnants of a star collapsed to a point of zero size. Since the laws of physics, in their mathematical expression, cannot accommodate infinite quantities, the logical conclusion was that these laws no longer apply at a singularity—and *literally anything can happen*. (We never see the laws break down because it happens inside the event horizon, from which nothing can escape.) The universe, according to some models, began with a singularity, which erupted into the Big Bang. Many physicists are satisfied with some version of this account. But Hawking realized you could never completely understand a universe that began at a point where anything could happen.

His journey, therefore, has taken him away from singularities, toward a theory that modifies the stark predictions of relativity through the application of quantum mechanics. He achieved this result in a totally abstract and mathematical form, by postulating a different kind of time, "imaginary" time as distinct from the "real" time that measures our days and years. ("Imaginary" is used here in a technical mathematical sense—meaning the square root of a negative number—it does not have its common-sense meaning of "illusory." And it is impossible to discuss it in ordinary physical terms; the question "How long is an imaginary year?" is meaningless.) In imaginary time, there are no singularities; the universe is finite, but without the boundaries that singularities imply, in the way the surface of the earth is finite but unbounded. In an hourlong interview, Hawking rises to the level of a paragraph on only one subject, this "no-boundary proposal": "I think that it really underlies science because it is really the statement that the laws of science hold everywhere. Once you allow that there could be exceptions to the laws of science, you couldn't predict anything . . . If the laws of science broke down at the beginning of the universe, they could break down anywhere."

And is this, then, the key that will unlock the true secret of the universe? The next two decades, Hawking has said, should hold the answer. Project Hawking's intellectual growth over the next 20 years and the possibilities are almost limitless; do the same with his physical deterioration and . . . There is a phenomenon of relativity known as time dilation, in which time appears to slow down almost to a stop for bodies that approach the speed of light. Hawking alludes, in his book, to what it might be like for an astronaut as he accelerates toward a black hole, as all eternity passes by outside in an instant of his time. There is a sense in which Hawking himself has experienced a kind of time dilation, an inexplicable slowing of a natural process that has added decades to his expected life span. The answer he seeks may be almost within his sight. But so, perhaps, is the event horizon. (pp. 58-9)

> *Jerry Adler, Gerald C. Lubenow, and Maggie Malone, "Reading God's Mind," in* Newsweek, *Vol. CXI, No. 24, June 13, 1988, pp. 56-9.*

Martin Gardner

Stephen Hawking opens with a marvelous old anecdote. A famous astronomer, after a lecture, was told by an elderly lady, who was perhaps under the influence of Hinduism, that his cosmology was all wrong. The world, she said, rests on the back of a giant tortoise. When the astronomer asked what the tortoise stands on, she replied, "You're very clever, young man, very clever. But it's turtles all the way down."

Most people, Hawking writes, would find this cosmology ridiculous, but if we take the turtles as symbols of more and more fundamental laws, the tower is not so absurd. There are two ways to view it. Either a single turtle is at the bottom, standing on nothing, or it's turtles all the way down. Both views are held by leading physicists. David Bohm and Freeman Dyson, to mention two, favor the infinite regress—wheels within wheels, boxes inside boxes, but never a final box. Hawking is on the other side. He believes that physics is finally closing in on the ultimate turtle. . . .

A Brief History of Time is Hawking's first popularly written book. Warned that every equation would cut sales in half, he has left out all formulas except Einstein's famous $E=mc^2$, which he hopes will not frighten half his readers. Hawking's prose is as informal and clear as his topics are profound. Work that he accomplished during what he calls his early "classical" phase—by "classical" he means work in relativity theory—is summed up in *The Large Scale Structure of Spacetime*, a book written with South African cosmologist George Ellis. Avoid it, Hawking advises; it is so technical as to be "quite unreadable." His

"quantum phase," begun in 1974, supplies the subject matter for his thoroughly readable *Brief History of Time.* (p. 17)

Einstein's model of the universe, the first to be based on relativity theory, is best understood as a three-dimensional analogue of the surface of a sphere. The sphere's surface is finite but unbounded. A plane flying in the straightest possible line across the earth's surface never reaches an edge, but eventually returns to where it started. In Einstein's model, space is the curved hypersurface of a four-dimensional sphere. The cosmos is finite in volume but unbounded. A spaceship traveling the straightest possible path would eventually circle the cosmos. To prevent gravity from collapsing his model, Einstein imagined a repulsive force that would keep the universe stable, but it was soon shown that stability would be impossible. His universe would have to be either expanding or contracting.

After overwhelming evidence was found that the universe is expanding, two influential models were proposed. The physicist George Gamow claimed that the universe started with what the astronomer Fred Hoyle derisively called the "big bang." Hoyle and his friends countered with a "steady state" universe, infinite in both space and time, that has always looked the same as it does now, and is destined to look the same forever. To maintain the overall structure, it is necessary to assume that hydrogen atoms are continually forming in space to provide the matter that keeps coalescing into stars.

The steady-state model was shot down by the discovery of background radiation that could only be explained as a remnant of a primeval fireball. Gamow's big bang became the standard model. For a while, cosmologists toyed with the notion of "oscillating" models in which the universe expands, reaches a limit, contracts to a small size, then starts over again with another explosion. Recent theoretical work, Hawking writes, makes such "bouncing" models extremely unlikely.

Before describing his new model of the universe, Hawking provides an artfully condensed overview of relativity theory and quantum mechanics. In Newton's cosmology, motion is "absolute" in the sense that it can be measured relative to a fixed, motionless space that nineteenth-century physicists called the "stagnant ether." Newton's time is also absolute in the sense that one unvarying time pervades the universe. Einstein abandoned both notions. Space and time were fused into a single structure. Light became the only nonrelative motion, its velocity impossible to exceed, and never changing regardless of an observer's motion. Gravity and inertia became a single phenomenon, not a "force" but merely the tendency of objects to take the simplest possible paths through a space-time distorted by the presence of large masses of matter such as stars and planets.

There is a curious mistake in Hawking's discussion of Newton's cosmology. We are told that Newton believed in absolute time but not in absolute space, and for this was sharply criticized by Bishop Berkeley. It was the other way around. Newton defended absolute space against the "relational" view of his archrival Leibniz, who argued that space is no more than the relative positions of objects. Inertial phenomena, such as the centrifugal force that turns the surface of water concave in a bucket rotating rapidly around its vertical axis, makes it necessary, Newton insisted, to view motion as relative to a fixed space. Berkeley argued that no body could move or rotate except in relation to other bodies—a striking anticipation of relativity theory.

Hawking also misleadingly attributes to Berkeley the belief that "all material objects . . . are an illusion." The Irish bishop did not think objects were illusions in any ordinary sense of the word. No one argued more cogently than he that the outside world is not dependent on human observations. For Berkeley, the structure of a tree or stone is maintained by the mind of God. He would have been delighted by quantum mechanics in which "matter" dissolves into mathematics. All material objects are made of molecules, but molecules are made of atoms, and atoms in turn are made of electrons, protons, and neutrons. And what are subatomic particles made of? They are quantized aspects of fields that are pure mathematical structures, made of nothing else. Applied to a field or its particle, the word "matter" loses all meaning. Nevertheless, for both Berkeley and a particle physicist, rocks are as nonillusory as they were for Samuel Johnson, who naively supposed he refuted Berkeley by kicking a large stone.

Hawking's chapter on the expanding universe centers on a famous paper he wrote with Roger Penrose, now at Oxford University. Penrose had been the first to show that if a massive star collapses into a black hole, a region of space-time from which light cannot escape, it must (if the laws of relativity hold "all the way down") produce a space-time singularity—a geometrical point of zero extension. At that point gravity would produce an infinite density and an infinite spatial curvature. When the variables of a law acquire infinite values, the law becomes meaningless. In plain language, physicists have no idea what happens at black hole singularities, if indeed they exist.

Hawking devotes two chapters to black holes. Although there is yet no decisive evidence that black holes exist, most cosmologists now are convinced that they do. (The best candidate for a black hole is the invisible part of a binary star system in the constellation of Cygnus, the swan.) Hawking's major contribution to black hole theory was showing that as a star's matter falls into a black hole, quantum interactions must occur and particles escape in what is known as "Hawking radiation." As the title of a chapter indicates, "black holes ain't so black." Mini-black holes are tiny structures that may have formed in great numbers after the big bang. Hawking showed that if they exist, radiation will cause them to evaporate and ultimately explode. When Hawking delivered his classic paper on this in 1974, the conference chairman, John Taylor, called the paper rubbish. Dennis Sciama, a British cosmologist, had an opposite reaction. He called the paper one of "the most beautiful in the history of physics."

A chapter called "The Origin and Fate of the Universe" is the book's centerpiece. About 1981 Hawking and Penrose became more and more impressed by the possibility that relativity ceases to apply on the quantum level. Just before the universe exploded there would be no singularity because quantum mechanics completely dominated the scene. Nor would there be a singularity if the universe contracted to the big crunch. These thoughts led Hawking to an elegant new model of the universe that he constructed with Jim Hartle, at the University of California, Santa Barbara.

It is hopeless to explain the new model in any detail here because it makes use of a special kind of time called "imaginary time," which plays a role in calculating the most probable paths of particles. It is called imaginary because it is measured by complex numbers—numbers of the form $a + b\sqrt{-1}$, where a and b are real numbers and $\sqrt{-1}$ is imaginary. [The clearest explanation of imaginary time I know of for nonspecialists is to be found in the late Richard Feynman's book *Q.E.D.,* which stands for quantum electrodynamics (Princeton University Press, 1985).] Like Einstein's model, the new model is finite in volume but not unbounded. Unlike Einstein's model, time is treated in exactly the same way as a space coordinate. Einstein's three space coordinates were closed in a circle, but his time was open at both ends. In Hawking's model, "real time" is replaced by imaginary time.

Hawking makes no attempt to explain his model except by a vague analogy. The universe is likened to a tiny region at the earth's North Pole. Think of the earth's axis as an imaginary time axis. The universe explodes and expands until it reaches its maximum size at the equator, then contracts to a tiny region at the South Pole. The two end spots are "singular" in the ordinary sense of being unique, but not in the technical sense of unextended points where the laws of science break down. Because the time axis is imaginary, it is not necessary to assume that the universe had a beginning or will have an end. The two spots are regions where disorder is total, the arrow of real time vanishes, and quantum events fluctuate aimlessly and forever in imaginary time.

From the standpoint of real time, the universe looks as if time began with the initial explosion and will cease after the big squeeze, but in imaginary time there are no singularities where time starts and stops. The universe emerged from a chaos that always was, and will go back to a chaos that will never cease. As Hawking puts it, the universe is eternal, "completely self-contained and not affected by anything outside itself. It would neither be created nor destroyed. It would just BE."

It is not clear whether Hawking is a determinist who thinks history has to be the way it is, or whether chance and free will intervene, although early in his book he raises a curious paradox. If determinism reigns it would impose the outcome of our search for universal laws, but "why should it determine that we come to the right conclusions from the evidence? Might it not equally well determine that we draw the wrong conclusions? Or no conclusion at all?" Because the search has so far proved increasingly successful, Hawking sees no reason to abandon Einstein's faith that the Old One may be subtle, but not malicious.

Space coordinates are symmetrical in the sense that they are the same in both directions and you can travel along them either way. But time is like a one-way street, with an arrow that points in only one direction. Hawking considers three foundations for the arrow: psychological, cosmological, and thermodynamic. The psychological basis is memory of the past. The cosmological basis is the expansion of the universe. The thermodynamic basis is the second law of thermodynamics, which says that events move in the direction of increasing entropy or disorder.

Our psychological arrow points the same way as the thermodynamic arrow, Hawking reasons, because our minds are parts of the physical world. We remember events in the order in which disorder increases. "This makes the second law of thermodynamics almost trivial. Disorder increases with time because we measure time in the direction in which disorder increases. You can't have a safer bet than that!"

Will the cosmological arrow ever reverse? That depends on the amount of mass in the universe. If it is below a certain ratio to the volume of the cosmos, the universe will expand forever and eventually die of the cold. If it is above the critical ratio, gravity will slow down the expansion and eventually reverse it. Early in his career Hawking defended the bizarre view that in a contracting universe time's other two arrows would turn around and human beings (if any still existed) would live backward like a motion picture run in reverse. It is impossible to reconcile this with consciousness and free will, but in any case Hawking now admits that this was a youthful blunder. His new model allows disorder to continue increasing throughout the contracting phase, although disorder would be too extreme to permit life. (pp. 17-19)

One of the big mysteries that remain is why after the big bang all but three space dimensions "compacted" into the tiny hyperspheres. On this question Hawking invokes familiar arguments that we could not exist in a universe with fewer or more than three dimensions. He includes a drawing of a two-dimensional dog showing how food digestion would be impossible because a tube from mouth to anus would split the flat dog in half. Evidently Hawking has not looked into A. K. Dewdney's fantastic book *The Planiverse* (Poseidon, 1984), in which methods of digestion in flatland are carefully worked out. As for dimensions above three, Hawking is quite right in saying that solar systems and atoms would be impossible, but the catch is that they are impossible only if based on laws we know. In my opinion Dewdney's book provides strong grounds for not ruling out the notion that universes could operate efficiently with laws we don't know.

"Even if there is only one possible unified theory," Hawking writes in his last chapter,

> it is just a set of rules and equations. What is it that breathes fire into the equations and makes a universe for them to describe? The usual approach of science of constructing a mathematical model cannot answer the questions of why there should be a universe for the model to describe. Why does the universe go to all the bother of existing? Is the unified theory so compelling that it brings about its own existence? Or does it need a creator, and, if so, does he have any other effect on the universe? And who created him?

Hawking wisely does not try to answer these questions. He does, however, say that if the ultimate theory exists it should eventually be understandable by everybody. We will then be able to get on with the superultimate question of why we and the universe bother to exist. "If we find the answer to that," writes Hawking in his book's final sentence (except for three idiosyncratic appendixes that capsule the lives of Galileo, Newton, and Einstein), "it would be the ultimate triumph of human reason—for then we would know the mind of God."

To me, a philosophical theist, there is not a chance of such a triumph. Even entertaining such a possibility strikes me as total folly. I firmly believe that it is not possible for science to discover any fact, or confirm any theory, that has the slightest bearing on why the universe bothers existing. As for time, I am among those who, like Augustine and Miguel de Unamuno, consider it the most terrible of mysteries. It is something given. You cannot even define it without smuggling time into your definition. The physicist John Wheeler is fond of saying that time is what keeps everything from happening at once. True, but this throws not a glimmer of light into the darkness. I have written elsewhere about why I believe time is bound up with other impenetrable mysteries such as free will and the foresight of God. I can imagine a possible world without time—just think of the universe as frozen to a halt—but I cannot conceive of you and me "existing" in such a world. (pp. 19-20)

> *Martin Gardner, "The Ultimate Turtle," in*
> The New York Review of Books, *Vol. XXXV,*
> *No. 10, June 16, 1988, pp. 17-20.*

Salman Rushdie

The most appealing account of the Big Bang I've ever read was written by Italo Calvino in his marvellous *Cosmicomics*. In the beginning, we're told by Calvino's narrator, the proto-being Qfwfq: 'Every point of each of us coincided with every point of each of the others in a single point, which was where we all were . . . it wasn't the sort of situation that encourages sociability.' Then a certain Mrs Ph(i)Nko cried out: 'Oh, if only I had some room, how I'd like to make some noodles for you boys!' And at once—bam!—there it was: spacetime, the cosmos. *Room.*

The idea that the universe might have been set in motion by the first truly generous impulse, the first expression of love, is rather wonderful, but it's certainly unscientific, and these days the creation of Creation is primarily the work of scientific, rather than literary or theological, imaginations. It's a hot story, and Professor Hawking's book [*A Brief History of Time*] is only the latest of a string of popularising bestsellers on the subject—fascinating books, full of exclamations.

To read this rapidly expanding universe of books is to come to see physicists as a highly exclamatory breed, longing above all for the moment when they get to cry Eureka. It's tempting to use a variant of the anthropic principle (the world is what it is because were it otherwise we wouldn't be here to observe that it was so) and propose that it's not surprising that such persons should have created a cosmos that begins with the biggest exclamation of them all.

Let us quickly concede, however, that there have been many astonishing discoveries, many genuine Eureka-opportunities, since Einstein's general relativity theory changed the world. Professor Hawking, striking a fine balance between the need to address himself to non-scientists and the danger of over-simplifying condescension, takes us for a canter over the territory. Here is general relativity itself, and Hubble's discovery of the expanding universe. Over there is the defeat of the steady-state theory by the big-bangers, and to the right (or maybe to the left) is Heisenberg's Uncertainty Principle. Just ahead are the great voyages into the heart of the atom, and out towards the black holes.

Hawking's near-legendary status confers immense authority on the text. Not only is he the fellow who showed that black holes leak, but it was his 1970 paper that 'proved' that the universe must have begun as a *singularity,* that is, a thing not unlike Calvino's single point. But the reason that this book gets steadily more engrossing as it approaches the heart of the subject is that it turns out that, on the question of Genesis, the Professor has changed his mind. Having applied the ideas of quantum mechanics—the study of the frequently irrational world of infinitely tiny things—to the condition of the universe before the Bang, he has decided that the singularity whose existence he 'proved' in 1970 needn't really have existed at all.

He now proposes that instead of a 'beginning' there was what Richard Feynman called a 'sum over histories'—a situation in which time was indistinguishable from directions in space, making redundant the concept of something out of nothing, of before and after. If this were so, he tells us, 'the universe . . . would neither be created nor destroyed. It would just BE.' It's a dazzling argument, ending with the dismissal of God himself: 'What place, then, for a creator?' Man proposes, God is disposed of . . . and Hawking is, as he makes clear, making no more than a proposal, a theory about a theory which he thinks will soon be worked out.

He is prepared, however, to draw an astonishing conclusion from his survey. He suggests that we're actually quite near the end of 'humanity's intellectual struggle to understand the universe.' There's a good chance, apparently, that a complete, unified theory of everything will be found 'within the lifetime of some of us who are around today, always presuming we don't blow ourselves up first.'

This sounds, I'm afraid, like a particularly bad case of Premature Eurekitis. Anyone who has followed Professor Hawking through his own changes of mind, who has learned, through him, the implications of the Uncertainty Principle—'one certainly cannot predict future events exactly if one cannot even measure the present state of the universe precisely'—or who has even the most rudimentary awareness of the history of human knowledge will find this notion of the proximity of the Ultimate Truth hard to swallow.

And, anyway, to all of us who aren't scientists—who are lay readers, or even writers—the real value of the ideas of the new physics and of quantum mechanics is precisely the same as that of Calvino's stories: namely, that they make explosions in our heads, and make it possible for us to dream new dreams, of ourselves as well as the universe.

It is impossible, however, not to admire the grand Quixotic conviction of Stephen Hawking's quest for the end of knowledge; while continuing to believe that the only permanent discoveries are those of the imagination. All theories eventually pass away, and are replaced by new ones; only Mrs Ph(i)Nko lives forever.

Salman Rushdie, "Head Bangers," in The Observer, *July 10, 1988, p. 43.*

Jeffrey Marsh

The title of Stephen Hawking's new book is unduly modest. *A Brief History of Time* is indeed brief, but it is considerably more than a history and it deals with a far wider range of topics than time. What Hawking has written is a concise, firsthand account of current scientific thinking regarding the nature of the universe as a whole, enlivened by his own insights into recent developments in the theories of general relativity and quantum mechanics. (p. 60)

Hawking's central theme is that the dogged pursuit of consistency, both between theory and observation and among different parts of the same theory, will eventually lead to a full understanding of the universe. Indeed, his scientific contributions as a whole have been characterized by an extraordinary intellectual determination to follow ideas to their logical conclusion, no matter how absurd that conclusion may at first appear.

Hawking is keenly aware that even the giants Newton and Einstein failed to pursue some far-reaching implications of their own insights. Newton did not realize that according to his theory of gravitation, a universe that was both infinite and unchanging could not exist: the force of gravity would inevitably cause it to collapse on itself. In fact, it took some 300 years before this was appreciated. And when at last Albert Einstein superseded Newton's theory with his General Theory of Relativity, according to which the universe would tend either to expand or contract spontaneously, he too assumed that the equations showing this result would have to be modified to allow for a static solution. (Einstein later declared this the worst mistake he ever made.)

According to Hawking, it was Edwin Hubble's 1929 discovery that the universe was expanding which, by destroying Newton's long-held assumption, began the modern study of cosmology and eventually led to general agreement that the universe came into existence at a definite time in the past. In simple terms, the beginnings of the current expansion can be traced back to a cataclysmic explosion, popularly known as the big bang. This was the moment of creation, the origin of the universe and of space and time. Depending on how much matter there may be in the universe (an issue of considerable dispute), the resulting expansion may either continue until eternity or reverse itself some time in the future, shrinking the universe until it once again approaches a state of infinite density—the "big crunch"—and the end of time as we know it.

Until the mid-1960's, the study of the origin of the universe remained something of a backwater within the field of astrophysics. An inconclusive debate pitted followers of the big-bang theory against others who believed on philosophical grounds that the expanding universe was kept in a steady state of constant average density by the continuous creation of matter at a slow rate. The latter theory was largely abandoned after 1965, about the same time Hawking was starting his career as a graduate student. As he describes it, having already survived longer than the two years' life expectancy he had been granted when his physical condition was first diagnosed, he had decided to marry and needed a Ph.D. to get a job. He came across an interesting thesis topic dealing with black holes, then a considerably more arcane topic than it was subsequently to become (thanks in no small part to Hawking himself).

Hawking's adviser, Roger Penrose, had shown that the collapse of a sufficiently massive star, the atomic structure of which was not strong enough to resist its own gravitational attraction, would result in a black hole. This, as devotees of popular science-fiction know, is a gravitational singularity occupying zero volume which is able to absorb anything closely approaching it but from which neither matter nor light can escape. Hawking soon realized that the logic of Penrose's argument could be reversed. In the first of his notable contributions, he proved that if the universe were indeed expanding, it must have *originated* in a gravitational singularity: the big bang.

Meanwhile, researchers in other branches of physics were also looking more closely into the early behavior of the universe. According to theories emerging in the 1960's and 70's, the subatomic particles—protons and neutrons—known since the early days of nuclear physics, were in fact made up of still more fundamental entities—quarks—which had the disconcerting property of being undetectable in isolation. To prove these new theories, it would be necessary to observe what happened to such subnuclear particles at extremely high energies, when (it was predicted) the considerable differences observed in their behaviors under normal conditions would disappear. Unfortunately, as Hawking remarks in one of his driest asides, an accelerator powerful enough to test the new theories "would have to be as big as the solar system—and would be unlikely to be funded in the present economic climate."

But there could be a substitute for such an experimental test: one could predict the composition of today's universe by making calculations on the basis of what should have happened immediately after the big bang, when both the density and temperature of the universe were sufficiently high. Considerations along these lines led to an ever growing acceptance both of the big-bang theory itself and of the unified theories of elementary particle physics.

In the 1970's, Hawking, who sometimes seems to be the Indiana Jones of mathematical physics, moved on to even less charted territory, the no-man's land between the theory of relativity, which deals with the universe on the largest scale, and the theory of quantum mechanics, which deals with the most microscopic aspect of reality. A reconciliation of these two theories, which in their present forms are inconsistent, is a prerequisite for a uniform theory covering all the laws of nature, the ultimate goal of physics.

There is a fundamental point of difference between classical physics, with its assumption of a strictly deterministic relationship between present and future, and quantum mechanics, where even in principle our knowledge can be no better than statistical. That point of difference is closely related to the Uncertainty Principle enunciated by the 20th-century German physicist Werner Heisenberg. To invoke the most familiar illustration of that principle, we cannot exactly specify both the position and the momentum of a particle: in other words, the more certain we are of the location of an object at one instant, the less we know about where it will be the next. Another less well known but equally surprising consequence of the Uncertainty Principle is that even a perfect vacuum is full of rapidly fluctuating electric and magnetic fields.

In the course of a dispute over thermodynamics, Hawking took note of this second consequence, and he was led by it to the totally unexpected, indeed shocking, conclusion that black holes, which supposedly can only absorb matter and energy from the outside world, actually spontaneously emit particles, with the greatest rate of emission coming from the least massive black holes. In terms as clear and simple as possible, and with the frequent use of witty and enlightening analogies, he explains in the book the reasoning that led him to this and other discoveries—discoveries that propel him to believe that "we may now be near the end of the end of the search for the ultimate laws of nature." Should we achieve this goal, he writes, the next step will be "the discussion of why it is that we and the universe exist. If we find the answer to that, it would be the ultimate triumph of human reason—for then we would know the mind of God."

What does Hawking mean by knowing "the mind of God"? Earlier, he has given us a clue to his own mind on this question when he cites the concept of imaginary time, a mathematical construct (obtained by multiplying time by the square root of minus one) frequently used by physicists. In the world of real time, experienced by real people, the universe, Hawking writes, "has a beginning . . . at which the laws of physics break down. . . . " But, he goes on, "maybe what we call real is just an idea that we invent." In such a case, the universe, though finite, "would be completely self-contained and not affected by anything outside itself. It would be neither created nor destroyed. It would just BE. . . . What place, then, for a creator?"

But if "what we call real is just an idea that we invent," what Hawking has given us here is not so much an insight into the "mind of God" as an explanation of why we cannot expect to have such an insight. His explanation is akin to a more familiar one given often by philosophers, though in his case it comes couched in the language of physics. Some may find it no more satisfactory for that.

"In all your ways, know Him," the Book of Proverbs tells us. Those ways extend beyond the intellectual. In particular, the "mind of God" may be thought to contain answers to two overwhelming questions touching upon the nature and purpose of the universe.

The first is implicit in a paradox expressed most pithily by Rabbi Akiva: "All is foreseen, but free will is granted." The reason that no merely human mind can fathom the answer to this paradox has to do with our necessarily imperfect knowledge of time. The second and more agonizing question is that of Job, and it concerns the justification of evil and suffering. To that question, our answer must lie in acceptance, which is not the same thing as resignation—and also in wonder at the example set for us by, among other marvels of the universe, the suffering and triumph of such as Stephen Hawking. (pp. 60-2)

> *Jeffrey Marsh, "Explaining the Universe," in* Commentary, *Vol. 86, No. 3, September, 1988, pp. 60-2.*

John Murray

In announcing his Berlin lecture of 1804, the German philosopher Johann Gottlieb Fichte promised his audience the "complete solution of the universe and of consciousness with mathematical certainty," presumably through *a priori* deduction. Similarly, in 1928 the German physicist and Nobel laureate Max Born, elated over Paul Dirac's new electron equation, told a group of visitors to Gottingen University that, "Physics, as we know it, will be over in six months." Now we have Professor Stephen W. Hawking, recently on the cover of *Newsweek* and holder of Isaac Newton's old chair of mathematics at Cambridge University, informing mankind that the yet-discovered Grand Unified Theory will permit the human race to "know the mind of God" and will bring about the end of physics. With all due respect to these three distinguished thinkers, such grandiose claims strike this humble humanist as pretentious at best and portentous at worst, and inevitably summon up Hamlet's line that "There are more things on heaven and on earth / Than are dreamt of in your philosophy, Horatio." Having made that observation, let me also say that *A Brief History of Time* is a highly informative book, written in the long British tradition of scientific popularizations, and provides the reader on either side of the Atlantic with a timely report on the current state of theoretical physics. . . .

There are, I believe, two problems with contemporary physics. The first is the historic antinomy between science and religion that began with the Inquisatorial trial of Galileo in 1616. As a result of this schism, science has ceased to have a firm basis in morality. A science without ethics, as we saw in Mary Shelley's feminist critique of male-dominated science, *Frankenstein,* is doomed to creating monsters and human misery: mushroom clouds, nerve gas, Agent Orange, dioxin dumps, and chlorinated fluorocarbons that break down the ozone layer. Similarly, of course, a theology that ignores scientific facts—whether Copernican heliocentrism, Darwinian evolution, or the necessity of population control to prevent the deforestation that is leading to global warming—risks fatal obsolescence not only among the intelligentsia but eventually among the middle class without whose support no religion can endure. Science, in short, is as much an imperative to human survival as religious faith, and unless a "grand unification" is affected between these two adversaries, the Western skies appear very dark indeed. The hubris of science needs to be tempered by humility as much as the doctrines of religion need to be consistent with the design as it has been discovered. Courses in ethics should be required of all science students, as science courses should be taken by all divinity students.

The second problem with physics today is the division between theoretical and experimental physics, a separation that began in the faddish 1960s when the academic branch of the sciences became a kind of philosophical Southern California. At that time such esoteric whimsies as superstring theory became dogma. The string theory, of which Hawking is an adherent, was invented as a theoretical effort to describe the strong force, and states, in his words, that "particles like the proton and neutron [can] be regarded as waves on a string." The theory is hotly contested by Hawking's peers, including Nobel laureate Sheldon Glashow, a professor of physics at Harvard University. . . . (p. 3)

There are two difficulties with Hawking's book: his endorsement of the anthropic principle and his ambivalent stance on determinism. The anthropic principle, currently popular among theoreticians, states that we live in an ob-

server-dependent, participatory universe in which all physical laws are dependent upon the presence of an observer to formulate them. Such a theory seems to me to be merely a resurrection of the old Judeo-Christian Doctrine of Final Causes (Genesis 1:28) which postulated that God created the universe for man. The homocentric fallacy was, I thought, pretty soundly repudiated by Copernicus, Newton, Darwin, and Einstein. Determinism, a system of thought espoused by the Marquis de Laplace in the early nineteenth century, states that, in Hawking's words, "there should be a set of scientific laws that would allow us to predict everything that would happen in the universe, if only we knew the complete state of the universe at one time." Laplace compared the universe to a clock that God created, wound up, and set to ticking with no further interference from him. The Heisenberg Uncertainty Principle, which postulated that it is impossible to know the position and velocity of a particle at the same time, led modern science to abandon determinism and its mechanistic *weltanschauung*. Hawking, though, seems to have a lingering fondness for this seductive model, as when he states that "most people have come to believe that God allows the universe to evolve according to a set of laws and does not intervene in the universe to break those laws." Similarly, "However, the laws do not tell us what the universe should have looked like when it started—it would still be up to God to wind up the clockwork and choose how to start it off." He concludes, with a telling qualification: "We now know that Laplace's hopes of determinism can not be realized, *at least in the terms* [emphasis added] he had in mind."

As a humanist, I took particular note of Hawking's discussion of specialization:

> In Newton's time it was possible for an educated person to have a grasp of the whole of human knowledge, at least in outline. But since then, the pace of the development of science has made this impossible. Because theories are always being changed to account for new observations, they are never properly digested or simplified so that *ordinary people* [emphasis added] can understand them . . . Only a few people can keep up with the rapidly advancing frontier of knowledge, and they have to devote their whole time to it and specialize in a small area.

To say that it is currently impossible for "an educated person to have a grasp of the whole of human knowledge" is not only false, it is dangerous, for it perpetuates a mythology about this being an "Age of Specialization" that is used to sustain mediocrity and subvert excellence as the standard of achievement both for students and professors at American and British universities. The fact of the matter is, many people in the three centuries since Newton have achieved as much universal knowledge as was possible in the Renaissance and Reformation: Mill, Huxley, Arnold, Whitehead, Russell, and Sagan, to name just a few. Furthermore, I can think of many professors in the humanities who read *Science, Scientific American,* and *Nature* as regularly as journals in the non-sciences, and *vice versa.* The myth of specialization must be exposed for what it is, and minds, such as Jonathan Miller, Isaac Asimov, and others taken as our models as much as Erasmus, More, and Sydney were the exemplars of an earlier age.

A Brief History of Time must, in the end, be given a partial endorsement. Its author is a celebrity, respected around the world for the extraordinary courage he has shown in battling the debilitating motor neuron disease. The book will certainly continue to be a bestseller, and that is good for the dissemination of knowledge. The book, however, has its inconsistencies and problems, and is pontifical in the way establishment science often is. Unlike Einstein's earlier popularization (*The Theory of Relativity,* London, 1924), Hawking's book also has several instances of personal aggrandizement and one unseemly personal attack on an American professor Hawking accuses of stealing a minor idea. Also, there are three puzzling statements on Galileo, Newton, and Einstein at the end of the book. All of these flaw an otherwise fairly well written and well edited book. The book contains a complete overview of the field for the general reader, but does not offer anything earth-shaking. Hawking and his colleagues will, despite their indications to the contrary, almost certainly never discover the quantum theory of gravity. The history of science teaches that *transcendental* breakthroughs—the conceptual metamutations that forever alter cultural DNA—are made by young and skeptical free-thinkers like Einstein, who was ostracized by his professors at Zurich's Ecole Polytechnique Federale for his revolutionary independence, or Newton, who was similarly isolated by his willingness to consider new ideas, and *not* by tenured dons who have become the risk-averse guardians of the received tradition on which careers are built and defended.

The reading of *A Brief History of Time,* finally, does not answer nearly so many questions as it raises. Until physics can answer these, and many other questions, it is about as close to "the mind of God" as the species was on the twilight plains of long ago, beating drums and watching sparks fly up into the stars. If the universe is infinite but bounded, expanding but destined to collapse, what possible meaning can human history, or the human experience have? How is it possible to have free will in a closed universe rigidly controlled by constants, values, principles, relationships, and laws? Doesn't his hybridized determinism inevitably lead toward atheism, as the French *philosophes* Holbach and Diderot showed of Laplace's determinism in the eighteenth century, and not, as Hawking suggests, to God? Are not evil, injustice, and suffering a contradiction to the "argument from design" proof of God on which some of his assumptions about creation and most of his speculation about current conditions are grounded? Is mind separate from matter? Is there a supernature? Don't the five senses limit apprehension and understanding of truth and reality? How does he reconcile the laws of physics with instances of reverse causality—of effects preceding causes—in cases of precognition? Does science really progress, or is it simply a succession of sciences, each capable of producing a technology that works, but each reflecting only a different milieu? Does not his taxonomically-resistant bestiary of subatomic particles violate Occam's Razor, the principle of economy and simplicity on which all successful sciences from Linnaeus to Lorentz have been based? Why suppose the universe came from one singularity—why not imagine that God, as with most gardeners, threw out a number of seeds? Having given us hell with nuclear weapons, is a guilty twentieth-century science now trying to give mankind heaven in its increasing reliance on God to explain everything mathematical physics can not? Who created the creator to whom Hawking makes reference? If matter can be neither created nor destroyed, where did the first matter come from? Is it possible that matter is alive, as the Roman Stoics believed, and that the ability to form complex life is a qualitative and quantitative property of matter, like rest mass, electrical charge, atomic weight, and the ability to form bonds? Will this latest generation of theories ever have any predictive or descriptive value—the ultimate test of any scientific theory—or will they simply be seen in retrospect to be pseudoscience, subjective idealism, and heuristic gnosticism? (pp. 3, 6)

> *John Murray, "Looking for the Mind of God,"*
> *in* The Bloomsbury Review, *Vol. 8, No. 5, Sep*
> *tember-October, 1988, pp. 3, 6.*

A. J. Ayer

Professor Hawking's **Brief History of Time** thoroughly deserves the praise with which it has been widely received. With only one formula, Einstein's celebrated $E = mc^2$, which he could just as well have put into prose simply by saying that energy is the arithmetical product of mass and the square of the velocity of light, Hawking gives a more lucid account than any that has yet come my way of such arcane matters as quantum theory and its wave-particle duality, the general and special theories of relativity, the blending of space and time into a four-dimensional continuum, the ways in which physicists measure the age and structure of the universe, the 'big bang' with which it is thought to have started, the reasons for holding that it continues to expand, the shrinkage of stars into 'black holes'. . . .

I am going not so much to take issue with him as to argue that there are one or two points in his exposition that need to be further clarified, and one or two assertions that have stranger implications than have been explicitly noted by him in his book or, so far as I am aware, by those who have reviewed it.

To begin with, it is not entirely clear whether Hawking takes a realistic or an instrumentalist view of physics. For the most part, his attitude seems to be realistic. Even when he speaks of the function of scientific theories as being that of relating qualities in the world to the observations that we make, the implication appears to be that the qualities are there, independently of our observing them. Moreover many of his accredited hypotheses, regarding the age and size of the universe, and the composition of its many galaxies, are related only tenuously to observation, which is not to say that our observations, such as they are, do not support them. On the other hand, his rejection of absolute time, on the basis of Einstein's theories of relativity, commits him to the view that an event has no temporal location except in relation to the positions and velocities of its observers, which need not coincide; and he also accepts the Copenhagen interpretation of quantum theory, according to which the impossibility of obtaining a precise measurement of the position and momentum of a particle at any given instant entails that to speak of a particle as being in such an undetectable condition makes no sense.

Hawking's tendency to oscillate at least between realistic and operational diction has one unhappy consequence for him. After introducing the concept of Euclidean space-time, as something measured by 'imaginary' numbers—

that is to say, numbers like   -1, which yield negative numbers when multiplied by themselves—and as something that differs from the subject of traditional Euclidean geometry in that it has four dimensions, with no difference between the direction of time and directions in space, Hawking reassures his readers, who may at this point have had some difficulty in following him, by saying that 'as far as everyday quantum mechanics is concerned, we may regard our use of imaginary time and Euclidean space-time as merely a mathematical device to calculate answers about real space-time.' On the very same page he initiates a discussion of the initial state of the universe in which his preference for a spatio-temporal surface which is finite but unbounded is based on his plumping for Euclidean space-time. Admittedly, he avoids self-contradiction by associating Euclidean space-time with 'quantum gravity' which goes beyond 'everyday quantum mechanics', but he just passes over the promotion of Euclidean space-time from a mathematical device to a physical reality. I am not convinced that the reasons he adduces for making this promotion are sufficient.

I am puzzled also by his saying that if he fulfilled Einstein's hope of unifying relativity and quantum theory he would be furnishing a description of the whole universe. What about the observations which would sustain the theory? They would need to be predictable, within quantum limitations, but would so abstract a theory actually describe them? What about the history of the universe? Would his theory account for the whole course of evolution with its chance mutations? Would they be derivable from quantum probabilities? Surely this needs to be shown.

Hawking distinguishes three arrows of time: the cosmological arrow, which is the direction in which the universe is expanding rather than contracting, the thermodynamic arrow, which is the direction of greater entropy, the passage from less to greater disorder, and the psychological arrow, which is the direction in which we experience the passage of time. He rather surprisingly identifies the thermodynamic and psychological directions, but he has given up his earlier belief in the possibility of our living our lives 'backward' because of his refusal to uncouple thermodynamic with cosmological time, his point being that if a reversal of entropy went with a contracting universe, there would be no human beings, since the physical conditions of our existence require us to dwell in an expanding phase.

This does not, however, prevent Hawking from accepting the possibility of time travel. He remarks, in a jocular aside, that it is just as well that 'cosmic censorship' would prevent astronauts who avoided falling into black holes from having the power to project themselves into the past. Otherwise, he says, 'not one's life would ever be safe: someone might go into the past and kill your father and mother before you were conceived.' Probably, if he had been speaking more seriously he would have spotted the non-sequitur. In the astronaut's time, events which occurred, according to an earthbound calendar, in the year in which my parents conceived me might succeed his approach to the black hole, but the events in question could be no more than a selection of the year's occurrences, arbitrarily chosen so as to define 'the past' and none of them entailing his presence, since he was not there. Since I was conceived he could not cause me not to have been. Of course my parents might have been killed before my conception: but for that we do not need an astronaut. A terrestial murderer would do just as well. This is quite an important point, because people are apt to wish that they could foresee the future in order to prevent whatever unpleasant things are going to happen to them. But if these unpleasantnesses do lie in the future they cannot be prevented. This is not fatalism. Perhaps they could be prevented if the proper steps were taken. But the premise that they actually lie in the future entails that they are not not going to be prevented.

A. J. Ayer, "Someone Might Go into the Past," in London Review of Books, *Vol. 11, No. 1, January 5, 1989, p. 6.*

FURTHER READING

Beardsley, T. "Cosmic Quarrel." *Scientific American* 261 (October 1989): 22.

    Explores reasons why *A Brief History of Time* became a best-seller in the United States.

Boslough, John. *Stephen Hawking's Universe.* New York: Morrow, 1985, 158 p.

    An introduction to Hawking's life, work, and ambitions, providing insights on his ideas. Also contains "Is the End in Sight for Theoretical Physics?," a lecture in which Hawking discusses the possibility of a complete, unified theory in the physical sciences.

Coyne, Patrick. "After the Bang." *New Statesman & Society* 1, No. 3 (24 June, 1988): 39.

    Review of *A Brief History of Time* and discussion of unification theories.

Dolphin, Ric. "Glimpses of God." *Maclean's Magazine* 101, No. 39 (19 September, 1988): 44-7.

    Feature article offering a biographical portrait of Hawking, discussion ideas presented in *A Brief History of Time,* and comments on the surprising success of this book.

Harwood, M. "The Universe and Dr. Hawking." *New York Times Magazine* (23 January 1983).

    Feature article on Hawking, discussing his life and work.

Krauthammer, Charles. "Absolute Density of Modern Physics." *Manchester Guardian Weekly* (18 December, 1988): 22.

    Speculates on why *A Brief History of Time,* which the critic calls "utterly incomprehensible," became a best-seller.

Osman, Tony. "Since an Earlier Big Bang." *The Spectator* 261, No. 8353 (13 August, 1988): 30-1.

    Laudatory review of *A Brief History of Time* that provides information on many of the theories discussed by Hawking.

Reeves, Hubert. "Universal Models." *Times Literary Supplement* 4, No. 464 (21-27 October, 1988): 1167.

Rucker, Randy. "A Mind that Roams the Universe." *Book World—The Washington Post* XVIII, No. 14: 7.
    Positive review of *A Brief History of Time* and explanation of some of the difficult topics explored in the book.

Shelby Hearon

1931-

(Born Shelby Reed) American novelist and biographer.

In her novels, Hearon often focuses on determinism, exploring the importance of lineage, environment, and regional culture in people's lives. Much of her fiction is set in the southern United States—chiefly Texas—and is populated by strong, unconventional female protagonists who struggle for a sense of identity amidst odd milieus. Hearon's intricately structured stories are related in a free-flowing style combining humor and irony. Although occasionally faulted for idealistic conclusions, Hearon is praised for her strong sense of place and vivid psychological insights. Marilyn Murray Willison commented: "[Hearon writes] with humor, pain, surprise and resolution in a single entertaining package. While we can identify with the characters, the situations are what strike us as outlandish. On reflection, of course, we find ourselves agreeing with Hearon's proposition that nothing that happens . . . is peculiar. What counts is how we deal with events, not the events themselves."

Hearon's first two novels, *Armadillo in the Grass* and *The Second Dune,* are semi-autobiographical treatments of the compromises and tribulations of love and marriage. *Hannah's House,* her first work to receive serious critical attention, probes the relationship between Hannah, a conventional nineteen-year-old, and Bev, her bohemian mother. When Hannah becomes engaged, Bev creates a "traditional" life for herself, which includes buying a house and conducting her affair with a married man with new discretion. While performing this conformist role to please her daughter, Bev remains very much in command of herself. Critics considered the heroine of Hearon's next novel, *A Prince of a Fellow,* not as amiable or dynamic as Hearon's previous protagonists. Avery, a Texas disc jockey, expects to find her ideal man through interviews on her morning talk show. Eventually she must choose between a kindly but unreliable novelist and the dependable but married mayor of San Antonio. Carole M. Lindsey asserted: "Ms. Hearon sees with a poet's preciseness; her dialogue's poignant, witty. . . . As a result *A Prince of a Fellow* is a fun romance cloaking a novel with much social comment."

Hearon's following work, *Painted Dresses,* chronicles a predetermined romance from the perspectives of both partners. Nell is a painter whose idiosyncratic vision sets her apart from her family, and Nick is a biochemist obsessed with the theory of predestination. Stifled by their respective family lives, the couple suffer marital woes and personal setbacks for twenty years prior to their fated union. Hearon again explores fate in *Afternoon of a Faun.* Harry, a rebellious homosexual, disowns his parents (whom he calls "the Roses Kennedy" because of their resemblances to the woman) and befriends a couple more to his taste, Ebie and Danny, who impulsively gave up a daughter years before. When Harry takes a job as a counselor at a summer music camp, he develops a rapport with fifteen-year-old Jeanetta and comes to realize that she is the couple's natural child.

In the critically lauded novel *Group Therapy,* Hearon's traditional Southern protagonist moves to Manhattan, offering witty, candid impressions of the city as well as sociological and personal insights into Northeastern customs. Lutie Sayre leaves her native Texas to teach in New York City and in the process discovers her true identity. Finally free of a whining ex-husband and an overprotective mother, Lutie joins a therapy group, copes with culture shock, and finds positive aspects in both the genteel South and the vibrant, animated North. Hearon returns to a Southern setting in *A Small Town.* The novel's title refers to Venice, Missouri, described as "a town so small that six china cups rattling from a shelf are a convincing apocalypse." Free-spirited Alma van der Linden illuminates Venice, narrating first through her childhood memories and then from an adult perspective after she has become part of the small-town malaise she witnessed growing up. Alma's numerous torrid affairs illustrate her ingenuous yearning for emotional, interpersonal connections. A critic from *Publishers Weekly* observed: "Generous, affectionate and unsentimental, this novel is darker than Hearon's earlier works, but it's a darkness that comes from exploring the shadows that lurk in her characters' lives as well as their spirited resilience."

The highly acclaimed work *Five Hundred Scorpions* centers upon a lawyer who leaves his wife and travels to Tepoztlán, Mexico, a mountain village where an Aztec god supposedly returns each year; it is also the place where disobedient husbands, fed a poison which renders them witless, are tethered to a rope and led around like sheep forever after. Reviewers admired the book's tight yet complex narration and strong sense of milieu. Lowry Pei commented: "Ms. Hearon builds this world with unobtrusive precision, sews it together with repeated images, hints at its secrets with a delicate touch, allows them to unfold inexorably and yet naturally; ironies lurk in the most innocuous lines of dialogue." Pei noted further that "the demonic and the domestic inhabit the novel together in a struggle that denies neither and intensifies both." In *Owning Jolene*, Hearon creates one of her most popular and critically praised protagonists. Having evaded a custody-seeking father for thirteen years, young Jolene is a master of disguises. Coached by her irrepressible mother Midge, Jolene has played, among other roles, a little boy, a child star, and an Indian. In myriad Texas suburbs where they hide, Midge poses as a piano teacher to remain inconspicuous. Finally, relatives intervene and take custody of Jolene until her nineteenth birthday. Regardless of who "owns" her, however, the tough yet vulnerable Jolene emerges as a witty survivor in control of her own life and astutely analyzing society's superficiality.

(See also *Contemporary Authors New Revision Series*, Vol. 18.)

PRINCIPAL WORKS

NOVELS

Armadillo in the Grass   1968
The Second Dune   1973
Hannah's House   1975
Now and Another Time   1976
A Prince of a Fellow   1978
Painted Dresses   1981
Afternoon of a Faun   1983
Group Therapy   1984
A Small Town   1985
Five Hundred Scorpions   1987
Owning Jolene   1989

OTHER

Barbara Jordan   (biography)   1979

Martin Levin

Hannah's House is constructed of quiet familial paradoxes. Hannah, a 19-year-old, lusts after conventionality—the outwardly tedious "signs of constancy" that are absent from her own background. Beverly, her mother, a 40-year-old divorcee, is as bohemian as life in a central Texas town permits. She has an easy relationship with her married lover, Ben, an anthropology professor, and no interest at all in mothers as a peer group. When Hannah gets married

Beverly manufactures an ambiance for the occasion, including a more respectable house for the wedding.

Shelby Hearon works up an interesting set of tensions among her characters: mothers, daughters, sisters, fathers, ex-spouses. Beverly's mother is a Philip Wylie-type Mom. Ben's daughter, Vanessa, is as deeply into Zen as Hannah is into *House & Garden*. Beverly's ex-husband, Roger, is a bounder, according to Beverly. Everything comes together on Hannah's wedding day in a white-gown ceremony complete with blue garter, bridal bouquet, old scores, false fronts and real tears.

> *Martin Levin, in a review of "Hannah's House," in* The New York Times Book Review, *June 15, 1975, p. 26.*

Janet Kammermeyer

Beverly Foster buys a house so that her daughter Hannah will have the proper setting for her year-long engagement to the very proper Eugene. *Hannah's House* is also the setting for Beverly's meetings with her lover Ben and a shared beer with drop-out Roy. In contrast to her conformist child, Bev remains very much her own person while playing out her roles of daughter, sister, mother, and ex-wife against the conflicting expectations of family and friends. Her thoughtful awareness of the public and private sides of her life adds dimension to this introspective novel of relationships.

> *Janet Kammermeyer, in a review of "Hannah's House," in* School Library Journal, *Vol. 22, No. 2, October, 1975, p. 111.*

Carol Gargan

Will Mary get Tom, will Julia get Jimmie? We meet and follow the first couple from the onset of [Shelby Hearon's novel *Now and Another Time*], up to the unconsummated resolution of their love, which occurs after Mary births a son, a reward from God Mary vows to pay for with fidelity to her unloved husband Alfred. The repercussions of this are echoed in Julia's and Jimmie's lives. We follow Julia, Mary's daughter, and Jimmie, Tom's son, through the unconscious disavowal of their love to the beginning of its realization. By then, Jimmie has long been married to a friend of Julia's and Julia long married to a friend of Jimmie's. Julia, by this time, has raised two grown daughters. Since she and Jimmie represent the median generation between those that didn't and those that do, we read waiting for the climax.

That may be all the incentive needed to complete the book. It isn't what made it worthwhile reading for me. Shelby Hearon's insights into people and their relationships with family and friends are what I found exciting—depressing for a large part, but quite real. Before the opening chapter quotes from R. D. Laing show the author is familiar with his theory of the mystification of experience—we do what we do or don't because mom and dad, grandma and pa, daughter or son expect this; all the world's a stage and we've been handed the script. It seems to me the demystification of experience is at least one of the concerns of the novel—getting at the "self." So, symbolically, will Julia have Jimmie like her mother never did Tom? I have my doubts about anyone knowing what she or he really is—or wants; we do not, cannot act alone: intercourse, the breakthrough in the novel, requires two. It is interesting to see at that point a statement by Julia: "It is not to whom you are born that determines who you are, it's who receives you," implying a partial realization of the emphasis on the family mystification element.

For Julia I wish all the emphasis hadn't been placed on the inevitable mating. Even though it is, for many of us, a physically gratifying attempt at self-discovery and has the common advantage of holding one's interest, it is a letdown. She is dealing with a problem that has to go further. I doubt if even Jimmie can fill "the space of her" for long. The space we have inside ourselves takes a lot more than a man or a woman to fill—they help, but the void demands more than that. What does Julia do now? For me the novel would start here.

Carol Gargan, in a review of "Now and Another Time," in Best Sellers, *Vol. 36, No. 7, October, 1976, p. 212.*

Anne Tyler

For some ten years, now, Shelby Hearon has been writing her slim, understated novels—all of them set in Texas, all revolving around strong female characters. But her first three (*Armadillo in the Grass, The Second Dune, Hannah's House*) possessed a certain particularity, a clear and sober tone of voice that was only Shelby Hearon's. *Now and Another Time,* her fourth book, moved away from that tone. It became wider and yet thinner, so to speak; there was broader landscape and a larger crowd of Texans, but we missed the unique women of the earlier novels. The women in *Now and Another Time* had something harsh and flip and trendy about them. You could meet several of their sort at any cocktail party.

A Prince of a Fellow, Shelby Hearon's latest novel, returns to the lone woman as center of the book. Avery Krause is a "frizzy-haired, washed-out princess looking for a prince," and by the age of 30 she is convinced that she will settle for just about anyone—even "some ordinary prince on a limping horse . . . just a third son of a minor king."

She does her prince-hunting on a morning radio show. Between recordings of "Getting High on Getting By" and "Amazing Grace," she interviews various local celebrities: everyone from the judge of a tobacco-spitting contest to the man who dumps green dye in the river on St. Patrick's Day. Two of these guests—an attractive young writer and a stuffy, boorish mayor with a wife and children—become her lovers. The novel follows the course of these two affairs, up until the time that Avery can tell us, revising her opening statement, that she is "not just any blonde with frizzy hair waiting for some bandy-legged rider to trudge into view." She has arrived, we're given to understand, at the point where she has a strong enough sense of self-worth that she can start refusing counterfeits.

But the problem with *A Prince of a Fellow* is that its heroine has valued herself so little all through the book that she's long ago lost our sympathy. Her affair with the mayor, which she reports in a wry and offhand tone, is in fact so debasing and unsavory that we dislike her for being

party to it. She wins a Congressman's friendship by pulling a political trick that is flatly dishonest, though she presents it as amusing; and she avenges herself on the mayor, finally, in a tawdry little scene that she seems to find comical. Throughout the novel (up to and including the end), she speaks to us in the slick, fake-tough voice of a ladies' magazine heroine. And, like any ladies' magazine heroine, she seems to believe that a quick fade-out with a handsome man will make us overlook the fact that they're really a very unsuitable couple.

If I seem too hard on Avery, remember that I'm comparing her to some exceptional people: the complex and original women of Shelby Hearon's first three novels. Struggling toward a means of self-expression or working through the problems of motherhood, wifehood, or daughterhood, these other heroines had a clarity and integrity that made their readers want to invite them over for a long walk. Avery, if she were invited, would probably dominate the conversation with a discussion of all the "hairy bellies" she's been acquainted with. (Avery has a real fixation about hairy bellies.)

There are some good moments in this book. The one virtue Avery shares with her predecessors is a talent for unexpected friendships—in this case, with a Mexican cemetery-sexton who puts on a German accent and lederhosen when moonlighting as a disc jockey, and with an educated black woman named Jane Brown who takes a perverse delight in appearing as the berobed and crowned Queen Esther of the Missionary Baptist Church. The bleached-out Texas countryside comes across well, and there are some wonderful scenes involving the feud between the German half of Avery's family and the Swedish half, as represented by Avery's pasty, stubborn mother.

In fact, everything *around* Avery is finely and convincingly drawn; it's Avery herself who's the trouble. Maybe we can form an axiom from all this: A book can have just about anyone for a heroine—even an outright villainess—as long as she assigns herself some worth that makes us want to identify with her. If she doesn't we stop caring.

Anne Tyler, "Lady of the Lone Star State," in Book World—The Washington Post, *April 2, 1978, p. E4.*

The New Yorker

Avery Krause, the heroine of Shelby Hearon's fifth novel [*A Prince of a Fellow*] is a morning radio disc jockey with a natural interest in the difference between how things appear or sound and what they really are—a curiosity that pertains to her hope, at thirty, of finding a true lover, to her unsettled family loyalties, and no less to the cultivation of her trade. The setting is a small town in central Texas founded by German immigrants, the population of which is now half German and half Mexican. ("Otto, my sidekick, who gives the news and weather in heavy German accent, is really a forty-five-year-old Mexican, with Pancho Villa mustache, who works afternoons . . . as the cemetery sexton.") The story, much of which unfolds in one or another of the town's nine graveyards, has to do with Avery's impulse to abandon a crummy though reliable illicit affair with the mayor of San Antonio in favor of a decidedly indefinite alliance with an elusive and dissembling writer. But the book is less important for its plot than for the thorough portrait of a woman that rises out of Mrs. Hearon's short and sweet account of most particular people living and working in a most particular place. (pp. 116-17)

A review of "A Prince of a Fellow," in The New Yorker, *Vol. LIV, No. 16, June 5, 1978, pp. 116-17.*

Margo Jefferson

[The bittersweet novel *A Prince of a Fellow*] is a fairy tale of sorts and, like all good fairy tales, it depicts the heroine's trials and tribulations much more vividly than the happy ending. The setting is Prince Solms, Texas, a small town whose feuding German and Mexican citizens both claim to be the original settlers, uniting only to condescend to the local Swedes and blacks. The would-be princess is 30-year-old Avery Krause, who conducts a local radio talk show. Her lover is the mayor of San Antonio—a dull, timid "burgher in white socks" for whom she feels no passion. She is Swedish on her mother's side, "sitting like a burr in the saddle of a large German family" that considers Swedes white trash. Self-mocking and self-hating, she is waiting for someone to change her life—preferably a prince.

He appears on her show in the form of a Texas novelist who has adopted the imposing name, Gruene Albrech ("Who reads books by Billy Wayne Williams?" he reasons). He is as reticent about his feelings as about his ancestry—convinced, like Avery, that "it was too easy to make a wrong move when you were being who you were." Hearon denies them a happily-ever-after relationship until Avery has learned that she can do better than play at being "a third-rate princess waiting in the wings of her garage tower" for a rescuer. Hearon writes with quick intelligence and a humor that is both tender and ironic. She understands that the nicest fantasies sometimes have a firm grounding in reality.

Margo Jefferson, in a review of "A Prince of a Fellow," in Newsweek, *Vol. XCII, No. 1, July 3, 1978, p. 80.*

Carole M. Lindsey

[The critic later published under the name Lindsey M. Bowen]

[A "woman's search for identity" book], *A Prince of a Fellow,* expounds the popular themes of reality vs. illusion (or "suspended disbelief" as Shelby Hearon phrases it), the heroine's search for truth, identity through heritage, and for her "Prince." Ms. Hearon writes with a comfortable, flowing style that creates a delightful story pierced with cynical insight into traditional Mid-American mores, bigotry, and life's general facades.

Thirty-year-old Avery Krause (named "Avery" after a large red grocery store sign by her Swedish mamma who refused to succumb to the German tradition of name-staining) is a female Holden Caulfield with her concern for phoniness vs. reality, but unlike Holden she accepts reality as forever being camoflauged by illusion:

If any appearance was the same in Kentucky, so was my manner of dealing with the world. I was a drama teacher, which, if you think about it, is not too different from what I'm doing now. In both settings I present illusions as real. In both theatre and radio the audience is let in on the hoax; together we share the thrill of belief suspended. Here, by consent, coconut shells pound into horses hoofs and squeaking doors signal mysterious entries and ominous departures. There, small white faces grow bold with greasepaint and eager hands slew dragons with broom handles.

Her prince has two identities: Greune Albrech, the Connecticut German writer returned to his homeland, and Billy Wayne Williams the Czech cowboy. Avery is unfluttered: "So it was fine with me if today's prince was after all a golden imposter, faking his German birthright; I too make my living by delusion."

Her personal life's also snared in delusion. She's entangled with a local mayor for whom she has no love, little respect, or intellectual interest. They meet regularly at his cabin where they share a cocktail and conversation about his sons. The last step in these rituals is the sex act. She isn't allowed to shower or sleep because she may leave evidence of her appearance.

Fringing Avery's snared existence is Avery's mother, who moves her dead husband's carcass from his German family's plot before a dying uncle (with whom she has an eternal feud) can lie beside him. In this Texas town even the cemetery's segregated, not only by the location of the plots, but by the tombstones. Laurel leaves mark German tombstones; shells mark the Swedes'. So it goes.

Ms. Hearon sees with a poet's preciseness; her dialogue's poignant, witty: "You're not right for radio. All your tricks are visual," Avery tells Minna, her newswoman friend. "Writers are so full of themselves they are like dogs looking for fire hydrants," Minna comments. As a result *A Prince of a Fellow* is a fun romance cloaking a novel with much social comment. (pp. 123-24)

Carole M. Lindsey, in a review of "A Prince of a Fellow," in New Letters, *Vol. 46, No. 1, Fall, 1979, pp. 123-24.*

David Guy

Painted Dresses is not a story of the bittersweet romance of two middle-aged lovers, though in the hands of another writer it might have been. Shelby Hearon throughout her fiction is concerned with the influences that shape us, our false starts in life, the paths that lead nowhere and our difficult return from them. *Painted Dresses* gives itself room fully to explore these matters. It opens some 30 years before the lovers meet, and in skillfully alternating segments traces their lives. The romance that the novel is really about does not take place until it is nearly over, though in another sense, as the ending makes clear, it was taking place all along.

One character after another in this novel is haunted by moments from the past. Nell Woodward, its painter-heroine, obsessively remembers the white china roses in the house of her aunts, and in some ways her whole artistic career is an attempt to recapture their purity. Nicholas

Clark is a biochemist whose career, as if to deny the power of the past, is devoted to refuting theories of predestination. Both have been stifled by early experiences in their family lives, and spend years trying to work them out. They exhibit what are described in a psychiatric paper in the middle of the novel as "Affects in Borderline Disorders," which are "characterized by a sense of longing for something (or someone) that is not merely absent but nonexistent, or at best undefinable, something that leaves one feeling empty or hungry, 'hopeful' in a very hopeless way."

Nell was raised in an extended family so ingrown as to be positively incestuous; her stepfather, as if to express its true spirit, abused her sexually when she was a child. Nell is the one member of the family who wants to remove herself from this tangle. She is an artist not just because she is obsessed with recovering shades of color from her remembered past, but also because she has always had her own peculiar vision of things. When she decides to pursue an artistic career she must leave her husband and child, a family and a social class that patronizes artists, and move to Santa Fe, where "it didn't matter." She is obsessed by a fantasy from her childhood, that her real father led an alternate life that she might have seen, and when she meets a rakish boozy journalist who reminds her of her father, she strikes up an affair that lasts through the years when she is establishing herself. He is a kind loving man, but his alcoholism makes him frequently absent even when they are together, a fantasy more than a real person for her.

Nicholas has perhaps been so obsessed by theories of predestination because his life has seemed predestined from the start, controlled by a malicious older brother and a family tradition of intellectualism. He too chooses a mate largely because of a childhood fantasy, though rather a more sexual one than Nell's, but his wife had previously been a girlfriend of his brother, and that fact dominates their relationship. She resents his work and seeks out men who give more of themselves to her, while he dreams of a relationship like that of an older couple he has admired, where both partners have their own work and a quiet domestic life beside it. It is hardly a surprise when, on a day that marks a highlight of Nicholas' career, his wife leaves him.

Like the lives she is describing, Shelby Hearon's narrative grows more satisfactory as it goes along; its early episodes can seem fragmentary and puzzling. Nell's family is too cutely eccentric to be believed—their rhyming names are especially annoying—and Nicholas' brother similarly seems too wicked. One can't help thinking that her lovers' paths, in two very different lives, cross once too often, though there is a thematic reason for having them do so: She is showing how stubbornly these people refuse to find each other. In this novel and in the earlier *A Prince of a Fellow,* Hearon has a tendency to connect things too neatly. One wishes for the comparative simplicity of her *Hannah's House,* a touching story of a mother and daughter.

Yet as in both these previous novels her heroine is an extremely engaging woman, who keeps picking up the pieces of her life and starting again. Though wrong at times about what she wants, she is persistent in trying to find it. Hearon's novels are intricately structured—their effortless flow is deceiving—and she writes with the buoyant

precise prose of a veteran novelist. If her story is unsatisfactory at first, it builds in momentum once her characters reach adulthood, and ends wonderfully. (pp. 8, 13)

Hearon is not saying something so simplistic as that her characters were made for each other, but that it took them half a lifetime to be ready to love, just as Nell, after years of painting the dresses that are really portraits of herself, is finally ready as the novel ends to turn to other subjects. It is right, too, that Hearon does not allow them some simplistic way to escape their pasts; she plops them right down in the middle of the whole mess. Nevertheless, they want to stay together. *Painted Dresses* is not so much the story of a love affair as of its prolonged beginning, and it does not suggest its lovers will live happily ever after. It does suggest that, after years of sorting through things they don't really want, they are ready at last to live. (p. 13)

David Guy, "Meetings at Midlife," in Book World—The Washington Post, *June 14, 1981, pp. 8, 13.*

Laura Cunningham

"I like a little extra touch," says a character in *Painted Dresses,* the sixth novel by Shelby Hearon. Although the line is spoken by a grandmother who loves appliquéd poodles, it's obvious that Miss Hearon enjoys "a little extra touch" herself. For it is her love of frills and detail that makes this double life story—a his-and-hers account of a love affair—into such a fancy collage. At first glance, it is difficult to see Miss Hearon's design: Her characters seem to miss one another for most of the narrative. They don't actually meet and make love until 20 years and 200 pages have passed.

Nicholas Clark and Nell Woodward, the two destined lovers, suffer years of separate marital and romantic misadventures. Nell flees a stodgy husband, has a long affair with a man who is too drunk to remember their fantastic sex, while Nick endures a long marriage to Virginia, who can't keep house but can flash a tattooed breast at the appropriate moment. One of the joys of this novel is that even the less appealing characters come off with verve and style: We don't mind Virginia sashaying her way through Nick's life, even though it hangs him up for a couple of decades. She's fun to watch.

Miss Hearon has applied herself to this novel with the same flair shown by her artist heroine Nell. Every scene is painted in color, and the outlines are drawn with equal care: We learn all about Nell's Texas clan of rhyming relatives: Estelle, Moselle and LaNelle herself. And we see Nick tackle his in-laws' over-cooked pot roast and try to pursue his scientific interest in DNA. But as I say, Nell and Nick finally do meet, share some doughnuts and then one another's lives. When Nick thinks, "It was absurd to expect another person to erase his painful past. . . . He could not expect her to stay," the reader may also wonder whether itchy-footed Nell really can settle down in Kansas City. So benign are the author's intentions that when Nell and Nick do bed down for keeps it seems a pleasant if unlikely conclusion. *Painted Dresses* has a variety of styles and sometimes turns chic or overly dramatic. Nick, seeing Nell's art work—a wedding gown painted "against a dark opacity"—thinks "the dress had no face. The face was hers!" Yet, viewed from a distance, the novel is more than a collection of odd-matched pieces—it's a very lacy Valentine.

Laura Cunningham, "Lovers and Movies," in The New York Times Book Review, August 2, 1981, p. 15.

Ingrid Rimland

Take a cryptic title, thin themes and an unlikely situation but tons of craftsmanship, and you have still a most enchanting little novel.

[In *Afternoon of a Faun*] Jeanetta, adopted teen-ager of rather dull but gushy parents, is told she was a "chosen" child; in retaliation, she treats herself to a minirebellion. Harry, somewhat older and with a chronic Oedipus grudge of his own, renounces his imperfect parents and "chooses" a set more to his liking—Ebie and Danny, middle-aged and rather unattractive folks who happen to have given Jeanetta away in an inexplicable spur of the moment. Fate forces those searching souls to meet.

One would not think much could be made of this plot. Yet the pruned style is captivating, and the undercurrents crackle. It's uncanny how the reader "knows" the people of this threadbare story line.

Take Harry, psyching out his grief:

> . . . The point was that I never lost either of my parents, I never had them in the first place. Certain causes had beat me to their attention by a full two decades. My dad, Wendell, lived and fed on his hatred of Franco's Spaniards: 'Oppressors who built their temples on the gnawed bones of separatists'—to pick a line at random from his anger. With equal obsession my mom, Marie, hated Unfair Labor Practices.

The reader comes to understand them all: Ebie's panic at another child; Danny's diffuse fury; Jeanetta's dense but doting parents; the narrow Kentucky setting; even minor characters such as " . . . a beanpole man with sprigs of hair that stuck straight up, and a clear crush on her, propelled her to the speaker's stand. He put a glass of water in her hand, they bent their heads to say a few things, then she shook her head, he wagged his finger, and she was on."

There are still writers who write so well they manage to be published for no other reason. That is a pleasure in itself.

Ingrid Rimland, "A Pleasure of Craft Sails Below a Story," in Los Angeles Times Book Review, April 3, 1983, p. 9.

Candace Flynt

In previous novels, especially her remarkable *Painted Dresses,* Shelby Hearon has written movingly about adults and children trapped in dead marriages or divorce. Unlike much rendering of the modern scene, the men and women Hearon creates want to connect with someone they can love on a permanent basis. They are self-concerned yet beyond narcissism.

It was perhaps a natural step for Hearon to give the children a chance to speak, to tell us what they think of the adults. So in her seventh novel, *Afternoon of a Faun,* we have the stories of two young people, Jeanetta Edna Mayfield, age 15 and adopted, and Harry James, who 15 years before the novel opens, decided to "adopt" new parents. His own parents, whom he refers to as the Roses Kennedy because they both look like her, have never paid him any attention.

Much of *Afternoon of a Faun* is concerned with Harry's memories of his experience with his "new" parents. At the time Harry chose them, he was a 19-year-old unprofessed homosexual, and a student at an Aspen music camp. He picked Ebie and Danny Wister out of a crowded restaurant because they were so normal-looking. Ebie and Danny were expecting a late baby to take the place of their little girl who died when she was 4. Harry followed the Wisters home, not knowing that Ebie's interest in him was not motherly. Mentally unstable, Ebie had already decided to give up this baby and leave her husband. Harry, she reasoned, could divert Danny while she was in the hospital giving away the baby and could keep him company when she left. Not a particularly propitious choice of surrogate parents, but then, as the novel progresses, we find out that perhaps Harry didn't want parents after all. Maybe he just wanted Danny. But Harry's uncertain motives are part of this novel's continuing confusion.

When *Afternoon of a Faun* opens, it is Jeanetta's 15th birthday, the day her adoptive parents have belatedly chosen to tell her of her origins. Jeanetta, who feels betrayed, withdraws from the close relationship she has had with them. Thinking it will do her good, they send her to summer music camp. There she meets Harry. Now a professed homosexual close to 35, he is recalling his youth by living with a 19-year-old camp instructor who has Jeanetta as a student. Soon Harry and Jeanetta become casual friends.

Although we are never sure whether Jeanetta is the same child whose parents Harry knew, this is one point that doesn't matter. The adopted and the adopter can still learn something from each other. But they don't. Instead, Harry summons Danny from New Mexico to see if he can recognize at a recital which of the student musicians is his daughter, a test which he fails. With this failure by Danny, and with his own memories of anonymous parents, Harry announces the theme of this book—how parents fail their children. . . .

The next day Jeanetta goes home.

Since this is a book about the failure of parents, perhaps Hearon thought it would be too easy a resolution to let the children learn something from each other. Jeanetta leaves camp, happy that she's made friends with a "real homosexual," but knowing no more about how to view her life than she did when the novel opened. Harry is stricken with grief for the love he feels he deserved but never received. He had the opportunity to mean something to Jeanetta but chose not to. When fiction fails to inform about what life either should or shouldn't be, it fails the reader, which is the sad plight of this novel.

Candace Flynt, "Generational Gaps and Gripes," in Book World—The Washington Post, April 10, 1983, p. 8.

Valerie Miner

[In *Group Therapy*], Lutie Sayre leaves Texas one autumn to become a visiting professor of sociology at the State University of New York at Purchase. Her heart swings between the fading gentility of the Southern family to whom she has promised to return and the caffeinated vitality of her new Northern friends. A dedicated self-improver, 32-year-old Lutie settles into Purchase with resolutions to exercise daily, to find a dressmaker who can copy Neiman-Marcus fashions and to enroll in group therapy. She succeeds on all counts. Indeed, in a surprisingly credible sequence of events, one of the therapists falls in love with her. Their romance generates the story's suspense—is she indelibly Southern or has she been seduced by the North? Shelby Hearon's eighth novel is intelligent, witty and tightly written. If anything, it is too compressed and needs more description of Lutie's work and her complex family. The choicest parts of the book are Lutie's candid impressions of herself in New York City. During the first evening of group therapy, she is mortified to find that one of the psychologists is slopping around in loafers with no socks while she has worn her best clothes, "overdressed in the biggest city there was." New York's impersonality, speed, vastness and expense continually confound Lutie. Yet by the end she has become a seasoned regular at Oscar's Restaurant in the Waldorf: "The five of them who were there, the waiter from Spain, the man who ate part of his ice cream, Jack Sprat and his worried wife, and Lutie, made a congenial group. She, restored and fed, felt a wave of happiness. The Waldorf, she decided, was like River Bend: a lovely place from the past which you could always count on."

> *Valerie Miner, in a review of "Group Therapy," in* The New York Times Book Review, *March 18, 1984, p. 18.*

Marilyn Murray Willison

[In *Group Therapy*] a Texas divorcee encounters New York, single living and emotional vulnerability all in one fall. Hearon writes much like a female Larry McMurtry with humor, pain, surprise and resolution in a single entertaining package. While we can identify with the characters, the situations are what strike us as outlandish. On reflection, of course, we find ourselves agreeing with Hearon's proposition that nothing that happens—to her characters or to us—is peculiar. What counts is how we deal with events, not the events themselves.

Lutie Sayre has survived divorce, an evaporated dream job at Vassar, separation from her beloved cat and her intimidating mother; her new connection is a group therapy session in Manhattan. It's a session where the attendees look and behave differently from their true selves, and where the leader, Joe, teaches them to meld the image with the substance. There are formidable obstacles here for most of Hearon's characters.

What really makes the book a moving experience is the main character, Lutie; she combines straightforwardness with a touching no-nonsense brand of vulnerability.

At one point, Lutie remembers the dying days of her ill-fated marriage—a trip to Italy with her struggling scholar husband. Instead of freeing them to rediscover romance or passion or even civility, travel brought on an onslaught of discontent from the man she had once deeply loved. She muses:

> I grew tired of his dissatisfaction. Let there be something that pleases you, I thought, here in the home of all your aspirations. One striated ciprollino column, one wild acanthus, one green smear of melted copper, one damp subterranean passage, one fresco's pale, thin colors. *Like something.* But no part of it could be right if the whole was wrong, and the whole made him sick. . . . So I went about my pleasures alone, as I had always done.

Hearon's books leave a warm, soft feeling of having shared chunks of the characters' lives. Her popularity will expand to match her talent.

> *Marilyn Murray Willison, "A Novel Exercise to Emotional Catharsis," in* Los Angeles Times Book Review, *May 27, 1984, p. 14.*

Jo Brans

I think I may be the world's foremost authority on Shelby Hearon's latest novel [*Group Therapy*] having read it now four—or is it five?—times. I keep reading it over and over for two reasons. First, from paragraph to paragraph as I read, I find nuggets of sociological insight that I am validating with my own experience. Like Hearon's heroine Lutie, I have myself recently made the trek from Texas to New York, and am learning the ways, as Lutie does, of the new environment. The other and perhaps better reason is just that I like it so much. Page for page, *Group Therapy* is everything that a novel of manners ought to be: perceptive, amusing, balanced, humane, and generous.

Lutie's New York corresponds to the one I have discovered. Like Lutie, I have learned "that it is a different world up here, and different rules apply." I too have at least once found myself embarrassingly "overdressed in the biggest city there is" because of not knowing that "in the South, people dress up when they go out; in the North, they dress down when they go off duty." Like her, I have puzzled over the etiquette of subways and cabs. And like her, I have wondered what to answer when asked my nationality, which isn't "a Texas question," as Lutie says. (p. 470)

The question of nationality is pertinent to the basic concerns of the book. Another way of phrasing it might be, To which group does Lutie really belong? Lutie is searching for a nationality of the heart, a group of her own. Her search takes her, and the reader, from Texas to New York to Rome to Georgia and finally north toward home, . . . to New York again. We aren't overwhelmed by the book's geography—all these places in less than three hundred pages—only because we are secure in Lutie's highly discriminating mind. Lutie is a civilizer. Just as her regular evening stroll encircles the plaza with the band and the picnickers and the listening crowd, she tries with tact and empathy and conscientious effort to draw a loving circle that takes all foreigners into its circumference. "You'll domesticate Hell itself," her ex-husband Dabney complains, and that is Lutie's ambition.

Some of her groups are a little hellish: the matriarchal southern world, for example, where houses have names like Redoaks, where descent is matrilineal, and where men recede into the background or disappear entirely. Dressed in big hats and silk blouses and antique jewelry, nibbling spoon bread and pound cake and clover-leaf rolls, Lutie's mother Florence and her Aunt Caroline shred their husbands and absorb their daughters. Immured in a world where only appearances matter, they systematically reject whatever is needy (Lutie's senile grandmother), unsightly (her fat cousin Nan), or not quite up to the mark (both their husbands). Lutie's frantic effort to make Redoaks seem pleasant and gracious for one of Florence's show-off parties becomes a metaphor for the decay of a way of life, as we glimpse the poor judgment in pumping vitality and charm into a structure where the plumbing doesn't work. "You should have married your mother," Dabney has hurled at Lutie. In a way Lutie has married her mother, and her divorce from Florence is much more traumatic than her divorce from him.

Lutie is married to Dabney for five years, and at the end she wonders if she ever really saw him; she can recall his clothes, his shoulders, his glasses, but not his face. Yet Shelby Hearon makes us see him, hear him, and hate him, and my sympathies are all with Lutie. His whining dissatisfactions with life are endless. . . . [He] is a despiser and Lutie is an enjoyer, and they never really join.

One of the nicest things about **Group Therapy** is, in fact, its unwavering hedonism. In a book that finds significance in the joys of daily living, Lutie moves toward pleasure as a sunflower turns toward light. She finds new friends: her lover Joe, himself a psychologist involved in creating groups; Mrs. Vaccaro, her seamstress, to whom she fetches buttermilk pies; Manuel, a waiter at the Waldorf; the butcher, the baker, the candlestick maker; especially Joe's black colleague, Sammy Davidson, who becomes her sidekick in the uneasy relationship with Joe. Not all of these characters are as vivid as Lutie. Ironically, Sammy is—ironically, because one of the author's jokes is that blacks in uniforms are invisible, and Sammy loves to put on uniforms to infiltrate the opposition. Yet Sammy is a fully active creation, capable of simultaneous parody and insight, as when he tells Lutie, "White mens is a figment in the South."

Other pleasures, just as real as these friends, are inanimate: new royal blue wool pants and a black jacket, a good seat for *La Forza del Destino,* a perfect glass of iced tea, banana and sweet potato soufflé, a poster of the Roman Forum, plumbing that works, the Waldorf, which, like her grandmother's home, is "a lovely place from the past which you could always count on." These things matter to Lutie, and Shelby Hearon makes them matter to us.

Joe grouchily compares her to Browning's Last Duchess, who "liked whate'er she looked on, and her looks went everywhere." Joe goes on,

> I figured out why the duke wrung her neck, and I thought I'd share it with you. It was after the tenth time he'd gone into her boudoir and begun to tell her that he was offering her his heart, and she told him the news about the seamstress's baby, and how the stableman was under the weather, and did he know that the cousin of the former duchess had run off with—

And he concludes passionately, "How can two people ever be a group?" Lutie shows him, turning so that his arms

encircle her and her arms encircle the rest of the turning world. It seems to work. (pp. 470-72)

> *Jo Brans, "She Liked Whate'er She Looked On," in* Southwest Review, *Vol. 69, No. 4, Autumn, 1984, pp. 470-72.*

Publishers Weekly

Hearon's ninth novel [*A Small Town*] displays again her eye for detail, her ear for the true messages of conversation and her fondness for characters with spunky good humor. Alma van der Linden's wry account of her life in Venice, Mo., reveals her to be as equal to confronting her interior misgivings as she is able to survive the external pressures of small-town existence. As a child, Alma spends a summer spying on her father to discover his affair with a cousin from Chicago. She also ferrets out the long-ago resentments that have split the branches of her family for generations. It takes longer than a childhood, however, for Alma to understand that her real search is for connection, even though she's always envied her older sisters, who had each other, and her friends, twins Reba and Sheba. Marrying the high school principal, Alma has children whom she calls "his," she feels so apart from them. She works on the weekly newspaper, has an affair with a visiting seismologist and, in the end, approaches family reconciliation and the fulfillment of her wish to have "someone of my own" in a satisfying, surprise conclusion. Generous, affectionate and unsentimental, this novel is darker than Hearon's earlier works, but it's a darkness that comes from exploring the shadows that lurk in her characters' lives as well as their spirited resilience. (pp. 65-6)

> *A review of "A Small Town," in* Publishers Weekly, *Vol. 228, No. 6, August 9, 1985, pp. 65-6.*

Elizabeth Tallent

Children in a Chicago suburb were once charmed by a certain game, played with locked hands whose spired forefingers touched, into tireless repetitions of the chant, "This is the church, this is the steeple; open the doors, and see all the people." Because the chant was unchanging, and nobody (no kid) was mocked by it (it wasn't like "Liar, liar, pants on fire"), its charm had to be found in the reiterated gesture of unfolding, which never failed to work on us, never failed to mean something. We loved it that *people*—meaning *adults*—who thought they were hidden could be exposed so simply, through words.

The essence of Shelby Hearon's ninth novel, *A Small Town,* is very similar: it aims to open the doors and show all the people—alike, distinct, quarreling or in love, but locked together in plain sight. The charm of this novel lies in the opening of the tight clasp of adult lives to a child, then to a woman with secrets of her own in Venice, Mo., a town so small that six china cups rattling from a shelf are a convincing apocalypse.

The narrator is Alma, who grows from an abused child with a Huckleberry Finn spunkiness into a high-school Lolita, from a principal's dutiful wife into a trailer-park adulteress, handling each role with an equanimity she never admits to. She keeps her voice modest, her approach open but scarcely confessional, veering off now and then into the wistful. *A Small Town* moves along at the speed of conversation—and not some rueful, elliptical 1985 dialogue, either—but an old-fashioned, "How nice to see you again, let me fill you in on all the details" conversation, with this drawback: it is sometimes slower than the speed of reading. . . .

This novel gossips brightly about its own small cast, wishing to engage, entertain and occasionally lecture the reader on Venetian manners and curiosities: "The rest of the country does not understand that *flood* is a touchy word around here. It does not, ever, flood in Venice. . . . Flood means the river overflows its banks; rain is not a flood." And often the narrative incorporates some bit of small-town print too good to be left out: a recipe for pretzel salad, an irate letter to the editor, passages from McGuffey Readers, an entire prayer of confession. These texts are fitted into the book with the patient affection that the poet William Carlos Williams showed for Paterson ephemera; they're the *objets trouvés* that coax the novel a notch nearer verisimilitude.

Yet it somehow fails in this respect because of a kind of mildness, even absent-mindedness, in treating Alma's character. She makes the transition from gnomic child with hair of "tan string" into a beauty toying with the principal by flirting her boyfriend's class ring in and out of the cleft between her breasts, with scarcely a psychic tremor; the narrative trips blithely to the brink of a seduction, but the actual scene is skipped, and within a page Alma has two children. At one point she is writing a novel, which sounds interesting, but which then vanishes from the story and is not mentioned again. When she refers to herself as "dumb," it startles the reader, who had thought Alma believed herself (rather endearingly) clever.

A Small Town is fine in dealing with the funny malaise of childhood, those small-town seizures of ennui, and at its gentle best there are sentences like this:

> We headed north to a borrow pit which had filled with spring rains and caught crawdads in old cling peach cans and toyed with letting them grab us with their pinchers for the thrill of it and then let them go—flopping onto our backs in a stretch of dandelions.

> Elizabeth Tallent, *"Venice Observed," in* The New York Times Book Review, *October 20, 1985, p. 22.*

Beth Levine

The prolific novelist [Shelby Hearon] again tackles her favorite theme in her latest novel—the effects of determinism on a person's life. How much do time, place and lineage affect what happens to our lives? . . .

Settling in for the afternoon, this lively, articulate woman can't wait to start talking, and not just about her latest novel, *Five Hundred Scorpions*. . . . Talking, she says, is her way of of processing and analyzing her thoughts. Leaning back in her chair from the dining-room table, against shelves full of books by and about Freud, his disciples and his patients, Hearon plunges right in.

Is there free will? Can you act? Can you change, or does your 'blank'—parents, family, hometown, race, class—determine you? I want the answer to be no, but I think we make a mistake if we don't deal with how much is determined.

The big three—Freud, Marx and Darwin—formed my thinking, and they are very much determinists. I'm still wrestling with the issue in my novels, although I'm tackling different sides of it. . . .

The determinist question is the reason 56-year-old Hearon started writing in the first place. She was born in Kentucky, raised in Texas and married after her graduation from the University of Texas in Austin. Following the birth of her two children ("Anne and Reed—I'd like their names to be in the interview"), the urge to write descended on her as a way of sorting out who she was.

"When my children were in nursery school, I felt the need to write out of that feeling of being both a mother and daughter. I was acting out of an idea that I was passing down family myths, passing on family scripts that I hadn't even read. Unless we are aware of what's going on, we can become unfulfilled wishes of the generation before us," she notes.

Despite the claims of being a mother and wife, she worked for five years on her first novel, *Armadillo in the Grass.* She had no formal education in creative writing, knew no agents and had no contact with other writers. She felt her way completely by instinct.

"I worked on the manuscript for two years," she recalls, "and then read it over and realized it was terrible. I threw it all away. I worked on it for two more years, read it over and felt I had 10 good pages. In the first draft everything was dead, but I couldn't see why. In the second draft, I knew those 10 pages were alive, so I could see what was wrong and what was right."

Upon completion, she submitted the work—unagented, in a plain brown envelope—to Knopf, where it was picked out of the slush pile and published to much critical acclaim. It was another five years before Hearon finished her next novel, *The Second Dune,* but agents were still intrigued by this unknown writer. (p. 56)

Her need to sort out and process her world has moved Hearon through five more novels and a coauthorship with former Congresswoman Barbara Jordan on Jordan's autobiography. It also has resulted in her winning grants from the Guggenheim, National Endowment for the Arts and Ingram Merrill and has made her much sought after as a lecturer and teacher. (She is spending this spring teaching at the University of California, Irvine campus.)

Hearon attributes her prolific nature to determination as well.

I start each book as a lab experiment. I propose a theory I hope to prove, usually dealing with the effect of time, place or family on people. But what I usually discover is that I have rigged my experiment. I'm testing something else I was not allowing myself to know about, and I sometimes don't realize that until I'm all done. These new issues lead me to a new book and a new experiment.

For example, in *Group Therapy* I was dealing with mothers and daughters. One of the characters in that book asks, 'Whatever happened to men?' My answer was *A Small Town,* in which I say, 'This is what happened to men—here are the father, grand-father, uncle.' It seemed a natural progression from there to deal more directly with men in *Five Hundred Scorpions.*

Actually, I got the idea for that book after watching the movie *Chariots of Fire.* I thought the real story there was, What happened to the runner after he got to China. Was he any different? What happens to someone who actually gets to where he wants to go? Does he grow, or is he only acted upon?

To compare Hearon's work to a lab experiment, however, is too cold an analogy to give full measure to the strong sense of place that suffuses her novels. Her characters are so much products of their environments that the setting often becomes a character itself. This is not happenstance, as Hearon is meticulous about her research. She travels to every town she writes about and often subscribes to its newspaper. She went to Mexico to find the town that would become the focus in *Five Hundred Scorpions,* spoke with townspeople to learn the legends, read several studies made of the place and even made the same tortur-ous climb up the Aztec pyramid that her Virginia gentle-man does in the novel.

"I always begin with place," Hearon explains, "because it is so determining. I always want to walk the ground and get a feel for its power, its limitations. From that I find out who would live there and what could happen there."

The issue of place—mental and physical—is a very crucial one for this transplanted Southerner in her day-to-day life as well.

"In *Group Therapy,* I posed the question, Can you run away? Are there times when you should stop dealing with a situation and just leave?" She continues: "I was not en-couraged to write in my first marriage. I was into role-playing anyway—being Betty Crocker in the kitchen, Brigitte Bardot in the bedroom and Maria Montessori in the nursery. I was very fragmented." (pp. 56-7)

The happiness that the author now exudes derives, no doubt in large part, from her relationship with second hus-band and philosopher Bill Lucas. He, too, found little en-couragement to work in his first marriage, so when the pair met, the attraction was instantaneous. . . .

In 1981, as a pledge to their commitment to each other's career, they left the South and moved to Westchester so Lucas could take a teaching post at Manhattanville Col-lege and Hearon could be nearer the publishing scene. An-other tangible symbol of their mutual support and encour-agement is the freestanding blackboard, chalked over with logic theorems, that takes up half of the living room.

"I got that for him because I wanted him to feel free to work in every room of the house," she explains. "He does, and I do, too."

She laughs, "We say that we used to have rich interior lives, and now we have rich exterior lives."

They work together a lot, processing, always processing.

> Bill's work is very different from mine so we have a fertilization, a synergistic effect. Since he's a phi-losopher, he starts with very specific instances and then builds a theory. I start with a theory, then

have to translate it into streets and faces. We get to the same bridge by different paths. It's wonderful to have a good home situation. I'm amazed at how much more productive and energetic we are.

Indeed, writer's block doesn't seem to be a problem Hearon faces much. Her novels have been coming out at a rate of about once a year. She is now in the midst of re-searching a novel set in San Antonio and, true to form, has a current subscription to the *San Antonio Light.*

Hearon leans forward intently. "I start out each book by collecting little pieces of paper in folders—stacks of notes, research from primary sources. I cut out photos of people and clothes. I try to find out what different people eat, what issues they'd be concerned with."

Another part of her research is to figure out each charac-ter's time frame.

> Maybe I read too much Proust and Mann at an early age, but I think everybody operates on a very different time cycle. There's a garden time, church time, political time, geological time, semester time. In my writing, I like to have a number of time cy-cles running concurrently to give the various levels to a book that we all have in our lives. It also gets back to my feelings about determinism because you are always bound by the time frame you go by.

> It all eventually gels in my head and has a Pygma-lion effect. I build to a center point, and then the characters come alive. When I finally see them, like a movie on the wall, I watch them for a while, and then I can start writing.

Hearon never moves onto a new novel until she is finished with the page proofs of the last one, so she won't "mess up the voice." But that doesn't mean she doesn't have ideas already kicking around. Other possible projects in-clude two sequels to *A Small Town,* which she is hoping to call *Merchants of Venice* and *The Doctor's Daughters.* (p. 57)

> *Beth Levine, "Shelby Hearon," in* Publishers Weekly, *Vol. 231, No. 13, April 3, 1987, pp. 56-7.*

Lowry Pei

Shelby Hearon's *Five Hundred Scorpions* is so many things at once that a listing of them risks obscuring the grace with which the novel is constructed. It is a bitter-sweet domestic comedy about a marriage threatened with dissolution, yet it peels away layers of intrigue like a spy novel, and puts some of its characters through a major natural disaster; it is thoroughly realistic, even chatty in parts, yet includes the magical and fantastic.

The book's two leading characters are Paul Sinclair, a Princeton-educated lawyer in Charlottesville, Va., and his wife, Peggy. In its opening pages, he leaves her, fed up with her short-lived enthusiasms, his older son's obsession with tennis and indifference to college, and his own feeling of "going through the motions of a life someone else had ordered for him." His destination is a Mexican mountain village called Tepoztlán, where the old Aztec god still re-turns each year to a ruined pyramid perched above the town, and where two female anthropologists have invited him to help with their study of adultery by village women.

The narrative shifts back and forth between Peggy in Tidewater, Va.—High Church, U. Va., old red brick, the comforts of the upper middle class—and Paul in Tepoztlán, where 500 varieties of scorpions live and almost nothing is what it at first seems. The sense of place and of social milieu is strong in both locales. Tepoztlán is both comic and sinister—a place where intolerable husbands are poisoned with a substance "which turns men into the dumbest sheep" and led, thereafter, by a rope around the neck. Paul is instantly attracted to one of the anthropologists, who doesn't entirely discourage his advances; the other one seems to dislike him on sight. He is given a Japanese-Mexican-American roommate who tells him, correctly, "What we don't know is why we are here, you and I"; he finds himself climbing a mountain in a downpour to witness the god's return. Meanwhile, back in Virginia, Peggy acquires a new friend, a man Paul went to Princeton with and made an enemy of. . . .

There's more—a great deal more, a tight, complex world of secret connections among the various characters, long personal histories, hidden motivations, manipulations, deceptions. Ms. Hearon builds this world with unobtrusive precision, sews it together with repeated images, hints at its secrets with a delicate touch, allows them to unfold inexorably and yet naturally; ironies lurk in the most innocuous lines of dialogue. The plot becomes an experience of human actions with deep reasons and inevitable consequences; the Sinclairs' victories—if they are victories—are as thoroughly, compellingly ambiguous as those in life itself.

Though its themes could easily have become lumpy with ideology—women's control of men, men's "lasting enmities" toward each other that "left women on the outside," what happens when mother- and father-dominated cultures meet—*Five Hundred Scorpions* is witty, fast-paced and oddly (given everything else) benign. If its narration sometimes becomes too benign, almost homey, that is directly related to the risk Ms. Hearon takes which makes this book unique: the demonic and the domestic inhabit the novel together in a struggle that denies neither and intensifies both.

> *Lowry Pei, "He Should Have Stayed in Charlottesville," in* The New York Times Book Review, *May 10, 1987, p. 7.*

Lennart M. Ginn

[In *Five Hundred Scorpions*] Paul Sinclair is abandoning his family in Virginia and heading south for Mexico. The reader wishes to climb on the plane with him to escape the ghastly similes of Mrs. Sinclair. "He began to make fists of his hands and butt them together, like two rams— punch, punch."

But what is Sinclair getting into? Two lesbian anthropologists, for the sake of science, are conducting an "unbiased" study of the microcosm located in Tepoztlán—a mountain village. Their work is to provide posterity with an unslanted view of matters. To penetrate the secrets of the male villagers, the female scientists need to recruit the services of two men. A WASP from Virginia and a little Japanese

man named Nakae. A perfectly logical team to infiltrate the villagers and gain their confidences.

Being a lawyer and brilliant academic scholar, the discerning Sinclair reads nothing but the most altruistic of motives. Nary a suspicion clouds his bright optimism towards this project. He is puzzled that he isn't having any luck scoring on one of the anthropologists, Helena. We are to believe that this successful lawyer is the only one in the book who hasn't figured out that Helena is gay.

All the men are depicted as one dimensional, adulterous and simple fools. One humiliation follows another. The action winding down and running out of ideas to debase men, Ms. Hearon introduces a devastating earthquake and a few scorpion stings to further demonstrate the ineptitude and cowardly weakness of men.

How does Mrs. Sinclair view her hero when she comes down to rescue her husband? "He had run off: the bad boy with all his belongings tied in a bandanna, who wants to come home when it gets dark."

Recommended reading for budding misogynists.

> *Lennart M. Ginn, in a review of "Five Hundred Scorpions," in* West Coast Review of Books, *Vol. 13, No. 1, May-June, 1987, p. 22.*

Dean Faulkner Wells

The first few chapters of Shelby Hearon's *Owning Jolene* are in many ways reminiscent of a toned-down version of Jay McInerney's *Story of My Life*. Both novels have a female first-person narrative voice, and both of the main characters are young (19 and 20, respectively) but far more worldly than their years warrant.

Both Hearon's Jolene and McInerney's Alison have a studied, casual attitude toward sex. At times they seem to watch themselves from a distance, voyeurs of their own lives, as if little connection exists between their bodies and their minds. Their voices are brash and grating as they recount their stories—the voices of driven young women who are desperate to find themselves.

But here the comparisons end. In their emotional makeup, Jolene and Alison are as far apart as are the settings for the two novels: Texas and New York. Alison is doomed to self-destruction; Jolene is a born survivor.

As the title of *Owning Jolene* may suggest, Hearon also addresses the serious, contemporary issue of child custody between estranged parents, although she does so with a surprisingly light touch.

Jolene repeatedly is a victim of zany, often outrageous kidnapings and kidnaping attempts on the part of her parents, Midge and Turk. Midge will go to any lengths to steal her daughter away from Turk. She is a master of disguises. . . . By the time Jolene enters school, she has been well taught in the art of deception and has learned to conform to Midge's cardinal rule: The best way to be invisible is to be conspicuous.

> I entered school a month late, with a pale face, dark curly hair, short ruffled skirt and sunglasses. I mean if you see a kid in third grade with shades on you think either that she's blind and wonder where

her dog has wandered off to, or that she's somebody really big. There were a couple of other touches, just to round the image off. One was an ankle bracelet Mom got at a thrift shop, the other was me wearing shoes with a heel to them. Are you getting the idea? Here was this Jolene, coming into class around Halloween, wearing this Lolita outfit, milk-white like she'd been kept indoors since the cradle, and nobody knew what to make of her, me, so they didn't make anything. Like Mom said, I was invisible.

Until Jolene turns 13, she and her mother are on the run all over Texas—attempting to lose themselves in one suburb after another, with Turk always in pursuit. Then her uncle and aunt intervene and take custody of her until she is 19. Through Uncle Brogan and Aunt Glenna, Hearon exposes middle-class values, Texas style, and the art world of oil-rich San Antonio.

Hiding from herself by assuming various disguises, Jolene becomes the model and lover of Henry Wozencrantz, a well-established Texas artist. After his showing of larger-than-life nude portraits of Jolene, she is thrust into the limelight—an affirmation, it would seem, of the Andy Warhol adage, "The day will come when everyone will be famous for 15 minutes."

Jolene's fame adds yet another dimension to her identity crisis. Who does "own" Jolene—Midge, Turk, Henry or the world?

Through her sometimes bizarre, sometimes touching relationship with Henry, Jolene is able to take control of her existence. She does, after all, comes to him well-trained in the art of dressing up, or down, to suit the occasion. So if Alison in McInerney's *Story of My Life* falls apart at the end, Jolene seems to have found her niche. We leave her posing for Henry wearing only a tiger mask and claws. She knows what will sell better than Henry himself does. (pp. 4-5)

> *Dean Faulkner Wells, "How a Wild Young Woman Finds Herself," in* Chicago Tribune— Books, *January 1, 1989, pp. 4-5.*

Tim Sandlin

Eliza Doolittle had it easy compared to 19-year-old Jolene Temple, or maybe it's Jackson, of Pass-of-the-Camels, Tex. Eliza had only one Henry Higgins grab her off the street and haul her away to create a new woman. Every time Jolene turns around, she finds herself nabbed by someone—generally a well-meaning relative—who wants to create and own her. One is even named Henry.

Jolene Temple/Jackson, as created by Shelby Hearon in her novel ***Owning Jolene,*** is something of a chronic kidnap victim. Each kidnapping forces her into a new role until Jolene has played so many parts she has no idea who inhabits the center of the mess that is her. Jolene could be called a literary Tar Baby, winning through passivity and stickiness.

One of the earliest roles Jolene recalls is that of a 7-year-old girl playing the part of a 4-year-old boy as her mother, Midge, sneaks her onto an airplane. "Now, Sonny, here's what you do," says Midge, telling Jolene to clutch her gen-

itals like a little boy and say, "I need to tinkle" as they are boarding. "They're looking for a girl. It's a subliminal trick, see?"

Midge Temple, master of a hundred disguises—all of them male, oddly enough—makes stealing and hiding her daughter a life's work. She cases Texas border towns, cruising for the suburb of all suburbs where she and Jolene can disappear into the boring.

Which I like. As a generalization, writers in the two middle time zones are afraid of suburbs. We like to think everyone is raised in small towns with names like Thalia or Chugwater, then either stays home or moves to Houston. Ms. Hearon makes a refreshing break from the noncoastal American myth in sticking her runaways somewhere in between.

At each hideout—Honey Grove Hills, Tierra Blanca Estates, Espiritu Santo Shores, Devil's River Bluffs—Midge hauls in a few pieces of furniture bought specifically for neighbors peeking through curtains, leases whatever car is most prevalent in the housing development and sets herself up as a piano teacher to prove she has nothing to hide.

Then she and Jolene wait patiently until Jolene's father, Turk Jackson, steals her back. Turk sells oil-field paraphernalia and is driven by a desire to give his daughter a "normal" childhood.

A lot is made of normal in ***Owning Jolene,*** maybe because no one in the book has a whiff of what the concept means. Occasionally, Jolene fantasizes about pretending normalcy, baking chocolate-chip cookies made with toasted pecans and condensed milk, wearing oven mitts as she rotates the pans, calling, "Come and get it, you all" while she pours tall glasses of cold milk for the family. But that role crashes down same as all the others.

Although the legalities remain fuzzy, Jolene's Uncle Brogan and Aunt Glenna Rose get hold of her for six years. Like everyone else Jolene meets, they are one thing (middle-class scammers) pretending to be something else (rich Texans on top of the situation). These two kinky characters enjoy having Jolene around as an audience and a vaguely interested third party. When speaking of Texas, which is as much a fraudulent character as anyone else in the book, Brogan says, "You think about yourself a certain way long enough, that's the way you got to be." (p. 10)

Ms. Hearon never tells us which of the observations she buys herself, but she sure serves up a host of entertaining people who see themselves as different than they are.

Jolene herself is the queen of the false pose. At various points she passes herself off as a little boy, a poet, an Indian, a stockbroker, a child star, a mugging victim, an acting student (the one role at which she bombs), a fashion model, an art dealer, a dead uncle's mistress, a famous nude model named Jolene and a Mexican skeleton wearing a tiger's mask. When her lover, Henry, tells her they will attend a gallery opening, Jolene says, "Who shall I be?"

Henry Wozencrantz is the famous painter Jolene poses for. Henry takes the reality-to-pretense theme and runs it backward. He was raised with a false name, Henry Kraft, by his own runaway mother, until he grew up, searched out the Wozencrantz roots and went back to his original name and identity.

Henry comes off as the nearly sane, wise character of the book, sort of. He enjoys making love by knocking over a vaseful of flowers at a crucial moment in foreplay.

All Henry's paintings of Jolene feature an artificial hand from the collection of his dead uncle's mistress. The fake hands mesmerize Jolene. She loves to pick them up and caress each one, saying it's "as if somebody had held on to the owner and wouldn't let her go, so she pulled loose and left her hand, the way animals, tearing themselves out of traps, leave a paw behind."

Now *there's* a symbol if I've ever read one, much better than later when Jolene complains that people "who have been a bone for more than a dozen years like me don't get excited when they see a couple of dogs about to fight over them."

When writing about a basically passive character, especially in the first person, there is a danger of creating a self-examining lump who just sits there waiting for colorful characters to come along. But, after 11 novels, Ms. Hearon has become very good at avoiding the pitfalls of passivity. Above all else, Jolene is likable. Somehow, out of the strangeness of her childhood, she has developed that mixture of toughness and vulnerability most of us strive for, both in fiction and in life. (pp. 10-11)

As in most novels, plot jumps over character toward the end and loose strings find themselves tied up more quickly than believably. In the last 10 pages Ms. Hearon pairs off characters à la Wodehouse or Shakespeare, but that is part of what makes a romantic comedy satisfying. (p. 11)

> *Tim Sandlin, "A Normal Life, with Oven Mitts," in* The New York Times Book Review, *January 22, 1989, pp. 10-11.*

Judith Paterson

Although she is concerned with family love and romance, Shelby Hearon spins her 11th novel, *Owning Jolene,* out of sheer *joie de vivre.* Novels—like life—she seems to be saying, are mostly for fun. And this one delivers.

The book begins just as 19-year-old Jolene is beginning to try to wrestle a grown-up life out of a childhood spent in the middle of a three-way tug-of-war between her divorced parents and a childless aunt and uncle over who "owns" her. She has spent most of her life being captured, rescued and recaptured by her unimaginative father and her ridiculously adventurous mother. In between, there are periods of respite in the home of the aunt and uncle who want not just to love her, but to have her as a bit player in their madcap business schemes as well.

Drawing on long experience with her mother's strategies of escape and disguise, Jolene sets out to live her life as if it were a series of masquerades. In a romp of a denouement, she is dramatically "unmasked" at a showing of nude portraits painted by her lover and then, in a high-spirited reversal of roles, pays mother back for all the bittersweet kidnappings of her childhood.

Owning Jolene is a funny, forgiving and tender look at what family life does to us all.

> *Judith Paterson, "Labors of Love and Loss," in* Book World—The Washington Post, *February 5, 1989, p. 6.*

Joseph Heller

1923-

American novelist, playwright, scriptwriter, and short story writer.

The following entry presents criticism on Heller's novel *Catch-22* (1961). For essays on Heller's other works, see *CLC,* Vols. 1, 3, 5, 8, 11, 36.

Heller is a popular and respected writer whose first and best-known novel, *Catch-22,* is considered a major work of the post-World War II era. Presenting existence as absurd and fragmented, this irreverent, witty novel satirizes capitalism and the military bureaucracy. Heller's tragicomic vision of modern life, found in all of his novels, focuses on the erosion of humanistic values and highlights the ways in which language obscures and confuses reality. In addition, Heller's use of anachronism reflects the disordered nature of contemporary existence. His protagonists are antiheroes who search for meaning in their lives and struggle to avoid being overwhelmed by such institutions as the military, big business, government, and religion. *Catch-22* is most often interpreted as an antiwar protest novel that foreshadowed the widespread resistance to the Vietnam war that erupted in the late 1960s. While Heller's later novels have received mixed reviews, *Catch-22* continues to be highly regarded as a trenchant satire of the big business of modern warfare.

Catch-22 concerns a World War II bombardier named Yossarian who believes his foolish, ambitious, mean-spirited commanding officers are more dangerous than the enemy. In order to avoid flying more missions, Yossarian retreats to a hospital with a mysterious liver complaint, sabotages his plane, and tries to get himself declared insane. Variously defined throughout the novel, "Catch-22" refers to the ways in which bureaucracies control the people who work for them. The term first appears when Yossarian asks to be declared insane. In this instance, Catch-22 demands that anyone who is insane must be excused from flying missions. The "catch" is that one must ask to be excused; anyone who does so is showing "rational fear in the face of clear and present danger," is therefore sane, and must continue to fly. In its final, most ominous form, Catch-22 declares "they have the right to do anything we can't stop them from doing." Although most critics identify Yossarian as a coward and an antihero, they also sympathize with his urgent need to protect himself from this brutal universal law. Some critics have questioned the moral status of Yossarian's actions, noting in particular that he seems to be motivated merely by self-preservation, and that the enemy he refuses to fight is led by Adolf Hitler. Others, however, contend that while *Catch-22* is ostensibly a war novel, World War II and the Air Force base where most of the novel's action takes place function primarily as a microcosm that demonstrates the disintegration of language and human value in a bureaucratic state.

Heller embodies his satire of capitalism in the character of Milo Minderbinder, whose obsessive pursuit of profits causes many deaths and much suffering among his fellow

soldiers. Originally a mess hall officer, Milo organizes a powerful black market syndicate capable of cornering the Egyptian cotton market and bombing the American base on Pianosa for the Germans. On the surface Milo's adventures form a straightforward, optimistic success story that some commentators have likened to the Horatio Alger tales popular at the turn of the twentieth century. The narrative line that follows Yossarian, on the other hand, is characterized by his confused, frustrated, and frightened psychological state. The juxtaposition of these two narrative threads provides a disjointed, almost schizophrenic structure that reasserts the absurd logic depicted in *Catch-22.*

Structurally, *Catch-22* is episodic and repetitive. The majority of the narrative is composed of a series of cyclical flashbacks of increasing detail and ominousness. The most important recurring incident is the death of a serviceman named Snowden that occurs before the opening of the story but is referred to and recounted periodically throughout the novel. In the penultimate chapter, Yossarian relives the full horror and comprehends the significance of this senseless death as it reflects the human condition and his own situation. This narrative method led many critics, particularly early reviewers, to condemn

Heller's novel as formless. Norman Mailer's oft-repeated jibe: "One could take out a hundred pages anywhere from the middle of *Catch-22,* and not even the author could be certain they were gone" has been refuted by Heller himself, and has inspired other critics to carefully trace the chronology of ever-darkening events that provide the loose structure of this novel.

Heller poignantly and consistently satirizes language, particularly the system of euphemisms and oxymorons that passes for official speech in the United States Armed Forces. Yossarian, who possesses a healthy skepticism, introduces Heller's theme regarding the fallibility of language in the opening scene of the novel. Assigned to censor the letters of the enlisted men while he recuperates, Yossarian capriciously deletes various parts of these letters and attributes his work to "Washington Irving." Many scenes in *Catch-22* are noted for the vaudevillian quality of the interactions between characters who are caught in a kind of verbal Catch-22. For example, Yossarian's prostitute girlfriend refuses to marry him because he's crazy, a fact evidenced by his desire to marry her. The Glorious Loyal Oath Crusade, instigated by Captain Black, is another example of the deterioration in value of language. When other officers institute their own requirements for loyalty oaths, Captain Black increases his demands to two and three oaths per transaction; when he later adds the Pledge of Allegiance and the "Star Spangled Banner," even routine communication fails due to the necessity of swearing lengthy oaths before the simplest action can be taken. In other scenes, simple words or phrases are repeated over and over to the confusion of all involved.

Conversely, in the world of *Catch-22* metaphorical language has a dangerously literal power. The death of Doc Daneeka is an example: when the plane that Doc is falsely reported to be on crashes and no one sees him parachute to safety he is presumed dead and his living presence is insufficient to convince anyone that he is really alive. Similarly, when Yossarian rips up his girlfriend's address in rage, she disappears, never to be seen again. Marcus K. Billson III summarized this technique: "The world of [*Catch-22*] projects the horrific, yet all too real, power of language to divest itself from any necessity of reference, to function as an independent, totally autonomous medium with its own perfect system and logic. That such a language pretends to mirror anything but itself is a commonplace delusion Heller satirizes throughout the novel. Yet, civilization is informed by this very pretense, and Heller shows how man is tragically and comically tricked and manipulated by such an absurdity."

(See also *Contemporary Authors,* Vols. 5-8, rev. ed.; *Contemporary Authors New Revision Series,* Vol. 8; *Contemporary Authors Bibliographical Series,* Vol. 1; *Dictionary of Literary Biography,* Vols. 2, 28; and *Dictionary of Literary Biography Yearbook 1980.*)

PRINCIPAL WORKS

NOVELS

Catch-22   1961
Something Happened   1974
Good as Gold   1979
God Knows   1985

No Laughing Matter   1986
Picture This   1988

PLAYS

We Bombed in New Haven   1967
Catch-22   1973
Clevinger's Trial   1973

Granville Hicks

Catch-22 tells many stories, but its central figure is a bombardier named Yossarian. The war has come to seem to Yossarian quite crazy. "Men went mad and were rewarded with medals. All over the world, boys on every side of the bomb line were laying down their lives for what they had been told was their country; and no one seemed to mind, least of all the boys who were laying down their young lives." Yossarian minds very much: "He had decided to live forever or die in the attempt, and his only mission each time he went up was to come down alive."

The chief obstacle to Yossarian's achieving his ambition is Colonel Cathcart, who constantly raises the number of missions his men have to fly. Cathcart is a simon-pure opportunist, a man who will stop at nothing to get promoted, who is constantly courting the favor of his superiors, who does not care how many men are killed if he can get a little favorable publicity. He is as stupid as he is unscrupulous, and his immediate superiors have little advantage over him in either intelligence or morality.

Cathcart, of course, is a caricature, and there are plenty of caricatures in the book. With Milo Minderbinder, the mess officer, Heller goes beyond caricature into the realm of satiric fantasy. Milo, a stalwart advocate of private enterprise, organizes a syndicate whose black market activities range all over Europe. He steals the carbon dioxide cylinders that are used to inflate life jackets, and takes the syrettes of morphine from first-aid kits. (He always leaves a mimeographed note saying, "What's good for M & M Enterprises is good for the country.") His greatest exploit is to hire himself out to the Germans to bomb his own airfield for cost plus 6 per cent.

Heller's satire cuts a wide swath. He takes after a variety of bureaucrats, makes fun of security checks, ridicules psychiatrists and army doctors in general. Sometimes he shoots way over the mark, but often his aim is good. There are several extremely funny passages, the humor usually rising out of the kind of mad logic that seems to Heller the essence of modern warfare. Here is a passage that exhibits the humor and incidentally explains the title:

> Yossarian looked at him soberly and tried another approach. "Is Orr crazy?"
>
> "He sure is," Doc Daneeka said.
>
> "Can you ground him?"
>
> "I sure can. But first he has to ask me to. That's part of the rule."
>
> "Then why doesn't he ask you to?"

"Because he's crazy," Doc Daneeka said. "He has to be crazy to keep flying combat missions after all the close calls he's had. Sure, I can ground him. But first he has to ask me to."

"That's all he has to do to be grounded?"

"That's all. Let him ask me."

"And then you can ground him?" Yossarian asked.

"No. Then I can't ground him."

"You mean there's a catch?"

"Sure there's a catch," Doc Daneeka replied. "Catch-22. Anyone who wants to get out of combat duty isn't really crazy."

This is amusing and pointed, and so is much else, but the book as a whole is less effective than it might be. Heller has introduced so many characters, tried to deliver so many knockout blows, and written in such a variety of styles that the reader becomes a little dizzy.

> *Granville Hicks, "Medals for Madness," in* Saturday Review, *Vol. XLIV, No. 40, October 7, 1961, p. 32.*

Richard G. Stern

Catch-22 has much passion, comic and fervent, but it gasps for want of craft and sensibility. A portrait gallery, a collection of anecdotes, some of them wonderful, a parade of scenes, some of them finely assembled, a series of descriptions, yes, but the book is no novel. One can say that it is much too long, because its material—the cavortings and miseries of an American bomber squadron stationed in late World War II Italy—is repetitive and monotonous. Or one can say that it is too short because none of its many interesting characters and actions is given enough play to become a controlling interest. Its author, Joseph Heller, is like a brilliant painter who decides to throw all the ideas in his sketchbooks onto one canvas, relying on their charm and shock to compensate for the lack of design.

If *Catch-22* were intended as a commentary novel, such sideswiping of character and action might be taken care of by thematic control. It fails here because half its incidents are farcical and fantastic. . . .

As satire *Catch-22* makes too many formal concessions to the standard novels of our day. There is a certain amount of progress: the decent get killed off, the self-seekers prosper, and there is even a last minute turnabout as the war draws to an end. One feels the author should have gone all the way and burlesqued not only the passions and incidents of war, but the traditions of representing them as well. It might have saved him from some of the emotional pretzels which twist the sharpness of his talent.

> *Richard G. Stern, "Bombers Away," in* The New York Times Book Review, *October 22, 1961, p. 50.*

Julian Mitchell

Joseph Heller's *Catch-22* is an extraordinary book. Its basic assumption is that in war all men are equally mad; bombs fall on insane friend and crazy enemy alike. But wherever bombs fall, men die, and no matter how often the process of bombs falling and men dying is repeated, it is always terrible. Ostensibly a black farce about an American bomber squadron stationed on an island in the Mediterranean towards the end of the Second World War, it is, in fact, a surrealist *Iliad,* with a lunatic High Command instead of gods, and a coward for hero.

Yossarian, the coward, is a rational man trying not to be killed in a wholly irrational world, forced to resort to even more irrational behaviour than that of his superiors in order to survive. He is an expert malingerer; he performs minor acts of sabotage on his own plane; he takes every possible form of evasive action. But he cannot succeed against the appalling Colonel Cathcart, who continually raises the number of missions the men have to fly before they can be sent home, solely to get a reputation as a tough leader of men. Whatever Yossarian does, there is always a catch—Catch-22: 'Catch-22 says they have a right to do anything we can't stop them from doing.' It is an unwritten law which is ruthlessly enforced.

Epic in form, the book is episodic in structure. Each chapter carries a single character a step nearer madness or death or both, and a step, too, into legend. The action takes place well above the level of reality. On leave or in action the characters behave with a fine disregard for the laws of probability. Yet they follow the law of Catch-22 and its logically necessary results. Within its own terms the book is wholly consistent, creating legend out of the wildest farce and the most painful realism, constructing its own system of probability. Its characters are as boldly unlikely as its events, but when they die, they die with as much pain as any 'real' men, and when they are dead, they are wept for with real tears. There is a scene in which Yossarian bandages the wounded leg of one of his crew, only to find that inside the man's flak-suit his vital organs have mortally spilled, a scene which is repeated again and again, each time with more detail and more dread. It acts as a reminder that *Catch-22,* for all its zany appearance, is an extremely serious novel. Against Catch-22 the man who does not wish to die has only his wits: war is not civilised, and to be caught up in it is to be reduced to a state of nature far worse than that visualised by Hobbes. *Catch-22* is a book of enormous richness and art, of deep thought and brilliant writing.

> *Julian Mitchell, "Under Mad Gods," in* The Spectator, *Vol. 208, No. 6990, June 15, 1962, p. 801.*

Daedalus: Journal of the American Academy of Arts and Sciences

Since books not worth reading are not worth reviewing and *Catch-22* is worthless, my review needs justification. I will supply it in conclusion. Meanwhile it may be viewed as a protest against the means by which I was fubbed, an advertisement containing twenty-three testimonials to the superlative quality of Mr. Heller's book. Four of these were anonymous quotes from mass media (*Time, Newsday, Newsweek, Associated Press*) which seemed to support the identified speakers with the voice of the people which is also the voice of God. Of the identified speakers, about half were professional wind-raisers for the publishing industry and its captive journals. I am not bitter about these. To sustain themselves in the needy world of book-page journalism they must review more books than they read, and no doubt end many a working day with plaintive speculations: surely there must be *some* way of earning an honest living. It was by the nonprofessional enthusiasts that I was, in all senses of the word, sold. One was A. J. Liebling, whom I had assessed as a man not easily exploited. Another was a professor who, by unlucky coincidence, shares a surname with one of Mr. Heller's asinine villains. I know him to be neither villain nor ass. Indeed none of the testifiers need be thought of as wicked or stupid men. They share in the prevalent confusion which I shall deal with at the end. And they are generous. It may not have occurred to them that, in supporting a raid on my purse and leisure, they were being generous with time and money not their own. (pp. 155-56)

Institutional rivalry has nothing to do with my estimate of *Catch-22.* Its author might have passed through my own university as he has through New York University, Columbia, and Oxford, unscathed by education. He is a phenomenon of our times, when a fair percentage of students prepare themselves to shape our culture by proving impervious to culture, and to use the tool of language by acquiring no skill with languages. A writer need not learn to write; he still can make his mark.

Before describing the theme of *Catch-22,* I must make this point which I trust will not be considered trifling—that its author cannot write. . . . [Let] the reader check, if he wishes, the fact that the specimens offered truly exist and are typical of the style of their context. In most of the book the question of style scarcely arises. Its pages are filled with dialogue of the type which television comedians blame on their "writers," with the skits linked by brief paragraphs in the simple-style-dogmatic of the post-Hemingway era. Flat assertions succeed each other with the engaging rhythm of a slapping screen-door. It is when the author aspires to vivid or "fine" writing that we get a taste of his quality. Journalese emerges as the basic language, whole sentences consisting of clichés punctuated by proper names: "Even though Chief White Halfoat kept busting Colonel Moodus in the nose for General Dreedle's benefit, he was still outside the pale." Inevitably there follows the car which "slammed to a screeching stop inches short" of something or other. The author's way of breaking the cliché barrier is to supply all nouns with adjectives, frequently in strings: "He was a sad, birdlike man with the spatulate face and scrubbed, tapering features of a well-groomed rat." If "spatulate" still means "broad and flat," it creates certain anatomical difficulties when used in connection with the "tapering features" of a rat; perhaps this is a form of ambivalence. Mr. Heller returns for another look at this face: "He had a dark complexion and a small, wise, saturnine face with mournful pouches under both eyes." Observe the helpful word "both"—serving those of us accustomed to faces with pouches under only one eye. Recalling the curious rat which this character resembled, we trust that the pouches were like the features, "tapered," and not like the face, "spatulate," and that they sagged under "both" beady eyes.

Mr. Heller's special genius is for selecting not the wrong word but the one which is not quite right, as when he describes one of his Italian beauties as having "incandescent blue veins converging populously beneath her cocoa-colored skin where the flesh is most tender." Obviously she was well-peopled with veins, but their "converging beneath" her skin leaves us puzzled about where they diverged—surely not, cilia-like, *above* her skin nor yet at her stout whore's heart. In any event she would have been, as all women were to Hungry Joe, a "lovely, satisfying, maddening manifestation of the miraculous." As women to Hungry Joe, so alliteration to Mr. Heller. (pp. 156-57)

The book tells no story. It alternates serially, by means of the "advanced" technique of fragmented structure, five standard routines: I, Hospital routine, with malingering soldiers and incompetent staff; II, Combat routine, with everything snafu, yet missions accomplished with negligent gallantry; III, Funny fraud routine, involving army supplies and G.I. tycoon; IV, Red tape routine, at training center and headquarters; V, Leave in Rome routine, with orgies. The last is the only one of a type unavailable to television viewers, the elder of whom must console themselves with fond memories of the penny-in-the-slot movie, "Ladies' Night in a Turkish Bath," where everyone ran around naked.

There are no characters. The puppets are given funny names and features, but cannot be visualized or distinguished from one another except by association with their prototypes. Sergeant Bilko, Colonel Blimp (and Captain Whizbang) are immanent and circumambient, their spirit, like Yossarian in his plane, moving over the face of the waters. The character-names range from the subtly whimsical (General Dreedle) to the mercilessly side-splitting (Milo Minderbinder and Dori Duz, who, as Mr. Heller and his publisher carefully explain, "does."). Alliteration is rife: General P. P. Peckem, Colonel Cathcart, Colonel Cargill, Colonel Korn, Major Metcalf. One character surnamed "Major" has received from his cruel father the given name "Major" and since he is now a Major in the army, he is Major Major Major. He must have picked up a middle name when my attention lagged since one of Mr. Heller's chapters is titled "Major Major Major Major" at which point our laughter becomes uncontrollable. In this world, of course, Texans are bores, Iowans rubes, chaplains feeble, doctors hypochondriac, and officers increasingly contemptible as they rise in rank until we reach generals, who are effete. The copying of every available stereotype, and the failure to find in the whole range of humanity anything new to draw illustrates the author's indifference to people. We can see no one because he has seen no one.

The forms of verbal wit are limited to two. The first consists of self-contradictory statement which may or may not be meaningful. This might be called the Plain Man's Paradox or Everybody's Epigram since the fact that a sally of wit has been attempted is inescapable: ". . . the games were so interesting they were foolish;" "Nately had a bad start. He came from a good family;" ". . . the finest, least dedicated man in the whole world;" "And if that wasn't funny, there were lots of things that weren't even funnier;" "Failure often did not come easily;" "He was a self-made man who owed his lack of success to nobody;" "He had decided to live forever or die in the attempt;" ". . . never sees anyone in his office while he's in his office;" ". . . she was irresistible, and men edged away from her carefully;"

"This . . . old man reminded Nately of his father because the two were nothing at all alike;" "He did not hate his mother and father, even though they had both been very good to him." This last, like several others of the hundreds in the book, comes near to being a hit, but Mr. Heller, as usual, kills it by the wrong kind of "milking." He proceeds to lambaste the mother and father for snobbishness. After gazing apathetically at the constant shower of sparks rising from Mr. Heller's "mordant intelligence" (Brustein [see *CLC*, Vol. 3]), we are amazed to come upon this:

> "My only fault," he observed with practical good humor, watching for the effect of his words, "is that I have no faults."
>
> Colonel Scheisskopf didn't laugh, and General Peckem was stunned.

General Peckem and Author Heller are brothers under the skin after all (as are Colonel Scheisskopf and I). The striving for paradox often takes the form of extended statement ending in a "snapper." A review of intellectual attainments will end "In short, he was a dope," or a list of virtuous traits with "I hate that son of a bitch." There is much multiplying of negatives, as in the comment on the farmer paid for not raising crops, which alone might well have been eight years in the making. It is designed for those who have never had this joke in a large enough portion.

Mr. Heller's other resource is echolalia. This is a device best illustrated in one of its traditional settings, the minstrel show:

> Interlocutor: Bones, who was that lady I saw you out with last night?
>
> Bones: Who was that lady you saw me out with last night?
>
> Interlocutor: Yes, Bones. Who was that lady I saw you out with last night?
>
> Bones: That was no lady. That was my wife.

Mr. Heller employs some form of echolalia on every page. Usually it is pointless:

> "You're a chaplain," he exclaimed ecstatically. "I didn't know you were a chaplain."
>
> "Why yes," the chaplain answered. "Didn't you know I was a chaplain?"
>
> "Why, no. I didn't know you were a chaplain."

Sometimes it italicizes a joke, on the remote chance that we have not heard it, like the one showing dignitaries so ignorant that they fail to recognize the name of a famous author:

> "Well, what did he say?"
>
> " 'T. S. Eliot,' " Colonel Cargill informed him.
>
> "What's that?"
>
> " 'T. S. Eliot,' " Colonel Cargill repeated.
>
> "Just 'T. S.—' "
>
> "Yes, sir. That's all he said. Just 'T. S. Eliot.' "

> "I wonder what it means," General Peckem reflected. Colonel Cargill wondered too.
>
> " 'T. S. Eliot,' " General Peckem mused.
>
> " 'T. S. Eliot,' " Colonel Cargill echoed with the same funereal puzzlement.

(Could this be what Professor Cargill has in mind when he testifies, "Heller writes the freshest dialogue since the advent of Hemingway thirty years ago"?) (pp. 158-60)

Nothing is easier than to blast a book, especially a sitting turkey, and, ordinarily, nothing more gratuitous. There will always be vulgar and noisy authors vulgarly and noisily praised, and ill-written, uncreative, and tedious books for which the proprietors can drum up a claque. What gives the present enterprise its special significance is the peculiar kind of pretentiousness involved, and the dislocation in literary and moral standards encouraging this kind of pretentiousness. The appalling fact is that author, publisher, and reviewers seem unaware that the book is destructive and immoral, and are able to add to their economic and other delights in it, gratifying sensations of righteousness. There is the real "catch" in *Catch-22.*

The identity of the book as non-art may be illustrated by a single detail. In the hospital where Yossarian malingers is a so-called "soldier in white" whose limbs are in traction and whose body is swathed in bandages except for holes where he breathes and where tubes enter for intravenous feeding and kidney drainage. Before he dies, this "soldier in white" becomes one of Mr. Heller's comic props. On page 10 we read:

> When the jar on the floor was full, the jar feeding his elbow was empty, and the two were simply switched quickly so that the stuff could drip back into him.

In a word, he is being fed his own urine. On page 168 this brutal fancy is repeated, in the usual two sentences where one would do:

> Changing the jars for the soldier in white was no trouble at all, since the same clear fluid was dripped back inside him over and over again with no apparent loss. When the jar feeding the inside of his elbow was just about empty, the jar on the floor was just about full, and the two were simply uncoupled from their respective hoses and reversed quickly so that the liquid could be dripped right back into him.

Catch-22, says Orville Prescott, "will not be forgotten by those who can take it." Why should we wish to take it?

The issue here is an artistic, not a moral, one. There is in art, current notions to the contrary, such a thing as decorum, propriety, fitness—a necessary correspondence between matter and mode. No kind of matter is denied the artist, providing he finds the right mode and possesses the right skills. Swift might have been able to adapt the matter of the "soldier in white" to the mode of satire as he adapted the idea of butchering Irish babies for the English meat market in his "Modest Proposal." Swift's persona is consistent and *serious,* the powerful thrust of the piece deriving from his frightening obtuseness; the material, as it must be in such a risky case, is under perfect control, the intention unmistakable. Heller, *pace* Leo Lerman, is not "our Swift." His conception of satire, if he has one, is that it is any mixture of the repellent and ridiculous, and so he keeps pelting us from his bag of merry japes. Suffering and death are not fit subjects for his mode and talents, and neither is juvenile pimping in Rome. It is not that we are horrified by his "soldier in white." We are a little disgusted and greatly bored. The jokes are there to prevent us from taking the figure seriously, and the figure is there to prevent us from taking the jokes as jokes even if they were good. The result is vacuum. Whatever else it may be, art may not be vacuous. (pp. 161-62)

Because Heller's book reads as if the pages of the manuscript had been scrambled on the way to the printer, it is viewed as experimental and "modern"—like the work of the painter who squirts colors on the side of a barn with a firehose and thus triumphs in a new "technique." The idea has still failed to penetrate that formlessness is not a new kind of form, and that true modern art is not formless. The ideal of excess is explicitly stated by one of Heller's contemporaries writing of another. Updike in praising Salinger has said that the mark of the true artist is the "willingness to risk excess on behalf of [his] obsessions." Our timid demurrer that a few true artists have risked moderation on behalf of their insights is irrelevant in the present context. The interest of Updike's dictum is the evidence it provides that artistry is being defined in terms of *differentia* and that *genus* is being forgotten. Artistry, we had supposed, was mastery of materials, the ability of certain unusual people to arrange the right things in the right order, words, or sounds, or colors and shapes; but if excess and obsession are its mark, we must revise our notions and accept the fact that membership in the society of artists is wide open. Although Updike and Salinger write far better than he, they will have to admit Heller. Perhaps it should be put the other way around. Salinger was one of those mentioned as incorporated in Heller. Updike did not make the grade.

Those who can mistake non-art for art can mistake immorality for morality. My word immorality applies, of course, to Mr. Heller's book, not his personal character or literary intentions. In assessing the response of the reviewers, I realize that I am dealing with excerpts, but I have made sure that these excerpts predicate; no amount of hedging in the unquoted portions of the critiques would alter the implications. The Associated Press excerpt contains the usual bullying sentence: "If you have no imagination you won't understand it." I have imagination and I understand it. I have observed that *Catch-22* contains trace elements of decency. Mr. Heller avoids scatalogical and homosexual humor, for which I thank him, and he dedicates his book to his mother, wife and children. Although during its "heartstopping moments" (West) my heart beat steadily on, I know where they are supposed to be—indeed, in my initial exposure to the book, was looking for them longingly, desperately. Yossarian sorrows over the death of rear-gunner Snowden in spite of the clever pun "Where are the Snowdens of yesteryear?" and the neat turn given the account of his wound:

> Here was God's plenty, all right, he thought bitterly as he stared—liver, lungs, kidneys, ribs, stomach and bits of the stewed tomatoes Snowden had eaten that day for lunch. Yossarian hated stewed tomatoes and turned away dizzily and began to vomit.

Yossarian wishes to rescue "Nately's whore's kid sister" from the brothel, even though earlier she has been hilariously portrayed as completely adapted to environment. The humble family visiting Yossarian in the hospital is kindly, even though they insist on mistaking him for someone else. Although Yossarian is quite the village atheist, Mr. Heller's pile-driver satire comes down less heavily on the chaplain than on other officials, divesting this man of God only of dignity. Mr. Heller's heart is no doubt in the right place; the trouble is with his head and the current notions which have addled it.

Catch-22 is immoral in the way of so much contemporary fiction and drama in being inclusively, almost absentmindedly, anti-institutional. This quality has become so pervasive that it now evades recognition. The codes of conduct subtending such institutions as marriage and family life are treated casually as if nonexistent or vestigial. Acts of adultery are presented as if it would occur to no one to object, with the betrayed partner usually the unsympathetic party—a natural concomitant of the new literary form of betrothal, not an exchange of vows but getting into bed. Indulgence emerges as a new ideal, with so cleanly a thing as sexuality consistently dirtied by association with ideas of violence, prowess, and proof of normality, and divorce from ideas of procreation of tenderness. By a new kind of stock response, profanity and obscenity are accepted as signature of the literature of the elect, reverberating more loudly in theatres than in bars. Every observant reader must be familiar with the mounting insistence with which he is made to stare at the same graffiti scrawled on different walls. In 1955 as distinct from 1961 the nation was not "ready" for *Catch-22.*

It now requires considerable temerity to write words like the above; they have become the only kind *unprintable* in literary media. The new conformity is there with its bludgeon, and hordes of hack reviewers ready to step forth valiantly to defend the autonomy of the artist. The question is, where is the autonomy and where are the artists? The lock-step is the lock-step, whether the march is forward or backward. Books are immoral if they condone immoral behavior inadvertently or otherwise. Because legal censorship of seriously intended works is wrong, as most intelligent men agree, it does not follow that moral considerations should be barred from critical discussion. If a book like *Catch-22* is offensive, we should say so. (pp. 162-64)

Catch-22 is immoral because it follows a fashion in spitting indiscriminately at business and the professions, at respectability, at ideals, at all visible tokens of superiority. It is a leveling book in the worst sense, leveling everything and everyone downward. It is chilling to observe the compulsive love of destruction that has gone into this presumed protest against the destructiveness of war. The only surviving values are self-preservation, satisfaction of animal appetite, and a sentimental conception of "goodness of heart." The "sane" view is live-and-let-live, as if it were as simple as that, and men had never died so that others might live. By stacking the cards so clumsily that they clatter, Mr. Heller is able to demonstrate that Yossarian does right by deserting: "That crazy bastard may be the only sane one left"—except for the other deserter, Orr. Selden Rodman says in his piece, "The preposterous morality of this world passes in review." Observe the grand inclusiveness. Presumably no distinction exists between the morality of the Nazis, who murdered non-Nordic countrymen because they were non-Nordics, and the morality of the Danes, who rescued non-Nordic countrymen because they were human beings—all the morality "of this world" is equally "preposterous." The American effort which Mr. Heller "satirizes" was not a crusade, but some Americans who died in it, perhaps even a few colonels, fought as they did because they hated cruelty. It is easy enough to be "sane" in a simple world of self, where the value of all actions can be judged in terms of personal convenience. Sanity of Mr. Heller's brand was evidently on the increase in Korea, among those who sold out their fellow prisoners for an extra handful of rice.

If it seems that this book is being taken too seriously—just a first book, and one that tries to be funny—have we not been told that it is "an intensely serious work" (Brustein)? When it was more recently advertised, the "sixth printing" was mentioned (with the usual reticence about the size of the printings), but the full page ads and the promises of dirt and delight have not yet succeeded in jacking it into the best seller lists in this country. The promoters claim to have done so in England, and this is not implausible. It has an ersatz American quality, like those imitations of hound-dog singing now making British music halls hideous. Europe has always imported our more dubious cultural products, and is in the market for surplus Beatism. Philip Toynbee has boarded the *Catch-22* bandwagon—"the greatest satirical work in English since *Erewhon.*" When the publishers run out of American boosters, there will always be an Englishman. The number of printings, six or six hundred, is quite immaterial—the book is what it is. Its author should know that there are some of us who see no distinction between a fraudulent military success like his Colonel Cathcart's and a fraudulent literary success like his own. (pp. 164-65)

> *A review of "Catch-22," in* Daedalus: Journal of the American Academy of Arts and Sciences, *Vol. 92, No. 1, Winter, 1963, pp. 155-65.*

Alex Cockburn

Catch-22 is a description of the characters and interactions of a few of the members of a USAF bomb squadron in Pianosa (actually an island eight miles south of Elba) during the second world war. Heller's method is to involve one gradually in the actions and motives of these characters; establishing each with great deftness and incision, presenting him in speech or action, and then sliding casually off on a different topic. The time scheme, now and then confusingly handled, is largely at the service of this hit and run technique of presentation. A character is described, a quick allusion is made to some event in his past history which has made him memorable; then he is left for 50 pages, until with equal abruptness Heller returns to describe the incident previously mentioned. We start the book in the position of someone looking at a half completed crossword puzzle; as we go on, the technique of cross reference and of abrupt clarification brings the whole construction into focus.

At the opening Yossarian is in hospital ("he had made up his mind to spend the rest of the war in hospital"); as yet we have no idea of why he has elected to go on sick leave; Heller chooses to keep the focus sharp and limited. To while away the long hours he is working on the letters he is required to censor:

> To break the monotony he invented games. Death to all modifiers, he declared one day, and out of every letter that passed through his hands went every adverb and every adjective. The next day he made war on articles. He reached a much higher plane of creativity the following day when he blacked out everything in the letters but *a, an* and *the.* That erected more dynamic intralinear tensions, he felt, and in just about every case left a message far more universal. Soon he was proscribing parts of salutations and signatures and leaving the text untouched. One time he blacked out all but the salutation 'Dear Mary' from a letter, and at the bottom he wrote, 'I yearn for you tragically. R. O. Shipman, Chaplain, US Army.' R. O. Shipman was the group chaplain's name . . . Most letters he didn't read at all. On those he didn't read at all he wrote his own name. On those he did read he wrote, 'Washington Irving'. When that grew monotonous he wrote 'Irving Washington'.

The passage is worth quoting *in extenso* because it exemplifies an important aspect of Heller's technique; the rapid development of quite a funny idea, which not only gives us a quick flash of Yossarian, half artful dodger, half victim of Catch 22 (whose final formulation [is], "Catch 22 says they have a right to do anything we can't stop them from doing") in the process of making a foray on the system, but also extends itself through the book. The effect of his tiny sabotage, his use of Shipman and Washington Irving, comes up sporadically throughout the story; spying emissaries from Them descend on the base to crossexamine, distort, and harass in their investigations; two other characters start to use the name Washington Irving themselves. In this way Heller uses jokes and absurdities initially of quite minor effect as points around which whole sections of the book revolve. This technique carries itself through the whole ordering of the story. The hospital where Yossarian and Dunbar, his mutinous ally, have fled is abandoned after the first chapter; and it is only 140 pages later at the end of a sequence antecedent in time to the first chapter that we discover why they are there.

For these reasons it is wrong to analyse the book in terms of plot. For at least the first three quarters of the book it is more a matter of gradual involvement with the characters, viewed from different angles in different situations. Heller refers to the same incidents again and again, each time slightly modified and elaborated in the characters' memories. Gradually, out of this mesh of incidents a pattern of events emerges. At the centre are the missions—the bombing raids to Orvieto, Avignon, and Bologna; and between these missions Heller stretches the main thread of continuity throughout the book: the continual raising of the number of missions required. As the number rises from 35 to 40, and from 40 on up to 75, the mutinous, the apathetic, and the stupid, are developed in terms of their reactions to these extensions of their duty. Interwoven among these focal points of military action are—as Heller would doubtless cheerfully term them—the sex bits. A gradually embellished picture is formed of the characters racing off to Rome for orgies, simple, violent, or confused in the quarters thoughtfully providing for them by a senior officer.

About three quarters of the way through the book, a reticent development takes place; as if Heller has accounted for the sum total of the actions and personalities of his protagonists and then allowed some sort of evolution to take place. The man who can't stand whores gets round to throwing one out of the window; the weak and the apathetic, the objectors and the carefree are killed, or make a motion of resistance, or flee.

This abstract resumé, disencumbered of illustration, could refer to a worthy war book, where the writer serves out the blood, the guts and the women straight from the shoulder. *Catch-22* is, of course, a satire, and it is Heller's techniques of presentation and narration that typify the nature of the book.

Naturally the satirist's task is to ridicule and expose; to arrive by means not at the ordinary novelist's disposal at what he imagines the reality of a given situation or ideology to be. (Sometimes it seems a pity that Swift is so often cited as the supreme satirist. Swift relies, over the moral base of his protest, on a superstructure of distorted event and motive. The tradition before him going back to Juvenal relied mainly on the presentation of the bare facts unencumbered with the rhetorical device of distortion.) Heller makes use of both these techniques, the straight exposé, and the abrupt distortion of reality to gain his effects. He is particularly fond of the surprise repeat; one of the simplest comic techniques:

> "Some of my very best friends are enlisted men, you understand, but that's about as close as I care to let them come. Honestly now, Chaplain, you wouldn't want your sister to marry an enlisted man, would you?"
>
> "My sister is an enlisted man, sir," the Chaplain replied.
>
> The colonel stopped in his tracks again and eyed the chaplain sharply to make certain that he was not being ridiculed. "Just what do you mean by that remark, Chaplain? Are you trying to be funny?"
>
> "Oh, no, Sir," the chaplain hastened to explain with a look of excruciating discomfort. "She's a master sergeant in the marines."

Heller deploys these techniques with great expertise; a variation is the surprise follow through; Heller is fond of using this in description of character: take the portrait of Major Major, accidently promoted through a faulty anode in an IBM machine:

> He never once took the name of the Lord his God in vain, committed adultery or coveted his neighbour's ass. In fact, he loved his neighbour and never even bore false witness against him. Major Major's elders disliked him because he was such a flagrant non-conformist.
>
> Since he had nothing better to do well in he did well in school. At the State University he took his studies so seriously that he was suspected by the homosexuals of being a Communist and suspected by the Communists of being a homosexual.

With the aid of this slick technique of paradox and dead-

pan follow-throughs, Heller is adept at fixing his characters on the reader's mind, so that after a page of description a firm idea of their attitude and the illusion of a complete portrait is left on the memory. . . . (pp. 87-9)

It is this deft technique that controls the book; the aptly presented contradictions, coincidences, antitheses that come out in the paragraphs quoted above govern most of the book, and control Heller's handling of time scheme and incident. It must lead one on straight away to Heller's satiric intention. What is the reference and anchor for his satire? How much is it a parody on war books, how much is it a satire of war? (p. 89)

One of the crucial texts in this respect is the passage where Milo Minderbinder gives his rationale of private enterprise and war. Milo has been put in charge of the mess tent. Business on the black market has boomed and soon he is trading all over Europe. In this spirit of free enterprise he accepts the German's lucrative offer to bomb his own base. Exposed to criticism Milo discloses that he has enough money to reimburse the government for the damage to its personnel and material: but

> The sweetest part of the whole deal was that there really was no need to reimburse the government at all.
>
> "In a democracy the government is the people," Milo explained. "We're people aren't we? So we might as well just keep the money and eliminate the middle man. Frankly, I'd like to see the government get out of war altogether and leave the whole field to private industry. If we pay the government everything we owe it, we'll only be encouraging government control and discouraging other individuals from bombing their own men and planes. We'll be taking away their incentive."

This could be taken as a moment of truth in the satire—the moment when Heller's view of the essential, or one of the essential, motives of war has been reached by the rhetoric of exaggeration and overstatement. But it is dangerous to do this. Heller is as likely to be parodying the play made with small time entrepreneurs in straight war books. Is Heller parodying what he considers to be false or initially overstated, or satirising towards what he considers to be the truth? It could be objected that the question of motive is irrelevant; that it is the effect of the passage that counts in criticism. But a decision has to be made, since the interpretation one puts on the passage bears on the rest of the book. This is a central ambiguity, one that ultimately becomes disturbing and dissipates the effect of the book.

Yet I found it a very funny book to read—over an extended period in short bursts—rather in the manner of listening to a weekly comedy series, and in view of my eventual impression, this manner of approach could be significant in itself. For, as I have suggested above, it is by the brief paradox that Heller makes his point, and it is by their sum total rather than by their sequential development that Heller achieves his impact—thus the importance of following closely the dodging narrative is doubled. (pp. 89-90)

This is really the full range of satirical machinery that Heller commands. Fundamentally he uses simply the technique of exaggeration: war books say that men in battle spend their spare time falling intensely in love; so present a character falling in love with a whore whose main idea of the service he can do for her is to allow her to sleep or sleep with other men. War is a satisfaction of personal ambition; so present the leading commanders entirely obsessed with efforts to please still higher commands, willing to nullify the effect of a bombing mission to obtain the perfect bomb patterns that the commanding officer finds so desirable. The method is frequently satisfactory, but in the end the tone that Heller sets for himself, of these brisk send-ups, weakens the book. He relies on keeping your attention shifting from absurdity to absurdity; but on the occasions when he focusses for a longer period on some central confrontation his stance shifts and the style seems to sag. There is a long passage where Nately, naive young patriot meets, in a brothel, an old Italian survivor, aged experience. The scene goes on for six pages; but it is limp. And with the demands of extended discussion the scene is repetitious and Heller's succinct paragraphs are dissipated in rather forced "home truths versus idealistic inexperience."

Near the end of the book Heller suddenly changes pace, and expands his style. The paragraphs become more sustained and the focus stays for longer on one incident. It is as if the evidence, the assemblage of facts has been completed and are at least brought to bear on Yossarian. The catalyst for this development is death. Nately dies. Dunbar, his close ally is "disappeared" by the CID. In a nightmare that is half a ferocious parody of the guts scenes in other war books Yossarian finally remembers fully the death of his flying companion Snowden, after he had bandaged up the wrong wound. Heller is more interested in the results of death on Yossarian than on the actual disasters themselves. They remain contained in the ironic narrative:

> He studied every floating object . . . prepared for any morbid shock but the shock McWatt gave him one day with the plane that came blasting suddenly into sight out of the distant stillness and hurtled mercilessly along the shore line with a great growling clattering roar over the bobbing raft on which blonde pale Kid Sampson his naked sides scrawny from even so far away leaped clownishly up to touch it at the exact moment some arbitrary gust of wind or minor miscalculation of McWatt's senses dropped the speeding plane down just low enough for a propeller to slice him half away.

McWatt flies off and:

> a great choking moan tore from Yossarian's throat as McWatt turned again, dipped his wings once in salute, decided, oh, well, what the hell, and flew into a mountain.

> Captain Cathcart was so upset by the deaths of Kid Sampson and McWatt that he raised the missions to 65.

Death comes on the same wry sentence-end fall as many of his earlier humorous paragraphs. Yossarian informs Nately's whore of his death and through the last chapters she dogs him round Italy, trying to murder him as representative of the slaughtering soldiery. He refuses to fly more missions; to counteract incipient mass mutiny his commanding officers offer to fly him home on condition that he plays the role of a war hero. Yossarian first accepts and finally refuses. The book begins to expand outwards

from military into civil life and it becomes apparent that his satiric aim has moved off the exclusively military plane. This change of emphasis is indicated by a shift in rhetorical intensity. It is no longer the military condition but the human condition that Heller is treating; and in a long chapter entitled "The Eternal City" he works this theme. . . . (pp. 90-1)

Yossarian walks through the town, a spectator of horrors that mount in intensity. A dog being beaten, a boy being beaten, finally back in his own quarters he meets Sergeant Aarfy who has just thrown a whore through a window. Horrified, Yossarian remonstrates; the police will seize you, he cries. Aarfy remains calm. The crash of MP's thundering up the stairs is heard. Aarfy becomes nervous. They leap in and arrest Yossarian for being in Rome without leave papers. Back at the base he hears that Orr, a previous flying companion of his, presumed drowned after a crash, has in fact managed to float his raft through the straits of Gibraltar round to Sweden and escape into neutral internment. He makes a similar choice to flee, and goes jumping spryly out of the book, pursued vengefully by the female victim of the war, Nately's whore.

Thus the end of the book represents an expansion of the area in which They can louse Us up. The choice of the hero, pointedly a man of no nationality, is to escape. However, the crucial jump from the military absurdities and savageries to the final civilian sequence is a failure. The idiom and method remain the same. The cumulative effect of the book is one of the artful dodger suddenly released; but the release seems mechanical and the finale arbitrary. The fault lies in Heller's basic intention. I mentioned earlier the difficulty of distinguishing between the satiric and the parodic in the book. The fundamental weakness of *Catch-22* seems to be that it *remains* parody and never really becomes satire. If one takes satire to be the operation of exaggeration and ridicule from a basic exterior moral referent, and parody to be an exercise firmly anchored in the object parodied, the distinction can be made clearer. Heller provides no moral referent for his ridicule; and it is because of this that the end seems to be a mechanical termination. All the way through, his treatment is parodic: he is ridiculing the conventional idea of war in experience and literature; and ridiculing it not from a standpoint of moral protest outside these experiences, but within their own terms. He does not offer a new evaluation of mens' actions and motives in wartime so much as a serial parody of the circumstances of war, and, as I have tried to point out, the techniques at the service of this procedure are limited in range. Hence outside the military context he fails because he has left behind the only referents that have sustained his ridicule. There is no wider position from which he can satirise the civil as well as the military condition.

Significantly the most successful "generalised' passages in the book are the two trial scenes where the military context is employed and the civil implied, using the most popular artistic props of our age, a table, three prosecutors and a victim. (pp. 91-2)

I kept wondering why Heller did not attack the question of why the men at Pianosa were fighting and confined himself to how they were fighting. He would probably dismiss the question as irrelevant to the point of his book which was about men in war, not men in war against Fascism.

From his angle war is war, be it war against the Fascists or not. And those who overcome Catch-22 are entitled to evade or desert either conflict. It is a moral problem he never discusses satisfactorily, or deploys sufficiently in the imaginative context of his book. Funny as much [of *Catch-22*] was, this depressing feeling of omission remained. (p. 92)

Alex Cockburn, in a review of "Catch-22," in New Left Review, *No. 18, January-February, 1963, pp. 87-92.*

Norman Mailer

[This essay originally appeared in *Esquire,* July, 1963.]

[*Catch-22*] is an original. There's no book like it anyone has read. Yet it's maddening. It reminds one of a Jackson Pollock painting, eight feet high, twenty feet long. Like yard goods, one could cut it anywhere. One could take out a hundred pages anywhere from the middle of *Catch-22,* and not even the author could be certain they were gone. Yet the length and similarity of one page to another gives a curious meat-and-potatoes to the madness; building upon itself the book becomes substantial until the last fifty pages grow suddenly and surprisingly powerful, only to be marred by an ending over the last five pages which is hysterical, sentimental and well-eyed for Hollywood.

This is the skin of the reaction. If I were a major critic, it would be a virtuoso performance to write a definitive piece on *Catch-22.* It would take ten thousand words or more. Because Heller is carrying his reader on a more consistent voyage through Hell than any American writer before him (except Burroughs who has already made the trip and now sells choice seats in the auditorium), and so the analysis of Joseph H.'s Hell would require a discussion of other varieties of inferno and whether they do more than this author's tour.

Catch-22 is a nightmare about an American bomber squadron on a made-up island off Italy. Its hero is a bombardier named Yossarian who has flown fifty missions and wants out. On this premise are tattooed the events of the novel, fifty characters, two thousand frustrations (an average of four or five to the page) and one simple motif: more frustration. Yossarian's colonel wants to impress his general and so raises the number of missions to fifty-five. When the pilots have fifty-four, the figure is lifted to sixty. They are going for eighty by the time the book has been done. On the way every character goes through a routine *on every page* which is as formal as a little peasant figure in a folk dance. Back in school, we had a joke we used to repeat. It went:

> "Whom are you talking about?"
> "Herbert Hoover."
> "Never heard of him."
> "Herbert Hoover."
> "Who's he?"
> "He's the man you mentioned."
> "Never heard of Herbert Hoover."

So it went. So goes *Catch-22.* It's the rock and roll of novels. One finds its ancestor in Basic Training. We were ordered to have clean sheets for Saturday inspection. But one week we were given no clean sheets from the Post laundry so we slept on our mattress covers, which got dirty. After inspection, the platoon was restricted to quarters. "You didn't have clean sheets," our sergeant said.

"How could we have clean sheets if the clean sheets didn't come?"

"How do I know?" said the sergeant. "The regulations say you gotta have clean sheets."

"But we can't have clean sheets if there are no clean sheets."

"That," said the sergeant, "is tough shit."

Which is what *Catch-22* should have been called. The Army is a village of colliding bureaucracies whose colliding orders cook up impossibilities. Heller takes this one good joke and exploits it into two thousand variations of the same good joke, but in the act he somehow creates a rational vision of the modern world. Yet the crisis of reason is that it can no longer comprehend the modern world. Heller demonstrates that a rational man devoted to reason must arrive at the conclusion that either the world is made and he is the only sane man in it, or (and this is the weakness of *Catch-22*—it never explores this possibility) the sane man is not really sane because his rational propositions are without existential reason. (pp. 13-15)

[At one point in the novel,] there is a discussion about God.

> ". . . how much reverence can you have for a Supreme Being who finds it necessary to include such phenomena as phlegm and tooth decay in His divine system of creation . . . Why in the world did He ever create pain?"
>
> "Pain?" Lieutenant Scheisskopf's wife pounced upon the word victoriously. "Pain is a useful symptom. Pain is a warning to us of bodily dangers." . . .
>
> "Why couldn't He have used a doorbell instead to notify us, or one of His celestial choirs?"

Right there is planted the farthest advance of the flag of reason in his cosmology. Heller does not look for any answer, but there is an answer which might go that God gave us pain for the same reason the discovery of tranquilizers was undertaken by the Devil: if we have an immortal soul some of us come close to it only through pain. A season of sickness can be preferable to a flight from disease for it discourages the onrush of a death which begins in the center of oneself.

Give talent its due. *Catch-22* is the debut of a writer with merry gifts. Heller may yet become Gogol. But what makes one hesitate to call his first novel great or even major is that he has only grasped the inferior aspect of Hell. What is most unendurable is not the military world of total frustration so much as the midnight frustration of the half world, Baldwin's other country, where a man may have time to hear his soul, and time to go deaf, even be forced to contemplate himself as he becomes deadened before his death. (Much as Hemingway may have been.) That is when one becomes aware of the anguish, the existential *Angst,* which wars enable one to forget. It is that other death—without war—where one dies by a failure of nerve, which opens the bloodiest vents of Hell. And that is a novel none of us has yet come back alive to write. (pp. 15-16)

Norman Mailer, "Some Children of the Goddess," in Contemporary American Novelists, *edited by Harry T. Moore, Southern Illinois University Press, 1964, pp. 3-31.*

Victor J. Milne

Most recent studies of *Catch-22* share the assumptions that the novel presents the world as absurd and chaotic, and that Yossarian's desertion reflects the currently widespread sentiment in favor of dropping out of a mad society. Thus Yossarian has been variously presented as an idealistic "puer eternis" who "refuses the traditional journey of learning in manhood," [see Pinsker, Further Reading list] and as the traditional comic rougue-figure who "never tries to change the society that he scorns." Although most critics are agreed on these points, their evaluative judgments run through the whole spectrum from laudatory to condemnatory, and the majority of them register some uneasiness about the moral perspective which they impute to Heller. (p. 50)

The intention of the present study is to substitute for these opinions a new and more positive interpretation of Heller's ethical and metaphysical perspective, and in so doing to justify the formal peculiarities of the novel as appropriate to the author's vision. At the root of the dissatisfaction with *Catch-22* lies a failure to recognize its epic inspiration, which not only explains its digressive structure but also constitutes the vehicle for Heller's moral vision. *Catch-22* uses the mock-epic form to dramatize a clash between two opposing moralities. The one ethic, exemplified by Yossarian, is a Christian ethic of universal benevolence, which, as the symbolic importance of Sweden suggests, expresses itself economically in terms of socialism and politically in terms of non-repressive government. The conflicting outlook, which will be referred to as the competitive ethic, is associated with capitalism, false patriotism, and the heroic code of the true epic and is exemplified by Colonel Cathcart and the other villains. The conflict between the two codes inevitably raises a second question: how is the man of good will to succeed or even survive in dealing with the unscrupulous adherents of the competitive ethic? Yossarian's desertion, seen in the context of the symbolism of the novel and the explicitly theological language of the last chapter, attempts to answer that question. The answer is a religious one, which is in harmony with classical Protestant doctrine, and which is most readily explicated in terms of the ethical teaching of a great modern theologian—Dietrich Bonhoeffer.

The parody of the epic is most apparent in the plot of *Catch-22,* which offers notable parallels to the *Iliad.* When Yossarian refuses to fly any more missions and marches "backward with his gun on his hip," Colonel Korn inquires, "Who does he think he is—Achilles?" Although this seems to be the only occasion in the novel on which explicit reference is made to the *Iliad,* it is sufficient to remind the reader that Yossarian's situation is identical with that of Achilles. Let us review briefly the relevant facts about the *Iliad.* The "argument" of the epic is not the fall of Troy but the wrath of Achilles, and the main plot is concerned with the efforts of the Greeks to bring Achilles back into battle, just as the main plot of *Catch-22* is concerned with the pressures put on Yossarian to fly more combat missions. The *Iliad* begins *in medias res* with the bitter quarrel between Achilles and Agamemnon, in which Achilles berates his commander for much the same flaws that are most prominent in Colonel Cathcart—acquisitiveness and cowardice. Achilles retires to his quarters to sulk, his friend Patroclus voluntarily goes into battle, and his death precipitates Achilles' reconciliation with Agamemnon, his return to battle, and consequently his death.

If *Catch-22* is carefully examined, it will be found to present a close parallel to these events. The novel opens *in medias res* at the point where Yossarian has "made up his mind to spend the rest of the war in the hospital." Nately serves as the Patroclus-figure, and since the novel provides a mirror-image of the values of the epic—that is, everything is seen in reverse, Nately's death precipitates Yossarian's firm resolve to fly no more combat missions. Paradoxically, this results in a reconciliation between Yossarian and Cathcart when Yossarian accepts the "odious" deal whereby he is to be sent home transformed into a hero for purposes of public relations. (A minor parallel is that both commanders are incompetent blusterers and must rely on their shrewd subordinates—Ulysses and Korn—to win over the recalcitrant warriors.) Yet the novel cannot end at this point, and the crisis of decision is repeated in Chapter Forty-One where Nately's place is taken by all of Yossarian's dead pals, and Yossarian tells Danby that he intends to break the odious deal.

From the foregoing account, Heller's novel is obviously far from a detailed reworking of an ancient legend. Inevitably, in accommodating the plot of the *Iliad* to a modern military situation, Heller has made considerable changes. . . . The only important change is dictated by Heller's need to make the plot of the *Iliad* serve his own moral vision. There must be two crises of decision in order to present Yossarian's flight to Sweden as an act of heroism and responsibility rather than of cowardice. Yossarian is free to choose the odious deal but does not, and Heller clearly indicates that his decision is motivated largely by loyalty to his dead friends: "Goddammit, Danby. I've got friends who were killed in this war. I can't make a deal now." The morally responsible nature of Yossarian's desertion is further underscored by Yossarian's allusion to a well-known biblical paradox when he tells Danby that the odious deal is not a way to save himself but a way to lose himself.

As well as parodying the plot of the *Iliad,* Heller makes use of some of the generic devices of the epic form. A characteristic feature is the digressive amplitude of the narrative, which confers the liberty of developing minor characters far more fully than their roles in the plot require. Several critics have been troubled by this violation of the strictest canons of structural unity in *Catch-22.* Yet the digressions make an essential contribution to the texture of the novel and the epic. In the *Iliad* an undertone of universal pathos is built up by the accumulated effect of the structurally irrelevant descriptions of the heroes' homelands and of the ways in which they came to join the Achaian host, and the end result is that the epic achieves cosmic significance. Heller, too, uses digressions to give his work a universal frame of reference so that war is treated not so much as a problem in its own right but rather as a symbol of the plight of modern western civilization, and this he accomplishes with a fine blend of pathos and comedy, appropriate to his mock-epic form, as, for example, in the digression on Major Major's upbringing and his induction into the army. (pp. 51-4)

George Steiner holds that the *Iliad* is the prototype of all tragedy, and he affirms that the essence of tragedy is doubt about the rationality and justice of the universe, an assertion "that the forces which shape or destroy our lives lie outside the governance of reason." The *Iliad* taken as a whole may be said to pose this root question of theodicy and to hint at a despairing answer, but none of the characters in the epic ever engages in such radical questioning. In this respect Yossarian goes beyond Achilles to become Job: "Good God, how much reverence can you have for a Supreme Being who finds it necessary to include such phenomena as phlegm and tooth decay in His divine system of creation." The question of the justice of the universe runs like a black thread through the novel, sometimes hyperbolically bitter as above, sometimes unrelievedly tragic, and sometimes transmuted into comedy as when one of the hospital patients observes: "There just doesn't seem to be any logic to this system of rewards and punishment. . . . Who can explain malaria as a consequence of fornication?" In *Catch-22* the tragic questioning of God's ways to men is prompted above all by the war, by the pointless extinction of one human life after another:

> Kraft was a skinny harmless kid from Pennsylvania who wanted only to be liked, and was destined to be disappointed in even so humble and degrading an ambition. Instead of being liked, he was dead. . . . He had lived innocuously for a little while and then had gone down in flame over Ferrara on the seventh day, while God was resting. . . .

Homer's tragedy is intensified because the Olympian gods provide "a comic background to the tragedy below." For example, Ares' complaint to Zeus when he is lightly wounded by Diomedes is comically outrageous in its insignificance following a battle in which scores of warriors stoically accepted death. In *Catch-22* the equivalent comedy is provided by the upper echelons of the military, who are safe from the dangers of combat, and who at all times act as though they had no share in mortality. Just as the gods urge whole armies into battle and doom certain men to death, all the while quarrelling jealously among themselves, so the headquarters staff in *Catch-22,* in the midst of their scramble for status, deliver pep talks and issue the orders that doom men like Nately to an unnecessary death. (pp. 54-5)

One other illuminating parallel between these two literary universes may be developed. Although all the other gods tremble at the words of Zeus almost as much as Colonel Cathcart does at the frown of General Dreedle, neither Zeus nor the Gods as a whole are supreme in the universe. They themselves must submit to the decrees of the *Moirai,* the impersonal fates that rule the cosmos. In the same way, Dreedle, Peckem, Cathcart, Korn and the rest do not really run the microcosm of Pianosa but merely ratify the decrees of Milo Minderbinder and ex-Pfc Wintergreen. As Colonel Korn explains in a moment of self-revelation, he and the other non-combatant officers are all helpless victims of the competitive ethic: "Everyone teaches us to as-

pire to higher things, a general is higher than a colonel, and a colonel is higher than a lieutenant-colonel. So we're both aspiring." The competitive ethic is the law decreed by omnipotent capitalism, personified in Milo Minderbinder, who, as his very name indicates, has the power to shackle thought and decent human feelings, and who, Heller makes plain, is to be conceived of as the supreme deity of this insane world: "Milo was the corn god, the rain god and the rice god in backward regions where such crude gods were still worshipped, and deep inside the jungles of Africa, he intimated with becoming modesty, large graven images of his mustached face could be found overlooking primitive stone altars red with human blood." Of course, from a Christian point of view the pagan gods are no more than devils, and Milo, whose "argosies . . . filled the air," does indeed represent the prince of the powers of the air. As we shall soon see, he is elsewhere unmistakably identified with Satan.

Heller, then, uses the mock-epic form to reject the pre-Christian (and sub-Christian) values of the military-economic complex, whose competitive ethic is another manifestation of the ancient heroic code. Yossarian, a twentieth-century man with a Christian attitude to the sanctity of human life, finds himself—up to the last chapter—plunged into the indifferent pre-Christian universe of the primary epic. . . . Whereas the warriors of the *Iliad* submit stoically to sudden death, Yossarian resolves "to live forever or die in the attempt." Whereas they chiefly prize fame won in battle, Yossarian answers with a negative Colonel Korn's question: "Don't you want to earn more unit citations and more oak leaf clusters for your air medal?" Yossarian categorically rejects the heroic code in his talk, but the definitive disavowal of these outworn values comes in the act of desertion. Thus above all else, the conflict between the competitive ethic and the humanistic Christian ethic determines the literary form of the novel as a "Bologniad," as a mock-epic embellished with comedy and horror, in which a modern Achilles says "baloney" to the demands of a corrupt society with its iniquitous heroic code requiring the sacrifice of human lives.

For the very reason that Yossarian opposes himself to the competitive ethic and its attendant heroic code we cannot view him as the traditional rogue figure who delights us by his impudent, self-centered indifference to conventional morality. Although he is concerned with his personal safety, he wants to save his life in both senses of the phrase. We have observed that Heller makes every effort to show that the desertion is a responsible, moral act; to this we must now add that he is not inconsistent in drawing attention to the moral perplexities involved in Yossarian's choice. . . . [Yossarian] is faced with a choice between two incompatible relative goods—a patriotism that is justifiable because his country is engaged in a just war and a rebellion against an inhumane system of exploitation, whereby Cathcart and Korn enjoy their meaningless triumphs of egotism at the expense of men's lives. The opposition between the two goods means that each good has an evil inseparably annexed to it. Rebellion against the American system of exploitation involves abandonment of the struggle against the inhumanity of the Nazi state; support of the American war effort entails supporting the evil system and being disloyal to the friends who have suffered under it. Although Heller leaves no doubt that the American system, which gives so much scope to the petty oppressors, is still a lesser evil than the frank tyranny of the Nazis, we are made to feel in the course of the novel that Yossarian must take a stand against the exploitation that confronts him. (pp. 55-8)

If Heller had implied that the question of an Allied victory in World War II was morally neutral, we should have despised such a shallow view of human affairs, and the lack of dramatic tension in Yossarian's choice would have rendered the novel boring. . . . Although the novel needs no defence beyond a demonstration that Heller has dealt faithfully with the moral complexities of his hero's situation, the recognition of the paradox inevitably does prompt the question whether there is a resolution within the novel. There is some evidence of such a resolution, and to understand it we must examine the theological background of the novel—particularly, the concept of guilt. (pp. 58-9)

From a theological viewpoint the novel presents exploitation and submission to exploitation as the two great sins. Exploitation, however, need not involve the imposition of physical hardships; it is better defined in Erich Fromm's phrase as "the reification of man." Thus Milo, viewing the men only as a market to be manipulated, exploits them fully as much in providing broiled Maine lobster as in trying to introduce chocolate-coated cotton to the menu. It is in this sense—the denial of humanity—that Milo, or capitalism, requires human sacrifice. The political system, as much as the market place, encourages the process of reification, and it is particularly noticeable in the idealists, Clevinger and Danby. Even though their actions are externally indistinguishable from those of men who have responsibly decided to serve a cause, they have, in fact, reified themselves in accepting the notion that their value resides only in their utility as cogs in the war-machine. The soldier in white, who functions only as part of a pipeline between two glass jars, and of whom life can be predicated only on the basis of a thermometer reading, is the perfect symbol of the reification of man. Yossarian, then, in insisting upon the unique value of his individual life, constitutes a focal point of resistance to exploitation. Milo and Colonel Korn both recognize his importance and treat him as the bellwether whom the rest of the flock will follow. If Yossarian will allow himself to be used in any way, even in accepting the odious deal, none of the others will refuse to fly combat missions.

In stripping off his clothes Yossarian is trying to deny his complicity in the evils of the world. However, in the chapter entitled "The Eternal City"—let us note in passing that Rome is the "Babylon" of the Book of Revelation, the epitome of the worldly lust for pomp and power—Yossarian acknowledges the guilt that he shares with the rest of humanity: . . .

> Yossarian thought he knew why Nately's whore held him responsible for Nately's death and wanted to kill him. Why the hell shouldn't she? It was a man's world, and she and everyone younger had every right to blame him and everyone older for every unnatural tragedy that befell them; just as she, even in her grief, was to blame for every man-made misery that landed on her kid sister, and on all other children behind her. Someone had to do something sometime. Every victim was a culprit, every culprit a victim, and someone had to stand

up sometime to try to break the lousy chain of inherited habit that was imperiling them all.

In this passage there is (in addition to a modern redefinition of original sin) a significant explanation for the puzzling attacks of Nately's whore: hers is the role of an accuser, almost a comic equivalent of the Eumenides. Interestingly enough, she succeeds only once in stabbing Yossarian, immediately after he commits his one unequivocally loathsome action in agreeing to the odious deal. Her attack is obviously the incident which jolts Yossarian into rejecting the deal: "Goddammit, Danby. I've got friends who were killed in this war. I can't make a deal now. Getting stabbed by that bitch was the best thing that ever happened to me." Thus Nately's whore is to be viewed in the latter part of the novel as an allegorical projection of Yossarian's own conscience, which will not let him come to terms with any form of exploitation.

At this point the moral dilemma of the novel is posed in its acutest form. If Yossarian were to accept the deal, he would be guilty towards his friends, who have been exploited by Milo and Cathcart. If he were to desert he would be guilty towards his country and the just cause in which it is engaged. If he were neither to accept the deal nor to desert, he would face a court-martial on trumped-up charges. A superficial application of Christian ethics would suggest that Yossarian could escape guilt by staying to face the false accusation. However, Yossarian's suffering could have no redemptive value for the other victims since, as Danby points out, all without exception will believe the charges. Yossarian's situation raises in a peculiarly acute form the question of passive suffering as against active resistance. By offering himself as a victim, by trying to keep his conscience spotless, Yossarian would really be helping the powerful exploiters of humanity. In other words, excessive scrupulosity can be dangerous, for it can too easily reconcile hope for social justice with a passive submission to the bluff of the authorities that "Catch-22" says "they have a right to do anything we can't stop them from doing." Thus Yossarian's decision to desert enacts Heller's ethical judgment that an individual has no right to submit to injustice when his action will help to maintain an unjust system, for the desertion is a positive moral act calculated to discomfort the exploiters, whereas facing the court-martial would represent a paralysis of the will, a desire to maintain purity of conscience at the cost of inaction.

To understand the problem more clearly and Heller's resolution of it, we must examine two subordinate characters, Chaplain Tappman and Major Major. So far as *Catch-22* can be allegorized, we may say that these two represent the Christian virtues as popularly conceived and in particular the disabling "virtue" of excessive scrupulosity. They are both men of good will, and they both submit patiently to all the indignities thrust upon them. Major Major, especially, is characterized by his adherence to the Decalogue and the moral teachings of Christ:

> He turned the other cheek on every occasion and always did unto others exactly as he would have had others do unto him. When he gave to charity, his left hand never knew what his right hand was doing. He never once took the name of the Lord his God in vain, committed adultery or coveted his neighbour's ass. In fact, he loved his neighbour and never even bore false witness against him.

The result of such characteristics is that Major Major and the chaplain are both exiled from human society and become ineffectual hermits unable to influence the world for good or evil. This is the price exacted by excessive concern with purity of conscience; one can avoid evil but cannot do good: "The chaplain was a sincerely helpful man who was never able to help anyone . . . ". In fact, the chaplain has become so paralyzed by his undeniable virtues that at the end of the novel Yossarian must urge him: "For once in your life, succeed at something." (pp. 59-62)

Catch-22 has seemed inconsistent to a number of critics because the theological substructure of the novel is in full accord with the paradoxical insights of classical Protestant thought. On the one hand, Protestant doctrine recognizes the sinfulness of all human endeavour, and on the other hand, it refuses to be seduced into ignoring the imperfect world of becoming in favour of the perfect world of being. On the contrary, Protestant theology insists on activism even though sin inevitably results; the principle is enshrined in Luther's startling maxim, *pecca fortiter*—sin resolutely. The same notion is expounded more thoroughly in a modern Protestant classic, Dietrich Bonhoeffer's *Letters and Papers from Prison,* a work which may be profitably read in conjunction with *Catch-22* as it also comes out of World War II and shows a remarkable affinity in temper to Heller's novel. (pp. 63-4)

It would be impossible to summarize Bonhoeffer's complex doctrine of responsibility which forms the core of his ethical thought. Basically, we may say that responsibility involves an acceptance of the need to relate all moral action to the concrete situation of mingled good and evil, and thus it is opposed to a Kantian affirmation of abstract ethical demands which are to be practised universally without regard to the concrete situation. Yossarian recognizes that he must make his choice in the real situation which offers only relative good and relative evil. Any choice will involve sinning against some abstract ethical principle. And according to Bonhoeffer's doctrine a choice such as Yossarian's is justified by God even if the greater evil is unintentionally chosen, for "if any man attempts to escape guilt in responsibility, he detaches himself from the ultimate reality of human existence" and "sets his own personal innocence above his responsibility for men." Yossarian, then, is the responsible man, in Bonhoeffer's sense, while Clevinger and Danby in their arguments with Yossarian show themselves to be Kantians who cannot understand his reluctance to affirm that an ethical abstraction must be honoured at all times and at all places and under all conditions.

Our theological perspective can be completed only by a consideration of the God of *Catch-22,* the true God who stands in opposition to Milo Minderbinder's demonic claims. One persistent motif in the narrative is the chaplain's progressive loss of faith in God. Like Yossarian the chaplain is led by the spectacle of meaningless death to question the justice of the universe, and after his failure to dissuade Colonel Cathcart from raising the required number of missions, he is ready to disbelieve "in the wisdom and justice of an immortal, omnipotent, omniscient, humane, universal, anthropomorphic, English-speaking, Anglo-Saxon, pro-American God." Why should he believe in such a God? This God has based his reputation on his abilities as a benevolent stage-magician who will always intervene on behalf of a right-thinking, humane Anglo-Saxon, but "there were no miracles; prayers went unanswered, and misfortune tramped with equal brutality on the virtuous and the corrupt." The chaplain's "atheism" may be regarded as an essential preliminary condition of true faith; he must reject the anthropomorphic idol invented to ratify the pretensions and prejudices of a particular culture if he is ever to believe in the mysterious Biblical God who impartially distributes temporal blessings and misfortunes. (pp. 64-5)

[The] chaplain never wholly loses faith in God but only in the man-made idol, and when the time comes, he is given a new revelation. The chaplain has rejected the stage-miracles of religious tradition, but he discovers that there is a different kind of miracle. When news of Orr's safe arrival in Sweden reaches Pianosa, he exclaims: "It's a miracle, I tell you! A miracle! I believe in God again." Orr's escape has a quite obvious religious significance, for seen in a theological context, his crash-landing in the Adriatic is a symbolic baptism and the sudden news of his safety gives the whole episode the quality of resurrection following death—a miraculous reversal of the seemingly irrevocable catastrophe.

Orr is an important figure but remains enigmatic up to the last chapter of the novel. To Yossarian he seems a comic figure, a sucker, the prototypal victim of all the forms of exploitation that Yossarian himself protests against. To him Orr is "a freakish, likeable dwarf with . . . a thousand valuable skills that would keep him in a low income group all his life," and he is convinced that Orr needs to be shielded "against animosity and deceit, against people with ambition and the embittered snobbery of the big shot's wife, against the squalid, corrupting indignities of the profit motive and the friendly neighbourhood butcher with inferior meat." Yossarian is wrong, of course, because, though seeing the qualities that lie behind Orr's apparent innocence, he does not understand their value. Orr is self-reliant ("a thousand valuable skills"), patient, enduring ("oblivious to fatigue"), and adaptable ("not afraid . . . of foods like scrod or tripe"). Above all, Orr is a doer rather than a contemplative like the chaplain, and he is admirably equipped to survive. The imagery identifies Orr closely with the natural world—he is "a gnome," "a dwarf," "as oblivious to fatigue as the stump of a tree" and has "an uncanny knowledge of wildlife." He may be seen as a mischievous and resilient earth-spirit like Puck or as the true embodiment of the seemingly naive but really shrewd and self-reliant archetypal Yankee farmer, of whom Major Major's father is a ludicrous parody. In any case, Orr is the personification of the qualities of intelligence and endurance which make possible the survival of humanity under the worst conditions of oppression and exploitation. While the chaplain engages in futile efforts to reason with Colonel Cathcart, while Yossarian carries on a futile and dangerous revolt, Orr quietly practises the skills that will ensure his survival. Only after Orr has acted can Yossarian grasp the possibility of escape that was and still is open to him, and then he realizes that he must imitate Orr in being "as wise as serpents and harmless as doves." . . . (pp. 65-7)

Throughout the novel, Yossarian, for all the verbal energy displayed in his revolt, has been paralyzed by his moral quandary. In the Snowden episode he was an impotent

laughed at the novel's "absurdities" but who came to look back with horror at what they were laughing at. This confirms that the novel's repetitions are the key to its meaning. Heller once said that he meant to expose "the contemporary regimented business society," and he does just that in his brilliant satiric caricatures of the senior officers, representative professional and business figures, and such remarkable examples of the capitalistic spirit as Milo and ex-P.F.C. Wintergreen. Yet Heller's portrait of this world did not require the elaborate system of repetitions that underlies the novel's complex structure. Heller added this feature because he wanted to make his crucial point about widespread complicity in the regimented business society. He wanted people to laugh and then look back with horror at what they were laughing at. They had to recoil from the *same* events they first laughed at because otherwise they might be tempted to trace the novel's darkening tone to changing circumstances within the fiction. Heller could not permit this, for it is essential to his argument that the world of *Catch-22* has *always* been what it is only belatedly perceived to be. By rendering the same events in such radically different ways, Heller encourages people to see that their problems involve more than life's destructive circumstances. Even more crucial is their failure to recognize these circumstances for what they are and to act accordingly. This is why one of the funniest of all novels is finally not very funny at all, for Heller arrests his reader's laughter and exposes the complacent beliefs he has shared with Yossarian.

Indeed, the greatness of *Catch-22* lies in Heller's ability to convert the tenets of a conventional liberalism into the informing ideas of a powerfully moving fable. Like such novelists as Theodore Dreiser, John Steinbeck, and Richard Wright, Heller dramatizes the crippling effects of modern society on the sensitive individual as in his portraits of Yossarian, Dunbar, the chaplain, Major Major, Clevinger, Nately, and Snowden. Yet he goes beyond his liberal predecessors to show that the enemy is not just the corporations and their authorities (in this case the military and its commanding officers). "They" are indeed amoral if not immoral; "they" are Korn, Black, Cathcart, Scheisskopf, Dreedle, Peckem, Aarfy, Wintergreen, and Milo. In a very real sense, however, M & M Enterprises is not the enemy, for someone like Milo only has the power he is allowed to have. As Pogo once remarked, memorably if ungrammatically, "we have met the enemy, and it is us." *Catch-22* is a masterful confirmation of Pogo's insight. (pp. 146-51)

> *Robert Merrill, "The Structure and Meaning of 'Catch-22'," in* Studies in American Fiction, *Vol. 14, No. 2, Autumn, 1986, pp. 139-52.*

FURTHER READING

Aldridge, John W. " 'Catch-22' Twenty-Five Years Later." *Michigan Quarterly Review* XXVI, No. 2 (Spring 1987): 397-86.

Overview of the critical response to *Catch-22*.

Blues, Thomas. "The Moral Structure of 'Catch-22'." *Studies in the Novel* III, No. 1 (Spring 1971): 64-79.

Evaluates Yossarian's dessertion at the conclusion of *Catch-22* in terms of the moral structure Heller has constructed throughout the novel.

Doskow, Minna. "The Night Journey in 'Catch-22'." *Twentieth Century Literature* 12, No. 4 (January 1967): 186-93.

Analyzes chapters 39-42 of *Catch-22* as a journey to the underworld analogous to that taken in such classic epics as *The Odyssey, The Aeneid,* and Dante's *Inferno.*

Goodwin, George. "The Pseudo-Victim." In his *The Poetics of Protest,* pp. 133-57. Carbondale and Edwardsville, Ill: Southern Illinois University Press, 1985.

Considers *Catch-22* a victim-of-society novel in which a pseudo-victim, Yossarian, exposes the vulnerabilities of the powerful military bureaucracy.

Gross, Beverly. " 'Insanity Is Contagious:' The Mad World of 'Catch-22'." *The Centennial Review* XXVI, No. 1 (Winter 1982): 86-113.

Defines and explores two antithetical forms of madness exhibited in *Catch-22.*

Kiley, Frederick and Walter McDonald. *A 'Catch-22' Casebook.* New York: Crowell, 1973, 403 p.

Selection of representative criticism including early reviews and analyses of form, structure, theme, and the relationship of *Catch-22* to Absurdist literature.

Meller, James M. "Heller's 'Catch-22'." In his *The Exploded Form: The Modernist Novel in America,* pp. 108-124. Urbana, Chicago, and London: University of Illinois Press, 1980.

Offers *Catch-22* as an illustration of several aspects of what Mellard terms the second phase of Modernism.

Merivale, P. " 'Catch-22' and 'The Secret Agent': Mechanical Man, the Hole in the Centre, and the 'Principle of Inbuilt Chaos'." *English Studies in Canada* VII, No. 4 (December 1981): 426-37.

Compares imagery, structure, and point of view in *Catch-22* and Joseph Conrad's *The Secret Agent.*

Merrill, Robert. *Joseph Heller.* Boston: Twayne Publishers, 1987, 153 p.

Surveys Heller's works as they reflect the themes and techniques utilized most successfully in *Catch-22.*

Nagel, James. *Critical Essays on Joseph Heller.* Boston: G. K. Hall, 1984, 253 p.

Anthology of criticism including essays by Kurt Vonnegut, Jr., Clive Barnes, and John W. Aldridge.

Perry, Nick. "Catch, Class and Bureaucracy: The Meaning of Joseph Heller's 'Catch-22'." *The Sociological Review* 32, No. 4 (November 1984): 719-41.

Sociological investigation of the source of the popularity of *Catch-22.*

Pinsker, Sanford. "Heller's 'Catch-22': The Protest of a 'Puer Eternis'." *Critique: Studies in Modern Fiction* VII, No. 2 (Winter 1964-65): 150-62.

Compares Yossarian to such literary figures as Ulysses, Tom Sawyer, and Holden Caulfield.

Pletcher, Robert C. "Overcoming the 'Catch-22' of Institutional Satire: Joseph Heller's 'Surrealistic' Characters." *Studies in Contemporary Satire* XV (1988): 20-7.

Analysis of Heller's satirical techniques in *Catch-22.*

Scotto, Robert M. *Three Contemporary Novelists: An Annotated Bibliography of Works by and about John Hawkes, Joseph Heller, and Thomas Pynchon.* New York and London: Garland Publishing, 1977, 97 p.

    First exhaustive Heller bibliography.

Seed, David. *The Fiction of Joseph Heller: Against the Grain.* London: Macmillan Press, 1989, 244 p.

    Surveys Heller's works from the early short stories to *Picture This* and explores their similarities.

Solomon, Jan. "The Structure of Joseph Heller's 'Catch-22'." *Critique* IX, No. 2 (1967): 46-57.

    Suggests that Heller's two main time schemes, focusing on Milo Minderbinder and Yossarian, create a structural absurdity that underlines his absurdist theme and technique.

Thomas, W. K. " 'What Difference Does It Make': Logic in 'Catch-22'." *Dalhousie Review* 50, No. 4 (Winter 1970-71): 488-495.

    Investigates Heller's use of illogic.

Elia Kazan

1909-

(Born Elia Kazanjioglou) Turkish-born American director, novelist, autobiographer, scriptwriter, and actor.

One of the most prominent and controversial filmmakers of the post-World War II era, Kazan is best known for his sensitive, astute direction of several of the most popular and critically acclaimed dramas and films of his time. In addition to receiving Tony Awards for his direction of Arthur Miller's plays *All My Sons* and *Death of a Salesman,* Kazan accepted Donaldson Awards for his productions of Tennessee Williams's plays *A Streetcar Named Desire* and *Cat on a Hot Tin Roof,* and Academy Awards for his films *Gentleman's Agreement* and *On the Waterfront.* Particularly noted for his skill in managing actors and producers, Kazan is credited with having developed many major acting talents, including Marlon Brando, Paul Newman, Geraldine Page, and James Dean. His plays and films usually feature strong, rebellious characters who affirm American values in their ability to overcome immense obstacles despite social or familial disapproval. Although his works have been variously faulted as opportunistic, sentimental, or polemical, Kazan is praised for his blend of social and psychological realism and for his strongly delineated characters. While Kazan's novels, written after he retired from directing in the early 1960s, have not garnered the critical praise of his theater productions, many of his books have attained wide popularity.

Born in Constantinople (now Istanbul) to an Anatolian Greek family living under tyrannical Turkish rule, Kazan was the son of a rug merchant who relocated to the United States and earned enough income to bring his family overseas just prior to World War I. After graduating from Williams College in Massachussetts in 1930, Kazan attended Yale Drama School but left after only two years to audition for the Group Theater in New York City. This prestigious troupe, led by Harold Clurman and Lee Strasbourg, included such notable playwrights and actors as Clifford Odets and Luther and Stella Adler. Although initially rejected, Kazan was admitted to the Group Theater in 1933 as a handyman and received the nickname "Gadg" or "Gadget" due to his ability to build and repair stage props and scenery. Gradually broadening his role in the Group, Kazan became a successful actor and learned the famous Stanislavski method, a technique in which actors connect a personal emotional experience with one to be simulated onstage.

In the mid-1930s, Kazan began directing plays for Broadway. Although his early productions attracted little notoriety, Kazan garnered acclaim in the 1940s beginning with Thornton Wilder's ambitious comedy *The Skin of Our Teeth.* This play, in which characters step in and out of their roles to personally address the audience, was lauded for its innovative staging techniques. Kazan established a reputation for dealing with controversial social problems for his direction of Arthur Miller's *All My Sons.* Two years later, Kazan again achieved high praise for his sensitive production of *Death of a Salesman,* another play by Ar-

thur Miller. Kazan began directing films in the mid-1940s. His first motion picture, *A Tree Grows in Brooklyn,* garnered accolades for its warm yet unsentimental portrayal of a sensitive young girl growing up in the slums of Brooklyn. Although Kazan's ensuing films of the 1940s are often regarded as conventional and complacent in their treatment of moral and social issues, he continued to be one of the few directors of this era to deal with volatile and controversial subjects, including anti-Semitism and racism, as evidenced in such films as *Gentleman's Agreement* and *Pinky. A Streetcar Named Desire,* a film adapted from Tennessee Williams's play, which Kazan had also directed on Broadway was his next major work. In this work, Kazan introduced a harsh yet poetic form of class-conscious realism to American cinema. Much of the film's success is attributed to Kazan's ability to combine the intense emotion of the Group Theater's celebrated method acting with the purely technical skill of traditional performance, which he believed to be characterized by "externally clear action, controlled every minute at every turn, with gestures spare yet eloquent."

In the early 1950s, Kazan and other members of the Group Theater were accused by Senator Joseph McCarthy and The House Un-American Activities Committee

(HUAC) of participating in a secret communist alliance. Called before the Committee in 1952, Kazan admitted to joining the American Communist Party in 1934 but claimed he had resigned in 1935 after refusing to comply with the decision of the Party's commissar, V. J. Jerome, that the Party take control of the Group Theater. Although Kazan initially refused to furnish HUAC with names, he later submitted, partially due to pressure from influential Hollywood producers who threatened his career. As a result of his presumed willingness to supply the Committee with the names of friends and associates in both Broadway and Hollywood, Kazan lost many friends, made many enemies, and was denounced by both the political left and right. Nonetheless, Kazan went on to direct many of his most highly acclaimed films and dramas. His next major film, *On the Waterfront,* is a collaborative effort written in association with Budd Schulberg, a Hollywood scriptwriter who also informed at the McCarthy hearings. Viewed by many as an apologia or vindication of the informer, *On the Waterfront* offers a realistic expose of union corruption and brutality on the New York harbor. Although several reviewers have faulted the film's political content as unconvincing, many concurred with A. H. Weiler, who called *On the Waterfront* "an uncommonly powerful, exciting and imaginative use of the screen by gifted professionals."

During the 1950s, Kazan also directed many of his most famous stage productions. These include Robert Anderson's *Tea and Sympathy,* Tennessee Williams's *Cat on a Hot Tin Roof,* and William Inge's *Dark at the Top of the Stairs.* In his later stage productions, including William's *Sweet Bird of Youth* and Miller's plays *After the Fall* and *Incident at Vichy,* Kazan attempted to create a more convincing sense of reality by eschewing the conventional staging and chronological arrangements of traditional drama in favor of disjointed shifts in time and place. Kazan's films of the 1950s subsequent to *On the Waterfront* also achieved consistent critical success. *East of Eden,* a classic of American cinema adapted from a portion of John Steinbeck's novel, garnered widespread praise for its lack of conventional melodrama and for Kazan's surrealistic use of sharply contrasted images. Kazan's ensuing films include *Baby Doll,* an erotic comedy by Tennessee Williams; *A Face in the Crowd,* a second collaboration with Schulberg; and *Splendor in the Grass,* a work adapted from William Inge's novel. Although Kazan stated he would not return to the cinema after retiring in the early 1960s, he directed *The Last Tycoon* in 1976, an adaptation of the uncompleted novel by F. Scott Fitzgerald.

Kazan initiated his career as a novelist with *America, America,* a work regarded by most critics as more an autobiographical vehicle for a screenplay than a novel. Set at the close of the nineteenth century, the book relates the story of Stavros Topouzoglou, a twenty-year-old Anatolian Greek living with his family under Turkish domination in Constantinople, who struggles to earn enough money to move to America. Nat Hentoff commented: "The language itself is uncommonly spare and exact, and the people who move in and out of Stavros' life are seen whole, however quickly." Kazan adapted the book, as well as his second novel, *The Arrangement,* for film in the mid-1960s. The latter work concerns a successful, middle-aged advertising executive who devises cigarette advertising campaigns and secretly writes social protest articles to relieve his guilt. After becoming involved with a beautiful, intelligent woman, he realizes he can no longer tolerate "the arrangement," the artificial web of social lies that constitute success. In *The Assassins,* a Mexican sergeant in the United States Air Force is unjustly acquitted for murdering a hippie drug dealer who seduced his daughter. While the novel was faulted by critics for its presumed lack of focus, inconsistent examination of moral issues, and use of stock characters, *The Assassins* achieved popular success.

In his next book, *The Understudy,* Kazan focuses on Sonny, a successful but undistinguished actor who had studied under Sidney Castleman, an older thespian whose popularity has waned. Sonny travels to Africa in an attempt to resolve his guilt over agreeing to ban Sidney from any further roles in his pictures due to the older man's unprofessional behavior. In *Acts of Love,* a spoiled woman taught to be "nothing more than a household pet" becomes disenchanted with her husband, a Navy officer, after realizing that he cannot tell her how to live her life. As a result, she becomes involved in a platonic relationship with her husband's father, a chauvinistic, old-world Greek American who convinces her to bear him a grandson. *The Anatolian,* a sequel to Kazan's first novel, *America, America,* focuses on Greek immigrant Stavros from 1909 to 1919. A poorly paid salesman for a New York rug merchant, Stavros brings his family to America and begins his own business while pursuing a beautiful, educated woman whom he hopes will enable him to ascend in American society. Christopher Lehmann-Haupt called the novel "the author's most accomplished work to date," and Eliot Wagner asserted: "[When] Elia Kazan is true to his dark vision of American immigrant life, which he is most of the way through *The Anatolian,* this is a vigorous and affecting novel."

In addition to his fiction, Kazan has also published a controversial autobiography, *Elia Kazan: A Life.* Written in a colloquial style, this book generated extensive commentary and controversy concerning Kazan's revealing descriptions of illicit love affairs and his HUAC testimony. Although some critics faulted the book as sensational, manipulative, or egotistical, many praised *A Life* for its insights into mid-century theater and for Kazan's comments on such figures as John Steinbeck, Budd Schulberg, and Thornton Wilder.

(See also *CLC,* Vols. 6, 16 and *Contemporary Authors,* Vols. 21-24, rev. ed.)

PRINCIPAL WORKS

PLAYS (DIRECTOR)

The Young Go First (with Alfred Saxe) 1935
Casey Jones 1938
Thunder Rock 1939
Cafe Crown 1942
The Skin of Our Teeth 1942
The Strings, My Lord, Are False 1942
Harriet 1943
It's Up To You 1943
One Touch of Venus 1943
Jacobowsky and the Colonel 1944

Deep Are the Roots   1945
Dunningan's Daughter   1945
All My Sons   1947
A Streetcar Named Desire   1947
Truck-line Cafe   1947
Love Life   1948
Sundown Beach   1948
Death of a Salesman   1949
Point of No Return   1951
Flight into Egypt   1952
Camino Real   1953
Tea and Sympathy   1953
Cat on a Hot Tin Roof   1955
The Dark at the Top of the Stairs   1957
J. B.   1958
Sweet Bird of Youth   1959
After the Fall   1964
But For Whom, Charlie   1964
The Changeling   1964
Incident at Vichy   1964
Marco Millions   1964

FILMS (DIRECTOR)

A Tree Grows in Brooklyn   1945
Boomerang!   1947
Gentleman's Agreement   1947
Sea of Grass   1947
Pinky   1949
Panic in the Streets   1950
A Streetcar Named Desire   1951
Viva Zapata!   1952
Man on a Tightrope   1953
On The Waterfront   1954
East of Eden   1955
Baby Doll   1956
A Face in the Crowd   1957
Wild River   1960
Splendor in the Grass   1961
**America, America*   1964; produced in Great Britain as
   The Anatolian Smile
**The Arrangement*   1969
The Visitors   1972
The Last Tycoon   1976

NOVELS

***America, America*   1962
***The Arrangement*   1967
***The Assassins*   1972
***The Understudy*   1974
Acts of Love   1978
The Anatolian   1982

AUTOBIOGRAPHY

Elia Kazan: A Life   1988

*Kazan also wrote the screenplays for these films, which were adapt-
   ed from his novels of the same titles.

**Portions of these novels, as well as two of Kazan's essays on film
   direction, were published in *A Kazan Reader,* 1977.

[The following entry presents criticism on Kazan's prose

works. For discussions of his complete career, see CLC,
Vols. 6, 16.]

Nat Hentoff

Elia Kazan has written his first book [*America America*],
and although it is now too late, the best I could have
wished for this arrestingly zany story is that it not fall into
the hands of Elia Kazan, the director. In this latter function, Kazan has become a chronic italicizer, twisting the
rhythms of the writer's language and characters into vivid
distortion. In his own scenario—and in form, this sinewy
odyssey is more a screenplay than a novel—Kazan's inexorable tempo is unhampered by contrived showmanship.

The tale set at the end of the 19th century, is that of
Stavros, a 20-year-old Greek who is obsessed with the
promise of America. In his bruising journey from his
home in Turkey to Constantinople and finally to America,
Stavros is toughened into a manic pragmatist. . . .

Kazan's incisively unsentimental exploration of the nature
of survival when the odds are toweringly negative achieves
its considerable cumulative power because of his remarkably distilled writing style. It is not only that every line in
the book is part of an action or leads directly to an act. The
language itself is uncommonly spare and exact, and the
people who move in and out of Stavros' life are seen whole,
however quickly. In a few early pages, for example, Kazan
makes chillingly immediate the core of terror and self-
corrosion in the Greeks of Turkey who endured their
overlords.

The pervasive tone of *America, America* is essentially
bleak. ("I have one idea for this world," says a doomed
humanist. "Destroy it and start over again. There's too
much dirt for a broom. It calls for a fire. It needs the
flood.") Nonetheless the book is also infused with regret
at what we could, but do not, become. Kazan, moreover,
does not indict all those who have become acclimated to
the world as it is. His evocation of the close family life of
a rich Constantinople rug dealer, for instance, succeeds in
making these particular domestic values almost palpably
comforting, even though they are not for Stavros.

There are other moments of hopeful softness in Stavros
himself and in those he meets; and while the book ends in
America with Stavros fitting all too well into the syn-
drome of acquisitive upper mobility, there is a stinging
recognition of what Stavros has lost in his migration to
manhood and to a land in which he had once hoped to "be
washed clean." . . .

I hope Mr. Kazan continues his writing, and tells us, for
one thing, what if anything Stavros will salvage from his
American "success," which is sure to come.

*Nat Hentoff, "Sinewy Odyssey to the Promised
Land," in* Books, New York, November 11,
1962, p. 4.

Herbert Mitgang

Elia Kazan, in **America, America,** has written and directed his own first book. He has chosen an important theme—the effort of a Greek youth to escape the poverty and persecution of Turkey, just before the turn of the century, and get to the United States by hook or crook. It is the story of the 20th-century immigrant, tagged and bundled, dreaming of the golden door. . . . , as underdog people (including some already here) still envision America.

The noted stage and screen director, following his bent, tells his story in pictorial and violent ways. The director overwhelms the writer in **America, America.** This accounts for the unusual form in which Mr. Kazan has written. Although there are no camera directions, the novel closely resembles an original screen "treatment." To call this a new form would be to conceal the fact that the book, is, in fact, the basis for a film the author is directing.

Yet **America, America** is not a non-book. It is (though without the novelist's grace) similar to Arthur Miller's book version of *The Misfits.* What Miller said in the preface of his book applies here: "It is a story conceived as a film, and every word is there for the purpose of telling the camera what to see and the actors what they are to say."

Elia Kazan knows how to pack emotion into a storyline, regardless of form, and he keeps **America, America** moving quickly. In rapid succession "we see" (a phrase repeated in the book) Turks stealing from Greeks, an Armenian church burned, shooting and stabbing, robbery and murder, mayhem in inns and belly dances by prostitutes. All these are "used" by the author—in flicking scenes with the in-and-out thrust of drama—to depict the obstacles on the road to America.

The emphasis on action dominates the story. The 20-year-old Joe Stavros is a tough egg, but Mr. Kazan makes the reader root for him. Other stark characters, from members of the family to various rug dealers, rich and poor along the way, play appointed roles. Characters are secondary to the scenes, and some of these scenes are purely theatrical and often unbelievable—such as the one where Stavros' grandmother (testing his mettle) dares the youth to stab her.

Still, this story of one man's migration to America has tension, structure and an admirable purpose. And that old line has relevance: it should be quite a movie.

> *Herbert Mitgang, "Immigrant in the Camera's Eye," in* The New York Times Book Review, *November 18, 1962, p. 66.*

William James Smith

"Gadg, baby, you're a nigger, too." So says James Baldwin in a jacket "puff" for Elia Kazan's scenario-novel [**America, America**] about a turn-of-the-century Armenian immigrant boy. The Honorable Robert F. Kennedy couldn't put it down. Nobel Prize-winner John Steinbeck found it EXTREMELY interesting and Archibald MacLeish EXCITING. Several other notables, including President A. Whitney Griswold of Yale University, contribute similar words of praise. Surely men of their stature can not

have been suborned. Besides, the book *is* good and the motion picture which Gadg envisions will be a splendid one indeed if ever he does direct it.

Whether the picture will ever be made is another matter. The scenario is not exactly box office material. The love story is not of a boy for a girl but of a boy for a country, one which he has never seen, at that. Stavros Topouzoglou is a twenty-year-old Armenian boy living with his family in terror of their Turkish rulers. His father has settled for bribing his way to some sort of precarious safety, but Stavros, once he has been the futility of insurrection, dreams only of the New World and its soaring towers. He is all innocence and servility and deprecating smiles, but a core of fanatic determination burns within him. He must get to America. No labor, no compromise, no betrayal of others or of himself is too great if he can realize his goal. Murder, slavery, prostitution he is willing to use as a means to his end. Eventually he drops even his name, his very personality, and assumes that of a friend who dies to save him. "America America" his Old World friends call him and eventually he attains the magic land. It is inevitable, given Mr. Kazan's brand of bitter irony, that America the country proves somewhat less miraculous than Stavros' dream. Stravros himself, however—and it is the best possible tribute to Mr. Kazan's real artistry—is unaware, as he shines shoes, of his author's wry brooding. Stavros, transmogrified into Joe, grabs his tips and cries, "Next! Come on, you, let's go, you! People waiting!" And the dimes go to bring his family to America, one by one. His joy has not been diminished by the discovery that his love is not perfect.

It is strange, as S. N. Behrman says in his introduction to **America, America,** that the theme of immigration has played so little a role in the fiction of the New World. Certainly future generations will look back to these vast movements of people with an awe difficult for us to comprehend—surging tides of humanity which are still washing around the shores of the world, dreaming of escape and clawing for a spot in a New Land. Much of it is grimmest necessity, then as now, and that may well be one reason for its rejection as creative material. It is something people put behind them and try to forget for a variety of reasons. It is the dark past, not the bright future, but we owe Mr. Kazan a vote of thanks for reminding us that it is there.

Tennessee Williams, with whom Mr. Kazan has been so prominently associated in a directional capacity, is said to have approached the manuscript version of **America, America** with the same sort of nervous misgivings that I believe I had, the doubts one has about a friend who has written a novel after thirty years in the garment industry. Well, not quite, but knowing that Mr. Kazan was a man of creative talent might even have made the approach more nerve-racking. A failure would be so much more distressing. Tennessee was delighted to discover then that it was GOOD. Without the emphasis, I go along with him. **America America** is not a "promising first novel." It is not a novel at all, for that matter. But it is an honest (what greater praise?) and well-turned piece of work. I hope that some day Mr. Kazan will be able to bring his other skills to bear on it and direct a film version. (pp. 261-62)

> *William James Smith, "The Immigrants' Miraculous Dream," in* The Commonweal, *Vol.*

LXXVII, No. 10, November 30, 1962, pp. 261-62.

Eliot Fremont-Smith

[Elia Kazan's novel *America, America*] was, in fact, an autobiographically inspired screenplay though without technical directions. . . . Mr. Kazan's new book [*The Arrangement*] is a straightforward novel—a long one—set in contemporary Los Angeles. It is chock-full of action, sex, punchy set-pieces, yards of conversation, all in a sort of amalgam of the styles of Norman Mailer, Hemingway and Harold Robbins—and it, too, should have few commercial worries. The best thing about the novel is its rollicking zest; Mr. Kazan simply never tires. The worst is that he doesn't. *The Arrangement* seems interminable, and for no particular reason other than Mr. Kazan's apparently unflagging determination to get everything in.

Everything includes all the clichés of style, thought and character one can readily recall. Yet—and this is the other source of the charm of his novel, the other face of its energy—Mr. Kazan employs clichés with the nerve of a true innocent, as if he had never heard of them before. It is disarming.

Eddie, the protagonist and narrator of *The Arrangement,* is a successful middle-aging advertising account executive who gets back at his job by writing social conscious pieces—"justice pieces," he calls them—for the intellectual monthlies, and who gets back at his overly rational and materialistic wife, Florence, and her "theory of limited objectives" by cautious philandering. "Over the years," he confesses early on, "I'd broken out and away from her more than a few times, yes, but never very far, and always with a return ticket in my pocket." . . .

The son of an Armenian immigrant who had changed his name from Seraphim Topouzoglou to Sam Arness, Eddie was baptized Evangelos Arness. When he married Florence he changed his name to Edward Arness, Eddie for short. The agency anglicized it to Edward Anderson. Florence suggested his intellectual pen name: Evans Arness. Thus, at work he was Eddie, his wife called him Ev, his mother called him E and his father called him Evangeleh and sometimes Shakespeare. He thinks of himself as Eddie, but clear as clear, an identity crisis is at hand.

Her name is Gwen; she's young, gorgeous, intelligent, ironic, wise and her own woman—a modernized, beautiful and sensualized version of the old noble prostitute. She's also the boss's secretary and it isn't long before she and Eddie cuddle up on his office couch. And suddenly, the arrangments of Eddie's life will no longer do. The revelation of her attitude about herself and her reaction to him makes another, freer kind of life suddenly thinkable.

What ensues is the saga of Eddie's breakout, his second chance at the race. It turns out to involve many emotional and material sacrifices, a lot of sex (and quite a lot of mooning about it), heartbreak and divorce, suicide attempts, dramatic scenes with friends, enemies, colleagues and movie people, acts of desecration (to the cigarette ads he thought up) and dedication (to writing) and finally a happy or at least contented, ending.

It does seem to take forever; Eddie does seem too often a bit of a boob (one must take on faith the quality of his writing) and none of the many characters is ever quite convincing. Yet *The Arrangement* is fun enough for however long one wants to or can stick with it, and it does deal with feelings and fantasies that are serious, contemporary and not uncommon. And occasionally Mr. Kazan stirs up from the bottom of his caldron tasty rewards—nice, subtle surprises of observation.

Eliot Fremont-Smith *"All about Eddie," in* The New York Times, *February 21, 1967, p. 45.*

The Times Literary Supplement

Kazan has written a novel [*The Arrangement*] which exposes his over-respect for reviewers. An important episode involves a Hollywood man who has read, with anguish, "what *Cahiers du Cinema* and *Sight and Sound* said about his films", and who therefore takes a mean revenge on a director who is "one of the chief darlings of the in-crowd". Mr. Kazan's narrator announces, as if defiantly eccentric, "I'd rather be a first-class mechanic than the editor-in-chief of the *New York Review of Books*". Discussing household economies with his wife, he lists a large number of journals, including the *New Statesman* and *Vogue,* adding: "Those are things that keep us in touch with the living world, and they'd be the last items I'd cut down. But I'd like to hear what you think: the item is $340." The author is presumably ironical, as he is when his narrator remarks of America's most admired reviewers (Clurman, Macdonald and Brustein): "We used to just run to get into bed and read their reviews out loud to each other." But when this narrator boasts of getting an article into the *Partisan Review* or admits modelling his appearance on that of the *New York Times* theatre-reviewer, we begin to suspect the author of reading more reviews than are good for him.

Mr. Kazan's films were more original and vital than this novel. It is fiction for the Sons of the Immigration—almost as predictable, though much more agreeably so, as the Daughters of the Revolution. Successful men of Mr. Kazan's kind write wild novels, "What's it all for?" their heroes yell,

> This world of alimony, Canadian Club and sneering W.A.S.P.s whose daughters I constantly marry? I am too tough a cookie for such ennui. My father was a fat, virile pasha—not the faggoty, wasp-waisted sun-lamp addict you all think me to be. Yet I am superior to my alien father. I know the score. I have a boxing-ring rigged in my private room, next to the circular bed; and my present wife uses the world's most expensive psychiatrist. I am as husky as a truck-driver and swear more readily, despite being a middle-aged headworker. So why do I feel so bad? It can't be capitalism. I haven't been a Red since I was in knee-pants.

The narrator is an advertising man who concentrates shamefully on protecting the cigarette image from the lung-cancer scare. This "Eddie Anderson" is of Anatolian extraction, born Evangelos Arness; his father was born Seraphim Topouzoglou. For reasons of self-respect, Eddie also writes exposures of millionaires for liberal journals, under the name of Evan Arness. One of the unconvincing things about this Greek is his deep interest in Jewishness, wondering how German Jews can bear to be survivors of the Camps; remarking that something is "without *tam,* as the Jews say"; referring to his boss, a man called Finnegan, as "Supergoy"; asserting that one Manfred von Stern is really Manny Stern and that Judge Ben Winston is really Beetle Weinstein.

Eddie's wife, Florence, has got "class" and Eddie wishes he could love her; but he is so good at sex, so near to a Harold Robbins or Ian Fleming action-man doll in his potent desirability, that no pulp-reader would wish him to remain monogamous. Only poor Florence can make him impotent. He muses, wide-eyed, about the superior honesty of his penis (for which he has many pet names) in comparison with the will or the conscience—or, rather, "the Arrangement", which is his label for the complex of social lies in which his life is trapped. Something of Strindberg's insane power would be needed to attach credibility to this passionate dream-man, as he writhes under the cruel plots devised by his wife and friends, burns down his father's house, destroys both his jobs, almost kills himself, lets his wife's doctor and lawyer take his money and certify him. Even Strindberg needed actors to vivify his fantasies; Elia Kazan needs "stars" of the kind he used to direct—Brando, Dean, Clift.

> All this talk about our Christian civilisation. We have a business civilisation. The idea is not to love your brother but to get the better of him. . . . But we live in pretence. . . . Well, I've stopped pretending.

This snatch of rhetoric is at the heart of the novel; and it has the blazing sincerity characteristic of many fine artists and of many forgettable best-sellers. Elia Kazan aims high, but his narrator can sink to a low level of naivety. About a German (prewar) immigrant:

> I'd come back, not too long before, from the Pacific, where I'd seen a lot of fellows die in a war that one of his countrymen had started, so I resented him immediately. Dale, who had been in London in 1941, wanted to kill Hoff on the spot. He vowed we'd get him.

There seems to be no saving irony here, no recognition of the childishness of such tough talk or of the feebleness of Dale's war record, ("ducking the Vs, one and two"). The prejudice is thought to be normal and honourable, the narrator supposed to be exceptionally noble in overcoming it, defending the German from verbal insults at a smart party. Admittedly, there is some discussion of the absurdity of "the problems of the middle-class sensitive soul" when compared with those of aliens in India "who lived in the weather and couldn't feed their bellies". But the argument is so quickly shelved, and the particular "middle-class soul" so insensitive, that it was scarcely worth starting. Such themes, suitable starting-points for more thoughtful novels, are mere parentheses within this strenuous, energetic, but trite fiction.

> *"The State of the Union," in* The Times Literary Supplement, *No. 3403, May 18, 1967, p. 413.*

Christopher Lehmann-Haupt

I think I see what Elia Kazan is trying to do in his latest novel, ***The Assassins.*** Reading over the two closing paragraphs again (after having stepped out of doors for a breath of cool air), I see that he has juxtaposed there descriptions of the rapid decomposition of a human body ("The bones powder, become part of the sand") and the slower disintegration of a bunch of airplanes, "the third largest air force in the world . . . the might of America, our answer to the challenge of history, our pride, our image, our identity, our names." There's meant to be some irony there, I think . . . something about people and machines in this country of ours . . . something uncomplimentary perhaps. And taking one precarious step further: to judge from the names of those airplanes—"Sky Raider," "Sky Hawk," "Globe Master," "Cougar," "Tiger" and so on—I gather Mr. Kazan is harking back to several earlier references in his novel to the law of the jungle. Which means that he is saying that life is a jungle game. Or that America is a beast of prey. Or that the ruling class of Amerika is a beast of prey. Or that idealistic enemies of the ruling class of America are beasts of prey in disguise. Or that . . . Well I guess I don't see what Mr. Kazan is trying to do in his latest novel, ***The Assassins.***

Why don't I? How is it possible to miss the point of a story in which an Air Force sergeant stationed on a base in New Mexico shoots to death his daughter's hippie boyfriend and is exonerated by the Establishment members of the community? That summary would seem to make the point of the ending clear enough: that military might has crushed the rights of citizens, it is supposed to defend. What's the matter with me?

Part of my problem redounds to Mr. Kazan's credit. For he has not simply told a didactic tale in black and white. He has colored his story with many subtler shadings. The hippies aren't all good and the squares aren't all bad. Moreover, there's a counterplot involving the murder-victim's best friend, Michael, the Christ-like leader of the flower children, who, when he discovers that justice is going to miscarry, takes matters into his own hands. And ends up assassinating not the perpetrators of the injustice, but the man he judges to be the real enemy, a young Air Force lieutenant who has tried to befriend Michael, but through lack of deep commitment to either side ends up betraying him. Things get complicated, see?

But what is most complicating are the things that work against the lucidity of Mr. Kazan's story.

To begin with, there is the question of whether the characters are meant to be real people or simply puppets of the author. Mr. Kazan seems to want it both ways. For instance, in order to make plausible the sergeant's murder of the hippie, Mr. Kazan endows him with a whole satchelful of motivations—a hot-blooded Latin temperament, an incestuous fixation on his daughter, an emasculating wife and the illusion (shared by us readers) that the boyfriend is thoroughly despicable. Yet when the novel settles down to its main business of demonstrating the injustice of the Establishment, Mr. Kazan asks us to recall an obscure and clumsily handled scene in which the sergeant's superior seems to be ordering the murder, and expects us to remember the murder victim with fondness.

And so it goes throughout. None of the characters behave consistently. They seem to put on whatever masks the business of sustaining the plot demands of them. This would be perfectly acceptable if the plot were well-made enough to establish a clear point. But the point always boils down to the behavior of characters too busy serving the plot to reveal themselves. We are led on a paper chase, the message of which seems to be that fate is the consequence of character, and character is formed by Mr. Kazan's zeal to keep the action boiling.

Then there is the befuddling quality of the book's language. Mr. Kazan has conceived his story visually, which is understandable considering what he has described in the past as his "filmic" imagination. One can "see" the story easily enough. But the language of the narrative, instead of serving this visual quality, actually obstructs it. Actions that would logically take up, say, one third of a scene are frequently described in a single sentence. Thoughts and impressions that would logically fleet through a character's mind are detailed at inordinate length (which, incidentally, reinforces the impression that Mr. Kazan is manipulating his people). This disjunction between action and language is most disconcerting. One finds oneself tripping over the simplest sentences and having to read them repeatedly to catch their meaning.

The cumulative effect of following the narrative and trying to keep the people straight is tiring. Long before one gets to those last two paragraphs one's mind has gone half to sleep. That's why I had to read them over after breathing some fresh air. That's why I'm still not sure what Mr. Kazan is getting at.

Christopher Lehmann-Haupt, "Misarrangement of Amerika," in The New York Times, *February 16, 1972, p. 37.*

James Boatwright

When the novelist takes on our national troubles, as Kazan does, he has a lot going for him. How can we not be interested in [**The Assassins**], a book dealing with drugs, hippies, the military mind, *machismo,* the generation gap, pollution, communes, drop-outs, middle-class prejudices, corrupt judicial systems? But suppose the author doesn't make us see and understand, suppose his perceptions aren't keen enough, his gifts great or fine enough? What he ends up with, unintentionally, is exploitation, a book-club bestseller, a rip-off, living off the lean of the land, making hay while the deadly rain falls. And more important, yet another masochistic pot shot at liberals and liberalism from an essentially liberal sensibility and conscience.

Quickly, the story. Master Sergeant Cesario Flores has a daughter, Juana, who keeps running off with a drug-crazed hippy. After subtle nudging from his superior, Colonel Dowd, Flores stages a showdown and murders his daughter's lover and a young black who is with him. The rest of the novel shows us the farcical workings of justice in Amerika. . . .

Newspaper headlines swim before one's eyes: this is familiar matter, another symptom of our disease, erupting at home and abroad with sickening repetitiousness. Understanding this phenomenon, working toward its cure is our urgent need, so when a writer fails, as Mr. Kazan mostly does, the loss is not only literary. But the causes of the failure are chiefly literary. First, an inadequate grip on language: painful solecisms, dialogue without the faintest breath of life, pointless detail. Then, a more ominous fault in a novel that laments our decaying humanity: most of the characters are ineptly drawn stock performers, cardboard cut-outs. A few of them—Flores, for instance, and the wife of Judge Breen—start out promisingly, with some of the complexity and density of actual human beings, but Kazan doesn't sustain them; they atrophy in front of our eyes.

One character is sustained, looked after, followed. It's clear that Alan is the pivotal figure in the novel; he's the character and it's his actions you should keep your eye on. Sophisticated, aloof, graceful, he wastes his time away on the tennis court (where else?), the best and most sensitive being the eastern establishment has to offer, and he's ripe for change. The change comes with the trial: at first, he's involved in the defense of Cesario, but the obvious fix repels him and he becomes a liberal. Not a radical like Michael with his muttering about guns and revolution, but a *liberal.* He perceives the rottenness of the institutions about him but thinks they can be changed. He sympathizes with much that Michael believes but thinks they can be changed. Unfortunately, Kazan isn't fair about this: he makes Alan a perfect patsy, the most awful wimp, whose language is ludicrous—or is it?

> I originally became a lawyer because I thought our way of justice was worth devoting a life to, excuse the corn. But gradually I forgot about it, married and settled into the air force, I played a hell of a game of tennis and made with the jokes, I didn't let myself look around and think about anything. Well, Michael started me up again. Anyway, it's come down, to this, either I'm full of it or I'm not, either I've spent my whole life lying to myself, or—you see what I mean, it's not him? It's me.

With this self-knowledge under his belt, he sets about trying to patch things up, to draw Michael (whose fineness Alan sees with great clarity; the reader may have some trouble) back into society. To do this he must collaborate with the sinister government agents and momentarily betray Michael, but it's all for his own good in the end. . . . What he gets for his efforts in this climactic scene is an embrace from Michael and then a bullet in his stomach. Thus, simply, neatly, is the voice of Hubert Humphrey stopped, liberalism indicted, for its compromises, its naivete, its pathetic hopes for operating within the system. Off the liberals!

If Alan's villainy hasn't been made clear enough to us, that's taken care of shortly afterward. Michael escapes to Mexico, the judge's son comes home for the summer. The judge is disturbed that his son takes it for granted that Michael killed Alan and that Michael is his son's hero.

> "What do you mean he made good on it?" Breen demanded of his son. . . . "He means," Sarah [his wife] told him later, "that while you were all exonerating a murderer, young Mr. Winter conducted his own trial, and imposed his own sentence." "But Sare, he shot an innocent man!" "Apparently he didn't think so," she said.

Which is brutal but tough-thinking, right? Alan isn't innocent because he was a stupid ineffective liberal and most deserved to die, deserved to die more than Cesario (who after all was an exploited product of his society), deserved to die more than the outright haters, the power-wielding big guns.

I find this muddy and dangerous morality, a put-up job, the sorry conclusion to a badly confused dramatic argument. It seems to me the self-laceration of a liberal conscience. What, after all, could be a more representative liberal response to our surrounding nightmare than to sit down and write a passionate *novel* about it, to seek out the energies of mind and imagination, to look for the possibilities of transformation in this great middle-class art form? What does Kazan do, despite his fable's meaning? He turns to precisely the same powers and forces Alan turns to, his faith in, and ultimately trusts: our rationality, our capacity to change, our essential worthiness.

> James Boatwright, *"Another Pot Shot at Liberals,"* in The New Republic, *Vol. 166, No. 11, March 11, 1972, p. 19.*

Anthea Lahr

If you were a macho Mexican Air Force sergeant and your favorite daughter was being turned on and fucked by a hippie dealer, what would you do? Sergeant Cesario Flores shot "the animal." Coldly and with premeditation.

Yet Flores too is a victim. Nowhere in Kazan's exciting and crisply written book [*The Assassins*] do we lose sight of Flores's humanity in the dilemma. He is a victim of both his Latin and American Air Force backgrounds. He sees his daughter, Juana, as a madonna, and feels compelled to protect her virginity. His military buddies regard long hair and drugs as anathema. To them hippies are animals, less than human. Flores was only reflecting the bias of his community.

Although this is an open-and-shut case of first degree murder, there is little doubt that "12 honest men" will find Flores not guilty. The jury will be a hand-picked team of burghers who bring with them all their prejudices—and in a military town in New Mexico, those prejudices would clearly favor a sergeant over a hippie. So it is the jury system and the entire American sense of justice that is on trial in *The Assassins.*

Alan Kidd, an Air Force lawyer originally assigned to the case, explains to Michael, a hippie he tried to befriend: "My father used to say that the jury system is based on an absurd premise which is that a fool is a fool, but 12 fools are wise."

The real iniquity in the American jury system is the way the lawyers can challenge prospective jurors, especially peremptorily. There is little chance of getting 12 random individuals who might have some diversity of opinion. Anyone with an unusual job, unsuitable clothes or an alien face is likely to be dismissed. Except for show. A visit to 100 Centre Street says their prosecutor wants one thing—a conviction. All the fine words from law school about justice and the rule of law are forgotten. As in *The Assassins,* justice means prevalence of local opinion, not recourse to a higher code of ethics.

After the murder, Kazan the director moves his characters round the courtroom, the base, the desert with exemplary skill. He can handle the diverse patterns of the lives of the lawyers, the hippies, the officers with breathtaking dexterity. The trial changes everybody's lives, and by the end of the book, Hope Wheeler and Alan Kidd are dead. . . . Alan Kidd is murdered by Michael.

As the exonerating verdict becomes increasingly predictable, the relationship between Alan and Michael becomes the focal drama of the book. Alan—tennis-playing, "a perfect six foot, 185-pound specimen, a Yankee classic, at 25 distinguished not because of anything he'd done, but because of what he was, a man aloof, protected by his passivity"—tries to be honest. The playing-out of the judicial farce revolts him. A lawyer only because his father was one, Alan develops a sense of justice. He was assigned to the case because his wife persuaded her colonel father that it would make Alan successful. As soon as Alan realizes the absurdity and the frivolity of the trial, ("Here were people trying murder, nothing less, in an atmosphere of twittering cordiality"), he is dropped.

This only increases his interest and his determination that someone care about the dead Vinnie and his black friend, who Flores arbitrarily kills at close range. But Alan is powerless. A lieutenant, he is at the mercy of his superiors and ridiculed by his supposed peers. Straight-arrow, he is distrusted by Michael and his friends. They are all as impotent as he is. Kazan shows the wave of inevitability rolling over them. As some sort of revenge Michael finally kills Alan, who is for him a symbol of oppression. Alan dies without a struggle—after all, his illusions have been shattered, he is truly homeless.

One of the remarkable aspects of this book is that Kazan, a middle-aged man, writes about Michael's America with sympathy, yet without condescension. (p. 37)

America is two nations. There are passports between the two such as drugs, sex, or politics, but what *The Assassins* so pessimistically emphasizes is the dichotomy of values. Bourgeois America, exemplified by Kazan in ambitious lawyers and their even more ambitious wives, thinks its children should, in the words of Michael's father, "get out of this place. It's stagnant water. Get out into the sea where it moves, where there are currents and storms, where the issues are being contested, where people are fighting for what they believe. Go somewhere." Michael's father's generation cannot understand that to drop out is to fight. Not to participate in society is action, because it arouses violence in the other side. Protesters going limp lead to police brutality.

Superficially the forces of law 'n' order win out. Michael is suspected of being the mastermind behind an assassination attempt on Flores. The police seize this opportunity to run in every barefooted young person in sight. Refugees flee across the desert, but they are really undefeated. Collins Air Force Base may temporarily be safe, but there is a continuous army of "un-Americans" ready to re-group.

Kazan's book ends with a display of American arms: "So here they stand, the might of America, our answer to the challenge of history, our pride, our image, our identity, our names . . . The F-8 Crusader, the F-9 Cougar, the F-11 Tiger, the F-24 Thunderstreak, the F-86 Saberjet, the F-89 Scorpion, the F-94 Star Fighter—and more."

But will there be men to fly them? (p. 52)

Anthea Lahr, "Twelve Fools are Wise," in The Village Voice, *Vol. XVII, No. 19, May 11, 1972, pp. 37, 52.*

Anatole Broyard

I have always hated the phrase "compulsively readable"—and not just for grammatical reasons—yet this is precisely what comes to mind when I try to sum up my feelings about Elia Kazan's new novel, *The Understudy.* It expresses my ambivalence about the book and also conveys the fact that I read it as if I had no choice. Though I hardly cared about any of the characters, though the main theme of the book did not interest me, I cannot say that I was bored by *The Understudy.*

How do I explain this? Well, I think that Mr. Kazan knows how to exert an influence. This may be a kind of charisma he has. He also has a great deal of savvy, which I would define as an ability to make things function smoothly, a characteristic that is most often acquired by running things or controlling people for a good long time. Savvy is not to be confounded with literary talent: it is more like an exalted form of salesmanship. As a novelist, Mr. Kazan is a brilliant director.

The Understudy is about a certain kind of actor. Again, I would use the word charismatic. Mr. Kazan says grand, which means the same thing for him. Sonny, the narrator, is an actor who has everything but this grandeur, and who is therefore a reluctant hero worshiper and victim of an older actor who carries ham to the point of sublimity. Though I don't believe in this kind of alchemy, in which the ego of the actor carries all before him, there are millions of people who do and they will probably adore old Sidney Schlossberg. . . .

When the book opens, Sonny is in the ascendancy and Sidney Schlossberg's star has faded. Racked by guilt, which seems to be the only emotion he can experience, Sonny is about to depart for an African safari. He feels guilty because, even with his considerable influence, he can no longer get understudy parts for Sidney in the plays in which he himself is the star. When Sidney did get these parts, he failed to show up at rehearsals, arrived drunk, insulted the director or the author, rewrote the script, and so on.

The generation before Sonny's used to go to Florida to repair the ravages of working for a living. Now Sonny goes to Africa, where he expects to find "the great chain of being" and clasp it around his wrist like a gold identification bracelet. You can't say the old fads aren't changing. The healing of sunlight used to be enough: now it must be nothing less than the annealing of epiphany. In Africa, during a bout of a mysterious fever, Sonny has the kind of conversation with a lion that he would have had, 20 years ago, with his psychoanalyst.

He returns a changed man. I'm not sure how he has changed, because he wasn't at all clear to me before. At any rate, he says he's changed. His wife, Ellie, who let him go with a minimum show of protest, has not changed. She is just as unconvincing as ever and so is her 11-year-old son by a previous marriage. It appears to me that Mr. Kazan has no time for bit parts like Ellie's. He is hooked, like a drug addict, on that old black magic called stardom.

Is it all worth it? I'm not sure. Perhaps *The Understudy* ought to be reviewed on the page where they do recipes. On the positive side, there is a lot of solid "inside" stuff about how acting and the theater work—at least Mr. Kazan's kind, which comprises a not inconsiderable part of the drama in America. I don't happen to like chicken fat, but Mr. Kazan will never go broke selling his brand.

Toward the end, *The Understudy* becomes congested with plot—exactly the way someone's face becomes congested with blood. Perhaps it even has a heart attack—or change of heart attack. As if he suddenly felt that Sidney and Sonny were not enough for today's cannibalistic readers, Mr. Kazan patches the script with a gangster who is going to play angel for Sidney's last strut on the boards. A couple of murders, some Grand Guignol—why not? Keep it moving, that's the idea.

The end of the book is bent to the author's purpose about as persuasively as that iron rod Rudolph Valentino bent across his bare chest in *The Son of the Sheik.* You can get away with things on the stage or in film that just won't go down in fiction. Somewhere in *The Understudy,* I believe Mr. Kazan says that you cannot lie on film, it shows everything up. I could not disagree more, but then I don't suppose he would see it my way either if I made the same claim for novels.

It is an odd feeling, gobbling up a book that does almost nothing that you believe good novels ought to do. It is enough to make you consider an agonizing reappraisal of your critical standards. Nor can *The Understudy* be dismissed as mere entertainment—it is both more and less than that.

Anatole Broyard, "On Compulsive Readability," in The New York Times, *December 19, 1974, p. 43.*

Julian Barnes

Given the films Elia Kazan has directed, one can be confident that his first novel about actors will avoid glossy thespiana. True, he gossips about Hollywood and Broadway glamour-boys (find out how Brando learnt to speak verse); and there are throwaways that one suspects may be in-jokes. But mostly, the background to *The Understudy* is resolutely glamourless, while its protagonist, Sonny, is presented as the sort of actor who never becomes a star. Though highly professional and well-paid, he is basically mechanical; there is never any danger (as a matinée idol of the previous generation notes) that he will cut loose and play a Rave Scene.

Sonny's problem is that his life is blowing all its fuses at the same time: his professional ability is called in question; his nervily-demanding wife is withdrawing from him; and his precarious relationship with an old-school actor and father-figure is beginning to sour. Mr. Kazan, though, is clearly out to do more than document just another backstage *crise de foi.* Indeed, apart from retailing some snappy theatrical *mots* . . . he is generally uninteresting on actors and acting. So when he packs Sonny off to Africa for a vacation, it becomes clear that they are both of them after Big Game. For the law of the jungle, as discovered on a bush trek, turns out to be nothing less than an elaborate parallel of the life of New York City. What, after all, are a predator's habits, if not a metaphor for urban violence; and why should men be repelled by a lion devouring a zebra foetus, when they themselves consume suckling pig? Much of the argument proceeds on this coarse and tendentious level, while Sonny ponders his civic and personal duties as a fairly fit survivor.

Humbled, he returns to the urban jungle, the pressures on him increase, and Mr. Kazan's resolution of them, disappointingly, is romantic in the purest celluloid tradition. Sonny, tormented by collapsing relationships and the problem of violence, finally plays his Rave Scene in real life, carries it over on to the stage, and is hailed by the newspapers as a star. In spite of Mr Kazan's knowledge of the external machinery of stardom, it is a climax that, from both psychological and aesthetic points of view, strikes one as altogether too glib.

> Julian Barnes, "The Greasepaint Jungle," in The Times Literary Supplement, *No. 3831, August 15, 1975, p. 913.*

Dan Wakefield

[*Acts of Love*] is the story of a spoiled young rich girl and the father of the man she marries.

No, the girl does not run off with her husband's father, nor does she ever have sexual relations with him. But it is her love for her father-in-law, and for the old order of values he represents, that forms the theme of the book.

Ethel Laffey is the adopted daughter of a well-to-do socialite surgeon in Tucson, Ariz., who dotingly raised her to be, as she charges him, "nothing more than a household pet." Ethel is bright, bored, attractive and rudderless, trying to find meaning in her own life through men she goes to bed with, and grasping at the promise of security in marriage to a Navy officer of a dominating temper. As she explains her attraction to the officer to a passive ex-lover: "I need someone to tell me how to be, what's right and wrong. He does that." . . .

Ethel longs for the "old time" of patriarchal rule, of "Me-Tarzan-You-Jane" relations, and her handsome young Navy husband doesn't live up (or down) to her masterly expectations. She tells him in frustration: "I wish you'd yell at me. I wish you'd beat me. Slap me around, if you're mad." There are times when Ethel seems not only sociologically out of date but also clinically disturbed.

She quickly tires of husband Teddy, but what holds her to the family (and holds her life in focus for a while) is his father, Costa. The old man is accurately described by another character as "the bigoted, but somehow lovable father from the old world who cannot be moved." Costa believes in which he calls "the proper way" of doing things, which is the "old-world" way that wants to know first if his son's fiancée is "clean" (virginal), if she can cook, and demands of her: "I want grandson my name."

One immediately sees Anthony Quinn in the role of this Greek-American, rough-hewn Florida fisherman turned bait 'n beer store owner on the Gulf Coast of Florida, Zorba-like in his talk and actions: "When the bill was presented, the old man reached into a shoe he'd taken off and produced some money."

Though Costa would have preferred that his son marry a nice Greek-origin girl and follow the dictum "Greek girl for family, American girl for pleasure," he takes a shine to Ethel, and develops a fatherly protectiveness toward her. She in turn invests him with the sort of strength she feels she has missed. To a poor little rich girl who saw *The Godfather* over and over and enjoyed it as a moral fable of an old patriarch who gave life to a family, Costa is a good stand-in for the Don Corleone-Brando figure. But as Ethel gains some measure of self-confidence and independence, her effort to fulfill Costa's image of her as an old-fashioned girl in the old-country sense leads to personal and cultural conflict that ends in tragedy.

The story tends toward melodrama, but the author's clear affection for the people he writes about makes the reader care.

> Dan Wakefield, *"Just Right for Anthony Quinn," in* The New York Times Book Review, *July 9, 1978, p. 14.*

John Leonard

[In *Acts of Love*], Ethel, with her big breasts and her reddish-golden hair, has many problems. People keep calling her kitten. She is an adopted child. Her adoptive father, a Tucson surgeon, and her adoptive mother, who is sickly and depressed, don't talk to each other. The men in Ethel's life—a mangy, "pathetic" bunch from every alley of life—seek in her body a cure for self-doubt or a vehicle of revenge or quick kicks. No wonder Ethel runs away to San Diego and talks herself into falling in love with Teddy Avaliotis, petty officer third class in the United States Navy, Mr. Nice Guy.

But before Ethel and Teddy can marry, Ethel must confront Teddy's father, Costa Avaliotis, who is very old-country Greek, a sort of Zorba the chauvinist. Before the red tide came to the Gulf coast of Florida, Costa used to dive bravely for the sponge. Now he sells bait and, in general, makes life miserable for his wife, Noona, while waiting around for a grandson. Costa proves to be the biggest problem in Ethel's feckless life.

For one thing, Costa disapproves of Ethel. She isn't Greek. For another, he insists on making all the wedding arrangements according to his own traditions, at the expense of anybody else's feelings. For a third, Ethel is fatally attracted to him. His pigheaded self-assurance, his masculine vitality, his redolent earthiness—indeed, his sweaty smell—and his muscle tone are just what Ethel seems to need in a man, a rock on which to dry her wings. Whether consciously or not, she courts him. If a grandson is what he wants, a grandson is what he will get, even if the child isn't Teddy's.

By the end of *Acts of Love*—after psychiatrists and policemen and maniacs, after Ethel's mother is dead and her father has run off with another woman, after Ethel has herself deserted from the Navy and gone to Mexico and returned to Florida, after Noona has been reluctantly liberated and Teddy finds somebody else and Costa has had several murderous tantrums, after countless sexual encounters that sound more like train wrecks than acts of love—everybody is in terrible shape, especially Ethel.

There's enough material here for several novels, and I'm not sure which one Elia Kazan wanted to write. Mr. Kazan, as everybody knows, is the director of stage and screen. As in his other novels, particularly *The Arrangement* his stage experience lends his fiction certain strengths and weaknesses. The strength in *Acts of Love* is dialogue, it is crisp and stressed, it twists the tail of the dramatic action. The weakness is a missing sense of place, for all the moving around in the novel—Florida, Tucson, Mexico—we seem always to be in the same overheated room, where people are shouting.

What are they shouting about? Costa and Ethel are equally annoying characters, equally incapable of coherent thought. Is Ethel supposed to exemplify the modern woman, in search of a definition of self that transcends the inconveniences of biology? Is Costa supposed to exemplify the old ethnic values, wiped out like his sponges by a red tide of assimilation and secular whoopee? But Ethel never gets out of her body, and Costa's primitivism is dangerous, and Mr. Kazan is ambivalent.

Perhaps Ethel is working out her incestuous longings for her father in the arms of Costa. But since her father was adoptive and Costa is merely an in-law, where's the taboo? Is sex a Greek tragedy? Perhaps, on the other hand, Mr. Kazan intends us to appreciate the damage that a deracinated demimondaine, a WASP on an affectless rampage, can cause when she meets up with Old World naïfs. And yet it is clear that Costa, with his violent superstitions, is even more damaging to Ethel than she is to him. Are we left, then, with nothing more than love gone wrong?

Novels, of course, don't require schemes, skeleton keys, crib sheets, Rosetta stones. They are entitled to their own logic. If, however, they are going to reverberate, they ought to refer in their particular emotions and consequences to a larger, more general world of emotions and consequences, a universal discourse. They must connect. *Acts of Love,* in which there is very little love, although there is plenty of sympathy, is content, almost smug, in its particularities. Here is what happens, it says, when you put one traditional Greek sponge diver in the same bedroom with one father-troubled sexy young semidaughter of a Tucson surgeon. Grief.

I agree that this is a recipe for grief. But what then, or next? Where is the resonance in an otherwise arbitrary confrontation? How do I care about a case history, an accident? *Acts of Love,* like an interesting radio program, just stops.

> *John Leonard, in a review of "Acts of Love,"* in The New York Times, *July 21, 1978, p. C23.*

Eliot Wagner

Things aren't what they used to be? Perhaps not in real life, but they are in Elia Kazan's grimly effective new novel, *The Anatolian,* which sees ambitious Greek-Turkish immigrant Stavros Topouzoglou and his world of antagonists through the decade ending in 1919. For the explosive Stavros, his mother, his brothers and sisters, his several bosses, his prostitutes and Althea Perry, his brilliantly delineated, Vassar-educated lover, 1909 and 1982 could almost be interchangeable. There is international unrest—Middle East wars now, Balkan wars then—the great powers are adrift and, then as now, there is much scheming to turn public conflict into private profit.

As this sequel to Mr. Kazan's *America, America* opens, 32-year-old Stavros is preparing to meet the freighter that is bringing his family to America. . . . After his arrival in New York, Stavros' labors become more genteel. He is a rug salesman and unwilling errand boy for an American carpet firm owned by Fernand Sarrafian and managed by a suburban Anglo-American, Morgan Perry. But it's a richer life that Stavros hankers after, something beyond the Saturday-night sexuality to which he initially restricted himself. With his family finally en route, he looks forward to returning responsibility to his father, moving to an apartment of his own and enjoying himself. His relatives arrive, however, without his father, who has died in Turkey just before the family's departure.

Stavros, now mired in conflict between his selfish desires and a sense of responsibility he does not want, becomes the head of the clan. Despite his reluctance, he discovers that ruling the family offers some satisfaction. Even though his brothers and sisters come to fear and resent him, his morally strong mother considers him the only real man her married life ever produced.

He sets up his siblings in a small family carpet business and molds them to his notions of success and propriety, but he continues to pursue his ambition of conquering America—that is, attaining the wealth and position that are his sole objective. He keeps his old job at the Sarrafian carpet firm, but, because of his gruff behavior, he is passed over for promotion when death or illness create opportunities.

Meanwhile he becomes involved with Althea Perry—the daughter of his despised boss Morgan—who has to prove herself with man after man. Although their relationship is as joyless as any in fiction today, Althea is nonetheless an engaging character. And since she hopes to spite her father and harridan mother, she couldn't have chosen a better lover than the man Morgan refers to as "that bow-legged Greek goat." That Stavros can imagine their shared resentment and sensuality to be love and that he can even want to marry Althea are signs of his demoralization. And the resistance of both his family and Althea's only sinks him deeper into confusion while increasing his resolve to have Althea.

Althea can absorb punishment, but after Stavros applies his Anatolian crede ("How she knows what's right, what's wrong, if I don't beat her?"), she ends her relationship with him in order to marry for the money her dying father can no longer supply. Stavros' own sharp business practices cost him his job with the Sarrafian carpet firm. And the family will not go along with a get-rich-quick scheme involving the business he has set up for them when their security is part of the risk. In a guilty bid for freedom he abandons his majority interest in the family business and, with it, the family.

This freedom leads him successively to cardsharping buffoonery, to pandering to the voyeuristic tastes of his former employer Sarrafian (the aged Armenian prince of manipulators whom Stavros aims to manipulate) and to actual pimping for the Armenian's English associate. Then a

Greek irredentist rally revives Stavros's moribund pride. And suddenly, the narrative veers.

There follows a crucial 80-page drop into mechanical contrivance that abruptly turns firm characters like Althea and the crafty, corrupt Sarrafian to putty. The conclusion rehashes Althea's acquisitive marriage and recasts Stavros as a kind of barber-Figaro master of ceremonies who, after acquiring a 40-percent interest in Sarrafian's business, sails off to Greece. Unfortunately, all of this seems to have been arranged in the interest of ending the book with Stavros on the road to success, or at least to further adventures.

This fabricated ending is a disappointment, but when Elia Kazan is true to his dark vision of American immigrant life, which he is most of the way through *The Anatolian,* this is a vigorous and affecting novel.

Eliot Wagner, "Conquering America," in The New York Times Book Review, August 15, 1982, p. 10.

S. S. Prawer

The cinema is dark, and so is the screen; all we hear is a pleasant speaking voice: "My name is Elia Kazan. I am Greek by blood, a Turk by birth, and an American because my uncle made a journey." The film which opens in this way is called *America, America,* and so is the novel based on the same material, written by the director himself; the central figure of both is modelled on the uncle who made the journey and who here appears under the name of Stavros Topouzoglou. Where *America, America* shows how the journey from Anatolia to the USA came to be made, Kazan's new novel, *The Anatolian,* shows how Stavros claws his way to some business success in his first ten years in the new country. We watch him perform many roles in the society to which he comes as an eager stranger: assistant in a large firm of rug-importers and founder of a small one; redoubtable head of a family struggling out of poverty; an immigrant who adapts to the American way without ever losing the consciousness that he does not feel at home; a man proud of his origins who . . . desires a woman of a quite different type and class—"American girls with golden hair, goddammit". Conscious that his unlovely physical appearance can be redeemed, in the eyes of the women he desires, by his strong sexuality, he has a love-hate relationship with the blonde and blue-eyed ones, with the WASPs who, as he says at one point, got to America first and therefore own it; an observation which elicits the reply: "This country belongs to anyone who takes it." And so we watch him make his way, alienated, lusting, out to get the other man before the other gets him, and take our leave of him at the end of the First World War, about to revisit Anatolia to make the business deal of his life as an "unredeemed" Anatolian at heart. The book, we note, is dedicated to "The Unredeemed".

As a novel, *The Anatolian* is no better and no worse than dozens of other lengthy fictions which draw on the American Dream for a sour tale of upward mobility. *What Makes Stavros Run* would be a reasonable alternative title. It reads like a book talked on to a tape-recorder and licked into shape by some practised New York editor: the relent-

less staccato of its short-breathed clauses carries the reader along, lurching occasionally into newspaper editorial English or into a passionate rant, but only once—in a humorous description of Graeco-Turkish food—offering anything in the way of stylistic distinction. Much of the book consists of talk in simplified immigrant's language; but we find little attempt to differentiate the characters by means of individual speech-patterns. What interest the novel has derives in the main from the fact that it is by Elia Kazan and that it represents yet another expression of the autobiographical impulse which has moulded so much of his work: first as an actor; then as a theatre-director; then as a director of films who continued to work for the New York stage and who, in the process, acquired more and more say in the scripting of plays and films; and finally as a novelist who is clearly working his way towards shedding the disguise of fiction in favour of an actual, acknowledged, autobiography. Stavros's obsession with the blonde and blue-eyed ones throws freshlight on the distinctive use Kazan has always made of fair-haired actresses with an outward reserve and an inner fire that could serve to warm, inspire and console his male protagonists: Deborah Kerr, Eva Marie Saint, Julie Harris, Kim Stanley, Barbara Bel Geddes, spring immediately to mind. Fernand Sarrafian, the successful rug merchant and dubious father-figure of *The Anatolian,* talks on occasions like Big Daddy in *Cat on a Hot Tin Roof,* while Stavros again and again appears to merge the characters Marlon Brando played in *On the Waterfront* and *A Streetcar named Desire.* Stavros constantly remembers the lessons he learnt as a *hamal,* a worker on the Turkish waterfront, at the mercy of stevedore bosses. As we watch Stavros becoming wise in the ways of American business, we cannot but recall Kazan's greatest stage success, his production of Arthur Miller's *Death of a Salesman.* How well Willy Loman would have understood what Sarrafian impresses on Stavros! "The first thing a salesman has to sell", he tells him at one point, "is himself. After that, it's easy". When, in the course of *The Anatolian,* a potential informer is killed before he can betray secrets ("He'd have given names when he was tortured") we remember not only *On the Waterfront,* but also the self-justifying impulse behind that movie, which attempted to make a hero out of a man who "named names" as Kazan had done when he appeared as a "friendly witness" before the House Committee on Un-American Activities. And when we hear Fernand Sarrafian, who becomes more and more the *raisonneur* of Kazan's new novel, declare himself astonished to find Stavros's convictions change into the opposite of what they were before, adding: "It seems that the only consistent thing about you is the level of your excitement"— then many readers will surely feel, as I do, that he has not only described Kazan's progress from his agit-prop and communist beginnings to his appearance as a "friendly witness", but also the cinematic and theatrical style which made him the ideal collaborator and interpreter of Tennessee Williams.

S. S. Prawer, "Un-American to All-American," in The Times Literary Supplement, No. 4193, August 12, 1983, p. 854.

Arthur Schlesinger, Jr.

Elia Kazan, storm-tossed and stormy, is one of the century's vivid American artists. . . . He was an admired actor in his youth, a best-selling novelist in later years. He has been a compulsive seducer of women; brilliant, passionate, generous, restless, discontented, angry, vengeful and a fount of creativity, resentment and controversy. He is relentless in self-revelation, introspection and confession, and his life, especially as recounted by himself [in *Elia Kazan: A Life*], makes a fascinating American story.

Mr. Kazan was born in Constantinople in 1909 to an Anatolian Greek family living under harsh Turkish rule in the Ottoman Empire. His father, a rug merchant, brought the family to America shortly before World War I. Elia Kazan attributes much to his Anatolian origins, especially his desire to ingratiate and his capacity to dissemble—"the Anatolian Smile" he so disliked in his father, "the smile that covers resentment."

Perhaps Anatolia deserves credit also for his hypnotic skills as a storyteller. James Baldwin had it right in his description of Mr. Kazan's novel *The Arrangement:* "the tale told by a member of the tribe to the tribe. It has the urgency of a confession and the stammering authority of a plea." Mr. Kazan addresses his readers, beguiles them, collars them, challenges and reproaches them. He is an effective rather than an elegant writer. His language—colloquial, sturdy and fluent—serviceably sustains the hard-driven pace of his narrative. Characterizations of people he has known—and he has known nearly everybody of consequence on Broadway and in Hollywood—are frank, incisive and penetrating. The structure of his tale is cinematic, with flashes forward and back, "twisting back and forth in time," as he puts it, "even though my life has been lived as yours is being lived, in a progression of days."

The author's effortless recall of scenes, conversations, confrontations and quarrels from the past is suspiciously total. Yet he draws to some degree on contemporaneous journals and letters, so that his recital is not entirely subject to the treacheries of memory. Also, the publication of memoirs while other witnesses are still around invites alternative versions of the same events, thereby enriching the historical record.

Ambitious from the start, the young Anatolian-American contrived in the late 1920's to get into Williams College in Massachusetts, where he spent four lonely years as an outsider, serving bar at dances in fraternities that denied him membership. "It was there, I suppose, that revenge began to be a motive in my life. It was at these parties that my obsessive attraction to other men's women was born and my need—it amounted to that—to take them away." But resentment was covered, in the Anatolian fashion, by the smile. "Our cunning taught us to be servile to the strong." By the time he moved on from the Yale Drama School to the Group Theater in New York, he had acquired the nickname he came to despise—Gadg, short for "gadget," a useful, handy, "ever-compliant little cuss." "You made yourself that way to get along with people, to be accepted, to become invisible—a Gadget!" John Steinbeck later told him. "What a neuter nickname! Useful for everyone, except yourself!"

The Group Theater was the most memorable of the Great Depression's experiments in radical theater. Dominated by Lee Strasberg and Harold Clurman, the Group attract-

ed bright young talents—Clifford Odets, Franchot Tone, Stella and Luther Adler, Elia Kazan—and instructed them in the famous Method, the theory that the actor must "take a minute" to experience internally the emotion he is about to simulate on the stage. The Method was exciting and revelatory, for a while.

But doubts arose. Serving as assistant stage manager for a Theater Guild production, Mr. Kazan saw an opposite theory at work. For the star, that splendid sardonic actor Osgood Perkins, "there was no 'take a minute' technique . . . in fact, there was no emotion. Only skill. In every aspect of technical facility, he was peerless." This was the external approach as against the Group Theater's internal approach; the professional technique as against the psychological technique. And it gave Mr. Kazan his guiding idea when he started directing.

> I believed I could take the kind of art Osgood Perkins exemplified—externally clear action, controlled every minute at every turn, with gestures spare yet eloquent—and blend that with the kind of acting the Group was built on: intense and truly emotional, rooted in the subconscious, therefore often surprising and shocking in its revelations. I could bring these two opposite and often conflicting traditions together.

This, as a director, he proceeded to do, and with brilliant effect. His comments on directing, scattered throughout the book, are almost invariably informative and astute. He is illuminating on picture, position, movement, pace, rhythm. He is also well aware of his own limitations. "I don't have great range. I am no good with music or with spectacles. The classics are beyond me," he says, and again:

> "I've had no training or experience to prepare me for such a task. There was no tradition here in this country from which I might have learned." In fact, "I am a mediocre director except when a play or a film touches a part of my life's experience. . . . I do have courage, even some daring. I am able to talk to actors . . . to arouse them to better work. I have strong, even violent, feelings, and they are assets."

The objectively observant tone of this passage is characteristic.

Mr. Kazan is especially interesting on the difference between stage and film. After winning an Academy Award for his fourth Hollywood movie, *Gentleman's Agreement,* he suddenly perceived that he was still only a stage director, excessively dependent on cameraman and cutter, that he really did not know how to make a movie; "I was inept at my profession." He then settled down to master the art of film making.

Film time, he soon learned, was different from stage time. In the theater time runs its normal course, the same on stage as it is in the audience. But film time is malleable; it can be slowed down or speeded up. Acting too was different in the movies. Some Group Theater colleagues were "too graphic—a nice way to put it—for the screen." You can fake emotions on the stage; the camera "penetrates the husk of an actor; it reveals what's truly happening—if anything, if nothing." And he now began to understand what John Ford had told him early on: "Tell it with pictures. . . . Direct it like you were making a silent."

"Photographed action," Mr. Kazan concluded, was the key.

His great Hollywood period was in the 1950's, and he gives an absorbing account of the making of his master-piece, **On the Waterfront,** with generous recognition of the contributions of Budd Schulberg, the writer; Sam Spiegel, the producer; and Marlon Brando. Experience as a director had now persuaded him that the Group Theater had it wrong: theater was not a collective art. A successful production expressed "the vision, the conviction, and the insistent presence of one person. It is best when it is undiluted by artistic cooperation."

He had abandoned the Group Theater in another way too—and one that caused him the greatest trouble in the decade of his greatest success. For not only was the Group politically radical, but it contained a secret Communist cell—a cell that Mr. Kazan joined for a year and a half in 1934-35. Then, when V. J. Jerome, the American Communist Party's cultural commissar, ordered the cell to seize control of the Group Theater, Mr. Kazan balked. At a special cell meeting, a comrade from Detroit laid down the line, denounced the obstructionist as a foreman type trying to curry favor with the bosses and called for repentance and submission.

Mr. Kazan resigned from the party that night. He had learned "all I needed to know about how the Communist Party of the United States worked. The Man from Detroit had been sent to stop the most dangerous thing the Party had to cope with: people thinking for themselves. . . . I understood the police state from him." Similar Communist attempts to discipline artists—successfully in the case of John Howard Lawson and Albert Maltz, two loyal party members, unsuccessfully with Budd Schulberg—confirmed him in his contempt for the party. Mr. Kazan remained a man of the left but was rather disengaged from politics.

Cut from 1935 to 1952. Senator Joseph McCarthy is in the ascendancy. The House Un-American Activities Committee is riding high. Mr. Kazan, summoned by the committee, refuses to name names. His future in films is at once in jeopardy. Hollywood grandees—Spyros Skouras, Darryl F. Zanuck, Bud Lighton—urge him to be sensible. He talks to his cherished friend Arthur Miller. (Mr. Miller in his fine memoir, *Timebends,* recalls this conversation as taking place after Mr. Kazan gave the committee names; Mr. Kazan, quoting his diary, says it took place after his decision but before his testimony. They agree on the substance of the conversation.) What, Mr. Kazan asks, would he be giving up his career for? "I said I'd hated the Communists for many years and didn't feel right about giving up my career to defend them. . . . Was I sacrificing for something I believed in?"

He named names. So did Clifford Odets. (Arthur Miller did not.) "The sad fact," Mr. Kazan writes, "is that what was possible for me hurt Clifford mortally. . . . He gave away his identity . . . he was no longer the hero-rebel, the fearless prophet of a new world." But the Anatolian had a gift for survival. Looking back, he insists that he has no regrets about his action; yet 35 years later he was "still worrying" about it. "What I'd done was correct, but was it right?" It remains hard for those who never faced the dilemma to pass judgment. I see a tendency today to regard the American Communists as heroes. But was it so heroic to conspire in secret, deny cherished beliefs, take the Fifth instead of emulating the Bulgarian Communist Georgi Dimitrov in the Reichstag trial and boldly declaring convictions? Why was it laudable for ex-Nazis or ex-Klansmen or ex-mobsters or ex-White House or National Security Council staffers to name names and contemptible for ex-Communists to do so? Yet doubts linger.

Mr. Kazan endured a storm of anger in the following years. Old friends cut him. Letters, often anonymous, reviled him. Even **On the Waterfront** was condemned as a glorification of the informer, the Kazan-Schulberg apologia for betrayal. But time passed. Friendships were repaired, though they were never quite the same again. Mr. Kazan made memorable movies, engaged in the effort to establish a repertory company in Lincoln Center, wrote novels and continued his lifelong struggle to understand and define himself.

Much of his book is the story, told with remarkable and at times excessive candor, of Mr. Kazan's turbulent personal life—his tangled feelings about his parents; his relationship, compounded of love, admiration and resentment, with his loving, intelligent and inflexible first wife, Molly Thacher; his beautiful and gifted second wife, Barbara Loden; his serene and reassuring third wife, Frances. There is very little, oddly, about his children, but much about his several psychoanalysts and perhaps too much about his innumerable girlfriends, some named, some not. Infidelity, he tells us, saved his life—a self-justifying claim, but maybe in this case there is something to it.

In the end, he believes, he finally learned to take off the mask of affability, to forget the Anatolian smile, not to contain his rage but to express it, not to deny his violent feelings but to respect them. He may overdo his claims of a lifelong silence in the face of intolerable provocation. His own narrative suggests a sufficient capacity for anger throughout his life. Nor does one get the impression that Mr. Kazan has entered into tranquillity at last. Self-revelation does not necessarily equal self-knowledge. (pp. 7, 9)

He anticipates that this book will bring about "another terrible fall from favor." Readers, he fears, will find it unfair, ugly, hateful, vulgar. Perhaps it is all those things at one time or another. It is also an indispensable account of American theater and film in our time and the impassioned testament of an artist who has done his valiant best to tell the truth about himself. (p. 9)

Arthur Schlesinger, Jr., "Behind that Anatolian Smile," in The New York Times Book Review, *May 1, 1988, pp. 7, 9.*

David Thomson

[In **Elia Kazan: A Life**], Kazan is a confessor-rascal, a limelit self-deceiver brandishing the open blade of candor in our faces. Thank God he's just on the page, as tortured and compelling as Whittaker Chambers. He doesn't seem possible or reliable as a real companion. He is not likable, yet he frets over a life torn between scorpion and nice guy. Esteemed for over 40 years as a director, he has never lost the paranoia of an actor who yearns to be noticed as a loitering, bristling outcast, dangerous and in love with danger. Those untamable characters played by Brando and James Dean were projections of Elia Kazan, or Kazanjioglou, from Constantinople and Kayseri. He was a Greek born in Turkey, already a cornered beast; and later he was known as Gadg, the Gadget, because he was the one in a coterie of artists and intellectuals who had the hands to fix common things when they broke. It was a patronizing name, goading his wish to be the leading man.

At the age of 78, from a decade of quiet following the wretched *Last Tycoon,* Kazan volunteers his *Life.* He is not so modest that he doesn't see it as a bequest, conceived in the spirit of Rousseau's *Confessions.* The gift is overwhelming; at 825 pages of story, it knows no decency of restraint. On page 782 he promises, "This is as far as I'm going," but requires the stopping space of a Ferrari on ice. I'd guess that editors gave up on his furious, beguiling idealizing of himself.

Make no mistake, he has the urgency and grabby stamina of a great gossip. This is an engrossing, shameless book, so compulsive, tasteless, and robust that it lurches along under its own weight. It strikes me as the most interesting and probably the most enduring achievement of Kazan's varied career. As autobiography, written with the zest of a proven popular novelist, it is as inadvertent an admission of the compromises in American show business as anything we have. It is also the self-portrait of an incorrigible sensationalist, a manipulative scene-maker and self-pitying bastard such as might turn his own stomach if he didn't heave and sigh with so many youthful ways of thinking well of himself. Without irony in its writing or its gaze, *A Life* prompts some pained mirth: How can all this frankness stay so unaware and feel so sly? The answer tells us a great deal about our respect for "sincere" and "raw" acting, a cult for which Kazan has been such a notable enforcer. (p. 34)

In early 1952 Kazan was 42 and without equal as a director working on stage and screen. The son of a rug dealer who landed in New York in 1913, he had made his own determined way, an ardent Anatolian outlaw, to Williams College and the Yale School of Drama—poor, ugly, small, and non-WASP, horny for the cool blond girls, and murderously inclined toward the social stiffs those girls preferred. He made it, on every count. By way of the Group Theatre, he developed as actor, godsend gadget, and director, thriving on the rivalry with Strasberg and Harold Clurman, marrying a lovely establishment blonde (Molly Thacher), electrifying audiences in supporting roles in *Waiting for Lefty* and *Golden Boy.* By the early 1940s he was directing on stage—*The Skin of Our Teeth, Harriet, One Touch of Venus, Jakobowsky and the Colonel.*

We might note the haphazard range of this material and Kazan's early charm with great stars: Tallulah Bankhead, Helen Hayes, Mary Martin. (In *A Life* he tells how Bankhead went from raging prima donna to naked candidate for his bed, comeuppanced at finding a younger actress warm there already.) When he took up the Hollywood offers, in 1944, he embarked on a string of films as impersonal as, but less deft than, his early stage work—*A Tree Grows in Brooklyn, Sea of Grass, Boomerang!, Gentleman's Agreement, Pinky, Panic in the Streets.*

Those movies are as dull and as dependent on quickly forgotten melodrama as [Kazan's novels]. . . . They are the work of someone ready to do anything to get a shot in pictures. At MGM, on *Sea of Grass,* Kazan went along with every studio concession to bogusness, to overweight, lazyminded stars, and to flatulent product: before shooting started, he knew he was about to make a hopeless, irrelevant picture. Yet a year later, when he was invited by Tennessee Williams and the producer Irene Mayer Selznick to direct the premiere of *A Streetcar Named Desire,* Kazan became the spearhead of a fresh poetic realism, of Method acting, of something wild and threatening thrown in the face of the audience.

Those who knew him then saw an uncanny, eroticizing inspiration with actors, a gadget's way of getting at the best fruit, as well as a careerist's indifference to material. Kazan was not shy about exulting in the Anatolian's hard-earned glory; the most groupish in the Group Theatre had always known that his wolfish ambition had to walk alone. In the 1930s he was a member of the Communist Party for less than two years. He resigned after a special meeting, in the Strasbergs' apartment, where he was berated and humiliated by a Party official from Detroit for independence of thought. (pp. 34-5)

And so, in 1952, after one HUAC session in which he had resisted it, Kazan named old friends. Why? It is one purpose of *A Life* to build an elaborate context in which Kazan sees (and saw) creative, critical instincts being stifled by the Party. He refers to Albert Maltz writing and then recanting a heretical article in *New Masses* in 1936. he mentions a later colleague, Budd Schulberg, refusing the Party's orders to turn *What Makes Sammy Run?* (1941) into a more "proletarian" novel.

But Kazan's justification hinges on two events much closer in time to his own informing. One is a meeting he and John Steinbeck had with the Mexican cameraman Gabriel Figueroa, about *Viva Zapata!,* the script of which Steinbeck had written and which Kazan wanted to film with Mexican assistance in Zapata's old territory. Figueroa took the script away and came back with a silent companion to decline it. Kazan imagined the dead hand of the Party in this, and he laughed off Figueroa's joke—"How would you like Mexicans in Illinois filming the life of Lincoln, in Spanish, with a Mexican actor?" The eventual *Zapata!*—muddled, picturesque, patronizing, half baked, with Brando as the Mexican leader, but filmed on the American side of the border—does nothing to suggest Kazan ever understood Figueroa's anxiety. His own "vision" was too precious to recognize Mexican concerns.

The other "warning" picked up by Kazan's greedy instincts was Arthur Miller's withdrawal from *The Hook.* This was a waterfront script they were working on, in which Zanuck wanted the gangsters to be changed into Commies. Again, Kazan regarded Miller's shift of mind as dictated by Party pressure. You can't trust anyone, Kazan seems to protest, as he gets ready for his own act of betrayal.

He says now, as he did then, that he named names to dispel secrecy, which offended him as the stealthiest and most corrupting force of communism. Within days of his HUAC session, Kazan ran an ad in the *New York Times* that attempted explanation. It is not quoted in *A Life,* though Kazan now reveals that it was written by his loyal wife, Molly, who had urged him to do whatever felt best in his heart. Briefly, the ad claimed that America deserved all the facts now and said that Kazan had delayed in revealing what he knew because of misguided attachments to old friends and unpopular opinions:

> Secrecy serves the Communists. At the other pole, it serves those who are interested in silencing liberal voices. . . . We must never let the Communists get away with the pretense that they stand for the very things which they kill in their own countries.

> I am talking about free speech, a free press, the rights of property, the rights of labor, racial equality and, above all, individual rights. I value these things. I take them seriously. I value peace, too, when it is not bought at the price of fundamental decencies.

> The motion pictures I have made and the plays I have chosen to direct represent my convictions.

> I expect to continue to make the same kinds of pictures and to direct the same kinds of plays.

Having read *A Life,* I venture to think that Kazan was no more afraid of Communism in 1952 than he was drawn to its principles in 1934. He has said that in the '30s he was red out of envy of Williams privilege. In the '50s, too, his actions are most explicable in terms of his own emotional needs. The "danger" in those he named had been overlooked many years by his silence. They were smaller people than Kazan, whose lives were made harder because of his testimony. Yet, in talk and in later works, he compared himself with reformed gangsters who gave evidence against the mob, or with decent soldiers who reported American massacres of the Vietnamese. Kazan could not see that his talking was a rather minor event, however much he felt like Lear on the heath. (pp. 35-6)

It was asserted, immediately, that Kazan's HUAC testimony permitted his new Hollywood contract. I don't believe that the linkage had to be so direct or so crass. Yet if he had declined to name people, Kazan could not have worked in Hollywood again for many years. He would not have directed **On the Waterfront, East of Eden, A Face in the Crowd, Wild River,** or **Splendor in the Grass.** And, contrary to Kazan's *New York Times* assurance, those pictures are not the same as he had been making. They are much better. A part of him soared on the danger, the notoriety, the attention.

What other daring could have come to Kazan as he informed? An answer may lie in the amazing underlife he confesses to in this book—though "confesses" is not quite the word. Now that two betrayed wives are dead, as well as those lovers he is prepared to name, he is pleased with the sexy scramblings in alleys, in the backs of cabs (a choice site for Kazan scenes), or on the floor of a theater dressing room. He insists to us, and to a third wife, that he is tranquil, ancient, and sleepy now. Yet he can hardly stop telling how inventively and recklessly he fucked around, and how adept he was at all the barefaced secrecy, the lies.

Kazan married Thacher in 1932. She died in 1963, suddenly, weeks after writing a famous poem on the death of JFK. Thereupon Kazan married Barbara Loden, the actress he directed in **Wild River** and **Splendor in the Grass** and, in 1964, in Miller's **After the Fall.** In that play, Loden

had the role of Maggie, generally regarded as a version of Marilyn Monroe, once Mrs. Miller—and before that? Yes, the mistress of Gadg. The actress Constance Dowling is another named affair. There are many others granted anonymity by this odd gentleman, because they are still living. Kazan is aggressively frank about his itch to take women from other men, about his attraction to slender blondes (the Anatolian opposite), about the abundant, compelling furtiveness that was his way of life. Indeed, he had had a son by Loden while Molly still lived. Yet the first wife and her four children by Kazan apparently knew it not. One comes away believing that Kazan could not do a play or a film without some conquest in its company.

At the same time, he claims that he never left, or would never have left, Molly; nor does he see how much kinder it might have been to quit. One longs to know what the wives thought. Not that they are neglected in this book. On the contrary, they are deeply felt objects of his affection, and Kazan is especially moving about the country toughness and acquired skepticism of Loden, about her defiance in the face of cancer, and about the one movie she directed, *Wanda,* the quality of which he never surpassed. But there is something repugnant in the revelling in affairs, and much that is blind to the author's own need for subterfuge. Kazan has a device—horribly overdone—of nudging us, of asking at his worst moments, Wouldn't we do the same? Aren't we really like that? The instinct may be shared, but what is special to Kazan is the relentless proclamation of it, the lust for coming clean that leaves all our water dirtier.

How could this horniness help account for the HUAC testimony? I can think of two ways, one speculative and marginal, the other much closer to his inner being. I have no evidence for the first, but it is possible that the committee was in a position to blackmail Kazan—if the FBI had any taste for boring surveillance, they must have seen something. The other point is that Kazan is destined to outflank the claims of loyalty. He is concerned to say that directors and actresses are inevitably drawn together sexually. But he doesn't notice what that implies about the narrow range of the material in which he did vital work; and he does not pause to consider how chilly, repetitive, and exploitative such ties can be. He assumes that the affairs are the heady, natural consequences of doing one creative chore after another. But that minimizes the process of promiscuity and the inability to sustain attachments. It is part of the erotics of gossip and informing.

It is in this area that Kazan's *Life* is most telling. How well he sees the human failure or incompleteness of Strasberg, Clifford Odets, Orson Welles, Nicholas Ray, Miller, Brando, Dean, Clift, and so on—he has known the best and often nursed their most vulnerable work into being. But he does not detect, or feel stricken by, shortcomings in himself. His own responses delight and monopolize him, as if they were extra hooks or screws on his great Gadget. He is quite sure that he has set his eyes on the highest targets: ultimate human mystery and ambiguity. He wants to borrow Jean Renoir's sense of every person having his or her own reasons, but he does not understand how dismaying or amusing that was to Renoir. An old man now, Kazan still has the exuberance of inexperience.

In his best work, Kazan has told versions of his own story. **On the Waterfront** is a blithe allegory on informing, and

East of Eden is a throbbing endorsement of male self-pity masquerading as sensitivity. Just consider how Kazan rigs the Steinbeck story so that Cal is a dear, dark boy and brother Aaron a stooge. Kazan doesn't seem to have liked Dean, but he gives no hint of realizing that his own psycho-dramatic legend set Dean in motion as a phenomenon.

It is hard to admire this Kazan; not that he leaves much room for others. The first impact of his films is their single power, and it is seldom long-lasting or comfortable when examined closely. The man he has disclosed in this book, with such panache and paternal pride, is as disconcerting as the special pleading of *East of Eden.* Yet this is an extraordinary book, and it will last as long as the twisting souls of show people are irresistible to us. Kazan's enemies have rich bait to rise to, and he may find his last years active with dispute. Perhaps he wants that. I suspect boredom—the need to shake his own life up—had a lot to do with the 1952 spilling.

In the end, the allure of Kazan's *Life* and the lesson in his work have to do with the way the manners and morality of acting, and of presenting drama, have invaded public life. This is one of those books that may show later generations when and how soul turned into performance, and why America began to prefer accomplished acting to awkwardness and difficulty. (pp. 36-8)

> *David Thomson, "The Scene-Maker," in* The New Republic, *Vol. 198, No. 19, May 9, 1988, pp. 34-8.*

Budd Schulberg

In my self-appointed role as a Hollywoodologist, I've tried to keep up with all the books by movie directors: Frank Capra, Billy Wellman, Josef von Sternberg, King Vidor. On the whole, they comprise a worthy literature on the men who finally take all those pages, and all those actors, and through the force of their talent, personality, and authority mold them into a cinematic whole (when they don't leave, as the best of them sometimes have, a cinematic hole).

While Capra was my neighbor in my childhood years at Malibu, Wellman my producer father's courageous choice for *Wings* . . . , Kazan was the only one with whom I worked. We spent more than two years on *On the Waterfront,* at least two more on *A Face in the Crowd,* and even longer on *In the Streets,* a script on Puerto Rican poverty that never made it to the screen because our prize-bedecked producer Sam Spiegel lost his nerve and walked out on us at zero hour.

So I would be dissembling if I pleaded impartiality in turning now to the latest, fattest, and most controversial of director's memoirs, *Elia Kazan: A Life.* When Kazan first approached me in the early fifties to write "a New York film with a social theme" (which became *Waterfront*), he heard my complaints about the low esteem in which the screenwriter was held in Hollywood and promised to treat my film script with the same respect he would bring to an Arthur Miller or a Tennessee Williams play: He would make suggestions, but only the writer would make changes. Although he's been accused of being selfish, ruth-

less, and only looking out for Number One, he always stood by his word and offered me genuine collaboration.

In the same spirit in which we agreed that we could not work honestly together if we did not level with each other, I plunged into his *A Life,* all 825 pages of it, everything you ever wanted to know (and sometimes even a little more) about the feisty, innovative, ambitious director. . . . (p. 55)

To learn how Kazan learned to belt even more effectively than Sinatra, "I did it *my* way!" (or, as Kazan says, "don't believe the meek will inherit the Earth"), we have to go back to his roots in Kayseri, Turkey, where his father's name was Kazanjioglou.

So many immigrants who came to America at an early age chose to cover up their foreign origins, to cleanse themselves, so to speak, of their dark beginnings, and to clothe themselves in their new American personalities. But Kazan . . . never cut those roots to Kayseri and his Greek relations living under Turkish oppression. Unlike successful assimilated Jews such as movie moguls Jack Warner and Harry Cohn, Kazan always maintained the ability to speak his native tongue—confirming that he was an outsider in an alien society in which the struggled first simply to survive, then to achieve, and finally to conquer.

It is the strength of the seventy-eight-year-old, internationally honored Kazan that he never forgets the little face with the big nose and the bad skin of the seven-year-old Elia:

> I've studied the faces of my two grandfathers. On Elia-pappou's face, I see that he was determined; crafty, stubborn, cunning, unwavering in desire, tough-hearted. He'd lived his life with his back to the wall and it shows. He had no time for gentle concerns. Kayseri was not a place for culture; the struggle was too severe. Elia-pappou passed those traits on to his eldest sons; I cannot remember my father reading a book.
>
> Equally I am the grandson of Isaak-pappou, a man who surrounded his children with love, who was, at one point in his life, glad to throw over a successful business so he could enjoy the more 'human' things in life, a man for whom family came first and who enjoyed the life of conviviality.
>
> (pp. 55-6)

[Throughout] his celebrated (if sometimes troubled) nearly sixty-year career, the determined and tough-hearted Elia-pappou and the human and life-giving Isaak-pappou would remain in contention. It was an arresting personality split that both served Kazan well and caused him loneliness and guilt, and inflicted pain on loved ones as well as devoted co-workers and friends.

Unlike Nixon and his promise to reveal himself "warts and all" (a half-truth, like everything else about our crafty thirty-seventh president), and unlike Lillian Hellman's well-written but clearly self-serving autobiographies, Kazan constantly exposes himself to the same tough-minded scrutiny he inflicts on famous colleagues and contemporaries such as Miller, Spiegel, Hellman, Bankhead, Lee Strasberg, Harold Clurman, Stella Adler, Clifford Odets, Darryl F. Zanuck, James Dean, the Hollywood playwright and Communist functionary John Howard Lawson, and the didactic party overseer (known at the time as the American cultural commissar) V. J. Jerome. All of these and more are given their comeuppance in Kazan's extended theatrical adventures.

Those who have worshipped the hallowed ground on which walked the living god Strasberg or the living legend (in Blackglama yet) Hellman will flinch at the irreverence, or worse, with which these saints of our twentieth-century arts are treated. Oh, there'll be cries of protest and "character assassination," "anti-anti-red-baiting," and "Who needs all that kissing-and-telling, bedding-and-unbedding?" There will be readers who slam it down with "Who the hell does he think he is?"

But to read this plain and bold chronicle carefully, the answer comes through with unusual, if not totally unexpected, clarity: He thinks he's Kazan, who has learned "what doesn't kill you will make you strong."

Confounding his party critics who felt he sold out to the McCarthy hysteria in 1952, Kazan, unlike other film masters, never surrendered his social zeal. The identification with the oppressed that brought him into the Communist Party during the depths of the Depression was to stay with him all his life, and would inspire and inform much of his best work. Yet, as he admits, there was always within him "the other Kazan," the intensely competitive Kazan, the individualistic and ruthless Kazan whose self-centered drive to achieve was one of his more positive, if not always socially appealing, characteristics.

Kazan simply refuses to flinch from his enemies. If they fault him for his cooperative testimony to the House Committee on Un-American Activities on his (and others') participation in the C.P. of the thirties, he faults them right back. Admitting that he agonized over whether he should cooperate, and at first torn between conflicting groups and ideas, he finally decided that the Communists had deliberately infiltrated and corrupted the left-liberals into thinking that anti-communism and anti-Stalinism were pro-fascism. Why, he asked himself, should he go on protecting secret membership in the party he had come to hate?

So Kazan went in there and gave names and was excoriated as a red-baiter and destroyer of fellow members of the Group Theatre. Denying the die-hard Hellman charge that "He did it for the money," Kazan hits back that "[Hellman] spent her last fifteen years canonizing herself." His own defense is uncharacteristically muted: "I did what I did because it was the more tolerable of two alternatives that were, either way, painful, even disastrous . . ."

So far, so good—or bad, according to your acceptance or rejection of Communist Party secrecy in the turbulent late thirties, when a Communist faction or caucus, within a democratic political or labor organization, was able to swing weight far beyond its numbers. I myself, as someone who felt the lash of Jerome even more directly than Kazan, and also felt obliged to describe my travail to a committee I didn't particularly admire (but preferred to Soviet death sentences for fellow writers), can sympathize with Kazan's wish to tear off the mask. Still, I question his extra step of taking out an ad in the *New York Times* to justify his position (actually written by Kazan's first wife, the steadfast, brainy, but inflexible Molly Thacher). A

paid ad hardly seemed a dignified way to react to one of the more complex problems of the McCarthy era.

In another significant confrontation, Kazan presents clear reasons for breaking with the co-founder and guiding spirit of the Actors Studio, Lee Strasberg, and his increasingly egocentric interpretation of the Stanislavski Method. In the beginning, Kazan believed in the Method as a liberating force from the tradition-bound American theater, but he finally came to see it as an orgone box in which the actor is trapped in his own introspections. In Lee Strasberg . . . he doesn't hesitate to smash an icon. The history of the Group Theatre and the Actors Studio is the history of new theater in America, and Kazan gives us that history in all its glory, and all its vainglory. If the latter seems to be the fault of Strasberg the starstruck ex-idealist, so be it. Kazan lets the chips—not to mention the chippies—fall where they may.

But if this sounds as if the book is all iconoclasm, getting even, and putting enemies and rivals in the stocks, the humanist, "Isaak-pappou" side restores a healthy balance, shoring the book securely against what Kazan's detractors may consider self-serving diatribe. There is no shortage of heroines and heroes in this *Life,* chief among them Kazan's first wife. Truly it was a mitzvah for Kazan, at that tender, even frightening moment when he was still the lonely outsider, to meet and eventually win a patrician and self-confident insider, a blue-blooded daughter of a Wall Street corporation lawyer; a woman of quality, of outstanding intelligence and moral character, who brought to the still painfully insecure son of a now-bankrupt and unloving father a new sense of worth, of identity, of acceptance, of purpose. Molly's choosing Kazan over the handsome and successful WASP straight arrows from the upper stratum into which she had been born was undoubtedly the major turning point of his life.

If it is a cliché to say that opposites attract, you may dust this one off and make it shine like silver, for Miss Insider, who seemed to have everything, fell for Mister Outsider at a moment in his life when he was acne faced, empty pocketed, and still unsure of the talent that Molly would recognize and nourish and support—and, yes, challenge, for her critical talents were sharply honed. Oh, could she challenge! The perfectionist in Molly was so highly developed that one of her greatest assets could eventually cross the line from highly informed constructive criticism to negative blockage. No script was ever "ready"—not Arthur Miller's, not Tennessee Williams's. After I had written my eighth (or was it tenth?) draft of *On the Waterfront,* when even Kazan and Spiegel were ready for the shoot, Molly still tried to hold up the starting date. Oh, it was very, very good, but not quite "ready."

Kazan would be (and is) the first to admit the major hurt he inflicted on her when he allowed heart (or passion) to displace mind and reason, and after many years of marriage moved out of Molly's ordered household and into the intense movable feast he enjoyed with the young blonde actress Connie Dowling. The plays and films Kazan would direct with such spectacular success would involve no emotional conflict more dramatic than his personal tug-of-war between home (Molly) and adventure (Connie). Kazan describes his inner torment without either Dostoevskian or Mailerish introspection. Again, as so often, the tone is "like it or not, this is what I did," although in this case he sounds somewhat more apologetic than usual about his eventual, rather cowardly escape from Dowling—simply leaving her a note and catching a train east. His motive, if not personally edifying, was artistically explainable: While the nights with Connie might fulfill every man's fantasy, the days were full of long silences in which they wondered how to spend the hours of light. And so it was back to Molly, and the home life to which his divided psyche would always return.

The home Kazan returned to was not exactly the conventional bourgeois union, but thanks to Molly's love and understanding it worked, at least much of the time. Kazan the loving husband and Kazan the admitted seducer of other men's wives somehow found a way to live in uneasy peace with each other, and through that emotional détente Kazan was able to establish himself first as a wonder boy of the theater and then as a major force in film after film.

As in his stage successes, Kazan brought to his films a brilliantly eclectic style. Learning on the job, with no Hollywood film experience, he directed *A Tree Grows in Brooklyn* and *Pinky,* and even won an Academy Award for *Gentleman's Agreement,* before he realized that he was still basically a stage director—guiding his actors with the energy and insight he had developed in the theater but leaving camera setups and movements to his cinematographer. After shooting the stodgy, Hollywoodized *The Sea of Grass* in an MGM hothouse, Kazan determined to break out—to film technique, to the use of the long shot (à la Ford, Stevens, and Hawks), to the power of the close-up, learning that "the camera is . . . a penetrating instrument . . . [that] looks *into* a face, not *at* a face."

In terms of direction (and here the book bristles with practical wisdom), Kazan emerges as a pragmatist, ready to draw from various disciplines. He never hesitated to do whatever was necessary to get what he was after. Twice, on *Waterfront* and *Face in the Crowd,* I saw him work with nonactors who were supposed to rise to such a level of rage as to cry with emotion. When rage was not forthcoming, Kazan walked up to his "actor," struck him sharply in the face, then stepped back and barked, "Action!" "I always wondered how the Method really worked," I teased him one time. And the homely but intense puss of the post-Stanislavski, post-Strasberg, dedicated pragmatist grinned. "Look, in this business, you take it any way you can get it."

Kazan, the ugly duckling, the little Greek Horatio Alger, may have had a roving eye, but he never took it off the ball when the ball was his work in progress. Yes, he took his share of shit in this world: early rejection (both in college and in the Group) until his now-legendary success in *Waiting for Lefty;* stonewalling from Hollywood producers afraid of the social conscience reflected in some of his more memorable films; the premature death of Molly. Another agony was the prolonged suffering of his talented, country-bred but street-smart second wife (and longtime mistress), Barbara Loden, who fought a gallant but losing battle with cancer. In the professional loss column was the turndown from Brando and his subsequent artistic differences with Kirk Douglas on the filming of *The Arrangement* (Kazan's painfully but liberatingly autobiographical best-selling novel), and his Hollywood decline with the strangely stilted (or Pinterized) *The Last Tycoon.* But again, Kazan fought back, with his will to establish himself as a novelist and his refusal to let poor and sometimes savage reviews shake his confidence or his exhilaration for his newfound love—writing.

It's all here in *A Life,* the living victories and what he aptly calls "the small deaths," like the mean reviews inflicted on his friend John Steinbeck at the end of his career: "exhausted voice," "a liberal betrays himself." Clurman, Odets, Williams, Bill Inge . . . in the closing chapters, Kazan seems obsessed with the number of friends who suffered such indignities. And despite all the glory days, Elia Kazan himself endured enough "small deaths" to bring down an elephant. But *A Life* is a 300,000-word shout of defiance at such deaths.

There is no way to win victory wreaths without risking and suffering deep wounds. It is to Kazan's credit that he makes no effort to hide either the wreaths or the wounds. *A Life* reads less like a literary memoir than a dead-honest last will and testament. Fault-finders may grumble, but who's to argue with Kazan's final cry of affirmation: "No tears. I've had one hell of a life, and I will go down, when I go down, satisfied."

Admirers will *kvell.* Enemies will yell. The book will sell. (pp. 56, 58-9)

> *Budd Schulberg, "Any Which Way He Could," in* American Film, *Vol. XIII, No. 9, July-August, 1988, pp. 55-9.*

David Denby

If manners can be said to serve as the mask of self-interest, then charming manners require that one create the illusion of interest in others. Most show-business people are determined to be charming, but whatever Elia Kazan's appeal in person (and from his own mouth one hears of much loyalty, many friendships), Kazan, as author, is ill-mannered, self-serving, and charmless. Now seventy-eight, Kazan has apparently kept note, through a long and very busy life, of every longing, slight, setback, and disappointment—and also of every rose of satisfaction. In *A Life,* he recalls some momentary defeat fifty-five years ago with the fresh outrage of unearned rebuff; he recounts a moment at a young actress's side as happily as a kid at camp who scores with a pretty girl on the first day of the summer.

Absurdly garrulous, and often coarse to the point of moral unconsciousness, Kazan tells so much—airing other people's critical opinions of his behavior as well as his own self-explanations and doubts—that he almost asks us to catch him fibbing, evading. He may be an egotist, but he is not vain, and his autobiography, for all its loutish demand on our patience, is also a soulful portrait of a man flailing about in a thicket of desire and guilt. Admitting his weaknesses and miseries, Kazan can be touching—a man longing to be a hero but uneasily aware that he may be a clown.

The book is not so much written as compiled. What makes it unusual, however, is Kazan's apparent conviction that rawness is itself a virtue. "After my family returned to New York to get the kids back to school [they had been visiting him on location], I bunked with a gentle, generous young woman who'd recently given birth; when we made love, her milk was all over my chest." A man of no ordinary foolishness wrote that awful sentence: the milk on his chest is both a badge of triumph and a challenge to the squeamish. Though of less artistic interest, *A Life* has the same pressured, slightly embarrassing emotional charge as Kazan's movies. The book offers the comic spectacle of an insatiable and shameless man. Part of the comedy is that while Kazan often sees himself as an artist driving for fulfillment, the reader is constantly amazed by, and sometimes admiring of, Kazan's astonishingly adroit careerism.

A Life is wonderfully instructive as an account of an American on the make. A powerful figure for years in both theater and film, Kazan was always watching, keeping his opinion to himself, charging in, winning or taking a beating, then, without much hesitation, picking himself up and moving on. He attained great success while remaining personally invulnerable—invisible almost—until the House Committee on Un-American Activities forced him, in 1952, to show his hand. He betrayed himself and others on that occasion, but then, in an astounding turnaround, used the ugly new cast of his personality to create his first distinctive work in the movies. . . .

According to Kazan, his father was a censorious and aloof man who never read a book. (Kazan says he has hated only two people in his life; the other person was . . . Tallulah Bankhead.) Fighting to establish himself in the face of his father's contempt, he became a crafty and calculating Anatolian in his own house. The odds against victory were steep. At his father's Fifth Avenue rug store, where Kazan was forced to work during summer vacations, George Kazan would praise to his customers the size of his nephew's—not his son's—penis. This indignity compounded a more serious worry. At the age of fourteen, he tells us, he contracted mumps, and the infection settled into his scrotum; by the end of the disease, one testicle had withered and died. He was short, bowlegged, he had a big nose and a big rump. He had one ball. At school, and later at Williams College, which he attended against his father's wishes, he lusted after girls, but only in secret.

Reading of this dolorous childhood in the way Kazan partly intends it to be read—as a warrant for later revenge—one grows a little suspicious. He tells us, for instance, that his problems with girls at school and college led to a desire to "score" that could be satisfied in later years only by pursuing the same type of blond, beautiful woman—generically, shiksas—that he had earlier failed with, or by taking women away from other men, particularly from good-looking actors or successful screenwriters. (In the case of Marilyn Monroe, however, he sounds pleased to have passed her on to his friend Arthur Miller and to have slept with her while she was considering Joe DiMaggio's proposal.)

But revenge can hardly account for all the fun he had. The book offers a proud and happy accounting of many quick boffs in limousines and hotels and dressing rooms (on the floor, before the matinee) as well as much lolling by swimming pools and within the breeze-caressed bungalows of Beverly Hills. Less a great sinner than a garden-variety cad, Kazan made a habit, for decades, of exploiting his power over young actresses. A few years after college, he married an accomplished girl from a good Yankee family, Molly Day Thacher, who seems to have assured him of his

sexual powers and his sense of his worth as a person, but his pursuit of young actresses never stopped; in fact, it increased. That some of the bundling may have been just for the fun of it, he doesn't admit. In his own eyes, he was a loser and an outcast screwing his way into the winner's circle.

After two years at the Yale Drama School, he left, dissatisfied, in 1932. "A saturnine young man of uncertain race," he was given a tryout by the revolutionary company that Cheryl Crawford, Harold Clurman, and Lee Strasberg had recently formed in New York, the Group Theater [and was accepted]. . . .

Falling, at first, under Strasberg's spell, Kazan quickly developed reservations about the great teacher's dictatorial and self-protecting way of imposing the "Method" on young actors, and he seems to have been interested less in the visions of the effusive Clurman than in impressing him with his own abilities. Here was a brilliant family with *two* disapproving fathers: he had to break into it. He was initially deemed untalented as an actor but was admitted to the permanent company when it became clear that he could set lights and build or repair anything backstage, a facility that earned him the nickname "Gadget," or "Gadge." From the beginning, he despised the name for what it revealed of his willingness to make himself useful to others. Amiable and compliant on the surface, he developed what can be amiability's internal echoes—anger, self-disgust, resentment.

His temperament, perhaps, would have led him to join a right-wing political movement. But in New York he was surrounded by left-wing actors and intellectuals. And so he visited dye plants in Paterson, went to the new Soviet films, and in the summer of 1934 joined the Communist party, becoming a member of a secret cell of actors within the Group. What can now be scarcely understood is that in 1934 Party membership could advance a young man's career in the theater. Kazan insists now that he was not then—or ever—genuinely political in his interests or instincts; and one can see that Party discipline was alien to a young man of his tumultuous ambition. (p. 37)

Despite the initial low estimate of his talents, Kazan succeeded as an actor. Playing gangsters and tough guys, he became a cult favorite, and even impressed Stark Young, the most discriminating critic of the time. But the value of acting for him, Kazan says, was that onstage he could drop the feigned sweetness and docility and express instead the anger he was feeling inside. (pp. 37-8)

According to Kazan's supply-side economy of the self, anything that adds to ego capital is useful: he defends the narcissism of actors on the ground that the self-approval derived from winning an audience's love can help liberate an actor's true self. His stage roles certainly did so for him, and now he began acting in life as aggressively as he had on stage. He started to direct plays, moving swiftly into prominence in the commercial theater, his early career culminating, in 1942, in the first production of Thornton Wilder's *The Skin of Our Teeth.*

A Life is a handbook of harsh but not cynical worldly advice, a shrewd primer in the skills of manipulating actors, producers, and agents (though not writers, whom Kazan generally reveres). For Kazan, these transactions are justified by an artist's need to gain the power to do what he wants. Directing the child actress Peggy Ann Garner in his first film, *A Tree Grows in Brooklyn* (1945), he was faced with the problem of getting a true emotion from Garner in the scene in which she must weep for her alcoholic father, who has died:

> [Garner] told me that she often dreamed of her father, who was overseas in the air force. When the day came in our schedule when she had to break down and cry, I talked to her about her father. Implicit in what I said was the suggestion that her father might not come back. (He did.)

Kazan got what he was looking for—and justice requires saying that the performance is extremely moving.

Later on, as an apostle of the Method, he would become friendly with actors, listening to their problems, trying to get hold of some psychological trait that could be mined for the performance. Mastery of the actor must be achieved one way or the other. During the rehearsals for the Wilder play, still a young man, he took control of the foul-tempered Tallulah Bankhead, who had repeatedly tried to get him fired, by screaming at her in front of the cast. He then won a stunning victory. Entering his hotel room one night during the road tryouts, she dropped her clothes, advanced to his bed,

> but stopped cold when she saw there was someone in it with me—also a member of the cast, but from a more modest salary level. Tallulah looked at me with a terrible fury, growled like an animal, pulled on her clothes, and left.

His pleasure in telling the story is obvious. But is he telling all? Did he anticipate Bankhead's offer and provide himself with a girl? In any case, after reading anecdotes like this, one begins to question Kazan's portrait of himself as a frightened outsider in America. He appears to have been able to look out for himself at any time in his life. But still:

> I trust authority—to be unfriendly. I feel I will be apprehended as much for my thoughts as for past deeds and omissions. I've done nothing for which I might be arrested, but that doesn't seem to make any difference.
>
> Even today, when I'm modestly affluent and recognized as a man of some achievement, I will be driving along or walking the streets or sitting at dinner, and suddenly I'll find myself in the grip of a fantasy in which I am defending myself—actually speaking the words, trying to wash myself of guilt. The police have me! I protest my innocence. . . . It seems I am constantly defending myself against an accusation of one kind or another.

One can't help noticing, however, that Kazan's neuroses, instead of blocking him, impel him upward. In *A Life,* the frequent passages of inward struggle are meant to enlist us in his drive to jettison the compliant side of his nature: Lord, let me be selfish so I can fulfill myself as an artist! But by the early Forties, far from having an artist's mission, he had established himself as a Broadway stage director with a pragmatic sense of what "works"; he was hardly a theater visionary like Meyerhold or Artaud. (p. 38)

Few people now have a good word to say for the Method—so inadequate for any classical play, so irrelevant to modernist work. But in the late Forties and Fifties, the Method's system of pulling large, ambivalent emotions

out of the actor's past experience was perfectly suited to the psychological themes—even the psychological clichés—of the new Miller, Williams, and William Inge dramas, whose characters were often dominated by buried secrets, illusions, and lies. Kazan was by training so much a Method man that he couldn't do his best work unless a play or playwright set off some emotional association in *his* memory. Willy Loman may have reminded many people of their own fathers (hence the generalizing weakness of *Death of a Salesman*), but the character, however hollowly symbolic, still had some specific private meaning for Kazan.

Williams, in *Streetcar,* was using much more idiosyncratic material than Miller, but Kazan decided that Williams was an outsider like himself, a fellow conspirator against bourgeois life, a restless prowler in sexual tenderloins. The character of Blanche Du Bois, Kazan thought, *was* Williams, and like Williams, who lived with an occasionally violent man and sometimes picked up rough trade, Blanche was attracted to a similarly violent force, Stanley Kowalski. Since everything, according to the Method, must proceed out of experience, Kazan, hoping to come closer to comprehending Williams's homosexuality, tells us he once had sex with a girl in Williams's apartment while the playwright in an adjoining bed had sex with a man.

Kazan gives no suggestion in his book that he had any particular ideas about theater. He was chiefly interested in the practicalities of casting and movement, in staging conflict and emotion. He directed *Streetcar* as a struggle to the death between Blanche and Stanley, and his heated production became a scandalous hit. It was only later, in the film version and on the page, that the play's literary quality became clear. Kazan infused his productions with the agitation of his resentful temper; onstage, he intended to intensify a play's erotic conflicts and psychological violence, bullying scenes to a climax, moving the line of emotion from a quiet low point to a frantic high. "We used to say in the theater: 'What are you on stage *for?*'" Kazan told the French critic Michel Ciment.

> "What do you walk on stage to get? What do you want?" . . . The asset of that is that all my actors come on strong, they're all alive, they're all dynamic—no matter how quiet. The danger of the thing may be a frenzied feeling to my work, which is unrelieved and monotonous.

He created a theater of sensation—more orgasmic than cathartic—that embarrassed those not immediately moved by it. Mary McCarthy, who admired neither Miller nor (alas!) Williams, decided that Kazan's work was merely violent and corny. There was too much broken furniture, too many weeping men, and Kazan himself was too much a "whip-cracking ring-master."

But Kazan's movie version of *Streetcar,* released in 1951, has many scenes of extraordinary delicacy in which Kazan lets the actors work quietly through lingering shots. Vivien Leigh especially, exploring the corners and shadows of Blanche's remarkable speeches, gives a sustained and beautiful performance. Throughout the rehearsals and tryouts for the stage production, Kazan had worried that Brando's Stanley was overwhelming the Blanche of Jessica Tandy. But in the movie, without reducing Brando's force in any way, Vivien Leigh's Blanche is allowed to dominate—and the poetry of the play comes through. In *A Life,* Kazan repeatedly deplores his own vacillating and compromising temperament, but perhaps this weakness added peculiar strengths to his skills as a director. Kazan could be sympathetic to both Stanley Kowalski's brute appetite and Blanche Du Bois's self-delusions perhaps because he saw both in his own character. A man of more coherent temper might not have understood the play so well. In his direction of Brando and Leigh, Kazan demonstrated at least the sensibility, if not the substance, of an artist.

He was on top of the world, a director highly successful and admired on both coasts (one of the few times this has happened). Still, he feared some impending disaster, the "Turk waiting in a shadow, with an unsheathed scimitar." But self-created myths don't necessarily tell you how to behave when disaster comes. Kazan's account of his lurching, inconsistent behavior in the McCarthy period is indelibly foolish, for he asks our approval of the good intentions he failed to honor as well as for the terrible things he actually did. At the beginning of the McCarthy period he had resolved not to give in to the House Committee on Un-American Activities. "I would not, under any pressure, name others. That would be shameful; it wasn't an alternative worth considering." In a preliminary executive session with the Committee, on January 14, 1952, he held to his resolution, admitting his Party membership but refusing to name others.

At a second session, however, on April 10—a session that he sought himself—he named the eight other members in the cell within the Group as well as a variety of other Communists he had known in such organizations as the League of Workers Theaters (later the New Theater League) and the Theater of Action. The sad pages of his testimony are a hapless, eager spilling of information, some of it asked for, some not. Kazan named front groups whose petitions he had not signed; he asserted "I did not support Henry Wallace for President," and so on. He appended to his testimony a bizarre *catalogue raisonné* of his work, describing how each play or movie was either anti-Communist in tendency or "not political."

From April 1952 on, in Victor Navasky's phrase, "Kazan emerged in the folklore of the left as the quintessential informer." What happened between the two appearances? For thirty-five years he has deflected interviewer's inquiries, promising to explain all in his own good time. But in *A Life,* though he labors heavily to re-create the events, his account is disjointed and unconvincing. Suddenly the man of candor evades and withholds.

He cites veiled threats to his career from Zanuck and Spyros P. Skouras but doesn't explain his behavior in the way that the book up to that point sets us up to expect—as the failure of nerve of an abnormally fearful child of immigrants. He now insists that he acted on principle, striking at a dangerous institution that also bullied writers and artists. . . . And Kazan was still angry about his humiliation in 1935 by the man from Detroit. Then, too, the Party thrived on silence and the squeamishness of liberals, who feared being accused of red-baiting. And so on. Underneath all this one can hear Kazan's outraged howl of disbelief: Why *me?* After all, he had never been a committed Communist like Maltz or John Howard Lawson. He had

joined as a career move. Were they now going to ruin him for it?

Kazan must have known at the time that what he was about to do was ugly, because he sought approval and forgiveness—or was it condemnation?—in advance. In scenes now famous, he absurdly tried to justify himself, a confused and masochistic suppliant, first to Arthur Miller in the Connecticut woods and then to Lillian Hellman in the Oak Room of the Plaza. Both have since expressed astonishment at his confused behavior. For he could have refused to testify and denounced the Party in speeches, articles, a book. There is no doubt that an uncooperative Kazan would have had a bad time of it in Los Angeles, but not in the New York theater, where his Communist past would have carried no stigma. And in Europe he would have been received as a hero. Despite everything he now says, there remains as large a gap as ever, in logic and in ethics, between assailing the Communist party as an institution and fingering eight old friends (as well as others), men and women who, with the exception of Paula Strasberg and Odets, possessed nothing like his fame or power.

More than once in *A Life,* he admits that naming names is a repulsive act (while defending it at the same time). But he doesn't re-create the eagerness of his prostration before the Committee; nor does he reprint the notorious ad he took out in *The New York Times* which attacked the Communist threat and defended his testimony, the text of which he says his first wife—dead since 1963—wrote for him.

After this shameful time in 1952, the jack-in-the-box sprang the lid again, and made a fast recovery that discomfited liberal moralists and others who prefer that personal fortune conform to virtue. Kazan now had real enemies, but this proved an invigorating experience that gave him—for the first time in his life, he insists—a strong sense of his identity. "I would be what I had to be—tougher than my enemies—and work harder." And he makes the defiant boast: "The only genuinely good and original films I've made, I made after my testimony."

This is true, and the second half of his book can be read as an elaborate defense of the act that Kazan is convinced transformed him into an artist. Without altering one's judgment of what he did in 1952, one has to admit that his life grows in moral interest as he begins, sometimes consciously, sometimes not, to convert his embattled new sense of himself into the material of his movies.

The irony is that one of his best movies, **On the Waterfront** (1954), reveals that he hadn't shaken the bad old Thirties. Remnants of the cloying, overexplicit tone of the left-wing theater haunt the shots of oppressed longshoremen, heads drawn together, like some choral grouping of players under a spotlight stage right; one hears that tone again in the hectoring speeches that Budd Schulberg wrote for Karl Malden's tough waterfront priest (a stand-in for the Thirties' tough labor leader).

But nothing from the American movies of the Thirties prepares one for the harsh, open-air look of the film, set in Hoboken, its sooty tenements taunted by the grandeur of Manhattan's towers. . . . There is nothing of the Thirties in the mixed shame and insolence of Brando's performance or in the beautiful and graceful sequence in which a guilty Brando hesitantly pursues a reluctant and suspicious Eva Marie Saint across the park in front of the church.

The romance between the guilt-stricken waterfront lout and the trusting convent girl is often mawkish, but in this scene the mingled abrasions of raw air and smoke support an almost painful sense of life unfolding at great risk. (pp. 40-2)

The delicacy is there again in the powerful sequence set in a saloon, in which Brando, a compromised prizefighter who has become the pet of a crooked union, exposes to his girl a self-disgust so pervasive that it sickens—Kazan had got himself on screen at last. Kazan imposed on Brando's Terry Malloy both his sense of unworthiness and, later in the movie, as Terry testifies before the Waterfront Crime Commission, his pleasure in destroying those who had dominated him. When Terry shouts, "I'm *glad* what I done!" he speaks for the Kazan who had taken a pasting in the liberal press.

Many commentators have said that *Waterfront,* a movie created by two informers (Schulberg had also cooperated with the Committee), offers a rationale in convoluted "moral" terms for ratting on one's friends, and of course this is true. But for Kazan more than self-justification may have been at stake. In the Fifties, many of his most successful colleagues were losing their morale or going under. Perhaps he feared that without asserting himself in some violent way he might have faded, too, as Odets and Williams, William Inge, Nicholas Ray, and Lee J. Cobb, each for his own reasons, did. Kazan, however, grew stronger. He was much in demand in the theater. Williams wanted him to direct all his plays, but Kazan found himself increasingly impatient with other men's work. The movies he made during this period appear to have as their subject different versions of himself—some ugly, some comical.

He is there in James Dean's resentful, unloved son in the biblical-Freudian *East of Eden* (1955), battling against the father who thinks he's worthless. Kazan's slyness, covetousness, and carnal resourcefulness show up in *Baby Doll* (1956), the erotic comedy that Tennessee Williams concocted for him out of two short plays, in which Eli Wallach, a cunning Sicilian in Mississippi, seduces the infantile but beautiful young wife of his business rival. *Baby Doll,* which caused a sensation at the time and was then mostly forgotten, is one of Kazan's films most worthy of revival. Williams's story has the structural elements of classical farce (virginal young wife, foolish middle-aged husband), but Kazan got the actors to play the characters as grotesques. . . .

Again, a mocking and undermining sense of himself comes through in *A Face in the Crowd* (1957), in which a back-country TV demagogue, rapidly rising to the top, experiences at the very peak of his success the unshakable sensation that he is a louse. Convinced that art and self-revelation were the same, Kazan eventually gave up on collaborators, telling the story of his family and himself in such memoirs and novels as *America, America, The Arrangement, The Anatolian.* This elderly self-absorption was perhaps the result of a lifetime's devotion to the Method—he has wound up talking only about himself. Still, Kazan's earlier films are among the more interesting American movies of the Fifties—coarse but emotionally

powerful. Kazan never became a moviemaker who expressed himself easily with the camera. Nevertheless, I emphasize his moments of delicacy because some of the best critics have never noticed them. Dwight Macdonald repeatedly called Kazan a vulgarian; Manny Farber saw nothing in his work but pretentious New York Freudianism and "hard-sell."

In France, Kazan as a director is revered as a master—even an obvious failure like *Wild River* (1960) is admired. To us, now, he seems an awkwardly powerful figure, a man both trapped by and expressive of the earnest, psychologically tormented side of the postwar years. His characters (sons, brothers, revolutionaries, betrayers) violently break through repressed feelings, sometimes literally ripping the doors from their hinges. Overwrought and often humorless, Kazan can also be courageous in ways threatening to the current taste for emotionally unengaged movies. Amid the dozens of teen movies of the last decade, none takes the miseries of adolescence with half the seriousness of *Splendor in the Grass,* a sustained piece of emotional filmmaking shot in velvety dark colors.

For all his Hollywood success, Kazan never quite became part of pop culture—his movies are too morose for that. But, like Robert Rossen, he flourished in the curious mannerist period between the easygoing, studio-produced genre films of the Thirties and Forties and the movie age of shopping-mall pop, both infantile and grandiose, that we live in now. Enraged, and flailing about, he often made people feel more than they wanted to at the movies. (p. 42)

> *David Denby, "Odd Man In," in* The New York Review of Books, *Vol. XXXV, No. 14, September 29, 1988, pp. 37-42.*

Dan Georgakas

[In *Elia Kazan: A Life,* an] Anatolian named Elia Kazan, ornery, charming, and unpredictable as ever, has used the genre of autobiography to force a reconsideration of his amazing career. Rekindling old issues with an energy belied by his seventy-eight years, Kazan offers unique insights into mid-century American film and theater. His approach to art is emotional rather than intellectual, and the wellspring of that emotionalism is an intense ethnic identity. Kazan aggressively articulates the often masked antipathy many white Christian ethnics feel toward mainstream culture, loathing it even as they triumph within it. Kazan reviews the family, educational, and cultural forces which left him feeling like an ugly outsider. He warns all that he has developed an Anatolian smile to mask his true sentiments which are a volatile compound of guile, ambition, and rage.

That rage found its most vivid expression in a brief stage/film acting career of eight years duration. Accounts of his stage work acknowledge both his limited range as an actor and his enormous power within that range. Rarely has the urban tough been portrayed so convincingly, an achievement that has been preserved in his supporting roles in films such as *City for Conquest.* (p. 4)

Kazan's greatest acting moment, however, was when he leaped on stage to denounce the company fink in the opening night performance of *Waiting for Lefty. New Masses* dubbed him the "Proletariat Thunderbolt." Kazan . . .

was amused by the tag. He also savored it, and his description of the cast's elation opening night sounds like a Sixties' New Leftist report on a demonstration that has exceeded the wildest expectations. Kazan asserts that the *Lefty* script still thrills him and he movingly evokes the ardor of the 1930s when he and his acting colleagues thought they would help bring socialism to America.

Kazan's shortchanging of his acting is linked to his association with the Group Theater. Rejected the first summer he applied for membership, he was kept the second summer only due to his ability to build scenery and serve as a handyman. The resulting nickname of "Gadget" or "Gadge" was a sobriquet he came to despise. Kazan now expresses doubt that the ensemble concept can work in America. Whether one agrees or disagrees, coming to grips with the issues from his perspective is useful. But in 1932 Kazan had no doubts. Lee Strasberg and Harold Clurman, the Group's leaders, seemed like demigods. No one could imagine that in less than a decade Kazan-as-director would eclipse them both.

When reflecting on his erstwhile mentors, Kazan is consistently generous yet hardnosed. He believes Clurman could dissect plays better than anyone in American theater but that he lacked the patience to hammer out the stage minutiae essential for outstanding productions. Strasberg is judged too cloistered and cerebral to be an effective director, and we are reminded of the irony that although Strasberg eventually achieved fame as a teacher of film stars, he always despised the star system and originally held film in contempt.

Once Kazan shifted his aspirations from acting to directing, his rise was meteoric. Beginning with *The Skin of Our Teeth*, he had a string of hits that made him Broadway's hottest director. He would originate nearly all of the most important plays of his time: *All My Sons, Tea and Sympathy, A Streetcar Named Desire, Death of a Salesman, Cat On a Hot Tin Roof, Dark at the Top of the Stairs*, and *JB*. The sweep of his stage work is a mini-history of mid-century American theater, beginning with the Group, moving to Broadway and worker action theater, swirling around the Actor's Studio and ending with the ill-fated Lincoln Center Repertory Company.

Kazan acknowledges that he has no sympathy for classical work and believes this is generally true of Americans. His observations on the training of American actors and the production realities of Hollywood and Broadway are told with an insider's savvy. His analysis of Clifford Odets, Tennessee Williams, and Arthur Miller is among the best to be found anywhere, and he has interesting, if less systematic, things to say about other writers with whom he worked on stage or film projects: William Inge, Franz Werfel, Thornton Wilder, Maxwell Anderson, John Steinbeck, and Budd Schulberg.

Hemingway once observed that writing was 98% perspiration. For Kazan, the perspiration ratio for directing appears to be 99.5%. In addition to having the sheer stamina required to realize even the best scripts, Kazan has always shown a special talent for handling actors. He remains the supreme director of Marlon Brando. His comments on why a Kirk Douglas fails in *The Arrangement* (film) or a Helen Hayes succeeds in *Harriet* (play) underscore his belief in the primacy of correct casting and how the right

actor may be better equipped to realize a script than the most insightful director.

Stage success led to the inevitable invitation to direct in Hollywood. Kazan's candor at how little he knew about film and how long it took him to grasp the medium's character is unaffected. If anything, he undervalues his early work. Whatever his lack of visual verve, his reliance on dialog, and his stage hangovers, his films often had an importance for their own time and a few have shown staying power. Of the earliest films, *A Tree Grows in Brooklyn* retains a certain working class and ethnic charm, *Gentleman's Agreement* was indeed the first direct assault on anti-Semitism in popular film, and even the disastrous *Pinky* took up the racial theme of 'passing for white,' a topic rarely addressed in popular films. Kazan admits to a certain fondness for the old studio system but differentiates between the hands-on producers like Darryl F. Zanuck and the bureaucrats at MGM. He also has some surprisingly positive things to say about the flamboyant Sam Spiegel, going so far as to assert that *On the Waterfront* bears Spiegel's imprint as much as it does that of Schulberg, Brando, and Kazan. (pp. 4-5)

Kazan's involvement with the Communist Party in the 1930s is hardly surprising. His original attraction to the CP was not like that of a college student who has ideological pretensions and wishes to help others but more like an angry worker looking for an instrument to fight with. Kazan never charges that he was duped or misled, and he writes affectionately of his involvement with radical theater. To this day he considers himself a socialist and thinks he is a better radical than his former comrades who lost their commitment to democratic procedures.

Kazan's break with the Party in 1935 involved his membership in the CP fraction within the Group. When his fraction was notified by V. J. Jerome, the CP cultural leader, that they must take control of the Group, Kazan was outraged. His problem was less with the proposal than with the process. The workers involved had not been consulted, much less asked to vote, and an organizer of auto workers was brought in from Detroit to socially intimidate the intellectuals and validate the directive. Kazan resigned from the Party but, unlike individuals who left due to events in the U.S.S.R., Kazan remained in the Party's social orbit. He thought the Hitler-Stalin Pact was a necessary evil and he did not become estranged from the policies of the U.S.S.R. until the late 1940s.

Hollywood's executives were always leery of Kazan, rightly judging him a social rebel with whom they had little in common. Nonetheless, his political views would have remained largely irrelevant if there had been no McCarthyism. During the first phase of the witch hunt, Kazan worked with other directors to preserve the integrity of the Screen Directors Guild. As the process moved to the federal level, Kazan's first impulse was to resist. He did not name names when first called. Nothing in his nature or culture made him a likely friendly witness. Why, then, did he capitulate when called a second time?

The decisive influence was his wife, Molly Day Thacher, who had come to a systematic critique of Communism. The early 1950s were not the Age of Glasnost but of *Darkness at Noon* and Big Brother, a time when murderous purges rent the ranks of Communist parties throughout

Eastern Europe. Molly thought it would be ridiculous for her husband to sacrifice his career to a movement that seemed ever more sinister and a Party he had left years earlier. Kazan had encountered more than one artistic conspiracy while in Los Angeles and New York and did not think it unlikely that similar cabals could exist in Washington. The strong anti-Communist statement that appeared in *The New York Times* over his signature was written by Molly, but Kazan assumes total responsibility for his decision to testify. His claim of being a premature anti-Stalinist isn't convincing. He could have made his views public, revealed his personal history, yet stood mute before the nation's inquisitors. He was not that brave. Nor were any others who shared his perspective.

Not only was Kazan denounced by the ideological Left, but actors like Brando also lost enthusiasm for working with him, novices at the Actors Studio gave him the cold shoulder, and his intimacy with Miller was shattered. Kazan writes with feeling that while he could withstand such ostracism, a person like Odets could not. Odets needed to be part of a political movement. Kazan's pride that his outsider's psyche allowed him to tough it out is a kind of bragging and an indirect suggestion that he too suffered. He is enraged by charges that he signed lucrative contracts as a result of the testimony and he condemns those who judge him without knowing the facts. He also believes that many critics seek an instant intellectual halo by attacking the friendly witnesses. What he refuses to come to terms with is that, unlike those who resisted, he avoided the blacklist and could continue to work.

His best films followed HUAC and were often linked to his testimony. He asserts that *Viva Zapata!* was anti-Communist in that the commissar is portrayed as a villain, but radical in extolling a revolutionary leader willing to abdicate power. That rendering of Zapata is not a Kazan-Steinbeck fantasy, as Zapata was greatly influenced by anti-authoritarian anarchist doctrine. Kazan also speaks of the problems generated by Communist-oriented unions when he thought of filming in Mexico. Given his background, his fears seem credible and respresent an aspect of left-led unions ignored by many progressive writers.

In regard to the testifying theme in *On the Waterfront,* Kazan says that was not what attracted him to a film that began as an Arthur Miller project. Once the film was underway, however, he exploited the testimony theme for his own purposes. He writes that when Terry shouts that he is glad he testified, it is the director speaking. Most readers' reaction may well be that the director doth protest too much.

The incredible success of *On the Waterfront* has obscured the breadth of Kazan's later film work. *A Face in the Crowd* certainly merits reconsideration as a warning about the emerging unholy alliance of politics and media. *Splendor in the Grass, Wild River,* and *Baby Doll* address contemporary issues in an engaging and often controversial manner. Kazan's favorite post-HUAC film, however, is *America, America,* the work which first placed his personal life at the center of his art.

America, America's assertion of ethnic roots was the fruition of Kazan's growing need to become an author. He understood that film authorship might belong to a distinctive actor like Cagney or an activist producer like Zanuck, but it usually belonged to the director, especially a director who authored or coauthored the script. He wanted to be such a creator and this intense need to put his distinctive imprint on his work eventually led him to abandon direction to become the ultimate author—a novelist.

As a prose stylist Kazan would be far more pedestrian than he ever was as a director, but some of his novels became best sellers and it is easy to believe him when he says he derives greater pleasure from his writing than he ever did from directing. We can posit that with this autobiography we have heard his individual voice more clearly than ever before. What is also apparent in the same work is that, despite his desire for personal authorship, Kazan's best work has been in intensely collaborative efforts, collaborations whose quality is rare in both theater and cinema. Had he not lost moral authority by his HUAC capitulation and alienated himself from those politically closest to him, one wonders what kind of collaborations might have been. Would he have had the same need to assert direct authorship?

The tumultuous sex life described in the autobiography has drawn as much attention as his comments on art. Fascinating as that topic is, it is largely irrelevant to the issue of evaluating his work. What is relevant is that when he writes about female colleagues such as Stella Adler, Irene Selznick, and Cheryl Crawford, ideological adversaries such as Lillian Hellman, and 'difficult' actors such as Tallulah Bankhead, the tone is not different or any less serious than when he writes about males. His discussion of Marilyn Monroe, whom he knew far better than most people who have written books about her, contains sensational details but is not exploitative. Instead he provides thoughtful observations on her relationship with Hyde, DiMaggio, Miller, and Strasberg. He also reveals his role in shaping the Monroe character in *After the Fall.*

While there is much about his parents, Kazan reveals virtually nothing about his own parenting. We are particularly frustrated not knowing the dynamics between Kazan and the son illegitimately born while he was still wed to Molly, and he drops a veil over his current marriage. The privacy he evokes in these areas stands out in a confessional autobiography that holds back on little else.

Considerable detail is given to his marriage with Molly. Long after their sexual life ended, they remained professional partners. Kazan writes with enormous compassion about his wife's failure to achieve her aspiration to become a successful playwright, but he does not deal with how his own needs and demands may have been a factor in her failure. The nature of their marriage will seem odd to most Americans but is not so unusual in Kazan's native culture.

Kazan also writes at length about his marriage to Barbara Loden who originated the Monroe character in *After the Fall.* He exhibits no artistic or sexual jealousy when he outlines her eventual efforts at independent film production with another man. What is truly heartrending is his account of her fatal struggle with cancer. His devotion to her at this time is as much a part of his inchoate emotional life as his incessant philandering. His adieu to Clurman, who died of cancer at the same time as Loden, is equally powerful.

Like all who write about themselves, Kazan has certainly colored events in his favor. Generally, however, one feels he has tried to remember honestly and to record his memories faithfully. The man is never fancy. He is no artistic pilot offering aerial tricks. He is infantry, an artistic grunt who files bloodstained reports from the front lines. Although he has garnered numerous honors, a certain critical silence continues to surround his work. Intellectuals who would be most sympathetic to the progressive content of his art remain estranged from him because of the HUAC role. Some who suffered during the 'scoundrel time' have forgiven him, most have not. Forgiveness is particularly difficult when he keeps insisting he did no wrong. There are also those who dare not praise his work for fear they will be labeled ideological traitors or softies.

Kazan, ever the audacious outsider-insider, has taken the matter of his intellectual shunning into his own hands. His preemptive self-evaluation of his times has catapulted him back into the consciousness of the film and theater worlds. Whether praised by Arthur Schlesinger in *The New York Times Book Review* [see excerpt above], savaged by Walter Bernstein in *In These Times,* or chided by Eric Bentley in *The Nation,* Kazan has forced the public scrutiny his work merits.

Perhaps the most appropriate response to Kazan was made long ago by Zero Mostel. Shortly after Kazan's HUAC appearance, Mostel met him on a New York street. Unlike others who had been blacklisted and now avoided the 'friendlies,' Mostel acknowledged Kazan's presence and agreed to share a drink. But before they entered a bar, Mostel put his arm around Kazan's neck, squeezing a bit too tightly to be simply friendly and said, in the most dolorous voice Kazan had ever heard, "Why did you do that? You shouldn't have done that." And how do we know about the tightness of that neck squeeze and the sadness in that voice? Kazan has recorded it in his autobiography. (pp. 6-7)

Dan Georgakas, "A Reconsideration of Elia Kazan," in Cineaste, *Vol. XVI, No. 4, 1988, pp. 4-7.*

Hugh MacDiarmid

1892-1978

(Born Christopher Murray Grieve) Scottish poet, essayist, editor, and prose writer.

MacDiarmid is generally considered the greatest Scottish poet since Robert Burns, although his uneven literary output and frequent use of the Scots dialect have resulted in general unfamiliarity outside of the United Kingdom. A zealous patriot, MacDiarmid glorified the Scottish people and landscape in verse praised for its controlled elegance and lyricism. Influenced by his country's traditional ballads and folk songs, MacDiarmid's forthright style combines wry humor, pathos, and vivid metaphorical language. Kenneth Cox contended: "His strength was in assertion: he spoke out straight and clear and could say almost nothing in a way that rang in the mind. When he lost grip he still kept going till he either startled or left gasping. He injected poetry with the rhythms and the vocabulary of prose, developing movements of torrential flow. He broadened its scope and made it interesting to everybody. He had the facility and the fallibility of the journalist and no finesse at all."

MacDiarmid was born in Langholm, Dumfriesshire, near the border of England. He became interested in literature when his family moved into a flat in the same building that housed the town library. He was educated at a local academy, where one of his teachers, Francis George Scott, a prominent songwriter of the era, later collaborated closely with MacDiarmid on his early poetry. MacDiarmid became a student teacher in Edinburgh in 1908, but soon gravitated toward journalism and started working at local newspapers. He also began a lifelong involvement with socialist politics, joining the Independent Labour Party at sixteen. In 1915, he enlisted in the Royal Army Medical Corps and served as a sergeant in Greece and France. MacDiarmid's experiences in World War I awakened a sense of national identity that he felt a need to express verbally. This desire and his vehement dislike of the English, resulting from having been required to speak and write in traditional English in school, led MacDiarmid to initiate the Scottish Literary Renaissance, a movement devoted to reviving interest in poetry written in the Scots dialect. Many critics assert that MacDiarmid's best poems were written in Scots. Diane Ackerman observed: "MacDiarmid is a poet of prodigious scope, astonishing reverent penetration, and a master of conventional English. His reasons for doing some poems in [Scots] have to do with elements in Scottish psychology which have seemed to him untranslatable, or incapable of being transposed."

MacDiarmid's first book, *Annals of the Five Senses,* was published under his given name before his involvement with the Scottish Literary Renaissance and contains poems and essays with visionary qualities. His critically acclaimed essay "A Four Years' Harvest" is a satirical and sensitive analysis of World War I. *Sangschaw* and *Penny Wheep,* MacDiarmid's first two collections of Scots verse, are chiefly comprised of short lyric poems. These early works examine ordinary events while metaphorically extending the scenes to metaphysical implications. In "Empty Vessel," for example, MacDiarmid uses the death of a child as a pretext to contemplate the limits of knowledge and the nature of language.

Critics assert that MacDiarmid found his voice with his third book, *A Drunk Man Looks at the Thistle.* The title poem, 2,685 lines long, was described by Diane Ackerman as "that effortless-looking, dynamic, and precarious feat of deep-sea diving into his own head." The work astonished the Scottish literati, wrote David Daiches, like "the shock of a childbirth in church." In turns comic, philosophical, ironic, and sexual, "A Drunk Man Looks at the Thistle" is presented as a high-spirited, stream-of-consciousness interior monologue by an inebriated person pondering Scotland's national emblem, the thistle. The poem, which celebrates and satirizes Scottish history and society, is widely considered MacDiarmid's masterpiece. His next work in Scots, the long poem *To Circumjack Cencrastus,* employed many of the same techniques used in *A Drunk Man* but is considered to lack the unity and energy of its predecessor. The short Scots verses in *First Hymn to Lenin and Other Poems* and *Scots Unbound and*

Other Poems include distinct political themes, while several other poems are written in conventional English. MacDiarmid discovered the Scots dialect to be a difficult medium in which to express his newfound aesthetic and scientific interests. Such poems as "Water of Life" and "Excelsior" combine the lyricism of Scots with speculative passages written in English. Many critics maintain that MacDiarmid's finest poem in English is "On a Raised Beach," included in the collection *Second Hymn to Lenin and Other Poems.* A sustained meditation on the beginning and end of creation—from the stones on a beach to humanity—"On a Raised Beach" offers an unaccommodating homage to all earthly forms in four hundred lines of free verse.

In the 1940s and 1950s, MacDiarmid began concentrating on writing what he referred to as "poems of fact," which contain enigmatic rhetoric, myriad styles that combine poetry and prose, and multiple ideas and prophesies. These epical poems are written in English and have been compared with Ezra Pound's *Pisan Cantos* and T. S. Eliot's *The Wasteland. In Memoriam James Joyce* and *The Kind of Poetry I Want* are two of the better-known "poems of fact" in which MacDiarmid attempts to present as many influential concepts and theories of society as possible. Neither volume received much critical recognition, and while MacDiarmid continued to write essays, autobiographies, and other prose works until his death, these later works failed to achieve the acclaim of the early Scots verse that established MacDiarmid as a distinguished contributor to the annals of Scottish poetry.

(See also *CLC,* Vols. 2, 4, 11, 19; *Contemporary Authors,* Vols. 5-8, Vols. 85-88 [obituary]; and *Dictionary of Literary Biography,* Vol. 20.)

PRINCIPAL WORKS

POETRY

Annals of the Five Senses [as C.M. Grieve]   1923
Sangschaw   1925
A Drunk Man Looks at the Thistle   1926
Penny Wheep   1926
The Lucky Bag   1927
To Circumjack Cencrastus: or, The Curly Snake   1930
First Hymn to Lenin and Other Poems   1931
Scots Unbound and Other Poems   1932
Tarras   1932
Selected Poems   1934
Stony Limits and Other Poems   1934
Second Hymn to Lenin and Other Poems   1935
Direadh   1938
Speaking for Scotland   1939
Cornish Heroic Song for Valda Trevlyn   1943
Poems of the East-West Synthesis   1946
A Kist of Whistles: New Poems   1947
In Memoriam James Joyce   1955
Poems   1955
Stony Limits and Scots Unbound and Other Poems   1956
The Battle Continues   1957
Three Hymns to Lenin   1957
The Kind of Poetry I Want   1961
The Blaward and the Skelly   1962

Bracken Hills in Autumn   1962
Collected Poems   1962
Poems to Paintings by William Johnstone 1933   1963
The Ministry of Water: Two Poems   1964
Six Vituperative Verses   1964
Two Poems: The Terrible Crystal, A Vision of Scotland   1964
The Fire of the Spirit: Two Poems   1965
Poet at Play and Other Poems, Being a Selection of Mainly Vituperative Verses   1965
Whuculls   1966
A Lap of Honour   1967
On a Raised Beach   1967
A Clyack-Sheaf   1969
More Collected Poems   1970
Song of the Seraphim   1973
Direadh I, II, and III   1974
The Complete Poems   1978
The Socialist Poems   1978

OTHER

Contemporary Scottish Studies: First Series   (criticism) [as C. M. Grieve] 1926
Albyn; or, Scotland and the Future   (political essays) [as C. M. Grieve] 1927
The Present Position of Scottish Music   [as C. M. Grieve] 1927
At the Sign of the Thistle: A Collection of Essays   1934
Five Bits of Miller   (fiction)   1934
The Islands of Scotland: Hebrides, Orkneys and Shetlands   (poetry and prose)   1939
Lucky Poet: A Self-Study in Literary and Political Ideas   (autobiography)   1943
The Company I've Kept   (autobiography)   1966

Hugh MacDiarmid   [in an interview with Alexander Scott]

[Scott]: *You were born and brought up in Langholm, Scotland, in the Borders. . . . Did you start writing poetry when you were still a boy in Langholm?*

[MacDiarmid]: Yes. I think I had my first attempts at verse published when I was about twelve, in the local paper, you know. I was always interested in poetry.

And, were they in English at that time?

They were in English, yes.

As a result of our educational system?

Well, at school—I think we all spoke Scots in Langholm, at home my parents spoke Scots—at school we were punished if we lapsed into Scots. We were supposed to speak what they would call "standard English," which is peculiar to Scotland, of course; you don't find it in England itself at all.

But you still spoke Scots, of course, the minute you escaped from it.

Well, I didn't come back to Scots until after the First World War when I was demobilized. (pp. 1-2)

[*When*] *you first came back, after the war, and settled in Scotland, in Montrose, you began to issue the anthology called* Northern Numbers *and at that time you yourself would be still writing in English.*

Yes, still in English, yes, yes.

And what turned your mind particulary towards writing in Scots, because I remember at that time you were actively hostile to the vernacular circle of the Burns Club in English and their attempts to revive the Doric, as they call it.

I have always hated the Harry Lauder type of thing Scots had degenerated into and I knew that the formation of vernacular circles under the auspices of the London Burns Club simply concerned to prolong that sort of thing and I wanted something entirely different. I had become interested in various European language movements by that time and I began to realize that something similar could be done in Scotland itself, you see.

And how did you start experimenting in Scots?

Well, by going to where the words were, you know. The dictionary. . . . That's what triggered me off—the words themselves actually triggered me off.

But of course some of the words weren't just in the dictionary, they were already in your own head and experience.

Oh yes. There had been a lot of lapsed vocabulary, you know, and it was necessary to reinforce the language with extended vocabulary very extensively.

But you began really with playing with the words.

Oh yes, oh yes.

So there was an element of the game, an element of fun.

Oh yes.

An element of deliberate . . .

No one took it seriously at first at all.

Until you discovered that this was the way that you wanted to go.

I discovered that I could write better poetry in Scots than I could in English.

And the first poems in Scots were on the whole short lyrics, weren't they?

Very short lyrics, yes. That was quite natural, of course, because nearly all English poetry is short lyrics, you see, and I hadn't begun to think in terms of anything else and realize that the lyric was no longer an adequate medium in the modern world with its big scientific developments and so on.

So very quickly your **Sangschaw** *came out, the first book of lyrics, in 1925, and the second book* **Penny Wheep,** *in 1926, already has extended poems in it.*

Yes, yes. They were leading to *A Drunk Man.* (pp. 2-4)

Now, of course, there are all kinds of stories around about the composition of **A Drunk Man,** *or maybe I shouldn't say the composition as there's no doubt that you composed it but about the organization of the material. There's this story about yourself and F. G. Scott putting it into its present*

order, shall we say. Is this story reasonably accurate or is it largely mythical?

It depends exactly what the story is, you know. Scott was invaluable to me, there's no question about that at all. He had a [greater] knowledge of Scottish literature, poetry in particular, than I had at that time; but it was simply the organization of the poem that he was mainly concerned with and I had written a great deal more than appeared in the final text, and a lot of it was below par, below the level of certain other things, and he helped me by suggesting that this and that and the other should be left out and the whole thing strengthened on the basis of the best, what he regarded and what I came to regard as the best things in the text.

Well, I believe he is also claimed to have provided the last two lines of the poem.

He claims that but I don't remember that as a matter of fact. I am quite willing to allow him the credit for that.

Well, I wish I had provided these last two lines. I have often wondered about the next long poem **To Circumjack Cencrastus,** *if it might not have benefitted by something of the same treatment—it's a very long poem with some marvelous things in it, but rather more unequal, shall we say, than* **A Drunk Man.**

That was written at a very bad time of my life when I was coping with what finished up as a divorce from my first wife, you know, and that was one of the reasons why I failed to concentrate as I should have done on the idea of the fundamental snake in the way that I concentrated on the idea of the thistle as a symbol. If I had been more realistic in the handling of the snake and so on, I could have brought the whole thing together in a better way, I think.

I think that's the difference between the two poems, that the thistle becomes protean, it becomes dozens of different things whereas the snake just lies there as a snake and never really develops into the various aspects that you want it to. However you went away from Scotland around that time. Do you think there is any connection between your departure from Scotland about 1930 and the fact that in the early 1930's you wrote so many poems investigating your own Scottishness and your own ancestry in particular.

Oh, probably. I was away from Scotland and that gave me a chance of seeing it better, you know and thinking about things. I wasn't very happy either in London or Liverpool and I wanted to get back to Scotland and I had to consider the pros and cons of whether it was worthwhile or not.

At the same time, or almost at the same time, as you were investigating your Scottishness, ironically your language was perhaps becoming less Scots and tending more towards an English kind of Scots.

That's quite true. That's quite true. In dealing with types of subject matter that hadn't been used in previous Scots poetry I had no precedents to pattern myself on, you see, so I had to fall back on a relatively unfamiliar field of English poetry which I never liked in any case, it never rang a bell with me, any moderrn English poetry at all. I was always very conscious of the psychological difference between myself as a Scot and anything English at all.

So you would say that your English is a very Scottish kind of English.

The English people—they refuse to recognize that I am speaking proper English at all, you see.

I think they have also, to their eternal disgrace, may I say, on the whole not recognized you as a poet in English, either to anything like the same extent, as for example, the Americans have recognized you.

It's much easier in America. I remember Professor David Daiches telling me that in various American universities, when he was acting as a professor he found his students had less difficulty in coping with Medieval Scots writing—Dunbar, Henryson, and so on—than they had in coping with the Augustan English poets—Pope and so on, because he said then that there were large dialectical differences in the United States themselves, and they were used to that kind of thing in a way that we had ceased to be in this country.

But in turning from Scots to English, was it a matter of Scots not any longer having the vocabulary to be able to cope with the subjects you were becoming more and more interested in?

That was the great difficulty, of course. It needed a considerable revival of obsolete language and you are always under a certain amount of pressure from friends to write in a Scots that would be intelligible to the ordinary person and I didn't think that was necessary at all; even now in certain quarters there is a desire to get back to spoken Scots. I'm not in favor of that at all. No. I don't see any advantage to be gained by it.

I agree with you there. That's like saying that a poet in England should give up the literary language and confine himself, say, to the patois of Liverpool. One says that one realizes what a ludicrous position that is. And in fact you would say I suppose that Denis Saurat is quite right in describing the Scots that you wrote in the twenties as synthetic Scots.

Oh yes. Undoubtedly. Saurat did a good deal to help the movement in the beginning putting in it proper content, delineating the potentialities of the movement in terms of European literature. I was never anxious to domesticate the issue at all and make it another slight development of local dialect or anything like that. I wanted to re-establish it as a language and work back to a complete cannon of the language. English was in a worse position than Scots. There are more dialect differences in England than ever were in Scotland, you know. They treat their dialects shamefully, the English.

Well, this is the reverse side of the coin, of course, of having a standard literary language which we did not have.

We didn't have, but they imposed a false standard that didn't arise out of the native circumstances except in a portion of the 17th century.

Yes, that's right, and if it was foreign to most of England it was even more foreign to us up here because whether we knew it or not we did inherit a literary language.

It had to be adopted; Northern English should have been adopted not the South Anglo-Norman English that was adopted as the basis of the common English language.

Well, certainly every time I read Barbour who is contemporary with Chaucer it is remarkable how much easier he is to read than Chaucer is. I'm not saying anything against Chaucer because I think he is a superb narrative poet but his language is difficult in a way that Barbour's is not, but of course the development of Scots as a literary language ceased abruptly in 1600 and you presumably were trying to start off again where the Medieval makars had left off.

Yes. Oh, quite. And I had realized also that it was impossible to achieve what I was aiming at without corresponding political developments. It was largely a political matter—even now in Yorkshire and Northumbria and Cumberland the dialect, and there are dialect societies, is very closely linked to Scots. Burns, the type of Scots that Burns uses in most of his work, doesn't fall strangely upon a Cumbrian or a Northumbrian ear or a Yorkshire ear.

Yes, I've noticed that there was a whole school of Cumbrian poets.

There were the dialect societies, and so on. As a matter of fact that was the basis of my argument that Scotland ought to extend to the Humber-Mersey line. (pp. 4-8)

Now, in the 30's, as you turned from Scots towards English the poetry becomes more philosophical, it becomes much more concerned with scientific fields, and it becomes a good deal more discursive. I recall from Kenneth Buthlay's book that you had a breakdown about 1934 and it has always seemed to me that there is a marked difference in style between the poetry before that period and the poetry after that period.

I think that was due to the difference of content, of course, difference of subject matter; I had become more and more political and I had become more and more influenced by certain developments in contemporary foreign literatures. I didn't want to do anything to encourage the continuance of Scottish local literature; I wanted Scottish literature to take its place in the development of literature generally with other comparable European countries.

And you wished to deal with themes that were of more than just Scottish relevance.

Oh yes.

And so this necessitated a change of style.

It was a necessity, because after all Scotland had practically ceased to have any peasantry. It had ceased to be primarily an agrarian country. It was one of the most advanced industrialized countries in Western Europe, and that difference, that development in Scotland required to be reflected in the literature of Scotland. We couldn't go back to the old peasant folk poetry. I think that's what's wrong with the present, in recent years, revival of Scottish folk poetry. They are simply molding themselves on forms that arose out of a different environment altogether. There is something spurious about it and it's not relevant to the requirements of the present day.

And yet it seems to be extremely popular at the moment.

It is very popular.

Do you think this is the old example of bad money driving out good?

I never knew a time, I don't think there has been a time, in literary history when poetry was otherwise than unpopular. It has always only appealed to a very limited section and it had popularity in inverse proportion to its poetic worth.

So in fact it takes a long time for a poet to make it.

Oh yes. Unless there are advantageous circumstances: Burns made it relatively quickly, but then he wasn't a solitary example; a man who made it much more quickly and still comes out in more editions than Burns, McGonagall, did appeal to a very broad mass of the people in a way that Burns, even Burns didn't.

Yes, they don't call him the great Burns, they call him the great McGonagall. I think in a way that the kind of ironic adulation of McGonagall is a reflection of the Scottish people's hatred of real poetry.

Of course it is.

*I've always thought it very peculiar that there's **A Drunk Man Looks at the Thistle** which seems to me to be the greatest extended poem in the whole of Scottish literature (and I've said this in print) published in 1926 and yet it doesn't go into a second edition until the 1950's, if I remember.*

[There are] about eleven editions now, I think.

That's right, but in the first place it took about a quarter of a century before it really got itself established, was recognized widely in literary circles, let alone anywhere else.

That's true. That was largely owing to the influence I think of the two main Scottish daily papers, *The Scotsman* and *The Glasgow Herald*. *The Glasgow Herald* reviewed it very unfavorably on its first appearance.

I thought they had published extracts . . .

Oh they did.

Before it appeared?

Yes. The review was very unfavorable and *The Scotsman* didn't review it at all.

Well, that's the kind of thing which shows that history repeats itself very frequently, because they certainly seem to be rather slow about reviewing Scottish books even now, and one sometimes wonders who the reviewers are that they choose to review Scottish books. Have you seen in general any improvement in your lifetime in the way Scottish books have been covered in Scotland?

Well, there's more space given to them, I think, in the leading papers, you know, but I should say the level of judgment on the part of the reviewers hasn't improved any.

But when you began, there really weren't any literary quarterlies in Scotland, you had to start them yourself.

There had been one or two abortive ones before I started, but I started them, yes. (pp. 9-12)

Now, all of the reviews which you personally edited, apart from Northern Numbers *which really comes before your rediscovery of Scots, as it were, all of them advanced the*

idea and sought to promulgate the results of the Scottish Renaissance.

Yes, yes.

Now, is there such a thing as the Scottish Renaissance apart from the poetry of Hugh MacDiarmid?

I think there has been. It has manifested itself in a lot of ways. There has been some very good Scottish poetry by a number of poets which I don't think would have come into being if it hadn't been for that general agitation, you know, and there's been a very considerable extension of the knowledge of Scots poetry and so on and teaching of it in schools and universities, and so on within recent years, and I think that was a direct product of the sort of ferment that we set going. I think not these periodicals that I started were mainly influential but I did a tremendous amount of syndicated work to all kinds of local papers, five or six columns a week appearing in an average of about 30 local papers for several years, plugging this idea of the possibility, of the desirability, of the Scottish Renaissance and I think they had a very considerable effect. (pp. 12-13)

So that all of this was happening in the twenties and the early thirties and the movement was given a sort of intellectual backbone by the ideas which you provided.

Yes, I think so. And I wanted something wider than that. I never believed in a real gulf between Scots and Gaelic. I thought that had been accentuated for reasons of divide and conquer, you know—British imperialism. After all, Scottish Gaelic literature is very largely a song literature and the actual lyric curve of Gaelic songs is almost identical with the best of Scots songs so there was no fundamental difference between the two and I wanted to see a unification and an understanding and very early when I started some of these periodicals promulgating the idea of the Scottish Renaissance amongst the first people who came to me were Gaelic writers—Sorley MacLean, George Campbell Hay, and so on. And of course that has gone on ever since.

But of course you yourself had to come to the Gaelic from outside, whereas you were able to come to Scots from inside.

Oh yes, they had it quite different. But there was no reason why we should be at each other's throat. The two things could be simultaneously encouraged and so on.

Well of course the poets in Scots and the poets in Gaelic do speak to one another nowadays.

At least most of them in my lifetime anyway.

In fact there has been quite a cross-fertilization because very evidently your poetry in Scots has had a strong influence on Sorley MacLean in Gaelic and then there's been a feedback into Scots because so many of his poems have been translated by Douglas Young and others into Scots from Gaelic.

Well, it digs both ways, and should do with the development of Scottish-Gaelic studies, this new Gaelic college in Skye and so on, I think the possibility of fruitful interaction will be developed.

Well this is unique, isn't it, in the history of Scottish literature; there seems to be very little feedback between . . .

Oh, there was antagonism, and that was fomented from outside, I think. The English discriminated in the punitive action they took against Gaelic; they didn't against Scots, you see. (pp. 13-14)

Well isn't it very difficult because of our educational system, and probably was even more difficult at the beginning of the twentieth century, for a Scotsman really to discover his own Scottishness because he gets over-laid so quickly with other . . .

There was everything to dissuade you from attempting to discover anything of the kind because you got thrashed if you lapsed into Scots in the school, and so on.

And presumably in your days at school very little Scottish literature would be taught at all.

Oh no, none. We didn't know anything about Scottish literature; it was all English literature.

Not even Burns?

Eh, you got an occasional thing of Burns I think by the time you got to about the sixth standard, but just one or two songs, that was all. And "Tam O'Shanter."

But the Scottishness was there nevertheless all round the school.

Yes. We learned nothing whatever about Dunbar, Henryson or any of the others.

So really your Scottishness came into you from the environment rather than from formal education.

It did; there was an antagonism to the English in the Borders at that time. To speak English was held to be aping the gentry, "speaking fine" you see.

"Pan loaf " as we say up in Aberdeen.

And of course the bulk of the population spoke Scots.

Well Scotch voices were not designed to speak English.

No.

I mean here we are speaking to one another in English but I think our voices go more naturally into the rhythms and cadences of Scots.

Well Burns didn't write any good English poems, did he?

Well I find it difficult to discover one.

I think I have, you see.

Yes, well would this not be because Burns never spoke anything else, I suppose, but Scots.

His reading was very largely English though.

That's true. Maybe it was because the models in English . . .

Yes, Shenstone and that sort of thing, you know, that was bound to be fatal to any potential Scotch poet.

And yet one could argue that contemporary English poetry is pretty thin gruel. (pp. 17-18)

[There's] no English poetry of any quality being produced at all. The English literary scene is sufficiently well organized that they keep on pretending that they have a whole range of poets, and I think all of them are extremely poor. When they want anybody who as a poet exemplifies the English language, potentialities for poetic expression of the English language, they get a Welshman and an Irishman and two Americans, not a single Englishman. Of course Hume, the Scottish philosopher, said long ago that English as a creative medium was on the way out; he foresaw the complete extinction of the long line of English literature. I think his prophecy has been realized in our time.

And yet you have written more and more poetry in English.

But it's not a kind of English that's recognized as proper English. The syntax and so on doesn't correspond.

Is it recognized as improper English?

It's improper, a good deal of it, but not in that sense.

*Now **In Memoriam James Joyce,** your longest published poem in English, is part of a much larger work called **"Mature Art";** does this work in fact exist as such?*

No, and not likely ever to exist either. As you know not only in regard to my English poems but in regard to my Scots poems at various times I promulgated ideas for a very large poem. In **"Glen Albyn"** I gave a complete scheme of what I was going to do there, and abandoned it, you see. [blank] . . . the same thing and it's certainly the same thing in **"Mature Art."** It's an impossible thing to realize; I've changed completely and am in the process of continual change. I want to write another long poem; six, seven thousand lines.

On what subject, on what theme?

That's the problem; I want a counterpart to **A Drunk Man** in Scots and I haven't got a key idea yet, but I think I will.

The thistle looks at the drunk man.

Well, we'll see. But I've got back again in my own thinking, in my own ideas, to Scots, you see. Scots is an impossible medium for any poems on scientific and modern subjects that I have been writing; you couldn't write **"On a Raised Beach"** in Scots at all, but you couldn't write it in English either, of course.

Well the kind of English you have written it in makes it a superb poem. I think myself that this is your finest poem in English.

I think it is one of my best poems, and certainly it evoked from an unexpected quarter the best critical essay on any of my work. Professor D. M. Mackinnon, Chair of Divinity, gave the Gifford Lectures in Edinburgh and then he published a small book summarizing the main points in his Gifford Lectures that he called *The Problem of Metaphysics*, and he devotes a whole chapter in that book to **"On a Raised Beach,"** and a very good one too. He is pointing out that there are a lot of people, and I know the late Helen Cruikshank was one of them, and her literary executor the Rev. J. B. Logan of Crieff say, "Oh well, Grieve writes—he says he's not a Christian—but his work is [blank] with Christian references and so on, he has written a Christian poem, he's a Christian without knowing it." However, Mackinnon puts that kind of thing in its place and justifies my atheism, you see. It's a very good essay. (pp. 18-20)

Now I would say that that poem in particular combines localism, being there in a particular place in Shetland, with a very wide outlook. Is this what you have been trying to do in your work throughout your career?

Yes. It's the most definitely atheistic poem that I've ever written. Materialistic if you care to use that term, which I don't. I think it's one of my best poems.

Yes, there are no ruined stones, I remember. And the fact that I remember something from it means that it has got no ruined stones. I am also fascinated by two things you said—in the first place you say that you haven't written these long poems because you have developed onwards so that you have got past the point of writing that particular long poem which I think is an ironic comment on Ezra Pound's The Cantos *because he tried to stick with it, so you have got a poem which changes course about ten times en route so that there is no poem.*

Ah yes, he lost the architectonic control of himself.

Absolutely.

I think it's a great poem nevertheless.

Well, there are certainly great things in it. Did Pound have any influence upon your writing of long poems?

Oh I think he had, because I corresponded with him and I finally went to Venice and saw him, and so on. I think Kulgin Duval and I are going to produce a little book of my various writings on Pound. I took part in a commemoration of Pound at Queen's University in Belfast and Olga Rudge with whom Pound was living thought that my tribute to Pound there was one of the best things that had ever been written about Pound by anybody and it was reproduced in that American Pound magazine *Pyuma Tyuma.* But I've got to write another essay, that's the problem, I'm getting old and lazy you see, and to make a sufficient bulk of a little book I need to write another one now—I haven't done that yet.

Well are you going to write that before or after you write the seven-thousand-line poem in Scots?

I don't know what I'll do first—if I do anything.

Well I think one of the most striking things you've done recently, since you were talking about the long poem in Scots, is the short poem in Scots that appeared originally in Akros and which your son Michael and I put in our anthology of your work—"A Change of Weather."

Oh yes.

That is one of your few poems in Scots in the last twenty years.

Oh I haven't written much in Scots, no.

Can you remember what started that one off?

There's another unpublished effort was in Scots; some of it has been revived recently in *Agenda* and in that little magazine that Manson brings out in Edinburgh *Waybock.* There's a whole lot of that stuff and I don't think most of it is good, but one or two of them are, and should be incorporated in some subsequent book. I'll certainly write a lot more of this if I . . .

God willing as they say; if I may say that to an atheist.

Unless I get lazier and lazier and don't do anything.

Well you've done such an immense . . .

It's all right a young man like you, you know, but at my age I want to rest on my oars a little.

Well you've certainly done enough in your time to entitle you to rest on your laurels.

Yes I think so, and then too much in some ways and too little in others. (pp. 20-2)

> *Hugh MacDiarmid and Alexander Scott, in an interview in* Studies in Scottish Literature, *Vol. XIV, 1979, pp. 1-22.*

Diane Ackerman

The dialect poet is a problem we are less and less able to cope with. Civilization has become increasingly centripetal, so much so that a dialect poet such as Hugh MacDiarmid runs a double risk, not only of seeming impenetrable but of seeming crankily out of the mainstream as well. Nothing, in his case, at least, could be further from the truth: MacDiarmid is a poet of prodigious scope, astonishing reverent penetration, and a master of conventional English. His reasons for doing some poems in Lallans have to do with elements in Scottish psychology which have seemed to him untranslatable, or incapable of being transposed; with the almost puritanical monopoly exercised by London English; the way in which dialect achieves idiosyncratic compression of shades and overtones; and the unique way in which vernacular embodies the lyrical and the ludicrous irrevocably fused. This is all very well; dialect poets always have good reasons for writing in their own way, but sooner or later our well—meaning willingness to puzzle through (which verges on literary altruism) conducts us to a dismal point at which we say, from within our own peninsula of standard usage, either this poet is so good he deserves a wider audience, or he doesn't matter and can be left to linger in Lallans, or whatever, as a quaint aberration, like the bagpipes, haggis, or Hogmanay.

Fortunately the Doric Donne, as MacDiarmid has been called, has written a generous amount in London English, though even this has failed to secure him a wide audience. Too far from London, too far east of New York, as some have said, he has won passionate devotees in the unlikeliest places, mainly among those who have read him, for to read him in bulk is to be astonished by the way in which he has raised to its highest power the peculiarly Scottish fondness for topsy-turvy collision, or, as Gregory Smith puts it in *Scottish Literature: Character and Influence* (1919), "the horns of elfland and the voices of the mountains . . . The sudden jostling of contraries. . . ." If indeed the twin poles of Scottish poetry *are* the real and the fantastic, we do not learn this from such a poet as Burns, who is a folk rhymer to MacDiarmid's cosmological imagist; but a pleasant discovery it is, and it suggests that what has held MacDiarmid back is his having a naturally metaphysical mind that coincided none too well with the kinds of poetry successively in vogue in London, from Thirties reportage to Apocalypse (such poetry as David Gascoyne's) to the clipped, dry, cautious, skeptically civil poetry of the so-called Movement. The taste that received

Dylan Thomas responded to the Welsh *hwyl*—histrionics from the heart—but not to the essentially intellectual work of a MacDiarmid, who might have risen on the tide induced by Eliot's essay on the Metaphysicals if only the *Criterion* and *Egoist* group of critics had heard of him; but they had not, and since then, having as it were missed the right boat, MacDiarmid has had to await his turn, blighted by Edwin Muir's accusation in 1936 that MacDiarmid had Europeanized Scottish poetry rather selfishly (after which he became, in his own words, less a man after Muir's heart than after Muir's blood). The whole fuss seems trivial, peripheral; a tribal poet and seer had broken loose from the clan and had soared on into nowhere, too bold mentally for the English, too cosmopolitan for the Scots. His *Collected Poems* (1962), published when he was seventy, enforced a final justice, informed to some extent by David Daiches's 1948 observation that MacDiarmid uses Scots not as an *alternative* to English but only for effects *unobtainable* in English. In 1962, Daiches clinched this by saying straight out that MacDiarmid is "one of the very great poets of our time."

It's probably true, and my purpose here is not to lament the lateness of his recognition but to explore three stages in his visionary career. Read his early lyrics, nearly all in Scots, and you find the Moon as a crow squatting in the crosswinds, the sun as a frog plunked down in a creambowl, the Earth as the bleached hulk of a beached whale. A cosmic euphoria blows through almost every poem, sometimes grotesque, at other times fusing primitive feeling with erudite conceits (**"Bombinations of a Chimera"** for instance). At this point in his career MacDiarmid already has a natural sense of the cosmic, and what he seems to labor at is getting words out of the dialect dictionary into the cosmic whelm, a bit like stuffed birds. One of the most startling poems, **"A Stick-Nest in Ygdrasil,"** links infinity and Ariadne, the space-time continuum and Eve, in easy transitions, at the same time arguing, with the radical, pell-mell candor that is the tune of Scottish talk, things like this:

> For what's an atom o' a twig
> That tak's a billion to an inch
> To a' the routh o' shoots that mak'
> The bygrowth o' the Earth aboot
> The michty trunk o' Space that spreids
> Rammel o' licht that ha'e nae end,
> —The trunk wi' centuries for rings,
> Comets for fruit, November shooers
> For leafs that in its Autumns fa'
> —And Man at maist o' sic a twig
> Ane o' the coontless atoms is!

A bit heavy going (inverted commas plague it), this is nonetheless the almost full-fledged metaphysical vision, rich with knowing savor and an almost voluptuous sureness of grasp. It was there in more garish, busily outrageous form in the poems he published in 1922, such as **"Water of Life":**

> Pool of the Holy Ghost
> In tides of light expand. . . .

and (more solidly) **"Spring, A Violin in the Void":**

> Spiders, far from their webs, with trembling feet
> Assemble on the ceiling, a charmed group,
> While the grey bow with many a swing and swoop,
> Draws from dim strings a music crying-sweet.

> Hard by the doorstep shelving to the street
> A fascinated lizard swells the troop
> Of mean hearts taken in a magic loop,
> From terror freed, and given a cosmic beat.

A disturbing and confident mind is at work here, as good at nimble metamorphoses as at sly juxtapositions, and it is clear that he knows how to handle himself. The weird thing is that he already has the "cosmic beat," a notion that widens in a later poem, **"Metaphysical Pictures of the Thistle,"** when God, made over into "a bobby," walks by outside, on his beat.

This unusual way of looking, of feeling deeply at home during all the tangential and integrative sorties of one's own mind, links MacDiarmid to Donne and Herbert. What startles others is as natural to them as inhaling, and that, I think, is why they are good poets, unlaborious and urbane and able to swerve around on a pin. Their shifts are organic, not out of Doctors Frankenstein or Moreau, and their "imitation" is not like Madame Tussaud's but demiurgic, in accord with the Coleridgean model. Who else in 1936 would take the trouble, or have the fruitful cantankerousness, to say . . . " 'Let there be light,' said God, and there was / A little: but he lacked the power / To light up more than part of space at once, / And there is lots of darkness that's the same . . . "? It's the sort of thing that interested Empson without intruding into his poems, whereas it pours through MacDiarmid's, conducting him past *A Drunk Man Looks at the Thistle*—that effortless-looking, dynamic, and precarious feat of deep-sea diving into his own head—to the long poem-declaration **"The Kind of Poetry I Want."**

I want now to look at what he "wants" and what, in another long poem, **"On a Raised Beach,"** he provides. What he wants can't be said shortly, that much is clear . . . and it's light years from Auden and those who came after him. Envisioning a poetry "the quality of which / Is a stand made against intellectual apathy" and founded on "difficult knowledge," he invokes "the innumerable dead" and "the innumerable to-be-born" under scientific auspices, say the glow-worm's "96 per cent efficiency" and then delivers his first arcane punch:

> Coleridge's esemplasy and coadunation
> Multeity in unity—not the Unity resulting
> But the mode of the conspiration
> (Schelling's *In-eins-bildung-kraft*)
> Of the manifold to the one,
> For, as Rilke says, the poet must know everything. . . .

Revelling in his own mind, in words and quotations, as he is, he's also bringing the world together to a unique rhythm. . . . [His] glosses don't matter half as much as his own awareness of *declaring intelligence,* more connectedly than Pound, more ecumenically than Eliot, more blatantly than Donne (though he echoes him in that each fit of far-ranging intellection seems to transmute his mind as he accomplishes it, sweeping it forward sea-changed along the "tensely flexible and complex curve" that represents his voice in the act of reading). This, we hear in every line, is the poet of specificity speaking about, and to, and for, the mainspring of life, which generates all our curiosity, from Madame Curie to Cézanne (whose "doubt" is famous), from the cedars of Lebanon to chalcolite, uranium mica, carnotite, tjujamunite, fergusonite, monazite sand, betafite, tobernite, and from there to "a Beethoven semitonal modulation to a wildly remote key" that feels like "the sunrise gilding the peak of the Dent Blanche / While the Arolla valley is still in cloud." What voracity! What patient, elaborate, yet genial-toned unfolding of the world—the savant's and the amateur's—from all its gnarled-up pleats! Rarely has hard thinking taken the form of discursive abundance with such lyrical felicity. An intellectual (an intellectual's) poem, it restored intelligence to a tradition (the British) from which it had too long been banned except in the form of riddles or puzzles. It may not be altogether reckless to suggest that MacDiarmid is a distinguished embodiment of an old Scottish tradition which prizes intellectual achievement above all and rejoices in the scholarships won by the sons of poor farmers to the Scottish universities, even, when fantasies come true, to Balliol College, Oxford.

Essentially, **"The Kind of Poetry I Want"** is an essay-toned plea for what he calls "wide-angle" poetry: not something prudent or glib, nor something pastoral only or *vers de société*, nor esoteric obscurantism, nor political tub-thumping, but poetry

> Taking in the whole which explains the part,
> Scientifically accurate, fully realized in all their details,
> As Prudentius's picture of the gradually deputrifying Lazarus,
> Or Baudelaire's of the naked mulatto woman,
> Or Pope's most accurate particularities
> In the Epistle to Lord Bathurst. . . .

which evinces that rare thing (since the late-Renaissance): "a many-sided active delight in the wholeness of things." Such a poetry may even be like "an operating theatre" in which the poet functions "as a nurse during an operation." I think the spirit of Whitman has here infiltrated itself into an alien tradition; such spaciousness, such grandeur, so basically synoptic a view of the poet's role, do not belong in the British tradition, not since early Auden, at any rate, and Auden (son of a nurse and doctor, as he pointed out in one poem) never achieved MacDiarmid's intellectual range, anymore than Yeats, say, achieved his ebullient relish of science. It may be argued, of course, that this doctrinal poem is too much of a tract, but a tract has never been so hungry, so delighted, so intricately attuned to a moment in the advance of knowledge, and in the end you have to read it as he meant it: as a celebration of mentality, with the poet an enraptured sponsor marvelling at all the random events that have hardened into something seen in the round as human history. The sheer force and elate gusto of the poem move it across the line separating tract from hymn; and, in a way that if you notice it at all is profoundly moving, it offers the crescendo of human evolution as something intrinsically poetic itself. In other words, the poetry he wants must be worthy of the Creator, must not short-change Creation, needn't be shy of the "profound kinship of all living substance," and had better be a poetry "abstruse as hedge-laying."

It should be noted that his notion of "kinship" really did extend to everything, not least to any given idea and its opposite, which is perhaps all right in a mystic, a cosmologist, a rhetorician, but puzzling to say the least in a self-professed Communist. MacDiarmid despised consistency, wanting everything all ways and round the clock. So, while it is useful to note that he declared himself a Communist in 1932, revolution as such was for him only one of many possible ways of bringing about something as high-sounding as *"epopteia"* (It means "supervision," so MacDiarmid wanted to *supervise* the development of the human race), the infusion of every human with genius. Politics to him is a stanza form to be used en route to the maximization of intellect under the auspices of a universe whose beauty consists in contraries (an idea he found in Marcus Aurelius). He joined the Communist Party in 1934, was expelled from it in 1938, and did not rejoin it until 1957—just when nearly everyone else was leaving it to show sympathy with the Hungarian Uprising. How typical of him. Always against the current, he vexed the Communists with his Scottish nationalism, the Scottish nationalists with his Communism, and saw himself as a superhumanitarian because he remained a Bolshevik:

> . . . I am like Zamyatin, I must be a Bolshevik
> Before the Revolution, but I'll cease to be one quick
> When Communism comes to rule the roost.

Something at once naive and cantankerous shows up here, and his vision of ultimate human fulfillment—with every mind tapping the mysterious vat of the race's genius—makes Shelley seem a pettifogging pragmatist. (pp. 129-35)

Oddly enough, the closest resemblance to MacDiarmid's meta-politics is Dylan Thomas' account of his own poetic process, in which he makes the poem from a host of warring images. In 1926 MacDiarmid said that "The function of art is the extension of human consciousness," and what you get from him is politics serving that end of poetry. His political manner is truculent and severe, but much of the time he has in mind "a sort of Celtic Union of Socialist Soviet Republics in the British Isles," and Eric Linklater said MacDiarmid preached Douglas' economics "for purely aesthetic reasons." Indeed, the *First* and *Second Hymn to Lenin* are more about poetry than about politics or Lenin, and we have to remember that he was an extremist prophet, envisioning the day when all men of whatever station would rise to a *norm* of genius, and—as if adding impersonality to the far-fetched because they belonged together—declaring that none of the views he expressed were necessarily his own since he was interested above all in "a big scheme" in which all points of view opposed one another and cancelled out. Anything that might speed up human evolution appealed to him, even cruelty and suffering. He is almost like an Olympian pondering how to shift a rock formation, having first of all exempted himself from the outcome. As a political thinker he is *homo ludens* raised to exponential maximum: the supreme player, bending the rules because he already knows from A to Z the universe they fit.

All this means is that MacDiarmid has a full cosmology to begin with: a given, so much so that, like some Monsieur Jourdain of lyricism, he talks cosmology before he quite knows what he's doing. Then he marshals what he knows of biology and geology, fleshing out his illustrious and cogitative overview (as in **"On A Raised Beach"**), and only in what might seem his third phase resolves to develop a full orchestration that amounts to "world-consciousness" via Whitman and Romain Rolland, whom he quotes, saying: "And before going to sleep in the anarchic and cruel world chaos where I hear the shock of colliding masses of diverse nations and differing spirits, I recall the wise and clear thought of Lenin. . . ." Lenin is something quite private and wholly serious to MacDiarmid, though he tends to walk him here and there like a barely-tamed pet; the ideologue doesn't matter, but the grievous identification with humanity—such as one might collect from reading the newspapers of any one day—matters enormously. The evolution of the stance is fascinating, and it goes something as follows. Cosmologically-minded to begin with, he at length recognizes how impersonal, or non-human, he might be, and spends the rest of his days—half a century—humanizing his vision: from star to cell to primitive man to his friend the writer Mary Webb. His advance is akin to the one he notes as having happened between Chaucer and Spenser, in which "floures white and rede" give way to things named in the April Eclogue, such as "pinks, columbines, gillyflowers, / Coronations, sopsin-wine, cowslips, / Paunce and chevisaunce." Yet nothing of what he progressively humanizes falls away; indeed, his sense of galaxy or space-time becomes more intense, and the epistemological augment of his heart piles up, not as detritus on the stairway of knowing but as a stairway itself. . . . Widening his heart and mind . . . , he perhaps lost the world's attention. Where the world wanted a teapot, he provided India and China. Where it wanted writers who wrote within the expectations of the public, he quoted Kierkegaard's "One can divide authors into two classes, those who write for readers, and the real authors—those who write for authors. These latter are unintelligible to the reading public, are looked upon as mad, and are almost despised. . . ." It chimes exactly with the end of **"The Kind of Poetry I Want"**:

> —A learned poetry wholly free
> Of the brutal love of ignorance;
> And the poetry of a poet with no use
> For any of the simpler forms of personal success.

Readers going to the misnamed and premature *Collected Poems* will find only a snippet of **"On A Raised Beach"** printed there (one reason for MacDiarmid's bringing out a *More Collected Poems* later on). I fix on this monumental slab of a poem, done ten years before **"The Kind of Poetry I Want"** . . . , not only because it takes up where Matthew Arnold left off, but because it is MacDiarmid at his least obliging, his most Kierkegaardian, honing an inclusive vision into language that physically enacts not only his meanings but also, through some extraordinary expressionism of the petrified, how he feels about geology. (When he went to live in the Shetlands, he spent a lot of time in the company of a geologist exploring the small islands around Whalsay.) Here are the opening lines, well worth bracing oneself for:

> All is lithogenesis—or lochia,
> Carpolite fruit of the forbidden tree,
> Stones blacker than any in the Caaba,
> Cream-coloured caen-stone, chatoyant pieces,
> Celadon and corbeau, bistre and beige,
> Glaucous, hoar, enfouldered, cyathiform,
> Making mere faculae of the sun and moon,
> I study you glout and gloss, but have
> No cadrans to adjust you with, and turn again
> From optik to haptik and like a blind man run
> My fingers over you, arris by arris, burr by burr. . . .

Newfound*land* indeed! Six lines further on, we run into a question mark, tiny reprieve for a reader whose head is aching with exegetical glosses, from discharge after child-

birth to stone-fruit, from the sacred black stone of Mecca to a city of Normandy where *chatoyer* means to have a changeable luster, like the stone named cat's-eye. . . . Yet it is a pleasurable pain, this cairn of "haecceity" or "thisness." One has, with line 25, a sense of coming out from under, and how appropriate that feeling is:

> Deep conviction or preference can seldom
> Find direct terms in which to express itself.
> Today on this shingle shelf
> I understand this pensive reluctance so well . . .

And the poem is off, tracking the only thing that moves: a bird, fondly plumbed:

> The widest open door is the least liable to intrusion,
> Ubiquitous as the sunlight, unfrequented as the sun.
> The inward gates of a bird are always open.
> It does not know how to shut them.
> That is the secret of its song. . . .

What ensues is an expansive act of homage to all forms of life, from mole to gorilla to girl, in fact to all the forms there are over and above the "ground bass" in which "There are no twirly bits." There are no ruined stones, either, he says, and "No visitor comes from the stars / But is the same as they are" (good going for 1934!). Then he tries the stones again, trying to get deeper into them through color and the use of old Norse words, but realizes that "These stones will reach us long before we reach them." All he can do (and this is very much a poem of the poet *in situ,* pondering his art in the presence of enigmatic stasis) is to review the metaphorical aspect of stones vis-à-vis common or garden notions of the truth. The reprise is close to Whitman, yet weirdly evocative of an earthbound St.-Exupéry:

> I am enamoured of the desert at last,
> The abode of supreme serenity is necessarily a desert.
> My disposition is towards spiritual issues
> Made inhumanly clear; I will have nothing interposed
> Between my sensitiveness and the barren but beautiful
>   reality. . . .

That just about sums him up. He sometimes goes on explaining when he might have clinched things with a salient metaphor, but his art is one of *sostenuto,* not of ellipsis, and he sometimes (as in the above) sets after an end-stop comma a phrase that lingers in brief apposition before taking off again as the subject of a parenthetical *da capo.* In other words, he does sculptural underlinings which themselves are strata in his "wide-angled" vision.

The poem ends with the formidable word *epanadiplosis,* which means "re-folding" and takes at least this reader back to his early poem about the bridegroom's "Gaining the lubric goal" and holding

> Earth, as a bridegroom holds his swooning, bare,
> Impregnate bride.

"Pleat your wild shiver on the quivering air," the poet exhorts him. Pleat or fold imagery is common in MacDiarmid: terrain or brain, it's much the same to him who, having a mind and unapologetically using it full blast, dignifies the stereoscopic variety of Creation while, in the keenest way, fulfilling his share of it. (pp. 135-39)

Diane   Ackerman,   "Hugh   MacDiarmid's

Wide-Angle Poetry," in Parnassus: Poetry in Review, *Vol. 9, No. 1, 1981, pp. 129-39.*

Kenneth Cox

[*The essay excerpted below was first published in* Scripsi, *Vol. I, Nos. 3 & 4, 1982.*]

Great writers resemble one another much less than small writers do. Some go clean contrary to established practice, follow traditions no longer respected and attempt things never done before. One such is the Scottish poet Hugh MacDiarmid.

The complete edition of MacDiarmid's poems now available contains work that does more than disregard standards readers may be accustomed to, it operates by virtue of qualities critics pronounce defects. Since the achievement is evident and there is no sign of perversity, it needs to be supposed the system of values is different. It is, and when this is recognized certain characteristics of the work are not mistaken for failings the author would have avoided if he could but are accepted as functions of the ideal towards which he is striving. Roughnesses remain but banalities and audacities become difficult to tell apart. At peaks they are indistinguishable.

Unless there are any whose response to poetry is at all times perfectly direct and simple, a poetry so different in kind would seem to be accessible only to two sorts of reader: to those who happen to share its unacknowledged assumptions and to those interested enough to identify and as far as possible suppress the preconceptions of their own that stand in the way of deeper appreciation. Deprejudiced readers are likely to become more numerous and more necessary now that the language is being used as a vehicle for the literature of various cultures.

Some will prefer appeal to a principle supposed universally valid. This may be possible but it cannot be taken for granted that universal principles exist, any that do will be difficult to discover and any discovered are likely to prove too vague to be much use. The fashionable test for 'authenticity' is no help either, for what it establishes is not the authentic, the sincere utterance of real people, but the ability to sound authentic and this is a verbal faculty whose relation to experience, if any, is retrograde and indirect.

Besides, in the case of MacDiarmid there are two special factors. Great writers usually combine the hypertrophy of some quality or qualities with a mastery of the particular skills that take the edge off the odd, assimilate it to other determinants of experience and enable it to appear after a while almost normal. MacDiarmid is hypertrophied all right and he rapidly acquired the skills he needed but they had to be re-invented and always lagged somewhat behind. The second factor is the method of synthetic composition. Not unique to MacDiarmid it is one much used in Scottish literature, many of whose most moving most vigorous and most 'authentic' works have been produced by translation, transcription, imitation, burlesque, parody, forgery or the refashioning of traditional songs. There is little point in examining such writing for verbal vestiges of firsthand knowledge: it is not that sort of thing.

In contradiction to a widely accepted opinion about the function of poetry MacDiarmid's may be said to have a palpable design on the reader. Its intention, if intention can be inferred from effect, is chiefly to exalt. To this end it uses a process of persuasion extending beyond all possibility of demur or misapprehension. Energy is provided by an ardent will to instruct and admonish: even when not engaged in polemic the writing tends to remain in one insistent tone and to exert a quasipedagig force. So far from assuming the presence of a sympathetic audience it sets out to overcome the resistance of one it expects to find if not hostile at least ignorant, indifferent or incredulous. It extends itself, emphasises, illustrates, reiterates, quotes. Values and quantitative: longwindedness for example becomes a merit (it may be renamed stamina) and excellence in general lies less in satisfying standards of workmanship, as in the crafts, than in breaking records and beating opponents, as in sport.

As to the content of what is being imparted, this is by no means easy to say. The form it takes may be political, though the chief notes of the politics are vision, recklessness and hero-worship, or ideological, though *it is not essential to believe that its ideas are perfectly true.* Essentially what the poetry asserts is its own poetic and in straining towards it or in striving to give it effect it attempts to establish the values of a possible future civilisation. As in the Cantos part of what it is intended to establish inheres however not so much in the substance as in the vehemence and velocity of its communication. But unlike Pound MacDiarmid uses no subtle involved allusive or otherwise sophisticated resources of language, he simply carries the ordinary ones to extraordinary lengths. Constantly urging himself onwards and continually changing approach— MacDiarmid repeatedly tries to convey something he knows can never be said direct, as though force and frequency and duration of attempt were the only but never adequate means of preparing people to receive an idea of it.

To object that MacDiarmid always points to an end he never attains would be to measure another's corn by one's own bushel: in MacDiarmid's poetry effort is everything. Dependent on self-propulsion and obliged to counter adversaries his poetry does not merely ignore alien values: it flouts them, attacks them. It tends in consequence to be alert and deliberate where poetry of an opposing kind remains ingenuous and unaware, and heedless where the other is cautious. Subjects modern and intellectual are treated in the manner of ancient and heroic poetry. Courage rates above delicacy, criticism is scathing, praise magnanimous, and the poetry realises itself in declarations of intent.

One of its procedures is to focus on facts, each of small scale and high definition, assert them with precision and emphasis and, stringing them on the thinnest and slackest of threads, work up to a vivacious climax. There is much expenditure of energy, strong flow with weak organisation, and much variety of pace, many twists and turns. The basic movement is a persistent undeviating drone interrupted by sharp bursts. The process is rational: the theme announced compels acceptance not by arousing emotion but by relentlessly and variously elaborating the cogent till this elates of itself. Analogues occur in Scottish dancing, piping and preaching.

The effect was described by Professor Gregory Smith before MacDiarmid was heard of but in a passage which

MacDiarmid made into a poem, **"The poetic faculty."** Here it is restored to prose:

> The completed effect of the piling up of details is one of movement, suggesting the action of a concerted dance or the canter of a squadron. We have gone astray if we call this art
>
> merely meticulous, a pedant's or a cataloguer's vanity in words, as some foolish persons have inclined to make charge against the 'antiquary' Scott. The whole is not always lost in the parts; it is not a composition impressive only because it is greater than any of its contributing elements, but often single in result and above all things lively.

Associated with such a result there is often a sense either of triumph or of outrage.

Pictish having died out Scotland has strictly speaking no language of its own. Of the other languages used at different times and in different parts of the country (Welsh, Irish, Norse, English, Flemish, French, Latin and others) only English and Irish remain. Irish, once dominant in the western isles and highlands and then called Scots, is now spoken by a small fraction of the population and called Gaelic or, more exactly, Scottish Gaelic. What is now known as Scots is in origin the northern dialect of English. Hardly any different from the midland and the southern dialects in structure, it differs from them partly in vocabulary but chiefly in sound. In Scotland the difference of sound is sharper and the vocabulary has been enriched by borrowings from the other languages once spoken there.

When Scotland was independent its variety of northern English came to be regarded as a distinct idiom, though it did not always receive another name. Following the political union with England the linguistic differences widened. Scots acquired its name but sank to the level of patois. Its dialects are divided into three main groups: 1. those of the central lowlands which constitute the basis of the old literary language, 2. the north-eastern, which owe to Scandinavian or other substrata distinctive features of vocabulary and phonology, and 3. the dialect of a small area in the extreme south which shares with the English spoken on the other side of the border a local system of vowels and intonation: speakers on the Scottish side object to its being called English and speakers on the English side object to its being called Scots. It was in this area, a few miles north of the border, that Christopher Grieve alias Hugh MacDiarmid was born and grew up.

MacDiarmid uses various languages or modes of language, both English and Scots, sometimes combining them and occasionally transposing one into the other, as a composer instruments music. For purposes of exposition (though limits rather than types) his instruments can be reduced to five or six:

1. His mother tongue, the speech of his birthplace and boyhood, perfectly natural and in some sense fundamental but varying in mood from raw tenderness to provincial bumptiousness.

2. Literary or as he called it 'synthetic' Scots, based on the central dialects but drawing vocabulary from all parts of the lowlands (hence sometimes called Lallans) as well as from the older literature. (In practice, principally from John Jamieson's *Dictionary of the Scottish Language,* pub-

lished in 1808 in four volumes quarto and later abridged in one volume octavo: the *Scottish National Dictionary* in ten volumes quarto was not completed till 1970.) Synthetic Scots is not an invention of MacDiarmid's. Writers in Scots have nearly always used a composite vocabulary: severe and sensitive users of a single sub-dialect like Garioch and Leonard are exceptional. But in the rapid amassing of a large and fantastical vocabulary no-one in modern times has been more daring than MacDiarmid.

3. Plain Scots, closer to the vernacular and keeping the features which distinguish it from standard English, only eliminating regional peculiarities. It is such a language as might have developed had a Scottish Mistral arisen to enhance prestige, establish usage, regulate spelling and compile a modern dictionary. In default of tutelage it appears in writing when obliged by policy subject or occasion, in prose infrequently and with individual variations. Often however it makes an appearance unnoticed and disguised: it appears as

4. Natural colloquial English with only some spelling conventions and a few differences of vocabulary to separate it from 3. At this limit the difference in sound may be no more than accent. Whether called Scots or English these are or this is MacDiarmid's most effective medium, vigorous and mature in expression and moving with a free swing.

5. The nameless nondescript English of journalists, universities and international communication: a cerebral lingo governed by printers' and editors' conventions but understood everywhere and able to accommodate the artificial vocabularies of science. It is a vehicle MacDiarmid felt at ease in and in it he composed some of his most stupendous work.

6. A stiff pedantic English learned in school and kirk. A ghost that haunts many Scots using English it walks in MacDiarmid's first work and appears as late as 1948 in *Glasgow is like the sea,* lines supposed to be spoken by a Hebridean. There was always a danger MacDiarmid might fall into this style and a few of its expressions became rather incongruous ingredients of his habitual vocabulary.

His beginnings were late and slow. At thirty he was still writing with the clumsy ardour of adolescence. The language he used then was a bookish Victorian English with inversion, apocope and latinate adjectives. Words revived in the 1890s for precious stones are found to fit the landscape of Scotland but in general the distance between ambition and resources is enormous. Were it not for its strong assertive thrust the writing would sound false. He perhaps lacked good models? Rather he seems temperamentally or theologically determined not to have models. He thinks he is God.

His second and third books are written in Scots, natural or synthetic, but their inspiration is German. A number of short poems see the earth as if from outer space and make high-flown far-fetched statements equating the terrestrial with the cosmic. Some of these poems have appeared in anthologies and become well known. The best have an eerie or a poignant beauty but many betray formula: a lilt, a word or two out of Jamieson, and away to the empyrean. Brevity is obtained not by compression but by premature ejaculation. Pairs of quatrains in the metre of the border ballads use the ballad device of elliptical narration: momentous things happen in the gaps between stanzas. But whereas in the ballads an event itself definite is left temporarily unstated in order to enhance effect, here the gap is a hollow in the conception, impossible to render positively even if the poet tried: instead he shies off to strike a superhuman pose.

It is in *A Drunk Man Looks at the Thistle,* published in 1926, that MacDiarmid finds his voice. Written in a rich natural Scots and in easy virile verse it is a series of poems in various measures, the metrical impulse perhaps from Dunbar, the most formal of the makars. Not political the work is a record of a man's struggle with himself and has more to do with marriage than with Scotland. It has in fact echoes of *The Waste Land,* a poem in other respects totally dissimilar. Frank and humorous in his sexuality MacDiarmid celebrates in his book a descent to earth, a wrestling both exhilarating and disturbing with the not-self for which the thistle is as they say a symbol. It has been called a classic but it is not that. It is a long ill-ordered high-spirited unstable and apparently spontaneous effusion, by turns witty and senseless, *but above all things lively:* nothing like it since Byron.

Initiation can only happen once and some struggles never end. In the turbulent and productive 'thirties MacDiarmid developed and abandoned various resources:

1. At the time his synthetic Scots was reaching its maximum in *Scots Unbound* (1932) he was transferring its procedure (the picking of rare words out of dictionaries) to scientific English. The method as such is as legitimate as synthetic Scots: there are no words in nature and not all that many in the mind. It matched the intensification of effort MacDiarmid was after and provided him with precise and as he liked to say *inoppugnable* detail. He sought out recondite words of exact meaning, technical terms and curious local names.

2. He emancipated himself from metre by adapting or adopting (actually transferring) passages of scientific prose. Its logically controlled periods and long words with many unstressed syllables enabled him to generate movements of exceptional celerity. Smaller in variation but higher in frequency and capable of longer duration than muscular effort they have the effect of literally quickening perception.

3. While abandoning Scots for international English he explored at the same time Scotland's Gaelic past. As well as a good deal of dubious celticry he found models for his poetry in its music dance and verse. Among other things he produced in 1935 a magnificent English translation of *Birlinn Chlann Raghnaill* (Clanranald's Galley), a description of a sea voyage by the 18th-century Scottish Gaelic poet Mac Mhaighstir Alasdair. The original is said by Professor Derick Thomson to be *the ultimate demonstration of Mac Mhaighstir Alasdair's hard, exact intellectual power.*

4. Throughout this period MacDiarmid was also exercising, mainly for polemical purposes, his vigorous colloquial style. Together these processes eventually resulted in a poetry of intellectual fervour, vast in scope and technical in detail, carried on loose-jointed long-drawn-out syntax and expressing itself in vivid direct colloquial English which

(abstruse and elaborate though the matter often is) makes the whole seem not composed but improvised.

To the 'thirties there also belong some occasional poems which do not develop method or try to. Limited in objective by some compelling subject or immediate purpose they simply place at its disposal the resources developed so far. They thus have an interest separate from the poetry's ultimate aim or outcome and lend themselves better to unprepared appreciation. Of the two now to be described by way of example one does not appear at all in the so-called 'collected' edition of MacDiarmid's poems published in New York in 1962 and revised in 1967, the other is cut in that edition to a stump. Both show a strong mind concentrated on a single subject, facility of utterance disciplined to a controlled eloquence, and technical deficiencies turned by an uncanny knack to functional advantage.

The first is called *Tam o' the Wilds and the Many-Faced Mystery.* It was dedicated to William Soutar and published in *Scottish Scene* (1934). Unusually for MacDiarmid it is a long poem in stanzas, 47 octets rhyming x a x a x b x b. Its subject is the 'Scotch naturalist' whose life was recorded by Samuel Smiles. He was a workingman who spent every moment he could spare from his job in the minute and tireless observation of nature, in all its weathers and in all its forms: birds, insects, fishes, plants. The poem is written in a fluent conversational style and its purpose seems at first only to record and commend an example of pure self-dedication. Rough versification and slapdash rhyming help convey Tam's makeshift means and his dogged persistence through difficulties and incomprehension. The language is everyday Scots except when cataloguing his collections, where names of species are English. The steady succession of stanzas regulates movement, so that the variety and intensity of his studies as well as the poet's interest and admiration are stabilised: mood is quiet, patient, determined. So the poem goes on, for 43 stanzas: 344 lines.

Suddenly the poet thinks of William Soutar, the friend to whom (the reader has forgotten) the poem is dedicated. Soutar, also a poet, was an invalid permanently confined to his bedroom. Yet he too lived a life of constant study and dedication, though outwardly as unlike Tam's as could be conceived. With the same steady patience as before, without pity or patronage, MacDiarmid contemplates the fates of these two men and contrasts both with the unthinking crowd. In the last stanza, still without change of tone, he turns to the author of the mystery that has produced two such different yet equivalent lives. With a short apostrophe in formal English he speaks to God in words which express part awe, part question and part the technical interest of a fellow-artificer, as who should say: Cannot two play at that game? The last four lines break the rhyme-scheme and the last line of all, as often in MacDiarmid, shoots off into the infinite and bursts, dislocating syntax.

The second poem, first published in *Stony Limits* (1935), is **"On a Raised Beach"**. It is a meditation on a beach in Shetland, the extreme northern isles where MacDiarmid then lived, on the nature and significance of stones. It begins as an evocation of stoniness, of matter as the elemental and everlasting substance of the universe. Against the stones it sets the evolution of life on earth and the possible future of mankind, a development in comparison with the stones precarious and insignificant. Among these concepts MacDiarmid moves with a sure foot and a cool head. For over 400 lines the poem is maintained at a level of speculation with scarcely a trace of deliberate terribilità, both subject and form conveying the patient inhuman mind of the artist-scientist. Apart from a short sequence using words in Norn (the Norse language of Shetland, now extinct) the language is English. The beginning and the end of the poem are each made up of rare scientific words, geological and other terms, built up like cairns. The verse is free with every occasional rhyme, like life fortuitous shock.

Several causes (including the second world war and MacDiarmid's personal circumstances but chiefly the character of the poetry itself) prevented his work from culminating in one completed opus. Parts remained unfinished, parts unpublished, parts were published at different times under different titles. The longest, *In Memoriam James Joyce,* appeared in Glasgow in 1955, when it was described as part of a work entitled *A Vision of World Language.* This still best indicates the nature of the work. Only the complete (London) edition of MacDiarmid's poems, compiled shortly before his death, contains all the parts and fragments that are preserved.

Into this last work MacDiarmid put his greatest effort. It is the nearest he got to the kind of poetry he wanted. It carried its characteristics to their extremes or rather (since these are by their nature limitless and any particular realisation is condemned to fall short) to the limited reach of his powers. It marks the last effort of a Promethean mind to extend means never adequate: sentences uniting abstract generalisation with remote particulars are stretched to breaking-point. It bears some resemblance to the late work of other great artists, though always unmistakably his own: huge in bulk, self-willed yet objective, contemptuous of carefulness yet curiously exact, unseductive yet extremely moving. It can put a thing as simply and easily as Pound or Zukofsky, yet like Joyce or Céline hold a voluminous body of material by the narrowest of margins just or not quite under control in a wild spree. (pp. 55-61)

Whatever MacDiarmid wrote he wrote out of a largeness of mind, with a superabundance of matter, from the furthermost reach of his thought. Few men can have been less petty or less prudent. Inseparable from writing others would blush to see in print is poetry nobody else could have written of a kind not many would have dared to attempt.

The authors he revered were Dostoyevsky, Hopkins, Doughty, Rilke, Shestov: a rum lot, but from none of them did he think of learning how to write. From each he took something of his own view of the world and in each he may have seen reflected something of his own isolation and purposefulness. He had an exceptional faculty for assimilating anything in which he glimpsed an affinity. With mystics and rebels he identified immediately. He was a passionate nationalist who followed the pioneer Marxist revolutionary John Maclean and the inventor of the new economics C. H. Douglas.

If not among the most intelligent of the poets he is among the least superstitious. His intellect was more capacious than acute, its range extremely wide, his knowledge of men not large, his emotional base rather narrow. He combined extension of cognition to the extremes of the known with expansion of sympathy to the extremes of deprivation but quickly turned pity for suffering into admiration for fortitude. He had a head for heights and was fascinated by the diversity of detail at the fringes. Brilliantly as his catalogues of particulars are written they are not, like those of Joyce or Rabelais, games of a mind exulting in its virtuosity but Whitman-like acts of humility and wonder. The middle-ground he was ignorant of and uninterested in.

Remoteness may have restricted his experience and exposed him to neglect but it protected him against more serious dangers. Can it really be that he revived, practised and developed a kind of poetry not known outside the north-west edge of Europe? So it would seem. He had no use for the Mediterranean tradition and none for the modern crazes. He was drawn to certain Asian systems of thought but took little interest in American writing and for most of what passes for literature in England had the utmost contempt.

On to his ancient and local kind of poetry he grafted modern universal science. This he treated not as an optional supplementary resource but as an indispensable foundation, *inoppugnable.* The function of science in his poetry is thus equivalent to the functions previously exercised in poetry by myth and metaphor and originally by language itself.

His strength was in assertion: he spoke out straight and clear and could say almost nothing in a way that rang in the mind. When he lost grip he still kept going till he either startled or left gasping. He injected poetry with the rhythms and the vocabulary of prose, developing movements of torrential flow. He broadened its scope and made it interesting to everybody. He had the facility and the fallibility of the journalist and no finesse at all.

He saw the English more clearly than others who knew them better, for he had no secret sentimental ties, but as satirist he was not so effective as might be thought. His hatred was pure but his observation was limited. His attacks have vivid phrases but tend to be long-range, ideological.

As a landscapist he was superb. Description of nature brought out his zest for existence, his delight in the most fleeting detail. He especially enjoyed rich colour, the sound of rushing water and the long swooping flight of the larger birds. This kind of poetry goes back through Thomson and Douglas to the medieval Irish.

Description was not his ultimate aim however. He depicted what he knew of the world in relation to an ideal recalled or potential. His poetry thus promotes change in the sense defended in the *Second Hymn to Lenin* (1935). Poetry of this kind, operating in the area between representation and action, has for essential function not the neutral manifestation of meaning but its utterance with force and clarity to persuade and inspirit, with the original energy art can canalise but not simulate. (pp. 63-5)

Kenneth Cox, "The Poetry of Hugh MacDiarmid," in Agenda, *Winter-Spring, 1987, pp. 52-65.*

W. S. Milne

[*Annals of The Five Senses*] is a reprint of MacDiarmid's first book (published in 1927), and in the English poems and essays here collected can be discerned perhaps the germ of all his subsequent writings, but particularly the work in Scottish—a distinct visionary, or metaphysical quality:

> I was a crystal trunk,
> Columnar in the glades of Paradise
> Bearing the luminous boughs
> And foliaged with the flame
> Of infinite and gracious growth,
> —Meteors for roots,
> And my topmost spires
> Notes of enchanted light
> Blind in the Godhead!
> —White stars at noon!

Although undoubtedly this is in a sense Grieve making himself anew, it is perhaps too fanciful to see this as the very moment when C. M. Grieve became Hugh MacDiarmid, as Alan Bold [author of the reprint's introduction] believes. It is rather the first and difficult stage in a long career as a writer of national and international significance—Grieve's last words in the book (written, like much of it, in the third person) being, 'And if I may be permitted just a word in the light of what I now know (and that incompletely) with regard to his subsequent career, it shall be simply this, that to my mind the storms of circumstance which have buffeted him so terribly are laden with this message: "And so shall our commission be accomplished which from God we had—to plague His heart until we had unfolded the capacities of His Spirit".' Well, it was never like MacDiarmid to be humble, never hesitating to aggrandize his spirit, or assign capitals to himself! Of course he was to continue in this vein, as in the poem, **"The Fool"** collected here:

> He said that he was God.
> "We are well met," I cried.
> "I've always hoped I should
> Meet God before I died."
>
> I slew him then and cast
> His corpse into a pool,
> —But how I wish he had
> Indeed been God, the fool!

—containing as it does the committed humanity, outraged dignity and proud humour we associate with the best of his work:

> Duncan Gibb o' Focherty's
> A giant to the likes o' me,
> His face is like a roarin' fire
> For love o' the barley-bree.
>
> He gangs through this and the neebrin' shire
> Like a muckle rootless tree
> —And here's a caber for Daith to toss
> That'll gi'e his spauld a swee!

Of all the prose pieces in the book, the best is undoubtedly **"A Four Years' Harvest"** (MacDiarmid would never have written 'Harvest' one feels, but 'Hairst'), especially in its satirical yet sensitive analysis of The Great War, seeing it as culmination of man's inveterate habit of pursuing complexity for its own sake—

Such a gallimaufry as it was of all that was frivolous, absurd, luminous, suggestive, depressing, exasperating and farcical! Such a mosaic of hot haste and fatigue, over-heated brains and mobs, overproduced nothingness, shams and jumbles! And through it all peered the faces of men and women, each one eager for acclamation and for gain. Moreover, to each of these things hung others, the odd fruitage and gleanings of this odd life, insane confidences, strange privileges, glimpses into bottomless horror, terror, emptiness, visions of sacrifice and heroism and endless glory and goodness.

As always MacDiarmid remains positive, right to the end.

The book is full of good things, as if we caught MacDiarmid in full conversational flow: "It is not healthy to live for ever in a mental cinema, least of all when you have, with slight differences in the screenings and accompaniments, seen all the films before, and over-familiarity with the technique of production has bred contempt"; "He was now quite certain that the imagination had some way of dealing with the truth, which the reason had not, and that commandments delivered when the body is still and the reason silent are the most binding that the souls of men can ever know"; "Truth, without the progressive belief of mankind in it, seemed vague and helpless. Of what little avail are the profoundest thoughts if they contain no germ of comfort!"; "So his tendency was always to the whole, to the totality, to the general balance of things . . . Here, probably, was the secret of the way in which he used to plunge into the full current of the most inconsistent movements, seeking—to find ground upon which he might stand foursquare"; "He was always fighting for the absent, eager for forlorn hopes, a champion of the defeated cause, for those portions of truth which seemed to him neglected . . . And thus his dreams were edged with the redeeming inconsistency, the saving dubiety, and he held with Browning the great central liberal feeling, a belief in certain destiny for the human spirit beyond and perhaps even independent of, our sincerest convictions . . . "

In his autobiography MacDiarmid said that this book contained 'the main ideas of all my subsequent work'—but the book is more than just a blueprint: it stands in its own right as the first published work of a first-class writer, and as we now know, his early prophecy proved indeed to be correct; "When the great music came it would not be such and such a bit of tone-colour, nor this or that sonority, but the soaring or tender curve of the themes, their logical yet ever new unfolding, the embodiment in the whole composition of richest variety with completest unity . . . "—a good description perhaps of the working method found in **"A Drunk Man Looks at the Thistle"**. Here we have "portions of his far-flung reading, certain recollections of landscape or house-furnishing, inflections of voices, smells, sounds, physical and mental sensations' which the writer returned to again and again in the course of his long and creative writing career.

This book is to be highly recommended, not only to readers of Scottish poetry, but to readers of poetry everywhere. (pp. 30-3)

W. S. Milne, "The Genesis of Hugh MacDiarmid," in Agenda, *Vol. 21, No. 3, Autumn, 1983, pp. 30-3.*

Wang Zuoliang

Hugh MacDiarmid is the pen name of Christopher Murray Grieve who came from the border between Scotland and England. Among his ancestors were tough men who sometimes committed robbery across the border; some were weavers of Scottish cloth. He proudly declared in one of his poems:

> Reivers to weavers and to me. Weird way!
> Yet in the last analysis I've sprung
> Frae battles, mair than ballads . . .

To many readers and critics MacDiarmid's most moving poems are those of his early years. About 1925 he and several of his friends initiated the "Scottish Literary Renaissance" movement, and he himself began to write poetry. During these years he wrote mainly lyrical poetry in a peculiar Scottish dialect called Lallans. Even today many people still enjoy these early poems such as **"The Watergaw," "The Bonnie Broukit Bairn," "The Eemis Stane," "Moonlight Among the Pines"** and **"Empty Vessel."** These are fresh, beautiful short poems, but not insubstantial ones. MacDiarmid always added something to a simple scene, to enlarge and deepen its significance.

In **"Empty Vessel,"** for instance, the poet describes a country woman's agony upon losing her baby. She is driven insane, singing to her dead baby. The four-line ballad form which the poet uses gives this ordinary scene a style of primitive simplicity and a sense of eternity. A transition appears in the second stanza; the country setting of the first stanza changes into a more general scene of nature. This poem is based on an eighteenth-century folksong, but MacDiarmid enlarges the woman's agony to encompass the whole universe.

"The Eemis Stane" is a meditation on time and life and death. If the world is unsteady like a stone in the wind, then life is simply capricious. Fame and history are only moss and lichen, covering everything. (This expression is novel—usually people say that fame will be buried by time, or that it will survive time and become immortal.) However, this is not a meditation in the abstract. The scene is concrete; it is surrounded in a sort of desolate atmosphere with strongly infectious power, and the primary images of stone, world, wind, sky and snow remind the reader of the universal circumstances of human existence.

"Moonlight Among the Pines" is a love poem of great momentum and tender feeling, in the fresh setting of the moon amidst the piney woods.

The poems mentioned above are only a few examples to prove that MacDiarmid's lyrics are among the most outstanding works of Scottish literature. Here a key element is the use of the Scottish dialect. MacDiarmid strongly protests the "English ascendancy" in Scottish literature, but at the same time he completely understands the predicament of Scottish poets. . . . He is dealing with Scottish subjects and they must be expressed in the Scottish idiom otherwise the content will be distorted. This conclusion is drawn from the work of many other poets as well as from his own experience. What kind of Scottish dialect should be chosen, then? Burns had provided an example for others, but the bitter experience following his death gives a warning. Writers trying to follow the Burns tradition added a too sentimental and vulgar atmosphere which

made the language sound more like that of a tipsy woman. MacDiarmid, however, would go a new way. He chose mainly the dialect from the lowland district of southeast Scotland, added some Scottish words and phrases collected from a dictionary of ancient dialects. . . . Consolidating these, he called it a "Lallans language," which he used as the language of his early poems. Using the Scottish dialect, absorbing the quintessence from the long tradition of Scottish country people, with the poet's modern sensibility which developed under the influence of the works of Mallarmé, Rimbaud and Rilke to correct any tendencies toward anarchism, these poems broke away from the English literary tradition and struck against the "English ascendancy" while displaying the brilliant genius of the Celts. This is the key element which makes MacDiarmid's lyrical poetry fresh and powerful.

MacDiarmid did not rest content with just repeating what he had done. The long poem **"A Drunk Man Looks at the Thistle,"** published in 1926, marked a further development of his poetic skill. The work consists of several independent poems, including lyrics such as the famous "O wha's been here afore me lass" which made Yeats feel, when he was shown it by a friend, "amazed that there should be such writing and he unaware of it." There are also satirical poems, comic poems, philosophical poems, extempore poems, epistles, translations, and imitations. He also wrote his first political poem, the **"Ballad of the Crucified Rose,"** which praised the General Strike of May 1926. What links the whole long poem is its theme: the condition of Scotland. The thistle is the symbol of Scotland, used as the pattern of the Scottish national emblem. It appeared in many places in the poem and the man who was observing it was a drunken person. The moonlight was very gentle, and everything was seen as dreamlike. The thistle underwent many marvelous changes in the drunken man's sleepy eyes. (For a while the thistle becomes an embryo in a test tube.) Each change represents one aspect of Scottish life, therefore while the drunken man was observing the changes, the poet was reflecting and criticizing the reality of Scotland. MacDiarmid's love for Scotland is beyond question. However, he is also aware of many of the weaknesses of his country. That is why his poetry is full of biting sarcasm and mockery particularly aimed at the upper-class Scottish people, castigating them for their neglect of traditions, their selfishness, conceit, apathy and self-deception. Even the withering of the red rose of the mammoth demonstration was imputed to the body of the plant itself:

> The vices that defeat the dream
> Are in the plant itsel',
> And till they're purged its virtues maun
> In pain and misery dwell.

MacDiarmid knew exactly what should be a Scottish poet's duty:

> A Scottish poet maun assume
> The burden o' his people's doom,
> And dee to brak their livin' tomb.

What is the way of salvation for Scotland? The poet, looking far into history, which appeared to him like "a huge moving wheel," observing the reality of Europe, found that an unprecedented struggle was taking place in Russia. He hailed Dostoevsky:

> I, in the thistle's land
> As you in Russia where
> Struggle in giant form
> Proceeds for evermair,
> In my sma' measure 'bood
> Address a similar task,
> And for a share o' your
> Appallin' genius ask

The conclusion was clear:

> —At a' events, owre Europe flaught atween
> My whim (and mair than whim) it pleases
> To seek the haund o' Russia as a freen'
> In workin' oot mankind's great synthesis.

The word "synthesis" will appear again in MacDiarmid's poems; here it represents the new political and social experiment, referring to the Soviet system of workers, peasants and soldiers. Influenced by John Maclean, the leader of Scottish workers, MacDiarmid put more and more political meaning into his lyrics; actually he was experiencing an important development in political thought. In addition to the Scottish nationalism which he espoused before, he began to cherish the ideal of communism, and he attempted to achieve a new "synthesis" between these two.

As a result, during the thirties, MacDiarmid wrote his three hymns to Lenin. The first and second were written and published in 1931 and 1932 respectively. The third hymn was written at an unknown date, but it apparently belongs to a later period to judge from its content and form and was published in 1955.

In the Soviet Union, long hymns like Mayakovsky's "Vladimir Ilyich Lenin" had been published. By the thirties the Soviet system was well established, but the capitalist world had been shaken by an economic crisis. It was an offense to the bourgeoisie to admire the leader of the world proletariat; it needed not only political courage but also artistic courage to do so, because there would be difficulties in determining what to praise and how to praise.

MacDiarmid solved these difficult problems in his own particular way. He did it neither by shouting hollow words like "long live," nor by loading his writing with fulsome flattery. As he said in the **"First Hymn to Lenin,"** his concern was to see "If first things first had had their richtfu' sway." The "first thing" is Lenin's position in human history. The poet compared Jesus with Lenin, and continued:

> Christ's cited no' by chance or juist because
> You mark the greatest turnin'-point since him
> But that your main redress has lain where he's
> Least use—fulfillin' his sayin' lang kept dim
> That whasae followed him things o' like natur'
> 'Ud dae—and greater!

> Certes nae ither, if no' you's dune this.
> It maitters little. What you've dune's the thing,
> No' hoo't compares, corrects, or complements
> The work of Christ that's taen owre lang to bring
> Sic a successor to keep the reference back
> Natural to mak'.

And the significance of Lenin is:

> Great things, great men—but at faur greater's cost!
> If first things first had had their richtfu' sway

> Life and Thocht's misused poo'er might ha' been ane
> For a' men's benefit—as still they may
> Noo that through you this mair than elemental force
> Has f'und a clearer course.

To MacDiarmid, nothing mattered so much as the development of people, and he especially extolled Lenin because the revolution that he had led enabled for the first time human beings to give full play to their own talents, not like "the traitors . . . through a' history" causing human beings to be bogged down forever in a state of childish ignorance.

In the **"Second Hymn,"** MacDiarmid discussed the relation between poetry and politics. The poem attracted a good deal of attention from western critics; some said that MacDiarmid claimed to be the equal of Lenin, and that poetry must be independent of politics. . . . Some quoted the concluding lines: "Ah, Lenin, politics is bairns' play / To what this maun be!" to show MacDiarmid's disrespectful attitude towards politics.

What did he mean by those words? If you reread the whole poem you will find that he was full of respect for and felt very close to Lenin, therefore he felt that he could come out with what was on his mind, comrade to comrade. He showed this attitude from the beginning:

> AH, Lenin, you were richt. But I'm a poet
> (And you c'ud mak allowances for that!)
> Aimin' at mair than you aimed at
> Tho' yours comes first, I know it.

The respect that the poet felt for Lenin was fully expressed in **"First Hymn"** and other poems written at the same time (e.g. **"The Seamless Garment," "The Skeleton of the Future"**). So when he wrote the **"Second Hymn"** one year later he felt no necessity to repeat himself. Instead he discussed poetry in depth. MacDiarmid held high hopes for poetry:

> tho' Joyce in turn
> Is richt, and the principal question
> Aboot a work o' art is frae hoo deep
> A life it springs—and syne hoo faur
> Up frae't it has the poo'er to leap

Judging by such criteria he found that the present situation of poetry was not satisfactory. He spoke first of his own poetry:

> Are my poems spoken in the factories and fields,
>   In the streets o' the toon?
> Gin they're no', then I'm failin' to dae
>   What I ocht to ha' dune.

> Gin I canna win through to the man in the street,
>   The wife by the hearth,
> A' the cleverness on earth'll no' mak' up
>   For the damnable dearth.

The situation was the same for other poets. They influenced "but a fringe o' mankind in ony way"; their topics are too cramped to attract large spirits; genuine great poetry should be "free and expansive."

Poetry, however, has good prospects, especially as it gains enlightenment from Lenin:

> Poetry like politics maun cut
> The cackle and pursue real ends,
> Unerringly as Lenin, and to that
> It nature better tends.

Wi' Lenin's vision equal poet's gift
And what unparalleled force was there!
Nocht in a' literature wi' that
Begins to compare.

Nae simple rhymes for silly folk
But the haill art, as Lenin gied
Nae Marx-without-tears to workin' men
But the fu' course insteed.

Organic constructional work,
Practicality, and work by degrees;
First things first; and poetry in turn
'll be built by these.

This shows solid and concrete admiration of Lenin. How, then, can one say that the poet was joking about Lenin? MacDiarmid's style was at once lively and serious. He considered that poetry must deal with really important subjects instead of getting bogged down in trifles. Such stupid matters should be cut off like a monkey's tail! The poet must be mature, no longer naive—one may recall that this was also stated in the **"First Hymn."** Now Lenin had given poetry an opportunity to be fully developed. As a result of the victory in the struggle which he led, human beings could for the first time be "Freein' oor poo'rs for greater things, / And fegs there's plenty o' them." . . . Thus MacDiarmid looks forward to a new role for poetry in the future, and if you visualize what this future poetry will be, "politics is bairns' play." MacDiarmid might be right or wrong, but he was not setting himself up as greater than Lenin. He was seeking a new "synthesis" between poetry and politics. It was precisely Lenin's October Revolution which carried human history to a new stage and so made that "synthesis" possible.

"First Hymn" and **"Second Hymn"** have different emphases, but they are completely consistent in spirit—in love for the revolutionary leader, in the central argument, even in key phrases (e.g. "first things first"), and both were written in Scottish dialect. In **"First Hymn"** each stanza consists of six lines (the shorter last line introduces a pause); in **"Second Hymn"** each stanza consists of four lines. These forms were chosen to suit MacDiarmid's free-flowing, lively style. The poems were not superficial and empty; in them he expounded some general principles of poetry. He wrote concretely but did not get bogged down in details; epigrams appear here and there; images are striking but not fantastic; his skillful use of rhythm takes full advantage of the subtleties of dialect. Thus these two hymns are outstanding in their artistry.

"Third Hymn to Lenin" was first published in *The Voice of Scotland* in 1955. The reason that it was mentioned as a work of a later period is that here MacDiarmid's style changes in comparison with the **"First"** and **"Second Hymn."** Scottish dialect and the short stanza disappear; this poem is characterized by free verse and standard English. Words and phrases gush out with a new tremendously eloquent momentum, revealing the poet's anxieties about the city Glasgow.

The poet introduces a seaman, then he asks rhetorically: Can a sailor know the flow of the waves as Lenin knew the flow of history? MacDiarmid then sings of Lenin:

You turned a whole world right side up, and did so
With no dramatic gesture, no memorable word.
Now measure Glasgow for a like laconic overthrow!
     . . .

After a long passage the poet proposes:

Be with me, Lenin, reincarnate in me here,
Fathom and solve as you did Russia erst
This lesser maze, you greatest proletarian seer!

What was the problem that Glasgow was facing? The poet painted this scene:

A horror that might sicken your stomach even,
The peak of the capitalist system and the trough of Hell,
Fit testimonial to our ultra-pious race,
A people greedy, lying, and unconscionable
Beyond compare.—Seize on this link, spirit of Lenin, then
And you must needs haul upwards to the light
The whole base chain of the phenomena that hold
Europe so far below levels worthy of its might!

Following this MacDiarmid described the stench of a Glasgow slum, and quoted a passage in prose from William Bolitho's (pseud. of William Bolitho Ryall) *The Cancer of Empire.* . . . [Despite] slums, however, many Scots were still content to leave things as they were:

So long as we avoid all else and dwell,
Heedless of the multiplicity of correspondences
Behind them, on the simple data our normal senses give,
Know what vast liberating powers these dark powers
     disengage,
But leave the task to others and in craven safety live.

As he did with the drunk men looking at the thistle, once again MacDiarmid mercilessly castigated those apathetic people: Labour M.P.'s, idle talkers, scholars and scientists. They allow the fascists to run wild and even help to spread their rumors. For example, MacDiarmid points to famous astronomers (e.g. Sir James Jeans) who, instead of carrying forward their research into scientific truth went back to the arms of the church. The poet shouted with rage at this situation: "This is the lie of lies—the High Treason to mankind."

Nor did MacDiarmid spare scholars and poets who aroused his disappointment and anger:

Michael Roberts and All Angels! Auden, Spender,
     those bhoyos,
All yellow twicers: not one of them
With a tithe of Carlile's courage and integrity.
Unlike the pseudos I am *of*—not *for*—the working class
And like Carlile know nothing of the so-called higher
     classes
Save only that they are cheats and murderers,
Battening like vampires on the masses.

A true poet, he pointed out, must be concerned with something completely different:

Our concern is human wholeness—the child-like spirit
Newborn every day—nto, indeed, as careless of tradition
Nor of the lessons of the past: these it must needs
     inherit.

But as capable of such complete assimilation and sur-
     render,
So all-inclusive, unfenced off, uncategoried, sensitive
     and tender,

That growth is unconditioned and unwarped . . .

In order to accomplish such a prospect, the poet again appealed to Lenin:

> . . . Ah, Lenin,
> Life and that more abundantly, thou Fire of Freedom,
> Fire-like in your purity and heaven-seeking vehemence,
> Yet the adjective must not suggest merely meteoric,
> Spectacular—not the flying sparks, but the intense
> Glowing core of your character, your large and splendid
>   stability,
> Made you the man you were—the live heart of all
>   humanity!
> Spirit of Lenin, light on this city now!
>
> Light up this city now!

This concludes the **"Third Hymn."** In short, in this poem MacDiarmid called for the awakening of the Scottish people and he considered that the way Lenin pointed out was the only way to eradicate poverty and disease in cities like Glasgow. He adopted a Whitmanesque free verse using language closer to spoken every-day expression, with rapid shifts in diction. The entire poem was written in English, completely abandoning the Scottish dialect. This became a characteristic of his later period.

The change in style first revealed itself in the mid-thirties. The collection entitled *Second Hymn to Lenin and Other Poems,* published in 1935, consisted of about fifty poems. All of them, however, were written in English except **"Second Hymn"**; among these were several outstanding pieces such as **"On the Ocean Floor," "The Storm-Cock's Song"** and **"Reflections in an Ironworks."**

In addition to these, several short English poems are also worth mention. **"The Skeleton of the Future"** (from *Stony Limits,* 1943) is usually included in selections of the poet's work. In it he used the terminology of geology to describe the solidity and glitter of Lenin's coffin chamber as well as the light which was reflected from the snow outside to represent the Russian land and people, to end with "the eternal lightning of Lenin's bones," a line both realistic (describing the light on Lenin's remains) and symbolic (representing Lenin's undying influence on mankind); the title itself reinforces this theme.

"Of John Davidson" (from *Scots Unbound,* 1932) is another impressive poem. Every line is permeated with deep emotion, although the author unemotionally describes how he observed Davidson's lonely figure walking up to the edge of the sea, but suddenly there is "—a bullet-hole through a great scene's beauty." The serene world was violently torn apart: a talented poet, like other beautiful things, ended in a single moment. Meanwhile MacDiarmid detachedly points out the reason for the tragedy: a short-sighted view of the future, finding the wrong spiritual sustenance. Compared to this deeply felt elegy, many other modern poems that mourn the dead seem to be perfunctory, composed only for the occasion.

It was, however, the long poem that formed the main feature of MacDiarmid's work in the later period. *In Memoriam James Joyce,* published in 1955, was one of them. The poem consists of 6,000 lines, but was only a part of a much longer poem, *A Vision of a World Language,* which was never completed. The content of *In Memoriam James Joyce* is complex; some parts of it are difficult to understand. At least two themes are clear: first, men must inherit and develop the whole human culture from ancient times to today (this has already been emphasized in **"Second Hymn to Lenin"**); secondly, a writer should bring his linguistic potential into full play as Joyce had done. MacDiarmid admired the Irish writer greatly. Many critics had frowned on the large number of new words which were created by Joyce in *Ulysses* and *Finnegans Wake,* but MacDiarmid fully supported Joyce's effort because he (MacDiarmid) considered language as "the central mystery / Of the intellectual life" and thought that a writer should seek the language which best conveys his sensibility:

> A language that can serve our purposes,
> A marvellous lucidity, a quality of fiery aery light,
> Flowing like clear water, flying like a bird,
> Burning like a sunlit landscape.
> Conveying with a positively Godlike assurance,
> Swiftly, shiningly, exactly, what we want to convey.

MacDiarmid considered that the attempt at originality which he and Joyce were making was significant:

> That is what adventuring in dictionaries means,
> All the abysses and altitudes of the mind of man,
> Every test and trial of the spirit,
> Among the débris of all past literature
> And raw material of all the literature to be.

This would be a kind of language that is understood by every nation, thus various cultures develop intercourse with one another and the development of human beings would be universal. It is evident that the poet's two themes are actually one, and that the first one is the prerequisite of the second.

MacDiarmid vigorously practiced what he advocated. *In Memoriam James Joyce* is a kind of embodiment of this theme. He frequently adopted foreign words and quoted foreign writers, scientists and thinkers. In one short section, for example, you can find Sanskrit, Greek, Finnish, and eastern European languages. . . . In using a broad range of quotations from ancient to modern times, from various countries, MacDiarmid is not doing exactly what T. S. Eliot did in *The Wasteland* and Ezra Pound did in *Pisan Cantos.* MacDiarmid was their friend, and he defended the *Pisan Cantos* in *The Company I've Kept.* He enjoyed the poetry of the French Symbolists and such modern German poets as Rilke, and displayed a perfect "modern sensibility" so sedulously cultivated by modernist poets. On two important points, however, MacDiarmid was different from the modernists. Eliot and others depend on knowledge coming from classical literature, whereas MacDiarmid's poetry spreads its roots in the tradition of Scottish folk-literature, which is an old but vital tradition. Eliot and Pound went back to the past, whereas MacDiarmid looked to the future. In his view, bringing the capacity of language into full play is an indispensable prerequisite for the universal development of human beings, and that is why he was so enthusiastic about it. (pp. 1-13)

MacDiarmid's works of the later period arouse various responses because many critics do not like his change of style. Readers enjoy the outstanding passages in these poems, but are puzzled by them as wholes. The poet himself clearly knew what he was doing and explained it in his usual forthright manner. For instance, he wrote:

> The greatest poets undergo a kind of crisis in their art,

A change proportionate to their previous achievement.
Others approach it and fail to fulfill it—like Wordsworth.

• • •

—I am forty-six; of tenacious, long-lived country folk.
Fools regret my poetic change—from my 'enchanting
    early lyrics'—
But I have found in Marxism all that I need—

He further declared in *The Kind of Poetry I Want:*

Utterly a creator—refusing to sanction
The irresponsible lyricism in which sense impressions
Are employed to substitute ecstasy for information,
Knowing that feeling, warm heart-felt feeling,
Is always banal and futile.

Here we can see that he no longer used the Scottish dialect, which is consistent with his abandonment of lyric poetry.

He clearly explained his reason for writing long poems in the essay **"Ezra Pound"**:

It is epic—and no lesser form—that equates with
the classless society. Everything else—no matter
how expressly it repudiates these in the mere logical
meaning of what it *says* against what it *is*—belongs
to the older order of bourgeois "values" . . .

MacDiarmid also used Heine as an example and pointed out how he had changed his style after the success of his early lyrics, and enlarged the range of his subjects, though his later poetry was not well received and had still not been correctly reassessed. The writing of epics is an inevitable trend, MacDiarmid thought. Epics were not created in ancient times only; today many progressive poets are writing them—Mayakovsky and Neruda, for instance, as well as "a Yugo-Slav shepherd [who wrote] *The Stormy Years of the 20th Century.*" They have all written magnificent epics. The appearance of the epic is inevitable, because "The grandeur of the time requires grand syntheses—not only in fine arts or music, but also in literature, not only in prose, but also in poetry."

However, what kind of epic is desirable? There does not seem to be any criterion, but certain tendencies may be seen in MacDiarmid's own later poetry, namely: "Marxization" of poetry—using poetry to attack and satirize class enemies with a violence hitherto rarely seen in verse, and placing one's hope in universal development, including a "greater synthesis" of human culture, which is what Lenin advocated.

"Scientificization" of poetry—for this MacDiarmid wrote "the poetry of facts", using many images drawn from science, frequently using scientific words.

Internationalization of poetry—for this he drew upon the quintessence of various cultures, quoting philosophical and literary works from various languages, and using large numbers of foreign words.

Establishing a new aesthetics—there are many discussions of poetry and poetics; he not only explained his own poetry and commented on others' poetry, but also explored the fundamental principles of poetry and art. He paid particular attention, as did many other modern poets, to the language of poetry, and he always strove to be original in his own poetic language.

Do these tendencies, or the subjects and artistic techniques used to accomplish them, necessarily lead to the production of epics? This requires further consideration. MacDiarmid's merit is that his poetic performance is far more brilliant than his theory; his practice often remedies the defects of his theory. His long poems may not be epics in the traditional sense—they are not even complete works; however, they represent an important poet's extensive experiments in art. Where experiments succeed, they succeed magnificently: his political poems blend power with beauty; he employs Whitmanesque free verse with cunning; his long stanzas are full of thrust; they shift continuously to express his sinuous thoughts; he assimilates materials from many sources, making of them a rich and unified poetry. He inserts brilliant comments: the passages in which he talks about art, poetry, language and his own experience and feelings are among the most outstanding in modern European poetry. His exploration of the relation between science and poetry shows a good grasp of important issues in the modern world. He has taken a large step in broadening the range of poetry, and that step is the beginning of his search for a greater synthesis of human culture.

What is our final impression? Among modern English poets MacDiarmid is a master from the North. He followed a road which was trodden by the masses and yet particular to himself—mass-based because of his revolutionary enthusiasm and Communist ideals; particular because of his art. Whatever he wrote carries his own hallmark; it would be almost impossible to imitate his poetry. Even when his poetry seems to be dull and redundant, suddenly a surprising image or epigram will light up the scene, or an unusual rhythm will soothe the ear. In his later poetry MacDiarmid wanted to repudiate his lyrical quality, but actually this is just the quality that makes him imperishable. This was evident not only when he wrote those enchanting lyrics but also when he wrote his later long poems. A poet's—any poet's—opinions may have great or small historical significance, but it is hard for anyone to escape from the ravages of time. Some scientific theories that MacDiarmid quoted in his long poems are obviously outdated now, and some of his understanding of Marxism may not be universally accepted, but the art of his lyrics will endure. These lyrics are not of a sweet, sentimental kind, but are of a higher order which has resulted from the fusion of deep feeling and an active imagination—the rhythm of a folksong wedded to a twentieth-century poet's sensitivity to language. This higher lyricism is to be found in his powerful eloquence, in the hymns to Lenin, in the homage to Joyce, in the prospect of the "greater synthesis" of human culture in the future.

Because he wrote with such lyricism his poetry will endure better than many modern English and American productions. When this great Scottish poet died in 1978 he had already seen that, with the publication of his **Collected Poems** in 1962, his poetry had finally broken through a long period of neglect and prejudice. Since then it has won more and more readers who wonder at its power and beauty. We can be sure that he laid down his pen with a final sense of triumph. (pp. 13-16)

Wang Zuoliang, "Reflections on Hugh Mac-Diarmid," in Studies in Scottish Literature, *Vol. XIX, 1984, pp. 1-16.*

FURTHER READING

Akros: Special Double Hugh MacDiarmid Issue 12, Nos. 34 & 35 (August 1977).
Includes bibliography and numerous critical essays.

Bold, Alan. *MacDiarmid: A Critical Biography.* London: John Murray, 1988, 482 p.
Comprehensive survey of MacDiarmid's personal life and career.

Boutelle, Ann Edwards. *Thistle and Rose: A Study of Hugh MacDiarmid's Poetry.* Loanhead, Scotland: Macdonald, 1981, 259 p.
General study and introduction to MacDiarmid's works, particularly poems written before 1935.

Buthlay, Kenneth. "Some Uncollected Poems by Hugh Mac-Diarmid." *Scottish Literary Journal* 12, No. 1 (May 1985): 70-6.
Discussions and reprints of eleven uncollected poems, including "Green Serene" and "The Miracle of Edinburgh."

Daiches, David. "Hugh MacDiarmid and Scottish Poetry." *Poetry* 72, No. 4 (July 1948): 202-18.
Survey of the poet's influence and achievement. Considered one of the most significant American studies on MacDiarmid.

Davis, A. C., and Scott, P. H., eds. *The Age of MacDiarmid: Essays on Hugh MacDiarmid and His Influence on Contemporary Scotland.* Edinburgh: Mainstream, 1981, 268 p.
Critical and personal discussion of MacDiarmid's poems and political life. Includes essays by David Daiches, Duncan Glen, and Iain Crichton Smith.

Glen, Duncan. *Hugh MacDiarmid and the Scottish Renaissance.* Edinburgh & London: Chambers, 1964, 294 p.
Biographical analysis of MacDiarmid's verse. Includes bibliography. Critically regarded as an excellent introduction into MacDiarmid's life and work.

McQuillan, Ruth. "The Complete MacDiarmid." In *Studies in Scottish Literature,* edited by G. Ross Roy, pp. 177-209. Columbia: University of South Carolina, 1983.
Detailed review of MacDiarmid's *Collected Poems.*

Roy, G. Ross. "The Thorn on Scotland's Rose: Hugh Mac-Diarmid." *World Literature Today* 56, No. 1 (Winter 1982): 58-61.
Analyzes several Scottish studies of MacDiarmid's works.

Singer, Burns. "Scarlet Eminence: A Study of the Poetry of Hugh MacDiarmid." In *Hugh MacDiarmid: A Critical Survey,* edited by Duncan Glen, pp. 35-57. Edinburgh: Scottish Academic Press, 1972.
Examines MacDiarmid's singular political attitude and his formation of the Scottish Literary Renaissance.

Alistair MacLean

1922-1987

(Full name: Alistair Stuart MacLean; also wrote under the pseudonym Ian Stuart) Scottish novelist, short story writer, scriptwriter, travel writer, and juvenile fiction writer.

A popular and prolific adventure writer, MacLean is regarded as a master of the suspense novel. He often pitted his protagonists against an adverse environment and their own internal terrors to illustrate the power of humanity's raw courage. MacLean's heroes struggle to overcome incredible dilemmas through a combination of intelligence and physical force. Although sometimes faulted for a melodramatic style and one-dimensional characters, MacLean is lauded for his swift narratives and labyrinthine plots. Martin Sieff asserted: "[MacLean's] novels are imbued with a powerful, uncompromising moral vision—that there is wickedness in the world and that it must be recognized and fought to the death, come what may."

MacLean spent much of his youth in the remote village of Daviot, Scotland, where his father was a parish minister. After attending school in Glasgow, he joined the Royal Navy in 1941 to fight in World War II, and his five years as a torpedoman informs much of his espionage fiction. In 1954, MacLean was working as an English teacher when his short story, "The Dileas," won a *Glasgow Herald* competition and caught the attention of editors at William Collins, a Glasgow publishing house. Several months later, the company printed MacLean's first novel, *H. M. S. Ulysses,* which was an instant best-seller and remained MacLean's personal favorite throughout his lengthy career. The story takes place in 1942, when the shortage of ships in the British navy led commanding officers to overextend their existing fleet, driving the crews to exhaustion, delirium, and sickness. At the novel's outset, the men of the *Ulysses* have already mutinied but are ordered back out to sea to assist a convoy crossing enemy waters. The courage they exhibit amidst the tension of constant attacks during the next five days is the novel's principal focus, as MacLean charts the crew's redemption.

MacLean considered the enormous success of *H. M. S. Ulysses* a fluke and continued to teach until the acclaim greeting his next book, *The Guns of Navarone,* convinced him to concentrate on his writing career. In time, it would prove to be his most popular novel. Like many of MacLean's works, *The Guns of Navarone* is comprised of a series of adventures occurring over a short amount of time. Five men, each with distinctive espionage talents, are brought together during World War II for a special assignment: they have four days to destroy huge German guns commanding an eastern Mediterranean channel so that British ships can pass safely. *Force Ten from Navarone* unites the three survivors of this venture with three new agents in a mission to blow up a dam in Yugoslavia. These works, which focus on the psychological consequences involved in such feats, prompted critics to note MacLean's use of such cinematic techniques as crosscutting to accelerate a story's pace. Accordingly, MacLean proved to be an accomplished screenwriter,

adapting several of his works for motion pictures, including both *The Guns of Navarone* and *Force Ten from Navarone.* Another novel successfully adapted to film, *Where Eagles Dare,* chronicles the World War II adventures of eight British spies who parachute into Germany to rescue an American general held prisoner by the Gestapo.

In *The Secret Ways,* a British secret agent is sent to Hungary to retrieve a scientist brainwashed by Soviets who want him to deliver an anti-British speech to a scientific conference. Reviewers praised MacLean's lucid rendering of the political and cultural atmosphere of the Cold War era. MacLean's next novel, *Night without End,* was regarded as his first wholly credible story. When a plane crashes near a Greenland weather station, the doctor based there rescues the survivors and discovers that the pilot was shot and the plane deliberately destroyed. After the station's radio is wrecked and its operator killed, the doctor realizes there is a murderer among the survivors. The group must hike to a settlement three hundred miles away, still unaware of the killer's identity. *Ice Station Zebra* also takes place at an arctic meteorological station, as an American submarine transports a crew to investigate a post where murder, arson, and other crimes have been committed. A critic from the *Times Literary Supplement* commented: "The story evolves in a succession of masterful puzzles as astonishing as they are convincing, and Mr. MacLean's method is ingenious . . . [There] is so much swift-moving action, so much clever innuendo and such a feeling for relevant detail that one cannot help but be fascinated by the mind at work here."

Bruno Wildermann, the protagonist of *Circus,* is typical of the superhuman characters populating MacLean's works. The greatest trapeze artist in the world, Bruno is also a judo and karate expert who possesses a photographic memory and clairvoyant powers. He is hired by the CIA and sent to Eastern Europe to steal the secret of "antimatter," a substance with extremely destructive powers. To enter the prison where the formula is kept, Bruno must cross a three hundred yard-long wire charged with two thousand volts of electricity. He discovers that his parents have been incarcerated at the prison for many years for political reasons. Several reviewers of *The Golden Gate* observed that MacLean's style and characterizations were becoming redundant and obvious. In this novel, a group of people kidnap the President of the United States in the middle of San Francisco's Golden Gate Bridge. The group's leader, a banker's son with an Ivy League education, becomes a folk hero for cleverly demanding a ransom of five hundred million dollars and a presidential pardon to avoid prosecution. *San Andreas* takes place aboard a British hospital ship during World War II. In this enigmatic drama, a saboteur has shorted out the ship's electrical system. Shadowed by two German U-boats, the *San Andreas* survives numerous acts of sabotage on its journey to Scotland, leaving the crew to ponder why the Germans want to seize the ship instead of sink it. In MacLean's last novel, *Santorini,* published a month after his death, a ship's crew watches a plane go down in flames in the Aegean Sea just as a nearby yacht catches on fire. Upon discerning that the submerged plane is carrying atom and hydrogen bombs, one of which is set to detonate, they display skill and courage in averting a great disaster.

In addition to his novels, MacLean wrote juvenile fiction, most notably the biography *All About Lawrence of Arabia.* His collection of short stories, *The Lonely Sea,* each of which were written early in MacLean's career, recount naval battles and examine the courage and strength of the people involved. Reviewers applauded many of the stories, including "The Dileas," the prize-winning work that first brought MacLean critical attention in 1954. This piece chronicles the relationship of two brothers who sacrifice their lives during a raging storm at sea. "Rendezvous," related in first-person flashback, is a classic tale of war and espionage possessing the vivid characterizations and the intensity of *The Guns of Navarone.*

(See also *CLC,* Vols. 3, 13, 50; *Contemporary Authors,* Vols. 57-60, 121 [obituary]; *Contemporary Authors New Revision Series,* Vol. 28; and *Something about the Author,* Vols. 23, 50.)

PRINCIPAL WORKS

NOVELS

H. M. S. Ulysses   1955
The Guns of Navarone   1957
South by Java Head   1958

The Last Frontier   1959; also published as *The Secret Ways*
Night without End   1960
The Dark Crusader [as Ian Stuart] 1961; also published as *The Black Shrike*
Fear is the Key   1961
The Satan Bug [as Ian Stuart]   1962
Ice Station Zebra   1963
When Eight Bells Toll   1966
Where Eagles Dare   1967
Force Ten from Navarone   1968
Puppet on a Chain   1969
Bear Island   1971
The Way to Dusty Death   1973
Breakheart Pass   1974
Circus   1975
The Golden Gate   1976
Goodbye California   1977
A Weekend to Kill   1978
Athabasca   1980
San Andreas   1986
Santorini   1987

SCREENPLAYS

The Guns of Navarone   1959
Where Eagles Dare   1969
Puppet on a Chain   1971
When Eight Bells Toll   1971
Caravan to Vaccares   1974
Breakheart Pass   1976
The Golden Rendezvous   1977
Force Ten from Navarone   1978

OTHER

All About Lawrence of Arabia (biography) 1962; also published as *Lawrence of Arabia*
Alistair MacLean Introduces Scotland (travel) 1972
Captain Cook (biography) 1972
The Lonely Sea (short story collection) 1985

E. B. Garside

Mr. MacLean's novel [*H. M. S. Ulysses*] opens with *H. M. S. Ulysses* laid in at Scapa Flow, under investigation by Admiral Starr of British naval operations. After the 5,500-ton light cruiser had made several trips, unbroken by shore leave, on the Murmansk run, a faction among the crew revolted. In quelling the mutiny marines have killed two men and wounded others.

In vain Captain Vallery tries to convince Starr that his men were simply driven beyond human endurance. Tuberculosis, brought on by bad food and damp cold between decks, is rife among the crew, and numbers have gone mad from strain. But Starr has to think of fighting ships as pawns. The time is 1942, a year when the Germans are to sink six and a quarter million tons of shipping, the bulk of it British. Starr coldly orders the *Ulysses* out again to assist a convoy crossing from St. John's.

The cruiser, with despair in the fo'c'sle and great tension in the wardroom, moves into the teeth of the great Arctic cyclone of 1942. In this monstrous gale, with winds up to 120 mph and below zero temperatures, the ice-sheathed flight deck of one of the accompanying carriers is torn up by the roots and bent back into a fantastic U-shape. Other vessels founder, or are forced to run for home. But the remnants of the escort rendezvous on schedule in mountainous seas off Northern Iceland.

During the next five days the *Ulysses,* chief target in the escort, is under constant attack, by subs, from the air, and by the Hipper, a much more powerful German cruiser: Captain Vallery dies of exhaustion; subordinates carry on. One by one gun turrets are ripped asunder. Gaping holes are punched into the *Ulysses'* compartments. The end comes off the Kola Peninsula. With her battle flag flying, she wheels, and heads for the Hipper, intending to ram at forty knots. But she cannot. An exploding magazine blows away her bows. Down she goes, at full speed, into the sea, her jack streaming in the wind. Meanwhile, of the original thirty-six ships in the convoy, seven have made it through.

For all its faults, this novel is a gripping thing. In it is not a trace of the cynicism and iconoclasm of so many of our American Navy stories. Dying in wartime is taken for granted. The characters are overdrawn, to be sure, the heroics rather windily described. Still, one feels instinctively that Mr. MacLean, former torpedoman, now a Scottish schoolmaster, has caught the bitter heart of the matter. It is refreshing to meet, through his writing, someone who quite openly believes in the value of courage.

> *E. B. Garside, "On the Murmansk Run," in* The New York Times Book Review, *January 15, 1956, p. 36.*

Taliaferro Boatwright

In the naval annals of World War II the Murmansk convoys occupy a place apart. To the cruel risks of warfare at sea elsewhere were added bitter, survival-inhibiting cold, next-door accessibility to air, submarine and surface attack, and a frightening history of attrition. From every aspect, they were harrowing ordeals. This was true for the virtually helpless merchant ships in the convoys; it was compounded for the escort vessels condemned by a ship-poor Admiralty to return again and again in a never-ending agony.

All the terror, appalling carnage and desperate heroism of the Murmansk convoys are concentrated into one nightmarish operation in [*H. M. S. Ulysses*] by Alistair MacLean, a young Scotsman. As the story begins, the *Ulysses,* a 5,500-ton light cruiser, flagship of 14th Aircraft Carrier Squadron, is in Scapa Flow. Her crew, driven beyond the edge of reason by constant exposure to fear, hunger, cold, danger and even disease (consumption), has mutinied. But the Admiralty refuses to understand, and orders the ship out again. . . . (p. 1)

In [the next five days] the officers and the men of the convoy are called upon to face every imaginable form of attack by the elements and the enemy. To catalogue the individual incidents would be to spoil the author's story, but the cumulative effect is one of almost unbearable tension for the individual members of the ship's crew.

Truth to tell, they are not so much individuals as types.

There are the gallant navigator, the keen-eyed seaman, the salty old First Lieutenant, the incredibly strong stoker, the gruff, Socratic surgeon, the tragic and competent petty officer. Above all, there is the Christlike figure of Richard Vallery, Captain of the *Ulysses,* coughing up his life even as he takes his ship out of Scapa Flow, but alone capable of lifting his crew to the heights of which they are capable. In the background is the inexorable, all-powerful Admiralty, the jealous God who has condemned them to wander, Ulysses-like, over the face of the earth.

H. M. S. Ulysses, then, is more a legend than a novel of real flesh and blood people. Like most legends, it is larger than life. This does not gainsay the truth of its elements. The endurance, the sacrificial bravery of the men who supplied our Russian allies across the top of the world command sympathy. The accuracy and vividness of the descriptions of the attacks on the convoy compel undivided attention, morbid or not. And despite one's foreboding of the denouement, despite even theatrical, sometimes melodramatic touches, the *Ulysses* and her officers and men come to have personal meaning. The result is a moving and thrilling book. (pp. 1, 8)

> *Taliaferro Boatwright, "Heroic Tale of the Murmansk Run," in* New York Herald Tribune Book Review, *January 22, 1956, pp. 1, 8.*

Time, New York

In a British film called *Kind Hearts and Coronets,* an admiral went down with his flagship, at full salute, unflinching as the waters closed over his beard. It was, of course, a British spoof of the proud Royal Navy, whose tradition of impenetrable reticence earned it the name "Silent Service." Now that the U.S. has become the world's greatest naval power, a certain relaxation of the stiff upper lip is in order. In overstated understatement, *H. M. S. Ulysses* is trying to show that the Royal Navy had a royal and rugged time of it in World War II—and that anything the U.S. Navy can do, the Royal Navy can do better. Specifically mutinies.

This is—novelistically—the British reply to *The Caine Mutiny.* It is a bloodier affair than just getting Queeg off his teetering bridge; some 50 sailors and Royal Marines are wounded, two die in a bloody free-for-all on the decks. The H. M. S. *Ulysses* is a 5,500-ton light cruiser, "the first completely equipped radar ship in the world," the seeing-eye watchdog of the Murmansk convoy run. Unlike that long-drawn-out, suspenseful business on the *Caine, Ulysses'* mutiny has already taken place, and this is the story of her glorious "redemption." This being the Royal Navy, the mutiny was a lower-deck affair, and the only officer-villain goes overside. It differs from the *Caine* mutiny in another merciful respect—the characters never get ashore into the arms of sea-fogged sex.

Ulysses ships up to 500 tons of ice topside; she is under constant threat of submarine wolf packs, is harried by Stukas, Condors and Heinkels snarling out of their Norwegian airfields. The crew is fed nothing but fear, lethal cold, and the slower death of the corned-beef sandwich. On this unhappy ship all is misery; she becomes a debating society, with the crew arguing their orders and the time and manner of their death. From stoker to captain, everyone is infected with what the British call "the Nelson touch," *i.e.,* an inspired disregard for orders. There is heroism, and men die well in these brutal waters, but the admiral cracks up and wanders crazed in his pajamas.

If the *Ulysses* crew are wooden, they are admiralty specification teak. Author MacLean, a schoolteacher who served five years in the Royal Navy, has brought to his first novel an ear as sharp as sonar. The Liverpool stokers blaspheme authentically, and about the story lies the fascination of precise technical information and service jargon—the grim grammar of war. (pp. 99-100)

> *"Royal Navy Raises Caine," in* Time, *New York, Vol. LXVII, No. 4, January 23, 1956, pp. 99-100.*

Daniel George

[In Alistair MacLean's *The Guns of Navarone*] we meet Captain Mallory, world-famous New Zealand climber of Himalayan peaks, who, it is said, talks Greek like a Greek and German like a German, summoned from exploits with the LRDG by Captain Jensen, to whom 'as the successful Chief of Operations . . . intrigue, deception, imitation and disguise were the breath of life.' The special job for which Captain Mallory is detailed gives him as companions Corporal Dusty Miller, who speaks American almost like the American he is said to be, and who had lied his way into the RAF, crashed outside Athens, and turned up, via Albania, in a force operating behind the enemy lines in Libya; Lieutenant Andy Stevens, RNVR, navigator, first-class Alpinist, fanatical philhellene; and Casey Brown, Petty Officer Telegraphist, in civil life a testing engineer in a famous yacht-builder's yard. Add to these Mallory's *alter ego* Andrea the Greek and two vouched-for natives and patriots of Navarone, and could anyone want a team more likely to provide thrills in the course of successful sabotaging operations against the precipitous island fortress?

> *Daniel George, in a review of "The Guns of Navarone," in* The Spectator, *Vol. 198, No. 6711, February 8, 1957, p. 185.*

Rex Lardner

Herculean feats of endurance, stoic acceptance of great peril and discomfort, self-sacrifice and bravado while in the hands of captors, ingenious plotting in a minuscule, but politically important, areas of World War II—these are some of the things taken up in the precipitative novel by Alistair MacLean. All the action—and *The Guns of Navarone* contains more than most—takes place in four eventful days. The focus here is small; the deeds fantastic.

Because German guns on the South Aegean island of Navarone commanded a channel through which British ships had to pass, the guns had to be destroyed. For the job, British Intelligence picked a lethal quintet of hatchetmen. They were: Keith Mallory, a New Zealander and the world's best mountain-climber; a huge man named Andrea, a former lieutenant colonel in the Greek Army, unmatched as a quick, silent killer; Casey Brown, who would act as engineer on the hulk that was to take them to a por-

tion of Navarone consisting of a vertical, seemingly unscalable cliff; Lieut. Andy Stevens, who spoke Greek, who was an experienced, if introspective, mountain-climber; and Cpl. Dusty Miller, a dour American who was the best man with explosives in southern Europe.

The team had been chosen well; where one man was weak, another specialist had more than enough strength or skill to cover for him; and all showed talent for acting and for improvising as unexpected traps were sprung. After a series of accidents, betrayals and games of hide-and-seek with the efficient German mountain troops occupying the island, the hatchetmen do what they have set out to do. It is a gripping, authoritative story.

> *Rex Lardner, "Lethal Quintet," in* The New York Times Book Review, *February 10, 1957, p. 30.*

Time, New York

Early in World War II a character called Alistair Digby-Vane-Trumpington (in Evelyn Waugh's *Put Out More Flags*) asked his wife if she would mind if he joined the Commandos:

> "They have special knives and Tommy guns and knuckle-dusters; they wear rope-soled shoes."
> "Bless you," said Sonia.
> "They carry rope ladders round their waists and files sewn in the seams of their coats to escape with. D'you mind very much if I accept?"
> "No darling. I couldn't keep you from the rope ladder. Not from the rope ladder I couldn't. I see that."

Like Digby-Vane-Trumpington, many writers cannot be kept from rope ladders; they love to swarm up the icy cliffs of fiction, creep up on reality in their rope-soled shoes and knock it out of commission with those knuckle-dusters. In the van of these shock troops is British novelist Alistair MacLean, who in *H. M. S. Ulysses* showed his ability to zero in with a battery of heavy clichés, fieldstrip and assemble a character in the dark, and tell an exciting story. MacLean displays the same talents in his current operation [*The Guns of Navarone*], dealing with the eastern Mediterranean in mid-World War II.

The Germans are set to wipe out the 2,200-man British garrison on the Greek isle of Kheros. The Germans control the air by day and the British the sea by night. Unless the British can silence a German battery on the neighboring isle of Navarone, nothing can save the Kheros garrison. Five men are selected to sail a caïque under the cliffs by night, scale them, and blow up the German guns. Largely because the five are led by a man so tough and tight-lipped that he would make Bulldog Drummond seem like a pacifist balletomane, they pull off this miraculous stunt. The superman is Captain Keith Mallory, a New Zealand mountaineer, "idol of the cragsmen," hero of legendary exploits in the Cretan resistance.

Before the action ends in a satisfactory bang, there is an uninterrupted spate of sinkings, gunplay, throat-slittings, cliff-hangings, captures and escapes, surrounded by sound technical information. For the young in heart it is great stuff—a first-rate derring-documentary. As in *H. M. S. Ulysses,* novelist MacLean sternly eschews sex. A man needs every ounce of strength to punch out novels like this.

> *"Derring-Documentary," in* Time, *New York, Vol. LXIX, No. 6, February 11, 1957, p. 102.*

Victor P. Hass

Alistair MacLean, who started out magnificently with the taut *H. M. S. Ulysses* and then lost some ground in his derring-do *Guns of Navarone,* loses another notch or so with . . . [*South by Java Head,* an] exciting but highly improbable tale of an escape from Singapore in World War II.

South by Java Head is fun, mind you, and MacLean is wizard at creating fighting men of almost superhuman stamp, but when you turn a page with the nagging notion that what you have just read defies belief, then enjoyment is impaired.

The story begins on Feb. 19, 1942—the day when Brigadier Farnholme, Britain's ace espionage agent in the far east, reaches flaming, falling Singapore with the complete plans, in films and photostats, of the projected Japanese invasion of Australia. There are no planes on Singapore and it is only by a miracle that Farnholme is able to take over a freighter commanded by a nefarious renegade Englishman.

The party he takes is large and consists of disabled soldiers and refugees. Their ship is blasted out of the water by Japanese bombers but, in the heart of a raging typhoon, they are taken off by the only other allied ship in the area, a British merchantman.

From that point the feats of valor mount incredibly, for that ship is shot out from under them and they whip a Japanese submarine with a carbine from a rowboat, survive a frightful landfall on Java, turn the tables on Japanese captors in all-but-unbelievable fashion, and find they have been harboring a nazi secret agent who is a better man than most of them, Gunga Din.

> *Victor P. Hass, "An Exciting Adventure, but Highly Improbable," in* Chicago Tribune, *January 5, 1958, p. 5.*

Taliaferro Boatwright

A Brigadier with stolen Japanese war plans that could save a continent, a drunken Muslim priest, a two-year-old boy, five oriental nurses, a squad of gravely wounded Highlanders, a hard-faced Dutchman, an elderly British gentlewoman—such was the passenger list of the Kerry Dancer, the last ship out of Singapore.

Brigadier Farnholme was determined to set his prize to safety. True, the colonel commanding at Singapore had given him an able-bodied detail of men as insurance. Nevertheless, the fate of the whole party was in the hands of Siran, the renegade who captained the rusty little tramp. And the Japanese commanded the Java Sea.

So Alistair MacLean sets the stage for his third novel [*South by Java Head*]. This time the author of *H. M. S.*

Ulysses has forsaken the semblance of reality in favor of an out-and-out thriller. This time he has written a pure escape novel, almost a formal exercise in espionage and counter-espionage, spiced by generous dashes of danger and violence.

The trouble is that the condiments are too generously applied. Farnholme and his shipmates undergo a succession of harrowing ordeals ranging from enemy attack by air, sea and land through storm, fire, thirst and shipwreck to treachery and deception, and even mangling by a clam. The effect is exactly like an old-time "serial" moving picture.

But the old "cliff-hangers" had a sovereign virtue: they required a week's wait between episodes. *South by Java Head* can be read in one sitting. The result is a dulling by repetition, coupled with a curious depersonalization, so that before long credence fails.

This is really a story of incidents, not of people. The interest lies almost entirely in what happens, not in the people it is happening to. The incidents involve people, of course, but almost without exception the people are figures (and usually time-tested stock figures). Not even the heroine, a beautiful Eurasian nurse, and the hero, a brave and resourceful ship's officer, are developed in depth. Added to that, the figures speak in stilted set speeches that are perilously close to parody.

The result is a book that will appeal only to the most voracious adventure lovers. In light of *H. M. S. Ulysses* it is a distinct disappointment.

> *Taliaferro Boatwright, "Last Ship Out of Singapore," in* New York Herald Tribune Book Review, *January 5, 1958, p. 5.*

Richard Philbrick

A distinguished English scientist, muddled and misled in his appraisal of communism, was about to make a speech in Hungary, harmful to the west, at an international congress of scientists. The mission of Michael Reynolds, British secret agent, was to remove him from the midst of his Russian hosts and return him to England.

[*The Secret Ways,* the] account of how Reynolds went about his assignment is, of course, a "spy story," and Alistair MacLean, author of *H. M. S. Ulysses,* has made it one of the scariest, most breathtaking books written in a long time.

There is no dawdling about even in the first few pages, not with Reynolds being pursued by "three trained Doberman pinschers, the most vicious and terrible fighting dogs in the world." And there is no letup in the fast pace until the last four paragraphs are at hand.

One of MacLean's triumphs is that he has struck a highly rewarding balance between Reynolds and his allies and their enemies, the secret police. For all their cleverness, Reynolds and the men in the underground have only a little the better of it in their attempts to extricate the scientist.

As in a game in which the lead is constantly changing, Reynolds' adventures are so unpredictable because of the strength of his opponents that the excitement builds up to a high pitch and is sustained there.

> *Richard Philbrick, "One of the Scariest Spy Stories in a Long Time," in* Chicago Tribune, *March 1, 1959, p. 3.*

The New Yorker

[In *The Secret Ways*] Michael Reynolds, an English secret agent, has put in eighteen months of special training for the job he now undertakes: he must make his way alone and in secret to Budapest to abduct an eminent elderly British scientist, Harold Jennings, who is in that city to attend the International Scientific Congress. Jennings has to be kidnapped, if he cannot be persuaded of the error of his ways, because he has gone over to Russia and has now come to Budapest from Moscow in order to deliver an inflammatory anti-British speech before the Congress. Reynolds' job is to get to Jennings before he can make the speech, and to accomplish this mission he must pit himself against the dreaded Hungarian Secret Police and other fearful forces. Most of the action takes place in Budapest, and Mr. MacLean shows alarming power in his ability to convey the terror of dark streets, suspiciously silent houses, and the constant presence of a patient, implacable enemy who never sleeps. This is an enthralling story.

> *A review of "The Secret Ways," in* The New Yorker, *Vol. XXXV, No. 8, April 11, 1959, p. 175.*

Taliaferro Boatwright

Looking for an escape novel? . . . [*The Secret Ways*] is a veritable Houdini, crammed with a succession of hairbreadth evasions of manifest fate and prodigious feats of endurance and physical dexterity that would do credit to the master illusionist himself. Furthermore, these are set in a background not only impressively *au courant* politically, but also Baedeker-perfect in its portrayal of behind the Iron Curtain flora and fauna. Unfortunately, like the exploits of Houdini their appreciation requires a suspension of disbelief. . . .

The Secret Ways is an espionage thriller. Its hero, trenchcoated Michael Reynolds, is a British agent, superbly trained, nerveless, ingenious, catlike. He is sent to Hungary with the mission of inducing a world-famous defecting British ballistics expert to return to England before delivery of a paper scheduled for an International Scientific Conference. To do so he must evade the AVO, the Hungarian Secret Police. As allies he can hope for only the few remnants of the Hungarian underground—if he can find them.

Michael's adventures carry him through secret hideaways, the cafes and hotels of Budapest, fortress prisons, and the deep snows of the Danubian plains. They lead him to incredibly efficient and brutally sadistic police agents, heroic resistance figures, and a girl who promises a new meaning for his life. Along the way too, he finds that there may be solutions to the cold war and the plight of the satellite countries other than total victory, "parachute diplomacy," or helping oppressed people to help themselves.

As he showed in *H. M. S. Ulysses.* Alistair MacLean has a flair for dramatizing the heroic. His principal faults are an addiction to the superlative and a tendency to theatrical characterization. In the never-never land of fictional foreign intrigue, these are not necessarily damning.

> *Taliaferro Boatwright, "British Agent in Hungary," in* New York Herald Tribune Book Review, *April 26, 1959, p. 10.*

Richard Philbrick

Far north on the Greenland ice cap the roar of an airplane mingled with the moaning of the Arctic wind. As the noise became louder it alerted the three men isolated in an international geophysical year station. An adventure began as though the first bullet had been fired from a belt of machine gun ammunition.

Five and one-half days later the adventure, which had engaged the entire attention of the military forces of at least three major nations, was over. Compressed as they are in that short span, the fragments of the suspense Alistair MacLean packs into his story [*Night without End*] explode with the impact of still another bullet in the ammunition belt.

The material from which he has constructed his novel is, for the most part, startlingly new. Geophysical research, trans-Atlantic air travel, guided missiles, and even the cold war are still fresh ingredients of fiction. Fused in this instance with extraordinary imagination and narrative power, they greatly enhance an excellent story.

The more common elements—danger, romance, courage, suspense, and the like—are handled with all the skill MacLean displayed in his first novel, *H. M. S. Ulysses,* and in *South by Java Head* and *The Secret Ways.*

The skill is apparent, also, in the depiction of Dr. Mason, the narrator in *Night without End.*

Though the adventure is suffused with mystery, Mason does not perform any extraordinary feats of deduction. He falls in love, but there is no real indication he will win the object of his affection. And for all he is both a surgeon and a scientist, he does not come up with any brilliant improvisations or last ditch miraculous operations.

Yet, because of the splendid design which the narrative follows, he emerges a hero. In the same way, the entire story is always credible, and amazingly powerful.

> *Richard Philbrick, "Powerful Narrative of Adventure in Greenland," in* Chicago Tribune, *March 6, 1960, p. 3.*

Margaret C. Scoggin

[In Alistair MacLean's *Night without End,* a] special BOAC flight with a few but oddly assorted passengers crashes on the Greenland Icecap near an isolated IGY weather station. Dr. Peter Mason, in charge of the camp, rescues the survivors. He discovers that the plane had been deliberately crashed after the shooting of the pilot and one of the passengers. When his radio is destroyed and the plane's wounded radio operator killed during the first night in camp, Dr. Mason realizes there is a murderer among them who will stop at nothing to accomplish his or her purpose, whatever it is. He knows, too, that their only chance for survival depends upon a desperate push to the nearest settlement over three hundred miles away. Danger is piled upon disaster almost—but not quite—to the plot's breaking point. It is a good hair-raising hunt-and-chase spy thriller, not to be taken seriously or recommended to the too sensitive. I like it better than MacLean's *South by Java Head* where the plot *did* break under the weight of disasters, although I'd rate it below his *H. M. S. Ulysses* and *Guns of Navarone.*

> *Margaret C. Scoggin, in a review of "Night without End," in* The Horn Book Magazine, *Vol. XXXVI, No. 3, June, 1960, p. 237.*

The Times Literary Supplement

[In *Ice Station Zebra*] Dr. Neil Carpenter, a fast-talking Britisher, boards the U.S.S. Dolphin, an atomic submarine ordered to the Arctic to rescue the survivors from fire-ravaged meteorological station Zebra, adrift somewhere on the polar ice cap. When Carpenter shows an alarming knowledge of atomic submarines and correctly analyses the source of an accident nearly fatal to the submerged Dolphin, it becomes distressingly clear that his mission is indeed dubious and that the meaning behind the fate of Ice Station Zebra has a greater than meteorological importance. The story evolves in a succession of masterful puzzles as astonishing as they are convincing, and Mr. Mac-Lean's method is ingenious. Carpenter is the narrator, and he withholds as much information about himself and his purpose from the reader as he does from the officers of the Dolphin. Although Carpenter sounds at times too much like an American private detective, there is so much swift-moving action, so much clever innuendo and such a feeling for relevant detail that one cannot help but be fascinated by the mind at work here.

> *"Totleigh Revisited," in* The Times Literary Supplement, *No. 3206, August 9, 1963, p. 605.*

Martin Levin

In *Ice Station Zebra* Mr. MacLean sends the American nuclear sub Dolphin on a mercy mission to the chilliest sector of the cold war—the polar ice cap, where a British meteorological station is having difficulties. Aboard the Dolphin is a slightly mysterious British physician, who may or may not be the frost-bite specialist he claims to be: and on the floating research center near the North Pole, there is evidently someone at large who is no Santa Claus—else how can you explain the incidence of murder, arson and sabotage? Why would anyone commit such excesses in a region where all nations have collaborated in the pursuit of scientific knowledge? Mr. MacLean has an intricate and ingenious explanation that comes at the end of a voyage that is in itself an exciting adventure.

> *Martin Levin, in a review of "Ice Station Zebra," in* The New York Times Book Review, *October 13, 1963, p. 48.*

John B. Cullen

A meteorological expedition burned out on the Arctic ice cap, a weak radio signal heard by a British trawler, long-range bombers from America and Russia, and the latest American nuclear submarines, add up to the author's growing list of thrillers. This reader reviewed MacLean's first success, *H. M. S. Ulysses,* based on his own experiences in the Arctic seas during World War II, and is pleased that the author has matured and polished his writing style, yet, has lost none of the gripping excitement conveyed in the action of . . . [*Ice Station Zebra*]. In addition to the vivid portrayal of man against nature and man against man, he has added the element of suspense.

Just as the *Dolphin* is about to leave the Firth of Clyde for rescue efforts under and through the ice, an English civilian doctor is taken abroad under questionable authority. Was the fire an accident? Are subsequent events on the sub accidents? Who is this doctor? A realistic trip under the ice on a nuclear sub, where once again MacLean portrays the naked emotions and reactions of men to danger, then the battle of men against the piercing ice storm as they cross the polar cap in search of the survivors.

The rescue and the return trip, when the answers to all mysteries are cleared up, put a fitting climax to a new class of novel, adventure and mystery. This is not history, but a fast-moving tale of fiction, which can be and is recommended to all readers searching for light diversion.

> *John B. Cullen, in a review of "Ice Station Zebra," in* Best Sellers, *Vol. 23, No. 15, November 1, 1963, p. 273.*

Bruce Cook

Alistair MacLean has gone back to mine the vein where he first struck it rich, and what do you know? He found a few nuggets of the real stuff still lying around at the bottom of the shaft. *Force 10 from Navarone* picks up the three survivors of the mighty blast that sent *The Guns of Navarone* tumbling to the bottom of the Aegean, then drops them smack-dab in the middle of Yugoslavia, where they are asked to blow up a dam.

They will in this way create a diversion that will (1) free a division of Yugoslav partisans from a mountain trap, (2) convince the Germans that an Allied invasion of Yugoslavia is imminent, (3) thus force the Germans to shift divisions of their own to that sector, (4) thereby assure the success of the Allied offensive next door in Italy.

I spell out all this as a service, for in the beginning the purposes of the mission are a bit foggy. But stay with it. The plot may confuse, the characterizations may seem sketchy, yet once Mr. MacLean finds his pace, the action fairly hurtles along. His secret, I think, is that better than any other practitioner of his craft, he has managed to translate into prose fiction the cinematic technique of cross-cutting—accelerating tempo by skipping among the various sectors of action in ever-shortening fillips of narration.

> *Bruce Cook, "It's a Great Year For the Fans of the Suspense-Fiction Field," in* The National Observer, *November 11, 1968, p. 23.*

The Horn Book Magazine

No sooner has that redoubtable New Zealander, Keith Mallory, destroyed the impregnable fortress of Navarone than he is summoned once again by British Intelligence. With cigar-smoking Andrea Stavros, poetry-reading Dusty Miller, and three Marine commandos he parachutes into Yugoslavia. There a handful of fearless Partisans block the passage of two German divisions through the vital valley of the Neretva, their fate lying in Mallory's agile wits and keen reflexes. [*Force 10 from Navarone*, the] long overdue sequel to *The Guns of Navarone* surges with the desperate courage of tough mountain men, who will never surrender, and with the steely aplomb of professional soldiers, who join them in an impossible mission. The novel is, beyond all else, a study in madness played out in the icy stillness of snow-laden plateaus, concrete escarpments, and a crucial bridge, which only Keith Mallory can destroy.

> *A review of "Force 10 from Navarone," in* The Horn Book Magazine, *Vol. XLV, No. 2, April, 1969, p. 194.*

Lalage Pulvertaft

In *Circus,* Alistair MacLean's new novel, two CIA men recruit a top trapeze artist for an intricate and hazardous mission in Eastern Europe: the objective is to capture the secret of "anti-matter", a substance with immensely destructive properties which has been created (by a German, of course) in the small Stalinist state of Crau. No sooner has the plan been outlined, and our sympathy enlisted by the CIA men who are to run the operation, than, forty pages in, the two fellows are both dispatched; one nastily shredded by a cageful of Bengal tigers, the other ventilated by that reliable standby, the icepick. Despite this evidence of infiltration, and a rising death-rate, the show must go on. Moral issues are kept pretty clear; and the prose is not exactly of the pussy-footing kind: "Sergius gave him a look more commonly associated with a starving crocodile which has just spotted lunch." But then one hardly reads Mr MacLean for the sophistication of his similes, and aficionados will not find this novel disappointing.

> *Lalage Pulvertaft, in a review of "Circus," in* The Times Literary Supplement, *No. 3822, June 6, 1975, p. 677.*

Martin Levin

All right, Foreign Intrigue fans. Here is a little suspense caper that will hold your undivided attention. It has characters who are crisply thumbnailed, the better to bemoan their passing or cheer their survival. It hinges on an espionage assignment of outrageous complexity. And it is all carried off with the breakneck speed essential to such narratives.

Circus dispatches Bruno Wildermann, the world's greatest aerialist (and mentalist), on a mission to purloin something of great scientific value from a redoubt in Eastern Europe that happens to be in his old home town. As a matter of fact, it's the town where his parents are longtime political prisoners. When Bruno reaches the place where the secret scientific stuff is, he needs all of his ability on the slack wire, plus the help of some circus buddies: a strong man, a trick rope artist and a knife thrower. From the moment a C.I.A. operative is thrown to a cage of circus tigers till the moment that finds 13 East European prison guards bound and gagged, the word *détente* doesn't come up even once. *This* is realism.

> *Martin Levin, in a review of "Circus," in* The New York Times Book Review, *September 14, 1975, p. 42.*

Joni Bodart

[In *Circus*] Bruno, a high-wire specialist, mentalist, clairvoyant, karate and judo expert with a photographic memory, is chosen to confiscate a revolutionary formula from a prison which can be reached only by a 300-yard wire charged with 2,000 volts of electricity. MacLean is skilled at pitting his hero against every possible hazard and then overcoming the obstacles, one by one, against incredible odds. A cliff-hanger for sure, this sustains credibility and suspense until the last pages when the evil mastermind, who has been attempting to foil Bruno from the outset, is finally revealed in an ending reminiscent of the author's *Ice Station Zebra.*

> *Joni Bodart, in a review of "Circus," in* School Library Journal, *Vol. 22, No. 3, November, 1975, p. 96.*

T. J. Binyon

Thrillers usually fall into one of two classes. In the first, the line of which runs through Bulldog Drummond to James Bond and beyond, the plot is always essentially that the hero, having got himself, through misplaced chivalry or sheer boneheadedness, into a situation where the diabolical villain . . . can gloat over his helplessness, then, taking advantage of an equal boneheadedness on the part of the villain, extricates himself by the use of his thews rather than his wit. In the second class, of which John Buchan's novels are an example, the hero is confronted with a more intellectual problem which he eventually solves through the equal exertion of brain and body.

Alistair MacLean's books belong to the second class rather than the first. He shares with Buchan a predilection for depicting men at the limit of physical endurance, while the plots of his novels are usually concerned with the hero's attempts to detect the bad apple among a closely knit group of characters and proceed, through a series of peripetias, to the final unmasking: *Where Eagles Dare,* one of his best stories, is a good example. He is a curiously old-fashioned writer: though a pretty girl appears in each cast list, sex is kept rigorously offstage. His heroes . . . are masters of meiosis, shrugging off danger and disaster with a terse quip or two; a characteristic which is thrown into relief by the author's own tendency towards heavy-handed overstatement: sofas are "so soft and comfortable that the overweight man possessed of prudent foresight would have thought twice about ensconcing himself in them, for regaining the vertical would have called for an apoplectic amount of will-power or the use of a crane".

Although Mr MacLean's gift for telling a story has not diminished, his latest books have seemed more and more to be parodies of his earlier ones: his heroes have become actors whose insouciance in the face of danger is not due to bravery but to their knowledge of the final page of the script, while the plots themselves are beginning to lose their capacity to astonish the reader.

In *The Golden Gate* a gang of crooks led by Peter Branson—one of the few arch-criminals with a PhD in economics—carry out an operation of "surgically military precision" to hijack a motorcade containing the President of the United States and the rulers of two major oil-producing countries as it is crossing the Golden Gate Bridge in San Francisco. For the release of their prisoners they demand a ransom of $500m. Luckily for the American taxpayer an FBI agent with a mind "as near ice-cold as any man's can be" is not too far away. *The Golden Gate* is still a difficult book to put down, but one turns the final page with some disappointment: there is no battle against the forces of nature, no real surprise in the plot—both hero and villain are obvious from the beginning. And the former no longer has to rely on his wits and his bare hands; he has a battery of devices to help him, ranging from miniaturized transceivers, through dart-firing felt pens, to military lasers which, in defiance of the laws of physics, can knock out searchlights and immobilize helicopters.

> *T. J. Binyon, "Masters of Meiosis," in* The Times Literary Supplement, *No. 3870, May 14, 1976, p. 592.*

Newgate Callendar

In Alistair MacLean's *The Golden Gate* we meet our old friend the supercriminal. This man has made over $20 million, is known to the police and has never appeared in court. He is too smart for the cops. He is a brilliant planner and organizer. It is also his boast that he has never taken a human life, nor does he ever intend to.

The supercriminal comes up with a supercaper in *The Golden Gate.* He dreams up and executes a scheme to hijack the bus of the President of the United States in the middle of the famous San Francisco bridge. In that bus are two superArabs—a king and a prince of two oil states. The supercriminal manages to accomplish his mission and then demands a superransom. He wants $300 million for his human cargo and $200 million for the bridge itself. Otherwise he will destroy President, king, prince and the Golden Gate.

There is also a neat gimmick. In addition to the money, the supercriminal demands a Presidential pardon. Then he and his men cannot be prosecuted. The gall—the super-gall—of it! The President fumes and sputters, but what can he do?

It is the misfortune of the supercriminal, however, to cross foils with a supercop from the F.B.I. This supercop is in the press entourage, disguised as a photographer. He does this and that, and is always one step ahead of the supercriminal, who has one defect in his armament. He does not really understand security, and the supercop takes advantage of that.

It's all nonsense, but agreeable nonsense. MacLean, author of such hits as *The Guns of Navarone,* keeps things

moving so fast that one does not have the time to question anything. The writing is lean and staccato, spraying action all over the place faster than the cyanide darts favored by the supercop. Yes, it's fun. But *The Golden Gate* is anything but a superbook.

> *Newgate Callendar, "Criminals at Large," in* The New York Times Book Review, *October 10, 1976, p. 34.*

Timothy J. Wood

Rising prices, declining quality, inflation: terms not restricted solely to describing the economy. In fact they all apply directly to Alistair MacLean's newest offering [*River of Death*], a mediocre short story inflated into a poor novel. In the past, typical MacLean characters have usually been one dimensional and current hero John Hamilton is no exception. His personality goes no deeper than the page he's printed on. Hamilton is an explorer who has discovered an ancient, lost city which contains the promise of gold and diamonds. Millionaire publisher Joshua Smith is willing to buy Hamilton's secret with the stipulation that Hamilton lead Smith's expedition to the city. Hamilton agrees. After numerous accidents, near fatal encounters with cannibals, anaconda, and piranha, the expedition finally arrives at the Lost City. After Hamilton's group overpowers the guards, they find what they were looking for—and much more. MacLean stories have always relied on fast paced action, and a twisting, turning plot that constantly leaves you guessing. In the surprises and dramatic revelations lays the pleasure. Yet here, the absence of any real surprises makes the action mere drudgery, leaving the shallowness of the characterizations too exposed.

> *Timothy J. Wood, in a review of "River of Death," in* West Coast Review of Books, *Vol. 8, No. 3, May, 1982, p. 27.*

Kirkus Reviews

There's more talk than action in . . . [*Partisans,* the] slim new WW II thriller from veteran MacLean—and much of the chatting is of the stiff-upper-flip variety, courtesy of cool, smartsy hero Peter Petersen. First met in Rome, Yugoslav-born Petersen would seem, by usual war-novel standards, to be a bad guy: with help from a Nazi Colonel, he's planning to sneak over to Yugoslavia and get crucial intelligence-data to the Royalist, anti-Partisan forces in the mountains. Also along for the trip: Petersen's two loyal cronies; twin brother-and-sister radio operators, supposedly seeking to join the Serbian Royalists; beautiful stranger Lorraine (who claims to be Italian but is really English); the enigmatic Giacomo (who may be Yugoslavian); and assorted other shady types—many of whom turn out to be working for Italian Intelligence. So, on the boat over to Italian-occupied Ploce, there are suspicious goings-on involving Petersen's envelope of top-secret data—as well as the budding of a mild romance between Petersen and radio-operator Sarina. And when the group heads into the hills and is captured by the Partisans, almost everyone—unsurprisingly—is revealed to *really* be on the Partisan side. (There are long speeches about the insanity of Britain's support of the Royalists.) The entire mission, in fact, turns out to be aimed at exposing the villainous anti-Partisan doings of an Italian Major—including the kidnap of Lorraine's little boy. But don't look for a thrilling rescue here, or much derring-do of any kind, for that matter: the liveliest action involves some semi-nasty interrogation/torture. And, with Petersen's occasionally amusing, often-tiresome banter at the forefront, this is likely to disappoint most MacLean fans. . . .

> *A review of "Partisans," in* Kirkus Reviews, *Vol. L, No. 23, December 1, 1982, p. 1307.*

Richard Freedman

Alistair MacLean (*The Guns of Navarone*) may be the most successful author of boys' adventure books since G. A. Henty regaled late-Victorian youth with such romances of derring-do as *Facing Death* and *The Bravest of the Brave*. In *Partisans* Mr. MacLean gives World War II the full Henty treatment: stilted writing about cardboard characters engaged in a desperate enterprise.

The time is 1943, the place Yugoslavia. The Nazis are still in control, although their Italian Fascist allies are fast crumbling. Into this chaos comes doughty Maj. Pete Petersen, a Yugoslav royalist who wants to see King Peter—currently sitting out the war in London—back on the throne. Helping him in this endeavor are fat George, a language professor at Belgrade University who resembles a Yugoslav Nero Wolfe, and a colorful cast of extras, one of whom may be a traitor.

From the very beginning, things seem to be going wrong. On the torpedo boat bringing Petersen home from Italy, a scruffy shipmate tries to poison him and is welded into his cabin for his pains. In Yugoslavia an Italian officer knows that the tiny force of royalist partisans has landed. Who tipped him off? Was it Josip, the friendly innkeeper, or the spoiled aristocrats Sarina and Michael von Karajan? Like their maestro namesake, they're "not accustomed to taking orders."

But as Petersen points out to an Italian major who has fallen into his hands, "The Royal Yugoslav Army takes orders from no one, and that includes Germans and Italians." Not taking orders is what *Partisans* is about if it's about anything at all. And when the novel ends one feels that if Mr. MacLean had been in charge, World War II wouldn't have lasted six days, let alone six years. (p. 33)

> *Richard Freedman, "Brothels, Spooks, War,"* *in* The New York Times Book Review, *March 6, 1983, pp. 10-11, 33.*

Rick Davis

[With *Partisans*], MacLean takes the reader back to the days of World War II and into Yugoslavia, and the camps of the Royalists, anxious to escape the rule of the tyrants who run the country. Italy has seen the handwriting on the wall and wishes to escape the toils of Berlin and assist the partisans to overthrow the Nazi stronghold settled into the frozen mountains of the Balkan states. Major Petersen heads a commando force to help the partisans who, despite their lack of numbers and shortage of firepower, have fought valiantly to save their King and coun-

try. He leads a small band of supporters into the Balkan mountains, running into double dealing and false leads all the way.

There is no smooth sailing in a MacLean plot line and this one is no exception. Set in an atmosphere of danger, intrigue and suspense, that is prime MacLean. In this book he returns to the scene of his former great successes, the vastness of the Balkan mountains, about which he writes so well.

> *Rick Davis, in a review of "Partisans," in* West Coast Review of Books, *Vol. 9, No. 2, March-April, 1983, p. 40.*

Alan Ryan

Alistair MacLean's *San Andreas* has . . . [few howlers], but since the howlers are the best part in a MacLean novel—he does not, for example, know the difference between "transmit" and "transport," thereby failing both English and Latin simultaneously—this one disappoints on all counts.

San Andreas is about a World War II hospital ship whose sole purpose seems to be to steam aimlessly through the most dangerous waters of the North Atlantic, inviting constant attack by enemy aircraft. The hellishly jumbled plot—about a saboteur on board and a gold store secretly used as ballast—has enough holes to earn it a watery grave.

Here's the captain in a tense moment: "He's an extraordinary seaman and he's never pestered anyone in his life. Let's have Janet along here to see if she bears out your preposterous allegations." Sounds like Gilbert & Sullivan to me. For drama, we get "My God, how foolish can I be! . . . Of course they've got radar on the island." Both dialogue and narrative are by turns pompous ("Bitter experience makes for a splendid conductor to belated wisdom"), meaningless ("They were useful planes and had their successes but were not particularly effective"), or simply hilarious ("Nothing like locking the door when the horse has ruined the stable").

MacLean's language cries out for quotation. "The foregoing," he writes, "may strain the bounds of incredulity or, at least, seem far-fetched." Indeed.

> *Alan Ryan, "Murder, Espionage and Mata Hari," in* Book World—The Washington Post, *October 6, 1985, p. 6.*

Caroline Moorehead

A couple of days after the publication of *H. M. S. Ulysses* in the autumn of 1955 Alistair MacLean opened a newspaper to see a long review of his book. It was terrible. The bleak account of the doomed wartime convoy to Murmansk was, complained the reviewer, an insult to the Royal Navy—in fact, the worst insult ever published.

From that day, MacLean has never read another review but it made no difference to his writing. "Then as now I write what I want to write", he says. "I don't ask anyone for comment."

This month over 30 years since *H. M. S. Ulysses* placed him at the top of the world best-seller lists, comes a 28th book of fiction, a collection of short stories called *The Lonely Sea.*

When *H. M. S. Ulysses* came out, MacLean was a reluctant teacher of English in a secondary school in a Glasgow slum, earning £650 a year and "feeling there was nothing I could teach the kids that made any sense." He was 32. Publication day this time will find him in Cannes, home for many years before a move to Dubrovnik five years ago, but still a town for which he retains great affection.

He speaks of his new book in a somewhat mocking tone, pointing out in his rather guttural, low Scots voice, that he himself keeps none of his own books, giving away any copies that come his way immediately he receives them. "I don't think any are very good. I'm slightly dissatisfied with all of them. I'm pleased enough if at the end of the day I produce a saleable product—and that I do."

Indeed he does. No book of MacLean's says Ian Chapman, his publisher, ever sells less than a quarter of a million copies in paperback alone. What distinguishes MacLean from other writers is not that today he ranks among the top ten world best-sellers, earning around a million pounds a year, but that he has been at the top for so long.

For a while, Ian Fleming with James Bond beat him in the league of those with books selling more than a million copies. He had 13. But then MacLean drew ahead—with 16. Nearly every book he has written has been a Book Club choice. Almost invariably, huge budget films, with star casts have followed. (He has never liked any of them.) He sells excellently in America but is best loved in Denmark, Norway and Finland, he says, because he understands about cold.

Something of MacLean's watchful and wary attitude towards the book world has obviously been with him unchanged since the beginning. Ian Chapman is fond of telling the tale of what he calls MacLean's fairy story. In the early 1950s, Chapman was working in the Bible department of Collins in Glasgow. One rainy Saturday, sitting over a manuscript at home, he noticed that his wife Marjory was in tears over a prize-winning short story she was reading in the *Glasgow Herald.* Having read and also admired it, he hunted down its author to a furnished flat on the other side of the city.

Over dinner, he learned that MacLean was the third son of a Gaelic-speaking clergyman, that he had spent five years in the Royal Navy as a torpedo man, that he had grown up on a farm outside Inverness, and later kept himself at university by working in the post office and sweeping the streets.

All that winter, Chapman kept urging MacLean to tackle a full-length novel. One day a brown paper parcel tied up with string was put into his hands: it was *H. M. S. Ulysses,* a highly autobiographical account of MacLean's own days on board a cruiser with the East Coast Convoy Escorts.

Seventy-two hours later, William Collins in London had offered an advance of £1,000—great riches for the 1950s. When Chapman, overwhelmed, hastened round with the news, MacLean stared at him unmoved. Finally, with re-

luctance, he stepped aside: "Och. You'd better come in." Within three months the book had sold 250,000 copies and was a Book Society choice. Of it, MacLean says now, with his mouth turning down in a thin smile: "I had a go, and the go went."

Far too cautious to view what he had done as anything but a fluke, MacLean refused to give up the teaching that so depressed him until, a year later, *The Guns of Navarone* met with the same acclaim. But then, after a pause in the south, he was off, to a villa built just outside Lucerne in Switzerland, with his wife Gisela—he had met her in a hospital in Surrey where he had been scrubbing the floors after demobilization—and the first of his three sons.

From the dining-room table, on a big electric IBM typewriter, rising early and working hard, MacLean produced success upon success. He never rewrote anything and resisted, with considerable stubbornness, even minor editorial changes proposed by Collins.

Momentarily at odds with his publishers, he chose to produce two books under the pseudonym of Ian Stuart, the name of the Chapmans' son, a joke designed to provoke. There are two versions of what happened next. Chapman maintains that the books sold 10,000 copies each, but that when reissued as written by MacLean their sales rocketed to their normal figures: MacLean, however, says that they were best-sellers all along.

Ten books on, however, and MacLean had had enough. He returned to England, bought a hotel on Bodmin Moor called Jamaica Inn and three others and became a hotelier. "Basically I'm a very idle man". But he grew bored. Four years later he was seduced back to the typewriter when an American film producer called Elliot Kastner asked him to write a script for *Where Eagles Dare.* That became a book.

With the ensuing inevitable success he returned to his yearly best-seller, writing solely, he will tell anyone who asks him, for money. But now that he cannot possibly need more money? MacLean, who speaks of himself only with the most tortured unwillingness, and has given no interview for nearly 10 years, will not be drawn. When he chooses to, he says nothing.

A shy, slight, stiff man, he speaks so quietly and with such a strong Scottish accent that he is not always easy to follow. He deflects questions and peers, almost sternly, over the top of enormous round glasses that slip slowly to the very tip of his nose, before he catches them as they are about to topple over. A wry look, and considerable courtesy, mitigate the severity.

He is as frugal as he is reticent, a trait of character that comes, say his friends to whom he is unfailingly generous, as much from the austerity of his childhood as from a feeling that it is morally wrong to earn so much.

His flat consists of a single floor, with a terrace covered in bougainvillaea directly above the sea, where he watches the liners and cargo ships coming into port. He has no servants. His eyesight is poor, so a friend drives his green Rolls-Royce. In Dubrovnik harbour there is a Chris Craft. These are his only luxuries; he has no interest in food except for fresh fish, no collection of pictures, no expensive clothes.

The only luxuries he has, that is, except perhaps for travel. In recent years 63-year-old MacLean has been to Peru, India, Brazil, Greece, Turkey, Jamaica and Kashmir. When he has to, he hires a private plane and he stays in good hotels. "I love travelling", he says, "and then I'm easily disappointed". What prompts him to set out? "Itchy feet, itchy feet, itchy feet."

He now has his mind on Tashkent, Samarkand and Bokhara, following the old silk routes. As he travels, he looks. He never takes notes. Later, details creep into the books, though he is firm about never doing any research. "The first books came from experience. The rest I invented. I have a fair degree of inventiveness, but not much imagination."

As a boy, MacLean read Scott and Buchan and Trollope but only, he says, because he was made to. He does not read thrillers or any of the authors who write as he does, saying that they are on the whole very poor and he feels he can do better. He once admitted to liking Raymond Chandler, but says that now he reads only newspapers. "I never read books, but I do read magazines, particularly scientific journals." Five arrive every week by post. Astronomy is the science he prefers, although he says that what he really wanted to become, when he was young, was a doctor but he had no money for the training.

These days, as in the first days of success, writing is done straight on to the IBM from early morning and is quickly finished. "I don't write the first sentence until I have the last in mind." He never corrects. "I don't even re-read. One draft and it's away."

The rest of life is determinedly solitary. Two of his grown-up sons live in Geneva, the third in London. His second wife, Marcelle, is dead, but they had parted some years before she died. His first wife is in Switzerland. He says that he has no desire, ever again, to return to Scotland: the condition of exile suits him.

That he is a success not even MacLean can easily deny, even if he prefers to deny all that could come with it. To a visitor, his days seem sparse. He lives what appears to be an inner existence unaltered over the years: inventing his invariably treacherous villains, his irreproachable heroes and his intricate but bloodless plots according to a formula once proved unbeatable and ever since adhered to. Only Agatha Christie, says Ian Chapman, has as strong a brand image.

But MacLean will only speculate as to why his books work: "All I do is write simple stories. There is enough real violence in the world without my adding to it." And then he adds: "I am lucky."

Caroline Moorehead, "The Man Who Outgunned James Bond," in The Times, *London, October 7, 1985, p. 11.*

M. S. Kaplan

Alistair MacLean's latest novel [*San Andreas*] begins with a factual prologue presenting, in almost textbook fashion, the "pitiable" state of the British Merchant Navy during World War II and the record of ruthlessness with which the Germans stalked and sunk the navy's ships. It serves as the book's dedication, really, paying tribute to the Merchant Navy's neglected role in the war effort while preparing the reader for the kind of plot twists and crisp action made famous by Mr. MacLean. Indeed, by the end of the first sentence, a saboteur has shorted out the electrical system of the *San Andreas,* a British Merchant Navy vessel converted into a hospital ship. By the end of the first chapter, the *San Andreas,* bound for Aberdeen, Scotland, has been bombarded by a German Condor in the Barents Sea. Taking command from the injured Captain Bowen is the gruff, blunt-speaking Bosun Archie McKinnon. As the acts of sabotage escalate, the members of the *San Andreas* learn that they are being shadowed inexplicably by German U-2 boats. So closely does the plot revolve around the bosun's craft and cunning that the boat itself becomes a key player in this seagoing cat-and-mouse drama. The mystery of why the Germans want to seize, and not sink, the *San Andreas* becomes more complicated with each enemy encounter. These episodes are among the most enthralling, but unfortunately everything in between stalls the suspense. It's difficult for a reader not to be impatient with McKinnon's matter-of-fact speeches, sounding as if they were transcribed from the same index cards used to prepare the prologue. Balancing the factual basis for the plot's plausibility with more vivid and diverse characterization would have evenly paced the suspense in this otherwise engaging adventure. (pp. 34-5)

*M. S. Kaplan, in a review of "San Andreas,"
in* The New York Times Book Review, *October 20, 1985, pp. 34-5.*

David Jordan

From the author of **The Guns of Navarone** and **Ice Station Zebra** comes [**The Lonely Sea,** a] collection of 14 tales of adventure on the high seas. At best, MacLean provides an accurate account of naval battles by an obviously knowledgeable reporter; however, without a Gregory Peck or a Rock Hudson to personify the "incredibly gallant men" of "indomitable courage" described in these yarns, we are left with a string of clichés which, try as the author might to revive them with overblown rhetoric, lie dead on the page.

The bulk of these stories were written during the Second World War, a time when a naval destroyer could capture the hearts and imaginations of a nation, when the mighty *Hood,* "thrusting the puny waves contemptuously aside," could symbolize "all that was permanent, a synonym for all that was invincible, held in awe, even veneration." To the handful of warship enthusiasts left today, these stories will have some appeal, but to the rest of us they are an anachronism, just as MacLean's plodding realism harkens back to a literary style long gone.

There are some notable exceptions to the hero-going-down-with-the-ship formula in this collection. For example, **"McCrimmon and the Blue Moonstones"** is a humorous account of a dockworker who attempts to smuggle gemstones out of Alexandria. Here again, however, MacLean's inflated verbiage stifles any chance of dramatic tension. Take for example the description of an Arab bodyguard, "chosen with a complete lack of the aesthetic viewpoint," to whom "the higher forms of etiquette were a closed book." All this to say he was an ugly brute.

In all fairness to the author, one must point out that MacLean has no pretensions of literary greatness. "Some day I might get around to writing a good book," the author tells us in a brief afterword to this edition. One can always keep hoping.

> David Jordan, in a review of "The Lonely Sea," in Books in Canada, Vol. 15, No. 3, April, 1986, p. 23.

Mason Buck

In 1954 Alistair MacLean began his writing career with **"The Dileas,"** the story of two brothers who bravely sacrifice their lives during a raging storm. More than half the stories in **The Lonely Sea** are set in World War II and they follow the pattern of **"The Dileas,"** the opening story in this collection. Each tale is named for a vessel in jeopardy, and follows the conduct of the endangered seamen. The crew of the British merchant ship Rawalpindi faces certain death against a formidable German fleet, but it is sustained until the end by a superhuman sense of pride. **"The Sinking of the Bismarck,"** the book's longest story, portrays the despair of Nazi officers who commit suicide when they see the battle is lost. The problem with all of these World War II narratives is that while they successfully describe the logistics of disaster at sea, the ships are populated with strictly one-dimensional passengers. The result is meticulous journalism that produces side effects accurately felt by the author afloat on the lonely sea ("We gradually settled down into a state of wakeful boredom"). Only in **"Rendezvous,"** told in a first-person flashback and with a vivid cast of characters, does Mr. MacLean come close to capturing the intensity of his major novels, such as **The Guns of Navarone** and **Where Eagles Dare.** The story deals suspensefully with war and espionage and illustrates that Mr. MacLean writes best when he uses sea or land battles as a backdrop and places his characters at center stage. (pp. 20-1)

> Mason Buck, in a review of "The Lonely Sea," in The New York Times Book Review, June 15, 1986, pp. 20-1.

Judy Bass

[In **Santorini,** preventing] "the biggest man-made explosion in history" is the task confronting some unflappable British naval officers in this adventure tale by the veteran suspense novelist Alistair MacLean, who died last month. As the technologically sophisticated NATO spy ship *Ariadne* cruises the Aegean, its crew notices two ominous, simultaneous occurrences—a flaming plane plummeting into the sea and a burning yacht about to sink. Comdr. John Talbot of the *Ariadne* isn't concerned until he learns that the submerged American plane contains hydrogen and atom bombs, one of which has begun ticking. If these weapons detonate, the consequences could mean an unprecedented number of casualties, as well as a volcanic eruption and earthquake beneath the nearby island of Santorini. While Talbot and his men explore solutions to this problem, the yacht's most nefarious passenger, the millionaire Spyros Andropulous, plans trouble for his rescuers. This potentially chilling and timely plot is regrettably unexciting as the author renders it. The book consists

more of talk than action, much of it tedious. Talbot and his associates always confer in a highly decorous, leisurely manner, despite their proximity to four and a half billion pounds of explosive power; their composure indicates either astounding imperviousness to danger or implausibly strong self-confidence.

> Judy Bass, in a review of "Santorini," in The New York Times Book Review, March 8, 1987, p. 20.

Heywood Hale Broun

E. M. Forster, who did not much like the work of Sir Walter Scott, had grudgingly to admit that, "He had the primitive power of keeping the reader in suspense and playing on his curiosity." Certainly it can be said of Sir Walter's fellow Scot, Alistair MacLean, that he had the primitive power of keeping the reader in suspense. Ticking bombs and booming guns were the modern tools with which he replaced Scott's dirks and claymores, but he kept us turning the pages with the appeal of, "and then? and then?," even though we knew, at some rational level, that the good guys, however outnumbered and outgunned, would triumph in the final chapter.

It is recorded of a turn-of-the-century writer of schoolboy serial fiction that he left his hero at episode's end manacled to a post and surrounded by lions. He solved the problem by beginning the next episode with the jaunty sentence "With one bound, Jack was free."

There are moments in the MacLean *oeuvre* when this technique is in evidence and there are moments, particularly in his vastly popular **Puppet on a Chain,** when a wave of silliness washes over the suspension of disbelief and drowns it.

Shortly before his death this year, MacLean had completed **Santorini,** a work with all the touches that sold millions of books in the 30 years in which he wrote, rising in good Scottish fashion in time to be at his desk at 5 a.m. and working through an honest eight-hour day and a completed novel in a month's hard writing.

MacLean is perhaps best known for **The Guns of Navarone,** in which an attractive assortment of adventurers, who talk as well as they fight, go against fearful odds to neutralize an important German stronghold in World War II. It was later made into a successful film with, among others, David Niven, Gregory Peck and Anthony Quinn. Film buffs will remember the scene in which the heroes, on the bridge of a small boat in a hurricane, succeed in drinking coffee without spilling a drop, even as they discuss the philosophy of violence without bouncing off the walls of the little wheelhouse.

Santorini is set on a somewhat larger vessel, and begins with MacLeanian brio as, in the opening pages, a burning airplane is observed overhead as simultaneously a luxury yacht is exploding and sinking on the horizon.

In the best tradition of *The Scarlet Pimpernel*, MacLean's protagonists are unflappable and where many of us might be inclined to gulp and yammer at the discovery that atomic weaponry is making funny noises a few fathoms under us, the officers of *HMS Ariadne* are ready with classical allusions and lighthearted quips along with a fairly staggering electronic expertise.

It is possible to discuss the plots of, let us say, the novels of Flaubert without lessening the reader's subsequent enjoyment of the work, but it's best to stop right here with the happenings in *Santorini.* Suffice it to say that the villains are not English, and that the Americans are given to cover-ups.

It should also be noted that those who like sex with their violence had best stick to Ian Fleming. Outside of Victor Appleton who never let Tom Swift kiss Mary Nestor, I cannot think of an adventure writer as sparing of romance as MacLean. There are two beautiful girls aboard the sinking yacht, but we sense early on that whatever may be lost in the possible disasters inherent in the world-imperiling situation in *Santorini,* it won't be the virtue of the two young women.

In this respect MacLean harks back to another distinguished Scottish adventure writer, John Buchan. The women in his books were good sports, and good comrades to the heroes who were as accurate in their quotations as they were in their marksmanship.

It was Ian Fleming who remarked some years ago that he attributed the success of his hero, James Bond, to the fact that, as England sank from its position as a world power, it would enjoy reading about an Englishman who changed the course of history with a karate chop or a well-aimed shot. It was a modest and ingenious argument but it did not explain the sale of so many Bond books outside the shrinking empire, nor does it explain the success of MacLean. That success is due to making the mixture bubble just enough.

Success in adventure fiction requires a rhythm of action that doesn't let the reader stop and think even as it avoids sating with increasing improbability. As gourmet diners are given to little tubs of sherbet between courses as a clarification of the palate, so good adventure writers like MacLean give us a rest between moments of suspense with bits of wit or sudden trips into mundane detail. John Buchan might spend two pages on the furniture in a club smoking room, just so that you are lulled by this realism into accepting, a page later, the news that somewhere there's an idol with a giant ruby in its forehead.

So, in *Santorini,* there are little stretches of what appears to be scientific education. As one whose grasp of that field stopped somewhere in the pages of *The Book of Knowledge,* I cannot say anything about its authenticity, but that doesn't matter. It sounds authentic—MacLean didn't spend years as a schoolteacher for nothing—and because it sounds authentic, it convinces us that all that other stuff about people behaving jauntily and efficiently in the face of doom, is equally authentic.

Alistair MacLean was in a grand Scottish tradition, and if he's not to be ranked with Robert Louis Stevenson, the master, he, in some writer's Olympus, is entitled to toast Sir Walter and, in turn, to be toasted.

Heywood Hale Broun, "The Final Adventure of Alistair MacLean," in Book World—The Washington Post, *April 12, 1987, p. 7.*

Boris Pasternak

1890-1960

(Full Name Boris Leonidovich Pasternak) Russian poet, novelist, short story writer, essayist, memoirist, and non-fiction writer.

Awarded the 1958 Nobel Prize in literature, which he declined under political pressure, Pasternak is regarded in the Soviet Union as among the foremost poets of the twentieth century. He garnered international acclaim, however, as the author of the novel *Doktor Zivago* (*Doctor Zhivago*). An epic portrayal of the Russian Revolution and its consequences, *Doctor Zhivago* ignited a political and artistic controversy that continues to overshadow Pasternak's achievements in other genres. While his complex, ethereal works often defy translation, Western critics laud his synthesis of unconventional imagery and formalistic style as well as his vision of the individual's relationship to nature and history. C. M. Bowra asserted: "In a revolutionary age Pasternak [saw] beyond the disturbed surface of things to the powers behind it and found there an explanation of what really matters in the world. Through his unerring sense of poetry he has reached to wide issues and shown that the creative calling, with its efforts and its frustrations and its unanticipated triumphs, is, after all, something profoundly natural and closely related to the sources of life."

The son of an acclaimed artist and a concert pianist, both of Jewish descent, Pasternak benefited from a highly creative household that counted novelist Leo Tolstoy, composer Alexander Scarabin, and poet Rainer Maria Rilke among its visitors. Encouraged by Scarabin, Pasternak began studying music as a fourteen-year-old, but abandoned this pursuit six years later over what he perceived as a lack of technical skill. He then turned to philosophy, eventually enrolling in Germany's prestigious Marburg University where he studied Neo-Kantianism. In 1912, however, Pasternak abruptly left Marburg when his childhood friend, Ida Vysotskaia, rejected his marriage proposal, compelling Pasternak to reevaluate his professional as well as personal choices. Deciding to commit himself exclusively to poetry, he eventually joined Centrifuge, a moderate group of literary innovators associated with the Futurist movement. Rejecting the poetic language of such nineteenth-century authors as Alexander Pushkin and Leo Tolstoy, the Futurists advocated greater poetic freedom and attention to the actualities of modern life. Pasternak's first two poetry collections, *Blitzhetz tuchakh* and *Poverkh barerov,* largely reflect these precepts as well as the influence of Vladimir Mayakovsky, Pasternak's close friend and among the most revered of the Futurist poets.

Partially lamed by a childhood riding accident, Pasternak was declared unfit for military service and spent the first years of World War I in the Ural Mountains as a clerical worker. When news of political turmoil reached Pasternak in 1917, he returned to Moscow, but the capital's chaotic atmosphere forced him to leave for his family's summer home in the outlying countryside. There he composed *Sestra moia zhizn: leto 1917 goda* (*My Sister, Life: Summer*

1917). Considered Pasternak's greatest poetic achievement, this volume celebrates nature as a creative force that permeates every aspect of human experience and impels all historical and personal change. Often uniting expansive, startling imagery with formal rhyme schemes, *My Sister, Life: Summer 1917* is lauded as an accomplished and innovative synthesis of the principal poetic movements of early twentieth-century Russia, including the Futurists, the Acmeists, and the Imagists. Pasternak's next poetry collection, *Temi i variatsi,* solidified his standing as a major modern poet in the Soviet Union. He also received critical acclaim as a prose writer with *Rasskazy,* his first collection of short stories, which includes the previously published pieces "Apellesova cherta" ("Apelles' Mark"), "Pisma iz Tuly" ("Letter to Tula"), "Vozdudhnye puti" ("Aerial Ways"), and "Detstvo Liuvers" ("The Childhood of Luvers").

In 1923, enthusiastic about the possible artistic benefits of the Revolution, Pasternak joined Mayakovsky's Left Front of Art (LEF), an alliance between Futurist writers and the Communist party that used the avant-garde movement's literary innovations to glorify the new social order. His work from this period, *Vysockaya bolezn', Deviatsot piatyi god, Leitenant Schmidt,* and *Spectorsky,* are epic poems that favorably portray events leading up to and surrounding the uprisings of 1917. However, socialist critics faulted the distinctly meditative, personal tone of the poems as bourgeois, a charge also leveled against *Povest* (*The Last Summer*), a novella, and *Okhrannaya gramota,* an autobiographical work. In this volume, Pasternak recalls the men who shaped his artistic sensibility, including Mayakovsky, Scarabin, and Rilke, while further outlining his concept of nature and its mystical role in the creative process. During the late 1920s, Pasternak grew disillusioned with the government's increasing social and artistic restrictions as well as with Communism's collective ideal that, in his opinion, directly opposed the individualistic nature of humanity. He then broke with the LEF, a decision finalized by Mayakovsky's suicide in 1930.

The following year, Pasternak divorced his first wife, Evgeniya Lurie, as a result of his affair with Zinaida Neigauz, whom he later married. Critics often cite this new relationship and the couple's friendships with several Georgian writers as the source of the revitalized poetry found in *Vtoroye rozhdenie*. A collection of love lyrics and impressions of the Georgian countryside, *Vtoroye rozhdenie* presented Pasternak's newly simplified style and chronicled his attempt to reconcile his artistic and social responsibilities in a time of political upheaval. Pasternak's newfound optimism, however, was subdued following the inception of the Soviet Writer's Union, a government institution that abolished independent literary groups and promoted conformity to the precepts of socialist realism. Recognized as a major poet by the Communist regime, Pasternak participated in several official literary functions, including the First Congress of Writers in 1934. He gradually withdrew from public life, however, as Josef Stalin's repressive policies intensified, and he began translating the works of others rather than composing his own, possibly incendiary, prose and poetry. His many translations include Johann Wolfgang von Goethe's *Faust* as well as the major tragedies of Shakespeare, which remain the standard texts for staging the plays in Russian.

Following the publication of *Vtoroye rozhdenie,* Pasternak reissued several of his earlier poetry volumes under the titles *Stikhotvoreniia v odnom tome, Poemy,* and *Stikhotvoreniia*. His new collections of verse, however, did not appear until World War II. *Na rannikh poezdakh* and *Zemnoy proster* reflect the renewed patriotic spirit and creative freedom fostered by the conflict while eschewing conventional political rhetoric. Suppression of the arts resumed following the war, and many of Pasternak's friends and colleagues were imprisoned or executed. Historians and critics disagree as to why Pasternak, who had publicly condemned the actions of the government, escaped Stalin's purges of the intelligentsia. While some credit his translation and promotion of writers from Stalin's native Georgia, others report that the dictator, while glancing over Pasternak's dossier, wrote "Do not touch this cloud-dweller."

In 1948, Pasternak began secretly composing his novel *Doctor Zhivago,* which he completed in 1956. Drawn from his personal experiences and beliefs, the novel utilizes complex symbols, imagery, and narrative techniques to depict the fortunes of the title character, Yury Zhivago, in the years surrounding the 1917 Revolution. Orphaned at the age of ten, Zhivago, whose name means "life," re-

sides with his uncle before finding a home with Alexander Gromeko, a Moscow intellectual. Eventually marrying Gromeko's daughter, Tonya, he becomes a doctor while privately composing poetry. Paralleling Zhivago's experiences are those of Lara Guishar, a dressmaker's daughter who becomes his greatest love and artistic inspiration. Several critics contend that Pasternak based the character of Lara upon his mistress, Olga Ivanskaya, whose liaison with the author endured for over fifteen years. According to one character, "everything that made our time, all its tears and insults, impulses, the whole accumulation of revenge and pride was ingrained in [Lara's] expression and in her carriage." While engaged to Pasha Antipov, an idealistic student and Communist party member, Lara is seduced by Victor Komarovsky, an unscrupulous lawyer and her mother's lover. Zhivago, however, only briefly encounters Lara in pre-revolutionary Moscow, once when he tends to her mother after her attempted suicide, and later when Lara shoots and superficially wounds Komarovsky at a ball Zhivago attends.

With the outbreak of World War I, Zhivago is drafted into the Tsarist army and sent to a remote military hospital, where he unexpectedly meets Antipov. She has become a nurse in hopes of finding Antipov, who joined the army when their marriage began to falter. While she and Zhivago establish a close friendship, they part when news of the Revolution compels him to return to Moscow. Zhivago initially supports the Communists, whose actions he regards as a just response to the corrupt, repressive policies of the Tsarist regime, but quickly becomes disillusioned as civil war breaks out and hunger spreads through the country. As conditions in the city worsen, Zhivago and Tonya leave for Varykino, a remote summer estate in the Ural Mountain district of Yuryatin. Living "an honest productive life" as a farmer, Zhivago is at peace until he recognizes Lara in Yuryatin. She becomes his mistress, but Zhivago is captured by Bolsheviks and taken to Siberia as a frontline physician. Released years later, he learns that Tonya has emigrated to France, and that Antipov has reappeared. Now a ruthless Bolshevik officer, Antipov has displeased his superiors and therefore endangers Lara's life. Taking her to Varykino, Zhivago convinces her to escape to the Far East with Komarovsky, who has resurfaced as a diplomat. Zhivago then drifts back to Moscow where he gradually abandons poetry and medicine as he grows contemptuous of his intellectual friends, now sycophants of the state. He then dies of a heart attack on a Moscow street. Lara, whose daughter by Zhivago disappeared in the chaos of the civil war, vanishes as well and likely dies "forgotten . . . in one of the innumerable mixed or women's concentration camps in the north."

When Pasternak submitted *Doctor Zhivago* to Soviet publishers in 1956, they rejected the novel for what the editorial board of *Novy mir* termed its "spirit . . . of nonacceptance of the socialist revolution." Pasternak then smuggled the manuscript to the West, where reviewers hailed the novel as an incisive and moving condemnation of Communism. In 1959, the Swedish Academy selected Pasternak for the Nobel Prize in literature, citing his achievements as both a poet and novelist. Nevertheless, the implication that the award had been given solely for *Doctor Zhivago* launched a bitter Soviet campaign against Pasternak that ultimately forced him to decline the prize. Despite his decision, the Soviet Writer's Union expelled

Pasternak from its ranks, and one Communist party member characterized the author as a "literary whore" in the employ of Western authorities. In memoirs he kept during the mid 1960s, however, Nikita Khrushchev, the Soviet premier who suppressed the novel in 1956, concluded: "I regret that I had a hand in banning the book. We should have given readers an opportunity to reach their own verdict. By banning *Doctor Zhivago* we caused much harm to the Soviet Union."

Evaluations of *Doctor Zhivago* in the years following "The Pasternak Affair" often disagree as to the novel's importance. Several critics regarded its many coincidences and Pasternak's distortion of historical chronology and character development as technically flawed. Other commentators compared Pasternak's thorough portrayal of a vast and turbulent period to that of nineteenth-century Russian novelists, particularly Leo Tolstoy. Additionally, the major themes of the novel, often distilled in the poems attributed to the title character, have been the subject of extensive analysis. Through Zhivago, critics maintain, Pasternak realized his vision of the artist as a Christ-like figure who bears witness to the tragedy of his age even as it destroys him. This idea is often linked to Pasternak's contention that individual experience is capable of transcending the destructive forces of history. It is this concept, commentators assert, that gives *Doctor Zhivago* its enduring power. Marc Slonim observed: "In *Doctor Zhivago* man is shown in his individual essence, and his life is interpreted not as an illustration of historical events, but as a unique, wonderful adventure in its organic reality of sensations, thoughts, drives, instincts and strivings. This makes the book . . . a basically anti-political work, in so far as it treats politics as fleeting, unimportant, and extols the unchangeable fundamentals of human mind, emotion and creativity."

Pasternak published two more works outside the Soviet Union, *Kogda razgulyayetsya*, (*When Skies Clear*), a volume of reflective verse, and *Autobiogratichesey ocherk* (*I Remember*), an autobiographical sketch, before his death in 1960. At his funeral, Pasternak was not accorded the official ceremonies normally provided for the death of a member of the Soviet Writer's Union. However, thousands accompanied his family to the grave site, which remains a place of pilgrimage in the Soviet Union. In 1987, under the auspices of Communist leader Mikail Gorbachev's policy of social reform, or *glasnost*, the Writer's Union formally reinstated Pasternak, and in 1988, *Doctor Zhivago* was published in the Soviet Union for the first time.

(See also *CLC*, Vols. 7, 10, 18; and *Contemporary Authors*, Vols. 116 [obituary], 127.)

PRINCIPAL WORKS

POETRY

Blitzhetz tuchakh   1914
Poverkh barerov   1917
Sestra moia zhizn: leto 1917 goda   1923
  [*My Sister, Life: Summer 1917,*   1967; also published
  in *My Sister, Life; and Other Poems,*   1976]
Temy i variatsi   1923
Vysockaya bolezn   1924

*Deviatsot piatyi god   1926
*Leitenant Shmidt   1927
Vtoroye rozhdenie   1932
Stikhotvoreniia v odnom tome   1933
Poemy   1933
Stikhotvoreniia   1936
Na rannikh poezdakh   1943
Zemnoy proster   1945
Kogda razgulyayetsya   1959
  [*Poems, 1955-1959,*   1960]

NOVELS

Doktor Zivago
  [first published as *Il dottor Zivago* in Italian, 1957; published as *Doctor Zhivago* in English, 1959; published in Russian, 1988]

OTHER

**Detstvo Luvors   1919   (short story)
  [*Childhood,*   1941; also published as *The Adolescence of Zhenya Luvers,*   1961]
**Rasskazy   (short stories)   1925
**Okhrannaya gramota   (autobiographical nonfiction) 1931
Povest   (novella)   1934
  [*The Last Summer,*   1959]
I Remember: Sketch for an Autobiography   (memoirs; from the Russian manuscript "Autobiogratichesey ocherk.")   1959
Sochineniya   (collected works)   1961
Lettere agli amici georgiani   (letters; from the Russian manuscript "Pis'ma k gurinskim druz'iam")   1967
  [*Letters to Georgian Friends,*   1968]
Slepaia krasavista   (play)   1969
  [*The Blind Beauty,*   1969]
Boris Pasternak: Perepiska s Ol'goi Freidenberg   (letters) 1981
  [*The Correspondence of Boris Pasternak and Olga Friedenberg, 1910-1954,*   1982]
Letters, Summer 1926   (letters)   1985

*Published together as *Deviastsot piatyi god* in 1927.

**Translated and published in *The Collected Prose Works of Boris Pasternak,* 1977.

C. M. Bowra

From their different angles the Futurists, the Acmeists and the Imagists [whose movements dominated Russian poetry in the early twentieth century], had some real contributions to make. While the Futurists stressed the call to a renewed language and a more vivid concern with actual life, the Acmeists stressed the virtues of a polished technique and the need to make vivid effects in a limited compass, and the Imagists aimed at the greater intimacy and charm which can be secured through a bold exploitation of imagery. Each school suffered from exaggerating its claims. The Futurists' love of violence excluded many legitimate effects, the Acmeists were too traditional for a revolutionary age, and the Imagists spoiled their work by turning a means of poetry into its chief end. What was needed was a poet who could pick up the different threads and combine them, correct the excesses of the various creeds and turn the modern movements to meet modern needs without giving too much emphasis to this or that claim of the competing antagonists. The man appeared in Boris Pasternak, who may be said to have seen almost from the start what truth there was in the several theories and what contribution each had really to make to the general problem of poetical composition. In his beginnings he had some association with the Futurists and was a member of a small association called "Centrifuga" which used to meet in Moscow. He was also a great admirer of Mayakovsky's early poetry. Pasternak's first verses show some traces of Futurist violence and over-emphasis in their abrupt movement and exaggerated effects, but this manner did not last long. When Pasternak was twenty-seven he had found his style and his own approach to poetry, and we can see how the different influences of his training had come together in a peculiar unity.

Pasternak was in full agreement with the new poets in his rejection of the mystical ideals held by the Symbolists. He was concerned not with some supra-mundane state but with the actual world that he knew. He did not however agree with the revolutionary rejection of the poetical past. He came from a family which represented in its highest form that devotion to the arts which cultivated Russians used to maintain with so unusual an accomplishment. His father was a painter of the Impressionist school; his mother was a brilliant musician. In his boyhood he not only learned what painting is but studied music with Scriabin. His culture spread outside his own country when, after taking a course in philosophy under Hermann Cohen at Marburg, he visited Italy and saw the great monuments of the European past. To an eye trained on painting and an ear trained to music he added a grasp of abstract problems and a natural gift for words which may have gained something from his study of foreign languages. . . . [He] learned that poetry must both be true to experience and as expressive as possible. He absorbed much from the past and formed his standards by it, but he was no slave to it and saw that a poet must create his own style and be faithful to his own outlook.

It was the need for a new style that drew Pasternak to the Futurists. It was because Mayakovsky really gave a new worth to words that Pasternak admired him. But this use of words reflected something else which Pasternak admired. On Mayakovsky's death in 1930 Pasternak compared him to Etna. It was this volcanic eruptiveness that he prized, the enormous elemental force which Mayakovsky put into words. Pasternak knew that he himself possessed a similar kind of force, even though it worked in a different way, and his intention was to make the most of this, to make his poetry as powerful as possible. Though his gifts were very unlike Mayakovsky's, and he ceased to admire Mayakovsky's work when it abandoned its first concentrated ecstasy, he cherished an ideal of a poetry which should be extremely expressive without breaking too violently with the traditions of Russian verse. Without going all the way with the Futurists and other advanced poets of his youth, he saw that they had something which older poets lacked, a fiercer approach to life, a greater power of giving an experience in its whole range, a readier and more sincere response to their creative inspi-

ration. In his long struggle with his art he has always kept true to this ideal, though he differs from the Futurists in the means which he uses and the kind of experience which he puts into poetry.

Pasternak's resemblance to the Imagists was more personal than intellectual. He was not of their number and was too good a craftsman to accept their extreme claims. But, like other modern poets, he saw that the image has a special part to play and that it is almost impossible to express complex states of mind without an adventurous and extensive use of it. It is customary to say that his use of images reflects the world of painting in which he grew up, but though Pasternak's visual sensibility is extremely keen, it does much more than mark and record. It carries with it something which is more than visual. Indeed we might say that his musical training has been quite as important as his knowledge of painting, since it has taught him to give a precise sensuous form to otherwise undefined feelings and to realise what strength can be added to words through combinations of sound. What he sees awakes in him so many remarkable trains of thought and sound that his poetry is packed and complex. It deals with many obscure states which might be material for a musician but are beyond the scope of a painter. Everything that he notices is fraught with mystery and meaning for him. He lives in the real world and observes it intently, but his rapt observation uncovers much more than meets the seeing eye. In the inextricable combination of his senses and emotions he both sees and interprets nature, both marks its manifestations and understands what they mean and what relations they suggest beyond the immediate "given". No doubt the Imagists hoped to do something of this kind through their cult of the image, but they defined its purpose too narrowly. Pasternak, consciously or unconsciously, has picked up their doctrine and shown how it should really be applied.

Pasternak did not burst into poetry in extreme youth. His early verses are not numerous and still show an experimental quality. At moments there are forecasts of his most mature manner, at others mere attempts to write like other men. Then in 1917 he flowered astonishingly and marvellously. His volume *My Sister Life,* which was not published until 1922, was written in the summer of 1917 and shows how perfectly Pasternak had found himself. The flood of inspiration in which he wrote this book continued for the next few years and produced the no less remarkable *Themes and Variations* in 1923. These two volumes are the essential core of his work, the climax of his first endeavours and the inspired product of his young manhood. In them his temperament and his circumstances combined to produce the new kind of poetry which was his to give and which his time needed. His later work contains many beauties, is always truthful and original, but it is sometimes too experimental, too much at war with his circumstances, to have the final harmony of these two books. In them Pasternak has done something which is unique in his time.

An outlook like Pasternak's demands its own technique, and he has found a form which is firm and concentrated and powerful. In an age of metrical experiments he normally uses stanzas of fixed length and regular rhythms. On the printed page his verses look perfectly normal. He also uses rhyme, though he goes far in his use of half-rhymes and assonances. While the formal plan of his verses binds its different elements together and reduces them to order, the unusual character of his contents is marked by his unusual rhymes. By this means Pasternak avoids that looseness of form which suits the surging moods of the Futurists but is unsuitable to a poet who wishes to give to a poem some of the balance and pattern of a painting or of a musical composition. Pasternak makes us feel that even the most complex of his themes has its own harmony and order and that, however surprising what he says may be, it has a controlling design. The strictness of the form adds dignity to the rich and unusual vocabulary which is in turns allusive, conversational and majestic, and does not shrink from elliptical expressions or from neologisms: it even controls the imagery which is always original and sometimes startling. The formality of Pasternak's verse holds the rebellious material together. Without it the complex themes would not be fused into a unity, and the final result would be far less satisfying.

In his instinctive knowledge of what poetry is, Pasternak is determined that his work shall be essentially and purely poetry. No doubt his standards owe much to the great Russian writers like Blok who brought poetry back to itself in the first decade of this century, but he must also owe something to the discriminating devotion to the arts which he learned in his family circle, especially from his father. If his determination to maintain always a level of pure poetry sometimes makes him obscure or even awkward, it also means that he never writes below a certain standard and never wastes his time on irrelevant matter. The close texture of his verse, which at times makes it difficult to grasp all his implications at a first reading, is an essential feature of his art. It helps him to convey his intense, concentrated experience and is a true mirror of his moods. He looks at objects not in isolation but as parts of a wider unity, marks their relations in a complex whole, and stresses the dominant character of a scene as much as the individual elements in it. His work is therefore extremely personal, but not so personal as to be beyond the understanding of other men. He assumes that others will recognise the truth of his vision and come to share it with him. For, in his view, what he gives them is not a scientific, photographic transcript of an impersonal, external reality but something intensely human, since reality and value are given to things by our appreciation of them and by our absorption of them into our consciousness. Man is the centre of the universe, and human consciousness is its uniting principle. Therefore he can say with perfect sincerity:

> Gardens, ponds and palings, the creation
> Foam-flecked with the whiteness of our weeping,
> Are nothing but categories of passion
> That the human heart has had in keeping.

Pasternak is a poet of sensibility in the sense that for him sensibility is both physical and intellectual, the means by which he gets a full and firm grip on reality, and that nothing counts but those moments when he has a vivid apprehension of something that happens both inside and outside himself.

To convey the results of this sensibility and this outlook demands a special technique. Since what the senses give us must be presented in its fullness, it is not right to use conventional means of description which presuppose an artificial arrangement of experience. The poet must convey his sensations exactly as they strike him. So Pasternak often presents a visible scene in a way which at first seems paradoxical but later reveals its essential truth and exactness. For instance he writes of a road so polished in summer by cart-wheels that it reflects the stars by night:

> By the road age-old midnight stands,
> Sprawls on the trackway with its stars;
> You cannot pass the hedge without
> Trampling upon the universe.

At first sight this looks like an imaginative trope, but it is really a truthful transcript of the poet's sensations. On crossing the road in such conditions he notices the reflected stars and for the moment believes that he is treading on them. That is the experience which inspires him, and that is precisely what he says. So somewhat differently, when he tells of a journey in a train at night, he assumes that, in his seat, he is the fixed centre of reality and that what he sees is a passing phenomenon. Everyone will know what he means and recognise how precisely he records it:

> And, with its third splash, off the bell goes swimming,
> Still making apologies: "Sorry, not here,"
> And under the blind the night passes flaming,
> And the plain crumbles off from the steps to a star.

The train has just left the station to the usual Russian signal of a bell rung three times. When the journey begins, the train seems to be fixed, and the night behind the blind to move, so that the country slowly disappears between the steps of the railway-carriage and the distant star which is relatively stationary. The description is careful and accurate. This is just what he feels in a train, and to put it differently would be to falsify it. But just because Pasternak sees it so clearly and knows exactly what it is, he is able to awake a delighted and surprised admiration at his exactness and truth.

The same art is applied to sensations other than visual and to these mental states which begin with sensations of eye or ear but contain something else in their mental appreciation of a situation. Pasternak, for instance, writes of a thunderstorm at the end of summer:

> Summer then to the flag-station
> Said good-bye. That night the thunder
> Doffed its cap and as memento
> Took a hundred blinding snaps.

The sight and the sound of the thunderstorm are inextricably mingled with the thought that the summer is over, and this combination comes out in original and consistent imagery. In Pasternak's poetry visible and mental things are closely associated, and he hardly troubles to distinguish between them. . . . The ultimate setting is in the poet's mind: this holds the phenomena together and gives them their character, but the physical sensations are none the less acutely felt and recorded. The watching mind observes them as they really are and sees their significance. Indeed the actual facts take on a symbolical importance and convey the character and atmosphere of the poet's state as he observes them. Pasternak's images deepen his meaning not merely because they give a greater exactness, but because they show the relation between a given event and other events not immediately connected, which are none the less of the same kind. They show that no event can be treated in absolute isolation but that any proper appreciation of it must take into account its universal qualities and relations.

This poetry is difficult just because it reflects the poet's sensations so exactly, especially when he advances beyond visual effects to the associations which they awake and with which they are inextricably united. Pasternak has a remarkable gift for giving shape and colour to these inchoate states of the mind in its moments of excited sensibility and uses vivid concrete images for much that poets usually leave undefined. He seizes on some significant trait in what he sees and relates it to something wider by his choice of a significant image. When, for instance, he writes:

> But people in watch-chains are loftily grumbling
> And sting you politely like snakes in the oats,

the primary effect is visual, but the scene, so clearly portrayed, suggests the character and habits of a class of persons who are coldly polite and use good manners to inflict wounds. So, more strikingly, in **"Spring"** Pasternak moves from the seen to the unseen, from an actual place to its character and meaning for him:

> It's spring. I leave a street where the poplar is astonished,
> Where distance is alarmed, and the house fears it may fall,
> Where air is blue just like the linen bundle
> A discharged patient takes from hospital,
>
> Where dusk is empty like a broken tale,
> Abandoned by a star, without conclusion,
> So that expressionless, unfathomable
> A thousand clamouring eyes are in confusion.

This is a real place with its street, its houses, its poplar, its sky with the colour of a blue bundle. But the visual effect is made more significant by the imaginative and emotional tone which it gets from the imagery. The poet leaves the place because it is somehow frustrated and incomplete. It has the confused pathos of an interrupted story, and this spreads to all who are interested in it and have hopes for its future. We all know how a visual scene may excite emotions in this way and contain in itself a power to move us to grief or pity. Pasternak describes such a state with admirable truth and appropriateness. He does not exaggerate his feelings, but passes with easy skill from one aspect of the situation to another until the short poem gives a complete and faithful picture of what has struck him.

This pictorial method enables Pasternak to deal with undefined and impalpable feelings and to give them a remarkable brilliance of colour and outline. He finds his images in what his eyes and ears have noted. These become his instruments for showing the obscure movements of the human soul. In particular when he tells of some action and wishes to show its full significance, he sometimes uses its actual feature symbolically. The symbols exist both in themselves and for what they represent, and a poem written in this way seems to call for understanding at two levels, literal and symbolical. One of his most quoted poems will show how Pasternak faces this technique with all its difficulties:

> Stars raced headlong. Seaward headlands lathered.
> Salt spray blinded. Eyes dried up their tears.
> Darkness filled the bedrooms. Thoughts raced headlong.
> To Sahara Sphinx turned patient ears.
>
> Candles guttered. Blood, it seemed, was frozen
> In the huge Colossus. Lips at play

> Swelled into the blue smile of the desert.
> In that hour of ebb night sank away.
>
> Seas were stirred by breezes from Morocco.
> Simoon blew. Archangel snored in snows.
> Candles guttered. First draft of *The Prophet*
> Dried, and on the Ganges dawn arose.

The last verse explains the whole. "The Prophet" is Pushkin's famous poem and Pasternak's subject is its composition. To this all the themes are related. In the first place we hear of the circumstances in which the poem is written. It is begun at night, and finished at dawn. The dark bedrooms, the guttering candles, the racing stars, are the accompaniment of composition. The geographical setting, from Africa to Archangel, from the Ganges to Morocco, places the poem in its wider, cosmic relations and sets its birth on the stage of the world. But each of the details serves a second purpose. They are symbols for the act of composition as it takes place in the poet. The storm at sea is his tumultuous energy, the freezing Colossus his state when the work begins, the listening Sphinx his expectant consciousness on the verge of starting, the swelling lips his joy that expands into creation, the snoring city of Archangel his indifference to all around him, and the dawn his final triumphant achievement. But though we may treat the poem at two levels, literal and symbolical, they are fused into a single result. The actual circumstances illuminate the significance of such an event and become symbols of its character. The composition of "The Prophet" is a display of creative energy in which the workings of the poet's inspiration have the power of natural forces and closely resemble them.

Pasternak uses imagery to give to his poems a high degree of exactness and individuality. For instance, he often writes about rain, but he distinguishes between its different aspects. At one time, on a summer evening, it advances through a clearing as a surveyor walks with his clerk: at another time a solid sheet of rain is like charcoal in a drawing: in **"Sultry Rain"**

> Dust simply soaked the rain in pills
> Like iron in a gentle powder.

The different parallels show variously the gentle approach of rain, its black torrential downpour, its disappearance in a parched landscape. When this art is applied to mental and emotional states, it gives a new significance and clarity to them. The unmarked passage of time becomes "the hour is scuttling like a beetle". A mood of quiet satisfaction appears as

> In fur-coat and arm-chair purrs the soul
> In the same way, always, on and on.

So the methods of the Imagists are given a new and much more impressive purpose. The image, as Pasternak uses it, is as rare and striking as they could demand, but instead of being given pride of place as the only thing that matters, it concentrates the poem's essence in itself and at the same time serves to make clearer the complex unity with which the poem as a whole deals.

The desire to make his imagery exact sometimes leads Pasternak into curious results. We may even feel that, like Apollinaire, he enjoys startling us by unexpected effects as when he says that a frosty night is "like a blind puppy lapping its milk" or that the dew "runs shivering like a hedgehog". But if we look closely at these, we see how apt they are in that a frosty night has really something primitively greedy about it and that the shivering of the dew is like the shivering of a hedgehog. The danger of this method is that the desire to make the image extremely precise may give it too great an emphasis and upset the balance of tone. . . . This is a minor fault, and there are not many instances of it, but it shows the difficulty of using images which are both striking and exact.

Pasternak uses this technique to convey his own vision of reality. He is perfectly at home in a real, physical world, but he sees it in a special way and gives his own interpretation of it. He believes that it has its own powers and forces and that it is for him to understand these and bring them into closer touch with himself. Just as the Futurist Khlebnikov believed that the earth is full of unacknowledged or neglected powers which he identified with the old Slavonic gods, so Pasternak, more realistically and more reasonably, sees in nature real, living powers with whom he can enter into some kind of communion and whose influence he can to some extent fathom. For him trees and flowers, skies and winds, clouds and light, are in their own way alive with a special energy and character of their own. Naturally he speaks of them in the language of human actions and relations, but his conception of nature is not simply of something akin to mankind. He sees that it works differently, and he is content to observe it as it is and to show how it affects him and other men. He can mark natural details as attentively as Tennyson, but he does more than this. He passes from his delighted observation of them to interpreting what they mean, what dramatic parts they play, what effects they create, what powers lie behind these common and apparently innocent phenomena. For him the natural world is a busy active place, full of strange forces and energies, which are often almost unintelligible but none the less exciting or disturbing. He feels that he stands in some relation to them, and tries to show what this means. Few poets have approached nature quite with these beliefs. Pasternak delights in it and feels that it is alive and powerful, but does not make a god of it or expect it to reveal oracular messages.

Pasternak is so at home with nature and treats it with so easy and affectionate a familiarity that we do not always notice how special his vision is and may even assume that his treatment of a natural subject is fundamentally conventional. (pp. 129-40)

This familiarity with nature passes into a deeper and more significant poetry. How much it can mean to Pasternak may be seen from **"Sparrow Hills."** Reduced to its lowest terms this is a variation on the old theme of *carpe diem:* since no pleasure lasts for long, let us enjoy what we can, and especially let us enjoy our youth. This is perhaps the fundamental theme, but the variations are what matter and give a unique quality to the poem. Pasternak tells of a real situation—the poem is in a section called "songs to save her from boredom"—and a real landscape. But in this actual scene he shows how close he is to nature and what it means to him: he starts with a hint of active love and shows how into this doubts break with their disturbing presage that this happiness will not last for ever. Even the pleasures of love may become monotonous, and he looks for an escape which shall be more satisfying and more exciting:

Kisses on the breast, like water from a pitcher!
Not always, not ceaseless spurts the summer's well.
Nor shall we raise up the hurdy-gurdy's clamour
Each night from the dust with feet that stamp and trail.

I have heard of age—those hideous forebodings!
When no wave will lift its hands up to the stars.
If they speak, you doubt it. No face in the meadows,
No heart in the pools, no god among the firs.

Rouse your soul to frenzy. Foaming all the day through.
It's the world's midday. Have you no eyes for it?
Look how in the heights thoughts seethe into white bubbles
Of fir-cones, woodpeckers, clouds, pine-needles, heat.

Here the rails are ended of the city tram-cars.
Further, pines must do. Further, trams cannot pass.
Further, it is Sunday. Plucking down the branches,
Skipping through the clearings, slipping on the grass.

Sifting midday light and Whitsunday and walking
Woods would have us think the world is always so;
They're so planned with thickets, so inspired with spaces,
Spilling from the clouds on us, like chintz, below.

This is Pasternak's *L'Invitation au Voyage,* but he invites his beloved not to an imaginary paradise but to a real wood in a real summer, and the renewal of life which he seeks is to come not from intellectual or artistic pleasures but from the presence of nature. The almost pantheistic language of the second verse, with its fear that the years may turn the poet's beliefs into illusions, prepares the way to the enhancement of the senses which is to be found in the woods, to the frenzy and the foaming which he believes to be at his command. In such an expedition the driving force is the belief that nature provides an invigorating relaxation, not supernatural peace but an enlargement of faculties in young lovers.

In nature, as Pasternak sees it, human beings are a constituent part. It interpenetrates their being and controls them in such a way that they are in some sense its creatures, swayed by the moods and subject to the influences of their surroundings. This interrelation raises many questions, and Pasternak sometimes forces us to look in quite a new way at man in his natural setting. For instance in **"In the Wood"** the scene is again a summer day in a wood, where a couple are asleep while the dusk gradually advances. What holds the poem together is the idea that, as they sleep, nature constructs a kind of natural clock which tells the hours, though the couple are insensible to the passage of time. We might almost say that the fundamental theme of the poem is that time flies for lovers while they do not notice it; but this flight is vividly expressed through the actual place where the lovers sleep. They, their sleep, and their surroundings are a single unity. . . .The poem begins with a suggestion of love satisfied. The lovers rest in a state bordering on sleep, in which the man is vaguely conscious of the woman at his side. Then gradually nature gets to work and builds in the sky its own kind of clock, and this sign of passing time is not marked by the couple who are now asleep. To this extent the poem is concerned with the state that follows the consummation of love, but just as other poets set love against the menace of fleeting time, so Pasternak makes the passing of the hours an element in the whole situation. Nature herself marks the time, though the human beings do not notice what they are losing.

Nature, which displays so many different moods to human beings, needs a different symbol or myth for each of them, and Pasternak, who has no fixed mythology, creates a fresh myth for each new manifestation of natural powers. Nature is alive with presences whose character cannot be fully known but whose actions are observed with keen curiosity. Spirits are abroad, but spirits of no common sort and with few familiar traits. They can be mischievous and arouse annoyance and even dismay. They have some of the malice of Shakespeare's fairies, but they move in a familiar world and are quite recognisable once our attention is drawn to them. Everyone, for instance, knows the disturbed and disturbing air that comes after the end of winter, and nowhere is the change of season more gusty and more trying to the temper than in the Russian thaw. At such a time uneasy spirits seem to walk abroad, and Pasternak tells of one:

> The air is whipped by the frequent rain-drops;
> The ice is mangy and grey. Ahead
> You look for the skyline to awaken
> And start; you wait for the drone to spread.
>
> As always, with overcoat unbuttoned,
> With muffler about his chest undone,
> He pursues before him the unsleeping
> Silly birds and chases them on.
>
> Now he comes to see you, and, dishevelled,
> The dripping candles he tried to snuff,
> Yawns, and remembers that now's the moment
> To take the hyacinths' night-caps off.
>
> Out of his senses, ruffling his hair-mop,
> Dark in his thought's confusion, he
> Leaves you quite dumfounded with a wicked
> Stupid tale that he tells of me.

The chief character is not named; he is simply "he" and is known from what he does. He rises out of the uneasy atmosphere, and his character and actions embody its untidy, restless, teasing spirit. He starts trouble not only by frightening the birds and making the candles flicker but in human beings. The poet feels the uneasiness spread to his companion and have the effect of a story told against himself. The season has in it a disturbing and grating presence, a kind of Puck, but a Puck who rises out of the time of year and is known only from his disorderly and malicious pranks.

This sense of natural powers at work in the world may even take on an almost tragic intensity. The Russian autumn has been sung by many poets, and Tyutchev more than once told of its melancholy character. In **"Spasskoye"** Pasternak does something of the same kind, but with a more poignant and more personal note. He takes the moment when the summer is over and autumn comes with falling leaves, the felling of trees, rising mists and anticipations of winter. What strikes him is the sense of decay and death, of lessened vitality and of painful separation. His imagery contributes greatly to the emotional effect; for each image adds something to the interpretation of the situation and suggests sickness and death. But behind the imagery and the description there is something which only Pasternak can convey, a situation in which man is so entangled in his natural surroundings that they dictate his moods and make him seem part of themselves:

> Unforgettable September is strewn about Spasskoye.

> Is to-day not the time to leave the cottage here?
> Beyond the fence Echo has shouted with the herdsman
> And in the woods has made the axe's stroke ring clear.
>
> Last night outside the park the chilling marshes shivered.
> The moment the sun rose it disappeared again.
> The hare-bells will not drink of the rheumatic dew-drops,
> On birches dropsy swells a dirty lilac stain.
>
> The wood is melancholy. What it wants is quiet
> Under the snows in bear-dens' unawaking sleep;
> And there among the boles inside the blackened fences
> Jaws of the columned park, like a long death-list, gape.
>
> The birchwood has not ceased to blot and lose its colour,
> To thin its watery shadows and grow sparse and dim.
> He is still mumbling,—you're fifteen years old again now,
> And now again, my child, what shall we do with them?
>
> So many of them now that you should give up playing,
> They're like birds in bushes, mushrooms along hedges.
> Now with them we've begun to curtain our horizon
> And with their mist to hide another's distances.
>
> On his death-night the typhus-stricken clown hears tumult,
> The gods' Homeric laughter from the gallery.
> Now from the road, in Spasskoye, on the timbered cottage
> Looks in hallucination the same agony.

The poem is built on a clear pattern. The first three verses set out the scene in its melancholy and decay. The actors are the natural features of the landscape—the echo, the marshes, the harebells, the trees, all of which are ailing and suffering. This sense of doom reaches its climax in the comparison of the trees in the park to an obituary column in a newspaper. In the fourth verse the purpose of this detailed setting emerges mysteriously and allusively. The undescribed "he" is surely one of Pasternak's natural powers, the genius of the place at this season who haunts and dominates the wooded park. It makes the poet feel as if he were again fifteen years old and again suffering from some childish melancholy and uncertainty with the sense that comes at such an age that life has lost its range and contracted its horizon. This feeling dominates the present moment and gives to the cottage and its surroundings a tragic air, as if it were being mocked by inhuman powers, like the people in the gallery of a theatre, in the hour of its death. The tense poignancy of the close is enhanced by the suggestion that the poet has been thrown back into his childhood and feels some old misery, awakened by the chance air of the season. All this is forced on him by natural powers at work in Spasskoye. He is their victim, and in their dealings with him they show the callous indifference which the ancient gods showed to men. His keen ears and eyes miss nothing in the scene, and everything which Pasternak gets from them starts something else in his mind, some parallel or illustration or symbol, which drives home with compelling precision his full response to the situation. Nature is the first source of his poetry and calls out his finest powers.

Pasternak's view of nature is central to his work, and his poetry illustrates his belief that a creative force is at work in everything and that elements in the natural scene are as powerful as those in man and closely connected with them. His special interest is in his contact or conflict with such powers. He sees himself and other men as moved by strange energies and influences which are not fully intelligible but can be grasped only through a special insight and represented only through myth or symbol. Even when he writes specifically about himself and his own feelings, his outlook is the same. He still treats of strange, undefined forces which sweep into or rush over him and are outside his control and full comprehension. This outlook, which rises from his acute sensibility, gives a special character to his poems of love. For him love breaks the ordinary rules of life and creates its own world. In **"From Superstition"** Pasternak shows how love transforms his circumstances and gives a new meaning to everything. For him "a box with a red orange in it" is all the lodging that he now needs: the dappled wall-paper becomes an oak-tree: the entry to this setting is gained by song: when he kisses his beloved, he tastes violets: her dress is like a snowdrop which chirrups a greeting to April. The casual encounter takes on all the charm of the country in spring, and it is not surprising that the poet feels as if his beloved has taken his life down from the shelf and blown the dust off it. Love imposes its laws on reality and makes the lover enjoy a state which is more real than the reality around him. A similar capacity to transform is more elaborately and more forcibly portrayed in **"Do not touch"** where what looks like a pretty trope takes command of the poem and gives to it an unusual power. . . . [In the poem], the transforming power of love is displayed in the image of the white light which comes from the beloved and changes the poet's world. And this power, which arises from what might seem to be an unhealthy or abnormal condition, exerts itself especially on the poet's melancholy until it makes even that luminous.

If love is like this, it is a little disturbing. Such an incalculable power is not to be welcomed lightly. It comes from unplumbed depths of nature and may well cause havoc. That is why Pasternak sometimes treats of the disintegrating effects of love and shows how afraid he is of them. In one poem he draws a strong contrast between the ordinary view of love and his own. While other people treat weddings as occasions to get drunk and to shut "life, that is like a pearly dream by Watteau, into a snuff-box", he finds that it releases primaeval energies in him:

> Chaos again crawls out upon the world
> As in the ages when the fossils lived.

Ordinary people are jealous of him and do not like it when he raises a girl from the earth "like a bacchante from an amphora". But against this critical opposition his own powers are all the more enhanced. The Andes melt in his kisses: it is like dawn on the steppe where stars fall in dust. The result is that in commonplace surroundings, amid the flat ritual of marriage, a strange, chaotic power is released. Pasternak sees love as brutal, irrational, and uncontrollable; it breaks into life and turns everything upside down. It is therefore appropriate that his most effective love-poetry should be the series called **"Rupture"** which treats love as a morbid condition in which the mind is infected with a kind of disease and the lovers are haunted by a sense of shame and guilt:

> O grief, infected with lies in its roots,
> O sorrow, leprous sorrow!

For a moment Pasternak may accept love's illusions and imagine that he and his beloved can escape, like Actaeon and Atalanta, into the woods, but the mood does not last, and reality soon asserts itself again. At the end the sep-

aration comes, quietly, but not without leaving a wound. . . . Pasternak accepts love and its results because it is a natural process, but he finds in it much that is disturbing and distressing.

Most of this highly personal and lyrical poetry was written by Pasternak at a time when his country was in great turmoil and confusion. *My Sister Life* was composed for the most part in the summer of 1917 between the February Revolution of Kerensky and the October Revolution of Lenin. *Themes and Variations* was written during the no less crowded and eventful period between the triumph of Bolshevism and the end of the Civil War. In these years, when the poetry of Mayakovsky and Khlebnikov was inspired by popular emotions and largely directed to revolutionary ends, Pasternak might seem to have kept himself detached and independent outside the battle. We might think that this time of violent changes made little impression on him: so faithful is he to his personal vision and to such themes as his immediate circumstances suggest to him. But this is to misunderstand him. Pasternak was neither unpolitical nor reactionary. As a boy of fifteen he had shared the revolutionary fervour of 1905. The Futurists were his friends, whose political aims and ambitions he shared. For him, as for them, the Revolution was a prodigious manifestation of natural forces which had hitherto lain dormant in Russia, and he could hardly fail to see that it answered to his own dynamic conception of life. In his own way his poetry contributes to the revolutionary period and owes much of its inspiration to the spirit of the time. But it is very much in his own way. Pasternak's manner of writing, sensitive, personal and lyrical, is quite different from the broken epics of Khlebnikov or the enthusiastic rhetoric of Mayakovsky. His genius forces him to assimilate his political experiences until they are part of himself and to present them precisely as he feels them. He understood the Revolution through his insight into the powers which stir in nature and in man, and it was this side of it that challenged his creative energies. It belonged to the same order of things as his other subjects, whether nature or love, and he wrote of it in the same way, as of something that touched him deeply in the roots of his being and was yet another sign of strange forces at work in the world.

The result is that Pasternak assimilates his political experiences so closely to his central outlook that he seems for the moment to detract from their importance and to reduce them to mere natural events. Yet this is precisely the importance that he finds in them. They are indeed natural events and therefore full of majesty and mystery. They are a special manifestation of the strange powers that can be observed in physical nature. Pasternak believes that, like other human actions, they rise naturally from the landscape and stand in some close relation to it. Even the Revolution is a natural event in the sense that it rises from the Russian soil no less than from the Russian soul. (pp. 141-50)

Pasternak is fully aware of the human side of the Revolution and sees that, though it holds out great promises, it also brings many anxieties and troubles. A hint of what he himself suffered in the first months after the Revolution and what solution he found may be seen in **"January 1918"** where he greets with relief the coming of a new year with its promise of better times. . . . [In the poem], as so often with Pasternak, the actual situation provides the symbols for something more abstract. After the suicidal terrors and deathly chill of the old year, the new year promises light and comfort and, above all, peace. Peace comes alike from nature and from men, both of whom are in their separate ways philosophers and know what it means. None the less the new year is not quite what is expected. It is noisy and vulgar and embarrassing. After the agonies and the sacrifices, after the bold Utopian hopes, reality gives something of a shock. But Pasternak accepts it with philosophic wisdom and cheerfulness and humour. The last two lines proclaim his trust in the future. The snow stands for the purifying forces which are abroad and will in the end produce a cure for present discontents. This poem shows the quality of Pasternak's detachment. He sees the events from his own point of view and is not afraid to say what he feels, but at the same time he appreciates their importance and foretells the good things that lie ahead.

The optimistic note on which this poem ends shows Pasternak's feeling towards his time. True to his trust that such an eruption of natural forces must in the end be right and prevail, he finds in them a source of vitality and energy. What matters for him is this release of nature's powers which bring man closer to itself. Pasternak is not a partisan of particular causes but a poet of the whole movement for liberation and a new life. That is why he is not too hard on his opponents. He feels that they have lost the battle and that they do not deserve too much attention. So he dismisses them ironically or contemptuously. He knows that there is a vast difference between his own exultant confidence and the straitened outlook of his adversaries, and that he has something which they cannot hope to have. What this means can be seen from **"May it be,"** written in 1919:

Dawn shakes the candle, shoots a flame
To light the wren, and does not miss.
I search my memories and proclaim
"May life be always fresh as this!"

Like a shot dawn rang through the night.
Bang bang it went. In swooning flight
The wads of bullets flame and hiss.
May life be always fresh as this.

The breeze is at the door again.
At night he shivered, wanted us.
He froze when daybreak brought up rain.
May life be always fresh as this.

He is astonishingly queer.
Why rudely past the gate-man press?
Of course he saw "No thoroughfare".
May life be always as fresh as this.

Still with a handkerchief to shake,
While mistress still, chase all about,
While yet our darkness does not break,
While yet the flames have not gone out.

The dawn symbolises the coming of the new order, and it breaks like a rifle-shot. The breeze shows that new movements are active, though their meaning is not fully understood and they do not conform to old proprieties and prohibitions. The poet welcomes the situation and knows that all will be well. In the last verse, the woman whom he addresses stands for the old ruling class which may for the moment continue its sentimental or authoritarian tasks but will before long have to change its ways. The poem is written in gaiety and confidence. What others may find frightening, Pasternak finds inspiring and exciting.

Pasternak's political poetry in the first years of the Revolution is nearly all composed in this special way. He tells how events strike him personally and what part they take in his scheme of things. But the Revolution called for more than this, and it was almost impossible for Pasternak to be deaf to it. Just as in these years Khlebnikov wrote heroic poems about Russian characters who fought for liberty, from the old rebel Stepan Razin to a nameless seamstress of 1917, so others felt the need to display the events of their time with a full sense of their grandeur. (pp. 151-54)

In nature, in love, in stirring political events Pasternak found the subjects of his mature poetry. In all of them was something primaeval and forceful which appealed strongly to him and echoed something in himself. This something was the spirit in which he composed poetry. He felt himself at home with such subjects because in them he saw powers at work which were closely related to his own powers when the spell of composition was on him. And just as these subjects excite his curiosity and vivid interest, so his own creative spirit is a burning question for him. He more than once writes about it and seems to have more than one view of it. Its aspects strike him differently at different times. He is so modest and truthful that we cannot expect him to produce a grandiose metaphysic of art or even to reveal his whole feelings about it. But his career shows how much it means to him and how he puts it first even when he feels a strong call to serve other ends. Sometimes when he speaks about poetry he seems to assume an ironical or paradoxical air as if he were on the defensive and unwilling to put forward his whole case. But this is the reflection of an extreme honesty which refuses to speak dogmatically about something which means a great deal to him but cannot really be grasped or explained. . . . Nor is he prepared to make vast claims for the mood in which the poet composes. There is nothing of Blok's "Artist" in what Pasternak says of his work, no timeless ecstasy or vision of Paradise. . . . He even denies that composition gives him any pleasure and says in **"Poetry"**:

You're summer with a third-class ticket,
A suburb and not a refrain.

It is as stifling as May or a crowded quarter of the town or a fort over which clouds pass. Even the final consummation is not claimed to be at all impressive or wonderful:

Poetry, when an empty truism,
Like a zinc bucket, stands below
The tap, is certain to be spouting.
The copy-book is open. Flow!

This is Pasternak's modest way of not claiming too much for his art. It is, it seems, a perfectly natural process and he must not pretend that it is more.

Yet it is a natural process and all that this means to Pasternak. Whatever difficulty he may find in explaining his art to others or in justifying its place in society, he is quite confident and explicit about what it means to himself. In one poem he admits that a poet is a peculiar kind of being, but insists that he follows a special destiny and wins special rewards. He looks back on childhood and tells how from the beginning he has known the magical power of words and found his own most vivid experiences through them:

> So they begin. With two years gone
> From nurse to countless tunes they scuttle.
> They chirp and whistle. Then comes on
> The third year, and they start to prattle.
>
> So they begin to see and know.
> In din of started turbines roaring,
> Mother seems not their mother now,
> And you not you, and home is foreign.
>
> What meaning has the menacing
> Beauty beneath the lilac seated,
> If to steal children's not the thing?
> So first they fear that they are cheated.
>
> So ripen fears. Can he endure
> A star to beat him in successes,
> When he's a Faust, a sorcerer?
> So first his gipsy life progresses.
>
> So from the fence where home should lie
> In flight above are found to hover
> Seas unexpected as a sigh.
> So first iambics they discover.
>
> So summer nights fall down and pray
> "Thy will be done" where oats are sprouting,
> And menace with your eyes the day.
> So with the sun they start disputing.
>
> So verses start them on their way.

This is Pasternak's apology. It tells how marvellous discoveries reward him for feeling that he is odd and unlike other men. His course follows an inevitable rhythm from the start, and though his early shocks are more violent than those of other men, his compensations are correspondingly great. He has his wonderful dreams, his moments of rapture and exaltation, his conviction that he is at one with nature and shares her strength. By such means Pasternak does more than defend himself against utilitarian or mechanistic notions of poetry: he shows that so far from being an artificial adjunct of society he is a magician who releases nature's powers through his art.

Pasternak responds to the special character of his calling by a special sense of the responsibilities which it puts upon him. He believes, above all, that everything that he writes must be a work of art, complete and independent with its own life, the final vehicle by which experience is selected and organised and transformed into a permanent shape. He also believes that no work of art has any value unless it is true in a rigorous and exacting sense, true not merely to fact but to experience, to all that the poet sees in it and feels about it. This double ideal is perhaps responsible for his complexities and roughnesses, but it is no less responsible for his final success and for his special importance. In a revolutionary age Pasternak has seen beyond the disturbed surface of things to the powers behind it and found there an explanation of what really matters in the world. Through his unerring sense of poetry he has reached to wide issues and shown that the creative calling, with its efforts and its frustrations and its unanticipated triumphs, is, after all, something profoundly natural and closely related to the sources of life. (pp. 155-58)

C. M. Bowra, "Boris Pasternak, 1917-1923," in his The Creative Experiment, *Macmillan & Co. Ltd., 1949, pp. 128-58.*

The Times, London

Is it another *War and Peace?* This question is immediately raised by the scope, the grandeur, the compassion and the beauty of Boris Pasternak's epic, [*Doctor Zhivago*]. Like Tolstoy, he searches deep into the meaning of life by tracing the loves, hopes, anguish and deaths of about a score of men and women during years of titanic struggle and upheaval in Russia. The superficial likenesses between the two books are many. As Tolstoy chose Pierre Bezukhov, the earnest and bewildered bystander and philosophiser, to be one of the pivots and interpreters of his story, so Pasternak has chosen Yury Zhivago, the poet, almost the quietist, who shrinks more and more from the October revolution and the civil war until he falls, worn out, into physical and moral decay.

Yet it would be wrong to pursue the parallels too far. Pasternak does not try to enter directly into the minds of the dynasts—the Kaiser or Hitler, or Lenin, Trotsky or Stalin—as Tolstoy spoke through the minds of Napoleon and Kutuzov. Indeed, one of the reasons why his book—already published in Italian and French, and now in English—has not yet been allowed in Russia is that he does not deal in any detail with the motives of the revolutionary leaders after 1917 or their material achievements. To that extent the book is truncated. The tragedy works itself out at a lower level of history than Tolstoy's. But that is because of Pasternak's own view of life. He denies that essential human life can be reshaped, and his chief concern is with the price that is paid in human misery when the attempt is made.

He is appalled (speaking through Zhivago and other characters) by the sequel to the revolution which they all had originally welcomed; appalled by the "spirit of narrowness" that set truth aside and demanded to be worshipped as holy itself; contemptuous of the limitations and self-centredness of Marxism; and horrified by mass direction. "The great misfortune, the root of all the evil to come, was the loss of faith in the value of personal opinions." Against it all he sets the Galilean message of love and compassion. "From that moment there were neither gods nor peoples, but only man." And at another place, "communion between mortals is immortal." The religious message burns with a clear flame in the twenty-five poems at the end. He asserts the duty of the intellectual, the poet, the believer, to pass judgment on the actions of men.

How misleading, though, to think of the book as a kind of fictionalized political treatise. It is a protest and a challenge certainly, but it springs from life itself, presented in the stories of quite ordinary men and women, Zhivago, Lara, Tonya, Strelnikov, and the rest. The developing theme through all the turmoil is awe-inspiring, a passionate and vibrant work of art that has the force, and the emotional power, of a symphony. . . .

Above all, there is the end of Lara. In this most Russian of novels Pasternak—perhaps to reinforce his message that life is concerned "not with peoples, but with persons"—has made his chief heroine the Russian-born daughter of a Belgian father and a Russianized French-woman. She lights up the whole story in every word and action. "One day Lara went out and did not come back. She must have been arrested in the street, as so often happened in those days, and she died or vanished somewhere, forgotten as a nameless number on a list which later was mislaid, in one of the innumerable mixed or women's concentration camps in the north."

An English reader may find the many Russian first names, patronymics and surnames a little perplexing. . . . He may also find something far-fetched in the coincidences which bring so many of the characters together after so many long journeys, spread over years. But these are small tribulations along the road. Pasternak has written one of the great books, courageous, tender, tragic, humble.

> *"A Modern Russian Novel on the Grand Scale," in* The Times, *London, September 4, 1958, p. 13.*

Irving Howe

Doctor Zhivago, the novel which climaxes the career of the Russian poet Boris Pasternak, is a major work of fiction; but it is also—and for the moment, perhaps more important—a historic utterance. It is an act of testimony as crucial to our moral and intellectual life as the Hungarian revolution to our political life. It asks for, and deserves, the kind of response in which one's sense of the purely "literary" becomes absorbed in a total attention to the voice of the writer.

The book comes to us in extraordinary circumstances. A great Russian poet who maintains silence through years of terror and somehow, for reasons no one quite understands, survives the purges that destroy his most gifted colleagues; a manuscript sent by him to an Italian Communist publisher who decides to issue it despite strong pressures from his comrades; the dictatorship meanwhile refusing to permit this book, surely the most distinguished Russian novel of our time, to appear in print—all this comprises the very stuff of history, a reenactment of those rhythms of brutality and resistance which form the substance of the novel itself.

Doctor Zhivago opens in the first years of the century, spans the revolution, civil war and terror of the thirties, and ends with an epilogue in the mid-1940s. On a level far deeper than politics and with a strength and purity that must remove all doubts, it persuades us that the yearning for freedom remains indestructible. Quietly and resolutely Pasternak speaks for the sanctity of human life, turning to those "eternal questions" which made the 19th Century Russian novel so magnificent and besides which the formulas of Russia's current masters seem so trivial.

The European novel has traditionally depended on some implicit norm of "the human." In our time, however, this norm has become so imperiled that the novel has had to assume the burdens of prophecy and jeremiad, raising an apocalyptic voice against the false apocalypse of total politics. (p. 16)

But where certain Western novelists have wrenched their narrative structures in order to reach some "essence" of modern terror, Pasternak has adopted a quite different strategy. With apparent awareness of the symbolic meaning of his choice, he has turned back to the old-fashioned leisurely Tolstoyan novel. His aim is not to mimic its external amplitude, as do most Soviet writers, but to recapture its spirit of freedom and then bring this spirit to bear upon contemporary Russian life. Given the atmosphere in which Pasternak must live and work, this kind of a return to the Tolstoyan novel comes to seem a profoundly liberating act.

Pasternak refuses to accept any claim for the primacy of ideological systems. Avoiding any quest for the "essence" of modern terror, he prefers to observe its impact upon the lives of modest and decent people. Again and again he returns to what might be called the "organic" nature of experience, those autonomous human rhythms which, in his view, can alone provide a true basis for freedom. The Tolstoyan narrative structure takes on a new and dynamic character, embodying his belief that everything fundamental in life remains inviolate, beyond the grasp of ideology or the state.

I do not mean to suggest that Pasternak permits a facile spirituality to blind him to the power of circumstances. He knows how easy it is to debase and kill a man, how often and needlessly it has been done; some of his most poignant chapters register the sufferings of the Russian people during the past forty years. Yet he is driven by an almost instinctive need to cling to other possibilities, and he writes about ordinary experience with such affection and steadfastness that, even under the blows of accumulating historical crises, it takes on a halo of sanctity. Not the fanaticism of the will, but existence as rooted in the natural world, seems to him the crux of things.

Yurii Zhivago, the central figure of the novel and in some ways Pasternak's alter ego, comes to this realization while still a young man. As he is driven from the battlefields of the First World War to revolutionary Moscow to partisan fighting in Siberia, and then back again to Moscow, Zhivago tries to keep hold of a few realities: nature, art, the life of contemplation. No matter how desperate the moment may be, he feels that the preservation of his inner identity is still possible if he can watch a cow grazing in the fields, read Pushkin's poems and speak freely to himself in the journal he intermittently keeps.

It is this effort to preserve the personal basis of reality which forms the main stress of Zhivago's experience—an effort always secured in a radiantly intense feeling for nature. One of the loveliest episodes in the novel occurs when Zhivago and his family, to avoid starvation during the civil war, decide to leave Moscow. They take a long journey eastward, and at one point their train becomes stalled in drifts of snow. For three days the passengers work in the open, helping to clear the tracks. A light of joy comes over them, a feeling of gratification for this gift: "The days were clear and frosty, and the shifts were short because there were not enough shovels. It was sheer pleasure."

Somewhat earlier in the book Zhivago reflects upon his life while traveling homeward from the First World War:

> Three years of changes, moves, uncertainties, upheavals; the war, the revolution; scenes of destruction, scenes of death, shelling, blown-up bridges, fires, ruins—all this suddenly turned into a huge, empty, meaningless space. The first real event since

the long interruption was this trip . . . the fact that he was approaching his home, which was intact, which still existed, and in which every stone was dear to him. This was real life, meaningful experience, the actual goal of all guests, this was what art aimed at—homecoming, return to one's family, to oneself, to true existence.

The novel begins with a series of clipped vignettes of pre-revolutionary Russia, apparently meant to suggest a Tolstoyan breadth and luxuriousness of treatment. A few of these vignettes seem hurried and schematic in effect, but many of them are brilliantly evocative, quick and sharp glimpses of another Russia.

But which Russia: the Russia of the Czars or of *War and Peace,* the country Pasternak remembers from his youth or the marvellous landscape of Tolstoy's imagination? The alternative, of course, is a false one, and I raise it merely to indicate the presence of a real problem. For in the mind of a writer like Pasternak, historical reality and literary heritage must by now be inseparable: the old Russia is the Russia both of the Czars and of Tolstoy. And as he recreates it stroke by stroke, Pasternak seems intent upon suggesting that no matter what attitude one takes toward the past, it cannot be understood in terms of imposed political clichés.

He is, in any case, rigorously objective in his treatment. He portrays both a vibrant Christmas party among the liberal intelligentsia and a bitter strike among railroad workers; he focusses upon moments of free discussion and spontaneous talk such as would make some contemporary Russian readers feel envious and then upon moments of gross inhumanity that would make them think it pointless even to consider turning back the wheel of history. Pasternak accepts the unavoidability, perhaps even the legitimacy of the revolution, and he evokes the past not to indulge in nostalgia but to insist upon the continuity of human life.

Once, however, the narrative reaches the Bolshevik revolution, the Tolstoyan richness and complexity promised at the beginning are not fully realized. Partly this is due to Pasternak's inexperience as a novelist: he burdens himself with more preparations than he needs and throughout the book one is aware of occasional brave efforts to tie loose ends together.

But mainly the trouble is due to a crucial difference between Tolstoy's and Pasternak's situations. Soaring to an incomparable zest and vitality, Tolstoy could break past the social limits of his world—a world neither wholly free nor, like Pasternak's, wholly unfree—and communicate the sheer delight of consciousness. Pasternak also desires joy as a token of man's gratitude for existence; his characters reach for it eagerly and pathetically; but the Russia of his novel is too grey, too grim for a prolonged release of the Tolstoyan ethos. As a writer of the highest intelligence, Pasternak must have known this; and it is at least possible he also realized that the very difficulties he would encounter in adapting the Tolstoyan novel to contemporary Russia would help reveal both the direction of his yearning and the constrictions of reality.

It is Pasternak's capacity for holding in balance these two elements—the direction of his yearning and the constrictions of reality—that accounts for the poise and strength of the novel. Like most great Russian writers, he has the gift for making ideas seem a natural part of human experience, though what matters in this novel is not a Dostoevskian clash of ideology and dialectic but Zhivago's sustained effort, amounting to a kind of heroism, to preserve his capacity for the life of contemplation.

Zhivago's ideas, it seems fair to assume, are in large measure Pasternak's, and as they emerge in the book, subtly modulated by the movement of portrayed events, it becomes clear that the central point of view can be described as a kind of primitive Christianity, profoundly heterodox and utterly alien to all dogmas and institutions. I would agree with the remark of Mr. Max Hayward, Pasternak's English translator, that Zhivago's Christianity "would be acceptable to many agnostics." Acceptable not merely because of its ethical purity but because it demands to be understood as a historically-determined response to the airless world of Soviet conformity. In such a world the idea of Christ—even more so, the image of Christ facing his death alone—must take on implications quite different from those it usually has in the West. Zhivago's uncle, his intellectual guide, suggests these in an early passage:

> What you don't understand is that it is possible to be an atheist, it is possible not to know whether God exists, or why, and yet believe . . . that history as we know it began with Christ. . . . Now what is history? It is the centuries of the systematic exploration of the riddle of death, with a view to overcoming death. That's why people discover mathematical infinity and electromagnetic waves, that's why they write symphonies. Now you can't advance in this direction without a certain faith. You can't make such discoveries without spiritual equipment. And the basic elements of this equipment are in the Gospels. What are they? To begin with, love of one's neighbor, which is the supreme form of vital energy. And then the two basic ideas of modern man—without them he is unthinkable—the idea of free personality and the idea of life as sacrifice.

Together with this version of Christianity, Zhivago soon develops a personal attitude toward Marxism—an attitude, I should say, much more complex than is likely to be noted by American reviewers seeking points for the Cold War. Zhivago cannot help but honor the early Bolsheviks, if only because they did give themselves to "the idea of life as sacrifice." His enthusiasm for the revolution dies quickly, but even then he does not condemn it. He is more severe: he judges it.

Unavoidably Zhivago also absorbs some elements of the Marxist political outlook, though he never accepts its claims for the primacy of politics. Indeed, his rejection of Marxism is not essentially a political one. He rejects it because he comes to despise the arrogance of the totalitarian "vanguard," its manipulative view of man, in short, its contempt for the second "basic ideal of modern man . . . the ideal of free personality." . . . Still more withering is Zhivago's judgment of the Soviet intelligentsia:

> Men who are not free . . . always idealize their bondage. So it was in the Middle Ages, and later the Jesuits always exploited this human trait. Zhivago could not bear the political mysticism of the Soviet intelligentsia, though it was the very thing they regarded as their highest achievement.

Such statements are plain enough, and their significance

can hardly be lost upon the powers in Moscow; but it must quickly be added that in the context of the novel they are much less abrupt and declamatory than they seem in isolation. Pasternak is so sensitive toward his own characters, so free from any intention to flourish ideologies, that the novel is never in danger of becoming a mere tract. The spectacle of Zhivago trying to reflect upon the catastrophe of his time is always more interesting than the substance of his reflections. His ideas are neither original nor beyond dispute, but as he experiences them and struggles to articulate them, they take on an enormous dignity and power. If ever a man may be said to have earned his ideas, it is Yurii Zhivago.

Zhivago's opinions reflect the direction of Pasternak's yearning, the long-suppressed bias of his mind; but there is, in the novel itself, more than enough counter-weight of objective presentation. Pasternak is extremely skillful at making us aware of vast historical forces rumbling behind the lives of his central figures. The Bolshevik revolution is never pictured frontally, but a series of incidents, some of them no more than a page or two in length, keep the sense of catastrophe and upheaval constantly before us— Zhivago fumbling to light an old stove during an icy Moscow winter while in the nearby streets men are shooting at each other, a callow young Menshevik "heartening" Russian troops with democratic rhetoric and meeting an ungainly death as his reward, a veteran Social Revolutionary pouring bile over the Communist leaders, a partisan commander in Siberia fighting desperately against the White armies. And as Zhivago finds himself caught up by social currents too strong for any man to resist, we remember once again Tolstoy's concern with the relationship between historical event and personal life.

Once Pasternak reaches the revolutionary period, the novel becomes a kind of spiritual biography, still rich in social references but primarily the record of a mind struggling for survival. What now matters most is the personal fate of Zhivago and his relationships with two other characters, Lara, the woman who is to be the love of his life, and Strelnikov, a partisan leader who exemplifies all of the ruthless revolutionary will that Zhivago lacks.

Zhivago himself may be seen as representative of those Russian intellectuals who accepted the revolution but were never absorbed into the Communist apparatus. That he is both a skillful doctor and a sensitive poet strengthens one's impression that Pasternak means him to be something more than an individual figure. He speaks for those writers, artists and scientists who have been consigned to a state of permanent inferiority because they do not belong to the "vanguard" party. His sufferings are their sufferings, and his gradual estrangement from the regime, an estrangement that has little to do with politics, may well be shared by at least some of them. Zhivago embodies that which, in Pasternak's view, man is forbidden to give to the state. (pp. 16-19)

[Some critics report] that Pasternak has apparently referred to Turgenev's Rudin as a distant literary ancestor of Zhivago. Any such remark by a writer like Pasternak has its obvious fascination and one would like very much to know exactly what he had in mind; but my own impression, for what it may be worth, is that the differences between the two characters are more striking than the similarities. Rudin, the man of the 1840's, is a figure of shape-

less enthusiasms that fail to congeal into specific convictions; he is the classical example of the man who cannot realize in action the vaguely revolutionary ideas that fire his mind. Zhivago, by contrast, is a man rarely given to large public enthusiasms; he fails to achieve his ends not because he is inherently weak but because the conditions of life are simply too much for him. Yet, unlike Rudin, he has a genuine "gift for life," and despite the repeated collapse of his enterprises he brings a sense of purpose and exaltation to the lives of those who are closest to him. There is a key passage in his journal which would probably have struck Rudin as the essence of philistinism but which takes on an entirely different cast in 20th Century Russia:

> Only the familiar transformed by genius is truly great. The best object lesson in this is Pushkin. His works are one great hymn to honest labor, duty, everyday life! Today, "bourgeois" and "petty bourgeois" have become terms of abuse, but Pushkin forestalled the implied criticism. . . . In *Onegin's Travels* we read:
> "Now my ideal is the housewife,
> My greatest wish, a quiet life
> And a big bowl of cabbage soup."

There is undoubtedly a side of Pasternak, perhaps the dominant side, which shares in these sentiments; but it is a tribute to his utter freedom from literary vanity that he remorselessly shows how Zhivago's quest for "a quiet life" leads to repeated failures and catastrophes. For Zhivago's desire for "a big bowl of cabbage soup" indicates—to twist a sardonic phrase of Trotsky's—that he did not choose the right century in which to be born.

The novel reaches a climax of exaltation with a section of some twenty pages that seem to me one of the greatest pieces of imaginative prose written in our time. Zhivago and Lara, who have been living in a Siberian town during the period of War Communism, begin to sense that their arrest is imminent: not because they speak any words of sedition (Zhivago has, in fact, recently returned from a period of enforced service as doctor to a band of Red partisans) but simply because they ignore the slogans of the moment and choose their own path in life. They decide to run off to Varykino, an abandoned farm, where they may find a few moments of freedom and peace. Zhivago speaks:

> But about Varykino. To go to that wilderness in winter, without food, without strength or hope— it's utter madness. But why not, my love! Let's be mad, if there is nothing but madness left to us. . . .
>
> Our days are really numbered. So at least let us take advantage of them in our own way. Let us use them up saying goodbye to life. . . . We'll say goodbye to everything we hold dear, to the way we look at things, to the way we've dreamed of living and to what our conscience has taught us. . . . We'll speak to one another once again the secret words we speak at night, great and pacific like the name of the Asian ocean.

From this point on, the prose soars to a severe and tragic gravity; every detail of life takes on the tokens of sanctity; and while reading these pages, one feels that one is witnessing a terrible apocalypse. Begun as a portrait of Russia, the novel ends as a love story told with the force and purity of the greatest Russian fiction; yet its dependence upon the sense of history remains decisive to the very last page.

Through a ruse Zhivago persuades Lara to escape, and then he returns to Moscow. He falls into shabbiness, illness and long periods of lassitude; he dies obscurely, from a heart attack on the streets of Moscow. Lara's fate is given in a fierce, laconic paragraph:

> One day [she] went out and did not come back. She must have been arrested in the street at that time. She vanished without a trace and probably died somewhere, forgotten as a nameless number on a list that afterwards got mislaid, in one of the innumerable mixed or women's concentration camps in the north.

Like the best contemporary writers in the West, Pasternak rests his final hope on the idea that a good life constitutes a decisive example. People remember Zhivago. His half-brother, a mysterious power in the regime who ends as a general in the war, has always helped Zhivago in the past; now he gathers up Zhivago's poems and prints them; apparently he is meant to suggest a hope that there remain a few men at the top of the Russian hierarchy who are accessible to moral claims. Other old friends, meeting at a time when "the relief and freedom expected at the end of the war" had not come but when "the portents of freedom filled the air," find that "this freedom of the soul was already there, as if that very evening the future had tangibly moved into the streets below them."

So the book ends—a book of truth and courage and beauty, a work of art toward which one's final response is nothing less than a feeling of reverence. (pp. 19-20)

> *Irving Howe, "Of Freedom and Contemplation," in* The New Republic, *Vol. 139, No. 10, September 8, 1958, pp. 16-20.*

Marc Slonim

At last we have the English version of ***Doctor Zhivago,*** the great novel from Russia that suddenly sprang into prominence last year in Europe and became the subject of passionate discussion among critics and readers. It is easy to predict that Boris Pasternak's book, one of the most significant of our time and a literary event of the first order, will have a brilliant future. It also has had an extraordinary past. (p. 1)

In the solitude of his bungalow in the neighborhood of Moscow, Pasternak wrote between 1948 and 1953 a long work in prose. "I always dreamt of a novel," he said, "in which, as in an explosion, I would erupt with all the wonderful things I saw and understood in this world." This novel, ***Doctor Zhivago,*** was accepted after Stalin's death by the State Publishing House; but following a closer examination of the manuscript (and instructions from higher party echelons), the work was barred. In the meantime Pasternak had sold the foreign rights to Feltrinelli, a Milan publisher. Moscow, seeking to prevent the publication of ***Doctor Zhivago*** abroad, compelled Pasternak to wire Feltrinelli, asking him not to publish the Italian translation of the novel and begging him to return the manuscript "for revisions." Feltrinelli's refusal brought about all sorts of pressure, including intervention by the Soviet Embassy. Nevertheless, the Italian version of *Doc-*

tor Zhivago came out in November, 1957, and immediately provoked a great stir (seven reprints in less than a year). Translations into most European languages followed and made the name of Pasternak universally known. The novel is still not available, however, in its original Russian text.

The central figure in the novel is Yurii Zhivago, son of a rich Siberian industrialist and orphan at the age of 10. He is brought up in the house of Moscow intellectuals and patrons of the arts and becomes a typical product of upper class, pre-revolutionary Russian culture. Yet as an individual, Zhivago cannot be so easily classified. An excellent physician, he studies philosophy and literature, and has decidedly personal views on many matters. He writes poems, and twenty-four of them form the ending of the novel. His main aim is to preserve his own spiritual independence. In a way he is an outsider, and does not become completely involved in current events.

Zhivago's refusal to become "engaged," however, is of an entirely different nature from the aloofness of a Camus "stranger": Zhivago loves life and lives intensely, but he does not want to be limited in his freedom. He welcomes the revolution, enjoying its stormy sweep, its dream of universal justice and its tragic beauty. Yet when the Communists begin to tell him how to live and how to think, he rebels. He leaves Moscow with his family and takes refuge in a forlorn hamlet beyond the Urals. To reach this haven he crosses the whole of Russia, going through burning cities and villages in uproar, through districts hit by famine and regions ravaged by civil war.

In the Urals he enjoys calm, but only for a short time. Soon his whole existence is upset by his passion for the fascinating Lara, whom he had met earlier, and by his wanderings in Siberia with the Red partisans, to whom he is forcibly attached as a physician. At the end of the civil strife he finds himself all alone; his family has been banned from Russia by the Soviet Government; his mistress has had to flee to Manchuria. Zhivago returns to Moscow, a broken man, to die in the street of a heart attack.

This vast epic of about 200,000 words has varied layers of narrative. Chronologically it encompasses three generations and gives a vivid picture of Russian life during the first quarter of our century, between 1903 and 1929 (its epilogue takes place at the end of World War II). It is primarily a chronicle of Russian intellectuals, but it contains some sixty characters from all walks of society. All form part of a complex and often symbolic plot, and the interdependence of individual destinies constitutes one of the main themes of the novel. Pasternak's heroes and heroines are shown not as puppets in a historical show, but as human beings obeying the laws of attraction and hatred, in an open universe of change and coincidence. This is particularly true of the love affair between Zhivago and Lara—a highly romantic and beautifully written story of chance, choice, joy and death.

Presented as a succession of scenes, dialogues, descriptions or reflections, ***Doctor Zhivago*** deliberately avoids any psychological analysis. Allusive and symbolic, fragmentary and impressionistic, the novel breaks away from the tradition of a well-structured "flowing narrative." It creates its own highly subjective form, with a peculiar mixture of dramatic and lyrical elements, with a combination of verbal simplicity, emotional complexity and philosophical depth. It has a strange, illuminating quality: a light shines in those beautiful pages (unfortunately dulled in an honest but uninspiring translation) in which realistic precision alternates with romantic, yet perfectly controlled, passion.

To those who are familiar with Soviet novels of the last twenty-five years, Pasternak's book comes as a surprise. The delight of this literary discovery is mixed with a sense of wonder: that Pasternak, who spent all his life in the Soviet environment, could resist all the external pressures and strictures and could conceive and execute a work of utter independence, of broad feeling and of an unusual imaginative power, amounts almost to a miracle. The Communist fiction of today always depicts man as a "political animal," whose acts and feelings are being determined by social and economic conditions.

In *Doctor Zhivago* man is shown in his individual essence, and his life is interpreted not as an illustration of historical events, but as a unique, wonderful adventure in its organic reality of sensations, thoughts, drives, instincts and strivings. This makes the book, despite all its topical hints and political statements, a basically anti-political work, in so far as it treats politics as fleeting, unimportant, and extols the unchangeable fundamentals of human mind, emotion and creativity. The main efforts of Zhivago, his family and his beloved Lara are bent toward protecting their privacy and defending their personal values against the distorting and destroying impact of events. They are victims and not agents of history, which is what makes their world so distinct and so contrary to that of revolutionary leaders. They are not reactionaries. Yurii Zhivago does not want to turn the clock back; he accepts social and economic changes brought about by the revolution.

His quarrel with the epoch is not political but philosophical and moral. He believes in human virtues formulated by the Christian dream, and he asserts the value of life, of beauty, of love and of nature. He rejects violence, especially when justified by abstract formulas and sectarian rhetoric. Only through goodness do we reach the supreme good, says Zhivago: if the beast in man could be overcome through fear and violence, our ideal would be a circus tamer with a whip and not Jesus Christ. Life cannot be forced into an artificial pattern by death sentences and prison camps, and it cannot be made better by legislation.

Zhivago laughs at the Partisan chief Liberius for whom "the interests of the revolution and the existence of the solar system are of the same importance." "Revolutionaries who take the law into their own hands are horrifying not because they are criminals but because they are like machines that have got out of control, like runaway trains," says Zhivago. And when a Communist speaks to him of Marxism as a science, he replies: "Marxism is too uncertain of its grounds to be a science. I do not know a movement more self-centered and further removed from the facts than Marxism. . . . Men in power are so anxious to establish the myth of their own infallibility that they do the utmost to ignore the truth. Politics do not appeal to me. I don't like people who don't care about truth."

Of course it would be wrong to attribute to Pasternak all the statements made by his protagonists and to identify the author completely with Doctor Zhivago. But there is no doubt that the basic attitudes of Pasternak's chief hero

do reflect the poet's intimate convictions. He believes that "every man is born a Faust, with a longing to grasp and experience and express everything in the world." And he sees history as only part of a larger order.

Every reader of *Doctor Zhivago* will be struck and enchanted by its beautiful descriptions of landscapes and seasons. Where time and space are the great protagonists of Tolstoy's *War and Peace,* nature is at the center of Pasternak's work. Before his death Zhivago "reflected again that he conceived of history, of what he called the course of history, not in the accepted way but by analogy with the vegetable kingdom." Leaves and trees change during the cycle of seasons in a forest, but the forest itself remains the same—and so does history with its basic immobility beneath all external changes. And so does life, which can be understood and felt and lived only within the framework of nature.

This organic, I would say cosmic, feeling gives a particular dimension to Pasternak's writing. Despite all the trials and horrors and death it depicts, despite the defeat of its heroes, his novel leaves the impression of strength and faith. It is a book of hope and vitality. And it is a book of great revelation. Even if we admit that communism represents a part of Russian life, mentality and history, it does not encompass all the Russian people and all the country's traditions and aspirations. A whole world of passion, yearnings, ideals and creativity exists next to or underneath the Communist mechanism. It lives, it stirs, it grows. Pasternak's novel is the genuine voice of this other Russia. (pp. 1, 42)

> *Marc Slonim, "But Man's Free Spirit Still Abides," in* The New York Times Book Review, *September 7, 1958, pp. 1, 42.*

B. Agapov and others

[*In the following letter, translated and excerpted by* The New York Times Book Review, *the members of the editorial board of the Soviet literary monthly* Novy mir *outline their reasons for rejecting* Doctor Zhivago.]

Boris Leonidovich:

We have read the manuscript of your novel *Doctor Zhivago* which you submitted to our magazine, and we would like to tell you with all frankness what we thought after reading it. We were both alarmed and distressed . . . The thing that disturbed us . . . is something that neither the editors nor the author can alter by deletions or alterations. We mean the spirit of the novel, its general tenor, the author's view of life, the real one or, at any rate, the one gathered by the reader. . . .

The spirit of your novel is that of non-acceptance of the socialist revolution. The general tenor of your novel is that the October Revolution, the Civil War and the social transformations involved did not give the people anything but suffering and destroyed the Russian intelligentsia, physically or morally. The burden of the author's views on the past of our country and, above all, the first decade after the October Revolution (for it is by the end of this decade—barring the epilogue—that the novel ends) is that the October Revolution was a mistake, that the participation in it of sympathizers from among the intelligentsia was an irreparable calamity, and that all that has happened since, evil.

To those who earlier had read your *Year 1905, Lieutenant Schmidt, Second Birth, Waves* and *Early Trains*—poetry which we, at any rate, thought imbued with a different spirit, a different tenor—your novel was a distressing experience. It would be no mistake, we think, to say that you regard the story of Doctor Zhivago's life and death as a story of the life and death of Russian intelligentsia, a story of its road to the Revolution and through the Revolution, and of its death as a result of the Revolution.

There is in the novel an easily discernible divide which, overriding your own arbitrary division of the work into two parts, lies somewhere between the first third of the novel and the rest of it. This divide—the year 1917—is a divide between the expected and the accomplished. Before it, your heroes expected something different from what actually occurred, and beyond it came what they had not expected and did not want and what, as you depict it, lead them to physical or moral death. . . .

On the one hand you admit—in a general, declaratory way—that the world of bourgeois property and bourgeois inequality is unjust, and you not only reject it as an ideal but actually regard it as unacceptable to the mankind of the future. But once you turn from general declarations to a description of life to actual people, these people . . . turn out to be, with extremely rare exceptions such as, for instance, the blackguard Komarovsky, the nicest, the kindest, the most subtle of spirits who do good, who seek, who suffer and who are actually incapable of hurting a fly.

This whole world of pre-Revolutionary bourgeois Russia, which you disclaim in general, turns out to be quite acceptable to you when you get down to a specific description of it. More, it turns out to be poignantly dear to your author's heart. The equally unacceptable thing about it is some general iniquity of exploitation and inequality which, however, remains behind the scenes while everything that actually happens in your novel turns out, in the final analysis, to be most idyllic: Capitalists donate to the Revolution and live honestly, intellectuals enjoy complete freedom of thought and are intellectually independent of the bureaucratic machine of the czarist regime, poor girls find rich and selfless protectors, while sons of workmen and yard keepers find no difficulty in getting an education . . . The novel gives no real picture of the country of the people, nor, consequently, does it explain why revolution became inevitable in Russia, nor reveal a measure of the intolerable suffering and social injustice that had led the people to it.

Most of the characters . . . talk about the Revolution . . . but they can also do very well without it, and there was nothing in their life before the Revolution that was intolerable physically or spiritually. And there are no other people in the novel (if we are to confine ourselves to characters who enjoy the author's sympathy and who are drawn with anything like a similar measure of penetration and detail). . . .

And then comes, or rather explodes, the Revolution. It explodes in the faces of your heroes unexpectedly because—for all their talk—they did not expect it, and when it comes, the Revolution and its working plunge them into amazement. In speaking of how the Revolution enters

your novel, it is even hard to distinguish between the February and the October Revolutions. In your novel it all comes out as pretty much the same thing, as 1917 in general, when at first the changes were not too abrupt and did not disrupt too noticeably the life of your "truth-seeking individuals," your heroes; and then, later, the changes went farther and cut deeper, more painfully. Their life became increasingly dependent on the tremendous, unprecedented things happening in the country, and as this dependence increased it infuriated them and made them regret what had happened. . . .

It is hard to imagine that first in the February Revolution and then in the October Revolution, which divided so many people into different camps, that the positions of the heroes of a novel about that period are not identified. It is hard to believe that the people leading an intellectual life and occupying a certain position in society would not identify their attitude in one way or another at that time in regard to such events as the overthrow of autocracy, the advent to power of Kerensky, the October uprising, the seizure of power by the Soviets and the dispersal of the Constituent Assembly.

And yet the characters in your novel do not openly state their views of any of these events, they do not give any straightforward estimate of the events through which the country lived at the period. . . .

The truth, to our mind, is that your "truth-seeking individuals" become increasingly furious with the mounting revolution not because they do not accept some of its specific forms, such as the October uprising or the dispersal of the Constituent Assembly, but because of the various kinds of personal discomfort they personally are doomed to by it.

Faced with an actual revolution . . . these "truth-seeking individuals" . . . to all appearances . . . continued to lead a spiritual life, but their attitude toward the Revolution, and primarily their actions, become increasingly contingent on the measure of personal discomfort brought about by the Revolution such as hunger, cold, overcrowded living quarters, disruption of the cozy, well-fed pre-war existence to which they have become accustomed. It is hard to name outright another work in which heroes with pretensions to higher spiritual values should, in the years of the greatest events, speak so much about . . . comforts and discomforts of life as in your novel.

Your heroes, and particularly Doctor Zhivago himself, spend the years of the Revolution and the Civil War in search of relative well-being and tranquillity, and this amid the vicissitudes of struggle, amid general devastation and ruin. They are not cowards, physically; you go out of your way as author to stress this. But at the same time their only goal is to preserve their own lives, and it is this that guides them in all their principal actions. It is the knowledge that their lives are not secure under the conditions of the Revolution and Civil War that leads them to a growing resentment of all that happens. They are not property-grabbers, gourmets or sybarites. They need all of this not for its own sake but merely as a means of safely continuing their spiritual life.

What life? Why, the one they led in the past, for nothing new enters their spiritual life and nothing changes it. They regard the possibility of continuing it without outside interference as the greatest blessing not only for themselves but for all mankind, and since the Revolution steadfastly requires them to act, to say "for" or "against," they turn in self-defense from a feeling of alienation from the Revolution to a feeling of active hostility toward it. . . .

So far we have not touched on the artistic aspect of your novel. . . . There are quite a few first-rate pages, especially where you describe the Russian nature with great realism and poetic power. There are many clearly inferior pages, lifeless and didactically dry. They are especially numerous in the second half of the novel.

Yet we would not like to dwell on this aspect since, as we have mentioned at the beginning of the letter, the essence of our disagreement with you has nothing to do with aesthetic wrangling. You have written a political novel-sermon par excellence. You have conceived it as a work to be placed unreservedly and sincerely at the service of certain political aims, and this—which is the main thing for you—has naturally focused our attention as well.

However painful it is for us, we had to call a spade a spade in this letter. It seems to us that your novel is profoundly unfair; historically prejudiced in the description of the Revolution, the Civil War and the post-Revolutionary years; that it is profoundly anti-democratic and alien to any concept of the interests of the people. All this taken as a whole stems from your standpoint as a man who tries to prove in his novel that, far from having any positive significance in the history of our people and mankind, the October Socialist Revolution brought nothing but evil and hardship.

As people whose standpoint is diametrically opposed to yours, we naturally believe that the publication of your novel in the columns of the magazine Novy Mir is out of the question.

As for your irritation with which the novel is written—and not your ideological position as such—we want to remind you, recalling that you have works to your record in which a great deal differs from what you have recently said, in the words of your heroine addressed to Doctor Zhivago: "You have changed, you know. Before you judged the Revolution not so sharply and without irritation."

But then, of course, the main thing is not irritation, because, after all is said and done, it is merely a concomitant of the ideas long rejected, untenable and doomed to perdition. If you are able to think about it seriously, please do so. In spite of everything, we wish that very much.

Enclosed is the manuscript of your novel *Doctor Zhivago.*

> *B. Agapov and others, "A Letter of Rejection: The Case against 'Dr. Zhivago',"* in The New York Times Book Review, *December 7, 1958, p. 6.*

Renato Poggioli

[Pasternak] was born in Moscow in 1890. His mother was a gifted pianist, his father a well-known painter, who illustrated Tolstoj's novel *Resurrection,* and taught at the local Academy of Fine Arts. The young Pasternak devoted himself to the arts cultivated by his parents, especially music, which he studied under no less a master than the famous composer Skrjabin. He also studied philosophy at the Universities of Moscow and Marburg. . . . He began his poetic career at a precocious age, in that feverish advance-guard atmosphere which marked the first prewar era. He was one of a special group of Moscow Futurists who were connected with Khlebnikov, but who also went back to other models, as recent as Ivan Konevskoj or as remote as Jazykov. That group took its name from the almanac *Centrifuga,* published in 1913, to which Pasternak contributed his earliest poems. The young poet was destined to keep a loose association with the Futurist movement, and later contributed to the *LEF* of Majakovskij. In 1914, he published his first volume of verse, **The Twin in the Clouds,** which remained unnoticed. His second book, **Above the Barriers,** appeared in 1917, and was already the work of an expert craftsman, although it did not bear the imprint of his more mature genius.

It was to be Pasternak's two succeeding volumes that would reveal the rarity and novelty of his gift. In 1922, when the poems collected under the title **My Sister, Life,** which had been written in 1917 and circulated for years in manuscript, finally appeared in book form, they marked the emergence of a major talent. In 1923, Pasternak published his second important collection, **Themes and Variations,** in which his style became at once more sober and more extreme. The best work from these two volumes, which exercised a perceptible influence not only on younger poets but also on the more established writers, was afterwards collected in **Two Books** (1927). After a long interval, Pasternak returned to lyric poetry with **Second Birth** (1933), which was followed in the same year by **Poems,** the first full collection of his verse.

It was in that period of time that the poet's ordeal began. He remained steadfastly loyal to his calling within a social order admitting no other loyalty than to itself. He had to fight singlehandedly a sustained rear-guard action in order to avoid surrendering unconditionally to the political pressure of the regime, augmented by the vicious attacks of sycophantic critics, by the whispering campaigns and the outright calumnies of enemies and rivals. The main accusations leveled against him were that he had committed the unspeakable crimes of individualism and formalism, and that he had shown indifference, and even hostility, to Marxist ideology. His stubborn refusal to obey the party's "general line," and to change his poetry into an instrument of propaganda, was branded as a betrayal. The literary press treated him as an outlaw; the writers' association, as an outcast.

Yet, in a spirit not of compromise but of humility, Pasternak tried to give poetical expression to his desire to connect himself with the will of the Russian people. He did so by trying to understand the Russian present through the perspective of history, and in 1926 he published his poem **Spektorskij,** in which, following similar experiments by Belyj and Blok, he used the protagonist's character, whose name gives its title to this work, as an autobiographical mirror, reflecting not only the poet's personality, but also the society and the age out of which he had come. In the same years Pasternak wrote and published (1927) a cycle of lyrical fragments, re-evoking, under the title **The Year 1905,** the political turmoil of that year. That rhapsody was followed by a long, simple episode, **Lieuten-**

ant Shmidt, more epic in tone and content, retelling the story of the mutiny of the battleship *Potemkin* in the Black Sea, with a naked power reminiscent of Ejzenshtejn's film.

It was in the same period that Pasternak composed his prose tales, which he collected twice, under the titles *Stories* and *Airways,* in 1925 and 1933. The most important of them is the opening piece, **"The Childhood of Ljuvers,"** written originally in 1918, in a tone and style that Western critics have compared to Proust's, although it is more reminiscent of *Malte Laurids Brigge* by Rainer Maria Rilke. (The Austrian poet had remained a lifelong friend of the Pasternak family from the time of his journeys to Russia, when the elder Pasternak had painted his portrait.) The theme of this story is feminine puberty, the foreshadowings of womanhood in the body and soul of a young girl, which the writer evokes with psychological subtlety and poetic insight. In 1931 Pasternak published his literary and intellectual autobiography, which he entitled, with enigmatic irony, **The Safe-Conduct.** The narrative is written in the first person, yet the ego of the narrator never intrudes and often retires into the background, giving way to a detached representation of persons and places, of ideas and things. The last part of the book is dominated by the figure of Majakovskij, acting like a mask or a ghost. In the finale, which recalls the official funeral of that poet, the palpable, almost bodily presence of that monstrous abstraction, "our Russian state," haunts the scene. Quite understandably, the authorities never permitted a reprint or a new edition of **The Safe-Conduct.**

In the following years, Pasternak managed to evade the required lauding of the regime and still function as a writer by devoting almost all his energies to translating. In his youth he had translated many foreign writers, especially German, from the Romantics to the Expressionists, but later he was attracted to more exotic models, and in 1935 published a rich anthology of poets from that Caucasian region which is called Gruzija in Russia, and Georgia in the West. More recently he tried his hand at the tragedies of Shakespeare, producing splendid versions of such plays as *Hamlet, Macbeth, King Lear, Othello, Romeo and Juliet,* and *Antony and Cleopatra.* Yet even then he never gave up his own writing, although very little of it appeared in print after the publication of his **Collected Poems** in 1932 and 1936. A decade later he took advantage of the short-lived calm after the Second World War to publish two slim collections (the second is but an expansion of the first), entitled **On Early Trains** (1943) and **The Vast Earth** (1946). They were followed by a long, silent spell which the poet broke by issuing his translation of Goethe's *Faust* and later by publishing a few new poems in literary periodicals, during the brief thaw following Stalin's death.

Despite its native originality and independent growth, Pasternak's poetry still seems to preserve the traces of its early connection with Futurism. What ties his poetry to the Futuristic experiment, and especially to the manner of Khlebnikov, is his conception and treatment of the word. While the typical Decadent or Symbolist poet seems to control the music of language by yielding to it, Pasternak masters his medium by doing violence to the very nature of poetic speech. His idiom is like a mosaic made of broken pieces. The fragments are shapeless, and if they finally fit within the pattern of a line, or within the design of a poem,

it is only because of the poet's will. The cement holding them together is either syntax or rhythm; more frequently, both. From his early beginnings, Pasternak tightened the syntax of Russian poetic speech as no modern poet had ever done. At the same time, in reaction against both the vagueness of late Symbolistic verse . . . , he chose to use, with strictness and rigor, duly regular and even closed metrical forms. In doing so he succeeded in reconciling within his poetry the demands of both the old and the new. Like all the most successful figures of the advance guard, Pasternak (who is its only surviving representative in Russia today) was thus able to prove that tradition also must play a role in the revolutions of art.

There is an obvious parallel between this historical function and the internal structure of the poetry of Pasternak. With terms taken from the vocabulary of our "new critics," one could say that his verse constantly aims at tension and paradox. His poems are equally ruled by passion and intelligence, or rather, by a reciprocal interplay of emotion and wit. This is why Prince Mirskij compared him to John Donne, by which that critic probably meant that Pasternak's poetry is "metaphysical" not in the original, but in the modern and revived, sense of that term. Yet his work is better understood if placed within the immediate and local tradition from which it sprang. If we do so, we may find that the concept of "transmental poetry" is the frame of reference we need. We know already that in their attempt to create a poetry purely verbal in essence, some of the so-called Cubo-Futurists wrote poems in what they named "transmental tongue," or in newly coined words without meaning, and with no other semantic value than that of their sound effects. The experiment was bound to fail; poetry can never become, at least in the sense that painting or sculpture can, an abstract art. Poetry cannot but be either expressionistic or ideational, and Pasternak made poetry nonrepresentational, so to speak, by forcing it to be both things at once. One could say that he succeeded where the Cubo-Futurists had failed, by using, instead of nonsense language, a highly complex linguistic mosaic, made of an interplay of denotative and connotative values: or, more simply, by employing a diction ruled at once by mental balance and emotional stress. It is only in such a context that one might define his style as a modern Baroque, reducing to sense and order a verbal matter apparently incongruous and absurd.

Pasternak's poetry, to quote a line from his favorite foreign master and friend, Rainer Maria Rilke, seems thus to lead *zum Arsenal den unbedingten Dinge.* Yet in the process it changes all the nondescript objects cluttering the world of experience not into abstract symbols, but into living, suffering, humanlike creatures. The anthropomorphic pathos of Pasternak's imagination brings him closer to the Romantics than any other of his immediate predecessors with the exclusion of Blok. The poet must have been aware of this since, unlike his great and distant contemporary, Khodasevich, who found a master in Pushkin, he sought a model in Lermontov, the Russian poet who felt and understood better than any other the tears of things, and who would perhaps have approved of Pasternak's claim that "one composes verses with sobs." It is equally significant that in recent times Pasternak has shown some interest in Shelley, whose vision he finds akin to that of Blok. Yet Pasternak's neoromanticism is strange and novel: so strange and novel that it can be compared only to some of the most novel works of modern art. (pp. 321-26)

The artistic game of Pasternak consists in a sort of balancing act: or in the attempt to fix in a precarious, and yet firm, equilibrium, a congeries of heterogeneous objects, of vibrant and labile things. His poetry seems to pass, almost at the same time, through two different and even opposite phases. The first is a moment of eruption and irruption, of frenzy and paroxysm; and second, which often overlaps the first, is the moment when matter seems to harden and freeze. Burning rivers of lava congeal at a nod. The sound and fury of lightning suddenly become, as in the poem so named, "a thunder eternally instantaneous." Fires are extinguished at a breath. Showers and thunderstorms abruptly stop; floods suddenly dry up. Often the same poem seems to be written now in hot, now in cold, blood. This dualism may perhaps be traced in, or symbolized by, the early education of the poet, which was both philosophical and musical. Yet, while his music ends in dissonance, and his logic leads to dissent, such a double discordance resolves itself into a harmony of its own.

The raw material of Pasternak's poetry is introspection. Yet Pasternak treats the self as object rather than as subject. . . . Sometimes he seems to treat the psyche as a neutral and an alien being, to be seldom, and if possible only indirectly, approached. Hence the negative hyperbole by which he claims, in one of his poems, to have appealed in prayer to his soul only twice in a hundred years, while other men do so at every instant. Pasternak, with the firm hand of a hunter or tamer, always holds his own spirit in his power, like a fluttering, wounded bird, and often encloses it in the solid cage of a stanza, from which the winged prisoner vainly tries to escape through the broken mesh of a rhyme.

Many critics have remarked that Pasternak looks at the world with the eyes of one newly born. It would be better to say that he looks at it with *reborn* eyes. As suggested by the title of one of his books, poetry is for him a "second birth," through which man sees again the familiar as strange, and the strange as familiar. Yet, whether strange or familiar, every object is unique. To give the effect of this uniqueness, the poet paints every single thing as if it were a monad, unwilling or unable to escape from the rigid frame of its own contours. Such an effect is primarily achieved through the harshness and hardness of his imagery, through the frequent ellipses of his speech, through the staccato quality of his meter. Rhythmically, he prefers a line heavily hammered, where no stress is blurred, and every beat is pounded as in a heel dance. He fails, however, to extend this rapid, metallic quality to rhyme. . . . (pp. 326-27)

Though some of his poems are romantically set against the lofty mountains of the Caucasian landscape, Pasternak usually prefers a restricted, bourgeois, and prosaic scenery, such as a city park, a country orchard, a home garden, or a villa in the suburbs. Yet even "back-yards, ponds, palings" are not mere backdrops, but, as the poet says, "categories of passions, hoarded in the human heart." His poetry thus leans toward a highly personal version of the pathetic fallacy, involving in his case not only nonhuman creatures, such as animals and plants, but also inanimate things, or manmade objects. For many of his poems Pasternak chooses, like Mallarmé in his *poèmes*

d'intérieur, indoor settings. Yet, unlike the French poet, the Russian introduces within the four walls of a room cosmic powers and elemental forces. This is especially true in the cycle "Themes and Variations," which is part of the book by the same title. In the third piece of this cycle Pasternak describes the now empty study where Pushkin has just finished writing his famous poem "The Prophet." Great geographical and historical landmarks, from the arctic city of Archangel to the river Ganges, from the Sahara to the Egyptian Sphinx, seem to witness in silence, along with the molten wax dropping from a burning candle, the drying of the ink on the manuscript.

In this, as in other poems, Pasternak surprises not only by a violent association of disparate elements, but by the even more violent dissociation of each one of them from the frame of reference to which it naturally belongs. The ripe pear which one of his poems describes while falling to the ground along with its leafy stem and torn branch can be taken as an emblem of his art. Hence the frequency in his verse of such words and ideas as "fracture" or "breach." At the end of the closing poem of the cycle **"Rupture"** (meaning here a lovers' quarrel, or their break), even the opening of a window is equated with the opening of a vein. In the same piece the poet transfers the trauma of life to an uncreated thing: for instance, to the piano, which "licks its foam," as if it were a human being in an epileptic fit. Yet even in metaphors like these the poet transcends both pathos and bathos, reshaping the disorder of experience into a vision of his own. If he succeeds in doing so, it is because in his poetry (as he said in **The Safe-Conduct**) the author remains silent and lets the image speak. In this ability to infuse words with passion, rather than passion with words, Pasternak has no rival among his contemporaries, and, among the poets of the previous generation, he yields only to Aleksandr Blok. (pp. 327-28)

Pasternak's [verse] is dramatic and pathetic, aiming at conveying the poet's vital experience in psychic terms. His metaphors tend to express the shock and wonder of being in abridged and concentrated form. In his recent **Notes on Translating Shakespearean Tragedies** (1954), the poet bases his theory of metaphor on the truth which the old saying *ars longa vita brevis* seems to have stated once for all; "hence metaphors and poetry," says Pasternak, and concludes: "imagery is but the shorthand of the spirit." As hinted in these words, Pasternak views metaphor not as an emblem or symbol, which suggests and conceals, but as a graphic scheme or a sketchy outline of the experienced thing. This may well be the reason why this artist has never indulged, like so many modern poets, in the false mystique of his own calling and craft. Poetry is for him not the revelation of a higher harmony, but simply the direct expression of "the dissonance of this word."

A poetry so understood gives the immediate sense of a reality endowed with no other glamor than that of being reality itself; poetry, as Pasternak says, is "a suburb, not a refrain." The dreams of such a poet are made of the stuff life is made of. One could then say that this artist has always unconsciously followed the principle which he has recently uttered through the fictional protagonist of his last book: "Art never seemed to me an object or aspect of form, but rather a mysterious and hidden component of content." Such a statement indicates the importance of that book, which is worth discussing at length, even though the medium in which the poet chose to write it is not lyric verse, but narrative prose.

It was in April 1945 that Pasternak announced in the Leningrad literary journal *The Banner* the imminent completion of a work in progress, entitled **Doctor Zhivago.** The author defined it as "a novel in prose," an obvious play on the subtitle "novel in verse" of Pushkin's *Evgenij Onegin.* The announcement was followed by a series of poems, supposedly written by the novel's protagonist. . . . Although the poet declared that the series was destined to close the novel as a fictitious appendix of posthumous papers or documents, through which the reader would understand better the personage to whom the writer attributed their authorship, everybody read those pieces as if their real author had written them in an autobiographical vein rather than in a fictional key. Later on, when the "thaw" which followed Stalin's death was already over, Pasternak submitted the complete draft to the Moscow literary monthly *New World,* but its editors (including such well-known writers as Konstantin Fedin and Konstantin Simonov) rejected the novel with a letter which convinced Pasternak that his book could never appear in Soviet Russia without changes so radical as to disfigure it. Shortly afterward the author handed the manuscript to a scout of Giangiacomo Feltrinelli, an Italian publisher with left-wing leanings. Notwithstanding his political sympathies, and despite official Soviet protests, Signor Feltrinelli managed to issue in 1957 an Italian translation of the original text. This was followed a year later by versions in French, English, and other languages, many of which became best sellers shortly after they appeared, making of the book a world-wide success. (pp. 328-30)

Doctor Zhivago, this new and challenging product of Pasternak's talent, is huge in size and broad in scope. The narrative rehearses the life and fate of its hero from his childhood to his premature death on the eve of the great Stalinist purge. Raised in the idealism of the early part of the century, Zhivago trains himself to become both a doctor and a poet, thus following the double call of charity and grace. He marries, but the Revolution forces him to settle in the Urals, where he is forever separated from his family and is made to serve as a medical officer in a Red guerrilla unit during the Civil War. His only consolation is his love for Lara, an old Moscow acquaintance, who represents in the novel the intuitive wisdom of life. When the crisis is over, he returns to Moscow, and in 1929 he dies there of a heart attack.

The narrative of Dr. Zhivago's existence merges with that of other, numberless characters, originally connected as neighbors, relatives, or friends, and who, in the course of the story, meet again in the most surprising circumstances. Although traditional in structure, the novel lacks a well-made plot: coincidence works beyond the limits of verisimilitude, taxing the credulity of the reader, and failing to raise the whims of chance or the writer's fancy to the level of either destiny or providence. Deprived of an epic or tragic design, the narrative unfolds as a rhapsody: and this explains why all its beauties are but fragmentary ones. There are many memorable episodes, but the novel's high point is the section describing the hibernation of the Red partisans in the wilderness of the far North, and the attempt by some of their wives to reach them by cutting a path through the snow and ice of a primeval forest.

The protagonist survives many physical trials, besides that of winter; yet he dies still young, worn out by an inner ordeal, wasted by the fever of life. Up to the end he faces each test with both the passive compliance of his will and the active resistance of his conscience. He acts at once like a witness and a victim, never like an avenger or judge. His mind often says "yea" to the reality to which his heart says "nay." Ivan Karamazov accepted God while rejecting the world He had created; Doctor Zhivago similarly accepts the postulate of the Revolution while rejecting many of its corollaries. From this viewpoint there is no doubt that the protagonist represents the author's outlook. The writer refuses, however, to intervene directly in the narrative; he thinks only with the thoughts of his characters, and speaks with no other words than theirs. Yet we hear his unique voice in the descriptive passages, and especially in those vivid images by which he constantly suggests to the reader that man, as well as time, is out of joint.

Perhaps the only characters who speak solely for themselves are those representing the younger generation in the novel's epilogue. The latter projects Russian life as seen now, twenty years after the death of the protagonist, in the immediate aftermath of the Second World War. There we meet again also some of the novel's main characters. The regime has recalled them before their term from deportation and exile; and they have rehabilitated themselves politically by defending the fatherland against the German invaders. It is difficult to say whether Pasternak considers these men and their sons as the children of the old bondage or the harbingers of a freer covenant. In a sense they seem to turn more toward the past than toward the future: perhaps they are also, as the author says of many others, naïve and innocent slaves who cannot help idealizing the slavery which is still their lot. Survivors of one upheaval, they may well disappear in the next one.

Despite all appearances to the contrary, it is this perplexing epilogue, more than any other parallel, which reveals that Pasternak wrote **Doctor Zhivago**—as other readers have already remarked—on the pattern of *War and Peace.* . . . Yet, despite its strong ties with Tolstoj's masterpiece, **Doctor Zhivago** is not a historical novel in the sense of *War and Peace,* since it deals with the contemporary age, an epoch not yet closed. Hence its epilogue is problematic rather than prophetic. Yet this difference is not important; whether or not it is a historical novel, **Doctor Zhivago,** like *War and Peace,* is written against history. What really matters is that Pasternak's protest rests on other grounds, and may well contain a message just the opposite of Tolstoj's. In *War and Peace* all the violence and cunning of history ultimately yield to the law of nature, to the universal principles of life and death, to the wars and peaces of being, which reduce strategy and diplomacy to senseless games, vainly attempting to shape the destiny of the human race. In Tolstoj's view mankind survives the ordeal of history in the wholeness and singleness of the species. The immortal cell of human life is the family, which triumphs, always and everywhere, over the destructive force of that monster which men call "reason of state." In Tolstoj's novel the issue is simplified, since the "reason of state" is symbolized by the aggressive imperialism of a foreign power; hence patriotism coincides with the moral and practical interests of that patriarchal household which for Tolstoj represents an ideal way of life.

Pasternak, however, sees the perfection of human existence in the person, in the inviolate integrity of its inner conscience. Such a form of being implies the refusal of all constraints, including the ties of blood and the bonds of the heart. This is why his hero must go his way even though against his own will, never to rejoin his wife and offspring; and perhaps his almost fleshless love for Lara should be seen as the sign of a personal destiny which must unfold itself in a cold and distant solitude, far away from the comforting warmth of the fireplace, from the charmed circle of the family nest. *Doctor Zhivago* differs from *War and Peace* in its view of the human condition; it differs, also, in its interpretation of the function of history. In Pasternak's novel history manifests itself as civil war and domestic strife, in a "permanent revolution" which is at once material and spiritual warfare, a total struggle without quarter or truce. Through technology, ideology, and social planning, history is now able to submit to its will the nation, the class, and the family—perhaps the world itself. But its weakest victim may be also its most elusive enemy, and that victim and enemy is the single person, the individual soul. Hence the voice protesting here is the one that says not "we," but "I." Here it is not Mother Russia, but one of her orphan children, who, like a fairy-tale Kutuzov, defends the homeland of the soul, the little realm of personal dignity and private life, first by trading time for space rather than space for time, and then by withdrawing into other dimensions than those. Such a stubborn retreat of the spirit, or, if we wish, the passive resistance of an inflexible soul which repels the temptation as well as the threat of all violence, is *Doctor Zhivago*'s main motif, perhaps its only one; and it is the exceptional nobility of this theme that turns Pasternak's novel, if not into a masterpiece, at least into a spiritual document of great significance, which brings to us a very different message from that of *War and Peace*. Nothing conveys better the sense of this difference than the two plants symbolizing the "tree of life" in each novel. In one we have the old oak which Prince Andrej suddenly sees rejuvenated by the sap of spring, with its once bare trunk and despoiled limbs covered by a crown of new leaves; in the other we have that evergreen thicket, almost buried by ice and snow, holding high a branch full of berries in the heart of the Siberian winter. Pasternak's "golden bough," unlike Tolstoj's, is thus a burning bramble that shines and consumes itself mystically and ecstatically in the desert of the self, in the cold land of the spirit.

Despite the urgency and immediacy of its message, *Doctor Zhivago* must be viewed as an old-fashioned novel even if looked at from a less superficial perspective than that of its conventional structure. Its spiritual quality may be conveyed by saying that [*Doctor Zhivago* fulfills] Goethe's definition of the novel form as a "subjective epos." . . . [Yet this] "subjective epos" fails to grow and ripen into a *Bildungsroman*. The reason for this is that its main character, who acts as if he were both accepting and refusing the lesson of history, seems already to know all too well the lessons of life. The novel treats all events or experiences as if they were not dreams or crises, but tests or ordeals, which the protagonist undergoes more like a martyr than like a hero, and which he overcomes with the help of a grace which is not of this world. This, as well as the fact that all its figures are not painted in the round but drawn like abstract, allegorical outlines, turns *Doctor Zhivago* into a kind of morality play. It is this quality of

the novel's vision that fully justifies Pasternak's use of religious imagery and Christian symbolism. Such imagery and symbolism need not be explained as polemical devices, or as the signs of the author's conversion to another creed. Like many a poet raised in another faith, or who lost his religious beliefs, Pasternak seems to have found no better language than the one which the Christian imagination shaped forever to convey the sacraments and the redemptions of the soul.

In an article published in *Partisan Review* immediately after the Italian edition of the novel, Nicola Chiaromonte described *Doctor Zhivago* as "a meditation on history, that is, on the infinite distance which separates the human conscience from the violence of history, and permits a man to remain a man. . . . " This is true, and well said, and it is no less true that the extension and depth of such a meditation represents something new in Pasternak's work. There is no doubt that in such poems as *The Year 1905* and *Lieutenant Schmidt* the poet had tried to come to terms with historical reality, rather than to face it as a critic and a judge. Only once did he express his sense of alienation from Soviet society: in that page of his long autobiographical essay *The Safe-Conduct* where he described Majakovskij's funeral, haunted by the weird presence of that state power which the dead poet had served only to be crushed by it. As for Pasternak's lyrical poems, they had often expressed in passing (and not without a sense of guilt) the poet's attempt to shun or to transcend the historical experience of his nation and time. Nothing exemplifies better such an attempt than an early piece dealing with the secluded workings of the poetic imagination, where the poet's voice suddenly bursts out with the question: "Children, what century is it, outside in our courtyard?" That question, both sophisticated and naïve, hints that the poet was then convinced that the artistic mind is innately indifferent to the dimension of time, to the category of history. Later, however, Pasternak seemed to realize that such an indifference is impossible, and that the self was bound to merge, whether willingly or unwillingly, with the historical process. He once conveyed the sense of this awareness in a famous line where he significantly spoke in the first person plural, although that plural refers to a few, rather than to the many: "We were people: we are epochs now." But it is true that in another poem he claimed that the poet could at least evade contemporary history by projecting himself into the future, or, as he said, by escaping like steam, through the chinks of fate, from the burning peat of dead time.

Many similar statements could be quoted from Pasternak's earlier and later verse: yet, taken together, all of them sound like apologies which the poet addressed not so much to the regime as to public opinion, or rather, to an elite able to understand equally the reason of poetry and the reason of state. Yet the poet seemed to know, at least in the depth of his heart, that any reconciliation between art and politics was fundamentally impossible. Hence that sense of both pride and shame in all of Pasternak's statements on the subject: the pride of his unconquerable loneliness, and the shame of being unable to pay the Revolution the tribute which all pay, and which may well be justly due it.

Pasternak continued to grapple with these questions during the long years of a silence which was at least in part self-imposed; and at the end of that period he reached the conclusion that lyrical poetry had become too limited and subjective a vehicle to allow him to express what was no longer a purely private attitude toward the problematics of revolution and the dialectics of history. After presenting his poet's case in verse, he felt that now he should present the case of man in prose. The writer was still in an apologetic mood, but the apology he now wanted to make was a far more universal one; and he wished to address it, beyond official Russia, to the Russian people, and even to his Western brethren. He felt that the proper vehicle for such an apology, which was also to be a protest, could be only fictional and narrative prose, the traditional tool of the Russian literary genius, which has found the master road of its ethos and art in that "classical" and "critical" realism of which Socialist Realism was but a monstrous caricature. If Pushkin's "poetry" had never denied "truth," so the "truth" of the "classical" and "critical" realists had never denied "poetry"; and this may help us to understand why, the first time Pasternak spoke in public of the novel he was then writing, he called *Doctor Zhivago,* with a formula which was not a mere pleonasm, a "novel in prose."

The poet himself recently explained this new aesthetic and moral view in a reply to a series of questions submitted to him by a South American magazine: "Fragmentary, personal poems are hardly suited to meditations on such obscure, new, and solemn events. Only prose and philosophy can attempt to deal with them. . . . " Here Pasternak seems to re-echo, unknowingly, Sartre's statement that prose, unlike poetry, should always be *engagée;* nor does it matter that *engagement* for Pasternak involves different, and even opposite values: not social obligations but moral ones. Pasternak seems to feel that such an *engagement* was impossible while he was only a lyrical poet; and this is why the author of *Doctor Zhivago* spoke disdainfully of his poetic work in his reply to that questionnaire. By doing so he merely underscored something at which he had hinted in the novel itself. Nothing in *Doctor Zhivago* has a more autobiographical ring than the comment on the literary career of the protagonist. According to his creator, Doctor Zhivago "had been dreaming of writing a book on life, in which to express the most wonderful things he had seen and understood in the world. Yet for such a book he was too young, and meanwhile he went on writing poems, like a painter who all his life draws studies for a painting still in his mind."

Yet if these words apply to the author himself, as the latter undoubtedly meant them to do, then what dictates the truth they may contain is not insight, but hindsight. It would be unfair to Pasternak both as man and writer to accept his retrospective claim that his poetic production was but a gradual preparation for *Doctor Zhivago,* which is a moral act and a psychological document of great value, but not the single culmination of his work. His poems are more than simple preludes to the novel; and though *Doctor Zhivago* towers over all Soviet fiction, this is due not only to Pasternak's stature as a novelist but also to the mediocrity of his rivals. What I prefer to emphasize is that this "novel in prose" proves more passionately and eloquently, yet in a less spirited and witty way than his poems, the same truth: that even in Communist Russia there are moral "corners" or spiritual "pockets" permitting the cultivation of the most bourgeois of all psycholog-

ical activities, which could be defined in literary terms as the "sentimental education" of the soul.

In his poetry and his earlier prose, no less than in this novel, Pasternak had asserted and defended the private rights of the spirit in a forthright manner, without a wrong idealization, or a false mystique. . . . He has always known, as he says in one of his poems, that when in contact with reality human passion cannot heed the warning which reads "Fresh paint: do not touch." In short, Pasternak has never longed after a purity which is not of this world. He is one of those who feel that the soul is too rooted in life to be disinfected, as if it were merely a wounded limb. We may "purge" the soul, rather than "cleanse" it; and this is the catharsis which *Doctor Zhivago* in the end finally achieves. Perhaps after such an act of purgation, the author might feel free to publish poetry again. Like a Jonas delivered from the whale, he may now walk again on the mainland of his art. If we must hope that he will do so, it is because Pasternak's poems are more vital and exciting than this novel, which lacks the inner tension of his previous works in verse or prose, so challenging in their inborn advance-guardism. (pp. 330-38)

In view of this, it is perhaps worth remarking that when the Swedish Academy decided, in October 1958, to crown Boris Pasternak with the second of the two Nobel Prizes ever granted to Russian writers, it chose to honor him as poet as well as novelist. That, after having gratefully accepted that deserved honor, Pasternak was forced by the vilifications of the Soviet press, and by such official acts as his expulsion from the writers' association, first to reject the greatest of all international literary awards, and then to address a pathetic and noble petition to Krushchev, lest the regime deprive him of his birthright, of the privilege to live, work, and die on his native soil, is another story. There is no doubt that it was this scandal, even more than the circumstances that had led the writer to publish his novel abroad, that stirred in the West the heated controversy now going under the name of Pasternak's case. Sad as it is, the tale cannot be forgotten, and should be retold again and again, not only in admiration, to bless the gift of the poet, but also in anger, to curse that party or state power which, like another Moloch, demands every day a new holocaust. Not content with the thousands of nameless victims on which it has built its jails, its fortresses, and its factories, the Soviet regime seems to require the public sacrifice of their life, liberty, or happiness even by those artists, who, like Majakovskij and Esenin, or like Akhmatova and Pasternak, either remained the loyal friends of the Revolution, or refused to become its active enemies. (pp. 338-39)

Renato Poggioli, "Poets of Today," in his The Poets of Russia: 1890-1930, *Cambridge, Mass.: Harvard University Press, 1960, pp. 316-42.*

Nicola Chiaromonte

According to Edmund Wilson, *Doctor Zhivago* is an elegiac poem rather than a novel. His knowledge of the original Russian text makes his judgment particularly persuasive. In translation, too, the rhythm of Pasternak's story is the rhythm of poetry: events do not take place in the dimension of ordinary time, which is proper to the novel, but are suspended somewhere outside time. The author tends to sing rather than tell, and he seems ill at ease in those parts of the novel in which he has to deal with the details of his story. In fact, his forte is not the representation and contrasting of character but evocative perception, the creation of an image or a situation—a moment seized and fixed at its most vibrant and luminous. His comments on the meaning of the events he is relating are a blend of the visionary and the sententious so that, more often than not, they are declamations rather than reasoned reflections.

Nevertheless, *Doctor Zhivago* was composed as a novel, and a novel it is, not only because it is written in prose, but because it sets out to tell the story of a given society at a given time, which is the principal aim of any novel.

In a short essay on the nature of poetry, Roger Caillois remarks that, 'poetry at its origin was everything one wanted to preserve intact in the memory. The rest was nothing but interchangeable words.' Let us say, then, that *Doctor Zhivago* attempts 'to preserve intact in the memory' that which time and violence threatened to wipe out—the great upheaval of the Russian Revolution as it was actually lived by the 'defeated'—all those who were cast on the scrap heap of history. That the aim of the novelist is to rescue them from oblivion explains the elegiac tone of the narrative.

But since this commemorative poem was also conceived as a novel, as a 'true story', the author does not shun the 'interchangeable words' that no story can do without, nor does he avoid polemics and moral discourse.

The ambiguity of the form of *Doctor Zhivago* reflects Pasternak's basic intellectual uncertainty, which we see in the shifting focus of his judgments, his analyses, and his attempted solutions of the problems of his time. But the novel is alive. With all its wavering and inconsistency, *Doctor Zhivago* remains the most passionate and most serious effort by a contemporary writer to represent with love and judge with equity the men and events into whose midst history has thrown him.

The novel encompasses fifty years of Russian history, from the beginning of the twentieth century, through the Second World War, to the death of Stalin, including the Revolution of 1905, the First World War, the Revolution of 1917 and the establishment of the Soviet regime.

It is a crucial period of contemporary history during which the fate of Russia became inextricably involved with that of Europe. The basic problems of conscience raised for Europeans by all that happened after 1914 are the same problems that confronted Russians with an even more devastating impact. And they are the same problems that confront us today.

The first one concerns history. Historical events appear to strike the individual from outside but actually burst forth from the innermost recesses of society, and hence from man's own nature. Is there an intrinsic rationality in these events that the individual is obliged to recognize and accept as he recognized and accepted necessity and the will of God in the past?

This central problem raises many questions, such as the importance of individual freedom in the face of the calamities that may befall the community as a whole; the meaning of the resurgence of force in a society in which the progress of reason and freedom seemed assured; the place of moral aspirations and simple human affections in a world ruled by the principle of violence; the possibility in such a world of the survival of some truth man can believe in and base his life on; and, finally, the resolution of the conflict between political aims and personal values, which underlines all the other questions.

All these issues are present in Pasternak's novel and actually form its substance—either as elements implicit in the situations the characters live through or as explicit considerations by the author-protagonist. In this sense, and apart from any comparison of the intrinsic value of the two works, one can say that *Doctor Zhivago* is a modern sequel to *War and Peace*. And this, one might add, was Pasternak's avowed intention.

In fact, Pasternak, like Tolstoy, was determined to rescue a crucial epoch in the story of the Russian people from the falsehoods of official history. Like Tolstoy, he was inspired by the conviction that history as we actually experience it is not a rational concatenation of events or the outcome of decisions in high places but a mass of infinitesimal accidents and unexpected incidents. 'No single man makes history. History cannot be seen, just as one cannot see grass growing,' says Yurii Zhivago.

This observation by Zhivago seems to echo Tolstoy's polemics against historians and philosophers of history and their cult of 'the great man'. But in the light of Tolstoy's great diatribe, Zhivago's observation appears equivocal on close examination. Tolstoy would probably not have objected to Pasternak's simile, but he would never have accepted the implication that a historical event was of the same order as a fact of nature. Tolstoy made a sharp distinction between social and natural fact and although he, too, maintained that history 'cannot be seen' . . . he would never have agreed that history was like growing grass. If the simile were to be taken literally it would lead to a conception of life very different from Tolstoy's, a kind of pantheism from which a return to a mild form of hero worship would be an easy step. For if we assumed the existence of some sort of preestablished harmony between the course of nature and the course of history, then great leaders might well be privileged individuals capable of perceiving, if not the growth of grass and the hidden changes in the social organism, at least the crucial moment of their developments, and might intervene and help the subterranean historical trend to manifest itself. Now this is precisely what Tolstoy denied. For he believed that human history obeyed a Force transcending any single will and any single fact of nature. (pp. 117-19)

Tolstoy's opposition of peace and war corresponds to Pasternak's contrast of nature and history. But while Tolstoy sees peace and war as antithetical, Pasternak is less categorical. He considers 'nature' and 'history' to be two aspects of the life of the universe (Spinoza's *natura naturans*). For him the crucial incompatibility is rather that of freedom and constraint, of sincerity and craftiness, and the chief evil of history (with its revolutions and wars) is its violation of nature and the 'natural'. In Tolstoy, on the contrary, both nature and peace are sharply opposed to history and war. The latter are manifestations of Fate, whose sphere lies outside nature.

For Pasternak, too, the distinguishing quality of periods of peace is 'naturalness'. And he gives a felicitous analysis of it in the first part of *Doctor Zhivago* where he describes travellers getting on and off the train at various stops in the course of a long journey.

> Every motion in the world taken separately was calculated and purposeful, but, taken together, they were spontaneously intoxicated with the general stream of life which united them all. People worked and struggled, each set in motion by the mechanism of his own cares. But the mechanisms would not have worked properly had they not been regulated and governed by a higher sense of an ultimate freedom from care. This freedom came from the feeling that all human lives were interrelated, a certainty that they flowed into each other—a happy feeling that all events took place not only on the earth, in which the dead are buried, but also in some other region which some called the Kingdom of God, others history, and still others by some other name.

This, for Pasternak, is peace. It is worth nothing, however, that it is seen (or rather reconstructed) *a posteriori*, according to the experience of its opposite, war, when the 'stream of life', which was once a unifying element, becomes a torrent that separates and destroys; when anxiety takes the place of lightheartedness; when the smooth functioning of interrelated human lives is thrown out of joint; when happiness finally becomes impossible and the 'other region', be it the Kingdom of God or history, no longer has meaning. Because war violently deprives us of that sense of happiness which gives meaning and life to ordinary events, war is truly 'hell'—the absence of inner and outer harmony. Pasternak portrays this hell in his description of the Zhivago family's journey from Moscow to Varykino across a country in the throes of the revolution.

But, as we have already seen, Pasternak considers 'peace', 'nature', 'history' and the life of the community as different facets of a single reality—universal life—that includes even war and excludes abstractions and lies, which to him are pure evil.

In *Doctor Zhivago* the life of society is so inextricably part of history and the lot of individuals is so dependent on it that, in the passage which ends with the observation that history can no more be seen than one can see grass growing, Pasternak-Zhivago does not hesitate to identify history with the world of nature.

> He reflected again that he conceived of history, or what is called the course of history, not in the accepted way but by analogy with the vegetable kingdom. In winter, under the snow, the leafless branches of a wood are thin and poor, like the hairs on an old man's wart. But in only a few days in spring the forest is transformed, it reaches the clouds . . . This transformation is achieved with a speed greater than in the case of animals, for animals do not grow as fast as plants, and yet we cannot directly observe the movement of growth even of plants. The forest does not change its place, we cannot lie in wait for it and catch it in the act of change. Whenever we look at it, it seems to be motionless. And such also is the immobility to our eyes of the eternally growing, ceaselessly changing history, the life of society moving invisibly in its incessant transformations.

Pasternak goes on to make an extremely revealing comparison between his conception of historical change and Tolstoy's.

> Tolstoy thought of it in just this way, but he did not spell it out so clearly. He denied that history was set in motion by Napoleon or any other ruler or general, but he did not develop his idea to its logical conclusion. No single man makes history. History cannot be seen, just as one cannot see grass growing. Wars and revolutions, kings and Robespierres, are history's organic agents, its yeast. But revolutions are made by fanatical men of action with one-track minds, geniuses in their ability to confine themselves to a limited field. They overturn the old order in a few hours or days, the whole upheaval takes a few weeks or at most years, but the fanatical spirit that inspired the upheavals is worshipped for decades thereafter, for centuries.

The extraordinarily beautiful descriptions of nature in *Doctor Zhivago* have their source in this vision of the world. Forests, clouds, stars and landscapes have the quality of apparitions that are both dramatic and calming. They are images of stability that emerge unexpectedly from the turmoil of events and create a pause. They are the poet's signs and symbols of the real history of the world and the real rhythm of life. Their contemplation is literally a state of ecstasy before the features of the divine.

But surely this notion of the interrelation of history and nature is a far cry from Tolstoy's. One cannot imagine the author of *War and Peace* attributing to Napoleon or any other leader or 'great man' the role of the 'organic agent' of life. As individuals he found such people more or less obnoxious but as 'great men' he considered them absolutely evil and deadly by definition. If life continued and flourished, it was in spite of them, not because of them. . . . [Nor would Tolstoy] have found Pasternak's characterization of famous leaders and revolutionaries as 'geniuses in their ability to confine themselves to a limited field' more acceptable. If those words have any meaning at all, they describe either saints or men of action so absorbed in the accomplishment of their aims that they are indifferent to everything that does not promote those aims as well as to the evil they entail. This is the picture of beings without humanity, beings whom Tolstoy could never have brought himself to admire.

The fact is that *up to a certain point* Pasternak-Zhivago identifies himself with the Russian revolution, the great historical event he lived through, and his judgment cannot but be equivocal. On the one hand, he considers that *fait accompli* not only inevitable but just; on the other, he cannot shut his eyes to its consequences or justify them by the ideology of Marxist historicism, an ideology whose only relation to real facts consists in having helped to bring about those facts. (pp. 120-23)

Because his allegiance to justice never wavers, Pasternak is forced to shift continually from total acceptance of what happens on the stage of the world to refusal to modify his judgment of living men and real events in the name of abstractions. These two attitudes cannot be easily reconciled, and in reading *Doctor Zhivago* one must take into account and examine them both.

For example, Pasternak does not consider 'war' an evil as long as it is a natural eruption of violence and does not become the means to an abstract end. When the tide of history reaches a critical point (or the course of nature erupts catastrophically), men can even feel exalted, as if by a kind of spring thaw of collective life. This, in fact, is Zhivago's attitude at the outbreak of the 1905 revolution.

> He hurried on as though his pace might hasten the time when everything on earth would be rational and harmonious as it was now inside his feverish head. He knew that all their struggles in the last few days, the troubles on the line, the speeches at meetings, the decision to strike . . . were separate stages on the great road lying ahead of them. But at the moment he was so worked up that he wanted to run all the way without stopping to draw breath. He did not realize where he was going with his long strides, but his feet knew very well where they were taking him.

During the very same period, we witness the rebirth of Lara, the woman who feels that she can be redeemed from the humiliation she suffered in peace time only by war and revolution. 'Lara walked swiftly, some unknown force swept her on as though she were striding on air, carried along by this proud quickening strength. "How splendid", she thought, listening to the gun shots. "Blessed are the downtrodden. Blessed are the deceived. God speed you, bullets. You and I are of one mind".'

There is something extremely ambiguous in this optimism, in this 'war' which is seen both as the road to happiness and life-fulfilment, that is, to 'peace' and as a violent, irrational explosion which is exhilarating just because it means the end of peace and normal existence. Pasternak seems to accept this ambiguity as inevitable, although as the story proceeds it becomes clear that he is troubled by it.

Those early critics who considered Pasternak's novel the nostalgic outpouring of an intellectual hostile to the revolution simply misread it. No Russian or non-Russian writer has found more eloquent language to exalt that event. 'Just think what's going on around us!' says Zhivago at the outbreak.

> Just think of it, the whole of Russia has had its roof torn off, and you and I and everybody else are out in the open. And there's nobody to spy on us. Freedom! Real freedom, not just talk about it, freedom, dropped out of the sky, freedom beyond our expectations . . . It was partly the war, the revolution did the rest. The war was an artificial break in life—as if life could be put off for a time—what nonsense! The revolution broke out willy-nilly, like a sigh suppressed too long. Everyone was revived, reborn, changed, transformed. You might say that everyone has been through two revolutions—his own personal revolution as well as the general one. It seems to me that socialism is the sea, and all these separate streams, these private, individual revolutions, are flowing into it—the sea of life, the sea of spontaneity.

It is obvious that the reflections and hopes expressed in this passage have little relation to the actual aims and real possibilities of any revolution, especially the Bolshevik revolution. The Bolshevik leaders certainly did not think of socialism as a 'sea' into which all those separate streams were to freely flow, but, if anything, as an artificial lake and gigantic dyke in which the energy of each 'stream' was to be locked and rationally exploited. But, in attributing

such thoughts to his hero, Pasternak evidently wants to show with what feelings a young Russian intellectual could hail the Revolution in the months from February to October 1917.

As the revolution gathers momentum, however, Zhivago's attitude changes. The sense of liberation in which he rediscovers the boundless freedom of nature is replaced by an acceptance of fate. 'He realized that he was a pygmy before the monstrous machine of the future; he was anxious about this future, and loved it and was secretly proud of it, and as though for the last time, as if in farewell he avidly looked at the trees and clouds and the people walking in the streets, the great Russian city struggling through misfortune.' (pp. 123-25)

In Pasternak, as in [André] Malraux, the sense of fatality is the dominant note. For both these writers observe the event not from within, or even from 'beneath', but from an imaginary point above whence their gaze can embrace and understand the general meaning, if not the law, of the event. And the meaning they find in it could be expressed in the statement: 'The event is "historical".' In other words, it has already been defined and its outcome decided, so that in its presence one can only feel a kind of religious dismay and bow one's head.

Suddenly, however, the October *coup d'état* and Lenin's resolute action changed everything. Religious dismay is replaced by admiration of an event that seems to have the quality of a work of art and of a phenomenon of nature. 'This fearlessness', says Yurii Zhivago, 'this way of seeing the thing through to the end, has a familiar national look about it. It has something of Pushkin's uncompromising clarity and of Tolstoy's unwavering faithfulness to the facts.'

This enthusiasm seems to be inspired by the brilliant and original creative act of an individual. And its value for Pasternak-Zhivago lies in its being part of the natural order of things, in which creation is not only an uninterrupted and invisible process but an abrupt and violent explosion.

> The real stroke of genius is this. [Zhivago is thinking aloud.] If you charged someone with the task of creating a new world, of starting a new era, he would ask you first to clear the ground. He would wait for the old centuries to finish before undertaking to build the new ones, he'd want to begin a new paragraph, a new page. But here they don't bother with anything like that. This new thing, this marvel of history, this revelation, is exploded right into the very thick of daily life without the slightest consideration for its course. It doesn't start at the beginning, it starts in the middle, without any schedule, on the first weekday that comes along, while traffic in the streets is at its height . . . only real greatness can be so unconcerned with timing and opportunity.

Here Pasternak is evidently trying to glorify a major historical event, Lenin's *coup d'état,* without glorifying the 'leader' or History, which would be an unpardonable sin in the eyes of Tolstoy.

But he fails, as we see at once by the way he takes refuge in the mystique of the 'everyday'. He falls into a trap he seems to have set for himself. There is something that smacks of Victor Hugo in the notion of 'someone' who had been 'charged with the task of creating a new world' and who, we do not know why, should have 'waited for the old centuries to finish' before undertaking the task, as if the 'old centuries' could not have ended without his deciding to start the 'new ones': all this is rhetoric.

Pasternak's attempt fails because it conflicts with his effort to bring out the prosaic, almost 'non-historical' character of Lenin's action, for it is simply impossible to look at a historical event both from the outside, as if it were a completely finished object presented to our view, and from the inside, which is the perspective of the individual who actually experiences it and whose vision is the only authentic one, according to Tolstoy and to Pasternak as well. 'History cannot be seen', Zhivago says. By what marvel or divine inspiration, then, is he suddenly able to see it and appraise its 'greatness'? Tolstoy, whom Pasternak invokes along with Pushkin, would never have made this claim.

It is not a matter of minimizing the importance of the roles played by Lenin and Napoleon but, on the contrary, of recognizing the grandeur and the very incommensurability of an event, realizing that it is the product of something more than the demiurgic will of certain individuals and the magic power of certain ideas.

Try as he may to find a rationalization of history either in nature or in Christianity, Pasternak, like Tolstoy, really believes that history is intrinsically absurd when it takes the form of war, revolution, or government action. And it is the images that capture with their sense of motionless stupor the essential absurdity of human situations that express most profoundly Zhivago's perception of history. Thus, for example, the account of an officer's attempt to quell a sudden mutiny of soldiers:

> At the very doors of the station, under the station bell, there stood a water butt for use in case of fire. It was tightly covered. Gints jumped up on the lid and addressed the approaching soldiers with an incoherent but gripping speech. His unnatural voice and the insane boldness of his gesture, two steps from the door where he could so easily have taken shelter, amazed them and stopped them in their tracks. They lowered their rifles. But Gints, who was standing on the edge of the lid, suddenly pushed it in. One of his legs slipped into the water and the other hung over the edge of the butt. Seeing him sitting clumsily astride the edge of the butt, the soldiers burst into laughter and the one in front shot Gints in the neck. He was dead by the time the others ran up and thrust their bayonets into his body.

Thus a 'clumsy' fall decides the fate not only of a man but of one of the innumerable attempts made after the February revolution to hold the Russian army together. On failures like this the fate of Russia hung. Does this mean that a simple misstep unleashed a collective act that might have been prevented by that one man's temerity? If so, then we are in the presence of the irrational as it appears in the elementary form of a simple accident. If, however, we look at the episode from the historicist's point of view, it can be construed as a sign of the fatal situation of the entire Russian oligarchy, from Kerensky's provisional government down to the lowest officer. Then Gints' clumsy fall becomes only a symbol of the clumsiness and impotence of a class trying to escape the fate to which history has already condemned it. But the historian's effort to 'explain' the accident and give it some semblance of rationality only renders it more irrational, since one has to assume the intervention of a Power who uses the slip of a leg to accomplish more or less preordained ends. Perhaps Pasternak's attitude to history is revealed even more clearly by Zhivago's reflections in the train carrying him home from the front:

> Three years of changes, moves, uncertainties, upheavals; the war, the revolution; scenes of destruction, scenes of death, shelling, blown-up bridges, fires, ruins—all this turned suddenly into a huge, empty, meaningless space. *The first real event* since the long interruption was this trip in the fast-moving train, the fact that he was approaching his home, which was intact, which still existed, and in which every stone was dear to him. This was real life, meaningful experience, the actual goal of all quests, this was what art aimed at—homecoming, return to one's family, to oneself, to true existence.

Here the Tolstoian peace motif is taken up again and carried to the extreme: 'War' (and 'history', in consequence) is presented as completely futile, and its events are depicted as completely unreal. The 'first real event' for Pasternak's hero is his return to his home, to family affection, to daily life. The facile retort that Zhivago's thoughts are nothing but the commonplaces of a bourgeois intellectual going back to his comfortable daily habits has no validity whatever. Except for the tone and the reference to art, the reactions of a peasant or a worker in the same situation would not be described differently.

The conclusions Zhivago draws from the historical events he has lived through and is still living through are suggested by the title he gives to the notes he keeps during the period between the February and October revolutions, before the storm closes in again. 'Playing at People, a Gloomy Diary or Journal Consisting of Prose, Verse, and What-have-you, Inspired by the Realization that *Half the People Have Stopped Being Themselves and Are Acting Unknown Parts*' (my italics).

This is perhaps the clearest and most concise expression of Pasternak-Zhivago's attitude to history-in-the-making. Later in the novel, Pasternak shows us Zhivago, a prisoner of the partisans, forcibly involved in one of the many chaotic engagements of the civil war. At first he is hesitant and passive, then he suddenly decides to behave exactly like a soldier in battle, since that is the role fate has assigned him. He begins to act his part by shooting at a tree trunk, but he kills a man instead. This episode, which was widely discussed when the book first appeared, was considered by some critics to prove that Pasternak's hero is a typical irresponsible bourgeois intellectual. In fact, it reveals much more than that when one remembers all the passages throughout the novel in which Pasternak struggles to describe and understand historical events without resorting to current ideologies. In the character of Zhivago Pasternak attempts to show as honestly as possible not only his fascination with the revolution but his early doubts and his final loss of confidence as well. The complexity and contradictions of Zhivago's thinking are patent, and in presenting them Pasternak is forced to come to grips with the problem of history. His answers remain unclear and sometimes contradictory, because, as I have already suggested, he seeks a solution in the notions of 'the life of the universe' and the process of nature. But the history of man cannot be explained, judged and justified by invoking the growth of trees and the rhythm of the seasons. It belongs to another order and obeys laws that are less easy to fathom. Attempting to explain the course of history in terms of nature tends to dismiss the enigma of history and nature and leaves one face-to-face with a Power that is superior to them both.

This is why Pasternak seizes on the message of Christ as marking the beginning of a new historical era and revealing the meaning of history itself. In Nikolai Nikolaievich's affirmation at the beginning of the novel we hear Pasternak's voice:

> It is possible not to know whether God exists, or why, and yet believe that man does not live in a state of nature but in history, and that history as we know it now began with Christ and that Christ's Gospel is its foundation . . . To begin with, love of one's neighbour, which is the supreme form of vital energy . . . And then the two basic ideals of modern man—without them he is unthinkable—the idea of free personality and the idea of life as sacrifice . . .

The interpretation of the Christian Gospel given toward the end of the novel by Sima, the peasant soothsayer, is not very different:

> Rome was at an end. The reign of numbers was at an end. The duty, imposed by armed force, to live unanimously as a people, as a whole nation, was abolished. Leaders and nations were relegated to the past. They were replaced by the doctrine of individuality and freedom. Individual human life became the life story of God . . . The basis of life is to be that inspiration which the Gospel strives to make the foundation of life, contrasting the commonplace with the unique, the weekday with the holiday, and repudiating all compulsion.

To see the key to the history of modern times in Christ's, rather than Hegel's or Marx's, teaching was undeniably the most flagrant of heresies, given the context of the novel and the period in which it was written. However, love of one's neighbour, the ideals of free individuality and of life as sacrifice, the belief that individuality and freedom should supplant the concept of nation, the repudiation of force in collective life—all these aspirations, whether or not they are part of the Christian Gospel (and here it is a question of idiom or emphasis), unquestionably constitute a personal creed, but they certainly do not provide an explanation of history.

Pasternak's passionate desire to reassert the validity of truth and to combat nihilism and bad faith is expressed with great force in Lara's account of her experiences with Antipov, the young revolutionary she had married.

> 'It was then that untruth came down on our land of Russia. The main misfortune, the root of all the evil to come, was the loss of confidence in the value of one's own opinion. People imagined that it was out of date to follow their own moral sense, that they must all sing in chorus, and live by other people's notions, notions that were being crammed down everybody's throat . . . This social evil became an epidemic. It was catching. And it affected everything, nothing was left untouched by it.'

And later, during the conversation between Zhivago and Strelnikov-Antipov, the author writes: 'It was the disease, the revolutionary madness of the age, that at heart everyone was different from his outward appearance. Everyone could justifiably feel that he was guilty, that he was a secret criminal . . . an undetected imposter.' In other words, the useful lie, the official truth 'crammed down everybody's throats', had become *the* truth, so that anyone who still had even the slightest notion of the humble reality of things could not help feeling 'guilty', like an 'undetected impostor'.

Pasternak's chief object in **Doctor Zhivago** is to make a stand against 'official' truth in the name of individual freedom and independent thought and to show how this stand can only lead to tragedy (as exemplified by Zhivago's wretched end).

As we have seen, his search for explanations leads him to attempt all the paths that seem possible, from the Tolstoian view of the world to that of a religion of nature combined with a rational-mystical interpretation of Christianity. But one wants to know what Pasternak's own final answer is. Is there a point in the novel where Pasternak, the artist and intellectual, gives the impression of having glimpsed an authentically personal truth?

The first reply that comes to mind, and it is perhaps the simplest and the fairest, is that Pasternak's truth lies precisely in his attempts to find answers and in his uncertainty as to the path that will lead to them.

There is, however, a scene in **Doctor Zhivago** where poetic image and a living, almost religious, message, coincide so strikingly that one cannot resist the feeling that some kind of revelation is involved, a revelation so puzzling and unexpected that the author himself seems unaware of its full significance. It is the scene in which Kubarikha, the soldier sorceress, exorcises the stricken heifer:

> The woman was saying: 'Aunt Margesta, come and be our guest. Come on Wednesday, take away the pest, take away the spell, take away the scab. Ringworm, leave the heifer's udder. Stand still, Beauty, do your duty, don't upset the pail. Stand still as a hill, let milk run and rill. Terror, terror, show your mettle, take the scab, throw them in the nettle. Strong as a lord is the sorcerer's word.
>
> 'You see, Agafia, you have to know everything—bidding and forbidding, the word for escaping and the word for safekeeping. Now you, for example, you look over there and you say to yourself: "There's a forest." But what there is over there is the forces of evil fighting the angelic hosts—they're at war like your men in Bassalygo's . . .
>
> 'Look over there where I'm pointing . . . You think it's two twigs that the wind has tangled together? Or a bird building its nest? Well, it isn't either. That thing is a real devil's work, a garland the water spirit started weaving for her daughter. She heard people coming by, that frightened her, so she left it half done . . .
>
> 'Or again, take your red banner. You think it's a flag, isn't that what you think? Well, it isn't a flag. It's the purple kerchief of the death woman, she uses it for luring. And why for luring? She waves it and nods and winks and lures young men to come and be killed . . . You thought it was a flag. You

thought it was: "Come to me, all ye poor and proletarians of the world."

'You have to know everything these days . . .
every single thing. What every bird is and every
stone and every herb . . . '

Yurii Andreievich was sufficiently well read to
suspect that Kubarikha's last words repeated the
opening passage of an ancient chronicle, either of
Novgorod or Epatievo, but so distorted by copyists
and the sorcerers and bards . . . Why, then, had he
succumbed so completely to the tyranny of the legend? Why did this gibberish, this absurd talk, impress him as if it were describing real events?

Because, one might easily reply, this gibberish suggests the
only verity to be found in the vortex of events which engulf
Zhivago and which he cannot understand or control any
better than the sorceress. The 'gibberish' is the 'gibberish'
of historical happenings—czars, angels, Mohammedans,
waterspirits, red flags that are not red flags but magic
handkerchiefs luring young men to death. The poor, the
proletariat, birds, stones and grass swirl in those words
like men caught in the hurricane of history. But that 'gibberish' is also poetry—not only because of the startlingly
original juxtaposition of words, images and ideas but because it is an echo, albeit a distorted one, of the folk voice
of ancient Russia.

Yet the sorceress' incantation is not only a savage image
of the turmoil of events; it is the voice of that arcane but
ubiquitous realm beyond the world of events; it summons
both demons and gods from the shadowy sphere of the sacred whose spell over men never ends.

Outside the boundaries of logic, speculation and morality,
and beyond attempts to judge or understand, this incomprehensible gibberish is pure and numinous reality, contact with the sacred and direct communion with the soul
of the people. In the outpourings of the sorceress the religion of nature and the speculations about history that Pasternak expressed through images and concepts in the story
of Yurii Zhivago are reconciled with an inspired simplicity. Although he has not given us the key to the riddle, he
has shown us where to seek it.

In a certain sense the book should end on the note of incantation. To be a perfect novel, it should perhaps have
been written—or rewritten—in the key of Kubarikha's
'gibberish'. For there moralism, orthodoxy, polemics and
absolutes all melt in a solvent that no 'untruth' and no
mask can resist. The only truth that remains is that of the
individual and collective soul, alone in its mad freedom.
(pp. 125-32)

> *Nicola Chiaromonte, "Pasternak, Nature and
> History," in his* The Paradox of History: Sten-
> dhal, Tolstoy, Pasternak and Others, *London:
> Weidenfeld and Nicolson, 1970, pp. 117-32.*

John Wain

When a major poet, towards the end of his life, decides to
break out in a completely new direction by writing a novel,
and a long and ambitious novel at that, there is reasonable
ground for surprise and curiosity. That T. S. Eliot, or Paul
Valéry, should have published an immense novel in his

sixties is hardly imaginable. That Pasternak should do so
was equally unimaginable, until he did it. Like Eliot and
Valéry, he was a distinguished member of the second generation of Symbolist poets, that generation who were born
in the late nineteenth century and revealed their gifts before 1914. Pasternak's importance in the European Symbolist movement was well recognized in every country in
which that movement flourished. . . . In Russia, the
Symbolist movement was frowned on by the Soviet authorities, and many of its most distinguished practitioners
were silenced, executed or driven to suicide. Just as one
of the historical functions of the Roman Empire was to
make martyrs for Christianity, so one of the historical
functions of the Soviet empire was to make martyrs for
Symbolism. The parallel is not a frivolous one, for Symbolism was not merely a strategy for writing poetry but an
attitude towards experience. It was the last great concerted impulse in European letters; it died with Pasternak, and
it left a hole that has never been filled.

Symbolist writing often uses exact description, but it is,
nevertheless, basically anti-realistic. Where the realist
holds that his duty is to reproduce faithfully the outer surface of life, in the belief that the inner essence will accumulate behind it just as it does in actual experience, the Symbolist is akin to the religious mystic in believing that the
surface of life is a mere carapace, that truth is essentially
mysterious and can be glimpsed only at moments of vision. It is the function of Symbolist writing to induce these
moments of vision, which it does by intense meditation on
symbols which are not symbols *of* anything that can be
produced and named, but rather instruments for bringing
the mind to an awareness of things that cannot be appre-
hended except by the intensely meditated symbol. Hence
the 'epiphanies' of Joyce, hence the 'image' of the Imagists, hence the consistent refusal of poets of the Symbolist
wing to provide 'explanations' of their poems or even to
confirm or deny these explanations when produced by others.

Within this framework, Pasternak's work as a poet was
well enough grasped and understood. Some of its qualities
even came over in translation, and his reputation was international. What no one knew, all this time, was that Pasternak was one day to come before the world as a major,
and perhaps the last, writer of the Symbolist novel; that
he was not only the equal of Yeats or Rilke but also the
equal of Joyce and Proust. His achievement thus over-
arches modern literature and makes him arguably the
greatest writer of the twentieth century. I say 'arguably'
because, not knowing Russian, I cannot argue it myself. I
read Pasternak in translation, and though I realize that
this is unfortunate, it is consoling to recall that this is how
the great Russian writers have always made their impact
on the outside world. (pp. 128-29)

> An old Russian folk-song is like water in a weir. It
> looks as if it were still and were no longer flowing
> but in its depths it is ceaselessly rushing through
> the sluice-gates and its stillness is an illusion.
>
> By every possible means—by repetitions and simi-
> les—it attempts to stop or to slow down the gradual
> unfolding of its theme, until it reaches some myste-
> rious point, then it suddenly reveals itself. In this
> insane attempt to stop the flow of time, a sorrowful,
> self-restraining spirit finds its expression.

This description of Kubarikha's song does not fit exactly the method of *Dr Zhivago,* but it certainly comes a good deal nearer than we should be likely to come if we started with conventional expectations based on the realistic novel. Pasternak was, it is clear, intensely interested in the novel as a form, especially in its still unexplored possibilities. But for the conventional rules and regulations of the novel, as developed over the last two hundred years, he seems to have felt a certain genial contempt. Most novelists have been studious of probability; Pasternak goes out of his way to introduce walloping coincidences. Most novelists keep their narrative fairly tidy, with large events in the foreground and small in the background; Pasternak will spend pages over a description of the weather, and bundle some major event into a couple of paragraphs.

Dr Zhivago is, however, a traditional, even an old-fashioned, novel in one important respect. It has a 'hero', a principal character whose thoughts and actions embody more or less exactly the values of the author. Even if we did not know a great deal about Pasternak from other sources, even if we did not have his other works and a record of many of his personal utterances, we should know that Yury Zhivago stands very close to Boris Pasternak; we should know it partly from the tone of the book itself, which is one of the very few major novels to make use of irony, and partly from the very important fact that Pasternak wrote, and published with the book, twenty-two poems supposed to be written by Zhivago, which are indistinguishable in tone, method and import from Pasternak's own mature work.

Dr Zhivago, then, has a hero whose values are substantially the author's, and whose experience embodies the lessons of the author's lifetime. Yury Zhivago is presented as a kind of Everyman; not a simple cardboard cut-out in peasant costume, but the kind of complex, all-suffering and all-knowing Everyman that Hamlet is, for instance. The word *zhivago* recalls the Russian words for *life, alive* and *living.* . . . Zhivago is Life; he embodies human consciousness in all its facets. Like Hamlet, he may be powerless to alter his destiny, but he is extremely sensitive in his awareness of it. Nothing escapes him and nothing leaves him unaffected. He is responsive to other people, to the physical world, to art, to history, to the whole shifting mass of human experience. It is natural that he should be shown as a poet, since the poet has traditionally made a virtue of his openness to miscellaneous experience, and it is also natural that he should cultivate the scientific way of looking at the world. He is a doctor with a special gift for diagnosis (an episode, specially designed to plant this, is provided in IV, 5). And diagnosis is the art of deducing the whole from a part.

The concern for wholeness, and the gift of divining it, are also the mark of Zhivago the poet, whose attitude to his art is bound up, as it must be, with his idea of human character and destiny. We find the first major statement of this in his speech to the suffering Anna Gromeko in III, 3. Anna is afraid of her approaching death, and Yury rises to the occasion by delivering, rather to his own surprise, an 'impromptu lecture' on the subject of life, death and immortality. Here is the central passage:

> Resurrection.—In the crude form in which it is preached for the consolation of the weak, the idea doesn't appeal to me. I have always understood

Christ's words about the living and the dead in a different sense. Where could you find room for all these hordes of people collected over thousands of years? The universe isn't big enough, God and good and meaning would be crowded out. They'd be crushed by all that greedy animal jostling.

But all the time life, always one and the same, always incomprehensibly keeping its identity, fills the universe and is renewed at every moment in innumerable combinations and metamorphoses. You are anxious about whether you will rise from the dead or not, but you have risen already—you rose from the dead when you were born and you didn't notice it. Will you feel pain? Do the tissues feel their disintegration? In other words, what will happen to your consciousness? But what is consciousness? Let's see. To try consciously to go to sleep is a sure way to have insomnia, to try to be conscious of one's own digestion is a sure way to upset the stomach. Consciousness is a poison when we apply it to ourselves. Consciousness is a beam of light directed outwards, it lights up the way ahead of us so that we don't trip up. It's like the headlamps on a railway engine—if you turned the beam inwards there would be a catastrophe.

So what will happen to your consciousness? *Your* consciousness, yours not anyone else's. Well, what are *you*? That's the crux of the matter. Let's try to find out. What is it about you that you have always known as yourself? What are you conscious of in yourself? Your kidneys? Your liver? Your blood vessels?—No. However far back you go in your memory, it is always in some external, active manifestation of yourself that you come across your identity—in the work of your hands, in your family, in other people. And now look. You in others are yourself, your soul. That is what you are. This is what your consciousness has breathed and lived on and enjoyed throughout your life. Your soul, your immortality, your life in others. And what now? You have always been in others and you will remain in others. And what does it matter to you if later on it is called your memory? This will be you—the you that enters the future and becomes a part of it.

And now one last point. There is nothing to worry about. There is no death. Death is not our department. But you mentioned talent—that's different, that's ours, that's at our disposal. And to be gifted in the widest and highest sense is to be gifted for life.

At first sight this looks like an activist doctrine resembling official Marxist and Communist attitudes to a human life. That we exist 'always in some external, active manifestation' of our identity, that 'consciousness is a poison when we apply it to ourselves', would meet with no dissent from official Soviet opinion, with its insistence on work and more work, its disapproval of psycho-analysis, its demand for objectivity and representationalism in art. Zhivago is quite willing to go along with such doctrines up to a point. He is no individualist, or at any rate not quite in our usual Western sense. He believes in 'the you that enters the future and becomes part of it'. A man's jealously guarded individuality, the little box of tricks and idiosyncrasies that set him apart from others, seems to him merely trivial. What is important is life, the one thing we all share, and the all-important thing.

Art, of course, is life: life in one of its most important manifestations. Jumping forward to IX, 4, we find Yury writing in his notebook, during that first period at Varykino, before the renewal of his relationship with Lara, when he is putting his thoughts in order and enjoying the quiet and solitude of rural life before his capture by the partisans, that art 'is not a category', that it is 'a principle which comes into every work of art', that it is in fact 'a hidden, secret part of content'.

He goes on:

> There is no plurality in art. Primitive art, the art of Egypt, Greece, our own—it is all, I think, one and the same art throughout, an art which remains itself through thousands of years. You can call it an idea, a statement about life, so all-embracing that it can't be split up into separate words; and if there is so much as a particle of it in any work which includes other things as well, it outweighs all the other ingredients in significance and turns out to be the essence, the heart and soul of the work.

Art is like life in two important respects: it is 'so all-embracing that it can't be split up', and it is the seed of ferment, transfiguring the whole if it is present even in 'a particle'.

If we hold these two statements in focus we shall not be surprised, on turning to Zhivago's more formal statements on his art as a poet, to find that he sees the poet's role as impersonal. The poet goes where life leads him, and the leading-string is language. In XIV, 8, where he has his greatest burst of creative activity during that blessed interval of peace with Lara and her daughter, in the second period of Varykino, Zhivago is visited by 'inspiration'. The whole passage is crucial.

> After two or three stanzas and several images by which he was himself astonished, his work took possession of him and he experienced the approach of what is called inspiration. At such moments the correlation of the forces controlling the artist is, as it were, stood on its head. The ascendancy is no longer with the artist or the state of mind which he is trying to express, but with language, his instrument of expression. Language, the home and dwelling of beauty and meaning, itself begins to think and speak for man and turns wholly into music, not in the sense of outward, audible sounds but by virtue of the power and momentum of its inward flow. Then, like the current of a mighty river polishing stones and turning wheels by its very movement, the flow of speech creates in passing, by the force of its own laws, rhyme and rhythm and countless other forms and formations, still more important and until now undiscovered, unconsidered and unnamed.
>
> At such moments Yury felt that the main part of his work was not being done by him but by something which was above him and controlling him: the thought and poetry of the world as it was at that moment and as it would be in the future. He was controlled by the next step it was to take in the order of its historical development; and he felt himself to be only the pretext and the pivot setting it in motion.

Several important matters are dealt with here, briefly but lucidly. The whole question of poetic form is illuminated not from the outside, as a matter of conventions, rules,

working arrangements and external standards, but from the inside, as one more part of the great shaping activity that we know as language. Any work of literature is a collaboration between the individual writer and the nation that has forged the instrument of his language and put it into his hands. . . . Language can 'think and speak for man' because he has, as we say nowadays, programmed it to do so; it is instinct with a life that man has breathed into it, and that life is capable of marvellous variations and extensions, among them poetic form and, for that matter, all other literary forms.

This absorption of the artist's individuality into the 'mighty river' of language is partly Pasternak's own variant of the traditional doctrine of poetic inspiration as we find it in Plato's *Ion,* and *passim* in western literature, and partly an extension of the basic idea that human fulfilment means diving into the life-giving current, going where the great impersonal forces lead you, rather than clinging on to the shreds and tatters of individuality. . . . One of the impersonal forces is certainly what the Marxist would call History. The 'thought and poetry of the world' is about to take the next step 'in the order of its historical development'. And we must assume that if Zhivago had not been writing poems, if fate had not granted him that interlude of threatened but perfect tranquillity in which his poetic genius might have its last and most joyful fling, then the essential work would still have been done by other poets here and there; the 'thought and poetry of the world' is an irresistible and impersonal force which will choose this or that individual to act through, but in any case cannot choose but act.

This view puts Pasternak squarely among those who believe that art is no mere icing on top of the cake, to be indulged in times of plenty but sternly omitted when more important matters claim priority; that it is, on the contrary, an elemental force, a condition of life as urgent as sex or hunger. From this it follows that an undue fastidiousness about technique, the relish of the 'formalist' for endless debate and agonizing choice among the competing ways and means of expression, is the mark of the minor artist, the dabbler through whom this mighty current does not flow strongly. If the 'mighty river' rolls strongly enough it cannot help polishing the stones; on the other hand, it will not stay to carve them into curious shapes. (pp. 130-36)

It all circles back to that sentence in Yury's 'impromptu lecture' to Anna: 'To be gifted in the highest and widest sense is to be gifted for life'. But this being 'gifted for life' does not involve the complete surrender of what we ordinarily think of as individuality. The artist's destiny is to surrender to the powers that move him, to speak with the voice of all humanity at the point of the historical process that has been reached. But he does this not by subscribing to some big general doctrine like Marxist-Leninism, but by simply and unselfconsciously accepting the things that happen to him as a person. Zhivago's poems, as we have them at the end of the book, are full of personal details, but even if we did not have them we should still know that this was his way of working. . . . (p. 136)

There is no need for the poet to go out and gather material. As for accepting material handed to him from outside, that is out of the question. 'Life', not only the broad impersonal force but his own personal life, made up of details and cluttered with seeming irrelevances, will send him his material. But by submitting to life, he will switch on something as old, as new, as wide, as deep, as humanity.

As diagnostician, as poet, Zhivago's values are founded on the idea of wholeness. In the story, the people to whom he is opposed are always those whose aim it is to substitute a part for the whole, to freeze off everything in life except the part that happens to engage them. There is a whole gallery of such figures, from the deaf-mute Yury encounters in the train on his way back from Melyuzeyevo to Moscow to the partisan leader Liberius and, most notably of all, Pasha Antipov, husband of Lara, who accepts the values of the revolution so completely that he restructures his entire character and makes himself over into the metallic Strelnikov, 'the Shooter'. Antipov/Strelnikov is worth examining in detail. As a young boy, he is shown as quick, bright and affectionate, with a special gift for mimicry with which he amuses his foster-mother Tiverzina, on whose protection he is thrown when his father is arrested in the upheaval of 1905. Later, as a young man at the university, he is headlong in love with Lara and entirely dominated by her. It is his nature to twine round a stronger being. This results in a marriage-situation which does not quite make him happy, and he also finds life in a country province narrow and boring. Lara enjoys it, because she has that deep sanity and wholeness within herself that is nourished by the fruitful rhythms of nature and the interests of ordinary human beings. The war provides Pasha's answer by giving him an acceptable reason for leaving home and trying out his manhood. But the trial results in a complete and unforeseeable change. (pp. 137-38)

No doubt Pasha's early gift for mimicry, his tendency to sink his own personality into something outside himself and stronger, points to an inner weakness which makes possible his later corruption by the poison of dogma, of schematic and partial thinking. Antipov is a brave and honourable man; his death, as we shall see later, is given the full tragic treatment in one of the book's finest passages. But for temperamental reasons, and also for reasons connected with the circumstances of his life, he falls victim to the spiritual scourge of dogmatism. This disease is diagnosed, and its effects noted, everywhere throughout the book. As Zhivago says, almost casually, in one of his conversations with the local fixer Samdevyatov:

> . . . You talk about Marxism and objectivity. I don't know any teaching more self-centred and further from the facts than Marxism. Ordinarily, people are anxious to test their theories in practice, to learn from experience, but those who wield power are so anxious to establish the myth of their own infallibility that they turn their back on truth as squarely as they can. Politics mean nothing to me. I don't like people who are indifferent to the truth.

This doctrine of wholeness, of respect of the 'unprincipled' heart for the truth in all its complexity, is never more beautifully stated than in Lara's meditations, after Yury's death, on the nature of the love between them.

> It was not out of necessity that they loved each other, 'enslaved by passion', as lovers are described. They loved each other because everything around them willed it, the trees and the clouds and the sky over their heads and the earth under their feet. Perhaps their surrounding world, the strangers they met in the street, the landscapes drawn up for them

to see on their walks, the rooms in which they lived or met, were even more pleased with their love than they were themselves.

> Well, of course, it had been just this that had united them and had made them so akin! Never, never, not even in their moments of richest and wildest happiness, had they lost the sense of what is highest and most ravishing—joy in the whole universe, its form, its beauty, the feeling of their own belonging to it, being part of it.

> This compatibility of the whole was the breath of life to them. And consequently they were unattracted to the modern fashion of coddling man, exalting him above the rest of nature and worshipping him. A sociology built on this false premise and served up as politics, struck them as pathetically homemade and amateurish beyond their comprehension.

Even in translation, one can see that the book's literary method is designed to express in every possible way this attitude, this reverence for the wholeness of life. The celebrated coincidences are primarily a way of reminding us of the extent to which our lives are woven in with other people's. The conventional novel avoids coincidences because it feels a need to demonstrate that character is destiny: or, alternatively (if it is that kind of novel) that social circumstances will shape a life inexorably. In either case, to allow chance into the story is to spoil the neatly ruled pattern. Pasternak delights in spoiling the pattern, or rather in opening it up to show the deeper pattern underneath. Since experience is indivisible, it does not flow unbrokenly from character nor from social circumstances. Chance plays just as large a part as anything else. It must have pleased him to begin the story with a large-scale coincidence; in Chapter I, the train that suddenly halts within earshot of Nikolai Nikolayovich, Yury, and Nicky Dudorov, and from which Yury's father has just thrown himself to his death, is carrying Komarovsky, Tiverzina, and Mischa Gordon and his father. Since Tiverzina is the foster-mother of Pasha Antipov, later to be the husband of Lara, the roll-call of the book's central characters is very nearly complete. Since life will in any case bring these people together, there is no need for Pasternak to contrive a situation in which they will be crowded on to the one canvas; he does so as a deliberate gesture away from realism and towards a symbolic presentation.

There are also a number of linking devices that bind the huge, episodic narrative into a unity. Sometimes these are almost Joycean in the feeling of circularity they create. The most obvious example is that Komarovsky brings Lara into Yury's life and in the end takes her out again. Equally important is the candle that burns in the window of Pasha Antipov's apartment in Kamerger Street. Lara, whose engagement to Pasha has been on and off several times, impulsively calls on him and tells him they must be married immediately. She is highly distressed, being on her way to that party at which she will shoot at Komarovsky, miss him and hit someone else, and in an effort to regain calm she asks him to light a candle and put out the electric light. He does so, and as the candle stands in the window it melts the thick frost and makes 'a black chink like a peep-hole'. Just then, Yury and Tonya drive past, on their way to the same party, and Yury notices the hole. 'Its light seemed to fall into the street as deliberately as a glance, as if the flame were keeping a watch on the passing carriages and waiting for someone.' Yury and Tonya have just allowed the dying Anna to 'betrothe' them; at the Sventitsky's party, Yury will see Lara for the second time. This crucial point of inter-section is also the theme of Zhivago's poem 'Winter Night'. And finally, this very room is the poet's last resting-place; Yevgraf hires it for him in his last attempt to bring some peace and order into his life and set him on his feet, and after Yury dies he is laid out, and Lara's great lyrical outburst of joy and grief is uttered over his body, in this room where the candle had shone. (pp. 139-41)

Everywhere the narrative is criss-crossed by these linking devices. With the inexorable logic of a dream, the characters crop up and meet each other in different circumstances and guises. (p. 144)

The imagery of the book also makes a steady and all-pervading contribution to the novel's insistent suggestion that life is indivisible, that there are not different kinds of life but only life and not-life. We first meet Nicky Dudorov as the imaginative boy who is possessed by the thought of a certain tree that grows in the courtyard of a house in Tiflis where he is taken for holidays. The tree is 'a clumsy, tropical giant, with leaves like elephants' ears which sheltered the yard from the scorching southern sky. Nicky could not get used to the idea that it was a plant and not an animal.' A little earlier we have had the simile of the sun, with its level evening rays, coming to look at the body of the suicide Zhivago as it lies beside the railway line, 'like a cow from a near-by herd come to take a look at the crowd'.

The small town of Melyuzeyevo, on a summer night, furnishes a cluster of these barrier-crumbling similes:

> Narrow, dead-end streets ran off the square, as deep in mud as country lanes and lined with crooked little houses. Fences of plaited willow stuck out of the mud like the tops of lobster pots. You could see the one-eyed glint of open windows. From the small front gardens, sweaty yellow heads of maize with oily whiskers looked in at the windows, and single pale thin hollyhocks gazed into the distance over the fences, like women in their night-shifts whom the heat indoors had driven out for a breath of air.

Even physical impressions are deliberately scrambled. The sound of church bells on Maundy Thursday sinks through the drizzle-heavy air 'as a clump of earth, torn from the river bed, sinks and dissolves in the water of the spring floods': an image that connects the religious festival with the natural rhythm of the seasons.

But Pasternak's method is far more complex than these random samplings would indicate. His English translators have been forced to simplify a good deal, but even in what remains we can see a densely woven texture. . . . (pp. 144-45)

It has frequently been noted that *Dr Zhivago* uses the New Testament in the same way that *Ulysses* uses the Odyssey. It is the screen on which the characters cast the giant shadows of their mythical dimension. But there the similarity ends. *Ulysses* is neat, logical, pegged out with the strong rational control that was Joyce's gift from his Jesuit education. *Dr Zhivago* uses the mythical dimension in a much more fleeting, tangential, multi-faceted, ungrasp-

able way. Where Joyce is constructing a formal shadow play, Pasternak is lighting a row of tapers and letting them cast multiple, flickering, persistent shadows, always changing shape before our eyes but never disappearing altogether.

Thus to say that Zhivago 'is' Christ would be absurd, even in the unfixable way in which Leopold Bloom 'is' Odysseus. Pasternak's method does not allow figure-for-figure identification at any point, though it is clear that Lara has some elements of Mary Magdalene and Komarovsky of Judas. The New Testament background to Zhivago's story is purposely made both vague and more all-pervading. They are alike in their central metaphors, in their atmosphere of poignancy and exaltation, of high tragedy seen against a dawning sky.

I do not know what was Pasternak's attitude to Christianity, but the attitude he gives to Zhivago is that the teachings of Christ were the greatest moral break-through in human history. Men are defined by what they choose to worship. Whether or not Christ was the Son of God, whether or not He actually said, 'Father, forgive them, for they know not what they do' as He hung on the cross, it was a break-through for humanity that men should believe these things and that they should use them to project their idea of the highest reach of moral beauty and courage, the ultimate good which deserved to be worshipped. If we compare that supreme moment of the Christian story with anything in the Graeco-Roman tradition, we see at once the tremendous stride that humanity had taken, even if the Christian religion contained no revelation and was simply a human fabrication.

I am not one of those who claim to have settled this question, and in those last few sentences I was giving my own opinion. But it is also the opinion that we find in *Dr Zhivago*. As early as I, 5 we find Nikolai Nikolayovich giving a long and passionate exposition of the view that human history begins with Christ. 'What you don't understand', he says to the uncomprehending social philosopher Ivan Ivanovitch, 'is that it is possible to be an atheist, it is possible not to know if God exists or why He should, and yet to believe that man does not live in a state of nature but in history, and that history as we know it now began with Christ, it was founded by Him on the Gospels.'

Nikolai Nikolayovich is an important character who fades out half-way through the story because there is no further need for him. His function is partly to act as an awakening influence on the young Zhivago's mind, rather as the composer Scriabin did on the young Pasternak's, and partly to have a mature character who can begin at once to voice the book's essential doctrine. It is one of the marks of Pasternak's indifference to conventional novelistic practice that he never shrinks from undramatized exposition of ideas; the book makes its points by the purest poetic means of suggestion and symbol, but also, when the author happens to feel like it, by great chunks of overt exposition. Undoubtedly the most important of these is in XIII, 17, when Yury and Lara are living in Yuryatin. A female character, Sima Tuntseva, is brought in solely in order to visit them and deliver a long discourse. Yury lies on the sofa in the next room, and listens through the open door; Lara, picking up her sewing, remarks: 'I like to listen to a long, wise discourse when it's snowing . . . Go on, Sima dear. I'm listening.'

Sima then states one of the most important of the book's sustaining ideas.

> I don't like such words as 'culture' and 'epoch'. They are confusing. I prefer to put it another way. As I see it, man is made up of two parts, of God and work. Each succeeding stage in the development of the human spirit is marked by the achievement over many generations of an enormously slow and lengthy work. Such a work was Egypt. Greece was another. The theology of the Old Testament prophets was a third. The last in time, not so far replaced by anything else and still being achieved by all that is inspired in our time, is Christianity.

She goes on to elaborate on this idea in a statement running to three pages, not a word of which should be lost by the attentive reader. . . . The change in humanity that came with a changed idea of the divine, the suddenness with which 'the reign of numbers was at an end' and 'the story of a human life became the life story of God and filled the universe', leads Sima to the beautiful meditation on the figure of Mary Magdalene. 'What familiarity, what equal terms between God and life, God and the individual, God and a woman!'

The pre-Christian idea of God was bound up with power in the obvious sense: masses, force, armies, nations. With Christ came the idea of divinity as individual self-realization, the unique soul flooded with light—in short, 'equal terms between God and life'. And Zhivago's disillusion with the thoughts and feelings of the post-revolutionary régime arises from the fact that these *exaltés* have turned the clock back, turned away from the idea of the free individual spirit and gone back to thinking in terms of masses, nations, vast general movements governed by theories, so that when the revolutionary attitudes have hardened into dogma he can look back sadly on the early days when 'everyone had gone mad in his own way.' What distinguishes Christ from earlier and cruder notions of God is precisely that Christ does not impose His will on life from the outside, but on the contrary submits to it. The object of Christian worship is a God who says to mankind: 'I will not thump you into submission to my will; far from it, I will suffer every humiliation and agony you can heap on me, and still emerge as a God, with my radiance undimmed by what you have done to me and to yourselves.' And Christ does this without pomp, modestly, unobtrusively, almost without volition, merely by being true to His nature.

Zhivago's poem 'Hamlet' is relevant here. (pp. 151-54)

True to Symbolist practice, the poem works through a multiple consciousness: the central figure is Hamlet, and also an actor playing Hamlet, and also Christ. (If we add 'and also Zhivago', this need not involve us in any crude over-literalness.) The actor has to nerve himself to face the audience; Hamlet has to face the tragic fact of his responsibility to the situation, the 'cursed spite' that he was 'born to set it right'; Christ wishes it were possible to 'let this cup pass from me', but knows that His destiny is what it is. The last line, as the translators explain, is a proverb: this has the effect of landing the poem squarely in the lap of the ordinary human reader who is neither tragic personage, actor, or God, but must bear some part of all three just by living a human life. In an essay commenting on his own translation of *Hamlet,* published in *Literaturnaya*

Moskva in 1956, Pasternak remarked that the fact that Hamlet's command came to him through a ghost was not important. What matters is that 'by the merest accident Hamlet should be chosen to sit in judgment on his time and become the servant of a remoter one'. Hamlet was put into his tragic position by the 'accident' of being the king's son, otherwise he could have lived the studious private life that would have made him happy. But Hamlet accepted this as his fate and did not struggle against it. Turning back to the novel, this should help to make clear what has puzzled some readers, especially in England where there are so many Boy Scouts: why does Zhivago make so little effort to resist his fate, why does he go down, accepting a long period of decline before his death, suffering himself to be robbed of everything that made life worth living? Why does he not accept Komarovsky's offer to get him away to Vladivostok and thence out of Russia altogether? Why does he make no effort to escape when, at Varykino, he is in constant danger of arrest and execution?

The answer to this is, *mutatis mutandis,* the same as the answer to the similar questions about Hamlet (who didn't abdicate) and Christ (who didn't come down from the Cross). To be truly human, to be 'gifted in the highest and fullest sense', which means also to be truly divine, is to accept what life brings, to play out the role assigned to you, without trying to escape. Compare Zhivago's outburst to Liberius about the folly of trying to reshape life:

> Reshaping life! People who can say that have never understood a thing about life—they have never felt its breath, its heart—however much they have seen or done. They look on it as a lump of raw material which needs to be processed by them, to be ennobled by their touch. But life is never a material, a substance to be moulded. If you want to know, life is the principle of self-renewal, it is constantly renewing and remaking and changing and transfiguring itself, it is infinitely beyond your or my inept theories about it.

Zhivago's poems are full of this idea. **"March"**, for instance, with its marvellous evocation of spring ('That strapping dairy-maid'), ends with the lines

> The culprit and the life-giver
> Is the dung with its smell of fresh air.

When the poem first appeared in a periodical, the reference to dung as the cause of life and growth was cut out; Stalin had recently died, and no doubt the editor felt it was no time to be making remarks about life growing out of death—a good example of the caution which Soviet life makes necessary for literary men. Actually as we can see in a larger perspective, the theme of resurrection, the image of death fertilizing life, is always uppermost in Zhivago's mind, and in the mind of his creator. (pp. 154-56)

Finally, in what sense is Zhivago himself resurrected? The answer is given in the last words of the novel, 'it seemed that the book in their hands knew what they were feeling and gave them its support and confirmation'. Yury's two lifelong friends, Mischa Gordon and Nicky Dudorov, are sitting together at a high window, 'five or ten years' after Zhivago's death (such vagueness shows that the exact time doesn't matter), and turning over in their hands 'a book of Yury's writings which Yevgraf had compiled'. Yevgraf, whose name is associated with ἐν γραφειν. To write well, plays an entirely symbolic role in the action; he appears at those times when Yury is on the point of being submerged by his material worries and in desperate need of peace and order. Except for the supremely joyful but doomed interlude at Varykino in Chapter XIV, when Yevgraf's function was taken over by Lara, he has acted as the guardian angel of that side of Zhivago the creative artist. No attempt is made to explain how Yevgraf lives, where he goes to in between his sudden appearances, how he can always get food and accommodation, how he attains the rank of Major-General in the war; it is simply a *donnée*. That Yevgraf should collect Zhivago's scattered writings into a book (presumably a typescript, since there is no mention of its having been published or existing in more than one copy) is in keeping with his role, just as it is in keeping with the roles of Gordon and Dudorov that they should treasure the book and feel united in the impulse of joy that it brings them.

After all that has been said about the use of the New Testament as back-projection for *Dr Zhivago,* the reader will hardly miss the parallel between Yevgraf's compilation and the Gospels. All through the book, although Yury is shown as taking his vocation as a poet with complete seriousness, he never expresses any ambition to have a literary career or to transmit his work safely to posterity. Like Christ, he makes it his concern to express the truth and leaves to others the task of collecting and preserving what he utters. Gordon and Dudorov, though unalterably his friends, are conventional and rather stupid; even, at times, cowardly; very like the disciples of Christ as we glimpse them in the New Testament. In a moment of irritation during his last conversation with them, Yury thinks, 'Dear friends, how desperately commonplace you are . . . The only bright and living thing about you is that you are living at the same time as myself and are my friends.' In this conversation, too, he tells them of his approaching death. 'I'm not pretending, you know. It's an illness I've got, sclerosis of the heart. The walls of the heart muscle wear out and get too thin, and one fine day they'll burst.' The Bridegroom will not be with them much longer.

'Five or ten' years later—that is, within the era of Stalin, of blood, terror and injustice on an unheard-of scale—Gordon and Dudorov sit at the window and feel 'a peaceful joy for this holy city and for the whole land'. Objectively, there is little enough to warrant these stirrings of happiness. But then, five or ten years after the Crucifixion, the Roman Empire seemed as inert, as immovable, as brutal as ever.

Zhivago, like Christ, has triumphed by submitting. He has allowed material circumstances to sweep over him and then come sprouting up like the seed from the earth. Just as there are various points in the Gospel narrative at which Christ could have stepped aside from the path that led to the Cross, so there are various points in Zhivago's story at which he could have turned away from the years of decline, the descent into anonymity and poverty, the heart attack on the tram, the fatal spasm on the pavement. But he chose consistently to stay on that path. 'You have no will,' says Lara to him in one of their profound and tender conversations. But in the larger perspective of the whole story, we, the readers, can see that Zhivago does what a wilful man could not do. He builds his whole life

on a deep act of choice, choosing his death and choosing his resurrection. (pp. 157-58)

> *John Wain, "The Meaning of 'Dr. Zhivago',"*
> *in his* A House for the Truth: Critical Essays,
> *1972. Reprint by The Viking Press, 1973, pp.*
> *128-60.*

Czesław Miłosz

For those who were familiar with the poetry of Boris Pasternak long before he acquired international fame, the Nobel Prize given to him in 1958 had something ironic in it. A poet whose equal in Russia was only Akhmatova, and a congenial translator of Shakespeare, had to write a big novel, and that novel had to become a sensation and a best seller before poets of the Slavic countries were honored for the first time in his person by the jury of Stockholm. Had the prize been awarded to Pasternak a few years earlier, no misgivings would have been possible. As it was, the honor had a bitter taste and could hardly be considered as proof of genuine interest in Eastern European literatures on the part of the Western reading public—this quite apart from the good intentions of the Swedish Academy.

After *Doctor Zhivago* Pasternak found himself entangled in the kind of ambiguity that ought to be a nightmare of every author. While he always stressed the unity of his work, that unity was broken by circumstances. Abuse was heaped on him in Russia for a novel nobody had ever read. Praise was lavished on him in the West for a novel isolated from his lifelong labors: his poetry is nearly untranslatable. No man wishes to be changed into a symbol, whether the symbolic features lent him are those of a valiant knight or of a bugaboo: in such cases he is not judged by what he cherishes as his achievement but becomes a focal point of forces largely external to his will. In the last years of his life Pasternak lost, so to speak, the right to his personality, and his name served to designate a cause. I am far from intending to reduce that cause to political games of the moment. Pasternak stood for the individual against whom the large state apparatus turns in hatred with all its police, armies, and rockets. The emotional response to such a predicament was rooted in deep-seated fears so justified in our time. . . .

The attention the critics centered on *Doctor Zhivago* has delayed, however, an assessment of Pasternak's work as a whole. It is possible that we are now witnessing only the first gropings in that direction. My attempt here is not so much to make a neatly balanced appraisal as to stress a few aspects of his writings.

I became acquainted with his poetry in the thirties when he was highly regarded in Polish literary circles. This was the Pasternak of *The Second Birth* (1934); the rhythm of certain "ballads" printed in that volume has been haunting me ever since. Yet Pasternak did not appear to his Polish readers as an exotic animal; it was precisely what was familiar in his poems that created some obstacles to unqualified approval. In spite of the considerable differences between Polish and Russian poetry, the poets who had been shaped by "modernistic" trends victorious at the beginning of the century showed striking similarities due to their quite cosmopolitan formation. . . . Now the fact is that in the thirties the poetics represented by those eminent figures was breaking down. The young poets who claimed the name of "avant-garde" paid lip-service to the recognized brilliance of their elders, but looked at them with suspicion and often attacked them openly. In spite of all the loose talk proper to so-called literary movements, some serious matters were at stake, though veiled by disputes over metaphor and syntax. Those quarrels proved to be fruitful and later gave a new perspective on the writers then in combat. Pasternak, however, to the extent that he was used as an argument by the traditionalists, partisans of the "sonorous" verse inherited from symbolism, had to share the fate of his allies, venerated and mistrusted at the same time by the young. (p. 215)

Of Pasternak's eminence, I have never had any doubts. In an article written in 1954 (before ***Doctor Zhivago***) I predicted that a statue of Pasternak would stand one day in Moscow.

The Image of the Poet. Half a century separates us from the Russian Revolution. When we consider that the Revolution was expected to bring about the end of the alienation of the writer and of the artist, and consequently to inaugurate new poetry of a kind never known before, the place Pasternak occupies today in Russian poetry is astounding. After all, his formative years preceded World War I, and his craft retained some habits of that era. Like many of his contemporaries in various countries, he drew upon the heritage of French *poètes maudits*. . . . A peculiar image was created by French poets of the nineteenth century, not without help from the minor German romantics and Edgar Allan Poe; this image soon became common property of the international avant-garde. The poet saw himself as a man estranged from a society serving false values, an inhabitant of *la cité infernale,* or, if you prefer, of the wasteland and passionately opposed to it. He was the only man in quest of true values, aware of surrounding falsity, and had to suffer because of his awareness. Whether he chose rebellion or contemplative art for art's sake, his revolutionary technique of writing served a double purpose: to destroy automatism of opinions and beliefs transmitted through a frozen, inherited style; to mark his distance from the idiom of those who lived false lives. Speculative thought, monopolized by optimistic Philistines, was proclaimed taboo: the poet moved in another realm, nearer to the heart of things. Thoeries of two languages were elaborated: *le langage lyrique* was presented as autonomous, not translatable into any logical terms which are proper to *le langage scientifique.* Yet the poet had to pay the price. There are limits beyond which the poet cannot go and maintain communication with his readers. Few are connoisseurs. Sophistication, or as Tolstoy called it, *utonchenie,* is self-perpetuating, like drug addiction. (pp. 215-16)

The image of the poet that we find in the early poems of Pasternak corresponds to the pattern dear to literary schools at the turn of the century: the poet is a mysterious, elusive creature living in accordance with his own laws which are not the laws of ordinary mortals. To quote Pasternak: "When a poet is in love, a displaced god falls in love and chaos crawls out into the world again as in the time of fossils." A man born with an ultraperceptive sensory apparatus gradually discovers that personal destiny which estranges him from the world and transforms a fa-

miliar reality into phantasmagoria: "Thus the seas, sudden as a sigh, open up flowing over the fences, to where houses should have stood; thus the iambs start." The weird, incongruous core of things unveils itself to the poet. He is overpowered by elemental forces speaking through him, his words are magical incantation, he is a shaman, a witch doctor. (p. 216)

Pasternak achieved perfection within the framework of traditional meter; one can also say that the wisdom of his maturity grew slowly and organically out of the image of the poet he shared in his youth with many poets. His poetry is written in rhymed stanzas, mostly quatrains. His experimentation consisted in inventing incredible assonances and in weighting every line to the breaking point with metaphors. Such a superabundance should have inclined him, it seems, to search for a principle of construction other than that of pure musicality. Perhaps Pasternak was afraid that his world of flickering bits of colors, of lights and of shadows would disintegrate if deprived of a unifying singsong. He is often a prestidigitator in a corset, which he wears as if to enhance his skill in the reader's eyes. It so happened that in this attachment to meter he fulfilled, at least outwardly, the official requirements. Strangely enough, in Russia meter and rhyme acceded to political dignity through the rulers' decision to freeze art and literature in their "healthy" stages of the past. Here an analogy between poetry and painting imposes itself: certain popular notions of the distinctive marks proper to the poet and to the painter have been carefully preserved; the poet is a man who writes columns of rhymed lines; the painter is a man who puts people and landscapes on his canvas "as if they were alive." Those who depart from that rule lack the necessary artistic qualities.

Pasternak's poetry is antispeculative, anti-intellectual. It is poetry of sensory perception. His worship of life meant a fascination with what can be called nature's moods: air, rain, clouds, snow in the streets, a detail changing, thanks to the time of the day or night, to the season. Yet this is a very *linguistic* nature. In the Slavic languages words denoting planets, plants, and animals preserve their ancient power; they are loaded with a prestige of their femininity or masculinity. Hence the obsessive desire to identify the word with the object. (pp. 216-17)

Pasternak gradually modified for his peculiar use his image of the poet as an exceptional being in direct contact with the forces of universal life. He stressed more and more passive receptivity as the poet's greatest virtue. The following pronouncement (from 1922) is characteristic: "Contemporary trends conceived art as a fountain though it is a sponge. They decided it should spring forth, though it should absorb and become saturated. In their estimation it can be decomposed into inventive procedures, though it is made of the organs of reception. Art should always be among the spectators and should look in a purer, more receptive, truer way than any spectator does; yet in our days art got acquainted with powder and the dressing room; it showed itself upon the stage as if there were in the world two arts, and one of them, since the other was always in reserve, could afford the luxury of self-distortion, equal to a suicide. It shows itself off, though it should hide itself up in the gallery, in anonymity." (p. 217)

Not all Pasternak's poems are personal notes from his private diary or, to put it differently, "Les jardins sous la pluie" of Claude Debussy. As befitted a poet in the Soviet Union, in the twenties he took to vast historical panoramas, foretelling *Doctor Zhivago.* He enlivened a textbook cliché (I do not pretend to judge that cliché; it can be quite close to reality and be sublime) with all the treasures of detail registered by the eye of an adolescent witness; Pasternak was fifteen when the revolutionary events occurred that are described in the long poems: *The Year 1905* and *Lieutenant Schmidt.* Compared with his short poems, they seem to me failures. The technique of patches and glimpses does not fit the subject. There is no overall commitment; the intellect is recognized as inferior to the five senses and is refused access to the material. As a result, we have the theme and the embroidery; the theme, by contrast, returns to its quality of a cliché.

Thus I tend to accuse Pasternak . . . of a programmatic helplessness in the face of the world, of a carefully cultivated irrational attitude. Yet it was exactly this attitude that saved Pasternak's art and perhaps his life in the sad Stalinist era. Pasternak's more intellectually inclined colleagues answered argument by argument, and in consequence they were either liquidated or they accepted the supreme wisdom of the official doctrine. Pasternak eluded all categories; the "meaning" of his poems was that of lizards or butterflies—and who could pin down such phenomena using Hegelian terms? He did not pluck fruits from the Tree of Reason. The Tree of Life was enough for him. Confronted by argument, he replied with his sacred dance.

We can agree that in the given conditions that was the only victory possible. Yet if we assume that those epochs when poetry is amputated, forbidden thought, reduced to imagery and musicality, are not the most healthy, then Pasternak's was a Pyrrhic victory. When a poet can preserve his freedom only if he is deemed a harmless fool, a *iurodivyǐ,* holy because bereft of reason, his society is sick. Pasternak noticed that he had been maneuvered into Hamlet's position. As a weird being, he was protected from the ruler's answer, and he had to play the card of his weirdness; but what could he do with his moral indignation at the sight of the crime perpetrated upon millions of people? What could he do with his love for suffering Russia? That was the question.

His mature poetry underwent a serious evolution. He was right, I feel, when at the end of his life he confessed that he did not like his style prior to 1940: "My hearing was spoiled then by the general freakishness and the breakage of everything customary—procedures ruling then around me. Anything said in a normal way shocked me. I used to forget that words can contain something and mean something in themselves, apart from the trinkets with which they are adorned." "I searched everywhere not for essence but for extraneous pungency." We can read into that judgment more than a farewell to a technique. He never lost his belief in the redeeming power of art understood as a moral discipline, but his late poems can be called Tolstoyan in their nakedness. He strives to give in them explicitly a certain vision of the human condition.

I did not find in Pasternak's work any hint of his philosophical opposition to the official Soviet doctrine, unless his reluctance to deal with abstractions, so that the terms *abstract* and *false* were for him synonymous, is a proof of his resistance. The life of Soviet citizens was, however, his

life, and in his patriotic poems he was not paying mere lip service. He was no more rebellious than any average Russian. *Doctor Zhivago* is a Christian book, yet there is no trace in it of that polemic with the anti-Christian concept of man, which makes the strength of Dostoevsky. Pasternak's Christianity is atheological. It is very difficult to analyze a Weltanschauung which pretends not to be a Weltanschauung at all, but simply "closeness to life," while in fact it blends contradictory ideas borrowed from extensive readings. Perhaps we should not analyze. Pasternak was a man spellbound by reality, which was for him miraculous. He accepted suffering because the very essence of life is suffering, death, and rebirth; and he treated art as a gift of the Holy Spirit.

We would not know, however, of his hidden faith without *Doctor Zhivago.* His poetry—even if we put aside the question of censorship—was too fragile an instrument to express, after all, ideas. To do his Hamlet deed, Pasternak had to write a big novel. By that deed he created a new myth of the writer, and we may conjecture that it will endure in Russian literature like other already mythical events: Pushkin's duels, Gogol's struggles with the devil, Tolstoy's escape from Yasnaya Poliana.

A Novel of Adventures, Recognitions, Horrors, and Secrets. The success of *Doctor Zhivago* in the West cannot be explained by the scandal accompanying its publication or by political thrills. Western novel-readers have been reduced in our times to quite lean fare, for the novel, beset by its enemy, psychology, has been moving toward the programmatic leanness of the antinovel. *Doctor Zhivago* satisfied a legitimate yearning for a narrative full of extraordinary happenings, narrow escapes, crisscrossing plots, and, contrary to the microscopic analyses of Western novelists, open to huge vistas of space and historical time. The novel-reader is a glutton, and he knows immediately whether a writer is one also. In his desire to embrace the unexpectedness and wonderful fluidity of life, Pasternak showed a gluttony equal to that of his nineteenth-century predecessors.

Critics have not been able to agree how *Doctor Zhivago* should be classified. The most obvious thing was to speak of a revival of great Russian prose and to invoke the name of Tolstoy; but then the improbable encounters and nearly miraculous interventions Pasternak is so fond of had to be dismissed as mistakes and offenses against realism. Other critics, like Edmund Wilson, treated the novel as a web of symbols, going so far sometimes in this direction that Pasternak in his letters had to deny he ever meant all that. Still other critics, like Gleb Struve, tried to mitigate this tendency, yet conceded that *Doctor Zhivago* was related to Russian symbolist prose of the beginning of the century. The suggestion I am going to make has been advanced by no one, as far as I know.

It is appropriate, I feel, to start with a simple fact: Pasternak was a Soviet writer. One may add, to displease his enemies and some of his friends, that he was not an "internal émigré," but shared the joys and sorrows of the writers' community in Moscow. If his community turned against him in a decisive moment, it proves only that every literary confraternity is a nest of vipers and that servile vipers can be particularly nasty. (pp. 217-18)

According to the official doctrine, in a class society vigorous literature could be produced only by a vigorous, ascending class. The novel, as a new literary genre, swept eighteenth-century England. Thanks to its buoyant realism it was a weapon of the ascending bourgeoisie and served to debunk the receding aristocratic order. Since the proletariat is a victorious class, it should have an appropriate literature: namely, a literature as vigorous as the bourgeoisie had in its upsurge. This is the era of socialist realism, and Soviet writers should learn from "healthy" novelists of the past centuries while avoiding neurotic writings produced in the West by the bourgeoisie in its decline. This reasoning, which I oversimplify for the sake of clarity, but not too much, explains the enormous prestige of the English eighteenth-century novel in the Soviet Union.

Pasternak did not have to share the official opinions as to the economic causes and literary effects in order to feel pleasure in reading English "classics," as they are called in Russia. A professional translator for many years, mostly from English, he probably had them all in his own library in the original. While the idea of his major work was slowly maturing in his mind, he must often have thought of the disquieting trends in modern Western fiction. In the West fiction lived by denying more and more its nature, or even by behaving like the magician whose last trick is to unveil how his tricks were done. Yet in Russia socialist realism was an artistic flop, and nobody heeded, of course, the repeated advice to learn from the "classics": an invitation to joyous movement addressed to people in straitjackets is nothing more than a crude joke; and what if somebody, in the spirit of spite, tried to learn?

Doctor Zhivago, a book of hide-and-seek with fate, reminds me irresistably of one English novel: Fielding's *Tom Jones.* True, we may have to make some effort to connect the horses and inns of a countryside England with the railroads and woods of Russia, yet we are forced to do so by the travel through enigmas in both novels. Were the devices applied mechanically by Pasternak, the parallel with Fielding would be of no consequence; but in *Doctor Zhivago* they become signs which convey his affirmation of the universe, of life, to use his preferred word. They hint at his sly denial of the trim, rationalized, ordered reality of the Marxist philosophers and reclaim another richer subterranean reality. Moreover, the devices correspond perfectly to the experience of Pasternak himself and of all the Russians. Anyone who has lived through wars and revolutions knows that in a human anthill on fire the number of extraordinary meetings, unbelievable coincidences, multiplies tremendously in comparison with periods of peace and everyday routine. One survives because one was five minutes late at a given address, where everybody got arrested, or because one did not catch a train which was soon to be blown to pieces. Was that an accident, Fate, or Providence?

If we assume that Pasternak consciously borrowed his devices from the eighteenth-century novel, his supposed sins against realism will not seem so disquieting. He had his own views on realism. Also we shall be less tempted to hunt for symbols in *Doctor Zhivago,* as if for raisins in a cake. Pasternak perceived the very texture of life as symbolic, so its description did not call for those protruding and all too obvious allegories. Situations and characters sufficed; to those who do not feel the eighteenth-century flavor in the novel, I can point to the interventions of the

enigmatic Yevgraf, half-Asiatic, the natural brother of Yuri Zhivago, who emerges from the crowd every time the hero is in extreme danger and, after having accomplished what he had to, returns to anonymity. He is a benevolent lord protector of Yuri; instead of an aristocratic title, he has connections at the top of the Communist Party. Here again the situation is realistic: to secure an ally at the top of the hierarchy is the first rule of behavior in such countries as the Soviet Union.

The Poet as a Hero. Yuri Zhivago is a poet, a successor to the West European bohemian, torn asunder by two contradictory urges: withdrawal into himself, the only receptacle or creator of value; movement toward society, which has to be saved. He is also a successor to the Russian "superfluous man." As for virtues, he cannot be said to possess much initiative and manliness. Nevertheless, the reader is in deep sympathy with Yuri, since he, the author affirms, is a bearer of charisma, a defender of vegetal "inner freedom." A passive witness of bloodshed, of lies and debasement, Yuri must do something to deny the utter insignificance of the individual. Two ways are offered to him: either the way of Eastern Christianity or the way of Hamlet.

Pity and respect for the *iurodivyĭ,* a halfwit in tatters, a being at the very bottom of the social scale, has ancient roots in Russia. The *iurodivyĭ,* protected by his madness, spoke truth in the teeth of the powerful and wealthy. He was outside society and denounced it in the name of God's ideal order. Possibly in many cases his madness was only a mask. In some respects he recalls Shakespeare's fools. . . . (pp. 218-19)

Yuri Zhivago in the years following the civil war makes a plunge to the bottom of the social pyramid. He forgets his medical diploma and leads a shady existence as the husband of the daughter of his former janitor, doing menial jobs, provided with what in the political slang of Eastern Europe are called "madman's papers." His refusal to become a member of the "new intelligentsia" implies that withdrawal from the world is the only way to preserve integrity in a city that is ruled by falsehood. Nevertheless, in Yuri Zhivago there is another trait. He writes poems on Hamlet and sees himself as Hamlet. Yes, but Hamlet is basically a man with a goal, and action is inseparable from understanding the game. Yuri has an intuitive grasp of good and evil but is no more able to understand what is going on in Russia than a bee can analyze chemically the glass of a windowpane against which it is beating. Thus the only act left to Yuri is a poetic act, equated with the defense of the language menaced by the totalitarian doubletalk or, in other words, with the defense of authenticity. The circle closes; a poet who rushed out of his tower is back in his tower.

Yuri's difficulty is that of Pasternak and of his Soviet contemporaries. Pasternak solved it a little better than his hero—by writing not poems but a novel, his Hamletic act. The difficulty persists, though, throughout the book. It is engendered by the acceptance of a view of history so widespread in the Soviet Union that it is a part of the air one breathes. According to this view, history proceeds along preordained tracks, it moves forward by "jumps," and the Russian Revolution (together with what followed) was such a jump of cosmic dimension. To be for or against an explosion of historical forces is as ridiculous as to be for or against a tempest or the rotation of the seasons. The human will does not count in such a cataclysm, since even the leaders are but tools of mighty "processes." As many pages of his work testify, Pasternak did not question that view. Did he not say in one of his poems that everything by which this century will live is in Moscow? He seemed to be interpreting Marxism in a religious way; and is not Marxism a secularized biblical faith in the final accomplishment, implying a providential plan? No wonder that Pasternak, as he says in his letter to Jacqueline de Proyart, liked the writings of Teilhard de Chardin so much. The French Jesuit also believed in the Christological character of lay history and curiously combined Christianity with the Bergsonian "creative evolution" as well as with the Hegelian ascending movement. (pp. 219-20)

The latent "Teilhardism" of *Doctor Zhivago* makes it a Soviet novel—in the sense that one might read into it an esoteric interpretation offered by official pronouncements. The historical tragedy is endowed with all the trappings of necessity working toward the ultimate good. Perhaps the novel is a tale about the individual versus Caesar, but with a difference: the new Caesar's might has its source not only in his legions.

What could poor Yuri Zhivago do in the face of a system blessed by history and yet repugnant to his notions of good and evil? Intellectually, he was paralyzed. He could only rely on his subliminal self, descend deeper than thought monopolized by the state. Being a poet, he clutches at his belief in communion with ever-reborn life. Life will take care of itself. Persephone always comes back from the underground, winter's ice is dissolved, dark eras are necessary as stages of preparation, life and history have a hidden Christian meaning—and suffering purifies.

Pasternak overcame his isolation by listening to the silent complaint of the Russian people; we respond strongly to the atmosphere of hope pervading *Doctor Zhivago.* Not without some doubts, however. Life rarely takes care of itself, unless human beings decide to take care of themselves. Sufferings can either purify or corrupt, and too great suffering too often corrupts. Of course, hope itself, if it is shared by all the nation, may be a powerful factor for change. Yet, when at the end of the novel friends of the long-dead Yuri Zhivago console themselves with timid expectations, they are counting upon an indefinite something (death of the tyrant?), and their political thinking is not far from the grim Soviet joke about the best constitution in the world being one that grants to every citizen the right to a postmortem rehabilitation.

However, Pasternak's weaknesses are dialectically bound up with his great discovery. He conceded so much to his adversary, speculative thought, that what remained was to make a jump into a completely different dimension. *Doctor Zhivago* is not a novel of social criticism; it does not advocate a return to Lenin or to the young Marx. It is profoundly arevisionist. Its message summarizes the experience of Pasternak the poet: whoever engages in a polemic with the thought embodied in the state will destroy himself, for he will become a hollow man. It is impossible to talk to the new Caesar, for then you choose the encounter on his ground. What is needed is a new beginning, new in the present conditions but not new in Russia, marked as it is by centuries of Christianity. Literature of socialist realism should be shelved and forgotten. The new dimen-

sion is that of every man's mysterious destiny, of compassion and faith. In this, Pasternak revived the best traditions of Russian literature. . . .

The paradox of Pasternak lies in his narcissistic art leading him behind the confines of his ego. Also in his reedlike pliability, so that he often absorbed *les idées reçues* without examining them throughly as ideas but without being crushed by them either. Probably no reader of Russian poets resists a temptation to juxtapose the two fates: Pasternak's and Mandelstam's. The survival of the first and the death in a concentration camp of the second may be ascribed to various factors, to good luck and bad luck. Still, there is something in Mandelstam's poetry, intellectually structured, that doomed him in advance. From what I have said about my generation's quarrel with worshipers of Life, it should be obvious that Mandelstam, not Pasternak, is for me the ideal of a modern classical poet; but he had too few weaknesses, was crystalline, resistant, and therefore fragile. Pasternak, more exuberant, less exacting, uneven, was called to write a novel which, in spite and because of its contradictions, is a great book. (p. 220)

Czesław Miłosz, "On Pasternak Soberly [1970]," in World Literature Today, *Vol. 63, No. 2, Spring, 1989, pp. 215-20.*

Peter Levi

Thirty years after the death of its author and the hushing of the storm it gave rise to, *Dr Zhivago* retains its freshness and its mystery. Critics have found it many-faceted and enigmatic, but as time passes that does not matter in the least. It is a vast, sprawling, beautiful book, symbolist at times, enormous in scope and range, able to focus finely and to turn on a sixpence. It is certainly a work of genius, but not a Tolstoyan novel, because its lucidity comes and goes, and so does its sense of history; it is not really a novel at all, in any received sense. Some of its most important events happen between sections or chapters, its coincidences are extraordinary, and its time-scale negligent. Somewhere in the course of writing, Pasternak has put in an extra year, but this does not matter at all to the ordinary reader. It is as vast in ambition as any novel ever written, yet at times it has the feel of an allegory or a morality. It strays towards autobiography and it does throw some light on the poet's life, but the light is equivocal because its roots in reality are not single but complex, and Zhivago is not exactly Pasternak. It is the most memorable of Russian novels since Tolstoy's *Resurrection* (1899), which is saying a very great deal, and, more than any other work of fiction, it is the monument of its epoch, though it does not succeed in describing that epoch, 'Russia over the past forty-five years', as he told his cousin Olga.

Gladkov makes a sensible point about it when he complains that it seems to discuss the eternal Russian soul, Bolshevism, Stalinism and the victory over Hitler, and, although it was 'received abroad as something that offered a key to these mysteries, it does not in fact throw real light on any of them.' *Dr Zhivago* is about the world, though, and about real life, though more about life's interaction with the individual and with his soul, and of course with his poetry. As a portrait of a poet or artist it is unique in the history of literature: it is brilliantly convincing, and Zhivago's poems both add to the mystery and intensify the reality. They are the explosive part of the bullet. 'The hero will be something intermediate between me, Blok, Yesenin and Mayakovsky.' He is not just a poet but a great poet, and that in itself makes the book unique. One has only to imagine Auden or Yeats or Eliot writing such a book. Pasternak's sense of predestination, which is both philosophic and religious in colour, makes his book possible where theirs are not, because he believes absolutely in the significance of his story, and he communicates just that.

Feminists object to the women characters, who are pale or play stiff, old-fashioned roles in Zhivago's central light. . . . The negative critics have come in time to look ridiculous. Akhmatova was often funny about *Dr Zhivago,* which she said contained 'quite unprofessional pages; I think they were written by [Pasternak's lover] Olga Ivinskaya.' The idiot Costello, a New Zealander who used to infuriate Pasternak in the forties by trying to persuade him to join the Communist Party, wrote after Pasternak's death, 'Do people still read *Zhivago?* No one can have read it twice.' Sinyovsky called it 'a weak novel of genius'; if he means weak as a technical construction it is a true but misplaced remark, because the weakness is a necessary part of its mysterious and memorable strength: one would not like to read it tidied up by a subeditor. Professor Kermode cleverly calls it 'a heroic if flawed effort to impose upon the matter of realistic fiction the form of a post-imagist poem', but the truth is that such an attempt on such a scale makes no sense at all, and like most separations of matter and form this criticism is itself flawed. What is true all the same is that individual sections are written like lyric poems, with the same symbolist techniques, though the end of one of these poem-like pieces does not necessarily or usually correspond exactly with the end of a section of the novel. The prose wanders off under merely rational control until one suddenly notices another lyric has been crumbled into it. This technique is quite close to Kermode's conception, and helps to account for the extraordinary lyric impetus of *Dr Zhivago,* and its tranquil freedom of spirit. It may well be that, for Boris Pasternak as a lyric poet, *Dr Zhivago* was the breaking of a dam.

This lyrical technique recurs, but I found it particularly noticeable in the first two chapters. . . . Chapter 1 is called 'The Five o'Clock Express', and the train is spectacular, but consider the blowing of the wind in the first sentence and then at the end of the section, then five times in the second section. The wind carries on the chanting at the funeral, bears down on the boy and lashes him with rain, carries the plaintive hooting of engines, makes the acacias dance and the light flicker; its climax 'almost as if the snowstorm had caught sight of Uri and conscious of its power to terrify, roared, howled. . . . The blizzard was alone on earth and knew no rival.' That is the end of the wind, which has served its lyric purpose. Later there are recurring birds, horses, and so on, and the narrative is sprinkled with bits of autobiography unrelated to the story except as symbols: the Kologrivov place in section 4 is just like Obolenskoye, and in Moscow there are addresses the reader [may] . . . recognise. The novel is in a way about the freedom of spirit necessary to write the novel, about the poet's poetry and love and soul, but not about his biography. Its realism is a huge advance on the early prose and on *Spektorsky,* but it is not the fictional history of modern Russia people were waiting for. As for the formal influ-

ences that may help to explain the mysterious construction of what he did write, the only one I can think of that critics have neglected is Charles Dickens's *A Tale of Two Cities,* which his cousin Olga notes was almost always on or near his desk while he was writing *Dr Zhivago.* 'It was the best of times, the worst of times . . . ' That treatment of the French revolution throws light on Pasternak's developed view of 1917.

He wrote in his awkward but oddly attractive English to John Harris in February 1959 about how the book is meant to work: 'There are aphorisms, definitions, statements in my novel. But the chief participation of thought in it does not lie in these open sentences (opinions uttered in dialogues, author's notes, etc. etc.) but in the hidden tendency which penetrates the very manner of my display of reality, of my description. Here, in my change of times, style of movement, character of colours, arrangement of groups is my latent unsaid philosophy. I could say more: my philosophy itself, as a whole, is in general rather an *inclination* than a conviction. . . . What matters in this case are not the different, separate notions and sayings, but the constant peculiar light in which everything is seen, lived, reflected and said.'

The light is surely that of Christianity and of poetry: details of the text constantly reflect particular bits of poems as of early prose. The death of the boy commissar Gintz, for example, becomes an allegory or a fable, however brutally it finishes, and the train that carries Zhivago homewards has shadows that leap across it and out of the opposite windows as the lights did earlier. The forest clearing where the soldiers encamp in the same chapter, with its wild strawberries and timber and abandoned huts, is not only idyllic: it is like a poem, though the poem is aborted: it is reduced to an elegiac note or two about the Tolstoyan rebels like English Levellers. The timber of the Cossack horse-vans, reduced by time to a close affinity with natural timber, is part of this lost poem. But Pasternak's letters make clear an overriding mystical and religious intention. I have felt this in many rereadings of the novel itself, even in its small-scale complexities and enigmas. In 1959, when he wrote to Harris, he was getting further away from the writing of the text, and he was a dying man; his interpretations of his book doubtless grew more intensely mystical than they might have been earlier. Still, one must accept both the sincerity and the reality of his vision of what gives meaning to *Zhivago,* and perhaps to life itself.

The epilogue confirms this: it is written in a despair curiously streaked with hope. Pasternak's political view of the first thirty years of his life had probably remained the same or intensified. When Zhivago went home to Moscow from the war, 'Here too were his loyalty to the revolution and his admiration for it, the revolution in the sense in which it was accepted by the middle classes and in which it has been understood by the students, followers of Blok, in 1905.' Later his experience became wide, and he saw human consequences work themselves out: hence the vast range of the book. But still 'civic institutions should be founded on democracy, they should grow up from below, like seedlings that are planted and take root in the soil. You can't hammer them in from above like stakes for a fence.' . . . His hope for Russia, and the meaning that he saw in history, could be more easily stated in religious or mystical terms than in any others. He wrote in August

1959 to Stephen Spender that he had seen nature and the world as a kind of painted canvas roof, pulling and blowing and flapping in the air, 'an unknown, unknowable wind'. In the same letter he says, 'there is an effort in the novel to represent the whole sequence of facts and beings and happenings like some moving entireness, like a developing, passing by, rolling and rushing inspiration, as if reality itself had freedom and choice and was composing itself out of numberless variants and versions.' This is not a Hegelian or a Marxist or any other classic philosopher's view of history; it is his own.

But the story, like every long story since the *Iliad,* consists of its details. The multiplicity of its characters is so dazing that at one point the Collins translation leaves them out. . . . (pp. 210-14)

After five or six full rereadings I still find it as hard to remember who is who in *Dr Zhivago* as in the *Iliad. Dr Zhivago,* like the *Iliad,* is based on earlier attempts, and in that way it can be studied as a development of themes. . . . The prose fragments written between 1937 and 1939, to which one may add the mastery of style in his wartime reporting, show a particular affinity with the novel . . . But only in *Zhivago* does he call Lenin 'vengeance incarnate' and Stalin a 'pockmarked Caligula', and deride Marxism as unobjective, uncontrolled, unscientific, and having something in common with mediocrities and 'victims of the herd instinct'. In the concrete, in terms of characters, he is less harsh and more penetrating. He is excellent at the old, embittered railwaymen, like grim and silent gods at whose feet the revolution laid its smoking sacrifices. No writer has been more conscious of the paths of young extremists or of the irony of events. Vignettes of characters tied loosely to the edges of history and of this book are like separate short stories, but their oblique, sometimes unspoken, commentary on the central narrative is essential.

What makes *Zhivago* different from other books and, as Boris Pasternak knew, quite different from his earlier lyric poetry is the fullness of its integrity and the range of its wisdom. There are awkward sentences in it, which Akhmatova swatted like midges, but no unreadable pages, no boring paragraphs. One reads and rereads it, continually enthralled, and entering into a world one cannot really know. Why? Because it is written in what Eliot called a 'condition of complete simplicity, costing not less than everything'. And what is this work about? Not religion, not even poetry, though his poetry is essential to it as the fine point of Zhivago's expression, and the assurance of his immortality. It is about suffering, about war, civil war, revolution and the hell of life, and among these the tracks of love, which are so painful and so moving and without which we could not live. It is a love story as his own life was: the women characters are multiple, but Tanya has a bit more of [Pasternak's second wife] Zinaida in her youth, and Lara more of Olga Ivinskaya in hers.

Before going through the book or the affair of Boris and Olga in any more detail, it would be best to look closely at the Zhivago poems. Some of them can be attached to precise places in the prose text, but some cannot, and it does not seem to matter, since they form a series, and they are all written by a mature poet who has turned his back on the state and intends to tell the truth about it. His simplicity has become stony and prose-like, but that only

means that one can feel the force of prose behind the force of poetry, as one often can in the mature poetry of Yeats. That analogy is worth pursuing, because they both had to extricate themselves from dream-worlds, from symbolism and from a prose habit which was relatively arty. (pp. 214-15)

The order of the poems is probably important, since it draws attention to a correspondence between the first poem and the last. We know independently that Boris Pasternak took a high view of Hamlet, whom he thought a noble character, no mere ditherer, and we know that his poem "Hamlet" was in a way prophetic of the storm that would break on his head when *Dr Zhivago* was published. The book was written knowingly, but Boris had early experience of the role of reluctant Hamlet from the twenties and thirties; it may even have been basic to his psychology. In these poems Hamlet is like Christ, and the series ends with Christ in the garden of Gethsemane, a Christ who is like Hamlet, longing for the cup to be taken away. But this restatement of the Hamlet theme, which obsesses several poems at the end of the series, adds a prophecy.

> The book of life has turned the page
> to what is holy and most precious to men,
> what is written shall be fulfilled:
> so be it. Amen.
>
> Look. Centuries of years like parables
> passed, each on fire as it went:
> in the name of its terrible majesty I shall go
> freely down to the grave through torment.
>
> And on the third day I shall rise again,
> like rafts going downriver, like a long line of barges
> they shall float down to me from their darkness
> to be judged, and I shall judge the centuries.

To take these last poems first, the whole Christian section is in the position of climax at the end. It begins with **"Christian Star"**, a long Dutch Nativity scene with the rhythm of a gentle snowfall, which we know from early in the novel to be a tribute to Blok. . . . The poem is original and surprising; it is a landscape poem and one that casually makes itself a position where there seemed no room, a poem that makes itself at home among all existing poems, yet with no concession to cliché. 'Angrier and wickeder the wind blew from the steppe', though there are no wolves. At the end, 'Gazing at the Virgin like a guest, the Christmas Star was standing in the doorway'.

Next comes **"Daybreak"**, a poem that expresses charity, a Christian outlook. It is a restatement of the title poem from *On Early Trains,* about travelling into Moscow on the community train. One might have taken **"Daybreak"** to express socialist warmth and camaraderie. 'All night I read your testament . . . I want to be among people . . . and bring them to their knees. . . . In me are people without names. Children, stay-at-homes, trees. I am conquered by them all, this is my only victory.' It goes deeper than the poem it restates, though that does not necessarily make it a better poem; the context makes it more powerful, that is all. **"The Miracle"** follows: it is the miracle of the barren fig tree that Christ cursed, here applied not to Israel but, I assume, to Russia. The next poem, **"The Earth"**, is about spring in Moscow. Zhivago (or Pasternak) feels his calling extends to a responsibility 'that the distances should not lose heart, the earth should not feel lonely'. So he gathers with his friends, 'and our evenings are farewells and our parties are testaments', like the Last Supper, we must assume, 'So that the secret stream of suffering should warm the cold of life.' This looks like another poem of applied Christianity, sandwiched like **"Daybreak"** between two mythological Christian poems. The series ends with **"Evil Days"**, which is about Christ when the crowd turns on him, then the two 'Mary Magdalene' poems, of Bach-like grief and redemption, and **"Gethsemane"**. The last stanza of **"Evil Days"** is about Christ's memory: the fluttering candle goes back a long way in Pasternak's poetry and life.

> And the poor in their hovel, gathering,
> and going down to the vault, candle lighted,
> and the candle in terror snuffing out
> when Lazarus stood up out of the dead.

Those of these poems that are not about fear like Hamlet's transformed to Christ's (a theme that first appears, I think, in *Lieutenant Schmidt*) are all touched with the Resurrection. They were all the more of a wonder in Russia, because this kind of poetry, which in England might almost have been written by a rural dean in the eighteenth century, simply does not exist in Russian. Its formal source for Boris Pasternak was probably in Lutheran hymns. Congregational hymns of that kind do not exist in Russian either. The Russians have splendid and far more exciting kinds of religious poetry. Pasternak has made native in his language a new kind of poetry, and done so with complete assurance. (pp. 215-18)

The poem **"Hamlet"** which opens the entire series and echoes right through it, is famous. (p. 218)

[It is followed by] a poem called **"March"** seething with rustic life, then **"In Holy Week"**, relating the natural countryside to the Orthodox liturgy and lightly tinged at the end with the coming Resurrection. It is not as forceful as the later Christian poems. **"White Night"** remembers Petersburg; it is a memory of a girl student from Kursk, 'daughter of a small landowner of the steppes'. I am unable to fit this poem exactly into the novel, but nor can I find poems to fit all the moments in the novel when Zhivago writes them. This poem is light and generous, and its nightingales are thunderously loud in the woods. **"Spring Floods"** has nightingales even more prominent, and linked with the nightingale of a famous and ominous folksong from southern Russia called 'Ilya of Murom and Nightingale the Robber'. 'Sparks and fire poured from his mouth and nostrils, he piped like a nightingale, roared like an auroch, and hissed like a dragon,' says the epic, and his whistle caused an earthquake that destroyed the city of Kiev. Pasternak was fond of him, and in this poem it seemed he would come out of his forest lair to meet the partisans. This poem and the next, **"Explanation"**, which is about a difficult love affair, can be more or less anchored in the novel; so perhaps can **"Summer in Town"**, which is about a woman, and **"Wind"**, if only because *Dr Zhivago* is full of wind-blasts and storms. (pp. 218-19)

The poems deliberately move on through seasons. After the slight love-epigram **"Intoxication"**,which is love in the open air, we come to **"Indian Summer"**, **"The Wedding-Party"** and **"Autumn"**. They are magnificently direct poems about happy days: they fit precisely into the novel. But after **"A Fairy Tale"** we are back to **"August"**. I had thought this poem was sad, even tragic, and that its un-

happiness probably placed it here. But the third part of it transforms all into an allegory of love overcoming dangers and lasting as it seems for ever. No doubt Zhivago is writing later, thinking back to the lost summer. After this comes one of the most mesmerising and beautiful of all his lyrics, **"Winter Night"**. (p. 219)

I despair of conveying the spirit of this simple and perfect poem. It is powerful in the same way as a Victorian poem, yet it is perfectly modern, indeed it is almost prose. It reads as if Zhivago has taken over from his creator and developed a life of his own, as so often happens to novelists, so that Pasternak was seeing with his hero's eyes. **"Parting"** and **"Meeting"** convey the same sensation, and then we come to **"Christmas Star"**. If I have dwelt a long time on the Zhivago poems it is not just because I think them so remarkable: they are not more remarkable than the prose text. But they give that text a powerful charge of emotional force, and of what I can only call inner life. By more directly expressing what Zhivago himself most deeply means they show you what the book means. They are arranged in a series in which his happiness in love reaches a climax in the summer and his deeper Christianity, which comes at the end, is more slowly achieved. Hamlet becomes Christ so slowly that one hardly notices. It may be worth adding that those who see *Dr Zhivago* as an epic novel (a phrase I personally find inappropriate) should consider the strange sub-epic narratives of Russian tradition, the folksongs of the Kiev cycle, which have had a more formative influence on Boris Pasternak than Homer and Virgil and Milton. 'Nightingale the Robber' is the only direct allusion, yet one often feels that folksongs are in the back of his mind. They may well have helped him attain the clarity of his narrative in *Dr Zhivago*, which is like spring water.

Dr Zhivago is written as a novel in two parts, with seven chapters in each, then a conclusion and an epilogue at the end of the second. The big division comes after the revolution, at the arrival near Varykino, far to the east, at the far side of the Urals. The first part is Zhivago's pre-war life, his marriage, the war and its consequences, including the revolution. But it is only in the second half that the poet finds himself; the lover follows a path far beyond normal matrimony, and it is fair to say that he both suffers and grows accordingly. The revolution also begins to sort itself out. The fact that old characters recur seems to me to mean only that this is what might become of such a type, such a person, a man in such a job, or such a man's son. Certain characters do remain enigmatic, though they are probably meant to be intelligible enough, such as Pasha Antipov and perhaps Yevgraf. Numerous events which were once taught in schools are now beginning to fade from memory, but Pasternak wrote for those who knew them; he wrote about what happened thirty years earlier, expecting much to be familiar. The names of characters are often apparent hints to their meaning, but are not systematic or very helpful. Yevgraf means 'good recorder' or 'evangelist'; he is possibly a sort of good angel. On the other hand Mikulin is named after a river. Zhivago means 'Life', or 'Doctor Lively', but I have been told Boris Pasternak found the name, however pleased he was by finding it, on the iron cover of a manhole somewhere in Moscow. The book may be pregnant with hidden symbolism, but not to me, so having recorded this aspect of the book I will now ignore it.

'The Five o'Clock Express' is a lyrical introduction to what were meant to be some principal themes of the entire book. New characters occur on every page, and we see a variety of provincial places and railway trains. The first section is the funeral of Zhivago's mother. He climbs on top of her grave and all but howls like a wolf. The wind and the rain lash on him, then his uncle Kolya, a distinctly unmotherly unfrocked priest, leads him off to a monastery where they spend the night. Kolya works for a progressive newspaper in a provincial town on the Volga. The evening is cold and spooky, and the snowstorm howls, roars and terrifies the poor child. He is ten years old, deserted by his father long ago in favour of 'wenching and carousing'. Two years later the boy is taken to see another progressive writer in the country, which he hears is ripe for revolution. Kolya becomes for a brief moment interesting, because he is a man going somewhere unknown: the books that will make him famous are still unwritten, he has been a priest, a Tolstoyan and 'a revolutionary idealist', his mind moves freely and 'welcomes the unfamiliar'. But the progressive writer, who lives on the estate of a progressive millionaire, is as dry as dust; his conversation has a period flavour, as Pasternak intended. Kolya explains how Christ has altered the meaning of death, and refers in passing to the deadness of Rome and the horrors of its pockmarked Caligula: surely Stalin.

Young Zhivago is twelve, but he weeps himself into fits for his mother, on his own in the woods. Meanwhile an express train has halted in the marshes, because of a suicide, which is actually that of his father, though no one knows that except the reader. The father was travelling with a 'thick-set, haughty lawyer' who will turn out to be Zhivago's evil genius, and the same train is full of characters we shall meet again. Misha Gordon is a Jewish boy, and with him the problem of Jewish consciousness is squarely faced, though it never gets developed. There is also an old woman whose husband was burned to death in an accident, and whose sons are engine drivers. We enter quite deeply into Misha and his problems, and into Nicky, a boy in the house, two years older than Zhivago and the son of a terrorist and a princess. Nicky tries to kiss a girl on a lake, but they both fall in. So far, almost none of these expansively sketched characters have met or talked to one another. It is as if Pasternak were merely experimenting, but that is the end of the chapter. Nicky's adolescence will have to do for Zhivago's, and Kolya and his writer friend will have to stand for a generation.

Writers do not have many themes or devices, they constantly re-use the same ones, so it is easy to pick up allusions to Boris Pasternak's own life, but at a deeper level: there is no tendency to autobiography here, rather the opposite. Why do both Zhivago's parents die? I think simply to get them out of the way. The riches that were lost are just romance: the smell in the woods reminded him of his mother at Antibes and Bordighera, and there was once an estate like an enchanted kingdom. You could tell your sleigh driver to take you there: can it have been Samarin's Peredelkino? 'The park closed round you as quiet as a countryside; cows scattered the hoar-frost as they settled on the heavy branches of the firs; their cawing echoed like cracking wood; pedigree dogs came running across the road out of the clearing where building was going on and where lights shone in the gathering dusk. Suddenly it all

vanished. They became poor.' How beautiful it is, and how strange, this extremely Russian paradise lost.

'A Girl from a Different World' begins in 1904 or 1905. It might as well be called 'Youth'. The wicked lawyer Komarovsky features here, and it all happens in Moscow: a mean hotel in Oruzheinyi Street, a repellent old dressmaker and her daughter Lara. In this chapter Zhivago becomes friendly with Misha and hears about his father's death. There seems to be a lot of Dickens in all this. The characters are so numerous they even include a canary in a cage called Kyril Modestovich. When Lara goes to sleep her thoughts are Boris Pasternak's, of the stuffed bears in the windows of the coachmakers' and the dragoons parading at the barracks. There are magnificent station scenes, and we meet Antipov's father, the track overseer, and an entire interlocking world of railway workers and their families. It was obviously Pasternak's intention to use these people, whom he knew from childhood, to show how the revolution had happened, and to people it with human faces. At times he overdoes the typical: 'As usual the old foreman, Pyotr Khudoleyev, was walloping Yusupka the apprentice.' But it is here and among railway workers that the plot begins to be gripping. We have had no high-life characters except the ghastly lawyer. The demonstration at the Arts School is formalised like a tale too often told, but the charge of the dragoons is brilliant, unexpected and sickening. Meanwhile Kolya has come to Moscow to write and sees the dragoons from his window. Zhivago now has lodging with a professor whose daughter is Tanya; Misha is close to them both. The young people read Tolstoy's *Kreutzer Sonata* and believe in chastity . . . and Komarovsky corrupts Lara.

In the middle of all of this, the Presnya rising takes place. Nicky and Pasha go to the barricades. People poured over them bucket after bucket of water, which froze immediately and must have made them formidable obstacles to horses. Nothing else could explain why determined cavalry was not able to clear the streets in an hour. 'The two boys were playing the most terrible and adult of games. . . . Good decent boys, thought Lara, it is because they are good they are shooting.' Zhivago really is just a boy, and he and Misha go with the doctor for fun for what turns out to be a gruesome visit to Lara's mother's attempted suicide. They are both embarrassed, but Zhivago's feelings are distinctly ambivalent; sex raises its head for him, and he has seen Lara. Throughout this chapter, as history and the novel gather pace, the most gripping element is the tiny details of railways and cold weather. Pasternak has not only created world beyond world of people but, more difficult still, a city. 'The air smelt of early winter in town—of trampled maple leaves, melted snow, and warm engine soot and rye bread just out of the oven (it was baked in the basement of the station buffet). Trains came and went and were shunted, coupled and uncoupled to the waving, furling and unfurling of signal flags. The deep engine hooters roared, and the horns and whistles of the guards and shunters tooted and trilled. Smoke rose in endless ladders to the sky, and hissing engines scalded the cold winter clouds with clouds of boiling steam.'

'Christmas Party at the Sventitskys' sees Tanya ready to graduate in law, Misha in philosophy and Yura Zhivago in medicine. His youth has therefore passed with only those incidents recorded which might have personal or do have historical significance. These experiences have been unpleasant, but it is hard to see that they make any difference to him in the future, since he emerges as sage, middle class, a doctor and a poet. Yet the book is cumulative, so one senses the suffering in its early chapters as if it were always present in him, and as if it somehow explained his quality of love, and the hidden impulse of his poetry. The superficial roots of poems occur in this third chapter, which begins and ends with death, resurrection in all its forms still being the conscious subject-matter of the whole work. Even in the dissecting room, Zhivago is thrilled by the mystery of other lives, and in section 3 he makes his first attempt at talking about the conquest of death. He is completely serious about this religious or philosophic comfort, of which Russia was deprived not by fashionable atheism but by the state. What he says therefore emerges with great force. No doubt that is also the point of the Christmas party. The roots of the poems appear superficial, yet the poems themselves are deeply felt. They are **"Winter Night"** and **"Christmas Star"**.

The melodramatic event of this chapter is Lara's shooting of Kamarovsky; it stands out even more vividly than the background rumble of history and the oddly beautiful process of the growing up of Lara and young Antipov, but the themes of life and burial are more deeply dramatic than any melodrama, and here they surround the shooting like heavy black edging on old letter paper. The wound is not at all bad. 'Well, you've been lucky. It's not even worth bandaging. A drop of iodine wouldn't do any harm though.' It is little more than symbolic, like a slap on the face, but the pistol no doubt derives from old stories about girls of the People's Will association in the last century, and the pistol-owning girl in ***Spektorsky.*** Yet as fiction it is perfectly judged, it seems the exact truth. One cannot imagine a Lara who would slap the lawyer's face, or a Lara who would be a good shot. The shooting gets a further revolutionary colouring from the presence of Kornakov, a prosecution lawyer against the railwaymen who in real life made a fanatical speech against them.

'The Advent of the Inevitable' takes us to 1917, to the excitements of the first revolution. Lara ends it remembering 1905, 'but how much more frightening it was now! You couldn't say, It's the children shooting, this time. The children had all grown up, the boys were all here, in the army.' It is interesting to what degree Lara rather than Zhivago is the consciousness and conscience on which the revolution registers. There is something persistently pure about the way in which she sees things: Zhivago by comparison is just a benevolent liberal, passive because he is a poet, no doubt. We begin with Komarovsky in the ruins of Christmas; Lara is ill and recovers, Pasha marries her and hears her past, so that he never recovers. The Antipovs move away to Yuryatin, where Lara's parents had lived, Zhivago is shown brilliantly at work in a hospital, his wife Tanya has a son. He goes on to the war, where he behaves with a patience and devotion we are beginning to recognise. The minor characters conduct their lives with passionate unsuccess. Antipov dislikes Yuryatin; he feels that what Lara loves is only her own heroism, and sets off on that ruthless intellectual journey which will transform him into the terrible civil war figure of Strelnikov.

But Boris Pasternak adores Yuryatin, so to dislike it is to fail as his reader. Lara loves it. . . . The war zone is treated as a vast, smouldering chaos, like that of the Orel front in 1943. It is magnificently awful, and its violence is unpredictable. Pasternak shows with intelligent economy how it becomes a way of life. Its astonishing coincidences are always connected with death, but it has unaccountable islands of safety. Pasternak has considered the styles of war journalism quite carefully, and in section 12 we get a sharp analysis of what is wrong with them, which turns to analysis of nationalism, Judaism and the gospels. 'Why don't the intellectual leaders of the Jewish people ever get beyond fashionable *Weltschmerz* and irony?' Why in fact are they not Tolstoyans? These two or three pages of powerful polemic are difficult to answer, and have therefore caused great offence; he is never so rude about Russians.

'Farewell to the Past' follows with stunning swiftness. The technique of leaving things to happen between chapters means that Pasternak seems to be bursting with things to say. The revolution was passed over with some criticism of the Tsar and a paragraph or two of shooting in Petersburg. 'Farewell to the Past' begins with Lara as a nurse and Zhivago as a doctor setting up the future affair which is going to consume them both. A lot of space is given to the strange but probably typical episode of the independent republic of Zabushino, which Pasternak links to the seventeenth century. It was a millennial kingdom set up by the local miller, who was a Christian of some strange sect and had corresponded with Tolstoy. It was an independent republic of one village and some armed deserters, ruled by a council called the Apostolic Seat. Of course it was crazy and doomed; it lasted just over two weeks in the June of 1917.

Its meaning for Pasternak is its comparative authenticity, its wildness and unregenerate peasant quality, on which the official revolution closes in. We see the machinery of repression beginning (inevitably of course) to operate. The death of the young commissar Glintz who falls into a water-butt, gets shot and then bayoneted to death, is its symbol. The tall and ghostly figures of the mounted Cossacks with swords drawn among the trees, standing in a circle round the clearing ready to move in, is equally unforgettable. From this episode Zhivago goes home to Moscow by train. He travels with a deaf-mute who gives him a duck, having been on a shooting expedition. Is this the same deaf-mute who took part in the brief republic? Who is he? The incident remains so far as I can see enigmatic, as if Zhivago were like a character in *The Magic Flute,* searching for the right way among events he was unable to decode.

All these seven chapters, even though they constitute half the book, were intended to set up Zhivago's adventures in the Urals, so both Yuryatin and the vivid forest clearing of Zabushino are foretastes. One has the impression that by the end of chapter 5 Pasternak was hurrying to get to the main unfolding of his story in part two. Chapter 6 is 'Moscow Bivouac': at the beginning Zhivago is in his slow train, and at the end he sets out for Yuryatin. 'It had seemed to Yuri that only the train was moving, that time stood still and it was still only midday.' In Moscow the squares were crowded but there was nothing to buy and they were unswept. 'Already he saw, shrinking against the walls, thin, decently dressed old men and women, who stood like a silent reproach to the passers-by, wordlessly offering what no one needed.' At home he finds 'streets dirty, roofs leaking, bellies empty. . . . There will be all sorts of horrors this winter, famine, cold . . . ' He loves his child but he finds himself isolated: even Uncle Kolya has come home as a Bolshevik, and Nicky is keen on Mayakovsky, though Zhivago is not. Maybe in real life Zhivago would have been closer to the Acmeists? But the scarcely submerged Christian and socialist disturbance of the Zhivago poems would have torn apart any formal surface: he was himself alone, and isolated. In section 4 we see that the revolution had not yet reached its flood-tide. (pp. 220-27)

Pasternak shows the breakdown of civilisation with exquisite precision. His hero rescues a street victim, who protects him; the author feels that is necessary in the suspicious world of 1917. Fighting breaks out in the street, and Soviet power is proclaimed in the papers. Zhivago reads about it by a streetlight in a snowstorm: an oddly unforgettable vignette. 'He was shaken and overwhelmed by the greatness of the moment, and thought of its significance for centuries to come.' He brings home this broadsheet, which he feels is a work of genius; 'Only real greatness can be so misplaced and so untimely.' It has Pushkin's directness, he says, and Tolstoy's bold attachment to the facts. These praises are in no way exaggerated; if the early weeks of the revolution gave us nothing else, they gave us an incomparable boldness of style, just as the American revolution did. But trouble of many kinds follows, including typhus. His enigmatic younger half-brother Yevgraf looks after him when he has fever, and advises the family to clear out of Moscow, so they set off for Yuryatin. (pp. 227-28)

The last chapter of the first part is about the journey east. It opens with an even more withering depiction of conditions in the new Soviet state. Even the sweet old family servant can no longer be trusted. 'At the militia post which he had selected as his political club, he did not actually say that his former masters sucked his blood, but he accused them of having kept him in ignorance all these years, and deliberately concealed from him that the world is derived from apes.' There really was a Tsarist decree against the dissemination of Darwinism. The party leave at dawn, in a fall of snow, to join the gypsy caravan of the long train. 'Tanya had never travelled in a freight truck before.' They have plenty of time to meet conscripts, co-operativists and peasants, whose intertwining stories we learn. It is as if by merely being on this train they are plunged into the heart of the Russian people. Any reader of Maurice Baring's account of Russian journeys twelve years earlier will recognise the truth of this, though in his day the first-class carriages had a library, a piano, and real bathrooms.

As they approach the end of their journey, the state of civil war begins to press around them. The signs of hope are natural: a morning of sawing in the forest, an overwhelming leafless wood with a mighty waterfall, a few wild cherry trees in blossom. But Yuryatin is under siege, and Zhivago has an ominous wayside conversation with Strelnikov, whose name means Shooter, though they nickname him the Executioner. Zhivago turns out to have been 'twice wounded and invalided out', which is new to us: Pasternak does not bother about such details until they seem useful or necessary. 'These are apocalyptic times,'

says Strelnikov, 'this is the Last Judgement. This is a time for angels with flaming swords and winged beasts from the abyss, not for sympathisers and loyal doctors.' Zhivago refuses to have it out with him, but the conversation, we are warned, is only postponed.

The second part of the book opens with chapter 8, 'Arrival', of which the climax is a conversation about Pasha Antipov, who was such a good science teacher, and was killed in the war. (In fact he was taken prisoner, as we already know.) 'Some people say this scourge of ours, Commissar Strelnikov, is Antipov risen from the dead. But it's only a silly rumour of course. It's most improbable. Though who can tell, anything's possible. A little more tea?' The chapter is not otherwise very exciting: they are swallowed up slowly into local interests and local perspectives before arriving. Zhivago makes his cutting and very important attack on Marxism to a local bigwig, and at the country station they are befriended by the ancient station master, who knows Tanya's family of course, though he warns them to be careful about mentioning that connection. They are driven to her confiscated parental estate by a white mare with a black foal, and for a moment life is lyrical. (pp. 228-29)

Chapter 9, 'Varykino', opens with the core of the entire novel, Zhivago's diary. At the end of it he has met Lara in Yuryatin, he knows who Strelnikov is, and as he rides home he is captured by the partisans in the forest. I do not know how far the analogy can be pressed, but if there is something in common between the circles of this novel, pressing spiritually inward and physically outward, and the circles of Dante's heaven and hell, then the circle of this chapter is a kind of paradise. When the partisans take him away, one thinks at once not of his fate or his deserted wife and child, but of the forest and of his love of the people. The scene for that feeling has been set by the old man who drove them from the station in chapter 8. His diary deals seriously with poetry. (p. 229)

The record of Zhivago's happiness and his hard, physical work recalls nothing in Boris Pasternak's life but Peredelkino. There he dug his own potatoes and cultivated what in England would be an allotment, and was often seen doing it. The others employed gardeners, but he really enjoyed the work. When someone toasted him not as a poet but as a working man, the stonemason of Russian literature with his sleeves rolled up, he cried out, 'That's right, that's what I am, a working man.' Lev Ozerov remembers the occasion, which anyway was not unique. I find Zhivago's diary, which is written with the laconic delicacy of which Boris was a master, the best part of the book. Everything that went before it was necessary in order that we should believe in such a man, writing such a diary as he writes, at such a time. For one thing, it brilliantly carries on the narrative, through what might have seemed static. 'We have been lucky. The autumn has been dry and warm. It gave us time to dig up the potatoes.' His potatoes have become more exciting to the reader than world politics. The diary is also extremely beautiful.

They re-read *War and Peace, Eugene Onegin,* all Pushkin's poems, Stendhal's *Le Rouge et le Noir,* Dickens's *A Tale of Two Cities* and Kleist's short stories. If ever there were a heavy hint about the formal origins of a book, no doubt this is it. . . . He comes on a nightingale in Pushkin which is conventional, but it excites him to quote 'The Nightingale the Robber'.

> At the nightingale's whistle, the wild forest voice,
> The grass was a-trembling, the petals were shed,
> And all the dark forest, it bowed to the ground,
> And all the good people were falling down dead.

He remembers Turgenev on the nightingale, and records its notes as he heard them: *Tyock-tyock-tyock*. At this point Yevgraf appears again as a *deus ex machina* with unexplained powers. I believe one must assume that is how Pasternak believed in his own protection and survival, not as the influence of Lunacharsky or Bukharin, still less of Scriabin's cousin Molotov, but as something magical. Or can it be that Yevgraf is an invented apotheosis of his younger brother Sasha, or that he had to invent Yevgraf, as I think most likely, in order to explain the survival of a poet unlike himself, one without acquaintance with Lunacharsky or Bukharin, a poet of absolute integrity? 'In the distance, where the sun was refusing to go down, a nightingale began to sing. "Wake up, wake up" it called entreatingly; it sounded almost like the summons on the eve of Easter Sunday: Awake O my soul, why sleepest thou?' He is going to meet Lara again, and Tanya's marriage is doomed.

Chapter 10 is called 'The Highway', chapter 11 'The Forest Brotherhood' and chapter 12 'Red Rowanberries'. This forest episode with Zhivago among the partisans is quite a large slice of the book, much more than a tenth. The episode is set among archaic Cossack villages along the old post road into Siberia. Pasternak remembers with awe the old political prisoners: tea, bread and pig-iron travelled one way, and prisoners in chains the other. Village to village, and town to town, the people were linked by friendship and by marriage. In the distant past before the railway came (not so very distant) the mail went by troika, and the condemned 'walked in step, jangling their fetters—lost, desperate souls as terrible as heavenly lightning—and around them rustled the dark, impenetrable forest.' When he wrote that, did Pasternak know the modern counterpart of these men, even more miserable? Undoubtedly he did. Zhivago arrived in a village on a Holy Thursday, and the narrative hints at the liturgy, but with no hope of the Resurrection. The partisan leader believes that 'only through the Soviets can the alliance between the town poor and the country poor be achieved', but we shall see that hope fail and the depths of Russia betrayed. The portrait of these peasant partisans is as full as *The Burghers* by Franz Hals: they are most carefully observed. The depiction includes an Easter feast, political argument and the dramas of the day. This tenth chapter might almost be by Thomas Hardy. (pp. 230-31)

The doctor has been a conscript, almost a prisoner with the partisans. In the transition between chapters, two years pass. He has tried to escape, but all attempts have failed. With typhus in winter, dysentery in summer, and more and more wounded, he is up to his eyes in work. The civil war is more ghastly than the war. . . . The partisans and the Whites, the anti-communist army, swing backwards and forwards in a deadly wrestle like Balin and Balan. Civil war is in the first place a shock. It is at least thinkable that it was with the Whites as much as the communists that Pasternak now intended to make his peace. That may be going too far, but he was deeply a Tolstoyan,

and in section 5 of 'Forest Brotherhood' Zhivago says so. In this encounter with the partisan leader, I have the impression that Zhivago's quarrel with the state reaches its deepest: it grounds on an absolute. He demands to be released. But the season moves slowly, creeping towards winter, and he remains enmeshed. The weather is still and dry, the woods are brilliant with ripe berries. An old man called Pamphil loses his wits and goes beserk with an axe.

'Iced Rowanberries' begins with the arrival of partisans' families, including a witch who interests Pasternak greatly. She must be drawn from life, but where and when? All these three astonishing chapters are written as if he had actually lived the life of Zhivago. They ring completely true, yet they are as distant from us, or far more so, than *The Mayor of Casterbridge* or *Under the Greenwood Tree*. Boris Pasternak has a freshness none of his contemporaries achieve. In 'Iced Rowanberries' the weather deteriorates. 'The rain skimmed and smoked over the pine-woods.' We hear the witch's spell, which ends with a bit of an ancient chronicle. Zhivago dreams of Lara, though earlier he dreamed of his wife. 'High winter came with its grinding frosts', and he escapes. 'Isn't that just like a gentleman's folly! Who's ever heard of picking berries in winter! Three years we've been beating the nonsense out of the gentry but they're still the same. All right, go and pick your berries you lunatic. What do I care?'

There are only two chapters left of the body of the novel. The thirteenth is 'The House of the Caryatids'. It begins when he gets into Yuryatin, and ends with a goodbye letter from his wife, who has got to know Lara and finally gone abroad. 'I am thankful to her for being constantly at my side when I was having a difficult time and for helping me through my confinement. I must honestly admit she is a good person, but I don't want to be a hypocrite—she is exactly the opposite of myself. I was born to make life simple and to look for sensible solutions, she—to complicate life and confuse the way.' This letter gives him a heart attack, and the few sentences I quote indicate the situation of Zinaida versus Olga Ivinskaya more than any other in the book. (pp. 231-33)

When Zhivago returns to civil life in chapter 13 he finds himself without papers and grossly disadvantaged. Nothing really happens except this tragedy working itself out; the good news is that he finds Lara. (p. 233)

The last chapter is called 'Varykino Again'. Komarovsky turns up, they flee to rustic solitude, and Zhivago writes poems. There he persuades Lara and her daughter to leave as Komarovsky suggested; in a sense, Komarovsky wins. There also Zhivago settles his account with Strelnikov, who is now perfectly friendly and a hunted man. The chapter ends with his death: Lara had been left alive only as a lure to him. If the diary was the core of this novel, then the poems Zhivago only now writes are its climax. The narrative is engrossing and swift, and Komarovsky as the devil's advocate gives it a smell of burning wheels. In section 8 Zhivago writes out his old, finished poems, 'which had taken the most complete shape in his mind', such as **"Christmas Star"** and **"Winter Night"**. He goes on to others, unfinished or only begun. 'After two or three stanzas and several images by which he himself was astonished, his work took possession and he experienced the approach of what is called inspiration.' Language itself took him over and 'turned wholly into music'. We are not told what he wrote in that state, which is fully described, but only of Zhivago's prayer to God, 'and all this is for me? Why hast thou given me so much . . . ?' He sees the white flame of light playing on the shadowless snow, and in the distance the wolves. One should notice that the creative moment for him is when language conforms miraculously to music.

In the next few days he goes on writing **"Fairy Tale"**; he must find a connecting theme; he cuts the rhythm to lose its pomp 'as you cut out useless words in prose. . . . He heard the horse's hooves ringing on the surface of the poem as you hear the trotting of a horse in one of Chopin's Ballades.' But the wolves disappeared and the moment was over and Lara went away. I take it that this sad desertion was planned from the first page of chapter 1. He loses Lara just as he lost his mother, and well he might howl like a wolf. 'Do you hear? A dog howling. Even two of them I think. Oh how terrible. It's a very bad omen. Well, bear it till morning, and then we'll go, we'll go.' Too late of course.

'Conclusion' is a dead-pan record, like the conclusions of Dickens. 'All that is left is to tell the brief story of the last eight or ten years of Zhivago's life, years in which he went more and more to seed, gradually losing his knowledge and skill both as a doctor and as a writer.' Had Pasternak known such people? One fears he had. Zhivago came back to Moscow in the spring of 1922; at first he wrote booklets which a peasant friend printed, then he drifted. Once again, Boris Pasternak has an extremely sharp eye for the downward social history of Moscow. Zhivago settles in with his servant's daughter and has two children by her; he meets Misha and Nicky again. 'People who have sufficient words at their disposal talk naturally and coherently.' He gets interested in a persecuted priest, and he hears from Tanya in Paris. He writes articles without end and incessant poems, and suddenly he dies.

'Perhaps the mysteries of transformation and the enigmas of life that so torment us are concentrated in the greenness of the earth, among graveyard trees and the flowering shoots that spring up from graves. Mary Magdalene not immediately recognising Jesus risen from the dead mistook him for the gardener.'

Lara finds him dead, and starts to sort out his poems. 'One day she went out and did not come back. She must have been arrested in the street, as so often happened in those days, and she died or vanished somewhere, forgotten as a nameless number on a list which later was mislaid, in one of the innumerable mixed or women's concentration camps in the north.'

How after that can there be an epilogue? Yet there is one, in 1943, on the Orel front. Misha is a lieutenant, Nicky is a major; they are talking over their extremely grim lives, and agreeing together that, whether one was in a university or a concentration camp, the war came as a relief. They consider cold-bloodedly how collectivisation was a mistake and how private judgement had to be stamped out. They discuss a horrifying tale of heroism. They still have hope, like an inextinguishable natural force. Yevgraf is a major-general, and his role now is to look after Zhivago's lost child by Lara, whom he discovers. No real summary is possible. 'A thing which is conceived in a lofty, ideal manner becomes coarse and material. Thus Rome came

out of Greece and the Russian revolution came out of the Russian enlightenment.' But that is not an adequate verdict, and Pasternak knows it is not. In Stalin's last few years, Misha and Nicky meet again. 'To the two ageing friends sitting by the window it seemed that this freedom of the spirit was there, that on that very evening the future had become almost tangible in the streets below. . . .' The final paragraph is moving, because somehow one believes it, God knows why.

Although I have travestied the plot of this book, I hope I have given its spiritual skeleton. There is nothing more to say about **Dr Zhivago** except that it is a great masterpiece in its queer way, beyond the reach of any other writer in this century, and an extraordinary monument to humanity and to poetry and to grief. One seems to experience in it without mediation things that are otherwise more obliquely conveyed. In spite of its faults, which are ludicrous and childish, it seems to me better and more tragic every time I read it. (pp. 233-35)

> *Peter Levi, in his* Boris Pasternak, *London: Hutchinson, 1990, 310 p.*

FURTHER READING

Barnes, Christopher. *Boris Pasternak: A Literary Biography, Volume One: 1890-1928*. New York: Cambridge University Press, 1990, 507 p.

> First installment of a proposed two-volume set providing the most comprehensive portrait of Pasternak's early life and career to date.

Borisov, Vadim, and Pasternak, Evgeni. "The History of Boris Pasternak's novel *Doctor Zhivago*." *Soviet Literature* 2, Vol. 491 (1989): 137-50.

> Translated excerpt from the Soviet periodical *Novy mir* written in part by Pasternak's son recalling the circumstances surrounding the novel's conception.

Burford, William S. "Boris Pasternak, The Talent for Life: *Doctor Zhivago* in Perspective." In *Six Contemporary Novels*, edited by William O. S. Sutherland, Jr., pp. 22-45. Austin: University of Texas, 1962.

> Explication of *Doctor Zhivago* concentrating upon Pasternak's synthesis of nature, history, and literature.

Carlisle, Olga Andreyev. "A Walk in Peredelkino," "A Conversation," and "Pasternak Remembered." In her *Voices in the Snow: Encounters with Russian Writers,* pp. 183-93, 194-212, 213-24. New York: Random House, 1962.

> Three chapters chronicling Carlisle's extensive visits with Pasternak in the late 1950s.

Chiaromonte, Nicola. "Pasternak's Message." *Partisan Review* XXV, No. 1 (Winter 1958): 127-34.

> Laudatory evaluation of *Doctor Zhivago* that commends Pasternak's incisive appraisal of the October Revolution and its consequences.

Danow, D. W. "Epiphany in *Doctor Zhivago*." *The Modern Language Review* 76, No. 4 (October 1981): 889-903.

Traces Zhivago's creative process and how it elicits moments of spiritual recognition throughout the novel.

de Mallac, Guy. *Boris Pasternak: His Life and Art.* Norman: University of Oklahoma Press, 1981, 450 p.
A valuable, detailed chronicle of Pasternak's life that extensively analyzes his poetry and prose.

Dick, J. W. "*Doktor Zivago:* A Quest for Self-Realization." *The Slavic and East European Journal* VI, No. 2 (Summer 1962): 117-24.
Argues that Pasternak's emphasis upon individualism and self-realization "may well foreshadow the beginning of a Russian cultural Renaissance."

Dreistadt, Roy. "A Unifying Psychological Analysis of the Principal Characters in the Novel *Dr. Zhivago* by Boris Pasternak." *Psychology* 9, No. 3 (August 1972): 22-39.
A Freudian interpretation of *Dr. Zhivago.*

Erlich, Victor. "The Concept of the Poet in Pasternak." *The Slavonic and East European Review* 37, No. 89 (1959): 325-35.
Contends that the "irreconcilable conflict between the outlook of the poet and the party activist lies at the core of *Doctor Zhivago* which is . . . [Pasternak's] first successful attempt to reach beyond the realm of lyrical emotion . . . towards the fundamental moral dilemmas of our time."

Fleishman, Lazar. *Boris Pasternak: The Poet and His Politics.* Cambridge, Mass.: Harvard University Press, 1990, 359p.
Critical study of Pasternak's career.

Frank, Victor S. "A Matter of Conscience." *The Dublin Review* 234, No. 485 (Autumn 1960): 222-26.
Links Pasternak's opposition to the Communist regime to a long history of conflict between Russian artists and government officials.

Harari, Manya. "Pasternak." *The Twentieth Century* 164, No. 982 (December 1958): 524-28.
An evaluation of *Doctor Zhivago* relating its political message to Pasternak's refusal of the Nobel Prize and expulsion from the Soviet Writer's Union.

Hayward, Max. "*Doctor Zhivago* and the Soviet Intelligentsia." *Soviet Survey,* No. 24 (April-June 1958): 65-9.
Contends that the experiences of Yuri Zhivago accurately reflect the plight of Russian intellectuals in the years following the October Revolution.

Jennings, Elizabeth. "Boris Pasternak: A Vision from Behind Barriers." In her *Seven Men of Vision: An Appreciation,* pp. 224-46. London: Vision Press, 1976.
Examination of the poems in *Doctor Zhivago* focusing upon their religious themes and imagery.

Kayden, Eugene M. Introduction to *Boris Pasternak [Poems],* by Boris Pasternak, translated by Eugene M. Keyden, pp. vii-xii. Ann Arbor: University of Michigan Press, 1959.
Evaluation of Pasternak's poetry focusing upon his poetic innovations and compassionate portrayal of humanity.

MacKinnon, John Edward. "From Cold Axles to Hot: Boris Pasternak's Theory of Art." *The British Journal of Aesthetics* 28, No. 2 (Spring 1988): 145-61.
Outlines the central features of Pasternak's theory of creativity, including "movement and interaction,"

"transformation and re-union," and "naming and the lyric truth."

———. "Boris Pasternak's Concept of Realism." *Philosophy and Literature* 12, No. 2 (October 1988): 211-31.
Contends that "successful art, for Pasternak, is necessarily realist, issuing each time from a selfless regard toward and a sustained caring for the world, for objects, and memories."

Magidoff, Robert. "The Life, Times and Art of Boris Pasternak." *Thought* XLII, No. 166 (Autumn 1967): 327-57.
A brief critical and biographical overview of Pasternak's career.

———. "The Recurrent Image in *Doctor Zhivago.*" In *Studies in Slavic Linguistics and Poetics in Honor of Boris O. Unbegaun,* edited by Robert Magidoff, et. al., pp. 79-88. New York: New York University Press, 1968.
Discusses Pasternak's use of such images as water, light, and wind.

Mathewson, Rufus W., Jr. "Pasternak: 'An Inward Music'." In his *The Positive Hero in Russian Literature,* rev.ed., pp. 259-78. Stanford: Stanford University Press, 1975.
Sets forth that the conflict between "the ethos of Revolution" and the "continuum of Life" lies at the center of *Doctor Zhivago.*

Mlikotin, Anthony M. "*Doctor Zhivago* as a Philosophical and Poetical Novel." *Australian Slavonic and East European Studies* 2, No. 1 (1988): 77-88.
Rejects formalistic approaches to *Doctor Zhivago,* contending that "only Pasternak's philosophical turn of mind and his poetical genius working hand-in-hand have given life and a sense of beauty to the novel."

Monas, Sydney. "A Miracle Is a Miracle." *The Hudson Review* XI, No. 4 (Winter 1958-1959): 612-19.
Review of *Doctor Zhivago* faulting its narrative style while praising its confrontation of the limitations and cruelties of Communism.

Mossman, Eliot. "Metaphors of History in *War and Peace* and *Doctor Zhivago.*" In *Literature and History: Theoretical Problems and Russian Case Studies,* edited by Gary Saul Morson, pp. 247-62. Stanford: Stanford University Press, 1986.
Compares and contrasts Tolstoy's "mechanical" vision of history with Pasternak's "biological" interpretation of past events.

O'Hara, Frank. "About Zhivago and His Poems." In *On Contemporary Literature,* edited by Richard Kostelanetz, pp. 486-97. New York: Avon Books, 1964.
Argues that *Doctor Zhivago* disproves the common contention that poets cannot write successful prose.

Pasternak, Evgeny. *Boris Pasternak: The Tragic Years 1930-1960.* London: Collins Harvell, 1990, 278 p.
Translated from the Russian text by Pasternak's son, this volume objectively recounts the author's rise to prominence in and subsequent rejection by the Soviet literary community.

Pasternak, Josephine. "Patior." *Russian Literature Triquarterly* (1974): 371-88.
Assessment of the character Lara by Pasternak's sister based upon events in her brother's life.

Stern, Richard D. "*Doctor Zhivago* as a Novel." *The Kenyon Review* XXI, No. 1 (Winter 1959): 154-60.

> Negative review of *Doctor Zhivago* that faults the narrative as weak and diffuse.

Steussy, R. E. "The Myth Behind *Dr. Zhivago.*" *The Russian Review* 18, No. 3 (July 1959): 184-98.

> Examines the concept of predestination in *Doctor Zhivago* and the allegorical role of certain characters.

Tarnaovsky, Kiril. "On the Poetics of Boris Pasternak." *Russian Literature* X, No. IV (15 November 1981): 339-58.

> Examination of Pasternak's poetic technique centering upon Pasternak's own description of his verse as "uniting the rapture with the ritual of everyday life."

Wilson, Edmund. "Legend and Symbol in *Doctor Zhivago.*" *Encounter* XII, No. 6 (June 1959): 5-16.

> Detailed explication of the complex symbolism pervading *Doctor Zhivago*.

Reynolds Price

1933-

(Full name Edward Reynolds Price) American novelist, short story writer, poet, playwright, essayist, memoirist, translator, and critic.

Best known for his acclaimed novel, *Kate Vaiden,* for which he received a National Book Critics Circle Award, Price is considered among the most accomplished contemporary authors of the American South. His novels and short stories, which are frequently set in the rural regions of his native North Carolina, are complex character studies that address such universal themes as the consequences of familial and sexual love, the need for independence, the effect of the past upon the present, and the mystique of place. Although some consider Price's use of symbolism and irony overwrought, many critics laud his unsentimental characterizations and acute depiction of regional traditions. While Price disclaims favorable comparisons made between his work and that of other Southern writers, particularly William Faulkner, critics frequently detect the influence of such authors as Eudora Welty and Flannery O'Conner in the spiritual and mythic subtext underlying Price's deceptively narrow regional settings.

The son of a traveling salesman, Price was born in Macon, North Carolina, where he continues to reside. After graduating from Duke University, Price attended Merton College, Oxford, as a Rhodes scholar. While residing in England, Price composed his first novel, *A Long and Happy Life.* Initially published in single issues of the British journal *Encounter* and the American magazine *Harper's,* this work drew wide acclaim for its memorable characters and graceful lyricism. The novel focuses upon Rosacoke Mustian, a sensitive young woman living in rural North Carolina, who pursues Wesley Beavers, an enigmatic, free-spirited man she has loved since childhood. During the course of the novel, Rosacoke becomes pregnant by Wesley and her dreams of a life with him are ironically fulfilled when he proposes marriage. Disillusioned by the knowledge that he does not love her, Rosacoke considers rejecting Wesley; however, upon portraying the Virgin Mary in a Christmas pageant, she begins to understand the imperfect rewards of marriage, and accepts his proposal. Rosacoke is also the protagonist of "A Chain of Love," a story included in Price's first volume of fiction, *The Names and Faces of Heroes.* This volume features such acclaimed stories as "Uncle Grant" and "The Warrior Princess Ozimba." Price's second novel, *A Generous Man,* details the sexual awakening of Rosacoke's older brother.

Love and Work differs in subject matter from Price's earlier fiction, as it focuses upon an academic who forsakes emotional involvement to pursue his literary ambitions. Following the death of his mother, the protagonist discovers letters written by his parents that reveal the love and compromise inherent in their marriage. Through their correspondence, he realizes the selfish nature of his work and begins to look to others for fulfillment. The tales featured in *Permanent Errors,* Price's second short fiction collection, attempt, in his words, "to isolate in a number

of lives the center error of act, will, understanding which, once made, has been permanent, incurable, but whose diagnosis and palliation are the hopes of continuance." This volume includes such frequently anthologized pieces as "Waiting at Dachau" and "The Happiness of Others." *The Surface of the Earth,* generally considered Price's most complex novel, begins with the elopement and subsequent estrangement of Eva Kendal and Forrest Mayfield, a couple whose aspirations and mistakes adversely affect four generations of their descendants. *The Source of Light,* Price's sequel to *The Surface of the Earth,* relates the story of their grandson Hutch, an aspiring poet who ultimately brings peace to his family. While some reviewers considered these works anachronistic, others concurred with Eudora Welty who, in defense of *The Surface of the Earth,* characterized the novel's admirers as those "who are able to accept the reality of other people, living or dead, who have spoken and acted and dreamed out of their own lifetimes, to ask for and to give and to receive and to generate, as they can, affirmation and love."

While composing his next novel, *Kate Vaiden,* in 1984, Price was diagnosed as having spinal cancer and was eventually confined to a wheelchair. Convinced that he would not live to see the book's publication, Price completed the

321

work while undergoing chemotherapy and radiation treatments. *Kate Vaiden* is a first-person narrative of the title character, a vibrant, fifty-seven-year-old woman who re-examines her unconventional past after learning that she has cervical cancer. During the course of the novel, Kate candidly relates her experiences as an orphaned child in rural North Carolina, as a teenaged mother who regretfully abandoned her illegitimate son, and as a free-spirited wanderer who avoided permanent relationships. Price professed that his curiosity concerning the early life of his mother, Elizabeth Rodwell Price, led to *Kate Vaiden*. While he did not intend the novel to be a faithful biographical portrait, Price drew upon several of her experiences and characteristics. By writing from Kate's point of view, Price also sought to challenge what he perceives as a feminist bias against male writers who depict female experience. According to critics, Price succeeded in creating a convincing protagonist whose engaging narration places her among the most memorable characters in contemporary fiction. Reviewers also lauded Price's deft use of language in the novel's picaresque narrative, which several likened to that of Daniel Defoe's *The Fortunes and Misfortunes of the Famous Moll Flanders.*

In addition to *Kate Vaiden,* Price composed several other works while receiving cancer therapy. *Good Hearts* returns to the protagonists of *A Long and Happy Life.* After twenty-eight years of marriage, Wesley suddenly leaves Rosacoke. Through diary entries, letters, and omniscient narration, Price traces their slow movement toward self-awareness and eventual reconciliation. Jill McCorkle observed: "As we and they discover, [Rosacoke and Wesley] are people equipped with the power to be good human beings, with the power to love. In revealing this, the tone and rhythms of Reynolds Price's language are masterful. *Good Hearts* is superb storytelling by an enduring craftsman. It is a study of life and the placement of individuals within life. In every sense of the word, it abounds with goodness." Price's next novel, *The Tongues of Angels,* is a first-person narrative in which Bridge Boatner, a successful middle-aged artist, examines his role in the death of a fourteen-year-old boy at the summer camp where he worked as a youth.

In addition to his novels and short stories, Price has published several collections of essays and biblical translations. *Things Themselves: Essays and Scenes* and *A Common Room* include pieces on the gospels and the status of contemporary Southern literature, as well as criticism of works by such authors as Eudora Welty, William Faulkner, Ernest Hemingway, and John Milton. Price also earned critical recognition for his plays *August Snow, Private Contentment,* and *Early Dark*—a drama based upon *A Long and Happy Life*—as well as for several volumes of verse. While the poems in *Vital Provisions* examine various subjects, including religion and history, those in the *The Laws of Ice* specifically address Price's struggle against cancer. In his recent memoir *Clear Pictures: First Loves, First Guides,* Price draws upon childhood events he recalled while undergoing hypnosis to control the pain caused by his illness. Robb Forman Dew observed: "This is a seductive book, in which one reads a bit and pauses to ruminate on the nature of the essential facts of one's own life. Mr. Price . . . is never strident in his reminiscence, and he leads us to conspire with him, to unravel the

separate threads of truth and invention in order to decide if there is a difference between the two and if it matters."

(See also *CLC,* Vols. 3, 6, 13, 43, 50; *Contemporary Authors,* Vols. 1-4, rev. ed.; *Contemporary Authors New Revision Series,* Vol. 1; and *Dictionary of Literary Biography,* Vol. 2.)

PRINCIPAL WORKS

NOVELS

*A Long and Happy Life 1962
*A Generous Man 1966
Love and Work 1968
The Surface of the Earth 1975
The Source of Light 1981
Kate Vaiden 1986
Good Hearts 1988
The Tongues of Angels 1990

PLAYS

Early Dark 1977
Private Contentment 1982
August Snow 1984

POETRY

Late Warning: Four Poems 1968
Lessons Learned: Seven Poems 1977
Vital Provisions 1983
The Laws of Ice 1988

SHORT FICTION COLLECTIONS

The Names and Faces of Heroes 1963
Permanent Errors 1970

OTHER

Things Themselves: Essays and Scenes 1972
Presence and Absence: Versions from the Bible (nonfiction) 1973
A Palpable God: Thirty Stories Translated from the Bible with an Essay of the Origins and Life of Narrative 1978
A Start (miscellany) 1981
A Common Room (essays) 1987
Clear Pictures: First Loves, First Guides (memoir) 1989

*These novels, along with the short story "A Chain of Love," were collected in *Mustian,* 1983.

Michael Ruhlman

Major events seem to happen to Reynolds Price on significant dates. He's proud of that, in an eerie way, as though such coincidences were proof that the world, like the novels he writes, is ordered by a single being with a curious sense of humor. In 1933, Price's mother went into protracted, nearly fatal, labor with him just hours after Hitler had become Chancellor of Germany. When Price reached manhood, when he was exactly 21 years and 21 days old, his father died. (p. 60)

So there was cause for some nervous chuckling on the day in May 1984 when, after noticing stiffness in his legs, Price checked into a hospital during an eclipse of the sun. He laughs now and says this was "something no self-respecting primitive would have done." The visit resulted in the discovery of a malignant tumor the size of a pencil twisting down the top of of his spine.

Between then and last November, Price endured three lengthy operations to remove the tumor and five and a half weeks of radiation therapy. For months, he woke at 4 A.M. or so, not knowing how long he would last. At one point, his doctors believed he had five weeks to live. He watched the use of his legs disintegrate and become permanently lost. He was in almost constant pain.

I had seen him only once since 1983, when I was a student in one of his English classes at Duke University. I remember how he would weave rapidly through throngs of students on the way to his office, an ebullient but enigmatic campus figure. Last February, when I arrived at his home near Durham, N. C., I saw, as he lifted himself from his wheelchair to stretch his upper body, that his fierce smile had not changed. He seemed to be testing the irreversible bondage that now held him. "Sizzle, zap!" he said. Then, lowering himself to the chair: "Sit you down, buddy."

He says that cancer has brought about only one major change in his life. He now does more of what he has been doing successfully for the last 30 years—writing.

Reynolds Price is the author of 14 books, including poetry, essays, plays, biblical translations and stories, but it is as a novelist that he has earned widest recognition. Working primarily in a Southern tradition reminiscent of Faulkner, Price's fiction depicts a rural and small-town South, mostly during the 1940's and 50's, the time, he says, "when I was coming onto the scene as an observing device."

Though the time and place do vary in his work—from turn-of-the-century North Carolina to modern-day England—what remain constant are Price's lyrical, obsessive voice and his dense prose. His Southern Gothic tales of families cohering and dispersing in the wake of suicide and murder, of lethal childbirth and romantic entanglements, are considered by some readers and critics to be forced, overly mannered and repetitious, but others praise their linguistic agility, their accuracy and power.

Critics generally agree, however, that Price is at his best when he writes from the point of view of his female characters, as in his last novel, *Kate Vaiden,* the story of an orphan woman who abandons her own child. The novel won the National Book Critics Circle Award for best fiction of 1986 and was Price's most commercially successful book. (pp. 60, 131)

Price's work attempts to shed light on the nature of human relationships. It shows how people, as they struggle awkwardly to understand their own position in the cosmos, love and harm one another. "All narrative artists," Price says, "are very much involved in telling the only story we really want to hear, which is: 'History is the will of a just God who knows me.' Now, that either is or isn't true. I hope it is."

Price's method in fiction is to establish thoughtful charac-

ters and then drop them into situations in which they must make choices. The choices may be prosaic—whether to leave home or stay—or more momentous—whether to have a child or not—but all of them have serious, sometimes fatal, consequences. The characters often attempt, however futilely, to expiate their past mistakes. In the end, many of them manage enough self-awareness to move forward in life with more care than when they began.

For many months after his treatment for cancer began, Price was able to do little more than sit in his own room obsessively drawing pictures, as he had done as a child. But then came a burst of work that, at least by his previous rate of output, was quite surprising. He finished the last two-thirds of *Kate Vaiden,* three plays, a volume of poems, a volume of essays [*A Common Room*] . . . , and his seventh novel, *Good Hearts*. . . . In *Good Hearts,* he returns to the characters he created in *A Long and Happy Life,* fixing his steady gaze once again on Rosacoke and Wesley. (p. 131)

"*Good Hearts* is a moral fable about the near destruction but rescue of a marriage," he says.

> It's very different from the other Mustian novels. It takes up with Rosacoke and Wesley when she's 48 and he's 50. They've been married for many years. They've lived the vast majority of their lives in a small American city, not in the rural agricultural countryside.

Price had not intended to write this novel, but in July 1986, while he was typing notes for a new, first-person novel, the Rosacoke-Wesley story dawned on him very powerfully. He dropped the first-person tale and dived in. "I don't know what made my unconscious mind leap off the track that I'd been trying to pursue onto an old one," he says. Rosacoke and Wesley "demanded to be watched again," he says, and he found that they had proceeded with their own lives much as he had his. They had acquired "a great amount of emotional resonance. They've become tools with which I can economically and rapidly do a lot of work."

Price believes that his imagination works inextricably with his unconscious. The unconscious mind, he feels, offers up to him the emotional content of past experience, although in a form no longer recognizable as experience. Part of Price's work as a writer has been to nurture this process. He goes about it as if he were an athlete training his body. "You train the unconscious mind," he says,

> to give you what you need by giving it the right amount of time and whatever nutrition and psychic conditions it needs for its own plans. I don't know that it lies awake at night and writes pages 1 through 15, but when I go to work, the material is simply there.

Price ascribes no mystical powers to the unconscious, but he believes that it exists, and that it never stops working, even while he is resting or watching movies. He gives his characters emotions from his own past, after the emotions have, as he puts it, "marinated" in his unconscious for many years. "In my case," Price says,

> it [the unconscious] has to turn the stuff from autobiography into fiction. My brain has to strip an event down, to find what the absolute bottom line is, what the real emotional spiritual narrative con-

tent of the experience is so that it can give that experience to characters who are not Reynolds Price and his friends.

As a result of his training, Price now relies on the trust that "if I make a propitious start with interesting characters at an interesting juncture in their lives, a story will be generated." But when he was less skilled and just starting out in his career, he needed to know in advance everything that was going to happen.

He tells, for example, how *A Long and Happy Life* came to be. In his digs at Oxford, in January 1957, the young Rhodes scholar was reading some newspapers his aunt had sent him from home. "My mind suddenly produced a picture," he says: a girl dressed as the Virgin Mary for a church play. As the vision gathered in his mind, he saw that the girl was Rosacoke Mustian, the heroine of his first published work, a short story that appeared in the British magazine *Encounter*. As he thought about her in his Oxford room, her image grew sharper, and Price saw that Rosacoke was pregnant. And there it was, the seed of his first novel. Price asked himself, "How did she get that way, and what's she going to do about it?"

To find out, he began a notebook that he would keep for 20 months. (Now, he can finish a whole book in that time.) Laboriously, he worked his way from the church play backward through events until the story was complete. This 1957 notebook reveals Price as extremely scholarly, but it also indicates his immaturity as a writer and inability to gauge an appropriate length for the material.

He wrote in the notebook:

> Oxford, 3 March 1957—Before there can be tragic vision, there must surely be certain self-knowledge or at least self-perspective. So Rosacoke must do a great deal of thinking about her mistake and her situation. The problem is how to do it naturally, but not in great long chunks of introspection. She's not that sort, nor am I. She thinks in bits and pieces, jarred into thought 1,000 times a day by a face or a voice or a picture or a bird's song.
>
> (pp. 132-33)

Or, after nearly 100 pages of notes and many months of believing he was writing a short story:

> 14 December 1957—Maybe this thing ought to be a novel.

In contrast, to begin his novel *Good Hearts* 29 years later, Price made notes for only a few days before he understood the act from which the novel would spring: Wesley Beavers would disappear after nearly 30 years of marriage. While writing the opening pages, he realized that after Wesley leaves, a violent attack would befall Rosacoke. Bang! The gates fly open and the story streaks off from there.

"The longer I go on writing fiction," Price says,

> the more I am conscious that it's a kind of metabolic activity of my particular brain. I don't want to have a tremendous amount of control over that activity at its earliest levels, just as one can't decide what one is going to dream. I want to see what patterns and curiosities my mind throws up.

Although most of Price's stories are concerned with peo-

ple and places of the South, he uses the term "Southern" guardedly and is critical of the connotations readers and reviewers now tend to give it. "They like to use 'Southern' as a diminutive pygmy pigeonhole," Price says,

> to make you easier to handle, easier to patronize and discard. If you're Southern, you're Southern in quotes, and you write about big-bellied sheriffs and little old ladies in cobwebby mansions serving tea to two gifted little sexually precocious boys. I've never done that, and I don't intend to.

"The number of times my novels have been described as being about hillbillies is amazing," he says. "Well, there's not a hillbilly anywhere in my work." He points out that Saul Bellow is not labeled a "Midwestern" writer nor John Updike a "New England" writer, and he believes that "Southern" is now invariably a facile and demeaning term that encourages people to ignore what is universal in novels concerning the South.

The region is still, Price says, "a fertile environment for the production of fascinating fiction," because of its unique mixture of dialects, races and religions.

> This part of North Carolina is where 95 percent of my emotional intensity has been grounded. My early childhood familial experiences, and all my later intense emotional experiences have occurred here. It's the most repeated cliché of writers that you're given your basic questions as a human being, the stuff you're obsessed by in your work, before you're pubescent. I happened to be here. Also, from my point of view, I'm the world's authority on this place. It's the place about which I have perfect pitch. I can't strike a false note when I'm writing about this part of the world.

Edward Reynolds Price was born in Macon, N.C., and reared in several small Carolina towns amid cotton and tobacco farmers and the omnipresent fear of financial ruin during the Great Depression. He attended high school in Raleigh, where he was first encouraged to pursue writing, and, thereafter, he received a full scholarship to Duke University.

Older writers were of fundamental importance during Price's apprentice years. He met Eudora Welty when he was a senior at Duke. She read his first story and, charmed by his personality and his prose, sent it to her agent, the late Diarmuid Russell, who later became Price's agent.

"What attracted me then to Reynolds," Eudora Welty says,

> is what attracts me now, what you can't help but feel—the power of his mind, his thoughts, his sympathy. Only a blind person could have missed the fact that in college he was a good writer already. And he has always advanced, grown. He's just one of our major writers.

After graduating summa cum laude from Duke, he began three years at Oxford, where he became friends with Lord David Cecil, the critic and biographer, the poet W. H. Auden, who was Professor of Poetry there at the time, and Sir Stephen Spender, the poet and critic who first published Price's work in *Encounter*.

"The thing about Reynolds when he was young," says Spender, "was that he was incredibly critically conscious in what he wrote; the effects were so conscious that other writers and editors couldn't decide whether it was very good or artificial. Some people absolutely hated it. Dwight Macdonald was infuriated by it and discouraged me from publishing it. It's very interesting and very much to his credit that a writer should provoke such a fury in some readers.

"He is unique, really," Spender goes on. "He ranks very high, with Eudora Welty and, I suppose, Faulkner. Reynolds's writing is a kind of writing that is actually poetry. The dialogue is like real dialogue, but it's been elevated into a special language which he carries through with great consistency. Reynolds persuades one that his characters not only speak in character, but also that they talk out of a whole culture. I was always hoping he'd become an English writer."

By that, Spender means that he hoped the young man would stay in England, but Price preferred to return to North Carolina. For one thing, he was obliged to help support his widowed mother and younger brother. Since high school, Price knew he wanted to be a writer who taught, so he found accommodation in a small trailer about 200 yards from where he lives now, began teaching at Duke and wrote his first novel.

The critical reception in 1962 of *A Long and Happy Life,* and of *The Names and Faces of Heroes,* a book of stories published the next year, allowed Price from then on to publish virtually anything he wanted to and to teach only one semester a year. Today, he is James B. Duke Professor of English and writer in residence.

Price finished the first third of *Kate Vaiden* the day before he entered the hospital, but in the months that followed, as he sat drawing pictures, he could not recapture his heroine's voice. Then, in November 1984, Hendrix College in Arkansas called Price wanting to commission a play from him. He says: "I just sort of took that as a tap on the shoulder from the Holy Spirit, and I told them, 'O.K., I'll do it. But here's the danger, I might not live to finish the play.'"

He did finish the play, *August Snow,* and its production in Arkansas was so successful and rewarding for Price that it triggered two more plays that winter. These make up a trilogy he calls *New Music.* . . . The trilogy comes nearly a decade after the production of Price's first play, *Early Dark,* at the W.P.A. Theater. Off Off Broadway, and after a second, *Private Contentment,* was written for public television's *American Playhouse* in 1982.

As he finished *August Snow,* the engines of his unconscious continued to crank, the voice of his heroine Kate Vaiden returned and he finished the novel. No change in tone is noticeable at the point where he broke off and then resumed work—between pages 120 and 121 of the book. But another work that bridges his life before and after cancer does show a distinct change in voice. It is a sequence of 35 poems called "Days and Nights," published in *The Laws of Ice* (1986). Unlike his fiction, Price's poetry addresses the actual physical and psychical events of his life, and, in "Days and Nights," he began sketches of events that would become, in effect, a journal of the discovery of the spinal tumor.

"Because my fiction has not fed directly off the daily events of my life," he says, "I began to feel, in my late 30's and 40's, that there was a tremendous amount of significant narrative emotional material that was slipping through the cracks of my work. An awful lot was happening in my life that never got into my fiction. I didn't want it all to be lost, and I began to try to weave nets to catch those things."

Though much of Price's work is concerned with the emotions and obligations of family, he has never felt the need for one of his own. He relates to the next generation through his students, many of whom have become novelists themselves—Anne Tyler, Josephine Humphreys, David Guy. (pp. 133-35)

Price has always maintained that writing is very much a physical act, that he makes his work out of his own body, a body recently, as he puts it, "sawed off at the waist." Outwardly, he seems, in the words of Anne Tyler, "to have that bounce and love of life that he always did have." And Price says that, because he had learned already how to sit down and stay put for several hours to write, he has limited the negative effects of the cancer on his life.

He is reluctant to speculate about how his writing will reflect his recent experience—the months he spent on what he thought might be his deathbed, the biofeedback and hypnosis techniques he is learning to control the pain that is common after surgery on the central nervous system. Perhaps, he says, none of this will ever show up in his fiction. He notes, however, the ancient belief that the gods may take something away from a person in order to give him more of something else. "I'm not saying that I got to be a better writer because my legs got effectively lopped off," he says. "But I do know that writing has come more freely and, perhaps, more richly now than it has at some other times in my life."

But, aside from what Price says, can a reader find a new sensibility in the form and the subjects of his work? It's probably too early to tell for certain, but *Good Hearts*—in fact, most of his work since the cancer—does indicate that he is writing more directly about his own beliefs and focusing more fixedly on the organization and mechanics of the universe.

In *Good Hearts*—his "moral fable"—he examines the connections between the supernatural and morality. People's actions have an effect on events that would normally seem coincidental. For example, Wesley Beavers deserts Rosacoke, and this does more than leave Rosacoke unprotected. The omniscient narrator implies that Wesley's leaving actually brings an intruder to the home he abandons, that Wesley's leaving causes violence.

In this latest novel, two people—a woman defined by her intellect and a man by his physical prowess—each undergo a physical alteration. Afterward, each must re-evaluate life in order to live married once again.

Does this, I asked my former teacher, mirror Price's own personal struggle with disease over the last three years? If it does, that's news to him, Price says. Interesting news. But then, any such parallel may be insignificant, merely coincidental—like the eclipse of the sun that occurred the day Price entered the hospital. (p. 135)

Michael Ruhlman, "A Writer at His Best," in

The New York Times Magazine, *September 20, 1987, pp. 60, 131-35.*

John Blades

There's nothing especially mysterious about why certain artists (writers, painters, musicians, et al.) are such perceptive critics, often better than those who make their living at the critic's trade. The crucial difference, the not-so-secret word, is "empathy." The moonlighting artist knows from experience how the work is done (and how hard it is to do), whereas the professional critic knows only how it should *not* be done. In any case, empathy is high among the virtues of Reynolds Price's *A Common Room* which consolidates three decades of his essays and permanently places him in the firmament of artist/critics, along with John Updike, William Gass, Virgil Thomson and Fairfield Porter.

As a Southern novelist (and critic), Price must inevitably confront the ghost of William Faulkner, to whom he devotes several chapters in *A Common Room,* including a surprisingly affirmative assessment of *Pylon,* usually considered Faulkner's second-worst novel. Perhaps more surprisingly, Price doesn't treat him with nearly the reverence (or empathy) that so many of his literary kinsmen do. He attempts to cast off the Faulkner "burden," which was attached to him by critics who detected echoes of the master's voice and style in his first novel, *A Long and Happy Life.* And he notes his "resentment at being looped into the long and crowded cow-chain that stretched behind a writer for whom I felt admiration but no attraction."

On the other hand, Price more than welcomes comparisons to Eudora Welty, whose influence (and career assistance) he gracefully acknowledges in several long and admiring but eminently level-headed considerations of her novels and stories, her "frightening gifts." . . .

Price doesn't confine his criticism to Southern writers and writing. Among his more renegade assertions, in fact, is that there is no such beast as the "Southern novel." The essay that provides the book's title is equally provocative, a survey of the "reversed gender novel," in which an author and his/her main character are of the opposite sex, as was the case with Price's award-winning *Kate Vaiden.* Price is also very astute and heterodox in his appraisals of Henry James, Graham Greene, Toni Morrison, Horton Foote and Ernest Hemingway, whose lifelong subject, he proposes with a certain perverse logic, was "saintliness."

Price has assembled *A Common Room* from a multitude of sources: prefaces to his fiction, speeches, letters, contributions to anthologies and magazines, big and little. He even reprints his first book review, a college paper on Thackeray's *Vanity Fair,* which he disliked. But as much as anything else, *A Common Room* is a work of autobiography, with uncommonly good personal essays on growing up in North Carolina, his childhood reading, the death of his loving, alcoholic father, and "all-but-daunting tales" of how his books came to be written. In his **"Letter to a Young Writer,"** Price starts by offering this advice: "If you can stop, you probably should," but he concludes with more encouraging words for those whose "reckless faith" prevents them from choosing a less hazardous path.

Because Price is a dedicated scholar (at Duke) as well as a fiction writer, poet, critic, journalist and essayist, there are some unavoidably turgid patches in the book: his lengthy recap of Welty's *The Optimist's Daughter,* for instance, which tends to indicate that what artist/critics have in common besides empathy is garrulity (and/or indulgent editors). Unlike most academics, Price has a lively prose style, a healthy scorn for academic criticism, and a ferocious wit, which he doesn't hesitate to direct at himself. He has such vast and humbling intellectual resources that they finally inspire something more than admiration and awe: To invert an old Southernism, you can't help but envy, even resent, him for having so many bricks more than a load.

John Blades, "Reynolds Price Balances Duties of an Artist/Critic," in Chicago Tribune—Books, *December 13, 1987, p. 3.*

George Core

Reynolds Price has always been precociously talented, as the reissue of *A Long and Happy Life* and the publication of [*A Common Room,* a volume of] essays, mainly critical but also occasional and autobiographical, remind us. To some readers his manifest talent and accomplishment may seem a matter of luck. . . . But this ample book, which contains 57 pieces and which runs from his senior year at Duke University in 1954 through 1987, shows that Price has made his own luck through fortifying his talent with vast reading and remarkable application.

The characteristic subjects mined here are wide and diverse: the novel, southern and otherwise (Cervantes, Thackeray, Faulkner, Hemingway, Graham Greene, Price's own fiction); the Bible, especially the Gospels; poetry (particularly Milton); classic music and art (Rembrandt, for instance). The modes vary: review, critical essay, preface, autobiography, report (chiefly on Jimmy Carter), commentary on the Bible and its translators, translation by the author himself.

Among the diverse strands that bind the book into a thick hawser of flexible strength and long reach are the distinct voice of its maker, the suppleness of his prose, the penetration of his critical judgments, and the repetition as well as the breadth of his interests and commitments.

That Price is a believing Christian who has read deeply in the Bible and its literature is but one such interest and commitment. His profound devotion to the importance of story in human life ("stories are vital," he says, "food for . . . lives, pledges of love") is the most striking of these interests, which encompass the natural world (nature is sentient, he tells us), memory, country life, politics, androgyny, food, love, reading, work, the South and more.

The author emerges as a complicated, believable and likable person of distinct humanity and wisdom. I like his autobiographical forays, but I think more highly of his criticism and wish his autobiographical presence were less insistent there. In addition to being a good essayist he is one of our best critics of contemporary fiction, of southern culture, and [of] his favorite authors, particularly James, Hemingway and Eudora Welty.

What I relish in reading this miscellaneous prose is its richness and accuracy. Price strikes one apt metaphor after another (of his family: "I was the axle of their world"); he often reforges tired expressions ("dead as pterodactyls"); and he endlessly turns poetic phrases ("tendrils of memory and hearsay"). His lapses as a stylist—use of cant language, overwriting—are rare.

As a critic Price sees literature from the inside, and he also thoroughly understands the mechanics and machinations of the literary marketplace (see **"Letter to a Young Writer"**). His insights into the nature of time and of narrative, especially in fiction, are dazzling (read **"Across the Lines"**). Price's voracious reading superbly informs all his criticism. My own predilections and prejudices, tastes and judgments are so much in agreement with his that I seldom oppose him. (I do wish there were fewer essays in this book and that they were arranged more by subject than chronology.)

To follow the course of Price's mind over such a considerable terrain, particularly his literary terrain, is to be instructed in writers whom you thought you knew thoroughly and to be informed about artists of every stripe whom you knew only glancingly or not at all.

Reynolds Price, like some of the writers whom he most admires—Robert Penn Warren and Eudora Welty, for example—takes the whole of literature as his purview. In a time when men and women of letters are a threatened species, his example is luminous. (pp. 6-7)

> *George Core, "Reynolds Price: Teacher, Novelist, and Man of Letters," in* Book World—The Washington Post, *February 14, 1988, pp. 6-7.*

Monroe K. Spears

When Reynolds Price was stricken with cancer in 1984, he felt an extraordinary renewal of inspiration. Since then he has produced three plays; a volume of poems; a remarkable collection of essays, **A Common Room;** and his most popular novel, **Kate Vaiden.** The present delightful and thought-provoking novel, his seventh, is the latest fruit of this renewal.

Though **Good Hearts** is a sequel to Price's first novel, **A Long and Happy Life,** published 26 years ago, it is almost twice as long and very different in style and tone. **A Long and Happy Life** was a pastoral, describing the courtship of Rosacoke Mustian, a simple but very intelligent country girl, and Wesley Beavers, her womanizing, motorcycle-riding, ex-Navy lover. She does what she thinks she needs to do to keep him. When she finds herself pregnant, Wesley is willing (but not eager) to marry her; the resolution of the novel comes when she, playing the part of Mary in a Christmas pageant, accepts her role.

Good Hearts takes up the same couple again, after some 30 years of marriage. In contrast to the pastoral isolation of the first novel, the characters in this one live very much in the contemporary world, in the small city of Raleigh. Rosa works as secretary to a university English department and Wesley as a mechanic (only on expensive foreign cars). Wesley, now 50, leaves Rosacoke and goes to Nashville, where he finds a mistress. Rosacoke is raped (in consequence, it is suggested). The story is pulled along irresistibly by suspense (will Wesley return? will Rosacoke take him back? will the rapist make another attempt?).

When Wesley does return after a few months, it remains uncertain whether or not he will stay and whether or not Rosacoke will take him back. As to the rapist, he does at last return, but as a guest in the house, and blesses the marriage.

Good Hearts is more readable than **A Long and Happy Life:** the style is simpler, closer to contemporary speech; there are not more long, dreamy sentences to evoke a pastoral world, no idyllic distancing, but more suspense and more dialogue. Price can write dialogue that seems natural but characterizes economically without awkwardness or dialectal spelling; Rosa, especially, is highly distinctive both in speech and in her writing in her diary. Whereas **Life** was told by an omniscient narrator, **Hearts** uses varied methods of narration: after an omniscient beginning chapter, Rosacoke tells her story through her diary, which alternates with the omniscient presentation of Wesley's story. When Wesley comes home the omniscient narration continues, but Rosa's diary has established her as the protagonist and as the articulate character, as opposed to Wesley, who doesn't like talking but has the touch for both machines and women.

The title, **Good Hearts,** is plausible enough for Rosa and Wesley; on the basis of both this novel and the earlier one, we readily agree with the omniscient narrator of the first chapter that they have "hearts as good as any you've met unless you meet more saints than most." Rosa has her flaws, but is a very sympathetic character, overcoming the comic archetype of woman as pursuer—which she embodies throughout both novels, in which from first to last she pursues Wesley. Wesley is gentle, incapable of causing deliberate harm (here he is unlike D. H. Lawrence's nonverbal men who have the touch); he causes Rosa pain, but his leaving her is, we are led to believe, a necessary result of his character. He feels, understandably enough, at 50, that he has always been essentially passive, has never defined himself. But Wesley remains a mythical character, somewhat enigmatic, not to be captured by language.

To make the reader believe in the goodheartedness of the rapist, Waverly Wilbanks, however, is the most difficult task Price has set for himself. Waverly believes that he is helping women by raping them; his motive is entirely altruistic and religious, and he requests thanks from his victims. In the final chapter, Wave explores Rosa and Wesley's bedroom just before they return to it. He finds a mysterious resemblance between himself and a picture of Rosa's father, and hears the voice of God telling him that what he has done has been right.

The sense of the supernatural is strong throughout; though never defined, it is felt as unquestionably real. There are mysterious connections and coincidences, as between Wesley's leaving and the rape, and Rosacoke's brother Rato's dream that tells him when Rosa is being hurt. Everybody in the novel prays regularly, though their beliefs vary widely. Wesley says of Rosacoke's profession of belief in the Apostle's Creed and the Lord's Prayer, "Don't be a damned missionary all your grown life," and of his own beliefs, "Oh, I guess there's a God. But it sure as hell looks like He's so far gone, He can't see us and barely hears even our loudest begging." (pp. 5, 10)

Price's characters seem real people that one can identify with and take seriously; they are responsible and make significant choices. They want to be good, do what is best for each other. If Waverly is not wholly convincing (at least to this reader) and Wesley remains somewhat remote, Rosacoke is fully realized and vividly present. She is not perfect, but she is warm and loving as well as dutiful and good, and she is intelligent and funny as well as shrewd. In the end she accepts Wesley's need to change, as he accepts her need for permanence.

While *Good Hearts* is self-sufficient, much is added to it if the reader goes back to *A Long and Happy Life,* for the later novel casts light on the earlier, as well as vice versa. At the end, the reader has the sense that all has been resolved and explained as well as may be in a universe that, if full of mysteries, still makes fundamental sense.

In the title essay in *A Common Room,* Price makes a plea for a kind of Authors Androgynous, for the novel as a common room for the understanding of both sexes. The heroine he has created, Rosacoke, is a triumphant example of such understanding. (p. 10)

> *Monroe K. Spears, "Scenes from a Marriage,"* in Book World—The Washington Post, *April 10, 1988, pp. 5, 10.*

Harry Mark Petrakis

I had not read *A Long and Happy Life,* the 1962 novel by Reynolds Price that began the story and characters he has now fashioned into this sequel [*Good Hearts*]. Reading both books intensified my pleasure and extended my admiration for his achievement. They are marvelous books, rich in a fluid and lyrical grasp of language, wise and compelling in their vision. He uses the landscape of Raleigh, N.C., and Nashville, Tenn., but it is his creation of the men and women he places against this terrain that gives his books their haunting beauty and power.

The earlier novel tells the story of the courtship and betrothal of Rosacoke Mustain and Wesley Beavers. From her girlhood, Rosacoke loved Wesley. Later, in remembering him, she would say, "Wesley was the name that came to me when anybody mentioned a boy's name and love or happiness."

Rosacoke comes to recognize in Wesley what we understand about him ourselves, that besides being a sensual and gentle man, he is a life force as well.

Good Hearts begins after Rosa (her name shortened for this novel) and Wesley have been married 28 years, having borne one child and lost another. They sleep together but their spirits have grown divided and a rejection of his attempt to make love to her one night makes Wesley leave Rosa. In the beginning she cannot fathom the reason for his leaving and cannot believe he won't return. . . .

The narrative alternates between Wesley and Rosa, their longings and fears and their dreams that sometimes spill over into the waking world, blurring where dream ends and reality begins. There are letters, memories, vivid scenes when characters meet. Rosa's mother, Emma, her brothers Milo and Rato, the girl, Wilson, who is lover to Wesley for an interlude, the strange man, Wave.

Soon after Wesley leaves, Rosa is raped one night in her home by an intruder. She does not report it to the police.

And the rapist rejoins the story, spinning a surprisingly complex and yet profound development to the plot.

Wesley leaves the girl, Wilson, and returns to his wife when he learns of the rape. But there isn't any swift embrace, no easy reconciliation. They approach one another with the hesitation and uncertainty of new lovers, having been made aware of suffering as an inescapable constant in any effort to love. One of the many wonderful scenes in the book takes place after Wesley has returned and goes to bed with Rosa for the first time. Both feel guilty and remorseful, both are trapped in their memories and fears:

> Then for the first time in all his years with women, Wesley lay on quiet and let Rosa work her own slow will—partly because he started so tired but also because he was gambling there might be something to learn.
>
> Rosa didn't share the hope. She'd learned all this, every move and sound, in her bedtime thoughts and dreams long ago. These were the ways she'd always loved Wesley, in her mind at least. The main thing she made was slow circles, small circles with her hand and (though she could only see a little) the syllables of tranquil comment and assurance that are most men's favorites of the sounds on earth.

The poet and novelist Thomas Wolfe wrote in "The Story of a Novel":

> I know the door is not yet open. I know the tongue, the speech, the language that I seek is not yet found . . . and I believe with all my heart, also, that each man for himself and in his own way, each man who ever hopes to make a living thing out of the substances of his life, must find that way, that language and that door—must find it for himself as I have tried to do.

From his struggle to find the door, the speech, the tongue and the language, Reynolds Price has created a miniature masterpiece that illuminates our solitary, mysterious journeys toward the repayment of a debt to death each of us incurs the instant we are born.

> *Harry Mark Petrakis, "Two 'Hearts' Revisited in Rich Sequel," in* Chicago Tribune—Books, *April 17, 1988, p. 6.*

Jill McCorkle

Reading *Good Hearts* is like returning home, calling to mind vivid memories and at the same time filling in the space of the years that have passed. In 1962, the publication of *A Long and Happy Life* established Reynolds Price as a major force in American literature. Now, many successes and 15 books later, he has returned to this source, taking up Rosacoke Mustian and Wesley Beavers after 28 years of marriage and long past the threshold where Rosacoke had once uttered her hopes for a long and happy life.

The child whose imminent advent prompted their marriage is now a grown man, and Rosa (her name now shortened) and Wesley have left the familiar rural landscape of Afton, N.C., for the city of Raleigh, where he is a mechanic and she a secretary. But although many changes have occurred, Mr. Price's characters never jar our familiar recollections. Instead, the rich voices and personalities of Wesley, Rosa and her family are made still stronger, as if they had never been left for a moment but had continued living and talking their way through each day leading up to this one.

Through Mr. Price's omniscient narration, the reader is allowed into Rosa and Wesley's bedroom and into their conflicting dreams. At 48, Rosa is content; she has that same gentle strength, that wise sense of herself and others that endeared her to readers 26 years ago. On the other hand, Wesley at 50 sees himself as a failure. He is troubled by the approach of the Christmas season, which represents not only the anniversary of his father's death at age 56 but also the anniversary of his marriage. On this night, when we are reintroduced to them, he has been sexually "faced with Rosa's polite refusal or at least her hope of separate rest."

Our sensation of hovering there, observing Rosa and Wesley's existence first as a couple and then as individuals with isolated dreams, is hauntingly powerful; the juxtaposition of her contentment and his restlessness brings an uneasiness to the silence. It is as if we have been given a minute to savor this life before the action that will change it begins. . . .

It is after this quiet moment of observation that the events of the novel, like dominoes, are set in motion. By the end of the next day, Wesley has left home. When a waitress in Asheville urges him to "streak it to Nashville," he takes her advice, hiding out in a hotel where on New Year's Eve he meets Joyce Wilson, a 26-year-old radiology technician. She asks Wesley if he loves his wife. His answer, "I must not," the verbalization of his doubt, occurs at approximately the same time that a man enters his home back in Raleigh and assaults Rosa. It is as if her vulnerability is as much the result of his denial of her as it is of his physical vacancy from their bed.

Wesley, who before his marriage had " 'used himself' (as he thinks of it now) with nineteen women and three men," is as sensuous as he was when Rosa first met him; he attracts both sexes, his "goodness" being his power. It is Wesley's honesty, his genuine desire to please "a clean kind soul that seems in need," that keeps his affair with Joyce Wilson somehow elevated above the typical middle-age-crazy response. He is driven sexually as he has always been, and yet he is very sensitive to the person behind the body. He is equally sensitive to men, which again keeps him from falling into a womanizing stereotype.

During his stay in Tennessee, Wesley also meets Stan, a gay lawyer. Stan is willing to give to Wesley in the same way that Wesley gives to him—to listen, simply to be there, while knowing that nothing will occur between them sexually. This section of the novel is a very touching and subtle handling of the AIDS situation and how it is affecting not so much society as the individual within society, the isolated desires of a single person. For Wesley can comprehend and identify with the loneliness of Stan's life.

Off and on throughout *Good Hearts,* we read bits of Rosa's diary as she addresses her thoughts to Wesley. And here, as in *A Long and Happy Life* and most recently in *Kate Vaiden,* Reynolds Price's handling of the female psyche is nothing short of brilliant. Not only is Rosa Mustian Beavers vibrant and believable, she is also one of the more endearing characters ever to hit a printed page. She is a tower of strength, wit and goodness, and her very accep-

tance of Wesley and her handling of the situation are an indication of the depth and complexity of her love: "I would die for you every instant of the day," she writes, "and you damned well know it—and don't forget, I am writing this three weeks after a lunatic fouled me head to foot and in your bed, Wesley, in a house we both paid for but that's in your name and that you left a month ago with no word of warning."

But Rosa is not the only figure who takes life within this book. All of Mr. Price's characters are vividly drawn; even the rapist receives the benefit of the author's compassion. Among the most distinctive characters is Rosa's mama, who cooks three meals a day, watches *The Young and the Restless* and "thought she knew more than Justice Holmes or John-the-damn-Baptist." Another is Rosa's brother, Rato, who has a premonition about the rape. He is both touching and humorous: "Whatever clouds blow through that mind," Rosa observes of him, "they blew on away and left him calm as a good April evening."

Unobtrusively, without histrionics either on their part or the author's, Mr. Price's characters move through the action of the novel to a larger understanding of themselves and others. As we and they discover, they are people equipped with the power to be good human beings, with the power to love. In revealing this, the tone and rhythms of Reynolds Price's language are masterful. *Good Hearts* is superb storytelling by an enduring craftsman. It is a study of life and the placement of individuals within life. In every sense of the word, it abounds with goodness.

> *Jill McCorkle, "Enhanced by Darkness," in* The New York Times Book Review, *May 8, 1988, p. 10.*

Vince Aletti

"The miracle is, you can last through time." That's Kate Vaiden, the tenacious heroine of Reynolds Price's last novel, talking, but it could easily be Rosacoke Mustian, the overripe, love-stunned country girl hurtling into adulthood in Price's first novel, *A Long and Happy Life.* Or Wesley Beavers, the boy who tips her over the edge. Rosacoke and Wesley are destined to be lovers from the moment she comes across him perched in the high branches of a pecan tree "like he was the eagle on money," and calls up, "Boy shake me down some nuts." But they seem unprepared for anything more. Rosa is avid, alert, hanging on Wesley's every move, he's reckless, taciturn, hovering just out of reach. Thinking she might hold Wesley by giving in to him, Rosacoke only gets pregnant, they lurch into marriage with no mention of love, no real proposal.

Price closes *A Long and Happy Life* with a quietly dazzling scene—set at a church Christmas pageant where Rosacoke plays Mary—that signals Rosacoke's acceptance of Wesley's abrupt invitation to "go to Dillon—you ain't got to wait for a license there." Price hints at love everlasting but also plants the seed of future discontent in Rosacoke's brooding about the elusive Wesley. "All this time I have lived on the hope he would change some day before it was too late and come home and calm down and learn how to talk to me and maybe even listen, and we would have a long life together—him and me—and be happy sometimes and get us children that would look like him and have his name and answer when we called." Knowing that he hasn't changed, Rosacoke says *yes,* whispers *yes* into the ear of the fitful baby Jesus, and studies love.

In *Good Hearts,* Price returns to his lovers 28 years later, when Wesley has turned 50, Rosa 48. They've settled in Raleigh, raised and married off their boy Horace, she's a secretary, he's a mechanic. In the book's opening pages, Price describes the couple falling off to sleep at the end of a day. Rosa, who dropped the country suffix, thinks of herself and her husband as "aging but content." When she dreams, it's about Wesley—a line from a poem she wrote him in high school: "Didn't we know that darkest brightness that can be?" But Wesley is far from satisfied; he's a man "with his nose flat against a blank wall of defeat," and he drifts off to dream of pride and failure. The next day, instead of returning from work, he gets in his car and just keeps driving.

Breaking the first half of *Good Hearts* into alternate chapters of entries from Rosa's diary and descriptions of Wesley's life away from home, Price seems at first to be crafting a more mature, more even-handed, slightly feminist *Rabbit Run* (the second day on her own, the wife says to herself, "Rosa, you can stand alone"). But Price isn't content to probe the muddied depths of this midlife crisis— the doubt, discontent, unresolved longings—and spread it before us with the impressionistic intensity that make *A Long and Happy Life* and *Kate Vaiden* so vibrant and affecting. He seems determined to thrust his characters (and himself) into a contemporary novel full of contemporary references (*People, Hustler,* Kenny Rogers, microwave ovens, Frederick's of Hollywood, AIDS) no matter how uncomfortable they all seem. So Wesley goes to Nashville and has an affair with a 26-year-old radiology technician in a trailer home and a soul-searching, sexless encounter with a gay man. Rosa is raped in her own bed on New Year's Eve and heads home to her family for comfort. Price stirs the plot up furiously, then gets on with his real concerns: memory, regret, family ties, friendship, aging, the persistence of love.

But if *Good Hearts* is essentially a love story, it's riddled with apprehension about the wisdom of romance, the impossibility of connection, and the uncertainty of life. Wesley, "dead at heart," feels trapped, "nailed to the floor" by his marriage. In Nashville, though, he's anxious and rootless and Rosa is always on his mind. His trailer home fling is plenty hot, but it doesn't stifle his "fear of death and a cold soft peter." "I've been a boy with no more troubles than a rock in the road," he says, "but lately the rock's been learning to worry." Rosa's diary—"a place I can come to and run and yell in at night"—is addressed to Wesley. A running account of her time without him, it's full of worries, entreaties, and best wishes, but utterly matter-of-fact about her rape and witty about modern notions of sex and marriage. Though her husband's disappearance baffles her, she thinks of him fondly as her only friend. "We had got to being like two old dogs in the same yard bumping up against each other at feeding time and curling up together in the cold night for warmth, not much else," she writes him in a letter. She longs for that simple state, and regrets it only if that's what drove him off.

Rosa's uninflected written description of her rape brings Wesley back and they begin a slow, wary readjustment. Rosa wonders how she can trust her husband again, much less continue to join him in bed at the end of the day. But maybe, she thinks, trust is more than she can ask. . . . Wesley, who came back not knowing what to expect or why, tells Rosa in bed one night that his life is "not the real best I've dreamed to have," but, without entirely denying his dreams, he doubts he'll ever find better. "I can trim my sails and live like a human," he says, "not an angel on fire gazing off toward God." In the end, these middle-aged lovers return from a refreshing, back-to-the-roots visit with Rosa's family to realize they are truly "Home, Safe again." Price doesn't toss flowers and flood the scene with shafts from heaven. Like Rosa and Wesley, his hopes are more modest—"small calm pleasures," and easeful death—and he simply notes "the unlikely choice of two normal creatures to work again at a careful life."

Good Hearts is not without its fumbles. Price's attempt to understand the inner life of Rosa's gentle rapist, and relate that boy's yearning to the universal quest for love, dissolves in fatuity. His picture of the New South is clouded by nostalgia and contempt that seem less his characters' than his own. But the book is studded with revealing, cropped-to-the-bone conversations—as always, Price's ear for laconic dialogue is so right that whole chapters snap into place. When he listens in on Rosa's family— especially her slow-witted brother, Rato, who really blossoms here (and deserves his own book)—the novel finds its natural groove and the reader fairly glides along. Woven into Price's scenes from a marriage, these glimpses of family life ground *Good Hearts* in rich domesticity. As Price writes in his preface to the *Mustian* collection, the continuing story of Rosa and Wesley offers a compellingly simple message: *The world exists. It is not yourself. Plunge in it for healing, blessed exhaustion, and the risk of warmth.* When Rosa and Wesley choose "The same warm house. Us same two old dogs, the same old basket," you're not in the least surprised. But you're more than satisfied to curl up there with them.

Vince Aletti, "A Song of Old Lovers," in VLS, *No. 23, June 7, 1988, p. 13.*

Jefferson Humphries

Reynolds Price published his first novel, *A Long and Happy Life,* in 1962. It received extraordinary critical accolades (after having been rejected by Jason Epstein at Random House) and won the William Faulkner Award for a notable first novel. Since then, in the course of twenty-five years, Price has published five novels, two books of poetry, two collections of short stories, two essay collections, two plays, and a book of translations from the Bible. None of those quite received the kind of unanimous ovation that had greeted the writer's first book until the appearance of *Kate Vaiden* in 1986. *Kate Vaiden* was also the first since 1962 to win a major national award (the National Book Critics Circle Award). . . .

[These] two books not only represent milestones of critical recognition in the writers career, but also are the only ones in which the chief protagonist is female (*Good Hearts* is not counted as a third because in it Rosacoke really shares equal billing with Wesley Beavers). *Kate Vaiden* is narrated in the first person by a woman, and the earlier book contains long letters written by Rosacoke Mustian, even though the whole story is not told by her. Why should these two, of all Price's very impressive body of work, have won such untempered praise? Could the fact of female point of view have anything to do with this?

A Long and Happy Life is in one sense a love story, a simple southern pastoral. Rosacoke Mustian, an unusually bright and sensitive country girl, loves Wesley Beavers, motorcycle salesman and youthful womanizer. Wesley may or may not love Rosacoke; it's hard to tell. He probably doesn't love anyone the way Rosacoke loves him. Nothing could be simpler or more timeless: unrequited love and its consequences. Rosacoke and Wesley do wind up tied together in marriage. Many readers were aware of a chilling irony in the novel's title, and those who have followed Price's career will know how strongly he has denied identification with Rosacoke and defended Wesley: what Price says in many interviews is that Wesley is just a good old boy who enjoys his freedom, to which Rosacoke puts an untimely end. If this describes the affinities of Price, it does not correspond to those of the novel's narrative voice, however. In any case, the novel's ironic, doom-charged title—like an inscrutable peal of distant thunder when the sky is blue—is emblematic of the book. The more disturbing possibilities—that life with Wesley may be far from happy though long, or neither long nor happy, and that similar romances and marriages may be similarly chilly corridors past childbearing and rearing towards the grave—are easy to ignore for the reader who would rather not see them. I would guess that most of *A Long and Happy Life*'s readers have chosen to ignore its darker side, and that would include the critics who objected to subsequent books like *Permanent Errors,* whose title and content are far less ambiguously pessimistic. Their lesson is one which Price says he got from reading Hemingway: "The lessons of one master, diffidently but desperately offered—*Prepare, strip, divest for life that awaits you; learn solitude and work; see how little is lovely but love that.*"

Good Hearts, which has just appeared, gives us a look at Rosacoke and Wesley in middle age, still married, but facing now the chasm of mutual strangeness that has separated them from the start, and which has rubbed both of them fairly raw without their knowing it. Rosacoke is a secretary for a college department office, and Wesley works as a mechanic. They live in Raleigh, North Carolina, and have had only the one child with which Rosa was pregnant at the end of *A Long and Happy Life.* He is an adult now, married and living a few hours away. Wesley, a few days before Christmas, goes off to work and does not return home. He has, we are told, left for as much as four days on more than one occasion before, sometimes leaving notes hidden in his sock drawer. This time there is no note, and the absence stretches on far beyond his prior record. How and why Wesley turns away from Rosacoke will evoke pangs of recognition from most people over thirty. She tells it herself:

> I know this much at least, that you'd turned away from me slowly but more and more. You were always courteous about it—but the fact is, you turned. It hasn't been all that hard for me to bear. I've been able to think it was a natural movement of time, working in both of us. But I can't help seeing all those old couples on t.v. saying they've never been happier with their bodies than now, when their children are grown and gone, and they can be alone in the house together. Not that you and I are

old, but we turned out not to know what to do alone together. That was one fault at least, and I bear at least fifty percent of the blame.

Rosa reacts, just as a reader of *A Long and Happy Life* would expect her to, by beginning a diary. Just as she spoke for herself in the earlier novel, not always but often—in first-person narration, letters, or out loud, to other characters—so she does now, twenty-eight years later. Her introspectiveness, her facility with words, which together make for a verbal compulsion to *make sense out of things*—things which usually don't make much sense—has not been good for the both of them, as it usually isn't when only one member of a couple has it:

> Wesley, you were always so slow to speak up for yourself that it took me long years to realize how I mowed you down time after time with all my orations and epistles. Of course I *didn't* mow you down. I never really won. You'd just tuck your square chin, nod, walk on off, and do your will in your own sweet time. But I wish I'd had the fairness to see years sooner how I shut you out of my own calculations and thought I was Miss Country Genius and Judge.

Is it too late now? To change, or make amends? As in the earlier novel, Rosa's eloquent candor makes her the star of *Good Hearts.* We love her because she has chosen us to confide in.

The more taciturn Wesley is shown to us in the third person, but we are made to understand here, as perhaps we were not in *A Long and Happy Life,* that Wesley is a genuinely *good* person, every bit as worthy of sympathy as Rosacoke. Price seems more concerned to tell Wesley's side of the story now than twenty-eight years ago, probably because of the one-sided view of the relation taken by so many readers of *A Long and Happy Life.*

The failure of both Rosacoke and Wesley to understand, to reach one another, to do whatever is necessary to keep their union living and vital, is in Price's vision an essential evil, as supernaturally *and* physically real as evil could possibly be. The lack of bad intention, of any will to harm on Rosacoke's part or Wesley's, does not make this evil any less what it is. Even though both Wesley and Rosa are essentially good and well-meaning people, a lack of vigilance is all it takes for them—for Rosacoke and their home—to become exposed: during Wesley's absence, Rosa must face Christmas alone, without Wesley or their son, and on New Year's Eve, she is attacked in their bed and raped. It is Wesley's abandonment of Rosa, and the accumulated wrong of their mutual estrangement, each taking for granted the other, that has left Rosa and their home open to such dark violence. This evil, though elemental, takes a firmly human form, as evil usually does. It does not have horns and breathe fire, or appear and disappear in a puff of smoke, but comes in the utterly ordinary shape of a deluded and disturbed though sane man—a rapist—who would never admit the evil, or even the wrong of his desires and acts, and who appears to be perfectly likable when under public scrutiny, completely unrecognizable—to all but Rosacoke—for what he is. He is also, like all real evil, finally ludicrous and pathetic. Price's depiction of this man is one of the most penetrating, believable, *true* portraits of evil I have ever seen or read, and is enough in itself to make this book extraordinary. In this case, and for the time being, evil does not prevail. This case, one feels, is given to us by the author as exemplary, one to emulate, not as a reflection of what usually happens in human relationships.

Good Hearts shows us two decent, kind people in deep, deep trouble as a couple. Facing the decision whether to let that trouble, stewing for so long, separate them, or try to face each other and reach over it (can any two people hope to reach *that* far?) is what this book is about. It is the most compelling and sensitive book Price has written. There cannot be a subject on which Americans of all ages living in 1988 more desperately need and crave (whether they know it or not) instruction: Can two good people live together for long without suffering or doing subtle, maybe invisible but nonetheless real, harm to themselves and each other—without "pecking each other bald," like two chickens nailed inside a single crate? If so, how?

This book is even more compelling in its subject matter than *Kate Vaiden,* I think, and the writing has the same quality as *Kate Vaiden.* In both of these books, there can be no mistake that we are in the hands of a master who has attained perfect ease in his art. You have the same feeling that the last Laurence Olivier could evoke on the stage: everything is effortlessly perfect. Do not worry, do not even think about how the artifice is accomplished. The perfection is so intense that it erases all trace of itself, and becomes apparently natural ease. One wonders why Price, who has always been one of America's great writers, should suddenly now transcend himself. The real wonder is that any artist, however great, manages to do so at all, ever. There is no answer to the question why. However and whyever, Price shows an ease with himself and with his readers that is the rarest quality in art. For example, in the opening page of *Good Hearts,* there is an aside by the narrator to the reader, like a parabasis in classical Greek drama—a moment in which the chorus of a play would remove their masks and step forward to speak directly in the author's name. The narration has been describing Rosa and Wesley in bed, about to fall asleep. Suddenly, there is this sentence: "You though, if you'd been transparent there, would have seen an apparently young married couple." Rosacoke is not the only one choosing to confide in us; the narrator is, too.

That Price should have returned, after so long, to his first and most popular characters is a surprise, perhaps to him as well as to readers who have followed his career closely. For many years he has replied to questions about what Rosacoke and Wesley might be doing now by saying that he had said all about them he knew in *A Long and Happy Life. . . .* But most surprising of all is how perfectly the Rosa and Wesley of *Good Hearts* dovetail with the depiction of their younger selves in *A Long and Happy Life.* One never doubts for an instant that these are the very same people. This is exactly and perfectly how they would have evolved. It could not have turned out any differently. On almost every occasion I know where a novelist has written a sequel to an earlier book, especially one in which the same characters are seen years later or earlier, the seams are too visible—there is a nagging discrepancy, beyond changes always wrought by time and events, between two characters which are supposed to be the same one. Here, that is not the case. I know of only one other modern writer who has accomplished this so well: Marcel

Proust, who of course did so on a rather grander scale in *A la recherche du temps perdu.*

Kate Vaiden is the intermediate step between Price's previous work and *Good Hearts. Kate Vaiden* frames the typically, and unambiguously, astringent vision of Price's mature work (*The Surface of Earth,* for instance) in first-person narration rather than the somewhat lofty omniscience of the writer's other novels, stories, and poems since *A Long and Happy Life.* It ties that vision to the circumstances of a narrating persona with whom anyone can sympathize or identify. This makes it more palatable to more readers and critics, I suspect, than *The Surface of Earth* and most of Price's other, earlier work. *Kate Vaiden* grew out of what Price has described as the impulse to write a fictional autobiography. He says that "as I advanced on into 1982-83, the impulse began to change in my mind to a woman's voice. I can only begin to understand the reason for that when I remember that at the same time I was beginning to do a great deal of thinking about my own mother." Kate's story is written by her late in life, when she knows that a cancer of the cervix will— perhaps?—soon kill her. This aspect of the story must have a great deal to do with Price's own recent bout with a cancerous spinal tumor, which interrupted work on *Kate Vaiden.* She tells the story of her life for a son abandoned when she was seventeen.

> Cervical cancer, no possible doubt. Seventy-two hours in near-solitary in a hospital room with radium seeds planted deep inside me, bombarding the guest. Except for nurses dashing in with my meals (which, since I couldn't raise my head, I couldn't eat), the only other human I saw was a man in a long pink smock who swore he was chaplain. I thanked him but said I dealt with God alone. A fool thing to say, but the pink smock threw me. I was dealing with death.
>
> I'd watched death at close range several times before but in other people's bodies. Like the average human, I'd assumed I'd escape. The absolute last invader I'd suspected was cancer *there.* But lying alone for two full days, with radium in me, I of course came round to the next deduction. I was punished at last in the place where I'd failed, the scene of the crime. Can you believe me if I say my first response was amusement? It seemed like a big tidy joke.

Kate Vaiden would be Rosacoke Mustian's polar opposite, at least in the way her desire expresses itself, without any of Rosacoke's fierce loyalty, determined bonding to one object of desire (Wesley) and unswerving commitment to see that bond through to the grave. Kate Vaiden is, as one reviewer put it, "a well-meaning betrayer." When Kate is a child, her father kills Kate's mother and himself after discovering that his wife has not been faithful to him. Kate loves many men, but is unable to commit herself to any of them. The very first, Gaston Stegall, might have been the exception if he had not been killed in training for World War II, or so Kate thinks. Of course, it's cheap to think so with the possibility firmly out of reach, and thinking so makes it easier to say no to others. As soon as anyone confesses his need of her, she takes the first opportunity to leave, usually without a word. This is not for lack of good will. Kate does not entirely excuse herself for being so simultaneously fickle and headstrong (though some readers will agree with Noony, Kate's black friend, mentor, and stern judge, that she comes too close), but she does not see, in retrospect, how she could have done any differently. She cannot contemplate spending the rest of her life, or even any large or indefinite portion of it, with any one other person. She abandons everyone who has ever loved or needed her, including her own illegitimate son. She believes, and may be right in believing, that she could not have lived any other way but alone. Still, she has damaged many lives by insisting on having things entirely her way—engaging in intimate relations while refusing the responsibility involved, never really accepting any responsibility for her own desire. When she begs Noony's pardon for her many sins toward the end of the book, Noony replies, "Too late." And many readers will agree. Nevertheless, to the end, Kate remains compellingly likable, even to Noony.

Kate's story, like Rosacoke's and all of Price's work, reflects a preoccupation with the difficult vagaries of desire between two, and sometimes more than two humans, the by turns healing and catastrophically rending force of love, all the more powerful and treacherous when it is sexual. I think Constance Rooke . . . was right when she said that Price's work is haunted by a double bind: the impossibility of living alone without desiring others, and the impossibility of being with others without sacrificing a large part of the self's autonomy, without mourning a (perhaps illusory) freedom. This would appear to be *the* moral dilemma which must confront every adult wishing to be responsible in her/his dealings with others, and I know of no writer who has plumbed it as deeply or thoroughly as Price. Kate's story, like Rosacoke's, is absolutely compelling because it could be anyone's, man or woman. And it is told in a prose which is both starkly simple and beautiful.

I don't know of any other writer who can come close to the piercing, lyrical clarity of Price's language. Many critics in the sixties and seventies called Price's style "overwrought," "artificial." It has taken us this long to appreciate it for what it has always been: meticulously, carefully crafted. His voice, or maybe I should say his voices, have been shaped by many things, early study of Milton, the translation of Biblical Greek, the rhythms of southern speech, and have been for a while so perfectly achieved that they completely transcend time and space, the modern upper South (North Carolina and Virginia) in which Price's characters usually move.

Nowhere is this style more visible or purer (distilled down to an even denser, more white-hot version of itself) than in the poetry which Price has been publishing since the early sixties. Two volumes of his poetry have appeared, the first, *Vital Provisions,* in 1982, the second, *The Laws of Ice,* in 1986. *The Laws of Ice* contains work dealing, as the title indicates, with morality and its consequences, the natural and supernatural dialectic of life and death. Many of these are poems dealing with Price's bout in 1984 with an astrocytoma, a malignant tumor on his spinal cord, which has left him confined to a wheelchair. The central section of the book, "Days and Nights: A Journal," comprises a poetic record of the days immediately before and after the discovery of that tumor. In one of those poems, Price meets in dream an avatar of death:

> I know he will make his thrust any moment;
> I cannot guess what aim it will take.

> Then as—appalled—I watch him quiver,
> He says "Now you must learn the bat dance."
> I know he has struck. It is why I came.
> In one long silent step, I refuse and turn toward
>   home.

> I will walk all night, I will not die of cancer.
> Nothing will make me dance in that dark.

Other poems narrate natural encounters, either with animals (a snake, for instance) or other humans, both of which seem to have supernatural import. The healing power of contact with human flesh, the mysterious balm of sex, is a recurring preoccupation. Dreams—always in Price's work potential messages from the sphere of the divine—and narratives expanded from Bible verses have both become leitmotifs of Price's poetry by now. Nowhere is it clearer that Price has somehow, miraculously, emerged from his maiming brush with premature death without any bitterness, without any diminution of his gifts as a person or a writer—on the contrary. *"I'm simply / The one happy man I know, / Assured of witness and judgement entirely / Beyond my power to guess or change."*

The same style, and the same preoccupations, are evident in *A Common Room, Essays 1954-1987.* Having written novels, stories, poetry, plays, and essays, Price is one of the only true "men of letters" in our culture. The essays are about everything from Milton's *Lycidas* to Jimmy Carter to southern cooking, and in them the vision reflected in the novels and poetry comes through as *credo:* "A line scored in the earth beneath this much at least of a career grounded in the beliefs described. Credos are dangerous coats to wear; they may alienate readers to whom the beliefs look absurd or excluding." That credo is the Apostles' Creed, an ancient and elegant affirmation of Christian faith—simpler, shorter, and less doctrinaire than the Nicene—well-known to Catholics and Anglicans. Price has always defined his vision as essentially Christian.

> The final help I can offer the proof-hungry is a reminder that virtually identical beliefs powered perhaps a majority of the supreme creative minds of our civilization—Augustine, Dante, Chaucer, Michelangelo, Durer, Milton, Rembrandt, Pascal, Racine, Bach, Handel, Newton, Haydn, Mozart, Wordsworth, Beethoven, Kierkegaard, Dickens, Tolstoy, Hopkins, Bruckner, Tennyson, Stravinsky, Eliot, Barth, Poulenc, Auden, O'Connor (to begin a long roll that includes only the dead). Pressed by their unanimous testimony to a dazzling but benign light at the heart of space, what sane human will step up to say "Lovely, no doubt, but your eyes deceive you"? Not I, not now or any day soon.

One of the best essays is the one for which the collection is named, **"A Vast Common Room,"** in which Price proposes a radical approach to the failure of understanding between men and women which may be worse today than it has ever been—ironically so, at a moment when both men and women are freer than ever before to criticize and change the culture's definition of "masculine" and "feminine." That freedom seems too often to have led women to answer traditional male misogyny with a mirror image, an excoriation of maleness, and men defensively to fear and scorn women all the more. Price's solution may be best illustrated by the three novels, *Kate Vaiden, Good*

Hearts, and *A Long and Happy Life,* and may answer in some degree the question I left unanswered at the beginning of this essay: why female point of view has produced the writer's most acclaimed fiction.

> Can we change? And should we? My own answer is an obvious Yes. Men should excavate and explore, however painfully, their memories of early intimacy with women, and attempt again to produce novels as whole as those of their mammoth and healing predecessors. More women should step through a door that is now wide ajar—a backward step, also painful but short, into the room of their oldest knowledge: total human sympathy.

What could be more obvious or more humane, but what other writer has said it?

Price, like Don DeLillo (unlike Price an urban and abstract novelist), is a writer working against the age. His realism, like DeLillo's, is in the service of a profoundly coherent and unique and *troubled,* though fervently hopeful vision of what it is to be human, and this means that it is a realism which does not defer to matter, does not stop at the material surface of things the way more popular writing does. While he has not been neglected, Price has not gotten the critical attention that more gaudily experimental novelists have, nor has he been very palatable to connoisseurs of a purely mimetic and material realism. But I don't know of any writer who has more important things to say, more really indispensable comfort and advice to offer, to a reader living in the second half of the twentieth century, or indeed in any time or place. (pp. 686-95)

> *Jefferson Humphries, "'A Vast Common Room': Twenty-five Years of Essays and Fiction by Reynolds Price," in* The Southern Review, *Louisiana State University, Vol. 24, No. 3, Summer, 1988, pp. 686-695.*

Jay Tolson

Any male Southern writer worth his grits must bear up under a certain amount of unfair and generally pointless comparison with William Faulkner. It comes with the territory, as they say. But Reynolds Price has had to tolerate more than his share, and for reasons largely irrelevant to his work. It began with a coincidence. Price's first novel, *A Long and Happy Life,* came out the same year Faulkner died, in 1962, a symbolic torch-passing for those inclined to see it as such. If that were not enough to give influence-hounds the scent, the same novel went on to win that year's William Faulkner Foundation Award.

For lazier reviewers, it was hardly necessary to read the novel: this was a Faulkner epigone, clear and simple. Those who bothered would have thought their suspicions confirmed by the novel's first sentence. A serpentine creature of almost 200 words, it looks as though it crawled straight out of Yoknapatawpha County. But the sentence deceives. It is the only one quite like it in the book. The prose that bodies forth the tale of Rosacoke Mustian and her barely requited love for Wesley Beavers is, for the most part, closely pruned, quite unlike Faulkner's sprawling verbal undergrowth.

Absent as well are other hallmarks of the Faulkner style—the incantatory iterations, the neologisms, the poetic infla-

tion. Price, in fact, favored a more clinched-in rhetoric, a rhetoric of understatement that owed more to Hemingway (an influence he acknowledges in one of the more self-revealing essays in *A Common Room*) than to Faulkner. Still, since Price was Southern, wrote about country people, and sometimes used dialect, the critics persisted. Over the years, Price complains, "It has been all but mandatory in discussions of my fiction to claim—and regret if not lament—the influence of William Faulkner."

Misleading as all this is, it is hardly necessary to rally to Price's defense. The 57 essays assembled in *A Common Room* do a more than adequate job on their own. Dating from 1954 to 1987 and spanning Price's productive career as a novelist, poet, playwright, and professor of English, they show how different Price's ambitions are—narrower, in a sense, but also more tightly harnessed to considerations of craft. The essays, variously personal, critical, and hortatory, also make for an illuminating *autobiographia literaria,* as revealing about Price's life and background as they are about his literary tastes and designs.

Price, one quickly learns, is a writer firmly rooted in "one dear perpetual place," that place being the gently rolling tobacco and cotton country of east-central North Carolina. To those who know it, it's pleasant enough country at the right season and the right time of day, but it can also turn dry, dusty, and red-clay mean during the long hot bake of summer. Hard country, in other words: it's the sort of place that doesn't leave people too much leeway, and for which, as a result, folks develop a wary, grudging love. Not surprisingly, it tends to lose many of its talented young to more hospitable climes.

What kept Price at home, or at least within a very short drive of his native Macon, was people, kith and kin. Among the former are the South's two extremes: overworked and underpaid blacks and the fading remnants of the old planter aristocracy. Both types serve as secondary characters in Price's novels, though not merely as thickeners of the social soup: they are always vivid presences, strongly individualized. Still, the people Price knows, and the ones who figure centrally in his fiction, are the white upper yeomanry. Small farmers (or former sharecroppers), skilled mechanics, shopkeepers, salesmen, and clerks—they are the people Jefferson idealized and, to a large extent, the people who still keep the South running.

Raised with modest social ambitions—the more driven or fortunate rise into the solid middle or upper middle classes, but even to them the yuppie creed of ever-upward is anathema—they live by the Protestant virtues of work and faith. If their lives often turn out to be bitterly hard and disappointing, they are not the kind to blame others or the system. They're far more likely to blame themselves, their moral failings; and if faith can't save them from guilt, they may turn in desperation to the bottle or to some other crutch to help them go silently to their graves. All is not a Vale of Tears, though. It sounds corny, but they live for family, even though the bonds of kinship as often strangle as sustain. Most also live with hope of grace, which more than anything else can make the hard life seem worth living.

Price has paid close attention to these people, his family early on becoming a source of fascination and mystery. There was, for one, an alcoholic father, an insurance salesman who struggled through the Great Depression and who, the night Reynolds was born, swore to give up the bottle if his wife made it through a particularly difficult labor. Price came to wonder what he owed this troubled but deeply loving man for keeping that difficult pledge. And, in one sense, Price's fiction is the answer: it is both a long meditation on sacrifice and indebtedness and an expression of gratitude.

Price owes perhaps an even greater debt to the women of his family (and also to a number of outstanding women teachers who quite literally changed his life). Of one particularly cherished aunt who, during all his childhood years of moving around North Carolina, remained a fixed point in Macon, the embodiment of rootedness and home, he recalls that she served "all the functions of an ideal grandmother—unquestioned love and generosity, without the riptides of parental love." The ties with his mother, like those with his father, were more complicated. In **"A Vast Common Room,"** an essay that explores the hermaphroditic nature of the artist, Price relates how his curiosity about his mother—"noted for youthful rebellion but then for impeccable loyalty to my father"—drove him one day "to write in a female voice, one whose atmosphere chimed in my ears with the timbre of my mother's lost voice, which I no longer remember." The book that issued from this compulsion was **Kate Vaiden,** to my mind Price's best novel to date, and powerful precisely because of the steady force of the protagonist's voice. As Price explains:

> However far my Kate ventured in rebellion and independence, she achieved in her voice and in all her acts a credible expression of my mother's own spiritual potential—a life whose courage and headlong drive I might have awarded my mother had I been able and were it not a life with even more pain than hers.

How we learn to handle the complicated "rip-tides" of love, and not just parental love, is Price's great theme, present from his first novel to his most recent. His constant attention to this question, and his quiet handling of its complex domestic ramifications, make him, finally, a very different writer from Faulkner. Faulkner's sights were set on something more grand, or grandiose: the creation of a mythic world in which a series of tragic destinies play themselves out. Price, more like Eudora Welty or E. M. Forster (two authors who are paid deep homage in *A Common Room*), is concerned with the problem of connecting.

What is more, as a number of these essays suggest, Price has found his own answer. It is work—steady, habitual attention to one's given trade. Work alone, he writes, "has freed me for the attempt to understand, if not control, disorder in myself and in those I love. It has even freed me at times to participate in the richest, most dangerous mystery of all—the love of what otherwise I should have feared and fled, a few human beings." In urging his solution on his readers and, no doubt, on his many fortunate students, Price sounds ever so much like the person I suspect his parents intended—the good, if unchurched, Protestant. (pp. 34-6)

Price's hard-earned Protestant wisdom is an admirable guide to self-sufficiency, and to much else as well. But as a foundation on which to build fictions, it poses problems.

A vision too strongly imposed upon the various world and its even more various inhabitants can lead to formula, a danger that threatens even Price's greatest gift, his powers of characterization. Price's characters, with occasional exceptions (notably the highly autobiographical protagonist of *Love and Work*) are shrewd rustics, blunt, funny and honest folk who talk about themselves and their plights with the same sort of light irony one finds in the better country music songs—the "work your fingers to the bone, what do you get? Bony fingers!" variety. But it's not the countriness that troubles. Price's populism is never condescending. The problem is that Price knows his characters almost too well. Lacking an inner opacity, they sometimes seem too dependent on their creator and the vision they were created to serve.

Yet for all that, Price makes us want to know his people. We want to, because they come across as attractive and nearly as wise as Price himself. Nearly, I emphasize, because they almost all have great difficulty connecting, a problem that stems from excessive expectations—theirs of others, others of them. We find these characters and the familiar blocked situations once again in Price's most recent novel, *Good Hearts,* which takes up the lives of Rosacoke and Wesley Beavers some 30 years after their rocky courtship in *A Long and Happy Life.*

The problem raised in that first novel was how a young woman of unusually subtle intelligence could resolve her unhappy love for a man who, while attractive and goodhearted, seems her intellectual and spiritual lesser. A standard variation on the classic small-town romance, in other words, but Price worked the familiar clay in quite marvelous ways, showing how a deep mutual attraction plays havoc with Rosacoke and Wesley's more obvious incompatibilities. The plot complicates when a tussle in the field leaves Rosacoke pregnant, and Wesley, and ex-Navy man and avid motorcyclist, unable to stay put in rural Afton, North Carolina, returns to the bigger lights of Norfolk, Virginia, unaware of what their lovemaking has produced. Even when he learns of Rosacoke's pregnancy and returns home to do the honorable thing, he cannot find the right words to satisfy Rosacoke. All seems doomed until both take part in a Christmas pageant at the Baptist church and Rosacoke is drawn by the laden symbolism of the occasion to see and accept Wesley for what he is. Marriage seems inevitable by novel's end.

To those readers who favor down-to-earth solutions, the conclusion of *A Long and Happy Life* may have seemed somewhat contrived: Was grace doing forced duty here? I, for one, felt that the resolution served as a fitting close to the book's larger theme: the mixed blessings of generation (there are other complicated births in the novel, both leading to deaths) and the mysterious claims and transformations involved in the engendering act. It also worked because Price convinced me that Rosacoke's perceptions and understanding were attuned to something more liminal than hard common sense. And furthermore, it was not, by any stretch, a snugly happy ending.

The novel left readers wondering about what might happen after this attractive though unevenly matched couple made it to the altar. *Good Hearts* tells us. Rosacoke (now Rosa) and Wesley have made their way from Afton to Raleigh, raised a son, and seen him settle into his own career and marriage. Rosa and Wesley both have respectable jobs—she as a secretary in a university English department, he as a car mechanic—and though both stand out at what they do, neither views work as the royal road to self-fulfillment. They don't even live vicariously through their son, who, though loving, is a bit on the dull side. (pp. 36-7)

Despite life's small disappointments, Rosa and Wesley seem to have found contentment. They appear easy with each other, comfortable with their routines. But then one day in late December of what seems a recent year, after a night of troubled dreaming, Wesley decides to leave Rosa without warning or explanation. The dream is of failure, and Wesley's journey westward, ending in Nashville (where so many songs of dashed hopes are made), is his last effort to fan some spark of significance before giving up on his life. Wesley, we learn, suffers from what at first seems absurdly monstrous vanity, a ludicrous (though not altogether unjustified) feeling that he is God's gift to women, and that, in his marriage with Rosa, he has wasted his specialness. Worse yet, he thinks, Rosa has insufficiently valued his gift—or never even needed it.

Wesley easily could seem a pathetic, even contemptible character, but Price's achievement is to make the wayward quest of this failed Golden Boy seem neither trivial nor vapid. Wesley comes across as at least as complex and dignified a character as, for instance, Rabbit Angstrom, Updike's *homme moyen sensuel.* Wesley's imagination is obsessively, almost demonically erotic, but we are shown that the ways of eros can lead to a kind of knowledge. Even more, Wesley recognizes the limits of his knowledge, and does so precisely because of what he has learned in his marriage with Rosa. Long exposure to her patient if sometimes scouring intelligence has left him with an ironic perspective on his fantasies. He knows that what he wants is crazy, but he is at war with himself, and the struggle is precisely what makes for his complexity.

Rosa doesn't feel the same urge as Wesley to set off on a journey of self-discovery and renewal; she has always been far ahead of him. At the same time, she knows that she has lived too much for Wesley's love, even while being unable to love him in the way that would make him happy. (This, obviously, is neither a character nor a predicament to send shivers of delight through militant feminists' hearts.) She yearns for Wesley's return but doesn't really believe that some fundamental change in herself is possible. Nor, after searching her heart, does she believe that one is called for.

The agency of resolution, here as in *A Long and Happy Life,* is the mysterious power of Providence. We are asked to accept a high, purposive design behind seemingly unrelated events (Wesley's departure and the attack of a rapist) as well as preternatural forms of communication (Rato Mustian, Rosa's extremely eccentric brother, has a dream hinting at his sister's violation). The usual laws of cause and effect collapse in the novel because the author, like his characters, is convinced that there is a divine purpose behind mortal affairs. There is even a theological premise at work in Price's novel—that we sin in order to be upbraided, and that by experiencing God's will in this way we draw closer not only to God but also to what he intends us to be. Price, again, is a very serious Reformed Christian.

And his novels, I would argue, are variations on a Christian pastoral theme. They evoke Arcadias peopled by fallen creatures who struggle to regain a lost happiness, and sometimes, through grace, succeed. Even though *Good Hearts* is set largely in cities (with occasional dashes to the country), the atmosphere—the moral atmosphere, one might say—is decidedly rural. The novel, in fact, offers a quiet comment on the tensions between rusticity and urbanity. The rural ethos of the characters, their countrified ways of seeing and saying things, is at odds with the surrounding urban world and the lost souls who occupy it. But one wishes Price did far more with this conflict. Instead, he leaves it in the background, focused, for example, in the tense relations between Rosa and her daughter-in-law.

Price's failure to address this tension more directly in *Good Hearts* is no small weakness. For one thing, it leaves the novel, despite its many strengths, with too little to do. The heavily psychological examination of Rosa and Wesley's troubles grows attenuated—indeed, the last part of the book labors 36 pages beyond what could have been the novel's more satisfying conclusion. Yet as closely scrutinized as the rupture and reconciliation are, Price never gives any strong indication that the larger culture (television, jobs, the nature of life in Raleigh) plays a part in the Beavers' crisis. Those elements of the larger world are present, but they have no power. As a result, Wesley and Rosa live in something close to a historical void.

In his essay **"Country Mouse, City Mouse,"** Price makes a very persuasive case for the importance of an "early and passionate relation between a writer and nature." Paraphrasing Wordsworth, he argues that it is only "permanent or permanently recurring objects which provide a sufficient reserve of imagery, an adequate sounding board for any but the most claustrophobic novel." He contends, moreover, that a number of otherwise excellent writers, including Baudelaire, Poe, and James, "maimed their work (or some portion of it)" by relying too narrowly on the imagery of city life. But Price's essay does not simply advocate rusticity for rusticity's sake. An intimate connection with rural life has provided the fullest writers, such as Dickens and Tolstoy, with the equipment to take on the larger world, the city as well as the country. Yet in Price's view (a view he might have revised since 1964), there have been since Forster no writers possessed of "the great whole rural-urban vision."

True or not, Price's remarks point to a shortcoming in his own work. Few contemporary writers of such consummate literary skill possess so enviably rich a grounding in the permanent world as Price. Yet he has insufficiently pressed his advantage. So far we have had sallies on the wider world, but no full-scale invasion. In *Kate Vaiden,* for example, the Great Depression and World War II swell into something more than background; they become palpable forces. Finally, though, Price seems to back away from a full exploration of their power over people and events. Doing so, he allows them to subside into devices of nostalgia, and we are left with a merely sentimental evocation of the past. This is the danger of a pastoral novel that lacks a firm historical vision. The novels that Price most admires chart not only the progress of the individual soul but also the progress of the age—and, indeed, the impingements of the latter upon the former. But using the still powerful idiom of the rural South, Price has brilliantly inscribed the story of the modern-day pilgrim's progress. He is our age's Bunyan. (pp. 37-9)

> *Jay Tolson, "The Price of Grace," in* The New Republic, *Vol. 198, No. 27, July 4, 1988, pp. 34-9.*

Robb Forman Dew

The adamancy with which a child's memory is challenged is universal—the first moment when he turns to some nearby adult and says, "*I remember.* . . . " Almost reflexively that aunt or uncle or mother or father dismisses the very idea: "Oh, no," with a note of tolerant fondness, "oh, no, that's not what happened at all! You simply *think* you remember it because you've heard us talk about it so much."

It's an edgy situation all around. The child is stunned and momentarily defeated in his careful construction of the truth of his own life. But that hapless adult also has taken a body blow. All at once this small child—perhaps the most recent addition to an extended family—has become yet another, perhaps untrustworthy, interpreter of family history and myth. So there they are, the two of them, perplexed, mulling over their separate versions of some shared moment, each suddenly perceiving the other as an adversary.

In the early pages of *Clear Pictures,* Reynolds Price's gentle, almost reluctant memoir, we are party to his first conscious memory—an idyllic moment when, as a 4- or 5-month-old infant, he was laid down on a sunny lawn with adults nearby and the family goat grazing beside his blanket, taking a great interest in the goat's attempt to make off with his diaper. Mr. Price feels certain that he does indeed remember this—that it is his own possession, a fact recalled—but it is a moment that occurs so much earlier than most adults can recall that he hedges a bit. Well, he concedes, that incident with the goat became part of family legend; it *could* could be that he has invested this tale—told frequently in his hearing—with the weight of imagination and only perceives it as memory. He grants that possibility with a sweet, understated modesty that pervades this volume, and we acknowledge it. We are that threatened adult anxious to deny such precocious recall, because we do not have similar knowledge of ourselves.

This is a seductive book, in which one reads a bit and pauses to ruminate on the nature of the essential facts of one's own life. Mr. Price . . . is never strident in his reminiscence, and he leads us to conspire with him, to unravel the separate threads of truth and invention in order to decide if there is a difference between the two and if it matters. About his first conscious recollection and about the mystery of memory itself, he says, "That scene is my earliest sure memory; and it poses all the first questions—how does a newborn child learn the three indispensable human skills he is born without? How does he learn to live, love, and die?"

This is not a book that reflects Mr. Price's astonishment at the remarkable coincidence of his own presence on the face of the earth, as too many memoirs do, and because of the serene authority with which he unfolds his recollections, it is immediately clear that he already knows who he is. The writing of this book is far more an homage to his teachers than it is a search for his essential self—it is a tribute to those people from whom he learned how best to live his own life.

He is the son of Will Price and the former Elizabeth Rodwell, both from Macon, N.C., where Reynolds Price was born on Feb. 1, 1933. He was an only child for eight years until the birth of his brother, Bill, and he and his parents had an unusual bond.

> Well before I was in school, I came to realize that they'd been together twelve years before my birth—six years of courtship and six years of marriage. And with that realization came a kernel of bitterness that I'd missed so much of them. . . . But the six years of marriage before my birth were all but tragic, Will's boyish taste for bootleg liquor . . . became a nightmarish and paralyzing thirst.

The difficult and nearly fatal struggle of his wife to give birth to his first son was undoubtedly the major turning point in Will Price's life. Near dawn, after a long night of labor with a breech baby, Elizabeth was near death, and the doctor told Will, "I'm losing them both."

> "More than once in later years," Mr. Price tells us, I watched [his father] hear the story of his next act from others; but I never heard him tell it. . . . It was far too weighty for public performance.

> He fled the house in the freezing dawn, went out to the woodshed; and there he sealed a bargain with God, as stark and unbreakable as any blood pact in Genesis—if Elizabeth lived, and the child, he'd never drink again.

Although the author did not learn of his father's desperate bargain until he was 5 years old, it is hardly surprising that this particular infant felt the scrutiny of his immediate world so intensely that at less than 6 months of age, lying in the sun with his parents close by, he became literally self-conscious. All children must perceive to some degree the fact that fate holds their parents hostage; how extraordinary for a child with the sensibilities of the author to be the object of such anxious surveillance. He was a much-cherished child, and his parents' overwhelming affection and their need that it be returned was a great gift but also, of course, an enormous burden.

And because of the peculiar nature of his parents' neediness, it is also telling that his first *sustained* memory was both a revelation of one of life's great secrets and also the key to a mystery that, once known, is fraught with responsibility. In the late spring of 1936, when Mr. Price was only 3, he was with his parents for a leisurely drive after supper though the cooling streets of the little town of Roxboro, N.C.

> Sometime in the ten-minute last leg of that ride—before we stopped in the drive by the white rock steps of our house on the hill on South Lamar Street, there on the rough cloth of a back seat—I knew for the first and final time that we were all married: Elizabeth, Will and Reynolds. . . . I watched this knowledge open inside me like a sudden strong flower. I knew that this thing in the car with us was what both Will and Elizabeth meant by a word they used several times a day and begged to hear from me. I'd heard the word hundreds of

times and never thought to wonder at its meaning, *love.*

Here again one is filled with momentary envy at the seemingly extraordinary life to be pondered, sorted out, made into a relatively linear experience until it slowly becomes apparent that what has been recounted is not particularly eventful, only miraculously observed and considered. And, as much as he loved his parents, even as a very young child Mr. Price was given to a need for moments of solitary contemplation. Early on he longed to be more of an observer than a participant.

He sought refuge from the gregarious, hectic intimacy of his two passionate and romantic parents in the company of various other adult friends and relatives, the most notable of whom was his mother's oldest sister, Ida Rodwell Drake.

> I sensed near the start that if I was going to learn solitude, the raw taste for which had come in my blood, I'd have to find a training ground other than home. . . . I'd need a long window onto the world and one understanding woman nearby. I found her early, the day I was born—the other lone soul in my mother's swarming family—and more than my parents, whom I loved maybe too much, that soul was the safest refuge of my childhood. . . . In the pristine wordless clarity of childhood, I knew that, in vital things, we were the same age. We were both worn-down and needed rest; we needed time alone to mend, to plan our defenses before the loud family called us again.

His recounting of his annual summer visits with his aunt in Macon is infused with the luxuriant dreaminess of a safe solitude in the long, heated days of Southern summers. One suspects that it is with Ida Drake that Mr. Price first discovered the pleasure and necessity of reflection.

It is a slow process, this development of real knowledge, and no sooner does he discover the evil of racism than he must struggle with that inevitable battle of any white Southerner born between 1930 and, say, 1970: how to justify loving those very people who, consciously or not, perpetuate such an abomination? Mr. Price also wrestles with the peculiar need of the artist to create, with the thirst of humanity for some sort of spirituality, with the definition of a life well lived. He settles these questions through association with and observation of those chosen few whom he adopts not only as teachers but as models of fortitude. He makes peace with the questions he has set himself to answer, and in the process he draws conclusions that are often quite particular, even arguable, but always vigorous and never dull.

Reynolds Price is indeed lucky to have perceived such clear pictures from his first loves and first guides; he is lucky to have had their company, and he quite rightly reveres his teachers—but essentially he needed none of them. He says of them:

> So I sit at this desk most days still, older than Will managed to be, in more or less steady thanks to them and a small clutch of others for basic training in independence, dependence, hunger, feeding, fireworks and damage control, awe at creation and its hid guardian. Maybe I see that the aim of their schooling was something as nearly impossible as *courtesy.* Courtesy in the broad continuous sense,

not the merely polite—knowing where to look and what to see, when to bow or kneel, when to leave or stay, how to stay alone if death clears the room.

(pp. 10-11)

Robb Forman Dew, "Learning the Three Indispensable Human Skills," in The New York Times Book Review, *June 4, 1989, pp. 10-11.*

David McKain

Since *A Long and Happy Life* appeared in 1962, Reynolds Price has published more novels and short fiction than any other contemporary Southern writer of note. Although Price does not attempt to account for his productivity in his memoir, *Clear Pictures,* we learn in the publisher's biographical sketch that his output increased significantly after he contracted spinal cancer in 1984. . . .

Grounded by "surgery, radiation and steroids," Price wrote this memoir after turning to imaging and hypnosis to reduce the pain of his cancer. As the pain receded, "a trickle of good memory began to replace it": a trickle that the author understandably encouraged until it became a gushing too good to be true. "All the memories were good," the author says in a promotional letter accompanying the reviewer's copy of the book: "No traumas, no fears."

I find it odd that Price boasts of his "brain's refusal to store painful early memories," as though the absence of pain in life might create the same salutory effect as the absence of pain in literature. No one blames a cancer patient for delighting in the solace of memories; but, as readers, we expect the author to recognize the imbalance and self-deception of such a claim. There are painful memories in *Clear Pictures,* but Price doesn't seem to be aware of them.

Rather than ask himself why "all the memories were good," the author decided to "see my early life, not as a road or a knotted cord but as a kind of archipelago—a ring of islands connected, intricately but invisibly, underwater." Unfortunately, Price does not fulfill the promise of the archipelgo image by diving down to explore what lies beneath the surface.

In the first seven chapters, Price records his evolving success as an artist; but only in the final chapter, dealing with the death of his father, does he record his development as a man. "As the meat of narrative," he admits in his Foreword, "most of my days were tepid broth." The result is an autobiography without conflict.

"I've tried to honor the family morals," he explains, and the result is an "endless dig for meaning, justification and forgiveness." We crave the search for meaning and forgiveness, but the attempt at justification undermines the search. The Price family was not better or worse than most white families in the upper South, but "the family morals" should not be unquestioned and honored in a memoir published in 1989.

Apologies for racism abound, partly because, in Price's childhood, whites and blacks were "so decorous that neither side began to explore or understand the other's hidden needs." Hidden needs? How could the needs of blacks be hidden unless those in the white majority closed their eyes? Poverty and suffering are visible. "I can't be far wrong in recalling that any number of skilled women would come into your house, cook three hearty meals, do a little cleaning and help with the children six days a week for maybe five dollars and edible leftovers. . . . " The sum of five dollars a week is revealing, for it is the exact sum of young Reynold's allowance, a boy who "never had a strenuous after-school or summer job."

Midway through high school, Reynolds once asked his father why the streets weren't paved in black neighborhoods, and "Will said 'Because they don't pay taxes, darling.' He honestly believed it." This is, for Price, justification enough, as though innocence were an excuse. "I accepted the facts of my culture as unchangeable," he writes.

The author accepts too much, not only of his culture but also of his family and of his own behavior. . . .

In the last chapter, "A Final Secret," Price witnesses the long ordeal of his father's death. "The inward pacific boy I'd been, a target for the love and hate of others, was standing at last in the white-hot eye of ultimate flame and—look—I was lasting, faithful and dauntless." On the last page he announces "I was more than ready to grow. . . . " But however moving the final secret might be, it comes too late.

The desire to distance oneself from pain makes human sense, but such distancing cuts the heart out of autobiography. Price's image of his life as a series of connected islands promises that we will explore their underwater depths, but in *Clear Pictures* we see little more than snapshots taken in the sun.

> *David McKain, "In His Memoir, Reynolds Price Would Rather Not Recall Pain," in* Chicago Tribune—Books, *June 11, 1989, p. 7.*

Paul West

"I'm as peaceful a man as you're likely to meet in America now," declares Bridge Boatner, the narrator of Reynolds Price's eighth novel, *The Tongues of Angels,* "but this is about a death I may have caused." So bald an opening sentence may be there only, as it were, to keep the meandering narrator on track or to remind him of his premise, like a pin stuck into a map. It reminded me of Camus's novel *The Fall,* in which a successful lawyer confesses his failure as a man—he failed to prevent a girl from drowning herself. Boatner certainly behaves like Jean-Baptiste Clamence, the *"Juge-pénitent"* who ceaselessly interrogates himself about the death *he* caused. A successful painter of the representational sort ("right through the abstract expressionist years"), he looks back 34 years and convicts himself of inattention or "plain lack of notice."

I wonder, though. What bothers Boatner is that, when he was a counselor at a summer camp in the Great Smoky Mountains of North Carolina, a 14-year-old camper was bitten by a timber rattler and soon afterward died of a stroke brought on by the exertions of climbing. Boatner puts his all into getting the boy, Rafe Noren, into the hospital and then into a placid frame of mind. After that, he lets himself think of other matters, although the boy's condition nags at him. Is he responsible for the stroke? I doubt it, except that Rafe Noren had gone climbing in order to

reach a hallowed prayer circle above the camp; it is this prayer circle that Boatner and Rafe jointly venerate in an intense relationship based mainly on Boatner's admiration of Rafe's gifts as an Indian dancer, and somewhat on Rafe's admiration of Boatner's paintings. In an atavistic, mystical way they go far beyond the customary camper-counselor duo. As much prey to mutual irritation as to esteem, they worry and argue their way—the 14-year-old boy and the 21-year-old man—through the 10-week intimacy of the camp, cut off from so-called civilization and therefore free, in terms they hold in common, to aim beyond the commonplace: into myth, art, ritual and pain. Reynolds Price deftly weaves them together, making Boatner, between his third and fourth years of college, seem increasingly Rafe's junior in both esthetic savvy and blood-consciousness.

If this relationship sounds a bit stilted, it is, but Mr. Price, whose novels include *Kate Vaiden* and *Good Hearts,* expertly leavens it with internal detonations of the pagan and the bawdy. Without such counterpoint, this would have been too diagrammatic a novel, like *The Fall* or something by Hermann Hesse at his most overt.

Early on, Bridge Boatner (how's that for allegory?) lets his blessedly visual mind work on compelling analogies for the book's apocalyptic blazing golden youth: "Imagine a tall girl stepping towards you from a Botticelli 'Spring' with your name on her lips, not knowing she's grander than the life all around. . . . Or the eighteen-year-olds on ancient Greek tombstones. They wave you in with what may be the start of a smile towards absolute rest."

There is a good deal of "towards" in this novel, from people turning towards one another to people en masse turning towards the sun or the mountain peak and an Amerindian vision that lies beyond. *The Tongues of Angels* is a book about how mystics, or would-be mystics, think mysticism makes them careless about their fellow humans, but also about how people think the mundane cuts them off from mysticism. Mr. Price, who is much shrewder and better educated than that, at one point slides into his text Jung's acute suggestion that "religion was a way to avoid having religious experiences." Watching Rafe dance almost naked, with a single feather and a breechcloth, the campers witness something otherworldly even though their minds are more on gunnysacks full of squirming rattlers to be gassed by the exhaust of the camp's station wagon. And, looking at Bridge's most ambitious painting to date (a mountain view after Cézanne), the whole camp population discerns another reason for being there, one having neither overtones of the Hitler Youth (as Bridge at one juncture worries) nor intimations of Christian morality. After 10 weeks, death is the one miracle that nobody is ready for, but it's part and parcel of the sylvan, Indian, primitive, part-violent reception of nature that Bridge and Rafe uneasily share.

My only concern with this chastely visionary novel is that, after the first 50 pages or so, Mr. Price and his narrator begin to know what the book means, adds up to: they were both more winning when they flailed around a bit, eidetic opportunists knowing they had a thick and luscious theme on hand that went beyond guilt about a young camper's reprieve and final death as he went up the mountain to plant his prayer stick in the magic circle. As a narrator,

Bridge improves as he goes, but he becomes more obvious too: more streamlined, better behaved. Maybe we all do.

No doubt of it, Bridge Boatner is a companionable wit when commenting on Lily Briscoe, Virginia Woolf's Sunday painter in *To the Lighthouse,* or on angels with "enthusiastic" genitals, or on why Southerners ask questions (not to pry but to make you feel cared for); he is "an agnostic mystic" with just a touch of "that built-in outlaw edge that clung to [Rafe's] every act." Rafe marked him—"Not a wound or a scar but a deep live line, like the velvet burr in the darkest shadows of Rembrandt etchings, the ones I've mentioned where demons lurk." The extraordinary thing about this novel is the way neither Bridge nor Rafe senses the bond developing, and then the way Bridge after Rafe's death still cannot quite believe its, as if the parts of themselves that sang together were mostly beyond everyday recognition but got recognized, and authorized, elsewhere by some recording angel both Indian and Biblical—whom Bridge tries to be, with the impassioned reluctance of all survivors.

Mr. Price reads that quandary to us with decorous, ventriloquial skill. Bridge is no ball of fire, but a brown, fretting dwarf, an American version of the self-doubting visionaries who haunt the fiction of Walter Pater and the early stories of E. M. Forster.

> Paul West, " 'A Death I May Have Caused',"
> in The New York Times Book Review, *May
> 13, 1990, p. 13.*

Reginald Ollen

One of my strongest camp memories dates from 1974, when all of us Christian campers were summoned back to our cabins. Each cabin had a small black-and-white television, on which we were told to watch the flickering President of the United States say farewell. Then we said a prayer and off we went to archery.

Understandably, I approached the new novel by Reynolds Price, **The Tongues of Angels,** with a bit of apprehension, this being the tale of a counselor and his campers in the 1950s, when boys spent the summer learning to be men. (At my camp, the boys learned how to tell pot smoke from burning leaves.) But my natural association of corruption and the decay of an empire with camptime did not interfere with my enjoyment of **The Tongues of Angels.** One comes away from this novel with the certainty that, regardless of what cultural baggage—or garbage—we carry into the forest, the majesty of nature and the mysterious spirit of our Native American past are things to carry home forever.

As is true of all Price's works, the telling is as important as the tale, the confessional power of the language evident from page one, paragraph one:

> I'm as peaceful a man as you're likely to meet in America now, but this is about a death I may have caused. Not slowly over time by abuse or meanness, but on a certain day and by ignorance, by plain lack of notice. Though it happened thirty-four years ago, and though I can't say it's haunted my mind that many nights lately, I suspect I can draw it out for you now, clear as this noon.

The American Indian plays a large role in the ensuing story, in the person of a Native American counselor named Bright Day, in the practice of Indian ceremonies at the camp and in the remarkable dancing skills of camper Raphael Noren, in whose death Price's narrator, Bridge Boatner, believes he was complicit. The frank ease with which Price calls forth his tale keeps the narration just short of gushing; *The Tongues of Angels* is thus sentimental, but in the older, more positive sense of the word, the sense that the word "liberal" once had.

Price sets his scene, and convincingly so, against a background of postwar bliss: The question of good and evil appears laid to rest, for the time being, as Hitler is dead and the summer is four months long. The story is narrated by aging artist Bridge Boatner, recollecting in tranquillity the summer when 21-year-old aspiring artist Bridge Boatner landed a job as a counselor and artist-in-residence at Camp Juniper.

What results is a small story of Bridge's friendship with Bright Day and the other counselors, respect for the camp's founder (the "Chief ") and his wife, and a strange affinity with the doomed camper Rafe Noren. This remarkable boy can see Bridge coming out as an artist, appreciates the large landscape Bridge develops layer upon layer as the summer progresses—and Bridge encourages the artist hiding in the youth. Rafe the child seems in many ways a greater artist than Bridge in either his summer or autumn years. At age 14, Rafe sparkles and dances, confounds and eludes any adult scrutiny. Rafe is Rimbaud to Bridge's Verlaine. He meets his death while imitating Bridge, climbing a mountain on the last day of camp rather than resting to recuperate from a snakebite that might not have proved fatal.

Bridge himself is mesmerized by Rafe and his "eagle dance," is much taken with the boy's possession of spirit. Longing to be let into Rafe's confidence, Bridge's parry and thrust with the boy goes on day and night. Beyond the enigma of the child, Bridge's obsession with the camper is traced to a shared pain: The artist had lost his father only a year before, slowly and with suffering. Rafe too had been witness to a tragedy only a few years beforehand—the murder of his mother—and Bridge could only marvel at his development:

> This was a boy who had some way managed to use an event that was dreadful on any scale, and that happened in his home, to build himself a man's mind and body. I quickly recalled myself at fourteen. I was smothering then in alternate gags of self-love and -hate, sexual claustrophobia and dreams of obscene private power.

Now, this is no Smoky Mountains *Death in Venice.* We all have known remarkable children, and sexual attraction is too simple, too easy a way to describe fascination, obsession and affection for a child who seems a step beyond precocious. (The closest that Rafe and Bridge come to bonding is in agreeing that Rafe will receive the canvas that is the work of the entire summer for Bridge.) Yet the whole novel seems rife with near misses, near sexual encounters between these two. Meetings at night, meetings in Indian ceremonies, meetings in the forest for Rafe to model as a cherub (resulting in the snakebite!). Bridge the narrator needs to tell one story, but Bridge the memory seems to act out something much more. (pp. 139-40)

Price seems to be playing a game with commitment—am I or am I not? Are these symbols or are these not? Will there be love or not? For most of the read this literary dance is intriguing; but ultimately, it is exasperating. An anticlimactic story line and the dwindling intensity of Price's language as the novel progresses leave one thankful for the digressions, as Bridge draws freely upon Jung, invokes the AIDS crisis and peels the skin off many a truth as he dogs his tale.

Stylistically, both Price's admirers and his detractors will find themselves thrown for a loop. Known for brandishing his literary weapons, Price merely adorns the parlor with them this time out. But this isn't the first time he has shifted gears at full speed. After kicking in the door at *Harper's* in 1962 with *A Long and Happy Life,* a first novel serialized in its entirety, followed by success with *The Names and Faces of Heroes* and *A Generous Man,* Price had established himself as among the most gifted and profound verbal acrobats of the South. These mad books of rural adolescence, passion and family, later to be grouped as the Mustian Trilogy, would influence (even if unacknowledged) a generation of writers, including the early Thomas McGuane, and Barry Hannah and Ken Kesey.

Perhaps the Southern Writer label alone led him to change, to wish to be recognized as more than a sound, a regional flavor or a condiment of phrasing, so in 1968 Price took a big chance with the somber *Love and Work,* and followed it a couple years later with *Permanent Errors,* a short-story collection that has never received its due praise. These works are moody, quiet studies of the insides of things rather than brash depictions of their outsides. With uncertain footing, critics gave a cool reception to *The Surface of Earth* and most of Price's other intense fictional creations of the 1970s. It was not until *Kate Vaiden,* in 1986, that he charmed his way back into the public eye. With that novel and the subsequent *Good Hearts,* some of Price's finest fiction to date, he articulated a percussive Southern sound that shifted his earliest, brightest voices several octaves in register, often employing delirious streams of dialogue or monologue that read with the madcap sensibility of a Preston Sturges screenplay.

Looking over Price's work, it seems a shame that Camp Juniper is not co-ed. He has always had a deft hand with female characters; many Price women have a touch of Rosacoke Mustian, his first creation and what remains his most enduring voice. In *Tongues,* the brief appearance of a single mother and her child at the home of Thomas Wolfe is, oddly, the most memorable incident in the novel. In this scene Bridge Boatner sees a friend of spirit, but a friend he must walk away from if he expects to go on with his life. She carries a baby and a sordid history that is all too familiar to Bridge, who sympathizes in a situation where confidence is tantamount to commitment:

> This was a deeply Southern transaction, even though she was mountaineer and I was piedmont. Many Americans would die naked in the road before they'd tell you what's hurt them the worst. But born Southerners will show you the cell in their heart that burns the hardest. They'll hold it right towards you, in their bare right hand. This girl had done that for me, Lord God.

It reads as if Reynolds Price is acknowledging his own debt to characters such as Rosacoke Mustian and Kate Vaiden, creations he is heart-to-heart with but that he must leave behind now and then to gain new perspective. Unfortunately, the confessional perspective Price adopts here doesn't quite burn hard. Although the departure in style is welcome, he has left behind too much of the energy that has become his mark as a writer. Even his darkest work seems to be actively waiting, like the timber rattler that bit Rafe. Reynolds Price does quite a turn around the campfire, but this is not his eagle dance. (pp. 140-41)

> *Reginald Ollen, "Indian Summer," in* The Nation, *New York, Vol. 251, No. 4, July 30-August 6, 1990, pp. 139-41.*

FURTHER READING

Crowder, Ashby Bland. "Reynolds Price on Writing." *The Southern Review* 22, No. 2 (Spring 1986): 329-41.

   Interview with Price conducted at the University of Arkansas in 1982 in which the author discusses his prose style and offers advice to aspiring writers.

Kimball, Sue Leslie, and Sadler, Lynn Veach, eds. *Reynolds Price: From 'A Long and Happy Life' to 'Good Hearts'.* Fayetteville: Methodist College Press, 1989, 154 p.

   Collection of essays by various critics examining Price's career.

Kreyling, Michael. "Motion and Rest in the Novels of Reynold's Price." *The Southern Review* 16, No. 4 (Autumn 1980): 853-68.

   Argues that Price's novels "share the theme of rest as the dream of human beings caught in the apparently deadly world of motion."

Upton Sinclair

1878-1968

(Full name Upton Beall Sinclair) American novelist, non-fiction writer, dramatist, autobiographer, and editor.

Best known for his controversial novel *The Jungle,* Sinclair is generally regarded as one of the most prominent "muckrakers," a group of early twentieth-century American journalists and writers who sought to initiate reforms by exposing social and political excesses and abuses. Sinclair saw no discrepancy between fictional form and polemical intent, which he often conveyed through arbitrary plots and characters who function as mouthpieces for his messages. Although he was variously labeled a romantic idealist and propagandist for his puritanical attacks on wealth and corruption and for his espousal of such liberal and political causes as socialism, pacifism, teetotalism, and women's rights, Sinclair was often praised for his social consciousness, meticulous research, and historical accuracy. Alfred Kazin commented: "[What] Sinclair had to give to modern American literature was not any leading ideas as such, but an energy of personal and intellectual revolt that broke barriers down wherever he passed. At a time when all the pioneer realists seemed to be aiming at their own liberation, Sinclair actually helped toward a liberation greater than his own by making a romantic epic out of the spirit of revolt."

Born into a noble Virginia family that became suddenly impoverished in the antebellum South, Sinclair was raised in Baltimore and New York City. The son of an alcoholic liquor salesman and an Episcopalian mother from a wealthy Baltimore family, Sinclair grew up in surroundings alternately characterized by either extreme wealth or poverty. To finance his undergraduate education at the City College of New York, he became a hack writer of jokes, stories, and juvenile novels. Inspired by the Romantic poets of the nineteenth century, particularly Percy Bysshe Shelley, Sinclair turned to writing serious literature in his twenties. While living in near destitution with his wife and child, he completed three sentimental novels, *Springtime and Harvest: A Romance, Prince Hagan: A Phantasy,* and *The Journal of Arthur Stirling,* which brought him scant critical or popular attention. To prepare for his next work, *Manassas: A Novel of the War,* Sinclair built a cabin on a small property outside Princeton University, where he purportedly read or scanned over a thousand books on the American Civil War. Conceived as a historical epic chronicling his family's past, the novel focuses on Alan Montague, the son of a plantation owner who becomes a proponent of abolition before and during the war. Although the book failed financially, *Manassas* attracted the attention of American socialists and later came to be regarded as a persuasive account of the growth of hostilities between the North and South. While studying philosophy and other disciplines at Princeton, Sinclair became interested in socialism and began contributing articles to socialist publications.

Sinclair's next work, *The Jungle,* established him as a leading social critic. This work is generally regarded as the

most powerful and convincing muckraking novel of its era. At the request of Isaac Marcosson, a reformative editor and publisher, Sinclair spent seven weeks investigating the Packingtown district of Chicago, where he observed the unsanitary living and working conditions of the meat-packing industry and talked intimately with workers. His goal was to write a tract for socialism as well as a romantic exposé of the betrayal of the American dream by focusing on Jurgis, a worker who tolerates squalid conditions to support his family. After becoming injured and attacking his supervisor for sexually harassing his wife, Jurgis loses his job and watches his family die as a result of health-related disorders. He becomes alternately a vagabond and a strike-breaker in the meat-packing plant strike of 1904 before discovering in the socialist cause "brothers in affliction, and allies." While some reviewers have faulted the novel's conclusion, in which Jurgis is captivated by the ideological doctrine of radical intellectuals, as didactic, simplistic, or unconvincing, the book garnered widespread praise from conservative and liberal reviewers for its candid exposure of social realities. Jack London commented: "[What] *Uncle Tom's Cabin* did for black slaves, *The Jungle* has a large chance to do for the wage-slaves of today." Ironically, however, the book's exposure of poverty prompted little controversy compared to a brief passage describing contaminated meat, which led to the establishment of the Meat Inspection and Pure Food and Drug Acts but resulted in scant improvement of workers' conditions. Sinclair commented: "I aimed at the public's heart, and by accident I hit it in the stomach."

Following the success of *The Jungle,* Sinclair used his royalty checks to organize Helicon Hall, a communal living center in New Jersey that was destroyed by fire in 1907. One year later, Sinclair completed the first of many full-length nonfiction works, *The Industrial Republic: A Study of the America of Ten Years Hence,* in which he argued for the humane institution of socialism as conceived by many optimists and early twentieth-century idealists. Wealth, corruption, and immorality are the targets of Sinclair's next two novels, *The Metropolis* and *The Moneychangers,* both of which feature Alan Montague, the protagonist of *Manassas.* These works respectively attack the bourgeois strata of New York society and the world of high finance as personified by a figure reminiscent of banker J. P. Morgan. They are generally regarded as unsuccessful combinations of propaganda and fiction. A similar blend of fact and narrative characterizes *Samuel the Seeker,* in which a young man becomes involved in the socialist cause and ends up a victim of police brutality.

For his next major novel, *King Coal,* Sinclair traveled to Colorado to research the coal miners' strike of 1913-1914 in the manner that he investigated the meat-packing industry in *The Jungle.* The novel is related from the perspective of Hal Warner, the son of a wealthy mine owner. Hal decides to live and work among the workers at a mine owned by his friend's father, where he is shocked by the exploitation of miners. After a mine explosion, the company seals the affected shaft off with men still inside to prevent fire from consuming valuable coal. Hal plans to lead a strike, which is averted after he persuades his friend to order the company superintendant to expedite rescue operations. Critics often attribute the fact that *King Coal* did not attain the status of *The Jungle* to its use of a protagonist who is a wealthy outsider rather than a representative member of the working class, and to its conflicting combination of social commentary and adventure story. Sinclair insisted, however, that the "book gives a true picture of conditions and events. . . . Practically all the characters are real persons, and every incident which has social significance is not merely a true incident, but a typical one. The life portrayed in *King Coal* is the life that is lived today by hundreds of thousands of men, women and children in this 'land of the free.' "

In 1917, Sinclair broke with the American Socialist party on grounds that the group opposed American intervention in World War I, which he favored because of Germany's military occupation of France. In 1918, however, Sinclair became critical of American attempts to intervene in the Bolshevik revolution in Russia. These concerns inform his next book, *Jimmie Higgins,* in which a member of the Socialist party is driven insane by the same situation Sinclair faced. Although the protagonist was deemed unconvincing by many reviewers, the novel is often considered to reflect realities of American Socialism during World War I. Sinclair also completed several controversial nonfiction works during this period, including *The Brass Check: A Study of American Journalism,* in which he denies the integrity and objectivity of the journalistic profession; the

Goose-Step: A Study of American Education and *The Goslings: A Study of the American Schools,* exposés of the control of education by the wealthy class and the resulting mediocrity of college and high school curriculums; and *Mammonart: A Study in Economic Interpretation* and *Money Writes!,* in which Sinclair denounces the use of literature for profit and decries narratives irrelevant to actual life. Sinclair's next major novel, *Oil!,* recounts the story of Bunny Ross, the son of a wealthy oil magnate who becomes involved in radicalism at a conservative college and who finances a group of American socialists, eventually becoming active in the cause himself. Although the novel's protagonist is often faulted by critics as only partially believable, some have contended that *Oil!* represents a considerable advance over the propagandistic thrust of Sinclair's earlier works in its sympathetic portrayal of wealthy individuals.

Sinclair attained considerable success with *Boston: A Documentary Novel of the Sacco-Vanzetti Case,* in which he uses his reportorial skills to create a historical account of the case of Nicola Sacco and Bartolomeo Vanzetti, immigrant socialists who were charged with murdering a paymaster and guard while robbing a shoe factory in Boston in 1920. Tracing the case from its beginnings in a pre-World War I labor dispute in Plymouth, Massachusetts, to the questionable executions of Sacco and Vanzetti in 1927, *Boston* focuses primarily on Vanzetti, who is portrayed as a contradictory blend of radical agitator and American idealist. Vanzetti is viewed from the perspective of Cornelia Thornwell, the fictitious widow of a banker and former governor of Massachusetts who meets Vanzetti after deciding to work under an assumed name as an unskilled laborer in a New England cordage factory. Like thousands of defenders of Vanzetti, Cornelia is aware of the upper-class fear of radicalism during the period after World War I and the Russian revolution, and regards the decision to execute Sacco and Vanzetti on the basis of circumstantial evidence a hypocritical attempt by Boston's wealthy elite to provide a compelling example to other radicals. However, Cornelia refuses to provide the defense with a false alibi for Sacco and Vanzetti and watches helplessly as the pair are destroyed by an unjust system. Although the novel was faulted for unbelievable characters and forced religious parallels, and for its unsuccessful blend of poetic and documentary realism, *Boston* drew praise for its accurate reportage and genuine pathos. Upon reading the book, Sir Arthur Conan Doyle called Sinclair "one of the greatest novelists in the world," and R. N. Mookerjee later summed up the critical consensus: "The abiding appeal of *Boston* remains undiminished to this day. No matter what our political views, the novel stands out as an epic document and will outlast even the memory of Sacco and Vanzetti."

During the 1930s, Sinclair wrote less fiction as he became more directly involved in politics. In 1933, he ran for governor of California, creating a plan to End Poverty in California (EPIC). This plan, in which he proposed instituting reforms that would have included greater taxation of the state's film industry, resulted in a Stop Sinclair campaign led by the Metro-Goldwyn-Mayer movie studio, which defeated his hopes of victory. The various stages of Sinclair's campaign are described in his books *I, Governor of California, and How I Ended Poverty: A True Story of the*

Future; The Lie Factory Starts; and *I, Candidate for Governor, and How I Got Licked.*

Following the entrance of the United States into World War II, Sinclair became convinced of the need for American radicals to support their nation during times of national crisis. As a result, he initiated a series of novels chronicling the period from 1913 to 1949 and featuring Lanny Budd, a self-proclaimed schizophrenic caught between liberalism and a pragmatic view of the world, who feels compelled by national necessity to defend traditional institutions. By posing as an art dealer and fascist sympathizer in Europe, Lanny pirates information from elite individuals and returns to America periodically to report and to advise the president of the United States. Despite the popularity of the series, the Lanny Budd novels were viewed by many liberal critics as a refutation of Sinclair's liberal idealism, and have not attained the critical stature of his earlier works. However, the series remains highly popular and receives continuing critical assessment. Sinclair regarded his Lanny Budd series as "the most important part of my literary performance," and received the Pulitzer Prize for the third volume of the series, *Dragon's Teeth.*

(See also *CLC,* Vols. 1, 11, 15; *Contemporary Authors,* Vols. 5-8, rev. ed., Vols. 25-28, rev. ed. [obituary]; *Dictionary of Literary Biography,* Vol. 9; and *Concise Dictionary of Literary Biography: 1929-1941;* and *Something about the Author,* Vol. 9.)

PRINCIPAL WORKS

JUVENILE NOVELS

Courtmartialed 1898
Saved by the Enemy 1898
A Soldier Monk 1899
A Soldier's Pledge 1899
Wolves of the Navy; or, Clif Faraday's Search for a Traitor [as Clarke Fitch] 1899
Clif, the Naval Cadet; or, Exciting Days at Annapolis [as Clarke Fitch] 1903
The Cruise of the Training Ship; or, Clif Faraday's Pluck [as Clarke Fitch] 1903
From Port to Port; or, Clif Faraday in Many Waters [as Clarke Fitch] 1903
Off for West Point; or, Mark Mallory's Struggle [as Frederick Garrison] 1903
On Guard; or, Mark Mallory's Celebration [as Frederick Garrison] 1903
A Strange Cruise; or, Clif Faraday's Yacht Chase [as Clarke Fitch] 1903
The Gnomobile: A Gnice Gnew Gnarrative with Gnonsense, but Gnothing Gnaughty 1936

NOVELS

Springtime and Harvest: A Romance 1901; also published as *King Midas: A Romance,* 1901
The Journal of Arthur Stirling 1903
Prince Hagan: A Phantasy 1903
Manassas: A Novel of the War 1904; also published as *Theirs Be the Guilt: A Novel of the War Between the States* [revised edition], 1959
The Jungle 1906

A Captain of Industry, Being the Story of a Civilized Man 1906
The Overman 1907
The Metropolis 1908
The Moneychangers 1908
Samuel the Seeker 1910
Love's Pilgrimage 1911
Damaged Goods: The Great Play "Les avariés" by Brieux, Novelized with the Approval of the Author 1913; also published as *Damaged Goods: A Novel About the Victims of Syphilus,* 1948
Sylvia 1913
Sylvia's Marriage 1914
King Coal 1917
Jimmie Higgins 1919
100%: The Story of a Patriot 1920; published in Great Britain as *The Spy,* 1920; also published as *Peter Gudge Becomes a Secret Agent* [abridged edition], 1930
They Call Me Carpenter: A Tale of the Second Coming 1922
The Millenium: A Comedy of the Year 2000 1924
Oil! 1927
Boston: A Documentary Novel of the Sacco-Vanzetti Case (two vols.) 1928; published in Great Britain as *Boston: A Novel,* 1929; also published as *August 22* [abridged edition], 1965
Mountain City 1930
Roman Holiday 1931
The Wet Parade 1931
Co-op: A Novel of Living Together 1936
No Parasan! (They Shall Not Pass): A Story of the Battle of Madrid 1937
Little Steel 1938
Our Lady 1938
*World's End 1940
*Between Two Worlds 1941
*Dragon's Teeth 1942
*Wide Is the Gate 1943
*Presidential Agent 1944
*Dragon Harvest 1945
*A World to Win, 1940-1942 1946
*Presidential Mission 1947
Limbo on the Loose: A Midsummer Night's Dream 1948
*One Clear Call 1948
*O Shepherd, Speak! 1949
Another Pamela: or, Virtue Still Rewarded 1950
*The Return of Lanny Budd 1953
What Didymus Did (Whether You Believe It Or Not) 1954; published in the United States as *It Happened to Didymus,* 1958
Cicero: A Tragedy of Ancient Rome 1960
Affectionately, Eve 1961
The Coal War: A Sequel to King Coal 1976

NONFICTION

The Industrial Republic: A Study of the America of Ten Years Hence 1907
The Profits of Religion: An Essay in Economic Interpretation 1918
The Brass Check: A Study of American Journalism 1920
The Book of Life, Mind and Body (two vols.) 1921-1922
The Goose-Step: A Study of American Education 1923
The Goslings: A Study of the American Schools 1924

Mammonart: A Study in Economic Interpretation   1925
Letters to Judd, an American Workingman   1926; also published as *This World of 1949 and What to Do about It: Revised Letters to a Workingman on the Economic and Political Situation* [revised edition], 1949
The Spokesman's Secretary: Being the Letters of Mame to Mom   1926
Money Writes!   1927
I, Governor of California, and How I Ended Poverty: A True Story of the Future   1933
Upton Sinclair Presents William Fox   1933
The Way Out: A Solution of Our Present Economic and Social Ills   1933
The Book of Love   1934
EPIC Answers: How to End Poverty in California   1934
The EPIC Plan for California   1934
The Lie Factory Starts   1934
I, Candidate for Governor, and How I Got Licked   1935; published in Great Britain as *How I Got Licked and Why,*   1935
We, People of America, and How We Ended Poverty: A True Story of the Future   1935
The Flivver King: A Story of Ford-America   1937; published in Great Britain as *The Flivver King: A Novel of Ford-America,*   1938
Terror in Russia?: Two Views   [with Eugene Lyons] 1938
Expect No Peace!   1939
What Can Be Done about America's Economic Troubles?   1939
Your Million Dollars   1939; published in Great Britain as *Letters to a Millionaire,*   1939
Telling the World   1940
The Cup of Fury   1956

PLAYS

**Plays of Protest*   [first publication]   1912
Hell: A Verse Drama and Photo-play   [first publication] 1923
Singing Jailbirds   [first publication]   1924
Bill Porter: A Drama of O. Henry in Prison   [first publication]   1925
†*Oil!*   [first publication]   1929
Wally for Queen!: The Private Life of Royalty   [first publication]   1936
Marie Antoinette   [first publication]   1939
A Giant's Strength   [first publication]   1948
The Enemy Had It Too   [first publication]   1950

OTHER

The Cry for Justice: An Anthology of the Literature of Social Protest   [editor]   1915, 1963 [revised edition]
American Outpost: A Book of Reminiscences   1932; published in Great Britain as *Candid Reminiscences: My First Thirty Years,*   1932
An Upton Sinclair Anthology   1934, 1947 [revised edition]
What God Means to Me: An Attempt at Working Religion   1936
A Personal Jesus: Portrait and Interpretation   1952; republished as *The Secret Life of Jesus,*   1962
My Lifetime in Letters   1960
The Autobiography of Upton Sinclair   1962

*These novels form Sinclair's "Lanny Budd" series.

**This volume contains the plays *The Naturewoman, The Machine, The Second-story Man,* and *Prince Hagan.*

†This play is adapted from Sinclair's novel *Oil!*

Granville Hicks

[*The following essay was originally published in slightly different form in 1933.*]

Upton Sinclair began his career as a serious novelist with a love story [**Springtime and Harvest: A Romance**], long since out of print, which he followed with **The Journal of Arthur Stirling,** a record of his own frantic struggles as a writer. Almost immediately after the publication of **The Journal,** he was converted to socialism, but his next novel was a story of the Civil War, **Manassas.** In 1904, however, he investigated labor conditions in the Chicago stockyards, and out of that investigation came **The Jungle.** This first venture in muckraking not only brought Sinclair success; it pointed out to him a path he could follow. He had always believed his books should serve humanity; after his conversion to socialism he knew what form that service should take. With **The Jungle** he became the novelist of the American scene, the recorder of great industrial movements, the fearless enemy of corruption and injustice. He wrote of millionaires, miners, socialists, labor spies. He dramatized the great struggles of his period: the Colorado coal strike, the war, the Mooney case, the Teapot Dome scandals, the murder of Sacco and Vanzetti. No such division of interests as deflected [fellow socialist] Jack London's purpose came between Sinclair and his career: what interested him as a socialist interested him as a novelist.

The Journal of Arthur Stirling reveals its author as an extremely sensitive young man, burdened down with the cares of the world but buoyed up by a sense of his mission and high destiny. Early in life, sharing his mother's fears for her irresponsible husband, Sinclair learned to take upon his own shoulders the obligations of others. The charity of rich relatives taught him something of the unequal distribution of wealth. His own struggles as an author showed him how little encouragement the callous world would give to noble purposes. All this ripened him for socialism: "It was like the falling down of prison walls about my mind; the most amazing discovery, after all these years—that I did not have to carry the whole burden of humanity's future upon my two frail shoulders." And his sensitiveness not only prepared the way for socialism; it became not the least of his literary gifts.

The great obstacle to Sinclair's development as a recorder and interpreter of the struggles between capital and labor was his lack of experience. Having lived in middle-class boarding houses, supported himself as a hack-writer, and frequently retreated to the Canadian wilds or the New Jersey countryside, he knew nothing at first hand of mines or factories or financiers' offices. But even before he began his career as a muckraker he showed his ability to accumulate the material he needed. To prepare for the writing of **Manassas** he read some five hundred books and examined at least five hundred more. As a result the novel is solidly

convincing in its account of the growth of hostility between North and South, and the characters have a firm
basis in the events of history. And, as *The Jungle* showed,
books were not the only sources of information on which
Sinclair could draw: in investigating the stockyards he visited workers' homes, wandered about the plants, and
talked with doctors, lawyers, politicans, and policemen.

The importance of this gift, this ability to accumulate the
necessary material, cannot be exaggerated. The novelist
who wishes to write about the complex structure of modern society cannot possibly have had all the different kinds
of experience he finds it necessary to describe: he can
scarcely have been both employer and employee, both
union member and scab, both ward boss and reformer. . . . If a novelist is to write about the great social
movements of his day, he must get some of his material
at secondhand, and he is fortunate if he can accumulate
it as accurately and as easily as Upton Sinclair has done.
Consider his use of the inside story of the panic of 1907
in *The Moneychangers,* his treatment of the Colorado
strike in *King Coal,* his portrayal of the activities of a labor
spy in *100%,* his introduction of the details of drilling,
piping, and selling in *Oil,* his handling of the Sacco-
Vanzetti records in *Boston.*

Sinclair knows what facts he needs and how to get them,
but unfortunately he is not so successful in assimilating
them. Perhaps no writer can subject the data of research
to exactly the same processes as he does the half-conscious
perceptions that are the basis of creation, and thus achieve
a perfect integration. Sinclair is far from perfection. In
Manassas, for example, there is a long passage, between
Allan's departure from the plantation after his father's
death and his return just before the outbreak of hostilities,
in which the method is simply that of historical exposition;
and the same eagerness to describe the action of social
forces, to present the facts as facts, is responsible for the
mechanical manipulation of the hero's movements that
makes him a witness of John Brown's raid, the firing on
Sumter, and the Baltimore riots. In *The Jungle* the reader
is less conscious of the documentation because, by virtue
of his own suffering at the time, Sinclair entered directly
into Jurgis' experiences, but there are nevertheless too
many passages in which the author, clumsily trying to
cover his tracks with some phrase about the tales of "an
old fellow whom Jonas had introduced," lays before us,
in the manner of a magazine article, the facts his investigation had uncovered. In *The Moneychangers* we settle
down to read an exposure of the causes of the 1907 panic
and the ways of the idle rich, and the adventures of the col-
orless hero seem merely an irritating interruption. *King
Coal* limits itself, for the most part, to aspects of the strike
that could have been present to Hal's experience, and *Oil*
also concentrates on the hero's rather than the reader's education, but both books bear the stamp of the outside in-
vestigator, and in *Boston* we again find long passages of
documentation. When critics complain that Sinclair is a
propagandist, they suggest that he is given to direct argu-
mentation. By and large the charge is not true, but he is
guilty—and this may be an even greater sin against the art
of the novel—of failure to assimilate the material he so
wisely accumulates.

All this would suggest that Sinclair is primarily a pamphleteer. His pamphlets are undeniably effective. *The
Brass Check,* despite its excessive preoccupation with the
author's own sufferings at the hands of the press, banishes
forever any lingering faith in the integrity of journalism,
and *The Goose-Step* reveals not merely the plutocratic
control of the universities but also the actual result of that
control in the timidity and dullness of most college teaching and the consequent indifference and ignorance of most
students. Even *The Profits of Religion,* with all its superficiality, builds a powerful case against the churches, and
Mammonart, however weak as criticism, does attack the
illusion that literature has no relation to life.

But, though Sinclair is a good pamphleteer, and though
the pamphleteer in him sometimes triumphs over the novelist, his novels deserve to be examined as novels. When
we examine them, we find that they are not weak because
they are sugar-coated pamphlets; their weaknesses are
both less reprehensible and more fundamental. Perhaps
the easiest way to understand his failure is to analyze his
choice of heroes and his treatment of them. In two of his
books his heroes belong to the working class, *The Jungle*
and *Jimmie Higgins.* The reason for his relative success
with Jurgis is suggested in *American Outpost:* "Externally
the story had to do with a family of stockyard workers,
but internally it was the story of my own family." And the
superiority of the first part of *Jimmie Higgins* to the second may be explained by Sinclair's knowledge of the affairs of a socialist local, on the one hand, and his ignorance, to say nothing of his false conception, of the war,
on the other. He could write effectively about workers
when he could draw directly on experience. But for the
most part the heroes of Sinclair's novels are chosen from
the middle class. Allan Montague in *The Metropolis* and
The Moneychangers is so feeble a character that we may
dismiss him at once. Hal in *King Coal,* however, is both
likable and comprehensible, the Bunny of *Oil* is real
enough to make us understand why millionaires' sons do
sometimes flirt with radicalism, and Cornelia [of *Boston*]
belongs with the not inconsiderable group of well-born
Boston women who have espoused unpopular causes.
There is no doubt that Upton Sinclair understands the
mind of the convert and all the processes of conversion.
Why should he not? He is himself a convert and, however
active he has been in propaganda and agitation, he has remained outside the working-class movement. Hal's attitude towards the coal strike was easy enough for Sinclair
to understand, for he had himself been an outside investi-
gator, surprised and shocked by what he saw. Bunny's
boyhood may have been very little like Upton Sinclair's,
but his attitude towards the exploitation of labor was precisely that of his creator. The Boston blueblood may not
be easy for a Californian of southern ancestry to understand, but obviously it is easier to understand her than it
is to understand an Italian anarchist, an I.W.W. lawyer,
or a communist agitator.

Sinclair's reasons for writing so often from the point of
view of the middle-class convert to radicalism are quite
clear, but it is also apparent that this convenient method
has its disadvantages. In *Boston* he had the greatest theme
of his career, but he could not master it. The significance
of the Sacco-Vanzetti tragedy was twofold: to enlightened
members of the bourgeoisie it was evidence that the ideals
of their class were being betrayed by the rulers of America;
to class-conscious workers it was a symbol of their lifelong
struggle and a call to battle. Sinclair, though a socialist,

devoted to the triumph of the proletariat, chose to emphasize the significance of the death of these two Italians for the bourgeoisie. Hence he chose Cornelia as his central character. She is skillfully presented, and, indeed, the whole account of life in Boston's ruling class is shrewdly perceptive. But Cornelia, with all that can be said for her and her kind, is a sentimentalist, and sentimentality pervades the entire book. We follow the adventures of the runaway grandmother, we see Vanzetti through her eyes, we read about the intrigues of the bankers and lawyers, we come upon long expository accounts of the conduct of the defense, and at the end we find the stark tragedy of the anarchists' death smothered in a description of Cornelia's mystic experience. The book is informing and at times moving, but the power, the significance, the dignity, that we have a right to expect, are missing.

What is true of **Boston** is true in some degree of all Sinclair's books. He is a socialist; he ardently desires the abolition of private property, and his loyalties are not divided as Jack London's were. But the conception of the class struggle, so fundamental in Marx's philosophy, the idea that the proletariat and only the proletariat will create the socialist state, has remained alien to him. His socialism has always been of the emotional sort, a direct response to his own environment, and, as a result of his failure to undergo an intense intellectual discipline, he has never eradicated the effects of his bourgeois upbringing. Though his aim has been socialistic, his psychology has remained that of the liberal. Therefore, whether he realizes it or not, he is always writing for the middle class, trying to persuade his fellows to take their share of the burden of humanity's future, to pity the poor worker and strive for his betterment. Even the pamphlets are aimed at the middle class: **The Brass Check** proposes a weekly newspaper under liberal auspices; **The Profits of Religion** calls on the devout to put the churches on a rational basis; **The Goose-Step** demands the reform of the colleges by means of a teachers' strike.

Sinclair has always been in too much of a hurry. To every good cause he has given his time and energy in abundance. But he has never taken the pains to prepare himself adequately for his task as socialist and novelist. He has remained essentially what he was in the days when he wrote **The Journal of Arthur Stirling,** a sensitive man, full of sympathy for the woes of the world and eager to alleviate them. He has not looked on life as a member of the class with which, by his conversion to socialism, he allied himself. He has not written as a member of that class; except on rare occasions he has not written convincingly about that class; and, whatever his conscious intentions, he has not written for that class. Socialism could have given him a definite point of view, a clear attitude towards life, and, thus equipped, he could have assimilated the material he accumulated. As it is, though he knows a great deal about the life contemporary Americans lead, he has very imperfectly related this information to his own beliefs and purposes. This material is not part of him, any more than he is part of the working-class movement to which he has, within the limits of his nature, been so loyally devoted. (pp. 196-203)

> *Granville Hicks, "The Years of Hope," in his*
> The Great Tradition: An Interpretation of
> American Literature Since the Civil War, re-
> *vised edition, Macmillan Publishing Company, 1935, pp. 164-206.*

Alfred Kazin

If Sinclair lives to survive all the bright young novelists of today and to publish a thousand books (and he may yet), he will remain a touching and curious symbol of a certain old-fashioned idealism and quaint personal romanticism that have vanished from American writing forever. Something more than a "mere" writer and something less than a serious novelist, he must always seem one of the original missionaries of the modern spirit in America, one of the last ties we have with that halcyon day when Marxists still sounded like Methodists and a leading Socialist like Eugene V. Debs believed in "the spirit of love."

Sinclair burst into fame with the most powerful of all the muckraking novels, **The Jungle,** and he has been an irritant to American complacency ever since. His life, with its scandals and its headline excitements, its political excursions and alarums, its extraordinary purity and melodrama, is the story of a religious mission written, often in tabloid screamers, across the pages of contemporary history. As a novelist, he has suffered for his adventures, but it is doubtful if he would have been a novelist without them. The spirit of crusading idealism that gave Sinclair his chance inevitably made him a perennial crusader as well, and if his books and career have become hopelessly entangled in most people's minds, they have been entangled in his own from the day he leaped to invest his royalties from **The Jungle** in the single-tax colony of Helicon Hall. That confusion has always given his critics the opportunity to analyze his works by reciting the adventures of his life, and it is inevitable that they should. For what Sinclair had to give to modern American literature was not any leading ideas as such, but an energy of personal and intellectual revolt that broke barriers down wherever he passed. At a time when all the pioneer realists seemed to be aiming at their own liberation, Sinclair actually helped toward a liberation greater than his own by making a romantic epic out of the spirit of revolt. From the first he was less a writer than an example, a fresh current of air pouring through the stale rooms of the past. Impulsive and erratic as he may have been, often startlingly crude for all his intransigence, he yet represented in modern American literature what William Jennings Bryan represented in modern American politics—a provincialism that leaped ahead to militancy and came into leadership over all those who were too confused or too proud or too afraid to seize leadership and fight for it.

Sinclair's importance to the prewar literature is that he took his revolt seriously, he took himself seriously—how seriously we may guess from his statement that the three greatest influences on his thought were Jesus, Hamlet, and Shelley. A more ambitious writer as such would never have been able to indulge in so many heroics; but Sinclair seems to have felt from the first the kind of personal indignation against society which could be quickly channeled into a general criticism of society, and that capacity for indignation gave him his sense of mission. The impoverished son of a prominent Baltimore family, he thought of himself from his youth as a rebel against the disintegration of the South after the Civil War, and he was determined to recite the argosy of his early tribulations for all the world to hear. Even after forty years he wrote with special bitterness, in an autobiography otherwise distinguished only by its immense cheerfulness, of those early days when he had dined with his aristocratic grandmother in great state on dried herring and stale bread, of his father's shambling efforts to peddle the liquor that he drank more often than he sold, of the flight to New York, his life on the East Side, and the unhappy years when he worked his way through college as a hack writer of jokes and stories. In those first years Sinclair was a foreshadowing of the kind of titanic Weltschmerz which Thomas Wolfe was to personify all his life, and like Wolfe he became such a flood of words that he began to write romantic epics around himself. His subject was the young Upton Sinclair and his world young Upton Sinclair's enthusiasms. He had many enthusiasms—he was intermittently enthusiastic about chastity, for example—and in that early period before he turned to Socialism, he gave full vent to his insurgence in lyrical early books like *Springtime and Harvest* (later republished as *King Midas*) and *The Journal of Arthur Stirling.*

These books were Sinclair's *Sorrows of Werther.* Living in great poverty with his wife and young child, humiliated by his obscurity, he wrote out the story of his own struggles in *The Journal of Arthur Stirling,* the furious romantic confession of a starving young poet who was supposed to have taken his own life at twenty-two. When it was disclosed that the book was a "hoax" and that Sinclair himself was Stirling, the sensation was over; but the book was more authentic than anyone at the moment could possibly know. "The world which I see about me at the present moment," he wrote there in the character of Arthur Stirling, "the world of politics, of business, of society, seems to me a thing demoniac in its hideousness; a world gone mad with pride and selfish lust; a world of wild beasts writhing and grappling in a pit." Like the imaginary dead poet who had learned Greek while working on the horsecars and written a frenzied poetic drama, *The Captive,* at the point of death, Sinclair was full of grandiose projects, and when his early romantic novels failed he planned an ambitious epic trilogy of the Civil War that would record his family's failure and make him rich and famous. He took his family to a tent outside of Princeton, where he did the research for the first volume, *Manassas,* and supported himself by more hack work. But when even his historical novel, a work which he had written with all the furious energy that was to distinguish him afterwards, fell on a dead market, he found himself in the very situation that he had portrayed with such anguish in the story of Arthur Stirling, the epic of the romantic genius who had stormed the heights and failed.

The Jungle saved him. Tiring of romantic novels which no one would read, he had turned to the investigation of social conditions, and in his article on **"Our Bourgeois Literature,"** in *Collier's,* 1904, he exclaimed significantly: "So long as we are without heart, so long as we are without conscience, so long as we are without even a mind—pray, in the name of heaven, why should anyone think it worthwhile to be troubled because we are without a literature?" Although he still thought of himself as a romantic rebel against "convention," he had come to identify his own painful gropings with the revolutionary forces in society, and when he received a chance to study conditions in the stockyards at Chicago, he found himself like St. Paul on the road to Damascus. Yet into the story of the immigrant couple, Jurgis and Ona, he poured all the disappointment of his own apprenticeship to life, all his humiliation and profound ambition. *The Jungle* attracted attention because it was obviously the most authentic and most powerful of the muckraking novels, but Sinclair wrote it as the great romantic document of struggle and hardship he had wanted to write all his life. In his own mind it was above all the story of the betrayal of youth by the America it had greeted so eagerly, and Sinclair recited with joyous savagery every last detail of its tribulations. The romantic indignation of the book gave it its fierce honesty, but the facts in it gave Sinclair his reputation, for he had suddenly given an unprecedented social importance to muckraking. The sales of meat dropped, the Germans cited the book as an argument for higher import duties on American meat, Sinclair became a leading exponent of the muckraking spirit to thousands in America and Europe, and met with the President. No one could doubt it, the evidence was overwhelming: Here in *The Jungle* was the great news story of a decade written out in letters of fire. Unwittingly or not, Sinclair had proved himself one of the great reporters of the Progressive era, and the world now began to look up to him as such.

Characteristically, however, Sinclair spent the small fortune he had received from the book on Helicon Hall, that latter-day Brook Farm for young rebels at which Sinclair Lewis is reported to have been so indifferent a janitor. In his own mind Upton Sinclair had become something more than a reporter; he was a crusader, and after joining with Jack London to found the Intercollegiate Socialist Society, a leading Socialist. "Really, Mr. Sinclair, you *must* keep your head," Theodore Roosevelt wrote to him when he insisted after the publication of *The Jungle* on immediate legislative action. But Sinclair would not wait. If society would not come to him, he would come to society and teach it by his books. With the same impulsive directness that he had converted Jurgis into a Socialist in the last awkward chapter of *The Jungle,* he jumped ahead to make himself a "social detective," a pamphleteer-novelist whose books would be a call to action. In *The Metropolis,* an attack on "the reign of gilt" which Phillips and Robert Herrick had already made familiar, Sinclair took the son of his Civil War hero in *Manassas,* Allan Montague, and made him a spectator of the glittering world of Wall Street finance. In *The Moneychangers* he depicted the panic of 1907; in *King Coal,* the Colorado strike; in *100%,* the activities of a labor spy. Yet he remained at the same time a busy exponent of the "new freedom" in morals, wrote the candid story of his own marriage in *Love's Pilgrimage,* "novelized" Brieux's famous shocker of the early nineteen-hundreds, *Damaged Goods,* and between pamphlets, fantasy plays, and famous anthologies like *The Cry for Justice* ("an anthology of the literature of social protest . . . selected from twenty-five languages covering a period of five thousand years") wrote stories of "the new woman" in *Sylvia* and *Sylvia's Marriage.*

Wherever it was that Sinclair had learned to write millions of words with the greatest of ease—probably in the days when he produced hundreds of potboilers—he now wrote them in an unceasing torrent on every subject that interested him. Like Bronson Alcott and William Jennings Bryan, he had an extraordinary garrulity, and his tireless and ubiquitous intelligence led him to expose the outrages of existence everywhere. He used his books for "social purposes" not because he had a self-conscious esthetic about "art and social purpose," but because his purposes actually were social. Few writers seemed to write less for the sake of literature, and no writer ever seemed to humiliate the vanity of literature so deeply by his many excursions around it. First things came first; the follies of capitalism, the dangers of drinking, the iniquities of wealthy newspapers and universities came first. "Why should anyone think it worthwhile to be troubled because we are without a literature?" His great talent, as everyone was quick to point out, was a talent for facts, a really prodigious capacity for social research; and as he continued to give America after the war the facts about labor in *Jimmie Higgins,* the petroleum industry in *Oil!,* the Sacco-Vanzetti case in *Boston,* Prohibition in *The Wet Parade,* it mattered less and less that he repeated himself endlessly, or that he could write on one page with great power, on another with astonishing self-indulgence and sentimental melodrama. He had become one of the great social historians of the modern era. Van Wyck Brooks might complain that "the only writers who can possibly aid in the liberation of humanity are those whose sole responsibility is to themselves as artists," [see excerpt in *CLC,* Vol. 15], but in a sense it was pointless to damn Sinclair as a "mere" propagandist. What would he have been without the motor power of his propaganda, his driving passion to convert the world to an understanding of the problems of labor, the virtues of the single tax, the promise of Socialism, the need of Prohibition, a credence in "mental radio," an appreciation of the sufferings of William Fox, the necessity of the "Epic" movement, and so much else? In a day when the insurgent spirit had become obsessed with the facts of contemporary society, and newspapermen could write their social novels in the city room, Sinclair proved himself one of the great contemporary reporters, a profound educative force. He was a hero in Europe, and one of the forces leading to the modern spirit in America; it seemed almost glory enough. (pp. 116-21)

> *Alfred Kazin, "Progressivism: The Superman and the Muckrake," in his* On Native Grounds: An Interpretation of Modern American Prose Literature, *Reynal & Hitchcock, 1942, pp. 91-126.*

Walter B. Rideout

Lincoln Steffens tells in his *Autobiography* of receiving a call during the early years of muckraking from an earnest and as yet little-known young writer.

> One day Upton Sinclair called on me at the office of *McClure's* and remonstrated.
>
> "What you report," he said, "is enough to make a complete picture of the system, but you seem not to see it. Don't you see it? Don't you see what you are showing?"

Having just been converted to Socialism, Sinclair was sure he "saw it," and in the late autumn of 1905 his friend Jack London was writing to the Socialist weekly *The Appeal to Reason* in praise of a new book which it was serializing.

> Here it is at last! The book we have been waiting for these many years! The *Uncle Tom's Cabin* of

wage slavery! Comrade Sinclair's book, *The Jungle!* and what *Uncle Tom's Cabin* did for black slaves, *The Jungle* has a large chance to do for the wage-slaves of today.

When *The Jungle* appeared in book form the following year, even the conservative literary critics agreed, with certain reservations, that at last an American was painting a picture "of those sunk in the innermost depths of the modern *Inferno."* Part of the novel's abrupt success among the public at large may have resulted, as Sinclair himself was to lament, from the unintended relevance of a brief muckraking passage on filthy meat; but no novel is read because of half a dozen pages, and this one was read internationally. The extent of the young writer's popularity is suggested by the remark of George Brandes, on his visit to the United States eight years later, that the three modern American novelists he found worth reading were Frank Norris, Jack London, and Upton Sinclair. (pp. 30-1)

The author of *The Jungle* was born in Baltimore in 1878 of a father and mother impoverished by the economic dislocations of the postbellum South, yet proud in their family ancestries. . . . Sinclair's father, a liquor salesman, was one of his own best, or worst, customers, was unable to support his family, and slowly and terribly drank himself to death. Sinclair later explained in his book of reminiscences, *American Outpost,* that one of his reasons for becoming a social rebel was his psychology as a "poor relation."

> Readers of my novels know that I have one favorite theme, the contrast of the social classes; there are characters from both worlds, the rich and the poor, and the plot is contrived to carry you from one to the other. The explanation of this literary phenomenon is that, from the first days I can remember, my life was a series of Cinderella transformations; one night sleeping on a vermin-ridden sofa in a lodging-house, and the next night under silken coverlets in a fashionable home. It was always a question of one thing—whether my father had the money for that week's board. If he didn't, my mother paid a visit to her father, the railroad official.

A second influence that assisted in guiding him ultimately to revolt was, Sinclair maintains, the Protestant Episcopal Church, since he "took the words of Jesus seriously," envisioning himself as a follower of "the rebel carpenter, the friend of the poor and lowly, the symbol of human brotherhood." Although he early lost faith in Christianity as anything more than a code of ethics, Sinclair has characteristically continued to hold Jesus as one of his heroes. In his own battle for Truth against Evil, he has made his life one long saga of St. George and the Dragon. An intense, sensitive boy, he was shocked into an ascetic denial of all indulgences by the decline and death of his father, whom he stood by loyally and through whose sufferings he discovered an important social fact, that behind the saloon-keeper loomed the politicians and Big Business. Disgusted with the ugliness of the world, he turned for escape to literature, where he found his spirit of revolt so strengthened that he came to suppose that literature made life. Like his character Thyrsis in the semiautobiographical *Love's Pilgrimage,* he read *Don Quixote* and *Les Misérables;* he loved George Eliot and was thrilled by the social protest of Dickens; he admired Thackeray most of all, for Thackeray saw the human corruption which lay at the heart of the world that he described. Significantly, the boy's favorite poets were the blind Milton and the revolutionary Shelley.

Two elements in the education of this social rebel still remained to take effect. The first was a prolonged acquaintance with what he later called "the economic screw." He supported himself for a year of graduate work at Columbia by hack writing, producing thousands of words of boys' stories each week. Then he broke away to write the Great American Novel, married the adoring Meta Fuller, and endured with her several years of drudging poverty. . . . In the autumn of 1902 he was rescued from this marginal existence by the kindness of George D. Herron, a gentle-minded Socialist writer and lecturer, who gave him financial support and, equally important in Sinclair's development, helped him to discover Socialism. Reading *Wilshire's* completed the conversion. Sinclair had more years of the economic screw to endure, but now he could gird himself for the fight with the whole armor of an economic and political philosophy.

> It was like the falling down of prison walls about my mind; the most amazing discovery, after all these years—that I did not have to carry the whole burden of humanity's future upon my two frail shoulders! There were actually others who understood; who saw what had gradually become clear to me, that the heart and centre of the evil lay in leaving the social treasure, which nature had created, and which every man has to have in order to live, to become the object of a scramble in the market-place, a delirium of speculation. The principal fact which the Socialists had to teach me, was the fact that they themselves existed.

Moving his family to a tent, later a shack on the outskirts of Princeton, New Jersey, he started work on *Manassas,* the first volume of a projected trilogy based on the Civil War, while the family's poverty continued and his unhappy wife passed through long periods of black melancholy. *Manassas,* though superior to his previous novels, sold scarcely better; but it was read by the editor of *The Appeal to Reason,* who enthusiastically wrote Sinclair that, since he had described the struggle against chattel slavery in America, he should now do the same for wage slavery. With an advance payment on the new novel, Sinclair spent seven weeks in the autumn of 1904 in the Packingtown district of Chicago, where the stockyard workers had just lost a strike. Horrified by the wretched conditions under which the inhabitants of Packingtown lived and labored, he collected his evidence with the zeal and care of any muckraking reporter. He returned to Princeton, worked incessantly for three months, began serializing the novel in *The Appeal,* and finally, in February, 1906, succeeded in having it brought out by Doubleday, Page and Company, a nonradical publishing house, after an investigating lawyer sent by the company had submitted a report substantiating Sinclair's findings against the practices of the meat-packers.

The Jungle is dedicated "To the Workingmen of America." Into it had gone Sinclair's heartsick discovery of the filth, disease, degradation, and helplessness of the packing workers' lives. But any muckraker could have put this much into a book; the fire of the novel came from Sinclair's whole passionate, rebellious past, from the insight into the pattern of capitalist oppression shown him by Socialist theory, and from the immediate extension into the characters' lives of his own and his wife's struggle against hunger, illness, and fear. It was the summation of his life and experience into a manifesto. The title of the book itself represented a feat of imaginative compression, for the world in which the Lithuanian immigrant Jurgis and his family find themselves is an Africa of unintelligibility, of suffering and terror, where the strong beasts devour the weak, who are dignified, if at all, only by their agony.

After their pathetically happy marriage, the descent of Jurgis and Ona into the social pit is steady. They are spiritually and, in the case of Ona, physically slaughtered, more slowly but quite as surely as the cattle in the packing plant. Disease spread by filthy working and living conditions attacks them, they endure cold in winter and clouds of flies in summer, bad food weakens their bodies, and seasonal layoffs leave them always facing starvation. When illness destroys Jurgis's great strength, he realizes that he has become a physical cast-off, one of the waste products of the plant, and must take the vilest job of all in the packing company's fertilizer plant. The forced seduction of his wife by her boss leads him to an assault on the man and thirty days in jail. Released without money, he returns to his family evicted from their home and Ona dying in childbirth. After being laid off from a dangerous job in a steel plant, Jurgis becomes successively a tramp, the henchman of a crooked politician, a strikebreaker in the packing plant strike of 1904, and finally a bum. Having reached the bottom of the social pit, he wanders into a political meeting to keep warm and hears for the first time, though at first unaware that he is listening to a Socialist, an explanation of the capitalist jungle in which he has been hunted. The sudden realization of truth is as overwhelming to Jurgis as it had been to Jurgis's creator. He at once undertakes to learn more about Socialism, is given a job in a hotel owned by a Socialist, and is eventually taken to a meeting of radical intellectuals where he hears all the arguments for the Industrial Republic which Sinclair wants his readers to know. Jurgis throws himself into the political campaign of 1904, the one in which the Party actually made such astonishing gains, and the book concludes exultantly with a speech first given by Sinclair himself, proclaiming the coming victory of the Socialists, at which time Chicago will belong to the people.

The "conversion" pattern of *The Jungle* has been attacked as permitting too easy a dramatic solution; however, aside from the recognized fact that many conversions have occurred before and since Paul saw the light on the road to Damascus, it should be noted that in *The Jungle* Sinclair carefully prepares such an outcome by conducting Jurgis through all the circles of the workers' inferno and by attempting to show that no other savior except Socialism exists. Perhaps a more valid objection to the book is Sinclair's failure to realize his characters as "living" persons, a charge which, incidentally, may be brought against many nonconversion novels. Jurgis is admittedly a composite figure who was given a heaping share of the troubles of some twenty or thirty packing workers with whom Sinclair had talked, and the author's psychology of character is indeed a simple one. Although in the introductory wedding scene Jurgis and the other major characters are sharply sketched as they had appeared to the writer at an actual wedding feast in Packingtown, during the remainder of the book they gradually lose their individuality, becoming instead any group of immigrants destroyed by the Beef Trust. Yet paradoxically, the force and passion of the book are such that this group of lay figures with Jurgis at their head, these mere capacities for infinite suffering, finally do come to stand for the masses themselves, for all the faceless ones to whom things are done. Hardly individuals, they nevertheless collectively achieve symbolic status.

Sinclair's success in creating this jungle world emphasizes by contrast what is actually the book's key defect. Jurgis's conversion is probable enough, the Socialist explanation might well flash upon him with the blinding illumination of a religious experience; but practically from that point onward to the conclusion of his novel Sinclair turns from fiction to another kind of statement. Where the capitalist damnation, the destruction of the immigrants, has been proved almost upon the reader's pulses, the Socialist salvation, after its initial impact, is intellectualized. The reader cannot exist imaginatively in Jurgis's converted state even if willing, for Jurgis hardly exists himself. What it means to be a Socialist is given, not through the rich disorder of felt experience, but in such arbitrarily codified forms as political speeches, an essay on Party personalities, or the long conversation in monologues about the Coöperative Commonwealth which comprises most of the book's final chapter. *The Jungle* begins and lives as fiction; it ends as a political miscellany.

The fact that Jurgis's militant acceptance of Socialism is far less creatively realized than his previous victimization is indicative of how Sinclair's outraged moral idealism is attracted more to the pathos than the power of the poor, and suggests his real affinity for the mid-Victorian English reform novelists. More specifically, *The Jungle* is reminiscent of the work of the humanitarian Dickens, whose social protest had "thrilled" the young rebel. There are frequent resemblances between the two writers in narrative method, in presentation of character, in the tendency of both to intrude themselves with bubbling delight or horrified indignation into the scene described. Whole paragraphs on the wedding feast of Jurgis Rudkus and Ona recall, except for the Lithuanian, the manner of Dickens with the Cratchits' Christmas dinner, and Madame Haupt, fat, drunken, and filthy, might have been a midwife in Oliver Twist's London. Finally, the temper of Sinclair's protest is curiously like that of Dickens. Where the latter urges only the literal practice of Christianity as a remedy for the cruelties he describes, Sinclair, to be sure, demands the complete transformation of the existing order of things by the Socialist revolution; yet the revolution that the orator so apocalyptically envisages at the conclusion to *The Jungle* is to be accomplished by the ballot and not by the bullet. Sinclair's spirit is not one of blood and barricades, but of humanitarianism and brotherly love. (pp. 31-6)

> *Walter B. Rideout, "Realism and Revolution," in his* The Radical Novel in the United States, 1900-1954: Some Interrelations of Literature and Society. *Cambridge, Mass.: Harvard University Press, 1956, pp. 19-46.*

John L. Thomas

In October, 1923, after his visit to the Charlestown prison, Upton Sinclair received a brief note from Bartolomeo Vanzetti thanking him for his efforts with his "golden pen" in behalf "of the truth and of the freedom" and assuring him that "what you have said about my innocence is but the truth." Then, as he was to do with so many of his new friends whom he suspected of canonizing him, Vanzetti added a disclaimer which continued to haunt Sinclair. "I understand the reasons by which you were advised to exalt me far beyond my little merit," he wrote. "If there is a little goodness in me—I am glad of it—but I do not deserve your praises. I think that there are some prisoners within these very four walls which exile me from society, which are much better than I am." Like all of his defenders who came to know Vanzetti in the course of his ordeal; Sinclair remained baffled by the deceptive simplicity of the man, the volatile mixture of artlessness and sophistication, passion and resignation, objectivity and outrage, contradictions left unresolved by his death four years later. Sinclair's decision to write a novel about the Sacco-Vanzetti case was made on the night of August 22, 1927, when word of the executions reached him in California. The result within a year was *Boston,* a sprawling 750-page novel which traces the history of the case from its beginnings in a prewar labor dispute in Plymouth to the disruption of the funeral procession on the outskirts of Roxbury twelve years later.

Boston is dominated throughout by the figure of Vanzetti, the man of "a little goodness" who seemed to Sinclair at once a genuine alien in a land of terror-stricken businessmen and a native radical agitator whose ideals lay deep in the American prophetic grain. If the real Vanzetti was indeed a study in contradictions, Sinclair's portrait of him derives its strength from just this sure sense of the contrarieties and contrapuntal qualities of the radical temperament, a recognition which makes *Boston,* despite its severe artistic limitations, a major document of the twenties and still a powerful novel.

To raise the ghost of Sinclair's esthetic failings at this late date requires a word of explanation. Those of us who read him in the late thirties and forties—studying *The Jungle* or *Oil!* in college surveys as examples of the muckraking novel and following the peregrinations of the eternal wanderer Lanny Budd—did so, I suspect, with distinct feelings of self-indulgence and the full knowledge that Sinclair was deliberately flouting all the rules for what we then called the "social novel." He insisted that literature was primarily a weapon in the class war, and charges that he idealized the workers and caricatured businessmen he airily dismissed with the reminder that since he himself had lived in both worlds he might be expected to know their inhabitants. Confronted with such ingenuousness, it seemed best simply to take him as we found him, knowing that he was impervious to criticism.

Such tolerance has no doubt increased in the intervening quarter-century which has seen the social novel reduced to shambles, art inverted in various "anti-" postures, politics replaced by ritual, and class consciousness supplanted by community. Approaching *Boston* as an esthetic experience is akin to examining *American Gothic* in terms of the canons of minimal art. Yet somehow the feeling persists that Sinclair's identification with Vanzetti places both of them in an established American tradition, and that assessing the strengths and weaknesses of **Boston** might help to illuminate those qualities peculiar to the American radical.

Sinclair defined **Boston** as a "contemporary historical novel" which he admitted was an unusual art form. So far as it concerns Sacco and Vanzetti themselves the novel is not really fiction but an attempt at history. Paralleling this account of the case, however, is a tale of high finance and business intrigue constructed out of fictionalized villains whose success in avoiding punishment for their misdeeds is intended to contrast vividly with the fate of the two anarchists. **Boston** is thus two novels: the first a bad romance composed by a self-proclaimed poet in the sentimental style of the Victorian age; the second a taut and carefully controlled account of the Sacco-Vanzetti case compiled by the historian-investigator who searches the records to find the meaning of their deaths.

The "fictionalized" novel opens on the funeral of Josiah-Quincy Thornwell, twice governor of the Commonwealth of Massachusetts, leading manufacturer and philanthropist, Republican spokesman and Brahmin par excellence, whose untimely demise has left his widow, the sixty-year-old Cornelia, in the clutches of the unloveliest set of daughters since Goneril and Regan. Driven from her gracious home by the squabbling of her family whose greed she has come to loathe, the "runaway grandmother" appears incognito in Plymouth where she . . . meets Vanzetti with whom she forms a deep and lasting friendship. "Nonna," as Bart calls her, comes to understand the basic injustice of the capitalist system and to respond to Vanzetti's vision of a world made totally free. She and her granddaughter Betty, a spirited suffragette whom the family has reluctantly consigned to her keeping, are in Europe drinking at the fountains of continental radicalism, when word reaches them of Vanzetti's arrest. They rush home and are immediately swept up in the swirling cross-currents of the case. Betty, converted to communism, sees in the case the promised end to liberalism. Cornelia, torn between her inherited and adopted worlds, rejecting the avarice of her family but not the liberal creed of men like William G. Thompson and Felix Frankfurter, is not so sure. Her own personal crisis comes early in the case with a defense request that she perjure herself by supplying Vanzetti with an alibi which the establishment in deference to her social position will not question. She refuses and can only watch helplessly as the judicial machinery crushes Sacco and Vanzetti. On the eve of the executions she visits Vanzetti hoping he will renounce violence when reminded of Comrade Jesus, only to be told that all he wants is justice "not for us, nor for vengeance, which is a wicked thing." Of his martyrdom Vanzetti says simply: "Tell our friends it is joy, not grief, it is success, not failure." Exhausted, Cornelia returns to her Beacon Hill apartment, the scene of a frenzied last-minute attempt to stay the executions, and tells the young militants: "Let me be quiet! I have been talking with God."

The flaws which mar all of Sinclair's fiction abound in **Boston:** a resolute refusal to create believable characters; overreliance on the "two nations" design with its heavy-handed irony; and repeated intrusions of the author as the amanuensis of "the Great Novelist who writes history." Rereading the "fictionalized" part of the novel today, we

sense nothing so clearly as the raw moralism of a mediocre Victorian novelist.

Yet if the fictionalized half of **Boston** returns us to the nineteenth century, so in an entirely different way does the "other" novel, the work of the journalist-investigator who shares with Vanzetti a native American radical tradition. Sinclair's Vanzetti is a romantic idealist—a tenacious true believer in "one of those high perfectionist doctrines which assume in human beings a quantity of virtue which few as yet possess." Vanzetti's enemies, no mere abstractions but the actual forces which kill him, are prejudice, exploitation, repression and power. His ultimate good is a fierce freedom which he knows experientially as the sole source of happiness. In an autobiographical passage borrowed from Vanzetti's real account (and couched in a dialect which quickly becomes wearisome), Sinclair has him explain his conversion to anarchism. "I come America," he tells Cornelia,

> "not for get rich, get little money, no work so hard, have time for read book. . . . I t'ink maybe I be socialist now, little bit socialist, sentimentale, genteel, good, ever'body be kind, make new world, ever'body be happy, maybe by vote. I come America for sooch pretty—what you say, dream."

The dream crumbles and iron enters Vanzetti's soul: he becomes an anarchist agitator whose whole life is centered on the crime of capitalism. . . . When Cornelia reads him William Lloyd Garrison's *Liberator* editorial—"I will be as harsh as truth"—Vanzetti says the name over and over again and then adds: "I never hear him before, but I feel him brudder; am joosta sooch man like him!"

Vanzetti, like Garrison, is Sinclair's ultimate hero—the man driven to act out his convictions. Garrison, is fact, is the prototype of Sinclair's new twentieth-century man. Like Garrison, Vanzetti has no use for politics ("Politeesh, he no work, liva good, dress a genteelman"). Scarcely less use for liberal reformers ("Riformista is—what you call it—trait'!"). Both men have an abiding fear of power ("Power and abuse of power are synonims"). Like the nineteenth-century moral reformer, Vanzetti finds in the role of the agitator a completeness denied him by the partial tasks assigned by society. He is similarly uncertain about the uses of violence. There will be no need for force in a world made over, but who, he asks, can deny its uses in making that world? Finally, there is a transcendentalist puritanism in Vanzetti which Sinclair respected, an urge to smash the toys of an acquisitive society and to return life to Thoreau's essentials—"a little roof, a field, a few books and food," as Vanzetti explains just after his imprisonment:

> "And more: The clearness of mind, the peace of the conscience, the determination and force of will, the intelligence, all, what make the man feeling to be a part of the life, force and intelligence of the universe. . . . "

It was the willful and premeditated destruction of the "man feeling" that so affronts Sinclair and makes this "other" novel a masterpiece of reporting and a forerunner of the novel-as-journalism which Norman Mailer has since perfected. Sinclair was forced to master the incredible detail of the case in order to know its real meaning. His mastery, well-nigh complete, shows on every page of this second novel: in his descriptions of an inept defense; in his masterful dissection of the legal reasoning of Webster Thayer; in lucid summaries of the endless series of defense motions; and not least in the scathing analysis of the report of the Lowell Commission. "I have tried to be the historian," Sinclair announced in explaining that his account of the case contained "no errors of real significance," a claim which Louis Joughin finds fully justified. Sinclair's poetic vision may have failed him in *Boston,* as it would countless times again, but his instincts as a reporter setting the record straight did not.

What, then, does the record show? What is Sinclair's verdict and what was the meaning of the case? It is clear, first of all, that he believed Sacco and Vanzetti innocent and knew that they had been denied even the semblance of a fair trial. More questionable, perhaps, is his view of the capitalist "system" suppressing dissent with single-minded ferocity. The apparent unity of the "establishment," as the more perceptive Bernard DeVoto makes clear in *We Accept With Pleasure,* dissolves under scrutiny into partial concerns, conflicting aims and cross-purposes. Welcome as Sinclair's analysis of the workings of power in the United States may be to a later generation properly disturbed by the malfunctioning of bureaucracy and fearful of all power, Sinclair's construction lacks the sophistication and the complexity of a really workable analytical model. What remains with us most clearly after rereading *Boston* are two legacies of nineteenth-century romantic reform: the idea of a "saving remnant" of middle-class liberals whose consciences drive them to strike out against social wrong; and, more important, the persistence of the radical vision in men like Vanzetti with their dreams of a perfect world commanding them to serve as "witness" with their lives. One senses that Sinclair himself was responding to some such categorical imperative—that he was serving as witness to his own beliefs—when he deserted the socialists in 1934 to present his EPIC plan to the people on the Democratic platform. And in our own time, when we read *Soledad Brother* and feel the impact of a different but equally strong radical imagination, we realize that these beliefs retain at least some of their original vitality. (pp. 24-5)

> *John L. Thomas, "Upton Sinclair's 'Boston',"*
> *in* The New Republic, *Vol. 165, No. 25, De-*
> *cember 18, 1971, pp. 24-5.*

Jon A. Yoder

At the mention of Upton Sinclair, college students dredge up an image of a Lithuanian falling into a vat to be turned into lard; history majors add hazy recollections about a gubernatorial campaign in California during the New Deal, with Roosevelt fortunately selling Sinclair short in some devious way. . . . Sinclair is one of those who never quite made it. He did not write The Great American Novel. There has been no Sinclair revival. He did not win the Nobel Prize. And as a prophet he now seems a bit silly:

> I will venture to put on record the prediction that
> students in high schools will be learning their histo-
> ry of the first and second World Wars from the
> Lanny Budd books long after Life and Time have
> ceased to be.

But for those who would read recent history in a way not

intended by Sinclair, this series—published from 1940 through 1953—can be almost as useful as Sinclair claimed. Eventually comprising what Sinclair considered "the most important part of my literary performance," these "eleven volumes, 7,364 pages, over four million words" sold well, with the first eight novels finding 1,340,139 buyers in the United States alone. But critics, when they deigned to take notice, were not overly impressed. As a reviewer for *Time* wrote:

> To the literary, the novels of Upton Sinclair . . .
> are not literature. To historians, they are not histo-
> ry. To propagandists, they are not propaganda. But
> to millions of plain people, they are all three of
> those things.

Consequently, if Sinclair was not a great writer in the sense of creating a series which would outlive its immediate readability, he may still be a fine reflector of the times in which he lived. The fact that Sinclair's sort of propaganda, American liberalism, was produced in annual and undiluted doses during a period when this ideology was going sour makes Sinclair an interesting case study of our national psyche.

The argument here will be that liberalism (and Lanny) failed because of curious weaknesses in the liberal mentality, weaknesses which make it impossible for liberalism to characterize periods of extreme stress in American history. Reduced to a generalization, the American liberal does not believe his own rhetoric. That is, whereas he wholeheartedly endorses all the ideals enumerated by Louis Hartz and John Locke, he also firmly believes that his first commitment is to what he mistakenly calls pragmatism. Moreover, in his *own* opinion, this presents a problem. For to be pragmatic, he feels, it becomes necessary to behave illiberally during a crisis. Thus one encounters the traditional suspension of liberal values "for the duration" of national emergencies, as the liberal's lack of ideological self-confidence becomes a self-fulfilling prophecy. And thus the liberal mentality is poorly equipped to lead a nation into a period of history where crisis will be continual.

Lanny Budd, the American liberal, is a self-diagnosed schizophrenic. Seeing himself as caught between his own idealism and his own definition of realism, he sacrifices the first for the second, fully expecting his acute discomfort to be temporary and anticipating the American post-war return to normalcy—the state of affairs in which one's schizophrenia is not so bothersome. However, shortly after World War II, Lanny and the Liberals enlisted as Cold Warriors. Selling their ideals for a mess of containment, American progressives became staunch defenders of the status quo during decades demanding rapid social change—and all in the name of pragmatism.

Never the most subtle of writers, Sinclair made no effort to disguise the fact that in Lanny Budd he had created a type character. Many critics objected to this at the time, but Sinclair (who had a gigantic, if genial, self-conceit) was undisturbed: "A type represents great numbers of persons and makes us aware of mass events. There are many novelists who are perfectly happy to portray individuals, and I leave it for them to do." . . . In the world set up by Sinclair, Lanny becomes every idealistic American's dream come true. Posing as an art broker with fascist sympathies, Lanny moves in and out of circles of elite Europeans, gathering priceless information; he returns periodically to the United States in order to advise his grateful President, write Roosevelt's most important speeches, and serve generally in whatever superhuman capacity requested. Primarily, Sinclair used his character to preach liberal propaganda. To his Marxist European friend, Lanny says: "First, you have to give up the class struggle; forget it absolutely. There's only one enemy now, and that is Hitler. Churchill has to be your friend, no matter how little you like him." Regarding the relationship between violence and social change, Lanny maintains that "these countries (England, France, United States) being 'democracies,' could bring about the changes peaceably. That was his way; he didn't want to hurt anybody, but to discuss ideas politely and let the best ideas win." (pp. 483-86)

But the author of *The Jungle* had always been considered a propagandist. In order to understand the liberal mentality of the period, it is necessary to take note of a curious critical response to the Lanny Budd series. While realizing that Sinclair was not sounding quite like the socialist muckraker of old, some critics confused a modification of tone with something academic liberals were determined to find in themselves—a transcendence of ideology altogether. For instance, [R. L. Duffus of] the New York *Times* concluded: "Mr. Sinclair has stepped out of the rather obvious role of a writer of moral tales with an old-line Socialist or new-line EPIC connotations. He has become a novelist. . . . "

In other words, as Sinclair's propaganda began to sound increasingly like their own, these critics decided that he must no longer be propagandizing. He must have withdrawn from the fray, and, therefore, he could be used as evidence for the ideology of objective neutrality, an ideology proclaiming loftily that ideology itself was a bore. Witness Warren French:

> Perhaps the most striking evidence . . . that some kind of terminal had been reached was that the American writer whose name had been for three decades most conspicuously linked with the kind of social novel that he could fairly be said to have invented decided suddenly in 1939 to abandon his efforts to reform the world and to retreat into reminiscence. . . . Sensing . . . that an end was coming, Sinclair decided to withdraw from his characteristically active involvement in affairs and to look back over the era. . . . With almost uncanny aptitude, he chose for the first book of the sequence that was to win more readers than his crusading novels of the thirties a title that is a slogan for the period: *World's End.*
>
> (p. 486)

This analysis of a changed Sinclair is deceptive because Sinclair's behavior in the Forties simply was not atypical for him. He supported the entry of the United States into World War I in precisely the same way as he supported his country during World War II and the Cold War. When his friends who felt compelled to stick by a Socialist Party analysis argued that American workers had no business helping British capitalists against their German counterparts, Sinclair withdrew from the party, contending that "the ability to think consists in the discovery of differences in things which appear alike. . . . It is fatally easy to say that all capitalist governments are alike, and that all must be opposed in the same way." In short, being lib-

eral meant for Sinclair being more nationalist than socialist whenever his nation was under attack.

Sinclair had always believed that a good liberal responds differently in periods of national emergency, a point he had made explicit in 1920: "*Except in time of war,* when a Nathan Hale may be a spy, spies are always necessarily drawn from the unwholesome and untrustworthy classes. A right-minded man refuses such a job." Since it is impossible to read the Lanny Budd series without concluding that Sinclair intends Lanny to be a symbol of right-mindedness, the implication is clear. Lanny and his creator had gone to war.

True to his conviction that the goal of the artist is to get the audience to swallow the message, in a letter to Einstein he referred to his novels as "not just entertainment" but "sugar-coated history of our times with an attempt at interpretation." And with his editor, he was even more candid: "What I am doing is giving the reader a great load of history and some propaganda, and I try to put in adventures as a sort of icing to the cake." Far from the withdrawal French asserts, Sinclair's conscious goal was to "create a set of characters and carry my message in the story." Far from abandoning his role as crusader in the Forties and Fifties, Sinclair merely modified his approach in order to help his country through a period of extreme stress.

This turn from critic to supporter, almost an automatic response by the American liberal when he sees the United States entering a period of emergency, has special implications after World War II because of basic changes in the nature of global conflict in a post-Nagasaki world. No longer able to drop liberal ideals "for the duration" with the intention of returning to the role of critic/reformer when things returned to normal, liberals such as Sinclair were caught flatfooted by the Cold War—by extreme stress becoming the normal and continuing condition to be endured by the American Way of Life. (pp. 487-88)

It has been contended above that Lanny, as a typical liberal, is plagued by a schizoid perspective. This suggests that although he might function adequately in society under normal circumstances, he cannot cope with extreme and extended duress. To illustrate the failure of liberals as Cold Warriors, then, it is necessary to make explicit the tendencies which had been generally undisturbed beneath the surface of Lanny's behavior throughout the series.

> There was one half of Lanny Budd—possibly a little more than half—which wanted to quarrel with an evil social order and to make sacrifices in the cause of truth-telling and justice; and there was another half, or near half, which liked to live in a well-appointed home, enjoy well-cooked food, be waited on, have a properly tuned piano—a long list of things which the world does not allot to its heroes, saints and martyrs.

Lanny's job had brought him close to that state known to psychiatrists as schizophrenia; two minds living in the same body.

With his role as a secret agent for Roosevelt constituting a living negation of the liberal ideal of seeing all sides of all issues while remaining free from dogmatic commitment, Lanny was simply unable to make his ideological theories come to life in his own particular case. He retained his stock in his conservative father's munitions company although his early version of liberalism concurrently saw these corporations as merchants of death. . . . It can, of course, be argued that nobody is capable of living up to his ideals; but in the case of the American liberal, continual capitulation to what appears to be the interest of the individual has added up to disaster on both personal and supranational scales.

For not only is Lanny unable to effect the sort of society he desires, but his constant sacrificing of principle for personal reasons eventually destroys his personality as effectively as it destroys those with whom he comes in contact. In *Dragon's Teeth,* a book for which Sinclair won the Pulitzer Prize, Lanny is willing to risk his own life to get a friend out of the hands of the Gestapo. Later in the series, when Trudi is captured by the Nazis [in *Presidential Agent*], he is ready to risk everything—not to defeat Nazism (merely), but to free his wife. He is, of course, successful in his effort to defy Nazi security precautions, but with the prison successfully entered and the escape route working brilliantly, the person in the torture chamber turns out to be someone other than the expected loved one (who had been sent to her death in a German concentration camp). So Lanny leaves the victim behind, escaping with his fellow liberators in such a way that the Nazis never know what had been attempted. He rationalizes his decision in terms of the larger cause: "There wasn't a thing those three intruders could have done; to have carried the man out would have given the whole thing away and ruined the career of a presidential agent."

Similarly, Lanny hides behind his own sexual conservatism to avoid taking the relatively small risk involved in saving the life of a German who literally meant nothing to him personally [in *Presidential Mission*]. Although he is a professional deceiver of Nazis, he rejects Rosika Diamant's suggestion that he marry her in Germany and thus help her avoid the fate reserved for beautiful Jewish women. Dismissing her suggestion, Lanny says: "I might do what you ask, but as it happens, I have a wife and baby in New York." . . . Lanny's sexual code of honor is not really at stake since Rosika makes it perfectly clear to him that she is more interested in her own existence that in anything sexual, assuring him that she will get the "marriage" annulled as soon as she is outside Germany. So Lanny rejects her plan even though Sinclair writes that his response constitutes "what both of them knew was a death sentence."

The implications of this go far beyond the importance of one character in a series of novels being unable to risk his larger cause unless he has a personal vested interest—in which case he does so vigorously. The point is that Sinclair cannot imagine his character acting in any other way even though he is aware of what this sort of selfishness does to the individual so concerned with himself. Depending on the degree of hostility one has toward this sort of liberal, one of the most touching or despicable scenes in the Lanny Budd novels involves Lanny's effort to reduce this incident to a joke—a gross effort at self-defensive humor which creates a taste of gall in the back of the mouth while a grin keeps trying to flash across the unhappy face:

> (Lanny) began to chuckle. "I have stayed too late, but you ought to hear the story of how I was tempted to commit bigamy. Perhaps you will give me

permission for that! Or is it in Colonel Donovan's department?"

> He told the story of Rosika Diamant, which wasn't really funny but horribly tragic when you stopped to think. Roosevelt laughed first and then he frowned.

It becomes increasingly clear that the liberal's concern for self runs at still deeper levels. For surely Sinclair is thinking of Lanny rather than Rosika when he uses the word "tragic." Surely it is the effect upon Lanny, his inability to do what [he] believes he ought to do, rather than the murder of Rosika that is intended to move us. So it is Lanny who must listen to what amounts to a message to the liberal mentality confronted with the 1940's and 1950's: "You are two men, and they are at war. Presently you will not know which you really are. Make up your mind, or it will go badly with you. I see a tragic fate in store for you." (pp. 488-90)

The story of the Cold War and the last part of the Lanny Budd saga delineate both the dehumanization of a liberal society supposedly based on humane ideals and the reduction of the liberal individual to an ineffectuality achieved by compromise with ideals in the name of pragmatism. Perhaps the most graphic way to trace this degeneration is to follow the arguments of the liberal in relation to the most extreme testing of his principles through the years—his response to the Soviet Union in general and to Stalin in particular.

Typical of the American liberal's response to communism in Russia, Sinclair moved from a perspective of early enthusiasm to a period of disenchantment immediately prior to World War II. This became a positive appreciation of a powerful wartime ally which turned into a more powerful antagonism when the alignments were redrawn for the continuation of a world at war. In the same way as liberal values are best tested under extreme stress, Sinclair is a good example of American liberalism because his response during each of these four periods was somewhat more extreme than the average.

This means that during the Thirties Sinclair was an ardent defender of what communists were attempting to do in Russia. Unlike some writers who joined the American Communist Party during this time, however, Sinclair argued only from the position of the libertarian:

> I am reluctant to defend any sort of dictatorship, because, as you know, I have been active as a Civil Liberties Unioner; but it does seem to me that the Russian proposition is a scientific one, that in proportion as they educate the workers and bring them into the Communist Party, they diminish the chances of opposition, and so the need of the state, in the sense of a police force and army, becomes proportionately less.

Sinclair would not advocate communism for his own country, but given the feudal circumstances of Czarist Russia, something as drastic as Leninism seemed to him to be required. Confronted by the cruelty of the Stalin regime, Sinclair argued that Russians had never had the liberties enjoyed by Americans and should be given time to learn how to live without resorting to totalitarian measures. Moreover, he pointed out, the country had been virtually at war for years, and no nation has a particularly good record regarding civil liberties during wars. So although Lanny was eventually to contend that there are no essential differences between Nazism and communism, at this time Sinclair was pointing the other direction: "It so happens that I believe one of these regimes is capable of progress and improvement, while I believe that the other means death to all hope of progress to mankind for all future time." (pp. 491-92)

[In a] debate with Eugene Lyons, Sinclair heaped scorn upon his opponent for imagining that Hitler and Stalin could join forces:

> You discuss various international possibilities and say: "Even a reshuffling that would place Russia and Germany on the same side of no-man's land is not, alas, beyond possibility." I would have thought that the shooting of Tukhachevsky and other pro-German generals might be taken to have settled that question for a long time.

However, in a notably short time there was a pact between the two, and Sinclair had to leapfrog into a prophecy which was geared toward proving that he had been correct all along:

> Chamberlain could have prevented the rise of Hitler, but he thought Hitler was going to defend capitalism and fight Communism. He could have had an excellent commercial arrangement with Russia, but he preferred Hitler. Now Stalin is gambling on pulling Hitler to the left, and my guess is that he will succeed in the end. It looks to me as if the war would be a stalemate and this will produce social revolution over a great part of Europe. I am waiting to see it happen and then put in [*sic*] into the third volume of this long novel I am writing.

But the third installment of the Lanny Budd series [*Dragon's Teeth*] would have to be made up of other things, for by November of 1940 Sinclair was writing: "As to Russia, it seems to me quite obvious that Stalin is today a prisoner of Hitler, and has to do what he is told, and is doing it."

This changing analysis was a response to pressure from other liberals who were making the big switch ahead of Sinclair after the invasion of Finland by the Soviet Union. Already in 1939 James T. Farrell had written to Sinclair to urge him to reconsider his position before the inevitable backing away became too embarrassing. Farrell pointed out that he had written two years previously asking about Sinclair's attitude toward the trials in Moscow and had been answered by Sinclair's public defense of them. He wanted to know if Sinclair still felt that the Soviet regime was the "best hope for the workers," if the Soviet Union was still "the most consistent defender of Peace," and if Sinclair had been surprised by the pact signed by Molotov and Ribbentrop. In conclusion, Farrell offered Sinclair a chance to save face by joining a mass movement: "Many persons have sought to reopen the question of the Moscow trials, and to ask all over again why were the defendants shot? Even staunch supporters of the Soviet Union changed their attitude." (pp. 492-93)

The apparent effect upon Sinclair appears in two letters which move him from the contention that Stalin had made a tactical error to the more basic admission that he could no longer use the Soviet Union as a model of social change to be defended in the United States and emulated in countries where democracy was not an immediate possi-

bility. . . . By April of 1940, Sinclair had advanced from the resentment of Soviet behavior in Finland to a criticism of communism as fraudulent in a more general sense:

> The appearance of the Communists as pacifists is pure fraud. They have shown us quite plainly in Finland that they are not pacifists. They are acting as pacifists in America at the present time because they are afraid that England may get into war with Russia and draw us in.

The third stage of the American liberal's progression into militant anti-communism involved the reaffirmation of the former faith in a currently valuable military ally. During the war, Sinclair never completely returned to his early enthusiasm for the Soviet Union, but he felt that it was "up to our statesmanship and the social science of our people to see to it that we conduct our international affairs openly, honestly and justly with those people who are now helping us to put down Nazism and fascism." Sometimes he made an effort to maintain that events were proving that he had been right in his analysis of Stalin from the beginning. . . . But more characteristic of Sinclair during this rather brief period of general good will toward Russia was his approval of efforts to get along with communists. . . .

> What I have seen and heard of the public's reaction to the Yalta conference seems to me very promising, and I believe that as time passes the actions of the Soviet Union will cause a spread of understanding in our country. I have high hopes for the future.

In Sinclair's fiction written during this period, Lanny expresses the same position in a conversation with James Stotzlmann [in *One Clear Call*]:

> "Winnie is a bulldog and never gives up. He argues, what is the good of winning the war if it leaves Stalin in the Balkans? The Boss, of course, wants to make friends with Stalin."
>
> "That's the difference between a Tory and a democrat," commented Lanny. . . .

But if good liberals were willing to try to live with the Russians, by 1947, when Sinclair was writing *One Clear Call,* this was done without exuberance. According to the hypothesis of Harry Hopkins, as expressed to Lanny:

> It appears to be a principle of revolutions that they degenerate, and I fear that Red Russia is no exception. All leaders think about themselves and their own power, and the longer they hold power, the more true that becomes.

Sinclair was moving rapidly to a position from which he could oppose the Soviet Union with even less qualification than he had once supported it, becoming increasingly ready to announce that he, though now wise, had been a fool:

> I have defended the right of the people of Russia to choose their own form of government, as long as I could hope they were choosing it. . . . The failure of the Soviet leaders to improve upon the inhuman regime of Czarist Russia has brought all the truly liberal forces of the world into danger. Russia's brutal Communist regime has made it all too easy for Fascism to proclaim that all brands of liberalism are dangerous and lead to despotism.

It is quite true that in *Presidential Mission* I portrayed Stalin and Mao and had them uttering "quite reasonable views." They were our Allies in the war against Fascism and I believed their promises of peace and world order afterwards. Now I know I was very naive.

It is possible to point out contradictions and rather wide areas of shallow thought in Sinclair's writing up through the Second World War. But mirroring only too completely the general postwar decay of American liberalism, his written thoughts, following that war, can only be said to reflect general incoherence. His contention that he could no longer defend the right of the people of Russia to choose their own form of government—because he no longer could imagine that they were, in fact, choosing it—is both logical and historical nonsense. Throughout Sinclair's lifetime, the Russians had *never* had a government based on popular election. But Sinclair could have, and as a liberal he should have, continued to defend ideals which may never have been actualized for the Russians but (as Locke said) remained their right because of their innate humanity. (pp. 494-96)

Sinclair's concern, like Lanny's throughout the series, seems to be controlled more by personal considerations than by ideological theory. He had defended Stalin during the decades when those in danger of summary elimination were Russian or German; but when the threat of what Stalin represented was *alleged* to be hovering over Pasadena, Sinclair took up the cry of outrage which has been ritualistically chanted for twenty-five years whenever American liberals have felt their life style to be at stake: This Time They've Gone Too Far. There was no time to investigate the real nature or extent of the allegation, for the commes were coming, the sky was falling, and it was high time to get more bang for the buck.

Since the conclusion of this analysis is that American liberals must now bring existential considerations into line with their ideological theories, Sinclair becomes a negative case study—a muckraking liberal who had been on the attack against social injustice within his own country for most of his life, but who became an ardent defender of the system to which he had once attributed the ills of the world, thereby fumbling his credibility, integrity, and effectiveness.

With respect to his credibility, as recently as *One Clear Call,* Sinclair had blamed capitalism for America's unnecessarily unhappy relationship with the Soviet Union. As Lanny says to Roosevelt:

It's puzzling, Governor, I admit. But the reason the Communists hate us Socialists is because they don't believe the changes can be brought about peaceably; therefore they call us betrayers of the workers' hopes. But if you once put industry on a cooperative basis, that attitude would dissolve. The attraction between the two systems (democratic socialism and communism) would be irresistible and they would be drawn into a truce. With capitalism, of course, there is no possibility of a truce, because capitalism is forced by its very nature to expand.

Somehow, between 1947 and the early 1950's, the natures of economic systems changed, and it was Czarism / Communism which was inherently expansionistic and imperialistic. (pp. 496-97)

Since it was now "obvious to all the world that the only thing which had so far kept the Soviet Union from taking possession of Western Europe was that supply of atomic bombs which the United States kept dangling over the Kremlin," Lanny began to make statements [in *The Return of Lanny Budd*] which sound curiously like those uttered by his munitions-making father early in the series: " 'I'm not calling for war; on the contrary, I think the only hope of preventing war is for us to rearm and do it quickly, to convince Stalin that he cannot take the rest of the world without war.' " It could be for this reason, then, that Sinclair decided that none of his earlier volumes would make appropriate reading for those who were now to be his new friends—a point he makes clear in a letter to J. Edgar Hoover:

You were kind enough to say that you would be interested to receive one of the "Lanny Budd" books from me. I debated which one to send you, and what I decided was that they are all out of date at present and that what I want you to read is the one I am just completing. This volume is concerned with the Communists and their whole bag of clever tricks. . . . This makes it a timely book, and I think it would be helpful to you as to many others.

(p. 498)

Inspired by patriotism of this sort, the degeneration of Lanny is reflected in [*The Return of Lanny Budd* in] the deterioration of dialogue between the agent and his Presidential Boss, with the man-to-man repartée between Roosevelt and Lanny becoming something simply sticky between Truman and the Spokesman for American liberalism:

"I won't be able to accomplish much with this new Congress the people have given me, but at least I'm going to make the demands and keep them before the public mind. I shall keep the flag flying."

Lanny smiled and said, "There was a song written about that, Mr. President; it is called 'The Star-Spangled Banner.' "

Degeneration of liberal self-confidence is concurrent. During the early stages of the Cold War, Sinclair was still convinced that the truth could win on its own merits:

I know that the Communists lie freely on principle. They think they get somewhere that way, and maybe they do in the short run, but in the end they defeat themselves. I believe in the truth, and I know that we can lick them with the truth.

But the following quotation illustrates the hypothesis that liberalism, according to liberals, continued to operate at a disadvantage during times of stress:

They have flooded our country with spies while we have very few, if any, in their country. More important yet, we have a conscience, while they have none. Therefore we have to wait for them to make the first attack.

(pp. 498-99)

Liberalism, Upton Sinclair, and Lanny Budd all became both dehumanized and ineffectual during the Cold War. Perhaps the saddest aspect of Sinclair's deterioration is his apparent unwillingness to realize what was happening to him as he was sucked into the mainstream current of American liberalism which was running swiftly downhill and to the right. In his letters, Sinclair tried to explain his apparent change of position by contending that while Russia had altered, he had remained ideologically consistent:

> In 1939 the deal between Stalin and Hitler put an end to my hopes forever. When Hitler made his attack upon Russia, I, of course, agreed with Roosevelt and Churchill in accepting Russia as an ally. . . . But, as you doubtless know Roosevelt was disillusioned before his death, and I learned of his disillusionment. I realized then that Russia had become an imperialist nation. . . . Ever since that time I have been heartily supporting the Truman-Acheson policies, with the result that I am now in the eyes of the Russians a "Wall Street's Lackey. . . ." My position is exactly what it has always been; my formula is "the social ownership and democratic control of the instruments and means of production." I use the word "democratic" in the true American sense, and not in the fraudulent Russian sense.

Actually, Sinclair tried to serve as Wall Street's lackey, but he was dismally ineffective. A man who had been remarkably open in his correspondence and fiction now had to learn to be specious, for Sinclair, whether he knew it or not, was producing a sort of propaganda differing from that which he had been publishing throughout his life, moving in lockstep with an American liberal mentality which had become reactionary. (pp. 499-500)

Liberalism cannot survive in an atmosphere where leading liberals equate cleverness with unscrupulousness, for the liberal ideal is to be effective in the world while retaining a humanistic outlook on life. What happened to Lanny in the last volume of the series demonstrates the dehumanization of the liberal individual who no longer believes in himself; and the failure of Sinclair with respect to this book gives clear indication of the ineffectuality of the liberal who begins to fight evil with evil. For the Lanny in Sinclair's final volume is a hard and cynical man, unaware that in his increasingly monomaniacal efforts to destroy communism, he has simply become an Ahab *sans grandeur,* a petty combatant for whom no holds are barred.

Early in the book, a Treasury agent is dismayed at Lanny's use of Fritz to spy on his own father—Lanny's boyhood friend, Kurt: " 'Mr. Budd,' said the other gravely, 'the Nazis used children to report upon their parents, and the Reds are doing it now. But it is not our practice.' " It soon became "our practice," however, as Lanny himself justifies a resort to totalitarian tactics in the name of the liberal cause. He receives an anonymous note informing him that Bess, his sister, is a Russian spy, a situation leading to the following conversation with his wife:

> "It is my plain duty to take it to the FBI."
>
> "Oh, Lanny, how dreadful! Could you bear to do it?"
>
> "Bess herself has given me the authority. You heard her say, 'The individual doesn't matter, only the cause matters.' You and I have a cause darling. Are we going to say it's less worthy than hers—that she can carry on secret war against us, and we have to lie down and take whatever comes to us? . . . No, the FBI are the people who know how to do this job, and it is the plain duty of every citizen to take them every scrap of information he may possess. To say that we must spare our own blood rela-

tives is simply to yield to a superstition and in effect to deny our cause."

Thus in order to support liberalism, one must accept the principle that the individual does not matter—a denial of the very basis of the liberal credo. Sinclair, who tends to make bald and explicit statements out of characteristics which more subtle liberals prefer to camouflage, received criticism from ideological colleagues who felt that liberalism should not present itself in quite so illiberal a way unless absolutely necessary. (p. 501)

Sinclair was unable to convince millions of Americans of the relevance of Lanny Budd's return. *World's End,* Sinclair's first effort of the series, eventually sold 23,669 copies within the United States; the next three volumes also sold approximately as well, but then sales climbed rapidly, reaching 86,000 with *Dragon Harvest.* However, a declining interest was reflected in lower sales for each successive novel in the last half of the series. But never was the decline so sharp as with *The Return of Lanny Budd.* For Sinclair's last gasp sold only 14,865 copies—about half the number sold of the novel immediately preceding it and far below the total with which he began the endeavor.

Sales figures are subject to differing analyses, but an additional indication of the degradation of Sinclair is to be found in his correspondence. There the man began to beg help from men whom he had once vigorously opposed on principle. In a mimeographed appeal for support, Sinclair argued that organizations traditionally opposed to communism should not overlook the contribution of their new ally:

> This statement is being sent to individuals and organizations which may be interested in opposing the "cold war" in the field of letters. The project has to do with a novel, *The Return of Lanny Budd,* just published by Viking Press. . . . (The author) is thinking of small and backward lands in which the message of this book is . . . urgently needed: Turkey, Greece, Israel, Egypt, Iran, Siam; the native languages of India, and Chinese via Hong Kong. The Communists are working diligently in all these lands, and this book is a weapon against them. The author invites some public-service group to finance this undertaking and he offers to donate the copyright. . . . Read the book, and see that it is a beacon light in a world threatened with darkness; a weapon in what William Blake calls "mental fight."

Sinclair had often served as his own public relations manager, but the people to whom he now addressed himself represent a rather vivid contradiction of his claim that he had not changed his position. In *Dragon Harvest,* Sinclair had stated that Henry Ford

> was, in all probability, the richest man in the world. . . . He had forbidden unions in his plants, and was fighting them by every means, not excluding criminal. But the New Deal was determined to break his will and force unions into all his plants. . . . As a result his plants swarmed with Nazis. . . .

Despite this, and despite the fact that Sinclair's first jailing resulted from his too explicit labeling of John D. Rockefeller as a murderer of miners, their wives, and children, Wall Street's would-be lackey offered himself and his new book to both the Ford and the Rockefeller foundations. (pp. 502-503)

The Army chose to pass the book from department to department, with rejections which amounted to thanks, but no thanks: Wendell W. Fertig, Acting Chief of Psychological Warfare, approved of the ideological content of *The Return of Lanny Budd,* but he indicated that since his endeavors were limited to actual combat areas Sinclair would have to seek another agency.

Allen Dulles reacted warmly to his advance copy of Lanny's *Return:* "I was particularly interested in the section dealing with Lanny's incarceration and the effort to extort a confession from him. You have made that unpleasant episode really live." But this letter contains a hint that Sinclair may not have been able to deceive himself completely about his own new political stance. For what reason other than shame could have induced the world's most compulsive collector of everything relating to Upton Sinclair to have written in the corner of this particular letter an apparently overlooked injunction to destroy the document?

Given this scrawled bit of information, there is no way of knowing how many other letters were destined to elude the Lilly librarians altogether. But it was Sinclair himself who was destroyed by the Cold War—both as a believer in humane liberalism and as an effective propagandist. Not until his writing career had finally ended did American liberals begin to make tentative efforts to deal realistically with their own ideals by encouraging those manipulating the American experiment to grant the liberal hypothesis the dignity of trial under stress. (p. 504)

> *Jon A. Yoder, "Upton Sinclair, Lanny, and the Liberals," in* Modern Fiction Studies, *Vol. 20, No. 4, Winter, 1974-75, pp. 483-504.*

James J. Storrow, Jr.

[For two people to agree on the major features of the case of Sacco and Vanzetti], they must first agree on much else. For many in that place and time, the execution on August 23, 1927 was the final vicious act of a decade of mounting hysteria and injustice. For an adolescent, as I was, it became a traumatic refutation of what one had been taught of morality and honor. Not just the Emperor (the Governor, the president of Harvard) was without clothes; their whole society seemed to have exposed itself.

Those good, responsible citizens of Boston who presided over the city saw a quite different skyline. The execution was, for them, an exemplary act of self-defense on the part of society. In the wake of the World War and the Russian Revolution—with a Communist Government in power!—with Socialism and Anarchism apparently on the march and a large population of foreigners (mainly Italians) in the Boston area, it only made sense for society to defend itself any way necessary. What matter whether those two Wops actually committed the crime? They were anarchists, weren't they? An example must be made of them!

Captain Dreyfus had a Zola to protest the injustices done him. Sacco and Vanzetti, likewise, found many to speak on their behalf, although less successfully in the end. One was Heywood Broun, who with fine fury wrote about the case in the New York *World* until he was fired for refusing to stop, and came to *The Nation.*

Another strong dissenting voice was that of Upton Sinclair. His *Boston* (recently reissued) describes itself as a "documentary novel" which, despite the laconic title, is an accurate account of the lives and deaths of the two men, as viewed by certain fictional people of Boston. It first appeared in 1928; it was written in as white a heat of anger as that in which Zola had written *J'accuse*—though this time the State in its majesty had already taken away what could never be restored.

Distancing in time, which has distorted or concealed the significance, for many, of the Sacco-Vanzetti case, has also had its effect upon the visibility of Upton Sinclair's achievements. He is largely absent from public consciousness. If he is thought of at all it is as the author of *The Jungle* and *Dragon's Teeth,* and as a quixotic social protester with a scheme for ending poverty in California. The reappearance of *Boston* will probably do little to rectify this neglect, though one may hope.

The central figure of *Boston* is Cornelia Thornwell, a rich, middle-aged, highly respected member of one of the city's oldest families, a "proper Bostonian" in every sense. Suddenly, at the age of 60 (the time is prior to World War I), she becomes disgusted with the pretentiousness of the family into which she had married, and the hypocrisy of the society among which they moved as leaders *primus inter pares*— what Sinclair happily refers to as a "system of feudalism in frock-coats." Seizing the opportunity afforded by a family gathering, she steals away, leaving two notes: one for the family and one for publication. Adopting an assumed name and with next to no money, she takes a menial job at the Plymouth Cordage Company and a tiny room as a paying boarder at the home of a poor Italian immigrant family named Brini. There Brinis were the actual family with whom Bartolomeo Vanzetti boarded; Cornelia Thornwell, alias Mrs. Cornell, encounters him almost at once, and fiction and fact are joined.

The mixing of the two is not entirely successful, and perhaps could never be so. Sinclair is concerned about all with faithful, undistorted recounting of historical events. His fictional characters appear stereotyped at times. He forces them to act unnaturally—but these were times of all sorts of unnatural acts, and it is perhaps the very truth of this story that most tests the reader's power of belief.

The novel-as-tract interferes, of course, with the novel as art. And blazing anger is no handmaiden to creativity, or to anything, for that matter. The portrait of Cornelia is at best two-and-a-quarter-dimensional. And "Bart" Vanzetti is so Christ-like that one expects momentarily to be told of nail marks on his hands. The pomposity, greed, and other unpalatable attributes of some of the Thornwell family make them—at times—like caricatures from a morality play.

But for all this, the story is lively, well-told, and truthful. In view of the book's purpose, one is surprised by the paucity of its editorial comment; the commercial messages, as it were, are so thoroughly commingled with lively action that the whole is absorbed without strain. Sinclair's brilliantly acerbic style makes this book easy, even pleasant reading. (pp. 281-82)

Upton Sinclair was clearly a writer of grace, style and talent, as well as of angry protest. **Boston** cannot be assigned to the highest pinnacle of fictional art but that was hardly its author's intention. As a work of research it is extraordinary; as a narrative it is gripping. Howard Zinn, in his introduction, quotes the chairman of the 1928 Pulitzer Prize Committee as saying that this book would have received the prize were it not for its "socialistic tendencies" and "special pleadings."

The book on its first appearance earned high praise elsewhere, but did not sell very well, apparently. We might put this down to a natural human tendency not to enjoy being reminded of shameful episodes and to wish to turn to happier matters. Whatever the reason, we are now afforded a second chance to read this important work. (pp. 282-83)

> *James J. Storrow, Jr., "Social Realism Reissued," in* The Nation, *New York, Vol. 228, No. 9, March 10, 1979, pp. 281-83.*

L. S. Dembo

In *The Radical Novel in the United States* Walter Rideout defended the long, didactic conclusion of Upton Sinclair's *The Jungle* by maintaining that the turn of the hero, Jurgis Rudkus, to socialism was carefully prepared for: Sinclair conducted Jurgis "through all the circles of the workers' inferno" and attempted to "show that no other savior except socialism exists" [see excerpt above]. The point is worth elaborating for it is crucial to an understanding of what Sinclair achieved in *The Jungle* and what he failed to achieve in most of his other novels.

Now, without the specifically socialist conclusion, Jurgis' story would be that of a naturalist man in a naturalist world. His repeated insights into the harsh terms of life in Packertown are never in themselves enough to free him. He arrives in America, for instance, with a naive faith in the ways of the world and a pride in his own powers; in reaching the inevitably disastrous decision to buy a house, he reasons: "Others might have failed at it, but he was not the failing kind—he would show them how to do it. He would work all day, and all night, too, if need be; he would never rest until the house was paid for and his people had a home." He eventually gains an understanding of his situation: "He had learned the ways of things about him now. It was a war of each against all, and the devil take the hindmost. . . . You went about with your soul full of suspicion and hatred; you understood that you were environed by hostile powers that were trying to get your money and who used all the virtues to bait their traps with."

This disillusionment does not make a socialist out of Jurgis. Quite the contrary, he accepts the state of affairs around him as a permanent reality, a given to which he must adapt himself. It is the naturalist, not the socialist, who declares the world a hopeless jungle. Thus Jurgis, still confident in his powers, goes no farther than determining on personal survival and the protection of his immediate family. His encounter with unionism teaches him that he has "brothers in affliction, and allies. Their one chance for life was in union, and so the struggle became a kind of crusade." But this sentiment, embryonic to begin with, does

not withstand the despair that overtakes him as he lies convalescing from an injured ankle.

It is in the misery of his imprisonment for assaulting his wife's seducer, however, that the vision of the world as a jungle in which all that matters is personal survival overwhelms Jurgis. Sinclair makes it explicit that frustration and rage, not social consciousness, underlie Jurgis' "rebellion." . . . This response is as far as Jurgis can go; on the death of his son, the last member of his immediate family, he can feel only the same kind of rage: "There should be no more tears and no more tenderness; he had had enough of them—they had sold him into slavery! Now he was going to be free, to tear off his shackles, to rise up and fight . . . he was going to think of himself, he was going to fight for himself, against the world that had baffled him and tortured him!"

Thoroughly disillusioned but still unenlightened—trapped by ignorance as well as rage—Jurgis gains a temporary respite by fleeing to the countryside, but returns to a life of street crime and, when the opportunity presents itself, political corruption. Nor is he averse to strikebreaking, an activity that earns for him, for the first time in the novel, Sinclair's sarcasm.

Regarded from a socialist point of view, Jurgis is the very man who, because of his sufferings, can appreciate the truth once it is made known to him. His conversion is explained in the same oration that illuminates him:

> there will be some one man whom pain and suffering have made desperate. . . . And to him my words will come like a sudden flash of lightning to one who travels in darkness. . . . The scales will fall from his eyes, the shackles will be torn from his limbs—he will leap up with a cry of thankfulness, he will stride forth a free man at last! A man delivered from his self-created slavery! A man who will never more be trapped—whom no blandishments will cajole, whom no threats will frighten; who from to-night on will move forward, and not backward, who will study and understand, who will gird on his sword and take his place in the army of his comrades and brothers.

An important point is easily overlooked in the flow of the rhetoric: revelation is only the first step in a socialist education; it must be followed by hard study and experience. The conclusion of *The Jungle* is optimistic not simply because it envisions a socialist victory at the polls, but because it marks the socialization of a man who without the doctrine would be wholly lost.

Never committing himself to a specific social theory, Zola emphasizes the baffling multiplicity of socialist solutions and at the end of *Germinal* he sends his hero, Lantier, off to Paris still uncertain of the path he should follow. Nothing is clear but the grim possibility of anarchic and apocalyptic uprising—the one sure means of ushering in a new world. Committed to socialism, Sinclair is anxious to show the diversity in socialist thought only to indicate that, contrary to the stereotype, socialists have no "cut-and-dried program for the future of civilization." And he does go on to list the fundamental principles on which all socialists agree. For Zola, "heredity" was as crucial an influence on character as environment: that fact was expressed in the belief that there existed a jungle within as well as without. Sinclair believed there was no jungle within except that created by the jungle without, that there was a specific criterion for enlightenment, and that socially conscious men, using rational means, could bring about change.

Unfortunately, the men and women who Sinclair believed met these standards—his heroes and heroines—frequently turn out to be not proletarians or foreigners but upper-class Americans. The implications of this preference are startlingly evident even in *King Coal* (1917), an account of conditions in the unorganized coal industry that was intended to be another muckraking bombshell. The trouble with this novel is not that it insists on presenting socialist propaganda in the guise of literature; to the contrary, it is socialist merely by inference. Its real failure lies in its focussing upon the experiences of an upper-class hero (Hal Warner, a mine owner's son who decides to spend a summer, disguised, in a mining camp not owned by his father, and soon finds himself championing the miners' causes). As he was to do in many of his succeeding novels, Sinclair, though intent on exposing the oppression of the working class by an avaricious and tyrannical capitalism, chooses as his means of narration the romantic clichés of popular fiction. The education of Hal is so simplistically and obviously rendered that *King Coal* cannot be justified by one's calling it a *Bildungsroman*. Although it is probably that Sinclair felt he could better enlist the sympathies of the bourgeois reader by presenting the story as he did—and in 1917 he may indeed have been right—an account of the heroic adventures and the noble, self-sacrificing behavior of a clear-eyed, red-blooded, rich young American among a group of down-trodden, confused, often inarticulate, and impotent foreigners not only appeals to the worst kind of sentimentality but confirms more prejudices than it dispels.

"The book," comments Sinclair,

> gives a true picture of conditions and events. . . . Practically all the characters are real persons, and every incident which has social significance is not merely a true incident, but a typical one. The life portrayed in *King Coal* is the life that is lived today by hundreds of thousands of men, women and children in "this land of the free."

This description may be accurate enough from a journalistic point of view but only from that point of view. Unlike the characterization in *Germinal*, or even in *The Jungle*, for that matter, that in *King Coal* is superficial and stereotypical. We are presented with a "representative" old Slovak, an Italian anarchist, a fiery Irish maid with an alcoholic father, and others—all of whom emerge precisely in their typicality, just as do the municipal and mine officials and their police.

We see these characters mostly through the eyes of a twenty-year-old youth, who is sensitive but inexperienced and still limited by many of the prejudices of his class. . . .

> Here was a separate race of creatures, subterranean gnomes, pent up by a society for purposes of its own. . . . Coal would go to the ends of the earth, to places the miner never heard of, turning the wheels of industry whose products the miner would never see. It would make precious silks for fine ladies, it would cut precious jewels for their adornment, it would carry long trains of softly upholstered cars across deserts and mountains; it would

drive palatial steamships out of the wintry tempests into gleaming tropic seas. And the fine ladies in their precious silks and jewels would eat and sleep and laugh and lie at ease—and would know no more of the stunted creatures of the dark than the stunted creatures knew of them. Hal reflected upon this, and subdued his Anglo-Saxon pride, finding forgiveness for what was repulsive in these people—their barbarous jabbering speech, their vermin-ridden homes, their bare-bottomed babies.

The speciousness of this passage is apparent in almost every line. The mine-owner's son finds "forgiveness" for the people whose exploitation has made him the "superior" person he is! It is easy enough for him to deride the "fine ladies" on "palatial steamships," quite another for him to realize that he is no less implicated. All of Hal's fine heroics on behalf of the poor—including his imprisonment in his bid to become checkweighman (a representative of the miners who makes certain that each man is credited by the company with the proper weight of coal he has dug)—are, without this knowledge, little more than adolescent adventures.

What is more, this lack makes Hal's heroism dangerously misleading. Because he is "educated" and "American," he is chosen as a leader and spokesman, and we are led to believe that he alone, acting on his own initiative, has the consciousness and capability to take effective action. Even the organizer from the miners' union is relegated to a passive role. As for most of the miners, we learn, "it was impossible to work so hard and keep . . . mental alertness . . . eagerness . . . and sensitiveness." This may well be true, but the activities of a Hal Warner, disguised as Joe Smith, are, from any social perspective that goes beyond romantic sentimentalism, irrelevant.

Hal persuades his college classmate, Paul Harrigan, son of the owner of the mine in which he is working, to order the superintendent to expedite rescue operations after an explosion (the mine had been sealed to prevent further property damage) and eventually, on the advice of union representatives, convinces his fellow-workers not to go ahead with their planned strike. After these exploits, he decides to return to his normal life and to marry the spoiled girl to whom he had been engaged; even from the beginning he had spurned the love of the Irish working-class girl whom he now leaves, as he leaves all his summer working-class friends, "with more than a trace of moisture in his eyes."

Sinclair means all this quite seriously; throughout the entire novel Hal's idealism and nobility are contrasted with the insensitivity and avarice of his relatives, friends, and the institutions they control. But because it lacks the sophistication and insight to develop the full implications of class relations, the work fails in social vision. Because it creates a stereotyped hero and not a character who undergoes an authentic moral development, it fails as a novel and remains at best a piece of muckraking journalism, at worst a sentimental tale.

A decade after he published *King Coal*, Sinclair wrote an exposure of the oil industry (*Oil!*, 1927) and once again chose to tell the story of an upper-class boy, this time Bunny Ross, the son of an oil magnate, who is torn between a devotion to his father and to a working-class friend, Paul Watkins, who perpetually is victimized by and reveals the horrors of the capitalist system in America. Bunny lives a dual life: captivated by the romance of oil exploration and eventually involved with a movie star, he remains partly true to his class; still he engages in radical activities at the conservative college he attends and befriends and gives financial aid to a group of socialists. After his father dies, he gives himself over more fully to the radical cause by founding a labor college and offering marriage to a Jewish socialist girl.

Unlike *King Coal,* which centers upon the tyranny exercised over an isolated mining camp, *Oil!* is a sweeping novel that, covering Bunny's life from boyhood in the 1900's through his youth in the 1920's, includes as part of its background the First World War and the Allied invasion of Russia in 1919, as well as the election of Harding and the subsequent oil scandals. Sinclair also comments on religious superstition in capitalist America through the story of Paul Watkins' brother, Eli (modelled on Billy Sunday), "Prophet of the Third Revelation," who rises to wealth and power. As always, Sinclair can be effective in describing social injustice, but he is still heavy-handed and unconvincing in creating a hero.

Bunny, it is true, is portrayed as an ambivalent figure—and as such is neither an outright hero or villain. Sinclair is explicit about Bunny's deficiencies: his extreme dependence on his father, his inclination to "lean on others," and his general fecklessness. On the other hand, he supposedly possesses the same "nobility" as Hal Warner in *King Coal;* he is depicted as being one of the rare men of compassion of his class and this quality is meant to redeem him. But unlike George Orwell, for example, Sinclair is interested in declassment not as a psychological, social, and ethical phenomenon but rather as a device for revealing the manners and conduct of the two classes through sensitive eyes. Bunny is chiefly an observer and sympathizer. Although he undergoes something of a socialist education, he is never made to experience the hardships of an oil worker. And like Hal, even when participating in radical activities, he holds the trump card of his identity as the son of a member of the ruling class; although occasionally baited by the press, he is never really brutalized.

That Sinclair is himself aware of these weaknesses in the position of his upper-class heroes is evident in *Boston* (1928), at once an account of the Sacco-Vanzetti case and a novel about the social and moral education of a Brahmin women, Cornelia Thornwell, who, upon the death of her wealthy and powerful husband, renounces her family (and all it stands for) and attempts to transform herself into a working-class woman. This so-called runaway grandmother does, in fact, undergo all the hardships that an unskilled worker in a New England cordage factory in 1917 would, but it is still not enough, as she learns in an argument with a French socialist:

> "Understand me, Comrade Thornwell, it is good of rich and cultured ladies to take an interest in the exploited workers; but you suffer always from the fact that you can't possibly realize how they actually feel."

> "Don't forget, Comrade Leon, I worked for a year and a half in a cordage plant, and lived on the wages."

> "I know. . . . and I never heard anything like it.

> But all the same, if you will pardon me, it wasn't practically real, because if you had been ill or out of a job, you'd have gone back to your family; it wasn't psychologically real, because you always knew you could, and you had the moral support of knowing you were a lady. No worker has that. . . ."

This revelation does not prevent Cornelia from committing herself to a socialist view of the world, nor does it in any way detract from Sinclair's obvious admiration for his heroine and her real-life models. What helps make her a sympathetic figure, not only to Sinclair but, insofar as she is credible at all, to his readers, is precisely what is lacking or at least unemphasized in the other heroes: a strength of character that perhaps goes deeper than politics or doctrine, and manifests itself in her desire to see and act upon the truth as it reveals itself, a quality that goes against the grain of her entire Brahmin upbringing in which decorum, maintained by repression and hypocrisy, is the chief value in social conduct, especially among women. Her education through the long ordeal that begins with her flight and culminates in the execution of Sacco and Vanzetti is intended to be that of the reader as well. *Boston* is Sinclair's *Vérité,* Sacco and Vanzetti, his Dreyfus. Like Zola, he argues for "objectivity" and historical accuracy in the reconstruction of the circumstances. "An honest effort," he tells us, "has here been made to portray a complex community exactly as it is. The story has no hero but the truth." (pp. 164-71)

[For all Sinclair's prodigious research, however, *Boston*] is impelled not by detachment but moral outrage. One can concede, I suppose, that Sinclair does explore certain morally ambiguous areas—as, for example, the dilemma into which Lee Swenson, the experienced, tough, radical lawyer, leads Cornelia when he informs her that she (and she alone) has the power to destroy the prosecution's case against Sacco and Vanzetti if she'll commit perjury; the implications and ramifications of this problem occupy Sinclair for several pages. Nonetheless, we neither expect nor find any sympathy whatsoever for those who have brought Sacco and Vanzetti to trial (the "rulers" of the Commonwealth of Massachusetts) or any hostility toward those who would defend them. By a "complex community," then, Sinclair in no way means one toward which, or in which, moral neutrality can have any place. What he does mean is a society divided into the oppressors and their henchmen and the oppressed; the former contains frequently antagonistic groups, such as the Back Bay aristocracy and the wealthy and politically potent Irish, but their commercial, legal, political, and social interactions are reducible to the common motives of avarice and lust for power. The latter are the poor, chiefly Italian, who are invariably portrayed in a favorable light; they are not Zola's Parisian poor (*L'Assommoir*) or his land-hungry peasants (*La Terre*). Whereas in Zola, family life on all social levels is dominated by envy and greed and therefore is in a state of disintegration, in Sinclair, Italian family life stands in ideal contrast to that of the Brahmins. Tolerance, generosity, kindness—an openness to life—characterize the relationships of the Brinis, with whom, as a boarder, Cornelia finds more than adequate compensation for the hardships she must endure as the laborer.

If Sinclair has presented an oversimplified image of the Italian family, it is not necessarily out of sentimentality that he has done so. Such an image logically underscores the view that, along with self-interest, an almost psychopathic paranoia marked the "American" attitude toward the Italians, all of whom it held to be potential bomb-throwing anarchists. Accordingly, Bartolomeo Vanzetti, whom Sinclair describes as a man of words rather than action, emerges as the perfect Italian hero, a saintly man incapable of taking any life, to say nothing of gunning down the paymaster of a shoe factory.

What is ironic in all this is that the socialist view of the anarchists—that is, the one expressed by Pierre Leon in his argument with Cornelia—actually justifies the anxieties of the capitalists who wish to jail, deport, or execute the "whole lot of them." . . . That Vanzetti as a dedicated anarchist could have committed the crime with which he has been charged is a possibility that Cornelia cannot accept—nor, in a sense, can Sinclair himself, since the effectiveness of his attack on the Commonwealth—the capitalist state—depends on Vanzetti's innocence, not only as a bandit but as a bomber. Equally important is that such innocence—carrying with it an inability to act—reaffirms the notion, ubiquitous in Sinclair's work, that the oppressed cannot save themselves—that somehow their salvation, if attainable at all, requires the appearance of enlightened American aristocrats who renounce or rebel against their class.

The wealthy, clean-cut American, sympathetic to the socialist cause but accustomed to privilege and material comfort, was to remain Sinclair's favorite hero to the end. Not only does he reappear in the simple propaganda piece about the Spanish Civil War, **No Pasaran,** but he is elaborated throughout the eleven-volume Lanny Budd series, Sinclair's epic and chronicle of the period 1913-1949. Written between 1940 and 1953, these novels can scarcely be called proletarian literature since they deal mostly with the haute bourgeoisie, the aristocracy, high government officials and leaders and with the diplomatic and political history of the West. Fascism, Nazism, and finally world communism emerge as the central evils; capitalism is attacked for generating these forms of tyranny or, at least, making it possible for them to flourish. Except for one episode concerning the slums of pre-World War I London, there is no attempt to delineate consistently the conditions that inspired the muckraking novels.

From the start Sinclair's reviewers were sensitive to the aesthetic weaknesses of the series. Pedantry, sentimentality, and an irritating facetiousness permeate the entire work. Wholly unaffected by the stylistic innovations of the twentieth century, Sinclair writes in what is often the worst rhetoric of another age. His treatment of personal relations, including Lanny's pallid romances, is superficial and contrived and the dialogue of his characters often banal and awkward. He is repetitious to the point of distraction, not only in his recitation of facts or his use of epithets for his characters, but in the plotting itself. (Lanny's adventures fall into basic types that appear cyclically: the interviews with political leaders, the rescue of prisoners or victims of the fascists, the participation in seances, art agent dealings, dealings with socialists. The many visits to Hitler or Roosevelt are identical in form, if not in actual subjects discussed, as are the other adventures within their categories.) Yet all these weaknesses conceded, there is no denying that Sinclair does have a genius for recreating historical events and portraying a seemingly endless variety of actual public figures. These portraits are not the ironic or idealized sketches that one finds in Dos Passos but convincing if limited life studies. In addition to Hitler and Roosevelt, Lanny Budd, playboy, art agent, and presidential spy, has protracted or numerous dealings with most of the major and many minor Nazi officials, Harry Hopkins, Hearst, Truman, Churchill, Laval, Petain; he has illuminating encounters with hundreds of others, including English, French, German, Italian, and Spanish aristocrats, industrialists, generals, scientists, and politicians. This plethora and scope led one reviewer to argue that Lanny was "an all-seeing eye, not a dramatic hero." From the viewpoint of technique Lanny is perhaps a device, but that does not mean we can avoid judging his character or considering his development as a socialist sympathizer and its actual significance.

The illegitimate son of Robbie Budd, an American munitions maker, and his first love, Mabel Blackless (called Beauty), whose marriage had been prevented by the Budd family, Lanny is born and raised on the Riviera by his socialite mother. He comes under the sway of his father, who visits him often and exposes him to his Darwinian views of society in the hope that Lanny will eventually take his place in the family business. Thus, justifying his trade, Robbie plants the seeds of a capitalist philosophy: " 'Men hate each other. . . . They insist upon fighting, and there's nothing you can do about it, except learn to defend yourself. No nation would survive for a year unless it kept itself in readiness to repel attacks from greedy and jealous rivals . . . ' " He sees the First World War as a "war of profits," in which the steel men were "selling to both sides, and getting the whole world into their debt" and international industrialists in general "had taken charge of the war so far as their own properties were concerned."

But Lanny finally is convinced no more by his father's conclusions than by those of his uncle, Jesse Blackless, the spokesman for violent world revolution. . . . Repudiating them both, Lanny sees himself at the age of eighteen, after his experiences at the peace conference, as "the man who loved art and beauty, reason and fair play, and pleaded for these things and got brushed aside. It wasn't his world! It had no use for him! When the fighting started, he'd be caught between the lines and mowed down." (pp. 171-74)

Content to roll through life "in a well-cushioned limousine," Lanny is confronted in the years 1933-1937 with the accession to power of the Nazis and the advent of the war in Spain. Through his boyhood friend, Kurt Meissner, pianist, composer, Prussian aristocrat, and Beauty Budd's former lover, he had come to know and love pre-Hitler Germany; he is fluent in the language and seems to be as much at home in upper-class German society as he is in French and English. In aiding another long-time friend, the Jewish speculator Johannes Robin, one of whose sons has married Lanny's step-sister, to escape, Lanny is given a direct insight into the realities of the new regime, and the fate of another son, Freddi, only increases Lanny's horror.

His commitment now takes the form of financial aid to a Socialist underground, whose representative, Trudi Schultz, a dedicated young Socialist and art student, Lanny makes several trips to Berlin to meet. Irma, who has grown less and less tolerant of his leftist activities, unsuspectingly accompanies him on one of his trips, and though she consents, in an emergency, to help smuggle Trudi, threatened by the Gestapo, out of the country, she has had enough. Characteristic of Lanny's double life is that part of the escape plan includes a prearranged visit to Hitler at Berchtesgaden, and here Irma's voluntary declaration of her admiration for the Nazis precipitates Lanny's final decision to divorce her.

What is thematically important in all this is that it signals the first real moral crisis in Lanny's life, and this crisis is accentuated when it becomes apparent that not only Irma, but most of Lanny's friends and acquaintances—the aristocracy and the ruling classes of western Europe, along with powerful groups in the United States, see in fascism and Nazism only a bulwark against the "Bolshevik menace." In *Wide Is the Gate* (vol. 4) ("Wide is the gate, and broad is the way, that leads to destruction") this thesis is dramatized repeatedly and offered as the basic reason that the Nazis were unchecked in the thirties. Whether talking to French industrialists, Spanish landowners, or highborn persons in the British Foreign Service, Lanny, when he is later gathering political information, knows just what politics will ingratiate him most quickly. But when he is sincere, as he must be with his father, now building aircraft, when after his experiences in Spain he comes to argue for a pursuit plane for the loyalist government, he finds himself in a hopeless deadlock with his own family. Robbie's intransigence, his bitter opposition to the Republican forces is a graphic enough demonstration of the chasm that has opened between Lanny and his class.

Whatever the depth of his commitment, Lanny, as it turns out, finds himself in a position that requires his continued existence as one of the privileged. As a "presidential agent," charged by Roosevelt with learning the intentions of the rich and powerful of Europe, he poses as a Nazi sympathizer pursuing his trade as an art agent. . . . [His primary] connection with the movement is through his continued relationship with Trudi Schultz, who refuses to give up hope that her husband, though captured by the Gestapo, is still alive, and, from Paris, slavishly devotes herself to composing anti-Nazi propaganda to be smuggled to German workers. Lanny, after a less than romantic courtship, marries her, admires her, and, when she is kidnapped by Gestapo agents in France, moves heaven and earth to locate and rescue her, until he is given confirmation of her death in Dachau.

With the exception of Rick (Eric Pomeroy-Nielson), another boyhood friend, who was crippled while flying for the R. A. F. during World War I and has become a liberal journalist and playwright, there are few members of the aristocracy with whom Lanny can express his real feelings. As he is to reflect after the Nazis are defeated. "He had been living in the enemy's country, not merely physically but ideologically; he had been living capitalism and luxury, while cherishing democracy as a secret dream." The fact remains, however, that despite some mental anguish and the personal risks involved in espionage, Lanny is never called upon to make any real sacrifices, never suffers unduly, and never abandons the habits, instincts, and outlook of the man of privilege. He tells Trudi that the force of property is "so overwhelming that only a small fraction of mankind has any chance of resisting it. I am

not sure if I myself am among this number; I feel myself struggling in a net, and just when I think I am out of it I discover that another fold has been cast over my head and I am as helplessly entangled as ever." This is a genuine insight, but its implications are not pursued. To Sinclair, Lanny is a wholly creditable hero whose essential high-mindedness is seriously presented: "No, he was not a Socialist, he didn't know enough to say what he was, but he knew human decency when he met it, and he had learned what it was for a modern state to be seized by gangsters and used by them to pervert the mind and moral sense of mankind." Lanny always speaks for "human decency," for the sound mind and moral sense of mankind. Thus, even though Sinclair has created a dichotomous position for his character, one that invites further inquiry into his motives and behavior, the subtleties involved have no part in Sinclair's design.

For example, it is of no thematic consequence that Lanny is a man who lives to ingratiate himself with others and that deception and manipulation are second-nature to him; that he is sanctimonious, condescending, and passionless; that his charm, his "famous smile," his ready wad of cash, his inside knowledge, his possession of credentials with intimidating signatures are his chief means of getting along in the world. Perhaps affected most by Trudi's kidnapping, and then not because he loved her but because he felt guilty for not having loved her enough (again the Moral Hero), he emerges physically and emotionally unaltered from every perilous adventure he has had, including torture by the Russians after the war. It is true he has risked much in helping relatives, friends, and allies escape from Germany, but he is wholly capable of turning down an appeal by strangers without much more than apt reflection on the sadness of the situation and perhaps a "tear in his eye."

The lack of psychological dimension in Lanny's character is no mere technical failing; it is a reflection of Sinclair's view of the world, which to its core is rationalistic and moralistic. . . . "Think more clearly, and so to organize and cooperate," "sufficient intelligence to persuade others"—these ideals are clearly the inspiration for the kind of liberal socialism that Sinclair espouses. They assume a simple human psychology and ethos in which reason and passion, intelligence and stupidity, are easily distinguishable from one another, as are good and evil, and they are founded on the hope that men can change themselves and the world by rational decision. (pp. 175-77)

Although, whatever its relation to capitalism, fascism presented its own forms of oppression and required a shift in perspective, it made a Manichean view even more credible. With the emergence of the Nazis, dragons appeared on the earth and dragon-slayers would have to be called upon to eradicate them:

> It was Lanny's fond dream that the whole people were wiser than any self-appointed leaders; that if they could once get power and keep it, they and the products of their toil would no longer be at the mercy of evil creatures spewed up from the cesspools of society. So long as such existed, so long as they could seize the wealth of great nations and turn them to fanaticism and aggression, they had to be fought . . .

Elsewhere, Lanny reasons, "It was really not the German

people who were perpetrating (the atrocities of Nazism), but a band of fanatics who had seized a nation and were perverting its youth and turning them into murderers and psychopaths. Germans would awaken someday as from a nightmare and contemplate with loathing and dismay the crimes that had been committed in their name." In this view, "evil" is not in the normal order of things and certainly not within oneself; it cannot belong to a whole people but only to the fanatics among them or to specific "creatures" who can be so designated. Wholly "other," it can be isolated and fought by the forces of reason and the men of "human decency."

These sentiments are perhaps more adequate as a call to action than as an explanation of the Nazi phenomenon. They are, in fact, too simplistic even for Sinclair's own portrayals of Nazi officials. In his dealings with these figures Lanny is so often caught up with them as personalities, that he must remind himself that they are perpetrators of atrocity. They come from all walks of life, represent a variety of temperaments, and more often than not are "typical" Germans. Ironically, one of the most fanatical of them is Lanny's old friend, Kurt Meissner.

The defeat of the Nazis did not, of course, satisfy Sinclair's moral sense; after bringing the series to a conclusion with *O Shepherd, Speak* (vol. 10) in 1949, he added a new volume in 1953, *The Return of Lanny Budd,* a work permeated with the attitudes of the Cold War. The Shepherd to whom Sinclair is referring is Roosevelt, whom Lanny has adulated and whose death he sees as leaving the world without strong moral leadership.

Having for over a decade regarded the idea of "the Bolshevik Peril" as a Nazi-propagated illusion, Lanny, after a flirtation with pacifism, now embraces it as a religious truth. The moral conflict that engages him is not between socialism and capitalism but between democratic socialism and revolutionary socialism, which Sinclair translates into a holy war between democracy and tyranny. Thus, explaining his view of the world situation to Truman, Lanny begins with what appears to be a straightforward socialist critique (Truman has asked what the U. S. has done to alienate the Soviet Union):

> "What we have done . . . is to be a bourgeois nation, the biggest and richest in the world. Our affairs are run by immensely wealthy capitalists who choose dummy legislators and tell them what to do. The capitalists are automatically driven by the forces of an expanding economy to reach out to every corner of the earth for raw materials and markets. We take these by purchase where possible, but where we encounter resistance we are ready to use force. By this means we reduce all colonial peoples to the status of peons and we keep them there." . . .

After more of this palaver in which Lanny draws a picture of hate-filled hordes using every possible means to bring about the destruction of the United States, Truman concludes that the country will have to rearm, but that having a large army will not be incompatible with social progress. Lanny goes away happy.

That the ideal of social progress per se is uppermost neither in Sinclair's mind nor his hero's at this time becomes all the more obvious when it is expressed by another sympathetic character, Professor Charles T. Alston, New

Dealer, foreign policy expert, and general insider. Speaking on the radio program sponsored by Lanny and Laurel's "Peace Foundation"—now sounding the alert on World Communism—he argues, "The only possible chance of defeating Communist dictatorship is by setting up industrial democracy by constitutional methods in which our political freedoms would be retained. That is one way we can gain and keep the support of the masses and bring the Red dictatorships to defeat."

Lanny's half sister, Bessie, always strong in her views, becomes in this volume one of the Communist "fanatics" against whom Lanny supposedly scores point after point in bitter debates (though she is too far gone to realize it), whom he sorrowfully denounces to the FBI as an espionage suspect, and whose long-suffering husband, Hansi, he not only sets free but provides with a more suitable mate. In his arguments with Bessie, Lanny seems never really to answer her charges but rather presents countercharges about Communist methods that are meant to be unanswerable. He has, in short, ceased being merely a bore and has himself become a zealot whose anti-Communist preaching fills several hundred pages. The conclusion of the Lanny Budd series in a grand peroration brings Sinclair's career full circle, a story of the triumph of moral ardor over the art of fiction. (pp. 178-80)

> *L. S. Dembo, "The Socialist and the Socialite Heroes of Upton Sinclair," in* Toward a New American Literary History: Essays in Honor of Arlin Turner, *Louis J. Budd, Edwin H. Cady, Carl L. Anderson, eds., Duke University Press, 1980, pp. 164-80.*

Christopher P. Wilson

As a rebel, lover of life, and devoted literary professional, Sinclair bore a striking resemblance to London, an author he admired, emulated, and eventually befriended. Of course, there were the obvious similarities of literary approach and style. Both men were intellectual Darwinists, popular naturalists, and internationally renowned socialists. Sinclair, in fact, remembered being thrilled by the discovery of London's *People of the Abyss* (1903) and its example of literary celebrity, and London—along with David Graham Phillips and Lincoln Steffens—soon became one of Sinclair's earliest supporters. Even more strikingly, there were similarities in how the two men first approached their vocation. Both had been driven to the literary life by an abiding fear of poverty. Raised mainly in a world where it was (as he later said) cheaper to move than pay rent, surrounded by bedbugs, street danger, and personal degradation, Sinclair had first tried to escape by devoting himself to reading. By adolescence, reading had become compulsive for him, as it had for London: "I read while I was eating, lying down, sitting, standing, and walking; I read everywhere I went—and I went nowhere except to the park to read on sunshiny days." Like London, Sinclair also employed the bootstrap of college—and had more success at it—and even went on to graduate work at Columbia; also like London, he found the college curriculum too slow for his omnivorous ambition and energies. Such similarities in social background, finally, interlocked with a remarkable likeness in temperament. Like London, Sinclair was prone to fits of enthusiasm and despondency, was an activist and yet a maverick, a compulsive workaholic who mastered the marketplace and yet also repeatedly muckraked it. Sinclair's literary output was equally remarkable. In a nineteen-year span, London would produce a half-hundred books, many articles, and a sizable correspondence; in the same period, Sinclair would write over a million words worth of dime novels, twenty-four books, and perhaps more articles—all only the start of a sixty-year career. Yet even more than Jack London, Sinclair seemed to epitomize the new political power bestowed upon authorship by the new marketplace. In 1906, with the hardcover publication of *The Jungle,* suddenly the modern author—and notably, a socialist one—commanded an unprecedented amount of American attention. More than any of his contemporaries, Sinclair seemed to turn ideas to praxis, to put the word at the service of politics. Moreover, his career exposed the paradoxical uses to which the new language of the marketplace could be put: he became a lifelong advocate of the workingman by mastering the skills of the modern cultural entrepreneur.

And yet, this new power was riddled with compromises and veiled ironies. At the very moment the marketplace vaulted American authors to the political platform, their own appearance signaled a change in politics itself: away from the partisan "armies" of the nineteenth century and into the managed media politics of the twentieth. Needless to say, the Progressive era is a far cry from our world of televised debates, packaged candidates, and pseudo-events in which literary celebrities mingle with political life—and where, in extreme cases, they even run for high office. But the early 1900s were in fact the years in which these possibilities, and their contradictions, were first entertained in the new limelight created by the advent of mass print media. We might momentarily consider that Jack London, once an anonymous street figure, ran twice for mayor of Oakland—and that, a few decades hence, Sinclair himself would become the first (alas, not the last) celebrity to run for the governorship of California. (pp. 114-15)

Although *The Jungle* is by now a fixture in the historiography of American Progressivism, its position has always been somewhat paradoxical. Literary critics commonly discredit the novel's formal characteristics—usually attributing its failings to Sinclair's political ideology—while historians usually credit external events, especially the political context, for the novel's popularity. In either argument, the novel comes out a loser—as it were, a kind of bridesmaid who gets neither the groom nor the bouquet. Yet neither attack, it might be pointed out, accounts sufficiently for the obviously dramatic response the book generated in its readers—nor, as well, why that reading might have led to misinterpretation. Alternatively, by viewing this book from a vocational standpoint—as an expression of Sinclair's synthesis of poet and dime novelist—we may recover a better sense of why the book had such a paradoxical impact. As with Jack London, we can trace the impact of Sinclair's vocational strategy within his style.

Sinclair himself seems to have conceived his book as a mix of popular media and political discourse, and frequently compared it to Harriet Beecher Stowe's *Uncle Tom's Cabin.* For instance, in his fourth novel, *Manassas,* the story of a Southerner turned antislavery advocate, Sinclair praises *Uncle Tom's Cabin,* calling it one of those books "which make their way into the world of literature from below, and are classics before the *literati* have discovered them." As if anticipating his own critics, he goes on to say:

> In truth, its literary faults are evident enough, its skeleton sticks through its very joints, but he who can read a hundred pages of it for the first or the twentieth time, with dry eyes, is not an enviable person. It was, when it appeared, and it has remained to this day, the most unquestionable piece of inspiration in American fiction.

(The breathlessness of dictation is visible even here.) In a typed outline that he gave to George Brett in 1904, Sinclair described his own plan as "to set forth the breaking of human hearts by a system which exploits the labor of men and women for profits," yet also to make "a definite attempt to write something popular." Later he said he had wanted to "portray how modern industrial conditions . . . were driving the workingman into socialism" and to make the book "as authoritative as if it were a statistical compilation."

Despite this naturalistic-sounding rhetoric, the more significant element in Sinclair's praise of Stowe was his highlighting of the grammar of self-projection practiced in both his poet and his cadet novels. In *Manassas* he wrote that the power of Stowe's depiction derived from her own sense of oppression as wife and mother. "Probably nowhere in the literature of all the world," Sinclair wrote with characteristic hyperbole, "is there a book more packed and charged with the agony and heartbreak of *woman.*" Describing his hero's reaction to the novel, he said it "is a mother's book, every line seemed to bring [his Southern protagonist] face to face with the very mother-soul. . . . a mother's passionate tenderness, a mother's frantic claspingness, a mother's terror at *destruction,* at cruelty and wounds and death." In sum, Sinclair now consciously believed that projection was not only a feasible technique but also a major source of literary power. (pp. 128-29)

[In preparation for *Manassas,* Sinclair] traveled north to Boston to interview abolitionists and their descendants, and spent months rummaging through Princeton's Civil War collection. This historical emphasis, in turn, had both tempered the narcissism of his earlier works and expanded the imaginative playground by giving it a larger and more topical canvas. Sinclair's surrogate in the novel, Allan Montague, acts out his personal conversion to abolitionist sympathy among figures like Abraham Lincoln and Frederick Douglass. The author's original plan for *The Jungle* was much the same: initially, Sinclair conceived it as the story of a well-born young man who "sinks" into the proletariat. Returning to the rhetoric of his dime novels, he formulated a style of activism first by exploring it imaginatively.

This pattern, however, subtly changed during the preparation of *The Jungle.* He arrived in Chicago in September of 1904; in fact, he later made a point of the fact that he arrived on his birthday, as if the date presaged another tale of conversion. How long he had planned to stay is unknown, but he wasted little time in settling in. Almost immediately, he arranged to take his meals at the University Settlement House (thereby spending much of his time with the reformer Jane Addams). On his very first night in the yards, he sat in the kitchen of a Lithuanian cattle butcher who had spent twenty-five years in Packingtown. This conversation apparently established Sinclair's decision to focus in on the Lithuanian community—an interesting decision since, as the novel explains, at the time these were the immigrants being displaced by the newer Slovak work force. Later, near the end of his seven-week stay, Sinclair witnessed a wedding celebration or *veselija*— and there found the family for his novel, as well as the setting for its famous first chapter. . . . [However], Sinclair did not put pen to paper immediately; he kept some notebooks, but again composed mostly in his head. Speaking of his younger self in the third person, he later wrote: "From four o'clock until nearly midnight he sat, making note of every detail and composing in his mind the opening chapter. . . . By ten years of practice he had learned to go over a scene and fix it verbatim in his mind. This opening chapter was not put on paper until the following Christmas, but it varied little from the mentally recorded vision." The actual text was written when he returned to his home-built cabin in Princeton.

During his Packingtown stay, Sinclair discovered that he could travel freely in the yards, much as he had at the military academies. The difference, however, was that now he had to wear old clothes and disguise himself by carrying a workingman's dinner pail. Sadly, as a poor and struggling author, he had worn old clothes because they were all he possessed. Apparently, what began to happen was that once again while composing, Sinclair began to parallel his own situation with that of his subject—here, that of the workingman. Consequently, when Sinclair returned to write in Princeton—burdened down with personal problems that included a declining marriage and meager income—he followed the dime-novel pattern and self-consciously projected himself into the novel. In fact, in describing the book's composition only months after its release, he made reference to the method, citing the pressures put upon his own youthful "delicate sensibilities" by the "commercial inferno" and "pit" of poverty. Looking back on the writing of the book, he said: "For three months I wrote incessantly; I wrote with tears and anguish, pouring into the pages all the pain that life had meant to me. Externally, the story had to do with a family of stockyard workers, but internally it was the story of my own family." This was the flip side of the term "proletarian author": Sinclair not only wrote about laborers, but now thought of himself as a brain worker. Even the speech of the socialist at the end of the book—which critics unanimously decry as needlessly tacked on—is actually a lecture Sinclair himself, once a college orator, gave at the end of his stay in Chicago. (In the 1914 film version of the novel, he played the role himself.)

Moreover, as if adopting Stowe's reputed method, Sinclair said that his identification with Jurgis's family was the source of the book's power. He called *The Jungle* an attempt to "put the content of Shelley into the form of Zola"—which might have been a synopsis of his own vocation. He said the "middle-class realists" worked with "infinite skill" and were "expert psychologists; but it is not part of their programme to live the life which they portray, and they do not feel obliged to share in the emotions of their characters. They do their work from the outside, and they resemble a doctor who is too much absorbed in the study of the case to sympathize with the patient's desire

to escape from his agony." Thus, Sinclair's emphasis on "heart" meant putting his own on the line.

Sinclair's sublimation of personal and poetic desire into his exploration of the American workingman created moments of brilliance as well as lapses. In its dramatic force, execution, and empathy, *The Jungle* was clearly Sinclair's finest work so far in his career. Even as he laid claim to realistic subject matter, his prose retained the heightened tones of his earlier allegories. The commonplace socialist division of capitalist society into two classes with "an unbridged chasm between them" neatly fit the dramatic polarity of his Nibelung parables. The allegorical motive, admittedly, created moments that may strike modern readers as artificial: Jurgis seems, at points, something of an Everyman in a nightmare, encountering an unrelieved stream of tragedies that were historically possible but perhaps not entirely credible as a narrative depiction of a single individual. On the other hand, Sinclair's poetic sensibility allowed him to capture the melancholy of an immigrant worker's wedding which only straps the newlyweds financially, to depict the anguish of encroaching destitution, to demonstrate the limbo of the tramp—in short, to vivify the lived experience of oppression. Dissecting the Behemoth with an unflinching gaze, Sinclair spoke openly in the narrative about having discovered sights and "words . . . not admitted into the vocabulary of poets"; but the hard-boiled exterior of "facts" is underwritten by that neo-Romantic concern for the soul. Capitalism is exposed as a system both of exploitation and of corruption: society as a whole is debased, degraded, infested. "I have known what it is to dare and aspire," the speaker at the socialist rally cries, "to dream mighty dreams and to see them perish—to see all the fair flowers of my spirit trampled into the mire by the wild beast powers of life."

Sinclair's mode of projection and preparation, however, did not always have positive consequences. First of all, many critics—including contemporary reviewers— complain that Sinclair's socialist politics led him to polemicize almost at will. But to be precise, Sinclair's digressive style, more an opening for polemical ideas than their by-product, was well in place before his conversion to socialism. More than anything else, the episodic character of the novel reflects Sinclair's vocational apprenticeship: specifically, the fact that the text is a relatively unreworked version of Sinclair's preparation—his visit to Packingtown. Robert Cantwell once said, and I think correctly, that Sinclair's plots are a little like land-grant railroads—they meander around, trying to encompass the social whole. But this is only because of his anticipatory strategy: he tended to reconstruct his novels after a preparatory visit, compose on the spot, and write later. In the text, however, it is apparent that Sinclair, reflecting the planned quality of his book, is often jumping the gun on his research. As if he is still holding in his head those on-the-spot compositions, in all too many instances we leap ahead of the narrative to a broader thesis. This is because Sinclair's dictation method opened him up not only to rhetorical flourishes but also to expounding in ways that fragment his narrative. For instance, he writes:

> They were common enough, [Tamoszius] said, such cases of petty graft. It was simply some boss who proposed to add a little to his income. After Jurgis had been there awhile he would know that the plants were simply honeycombed with rotten-

ness of that sort. . . . Warming to the subject, Tamoszius went on to explain the situation.

> Jurgis would find out these things for himself, if he stayed there long enough; it was the men who had to do all the dirty jobs, and so there was no deceiving them . . . he would soon find out his error—for nobody rose in Packingtown by doing good work. . . .

Here it is as if Sinclair's dictation method has led him not only to digress but to telegraph the punch of his narrative. Time is practically suspended in these passages—at worst, we lose the narrative frame altogether. Nor are we sure whose wisdom we are hearing: Sinclair's, Tamoszius's, or Jurgis's own. Sinclair rushes to his case repeatedly, and the sum effect is that the flow of the narrative is recurrently interrupted. Here we feel a tangible consequence of the market's premium on anticipation.

Of course, this might seem mere sloppiness on Sinclair's part—and some of it was. In several places it seems that we are simply rehashing Sinclair's own initial reactions to industrial life upon coming to Packingtown. Even this effect, moreover, was fundamentally a by-product of his projection technique. Sinclair's conscious decision to graft his own visit onto the Lithuanians' initiation, in other words, also had direct textual consequences. In fact, within the novel Sinclair draws an explicit parallel between the introduction of the Rudkis family to Packingtown and the initiation of an unnamed "visitor" referred to by the narrator. However, this tactic automatically gives the text a rather elliptical quality, derived from two different narrative positions: one of empathy, and yet one—not surprisingly—like an excursion. For instance, we encounter passages like the following:

> Those [streets] through which Jurgis and Ona were walking resembled streets less than they did a miniature topographical map. . . . In these pools the children played, and rolled about in the mud. . . . One wondered about this, as also about the swarms of flies which hung about the scene, literally blackening the air, and the strange, fetid odor which assailed one's nostrils, a ghastly odor. . . . It impelled the visitor to questions. . . . Was it not unhealthful? the stranger would ask, and the residents would answer, "Perhaps; but there is no telling."

> One stood and watched, and little by little caught the drift of the tide, as it set in the direction of the packing houses. . . . Our friends were not poetical, and the sight suggested to them no metaphors of human destiny; they thought only of the wonderful efficiency of it all. . . .

Valiant as the attempt may be, this "visitor" undercuts Sinclair's goal of empathy. As a literary vestige both of the originally conceived well-bred youth and of Sinclair himself, the visitor is an intelligence who is affected by Packingtown (smells, cattle slaughter, billboards) in a way we cannot be sure Jurgis and his co-workers are. Sinclair hoped to make his own initiation contiguous with Jurgis's, but in fact the visitor is either too far ahead of his subjects ideologically or too far behind them experientially. His projection never fully integrates into workers' emotive lives; despite Sinclair's professed intentions, this is not a novel written entirely from the "inside."

Furthermore, these passages about the visitor resonate

with the dominant imagery of the novel, having the cumulative effect of reaffirming the lines of kinship between visitor and narrator. Inevitably, then, the novel's primary case is shifted to the visitor's perspective, not the workers'. One can be easily misled by the narrative camouflage which insists, consistent with Sinclair's vocational mythology, that "poetic" consciousness has been eliminated by his own rite of passage. But in fact, as the presence of the visitor attests, the text is riddled with metaphorical and analogical passages and sequences. The visitor's poetic consciousness dominates the balance of the narrative's expository images: "flowers" trod under the feet of capital, cattle prepared for slaughter, souls denied their spiritual "blossoming." The end result is inconsistency. For instance, in the opening depiction of the marriage *veselija*, Sinclair's visitor is absent, as the scene foreshadows the plot by attending to the changing music of the wedding celebration. The Lithuanian musicians play frenetically, answering the desperate please of the older immigrants; but soon the older tunes are shouldered out by a crass, exploitative American ragtime. The ominous mood this particular movement generates is quite effective, because here Sinclair's empathy is truly remarkable: it is one pure scene where he witnessed well. But quite a different thing occurs when the visitor reappears to compare, in his own mind, the fate of slaughtered cattle to that of the workers:

> One could not stand and watch very long without becoming philosophical, without beginning to deal in symbols and similes, and to hear the hog-squeal of the universe. . . . Each one of these hogs was a separate creature. . . . And each of them had an individuality of his own, a will of his own, a hope and a heart's desire; each was full of self-confidence, of self-importance, and a sense of dignity. And trusting and strong in faith he had gone about his business, the while a black shadow hung over him and a horrid Fate waited in his pathway. . . . Perhaps some glimpse of all this was in the thoughts of our humble-minded Jurgis, as he turned to go on with the rest of the party, and muttered: "*Dieve*— but I'm glad I'm not a hog!"

Not only is this a form of telegraphing; more important, it is in passages like these that the competing consciousnesses of the novel fail to mesh. Although elsewhere (as cited earlier) Sinclair admits that Jurgis and his cohorts are not likely to wax philosophically, here he hopes that they do.

The splintering of the text, moreover, is partly why the conclusion of the novel seems literally forced. Many critics have rightly emphasized the parablelike or "morality play" quality to the plot: Jurgis is led, again like a modern Everyman, through a series of earthly tragedies before finding salvation in socialism. Indeed, the closing sections—in which, in a disturbing echo of the cadet novels, Jurgis is eyed by a beautiful young lady waiting in the wings—are the novel's weakest. But again, this wishfulness is not entirely a matter of Sinclair's naiveté. As Michael Folsom has shown, Sinclair actually also wrote a more pessimistic resolution. Nor is the pat solution merely the result of his "ideological" cast of mind. Rather, it resulted primarily from his conscious strategy of projection. The choice of the Lithuanians was indicative: grafting on his own fears of déclassé status, Sinclair had chosen an immigrant community itself experiencing declension and humiliation. Thus, when Jurgis has his own moment of socialist vocation, it echoes Sinclair's own: "in one awful convulsion . . . there was a falling in of all the pillars of his soul, the sky seemed to split above him—he stood there . . . gasping, and whispering hoarsely to himself: 'By God! By God! By God!' " Clearly, moments like this were bred in the politics of culture, and not the other way around. Despite his claims to narrative empathy, the residual presence of Sinclair's literary practice often deflected the novel away from the day-to-day thoughts of workers.

In fact, it may have been his poetic imagery, rather than his realism, that opened the book up to misinterpretation. The dominance of Sinclair's own analogical thinking had the effect of placing the degradation of meat in the figurative center of the novel. His metaphorical musings, in sociological terms, compared producers to products, workers to slaughter cattle. Sinclair presented his case not just in terms of exploitation but in metaphors of declension, corruption, and infestation: the workers' degradation seems, in fact, to stem from the poisonous world they inhabit. Ultimately, this metaphorical dimension, when combined with the essentially elliptical quality of the narrative, may explain why contemporary readers could find so much vicarious power in the text and yet finally misread its motives. As with earlier writers like Charles Dickens and Jacob Riis, part of Sinclair's effectiveness may have derived from the way his anonymous visitor orchestrated the reactions of more timid readers. But by the same token, middle-class readers may have interpreted the worker's embrace of revolution as a warning to implement liberal reforms before it was too late—as had been the intention of both [Dickens's] *Hard Times* and [Riis's] *How the Other Half Lives.* My point here, again, is that it may not have been simply a revulsion from the realism of the text that explains contemporary misreadings; if that were the case, one has the popularity of the novel to explain. Rather, it may have been that readers were carried along quite powerfully, but only from the guarded position of the visitor. In short, Sinclair's readers may have heard more of his heart than he suspected: at some level, they may have responded only to the echoes of his own vocation.

Perhaps Sinclair's mistake is not an uncommon one among American intellectuals, who have habitually seen the masses responding to matters of head and heart rather than to more tangible daily needs. But in this instance it was clearly also symptomatic of Sinclair projecting his own needs onto the worker. Most of all, Jurgis's soul, more than his stomach, needs answering; socialism becomes a form of belonging. Sinclair's dedication to social justice is not be taken lightly, nor is the genuine empathy of his mind. But there is a utopian strand in his political imagination that was itself partly a by-product of his vocational strategy. The socialist solution loomed out in front of him as a promise of respite from the regimen he had chosen—and end to the hard life of the crusader, the sweat and strain of his professional devotion. For both Sinclair and Jack London, who turned briefly back to politics after *Martin Eden,* a socialist future offset the isolation and wear of professional literary dedication.

The Jungle's public career, of course, was what earned Sinclair his continuing fame and ignominy; here was where his bridesmaid status really took hold. Once again,

however, viewing the novel in relation to the literary marketplace can explain more of its paradoxical history. The novel had been designed as a weapon: the immediate stimulus for the book, in fact, had come from Fred Warren, one of Sinclair's new socialist comrades and editor of the *Appeal to Reason.* But when the book skyrocketed to bestseller status, it seemed to be co-opted by the campaign to upgrade the sanitary conditions surrounding the packaging of meat—a cause Sinclair himself did not think helped workers at all. (Any close look at the novel reveals that Sinclair thought federal inspection a sham.) By our standard accounts, Progressive readers apparently took literally the symbolic degradation of meat, which Sinclair had probably employed primarily to emphasize the degradation of labor. Under the direction of Roosevelt and Senator Albert Beveridge, *The Jungle* was mobilized for both the Meat Inspection and Pure Food and Drug Acts, which, some historians have suggested, may have actually strengthened the market position of large packers. Sinclair's apt summary, because it is so often taken at face value, is also often quoted: "I aimed at the public's heart, and by accident I hit it in the stomach."

Sinclair's own socialist standard of value, of course, reflected the purism of his earlier romanticism; certainly, the lives of even workers themselves had been bettered by the new legislation. Nonetheless, to speculate about the meanings received by his audience, as Sinclair himself did, is naturally to invite the perils of "affective" criticism. Literally speaking, we cannot know precisely how Progressive-era readers actually responded. Unfortunately, reviews from the era are not much help either. Although it does seem that earlier reviews understood Sinclair's socialist intentions better than later commentary, this reflected only that the public controversy followed close upon the book's release, thereby shaping the content of the reviews. For this reason, reviews hardly provide a pure or unmediated sampling of contemporary reading. But we can know about the ways in which *The Jungle* was packaged for readers. To use the language of modern merchandising, we can discover what "bundles of attributes" were attached to the novel as it was promoted. This promotional dimension was itself an intrinsic part of Sinclair's vocational strategy—again, part of his decision to fight the world with its own weapons. In fact, conceiving the novel itself as a weapon was an implicit, if paradoxical, acknowledgment that popular impact—and by implication, adaptation of the modern best-seller system itself—was an indispensable component of even the most "proletarian" literary practice.

The Jungle campaign was the brainchild of Isaac Marcosson, one of the new progressive editors and publishers of the era. . . . In his memoir *Adventures in Interviewing,* Marcosson spoke proudly about having used *The Jungle* to take the book industry from the antiquated conventions of the Gilded Age into modern merchandising. Although in his own privately printed account Frank Doubleday himself said that he had actually found *The Jungle* quite revolting and its author something of a crank, he claimed that the firm had proceeded with the book in order to assert its independence under pressure from threats by Armour to withdraw advertising from the house periodical *World's Work.* But apparently what really happened was that prior to the novel's hardcover publication—as if alerted by Armour's threats—the publishing house decided to take its own steps to protect its investment and take advantage of the coming controversy. What Marcosson did, well prior to publication, was to investigate Sinclair's more serious allegations. Lest we lapse into conspiracy theory here, the important point is that Marcosson really felt he was supporting his author. In the language of the military campaign that was so common to merchandisers in these years, he later called it "bulwarking," or "fortifying" Sinclair's position.

Obviously fearful of legal repercussions, Marcosson himself—and Doubleday lawyer Thomas McKee, also involved in the *Sister Carrie* episode—traveled to Packingtown to do their own work. Intriguingly, Marcosson's investigations paralleled the visit of Sinclair, with an important twist. The promoter also disguised himself to enter the factories, but this time not as a worker but as a meat inspector. Subsequently, he interviewed Dr. W. K. Jaques, formerly city bacteriologist and head of meat inspection in the stockyards, and Dr. Caroline Hedger, a physician. Obviously, what Doubleday was most interested in were the book's charges about sanitation, not labor.

From this point on, Marcosson followed through with a trend-setting promotional effort. He sent advance page proofs of the novel to the editors of major papers (and hence to reviewers), to the UPI, and to the AP. He later claimed that one Chicago paper devoted two full pages to the book's charges. He also sent advance proof to Theodore Roosevelt, who invited Sinclair down to the White House, carried on a correspondence with the author about the book, and followed through with backing of the relevant bills. Sinclair himself was channeled easily into the promotion effort, keeping the issue alive by writing followup letters to newspapers and backup articles in *Everybody's.* In a June 1906 interview in the *Arena,* moreover, Sinclair admitted that he had gone over the manuscript with McKee after the lawyer returned from his own investigation, and cut out every line or phrase which McKee considered an exaggeration. Marcosson, meanwhile, again invoking the military metaphor—to which the former cadet novelist must have responded—said he kept Sinclair "shoulder to shoulder" in the "front lines of publicity," down in the "trenches" with other "allies" like T. R. Doubleday as a whole, it should be pointed out, was hardly concerned with *heading off* controversy. On the contrary, using a practice that really took hold in the Progressive era, Doubleday ads consciously fanned the flames of debate by using presolicited reactions pro and con. (Marcosson proudly said he had done the same thing for Thomas Dixon's *Clansman*). In fact, Doubleday used its own verification scheme as a hint that the book's charges were sensational. Commentary in the house periodical likewise emphasized the sanitation charges.

My point here is not the oft-repeated one that T. R. and the Progressives appropriated the novel for their own ends, though that was certainly the case. T. R. and Doubleday, for instance, actually conferred about the book, hoping some of the socialist material could be removed from the serialized version (which had appeared in *Appeal to Reason*) before going to hardcover. (As Robert Crunden has recently shown, neither Doubleday nor Roosevelt had much affection for Sinclair personally, or for his socialism, but early efforts to edit the book fell short of their plans.) Marcosson clearly recruited allies that Sin-

clair might not have on his own. But the more essential point here is that Marcosson's own attempts at "bulwarking" had set the terms of public debate about the book—and hence, for much of its reception. In other words, his own attempts to "fortify" the author had actually resulted in encircling a more narrow meaning in the text, an effect which only contributed to the book's public distortion. Because Doubleday's fears were themselves more middle-class; because the firm feared Armour's retaliation, and Armour was more concerned about consumer confidence; and because legal anxieties caused Marcosson to center his own investigations around what were to him the most sensationalistic aspects of the text—because of all this, the public misfire of the book was understandable. As one more bit of evidence, we might note that when Doubleday translated the novel into French, the new title they created was *Les Empoisonneurs de Chicago.* Perhaps not too surprisingly, then, there is even the intimation throughout Marcosson's account that he felt he had *improved* upon the case of his author. Marcosson notes proudly that even a meatpacker admitted that the book had resulted in greater consumer confidence. Whatever Sinclair's "proletarian" intentions, Marcosson felt more comfortable—and compatible—with the interests of his own class.

Here, then, was the outcome of Sinclair's decision to use the weapons of the modern literary marketplace for his own ends. Lured to topicality and popularity, he found his book channeled into what publicity men, the press, and politicians construed as his real message. One recalls a vivid message in *Martin Eden:* London lamented how, upon the death of that would-be singer Brissenden, the identity of a "famous writer" could be like a vapor created by the public mind, and then injected back into the real man. This analogy typified a recurring theme in a celebrity-conscious society: the persistent fear in the celebrity himself that he is imprisoned by his image—and, moreover, that his political identity is but a shadow cast by the steady glare of promotion. To paraphrase a recent critic of the media-made New Left, it is the problem of trying to make politics with mirrors. Along with the divided consciousness of its narrative text, the promotion of *The Jungle* illustrated the considerable cultural "meanings" bearing upon Sinclair's literary vocation—and hence, upon the reception of his novel. Sinclair's own projection into his story, the narrative splintering of the text, and his public packaging only crowded the text with voices: proletarian, poet, visitor, promoter.

To Sinclair's credit, he himself recognized much of this. We often overlook the vocational confession at the core of his famous quote: thinking that a book could be a weapon that could be "aimed," he failed to account for matters—within the text and without—over which he really had little control. Likewise, even when he spoke most proudly of his new literary program, we will mistake his hard-boiled hubris if we do not hear, at least partly, a lament as well. We might, in other words, hear an echo of Martin Eden's quest for knowledge. When Sinclair spoke of the "well-springs of joy and beauty" being dried up, or becoming "like a soldier upon a hard campaign"—Sinclair seemed to be acknowledging a price to the path he had chosen. (pp. 130-40)

Christopher P. Wilson, "Would-Be Singer: Upton Sinclair," in his The Labor of Words:

Literary Professionalism in the Progressive Era, *The University of Georgia Press, 1985, pp. 113-140.*

R. N. Mookerjee

The great success of *Oil!* [1927] and its enthusiastic reception both in socialist and literary circles after nearly a decade of indifferent and mediocre writing since *King Coal* (1917), restored Sinclair's confidence in himself as a novelist. He now felt that he could effectively use fiction for spreading his message and move people to work for social justice. The opportunity for writing another such powerful novel came soon when Sinclair found it impossible to resist the temptation of exploiting the Sacco-Vanzetti case that was then rocking the nation. Here, he felt, was an opportunity of exposing the utter hollowness and injustice of the American judicial system. It would also enable him to highlight the greed, corruption, pettiness, and inhumanity of the upper class, which controlled all segments of the capitalist economic system. (p. 94)

In *Boston,* published in book form on November 11, 1928, Sinclair showed even greater mastery over historical fiction, which, more than anyone else, he had invented and adapted to express contemporary records and events in all their details as a creative artifact, a kind of "news novel" as the British reviewer of *Boston,* John Strachey, called it.

Boston won for Sinclair many admirers from among those literary critics who had thought rather poorly of his artistic talents. Even Lewis Mumford, the doyen of American letters at the time, who had been highly critical of Sinclair in the past, now felt so happy with his latest novel that he wrote him:

> It is not merely your own final achievement: it is nothing less than an epic document, and it will last as long as the memory of Sacco-Vanzetti themselves. Your imaginative history of the American tragedy must supplement every other work, for it has the finality of truth and art.
>
> (pp. 94-5)

Boston, indeed, in a real sense marked a change in Sinclair's career as an artist. The novel in many respects is undoubtedly superior to all his earlier novels. Apart from almost continuously round-the-clock work for nearly fourteen months, which Sinclair put in for this novel, one also finds other significant departures in his approach and writing processes. An account of the writing of *Boston,* therefore, considerably helps in making us aware of the difficulties Sinclair faced and how he overcame them.

"The decision to write *Boston,*" said Sinclair, shortly after the book's publication,

> was taken on August 22, 1927 at half-past nine in the evening (Pacific Coast Time) on receipt of a telephonic message from a local newspaper . . . that Sacco and Vanzetti were dead. It seemed to me the world would want to know this story.

Not that the world did not know of what had been happening to these two unfortunate Italian immigrants for over seven years. Through the radio and the press, the American people had been kept informed of the various stages of their trial. But what Sinclair wanted to do was something more: "to make a picture of a civilization so that the world may understand the roots from which the Sacco and Vanzetti case sprang." Since the mass of conflicting reports spread over a long period of time had blurred the real issues, another objective of Sinclair was to present in the more lifelike form of a novel "an exact and honest picture of the Sacco-Vanzetti case, studied and recorded by a careful historian."

The Sacco-Vanzetti case, like the later Scottsboro trial in the South, held the attention of the American intelligentsia as few cases had. Nicola Sacco and Bartolomeo Vanzetti were arrested in Brockton, Massachusetts, on May 5, 1920, on charges of robbery and murder of a shoe factory paymaster and his guard. After a trial that attracted hardly any attention, they were sentenced to death in July 1921. Before the appeals could be disposed of, the editors of the *Liberator* gave publicity to the case and, in 1923, published an appeal by two Italians, Joseph Ettor and Arturo Giovannitti, who were similarly charged ten years earlier but were freed on appeal by the Italian government. These two Italians had formed a Sacco-Vanzetti Defense Committee and were campaigning for funds. Gradually, the case began to attract attention, and, by 1926, prominent writers like H. L. Mencken and John Dos Passos agreed to serve on the committee. Sinclair himself had as early as 1922 published a sympathetic article on Vanzetti, **"Vanzetti—A Tribute and an Appeal,"** and a year later written a review of Vanzetti's memoirs of his first year in jail. In the spring of 1927, Sinclair also formally joined the committee, but the massive support of almost all American artists and intellectuals came only in the wake of an appeal sent out by the committee on August 8, 1927, just two days ahead of the original date of execution. The appeal succeeded in getting a 12-day reprieve, but failed to change the death sentence. Michael Gold described the mood in Boston thus: "[Boston authorities] possessed with the lust to kill. The Frock coat mob is howling for blood—it is in the lynching mood." The efforts to save the two men gathered momentum very quickly, and on August 11, a large group led by Dos Passos, Katherine Anne Porter, Edna St. Vincent Millay, John Howard Lawson, Grace Lumpkin, and others picketed the State House in Boston. Sinclair, too, was deeply concerned about the fate of the two men, one of whom, Vanzetti, he had met in jail in Boston the previous year. Sinclair could not come from California, but was eagerly hoping for a favorable turn in the events when he got the shocking news of their execution. This act of "judicial lynching," as Edmund Wilson called it, shook American intellectuals and "made liberals lose their bearings." The case had shattered people's belief in the impartiality and justness of the American judicial system and "produced a spate of plays, poems, and novels, many written by men and women whose radicalism was first kindled by the death of the 'Dago Christs.'"

It was only to be expected that Sinclair, having established his mastery in this genre—fusing documentary and reportorial materials in fictional form—should take the first opportunity of using it. More so when this would also enable him to expose the injustice and inhumanity of the capitalist conspiracy and evoke sympathy for socialism and spread its message among thousands of readers at home and abroad. But this had to be done as early as possible while public interest in the case remained. Sinclair at once set to work. . . . [He] signed a contract with Seward Collins according to which the proposed novel was to appear serially in *Bookman* for 15 months, beginning in February 1928. This was rather unusual for Sinclair, for, in the past, he had his novels serialized only after he had completed the manuscript. In book form he could make only minor changes and could do nothing about the enormous length the serial had run. Because of its length, the novel was finally published in two volumes with a total of 755 pages.

It must be said to Sinclair's credit that, despite the urgency and haste, he took great care in the writing of the novel. He set before himself two guiding principles that he tried to adhere to even against heavy odds: (1) strict veracity of all accounts, thus making for historical accuracy; and (2) impartiality (to the extent he was capable of !) in his treatment of the materials, particularly pertaining to the Boston upper classes. As he said in his preface: "I wish to make clear that I have not written a brief for the Sacco-Vanzetti defense. I have tried to be a historian." This helped him to produce a novel that was artistically more satisfying than any of his earlier efforts. Another important departure in the writing of *Boston* was that, for the first time in his career, Sinclair sent manuscript chapters for comments and criticism to nonliterary persons who had personal knowledge about the facts of the case, and he then revised his work in light of corrections and suggestions. These measures considerably enhanced the over-all quality of the book in terms of both his previously mentioned objectives.

Though inspired to write *Boston* primarily because of the Sacco-Vanzetti case, Sinclair had also from the very beginning planned to include in his novel another important case dealing with the financial scandal of the Boston upper class. As he said in his preface: "Paralleling the Sacco-Vanzetti case throughout the book is a story of business and high finance which will be recognized as a famous law case recently carried to the United States Supreme court." This was obviously a reference to the Willet case of 1921, about which Sinclair tried to obtain accurate information since, in this part of the story, too, he would be "describing the events exactly as they happened but attributing them to imaginary characters." In the Willet case a group of Boston lawyers and bankers were found to have used their financial power to ruin an independent businessman, but they were let off. Sinclair made skillful use of this factual material to contrast the law governing the rich with that governing the poor. This polarity, as in Galsworthy's play *Silver Box,* is used effectively to show the double standards followed by the law courts.

For his facts concerning Sacco and Vanzetti (over a long seven-year period), Sinclair left no source untapped. He had the 3900 pages of the entire Dedham trial testimony and obtained from other sources the records of the Plymouth trial, which were officially denied to him, and wrote literally hundreds of letters seeking information and checking authenticity. After these efforts, he could confidently declare:

> So far as concerns the two individuals, Nicola Sacco and Bartolomeo Vanzetti, this book is not fiction but an effort at history; everything they are represented as doing they actually did. . . . The story contains no errors of any real significance.

By April 1928, Sinclair had written the first ten chapters. Simultaneously, he was also collecting materials for the other chapters, particularly regarding the legal issues involved in the trial. A faithful rendering of the settings and events presented him with no problems, but soon he was faced with what he called the "most difficult problem I have ever had to deal with in my life" and candidly wrote to a friend:

> I have been wrestling with it consciously and unconsciously for the past six months. . . . The upshot of the whole matter in my mind is that I do not know they (Sacco and Vanzetti) are guilty and I do not know they are innocent, and I can't say that I know either without lying.

He got over the problem when it dawned on him that he was really not required to pass any judgment; as a faithful chronicler his duty was only to present what he knew. (pp. 95-9)

Boston begins with the "fictional" or "invented" part of his story, dealing with upper-class Boston society—the death of old Josiah Thornwell "seated at his desk, his head fallen forward upon his arms," and the "release of Cornelia Thornwell, the grand old lady of the novel. The books cover roughly a period of 12 years in its re-creation of the background and circumstances preceding the trial, the trial itself, and its aftermath. Cornelia cuts herself loose from family ties and traditions and does what she had long wanted to do—experience for herself the outside world. While the sons and daughters of aristocracy are wrangling over Josiah's will and property, she sneaks away to Plymouth and gets a job in a cordage plant (chapter II). Gradually, Cornelia wins the confidence of Italian workers, who affectionately call her "Nona" and gets a first-hand knowledge and understanding of their problems. Soon she is joined by her granddaughter, the young Elizabeth Advin (Betty), who is well read in radical literature and is sympathetic to the cause of workers. (p. 100)

[After returning to their former lives, Cornelia and Betty, while in Italy], receive the news that Sacco and Vanzetti have been arrested and thrown into prison, charged with the payroll robberies. Cornelia and Betty return at once, joined a little later by Pierre Leon, a French Communist and editor, and Joe Randall, the American socialist journalist. They combine to organize the defense for Sacco and Vanzetti. Along with this story line, is also the immensely complex web of crooked finance, politics, and blackmail.

Cornelia is told that if a sum of $50,000 is paid as graft, the case could be withdrawn. She is shocked, and flatly refuses. The defense lawyer, at first quite hopeful, later realizes that the case could be strengthened only if Cornelia swears in court that, at the time of the crime, Vanzetti was with her. But this, too, she could never agree to—committing perjury was out of question for her.

The second volume of *Boston* begins with the trial scene in the court of Judge Thayer (chapter XIII), who gives an adverse judgment. Paralleling this story is the suit of Jerry Walker against Rupert Alvin and other bankers, with all the revelations the case brings out about Boston high finance and its large-scale banditry. However, in this case, tried by the same court, despite indisputable evidence, judgment is given in favor of the bankers, thus displaying the double standards followed by law courts.

Harvard President Lowell, in charge of a citizen's committee reviewing the Sacco-Vanzetti case, and Governor Fuller, could have set aside, or at least modified the findings of the prejudiced trial, but they both refuse to act. The defense committee prefers an appeal, but every effort fails. The two men, who would not have been found guilty on the basis of the available evidence by an impartial court, are executed in spite of appeals by the American masses and liberal intellectuals. The novel ends with Sacco and Vanzetti as martyrs of the U. S. judicial system.

This brief outline of *Boston*'s plot shows that, in narrating his story, Sinclair, unlike his practice in *The Jungle* and *Oil!* where he had often taken recourse to the flashback technique, uses a straight chronological account more in keeping with his aim of presenting history. However, in his use of the device of unfolding his story through the medium of one single major character, there is no change in Sinclair's technique. Like Jurgis in *The Jungle,* Hal Warner in *King Coal,* and Arnold Ross in *Oil!* it is Cornelia Thornwell "the run-away Grandmother" who "furnishes the fictional hub of the books." In some sense, *Boston* can be read as an account of Cornelia's attempt to withdraw from the meretricious physical and mental sloth of her group and come closer to the realities of life. By making her lodge in the same family as Vanzetti, Sinclair skillfully manages to proceed without much difficulty in linking his main plot, concerning Sacco and Vanzetti, and the subplot, involving the world of Boston high finance, while avoiding an illogical or forced connection.

It is through this close association established early in the novel (chapter III) that Cornelia's story becomes identified with Vanzetti's and the trial, imprisonment and execution on the one hand, and the goings-on and corruption of the ruling aristocracy of Boston on the other. By this device Sinclair achieves the fictional justification for making *Boston* the story of the Sacco-Vanzetti trial, while at the same time, through Betty and Cornelia, he is able to depict in vivid detail the immensely complex web of politics, blackmail, and bigotry that plagues the highest stratum of Boston society. To have succeeded in this with balance is in itself no small achievement for Sinclair, a point that seems to have been missed by some critics. One recent critic, for instance, has found the structure of *Boston* seriously flawed because although beginning with Cornelia in the first half of the first volume, the book becomes the story of Sacco and Vanzetti in the second volume, and there is "continual movement from the case of the two Italians to the upper reaches of Boston society," which he finds disturbing. Such criticism shows a rather casual reading of the novel, for Vanzetti is very much there at the beginning of the novel. From chapter II, where he is introduced first, to the end of the novel, he is present off and on. Similarly, Cornelia and Betty, with their intense campaigning on behalf of Sacco and Vanzetti and their world of Boston aristocracy are hardly forgotten in the second volume. In fact, the whole of the Jerry Walker case involving the upper-class friends of Cornelia is treated in this volume. The paralleling of the two accounts concerning the workers and the financiers, far from being a handicap, has been used as an effective device for structuring the novel. In this respect, therefore, Sinclair's combination of the "fictive" part (the invented story) and the "historical" part (the documentary case record and evidence) constitutes an artistic triumph for him.

However, such a device did impose limitations of another kind of his art. For while he felt free to invent and create in the "Cornelia-Betty-upper-class plot," which comes out more fully in the "Sacco-Vanzetti" main plot, he was obliged to restrict himself only to what he knew and what his documents would establish. Even when he felt that some of his scenes were inadequate, he did not, as he said, "feel justified at making imaginary scenes where I am dealing with real persons." Some of the confusion and inadequacy of the scenes, particularly in chapters XII and XIII, are to be attributed to this handicap.

The tagging on of a purely fictive set of characters, events, and speech to what is essentially a real account of persons and events in a historical context created another problem for the reader. In his preface, Sinclair gave a simple guideline: "the characters who are real persons bear real names, while those who bear fictitious names are fictitious characters." But how are readers, except for those who followed the case, to know who the real persons in the novel are? Are they to be expected to read a factual account of the Sacco-Vanzetti case first? Again, in practice, the mix-up of fictional and real characters is not simple at all when the fictional characters are brought into vital and dramatic contact with the real people. As a reviewer pointed out, it is well enough to give to Cornelia's last-hour visit to Vanzetti words actually spoken during W. G. Thompson's final interview with the doomed men, but when Cornelia protests to Governor Fuller that the trial was not a fair one, and Fuller replies that he has secret knowledge of their guilt and is, therefore, indifferent to its fairness, we (the readers) want to know whether he did actually say these words, and, if so, to whom. The reader's real interest is in the case and not the character, and at that moment Cornelia is more of a nuisance than a help.

Despite the limitations of Sinclair's method, he had introduced in the novel of contemporary history, destined to become the historical novel in course of time, a unique fictional device for narrating historical events against a contrasting background. Thus, in this mingling of the actual and the fictitious, both in events and characterization, Sinclair enriched this genre and created a new form of realism.

One of the strongest points of *Boston* is the enormous power and effectiveness with which Sinclair created the appropriate setting for the main drama and organized the massive records of the legal battle that raged for seven long, hectic, and tumultuous years. This needed an elaborate background that Sinclair provided very successfully in the first half of the novel. The Massachusetts and New England social life of the ruling classes is presented through the story of the Thornwells in great detail. . . . It is significant that Sinclair titles the novel as *Boston* and not after Sacco or Vanzetti. This he did deliberately to highlight the social background: Boston, the original citadel of the ruling aristocracy, and its corruption. In the first volume of the novel, which comprises 12 chapters and a little less than one-half of the entire novel, Sinclair brings his story down to the Plymouth trials, with chapters thrown in on the "graft ring" of upper-class Boston. The second volume, again with 12 chapters, begins with the Dedham trial and the activities of the Defense Committee. In many of the chapters in both volumes are devoted long passages to the plight of the exploited workers, the activities of strike-breaking police, the role of the capitalist press, and the Coolidge administration. He writes of Calvin Coolidge's "political and financial boss . . . a great lord of cotton-mills in New England, soon to be made a United States senator" who opposed an amendment to ban child labor and "led this campaign, and rallied the business men and bankers, the criminals, the hierarchy of the Catholic Church." He also writes of the Harvard intellectual circle, with its highbrow attitudes and total indifference to community life. These accounts, far from being out of place, build up gradually the historical context against which the trial takes place and enrich the setting as well. (pp. 100-04)

Sinclair's fusing of the facts and evidence into the narrative is superably done. Though running into 755 closely printed pages, [according to a reviewer from *The Times Literary Supplement*], he "handles his material with the utmost ability, and creates as the end draws nearer a gathering and painful intensity." Despite its length, the novel does not make burdensome reading and is not clogged with sentimentality. Mostly, the third-person, omniscient point of view is followed, and there is very little dialogue or direct speech by the characters. Sinclair's inborn reportorial skills and diligence coupled with a fine analytical intelligence are largely responsible for his achievement in mastering the monstrous welter of facts. Like Crane, Dreiser, Norris, and, later, Dos Passos, who made extensive use of newspaper reportage in their novels, Sinclair also incorporated in *Boston,* rather liberally, contemporary newspaper reports on the two Italians as well as on the trial and public reaction. In a letter to Michael Gold, he openly wrote that he intended to use some of his (Gold's) "vivid phrases and little glimpses of things as they happened" from his newspaper writings and declared that he considered "all other newspaper stuff as so much grist to be ground up into my story."

In his descriptions of the places and physical surroundings of the Sacco-Vanzetti part of the novel, Sinclair adhered to actual locations as far as possible for the sake of historical accuracy. In such episodes and scenes, he did not bother to think whether his accounts turned out to be convincing or not. This is the historian's approach. Against criticism of his description of the death house in Charlestown, he defended himself by saying:

> I wrote down the description of the death house word for word from the statement of Musmanno who spent a great deal of time in it and even drew me a diagram. . . . I read other descriptions in Boston newspapers and they appeared to fit exactly what Musmanno had given me. What is wrong with it?

(pp. 104-05)

The scenes concerning upper-class life, by contrast, are not realized so fully or faithfully, perhaps because Sinclair, apart from a few visits to wealthy relatives as a boy, had hardly any firsthand experience or knowledge of such life. His ingrained antagonism to this class was another reason for his lack of desire to know more about these people, even if solely for artistic purposes.

Boston gave Sinclair all the opportunity and scope to do what was dearest to his heart without damaging the artistic structure of the novel: to spread the message of socialism and plead for the cause of workers, since the major preoccupation of the book is the life and work of two socialist, anarchist workers. Here he had two characters expressly designed to personify the struggle. Unlike in *The Jungle,* where he had to concoct characters to dramatize his view of the social and economic condition, *Boston* grew out of intense human drama. In fact, the story was chosen precisely because it demonstrated Sinclair's view of the social situation. In *Boston,* therefore, there was no question at all of subordinating characters to propaganda—the usual charge made against Sinclair as an artist.

The debate and discussion of political ideology starts early in the book when Vanzetti calls himself an "anarchio individualista" and would approve no kind of organization except of a purely temporary kind. Through the numerous dialogues between Vanzetti and Pierre Leon on the one hand, and Cornelia and Betty on the other, Sinclair presented both the anarchist and the socialist points of view. The most powerful argument on behalf of the anarchists is put forward by Pierre Leon when he tells Cornelia:

> "What you have to get clear is the central doctrine of anarchism, that property used for exploitation is theft that makes capitalist society a gigantic bandit raid, a wholesale killing; any killing you have to do to abolish it, or to cripple it, always is a small matter in comparison."

Cornelia, however, is not convinced that anarchism is the right course for bringing about social change and expresses her faith in the power enlightened opinion as a means of enforcing justice and fair play. However, with her failure to get justice for the two Italians even after long years of struggle, she is left brokenhearted and exclaims, "Seven Years! . . . Seven Years!" . . . [Cornelia] is shocked and disappointed, but is certainly not converted to violence and bloodshed. Her remarks towards the close of the novel more or less echo Sinclair's own attitude that he had, in a letter to Gold, unambiguously stated just after completion of the novel:

> I do not deny that the Revolution may come in this country by violent means but I am not going to advocate that it should come that way and I think it is a great practical blunder and a great waste of moral force to commit or promote the first act of violence. . . . I can suggest a number of constitutional methods by which the workers might get control of industry. And it seems to me the part of wisdom to advocate these methods and try and apply them. . . . I look at Italy and see the frightful results of premature action by an armed proletariat and I think it is a lot better to wait a while and use such freedom as we have, freedom of propaganda to educate the workers and form them into great solid unions thoroughly instructed and aware of what they want. I am aware that that seems an old-fogyish idea to many impatient young comrades, but it is the way I feel.

Having conceived the character of Cornelia, Sinclair could have maintained a kind of artistic distance in his treatment of the subject. Cornelia is in an excellent position to serve as the narrator and commentator representing Sinclair's own point of view while at the same time not seeming unduly intruding. However, as in his other novels, Sinclair keeps on intruding through his voluminous authorial comments that are quite often repetitive and seemingly biased. This method, while it allows him full play for expressing his own ideas, weakens rather than strengthens his case. Had he left this task to Cornelia, who is well qualified to contrast the manners and interests of the rich and the poor, readers would have found themselves equally sympathetic, and this would have made the novel artistically more satisfying. But Sinclair could not help resorting to the journalistic, reportorial technique that he had been following for a quarter of a century. He follows the third-person, omniscient point of view with a minimum of dialogue.

In character delineation, too, never one of Sinclair's strong points, the nature of his theme proved an advantage. His interest being primarily in ideas, and his great skill being in reporting, the two main characters in the novel, Sacco and Vanzetti, caused him no difficulty in full and faithful presentation. The mass of records and information about these two "already made characters," who were to be portrayed as near their actual personalities in real life as possible, helped Sinclair to make Sacco and Vanzetti far more convincing characters than he had been able to create so far. For this achievement, he claimed no credit for himself. At the height of *Boston's* immense success just a month after its release, Sinclair frankly said,

> I did not make Vanzetti anything; I merely went among his most intimate friends and asked them to tell me what Vanzetti was and I set down the stories they told me without any change whatsoever, and without inventing a single incident. . . . I am not claiming any great virtue or skill as a historian when I assert that the Vanzetti in my novel is the real Vanzetti and as exact as anyone could make him.

Though Sinclair got a lot of information about Vanzetti from the Brinni family with whom Vanzetti had lodged for eight years, it certainly goes to Sinclair's credit that he could transform this mass of material into a convincing picture of a simple but passionate revolutionary. As Frank Swinterton had remarked, the way he makes

> the lives of his characters so real and so moving is astounding. Although one knows what the end is to be, since that is known all over the world, one reads as breathlessly as if the end were still in doubt—and certainly with as painful suspense as if the people of the book were personally known to me.

The other major character—in a way Sinclair's principal character, since it is she who keeps the structure of his long narrative from falling down—Cornelia Thornwell, too, Sinclair tells us, was based on a real person, a Mrs. Burton. He had, of course, invented the story of her conversion to radicalism and her role in the defense case. Her character is carefully developed from the very first page of the novel, and her actions seem nowhere inconsistent with her background. She desires to become a working woman, but Sinclair does not commit the mistake of showing her as successful in this. She, however, succeeds in becoming a friend of the working classes and puts up a heroic fight for justice. Also, as William Bloodworth points out, it is through Cornelia, who refuses to perjure, that Sinclair makes a case for truth itself and thus "introduces a universal element."

However, when it comes to delineation of personal relationships in the fictive part of the story . . . the members of the Thornwell family, especially between Betty and her parents and Betty's love life, Sinclair is not successful. A good example of the lack of human interest on his part is in the scene where Betty's pregnancy is revealed, and she is made to take it in a cool and disinterested manner. The whole of this matter is dismissed in just a page and a half ! Floyd Dell's view that "*Boston* is better than *Oil!* in its less sketchy treatment of . . . personal affairs" is valid only for the Sacco-Vanzetti part of the novel and not for the story woven around upper-class Boston life, in which personal relationships play an important part. Men and women as living human beings with intimate personal emotions are missing in Sinclair, and one has to admit that this lack constitutes a serious shortcoming in his characterizations.

Boston shows superb command over language. Though Sinclair, like Dreiser, wrote long sentences without much concern for economy, he had over the years come to acquire a distinctive style suited to his purpose and readership. A story like *Boston,* which attempted to re-create some of the most turbulant years of American history and mass upsurge, required powerful, moving prose to rouse the conscience of the nation. It is a measure of Sinclair's success that with his carefully chosen word pictures and easy flowing style, with occasional use of exaggerated and hyperbolic language, he wins the attention of the reader throughout the book. He is particularly brilliant when describing scenes of mass agitation. The protest of the Italian workers is described thus:

> Ten million protestants marching, singing, carrying banners in a hundred foreign tongues. Mobs roared their fury, shrieked their imprecations; bombs exploded, sheets of plate-glass were shattered; cavalry charged, clubs fell on human heads, sabers clove human flesh, men fled and bled and died—and of all that tumult not one sound reached the deaf ears, not one glimpse penetrated the blind eyes.

Sinclair's use of broken English for the Italian characters, particularly Vanzetti, who speaks extensively all through chapters III to VI and again in the second volume, is in keeping with his aim to be as realistic as possible. Vanzetti's usage is consistent in its incorrect usage, and there are hardly any discrepancies in the choice of words. His improving command over the language is also gradually and convincingly brought out. In this respect, Sinclair's success reminds one of Mark Twain's use of language in *The Adventures of Huckleberry Finn.*

Boston also shows a more varied and extensive use of imagery. Sinclair often uses appropriate images and symbols to give weight to an argument or drive home his point instead of the plain statement of his earlier writings. A striking example of this device is his portrayal of Mr. Katzmann's cross-examination of Sacco in the court of Judge Thayer:

> [The scene] made Cornelia think of a deer in a forest, when a wolverine or lynx or other fierce creature drops upon him from a tree, and chews into his neck as he runs. That is a common event in nature; but in this case appeared a phenomenon unknown to Zoology—another animal running alongside the fleeing deer, to keep anyone from interfering with the neck-chewing process. This creature went by the name of Webthayer.

Sinclair continues with this imagery and writes, "there followed upon this a phenomenon never observed in any forest; the Wolverine or lynx desisting from his neck-chewing, and letting the Webthayer take his place on the victim's back!" The imagery is continued in the three pages of faithful recording of the trial proceedings in the shape of Cornelia's commentary of what she was watching before her. The account ends thus: "he (Thayer) and Katzmann like two skillful basket-ball players, keeping the ball in play between them and working it down the field to the goal." Sinclair could, therefore, if he chose, present such scenes without any authorial intrusion and reach a fair measure of artistic excellence. From the point of view of fictional craftsmanship, *Boston* remains Sinclair's best-conceived and best-executed novel.

The enthusiastic reception from the critics and the enormous sales of the book in its very first month of publication amply justified Sinclair's high hopes for *Boston.* The novel was reviewed by most of the important newspapers throughout the United States, and, like *The Jungle,* attracted national attention. The entire first printing was immediately sold out. Almost simultaneously the novel was translated into French, German, Russian, Polish, Swedish, and Czech and a little later into Bulgarian, Danish, Spanish, Yiddish, Hindi, and Tamil (the last two being Indian languages). Sinclair was thus eminently successful in his objective of letting the world know the truth behind the executions and evoke public sympathy for the cause for which Sacco and Vanzetti had lived and died, a cause equally dear to Sinclair's own heart.

As a novel dealing with an actual case history, *Boston* occupies a unique position in its transformation of documentary material into the fabric of art, making it a compelling and disturbing piece of writing. For its accuracy and faithful reporting, *Boston* has received unqualified approbation from historians of the period. Louis Joughin and Edmund M. Morgan, who worked on a detailed study of the Sacco-Vanzetti case, for instance, unhesitatingly praised the novel for its historical authenticity:

> It is accurate in detail to the degree that one would expect of a scientific study, and it has qualities of proportion in its judgments which indicate careful thinking. This combination of completeness, accuracy, and penetration places *Boston* in the front rank of historical novels.

It was therefore only to be expected that of the novels published in 1928, *Boston* would be a serious contender for the Pulitzer Prize. The novel was indeed considered, and would have got it, but for what was regarded as its "special pleading and socialist propaganda." Though Sinclair did not get the award (he was later awarded the Pulitzer for a much inferior novel, *Dragon's Teeth*), *Boston* gave a tremendous boost to his reputation as a novelist. Impressed by his organization and marshaling of details in the investigative portion of the story, Arthur Conan Doyle, the great British writer of detective fiction, called Sinclair "one of the greatest novelists in the world." . . . In America itself, then, as years later, writers as disparate as Leslie Fiedler, Theodore White, and Norman Mailer were powerfully influenced by *Boston.* As Fiedler recounted years later: "the one book of his that moved me as a kid, helped in fact to confirm my lifelong interest in problems of guilt

and innocence and the 'demonstration trial' was his *Boston.*"

The abiding appeal of *Boston* remains undiminished to this day. No matter what our political views, the novel stands out as an epic document and will outlast even the memory of Sacco and Vanzetti. (pp. 105-12)

> *R. N. Mookerjee, in his* Art for Social Justice: The Major Novels of Upton Sinclair, *The Scarecrow Press, Inc., 1988, 151 p.*

FURTHER READING

Bloodworth, William A., Jr. *Upton Sinclair.* Boston: Twayne, 1977, 178 p.
  Analysis of Sinclair's works as they reflect his stance as muckraker, propagandist, and political figure, particularly focusing on his theme of "idealistic opposition to an unjust society."

Brevda, William. "Love's Coming-of-Age: The Upton Sinclair-Harry Kemp Divorce Scandal." *North Dakota Review* 51 (Spring 1983): 60-77.
  Biographical sketch of Sinclair's friendship with Harry Kemp, an indigent known as the "boxcar poet" whom Sinclair met and supported prior to World War I.

Buitenhuis, Peter. "Upton Sinclair and the Socialist Response to World War I." *The Canadian Review* 14, No. 2 (Summer 1983): 121-30.
  Analysis of Sinclair's resignation from the American Socialist movement prior to World War I on the grounds that the party opposed United States' involvement in the war. Sinclair's advocacy of American intervention, which stemmed from Germany's occupation of France, is said to be reflected in Sinclair's novel *Jimmie Higgins.*

Cantwell, Robert. "Upton Sinclair." In *After the Genteel Tradition: American Writers, 1910-1930,* edited by Malcolm Cowley, pp. 37-47. Carbondale, Ill.: Southern Illinois University Press, 1964.
  Sympathetic biographical portrait of Sinclair in which Cantwell argues that he "has done more than any American novelist toward breaking the path for a full and realistic treatment of working-class life in fiction." See excerpt in *CLC,* Vol. 15.

Chalmers, David Mark. "Upton Sinclair and Charles Edward Russell." In his *The Social and Political Ideas of the Muckrakers,* pp. 88-103. New York: Citadel Press, 1964.
  Biographical examination of Sinclair's involvement in socialism. Includes a brief analysis of *The Jungle.*

Cook, Timothy. "Upton Sinclair's *The Jungle* and Orwell's *Animal Farm:* A Relationship Explored." *Modern Fiction Studies* 30, No. 4 (Winter 1984): 696-703.
  Comparative essay in which Cook asserts that Orwell's "*Animal Farm* owes more of a debt to Sinclair's best-known novel than it does to any preceding beast fable or animal story."

Dell, Floyd. *Upton Sinclair: A Study in Social Protest.* New York: Albert and Charles Boni, 1930, 194 p.

The earliest biography of Sinclair by a fellow novelist and socialist, offering a sympathetic analysis of the author's life and best-known works.

Gottesman, Ronald. *Upton Sinclair: An Annotated Checklist.* Kent, Ohio: The Kent State University Press, 1973, 544 p.

Detailed bibliography of Sinclair's works in both English and foreign editions. Includes additional bibliographical sources and an itemized list of secondary sources, as well as notes on unpublished material on Sinclair.

Grenier, Judson A. "Muckraking the Muckrakers: Upton Sinclair and His Peers." In *Reform and Reformers in the Progressive Era,* edited by David R. Colburn and George E. Pozzetta, pp. 71-92. Westport, Conn.: Greenwood Press, 1983.

Examination of Sinclair's ambivalent relationship to the muckraking journalists of the Progressive Era.

Harris, Leon. *Upton Sinclair: American Rebel.* New York: Crowell, 1975, 435 p.

Extensively researched biographybot Sinclair.

Wilson, Christopher. "The Making of a Best Seller, 1906." *The New York Times Book Review* (22 December 1985): 1, 25, 27.

Retrospective analysis of the circumstances surrounding Sinclair's novel *The Jungle.*

Yoder, Jon A. *Upton Sinclair.* New York: Ungar, 1975, 134 p.

Brief investigation of Sinclair's life and works in which the author's socialist tendencies are viewed as a justified response to the social and political conditions of his era.

Youdelman, Jeffrey. "In Search of Lanny Budd." *San José Studies* 6, No. 1 (February 1980): 87-94.

Analysis of Sinclair's leftist view of World War II as reflected in his "Lanny Budd" series of novels.

Gloria Steinem

1934-

American journalist, editor, and biographer.

Steinem is one of the most vocal and influential leaders in the American feminist movement. A successful free-lance reporter in New York during the 1960s, Steinem helped found *Ms.* in 1972, the first national magazine operated by women for the advancement of women's causes. Although much of her time is consumed with editorial tasks at *Ms.* and speaking engagements throughout the country, Steinem has published many essays, some of which are collected in *Outrageous Acts and Everyday Rebellions.* This anthology reflects Steinem's position over a period of twenty years, ranging from the early, notorious "I Was a Playboy Bunny" exposé, to the later, more ideologically-oriented pieces she wrote for *Ms.,* including the comical yet incisive "If Men Could Menstruate." In *Marilyn,* illustrated with photographs by George Burris, Steinem discusses actress Marilyn Monroe—the quintessential American sex symbol—from a feminist perspective, portraying her as a victim of her own beauty and of insecurities bred by her childhood experiences. Several critics charge both *Marilyn* and *Outrageous Acts and Everyday Rebellions* with representing only the more pleasant, non-threatening elements of the feminist perspective. Steinem is nearly universally credited, however, with a lucid, well-written, and entertaining reportorial style, and for making feminist issues both accessible and familiar to the public.

(See also *Contemporary Authors,* Vols. 53-58; and *Contemporary Authors New Revision Series,* Vol. 28.)

PRINCIPAL WORKS

Outrageous Acts and Everyday Rebellions (essays) 1983
Marilyn [with photographs by George Burris] (biography) 1986

Angela Carter

Dog should not eat dog, nor feminist bad-mouth feminist, and nothing that follows in this review [of *Outrageous Acts and Everyday Rebellions*] should be taken as demonstrating on the part of the reviewer any lack of sympathy with Gloria Steinem's philosophy of social justice for women. (p. 1)

The essays [in this collection] span some 20 years of social change in the United States, a period that has amply demonstrated the truth of the "three steps forward, two steps back" theory of history. Gloria Steinem starts out as a blithe young girl reporter, undertaking an assignment which involves signing on as a Playboy Bunny. There could be no more nostalgic reminder of the early '60s. Per-

haps those Bunnies that remain should be preserved by the World Wildlife Fund. We girls in boots and dungarees have all but put them out of business and Steinem has done her bit towards that.

However, she seems a bit sheepish about this excellent, ironic, illuminating bit of reporting [**"I Was a Playboy Bunny"**], carried out in 1963. She adds a 1983 comment, how she came to realize that "All women are Bunnies." This is a problematic statement: it is impossible to imagine Emma Goldman, a heroine of Steinem's, resembling a Bunny in any way. Rosa Luxembourg? Djuna Barnes? Precision of thought is the enemy of polemic but that is no reason why ideologues should eschew it. But obviously the idea that all women are Bunnies means a lot to Steinem because she adds: "Since feminism, I've finally stopped regretting that I wrote this article."

But why the regrets, anyway? The piece is as full of feminist consciousness as some of the later reportage, and if it is implicit rather than explicit, it is no less powerful for that. It has a cocky bounce and brio, an endearing "look at me!" quality. If she doesn't dot the i's and cross the t's of the Bunny condition, because she doesn't yet know quite how, she lets Bunnydom sufficiently reveal its true nature.

And, here, she is rather more adventurous and illuminating in describing the complexities of women who work as objects of sexual display than she is in the piece about Linda Lovelace, dated 1980. In it Steinem is so straight-jacketed by her own ideology that she cannot perceive Linda Lovelace, erstwhile porno queen, now housewife and mother, as anything but an object, any more than the male customers for Lovelace's porno films could.

A different kind of object, of course—object of male sadism, rather than spurious representation of gratified desire. But an object, all the same, and one which Steinem helplessly finds herself selling, this time to an audience of concerned women.

The early pieces of journalism—the Bunny piece, the pieces on politicking about McGovern, McCarthy, Martin Luther King and others—are, in fact, far more persuasive toward the liberalism from which Steinem's feminism sprang than are the lay sermons reprinted from *Ms.*, which often suffer from such smug glibnesses as: "Now, we are becoming the men we wanted to marry." Speak for yourself, Gloria! I'd hope to do better than that.

An otherwise most moving account of her mother, **"Ruth's Song (Because She Could Not Sing It),"** is subtly warped by this self-satisfaction. For what right has Steinem to assume she knows what song her mother would have sung, had the women's movement existed at that time to provide the score? There is, throughout the essays, a curious blindness to history—to the economic forces that created the conditions for the emancipation of women in industrialized countries in the 19th century, and the way those same forces have determined the nature of the struggle since then. Steinem's suffragist grandmother, the vegetarian who prepared meat meals for her menfolk, was not denying her feminism as she did so, as Steinem seems to imply. She had no other option. Further, Steinem's ahistoricism makes her positively silly about Freud, whom she seems only to have read in quotations or in the glosses of other anti-Freudian feminists.

The final essay in the book, **"Far From the Opposite Shore,"** is, in effect, a prescriptive, inspirational tract exhorting women to stay true to the cause in the teeth of the right-wing backlash. Amongst other things, she prescribes performing "one outrageous thing" each day, in the cause of justice. These "outrageous acts" turn out to be such things as leaving a violent partner, reverting to a birthname, challenging a woman-hating joke. I trust she uses the adjective "outrageous" ironically. And nothing could be less apt a title for her book than: "Outrageous Acts and Everyday Rebellions." Which is a come-on, and a nod and a wink to the idea that some people feel menaced by that appeal to good sense and natural justice which is what feminism is all about. Many people do fear justice, of course. Only the innocent need not. But Steinem isn't the type to threaten apocalyptic judgment or the wrath to come. She is far too wise, tolerant and humane to do that, more's the pity. Too tolerant by far, in fact.

In her introduction, a review of her life as writer and feminist over the last 20 years, she cites among the emotional rewards of her career "meeting a midwestern Catholic priest who prays to 'God the Mother' as some reparation for five thousand years of patriarchy." What is she up to, approving of such a display of sentimental hypocrisy? She

conjures up a scene worthy of a Luis Bunuel movie, yet seems to feel she has to applaud this half-baked attempt to get right with God in case She is a woman as evidence that the priest in question has his heart in the right place. This is blatant Uncle Tomism. (pp. 1-2)

> *Angela Carter, "Gloria Steinem: From Miss to Ms.," in* Book World—The Washington Post, *October 9, 1983, pp. 1-2.*

Leah Fritz

How far we have come—and how much further we need to go—is the central message of Gloria Steinem's new book, *Outrageous Acts and Everyday Rebellions,* in which she continues her confident and faithful outreach to those millions of women (and men) who still have trouble accepting feminism as a serious political philosophy.

How far we have come as a movement is largely a matter of intangibles. Feminism is a recognized political entity. It has changed the attitudes of millions of women regarding their own importance in the world and the forces ranged against them. It has enlarged many women's aspirations. And, as Steinem points out in an essay on words, it has exerted an interesting pressure for change in vocabulary here in the United States. Just today I read in the New York *Times* that, worried about the "gender gap," Ronald Reagan has ordered the White House staff to use the word "humankind" instead of "mankind." Now *that's* and *advance.*

In a chapter called **"Sisterhood,"** written in 1972, Steinem traces how contact with other feminists altered her, from an individualistic woman hell-bent on making a career and a name for herself in the male-dominated profession of journalism (all the while retaining her feminine image) to a woman who could identify and work with other women for their common good. She writes:

> . . . I finally understood why for years I inexplicably identified with "out" groups: I belong to one, too. And I know it will take a coalition of such groups to achieve a society in which, at a minimum, no one is born into a second-class role because of visible difference, because of race or sex.

Personal change for Steinem, as for so many other women, *was* tangible: feminism altered the direction of her life. Although, given her subtle, quick intelligence, her articulateness, her drive, and her grasp of political nuance, she surely would have succeeded in her pre-feminist ambitions, it is hard to imagine a women's movement so immensely popular and vital at this time without her efforts. And that popularity and vitality have already begun to translate into power, if only, at the moment, in the negative sense of a countervailing force to the extreme Right. Her influence, then, will undoubtedly help decide how much further we all succeed in going—which is the more compelling concern of this book.

Steinem is as determined as ever to forge coalitions, though these days she uses the more disarming and trendier term "networks"—and for the present, they are mainly among groups of women. But as a political realist who, on journalistic assignments for *New York* Magazine, came in close contact with such leaders and politicos as George

McGovern, Eugene McCarthy, Martin Luther King, Jr., John Lindsay, Nelson Rockefeller, Robert Kennedy and Richard Nixon, she can be expected to extend this networking, at least on a *quid pro quo* basis, to the male liberal establishment. Grounding her strategic flexibility in feminist history, Steinem reminds us of the variety of approaches used by the Suffragists:

> Chaining themselves to the White House fence, going to jail, declaring a hunger strike, being cruelly force-fed: those events are now famous. But the range of tactics included humor, theatrics, passive resistance, persuasion, and whenever possible, the subversion of Establishment contacts and wives. . . .

[The] term "subversion" gives the reader a clue as to how Steinem views her role as political advocate, and how to correlate her various postures within this work. There is a noticeable difference, for instance, between the tightness and distance of her style once she began to think of herself as an influential public figure, and the open spontaneity of her earlier pieces. This cannot totally be accounted for by the onset of maturity and her entrance into the women's movement, although both factors must have played a part. In the excerpts from her profiles on the male leaders, Steinem is a shrewd observer and provides very candid, shifting impressions. These men emerge three-dimensional, and as a result, fascinating. We see in these pieces, too, the author's character evolving. When the person was not so political, Steinem was less cautious.

Again, in the article, **"I Was a Playboy Bunny,"** she reveals an untendentious sense of fun missing in her *Ms.* essays, where the humor is always politically relevant. The other "bunnies" Steinem met in the course of researching Hugh Hefner's exploitative practices are caricatured with a light irony that would never pass her "sisterly" censor now.

When anger at a woman threatens to break out in more recent pieces, such as one on a college reunion at Smith, she cannot summon up the laughter that made waiting on tables at the Playboy Club, tight costume, plastic-bag-stuffed bosoms and all, such a bittersweet delight to read about. In the **"Playboy"** article, her absolute fury at the waitress who boasted that she didn't need any padding gives that petty adversary life, whereas the envious Smith graduate who inaccurately called Steinem "an anachronism from the 1970s in size-six designer jeans talking sisterhood" receives political analysis and cold scorn. Even this is an expression of emotion in an article otherwise bound up by the contradictory desire to be amusing, but really at nobody's expense.

Steinem admits her difficulty with expressing anger openly, a common problem among feminists who tend to sentimentalize sisterhood and to ignore sibling rivalry. Honest disagreement or irritation with other women inspires fears of being disloyal or divisive and may be equated in a feminist's mind with "trashing." But the advice we were given as children, to say nothing if you can't say anything nice, can paralyze a movement or a woman for whom truth is fundamental to progress. (p. 7)

Steinem savors diversity and admires the outrageous, but in her desire to popularize feminism she anxiously smooths the rough edges of women who defy the strictures of femininity. In the short run, this "image-tidying" may achieve her purpose. In the long run, however, an unexpurgated display of our divergence from ladylike "norms" might inoculate her followers against a disillusioned, hostile reaction later on.

In the section called "Five Women," four of the sketches are dampened by Steinem's refusal to acknowledge the wilfulness in her subjects, a quality which the world may consider wholly negative in women, but which feminists ought to respect.

In her sketch of Marilyn Monroe—**"The Woman Who Died Too Soon"**—she admits to a prefeminist hatred for the actress' screen image. Instead of accepting this feeling as envy of Monroe's beauty and obvious talent, an envy multitudes of women and men shared, Steinem, with her newly incorporated sisterlines of 1972, blames her former hatred on Monroe's vivid vulnerability, a vulnerability Steinem says she herself resisted expressing in her prefeminist existence. But then she recalls having met Monroe while auditing one of Strasberg's classes at the Actors Studio, and how sorry she felt for this woman so humbled before the famous teacher. It was Monroe's real vulnerability, ultimately so *non-threatening,* which in fact won Steinem over, and which makes her portrait of a powerfully ambitious woman incomplete. The devil in each of us *wants* her due, in balanced proportion with the angel. It was the devil in Monroe, alive and dead, that Steinem rejected, and thus the devil in herself remained disguised.

Likewise, Steinem wants to deny that making money was a motivation for Linda (Lovelace) Marchiano's promotion of her book *Ordeal.* Certainly, Marchiano was heroic in speaking out about her terrible experience as a sexual slave. She is fully conscious of the importance of her book to our understanding of pornography as a business that uses and throws away women. But to help her make her new start in life, she did need money, and had even thought to act in a legitimate film, until it turned out that nudity would be required of her there, too. The former star of *Deep Throat* would never again take off her clothes for money. The offer she received from a reporter to turn her story into a book must have struck her as an honorable way to accomplish both her ambitions: to get the truth out and to give her some financial security. As it turned out, she was cheated of her earnings by legal maneuvers on the part of her former husband, and more's the pity. But Marchiano's determinedly patient handling of the press does not simply argue a "core of strength and stubbornness" as a "microcosm" of that which exists in the generality of women, as Steinem would have it.

Marchiano's competence with the media was born of a unique intelligence and the same healthy ambition that gave her the courage to escape from her slavery and to talk about the experience publicly in the first place. (pp. 7-8)

Recognizing this does not take away from Marchiano's feeling for justice and her own responsibility in achieving it, any more than recognition of Steinem's personal ambition takes away from the extraordinary gifts which she has put generously at the service of the women's movement. The women's movement *itself* is immensely ambitious and will succeed insofar as it expresses the personal intelligence, inventiveness, and ambition of each of its members. So long as fame and fortune exist in the patriarchy, they will remain goals to bring out the best and the worst in individuals. Channeling these aspirations to bring out the best requires an open acknowledgement of their importance to each and all of us, in the here-and-now. We will know that our feminist utopia has arrived when the values of success and failure cease to move us, when the need for and the idea of both individualism and group affiliations stop forcing us to cover our naked souls. In the meantime, if we are ever to move in that visionary direction, we had better recognize and use well what is.

The pity and excuses Steinem bestows on individual women are blessedly absent from her comments on patriarchal institutions. She goes after the hypocrisies of organized religion, the so-called democratic process, the right-wing construct of "the family," and the romantic view of marriage with a wit that devastates. By confronting these mighty targets with humor, she evidently hopes to enlist women who, until they read her words, might subscribe unthinkingly to conventional orthodoxies. She is at her devilish missionary/subversive best in these passages. In **"Night Thoughts of a Media Watcher,"** she observes that if few women are casino-gamblers it is probably because marriage satisfies most women's "total instinct for gambling." She says, " . . . consider just how tough it is to know that the person you are about to marry . . . really is going to have the law career or foreman's job or political office you want for yourself and for your security . . . "

If ambition expresses itself through individual drive for upward mobility and through cooperative efforts for the success of a group, it also finds an outlet, especially for women whose own talents are so often brushed aside, in marrying into (relative) money and power. According to feminist logic, then, one would think that what a woman wins in the marriage gamble legitimately belongs to her, as a wife, divorcee, or widow. She has a right and even perhaps a duty to use it for what she believes in. And yet Steinem proffers this passage on Jacqueline Onassis:

> . . . Part of her uniqueness [Onassis, at least, is seen to be unique] is an ability to distance herself from her public image, to ignore the obsessive interest of strangers, and to refuse to read most of what is written about her.
>
> Certainly, this ability has helped her to survive with her sanity and humor pretty much intact. Probably it is the habit that most frustrates those who wish she would use her public power for various political ends. (I, for instance, wish with all my heart that she would use some of her *derived influence* to work publicly for the issues of powerless groups in general and women in particular.) But wanting her to use that *power from her other lives* may be unfairly close to wanting to use her, however worthwhile the cause.

Steinem goes on to say that Onassis supports a Kennedy philanthropy in Brooklyn's Bedford-Stuyvesant section and continues to be devoted to the arts. Her involvement in the women's movement is limited to some quiet financial contributions, her personal career as an editor first at Viking and now at Doubleday (she doesn't just party), and encouragement of other rich women to find themselves jobs.

These are *choices* Onassis has made, and she has a right to them. But it is nonsense to speak of her "derived influ-

ence" or "power from her other lives." Although she had two husbands, like the rest of us she has only one life. And if the bulk of her money and power came from those husbands, it is no more "derived" than that of any other widow who manages to participate in an openly political context as a feminist.

It is her status as "Most Famous Woman in the World" that confers "uniqueness" on Jacqueline Onassis in Steinem's eyes—in 1979. (How far we have come.) And it is her uniqueness that excuses her from being "used" for the movement like the rest of us ordinary mortals.

For Steinem does not similarly excuse radical feminists who give half-hearted support to the ERA. It is no wonder that many radical feminists do not give it top priority, when we consider that NOW has collected millions of dollars and the energies of mainstream women everywhere in support of this abstraction (a constitutional amendment that Steinem herself admits might take yet another ten years to pass), while other, more immediate, women's needs, like shelters for battered women and child-care centers, have gone begging.

On the other hand, Steinem's astute reading of parallels between the anti-feminist backlash in Nazi Germany and the present danger of imminent fascism makes an excellent case for feminist unity on a different level. The kind of political unity she is proposing here would not diminish our diversity but simply protect our freedom to be diverse. On this level, our most potent reaction to the common crisis is to stand by our various struggles as if we still have options.

Outrageous Acts and Everyday Rebellions is an exciting and provocative book, as anyone can determine from the arguments I am picking with it. We will have to wait for another book by Gloria Steinem to find out how she does what she does so that those of us who see her as an effective feminist role-model can learn to follow in her footsteps. (Her essay, **"Houston and History,"** for instance, connects the National Women's Conference to the suffrage and abolition movements, but does not describe Steinem's own experiences in helping to organize the outcome.) Her many organizational suggestions throughout the book, and particularly at the end, should prove helpful for the time being.

The essay **"Erotica vs. Pornography"** is a useful and concise description of one of feminism's most basic and complex struggles. Her analysis of feminist conservatism in young women also offers valuable insights; in sum, the book provides a readable overview of feminist issues that should also recommend it for courses in Women's Studies. (p. 8)

> *Leah Fritz, "Rebel with a Cause," in* The Women's Review of Books, *Vol. 1, No. 3, December, 1983, pp. 7-8.*

Peter Conrad

At her college reunion two years ago, Gloria Steinem hoisted into the air a placard announcing 'Women get more radical with age.' She herself has ripened into a revolutionary, and her collection of journalism from the last two decades [***Outrageous Acts and Everyday Rebellions***] records that progress—from a timid creature paralysed by her fear of public speaking to a rallying rhetorician; from a servant of male interests and egos to her own proud person. Her journey reprises a phase of history: she writes, she says, about 'the distance travelled' by herself as a representative of all her sex. . . .

Steinem's first journalistic coup was her undercover and undressed insinuation of herself into Hugh Hefner's furry harem in 1962. Renaming herself Marie Catherine Ochs, she got herself recruited as a simpering cotton-tailed hostess at the Playboy Club in New York, and for a couple of weeks tottered about on vertiginous heels, praying that she wouldn't tumble out of her cantilevered *décolletage* as she fetched and carried cocktails while fending off the importunities of her customers and stowing their tips in disused bodily apertures.

Reduction to witless Bunnydom was her course in political enlightenment. It taught her that the body she had been made to pad, corset and lewdly wiggle for the delectation of men belonged to her, and could be granted or withheld as she saw fit. Now she chooses to exhibit it in the steam rooms of health spas, among a supportive sorority. And the new body in question is the body politicised, trained for self-delight and combat duty against male assailants. . . .

It's on the subject of the indignities suffered by the body that Gloria Steinem is most angrily eloquent. She begins with the Playboy Bunny's transformation of herself into a kewpie doll, with a coiffure of candyfloss. Those portentous, pointy breasts turn out to be disposals of whatever refuse lies to hand: they're augmented with plastic dry-cleaning bags, Kleenex tissues, Kotex halves, gym socks, and transplanted asbestos Bunny pom-poms. Probed internally by a seamy doctor before being hired, Bunnies are then castigated if they allow their ears to droop, or don't keep their tails in good order. Ms. Steinem herself retains a legacy of her brief servitude: 'feet permanently enlarged by a half size by the very high heels and long hours of walking with heavy trays.'

If Ms Steinem—who volunteers for this mistreatment as an experiment in sisterly empathy, and writes about it with such mocking rage—is the book's comic heroine, its tragic victim is Linda Lovelace, the omnivore of *Deep Throat,* maintained in sexual serfdom by her manager, beaten when she weeps during a gang-bang and causes one of her rapists to default on payment, required to suffer on film the embraces of a dog. . . .

Behind her throng nameless others, mutilated into submission—the 30 million women who have been made to undergo Sunna circumcision, clitoridectomy and infibulation; a decapitated prostitute left to rot in a Times Square hotel room; the unmarked graves of the starlets eviscerated in performance by a Californian maniac who specialised in snuff movies. There are also those who deludedly mutilate themselves. One of Ms Steinem's most sober and perceptive essays interprets trans-sexualism as punitive self-hatred. Instead of altering a society which oppresses them with its false categorisations, these people deform themselves in the desperate hope of at last qualifying to belong to that exigent society.

Most touchingly of all, there is a chorus of muffled or silenced voices, on whose behalf Ms Steinem speaks out.

Marilyn Monroe is one of them, observed at a Strasberg acting lesson shyly lamenting what she took to be her own talentlessness. On a campaign plane in 1968, Steinem interrogates Patricia Nixon. At first she's palmed off with polite formulae; finally she provokes a long self-lacerating plaint about Mrs Nixon's aborted hopes and her subservience to a husband who commended her in his Checkers speech as 'a wonderful stenographer.'

The best piece in the book ["**Ruth's Song (Because She Could Not Sing It)**"] records another line of quiet desperation: that of Ms Steinem's mother, so corroded by anxiety that she had to keep herself stupefied with an elixir of chloral hydrate, so insecure that she always, when in her sixties, told taxi drivers she was eighty in the hopes that they'd compliment her on her state of preservation, and at theatre box offices pretended to be deaf, trusting that the ticket sellers would pity her and give her seats in the front row.

Despite her book's title, Gloria Steinem's talent is not for outrage. That she should leave to Germaine Greer, whom she remembers taunting a talk-show host by demanding, as he laid down the law about monthly emotional changes and female unreliability, 'can you tell me if I'm menstruating right now—or not?' Ms Steinem's gift is for tender, grieving commiseration and commemoration. Her book is an anthem for brutalised bodies and for wasted lives.

> Peter Conrad, *"The Body Politic,"* in The Observer, *April 8, 1984, p. 23.*

Sandra M. Gilbert

In **"If Men Could Menstruate"**, a witty essay included in her book *Outrageous Acts and Everyday Rebellions,* Gloria Steinem speculates that if "men could menstruate and women could not . . . menstruation would become an enviable, boast-worthy, masculine event". Indeed, she observes, the fact of male periodicity would be used to exclude women from all the public positions and privileges that female sexuality has in the past kept them from: "Generals, right wing politicians, and religious fundamentalists would cite menstruation ('*men*struation') as proof that only men could serve God and country in combat ('You have to give blood to take blood'), occupy high political office ('Can women be properly fierce without a monthly cycle governed by the planet Mars?'), be priests, ministers, God Himself ('He gave this blood for our sins'), or rabbis ('Without a monthly purge of impurities, women are unclean')."

Exuberantly sardonic, Steinem's comic fantasy nevertheless summarizes the serious battle over sexual modes, manners, and morals that her collection of essays— together with Germaine Greer's *Sex and Destiny* and Mary Midgley and Judith Hughes's *Women's Choices*— undertake s to analyze. What are the implications of the female reproductive cycle for human societies around the world? To what extent is it appropriate for modern technology, offering new and diverse methods of contraception and abortion, to intervene in that cycle? How should we feel about nuclear families and about the larger institution Greer calls the "Family"? What are our obligations to children and to their mothers (and do the rights of those two groups conflict)? These are questions to which all four authors address themselves, though often in such striking-ly different ways as to offer interesting evidence that what nineteenth-century thinkers called "the Woman Ques-tion" remains in our time a vexed and vexing one. . . .

After the passion of Greer and the dispassion of Midgley and Hughes, it is a relief to turn to the straightforward ac-tivism of Gloria Steinem. *Outrageous Acts and Everyday Rebellions,* the first collection of essays by the founding editor of the important American feminist journal *Ms,* is lively, witty, and modest—which is to say that Steinem is not grandiose; she does not try to prove that whatever is, is right, or that whatever is, is wrong; she does not make large-scale accusations and dire pronouncements or put forward compromises. Presenting herself, quite properly, as someone caught up in an exhilarating process whose end is not yet clear (though its goals are), she has pro-duced a book whose pleasures reside, at least in part, in its author's "negative capability"—in her talent for "being in uncertainties, mysteries, doubts, without any irritable reaching after fact and reason". She writes sympathetic profiles of such radically unlike and sometimes (for a femi-nist) unlikely figures as Alice Walker and Marilyn Mon-roe, Jackie Onassis and Linda Lovelace; and her pieces on "male menstruation" and female clitoridectomy, along with her analysis of the false parallels drawn by Right-To-Lifers between abortion clinics and Nazi gas-ovens, ad-dress specific issues with energy and intelligence.

Sometimes, to be sure, Steinem's journalistic vigour grows wearisome; like so many other lively writers for the mass media, she suffers from what one critic has called "dotul-ism"—the disease of over-elaborated parallel construc-tions (her mother was "a woman who . . . a woman who . . . a woman who . . . "). Nevertheless, in the con-text of theories that, like Greer's, would repudiate many of the important ideas of Western feminism as narcissistic or ethnocentric, or that, like Midgley's and Hughes's, would reject many of the crucial concerns of modern femi-nism as, somehow, non-existent or nonsensical, Steinem's acts and rebellions reveal a sensible and often selfless con-cern for all the world—first, second and third—in which women must really live.

In this respect, Steinem continues a tradition of lucidly vindicating the rights of women that goes back as far as Mary Wollstonecraft and which was carried forward earli-er in our own century by writers like Virginia Woolf and Dora Russell. In "Jason and Medea: Is There a Sex War?", the first chapter of her *Hypatia* (1925), Russell de-clared that "When I can open my newspaper to-day and read of mothers desperate with hunger, misery, or rage drowning themselves and their children, I cannot bring myself to look upon Medea as some elemental being from a dark and outrageous past". And she answered her own question "Is there a sex war?" with the unequivocal state-ment that "There has been." That there has been such a war—and, as Steinem would no doubt insist, there still is—is a point that should not be forgotten by those fight-ing in the battle of sex. Women and children have not al-ways had "riotous good fun" in the Harem [as Greer states in her *Sex and Destiny*];—or anywhere else; clitori-dectomies probably aren't any good for anybody; and even if the cause of misogyny is male anxiety, it doesn't follow that misogyny "ceases to offend". We need people like

Gloria Steinem—and Dora Russell—to remind us of these truths.

Sandra M. Gilbert, "New Strategies in the Sex War," in The Times Literary Supplement, *No. 4236, June 8, 1984, p. 645.*

Spencer Brown

[Gloria Steinem's message in *Outrageous Acts and Every-day Rebellions*] is unburdened by lead. In her brisk, com-petent (she even uses the word *decimate* in its proper meaning) standard journalism the message shouts "We've come a long way, baby, and let's give 'em hell." (Of course *'em* means all men.) Steinem is intensely personal: she al-leges that she was not always so vigorously and virtuously belligerent. But her whole life has been first the prepara-tion for and then the practice of feminist crusading. Even in an earlier timid phase Gloria Steinem could have scared the daylights out of a wolverine.

Outrageous Acts and Everyday Rebellions is a collection of essays and reports, all to one clear harp in divers tones. Even her portrait of her mother, a confused but moving reminiscence called **"Ruth's Song,"** is in large part a saga of women's troubles. The political reports—an interview with Pat Nixon and accounts of the Nixon, McCarthy, and McGovern campaigns—relate enthusiasms and hos-tilities predictably leftist but made individual by her slant-ing them toward feminist issues. The longest piece, **"I Was a Playboy Bunny,"** is a fairly amusing story of Steinem's infiltration into the sexist mecca of the Playboy Club—an arrangement for the Bunnies and the cretins who are their patrons and tormentors that seems to quadruple the ex-pense and inconvenience of prostitution with little of its satisfaction. She emerges from the experience with perma-nently enlarged feet (high heels and heavy trays) and the realization that "all women are Bunnies."

In a sentimental vignette of the steam room in a women's spa, **"In Praise of Women's Bodies,"** Steinem exults that here is achieved the counterpart of the "casual togeth-er-ness" of a men's locker room—something that I, at least, never particularly treasured. "Instant sisterhood" is evi-dently promoted by the variety of figures—a nonflat stom-ach or a perfect egg-shape or bellies scarred from opera-tions. "Stretch marks and Cesarean incisions from giving birth are very different from accident, war, and fight scars. They evoke courage without violence, strength without cruelty, and even so, they're far more likely to be worn with diffidence than bragging. That gives them a moving, bittersweet power." Steinem might have mentioned Medea's "I would rather stand three times in the front rank of their battles than bear one child."

Much of Steinem's feminist crusade evolves into political activism not specifically feminist, and some political activ-ism is given an unnecessarily feminist slant. For example she links to sexual hostility the political resistance to food stamps and adequate welfare payments; but of course she knows, and would say elsewhere, that this resistance is rooted in the selfishness of the rich. "We have to uproot the sexual caste system that is the most pervasive power structure in society." So much for the power of money. Bella Abzug lost at the polls only because she was aggres-sively feminist—but there is not a word about Abzug's long-standing prominence as a fellow traveler. And the essay **"Campaigning"** produces some embarrassing adulation of Eugene McCarthy and McGovern even though these heroes waffle on women's rights and are unadmirable in other ways.

Steinem's writings have been highly praised—and with some justice. **"The International Crime of Genital Mutilation"** effectively exposes the horrors of clitoridectomy inflicted on millions of women as well as the general Arab and African resistance to reform. Elsewhere she makes clear the importance of male domination for Nazism. Hitler's crushing of feminism was one of his steps to power. On pornography Steinem is a better guide than [Susan] Sontag, though she does leave a door (or peephole) open for *erotica,* which suggests pleasure without aggression or sadism. Her essay on Linda Lovelace is a real-life shocker: Linda was tortured and enslaved by the makers of *Deep Throat.*

The late Irving Babbitt used to say "The Jesuits call repetition the mother of learning; and to that I add exaggeration and paradox." By Babbitt's criterion Steinem is the ideal teacher. She batters us until we are convinced . . . [Moreover] she can employ a light touch and can please as she preaches and wallops. She even includes a jolly romp called **"If Men Could Menstruate."** (pp. 658-59)

For a last word on Steinem, a mild demurrer to the sisterhood from a square male: is it true, as she alleges, that aging is "a greater penalty for women than men"? Do men really talk more, and are more stridently, than women? "Clearly," she adds, "male silence (or silence from a member of any dominant group) is not necessarily the same as listening. It might mean a rejection of the speaker . . . or a decision that this conversation is not worthwhile." (Damned if you talk, and damned if you shut up.) Are *all* households dominated by men? . . . Steinem holds machos responsible for all wars and aggressions; women would solve such unpleasantness. The truly devout fems revise Gibbon's melancholy dictum to read that history is little more than the register of the crimes and follies of men and the misfortunes of women. One cannot but wonder if Steinem has ever thought of Medea or Clytemnestra or Lady Macbeth—or even Mrs. Bennet or Mrs. Proudie or the Wife of Bath—or, if we cannot trust literature to represent life, Catherine the Great or Charlotte Corday or Queen Elizabeth I.

Yet as repetition, exaggeration, and paradox are noted and allowed for, and smoldering rage and sex-chip on shoulder are recognized as understandable in the light of past and present injustice and long-delayed reform, I should like to suggest a nonbelligerent view neither macho nor fem. Let me revert to a remark by another, and better, critic. . . . When asked "Which is more intelligent, man or woman?" Dr. Johnson replied "Which man? Which woman?" (p. 660)

> *Spencer Brown, in a review of " 'Outrageous Acts and Everyday Rebellions',"* in *The Sewanee Review, Vol. XCII, No. 4, Fall, 1984, pp. 658-60.*

Mandy Merck

Monroe's métier was the sex comedy, not the melodrama, and her image—despite the notoriously pneumatic breasts—anything but maternal. Those critical taxonomies which oppose her to wholesome blondes like Doris Day ignore the self-parody in both their performances, but much of that was lost on the children of the Fifties. Gloria Steinem remembers being embarrassed as a teenager watching the star on screen, 'mincing and whispering and simply hoping her way into love and approval'. Some of us were just scared. Marilyn Monroe seemed a man's woman, first and foremost, with a specifically heterosexual attractiveness polished to such a high gloss that it threatened to leave the rest of us in the dark—unless we too accepted the corseting and cosmetics and constraints that this femininity required.

Yet in the quarter-century since her death Monroe has become a tragedienne and, recently, a figure reclaimed for feminism. It's amazing what death can do for a girl. Among other things, it's a prerequisite for martyrdom. The taste for hagiography runs rampant in the modern women's movement and, if a star is torn, she becomes a suitable case, like Janis and Bessie and Judy, for canonisation.

The talent and the tragedy of these women's lives may be indisputable, but so is the current emphasis on the second term at the expense of the first. Despite the lip-service to Monroe's concern for her craft, Steinem is much more interested in 'the endlessly vulnerable child who looked out of Marilyn's eyes'. Suitably infantilised, Monroe's life can be rendered as one of persecuted innocence—the classic melodrama scenario—in which poverty, desertion, sexual abuse and narcotics take their terrible toll.

Sadly, all of these things probably happened to Marilyn Monroe, although Steinem's efforts to verify conflicting stories (including those of her subject) are unimpressive. Despite the addition of photojournalist George Barris' unpublished interview from Monroe's last summer of '62, this is a compilation of secondary sources, designed to supplement the scores of photographs taken by Barris and his predecessors over the years. As such, it occupies a peculiar place in the literature of stardom, a sort of moral fanzine or consecrated coffee-table book.

This is a difficult balance to maintain, threatening to topple over into the unfeminist eroticism of the pin-up on the one hand (the famous calendar nude is notably absent) and the *Hollywood Babylon* death scene on the other (only one black and white of Monroe's dishevelled bedroom is included). In between, the book displays a large number of Barris' contrived candids (Marilyn playing on the beach, sticking her tongue out, leaning on her elbow) which, given the rounded contours of her 36-year-old face and figure, do look rather childlike. They reminded me strongly of the redeemed stripper in *Not A Love Story,* also filmed draped with seaweed at the end of her odyssey through the porn industry. In both cases the subjects seem to have lost, along with their exposure to the skin trade, the wit and intelligence they employed against it.

In this book Steinem confesses to a fantasy of saving Monroe from her tragic fate, and also to an interest in (strictly non-Freudian) psychology. The much-disparaged Freud would have reminded her that the jealous child's desire to rescue mother from the degradation of sex with daddy also includes a measure of revenge. In appropriating Marilyn

Monroe to the conventions of melodrama, in which suffering becomes the major evidence of merit, we may be paying one of the most influential actresses of our century a rather mean tribute. (p. 29)

Mandy Merck, *"A Life in Pictures,"* in New Statesman, *Vol. 113, No. 2917, February 20, 1987, pp. 28-9.*

Julian Barnes

In *Some Like It Hot* Marilyn Monroe makes her entrance, late and lustrous, at Chicago main-line station. Her face empty of expression, her skirt brimmingly tight (at the time Western men went in for the knee-binding of their women to emphasise the calves and bottom), she carries a ukelele—a toy, joke instrument for a toy, joke woman. As she sashays provokingly past, Jack Lemmon turns to Tony Curtis and remarks wolfishly, 'Look at *that.*'

That: the routine male depersonalising pronoun; but less inaccurate than usual here. For Monroe, besides being 'built,' as they say, was also constructed; not unlike an Oldsmobile. Her name was invented, her hair artificially coloured, her jaw (and possibly nose) amended by plastic surgery, her voice desqueaked; and though she was still in her thirties her body was already being filled with antiageing hormones. Even that seductive walk was allegedly the produce of a technical fiddle: one of her high heels was slightly shorter than the other. . . .

It's a measure of her vivid status as an American symbol that she is still written about as though it was not too late to bring her back to life. If Norman Mailer's *Marilyn* (1973) was the long, brawling amour he never had with the actress (luckily for her), then Gloria Steinem's *Marilyn* is a rescue bid 25 years after its subject's death.

Marilyn as feminist heroine? No, but certainly Marilyn as emblematic female victim: constructed for men, used and abused by men (and for the most part written about by them too). This is not a movie buff's book (indeed, it has oddly little to say about the films). It is a personal book, an act of retrospective support, a lament for a woman embroiled in the sexual attitudes of a pre-feminist age. It is strong and trenchant on subjects like the long-term effects of child neglect, the psychological cramping of women by male expectations, and the nature of female sexuality.

One of the abiding ironies of Marilyn Monroe's case is that the sex life of this erotic goddess was a shambles, and her body—that primped, sleek, rejigged body—a surgeon's battlefield which brought her little pleasure. She rarely had an orgasm; she suffered extreme menstrual pain; and the hourglass figure, that parodic exaggeration of childbearing hips and milk-giving breasts, knew a dozen abortions, plus false and ectopic pregnancies, and miscarriages.

Steinem puts the dozen abortions down to a dizzy spontaneity about sex, but it sounds even more extreme—as if she was the only person on earth except the Tully River Blacks who was unable to connect coition with pregnancy. And this dizzy spontaneity had its limits: immediately after making love she used to put her bra back on so that her muscle tone wouldn't slacken.

She came from a family stained by madness and suicide; she was fostered, put in an orphanage, sexually abused. Yet she became a huge star, married famous men, slept with a President. Yet—again—she blew it all, boozed and pilled and screwed it away, losing her job and her husbands.

Is it a moral tale about American success? A tragic parable about genetic and social determinism beating down the frail murmur of free will? Or does it have no more significance than itself—just another sad life, with enough blankness at its centre for a range of judgments to be possible. . . .

Ms. Steinem's book, forceful as it is on elements of Marilyn's wrecked soul, is disappointingly difficult to read. Part of the cause is technical and self-inflicted: writing a text to go with an overstretched portfolio of patchy photos by George Barris, Steinem decided on a 'non-linear' approach. Her seven chapters are to be read in any order; each contains 'a microcosm of Marilyn's life,' and the hope is that just as superimposed photos may build up into a holograph, so her free-standing chapters, which are allowed to repeat the same information, will produce 'a factual and emotional holograph of a real person.' This doesn't even sound like an idea for an idea, let alone an idea for a book; and Steinem, admirable polemicist though she is, simply doesn't have the literary technique to get the strategy off the page. Repeating information comes across as just repeating information.

The other difficulty is equally crucial, and comes from Steinem's good-heartedness, from her laudable desire to offer Marilyn the unconditional love and devotion she never got (or never got enough of) in life. This is a no-fault biography, like a no-fault divorce. Marilyn had such a sad and painful time that Steinem cannot bring herself to criticise her. Marilyn was so terrified of being thought a joke that Steinem will always take her seriously.

Thus, many of Marilyn's utterances about her work are standard Hollywood guff of the sort you might hear from Joan Collins on any old chat show, but they are here reverently transcribed. Her prima donna antics when on set are treated with the same awe: on 'The Misfits' she famously kept Clark Gable (who had a severe heart condition) waiting for hours; and later wondered, with a glazed self-regard which Steinem doesn't question, whether she wasn't subconsciously punishing the father who decades previously had deserted her. Well, maybe she was, but what she was mainly doing was keeping Gable waiting. He was to die 10 days after filming stopped.

The funniest moment of over-sympathetic authorial dereliction comes when Steinem is listing examples of Marilyn's spontaneous generosity: 'She gave personal gifts to hairdressers and others who worked for her, even making sure to keep Chivas Regal on hand for the cleaning woman.' If that isn't the way to get wonky hoovering, I don't know what is. But Steinem is too loyal to notice the comic hopelessness of the gesture. Her book is more an act of friendship than a biography; as if to forgive all were to know all.

Julian Barnes, "Requiem for a Goddess," in The Observer, *February 22, 1987, p. 29.*

Maureen Quilligan

It may seem strange to juxtapose Gloria Steinem's *Marilyn/Norma Jean* (1986) to a biography of Lillian Hellman. No two women could seem further apart. Simply to conjure in the mind the contrasting images of the ravaged Lillian Hellman's monstrous (parodic?) appearance in the Blackgama mink advertisement, and the famous pictures of the thirty-six-year-old Marilyn Monroe taken by George Barris during the last month of her life—pictures which are the centerpiece for Steinem's seven brief essays—is to sense the extreme variety with which individuals can fulfill the conditions of "successful" womanhood. Yet Hellman and Monroe did in fact share close connections to the same American entertainment industries; moreover, in their personal and political lives, both stood by their liberal men when questioned by the House Un-American Activities Committee; and, significantly, neither had children. It is something of a shock to our own stereotypic conceptions to realize that sexually, the rather homely Lillian Hellman seems to have been far more successful than Marilyn Monroe, if one measures success in personal satisfaction. This paradox is perfect for a certain kind of feminist position: the self-actualized Hellman was a more successfully sexual woman than the male-created sex goddess Monroe. The irony may be, however, that Hellman's liberated promiscuity may only have been so "successful" because Hammett (himself a devotee of prostitutes) was a better mentor in such matters than any of Monroe's lovers. As well as a better coach for a career. Had, for instance, Arthur Miller been willing to sacrifice his career to hers, as Hammett did for Hellman's (he never wrote anything else after Hellman's first success at age twenty-nine), had Joe DiMaggio devoted himself to his wife's film work, perhaps Monroe would have received the focus and support Hellman apparently did.

Gloria Steinem may usefully serve as an exemplary feminist; her approach to Marilyn Monroe is feminist discourse pared away to its journalistic essentials. That her book provides no more than these bare essentials is its virtue and its vice. What is perceivably different from the outset is that Steinem is writing specifically for women, taking herself as representative of a gendered response to the subject. She tells us that at age twelve she walked out of Monroe's film *Gentlemen Prefer Blondes* in profound embarrassment: "How dare she be just as vulnerable and unconfident," Steinem confesses, "as I felt?"

Monroe's much-publicized vulnerability and lack of self-confidence is the hallmark of Steinem's goddess. The title of her book is significant; nested within, and almost typographically invisible in the block letters of its title, is Marilyn Monroe's real name, Norma Jean: "As you read and think about Marilyn," Steinem cautions her reader, "remember Norma Jean." That vulnerable, unmothered child is Steinem's focus. The question she asks is: what would Marilyn/Norma Jean have been if she had lived to see the dawn of the women's movement? Could sisterhood have possibly supplied the missing parenting, could it have nurtured Marilyn as she was never sufficiently mothered by the unconditional love she sought from men? "When the past dies, there is mourning, but when the future dies our imaginations are compelled to carry it on." If Marilyn Monroe is the ultimate popular cultural product of masculine imaginings, then it makes perfect sense for a popular

culture feminist like Steinem to undertake an ideological rewrite of the icon. If Norman Mailer used his biography of the star to tell us he felt that he individually—as an artist and lover—could have saved Marilyn Monroe, it is perhaps not surprising that Steinem tells us she feels the sisterhood could have collectively done the same. Steinem's propagandistic capture of the icon of Marilyn is, logically, to imagine a mature, even elderly, autonomous Marilyn Monroe engaged in some useful philanthropic activity (the proceeds of the book are destined for just such a cause). As a biographer, Steinem reads the life-as-lived in a way that allows for an ultimate, politically active development.

Nor is it surprising that the biographical background against which Steinem writes is specifically Norman Mailer's *Marilyn*; Mailer offered the masculinist vision from which the icon must be rescued. Thus Steinem reminds us that Mailer dismissed Norma Jean's mother as simply callous toward her children when she listed her earlier babies as "dead" on Norma Jean's birth certificate. Steinem, in contrast, considers at some length that mentally ill woman's trek to find her first children. When she eventually discovered them happily ensconced in a foster home in Virginia, she sacrificed her motherhood to their welfare, relinquished her rights, and allowed them full freedom from the burden of knowing her own marginality. Whereas Mailer doubts Marilyn's claim that she was sexually abused as a child because her first husband reported her a virgin, Steinem points out that it was all too statistically possible that she was telling the truth, and that sexual abuse does not require penetration to be psychologically damaging. To Mailer's charge that Monroe's refusal to marry an elderly wealthy man only proved how fully she was the "Great Castrator," Steinem answers that however many sexual favors the actress might have bestowed in order to obtain jobs from studio heads (or to obtain affection, for however brief a time), Monroe knew she risked losing herself if she married for jobless security: "Marilyn supplied sex so that she would be allowed to work, but not so that she wouldn't have to work." Such a celebration of self-determined vocational definition is, of course, a mainstream *Ms.* magazine virtue. Whatever sociological purpose this glorification of autonomous work now fulfills, it makes the case that if one's work is to be a sex goddess, then that self-defining work is acceptable, and Monroe can be a protofeminist because she was a working woman, even if her work produced such embarrassing results as *Gentlemen Prefer Blondes*.

While Steinem's constant quibbling with Mailer tends to make her slender biography seem like some Billie Jean King vs. Bobby Riggs tennis match with Marilyn Monroe as the tennis ball, it also reveals how ideologically loaded any biography can be. In the biography of a public figure such as Marilyn Monroe, who—as an actress—enacts a culture's fantasies, such ideological manipulation is perhaps all the more logical and even legitimate. A self-conscious cultural construct to begin with, a film star provides the occasion not only for the story of a life, but of a time. Steinem's book, then, however deficient as a study, is the genre pared to its purpose ideological skeleton, happily pointing at an equally skewed, personal, and ideological male-authored biography. Feminist biography does not expect to learn the "truth" of a character in the old sense of the term, because the "truth" of the individual belongs to a different ideology: one that posits that there is some bedrock of noncultural, unscripted private character accessible to anyone who can ferret out these "facts," especially after the life is over. A life, as Virginia Woolf observed, is only given its shape after it has ended. Insofar as Steinem is in part conscious of what she is doing with Marilyn Monroe politically, she is interesting to watch. Unfortunately, her manner does not allow her always to be so self-conscious, and her popular psychologizing about Monroe's famous deprived childhood, for instance, makes the sentimentalized material ultimately unilluminating.

But what is finally unforgivable about Steinem's analysis is that she simply does not take Monroe's work seriously. As a betrayal of feminism's own terms, and the terms in which Steinem herself wishes to praise Monroe, the oversight is devastating. Steinem may perhaps be forgiven for not commenting on the dumb-blonde roles Monroe played in various studio films, but when she does not say a word about the content of the two films Monroe made after forming her own production company—*Bus Stop* and *The Prince and the Showgirl*—she must be seen to have missed an ideal opportunity to find Monroe's own commentary on her work in the language Monroe chose to speak: film acting. To take seriously Monroe's self-directed manipulation of her persona in these two scripts, to pay at least a modicum of attention to her achievement, her film acting (which is on record), would have been a fine corrective to the endless sentimental lamentations about Norma Jean. Steinem ultimately leaves Monroe a victim—of her mother's insanity, the Kennedys' callousness, the general insensitivity of the studios, and American macho mentality. She does not give us the woman of whom fellow artist Ella Fitzgerald said—in gratitude for Marilyn's daring political act of sisterhood in securing her right to perform in a Los Angeles club—"She was ahead of her time." (pp. 265-69)

> *Maureen Quilligan, "Rewriting History: The Difference of Feminist Biography," in* The Yale Review, *Vol. 77, No. 2, Winter, 1988, pp. 259-86.*

Diana Trilling

[Gloria Steinem's *Marilyn* is a] thoughtful and absorbing biography of the actress.

Whether Marilyn Monroe, a chronic insomniac, intended to kill herself, or only to get some rest, will probably never be known, though we learn from Ms. Steinem's careful investigation that Marilyn's achieved death followed seven or eight near misses. Still a young woman, she had said of herself, "Yes, there was something special about me, and I knew what it was. I was the kind of girl they found dead in a hall bedroom with an empty bottle of sleeping pills in her hand."

She didn't die in a hall bedroom but the empty pill bottle is everywhere in Mr. Barris's [accompanying] pictures of her, perhaps especially when, below vacant eyes, she forces her famous smile, radiant and full of promise. (p. 1)

It is questionable if Monroe had ever had a gift for acting, other than as an overflow of her good humor—professional opinion would seem to have been divided in the matter. On the positive side, according to Ms. Steinem's account, Lee Strasberg rated her with Marlon Brando as "one of his most talented pupils." And John Huston said, "She went right down into her own personal experience for everything, reached down and pulled something out of herself that was unique and extraordinary. She had no techniques. It was all the truth, it was only Marilyn."

But whatever her talent or its absence—and certainly a capacity, like Marilyn Monroe's, for self-irony is a great asset in a comedian—movies and movie making were at the heart of her life. She had been born and raised in Hollywood. She was an illegitimate child; her father had run off before her birth—when Marilyn wanted to create this parent she visualized him as Clark Gable. During the brief periods that she was able to be with her daughter, before disappearing forever into a mental hospital, Marilyn's mother was employed in film studios. Shunted as a child between orphanage and foster homes, all Marilyn could turn to were the movies to instruct her in a world that offered more than barrenness. . . .

Gloria Steinem's biography is a quiet book; it has none of the sensationalism that has colored other purportedly serious books about the film star, Norman Mailer's in particular. But it necessarily reports on Marilyn's sexual life. Although Marilyn Monroe cannot fairly be said to have slept her way to the top, she did at the start of her career sleep her way to the opportunity to work. After that, world famous, she continued to be vastly compliant: she slept with men, and on occasion even with another woman, in order to please—perhaps also to feel herself made real by their desire for her. Apparently the ability to give rather than receive pleasure in sex was the whole of her delight. Practiced in the arts of accommodation, she flattered many men into believing that they were the first to satisfy her. It was her boast that she had never been kept. . . .

[In addition to her three husbands,] her later lovers, conspicuous among them Frank Sinatra and Robert Kennedy, were similarly inappropriate. Delving more closely than Arthur Schlesinger does into Marilyn's relation with Robert Kennedy, Ms. Steinem gives us a pitiful picture of Marilyn trying to convince herself that she will soon marry the Attorney General. She obviously pleased Robert Kennedy just as, during the 1960 Presidential campaign, she had pleased his brother Jack. But Marilyn Monroe was designed for wish-fulfillment, not for wifehood or public companionship with government leaders. . . .

Nor, it would appear, was she designed for motherhood. She longed for children and had great empathy with them; perhaps this was because she was herself always a child, essentially unmarked by her experience—no doubt her "innocence" had much to do with her unparalleled appeal to people in all walks of life. Laurence Olivier, who played with her in *The Prince and the Showgirl*, said of her, "Look at that face—she could be five years old." One of her suicide attempts followed a miscarriage during her marriage to Arthur Miller. But she had had a dozen or more abortions. . . .

In writing about Marilyn Monroe, Gloria Steinem for the most part admirably avoids the ideological excess that we have come to associate with the women's movement—Monroe emerges from her book a far more dimensional figure than she would have been if she had been presented as simply the victim of a male-dominated society. It is only when she deals with Monroe's quest for help with her emotional problems that Ms. Steinem becomes incautious and passes unfounded critical judgments.

That Freud regarded women as the second sex, charmingly puzzling but inferior to men, is scarcely arguable. This sexual bias cannot be overlooked by any prideful woman but it does not account, as Ms. Steinem would have it do, for the failure of Freudian psychoanalysis to cure Monroe. Marilyn Monroe was in the care of Freudian psychoanalysts but she was not being psychoanalyzed; she was in psychoanalytically derived supportive treatment. The distinction is important. Patients with her emotional affliction are not available to orthodox analysis. . . .

Unhappily, medicine has not yet found a cure or even a confident therapy for Marilyn Monroe's personality disorder. Ms. Steinem quotes extensively from a work by Dr. W. Hugh Missildine, *Your Inner Child of the Past*: it seems to serve as her psychiatric authority. While these passages sensitively report on how people behave when they have been neglected in childhood, they propose no method of treatment.

Even Ms. Steinem's well-researched book falls short of fully documenting the role of heredity in Marilyn's psychic illness. It isn't only that Marilyn Monroe was manic-depressive and had a severe character disorder; by her own account in "My Story" her mother died insane, her mother's father died insane, her mother's grandmother died insane, her mother's brother killed himself. But our culture is a blame culture. It prefers to address only those ills that excite our moral indignation and to ignore the terrors of fate.

Marilyn Monroe didn't view herself as a tragic figure; she didn't give herself that much weight. But she begged to be taken seriously and to be regarded as someone with ideas and opinions worth hearing. One of her most moving requests was made of an unnamed interviewer near the close of her life; it was not granted but it is remembered by her press secretary. "Please don't make me a joke. End the interview with what I believe."

One can wish that she had been told she wasn't a joke: a sex idol who read books! The truth is that she was unusually intelligent. Indeed, as uneducated as she believed herself to be, she gave distinct signs of literary gift. Professional writers might envy the terse description of her ill mother in *My Story*: "Even the sound of a page turning made her nervous." Surely we are reminded of the everyday luminousness of F. Scott Fitzgerald and the strange sorrow that overhangs his work when Marilyn Monroe remarks of herself, "I am not interested in money. I just want to be wonderful." . . . (p. 23)

Diana Trilling, " 'Please Don't Make Me a Joke'," in The New York Times Book Review, *December 21, 1986, pp. 1, 23.*

Tom Stoppard

1937-

(Born Tomas Straussler) Czechoslovakian-born English playwright, novelist, short story writer, scriptwriter, critic, translator, and journalist.

The following entry presents criticism on Stoppard's play *Rosencrantz and Guildenstern Are Dead* (1966). For an overview of Stoppard's career, see *CLC,* Vols. 1, 3, 4, 5, 8, 15, 29, 34.

Stoppard is a leading playwright in contemporary theater. Like George Bernard Shaw and Oscar Wilde, with whom he is often compared, Stoppard examines serious issues within the context of comedy, often conveying weighty moral and philosophical themes through such comedic devices as word games and slapstick. Because Stoppard uses humor while addressing complex questions pertaining to authority, morality, the existence of God, the power of words to represent reality, and the role and function of art, his style of drama has been termed "philosophical farce." Stoppard's productions occasionally draw upon Shakespeare's plays for a framework in which to present modern concerns. His works also reflect the influence of Wilde in their use of comedy, of Samuel Beckett in their absurd view of existence, and of Luigi Pirandello in their use of drama as a means of probing the nature of illusion and reality. Although some critics consider Stoppard's theatrical devices to be a smokescreen concealing a lack of profundity, most praise him for his wit and technical virtuosity.

When the Nazis invaded Czechoslovakia in 1939, Stoppard's family fled their homeland and settled in Singapore. They were forced to relocate in India in 1942 because of advancement by Japanese forces. Dr. Eugene Straussler, Stoppard's father, remained in Japanese-occupied Singapore and was killed. After Straussler's widow married Major Kenneth Stoppard in 1946, the family moved to Britain. Stoppard was educated at Yorkshire public schools but dropped out at the age of seventeen to become a journalist. During the 1950s and 1960s, he worked on the Bristol *Evening World* and the *Western Daily Press* as a drama critic while composing radio and television plays. In 1963, a casual discussion with his agent, Kenneth Ewing, changed Stoppard's life. Ewing's query as to whether or not Lear was King of England during the time frame of Shakespeare's *Hamlet* prompted Stoppard to write a one-act play in verse, "Rosencrantz and Guildenstern Meet King Lear." In the next three years, the work evolved into Stoppard's first major production, *Rosencrantz and Guildenstern Are Dead,* which was an immediate popular and critical success.

Exploring such themes as identity, fate, freedom, and death, the play centers on two minor characters from *Hamlet.* While waiting to act out their roles in Shakespeare's tragedy, the courtiers Rosencrantz and Guildenstern pass the time by telling jokes and pondering reality, much in the same way that the two tramps occupy themselves in Samuel Beckett's *Waiting for Godot.* Rosencrantz and Guildenstern's original function—to transport Ham-

let, and the letter ordering his murder, to England—remains intact in Stoppard's rendering, as do their inevitable deaths when Hamlet alters the letter to command their executions. *Rosencrantz and Guildenstern* depicts the absurdity of life through these two characters who have "bit parts" in a play not of their making and who are capable only of acting out their dramatic destiny. They are bewildered by their predicament and face death as they search for the meaning of their existence. While examining these themes, Stoppard makes extensive use of puns and paradox, which have since become standard devices in his plays. Upon its London stage debut, *Rosencrantz and Guildenstern* was hailed by Harold Hobson as "the most important event in British professional theatre of the last nine years." The play received similar acclaim in the United States, winning the Tony Award as well as the New York Drama Critics Circle Award for best new play of 1968. Clive Barnes asserted: "This is a most remarkable and thrilling play. In one bound Mr. Stoppard is asking to be considered as among the finest English-speaking writers of our stage, for this is a work of fascinating distinction. Rosencrantz and Guildenstern LIVE!"

Stoppard was not the first playwright to discern dramatic possibilities in Hamlet's two courtiers. In 1891, Sir W. S.

Gilbert, librettist of the acclaimed composing team Gilbert and Sullivan, wrote a short burlesque comedy titled *Rosencrantz and Guildenstern.* Like Gilbert, Stoppard views the pair as confused pawns. He explained: "As far as their involvement in Shakespeare's text is concerned they are told very little about what is going on and much of what they are told isn't true. So I see them much more clearly as a couple of bewildered innocents rather than a couple of henchmen, which is the usual way they are depicted in productions of *Hamlet.*" Throughout Stoppard's version, when the plot becomes deeply embroiled with Shakespeare's original design, quotes directly from *Hamlet* further serve to illustrate the inconsequential status Rosencrantz and Guildenstern cannot elude. Stoppard's first variant in the text is the creation of fuller personalities for these previously minor characters. The leader of the pair, Rosencrantz, is more the intellectual; he expects his world to be coherent and becomes frustrated when meanings are vague. Guildenstern is simple-minded, curious, and more sympathetic of other people's plights. The duo is frequently compared to Vladimir and Estragon in Beckett's *Waiting for Godot.* Clive Barnes observed: "Like Beckett's tramps, these two silly, rather likable Elizabethan courtiers are trying to get through life with a little human dignity and perhaps here and there a splinter of comprehension. They play games with each other and constantly question not their past (probably only heroes can afford that luxury) but their present and their future. Especially their future." Like Vladimir and Estragon, Rosencrantz and Guildenstern seem to lack free will and understanding of their situation, but, unlike Beckett's two tramps, they ultimately receive answers to their questions.

As the play opens, Rosencrantz and Guildenstern are on a deserted road en route to the palace of Claudius, the new king of Denmark. They have been summoned to investigate Prince Hamlet's apparent mental illness. They relieve the monotony of their trek by tossing coins, which land "heads-up" every time. This immediately establishes that the ordinary laws of chance have been abandoned and foreshadows the predetermination that governs the rest of the duo's lives. They meet the "tragedians," a travelling acting troupe who serve as telling metaphors for Rosencrantz and Guildenstern's dilemma. For example, the Player, the troupe's leader, readily admits that the performers have no control over their lives: they have no idea where they will perform next, what the show will be, who will be watching, and how they will be received. Rosencrantz and Guildenstern grasp that they too are merely actors performing predestined roles, but, unlike the tragedians, who accept their situation passively, the courtiers consider their inability to control their actions a form of spiritual death. Their confusion and helplessness mirror Stoppard's ambivalent theatrical approach. He acknowledged: "My plays are a lot to do with the fact that *I just don't know.*" Numerous critics have maintained that it is his characters' bewilderment through which Stoppard obtains his psychological insight. J. Dennis Huston commented: "[From] their powerlessness the playwright derives his power; in their confusion, he finds vision. Out of apparent chaos he shapes an imaginative world logically disordered by its blurred dramatic perspective but thematically coherent and theatrically compelling."

After engaging in some role-playing—Guildenstern pretends he is Prince Hamlet, and Rosencrantz questions him about his distress following his father's death, his mother's marriage to his uncle, and his uncle's usurpation of the throne—the two decide that Hamlet's precarious mental state is merited. They encounter the Prince on the road, and Hamlet mistakes his "excellent good friends" for each other. This mistake of identities recurs in *Rosencrantz and Guildenstern Are Dead;* the courtiers often cannot even distinguish themselves. Several critics have maintained that while Stoppard has given Rosencrantz and Guildenstern distinct personalities, he also allows them the realization that no one else is conscious of their identities. To other characters they are not whole, and are often interrupted or pushed aside. As Rosencrantz complains, "Incidents! All we get is incidents! Dear God, is it too much to expect a little sustained action?!"

Rosencrantz and Guildenstern accompany Hamlet back to the palace, where the tragedians will be performing several plays. The Player slyly insinuates that he knows the story of *Hamlet* and informs Rosencrantz and Guildenstern of their imminent demise. After viewing *The Mousetrap,* in which the tragedians reenact the murder of Hamlet's father as per Hamlet's request, Claudius realizes that Hamlet is aware of his involvement in the slaying and orders Rosencrantz and Guildenstern to find the prince and transport him to England. On the boat, the courtiers read Claudius's letter, which orders Hamlet's beheading, and decide not to defy the king. When pirates attack the ship, everyone on board hides in barrels, and Hamlet disappears. When Rosencrantz and Guildenstern later reread the letter of execution, they discover that it has been changed by Hamlet and now states that *they* will be slain. They go to their deaths willingly, finally understanding that their only role in life is to die and that they will be repeating this cycle endlessly in other performances. As they exit, the last scene of *Hamlet* begins, as an Ambassador from England reports that "Rosencrantz and Guildenstern are dead" and darkness overtakes the stage.

While praising the tragicomic and thematic elements in *Rosencrantz and Guildenstern,* reviewers were impressed with Stoppard's adroit recreation of such a complex work as *Hamlet,* noting that his existential perspective on humanity translates well to Shakespeare's study of alienation and anguish. C. W. E. Bigsby asserted: "The wrenching of object from setting, of events from context, results not merely in a revealing absurdity but in a perception of the contingent nature of truth." *Rosencrantz and Guildenstern* has generated extensive commentary; among numerous concepts, critics have discussed the play's philosophical themes, its theatricality, its artistic design, Stoppard's use of black comedy, and his successful manipulation of logic and language.

(See also *Contemporary Authors,* Vols. 81-84; *Dictionary of Literary Biography,* Vol. 13; and *Dictionary of Literary Biography Yearbook:* 1985.)

PRINCIPAL WORKS

PLAYS

The Gamblers   1965
Tango   1966
Rosencrantz and Guildenstern Are Dead   1966

John Weightman

In ***Rosencrantz and Guildenstern Are Dead,*** Mr. Tom
Stoppard has had, or appears to have had, a brilliant idea.
It has always been said, at least by the old-fashioned critics, that Shakespeare's characters "go on existing" after
they have left the stage, whereas those of the classical
French dramatists—Racine's or Molière's, for instance—
do not. A Shakespeare play is not, primarily, *une pièce*
bien faite, a dramatic machine with a sleek and visible
mechanism, although the mechanism may be there all
right. It is more like a hunk of material ripped out of life.
You feel that if it were put back into place, it would at
once link up again in all directions, so that we could know
how many children Lady Macbeth had and how the poem
"Childe Roland to the Dark Tower came" actually goes
on. Mr. Stoppard has walked off into the wings to imagine
the extra-textual reality of two characters in *Hamlet,*
whose Shakespearian appearances are tantalisingly incomplete. Rosencrantz and Guildenstern never come on
to the stage, and are never referred to, except as a couple,
as if their psychological charge were too slight to allow
them to exist separately. Hamlet greets them warmly as
old friends and then, a little later, sends them off without
compunction to their deaths. They appear fitfully, do
nothing very much, and then disappear. This being so, Mr.
Stoppard has decided that they can be developed as modern anti-heroes. They are siblings in nonentity, sharing a
ridiculous Tweedledum/Tweedledee part; they never fully
get the hang of the situation and they are swatted like flies
through being accidentally caught up in the tragedy.

Before setting to work, he has obviously read his illustrious predecessors in the contemporary theatre, since the
text abounds in allusions. At times it seems as if he has put
Waiting for Godot inside *Hamlet,* and one admires the
courage of a young man who has the nerve to do this. His
characters needle each other in a vacuum. . . . Their
prose is occasionally disguised Eliotish verse, with a note
of ponderous, philosophical inquiry which may, or may
not, be taking itself seriously. . . . The stage business becomes reminiscent of the mirror-like complexities of
Genet, when the Players put on for them a play within the
play within the play. All these echoes reinforce the up-to-
date nature of this comedy team—one skinny, the other
rather plump, one intellectual, the other rather dim, one
slightly hysterical, the other quite robust, etc. If Hamlet
himself can be looked upon as the great pre-Existentialist
hero in European drama—bastardised by his uncle's usurpation, puzzled by contingency, uncertain about how to
exercise his freedom, distressed to the point of craziness
by the absence of essences—Rosencrantz and Guildenstern, when treated like this, become little Hamlets, whose
uneasiness is a wry, apologetic modern echo of the
Prince's splendid Renaissance melancholia.

The idea is brilliant and produces a certain amount of fun,
but I don't think it is worked out with complete success.
The action is not a legitimate extension of the minimal
identity that Shakespeare gives Rosencrantz and Guildenstern in *Hamlet,* and so Mr. Stoppard's play operates at
an uncomfortable tangent to Shakespeare's. To reduce, or
elevate, his protagonists to the status of "outsiders" with
whom we can sympathise, Mr. Stoppard has to curtail
their biggest Shakespearean scene, because in it they appear as rather silly time-servers, at the opposite pole from
Horatio, the friend of sterling quality. Also, he has to put
them into a limbo which is largely gratuitous.

We first see them during a pause in their journey to court,
and they are presented as having uncertain memories of
their past identity. Of course, Existentialist anti-heroes are
frequently amnesiac or semi-amnesiac, since their anguish
comes partly from living in the ever-moving present, with
the past constantly crumbling into nothingness behind

them. But Rosencrantz and Guildenstern cannot come out of the void into the action of *Hamlet;* they would only obey the summons if they understood it, and it seems portentous to surround them with questionings as if they were the Magi en route for an unknown Bethlehem or Vladimir and Estragon really waiting for Godot. Similarly, once they get to court, they would know what was going on there since, as courtiers, they would be in the thick of the gossip. On this point, Mr. Stoppard wobbles; he both shows them as understanding the situation to a certain extent and as deliberately killing time in limbo when they are not taking part in the action. Every now and again, the plot of *Hamlet* swirls in and around them and they fall into their Shakespearean roles in Shakespearean English, whereas before they had been talking in 20th-century voices. But it is as if they were members of the audience seeing only those snatches of *Hamlet* in which they themselves are involved, the rest of the play remaining a closed book ("I don't pretend to have understood. . . . If they won't tell us, that's their affair"). If this is meant as a symbol, it can only signify that we see our lives as an intermittent, incomprehensible dream, of which we never grasp the plot. But even those people most subject to *Angst* are never as much in the dark as this, except perhaps about collective, public events beyond their range. It may be true of thorough-going schizophrenics, but Rosencrantz and Guildenstern are not made as pathological as that.

In any case, at one point Mr. Stoppard completely contradicts this general impression of ignorance by making Rosencrantz and Guildenstern impersonate Hamlet and envisage the situation very penetratingly from his point of view:

> Ros: To sum up: your father, whom you love, dies, you are his heir, you come back to find that hardly was the corpse cold before his young brother popped on to his throne and into his sheets, thereby offending both legal and natural practice. Now why are you behaving in this extraordinary manner?
>
> Guil: I can't imagine!

This is a witty demolition of Shakespeare's plot. There would be no *Hamlet,* if the Prince, instead of feigning madness and complicating all the issues, took the obvious course and denounced his uncle publicly from the start as an arrant usurper, which is what he would have done, had he been a character in one of the historical plays. The Ghost, the Players, the interview with Gertrude, the trip to England are all, strictly speaking, unnecessary, and Shakespeare does nothing to justify them, apart from making them the occasion of splendid poetry. All those marvellous words cover up much ado about nothing. The King should not need Rosencrantz and Guildenstern to tell him why Hamlet is uneasy; his problem is rather to know why, in the circumstances, Hamlet has not already begun to topple him from the throne. However, I don't think we worry about this as we watch *Hamlet.* We take it for granted that neither the Prince nor the King does the straightforward, rational thing, because, if they did, Shakespeare would not have been able to give us this extended lament on the puzzling nature of human existence. But we do worry, or at least I worry, about the fact that Mr. Stoppard's heroes are not properly connected up to *Hamlet,* because *Hamlet* is, after all, where they come

from. The other alternative is to say that ***Rosencrantz and Guildenstern Are Dead*** has nothing to do with *Hamlet,* but is a dialogue between two near-Existentialist heroes, occasionally decorated with quotations from Shakespeare in an inconsequential, Pop-art manner.

Even if this interpretation is the correct one, it is still difficult to see at times on what level the author wishes us to understand his text. The play opens with a long scene in which Rosencrantz and Guildenstern are whiling away the time by spinning coins. The result has been heads in about a hundred throws in succession. This is, of course, a miracle, which is presumably intended to enhance the sense of awe surrounding the summons to the court. Yet these intimations of Someone pulling strings from the Beyond for an Ultimate Purpose are not backed up by any metaphysical beliefs. Shakespeare can use the Ghost in his first scene, because the supernatural was still part of his accepted stock-in-trade. Eliot and Claudel are on weaker ground when they introduce miracles into their plays, since stage thaumaturgy costs nothing and proves nothing, but one could argue that, being convinced Christians, they no doubt believed in miracles, and therefore were free, as between Christians, to use imagined miracles for poetic effect. But Mr. Stoppard's miracle is a sort of *hors d'oeuvre,* a mere incidental theatrical gimmick, which gives an excuse for some mildly entertaining back-chat and funny stage-business, but has no significance beyond itself.

Perhaps the whole play is just intellectual fooling around, with occasional stabs at seriousness. Now and again, one suspects that Mr. Stoppard is trying to be genuinely poetic and is inviting us to commune with Rosencrantz and Guildenstern in some emotion. Since the performers are attractive, we allow ourselves to be beguiled and then are suddenly let down, because the poetry is spurious. For instance, Rosencrantz and Guildenstern are pleased to meet up with the Players, who offer an unexpected distraction during the initial period of waiting. But the troupe turns out to be a sorry band, scraping a living by doing obscene pantomimes and forcing their least unattractive member to function as male whore. On discovering this, Guildenstern, "shaking with rage and fright," exclaims passionately at the disillusionment of the chance encounter:

> . . . it didn't have to be *obscene.* . . . It could have been a bird out of season, dropping bright-feathered on my shoulder. . . . It could have been a tongueless dwarf standing by the road to point the way. . . .

The bird out of season and the tongueless dwarf are surely *kitsch,* but are we meant to appreciate them as being symptomatic of Guildenstern's camp vibration, or to enjoy them as poetry? I guess that Mr. Stoppard is hoping for the latter reaction but would settle for the former, and so the former it inevitably is. When, at the end, Rosencrantz and Guildenstern go wittingly to their deaths "to give their lives a meaning," the effect is equally thin and camp.

As the play progresses, we see that the only other characters Rosencrantz and Guildenstern commune with in their limbo are the Players and, in fact, the leading player almost steals the show. This is another Existentialist commonplace; if the average person is so befuddled by contingency that he can only give himself an identity by accepting this or that form of "bad faith," then the actor can become the modern hero, since he sits loose to all identities and plays with them at will. At the same time, he only becomes "subject" by deliberately making himself "object" for contemplation by others; if the others stop watching, his identity as subject/object sputters away like a collapsing balloon. This is beautifully expressed in one of the speeches by the leading Player when he complains about Rosencrantz and Guildenstern asking his troupe to put on a show and then not staying to see it through. These exchanges between the Player and Rosencrantz and Guildenstern seem to me to be the best bits in the work. The Player has a strong presence, because he accepts only two basic forces, greed and lust, and looks upon all the superstructures as provisional and interchangeable; this is a rudimentary philosophy which works up to a point. Rosencrantz and Guildenstern have likable non-presences; they are comparable to actors who haven't yet been adequately briefed about their parts and who are playing word-games or indulging in random reflections until the playwright or the director makes up his mind. Curiously enough, the newspapers say Mr. Stoppard was a journalist until he became a dramatist. He strikes me as being a born man of the theatre, but whether the expression is to be taken in its very good, or its less good, sense, I would not yet like to bet. (pp. 38-40)

John Weightman, "Mini-Hamlets in Limbo," in Encounter, Vol. XXIX, No. 1, July, 1967, pp. 38-40.

Clive Barnes

It is not only Hamlet who dies in *Hamlet.* They also serve who only stand and wait. Tom Stoppard's play ***Rosencrantz and Guildenstern Are Dead*** . . . is a very funny play about death. Very funny, very brilliant, very chilling; it has the dust of thought about it and the particles glitter excitingly in the theatrical air.

Mr. Stoppard uses as the basis for his play a very simple yet telling proposition; namely that although to Hamlet those twin-stemmed courtiers Rosencrantz and Guildenstern are of slight importance, and that to an audience of Shakespeare's play they are little but functionaries lent some color by a fairly dilatory playwright, Rosencrantz and Guildenstern are very important indeed to Rosencrantz and Guildenstern.

This then is the play of *Hamlet* not seen through the eyes of Hamlet, or Claudius, or Ophelia or Gertrude, but a worm's-eye view of tragedy seen from the bewildered standpoint of Rosencrantz and Guildenstern.

We first see them on a deserted highway. They have been summoned to the King's palace; they do not understand why. They are tossing coins to pass the time of day. The ordinary laws of chance appear to have been suspended. Perhaps they have been. Destiny that has already marked out Hamlet for such a splendid, purple satin death, is keeping a skimpy little piece of mauve bunting for poor Guildenstern and gentle Rosencrantz. They are about to get caught up in the action of a play.

Their conversation, full of Elizabethan school logic and flashes of metaphysical wit, is amusing but deliberately

fatuous. Rosencrantz and Guildenstern are fools. When you come to think of it, they would have to be. Otherwise they might have been Hamlet.

As they talk, the suspicion crosses the mind (it is a play where you are encouraged to stand outside the action and let suspicions, thoughts, glimmers and insights criss-cross your understanding) that Mr. Stoppard is not only paraphrasing *Hamlet,* but also throwing in a paraphrase of Samuel Beckett's *Waiting for Godot* for good measure. For this is antic lunacy with a sad, wry purpose.

Like Beckett's tramps, these two silly, rather likeable Elizabethan courtiers are trying to get through life with a little human dignity and perhaps here and there a splinter of comprehension. They play games with each other and constantly question not their past (probably only heroes can afford that luxury) but their present and their future. Especially their future.

On the road they meet the strolling players, also, of course, for the plot is a mousetrap seen from the other side of the cheese, on the road to Elsinore. The leading Player, a charming, honest and sinister man, invites the two to participate in a strolling play. They, with scruples, refuse, but in fact they cannot refuse—because in life this precisely is what they have done.

Mr. Stoppard seems to see the action of his play unfolding like a juicy onion with strange layers of existence protectively wrapped around one another. There are plays here within plays—and Mr. Stoppard never lets us forget that his courtiers are not only characters in a life, but also characters in a play. They are modest—they admit that they are only supporting players. But they do want to see something of the script everyone else is working from.

It is one of Mr. Stoppard's cleverest conceits of stagecraft that the actors re-enacting the performance of *Hamlet* that is, in effect, dovetailed into the main section of the play, use only Shakespeare's words. Thus while they are waiting in the tattered, drafty antechamber of the palace for something to happen, we in the audience know what is happening on the other side of the stage. As one of them says, "Every exit is an entry somewhere else."

Finally reduced to the terminal shrifts of unbelief, it seems that Rosencrantz and Guildenstern realize that the only way they can find their identity is in their "little deaths." Although on the final, fateful boat they discover the letter committing them to summary execution in England, they go forward to death, glad, even relieved.

It is impossible to re-create the fascinating verbal tension of the play—Mr. Stoppard takes an Elizabethan pleasure in the sound of his own actors—or the ideas, suggestive, tantalizing that erupt through its texture. Nor, even most unfortunately, can I suggest the happy, zany humor or even the lovely figures of speech, such as calling something "like two blind men looting a bazaar for their own portraits." All this is something you must see and hear for yourself. . . .

This is a most remarkable and thrilling play. In one bound Mr. Stoppard is asking to be considered as among the finest English-speaking writers of our stage, for this is a work of fascinating distinction. Rosencrantz and Guildenstern LIVE!

Clive Barnes, in a review of "Rosencrantz and Guildenstern Are Dead," in The New York Times, *October 17, 1967, p. 53.*

Walter Kerr

After all these years of prattling on and on about Revenge Tragedy (with *Hamlet* as the supreme example of the good play that can be born of a merely bloodthirsty tradition) we have finally arrived at its dead opposite: Revenge Comedy.

Tom Stoppard's *Rosencrantz and Guildenstern Are Dead* . . . is a Revenge Comedy in two senses of the term. On a superficial, and quite pleasant, level, the comedy takes its revenge on all of those people who have, for 400 years, obstinately announced that they couldn't tell Rosencrantz and Guildenstern apart. Mr. Stoppard makes it clear that Rosencrantz and Guildenstern couldn't tell themselves apart, either.

On a much more serious, and finally most impressive, level, the comedy takes its revenge on that dirty trickster, Life, for being built the way it is. It is built like a honeycomb that is mostly plugged up, defying all the busy little bees who must live with it to get at it.

Rosencrantz and Guildenstern must live with the honeycomb that is Hamlet's house. They have been summoned by a messenger who came so early in the morning that they can scarcely remember what he looked like or what he said. Having arrived at a castle that seems so much melted-down wax, they are welcomed and then abandoned, left to toss coins in drafty corridors while the urgent business of the hour goes on in other rooms without them. They do not understand the task they are to perform, much less the crisis that has overtaken the occasional fugitives who slip by them to scream silently or perhaps to make an incomprehensible joke about knowing a hawk from a handsaw.

Guildenstern, a spare, gangling, fretful fellow who looks like both a hawk and a handsaw, is exasperated that he should so become "intrigued without ever being enlightened." Guildenstern expects something of the world he inhabits. He expects coherence, a pattern in which "each move is dictated by the previous one—that is the meaning of order." But here there are only fragments: Hamlet yanking at Ophelia's blond hair to whip-saw her head about, for no known savage reason: touring players rehearsing a dumb-show in which the dead are blown away on the wind like nameless November leaves.

Rosencrantz is, for a time, more easygoing, if only because all the coins he tosses keep coming up heads: the probabilities, which no one can fathom, seem to be in his favor. Gradually, though, it becomes apparent that the universal drift is toward death—and toward a death that will come before anyone has quite grasped life. "Incidents! Incidents!" he cries out, shaking his fist at empty heavens as he begins to scent the woodsmoke of his own funeral pyre. "Dear God, is it too much to expect a little sustained action?"

The principal touring player gives neither of them comfort. He has long since ceased trying to make any sense of himself as a man; he is resigned to being nothing more than an actor, a creature of no settled identity. But he doesn't really suppose that acting is going to impose any shape on his wayward passage. He has long ago been "tricked out of the single assumption that makes our existence tolerable—that someone is watching." The play goes on, blindly, piecemeal. All of us are caught up in it. But it is being performed to silence. Rosencrantz shakes his fist at no one.

The play is of course yet one more document in the unreeling existentialist catalogue. If I have anything against it, apart from its somewhat crushing overlength, it is that Mr. Stoppard himself is watching too closely, is too much with us. His two principal figures are not baffled and lost in their own ways. They are baffled and lost in his, speaking his words for him, placarding his thoughts. Thus there is a steady barrage of philosophical finger-pointing: "Which way did we come in—I've lost my sense of direction." "What have we got to go on?", "We're slipping off the map." "What does it all add up to?" The effect is to remove Rosencrantz and Guildenstern not only from the buzzing life that is rumored about them but also from the arbitrary play that is surely going to execute them. They stand outside both, ignorant and omniscient at once, intellectualizing for their author. What this ultimately suggests is a Presence in the wings after all, a designer, a dictator, a listening God of some sort—and it tends to undercut the play's own premises.

But the evening's compensations grow upon one steadily as the stage lights turn from an autumnal gold to a tidal wave of blood-red. When Mr. Stoppard puts himself to digging beneath the skin of human experience, he is capable of bringing back chilling bulletins from the unknown front. Rosencrantz seems to catch his breath as from an invisible, sickening blow as he realizes that he cannot for the life of him recall when he first heard about death. Someone must have told him, undoubtedly when he was a child. News of such import must have lodged somewhere in his head. But it hasn't. Does anyone remember the moment of that first staggering announcement that he is destined to die? No, probably not. With his mouth scarcely able to form the necessary syllables, pallid from the implications he is trying to sort out in his brain, Rosencrantz makes the obvious deductions. No one remembers first hearing the news because everyone was born knowing it. A baby's first bleat rides on the breath of "an intuition of mortality." The written moment . . . [is a] brilliant stroke of theater.

So is the fidgety scurry of . . . [Guildenstern's slippered feet as he] tries, with caterpillar tactics, to evade the sound of what his companion is saying, huddling his toes together and clapping his hands over his ears as though his entire body could be blinded if he exerted himself enough. Again, the desperation with which [Rosencrantz] struggles to imagine England when he has not yet got there is original and telling exploration of the human psyche, reminding us of those hundred half-forgotten—perhaps wilfully forgotten—sensations we've had of the insubstantiality of all that is most familiar to us, of the images that wantonly dissolve the minute we decide to force them into sharp focus. And humor is, in Mr. Stoppard's hands, the easy handmaiden of the frustrations we live with as we keep hot on the heels of a promised clarity. Either Rosencrantz or Guildenstern (it *is* hard to say which) wants to know why the players bother with a dumb-show before the spoken play proper. The chief player explains that the unspoken is a good deal clearer. "You understand," he adds with a bitter flourish, "that we're tied down to a language which makes up in obscurity what it lacks in style." (pp. 1, 3)

Walter Kerr "Taking Revenge on Life," in *The New York Times, October 29, 1967, pp. 1, 3.*

Tom Stoppard (Interview with Giles Gordon)

[*The interview excerpted below originally took place in March, 1968.*]

[Gordon]: *Why do you choose Hamlet? Why Rosencrantz and Guildenstern?*

[Stoppard]: They chose themselves to a certain extent. I mean that the play *Hamlet* and the characters Rosencrantz and Guildenstern are the only play and the only characters on which you could write my kind of play. They are so much more than merely bit players in another famous play. *Hamlet* I suppose is the most famous play in any language, it is part of a sort of common mythology. I am continually being asked politely whether I will write about the messenger in *Oedipus Rex,* which misses the point.

But in a way it is difficult to see the point. It is all very well for you to say that, but it was brilliant insight on your part to see that you could—or someone could—write a play about Rosencrantz and Guildenstern.

But as I said they are more than just bit players in another play. There are certain things which they bring on with them, particularly the fact that they end up dead without really, as far as any textual evidence goes, knowing why. Hamlet's assumption that they were privy to Claudius's plot is entirely gratuitous. As far as their involvement in Shakespeare's text is concerned they are told very little about what is going on and much of what they are told isn't true. So I see them much more clearly as a couple of bewildered innocents rather than a couple of henchmen, which is the usual way they are depicted in productions of *Hamlet.*

And this presumably is why you wanted to write about Rosencrantz and Guildenstern?

Yes, it presumably is. I can't actually remember.

This is why to the playgoer, at least to myself, the play is the first post McLuhan (if that means anything), post Beckettian drama because the two protagonists are bewildered innocents rather than henchmen, and their anonymity is magnified to such an extent that they become positive people. Do you feel that either Rosencrantz or Guildenstern corresponds to you at all? What you were saying earlier about your distrust of self-revelation seems to fit here.

They both add up to me in many ways in the sense that they're carrying out a dialogue which I carry out with myself. One of them is fairly intellectual, fairly incisive; the other one is thicker, nicer in a curious way, more sympathetic. There's a leader and the led. Retrospectively, with all benefit of other people's comments and enthusiasms

and so on, it just seems a classic case of self-revelation even though it isn't about this fellow who wrote his first novel . . . But of course the saving thing is that I'm the only person who really knows to what extent and at what points the play reveals me. There's a great deal, of course, which has nothing to do with me, which satisfactorily obscures the photograph.

Nobody can write anything which doesn't reveal a certain amount about himself.

That's perfectly true. It's merely the difference between reflecting one's experience and reflecting one's personality. (pp. 19-21)

Did you do a lot of rewriting of **Rosencrantz?** *The words and nuances seem very precise.*

I rewrote a great deal before I reached a final draft, but having got to a final draft I did comparatively little, though I did change the ending. We worked a lot on the ending with the National Theatre actors in the last two or three weeks of rehearsal. And, furthermore, between Edinburgh and London I wrote . . . [an entirely new scene]. It was suggested by Sir Laurence [Olivier], who pointed out that I had omitted a key scene in *Hamlet.* This is the scene where Rosencrantz and Guildenstern accost Hamlet after he has hidden Polonius's body. It arose because Olivier pointed out that when Claudius came on and instructed them to find Hamlet, who happened to have killed Polonius, it was the one time in the play when they were given an actual specific duty to fulfill, and it was a pity that it had been lost in the sort of cinematic cut we had then. So I wrote that scene. It's there, and I'm glad it's there.

The only scene which reveals them in action.

Though it's not very active for all that.

Who do you feel you've been influenced by as a writer, or don't you feel it's important?

It's not important to me, but I suppose it's interesting. Influences such as appear in **Rosencrantz,** and any play of anybody else's, are I suppose admirations that have been unsuccessfully repressed or obscured. I don't mean consciously! But, of the influences that have been invoked on my behalf, and they have been Beckett, Kafka, Pirandello of course, I suppose Beckett is the easiest one to make, yet the most deceptive. Most people who say Beckett mean *Waiting for Godot.* They haven't read his novels, for example. I can see a lot of Beckettian things in all my work, but they're not actually to do with the image of two lost souls waiting for something to happen, which is why most people connect **Rosencrantz** with *Waiting for Godot,* because they had this scene in common.

Beckett's novels are mainly about one lost soul waiting for nothing to happen.

I wasn't thinking so much of what they are about so much as the way in which Beckett expresses himself, and the bent of his humour. I find Beckett deliciously funny in the way that he qualifies everything as he goes along, reduces, refines and dismantles. When I read it I love it and when I write I just guess it comes out as other things come out. As for Pirandello, I know very little about him, I'm afraid. I've seen very little and I really wasn't aware of that as an influence. It would be very difficult to write a play which was totally unlike Beckett, Pirandello and Kafka, who's your father, you know? (pp. 22-3)

I have the impression, from **Rosencrantz** *and from what you've been saying, that you're more interested in form than content.*

No, I'm not actually hooked on form. I'm not even hooked on content if one means message. I'm hooked on style.

I wonder if we don't mean the same thing by style and form. Style to me is modish, more superimposed than form, which is structural, integral. To me **Rosencrantz** *is formal, and has style;* Look Back in Anger *has neither, though it has a lot of other things.*

I think it has both. It is as formal as a quadrille, if you can have a quadrille with two girls and a man—you could draw that play on graph paper, with lines for Jimmy, Alison and whatsername—Helen?—crossing and recrossing in a formal construction. And although at first glance it has a sort of freebooting, free-associating flow of a compulsive talker with a certain wit and coherence, it is in fact constructed with an intense and ever-present recognition of the fact that it has got to be done in front of an audience and work in a particular way, and this concern for structure pops through to the surface at key points. The way that, for example, you end an act on a point where Jimmy and Helen, whom he has despised for the previous twenty minutes, come to a clinch—she hits him and he kisses her—act! It's exactly the same thing as ending a serial in a woman's magazine at a point where the reader is intrigued to buy it next week. As for style—the play seems merely emotional, but you can't really talk like that in real life without feeling self-conscious. And the reason you feel self-conscious is that you are aware that you are doing it with style, with just as much style as an Oscar Wilde character contriving to speak exclusively in epigrams. (pp. 25)

> *Tom Stoppard and Giles Gordon, in an interview in* The Transatlantic Review, *No. 29, Summer, 1968, pp. 17-25.*

Clive Barnes

Three Broadway seasons ago, Tom Stoppard's **Rosencrantz and Guildenstern Are Dead** was a hit, winning the Tony Award for the season as the best play, and enjoying a decent run. Someone, however, once characterized it as "a snob-hit," meaning, if I recall correctly, that he personally, in common with the majority Broadway audience, couldn't understand it, and that therefore it was out of place on Broadway.

The man might have been right—although he underestimated the potentiality of Broadway taste—for Stoppard's play is not the normal, undemanding Broadway fare. Now it has cropped up again, not on Broadway, not even off Broadway, but off off Broadway at the Classic Stage Company's Repertory Theater. . . .

C.S.C., which is one of the most enterprising and most ambitious theatrical projects around town, has put **Rosencrantz and Guildenstern** in repertory with its production of *Hamlet*. It saves on costumes, it saves on settings and, taken together, it must offer a perfect insight into Mr.

Stoppard's existential view of private tragedy and public comedy.

Rosencrantz and Guildenstern is a marvelous, mindbopping play. I have seen it two or three times with Britain's National Theater and a couple of times on Broadway. The C.S.C. version, totally understandably, was not as good as any of them. But the play, decently treated, easily survived, and I thoroughly enjoyed myself.

Mr. Stoppard's play, in a way, combines *Hamlet* with *Waiting for Godot,* which is not an unformidable combination. It is very much at home away from the Broadway ambiance. Its enthusiastic young audience laughs delightedly at all the jokes, quite unaware that it is seeing "a snob-hit" and simply accepting the play as true and funny.

Rosencrantz and Guildenstern are the greatest patsys in drama. They wait in an underdeveloped anteroom of literature. Occasionally, their eyes blinded by the spotlight of dramatic inevitability, they are permitted to come on stage where Hamlet, himself, smiling grimly, makes perfectly adequate fools of them. Later they are killed, almost as a joke or a dramatic curlicue. Yet before Rosencrantz and Guildenstern went to it and died, they lived. They were real. They were stupid, scared, irresolute and very fond of party games and logic. Nor did they really want to die. They were, after all, rather dragged into the play by Shakespeare, who never once consulted them. . . .

Of course there are faults. But the play remains fun, it teases the mind, it offers a load of belly laughs, and when everything is over you realize that this is a very complex play being sympathetically given.

> *Clive Barnes, in a review of "Rosencrantz and Guildenstern Are Dead," in* The New York Times, *November 19, 1970, p. 39.*

Normand Berlin

Tom Stoppard's **Rosencrantz and Guildenstern Are Dead** entered the theater world of 1966-67 with much fanfare, and in the ensuing years it has acquired a surprisingly high reputation as a modern classic. It is an important play, but its importance is of a very special kind up to now not acknowledged. The play has fed the modern critics' and audiences' hunger for "philosophical" significances, and as absurdist drama it has been compared favorably and often misleadingly with Beckett's *Waiting for Godot.* However, its peculiar value as theater of criticism has received no attention. To help recognize this value I offer the following discussion.

Rosencrantz and Guildenstern Are Dead is a derivative play. . . . It feeds on William Shakespeare's *Hamlet,* on Luigi Pirandello's *Six Characters in Search of an Author,* and on Samuel Beckett's *Waiting for Godot.* Stoppard goes to Shakespeare for his characters, for the background to his play's action, and for some direct quotations, to Pirandello for the idea of giving extra-dramatic life to established characters, to Beckett for the tone, the philosophical thrust, and for some comic routines. The play takes Shakespeare's Rosencrantz and Guildenstern—timeservers, who appear rather cool and calculating in Shakespeare, and whose names indicate the courtly decadence they may represent—and transforms them into garrulous, sometimes simple, often rather likable chaps. Baffled, imprisoned in a play they did not write, Rosencrantz and Guildenstern must act out their pre-arranged dramatic destinies. Like Beckett's Vladimir and Estragon, they carry on vaudeville routines, engage in verbal battles and games, and discourse on the issues of life and death. However, whereas Beckett's play, like Shakespeare's, defies easy categories and explanations, and remains elusive in the best sense of the word, suggesting the mystery of life, Stoppard's play welcomes categories, prods for a clarity of explanation, and seems more interested in substance than shadow.

Stoppard's play is conspicuously intellectual; it "thinks" a great deal, and consequently it lacks the "feeling" or union of thought and emotion that we associate with *Waiting for Godot* and *Hamlet.* This must be considered a shortcoming in Stoppard's art, but a shortcoming that Stoppard shares with other dramatists and one that could be explained away if only his intellectual insights were less derivative, seemed less canned. To be sure, plays breed plays, and it would be unfair to find fault with Stoppard for going to other plays for inspiration and specific trappings. In fact, at times he uses Shakespeare and Beckett ingeniously and must be applauded for his execution. But when the ideas of an essentially intellectual play seem too easy, then the playwright must be criticized. Whenever Stoppard—his presence always felt although his characters do the talking—meditates on large philosophical issues, his play seems thin, shallow. His idiom is not rich enough to sustain a direct intellectual confrontation with Life and Death. Consider, for example, Guildenstern's question: "The only beginning is birth and the only end is death—if you can't count on that, what can you count on?" Put in this pedestrian way, the idea behind the question loses its force. Or take Guildenstern's remarks on Death: "Dying is not romantic, and death is not a game which will soon be over . . . Death is not anything . . . death is not . . . It's the absence of presence, nothing more . . . the endless time of never coming back . . . a gap you can't see, and when the wind blows through it, it makes no sound. . . ." Examples of this kind of direct philosophical probing can be found throughout the play. We hear a man talking but do not feel the pressure of death behind the words. The passage seems false because the language does not possess the elusiveness and the economy that are essential if a writer wishes to confront large issues directly.

But there are indirect ways to deal with life and death, and here Stoppard is highly successful. And here we arrive at the heart of the discussion of Stoppard's art. According to Stoppard himself, his play was "not written as a response to anything about alienation in our times. . . . It would be fatal to set out to write primarily on an intellectual level. Instead, one writes about human beings under stress—whether it is about losing one's trousers or being nailed to the cross." Stoppard's words run counter to our experience of the play and indicate once again that writers are not the best judges of their own writing. Like all writers of drama, Stoppard wishes to present human beings under stress, but he does so in the most intellectual way. In fact, there is only one level to the play, one kind of stance, and that level is intellectual. The audience witnesses no forceful sequence of narrative, since the story is known and therefore already solidified in the audience's mind. One could say that the audience is given not sequence but status-quo, and status-quo points to a "critical stance—a way of looking at the events of the play as a critic would, that is, experiencing the play as structure, complete, unmoving, unsequential.

In the act of seeing a stage play, which moves in time, we are in a pre-critical state, fully and actively engaged in the play's events. When the play is over, then we become critics, seeing the play as a structural unity and, in fact, able to function as critics only because the play has stopped moving. In the act of seeing *Rosencrantz and Guildenstern Are Dead,* however, our critical faculty is not subdued. We are always *observing* the characters and are not ourselves participating. We know the results of the action because we know *Hamlet,* so that all our references are backward. Not witnessing a movement in time, we are forced to contemplate the frozen state, the status-quo, of the characters who carry their Shakespearean fates with them. It is *during* Stoppard's play that we function as critics, just as Stoppard, through his characters, functions as critic within the play. It is precisely this critical stance of Stoppard, of his characters, and of his audience that allows me to attach the label "theater of criticism" to the play, thereby specifying what I believe to be Stoppard's distinctiveness as a modern dramatist.

We recognize and wonder at those points in Shakespeare's plays where he uses the "theater" image to allow us to see, critically, the play before us from a different angle, where, for example, we hear of the future re-creations of Caesar's murder at the very point in the play where it is re-created, or where we hear Cleopatra talk about her greatness presented on stage "i' th' posture of a whore" at the moment when it is presented in that posture. At these moments Shakespeare engages us on a cerebral level, forcing us to think, stopping the action to cause us to consider the relationship between theater and life. These Shakespearean moments are expanded to occupy much of Stoppard's play, just as Shakespeare's minor characters are expanded to become Stoppard's titular non-heroes.

I have indicated Stoppard's shortcomings when he wishes to express truths about Life and Death. However, as critic discussing *Hamlet* and Elizabethan drama, he is astute, sometimes brilliant, and his language is effective because it need not confront head-on the large issues that only poetry, it seems, is successful in confronting directly. In a *New Yorker* interview with actors Brian Murray and John Wood, who played Rosencrantz and Guildenstern in the New York production of Stoppard's play, Murray says: "I have been an actor most of my life, and I've played all kinds of parts with the Royal Shakespeare Company, but I never realized how remarkable Shakespeare is until I saw what Tom Stoppard could do with a couple of minor characters from *Hamlet.*" This fleeting statement in a rather frivolous interview pinpoints what Stoppard does best: what he can "do with" Shakespeare's minor characters to help us realize "how remarkable Shakespeare is." That is, Stoppard helps us to see more clearly not "human beings under stress" but Shakespeare. The actor Murray is applauding a critical function, and as we thread our way through the play Stoppard must be praised for precisely that function.

Here is an exchange between Rosencrantz and Guildenstern in which Guildenstern, pretending to be Hamlet (or, to put it better, *playing* Hamlet), is being questioned by Rosencrantz.

> Ros. Let me get it straight. Your father was king. You were his only son. Your father dies. You are of age. Your uncle becomes king.
>
> Guil. Yes.
>
> Ros. Unorthodox.
>
> Guil. Undid me.
>
> Ros. Undeniable. Where were you?
>
> Guil. In Germany.
>
> Ros. Usurpation, then.
>
> Guil. He slipped in.
>
> Ros. Which reminds me.
>
> Guil. Well, it would.
>
> Ros. I don't want to be personal.
>
> Guil. It's common knowledge.
>
> Ros. Your mother's marriage.
>
> Guil. He slipped in.
>
> Ros. . . . His body was still warm.
>
> Guil. So was hers.
>
> Ros. Extraordinary.
>
> Guil. Indecent.
>
> Ros. Hasty.
>
> Guil. Suspicious.
>
> Ros. It makes you think.
>
> Guil. Don't think I haven't thought of it.
>
> Ros. And with her husband's brother.
>
> Guil. They were close.
>
> Ros. She went to him—
>
> Guil. —Too close—
>
> Ros. —for comfort.
>
> Guil. It looks bad.
>
> Ros. It adds up.
>
> Guil. Incest to adultery.
>
> Ros. Would you go so far?
>
> Guil. Never.
>
> Ros. To sum up: your father, whom you love, dies, you are his heir, you come back to find that hardly was the corpse cold before his young brother popped onto the throne and into his sheets, thereby offending both legal and natural practice. Now why exactly are you behaving in this extraordinary manner?
>
> Guil. I can't imagine!

This dialogue says as much about Hamlet's dilemma—

crisply, comically—as many a critical essay, and it makes T. S. Eliot's search for an objective correlative in *Hamlet* seem academic. How effectively Stoppard repeats that phrase "He slipped in" to cover Hamlet's concern with both politics and sex. How precisely Rosencrantz's low-key "It makes you think" characterizes Hamlet's usual mode of behavior. How brilliantly Stoppard brings together the warmth of a newly dead body and the heat of a mature woman's body, Hamlet's two main preoccupations. Not that Stoppard in a few words has reached the heart of Hamlet's mystery; it never will be reached. But he allows us to place the mystery within a refreshingly clear framework. At the same time, by having Guildenstern play Hamlet, by having him put on that theatrical mask—calling to mind the various maskings of the Player—Stoppard allows us to think of man's usual condition: "Give us this day our daily mask." (pp. 269-73)

Stoppard confronts another critical crux in *Hamlet* when he has the Player present this brief statement on the dumb show: "Well, it's a device, really—it makes the action that follows more or less comprehensible; you understand, we are tied down to a language which makes up in obscurity what it lacks in style." Again we find that an attempt to answer the kind of question a critic would ask leads to a larger statement about the inability of language to communicate.

Quotations as evidence of Stoppard's critical examination of *Hamlet* can be multiplied. His critical interest, however, is wide and takes in Elizabethan drama and theatrical art in general. I offer only one example, an interesting dialogue on tragedy:

> Guil. You're familiar with the tragedies of antiquity, are you? The great homicidal classics? Matri, patri, fratri, sorrori, uxori and it goes without saying—
>
> Ros. Saucy—
>
> Guil. —Suicidal—hm? Maidens aspiring to godheads—
>
> Ros. And vice versa—
>
> Guil. Your kind of thing, is it?
>
> Player. Well, no, I can't say it is, really. We're more of the blood, love and rhetoric school.
>
> Guil. Well, I'll leave the choice to you, if there is anything to choose between them.
>
> Player. They're hardly divisible, sir—well, I can do you blood and love without the rhetoric, and I can do you blood and rhetoric without the love, and I can do you all three concurrent or consecutive, but I can't do you love and rhetoric without the blood. Blood is compulsory—they're all blood, you see.
>
> Guil. Is that what people want?
>
> Player. It's what we do.

Stoppard, a drama critic before turning playwright and in this play a playwright as drama critic, crisply pinpoints the characteristics of Greek and Elizabethan tragedy and, enlarging the range of his criticism, uses these tragic characteristics to indicate what "we"—players and audience—do.

I am arguing that Stoppard is most successful when he functions as a critic of drama and when he allows his insights on the theater to lead him to observations on life. He is weakest, most empty, when he attempts to confront life directly. Stoppard is at his artistic best when he follows the advice of Polonius: "By indirections find directions out." This is as it should be, I think, because Stoppard's philosophical stance depends so heavily on the "play" idea, the mask, the game, the show. Not only is the entire *Rosencrantz and Guildenstern Are Dead* a play within a play that Shakespeare has written, but throughout Stoppard uses the idea of play. Rosencrantz and Guildenstern, and of course the Player, are conscious of themselves as players, acting out their lives, and baffled, even anguished, by the possibility that no one is watching the performance. All the world is a stage for Stoppard, as for Shakespeare, but Shakespeare's art fuses world and stage, causing the barriers between what is real and what is acted to break down, while Stoppard's art separates the two, makes us observers and critics of the stage, and allows us to see the world through the stage, ever conscious that we are doing just that. The last is my crucial point: Stoppard forces us to be conscious observers of a play frozen before us in order that it may be examined critically. Consequently, what the play offers us, despite its seeming complexity and the virtuosity of Stoppard's technique, is clarity, intellectual substance, rather than the shadows and mystery that we find in *Hamlet* or the pressure of life's absurdity that we find in *Waiting for Godot*. Of course, we miss these important aspects of great drama, and some critics and reviewers have correctly alluded to the play's deficiencies in these respects, but we should not allow what is lacking to erase what is there—bright, witty, intellectual criticism and high theatricality.

I present one final example, taken from the end of the play, to demonstrate Stoppard's fine ability to make criticism and theater serve as a commentary on man. In this incident—"Incidents! All we get is incidents! Dear God, is it too much to expect a little sustained action?!"—Guildenstern, who all along has shown contempt for the players and for their cheap melodrama in presenting scenes of death, becomes so filled with vengeance and scorn that he snatches the dagger from the Player's belt and threatens the Player:

> I'm talking about death—and you've never experienced *that*. And you cannot *act* it. You die a thousand casual deaths—with none of that intensity which squeezes out life . . . and no blood runs cold anywhere. Because even as you die you know that you will come back in a different hat. But no one gets up after *death*—there is no applause—there is only silence and some second-hand clothes, and that's—*death*—

He then stabs the Player, who "with huge, terrible eyes, clutches at the wound as the blade withdraws: he makes small weeping sounds and falls to his knees, and then right down." Hysterically, Guildenstern shouts: "If we have a destiny, then so had he—and if this is ours, then that was his—and if there are no explanations for us, then let there be none for him—" At which point the other players on stage applaud the Player, who stands up, modestly accepts

the admiration of his fellow tragedians, and proceeds to show Guildenstern how the blade of the play dagger is pushed into the handle.

Here we seem to witness, for the only time in the play, an *act* being performed, a *choice* being made, not dictated by the events of Shakespeare's play—only to discover that we have witnessed playing, theater. Guildenstern and Rosencrantz are taken in by the performance of a false death, bearing out the Player's belief, stated earlier in the play, that audiences believe *only* false deaths, that when he once had an actor, condemned for stealing, really die on stage the death was botched and unbelievable. What we have in Guildenstern's "killing" of the Player, therefore, is a theatrical re-enforcement of the earlier observations on audiences by the Player as critic. As we spectators watch the event—Rosencrantz had remarked earlier that he feels "like a spectator"—we intellectually grasp the fact that we had no real action, that no choice was made, Stoppard thereby making his philosophical point indirectly and with fine effect. In Stoppard a condition of life is most clearly understood, it seems, only when reflected in a critical, theatrical mirror.

In *Rosencrantz and Guildenstern Are Dead* we do not have the kind of theater characterized by such phrases as direct involvement, emotional, pre-critical, theater of the heart, but rather a theater of criticism, intellectual, distanced, of the mind. In a very real sense, Stoppard is an artist-critic writing drama for audience-critics, a dramatist least effective when he points his finger directly at the existential dilemma—"What does it all add up to?"—and most effective when he confronts the play *Hamlet* and Elizabethan drama and theatrical art, thereby going roundabout to get to the important issues. Stoppard's play, because it feeds on both an Elizabethan tragedy and a modern tragicomedy, gives us the opportunity to consider the larger context of modern drama, especially Joseph Wood Krutch's well-known and ominous observations on the death of tragedy and his prediction of the devolution of tragedy from Religion to Art to Document [in *The Modern Temper*]. Krutch finds an interesting answer, I believe, in *Rosencrantz and Guildenstern Are Dead.* Using Krutch's words, but not in the way he uses them, we can say that *Rosencrantz and Guildenstern Are Dead* is art that studies art, and therefore serving as a document, dramatic criticism as play presenting ideas on *Hamlet,* on Elizabethan drama, on theatrical art, and by so doing commenting on the life that art reveals. That is, Stoppard's play is holding the mirror of art up to the art that holds the mirror up to nature.

This double image causes the modern audience to take the kind of stance often associated with satire. And yet, Stoppard's play cannot be called satirical, for it makes no attempt to encourage the audience into any kind of action, as do Brecht's plays, or to cause the audience to change the way things are. The play examines the way things are, or, more precisely stated, it intellectually confronts and theatricalizes the condition of man the player and the world as theater. By the pressure of its *critical* energy, the play awakens in the audience a recognition of man's condition, not in order to change that condition, but to see it clearly. In short, by presenting a theatrical, artistic document, Stoppard makes us think—the words "document" and "think" pointing to the modernity, the impoverishment, and the particular value of *Rosencrantz and Guildenstern Are Dead.* The play presents not revelation but criticism, not passionate art—Hamlet in the graveyard— but cool, critical, intellectual art—Hamlet playing with the recorders. *Rosencrantz and Guildenstern Are Dead,* in its successful moments, brilliantly displays the virtues of theater of criticism, and perhaps shows the direction in which some modern drama will be going—"times being what they are." (pp. 274-77)

> *Normand Berlin, " 'Rosencrantz and Guilden- stern Are Dead': Theater of Criticism," in* Modern Drama, *Vol. XVI, Nos. 3 & 4, Decem- ber, 1973, pp. 269-77.*

Douglas Colby

As the curtain rises on the first scene of Tom Stoppard's *Rosencrantz and Guildenstern Are Dead,* the two title characters are passing the time by betting on the toss of a coin. Waiting in Elsinore to be summoned by the king and having nothing better to do, these Elizabethan court- iers engage in a bit of friendly gambling. Rosencrantz, ap- parently, is already winning: his money bag is virtually full, while his companion's is nearly empty. Furthermore, as the action continues, it soon becomes evident that he is not about to lose. Every time that Guildenstern tosses a coin, Rosencrantz guesses "heads" and without fail proves to be correct. In total, he is right ninety-two times, a number that seems impossible. Despite the law of proba- bility, not a single coin lands "tails up."

In this, the opening scene of the play, Stoppard presents a multileveled visual metaphor that encompasses the four major themes of the play. The tossing of a coin and the re- sulting run of "heads" is a symbolic action that introduces the ideas that the rest of the play develops.

The first of these themes, which stems from the idea that there are two sides to every coin, is that there are also two sides to the story of Rosencrantz and Guildenstern. That is, the two existing plays which tell the history of the two courtiers tell it from perspectives that are the reverse of each other. (In addition to the full-length plays *Hamlet* and *Rosencrantz and Guildenstern Are Dead,* there is a short burlesque titled *Rosencrantz and Guildenstern* that records events in the lives of the two courtiers. Written by W. S. Gilbert of Gilbert and Sullivan, it was first produced on June 3, 1891, in London.) In *Hamlet* the action focuses on the prince of Denmark, Claudius, Gertrude, Horatio, and so forth; Rosencrantz and Guildenstern are only minor characters whose story is unraveled incidentally, when they cross the paths of the central characters and thereby step into the unfolding plot. In contrast, in *Rosen- crantz and Guildenstern Are Dead* the action spotlights the two courtiers; Hamlet, Claudius, Gertrude, Horatio, et al. are now the peripheral figures whose story is told in passing. In Shakespeare's play Rosencrantz and Guilden- stern are insignificant pawns in Claudius and Hamlet's great game of political intrigue, while in Stoppard's they are "important" characters in their own right.

Stoppard reinforces the idea that his play (meaning that part of the play he has written, therefore excluding the scenes he has borrowed from *Hamlet*) is the reverse side of Shakespeare's by employing an intricate symbolic de-

vice. He uses the appearance of opposite sides of the coin to point out that dramas which are flip sides of each other are being juxtaposed in *Rosencrantz and Guildenstern Are Dead.* At the beginning of the play, when Stoppard's ma- terial is being performed, Guildenstern tosses only "heads": one side of the coin appears in conjunction with the acting out of a single author's work. Just as a scene from *Hamlet* is about to be staged, however, Rosencrantz, replacing Guildenstern as tosser, flips a coin that lands "tails up": the appearance of the other side of the coin sig- nals that *Hamlet,* the flip side of *Rosencrantz and Guil- denstern Are Dead,* is about to be performed.

Not only is Stoppard's play the reverse side of Shake- speare's, but also it is the complementary one: it is the missing half that completes the whole Elizabethan tale. When Stoppard interpolates speeches from *Hamlet* into the action of his own play, he often attaches additional meanings to them. Such a speech is that delivered by Clau- dius upon his becoming suspicious of the Danish prince's recent change in character.

> Something have you heard
> Of Hamlet's transformation, so call it,
> Sith neither th' exterior nor the inward man
> Resembles that it was.

In the context of *Hamlet,* "exterior" versus "inward" man describes the Danish prince's physical appearance as dis- tinquished from his inner feelings. In *Rosencrantz and Gildenstern Are Dead,* however, these terms also refer to his visible versus his hidden existence. We are made aware that dramatic characters lead two lives, one which the playwright shows us in his work, the other which he lets remain unseen. That of the "exterior" man is presented for viewing before the audience. That of the "inward" man, undramatized, goes unrecognized by us. It is known to the character alone, in his inner mind.

The reference to these different existences is made not so much to explain the condition of Hamlet as to cue us that Rosencrantz and Guildenstern have a life outside the neg- ligible one that Shakespeare presents. They continue to exist even after they have completed their scenes in *Ham- let* and exited from Shakespeare's world. In his own play Stoppard displays this other life and thereby supplies the complementary half of the courtiers' total existence. He presents a world on the other side of the looking glass, in which Rosencrantz and Guildenstern "do on stage the things that are supposed to happen off. Which is a kind of integrity, if you look on every exit as being an entrance somewhere else."

It must be noted that by writing his play and making this complementary existence visible to an audience, Stoppard renders that previously "interior" existence "exterior." Consequently, the life of the two courtiers shown in *Ham- let*—a life which is the reverse of that portrayed in *Rosen- crantz and Guildenstern Are Dead*—necessarily becomes "interior." (pp. 29-32)

The second theme introduced in the opening visual meta- phor—a theme that is also suggested by the two-sidedness of a coin—is that Rosencrantz and Guildenstern are es- sentially two sides of the same person. Because they are only minor characters in *Hamlet,* included primarily as a tool to forward the plot, Shakespeare has spent little time developing and differentiating their characters. They are granted only intermittent involvement in the play's action

> Ros: Incidents! All we get is incidents! Dear God, is it too much to expect a little sustained action?!

and a single voice through which to speak: their lines emerge from the linked pair, not from separate individuals.

> Ros: Both your majesties
> Might, by the sovereign power you have of *us,*
> Put your dread pleasures more into command
> Than to entreaty.
>
> Guil: But *we both* obey,
> And here give up *ourselves* in the full bent
> To lay *our* service freely at your feet,
> To be commanded.

As a result, these sadly neglected *dramatis personae* are virtually indistinguishable from each other. We, the audience, have trouble discriminating between the two, and so do characters within the play. . . . [The] two characters function as a single identity, the boyhood friend of Hamlet who is commissioned to escort the Danish prince to England.

In *Rosencrantz and Guildenstern Are Dead,* Stoppard maintains the integrity of Shakespeare's minimally drawn characterizations. The two courtiers are again like Tweedle Dee and Tweedle Dum, twin characters who seem to be identical and also add up to only one identity. As Stoppard comically reveals, Rosencrantz himself has great difficulty distinguishing between himself and his companion.

> Ros: My name is Guildenstern, and this is Rosencrantz. (Guil *confers briefly with him.*) (*Without embarrassment.*) I'm sorry—*his* name's Guildenstern and *I'm* Rosencrantz.

Here too they are a tied pair who speak as one: much of the dialogue between them consists of lines that flow into each other as if originating from one source.

> Ros: He's the player.
>
> Guil: His play offended the King—
>
> Ros: —offended the King—
>
> Guil: —who orders his arrest—
>
> Ros: —orders his arrest—
>
> Guil: —so he escapes to England—
>
> Ros: —On the boat to which he meets—
>
> Guil: —Guildenstern and Rosencrantz taking Hamlet—
>
> Ros: —who also offended the King—
>
> Guil: —and killed the King—
>
> Ros: —and killed Polonius—
>
> Guil: —offended the King in a variety of ways—
>
> Ros: —to England. (*Pause.*) That seems to be it.

While the two courtiers are uncannily similar, however, they are also notably different. It is true that they are two sides of the same coin, but just as "heads" and "tails" are distinct from each other, so too are Stoppard's versions of Rosencrantz and Guildenstern. Guildenstern, who tosses only "heads," is characterized as the brains. Rosencrantz, who flips only "tails," is marked the ass.

This polarity is illustrated first by Guildenstern's success and Rosencrantz's failure at correctly identifying which courtier is which. It is delineated secondly by the characters' contrasting responses to their coin tossing. Guildenstern, recognizing that the phenomenal results of their gambling must have some great implication for them, systematically and logically examines several possible explanations.

> Guil: It must be indicative of something, besides the redistribution of wealth. (*He muses.*) List of possible explanations. One: I'm willing it. Inside where nothing shows, I am the essence of a man spinning double-headed coins, and betting against himself in private atonement for an unremembered past. . . .
>
> Two: time has stopped dead, and the single experience of one coin being spun once has been repeated ninety times. . . . On the whole, doubtful. Three: divine intervention, that is to say, a good turn from above concerning me, cf. children of Israel, or retribution from above concerning me, cf. Lot's wife. Four: a spectacular vindication of the principle that each individual coin spun individually . . . is as likely to come down heads as tails and therefore should cause no surprise each individual time it does.

Rosencrantz, on the other hand, acts like a fool when he tries to assist in the investigation. All he can do to help is cite totally irrelevant and absurd information about the growth of fingernails and beards during life and death.

> Ros: (*Cutting his fingernails*): Another curious scientific phenomenon is the fact that the fingernails grow after death, as does the beard.
> . . . The fingernails also grow before birth, though *not* the beard.

Throughout their ardent pursuit of answers that will make sense of their situation, the thinking Guildenstern with his proposal of cogent theories is always "ahead," while the mindless Rosencrantz with his inane mimicing or attempts at substantiation of these theories is forever "behind."

> Guil (*Turning on him furiously*): Why don't you say anything original! No wonder the whole thing is so stagnant! You don't take me up on anything—you just repeat it in a different order.
>
> Ros: I can't think of anything original. I'm only good in support.

The third theme introduced in the opening visual metaphor stems from the reality that Guildenstern's consistent tossing of "heads" is more than the result of luck. Ninety-five "heads" in a row, a more than unlikely event under the law of probability, can only be the product of fate. Similarly, all the other experiences that Rosencrantz and Guildenstern undergo are predetermined, predetermined by Shakespeare and Stoppard. One of the central ideas in *Rosencrantz and Guildenstern Are Dead* is that characters in any play are predestined by its author. From the moment it begins until the last scene is ended, that play can head in only one direction, the one prescribed by the script. The characters, who are swept along by the plot, have no free will. The playwright has chosen a course for them, and they are forced to follow it.

> ROS: We've been caught up. Your smallest action sets off another somewhere else, and is set off by it. Keep an eye open, an ear cocked. Tread warily, follow instructions. . . . There's a logic at work—it's all done for you.

Therefore, as Shakespeare and Stoppard dictate in the texts of their plays: the two attendant lords will be summoned to the king's court, given orders to accompany the prince of Denmark to England, and ultimately be executed upon delivering the letter that seals their death. Their end is fixed from the very moment either play begins, and they have no power to evade it.

> ROS: They had it in for us, didn't they? Right from the beginning.

From Shakespeare and Stoppard's viewpoints, Rosencrantz and Guildenstern are little more than their own, not just Claudius and Hamlet's, private game, for the two courtiers are only chess pieces they take pleasure in maneuvering and, in another sense, victims of the deadly fate they have chosen to hunt them down. (pp. 32-6)

Although Rosencrantz and Guildenstern are fated to die during both *Hamlet* and *Rosencrantz and Guildenstern Are Dead,* they are also set to be reborn as soon as either of these plays begins to be performed again. The life of a play is cyclical in that the end of one performance leads into the beginning of another; the characters involved in the play repeat the same actions from one performance to the next. . . . Therefore, although the two courtiers expire temporarily by the end of each play, overall they are immortal, for they continue to come alive after every death. Following every execution and a brief nonexistence in between performances, they are reborn—when the same man, who has always done so, once again awakens them from death to let them begin their lives once more.

> GUIL: Practically starting from scratch. . . .
> An awakening, a man standing on his saddle to bang on the shutters, our names shouted in a certain dawn, a message, a summons.

One important device that Stoppard uses in his play is to have his protagonists not only encounter their destiny, but also recognize that it exists. He lets them temporarily step outside themselves and their worlds to see objectively that they are caught up in the wheel of fate (which for them is the action of a play) and that they cannot extricate themselves from its centrifugal force.

> GUIL: Wheels have been set in motion, and they have their own pace, to which we are . . . condemned. Each move is dictated by the previous one—that is the meaning of order.

They know that they have lived and died before, during past performances, . . . that they are headed toward death in the present one, . . . and that they are forever doomed to replay the same scenes in future performances.

> GUIL: We move idly towards eternity, without possibility of reprieve or hope of explanation.

Because Rosencrantz and Guildenstern realize that they are to be "resurrected" in the next performance, they are also aware that corporeal death for them is not really tragic. Even at the climax of the play, as they are about to be executed, they are looking forward to their next life, facing their approaching death calmly. (pp. 36-8)

However, because Rosencrantz and Guildenstern also recognize that they lack free will, they see that they are in a perpetual state of spiritual death—a state that is genuinely tragic because there is no possibility of escape. That they themselves consider their inability to control their actions a form of spiritual death is most clearly revealed in the last act of the play. Rosencrantz and Guildenstern are on a boat that transports them and Hamlet to England. Although the two courtiers can move around as they wish within the confines of the moving vessel, they have no choice in determining their final destination. The boat, which is carrying them inexorably toward their execution, represents fate—a fact that Guildenstern himself recognizes.

> GUIL: Free to move, speak, extemporize, and yet. We have not been cut loose. Our truancy is defined by one star, and our drift represents merely a slight change of angle to it: We may seize the moment, toss it around while the moments pass, a short dash here, an exploration there, but we are brought round full circle to face again the single immutable fact—that we, Rosencrantz and Guildenstern, bearing a letter from one king to another, are taking Hamlet to England.

On the boat, they "toss a moment" as they would a coin, hoping that any outcome is possible. Yet they hope in vain, for just as their coin can end up landing on only one side, so too their time spent on the vessel can result in only one conclusion. (Stoppard creates an even stronger connection between the fated courtiers and the predestined coins they toss by subtly revealing that these coins are probably guilders, a word that shares the same root as *Guildenstern* and, by association, objects that share a similar life. The playwright never explicitly indicates that this is the type of change they flip, but he does imply, through the disclosure that it costs ten guilders to see a performance by the traveling tragedians that guilders were widely used medieval currency and therefore likely to be the coins with which they gamble.)

In addition to Guildenstern's coming to his realization, Rosencrantz recognizes that the boat also represents spiritual death. When he asks: "Do you think death could possibly be a boat?" he refers not only to his feeling that the boat, which carries them toward the hangman's noose, is the agent of physical death, but also to his sense that to be on the boat and lack free will is to be a hollow puppet controlled by the strings of external forces and therefore spiritually dead.

Finally, by associating both fate and spiritual death with the boat, the courtiers, together, implicitly link the two as well. They, as one identity, realize that because they lack free will, Rosencrantz and Guildenstern are dead.

Given the horrifying prospect of not only being in, but also knowing that they are in, a state of living death, Rosencrantz and Guildenstern would seem to be characters existing in a perpetual hell. Yet this is not the case. Stoppard has given them a defense mechanism that turns what would otherwise be a totally tragic existence into one that is half-tragic, half-comic. He lets them partially block from their minds the reality of their condition so that they are only semi-conscious of it. The result is that for them and for us the dark element of their existence is considerably lightened.

This delicate balance between awareness and ignorance is evidenced in the series of double entendres throughout the play. These remarks (unrecognized as two-sided by the courtiers) emphasize that Rosencrantz and Guildenstern view their situation from two separate perspectives, perspectives that work together to create an overall vision that is uncertain.

> Ros: "Question and answer" . . . Hamlet was scoring off us, all down the line. . . . He murdered us.

From one angle, Rosencrantz remembers that Hamlet slaughtered them in a game of question and answer; from the other, he recalls that the Danish prince was responsible for their death in the previous performance. . . . Rosencrantz complains that for two attendant lords, they have very little attending to do; he also foresees that they will soon be dangling lifelessly from the gallows. . . . [He] again laments the sporadic nature of his work at the court; he also questions Shakespeare, the source of his creation and therefore his God, as to why he and Guildenstern were not blessed with a more constant existence in *Hamlet*.

> Guil: We must have gone north, of course.

Guildenstern remarks that their boat, clearly, has digressed and is currently heading northward; he presumes that it is moving in that direction because that is the course that fate has assigned to them.

This dual vision is what ultimately lets the courtiers maintain their sanity as they are eternally propelled through the two plays. Whenever they face an approaching death, they calm themselves by leaning toward an awareness of being immortal and having a next performance. . . . Whenever they realize that they are immortal only because they are characters in a play, who are also spiritually dead, they sway back to a belief that they are everyday people who have free will. (pp. 38-41)

The fourth theme, which again arises from the notion that there are two sides to every coin, concerns two more complementary sides of the two courtiers. Both are characters in a play and also spectators of another play: they are *dramatis personae* in *Hamlet* and ***Rosencrantz and Guildenstern Are Dead*** as well as the audience watching the drama performed by the traveling tragedians. At one point the Player remarks: "For some of us it is performance, for others, patronage. They are two sides of the same coin." For Rosencrantz and Guildenstern, however, it is both.

Significantly, the dual role-playing of the two courtiers has

implications that extend beyond the world of the drama. Their double identity indirectly suggests that we, the audience of Stoppard's play, are also characters in some all-encompassing, cosmic drama. Indeed, if we analyze the different relationships that Stoppard sets up between audience and dramatic character, we eventually arrive at this conclusion: the characters in the play-within-a-play (that of the tragedians) are being watched by Rosencrantz and Guildenstern, the spectators; Rosencrantz and Guildenstern, in turn, are characters in a play who are being watched by us, the audience; we, in turn, are *dramatis personae* in a larger drama.

Not only does Stoppard suggest this idea through the structure of his play, but also Guildenstern implies it verbally. At one point, after the courtier has stated that "Wheels [symbolic of plays and their cyclical course] have been set in motion," he further remarks that "there are wheels within wheels, etcetera." In addition to the fact that one play is being performed over and over again, it is also true that that play is one of an infinite number of concentric plays, all of which repeat themselves endlessly. We, the audience of one of them, are characters in another.

Stoppard, perhaps realizing that our immediate reaction to his idea is to dismiss it as intriguing in theory but far-fetched in reality, playfully bombards us with an additional argument, intended to make us reconsider his proposition. In the play performed by the tragedians, there are two characters who are mirror images of Rosencrantz and Guildenstern (in fact, the entire drama that the tragedians act out is a reflection of *Hamlet*). The two courtiers, however, fail to recognize themselves in their counterparts. Although here art mirrors reality, they do not see that it does.

> . . . *Under their cloaks the two* SPIES *are wearing coats identical to those worn by* ROS *and* GUIL, *whose coats are now covered by their cloaks.* ROS *approaches "his"* SPY *doubtfully. He does not quite understand why the coats are familiar.* ROS *stands close, touches the coat, thoughtfully . . .*
>
> Ros: Well, if it isn't—! No, wait a minute, don't tell me—it's a long time since—where was it? Ah, this is taking me back to—when was it? I know you, don't I? I never forget a face—(*He looks into the spy's face*) . . . not that I know yours, that is. For a moment I thought—no, I don't know you, do I?

If we, like Rosencrantz and Guildenstern, reject the proposition that we are dramatic characters as well as spectators, then we too fail to recognize that art mirrors reality. We are as impervious to the truth as the two courtiers.

The first three themes introduced by the opening visual metaphor are all concerned with the nature of drama and dramatic characters. These ideas do not, by themselves, relate to the actual world. However, when they are associated with the fourth theme—that we are all characters in a play—they suddenly pertain to our own condition. If we are characters in a play, then all the aspects that the first three themes attribute to *dramatis personae* should also be applicable to ourselves. First, in some unknown sphere, the history of our lives is being told in a drama that is the reverse and complement of the one we are in. Secondly, everyone in "our drama" may be one of two sides of the same person. Thirdly and most importantly, we, being characters in a play, have all our actions predetermined for us by fate.

Not only does the play's structure inform us of this last reality, but Rosencrantz and Guildenstern do as well. Throughout the drama, we, the audience that includes Stoppard, sit back and analyze from a safely removed distance the semitragic state of the two courtiers. In one brief, but triumphant moment, however, Rosencrantz and Guildenstern have their opportunity to retaliate and tell us that we are predestined too. In the opening, coin-tossing scene, the two courtiers engage in another conversation that has two levels of meaning.

> GUIL: (*Flipping a coin*): There is an art to the building up of suspense.
>
> ROS: Heads.
>
> GUIL: (*Flipping another*): Though it can be done by luck alone.
>
> ROS: Heads.
>
> GUIL: If that's the word I'm after.

On one level, Rosencrantz and Guildenstern delight in their ability to create tension as they toss one coin after the other and anticipate results. On the other, they, peering out into our world, tell Stoppard that his playwriting is controlled by the forces of predestination. His "art to the building up of suspense" is not an endeavor that he undertakes out of his own free will. Rather, it is one forced upon him by "fate," the word they constantly search for as the correct substitute for "luck."

We in the actual world, as represented by Stoppard, are predestined in every step we take. Although we seem to have free will, the appearance of our having control over ourselves is only an illusion. Like Rosencrantz and Guildenstern, we are characters caught up in a drama, doomed to replay the same scenes and therefore relive the same lives over and over again. We too, condemned to the wheel of fate, are spiritually dead. (pp. 42-5)

> Douglas Colby, " 'The Game of Coin Tossing':
> 'Rosencrantz and Guildenstern Are Dead' by
> Tom Stoppard," in his As the Curtain Rises:
> On Contemporary British Drama 1966-1976,
> Farleigh Dickinson University Press, 1978, pp.
> 27-46.

Robert Egan

To quote one of its own phrases, Tom Stoppard's first major work is "gathering weight as it goes on." While we have been variously intrigued and entertained by *The Real Inspector Hound, Jumpers,* and *Travesties,* considered responses to these plays are still being formed. Yet *Rosencrantz and Guildenstern Are Dead* is apparently finding a stable place in our shared opinion. Now over ten years old, the play is still very much with us, as its many recent revivals and its persistence on college reading lists attest. The passage of another decade or two may well find it a modern classic. (p. 59)

I would like to point out that, whatever its affinities to earlier modern drama may be, *Rosencrantz and Guildenstern Are Dead* is not, essentially, a recasting of *Waiting for Godot* in Shakespearean terms. Stoppard's is a consciously literary style of playwriting: his scripts are dense with allusions to his artistic predecessors, both by quotation and parody. And certainly, at several points Rosencrantz and Guildenstern recall Beckett's two tramps, both in their relationship to one another and their responses to the world at large. But their world is not that of *Waiting for Godot.* To begin with, the equivalent of Godot for Rosencrantz and Guildenstern arrives early in the play. A messenger has summoned them, a coin has come up heads eighty-five times in a row, and the open space in which they are passing the time will shortly be filled with a welter of characters and events. Moreover, in contrast to Beckett's play, the universe in which Rosencrantz and Guildenstern find themselves discloses a manifest sense of order, plan, and predictability.

Of course, they are no less unhappy and disoriented in their ordered world than are Didi and Gogo in their vacant wasteland. Rosencrantz and Guildenstern view the world of *Hamlet* from a perspective that is a dark converse of Hamlet's own ultimate vision. Shakespeare's protagonist struggles through social disorder, psychological crisis, and metaphysical confusion to an affirmation of an order operating through all things, a "divinity that shapes our ends, / Rough-hew them how we will" (V.ii. 10-11). With this realization of "special providence in the fall of a sparrow" (V.ii. 219-220), his spiritual suffering is at an end. He resigns himself to enacting his given role in the divine plan, and immediately afterwards everything he has sought throughout the play comes to pass: the exposure of Claudius's villainy, the purging of Denmark's throne, the avenging of Hamlet Senior and the quietus of Hamlet himself.

Adrift in this same world, Stoppard's central characters by degrees sense its providential plan moving around and through them. Yet what dawns on Hamlet as an epiphany comes to Rosencrantz and Guildenstern as a visitation of terror; for they have no assurance that the grand scenario in which they are caught up has anything to do with their desires or welfare. And since we, as audience, already know the plot of *Hamlet,* we are aware that their worst fears are thoroughly justified. . . . The script that will culminate in the apotheosis of Hamlet has foreordained them to manipulated lives and obscure deaths.

Rosencrantz and Guildenstern Are Dead does not present us, then, with figures in a Beckettian vacuum, at liberty to wait for a Godot who does not arrive. But neither is the play an ironic account of human marionettes, utterly without access to hope, insight, or meaningful action. In this study, my chief point of focus will be the Player and his Tragedians. My contention is that the actions of the Tragedians and the comments of the Player together constitute a source of meaning that counterweights the play, significantly offsetting what would otherwise be its closed, fatalistic perception of existence. My perspective is a slanted one, having been shaped by my experience of performing the role of the Player. Consequently, much of the interpretation that follows derives from a view of the play as seen by one actor through the eyes of one character. Yet, such a bias may prove helpful to the central concerns of this essay. For the essence of the Player's philosophy lies in a particular concept of play; and I would hope that what I learned in playing the role afforded me a practical hint, at least, of what that philosophy is.

For some ten minutes of stage time Rosencrantz and Guildenstern have been tossing coins and waiting, confined *"in a place without any visible character."* Guildenstern, the intellectual of the two, feels a frustrated suspense that mounts with each call of "Heads." Then, "on the wind of a windless day," they hear "the sound of drums and flute." Thus, the approaching music of the Tragedians seems to promise relief from their predicament. Guildenstern, in fact, hopes for a mystical encounter of some sort. (pp. 59-61)

When the Player and his band finally straggle on stage, Guildenstern is bitterly disappointed: "It could have been—it didn't have to be *obscene*. . . . It could have been—a bird out of season, dropping bright-feathered on my shoulder . . . It could have been a tongueless dwarf standing by the road to point the way . . . I was *prepared*. But it's this, is it?" He has hoped for an omen, such as the hero of a romance might receive at the outset of his quest. Bad enough, given his expectations, to be confronted by "a comic pornographer and a rabble of prostitutes"; but worse still is the implication that the Tragedians do indeed constitute a kind of obscene anti-omen, a grotesque reflection of Guildenstern's worst fears about his and his friend's place in the order of things. At the outset, the Player hails them both "as fellow artists," and this seems to be a kind of jeering *tu quoque* jest. Shabby and unheroic, traveling in a random direction toward an unknown goal, the Tragedians play out the roles predetermined for them by the gory melodramas of their repertoire. We immediately sense a metaphor here for the plight of Rosencrantz and Guildenstern, soon to enact the parts dictated to them by Shakespeare's script. Guildenstern himself senses a connection: "You said something—about getting caught up in the action." The Player replies by presenting them with an even more explicit and tawdry emblem of their condition: poor Alfred, whose role, no matter what the script, must be that of the helpless and used victim. What happens to Alfred literally in *The Rape of the Sabine Women* reflects figuratively what will happen to Rosencrantz and Guildenstern as they are "caught up in the action" of *Hamlet*.

Yet Guildenstern, in his aversion to the Tragedians, misses the full significance of what they do and what they are. For, despite their sorry condition, the Player and his troupe are that very hint of magic for which Guildenstern has been looking. Of course, we as audience are in no way disappointed or disturbed by the Tragedians. For us, they are a welcome addition to the show; their incessant slapstick and mock histrionics infuse the stage with playfulness. In fact, in all their onstage moments they call attention to and celebrate the practice of dramatic play itself. The Player's entering cry, "An audience!" not only expresses the character's response to finding Rosencrantz and Guildenstern; it affords the actor playing the Player an opportunity to voice all the joy, fear, and anticipation that accompany his first step into our presence. (pp. 61-2)

The behavior of the Tragedians, however, runs beyond the boundaries of what we normally consider theatrical circumstances; and this pertains to more than the services

they are prepared to render. Their playing is all-encompassing and nonstop. Always in character, never out of costume, they recognize no limits to the time and place appropriate to dramatic play, and in this they profess "a kind of integrity, if you look on every exit being an entrance somewhere else."

More than a profession, then, the acting of the Tragedians is in effect a way of living. Thus, the importance of their metaphoric relationship to Rosencrantz and Guildenstern runs deeper than the ironic joke it has seemed to be. Like them, the Player and his band are doomed to act in scenarios not of their own devising. Yet unlike the protagonists, who at this point fear to recognize, let alone come to terms with, the truth of their situation, the Tragedians accept from the outset their dislocated and unfree condition. Acknowledging that they exist within a dramatic plan over which they "have no control," they "take [their] chances where [they] find them," playing their roles as best they can, wherever and whenever they must play them. . . . (p. 62)

This first encounter with the Player and his company ends in a flourish of stage magic. The Player agrees to perform number "thirty-eight" in their repertoire and then follows his men offstage, after indicating entrances and a playing area. Rosencrantz picks up the coin the Player has just been standing on and discovers that it has come up heads. Immediately afterward, a lighting change transforms "a place without any visible character" to the interior of Elsinore, and Ophelia runs on, pursued by Hamlet. There is a two-fold implication here. On one level, our attention is being called to the power of play in the theatre: through their art, actors on a stage *can* change one place into another, end one action and begin a new one. But within Stoppard's fiction, the fact that they have so totally transformed the conditions of reality as Rosencrantz and Guildenstern have known it until now gives the Tragedians new authority and attaches a special significance to their playing. Like the sign Guildenstern had hoped to find by the road, the Tragedians do indeed "point the way." The greeting of "fellow artists" has in fact been an invitation, in which the Player has held out to Rosencrantz and Guildenstern, for the first of several times in the play, a valid mode of action and being.

In the course of Act 2, the Player and his troupe progressively clarify and demonstrate the approach to existence they represent. Late in the first act, however, Rosencrantz and Guildenstern themselves begin to experiment with the key to that approach, with play as a means of ordering and coping with reality. As Guildenstern puns idly on the subject of the King's memory, Rosencrantz, repeating an earlier line of the Player's, asks, "What are you playing at?" The reply: "Words, words. They're all we have to go on." The notion that language itself is a form of play, a system of artificial counters that can be manipulated and rearranged to improvise meanings, leads them to explore its possibilities as such in the competitive game of "Questions and Answers." Subsequently, they go on to another game, in which Guildenstern plays the role of Hamlet while Rosencrantz interrogates him. Thus, from word-association to dialogue to dramatic *mimesis*, they explore progressively more sophisticated modes of play, and in the process they manage not only to remember their own names but to anticipate and rehearse their approaching encounter with Hamlet.

Of course, they forget their names again moments later, and their actual interview with Hamlet is a shambles (Rosencrantz scores it twenty-seven to three in Hamlet's favor). The point is that they are not yet experienced players; repeatedly, their attempts break down in confusion, and they are left to ask, "What's the game? What are the rules?" Nevertheless, their very lack of success at meaningful play prepares them to recognize the authority of the Player, and on their second encounter Guildenstern pays him that recognition, however reluctantly. . . . Being in the business, he is a past-master of playing, both as a theatrical art and a way of existing, and he proceeds to educate them in what is interchangeably an aesthetic and a philosophy. Nearly all his maxims do indeed operate "on two levels," since they rest on the assumption that truth onstage is indistinguishable from truth offstage:

> GUIL: I'd prefer art to mirror life, if it's all the same to you.
>
> PLAYER: It's all the same to me, sir.

The Player's instruction begins, properly enough, with a dialogue on the subject of acting:

> GUIL: But for God's sake what are we supposed to *do?!*
>
> PLAYER: Relax. Respond. That's what people do. You can't go through life questioning your situation at every turn.
>
> GUIL: But we don't know what's going on, or what to do with ourselves. We don't know how to *act.*
>
> PLAYER: Act natural. You know why you're here at least.
>
> GUIL: We only know what we're told, and that's little enough. And for all we know it isn't even true.
>
> PLAYER: For all anyone knows, nothing is. Everything has to be taken on trust; truth is only that which is taken to be true. It's the currency of living. There may be nothing behind it, but it doesn't make any difference so long as it is honored. One acts on assumptions. What do you assume?

The verb "to act," of course, is used here in both its senses, the histrionic and the literal. Either way, the principle is the same: if we are cast irrevocably in a scenario over which "we have no control," a dramatic plan whose inherent significance and purpose we can neither know nor be certain exist, our only valid option is to accept our roles within that plan and act them "on assumptions." For all anybody knows, nothing is true, but if, in our acting, we honor what we assume to be true, what in other words we decide *ought* to be true, we can, in effect, create that truth through the artistry and conviction of our performances. Through playing, we can endow the script that confines us with a meaning of our own devising.

Yet any assumptions which are to be acted into truths must be measured against the single, absolute certainty that circumscribes all acting; and the Player holds out no

optimistic illusions as to what that certainty is: "It never varies—we aim at the point where everyone who is marked for death dies. . . . We're tragedians, you see. We follow directions—there is no choice involved. The bad end unhappily, the good unluckily. That is what tragedy means." Whatever actors may do, everyone who is marked for death dies, and everyone, like Rosencrantz and Guildenstern, is marked for death. It follows that a valid attempt to create meaning through play must take death into account; death itself must be made an object of play. And playing at death is precisely what the Tragedians concentrate on doing. Death, as the Player says, "brings out the poetry in them": "It's what the actors do best. They have to exploit whatever talent is given to them, and their talent is dying. They can die heroically, comically, ironically, slowly, suddenly, disgustingly, charmingly, or from a great height." Their craft is thus a literal *ars moriendi,* and like its medieval counterpart it is an *ars vivendi* as well; by incorporating death into their playing, they can also incorporate and give meaning to life.

The option that the Player represents is not, as some critics have suggested, a form of self-defense, a retreat from reality into empty histrionics. The playing of the Tragedians in no way insulates them from the pain and fear of existence as Rosencrantz and Guildenstern experience it. On the contrary, playing lays greater demands on the Tragedians and renders them that much more vulnerable. They must enact every aspect of their lives on "the single assumption which makes [their] existence viable—that somebody is *watching.*" They must "pledge" their "identities" to the principle that every detail of their emotions, sensations, and actions, however intimate, is worth making manifest with all the style and form they can muster. And they must have the courage to do so in spite of the constant possibility that no one is watching, that they are playing in a silent, unresponsive void, "stripped naked in the middle of nowhere . . . every gesture, every pose, vanishing into the thin, unpopulated air." (pp. 62-5)

Finally, Guildenstern rejects what the Player has offered him, lashing out at all the Tragedians represent: "Actors! The mechanics of cheap melodrama!" In particular, he refuses to recognize the worth and validity of what they claim as their greatest talent: "No, no, no . . . you've got it all wrong . . . you can't act death. The fact of it is nothing to do with seeing it happen—it's not gasps and blood and falling about—that isn't what makes it death. It's just a man failing to reappear, that's all—now you see him, now you don't, that's the only thing that's real: here one minute and gone the next and never coming back—an exit, unobtrusive and unannounced, a disappearance gathering weight as it goes on, until, finally, it is heavy with death." He denies, then, that death can be acted, that it can be accommodated into play and so endowed with man-made significance. And in denying this, he denies the same of life, insisting upon the dumb, blank illegibility of all existence: "now you see him, now you don't, that's the only thing that's real."

But Guildenstern has failed to grasp what has just occurred in his presence, the Tragedians' second major stroke of stage magic. What began as their dress rehearsal of *The Murder of Gonzago* has metamorphosed in the playing to *The Life and Death of Rosencrantz and Guildenstern.* The action of the "cheap melodrama" has, impossibly, outstripped the present tense of the *Hamlet* plot and become a prophetic mirroring of Rosencrantz's and Guildenstern's future: their deputation by Claudius to escort Hamlet to England, their sea voyage, and finally their deaths at the hands of the English king. Thus the very sort of magic that the Player describes has come to pass. He and his troupe have, by their playing, created "a thin beam of light" and trained it on the fact of Rosencrantz's and Guildenstern's mortality, offering to "crack the shell" of its mystery. Lodged in the corny rhetoric of the playlet's closing chorus—"Traitors hoist by their own petard?—or victims of the gods?"—is a very real assertion of the significative possibilities of their deaths. "Victims of the gods," after all, bespeaks a tragic death, one in which some version of self or purpose has been expressed, while the alternative epithet indicates an ironic death, without dignity or import. But Guildenstern, confronted with a dramatic vision of his own death in a context of potential significance, denies that such a vision, or such a death, can be. The implications of that denial will become crucially clear in the third act. Meanwhile, face to face with a unicorn, he insists that he sees only a horse with an arrow in its forehead.

Although Guildenstern rejects the substance of the Player's advice, he and Rosencrantz do not cease to play. Midway through Act 3, in fact, they play their most important game of all. Finding themselves on a boat to England and moving irreversibly into darkness, they experience an uneasiness about their approaching destination, an inability to picture England as anything but a blank. We, of course, know that their premonition is fully warranted, that for them England will be the undiscovered country from whose bourn no traveler returns, the ending of their lifescript. In the face of their growing anxiety, they resort once again to play, this time a dramatic acting-out of their arrival in England. Significantly, they need no preparatory discussion or agreement on the rules, as they did in the first act. Through their repeated contacts with the Tragedians, their playing has grown to be a spontaneous and intuitive activity. As they ponder what to say upon arriving, Rosencrantz instinctively assumes the role of the English king, and the dialogue begins. Their improvised scene quickly gathers momentum, and before either of them realizes what has happened, Rosencrantz, in the heat of his performance, has torn open and read aloud Claudius's order for Hamlet's death.

Thus, Rosencrantz and Guildenstern reach their point of crisis as protagonists. In effect, they have managed to duplicate the sort of magic the Player has spoken of and demonstrated. Through the energy and commitment of their play-acting, they have created "a thin beam of light" that has momentarily illuminated the shadowy workings of the script containing them. Suddenly, miraculously, they have what they had despaired of having: choice and the capability to act. Perhaps they are not Prince Hamlets nor were meant to be; perhaps anything they do to turn aside the course of events will prove futile, and the boat will carry them to England and death in any case. Nevertheless, their playing has made available to them the opportunity to define significant versions of self through a concrete moral decision and a subsequent action, even if a useless action. If the script has predestined them to obscure deaths, better to perform those deaths as victims of the gods than as traitors hoist by their own petard.

Yet, once again, and this time irrevocably, Guildenstern refuses the option that play has offered him:

> GUIL: We are little men, we don't know the ins and outs of the matter, there are wheels within wheels, et cetera—it would be presumptuous of us to interfere with the designs of fate or even of kings. All in all, I think we'd be well advised to leave well alone. Tie up the letter—there—neatly—like that.—They won't notice the broken seal, assuming you were in character.

> ROS: But what's the point?

> GUIL: Don't apply logic.

> ROS: He's done nothing to us.

> GUIL: Or justice.

> ROS: It's awful.

> GUIL: But it could have been worse.

Guildenstern deliberately looks away from what the thin beam of light has shown him. He denies that he is capable of knowledge and the responsibility that goes with it. He insists on being a little man, without choice or significance. And Rosencrantz goes along with him; moments later, he declares that they "don't know what's in the letter." Thus both of them specifically opt for a mode of life without meaning, even if at the expense of someone else's illogical and unjust death. In a sense, all that follows is anticlimax where Rosencrantz and Guildenstern are concerned. They have passed their crucial moment and they have chosen to be traitors—much more to themselves than to Hamlet. They will play out their arrival in England once more, only to discover that in denying their significance as actors they have acceded to insignificant deaths. But prior to that, Rosencrantz realizes that, dead or alive, they have willed their own nonbeing: "If we stopped breathing we'd vanish."

One more significant episode remains. If the action involving Rosencrantz and Guildenstern is effectively over, the ongoing dialectic between Guildenstern and the Player stands unresolved. And so, for a final time, Rosencrantz and Guildenstern encounter the Tragedians. After reading the letter that seals their deaths, Guildenstern once more protests their helplessness and bewilderment as little men: "But why? Was it all for this? Who are we that so much should converge on our little deaths? (*In anguish to the Player:*) Who are *we*?" That question is meant to be rhetorical, but the Player will not let it go unanswered:

> PLAYER: You are Rosencrantz and Guildenstern. That's enough.

> GUIL: No—it is not enough. To be told so little—to such an end—and still, finally, to be denied an explanation—

> PLAYER: In our experience, most things end in death.

> GUIL: (*Fear, vengeance, scorn*): Your experience!—Actors!

> *He snatches a dagger from the Player's belt and holds the point at the Player's throat: the Player backs and Guil advances, speaking more quietly.*

I'm talking about death—and you've never experienced *that*. And you cannot *act* it. You die a thousand casual deaths—with none of that intensity which squeezes out life . . . and no blood runs cold anywhere. Because even as you die you know that you will come back in a different hat. But no one gets up after *death*—there is no applause—there is only silence and some second-hand clothes, and that's—*death*—

And he pushes the blade in up to the hilt.

Again, Guildenstern denies that death can be acted, can in any way be encompassed or rendered legible by human means. At this point he *must* deny such a possibility, having foregone the chance to act his own death into meaning. Now, however, he intends not only to prove the Player wrong but to set a terrible certainty on his proof by inflicting on the Player a death as meaningless as he anticipates his own will be.

Yet, far from putting a stop to all playing, Guildenstern has set the stage for the Player's best performance. He recoils *"with huge, terrible eyes,"* falls to his knees and then to the floor, suffers his death agony and *"finally lies still."* A silence passes, the Tragedians *"start to applaud with genuine admiration,"* and suddenly the Player bounces up to receive the congratulations of his fellow actors. It is a trick, of course. The Player has not in fact died and come back to life; freely, he demonstrates the retracting knife-blade. But there is much more significance to this, the play's ultimate stroke of stage magic, than that it was done with mirrors. The character of the Player, and the actor playing that character, *have*, literally, acted death, and the meaning of this accomplishment lies to a considerable extent in its dimension as performance. "There's nothing more unconvincing," the Player has earlier confided, "than an unconvincing death," and he might have added that there is nothing more difficult than a convincing one. This, then, is the most crucial point in the onstage career of the Player. (pp. 65-8)

If the moment makes supreme demands on the actor, it can also evoke a peak of response from the audience. We are not duped to the extent that Guildenstern is; we do not actually believe that a man is dying onstage. We do, however, assume that a character called the Player is dying and that the actor playing him is bending all his abilities toward portraying that death. If the performance is a successful one, we pay it the tribute of our most serious attention. When the Player jumps to his feet again, we are shocked—not so much by the unexpected as by the sudden affirmation of what we already know. Simultaneously, both performer and character focus our awareness on the same truth. Through play, each has encountered the reality of death and accommodated it into the realm of human experience—as far as is humanly possible—by rendering it subject to artistic form.

Stoppard does not provide a formal resolution to the debate of Guildenstern and the Player. At the end, their opposing views, and the opposite approaches to existence they represent, are recapitulated side by side. The Player disappears into the gathering darkness on a characteristic note: *"(Dying amid the dying—tragically; romantically.)* So there's an end to that—it's commonplace: light goes with life, and in the winter of your years the dark comes early. . . ."* As always, death brings out the poetry in

him. It's commonplace, he says, but he expresses that commonplace lyrically. And the commonest fact of all, enacted "tragically, romantically," becomes something rich and strange, a miracle of art. Guildenstern's reply is equally characteristic: "No . . . no . . . not for *us,* not like that. Dying is not romantic, and death is not a game which will soon be over . . . Death is not anything . . . death is not . . . It's the absence of presence, nothing more . . . the endless time of never coming back . . . a gap you can't see, and when the wind blows through it, it makes no sound. . . ." Guildenstern, too, retains an eloquence at the end, as well as a sad, stubborn insistence on the truth as he sees it. Stoppard does not unduly weight the case against him. It is plain enough that if we side with the Player we follow much more in the way of faith than of reason—everything, as the Player himself has said, has to be taken on trust—whereas Guildenstern's despair is born of an uncompromising empiricism.

Yet it seems to me that the play's ending is suffused with an unmistakable, if unstated, sense of resolution. Ultimately, Guildenstern does die the death he has opted for. His repeated insistence on the meaninglessness of death (and thus of life) becomes a self-fulfilling prophecy. He is, in fact, echoing an earlier phrase of his when the light unceremoniously winks out on him: "Now you see me, now you—*(and disappears)*." In every sense, his own words are his epitaph. By contrast, the Player has shown us the possibility of a significant mastering of death and life through play. He has insisted that it is "enough" to be Rosencrantz and Guildenstern; that one's given name, even if a choice between interchangeable and objectively meaningless names, is enough with which to create one's own meaning. Finally, the play option is vindicated not only by the words and actions of the Player but also by the accumulated experience of the play itself in performance. The actors playing Rosencrantz and Guildenstern, too, have acted death and life; and we ourselves, by our presence in the theatre and our assistance as audience, bear an active witness to the validity and centrality of play as an indispensable—perhaps *the* indispensable—human skill. (pp. 68-9)

Robert Egan, "A Thin Beam of Light: The Purpose of Playing in 'Rosencrantz and Guildenstern Are Dead'," in Theatre Journal, *Vol. 31, No. 1, March, 1979, pp. 59-69.*

Simon Varey

In the mid-1950s Tom Stoppard "started wanting to write for the theatre." "After 1956," he says, "everybody of my age who wanted to write, wanted to write plays—after [John] Osborne and the rest at the Court." In 1977 Stoppard said "I used to feel out on a limb, because when I started to write you were a shit if you weren't writing about Vietnam or housing. Now I have no compunction about that." Ronald Hayman, a fervent admirer of Stoppard, thinks that in the early 1960s, after the influence of Beckett and Brecht, and of Osborne and other angry young men, the theatregoing public was prepared to accept drama without noble heroes, but without working-class anti-heroes like Osborne's Jimmy Porter [in *Look Back in Anger*]. Hayman therefore argues that the public was prepared for a play in which two attendants who are frequently omitted altogether from productions of *Hamlet* should be cast in leading roles.

This may be true, but it is not an influence that Stoppard chooses to emphasise very much. When a student in California asked him, "Did you get into the theatre by accident?" he replied characteristically, "Of course. One day, I tripped and fell against a typewriter, and the result was *Rosencrantz and Guildenstern.*"

But there is a more precise, though equally accidental origin of this play. Stoppard's agent, Kenneth Ewing, was idly wondering one day who was King of England when Rosencrantz, Guildenstern and Hamlet were on their way from Elsinore. Might it have been Lear? And if so, did they meet him raving mad at Dover? Stoppard started to work with this idea, and after early drafts including a one act verse play, which he calls "just a sort of Shakespearian pastiche . . . I mean, the whole thing was unspeakable," he came up with the play we now have as *Rosencrantz and Guildenstern Are Dead.* Any connection with Lear soon vanished, as Stoppard explains in his account of the transition from one play to the other, where his problem was a practical one:

> if you write a play about Rosencrantz and Guildenstern in England, you can't count on people knowing who they are and how they got there. So one tended to get back into the end of *Hamlet* a bit. But the explanations were always partial and ambiguous, so one went back a bit further into the plot, and as soon as I started doing this I totally lost interest in England. The interesting thing was them at Elsinore.

And the point of the play, he says,

> was to exploit a situation which seemed to me to have enormous dramatic and comic potential—of these two guys who in Shakespeare's context don't really know what they're doing. The little they are told is mainly lies, and there's no reason to suppose that they ever find out why they are killed. And probably more in the early 1960s than at any other time, that would strike a young playwright as being a pretty good thing to explore. I mean, it has the right combination of specificity and vague generality which was interesting at that time to (it seemed) eight out of ten playwrights. That's why, when the play appeared, it got subjected to so many different kinds of interpretation, all of them plausible, but none of them calculated.

Stoppard's object was to entertain audiences, which he succeeded in doing on a scale he could scarcely have dreamed when the play stuttered into its first performance, on the Edinburgh Fringe in 1966. But it was soon realised that this play, whatever its origins, was strikingly different. It was neither political nor social: as Stoppard was to write in the [London] *Sunday Times,* "Some writers write because they burn with a cause which they further by writing about it. I burn with no causes." In addition, this play, despite its obviously large debt to Samuel Beckett, did not belong to the Theatre of the Absurd. Speaking of his play during an interview in [the *Theatre Quarterly* in] 1974, Stoppard said:

> I tend to write through a series of small, large and microscopic ambushes—which might consist of a body falling out of a cupboard, or simply an unexpected word in a sentence. But my preoccupation as a writer, which possibly betokens a degree of insecurity, takes the form of contriving to inject some sort of interest and colour into every line, rather than counting on the general situation having a general interest which will hold an audience.

This is not the first time Stoppard has spoken of his insecurity or uncertainty. In the same interview he said "My plays are a lot to do with the fact that *I just don't know*" and he is also reported to have said that his favourite line in modern English drama comes from Christopher Hampton's play, *The Philanthropist:* "I'm a man of no convictions—at least I *think* I am."

We can see this attitude in the characters of Rosencrantz and Guildenstern early in Act One, where they are both ignorant about why they are "there," and uncertain as to how they got there or where they are to go:

> Ros. We haven't got there yet.
>
> Guil. Then what are we doing here, I ask myself.
>
> Ros. You might well ask.
>
> Guil. We better get on.
>
> Ros. You might well think.
>
> Guil. We better get on.
>
> Ros (*Actively*). Right! (*Pause.*) On where?
>
> Guil. Forward.
>
> Ros (*Forward to footlights*). Ah. (*Hesitates.*) Which way do we—(*He turns round.*) Which way did we—?

We see uncertainty at once on a larger scale, in Guildenstern's hesitant assertion, which finally dissolves altogether:

> We have not been . . . picked out . . . simply to be abandoned . . . set loose to find our own way. . . . We are entitled to some direction. . . . I would have thought.

One thing of which they apparently can be sure is that they are attendants: marginal characters, unimportant little men unable to take any decisions. The player tells them "You're nobody special" and Rosencrantz, a few minutes later, remarks peevishly:

> Never a moment's peace! In and out, on and off, they're coming at us from all sides.
>
> Guil. You're never satisfied.
>
> Ros. Catching us on the trot. . . . Why can't *we* go by *them?*
>
> Guil. What's the difference?
>
> Ros. I'm going.

But this brave decision evaporates, for Hamlet is coming, and Rosencrantz, knowing he cannot leave, rushes straight back. Their secondary function is nowhere better illustrated than in this scene:

> Ros. They're taking us for granted! Well, I won't

stand for it! In future, notice will be taken. (*He wheels again to face into the wings.*) Keep out, then! I forbid anyone to enter! (*No one comes— Breathing heavily.*) That's better. . . .

(*Immediately, behind him a grand procession enters, principally* CLAUDIUS, GERTRUDE, POLONIUS *and* OPHELIA)

So Rosencrantz's assertive gesture is destroyed at once, and they fall into their subservient roles. Near the end of the play, they recognize their insignificance. . . . And as the play reaches its climax:

Ros. They had it in for us, didn't they? Right from the beginning. Who'd have thought that we were so important?

GUIL. But why? Was it all for this? Who are we that so much should converge on our little deaths? (*In anguish to the* PLAYER.) Who are *we?*

By this late stage of the play, we have already seen their insignificance in different ways, such as their discussion of their total failure to get any information out of Hamlet, who has beaten them at their own game of question and answer. In one of the funniest scenes of the play, Guildenstern tries at first to salvage some of their lost pride:

GUIL. I think we can say we made some headway.

Ros. You think so?

GUIL. I think we can say that.

Ros. I think we can say he made us look ridiculous.

GUIL. We played it close to the chest of course.

Ros (*Derisively*). "Question and answer. Old ways are the best ways"! He was scoring off us all down the line.

GUIL. He caught us on the wrong foot once or twice, perhaps, but I thought we gained some ground.

Ros (*Simply*). He murdered us.

GUIL. He might have had the edge.

Ros (*Roused*). Twenty-seven—three, and you think he might have had the edge?! He *murdered* us.

GUIL. What about our evasions?

Ros. Oh, our evasions were lovely. "Were you sent for?" he says. "My lord, we were sent for . . ." I didn't know where to put myself.

GUIL. He had six rhetoricals—

Ros. It was question and answer, all right. Twenty-seven questions he got out in ten minutes, and answered three. I was waiting for you to *delve*. "When is he going to start *delving*?" I asked myself.

GUIL. —And two repetitions.

Ros. Hardly a leading question between us.

GUIL. We got his *symptoms*, didn't we?

Ros. Half of what he said meant something else, and the other half didn't mean anything at all.

GUIL. Thwarted ambition—a sense of grievance, that's my diagnosis.

Ros. Six rhetorical and two repetitions, leaving nineteen of which we answered fifteen. And what did we get in return? He's depressed! . . . Denmark's a prison and he'd rather live in a nutshell; some shadow-play about the nature of ambition, which never got down to cases, and finally one direct question which might have led somewhere, and led in fact to his illuminating claim to tell a hawk from a handsaw.

This dialogue then characteristically tails off into a seemingly inconsequential conversation about the way they came in, reaching the conclusion once again that they have lost their direction. They are powerless, indecisive, confused and ignorant. They are manipulated in argument by Hamlet, and in general by something they cannot define and cannot defend themselves against. Guildenstern makes their position clear when he says "We only know what we're told, and that's little enough. And for all we know, it isn't even true." Much of their dialogue concerns the nature of fate, or chance, or whatever it is that manipulates them, and much of their confusion derives from their uncertainty about it.

Their ultimate confusion, and a theatrically striking one, is the confusion of their names and identities. In *Hamlet,* these two are so nearly indistinguishable that in modern productions Claudius and Gertrude are made to mistake one for the other, but here they get their own identities wrong as well. At the end of the play they are no nearer getting this right than they were at the beginning.

On a slightly simpler level—the level of Stoppard's ambushes—Rosencrantz and Guildenstern confuse language, in a way that recalls Harold Pinter. But where Pinter's characters think and speak at such different speeds that [to quote Martin Esslin's *The Theatre of the Absurd*] "the slower-witted character is constantly replying to the penultimate question while the faster one is already two jumps ahead" so that communication becomes almost impossible. Stoppard's characters play a different kind of game. Rosencrantz and Guildenstern misinterpret language, frequently, recognise only one meaning of a word or phrase, and see no other. . . . In a pattern that later becomes virtually Stoppard's hallmark, Guildenstern, usually the more rational of the two, comes near to being persuaded that he is irrational. I do not think we need to attempt to find grand philosophical implications in such exchanges of linguistic confusion: they can be explained as logical arguments conducted by people who do not know enough to control them, and so they become illogical. "The funniest joke in the world" to Stoppard is one found in Beckett's work: "it consists of confident statement followed by immediate refutation by the same voice." For example:

GUIL. We are not restricted. No boundaries have been defined, no inhibitions imposed. We have, for the while, secured, or blundered into, our release, for the while. Spontaneity and whim are the order of the day. Other wheels are turning but they are not our concern. We can

breathe. We can relax. We can do what we like
and say what we like to whomever we like, without restriction.

Ros. Within limits, of course.

Guil. Certainly within limits.

If any of this works at a philosophical level, Stoppard's
brand of semantic comedy that dazzles us right through
the play effectively prevents our taking it very seriously,
as when Guildenstern tries to establish what reality is and
how we recognize it. He decides, with an amusing distortion of logic, that the more witnesses there are to an experience, the closer it comes to reality, "the name we give
to common experience." But when the player declares
"Everything has to be taken on trust; truth is only that
which is taken to be true," nobody laughs.

There are, of course, other elements that help to make the
play provocative, funny, and in places startling. A repeated example is the mockery of the conventions of the theatre, with Rosencrantz and Guildenstern looking into the
auditorium, yet seeing nobody. The dominant metaphor
in the play is a theatrical one. We are reminded frequently
that plays are mirror images of life, as the player says "we
do on stage the things that are supposed to happen off.
Which is a kind of integrity, if you look on every exit being
an entrance somewhere else." It is particularly interesting,
though, that this theatrical metaphor, and the coin tossing, and the word games, and the philosophical speculations about life and death, are all related to memory.

Memory is a subject on which Rosencrantz and Guildenstern continually dwell. During the totally pointless game
of coin tossing, within the opening minutes of the play,
Rosencrantz demonstrates that he has no memory:

> Ros. —we've been spinning coins for as long as
> I remember.
>
> Guil. How long is that?
>
> Ros. I forget.

Immediately afterwards, Guildenstern starts looking for
an explanation of the sequence that has brought the coins
down "heads" ninety-two times in a row. Of his list of possibilities, the fourth is correct, although it cannot "explain" such a sequence:

> a spectacular vindication of the principle that
> each individual coin spun individually is as like-
> ly to come down heads as tails and therefore
> should cause no surprise each individual time it
> does.

Mathematically speaking, this is true. Coins tossed in the
air are subject entirely to chance, and in the laws of probability this fact is sometimes stated as "a coin has no memory." Rosencrantz, who proves dozens of times that he too
has no memory, is similarly subject entirely to chance, and
the next time we see his memory at fault is within seconds
of Guildenstern's explanation. Guildenstern asks "What's
the first thing you remember?" Rosencrantz cannot answer, and quickly admits that he has forgotten the question. Guildenstern's memory proves equally faulty, and
between them they can remember only vaguely that they
were sent for as recently as the morning.

Gradually, memory—or rather, lack of it—comes to be
associated with uncertainty. This is only to be expected if
having no memory means being at the mercy of chance.
The player underlines this association when he tells
Rosencrantz that their meeting is timely, for

> by this time tomorrow we might have forgotten ev-
> erything we ever knew. That's a thought, isn't it?

but by that time tomorrow the players might be anywhere
(like Rosencrantz and Guildenstern, directionless), playing before they know not whom:

> We have no control. Tonight we play to the court.
> Or the night after. Or to the tavern. Or not.

The actors may forget what is familiar to them, and at the
same time it is a matter of chance where they will be at
any moment. Rosencrantz and Guildenstern too forget
the familiar—most obviously when Rosencrantz forgets
his name. When their names have been confused again,
with the members of the court, the two are left alone, confusing all the clichés they are trying to express, and Guildenstern suddenly asks:

> Has it ever happened to you that all of a sudden and
> for no reason at all you haven't the faintest idea
> how to spell the word—"wife"—or "house"—
> because when you write it down you just can't re-
> member ever having seen those letters in that order
> before . . . ?

Once again it is a matter of forgetting the familiar, and he
phrases his question in terms of outside influence—"Has
it ever *happened to you?*" It is obvious that they move in
a world where they have no free will. To round off this
point, Guildenstern declares:

> We'll be all right.
>
> Ros. For how long?
>
> Guil. Till events have played themselves out.
> There's a logic at work—it's all done for you,
> don't worry. Enjoy it. Relax. To be taken in
> hand and led, like being a child again, even with-
> out the innocence, a child—It's like being given
> a prize, an extra slice of childhood when you
> least expect it, as a prize for being good, or com-
> pensation for never having had one. . . . Do I
> contradict myself?
>
> Ros. I can't remember.

Later, Rosencrantz "can't remember" a moment that
ought to have been shattering, the moment when he first
became aware of death; "there's only one direction," he
says, "and time is its only measure."

Rosencrantz and Guildenstern apparently have no past,
no memory, like the coins; however, they recognise that
they do have a future, but they are uncertain about it. All
they can do is to reckon the future as a sequence of moments in time:

> Guil. Yes, one must think of the future.
>
> Ros. It's the normal thing.
>
> Guil. To have one. One is, after all, having it all
> the time . . . now . . . and now . . . and
> now . . .

Ros. It could go on for ever. Well, not for *ever,*
I suppose.

The only thing they know about the future is that it ends
in death. But Rosencrantz's speech about coffins demonstrates that his confused concept of lying dead in a coffin
is actually only lying alive in a coffin—and not enjoying
it very much. When, in Act Three, they are on the boat
to England, a similar pattern develops: confusion (about
the letter they are carrying), failure to remember, and
Rosencrantz's inability to envisage England—their future
destination. This time again, the pattern is completed by
another suggestion of death: "We're slipping off the
map"—another way of saying that they have no direction—but they do not know what death is. They *just don't
know.* To Guildenstern, death is "not-being." The pair of
them have already failed to recognise their own deaths in
the mime and Guildenstern has said that to him death is
like a theatrical exit. Real death, they learn from the player, is very unconvincing on the stage, theatrical death
much better than the real thing. Furthermore, death is virtually the purpose of the players' existence: it governs
their repertoire:

> Deaths for all ages and occasions! Deaths by sus-
> pension, convulsion, consumption, incision, exe-
> cution, asphyxiation and malnutrition—! Cli-
> mactic carnage, by poison and by steel—! Dou-
> ble deaths by duel!

Add to this the player's words which parallel Guildenstern's idea that there is a logic at work:

> PLAYER. There's a design at work in all art—
> surely you know that? Events must play them-
> selves out to aesthetic, moral and logical conclu-
> sion.
>
> GUIL. And what's that, in this case?
>
> PLAYER. It never varies—we aim at the point
> where everyone who is marked for death dies.
>
> GUIL. Marked?
>
> PLAYER. Between "just desserts" and "tragic
> irony" we are given quite a lot of scope for our
> particular talent. Generally speaking, things
> have gone about as far as they can possibly go
> when things have got about as bad as they can
> reasonably get. (*He switches on a smile.*)
>
> GUIL. Who decides?
>
> PLAYER (*Switching off the smile*). Decides? It is
> *written.*

It becomes obvious that Rosencrantz and Guildenstern
are exactly parallel to the player, nobody special, without
free will, enacting death, and governed by a written design:

> We're tragedians, you see. We follow direc-
> tions—there is no *choice* involved.

Rosencrantz and Guildenstern cannot know anything for
certain, because they are not people; as the player says:

> Don't you see? We're *actors,* we're the opposite
> of people!

We witness on the stage a play about a play: Rosencrantz

and Guildenstern have no free will, or independent existence, or knowledge, because they are manipulated not by
chance, fate, or God, but by the playwright. But we are
told that the actors present on stage what is supposed to
happen off, with obvious implications for the audience. It
is a play about a play, but also a play about how minor
characters like ourselves might care to look at life, perpetually waiting in the wings, passing the time between the
only two certainties, birth and death. We cannot remember birth, and we cannot envisage death.

When I said just now what I think the play is *about,* I left
something out. It is *about* particular people in a particular
situation: this does not prevent the play from containing
metaphysical and philosophical implications, but these are
not the "subject" of the play: if they were, it would probably be boring. To be about particular people in a particular
situation is, in the author's words, "the level on which a
play lives or dies." Even Tom Stoppard's sleight of hand
could not convert that remark into a statement that his
play is about life or death. (pp. 20-31)

> *Simon Varey, "Nobody Special: On 'Rosen-
> crantz and Guildenstern Are Dead'," in* Dutch
> Quarterly Review of Anglo-American Let-
> ters, *Vol. 10, No. 1, 1980, pp. 20-31.*

Manfred Draudt

When . . . [*Rosencrantz and Guildenstern Are Dead*]
opens we see two characters, Rosencrantz and Guildenstern, passing their time as they wait by tossing coins. This
nonsensical game defies the rules of chance and causes bewilderment in Guildenstern's more probing mind. After
some discursive rambling he at length concludes with the
existential commonplace: 'We have not been . . . picked
out . . . simply to be abandoned . . .'

Although the Beckettian echoes and parallels of this situation have been duly noted, both favourable and unfavour-
able critics seem to have failed to realize that the game of
coin-tossing has a deeper significance.

Particularly at crucial moments this game is taken up
again and again, as can be seen, for example, when Rosencrantz and Guildenstern meet the players. Rosencrantz's
attempts to pick up the coin hidden under the Player's
foot, which seem to be merely a comic routine, dramatize
the way he and Guildenstern gradually lose their grip on
reality. Whereas in the first instance Rosencrantz was able
to snatch away the coin, he is not only frustrated but even
injured when he tries to repeat his previous success later
on. And a third 'game' with coins provides another telling
comment on their increasing insecurity. When Guildenstern taps Rosencrantz's fists and finds both hands empty,
his genuine consternation is clearly reminiscent of that
caused by the impossible run of 'heads' at the beginning
of the play. Later on, however, Rosencrantz keeps coins
in each hand to comfort his distressed friend. By playing
this trick he is, as it were, making a naive attempt to cheat
the malevolent 'chance' whose incalculable caprice had
initiated their journey into the unknown, which, eventually, will end in their deaths.

The use of coins also reinforces our impression that in the
course of the play the two attendant lords assume the mercenary status of the players. Whereas at the beginning it

is the actors who receive money from the patronizing pair, towards the end the courtiers are on the receiving end, being in Claudius' pay.

Much more remarkable, however, is the fact that the coin seems to be one of the principal keys to an understanding of Stoppard's play. Though it is only occasionally employed as a metaphor, the image of the coin is basic to the concerns, form, and structure of the play, for it epitomizes the idea that two different aspects, or even separate identities, can meet in one and the same thing. The coin, whose two sides belong together but are yet opposed one to another, embodies a paradox: the dichotomy and identity of two opposites.

> For some of us it is performance, for others patronage. They are two sides of the same coin, or, let us say, being as there are so many of us, the same side of two coins.

The idea that the human race can be divided into actors and spectators is certainly not what Stoppard wants to say, yet such a classification does elucidate the complex and shifting relationship between Rosencrantz and Guildenstern and the players, who are the only people with whom they can successfully communicate: GUIL: 'The truth is, we value your company, for want of any other.' Because Stoppard significantly expanded their roles, the actors, and particularly their relationship with Rosencrantz and Guildenstern, merit a more detailed analysis.

When Rosencrantz and Guildenstern encounter the troupe of players for the first time, they insist on the distinct division into actors and spectators (ROS: 'I thought we were gentlemen.'), and they are convinced of their own superiority over the low 'rabble.' They are shocked at the suggestion of taking part in a 'performance' of *The Rape of the Sabine Women* and adopt a patronizing air towards the players:

> GUIL. Perhaps I can use my influence.
>
> PLAYER. At the tavern?
>
> GUIL. At the court. I would say I have some influence.

Although the Player by his retorts deflates their hollow-sounding protestations, he plays up to their condescending attitude and treats Rosencrantz and Guildenstern as his prospective patrons. Nevertheless, the Player's critical remarks and his 'faux pas,' 'I recognized you at once—as fellow artists,' has made us aware that Rosencrantz and Guildenstern may not be spectators only. In the course of the play we shall see how they desperately try to avoid becoming embroiled in the action in order to maintain their positions as 'spectators,' never realizing that actor and spectator are interchangeable roles, that is, two sides of the same coin.

Throughout the play Rosencrantz and Guildenstern remain unaware that, like the players, they are being employed at the court of Elsinore, whereas the audience clearly sees how they constantly betray their real natures:

> GUIL. Give us this day our daily mask.
>
> They've got us placed now—
>
> We don't know how to *act*.

Give us this day our daily cue.

Not only their words but also their actions and games enhance this dramatic irony by showing them as actors. Just as the players rehearse *The Murder of Gonzago*, Rosencrantz and Guildenstern practise for their encounter with Hamlet (Guildenstern assuming the identity of the prince) and perform the scene of their arrival and welcome in England, Rosencrantz playing the English king. Thus they unconsciously assume the role of 'actor' which they have resisted earlier.

The scene in which Rosencrantz and Guildenstern watch the rehearsal of the *Mousetrap* is the most significant moment in the play, about which the action turns. The Player's request, 'Now if you two wouldn't mind just moving back . . .', tellingly suggests that actors and spectators have changed positions. Having given up their former pretentiousness, Rosencrantz and Guildenstern have become more and more insecure, while the disreputable players have successfully established their superiority:

> PLAYER. I can come and go as I please.
>
> GUIL. You're evidently a man who knows his way around.
>
> PLAYER. I've been here before.
>
> GUIL. We're still finding our feet.
>
> PLAYER. I should concentrate on not losing your heads.

Even when they are face to face with their mirror-images, viz. the two Spies, Rosencrantz and Guildenstern are unable and, it seems, unwilling to recognize their real selves. . . . They insist on being spectators, ironically even clapping at the performance that anticipates their own tragic destiny. It is this illusion about their own status, this discrepancy between what they think they are and what they really are—mere pawns in the hands of the Danish court—that blinds them to reality and makes them stumble helplessly towards a fatal end, while the players, in contrast to them, just go on playing—and living. In this key scene Stoppard heightens the dramatic irony by means of the identical coats worn by the two Spies and by Rosencrantz and Guildenstern, and by having them '*sprawled on the ground in the approximate positions last held by the dead* SPIES' (thus emphasizing for us an identity which the two characters do not themselves recognize); yet he also skilfully demonstrates that reality and illusion, real and acted life, rehearsal and performance, spectator and actor, are simply two sides of one and the same coin. In contrast to Rosencrantz and Guildenstern, the actors accept this paradox as a fact: 'We do on stage the things that are supposed to happen off.' In this conversation with the pair, the Player ironically seems to support their idea of a dichotomy:

> . . . [we are] demented children mincing about in clothes that no one ever wore, speaking as no man ever spoke, swearing love in wigs and rhymed couplets, killing each other with wooden swords, hollow protestations of faith hurled after empty promises of vengeance— . . . Don't you see?! We're *actors*—we're the opposite of people!

Yet Stoppard portrays him as somebody who does *not* differentiate between his persona as an actor and his off-stage life:

> GUIL. Well . . . aren't you going to change into your costume?
>
> PLAYER. I never change out of it, sir.
>
> GUIL. Always in character.
>
> PLAYER. That's it.

This identification of the two normally incompatible positions of spectator and actor is, however, more than 'the working out of an intellectual conceit'. Because Stoppard expresses this idea in a play to be performed in front of an audience, the recognition of this paradox must be deeply disturbing to any perceptive spectator. The mood of complacent detachment in which we have been watching the ridiculously confident bearing and the childish games of the two protagonists will gradually give way to a feeling of unease, for we cannot but see a parallel between ourselves and these petty actors who stumble through the unknown towards death. (pp. 348-52)

The disreputable actors, on the other hand, 'know which way the wind is blowing' and therefore can offer advice to the respectable courtiers, who are more and more at a loss.

> GUIL. But for God's sake what are we supposed to *do?!*
>
> PLAYER. Relax. Respond. That's what people do. You can't go through life questioning your situation at every turn.
>
> GUIL. But we don't know what's going on, or what to do with ourselves. We don't know how to *act.*
>
> PLAYER. Act natural. . . . Everything has to be taken on trust; . . . One acts on assumptions.

Thus their continuous questioning is exposed as being negative. It is also clear that the initial relationship has been reversed, the players now being the 'heads,' whereas Rosencrantz and Guildenstern have become the 'tails'.

Although they are 'All in the same boat'—or of the same coin—the actors, in contrast to Rosencrantz and Guildenstern, appear to have the right strategy for survival. Even being dismissed in disgrace or forced to hide as stowaways does not worry them, for they 'take [their] chances where [they] find them' and unquestioningly submit to misfortunes, just as they accept death.

> PLAYER. We follow directions—there is no *choice* involved. The bad end unhappily, the good unluckily. That is what tragedy means.

Guildenstern's remark, 'I'd prefer art to mirror life . . .', indicates that, because of their disastrous narrowmindedness, they again fail to see the obvious identity of art and life, play world and real world.

The Player's thrilling mock-death, which finally gives drastic emphasis to this point, cunningly tests—because of its seeming reality—not only Rosencrantz and Guildenstern's but also the audience's awareness of reality; it occurs after a violent clash has again displayed the difference in their range of vision:

> PLAYER. In our experience, most things end in death.
>
> GUIL. Your experience!—*Actors!*

In Stoppard's 'comedy,' just as in Shakespeare's tragedy, death is the central problem, appearing in almost every conversation until its final physical impact is felt with the disappearance of Rosencrantz and Guildenstern. Of course, death has different associations and implications in a sixteenth- and a twentieth-century play, but it would be wrong to assume that the existentialist philosophy of the 'absurd' dramatists has been absorbed uncritically, or is the only view expressed in Stoppard's play; evidently, it is only one side of the coin. (pp. 352-53)

Rosencrantz and Guildenstern are two individuals, but also a team—the 'straight man' and the wit; although clearly distinguishable, they are also mutually exchangeable, not only in regard to the roles they play but also in the eyes of the others who mix up their names; furthermore, they are inseparably linked by a common fate. The mixing up of their identities becomes even more confusing—and hilarious—when Rosencrantz and Guildenstern rehearse their prospective meeting with the prince. Rosencrantz, who has always found it difficult to discriminate between his own and his friend's name, is completely perplexed by Guildenstern's assuming of Hamlet's persona:

> GUIL. I don't think you quite understand. What we are attempting is a hypothesis in which *I* answer for *him,* while *you* ask me questions.

Rosencrantz's question, 'Am I pretending to be you, then?' is not simply a funny line but indicates his naive attempt to carry the game of 'exchanging identities' to its logical conclusion.

A further complicating factor is Hamlet's unbalanced mind, which makes his persona as elusive as the identities of Rosencrantz and Guildenstern.

> ROS. He talks to himself, which might be madness.
>
> GUIL. If he didn't talk sense, which he does.
>
> ROS. Which suggests the opposite. . . .
>
> GUIL. I think I have it. A man talking sense to himself is no madder than a man talking nonsense not to himself.
>
> ROS. Or just as mad.
>
> GUIL. Or just as mad.
>
> ROS. And he does both.
>
> GUIL. So there you are.
>
> ROS. Stark raving sane.

Madness and sanity, Rosencrantz and Guildenstern, actor and spectator—these are all complementary but also interchangeable counterparts, different manifestations of one and the same principle.

Finally, it remains to demonstrate that the coin image is also related to the aspects of language and structure. Rosencrantz and Guildenstern's favourite occupation, their playing with words, shows that words, too, are items easily interchanged:

> ROS. I'm out of my step here— . . .
>
> It's all over my *depth*— . . .
>
> —out of my head— . . .
>
> —over my step over my head body!—I tell you it's all stopping to a death, it's boding to a depth, stepping to a head, it's all heading to a dead stop—

In this instance, as well as in the great number of puns which exploit the ambiguity of language ('England! *That's* a dead end.'), a playful and comic façade hides a menacing reality.

> GUIL. I have influence yet.
>
> PLAYER. Yet what?
>
> (GUIL *seizes the* PLAYER *violently.*)

In the first quotation the freely associating mind is somehow driven towards 'a dead stop,' which is a very telling anticipation of Rosencrantz and Guildenstern's rambling course through life that also heads towards and ends in death. In the second quotation, the Player's twisting of 'yet' exposes their pomposity and pathetic illusions of safety. Under the commonplace phrase or everyday situation there lurks the unexpected shoal, and the absurdly comic surface very often conceals a serious implication or even a tragic aspect. Almost simultaneously we laugh at and feel pity for the two struggling protagonists, because the play successfully demonstrates that comedy and tragedy, too, are opposite sides of the same coin.

As has been demonstrated above, the image of the coin is related to structure in the way that it expresses in dramatic form the 'head/tail' sides, i.e. the relationships of spectator/actor, real/play world, reality/illusion, etc. But structurally even more significant is the fact that the coin is also basic to the ingenious idea around which Stoppard built his play; the Player's assertion, 'every exit [is] an entrance somewhere else', helps us to understand this idea more clearly. By focussing on and dramatizing the off-stage life of two characters from *Hamlet,* Stoppard can be said to have taken the Player's statement literally: practically every exit in *Hamlet* is an entrance in *Rosencrantz and Guildenstern Are Dead.* Within such a concept based on reversals it is logically coherent that minor characters should become the new protagonists and that Shakespeare's enigmatic hero should be reduced to a figure in the background, from where he silently delivers his famous soliloquy.

By constructing his play around one paradoxical concept, which is the basis of both the play's meaning and form, Stoppard has shown that the force of Rosencrantz and Guildenstern's insistent entreaties, 'Consistency is all I ask', has not been lost on their creator. (pp. 355-57)

> *Manfred Draudt, " 'Two Sides of the Same Coin, or . . . the Same Side of Two Coins': An Analysis of Tom Stoppard's 'Rosencrantz and Guildenstern are Dead'," in* English Studies, Netherlands, *Vol. 62, No. 4, August, 1981, pp. 348-57.*

Joseph E. Duncan

In the decade after the first productions of Tom Stoppard's *Rosencrantz and Guildenstern Are Dead,* critics frequently remarked on the similarities between it and Samuel Beckett's *Waiting for Godot.* Strong similarities exist, chiefly in characterization, but Stoppard's two courtiers encounter a predicament and represent an experience essentially different from those of Beckett's two tramps. While Beckett's characters face interminable waiting, Stoppard's face sudden and inexplicable change. One of the most important distinctions is that in Stoppard's play Godot (as interpreted by various of Beckett's critics) comes.

Critics have seen the lives of Rosencrantz and Guildenstern as paralleling those of Beckett's Vladimir and Estragon. . . . [In his book-length study *Tom Stoppard*] C. W. E. Bigsby characterizes the play as "a kind of *Waiting for Godot* in which Vladimir and Estragon have become university wits" who follow Beckett's characters in playing Wittgensteinian games, seeking security in conversation, and reaching out to one another. Recently [in *The New Yorker*], Kenneth Tynan has observed that "the sight of two bewildered men playing pointless games in a theatrical void while the real action unfolds off stage inevitably recalls Beckett" [see Further Reading list].

Rosencrantz and Guildenstern Are Dead seems to show some strong influence from *Waiting for Godot.* Both plays present two little men, lacking knowledge and power, who are trying to grapple with a universe full of uncertainty. Similarities in characterization and in the relationships between the two main characters in each play are particularly striking. Guildenstern resembles Vladimir, or Didi, who is more head, while Rosencrantz resembles Estragon, or Gogo, who is more body. Didi experiences anguish in waiting for Godot and tells Gogo that he perceives things which his friend misses; Guildenstern shows great strain and fear at the long run of "heads" at the beginning of the play, does most of the philosophizing, and is much more mentally alert than Rosencrantz. Gogo is concerned with food, his feet, erections, and sleep; he has been a poet, has dreams, but forgets about Godot. Rosencrantz is indifferent to the run of "heads," but is aroused by the players' suggested pornographic exhibition; he is the first to voice an intuition of his own and Guildenstern's approaching deaths and later the first to voice acceptance. A very poor memory is characteristic of both Gogo and Rosencrantz. Didi and Guildenstern are the dominant members of these duos. Both Gogo and Rosencrantz frequently want to leave, but Didi and Guildenstern think they should remain, waiting for Godot or waiting on the King. Gogo has difficulty in understanding how to play at Pozzo and Lucky, and Rosencrantz has even more difficulty in understanding how to play at questioning Hamlet. The scenes in which Guildenstern plays the "nursemaid" to Rosencrantz are reminiscent of the way Didi comforts and sings to Gogo, and Rosencrantz's plea to Guildenstern, "Don't leave me!" when the Player steps on his hand seems an echo of Gogo's "Stay with me!" after he has been beaten. Didi can become irritated at Gogo's uncertainty and "whining," while Guildenstern becomes increasingly angry about Rosencrantz's lack of perception and initiative and finally "smashes him down." Stoppard has departed from *Hamlet,* where the two friends are virtually indistinguishable, to follow the dominant patterns of the characterization of the principals in *Waiting for Godot*.

Because Stoppard seems to be following Beckett very closely in some aspects of his play, the differences between ***Rosencrantz and Guildenstern Are Dead*** and *Waiting for Godot* are particularly important. If Stoppard consciously depended on Beckett and expected his audience to be aware of the dependence, he was also presenting thought, action, and a theatrical experience distinctively different from that in *Waiting for Godot*. "Nothing to be done," "Nothing ever happens" are the cries of Didi and Gogo, but in Stoppard's play a great deal happens very rapidly. Time hangs very heavy for the two modern tramps, but the two courtiers seldom refer to the passage of time, think time may be an illusion, and at times find "Never a moment's peace!" They do resort to games to pass the time and avoid facing their own predicament; however, they are at the same time trapped in the fast-moving, eventful *Hamlet* plot and are becoming increasingly anxious about their entrapment. Didi and Gogo are concerned about guilt and salvation, but make no assured contact with anything beyond themselves. Guildenstern and Rosencrantz are concerned chiefly with freedom of action and are amazed that the "they" who had it in for them found them so important. Beckett's play, in short, is about the uncertainty and frustration felt by Didi and Gogo in their interminable waiting in limitless time. Stoppard's is about the uncertainty felt by Rosencrantz and Guildenstern in trying to understand the origin and meaning of events which they come to realize are carrying them to their deaths.

If Rosencrantz and Guildenstern have existed in boredom and waiting up to the time of the summons, as the play suggests, with the summons their lives are transformed. The summons, the impossible run of "heads" in the coin tossing, their being "caught up" with the players, the entrapment in the action of Hamlet, and the deaths—all are intricately intermeshed and are part of a pattern which they enter, or which encloses them, at the time of the summons. . . . Though the two courtiers were sent for in *Hamlet,* the details of the summons are Stoppard's. Their names were called and they were awakened in the dawn—to a new kind of life. They are "practically starting from scratch," "with an extra slice of childhood when you least expect it." In *Waiting for Godot* the boy messengers address Vladimir as Mr. Albert, and it is uncertain if they are really from Godot and if they carry the two tramps' messages correctly, but in any case the messages result only in continued waiting. However, in ***Rosencrantz and Guildenstern Are Dead*** the messenger calls the names of the two courtiers and delivers the "royal summons." It results in their galloping off "headlong and hotfoot across the land, our guides outstripped in the breakneck pursuit of our duty. Fearful lest we come too late!!" Amidst the uncertainties of Elsinore, Guildenstern observes, "That much is certain—we came."

The summons functions much as a leitmotif in the play and becomes associated with the run of "heads," the *Hamlet* pattern represented by the Tragedians, and the deaths of the principals. These elements are brought together and their interrelationships suggested in two key passages. In the first passage, Guildenstern makes the second reference to the summons in his speculation about the impossible run of "heads":

> The sun came up about as often as it went down, in the long run, and a coin showed heads about as often as it showed tails. Then a messenger arrived. We had been sent for. Nothing else happened. Ninety-two coins spun consecutively have come down heads ninety-two consecutive times . . . and for the last three minutes on the wind of a windless day I have heard the sound of drums and flute. . . .

The music heralds the Tragedians, the first characters from the entrapping *Hamlet* plot whom Rosencrantz and Guildenstern meet, and the plot of course includes the players' production which results in the two being sent to England and their deaths. Rosencrantz's next remark to Guildenstern, that the fingernails and beard grow after death—the first reference to death—is only seemingly a *non sequitur*.

A second key passage occurs a few minutes later:

> GUIL. Practically starting from scratch . . . An awakening, a man standing on his saddle to bang on the shutters, our names shouted in a certain dawn, a message, a summons . . . A new record for heads and tails. We have not been picked out . . . simply to be abandoned . . . set loose to find our own way . . . We are entitled to some direction . . . I would have thought.
>
> ROS. (*Alert, listening*) I say—! I say—
>
> GUIL. Yes?
>
> ROS. I heard—I thought I heard—music.

Guildenstern's comment about lack of direction has been cited to show the loneliness and frustration of absurd man. And indeed the two characters are generally lonely and frustrated. But the words are ironic in their dramatic context, for their lives will not be without direction. The music announces the players and the dramatic pattern represented by the players in which Rosencrantz and Guildenstern will be "caught up" and swept along. They will be directed to England and their deaths. The "direction" which they receive includes the meaning of the direction of actors in a play. As the play progresses, Rosencrantz and Guildenstern are more bewildered by the direction which they are receiving than by the lack of it. A similar linking between the summons and the music of the players occurs at the court; and on the boat, just as Rosencrantz complains of lack of help, the sound of a recorder announces the Tragedians.

The coin tossing not only provides a protracted opening scene, but is referred to frequently in the play, and extends into the first meeting with the Tragedians. The fantastic run of "heads" involves the problem of chance, freedom, and determinacy, which is central to Stoppard's examination of the lives of these two minor characters from *Hamlet*. Critics have given relatively brief but diversified interpretations of the coin tossing and its relation to the play as a whole. . . . The coin tossing does tell us something about the fate of Rosencrantz and Guildenstern. It does not seem to predict monotony or continued waiting; rather, as some of these critics indicated, it marks a change.

When the play opens, Rosencrantz announces after a few onstage tosses that the score is seventy-six-love. The game is continued with the players and the final string of "heads" comes to ninety-two. This is a change from their past experience. Guildenstern observes "with tight hysteria": "We have been spinning coins together since I don't know when, and in all that time (if it *is* all that time) I don't suppose that either of us was more than a couple of gold pieces up or down." This has happened only after the summons, indeed on the same day as the summons, and has been continued into the meeting with the players, who introduce the controlling *Hamlet* plot. The series is not infinite, since "tails" finally comes up.

Guildenstern observes that the "fortuitous and the ordained" formed "a reassuring union which we recognized as nature . . . Then a messenger arrived." The coin tossing marks the two courtiers' apparent departure from what they and the audience have regarded as the normal realm of law, chance, and nature and their entry into a realm where happenings seem both capricious and deterministic. The long run of "heads" is a kind of epiphany, revealing an absurdist universe and foreshadowing the unbreakable chain of events in the *Hamlet* pattern which will catch up Rosencrantz and Guildenstern and sweep them along to their deaths. The events which will entangle them are as different from their previous eventless existence as this coin tossing is from earlier games. The ambiguous "they," who Rosencrantz and Guildenstern feel "had it in" for them from the beginning, becomes a personification for the order or disorder that causes or permits coins or courtiers to become fixed in unexpected patterns. More fundamental than the seemingly "natural" laws of mathematical probability is the law that all the world's actor-spectators have no real control. While "almost anything can happen," all are caught in whatever happens in the same way. The coin tossing also provides an image of life as a game in which one may lose suddenly and inexplicably; tossing or choosing coins, "questions," or entering a plot one did not write, far from being monotonous, may be filled with terrifying implications. This opening scene is parodied as Rosencrantz presents both fists empty several times and then holds a coin in both fists so that Guildenstern, again anxious, chooses the "correct" fist six consecutive times. Rosencrantz may be a parody of the absurdist god revealed in the run of "heads," but it is also implied that the absurdist god may be like him. The difference between this deity and Hamlet's "divinity that shapes our ends" defines the difference between the universe which Shakespeare's Hamlet and Stoppard's Rosencrantz and Guildenstern seek to understand.

The summons and the coin tossing, both with each other and with the Tragedians, lead to the two courtiers being "caught up in" the *Hamlet* pattern. . . . Formerly nonentities who do not recall anything about their previous existence, they gain their only memorable experience and their only identity through their involvement in the events of *Hamlet*. The players appropriately represent the entrapment which makes them participants in a play they did not write. The Tragedians include sex shows in their repertory and tell Rosencrantz and Guildenstern that "it costs little more if you happens to get caught up in the action." Guildenstern understands the implications before Rosencrantz and asks further about being "caught up" and the players prepare to catch them up. The figure suggests the ambiguous relationship between control and consent and between player and spectator as well as the tenuous distinction between being "caught up" and "caught."

Later, in the midst of their efforts to "glean" from Hamlet, Guildenstern says, "We've been caught up. Your smallest action sets off another somewhere else and is set off by it." When they are practicing the questioning of Hamlet, Guildenstern tells Rosencrantz to "catch me unawares." Also the players who are catching them up in the action are catching up with them in the journey. Finally, in a speech that anticipates the conclusion of the pattern in which they are caught, Guildenstern tells the Player that he doesn't "catch them [the spectators] unawares and start the whisper in their skull that says—'One day you are going to die.' " The Player maintains that he does. Three times the entrapment of Rosencrantz and Guildenstern in the play—or the play as life—is revealed by the players. As the Tragedians enter for their fateful performance before the King, Rosencrantz "breaks for the opposite wing" only to encounter two more approaching Tragedians. Immediately after the two courtiers have discovered the letter ordering their deaths, "the players emerge, impossibly, from the barrel, and form a casually menacing circle round ROS and GUIL." Desperately, Guildenstern tries to kill the Player, but discovers that his "death" was just a competent job of acting.

While at court and on the ship, Rosencrantz and Guildenstern, like Didi and Gogo, experience uncertainty and frustration. Beckett's characters, particularly Didi, are uncertain about what Godot is like, whether he will come, and whether the boys will carry the messages; Stoppard's characters, particularly Guildenstern, are uncertain about the King's motives and intentions, their assignment from the King, their own safety, and death. The principal characters in both plays are frustrated because of lack of success. But Rosencrantz and Guildenstern are not bored and are not existing in a void of endless time and space. They are primarily concerned with escaping from the *Hamlet* pattern in which they have been "caught up." So much is happening that Rosencrantz repeatedly wants to go home. Guildenstern tries to thinks that they will come through "all right" if they "tread warily" and "follow instructions," but that being "arbitrary" might cause a "shambles," and "If we go there's no knowing." They are blocked in time by an unbroken series of fast-moving events and in space by other characters. They have some time between *Hamlet* scenes to practice how to act with Hamlet (who always comes), but they are imprisoned within the *Hamlet* plot and within twenty-four hours arrive at Elsinore, receive instructions, try to "glean" from Hamlet, witness the play (including the foreshadowing of their own deaths) and the King's agitation, become involved in the slaying of Polonius, the arrest of Hamlet, and are sent off to England with Hamlet. Only for a "fractional moment" is there a possible escape from this pattern. Along with the confrontations with the Tragedians, Rosencrantz and Guildenstern feel trapped by other characters: "In and out, on and off, they're coming at us from all sides," and "As soon as we make a move they'll come pouring in from all sides. . . . " They vaguely hope for not just anything to happen, but for something that would bring an explanation or release. Ironically (very much as when the Tragedians' music is first heard), Guildenstern thinks the sound of a pipe aboard the ship "could change the course of events," but the music again heralds the players, who personify the ineluctable pattern of events.

Two young courtiers, then, have been suddenly awakened

by a summons from uneventful and directionless lives, coins turn up "heads" one hundred consecutive times in an absurdist epiphany, and the courtiers become part of a pattern of events—whose cause or purpose they do not understand—which they cannot or will not escape and which both gives them their only identity and carries them to their deaths. In this sense Godot comes in *Rosencrantz and Guildenstern Are Dead.* (pp. 57-65)

After the summons, Rosencrantz and Guildenstern, particularly the latter, feel that they are experiencing an un-, sub-, or super-natural force. In Act I Guildenstern feels afraid because the run of "heads" seems to mean the end of a natural order and the presence of a deity or force that permits or causes the fantastic to become inescapable. Guildenstern, "desperate to lose," experiences the same fear when he chooses the fist with the coin six consecutive times—only to learn that Rosencrantz had a coin in both fists. On the ship Guildenstern feels that they are caught in an incredible chain of events: "And it *has* all happened. Hasn't it?" The two feel more and more that their fate is determined. Guildenstern expresses it best: "Where we went wrong was getting on a boat. We can move, of course, change direction, rattle about, but our movement is contained within a larger one that carries us along as inexorably as the wind and current . . ." Also, more and more they see the forces controlling them as personified and hostile. They see themselves as intended victims but also as gaining importance. Their lives, they feel, are being directed and ended by an unseen "they" which sometimes suggests the King and the court, but which increasingly means some un-, sub-, or supernatural agency: "They don't care," says Rosencrantz. Again, jumping overboard "would put a spoke in their wheel," Rosencrantz says. "Unless they're counting on it," Guildenstern replies. Assume, Guildenstern remarks later, "that they're going to kill him": (i.e., Hamlet). As they near the coast of England, Rosencrantz sums up the courtiers' perception of "they": "They had it in for us, didn't they? Right from the beginning. Who'd have thought that we were so important?" Ironically, Rosencrantz says, "They'll just have to wait," before he disappears at the end. Though this agency does not appear in person, Rosencrantz and Guildenstern are convinced that "they" have seized control of their lives and swept them to their deaths. They do not feel, like Didi and Gogo, that they have been abandoned, but that they are receiving a disproportionate amount of attention.

In keeping with the different fates of the principals in relation to their Godots in *Waiting for Godot* and in *Rosencrantz and Guildenstern Are Dead,* the two plays differ structurally in at least two important respects. The structure of *Waiting for Godot* reflects the process of waiting and is basically circular and repetitive. . . . [Critics] have generally recognized that the play's two acts suggest a repeated rather than a completed action and that the second act does largely repeat the first. On the contrary, the first act of Stoppard's play is concerned with sudden change, and the play presents a completed action within a structure that is basically linear. The summons leads to the involvement in the *Hamlet* plot, which leads to the deaths of Rosencrantz and Guildenstern. Another structural difference is that in *Waiting for Godot* the two tramps generate their own action of waiting (whether Godot can or cannot come), whereas in Stoppard's play the two court-

iers are trapped in the *Hamlet* plot through what seems to them to be a supernatural agency. (pp. 67-8)

If we compare *Rosencrantz and Guildenstern Are Dead* with *Waiting for Godot,* we see in Stoppard's play two characters strikingly similar to Didi and Gogo who find themselves in a predicament essentially different from that in *Waiting for Godot.* Didi and Gogo, Rosencrantz and Guildenstern, are all representatives of humanity, and feel uncertain, frustrated, and powerless to change their situation. Didi and Gogo are desperate, but always wait for some resolution and explanation tomorrow. Rosencrantz and Guildenstern are bewildered by fast-moving developments—the *Hamlet* pattern, the revelation of the "they" who had it in for them, and their approaching deaths. From the run of "heads" to their plaintive wondering at the end if they had done anything wrong, they cannot understand why these sudden and unforeseen changes have come to them. Whereas Didi and Gogo represent the universal experience of waiting, Rosencrantz and Guildenstern represent the universal experience of feeling caught up by an incomprehensible force in a bizarre tragedy, written by an unknown author, "where everyone who is marked for death dies." (pp. 68-9)

Joseph E. Duncan, "Godot Comes: 'Rosencrantz and Guildenstern Are Dead',' in Ariel: A Review of International English Literature, *Vol. 12, No. 4, October, 1981, pp. 57-70.*

John M. Perlette

The last act of Tom Stoppard's *Rosencrantz and Guildenstern Are Dead* presents its audience with an exceptionally peculiar incident which has, to my knowledge, elicited no comment from critics of the play. Yet the text repeats the incident, presenting it not once but twice, and not merely as a simple repetition but as a repetition with a difference, taking the form of a chiastic inversion. On a ship bearing Hamlet to England, Rosencrantz and Guildenstern's efforts to decipher their role in the play's events and the implications of this trip for their future degenerate into another inscrutable dead end. Exasperated and depressed, Rosencrantz finally professes himself unable to believe in England:

> GUIL. (*Leaping up*) What a shambles! We're just not getting anywhere.
>
> ROS. (*Mournfully*) Not even England. I don't believe in it anyway.
>
> GUIL. What?
>
> ROS. England.
>
> GUIL. Just a conspiracy of cartographers, you mean?
>
> ROS. I mean I don't believe it! (*Calmer*) I have no image. I try to picture us arriving, a little harbour perhaps . . . roads . . . inhabitants to point the way . . . horses on the road . . . riding for a day or a fortnight and then a palace and the English king. . . . That would be the logical kind of thing. . . . But my mind remains a blank. No. We're slipping off the map.

Rosencrantz is the apostate here, whereas Guildenstern

attempts to shore up the faith. The forms of their different approaches to the question are important. For Guildenstern, England is real or credible, and defensibly so, as long as it is an abstraction, an idea, susceptible to the cartographer's symbolic representation. In contrast, when Rosencrantz attempts to realize the abstraction, to imagine the reality of England, he finds himself incapable of doing so. And this is not for Rosencrantz a matter of choice, some merely petulant refusal to believe. He is, as he explains, incapable of believing in his destination.

Shortly thereafter, we encounter the chiastic repetition; Guildenstern is now presented as the anxious nonbeliever with Rosencrantz attempting to reassure him:

> ROS. . . . We'll be all right. I suppose we just go on.
>
> GUIL. Go where?
>
> ROS. To England.
>
> GUIL. England! *That's* a dead end. I never believed in it anyway.
>
> ROS. All we've got to do is make our report and that'll be that. Surely.
>
> GUIL. I don't *believe* it—a shore, a harbour, say—and we get off and we stop someone and say—Where's the king?—And he says, Oh, you follow that road there and take the first left and—(*Furiously*). I don't believe any of it!
>
> ROS. It doesn't sound very plausible.

Guildenstern precisely reiterates Rosencrantz's inability to imagine the reality of England. But more profound implications are triggered by Guildenstern's menacingly loaded remark "England! *That's* a dead end," because both of these moments in the play are marked by explicit discussions of death. Immediately after Rosencrantz has explained his inability to imagine England, the following exchange occurs:

> ROS. We drift down time, clutching at straws. But what good's a brick to a drowning man?
>
> GUIL. Don't give up, we can't be long now.
>
> ROS. We might as well be dead. Do you think death could possibly be a boat?
>
> GUIL. No, no, no. . . . Death is . . . not. Death isn't. You take my meaning. Death is the ultimate negative. Not-being.

We can see in Rosencrantz's question, and Guildenstern's answer, the same kind of struggle to realize an abstraction that was present in Rosencrantz's futile effort to imagine England. In the second instance, Guildenstern's protestations of disbelief in England are immediately preceded by his remarking: "We've travelled too far, and our momentum has taken over; we move idly towards eternity, without possibility of reprieve or hope of explanation." And shortly thereafter he returns to this theme:

> GUIL. But why? Was it all for this? Who are we that so much should converge on our little deaths? (*In anguish to the* PLAYER) Who are *we*?

> PLAYER. You are Rosencrantz and Guildenstern. That's enough.
>
> GUIL. No—it is not enough. To be told so little—to such an end—and still, finally, to be denied an explanation. . . .

England is a dead end—end of their function, their mission, their journey, their lives—in more than one sense. Yet their destination ultimately makes no sense; it can be neither imagined nor explained.

The final symmetry (but again, a repetition with a difference) between these two moments makes explicit the connection between England and death as destination. Each involves a letter. Just after Rosencrantz's statement of disbelief, the pair open and read the letter ordering the execution of Hamlet. Just after Guildenstern's statement of disbelief, the pair open and read the (rewritten) letter ordering the execution of Rosencrantz and Guildenstern. "England" has become (both metaphorically and metonymically) "death," and consequently we may understand Rosencrantz and Guildenstern's repeated inability to believe in England as a displacement (a repetition with a difference) of their inability to believe in their own deaths. This inability is significant of the mind having run right up against one of its ultimate limits, that is, the psychological impossibility of truly imagining one's own death as nonexistence.

Freud acknowledges the commonplace human "tendency to 'shelve' death, to eliminate it from life . . . to hush it up . . ."; and he argues that this tendency is rooted in a psychologically structural inability to believe in our own death: "Our own death is indeed unimaginable, and whenever we make the attempt to imagine it we can perceive that we really survive as spectators. Hence the psychoanalytic school could venture on the assertion that at bottom no one believes in his own death. . . ." The problem, as Freud sees it, is that: "What we call our 'unconscious' (the deepest strata of our minds, made up of instinctual impulses) knows nothing whatever of negatives or of denials—contradictories coincide in it—and so it knows nothing whatever of our own death, for to that we can give only a negative purport." (pp. 659-61)

If we can perceive Rosencrantz and Guildenstern's inability to believe in England as a displaced version of their inability to believe in their deaths, we can relate Freud's insight to a number of other significant aspects of the play. For one, we can recognize that the incidents we have been focusing on are themselves displacements—repetitions with a difference—of a crucial scene encountered earlier. In Act Two, a reference to the future leads Rosencrantz to ask: "Do you ever think of yourself as actually *dead*, lying in a box with a lid on it?" Guildenstern, wanting no part of these morbid speculations, responds with a curt "No." But the decidedly less sensitive Rosencrantz blunders on in a series of mutually self-canceling statements—and questions:

> ROS. Nor do I, really. . . . It's silly to be depressed by it. I mean one thinks of it like being *alive* in a box, one keeps forgetting to take into account the fact that one is *dead* . . . which should make all the difference . . . shouldn't it? I mean, you'd never *know* you were in a box, would you? It would be just like being *asleep* in

a box. Not that I'd like to sleep in a box, mind you, not without any air—you'd wake up dead, for a start, and then where would you be? Apart from inside a box. That's the bit I don't like, frankly. That's why I don't think of it. . . .

Guildenstern remarks that "Death followed by eternity . . . *is* a terrible thought," and so it may in some sense be, even as a complete abstraction ("death" here is linked to the equally amorphous "eternity"). But Rosencrantz's confused formulations indicate that it is an entirely unattainable thought, a literally unthinkable thought, imaginatively considered. At one point in these confused ramblings, Rosencrantz says that although he is aware of death, that awareness is entirely nonspecific: "Whatever became of the moment when one first knew about death? There must have been one, a moment, in childhood when it first occurred to you that you don't go on for ever. It must have been shattering—stamped into one's memory. And yet I can't remember it. It never occurred to me at all." Rosencrantz is simply unable to realize imaginatively his own death: " . . . one thinks of it like being *alive* in a box . . . like being *asleep* in a box . . . you'd wake up dead, . . ." His contortions and contradictions here anticipate his inability to imagine England. (pp. 661-62)

Guildenstern's insistence upon dissociating death from "seeing it happen" . . . is not simply a recognition that nothing can represent the abstract negativity of death to us. It also confirms Freud's recognition of the structural key to this impossibility, namely that every representation (imaginative image or dramatic spectacle) falls short because, by the very act of witnessing it, "we really survive as spectators." "Spectators," of course, is a theatrical term which forces us to recognize that *Rosencrantz and Guildenstern Are Dead* is concerned not merely with a psychological curiosity, but also with the limits of theatrical representation. And this concern is focused not merely upon some momentary deficiency of imaginative or representative power, but rather on the structural limits of the medium itself.

Criticism has almost universally recognized the reflexive, self-conscious, or metadramatic aspects of this play. The self-consciousness of its relationship with *Hamlet,* the constant "playing" with the players, the reiteration of the play-within-the-play, and the treatment of Rosencrantz and Guildenstern as characters who are servants of the script have made inescapable the conclusion that this play is at least as much "about" itself (play, theatre, drama) as it is "about" anything else. I would like to suggest that two aspects of this reflexivity become doubly meaningful when viewed from the perspective of Freud's remark about surviving as spectators. The first is the notion of Rosencrantz and Guildenstern as audience (witnesses, spectators, "survivors") of *Hamlet.* (*Hamlet* is not only the play-within- but also the play-without-the-play in this play; that is, not only the play twice mimed by the players but also the controlling "frame" of events witnessed by Rosencrantz and Guildenstern.) Their role as spectators is established early, in their first meeting with the players, when Rosencrantz inquires about what it will cost "To watch." Later, Rosencrantz announces, during a lull in the action, "I feel like a spectator. . . . " And again, when the players commence their "rehearsal" of *Hamlet,* Guildenstern warns, "Keep back—we're spectators." These explicit references to the role of Rosencrantz and Guildenstern as spectators are implicitly reinforced for the audience (the spectators) at those moments when Rosencrantz and Guildenstern are represented as spectators of the events of *Hamlet* and of the plays-within-the-play.

This emphasis and structure have, I believe, the potential to create a curiously contradictory effect. We share with Rosencrantz and Guildenstern the role or position, the locus or site, of spectators. As Thomas Whitaker has remarked [in his book *Tom Stoppard*]: "Indeed, when Rosencrantz and Guildenstern emerge from that Shakespearean scene, they seem yet more emphatically with us." And we with them, at least when we share a "real time" moment of (spectatorial) experience with them. There would seem to be possible, therefore, a moment of immediacy, of direct contact here. Yet at the very moment when we share their place and function, "identifying" with them, what we witness is their inability to identify with what they are seeing. The essence of their spectating, after all, is to be spectators of their own deaths, with which they are unable to identify. As spectators (and this is Freud's point), they are forever cut off from any direct or unmediated access to their own ultimate reality. All they have are (reiterable) representations and mediations which, first, are incapable of rendering the "thing-in-itself" of death, of providing its fully felt realization, and, second, always have the effect of leaving them (as spectators) on the outside looking in. Through them, perhaps, we (also spectators) can intuit the inescapable distance or difference, alienation or artifice, alterity or otherness between "ourselves" and our representations. Cut off irretrievably from our most pressing reality, we can perhaps understand the inadequacy yet inevitability of representations which, though constructs or fictions, are as close to reality as we can come.

Perhaps. But now the abyss looms wide, as it always does when a discourse attempts to discuss itself, when a definition contains what it would define, when a medium, like the theatre, turns to itself. We must recognize that any insight, truth, or reality we would be tempted to derive here is thoroughly undermined. I shall put—not simply to be sure, but as directly as I can—the system created by the play, not of paradoxes (they are stronger than that), but of flat contradictions:

1. when we share the position of spectators with Rosencrantz and Guildenstern, we are put into the position of identifying with their inability to identify;

2. we are expected to be "satisfied" with the adequacy of a representation representing the inadequacy of representation;

3. we are asked to see a certain reality in the representation of Rosencrantz and Guildenstern's recognition that representations do not give them reality.

This kind of reflexivity doubles back on itself and erases its own tracks as it produces them. Like any work or system operating at the extremity of its own limits, this one calls into question its own premises and renders unstable its own language. The play giveth and the play taketh away.

Nor are these contradictions, these *aporia* or *insolubilia,* meant to be resolved or reconciled. They are the structural counterpart of the play's thematic of uncertainty, the latter, at least, attested by Stoppard himself. As almost all critical commentary recognizes, Stoppard has promoted contradiction as the central formulaic device of his work:

> . . . there is very often *no* single, clear statement in my plays. What there is, is a series of conflicting statements made by conflicting characters, and they tend to play a sort of infinite leap-frog. You know, an argument, a refutation, then a rebuttal of the refutation, then a counter-rebuttal, so that there is never any point in this intellectual leap-frog at which I feel *that* is the speech to stop it on, *that* is the last word.

Also popular among critics is Stoppard's statement: "I write plays because dialogue is the most respectable way of contradicting yourself." But perhaps most interesting in our context is an assertion made by Stoppard to A. C. H. Smith: "I am a very hedgy sort of writer. What I think of as being my distinguishing mark is an absolute lack of certainty about almost anything." "An absolute lack of certainty" is not just a statement about Stoppard's use of contradictions, but also a contradiction. It does what it serves as a reason for doing: it contradicts itself. And it brings us back to the point where a limit is reached (the certainty of uncertainty) as a statement folds in upon itself, undoing itself in the process.

This certainty of uncertainty certainly carries over to Stoppard's creatures. Throughout the play, Rosencrantz and Guildenstern are haunted by a nagging uncertainty which is pervasive and characteristic, and which takes many localized forms (from the inexplicable run of heads to the confusion of their identities to the mysteries of Hamlet). But this uncertainty centers ultimately on what Rosencrantz refers to as his "intuition of mortality." Guildenstern, especially, "knows" there is something (really no-thing) called death which is neither imaginable nor knowable, and which he finds profoundly disturbing. Significantly, it is in his moment of most obviously fraudulent evasion, when he is sophistically rationalizing Hamlet's fate and his part in it, that he says: "And then again, what is so terrible about death? As Socrates so philosophically put it, since we don't know what death is, it is illogical to fear it." But the dread (*Angst*) of the nothingness of death is what it is precisely because of its indeterminacy, its lack of an object. (pp. 663-65)

The certain uncertainty of death figures in the second aspect of dramatic reflexivity which I wish to mention here. That is, the Player's penchant for discussing the limitations of his audience. (And let us recall that in the matter of death we are all, and always, the audience—spectators.) He is insistent upon the point that the "spectacle" of death as artificial illusion which keeps its audience at a safe distance and leaves them surviving as spectators is the only kind they can appreciate. Driven by his nagging intimation and dread of the (known) unknown, Guildenstern berates the Player for blithely representing death: "Actors! The mechanics of cheap melodrama! That isn't *death!* . . . You die so many times; how can you expect them [audiences] to believe in your death?" Absolutely unruffled, the Player confidently responds: "On the contrary, it's the only kind they do believe." He knows that direct and immediate access to the reality of death is simply beyond the capacity of his audience. It is with doleful aversion born of difficult experience that he goes on to recount what happened when he had an actor-turned-thief actually hanged

in one of his plays. The audience were totally unable to relate to the event: " . . . you wouldn't believe it, he just *wasn't* convincing! It was impossible to suspend one's disbelief—and what with the audience jeering and throwing peanuts, the whole thing was a *disaster!*" Facing the reality of death, the audience maintain their primordial disbelief. Illusions known to be illusions are the only acceptable forms. "Audiences know what to expect," says the Player, "and that is all that they are prepared to believe in."

Strangely enough, this apparent disagreement between Guildenstern and the Player, which is repeated at the end of the play, turns out, in terms of the perspective we are providing here, to be no disagreement at all. In fact, their respective positions are corollaries of each other. It is important to note that when Guildenstern insists that no acting, no representation can give us a genuine vision or version of death, the Player does not refute this opinion. The Player does not protest that, yes, this is what death is like. On the contrary, he simply points out that illusory spectacles of death (known to be such and leaving us intact as spectators) are the only kinds in which we are prepared to believe. These positions are actually complementary, opposite sides of the same coin, each in its way a recognition of the fact that we have no direct access to the reality of death.

As a final joke, the inevitability of the illusory is once again brought home to Guildenstern (and to us) at the end of the play by the Player. Guildenstern's frustrated effort to convince the Player that acting is not death finally leads him to attack the Player, stabbing and apparently killing him. The Player's death is totally convincing. But no sooner are Rosencrantz and Guildenstern (and we) convinced that the Player is dead than his cohorts, now his audience, begin to applaud and the Player pops up again to proclaim: "You see, it *is* the kind they do believe in—it's what is expected." He is absolutely right. As audience, we will have been thoroughly caught up in the moment . . . investing it with our belief. But we need to look closely at what is being demonstrated here. To put it bluntly, we "believe" because we do not believe. To understand this statement, we need only imagine the incredulity and total alienation with which we would react to a real death on a theatrical stage. We can entertain and be entertained by these illusions only because they are illusions and because we are distanced (protected) from them by a fundamental disbelief. We can "believe" by suspending our disbelief only if that disbelief is there to be suspended in the first place. This illusion, as Freud pointed out, is the essence and limit of our approach to death. This, as Guildenstern has been insisting, is the cheat at the heart of representations of death which renders them inadequate. And this, as the Player has been protesting, is the only kind of death in which we are really prepared to believe. . . . What we already know ("Audiences know what to expect") is that the Player's death is a theatrical trick, and we know this before we know anything about the trick knife. The resurrection of the Player is a pointed reminder of the fact that we knew all along that his representation of death was not real. Our "serious attention," however momentarily genuine, is completely deflated, and the joke is, after all, on us. Once again, the play has gone out of its way to make us aware that the reality of death is simply inaccessible to us.

The play's last testament to this idea is, characteristically, a similarly playful one. In spite of everything he has seen (without seeing) and known (without knowing), Guildenstern's last line in the play is: "Well, we'll know better next time. Now you see me, now you—(*and disappears*)." Next time. Sure. Even at the last moment, Guildenstern is as unconvinced of his own death as we are, and maybe even more so. This situation has to strike us as amusingly absurd, and it is because of this resurgence of levity, this continuous deflation of seriousness, that we leave Rosencrantz and Guildenstern, not with any oppressive sense of death, but rather with a bemused sense of having been exposed to our own limits—logical, psychological, and theatrical. (pp. 666-67)

> *John M. Perlette, "Theatre at the Limit: 'Rosencrantz and Guildenstern Are Dead',"* in *Modern Drama, Vol. XXVIII, No. 4, December, 1985, pp. 659-69.*

J. Dennis Huston

Tom Stoppard's **Rosencrantz and Guildenstern Are Dead** does to critical categories what it does to *Hamlet*: it skews perspectives and disrupts expectations. Like Falstaff's Mistress Quickly, it seems neither fish nor flesh, and the critic knows not where to have it; for it mixes genres, times, places, and characters into what may seem only a confusing dramatic amalgam, composed of odd bits and pieces from *Hamlet, Waiting for Godot, Six Characters in Search of an Author* . . . to name only the most notable sources and influences cited by the critics. With alarming swiftness—and often with no explanation—Stoppard moves his action, as if in dramatic hyperspace, through the world of Elizabethan tragedy, burlesque humor, monomythic narrative, comic pornography, contemporary metadrama, modern philosophy, critical theory, and black comedy.

The apparently arbitrary, pastiche-like structure of the play, however, belies both its ambitiousness and its originality, for in it Stoppard attempts a literal revision, a modern "misreading," of *Hamlet*. In so doing he not only borrows ingeniously from pieces of Shakespeare's play, fundamentally changing its context while still preserving the letter of its text, but he also partly challenges Shakespeare's achievement by offering his audience a revised, contemporary view of the *Hamlet*-world, skewed from the perspective of the originally insignificant Rosencrantz and Guildenstern. When Stoppard arbitrarily manipulates and "misreads" *Hamlet*, then, he consciously dramatizes both the modern playwright's bondage to and rebellion against Shakespeare's imposing presence. That bondage Stoppard emphasizes by appropriating parts of *Hamlet*; that rebellion he enacts by resituating Shakespeare's text and reconstituting his characters and dramatic world. Metamorphosed into representatively modern anti-heroes, Stoppard's Rosencrantz and Guildenstern bemusedly observe small pieces of *Hamlet* from its periphery and confusedly live even small pieces of it from its vortex. Powerlessly, they confront a universe apparently arbitrary and incomprehensible. But from their powerlessness the playwright derives his power; in their confusion, he finds vision. Out of apparent chaos he shapes an imaginative world logically disordered by its blurred dramatic perspective but thematically coherent and theatrically compelling.

As a way of exploring both Stoppard's "misreading" of *Hamlet* and his ingenious manipulation of dramatic perspective, I mean to address in this essay three aspects of **Rosencrantz and Guildenstern Are Dead** which critics of the play have ignored: the ambiguity of the title, the preponderance of magic in the work, and the simultaneous presence in it of two *Hamlets*—Shakespeare's and Stoppard's. These three aspects of the play variously reflect problems of shifting, ambiguous perspective which characterize this work and contribute to its richly complex nature.

Because it is a quotation from *Hamlet*, the title announces the direct ties between this play and Shakespeare's, but it also introduces and embodies the self-contradictoriness and slippery relativism of Stoppard's dramatic world. For although this title may seem initially simple and clear, its meaning expands into complexity and collapses into self-contradiction as soon as we try to situate it precisely. (pp. 47-8)

To begin with the most obvious problem posed by the title: What time does it define? The tense of the statement is present, but in the present depicted by the play Rosencrantz and Guildenstern are certainly not dead. Therefore, the Rosencrantz and Guildenstern referred to in the title cannot be the Rosencrantz and Guildenstern of this play; they are rather the Shakespearean characters killed long ago in an Elizabethan revenge-tragedy. The event thus denoted by the phrase "are dead," though it reaches out to touch the present, has as its principal effect the differentiation of Stoppard's Rosencrantz and Guildenstern from Shakespeare's: the characters belong to different dramatic worlds and times.

Or do they? What happens, for instance, if we read "are dead" as truly present tense? Then at least two more possible meanings emerge. First, the word "dead" may refer to Rosencrantz and Guildenstern metaphorically, as roles rather than as characters: for actors these parts in Shakespeare's play are "dead"; they offer little in the way of range, challenge, or audience-appeal. But although Shakespeare may have created in Rosencrantz and Guildenstern two "dead" theatrical parts, Stoppard may outdo Shakespeare—within this limited context—by resituating those characters in a play which brings them to life. In this case his title becomes ironic, for it asserts as fact a situation he intends to alter dramatically; it challenges Shakespeare's presentation of Rosencrantz and Guildenstern as characters without much dramatic life. Stoppard's title and his play, then, announce simultaneously the playwright's aspirations and his anxieties. He means to revise the work of the world's greatest dramatist, but he chooses as his center of attention the confused comings and goings of two minor characters, who seem to have gotten little more consideration from Shakespeare than they got from his principal character.

The second possible meaning which emerges from a reading of "are dead" as truly present tense suggests close correspondence, rather than differentiation, between Shakespeare's and Stoppard's Rosencrantz and Guildenstern. For if the force of the verb is essentially upon the present, the title implies that Stoppard's characters are as good as dead; i.e., they are doomed by some judgment already passed upon them. Because in *Hamlet* Rosencrantz and Guildenstern are sent to their deaths near the end of the drama, the fate of Stoppard's characters, who now find themselves unaccountably called forth to play their parts in *Hamlet,* is sealed: Rosencrantz and Guildenstern are dead; their end is inescapable.

Such an interpretation of the title has, of course, radically different implications than the reading which distinguishes Stoppard's Rosencrantz and Guildenstern from Shakespeare's in world and time. Instead of differentiation, we find identification. What happened to Shakespeare's characters is happening to Stoppard's, who mirror them—bearing their names, speaking their lines, encountering the mad Prince Hamlet on behalf of King Claudius, and ultimately suffering their ignominious demise. And because in this interpretation of the title Rosencrantz and Guildenstern are perceived as dramatic characters contained timelessly in an imaginative world, time remains eternally present tense. What happened in the past is happening again in the present and will continue to happen, again and again, in the future.

This interpretation of the title depends partly on an audience recognizing it as a quotation from the closing moments of *Hamlet.* For then Stoppard encourages us to feel both correspondence and tension between the design of *Hamlet* and of this play: he makes us anticipate the moment when the words from *Hamlet,* as a judgment upon Stoppard's Rosencrantz and Guildenstern, shape their tragic end. The words of the title thus become something we as an audience wait for near the conclusion of the play, when Rosencrantz and Guildenstern's fate in Stoppard's dramatic world will be fitted somehow to their fate in Shakespeare's. By the example of a dramatic event known to us in *Hamlet,* the words promise a future remorselessly pressing upon the present: we know that inevitably, near the end of the play, we will hear that "Rosencrantz and Guildenstern are dead."

But what we do not know is whether, when we hear these words, they will be nullified by their context. For so cleverly and imaginatively does Stoppard play with the Shakespearean text he appropriates that we may wonder throughout the work if Rosencrantz and Guildenstern can escape their *Hamlet*-shaped fate. Because Stoppard can find ways of fundamentally altering Shakespeare's dramatic context, even while still retaining his language, he may also be able to deliver Rosencrantz and Guildenstern from death by creating a new context in which to announce it. The extent to which he and his principal characters are bound by the language, action, and overall outlines of *Hamlet* is never clear, because Stoppard plays fast and loose with his source.

Stoppard's title, then, in spite of its apparent clarity and simplicity, is neither clear nor simple. The Rosencrantz and Guildenstern it describes may be any one—or all—of four different Rosencrantzes and Guildensterns: the characters who appear in Shakespeare's play and are to be differentiated from Stoppard's Rosencrantz and Guildenstern; two contemporary anti-heroes recognizably different from Shakespeare's figures; two characters, identifiable with Shakespeare's, who are caught in a dramatic time warp where past, present, and future exist simultaneously; or the actors' roles, Rosencrantz and Guildenstern, which Shakespeare created, apparently with cursory attention, but which Stoppard reconstitutes, newly infused with theatrical life. Even the seemingly unambiguous word "dead"

in the title proves slippery in meaning. For its implications may be literal or metaphorical, and its point of reference, Shakespeare's play or Stoppard's. "Dead" describes a fate either identifying or differentiating Stoppard's and Shakespeare's characters, but which of these alternatives it will be, the play does not reveal until its conclusion. Even after Hamlet has disappeared from the boat late in act three, Stoppard offers ambiguous evidence about the "dead"-ness of Rosencrantz and Guildenstern:

> Ros. He's dead then, He's dead as far as we're concerned.
>
> Player. Or we are as far as he is.

This exchange may suggest that death is sometimes only a matter of perspective: as far as Rosencrantz and Guildenstern are concerned, Hamlet, because he is absent from them, is "dead," and vice-versa. Death may be sometimes a relative, as well as an absolute, condition. But this exchange may also suggest a chillingly different and absolute meaning. By writing the letter which orders Rosencrantz and Guildenstern's execution, Hamlet has assured their eventual murder: his concern for them has been for their death.

In ***Rosencrantz and Guildenstern Are Dead*** nothing escapes the swirling rush of Stoppard's shifting dramatic perspective, in spite of the heroes'—or the critics'—attempts to situate meaning precisely. Early in act three Guildenstern tries desperately to locate some "fact" which gives understandable purpose to his present circumstances: " . . . we are brought round full circle to face again the single immutable fact—that we, Rosencrantz and Guildenstern, bearing a letter from one king to another, are taking Hamlet to England." But even this "fact" dissolves as Guildenstern tries to give it expression, for his assertion contains not a "single immutable fact" but two: Rosencrantz and Guildenstern are taking Hamlet to England; and they are bearing a letter from one king to another. Nor does the statement, as Guildenstern claims, prove immutable, since they are actually taking Hamlet not to England but into the company of pirates—or into a disappearing barrel, whichever applies. In addition, the letter they bear will eventually become a letter not from one king to another, but from a prince to a king—again whichever applies. In a world where one fact proves to be two, and one letter, another, a statement like "Rosencrantz and Guildenstern are dead" confounds absolutist interpretation by engendering four Rosencrantzes and Guildensterns, a stereoscopic array of verbal references, and no sure definition of "dead," which may prove literal, metaphorical, or merely mistaken.

Such shifting meanings may partly account, too, for the preponderance of magic, another source of ambiguous perspective, in this play. For magic, like language in Stoppard's dramatic world and like the theatrical medium itself, works transformations. It changes one thing into another—even when that change is from something into nothing, as is often the case in ***Rosencrantz and Guildenstern Are Dead.*** That is because all the magic tricks in the play deal with surprising appearances and disappearances: Rosencrantz makes a coin vanish, so completely that not even he can find it; at another time one coin in his hands becomes two. In act three the players make their entrance out of barrels, like clowns unfolding themselves from a circus car. Later, in the darkness following the pirate attack, one of the barrels disappears; and then the Players, Rosencrantz, and Guildenstern surprisingly emerge from different barrels from the ones they have just fled to. Near the end of the play the knife blade Guildenstern means to drive into the Player instead harmlessly disappears into its handle. And finally, Rosencrantz and Guildenstern make their final exits simply by disappearing from the stage.

All of these magic tricks are, of course, only stage devices, sleights of hand worked by actors (and/or the characters), the stage crew, or the set designer. And perhaps they ought to be transparently obvious in their trickery. In that way, they would contribute to other "alienation effects" in the play, other moments which intensify an audience's awareness of themselves as an audience to a theatrical performance. Like the principal characters' periodic sense that they face an audience, . . . the stage magic would ask an audience to experience the work intellectually as well as emotionally. For only then can the audience remain alert to the fact, implicit both in Stoppard's title and in his use of magic, that meaning in theater, language, and world is embedded in structures so complex and anamorphic that they not only confound certain interpretation; they also encourage, indeed almost demand, fundamental self-contradiction. "I write plays," Stoppard has claimed, "because dialogue is the most respectable way of contradicting myself." (pp. 49-54)

The magic tricks in this play do not, however, have to be transparent, nor is Stoppard's artistic power necessarily compromised by Shakespeare's achievement. As earlier we saw Stoppard's title embodying the self-contradictions of his dramatic world, so here we see his focus on magic in the theatrical medium reflecting this same thematic concern. For what from one perspective is a world constrained by convention, whose magic is all overworked stage business, is from another perspective a world vitalized by imagination, whose magic is genuinely transformative. The claim of the magician, after all, is that he has access to forces operating beyond the pale of the natural world, and that these forces give him unusual control over ordinary, everyday occurrences. In a way, the playwright can make similar claims, since he, too, may exercise magical powers. Within the charmed circle of the theater world he may, if his play is successful, temporarily set aside the laws governing the movement of things in time and space. A play may be artificial in form, constrained by convention, enacted by players, dependent on obvious stage devices, and transparently derivative. But that same play may also magically transcend its artificiality, limiting conventions, and derivativeness by making its audience see old things in new ways. Two minor characters from *Hamlet,* for instance, take on vital dramatic energies when they are viewed, sometimes simultaneously, sometimes consecutively, from at least three different perspectives: as participants in a radically skewed version of *Hamlet;* as contemporary anti-heroes trapped in a universe they cannot understand or affect; and as characters inextricably caught up in some discontinuous, deenergized play that they can neither enliven nor abort, no matter what they do, or do not do.

Such perspectives, as Stoppard presents them, work a kind of magic on Rosencrantz and Guildenstern, transforming them from theatrically insignificant Elizabethan nonentities to, paradoxically, powerful dramatic representations of modern impotence. Between these two views of the characters there are, of course, correspondences, which Stoppard emphasizes by appropriating Shakespearean characters to his particular purposes. But there are also crucial differences between these two views, a fact which criticism of the play has generally ignored. For Stoppard's Rosencrantz and Guildenstern are not, as critics claim, trapped in the *Hamlet*-world; they are rather trapped in Stoppard's dramatic world, which is quite a different thing—even if Stoppard's theatrical magic periodically conjures up pieces of the *Hamlet*-world. Magic in **Rosencrantz and Guildenstern Are Dead**, then, serves partly as an image for the playwright's and the principal characters' limits, since both dramatist and characters are bound, though in different ways, by the stage tricks indigenous to the dramatic medium. But partly, too, Stoppard's stage magic calls attention to his powers as a playwright by paradigmatically embodying those powers, all successful drama being a kind of stage magic.

One notable example of such dramatic power is his complex and deliberately self-contradictory revision of the *Hamlet*-world. On the one hand, the literal presence of *Hamlet* in **Rosencrantz and Guildenstern Are Dead** emphasizes the shrunken trivialities of the modern condition. Its principal dramatic figures are no longer recognizably tragic heroes, summoned to terrible tasks by supernatural forces, but merely minor characters living on the edges of some ineluctable, death-dealing action, which alternately swirls around and by them. And from this perspective, the language of *Hamlet* dwarfs the petti-fogging idiom with which Rosencrantz and Guildenstern confront the conundrums of their world. But on the other hand, *Hamlet* is trivialized by **Rosencrantz and Guildenstern Are Dead**, as the young playwright enacts his dramatic revenge on the oppressive figure of the father-playwright. In the context of Stoppard's dramatic world, Shakespeare's verse may sound as archaic and artificial as the language of *The Murder of Gonzago* sounds in *Hamlet;* instead of grandness, it may attain only to bombast. In addition, the broken, discontinuous events of Shakespeare's play as it appears in Stoppard's reduce it to a comic pastiche, an effect further emphasized by radical changes in stage directions. And finally, when Stoppard at last moves his Hamlet outside the literal boundaries of Shakespeare's text, the character appears grotesquely modern: lounging under a beach umbrella like some contemporary vacationer, with nothing surviving of his capacity for brilliant, self-excoriating soliloquies but the mindless, inarticulate act of spitting into the wind.

In effect, then, there are really two Hamlets contained within the world of **Rosencrantz and Guildenstern Are Dead.** The first is Shakespeare's play, from which Stoppard borrows his title, principal characters, and whole sections of text, at least partly for the purpose of reactivating his audience's knowledge of that play. He chooses *Hamlet* as the basis of his plot and action for much the same reason that the Greek playwrights chose to build their plays upon myths: so his audience will bring into the theater already-formed impressions about his dramatic characters and action. But unlike the Greek playwrights (Euripides sometimes excepted), Stoppard wants to use his audience's impressions disruptively, in at least two ways. By implicitly contrasting Shakespeare's *Hamlet* with his own play, he emphasizes that tragic action, character, and language have been reduced in the contemporary theater and world to trivial, confused inaction. And by "ambushing" the audience's expectations—creating a second *Hamlet* by distorting the meaning even of the sections he borrows *verbatim* from Shakespeare—he loosens the audience's hold on the foundations of their perceptions, skewing their perspective. In this dramatic world coins, barrels, and characters disappear magically. And even such certainties as the written text of *Hamlet* and our knowledge of its plot—dissolve before our eyes.

As an audience we may persist in thinking that Rosencrantz and Guildenstern are trapped in the *Hamlet*-world. From our detached position as spectators who know what happens in *Hamlet,* we think we know also what will happen in **Rosencrantz and Guildenstern Are Dead.** But Stoppard keeps surprising us by the way he uses and abuses Shakespeare's play until we, too, may begin to feel almost as confused as his principal characters. Rosencrantz, trying to decipher King Claudius' instructions about gleaning what afflicts Hamlet, remarks: "He's not himself, you know." And we share his opinion, though our perspective makes us conscious of implications not available to Rosencrantz; for Hamlet is "not himself" in at least four ways: because he is apparently mad, because Guildenstern has assumed his part in a practice exchange with Rosencrantz, because Hamlet is always just a role played by an actor, and because this play in which he appears is not *Hamlet.* And since it is not, our assumed "knowledge" of the fate which awaits Stoppard's characters, as if they were Shakespeare's, may be fallacious.

Such uncertainty of perspective is further compounded by the fact that Stoppard himself seems differently bound to Shakespeare's text at different times: sometimes he reproduces it literally; sometimes he cuts it radically; and sometimes he departs from it altogether. Thus when Rosencrantz says at the end of act II, "And besides, anything could happen yet," the meaning of his words remains indeterminate. Is the speech ironic: Rosencrantz desperately trying to cheer himself up in the face of deeply felt danger? Or is it ironic in a different way: stressing the difference between Rosencrantz's optimistic way of viewing his situation, as almost infinite in possibility, and the audience's way of viewing it, as circumscribed by his inalterably fated death in England? Or, again, is the speech essentially Stoppard's metadramatic commentary on his characters' situation, which the playwright may bring to a conclusion in any way he likes? The reason why Stoppard concludes act II in this way, I think, is to emphasize dramatically his audience's, as well as his characters', confusion: perhaps anything *could* happen yet, the play being Stoppard's to shape as he wishes, but perhaps the conclusion is already predetermined by the outlines of *Hamlet,* to which Stoppard feels necessarily bound. In the third act of his play, however, he makes clear that the dramatic world which confines his principal characters is not Shakespeare's but his: Rosencrantz and Guildenstern are trapped not by *Hamlet* but by Stoppard's **Rosencrantz and Guildenstern Are Dead,** which means that anything *could* happen yet.

In that third act the basic elements of Shakespeare's plot still remain. Rosencrantz and Guildenstern, accompanying Hamlet by boat to England, carry from Claudius to the English king a letter ordering Hamlet's death; Hamlet reads the letter and substitutes for it one ordering their execution; and then Hamlet disappears from the boat during a pirate attack. But Stoppard, who has earlier been constrained by the written words of Shakespeare's play, now works entirely beyond its textual boundaries, inventing ridiculous correspondences between the particulars of his text and the implications of Shakespeare's. Hamlet travels in a deck chair under a gaudy beach umbrella; and later during the pirate attack he disappears not by boarding the pirate ship but by diving into a barrel. Rosencrantz and Guildenstern open the letter to the English king—twice—thereby learning of the order not only for Hamlet's death but also for their own as well; and yet they do nothing to try to nullify the actions commanded by the letters. They apparently cannot even choose to avoid delivering the letter which orders their own deaths.

With the opening of this second letter, Stoppard's play breaks completely free from the constraining logic of Shakespeare's plot. For no reader of *Hamlet* before Stoppard, I suspect, ever imagined that Rosencrantz and Guildenstern open and read the letter they deliver to the English king. Within the context of the *Hamlet*-world the thought is unimaginable. But within **Rosencrantz and Guildenstern Are Dead**—at least in the third act—"anything [can] happen," even, in a sense, the unimaginable. To be sure, such an event is no longer unimaginable once it happens, because it serves as a defining part of the dramatic world which contains it: their inability to act even when threatened by an imminent sentence of death—written into a letter they possess and could destroy—becomes the ultimate expression of Rosencrantz and Guildenstern's powerlessness, confusion, and imprisonment in the world Stoppard has shaped for them. Their paralysis, though, is a measure of Stoppard's power. Throughout this play he has found ways of moving freely within the apparently constraining form of his medium and his model. Now he has discovered how to explode dramatically the logic of Shakespeare's plot while yet choosing to abide by its ending; he replaces the logic of tragic inevitability with the irrationality of incomprehensible arbitrariness. And in the process he brings to dramatic fruition a theme originally sounded at the beginning of the play.

There instead of the *Hamlet*-world the title has encouraged us to expect, we encounter a world modeled on *Waiting for Godot.* Nobody comes; nobody goes, and two characters, waiting for some undefined event of importance in the future, pass the time in trivial activity—in this case, flipping coins. But their trivial activity takes on portentous importance because the coins defy the law of averages. . . . [The] trivial proves portentous; and, as the pastiche-like scenes from *Hamlet* shortly prove, the portentous is trivialized. Nor do the usual laws of dramatic exposition or characterization apply here: for almost twenty pages of text the characters remain nameless and, when they are at last identified, they prove to have no past which they can remember before that morning.

What Stoppard dramatically sets up by this disorienting beginning, he brings to thematic consummation in the scene when Rosencrantz and Guildenstern open the letter ordering their own executions. The force which arbitrarily shapes Rosencrantz and Guildenstern's destiny, then, is a play whose particulars they do not understand, but that play is not *Hamlet*; it is **Rosencrantz and Guildenstern Are Dead**. To them this difference may be insignificant, for both Shakespeare's Rosencrantz and Guildenstern and Stoppard's are prevented by their perspectives from understanding what eventually happens to them. But from the audience's perspective the distinction is crucial, because in Shakespeare's dramatic world there is a logical explanation to be discovered:

> Their defeat
> Does by their own insinuation grow.
> 'Tis dangerous when the baser nature comes
> Between the pass and fell incensed points
> Of mighty opposites. (*Hamlet* V. ii.)

In the world of **Rosencrantz and Guildenstern Are Dead**, however, no such explanation is forthcoming because no such logical order obtains. There shifting surfaces cover not villainy or a disoriented sense of self, as in *Hamlet,* but only indeterminate meanings, dramatic embodiments of a world without any secure foundations: where language derives its logic from ephemeral and often irresolvably confusing speech acts: "Yes, it's lighter than it was. It'll be night soon"; where the identity of the King of England is unknowable; where coins, barrels, and even characters inexplicably disappear; and where not even the text of *Hamlet* escapes trivialization. For such events we can, of course, posit meanings, though Stoppard's point, I think, is that these meanings never prove fully verifiable and are often self-contradictory; their shapes change with Stoppard's shifting dramatic perspective. And none of these changes in perspective proves more elusive and self-contradictory than the ones attending the trivialization of *Hamlet,* which serves Stoppard's purposes in richly varied ways. It radically reduces the power of Shakespeare's play by a "misreading" so that Stoppard, as a modern playwright, will not be intimidated into silence by the magnitude of Shakespeare's achievement. It demonstrates the fundamental difference between earlier, heroic conceptions of tragic action and the shrunken, contemporary view of it. It calls attention to his own dramatic brilliance, in radically altering Shakespeare's meaning without altering any words of his text. It "ambushes" his audience by using their expectations against them. And finally, it emphasizes the absence of any secure foundations for meaning in his dramatic world by dislocating the apparent bedrock source of plot and action in his play. That Stoppard thus succeeds in trivializing *Hamlet* without depriving it of crucial thematic importance in his work, that he also effects a kind of dramatic magic which metamorphoses the trivial into the portentous, and that he ultimately creates a dramatic world at once both logically impenetrable and thematically coherent, are important measures of his achievement in **Rosencrantz and Guildenstern Are Dead.** (pp. 54-62)

J. Dennis Huston, " 'Misreading' 'Hamlet': Problems of Perspective in 'Rosencrantz and Guildenstern Are Dead'," in Tom Stoppard: A Casebook, edited by John Harty, III, Garland Publishing, Inc., 1988, pp. 47-66.

FURTHER READING

Babula, William. "The Play-Life Metaphor in Shakespeare and Stoppard." *Modern Drama* XV, No. 3 (December 1972): 279-81.

Examines the conscious theatricality of *Rosencrantz and Guildenstern Are Dead.*

Brassell, Tim. "In the Off-Stage World: *Rosencrantz and Guildenstern Are Dead.*" In his *Tom Stoppard: An Assessment,* pp. 35-67. London & Basingstoke: The MacMillan Press, Ltd., 1985.

Discusses the subtle and blatant differences in Stoppard's rendering of Shakespeare's *Hamlet.*

Corballis, Richard. "Extending the Audience: The Structure of *Rosencrantz and Guildenstern Are Dead.*" *Ariel* 11, No. 2 (April 1980): 65-79.

Explores the "very sophisticated strategy" used by Stoppard to present his ideas in the play.

Gianakaris, C. J. "Absurdism Altered: *Rosencrantz and Guildenstern Are Dead.*" *Drama Survey* 7, Nos. 1 & 2 (Winter 1968-69): 52-8.

Suggests that while the play's format is reminiscent of absurdist drama, it has stronger ties to black comedy.

Gruber, William E. " 'Wheels within Wheels, Etcetera': Artistic Design in *Rosencrantz and Guildenstern Are Dead.*" *Comparative Drama* 15, No. 4 (Winter 1981-82): 291-310.

An overview of the literary qualities and allusions to classical tragedy that abound in *Rosencrantz and Guildenstern Are Dead.*

Guppy, Shusha. "Tom Stoppard: The Art of Theater VII." *The Paris Review* 30, No. 109 (Winter 1988): 27-51.

Lengthy interview that almost exclusively deals with aspects of Stoppard's writing career.

Harty, John III, ed. *Tom Stoppard: A Casebook.* New York & London: Garland Publishing, Inc., 1988, 394 p.

Contains essays on many of Stoppard's works, including three on *Rosencrantz and Guildenstern Are Dead* that focus on the play's artistic design, perspective, and ostensible lack of plot.

Keyssar-Franke, Helene. "The Strategy of *Rosencrantz and Guildenstern Are Dead.*" *Educational Theatre Journal* 27, No. 1 (March 1975): 85-97.

Asserts that Stoppard's play is successful because he comprehends audience awareness, and that the work is "a probing of the nature of the meaning and experience of theatre, past and present."

Kuurman, Joost. "An Interview with Tom Stoppard." *Dutch Quarterly Review of Anglo-American Letters* 10, No. 1 (1980): 41-57.

An interview from March, 1979 in which Stoppard comments on his childhood, his writing methods, and his reactions to criticism of his plays.

Levenson, Jill L. "*Hamlet* Andante/*Hamlet* Allegro: Tom Stoppard's Two Versions." In *Shakespeare Survey: An Annual Survey on Shakespearian Study and Production,* edited by Stanley Wells, pp. 21-8. Cambridge: Cambridge University Press, 1983.

Examines the manipulation of logic, language, and philosophy of Shakespeare's *Hamlet* in *Rosencrantz and Guildenstern Are Dead.*

Salter, Charles H. *"Rosencrantz and Guildenstern Are Dead."* In *Insight IV: Analyses of Modern British and American Drama,* edited by Hermann J. Weiand, pp. 144-50. Frankfurt: Hirschgraben-Verlag, 1975.

> Designed as a handbook for teachers. Includes concise, detailed synopsis of play, notable themes and allusions, and a list of possible questions for class discussions.

Tynan, Kenneth. "Withdrawing with Style from the Chaos." *The New Yorker* LIII, No. 44 (19 December 1977): 41-6, 51, 54, 57, 60, 65-6, 68, 71-2, 74, 79-80, 82, 85-6, 88, 93-4, 96, 99-102, 107-11.

> Excellent, detailed article on Stoppard that includes much biographical information. Also discusses in depth his career and various criticisms of his plays.

Lewis Turco

1934-

(Full name Lewis Putnam Turco; has also written under the pseudonym Wesli Court) American poet, critic, playwright, short story writer, and author of children's books.

Turco's finely crafted verse features resonant language, playful use of words, and experiments with conventional poetic forms. His poems usually present a speaker whose imagination is aroused by nature or actions, events, and objects of everyday life, leading to descriptions, impressions, and observations in which subtle meanings are developed. In *First Poems,* Turco employs traditional forms and techniques while meditating on such topics as the art of poetry, relationships, and the passage of time and seasons. These concerns are further explored in *Awaken, Bells Falling: Poems, 1959-1968,* a collection in which sense of vision has primary importance. In a review of this volume, a critic for *Virginia Quarterly Review* stated: "[Turco's] view of things is quiet and dark; he accepts rather than affirms, acknowledges rather than celebrates. But the poems have a solidity beyond acceptance, for he knows the music of the day's events and remembers the way the ordinary can often glow and blaze."

Turco's later verse is less formally structured and offers a more expansive development of themes. *The Inhabitant* comprises a series of poems relating the psychological impressions of a man as he walks about his home. *Pocoangelini: A Fantography and Other Poems* contains a series of pieces describing or spoken by the title character, an imaginative and humorous trickster. Evocations of natural phenomena and human structures in *American Still Lifes* lead to ruminations on such topics as time, cyclical patterns, and various connotations of the word "fall." Turco's interest in poetic forms and techniques is also evident in *A Book of Forms: A Handbook of Poetics,* which offers an introduction to poetry, and *Visions and Revisions of American Poetry,* in which Turco discusses the history of American poetry as a professional craft.

(See also *CLC,* Vol. 11; *Contemporary Authors,* Vols. 13-16, rev. ed.; *Contemporary Authors New Revision Series,* Vol. 24; and *Dictionary of Literary Biography Yearbook: 1984*).

PRINCIPAL WORKS

POETRY

First Poems   1960
The Sketches of Lewis Turco and Livevil: A Mask   1962
Awaken, Bells Falling: Poems, 1959-1967   1968
The Inhabitant   1970
Pocoangelini: A Fantography and Other Poems   1971
American Still Lifes   1981
The Compleat Melancholik: Being a Sequence of Found, Composite, and Composed Poems, Based Largely upon Robert Burton's 'Anatomy of Melancholy' 1985

NONFICTION

Poetry: An Introduction through Writing   1973
*The New Book of Forms: A Handbook of Poetics   1986
Visions and Revisions of American Poetry   1986

*Expanded edition of *The Book of Forms,* published in 1968.

Philip Legler

Most of the thirty-eight pieces which make up Lewis Turco's **First Poems** show a brilliant sense of technique and an imagination that loves to court the language. Turco has undergone rigorous training in achieving his craft. (He knows traditional forms so thoroughly he might well take time away from his studies at Iowa and write a poet's modern handbook.)

In **"A Note"** he can playfully sing

> You wonder why I write, Maureen?—
>   stop wondering,

it's merely spring.
Your hair's done up
   in pincurls, and your breasts
   fall free like two white clouds.

But in **"Chant of Seasons"** he rushes on to what, for him, is spring's conclusion:

What's to be done when winter's loose,
   When winter's loose?
Sense then the sharpened stars and know
The bold immensity of snow;
   Grant bone a glimpse of the abstruse
   Finis that it must undergo. . . .
   When winter's loose.

Here is his major theme, his fun, his sadness—the passing of youth into age, of spring and summer into winter: **"An Old Gourd," "Letter from Campus," "Song of the Black-bird," "A Pastorale of Sorts,"** and **"Sabrina"** play with the sense of loss—for Turco is not always convincing. Many of his rhythms suggest a fondness in the idea for what he can make out of it rather than a real concern with age and death and the end of love.

But why not! If he sometimes overindulges, he can afford his pleasure: at twenty-seven, he has just begun. There is plenty of time for singing painful tunes. (pp. 186-7)

Philip Legler, in a review of "First Poems," in Poetry, *Vol. XCIX, No. 3, December, 1961, pp. 186-87.*

William Stafford

Awaken, Bells Falling—the title itself—indicates that Lewis Turco [identifies with a line of creation carried on by other poets, persons who respond to a role and the current language of a group]. This book is dedicated to John Malcolm Brinnin and Don Justice; there is a poem about writing, and one addressed to W. D. Snodgrass. This envelopment in a group permits a certain gain . . . : the presence and the influences of known subjects and writers enable the page to carry reverberation and allusion, for any reader programmed for such content. That there are hazards in this in-group communication, we could all probably agree, but Mr. Turco is not limited because of his interest in the work of others; . . . his concerns swing his book toward the topics of a common life shared with a special group.

That Turco's ways are individual and vigorous is evident. A good example is the end of **"An Ordinary Evening in Cleveland"**:

There is nothing but the doorway
sighing; here there is nothing but the wind
   swinging on its hinges, a fly
dusty with silence and the house on its
   back buzzing
      with chimneys, walking on the sky

   like a blind man eating fish in an empty room.
                                                      (pp. 423-24)

William Stafford, "Books That Look Out, Books That Look In," in Poetry, *Vol. CXIII, No. 6, March, 1969, pp. 423-24.*

Henry Carlile

Turco generally chooses words carefully and keeps the emotions clean. His syllabic verses are neatly turned and, at their best, compassionate and sensitive. . . . (p. 127)

On the other hand, Turco has a fondness for negative declarations which tend almost to negate themselves in process. The following is a fair example:

There is nothing but the doorway
sighing; here there is nothing but the wind
   swinging on its hinges, a fly
dusty with silence and the house on its
   back buzzing
      with chimneys, walking on the sky

   like a blind man eating fish in an empty room.

(**"An Ordinary Evening in Cleveland"**)

Aside from the mixed metaphor, which seems to me contrived, one might ask: if nothing is happening why write about it? Obviously something *is* happening, and it is only the rhetoric of nothingness and silence which goes beyond mood to erode the poem itself. In **"The Burning Bush,"** for another example, the spheres make "no music," there is "no short anywhere," "no cane's cellophane" is caught in anything, glass is "no conductor," there is a wind the protagonist "had not heard, / nor wished to hear." Other examples abound.

But a profusion of negatives and an occasional strained metaphor cannot spoil the entire book. *Awaken, Bells Falling* contains many excellent poems. **"Burning the News"** is one of them, and a good piece to end on.

The fire is eating
the paper. The child who drowned
is burned. Asia is in flames.
   As he signs his great
bill, a minister of state chars

   at the edges and curls
into smoke. The page rises,
glowing, over our neighbor's
   roof. In the kitchens
clocks turn, pages turn like grey wings,

   slowly, over armchairs.
Another child drowns, a bill
is signed, and the pen blackens.
   The smoke of Asia
drifts among the neighbors like mist.

It is a good day for burning.
The fire is eating the news.
                                                      (pp. 127-28)

Henry Carlile, in a review of "Awaken, Bells Falling," in Northwest Review, *Vol. 10, No. 2, Summer, 1970, pp. 127-28.*

Lewis Turco [Interview with Gregory Fitzgerald and William Heyen]

[Fitzgerald]: *Do you regard [**"Burning the News,"** from* **Awaken, Bells Falling**], *as a political poem in any way?*

[Turco]: Perhaps political in the sense that it is relevant to current events—but in the larger sense, not really, because I think it would be relevant to almost any period in recent history.

[Heyen]: *Is there a danger in bringing up politics specifically into a poem?*

When anyone writes on a subject that's specifically of contemporary import, I think he runs the risk of seeing his poem become obsolete. However, one can simply use the contemporary event as a takeoff point for a larger statement.

[Fitzgerald]: *You mean something like Whitman's "When Lilacs Last in the Dooryard Bloom'd"?*

That was about an event of import not only for that moment but for all of American history. But I'm talking about something like an ode on the sinking of the battleship *Maine,* for instance; something that has a lot of import for a moment, but not so much for later on.

[Fitzgerald]: *You mention the* Maine. *There is, of course, a poem by Hopkins, "The Wreck of the Deutschland," which is a pretty fine poem, although I think it does, as you say, just take off from the event.*

Yes, it's not merely something like, "O *Deutschland,* thou art gone," you know. It makes a bigger statement. And I do think poems that try to make larger statements have more chance of surviving than poems that are specifically of the moment.

[Heyen]: *In regard to* **"Burning the News"** *again, these lines—"The smoke of Asia / drifts among the neighbors like mist" are very intriguing lines. You've said elsewhere that the mass media really hide or remove us from current events rather than bring us closer to them. But in this poem the neighbors seem to be breathing in the mist of Asia's burning rather better than they do by means of the newspapers.*

I wrote the poem after I'd come in from the back yard where I'd been burning newspapers one day. The inciting incident for the poem was a game I used to play to keep myself amused while I burned the papers. I used to put the newspapers in the trash burner, and then I'd take two matches; I'd light them, lay one on one side of the burner, and the other on the other side. Then I'd pretend that these fires were two opposing armies, and I'd watch to see which army gained the most newsprint territory in the least time. One day, when I was playing this game, I thought, "That's real. That's the way it is, and it's happening now." So the metaphor took on the color of the moment, of the neighborhood scene. The smoke of the burning newspapers both literally and figuratively permeates the neighborhood just as the news about the war in Vietnam floats through the air, and we watch it on television, and nobody does anything about it—it's there all the time, suffocating us.

[Heyen]: *Our perception is dulled rather than increased.*

That's right. And if the poem works, it works because both levels of the poem are real—both the actual, everyday situation, including the game I was playing, and the allegorical level: the news of war stifles us and makes us impotent as human beings. We become mummies removed from the real world where men are being killed. What we don't realize is that we are ourselves men being killed—not by bullets, but by a willed, safe, anesthesia of the imagination, of the rational mind. We are spectators in the death of ethics and morality, of consciousness and action—our own death, as well as the death of armies.

[Fitzgerald]: *You know, of course, that there have been a lot of changes in your poetry since the days when I reviewed your book* **First Poems** *[in the Iowa Defender, October 10, 1960]. I wonder if you would care to comment on the ways in which your poetry has changed. I remember, for instance, an enormous concern with rhythms, with things like alliterative verse. I wonder about your later book* **Awaken, Bells Falling**—*I wonder whether or not you feel there are great differences between the early mode and your current mode of writing.*

Most of the pieces in ***First Poems*** were written in traditional styles while I was experimenting in various ways—trying to learn how to write, really. Somebody's called them exercises, but I think that perhaps a few are better than that. Those poems that I felt never rose above the level of exercise were thrown away. At the time, I felt that the pieces in the book were relatively successful, in terms of the forms I was experimenting with. In the summer of 1959 I began to experiment with syllabics, and since that time a good many of my poems have been written in syllabics rather than in accentual-syllabics. (pp. 240-42)

I tried to give *Awaken* some kind of continuity as well as relevance; I tried not only to pick out the best syllabic poems I'd written between 1959 and 1967, but to arrange them in such a way as to give the book some kind of overall structure. I tried to do this in two ways: by following the seasons, and by following people. (pp. 240-42)

[Fitzgerald]: *[Would you discuss]* **"Lines for Mr. Stevenson"?**

This is an elegy. I got the idea from listening to Eric Sevareid just after Adlai Stevenson had died. Sevareid quoted a sentence Stevenson had spoken a few days before he was stricken. These words caught my ear and my attention, and I invented some more lines to be put into Mr. Stevenson's mouth, to try to sum up his life and his point-of-view at the end of his life. So this is called **"Lines for Mr. Stevenson"**—they are lines *for* him, in his memory; and they are also lines fo *him* to speak, at the end of his career. The last lines of the poem are actually Stevenson's as quoted by Eric Sevareid. . . . (p. 243)

[Heyen]: *The speaker of* **"The Burning Bush"** *also wants to hear another kind of music. We have the himanist Adlai Stevenson, trying to improve this life; now, in* **"The Burning Bush"** *(which is a Christmas tree), the speaker wants to find some kind of music out there. This poem ends very ironically, and I think this is another one of your voices.*

I think we *do* want to understand ourselves, at the same time that we're afraid to find out what we are. We'll make a half-hearted gesture, perhaps, toward attempting to find out what we are at root. Finally, perhaps, at the end we cop out. The man in **"The Burning Bush"** is like that. (p. 244)

[Fitzgerald]: *I want to change the pace a bit here and ask you about another of your books,* **The Book of Forms,** *which is a book about the techniques of poetry. I think most of us know your immense interest in these techniques, and*

I wonder if you would tell us in what ways your own poetry mirrors these interests that you have.

I suppose one of the reasons I did *The Book of Forms: A Handbook of Poetics* is that I got interested, when I was just starting to write seriously, in how to write. I was in the Navy from 1952 to 1956 (I'd gone in right out of high school). I had no teachers, and I had no one around me of whom I could ask questions. Boatswain's mates don't know too much about poetry. So I managed to get hold of some books that had been recommended to me by a magazine editor, and I simply went through them, and from that got interested in the various and sundry ways one could write. There isn't any one way of writing, I figured that the more I could learn, the more possibilities there might be for me to be able to do what I wanted to do. (pp. 246-47)

[Heyen]: *Are you more comfortable in one particular form than in another?*

No. I continue to write in various ways. I think that if you have at your command a range of technique, you can choose those elements you need to use for any particular poem you are driven, or—an old-fashioned word—inspired to write. If you have nothing to work with, you will produce nothing. (p. 247)

> *Lewis Turco, Gregory Fitzgerald, and William Heyen, in an interview in* Costerus, *Vol. 9, 1973, pp. 239-51.*

Morris Rabinowitz

The New Book of Forms is the most informative, easy-to-use, and most attractive book about poetics and verse forms that I have seen in 20 years of looking at such texts, both as teacher and librarian. Part I, the first third of the book, discusses four levels of prose and verse modes (typographic, sonic, sensory, and ideational) using examples to illuminate (hyperbole as calculated exaggeration: her eyes were as big as moons; metonymy as a way of describing by using a word related to a word rather than the original word itself: the *heart* will find a way, rather than *love* will find a way). Part II, using examples of poems written in different forms by poets from different periods, is an alphabetical compilation of over 300 verse forms. An analytical outline of topics covered in Part II, an index of authors and titles, and a valuable index of terms conclude the book. This is an indispensable work for anyone interested in poetry.

> *Morris Rabinowitz, in a review of "The New Handbook of Forms: A Handbook of Poetics," in* Kliatt Young Adult Paperback Book Guide, *Vol. XXI, No. 1, January, 1987, p. 20.*

Penelope Mesick

This rich and enthralling volume of poetic forms [*The New Book of Forms: A Handbook of Poetics*]—an expanded version of the author's *Book of Forms*—is both detailed and imaginative, a repository of arcana and an outward sign of Turco's delight in poetry. It distinguishes itself as a handbook by the inclusion of "examples of poems written in each form by poets of all periods" and a "formfinder" that tells the baffled reader exactly what a nine-line, alliterative anapestic stanza *is*. One must quibble with Turco's brave attempt to define poetry, to herd the verses into one pen and the prose into another, from which they will forever after flow unmixed, but the awkward matter of initial definitions aside, this is not only an extremely intelligent and useful work, it is a likeable, playful one as well. It is a pleasure, for example, to see Turco's "composite poem" of lines taken from Emily Dickinson's letters, which begins "One is a dainty sum!" illustrating syllable prosody. It is the great joy of this volume that it is on the juicy rather than the dry side, even while providing a wealth of technical information.

> *Penelope Mesick, in a review of "The New Book of Forms: A Handbook of Poetics," in* Booklist, *Vol. 83, No. 9, January 1, 1987, p. 678.*

Margaret Dickie

Revised essays published over two decades, the chapters in [*Visions and Revisions of American Poetry*] attest to Lewis Putnam Turco's long-term interest as a poet and an autodidact in the profession of poetry in America. Although he tracks the book's inception to two events of 1968—his publication of the handbook *The Book of Forms* and his reading of Hyatt H. Waggoner's *American Poets from the Puritans to the Present*—in fact, this book is neither about form nor about the Emersonian tradition in American poetry that Waggoner sets out in his monumental study. It is rather a study of professional poetry in America, a tradition older than the Emersonian and one which Turco identifies with Anne Bradstreet, Phillis Wheatley, Marianne Moore—all poets, like himself, who chose their profession, worked at it, and took pride in the craft.

This professionalism has always been suspect in America where such consciousness about craft has been considered a characteristic of European art and contrasted with the nativist tradition of inspired and visionary poetry. Vision in Turco's title then may refer to those poets from Whitman to the Beats for whom technique is secondary, if not totally irrelevant. Against this vision (also identified here with Waggoner's view of American poetry) is Turco's revision which attends to the other line of poets who were themselves interested in craft and so obviously like Turco himself revisionists. Besides the women—Bradstreet, Wheatley, Moore—Turco admits to this line Bryant (who wrote the first great professional poem in America, "Thanatopsis"), Robinson, and Frost. He adds too a third line that he calls the agonists. The amateurs use poetry as a means to a larger end such as the achievement of religious experience; the professionals are those who devote their lives to writing poetry; the agonists are poets who spend much of their time constructing a theory of poetry. Wallace Stevens is the most obvious example of the agonist although John Crowe Ransom fits here too.

Unlike Waggoner or Roy Harvey Pearce who combine literary history with close analyses of individual poems and whole careers, Turco presents his theories in a variety of engaging, if overlapping, discussions that circle around the same points and examples. He has convictions, opinions about certain poets, an earnest concern about poetic matters, and a wide knowledge of certain poems. In addition, he has some favorite authors (Manoah Bodman, for example) and some favorite poems (Longfellow's "The Ropewalk") that do yeoman service in his commentaries. Finally, he writes as a poet himself, conscious of his own work and anxious about his position in the traditions he enumerates, and as a teacher of poets. Director of the Writing Program at SUNY Oswego, Turco is himself training students to be American poets. Thus, the imperative to revise, to consider writing a craft, to work at it all your life stems from his efforts to convince students that their genius will not be destroyed by careful attention to prosody.

As literary history, this study is too sparse to stand up against its predecessors written by professional scholars. As one poet's testimonial, it draws together more than two decades of thinking about what it means to write and to be devoted to writing. It is then a different kind of literary history from the scholars'—one that should be of interest to all students of American poetry. It testifies to the persistence among American poets in searching for a usable past, in revising that past according to contemporary needs, and in affirming one poet's practice.

Margaret Dickie, in a review of "Visions and Revisions of American Poetry," in American Literature, *Vol. 59, No. 1, March, 1987, pp. 138-39.*

Mark Ford

[*Visions and Revisions of American Poetry*] is a fiercely formalist rejection of the whole conception of organic poetry as it derives from Emerson. [Turco considers Whitman] a large and costly mistake. The roots of his thesis, though, extend back to the earliest period of American poetry when the professional versus amateur debate, the "makers" against the "visionaries", was already being entered by Anne Bradstreet and Edward Taylor. A century later Phyllis Wheatley struck a blow for the professionals—all women are professionals, as only men can get away with the effeminate slop of Transcendentalism—but with the emergence of Bryant and Emerson in the earlier nineteenth century, the noose was complete. And that Emerson and Whitman triumphed at all was due mainly to public relations and the tandem strategy they lifted from Wordsworth and Coleridge—agonist and poet, publicist and product. Not until the arrival of that other fearsome duo, Eliot and Pound, were the tides to be rolled back. Turco bounces his themes off unlikely texts—principally Alfred Kreymbourg's *Our Singing Strength* (1927) and the work of Hyatt Waggoner. They add an illusion of solidity to his arguments, and act as a launching-pad for his dizzier speculations.

It is possible to disagree with everything Turco says and still find this book superbly engrossing. In this he is like Bateson, and these are really essays in critical dissent. The heresies are innumerable, and not always explained: "Dryden was a rather uniformly bad writer. . . . It is patent that Samuel Johnson was not a great writer . . ." and so on. His discussions of Stevens is particularly wilful; it sets him first "at the opposite pole from Emerson", rejects his later work as "sterile", and finally prefers Conrad Aiken altogether. That should go down well in New Haven. Yet

in the process he says a great many interesting things. This is typical of a book that is brilliantly written, continually challenging, and almost always wrong.

Mark Ford, "Jocks and Jockeying," in The Times Literary Supplement, *No. 4390, May 22, 1987, p. 557.*

Alfred Dorn

Visions and Revisions of American Poetry is one of the most thought-provoking books of literary criticism I have come across in a long, long time. Though one cannot agree with all of Mr. Turco's judgements, I find myself in basic agreement with his premises, and I also concur in many specific points.

I do not rate Marianne Moore as highly as Turco does. . . . Though one may like *some* of her poetry, much of it leaves this reader, at least, rather indifferent. William Blake is often a first-rate poet, especially in his *Songs of Experience* (1794); however, I would not place him, as Turco does, above Alexander Pope, whom I regard as one of the top ten English poets writing before 1900.

But these are minor disagreements compared to the major areas of our agreement. Turco is right about Walt Whitman, whose long poems are generally boring. Many people, I find, actually *enjoy* only a few of Whitman's poems, and most of those are short. Turco is right, also, about William Cullen Bryant, who is one of the best American poets in the 19th century; indeed, I would credit Bryant with having written more than the three superb poems the critic is willing to grant him, but Turco is entirely accurate in his observations on Robert Frost and Edwin Arlington Robinson, those great pre-Modernists who put craft on an equal footing with content. Having read all of Robinson's poetry, including the long pieces in blank verse, I am tempted to rate him even above Frost—*The Man Against the Sky* is one of the supreme achievements in American poetry.

One of the best things about *Visions and Revisions* is the section on Conrad Aiken, who deserves all the high praise Turco has bestowed upon him. Aiken may yet emerge from the obscurity to which he has been relegated, for he was a master. Frankly, I prefer Aiken to Wallace Stevens, with whom Aiken is compared, though Stevens was also a major poet. And Turco's analysis of the Eliot-Pound relationship is also admirable.

Turco is a highly perceptive critic, an opinion which was shared by Donald Davie when, acting as judge in 1987, he chose Mr. Turco's book to receive the Poetry Society of America's Melville Cane Award as the best prose book on the subject of poetry to be published in the years 1985-86. Davie's citation reads, "Mr. Turco's book offers not revisions but one thorough-going and far-reaching revision—of the course of American poetry through centuries, as commonly understood. It is polemical but good-humored, lightly and racily written but with passion, deeply serious, disconcerting and timely." If one reads *Visions and Revisions* carefully, one will derive a great deal of stimulus from it. (pp. 10-11)

Alfred Dorn, in a review of "Visions and Revisions of American Poetry," in The Hollins

Critic, *Vol. XXV, No. 5, December, 1988, pp. 10-11.*

Diane Wakoski

[In *Visions and Revisions of American Poetry*] Lewis Turco writes with the mania of a poet in the intuitive Emersonian tradition (which somewhat troubles him) and with the erudition, wide-reading, knowledge and facts-at-the-tips-of-the-fingers of a scholar, to present his rather wonderful, sometimes terrible, and always interesting theories about American poetry and its history. Often whole pages of his chapters read like eccentric letters-to-the-editor of a 19th century English newspaper; at other times, however, this reader held her breath at the accuracy and pungency of his observations. For instance, his argument about American poetry having its reality in a feminine, female set of models is remarkable. His observations about Whitman and his place in history, the present history scene, and tradition are unusual but breathtakingly accurate, whereas his constant inveighing against his personal *betes noirs* in contemporary academia and the world of poetry become predictable at times, and often discredit the real arguments when his axe becomes clumsy and brutal, destroying the skillful work of the sharp knife of his scholarly observations.

However, as I continued to read this eccentric and engaging book, I began to think that everyone who teaches college English should have to study the history and craft of versification with Lewis Turco or one of his disciples. Like a good old fashioned English teacher he would straighten us out about the differences between *genre* and *mode,* would teach us what the phrase "prose poetry" really means, and what the historic and rigid realities of metrics are. If you love order, you will love Turco's passion for order. (Maybe you will even long to elect him president.)

One of the problems of Turco's somewhat martinet-ish (or curmudgeon-ish) arguments is that they seem to come too late on the American poetry scene to "straighten out" most of us writing and/or teaching American poetry in American universities these days. One feels that his arguments with everyone from Rexroth to Shapiro ought to have been carried on with the Modernists at least 60 years ago. In fact, he is saying much of what Pound said for much of his lifetime, and in spite of the immense influence Pound has had (and Turco really is persuasive and brilliant on this subject), here we all are, dithering about without his enlightenment.

What is basically the problem with this wonderful little book is that it is written with the belief that perhaps a review of history can change it. Many of his arguments read like an historian telling us why we should not have fought the Vietnam War. No matter how right they are, we did fight it, and we have to live with the twists and turns that reality now brings us.

To be distinct, American poetry had to shed its European conventions, including some formalist conventions. To me, the interesting thing about Emerson is that he used an anti-intellectual doctrine to produce new possibilities of

intellectual discourse. We can't just go back and deny or obliterate this anti-intellectualism in our culture, no matter how distasteful we might find it. We do need some revisions of American poetry, such as the very sound one Turco suggests about the female-ness of the American poetic tradition; in fact, the whole book is worth reading for his second chapter, "The Matriarchy of American Poetry." But one longs to hand him a cup of hot tea with a shot of rum and say, "Calm down. It's not that bad. We're not all illiterates and fools." There is a school-boyish stubbornness to the arguments, even when they are sound and perceptive, which finally makes the reader wonder if Turco can possibly be right. In spite of this, I still recommend this book for any Ph. D. candidate whoever plans to teach poetry.

One of the nicest aspects of this book, if you are a connisseur of forms, as I am, is that Turco constantly shows you that there is "nothing new under the sun." And one cannot help but enjoy vagaries such as his very ballsy comparison of Wallace Stevens to Conrad Aiken, in which Aiken wins hands down. The man views history imaginatively. And he *knows* his prosody. (pp. 228-29)

Diane Wakoski, in a review of "Visions and Revisions of American Poetry," in The Centennial Review, *Vol. XXXI, No. 2, Spring, 1987, pp. 228-29.*

FURTHER READING

Courson, Herbert R. Jr. "A Certain Slant of Life." *Bartleby's Review,* Vol. 1, (Fall 1972): 39-43.

    An analysis of *The Inhabitant.*

Harder, Kelsie. A review of *The Inhabitant. Kamadhenu,* Vol. 2, nos. 1 & 2 (1971).

    Discussion of *The Inhabitant,* which the critic views as Turco's finest collection to date.

Masterson, Donald J. "Making the Language Dance and Go Deep: An Interview with Lewis Turco." *Cream City Review,* Vol. 8, nos. 1 & 2 (1983): 108-17.

Miles, Josephine. "The Home Book of Modern Verse, 1970." *The Massachusetts Review,* Vol. XII, no. 4 (Autumn 1971): 689-708.

    A survey of poetry volumes published in 1970 that includes brief, laudatory remarks on *The Inhabitant.*

Turco, Lewis. "The Process of Revision: Turning and Old Poem into a New One." *Contemporary Poetry,* Vol. 4, no. 1 (1981): 40-45.

    Reveals the evolution of Turco's poem "The Last Schooner" as an example of how "No poem is ever cast in concrete."

Mona Van Duyn

1921-

American poet and short story writer.

Van Duyn is respected by critics for verse that reflects intense emotions and thoughts beneath the placid surface of domestic life. In strictly metered poems that often recount such mundane events as trips to the zoo, hospital visits, and grocery shopping, for example, Van Duyn reveals a constant struggle with time and relationships. The poet commented in an interview: "[I began to see] that one of my major obsessive themes was the idea of time as a taking away of things and love and art as the holders and keepers of things." In her work, Van Duyn endeavors to perfect both love and art, thereby maintaining the aspects of life that time erodes. Although they often address such topics as a failing marriage and stressful interactions with one's aging parents, Van Duyn's poems remain essentially optimistic, focusing on the preservation rather than the devastation of relationships. While occasionally rendered in a colloquial voice, Van Duyn's verse is most often distinguished by references to classical and eighteenth-century poetry, long lines, and complex rhyme schemes.

In her first collection of poetry, *Valentines to the Wide World,* Van Duyn introduces many themes that she would develop throughout her career. In the title poem, which addresses a child's loss of innocence, the speaker discusses the possibility of rebuilding that remembered world of hope and trust through art; Van Duyn suggests that an artist can recapture that which has been lost simply by re-creating it. The world of art, Van Duyn implies, can therefore justify the trials and disappointments of life. The poet also explores her recurring theme of marriage in *Valentines to the Wide World.* In "Toward a Definition of Marriage," for example, she describes wedlock as a "duel of amateurs" that should endure despite hardships, emphasizing her belief that marriage is an essential component of civilized society.

The title poem of Van Duyn's second volume of verse, *A Time of Bees,* relates the story of bees that have died in the walls of a married couple's house. As the husband and a scientist-friend sift through the dead insects, collecting enzymes from their flight-wing muscles for an experiment, the wife watches, identifying with the few bees still fighting to live. The speaker views this episode as a clear illustration of the irreconcilable differences between men and women. Other poems in *A Time of Bees* deal with friendship, gardening, and mental illness. Many critics labeled this collection "domestic," including James Dickey, who observed: "[Van Duyn] is a master . . . of the exasperated-but-loving, intelligent-housewife tone."

Considered until *A Time of Bees* as a "poet's poet," Van Duyn gained a wider audience with her next book, *To See, To Take,* which won the National Book Award for Poetry. The best-known poems in this collection are written in response to W. B. Yeats's sonnet "Leda and the Swan." "Leda" and "Leda Reconsidered" paint a less romantic picture of the myth than Yeats's elevated version. Van

Duyn's lovers are perpetual strangers, destined to wrestle with the complexities of their relationship. Again, man and woman have little in common, but submit to love and its inherent difficulties. David Kalstone noted: "Every poem [in *To See, To Take*] staves off the executioner, like the home canning to which [Van Duyn] compares her work." In "Proust of the Pantry Shelves," canning is the "humble" art through which Van Duyn defies time. *To See, To Take*'s straightforward, often wry poems prompted Thomas H. Landess to dub Van Duyn a "tough-minded" poet. He added: "I can think of no contemporary poet who looks at the world with a steadier eye than does Mona Van Duyn. Not only does she fail to flinch in the face of what is distasteful or awry, but more importantly she never has visions."

Letters From a Father, published twelve years after *To See, To Take,* reinforced Van Duyn's reputation as a "tough-minded" poet. The title poem, written in the form of six letters, describes in candid detail the physical ailments of the poet's aging parents and the symptoms that foreshadow their imminent death. A gift from their daughter, however, restores their interest in life. Robert Hass noted that the "detail [in *Letters to a Father*] is potentially gruesome, the story potentially sentimental, but there is something in the implied attitude of the daughter—her clear eye, amusement, repugnance, fidelity—that complicates the whole poem and brings it alive, and it gets at an area of human experience that literature—outside of Samuel Beckett—has hardly touched."

(See also *CLC*, Vols. 3, 7; *Contemporary Authors*, Vols. 9-12, rev. ed.; *Contemporary Authors New Revision Series*, Vol. 7; and *Dictionary of Literary Biography*, Vol. 5.)

PRINCIPAL WORKS

POETRY

Valentines to the Wide World   1959
A Time of Bees   1964
To See, To Take   1970
Bedtime Stories   1972
Merciful Disguises: Published and Unpublished Poems
   1973
Letters from a Father, and Other Poems   1982
Near Changes   1990

Robert Mazocco

Faulkner spoke of the novelist as a "failed poet." In a provocative sense, not necessarily nasty, the reverse may be said of Mona Van Duyn. Blending the light (Phyllis McGinley, Elizabeth Bishop, the later Auden) with the dark (Modern Literature, the "complex fate"), sprinkling summery particulars and sour after-thoughts, funny yet compassionate, working with slant rhymes, a sestina, couplets (end-stopped and enjambment), her poems [in *A Time of Bees*], so rattlingly well assured, are less poems (they can all be easily paraphrased, for one thing), than a series of sketches, essayish anecdotes of experience, the Thorny Way as a Liberal Education, or vice-versa. The epigraphs from Santayana, a biologist, the St. Louis Post-Dispatch; the portraits of a doctor, a paratrooper, the next-door bore, or a Texas aunt (the evangelical nut sending news of Armageddon); the notes **"Toward a Definition of Marriage"**; the scene outside one's window, the thoughts while in one's kitchen ("I'll never climb Eiffels / see Noh plays, big game, leprous beggars, implausible / rites, all in one lifetime. My friends think it's awful. / It leads to overcompensation"); or the confessional in one's head (the crackup, the hospital, the Frommian beatitudes: "And now, in the middle of life, I'd like to learn how to forgive / the heart's grandpa, mother and kid, the hard ways we have to love")—all very contemporary subject matter, a day-to-day, mildly at-loose-ends world. For politics: a wry anti-utopianism; for philosophy: Camus's Mediterranean *mesure*, only domesticated, flat-chested hedonism, unillusioned, responsible.

I may seem grudging but even in Miss Van Duyn's rigorous, rather splendid title-poem [**"A Time of Bees"**] about the death of bees that had been nesting within the walls of her house, which is really a parable on the necessity of civilization to kill the instinctive life—even there, something's hokey. A scientist-friend comes over. "He wants an enzyme in the flight-wing muscle." He fiddles with the

bees. Miss Van Duyn draws back. "I hate the self-examined," she exclaims, "who've killed the self." Deft touch—but I don't believe it. In her poems of such knowing equanimity, Miss Van Duyn crosses all her t's, dots all her i's; there's no intensity, no confrontation here, only the idea of such things. The idea is always around, like road signs. In the end, I'm afraid, I respond as I do to the dénouement of a finely wrought, untroubling piece of fiction. "Her whole Life is an Epigram, smart smooth & neatly pen'd / Platted quite neat to catch applause with a sliding noose at the end." Thus Blake, on another occasion.

> *Robert Mazocco, "Mixed Company," in* The New York Review of Books, *Vol. IV, No. 5, April 8, 1965, p. 18.*

Richard Howard

Like Emerson, Mona Van Duyn, whose poems are about what passes for ordinary life—marriage, cooking, gardening, teaching, reading—prefers a tendency to stateliness to an excess of fellowship ("We can hide / nothing personal but the noises of sex and digestion and boredom, can leave each other only when we go to bed / or to work"). To institute an order in that "suburban heart" of hers, she generally invokes some technique of distancing—alexandrine, triple rhyme, sestina, parody, quotations from Plato and seed catalogues on which to suspend, in both senses, her voluble ardors—a device of modesty, as if she couldn't have thought up such things without a newspaper clipping or a child's letter to start them off. Formalities are to remind us, here, that the poem is achieved against and out of mess, that only when the imagination is tempered can it make itself heard over the noise of life:

> Complicity I understood. What human twig isn't bent
> By the hidden weight of its wish for some strict covenant

It is gratifying that so many technical demands, so industriously met, have not dimmed the idiosyncrasies of this poet's voice: wordy, appalled, anxious, confiding, she offers a fresh amalgam of the academic and the housewifely in her imaginative gestures. (pp. 301-02)

Emersonian, too, is Mona Van Duyn's interest in what really goes on inside of us all day long, rather than in what is forcibly created by an act of will. Life, the Sage of Concord once said, "consists of what a man is thinking of all day". And this poet, by the tension set up between what she knows she feels:

> And now, in the middle of life, I'd like to learn how to forgive the heart's grandpa, mother and kid, the hard ways we have to love.

and what she feels she knows:

> . . . Pebbles, we swell
> to planets, nearing the universal roll,
> in our conceit even comprehending the sun,
> whose bright ordeal leaves cool men woebegone.

engrosses such a definition. She chatters on, hurt and beguiled by the world, a truly interested and disinterested mind, in whose words we discover, with her, "that our lives are meaningful, and can speak". (pp. 302-03)

> *Richard Howard, in a review of "A Time of*

Bees," in Poetry, *Vol. 106, No. 4, July, 1965,*
pp. 301-03.

Richard Howard

> Before you leave her, the woman who thought you lavish,
> whose body you led to parade without a blush
> the touching vulgarity of the nouveau-riche,
>
> whose every register your sexual coin
> crammed full, whose ignorant bush mistook for sunshine
> the cold brazen battering of your rain,
>
> rising, so little spent, strange millionaire
> who feels in his loins' pocket clouds of power
> gathering again for shower upon golden shower . . .

That is the opening of **"Advice to a God"** [from *To See, to Take*], and that is how Mona Van Duyn will keep her sentence running through ten sets of such triplets—by refusing to let the mind or the ear *settle,* though she chides her utterance (diction, vocabulary, references, wit) into a presentment of drastic order. Alluding to Josephine Miles, a poet she thoroughly admires, Miss Van Duyn states her case for the poem as well-made cantilever: "the 'good outward and intent construction,' built over whatever inner hells and abysses, may very well be the single sign of our greatness." Not our greatness, notice, but the *sign* of it: hers will be poems of oblique conviction in which the lacerated but laced-up rhymer administers, as she perfectly puts it, "eyeful by eyeful the exact, extensive / derangement."

For all their contraption, Mona Van Duyn's poems are pitched below the tension of the lyre, not an instrument likely to be lying around the house—there is a mocking drop in her voice, not a learned but a *knowing* resonance in her voice; it is parlor speech not platform style, utterance which intends to accommodate alternative likelihoods:

> . . . The world itself creates
> possibility after possibility,
> constantly erupts, and quiets.
>
> When shape and shapeliness come together
> in a quiet ceremony of chance,
> page after page will finally be delivered
> into the perfect hands.

Possibility, that is her word. She uses it about ten times in this wise, talkative book, and there is in its insistent deployment a refusal to renounce. Life, our needs and diseases, our loves and compromises—life defines us, imposes on us, constricts, she says, but there is possibility, "the sweetest dream the human creature / can have." Her familiarity with failure, with "the dark particular," is just what allows, what urges this poet to allow for and to urge upon herself the hope of a difference, "the slow, awful return / to possibility" before everything "melts away in the storm of everyday life."

In her previous book, the brilliant though less organized, less composed collection, *A Time of Bees* (1964), Mona Van Duyn seemed so concerned with "the making and breaking of form and measure," with what she distanced, or outdistanced, as "the transformations of poetry, small, desperate and precious," that I found her only too willing to let the world offer her occasions, extend invitations to

speak up. She is much less diffident now about her making, and there are nowhere near so many poems that "take off," as the saying goes, from news items or seed catalogues. She trusts herself more, or at least entrusts herself to her poems, and her occasions are now centripetal—matters of biography, intimacies of memory and desire awesomely disciplined by the strict covenant of her discourse. In **"First Flight,"** enduring the plane's vibrations, she confesses the converse appeal:

> If the poem were to speak without its syllables,
> and love's spirit step out of its skin of need,
> I would tremble like this.

It is the old and, here as everywhere, eschewed temptation she registers: the temptation to put off the integument, the armor of mere poetry in order to "reach, finally, a plain absolute place, / and stand in the center, saying to someone, / 'Believe. Believe this is what I see.' " But Mona Van Duyn, though she offers and even exposes herself, never exhibits, and so never condescends. She does not ask us to believe what she sees, she lets us see it.

She has found a relish in her art, "the sugar and gall of language," which saves her from the waste of confession, of the confessional. "Women . . . are allowed a great deal more freedom than men to express their feelings in public," she remarked lately in a review of women poets, "but in poetry they must submit the tears, outrage or whatever to standards of freshness, relevance and excellence that apply to all poets." She has done just that, has submitted, has survived, has prevailed, and her recompense is the apparently bland one of being, invariably, interesting—not merely credible but interesting. It would be patronizing to praise Mona Van Duyn for being, as I have called her, wise and daring and profound. But it is within the critical province, I believe, to praise her for being interesting, since the interest of her poems—their capacity to be at the center (which is what the word *interest* means)—is a moral decision, a choice made beyond the mere dictates of nature.

The choice obliges a renunciation, for it means trusting to appearances, using the senses, the wits, even the record, which we call *the past,* of the senses and wits of others. These are unfashionable utilizations in our poetry, and they imply an abandonment of certain ecstatic potentialities. There is a moment at the end of her final, finest poem, **"Marriage, with Beasts,"** when Mona Van Duyn suffuses with her rueful wit that very abandonment, and articulates precisely those defeats which the trust in possibility rises from.

Having considered the various "bestial uses" of love, the animal analogies—flamingos, ungulates, monkeys, sparrows, some modern poets—that dramatize her sense of herself, of her marriage, the poet and her husband enter the lion house. A mountain lion comes up to the bars and meets her gaze. Here, as Lévi-Strauss confirms in the last lines of *Tristes Tropiques,* she suffers the ultimate encounter which is beyond language or love, the encounter with what is not herself, not mediated, other. And she draws it all together into the one poem, the lion, the man beside her, the life lived and still to be lived, the ecstasy renounced in favor of the expression:

> What can it be that comes without images?
> An eye, nothing in it but what he is,

the word, then,
after all this,
not love but

LION?
The slit widens. There. Illiterate.
Perfect. lion. without adjective.
lion lionlionlion it ceases
to be a word

but I get away, turning to where you are.
I'm shaking. Now take what you've seen of me home, and
     let's
go on with our heady life. And treat me, my pet,
forever after as what I seem; for it seems,
and it is, impossible for me to receive,
under the cagey wedlock of your eyes,
what I make it impossible for you to give.

To have had that illumination and to forgo it; to have chosen semblance for its human possibility; to have discovered that one's selfhood makes a pure experience of another impossible and yet not to discard one's selfhood—and to have done these things by just that submission to standards of freshness, relevance and wit by which she asks to be judged—make Mona Van Duyn a heroic figure in our literature. (pp. 536-38)

> *Richard Howard, "Possibility After Possibility," in* The Nation, *New York, Vol. 210, No. 17, May 4, 1970, pp. 536-38.*

Thomas H. Landess

Despite its breathless title, *To See, To Take* is a collection of remarkably tough-minded lyrics. As a matter of fact, I can think of no contemporary poet who looks at the world with a steadier eye than does Mona Van Duyn. Not only does she fail to flinch in the face of what is distasteful or awry, but more importantly she never has visions. I have the feeling that she could wring a chicken's neck or kill a hog with a degree of equanimity. . . . (pp. 150-51)

I do not wish anyone to think that she is callous or insensitive to the hardships and nuances of human existence. On the contrary, her chief province is the world of everyday experience, of birthdays and minor illnesses, of the pantry and the zoo—a world of feeling which she sees as subtle and various. Yet the feeling she treats is always related to events which are substantial, palpable; and in this respect she is remarkably unspoiled by those abstractions which plague too many of her contemporaries. She tends to think in terms of models rather than paradigms; hence she is not forever trying to correct the condition of man to an ideal which exists only by inference in the "angelic imagination".

For this reason the secular puritans of our time may want to conclude that Miss Van Duyn's poems, with their well-cut images, domestic scenarios, and political unconcern, are less than demanding, that she is merely doing the kind of thing that Alexander Pope said a poet ought to do. Yet I believe she is much closer to Wordsworth's poet than to Pope's, possessed as she is of more than usual organic sensibility. As an illustration of a poem which reveals how deceptively unpretentious are her talents I would offer **"In the Hospital for Tests"**. The details in this selection are familiar enough: they form a portrait of Everyhospital

with its perfunctory staff, its maddening routine, its charts, instruments, and odors. To be sure, these images are heightened by the poet's keen eye and wit: "In twenty-four hours, the hefty nurse, all smiles, / carries out my urine on her hip like a jug of cider, a happy harvest scene." But there is more to this poem than technique; for interwoven with its busy texture is an awareness of the horror and irony of such an environment, where all the "case histories" suffer their dark nights of the soul as cheerful internes make examinations, run tests. Thus the speaker of the poem leaves the hospital with a sense of guilt as well as relief, knowing what pain and terror she has escaped, what it means to be mortal and to receive grace. Such a poem may seem irrelevant; but in its rendition of human truth it reaches beyond the temporal limits it seems to set for itself, beyond the limits of any purely social or political verse.

As for Miss Van Duyn's relationship to the new poetics, she is, as she puts it in **"A Quiet Afternoon at Home"**, "speaking up for a more visceral poetry". Yet she never simply dishes up raw experience for indiscriminate consumption. To be sure, like Berryman and Dickey she deals explicitly with matters sexual, but she does so in the context of some larger thematic concern, either philosophical or mythological. Twice, for example, and in deference to Yeats, she uses the image of Leda to define the archetypal relationship of woman to man, so that in **"Leda Reconsidered"** we are not quite sure whether the character is a woman receiving a mortal though god-like man or whether she is indeed the Earth Mother herself. Thus in the tension between the two levels the poet is able to have it both ways—a poem rich in sensuous and emotional values yet effectively guarded against the charge of excessive intimacy. And at other times she has the good aesthetic sense to treat sex with a certain good-humored wit, as in **"Eros to Howard Nemerov"** and **"Billings and Cooings from 'The Berkeley Barb' "**. I would deduce from the tone of these and other poems and from the techniques she uses to formalize and control such experience that Miss Van Duyn is committed to a more traditional ontology than one generally finds informing the poetry of the 'sixties and 'seventies.

Yet in most of her work she chooses to adopt the current rhetoric, as she herself suggests at the beginning of **"What I Want to Say"**:

> It is as simple as can be.
> I will leave off my clothes
> (which is a kind of leveling, isn't it?)
> and address you as nakedly
> as anyone can.

This passage is taken out of context and therefore is something less than an authoritative credo, but it does tell us something about the poet's involvement with the problem of poetic language and her inclination in this instance (and in others) to confront her subject matter without the protective adornment of a complex style. Occasionally she will adopt an older rhetorical mode, as in **"Homework"**, a poem faintly Elizabethan in its compact phrasing and elaborate metaphor:

> Oh I know, I know that, great or humble, the arts
>
> in their helplessness can save but a few selves
> by such disguises from Time's hideous bite,

and yet, a sweating Proust of the pantry shelves,
I cupboard these pickled peaches in Time's despite.

In other selections the flat tone and sparse diction of **"What I Want to Say"** give way to a verbal intensity reinforced by the crowded montage of well-honed images. In **"Remedies, Maladies, and Reasons"** these techniques are pushed to their limits in order to suggest the obsession of a mother with illness and its abundant symptoms.

There's never been any other interesting news.
Homer of her own heroic course, she rows

through the long disease of living, and celebrates
the 'blood-red' throat, the yellow pus that 'squirts'

from a swelling, the taste, always 'bitter as gall,'
that's 'belched up,' the bumps that get 'sore as a boil,'

the gas that makes her 'blow up tight as a drum,'
the 'racing heart,' the 'new kind of bug,' the 'same

old sinus,' the 'god-awful cold'—all things that make
her 'sick as a dog' or 'just a nervous wreck.'

To summarize, Mona Van Duyn is clearly a poet who has found her voice, and for this reason she comes to the reader with confidence and authority. She may alter her tone from poem to poem, vary her diction to accommodate a change in mood or situation, but she is always herself—present and accounted for in every line. And by "present" I mean the whole person: heart, mind, and body. For this reason the appearance of *To See, To Take* is an important event, worthy of notation on anybody's literary calendar. It would be hard to find a recent volume which contained so many excellent poems. (pp. 151-53)

> *Thomas H. Landess, in a review of "To See, To Take," in* The Sewanee Review, *Vol. LXXXI, No. 1, Winter, 1973, pp. 150-52.*

Harvey Shapiro

Mona Van Duyn's poems, crammed with reality, present a curious case. She has been much honored by the academy—a National Book Award and a Bollingen—but among the poets in New York she has few readers. That has to do with the nature of her reality. She writes as a wife, indeed as a housewife, putting up poems as another good woman might put up peaches (she can begin **"An Essay on Criticism"** with a description of making prepared onion soup). Her poems describe vacation trips to the mountains or the shore. She writes about female friends, children, relatives. All of this is patently unfashionable. Unfashionable also is the fact that her poems have subjects. More damning than that, there is the basic assumption in her work that it is possible to elicit meaning from the world.

The early poems sometimes wobble unsteadily (reading [*Merciful Disguises*], a collection of all her work to date, is a bit like watching an ungainly girl grow into a graceful woman) because of the disparity between the prosaic, even folksy, detail and the very learned, literary and skilled mind alive in the language, propelling the poem. The effect is of the rhetoric sometimes jumping away from the detail into its own orbit. This plus excessive detail makes the poems difficult to take in. I assume some of this is intentional—modern metaphysical—but it misfires.

> *Harvey Shapiro, "As Three Poets See Reality," in* The New York Times, *September 22, 1973, p. 29.*

Louis Coxe

What Mona Van Duyn writes about strikes one at first as ordinary and on its face rather dull. Tone is everything; and the poet shifts easily from the ominous, the portentous, to wry humor and self-deprecation. At times one is perhaps too conscious of influences—Ransom, Marianne Moore, to both of whom she pays a witty compliment in a poem. But she is really under the influence of James Dickey, particularly prosodically, if that's the word. The basic "beat" is the thumping anapest looped over long lines; I think this beat or cadence has a tendency to coarsen the line as well as the texture of language. Certainly it encourages the tendency toward a kind of garrulousness, of elaborate wind-up before the pitch. Metaphor is so extended that it finally trails off into not much of anything. The poet seems unwilling to quit while she's ahead and goes on telling us past the point of interest or charm.

Yet charm is in many ways the key to her success: one's not in [*Merciful Disguises*] for a lot of poems nor a series of made objects but for a written-out diary of the poet as one of us: humorous, observant and lively—as we'd all like to think we are. Mona Van Duyn, if she never tries us very much, never really falls flat. The poems, nearly all of them, are interesting to read because of her company, her persona summed up in the last line and a half of the first poem: ". . . that serious recreation / where anything is still possible—or almost anything." The poet as actor or character is her chief strategy. The poet as woman and vice versa comes before us as the occasion and subject of most of the poems. But the strategy is not offensive or tedious as we might expect; both poet and woman are worth knowing. Together they tell the story of the days and occasions of their lives together, a narrative full of incident. She is at her best in poems such as **"The Fear of Flying"** and **"A View"** where she talks rather than addresses. The loose line, the casual air and colloquial tone seem suitable, and the poems build to a climax that is also anti-climax, as in life. (p. 28)

> *Louis Coxe, "A Clutch of Poets," in* The New Republic, *Vol. 169, Nos. 13-14, October 6, 1973, pp. 26-8.*

Herbert Leibowitz

Mona Van Duyn's poems in *Merciful Disguises,* a fine gathering of three decades' work, are comedies of definition. Though she often stands before us in her "skin of need," she is not a confessional poet fingering her emotional sores, for even when she writes about mental illness, "the whole monstrous ferny land of my nerves," she keeps the delicate propriety of distance. Self-exposure rhymes with a "ceremonious self-enclosure." A bravura actress, she takes from her verbal trunk the "merciful disguises of metaphor" and plays a repertoire of roles—wife, godmother, recluse, Leda, poet, counseling friend, the "outlandish agon" of love and loss—with a "touch of tart malice" and the quiet penetration of a Missouri Molière.

She is a brainy poet. Mistrusting stridency, she surveys the "shifting and lustrous" perimeters of the moral life where passion and reason cross, unearthing motives, defining value, noting how character survives intolerant time.

The occasions for her poems are often domestic and suburban; . . . her tone is a tough, scared humor or a weathered garrulity. The center of gravity—and dread—lies elsewhere, in the trenches of marriage, where routine narrows possibility and familiarity breeds an icy, stricken candor. Mona Van Duyn is a love poet, not of courtship or sexual windfalls, but of the bittersweet aftermath, the slow dying of feeling and its fitful replenishments. In such poems as **"Marriage, With Beasts"** and **"Fear of Flying,"** the politics of love and marriage are frayed, rife with feud, tedium, insult and a sense of bereavement, but also buoyed by a sardonic gaiety. . . .

In reporting the spectacle of marriage, that medley of guile, anger and courtesy, *Merciful Disguises* includes the rankness of animal life, the human mess, for Miss Van Duyn knows the dangerous poverty of not living in the physical world. In a fallen world, her poems contend, against "brilliant wasting" and death, man can marshal "shapes, storms of fresh possibilities." By which she means the hilarious masks of Eros, the wry benedictions of love. And the power of words, "both birthright and blessing":

> Once out of Eden, love learned its deviousness
> and found in Word its wiliest metaphor;

When love poems fail to find the fit words, creation is undone. But through the charity of the imagination, the process of "simultaneous discovery and reminscence," the self can be stabilized and we can repair the holes in our nature out of which feeling leaks.

Mona Van Duyn is a wily master of extended images. She hives the honey of metaphor. Her mischievous quatrains and slant rhymes artfully escape from the traps of regularity. As her syntax opens large spaces in which her speculative intelligence can play, as the "half-demented 'pressure of speech' " relaxes into light irony, the textures of experience—the world's "motley and manifold"—find their comely form. To examine the linked atoms of desire and disguise with clarity of analysis, as Miss Van Duyn does, is to be an expert in moral optics and an artist of "difficult wholeness." . . .

> Herbert Leibowitz, "Merciful Disguises," in The New York Times Book Review, December 9, 1973, p. 4.

Stephen Yenser

From the beginning, Mona Van Duyn has been writing poems no doubt too easily labeled "domestic"—poems rooted in the garden, set in the kitchen, discovered in the neighborhood, involving fertilizing the grass, sunbathing on the patio, getting the morning paper—and she has made herself our mistress of the mode. The suburban housewife is not by any means her only disguise, but it is one which permits many of her most intense meditations on love, poetry, and friendship, and one which she often assumes when confronting her other favorite subjects (even nature, into which she advances with an acknowl-

edged naiveté and a stock of homemade metaphors). Only an unconscionable stretch of the imagination could locate domestic elements in such exuberant *tours de force* as **"What the Motorcycle Said, A Small Excursion,"** and **"Billings and Cooings from 'The Berkeley Barb' "** or such variously rich occasional poems as **"Eros to Howard Nemerov, A Day in Late October,"** and **"To My Godson, on His Christening."** But the domestic manner is her bread and butter, and often the stuff of her *pièces de résistance* as well. . . . (p. 167)

[How] at home Van Duyn is in a poem like **"Walking the Dog: a Diatribe,"** with its rhythms buffeted between anapest and iamb, its imagery modulated from grand effect into delicate observation, its marvelous orchestration:

> I have never seen a cicada, but nothing so pollutes
> the night with noise as those self-absorbed, ear-baiting
>   singers,
> even in the night of a big wind, not the blurbs
> of trees, shaking and shouting their leaves at each other,
> not the girlish swish of tires on a street distorted to high-
>   way,
> nor, in gusts, all the clattery trash set out at curbs;
> there is nothing so loud, not the *Boo! Wawboooo!* of a
>   coonhound,
> whose throat, shaped for sounding the hunt through miles
>   of thicket,
> is leashed to the suburbs.

The opportunities to match Mona Van Duyn with Ginsberg and Whitman are rare, but we might well go to "Howl" and "Song of Myself" for comparable varieties of language and image in catenations of detail. Why, one would like the walk to go on and on, except that the conclusion (which will make the reader who looks it up wonder how anyone could call this poem domestic) is so worth getting to.

When she turns from her present to the past and myth, Van Duyn usually retains a homely view of things. In **"Leda,"** responding to Yeats's famous enigma ("Did she put on his knowledge with his power / Before the indifferent beak could let her drop?"), she adopts the no-nonsense tone of a woman who at least knows her ancestor and thus knows better. "Not even for a moment", she asserts; and she concludes with a wry twist of Yeats's lines:

> She tried for a while to understand what it was
> that had happened, and then decided to let it drop.
> She married a smaller man with a beaky nose,
> and melted away in the storm of everyday life.

In the wonderful recent poem, **"The Cities of the Plain,"** a down-to-earth, grub first and ethics later concern with the things of this world pervades Lot's wife's idiom and argument:

> Their sex life was their own business,
> I thought, and took some of the pressure off women,
>
>   . . .
>
> And there were plenty of the other kind—
> the two older girls got married when they wanted to.
> The riot in front of our house that evening,
> when a gang of young queers, all drunk and horny,
> threatened to break in, yelling
> for the two strangers, our guests, handsome
> as angels, to come out and have some fun. . . .

The speaker, the true opposite of Kirkegaard's Knight of Faith, does not understand the reason for the consequences ("The two strangers, it turned out, were Inspectors"), but she does not need to understand to know that the obliteration of "every single miracle of life / on the whole plain" was "blasphemous". Representing in her anonymity "nameless women / whose sense of loss is not statistical", she is also (although she does not realize this) the salt of the earth. (pp. 167-68)

Implicitly distinguishing between the power of women and that of men (who "are always being turned to stone by something"), this poem touches on one of Van Duyn's most surprising themes. **"A View"** deals with it in transparently symbolic terms, as the speaker, with a man at the wheel, rides through a "landspread" dominated by a majestic mountain and, "lying at his feet, his own foothill":

> wrinkled, blue, balding, risen-above,
> her back all sore from trails, child-ridden, shoved
>
> to the ground in a dumpy heap, mined-out,
> learned-on by the high one until that
>
> moment he knew his own destiny, donned
> a green-black cloak, rose up. . . .

The weakness in the conception (the mountain must be limited to a single proximate foothill) disappears behind the fine execution of the particulars, the unobtrusive ambivalences and the wise insistence on the literal. And it gets better, as she looks away from the foothill, "used all over" and "glad to be taken", to the "god":

> He stands nearby, unmoved. He knows
> how not to be. Even at sundown he flourishes.
>
> He can sway in aspen, and tender seedgrass
> in his low meadows, wearing the disgrace
>
> of his early delicacy still, when blue grouse,
> calliope hummingbird, rosy finch rise. . . .

A poem which might have become a polemic is suddenly ruffled by a breeze from the Song of Songs and the tone complicates itself into an extraordinary achievement. It is not just the sex of the writer that keeps us from confusing this position with that epitomized in Milton's "He for the god, she for the god in him". The poem's distinction and force reside in its conversion, by means of the equation of its maker with the foothill and the eulogy with no irony but the inevitable of the masculine mountain, of the capacity "to be *taken*" into real strength. Which is to say simply that one can only praise, not as a minor virtue or one with a masochistic edge but precisely above all, this ability to praise. "*O sage, Dichter, was du tust?—Ich ruhme.*"

Such poems ramify and even clarify—the prerogative of a collection—such earlier and first-rate work as **"A Time of Bees"** and **"Leda Reconsidered."** The former, which exposes the difference in attitude of the speaker and her husband toward the invasion of their house by a swarm of bees, ends with the husband and a friend picking over (in the interest of science) a mass of the dead and dying insects:

> under their touch, the craze
>
> for life gets stronger in the squirming, whitish kind.
> The men do it. Making a claim on the future, as love
> makes a claim on the future, grasping. And I, underhand,

> I feel it start, a terrible, lifelong heave
> taking direction. Unpleading, the men prod
>
> till all that grubby softness wants to give, *to give.*

One often admires in Van Duyn's conclusions the refusal to simplify. The indispensability of the men whose actions are nonetheless revolting, the suggestions of both postdigestive and sexual acts, the inextricability of living, suffering, giving: she insists on all of this.

The phrase *"to give"* (which like its complement, "to take", has an odd ambiguity, implying both passivity and activity) ends the volume entitled *A Time of Bees* and links up with the title of the next volume, *To See, To Take,* which comes from **"Leda Reconsidered,"** in which, however, the pivotal lines are these:

> Deep, in her inmost, grubby
> female center
> (how could he know that,
> in his airiness?)
> lay the joy of being used,
>
> . . .
>
> . . . to give up was an offering
> only she could savor,
> simply by covering
> her eyes.

To give up is also to receive. In **"The Voyeur,"** a woman stands naked before an uncovered cabin window, so that an unknown watcher's eyes might "find the / pure recipience she has turned to / and bring it . . . what? Anything, / sweet, sacred, or evil, / in his attention".

Of course the attentive reader finds more than recipience and surrender. Give-and-take, rather than the giving that is taking, is the subject of **"Toward a Definition of Marriage."** This poem begins perfectly, ends irrefutably, and hardly has a weak line in the ninety-some that intervene. In its center, we come on this passage, which exemplifies *anything but* surrender:

> Or, think of it as a duel of amateurs.
>
> . . .
>
> Now, too close together for the length of the foils,
> wet with fear, they dodge, stumble, strike,
> and if either finally thinks he would rather be touched
> than touch, he still must listen to the clang and tick
> of his own compulsive parrying.

Later poems involve similar encounters. In **"Open Letter, Personal,"** "Friendship" is defined as a "sweaty play"; and in **"Homework,"** the poet appears as "a sweating Proust of the pantry shelves". The fullest expression of this struggle is **"Outlandish Agon,"** which describes an all-night wrestling match with a "baby-faced boy", a rubbery *puto* "so slippery with sweat I couldn't keep hold, even with my nails", who is at once Eros, Jacob's angel, and, with his power "beyond the power of words", the poet's nemesis, the unarticulated, that with which she must come to grips and upon which she therefore depends.

Sometimes, too aware of the struggle, one wishes that she would give herself up more often, that her perseverance blurred less frequently into a "compulsive parrying", that a poem on one element did not lead inexorably to poems on the other three ("Elementary Attitudes"). In **"A Seri-**

ous Case," she makes Plato's Republic a mental institution, and it is a clever conceit, but then she characterizes the inmates, designated by the letters of the alphabet, from A to Z. Especially in the earlier poems, she is obviously the daughter of her mother, whose obsession with bodily fluids and functions is catalogued relentlessly (the rhetorical term might be the appeal *ad nauseam*) in **"Remedies, Maladies, Reasons."**

True, her "hard, heavy work" is part and parcel of **"The Creation,"** a remarkable elegy in which the poet tries, "like Rauschenberg, / to rub out, line by line" a memory of her dead friend's face and in so doing recreates her. Still, the poems that are allowed to have their heads make some of the finest discoveries. In **"West Branch Ponds, Kokadjo, Maine,"** the speaker steps over "burned pizzas / dropped among blooms by the lone cow". Later, she enters, "peeling, bobbing on top, grim, / the cookpot of the trout pond, with its scalloped, / smoky rim. / Now we are all together in the stew". Even here, isn't she too persistent?

Perhaps. But in its very doggedness, even such a passage displays the "waggish / invention" lauded and embodied in **"With Warm Regards to Miss Moore and Mr. Ransom,"** in which we are given some "clues to the imaginative journey / by which something deep, and with difficulty dug up, was led / from gross root to dish". The analogy is as apt as it is apparent. But after all, one need not argue that Mona Van Duyn is most characteristically a gross roots poet to make the important points: that she is one whose work any lover of the piquant and tangy should have on hand, and that our response ought to have something in common with hers:

> you thank the man who discovered horseradish,
> yield to what he must have been thinking of,
> and spread it with care over the solids of the day
> like married love.

(pp. 169-72)

Stephen Yenser, "To Give, To Take," in Poetry, *Vol. CXXVI, No. 3, June, 1975, pp. 167-72.*

Mary Kinzie

Mona Van Duyn is a poet both forcefully grim in confronting reality and formally grotesque. There is a quality about her most ambitious work that is perversely unpoetical, as if she were determined to suffer all over again the eclipse of stress by syllabel-stress metre, and the emergence of blank verse from the overhanging eaves of rhyme. Thus she will posit an alternating rhyme scheme for pentameter quatrains and then do her best to make what results sound like untutored (not to mention unmetred) prose. The title poem of *Letters from a Father* shows the poet's parents during their last year (both died in 1980), the mother senile and incontinent, the father ailing and irascible. What brings father and daughter together in their letters now is birdwatching, or rather, bird feeding, to which the father is won over only with strenuous effort on both their parts:

> You say you enjoy your feeder, I don't see why
> you want to spend good money on grain for birds
> and you say you have a hundred sparrows, I'd buy
> poison and get rid of their diseases and turds.

These packed and battered quatrains are designed to render a gruff rustic's bedrock earnestness, but I do not find the method compelling as poetry. Van Duyn has given us indeed pitiable portraits of her parents, and of her irreducibly unromantic childhood (though it may be that she simply remembers the cruel and ambiguous dullness of childhood with a clearer head than the rest of us do). But owing to autobiographical confidences no reader can help noticing and being moved by, the poet *corners* us with the same threatening intensity that marked the ancient mariner. It would be inhumane to dismiss the suffering or the persons; but the title poem is not excused by the mimetic fallacy, merely organized by it.

The blank-verse **"Photographs"** is less rough, whether because rhyme is no longer under attack, or because the poet-narrator is present in the scene, negotiating the descriptive and historical transitions that give a sense of continuing conscious life and sympathy when the father loses interest in one or another snapshot; the mother is in another sphere throughout. . . . (pp. 41-2)

Van Duyn has also written an elegy for her mother, called **"The Stream,"** which is one of her finest works. Composed in forty-five rapid-running couplets, it recounts her last visit with her mother in the nursing home the week before her death. The poet doesn't balk at references to "peeing" and "dugs"; in fact she works the least decorous details into the main Freudian symbol patterns of the poem, the mother as the daughter's child, her mature features having shrivelled back against the body, and the diuretic flood of tears that, in the main metaphor of dowsing, is produced by grace from the ground. The mother apparently expressed love only seldom, but does so directly now, at the end of her life, in one of those lucid intervals peculiar to those who are failing fast. "What is love?" the poet asks; "Truly I do not know":

> Sometimes, perhaps, instead of a great sea,
> it is a narrow stream running urgently
>
> far below ground, held down by rocky layers,
> the deeds of father and mother, helpless sooth-sayers
>
> of how our life is to be, weighted by clay,
> the dense pressure of thwarted needs, the replay
>
> of old misreadings . . .

Above these hardened layers of possibility and mistake runs "another seeker" in scatterbrained, will-less fashion, moved by a dowsing-wand

> which bends, then lifts, dips, then straightens, everywhere,
> saying to the dowser, it is there, it is not there,
>
> and the untaught dowser believes, does not believe,
> and finally simply stands on the ground above,
>
> till a sliver of stream finds a crack and makes its way,
> slowly, too slowly, through rock and earth and clay.
>
> Here at my feet I see, after sixty years,
> the welling water—to which I add these tears.

The upwelling of water betokens expression and release; what was so long thwarted and misread is now sped and numinously transparent. And yet the language never becomes intrusively literary; the guise of naturalness is maintained and, espcially here at the end, aggrandized. At the same time as the diciton is "natural," the rhythms have rounded more flexiby and formally, like wild-looking vines, about the symmetrical oak of the heroic pentameters. Technically speaking, she is using the favorite trick of Robert Frost, the folksy sound produced by two slacks in a row (trochaic and anapestic substitution both provide this in an iambic poem), which, instead of sounding rough, quick, *or* anapestic, becomes with clever handling the regular couterpoint-rhythm to the abstract binary iambs. The resulting melody is well-suited to a speaker at once unpretentious in style and overbearing in feeling.

Although **"The Stream"** earns my admiration, there is still about it something slightly forced, which does not arise in idler, less embattled poems. For example, **"Moose in the Morning, Northern Maine"** provides the old tenaciousness of subject (few poets are more dissatisfied with imagism; the languid apercu, few better disciplined at tracking an implicaiton down); her totally wacky and off-kilter viewpoint; stemming from this, her skill at amalgamating poems out of widely disparate languages but in such a way that, although there is always some oscillation between low and high ("A ton of monarch, / munching, he stands"), the oscillation doesn't sound like a coat of old mythologies. The moose poem invokes old friends, fellow artists, the comedies of rustic discomfort, and the nervous avoidance the poet feels compelled to enact against her own hard-earned and pent-up need to make, while she can, anything and everything into a poem. . . .

> The world is warming and lightening
> and mist on the pond
> dissolves into bundles and ribbons.
> At the end of my dock there comes clear,
> bared by the gentle burning,
> a monstrous hulk with thorny head,
> up to his chest in the water,
> mist wreathing round him.
> Grander and grander grows the sun
> until he gleams, his brown coat
> glistens, the great rack,
> five feet wide, throws sparks
> of light. A ton of monarch,
> munching, he stands spotlit.
> Then slowly, gravely, the great neck lowers
> head and forty pounds of horn
> to sip the lake.

I must refer to one last poem, the utterly engaging dissertation on Nero Wolfe's cuisine. Van Duyn like many poets is rather fixated upon the catalogue. What is always refreshing about her work is that livid glare of self-knowledge: she *knows* she is tempted by lists and inventories, linear recitations and the tapeworm of time. So she will turn to those of her avocations and expertises that permit her (as cookery does here) to indulge a weakness for recital as she emblazons it with wit. I recommend **"A Reading of Rex Stout."** (p. 42)

> *Mary Kinzie, "Haunting," in* The American Poetry Review, *Vol. 11, No. 5, September-October, 1982, pp. 37-46.*

Elizabeth Frank

In its wisdom, its humor, its plainness, *Letters From A Father* is moving the way Van Duyn's *Bedtime Stories* is moving. Like that sequence, which transcribed and distilled the poet's grandmother's speech, it remains staunch-

ly unliterary. Harnessed in coarse and grainy slant-rhymes, the vernacular carries everything: the dignity and reality of common life, the sufferings of someone loved and the claustrophobia of love itself. Through the tender, common-sensical gift of the bird feeder—not through art—the poet has gambled on renewal and won. But renewal is by no means a sure bet. In **"Photographs,"** Van Duyn watches in helpless sadness as her parents discard old photos of themselves, abandoning all that is left of their private selves. She is, as she says, "one witnessing heart," who cannot keep oblivion away.

The recognition of this helplessness is nowhere more apparent than in **"The Stream."** Using slant-rhyming couplets and ordinary speech, she describes her last visit with her mother, now a widow and confined to a nursing home:

> On the last night I helped you undress. Flat dugs
> like antimacassars lay on your chest, your legs
>
> and arms beetle-thin swung from the swollen belly
> (the body no more misshapen, no stranger to see,
>
> after all, at the end than at the beloved beginning).
> You chose your flowered nightgown as most becoming.

The lines sum up a life with words Whitman might have used, although their intimacy, their focus upon one individual human being, would have been unbearable for him. But why love makes courage possible, or just what love is, the poet does not pretend to know.

The poems in the second section, which are mostly about places, are disappointing. In the past, Van Duyn has made distinguished contributions to the observation-and-description poem, that line perfected by Elizabeth Bishop in which a kind of *National Geographic* curiosity and detachment yield detailed celebrations of the external world. In **"Postcards From Cape Split,"** for instance (in *To See, To Take*), Van Duyn anchors a place so securely in its facts that its completeness of being, its *thereness,* stands as proof of the world's reassuring thereness too:

> Everything looks like the sea but the sea.
> The sea looks like a lake
> except when fucus is dumped on its low-tide border
> like heaps of khaki laundry left out to rot—
> this seems a capacity for waste that is worthy of an ocean.
> But the diningroom floor looks like the sea,
> wide old boards, painted dark green,
> that heave and ripple in waves.
> Light hits the crest of each board and gives it a whitecap.

The new poems about places lack movement and definition. The sharp, crisp language of **"In the Missouri Ozarks"** remains merely well tooled, while the details fail to tell us anything new about its by-now standard subject, the American highway. Usually rigorous, Van Duyn lapses into cuteness at the end of **"Moose in the Morning, Northern Maine,"** describing a row of finches on a telephone wire as "little golden bells" and rejoicing "as that compulsive old scribbler, the universe / jots down another day." **"Madrid, 1974"** is labored and discursive, while **"Madrid, May, 1977,"** about Spain on the eve of its first post-Franco election, is spoiled by flat, lifeless language. A man dickers over a litter of puppies with three possible customers,

> each of whom has for a moment forgotten
> that, in a few weeks, having placed

a slip of paper in a plastic urn,
into his empty right hand will fall
responsibility for his own life
and a share of responsibility for the world.

This is sincerely felt, no doubt, but it sounds pompous and didactic. Wit and tough-mindedness return, along with lively colloquial speech, in **"At Père Lachaise,"** an account of a cold and rainy excursion through the great Parisian cemetery—a "spooky pilgrimage" indeed—that becomes hallucinatory when a friend cries out at the sight of

two of the great dun tombs
. . . dappled with color, with cats,
more cats than I can believe . . .
Grimalkins, grandpas,
lithe rakes, plump dowagers,
princes, peasants, old warriors, hoydens,
gray, white, black, cream, orange,
spotted, striped and plain—

One of Van Duyn's powers as a poet is just this capacity for finding live cats on marble tombs. (pp. 563-565)

Van Duyn's light verse is comely and unfailingly generous, yet she is not, I think, essentially a light poet. She writes in a bleak oracular style, in **"The Learners,"** of what happens to young artists when they put their apprenticeship behind them and enter the world. She exposes outright philistine stupidity and cruelty in **"The Vision Test,"** a complex rhyming fable about one of those *nice* ladies who administer driver's-license vision tests and call everyone "Honey" and "Dear." In this instance, having asked Van Duyn's profession, she breaks into mocking laughter when the poet answers that she is, in fact, just that—a poet. Of course it is Van Duyn who has failed the "vision test" by allowing herself to believe in the bureaucrat's benevolence.

My own favorite poem in the new book, **"Ringling Brothers, Barnum and Bailey,"** is simple in structure and statement. Watching a circus aerialist spinning fifty death-defying times, Van Duyn overhears a child sneering, "That's easy, / I could do that." The poem illuminates large subjects—art and the enemies of art, as well as life and death—without ever straying from its immediate circus setting. It is a more compressed poem than Van Duyn usually writes, as well as an unambiguous and defiant *No* from a poet who usually tries harder than many of her contemporaries to coax affirmation out of the waste and exhaustion of modern life. (p. 565)

Elizabeth Frank, "Gambling on Renewal," in The Nation, New York, Vol. 235, No. 18, November 27, 1982, pp. 563, 565.

Cynthia Zarin

In *Near Changes,* a title that brings to mind *Merciful Disguises,* the title of [Van Duyn's] collected poems published in 1972, certain self-restraints have been loosed, and there is no doubt about the security of her own crown. Changes—and Van Duyn's are Ovidian—go a step further toward the truth than even the most artful disguises.

Since 1953, with the publication of *Valentines to the Wide World,* Van Duyn has been hard at work writing poetry

notable for its formal accomplishment and for its thematic ambition. The searching intelligence of the personal we have learned to know in her poems—the well-educated wife, good friend, and daughter—combined with the humor, technical ease, and the blend of the abstract and the quotidian that the poet has made her own have resulted in that rare good thing: a strong, clear voice, original without eccentricity.

From the start Van Duyn has been a topical poet. A list of her subjects could serve as a guide to the preoccupations of the decades her work has spanned: paratroopers, suburbia (for which Van Duyn serves as a backyard Boswell), assassinations, lakeside vacations, marriage (as a state of being), motorcycles, and psychiatrists are only a few. In the tradition of her fellow Midwesterners, Thornton Wilder and Edgar Lee Masters, Van Duyn (who was born in Waterloo, Iowa, and has lived in St. Louis since 1950) has been a master of ventriloquism. *Bed Time Stories,* published in 1976, consists of fourteen poems in the voice of her grandmother, who came West at the turn of the century; and among the many poems about her parents in her last book, *Letters From A Father,* the title poem movingly re-created her father's report on the gift of a bird feeder. . . . (pp. 36, 38)

Chief among her subjects have been the roles of daughter and granddaughter: the feeder the speaker is reporting on is a gift from the writer, who has earlier in this long poem been excoriated for her extravagance, as her parents "won't be living more than a few weeks longer." Van Duyn's mother and father both died in 1980, and the first poem in *Near Changes,* called **"Birthstones,"** set off as a prologue to the main text, was written in 1966. Interestingly, it was left unpublished until now, perhaps because its closing mood of freedom set it apart from the earlier poems Van Duyn wrote about her parents—especially her mother—in which that relationship seemed a stultifying rather than instructive bond. The poem begins:

When I was young and we were poor
my mother showed me a ring some old love
    gave her,
and said, "I'll have your birthstone set in
    it."

And said, "Don't ever lose it. The jeweler
offered to sell me half-glass, half-emerald,
but I'm giving you the real jewel."

I wore it as if she had given me the world.
I had no notion what things cost.
I thought she'd love me if I could be good
    at last,

but I never was . . .

The stone proves, of course, to be all glass, and Van Duyn's synthetic, seemingly casual rhyme scheme sets up the framework for what turns out to be the usefulness of her mother's betrayal. "Poor" is rhymed with "her," and then in the second stanza with "jeweler"; a rhyme that is carried over, turned into interior assonance, in "emerald," which is itself, in the third stanza, rhymed with "world," so that phonetically, "poor" has translated with Nabokovian ease into "world" in eight lines. Poor world, in which lies are told for love! One hears, too, the tsk-tsk of the t-rhymes: it, cost, and last. All this in three stanzas. . . .

In [*Near Changes*], there are poems that seem to partner her early work, as if a second skater—one who not only made the intricate figures but saw in those figures a pattern—had joined the younger one on the ice. The poems I am thinking of have mainly to do with Van Duyn's view of a particular child, who may or may not be herself. . . .

In the central section of [**"Three Valentines to the Wide World"** in Van Duyn's debut volume], this disorganized child asks her mother whether love "is God's hobby." . . . Discovering "a fit instrument" for that question has been one of the forces at play in Van Duyn's strict husbanding of her verse, and the child whom the speaker describes can be read, I think, not only as lost time but as a correlative to her perception of the generation and possibilities of poetry. (p. 38)

But then here is the child again, decades later, in the middle of the poem, **"First Trip Through the Automatic Car Wash,"** in *Near Changes:*

> . . . dark leaves wrap her in a wild
> and waving threat, a typhoon that is all hers,
> swabbing to get in, as the storms of a child
> threaten the very skin of the child, its frail
> shell of self-regard.

This stage of the car wash, a "snail-spin, in neutral," seems "To destroy the customary in order to let in / something unwitnessed yet." The poem continues:

> Something refuses to be withstood.
> Its untamed, zigzag, dark rubbing will break
>   through.
> You *will* change, it squeaks, I replace old
>   selfhood.

The word "selfhood" clunks here—Van Duyn sometimes slips into an over-literalness, a colloquialism that mirrors the banality, rather than the poetry, encased in contemporary language—but the rest is marvelous, and the squeaky voice echoes that first child's squeak, in **"Three Valentines to the Wide World,"** as she asks her innocent, piercing question about God. But the truth of that child is that even she is not inviolate. . . . She has already been intruded upon and hurt. Change is after all a kind of death. But a kind of insistence on change from within, as when the body out of its own self makes new skin over a wound, transforming the flesh, runs through this book.

A slight millennial streak runs through it too—a new sense of the unknown beyond the bend, terrible but beautiful. The eon at its close is for Van Duyn a personal one: the end of her role as a daughter and, with that, an urgent sense of her own mortality. This streak can be traced back, I think, to a wonderful, enduring poem called **"The Stream,"** from Van Duyn's transitional book, *Letters From A Father.* It is about the death of the poet's mother, the difficult, overweaning figure who proffered glass emeralds. In the poem, something subterranean—a foreshadowing of the thing trying to break loose, and the fear of it, that surface in *Near Changes*— takes place in Van Duyn's work, and a less sure, questioning voice appears. . . . [In **"The Stream"**], yoked couplets carry the speaker forward. Trying to find the answer to the question, "what is love?" (she's now moved beyond wondering whether it is "God's hobby"), she becomes a dowser, in search of the wellspring, which by the end she has discovered:

> Here at my feet I see, after sixty years,
> the welling water—to which I add these
>   tears.

That well of water, found only after the death of the poet's mother, is the source for the poems in *Near Changes,* which demonstrate a new, even higher level of accomplishment. One thinks of that first young girl, probing the mystery of new flesh and learning about the miracle of regeneration. One is never oneself as one was before, and if there has been a problem with Van Duyn's work up until now, it was, to this reader, an absence of lyric discovery. Van Duyn has no equal in her ability to see the world objectively (her third book, which won the National Book Award in 1971, was called *To See, To Take*), and she unfailingly places what she sees in her own, wide-ranging context: she has a periscope gaze, with a fish-eye lens.

Still, there were poems in which it seemed that Van Duyn thought perhaps *too* hard before she spoke. The labor was a little too apparent, and in some cases the poems simply went on too long, as though Van Duyn didn't trust the sense of her impulses to come across to the reader without a gloss. That Van Duyn has been aware of this I am sure. One of the themes she has engagingly come back to on several occasions is her fear of airplane travel: this is a writer who doesn't trust a vehicle to stay up in the air without her hand on the controls.

But at least two new and exciting strains have now appeared in Van Duyn's work. The first, briefly, is that her poems now seem to be propelled by inner necessity rather than by a premeditated structure, by the imagination rather than by its aftermath, logical reduction. One sign of this new strength is a striking, associative use of language, especially noticeable in the remarkable sestina **"Memoir."** (pp. 38-9)

Second, without any lessening of her objective eye, Van Duyn seems in her new book to apprehend the physical world around her with an even higher level of lyric economy. It is as if having thrown off the many-layered disguises—specifically the role of the dutiful daughter, which inevitably entails a certain amount of hemming and hawing and for this writer seemed at times to mask her true identity—Van Duyn is now able to present some of the best images of her career. When working at the top of their powers, all poets are orphans. (p. 39)

Cynthia Zarin, "Periscope Gaze," in The New Republic, *Vol. 203, No. 27, December 31, 1990, pp. 36-40.*

Jessica Greenbaum

Van Duyn, with Adrienne Rich and a handful of other women—including Marie Ponsot, Carolyn Kizer and Gwendolyn Brooks—is just now being recognized for her lifetime of work. Since 1956 she has been garnering major honors, including the National Book Award, the Bollingen Prize and a chancellorship from the Academy of American Poets. Her work is instantly recognizable for the intelligence with which it juggles rhyme, wit, formality, storytelling, analysis and emotion. Her poems are at once slightly Shakespearian and (discriminatingly) quotidian—sly and sometimes scholarly in their use of language, but well-anchored in the world we know, and well-versed in the ironies of the human character. . . .

In *Near Changes,* the 69-year-old poet makes a study of the transformations in her approach to her own mortality, while glancing backward at the trail of life behind. Since, as the book's dedication tells us, Van Duyn's life did not include having children, the reader senses the poet's personal obligation to record her life's poetics: no one else will do it afterward. Although it may seem impolite to call this, as one admirer of hers did, "an old woman's book," the term conveys the essence of the collection (for those of us who respect old women). "A sage's book" may carry less ageism, but may not include the sense of pathos braided in the poems.

"The Block," for instance, traces the cycles of life as the speaker and her husband witness them from their long-time neighborhood home. The couple's slightly ironic status in relation to their neighbors gives the simply-stated poem its more complex dimensions. In primo Van Duyn style (hearty of detail, but still spare as heck), the poem's five stanzas simultaneously outline a little history of contemporary middle-class America. . . .

[One] dimension of Van Duyn's gift [is] her ability to unify the past and present. The lines have a seventeenth-century echo in their formality of rhyme and rhythm, in their extended metaphors and in their puckish exploration of the multiplicity of a word's meaning. Van Duyn presents us with words as if each were a moon; she first shows us the lit side, the obvious meaning, then throws the light of her mind on meanings we had not seen. . . .

As a whole, *Near Changes* depicts a writer who is a voracious reader and who carries her own readers with her to such various places as a ferris wheel, the grocery store, the opthalmologist's office, the zoo, inside the car wash, watching the news, gazing at an inflatable globe and, of course, in bed with a book.

The collection includes some formal poems—two villanelles, one sestina, two of Van Duyn's "minimalist" sonnets, two poems in couplets and near-couplets, and a variety of poems with uniform stanzas and rhyme schemes, among others. The range of subject and form encompasses a range of tone as well. In some of the most formal poems, the couplets for instance, we find Van Duyn's most everyday tone. . . .

["Pigeon Eggs"] manages to tell a long shaggy dog story in the voice of a neighbor describing a stranger-than-fiction day in which she inadvertently comes to the aid of four animals. There is a subplot to the narrative that talks about the relationships between love, resurrection and death, that comments on the world's "funny ways." The experience of reading such a poem is not so much that we discover more than one surface; the experience is that we find Van Duyn writing on a surface between the ones we most easily recognize and expect.

Sometimes, in fact, the language is intensely codified and requires uncoiling, as in "On Receiving a Postcard from Japan" or the sestina called "Memoir." In the latter, the meaning seems as hidden and tightly coiled as the principles of a nautilus shell. It begins: . . .

> As the conch tells the human ear,
> silence wants to be sound,
> so the earshell beseeches the eye
> to find the sounds it would lose,
> and the eye prays that flying words
> will be trapped in the amber of print.

I am still a stranger to "Memoir" by its end, but I suspect there are many readers out there . . . who delight in such a puzzle.

I am more drawn to those poems in which the speaker sounds like a possible peer, suddenly bonked on the head by a revelation about the human condition, or by an undeniable metaphor, as in (unlikely as it seems) "First Trip Through the Automatic Carwash" or "Falling in Love at Sixty-Five." . . .

One gets the feeling from *Near Changes* of Van Duyn's thorough participation in life—something we don't always need from writers. But in her work, that participation spawns revelation as Van Duyn's prowess reveals the full dimensions of truth, the light and dark sides of the moon. Like her inadvertent predecessor, Elizabeth Bishop, she is an expert, original observer, and an openhearted one. I look forward to what else she will bring us. In these hands, which borrow from the studied past and reach into the untried future, poetry is superbly nurtured.

Jessica Greenbaum, "Intimations of Mortality," in The Women's Review of Books, *Vol. VIII, No. 4, January, 1991, p. 14.*

August Wilson

1945-

American playwright.

Wilson emerged in the 1980s as a significant voice in American theater. His dramas, for which he has variously received such coveted prizes as the Tony Award, the New York Drama Critics Circle Award, and the Pulitzer Prize, are part of a planned play-cycle devoted to the story of black American experience in the twentieth century. "I'm taking each decade and looking at one of the most important questions that blacks confronted in that decade and writing a play about it," Wilson explains. "Put them all together and you have a history." The leisurely pace and familial settings of his dramas have evoked comparisons to Eugene O'Neill's works. Praised for their vivid characterizations, Wilson's plays often center upon conflicts between blacks who embrace their African past and those who deny it. His rich yet somber explorations of black history prompted Samuel G. Freedman to describe Wilson as "one part Dylan Thomas and one part Malcolm X, a lyric poet fired in the kiln of black nationalism."

Wilson grew up in a Pittsburgh, Pennsylvania ghetto called the Hill. He gained an early pride in his heritage through his mother, who worked as a janitress to support her six children. Frustrated by the rampant racism he experienced in several schools, Wilson dropped out in the ninth grade, thereafter deriving his education from his neighborhood experiences and the local library. In a collection of books marked "Negro," he discovered works of Harlem Renaissance and other African-American writers. After reading such authors as Ralph Ellison, Langston Hughes, and Arna Bontemps, Wilson realized that blacks could be successful in artistic endeavors without compromising their traditions. In his early writings, Wilson was so heavily influenced by other styles that it was difficult for him to find his own. In 1968, inspired by the civil rights movement, Wilson cofounded Black Horizon on the Hill, a community theater aimed at raising black consciousness in the area. The playhouse became the forum for his first dramas, in which Wilson purposely avoided the study of other artists in order to develop his own voice.

Wilson's first professional breakthrough occurred in 1978 when he was invited to write plays for a black theater founded by Claude Purdy, a former Pittsburgh director, in St. Paul, Minnesota. In this new milieu, removed from his native Pittsburgh, Wilson began to recognize poetic qualities in the language of his hometown. While his first two dramas garnered little notice, his third, *Ma Rainey's Black Bottom,* was accepted by the National Playwrights Conference in 1982, where it drew the attention of Lloyd Richards, the artistic director of the Yale Repertory Theater. Upon reading the script, Richards recalls, "I recognized it as a new voice. A very important one. It brought back my youth. My neighborhood. Experiences I had." He directed *Ma Rainey* at the Yale Theater and later took the play to Broadway. Since then, with Richards in the role of mentor and director, all of Wilson's plays have had their first staged readings at the Playwrights Conference

followed by runs at the Yale Repertory Theater and regional theaters before opening on Broadway.

Set in the 1920s, *Ma Rainey* is an exploration of the effects of racism. It is based on an imaginary episode in the life of legendary black singer Gertrude (Ma) Rainey, regarded by some artists as the mother of the blues. The action takes place in a recording studio and focuses mainly on four musicians who are waiting for Ma's arrival. As the details of the musicians' lives unfold, the audience becomes aware of the racism that these successful black performers have had to face throughout their careers. The attitudes of the group's white manager and the owner of the studio reveal continuing exploitation of Ma and her band. The play climaxes when one of the musicians, Levee, vents his frustrations on the others. Critics praised Wilson for the vitality of *Ma Rainey's Black Bottom,* as well as for the authentic, lively dialogue. In his next play, *Fences,* Wilson again examines the destructive and far-reaching consequences of racial injustice. Set in the late 1950s, on the eve of the civil rights movement, *Fences* revolves around Troy Maxson, an outstanding high school athlete who was ignored by major league baseball because of his color. Struggling through middle age as a garbage man, Troy's bitterness results in family conflicts. His son, who also aspires to an athletic career, must battle his father's fear and envy of him, and Troy's wife is humiliated by his adultery. Describing the two plays, Wilson commented: "My concern was the idea of missed possibilities. Music and sports were the traditional inroads for blacks, and in both *Ma Rainey* and *Fences,* with both Levee and Troy, even those inroads fail."

A new play by Wilson, *Joe Turner's Come and Gone,* debuted while *Fences* was still running on Broadway, a rare accomplishment in the New York theater. *Joe Turner,* which is generally regarded as more mystical than Wilson's other works, centers upon the struggles of migrants in the post-Civil War North. The play takes place in 1911 in the Pittsburgh boardinghouse owned by Seth and Bertha Holly. Following seven years of illegal bondage, Herald Loomis, a black freedman, travels to Pennsylvania in search of the wife who fled north during his enslavement. The critical issue of white oppression is symbolized in Herald's haunted memories of Joe Turner, the infamous Southern bounty hunter who captured him. His sojourn ends at the Holly boardinghouse, where the black residents are also searching for some kind of connection and wholeness in their lives. Partially assimilated to white America, they nevertheless embrace the African traditions of their past. At the play's end, the boarders sing and dance a *juba,* an African celebration of the spirit. Their shared joy represents an achievement of unity, having come to terms with the trauma of slavery and the harsh reality of white persecution. Herald, however, is unable to accept these truths, and does not join in the *juba. Joe Turner* was an immensely popular and critical success, and reviewers lauded Wilson's metaphorical language and tragicomic tone.

The Piano Lesson, which examines the confrontation of black heritage with the possibilities of the future, won the Pulitzer Prize before appearing on Broadway. A piano serves as a major element in this play, which is set in 1936 in Doaker Charles's Pittsburgh home. Decades earlier, the white master of the Charles family traded Doaker's father and grandmother for the piano, and the grief-stricken grandfather carved African totems of his wife and son in the piano's legs. Later, Doaker's older brother was killed in a successful conspiracy to steal the piano, which now sits in Doaker's living room untouched and revered. Conflict arises when Boy Willie, the son of the man who stole the piano, wants to sell it to purchase the land on which his ancestors were slaves. Frank Rich asserted: "Whatever happens to the piano, . . . the playwright makes it clear that the music in *The Piano Lesson* is not up for sale. That haunting music belongs to the people who have lived it, and it has once again found miraculous voice in a play that August Wilson has given to the American stage."

(See also *CLC,* Vols. 39, 50; *Contemporary Authors,* Vols. 115, 122; and *Black Writers.*)

PRINCIPAL WORKS

PLAYS

Black Bart and the Sacred Hills 1981
Jitney 1982
The Mill Hand's Lunch Bucket 1983
Ma Rainey's Black Bottom 1984

Fences 1985
Joe Turner's Come and Gone 1986
The Piano Lesson 1987

Samuel G. Freedman

During the early 1960's, as August Wilson was reaching manhood, the church of St. Benedict the Moor took up a collection for a statue atop its steeple. The church straddled the border between the Hill, the black Pittsburgh slum where Wilson grew up, and the city's downtown district. And when the statue was unveiled, Wilson remembers, Saint Benedict was opening his arms to the skyscrapers and department stores, and turning his back on the Hill.

A generation later, as August Wilson walks its streets on a visit home, the Hill looks godforsaken indeed. Gone are Lutz's Meat Market, the Hilltop Club and Pope's Restaurant. The New Granada Theater is closed. An abandoned truck rusts in a weeded lot and a junkie lurches up the street, hawking a stolen television set. Beyond the decay, past the plywood and charred bricks, rise the new glass towers of Pittsburgh, glistening like shafts of crystal.

"Hey, professor," a man in a worn overcoat says to Wilson, extending a calloused hand for a soul shake.

"Hey, man," Wilson says, meeting his grip.

This passing moment is the ultimate compliment, for if August Wilson has wanted anything in his career as a playwright it is to be recognized by the people of the ghetto as their voice, their bard. Wilson gives words to trumpeters and trash men, cabbies and conjurers, boarders and landladies, all joined by a heritage of slavery. Their patois is his poetry, their dreams are his dramas. And while Wilson's inspiration is contained—a few sloping blocks in Pittsburgh—his aspiration seems boundless. He intends to write a play about black Americans in every decade of this century, and he has already completed six of the projected 10.

Fences, a drama set in the 1950's, is the second of the cycle to reach Broadway. It was preceded by ***Ma Rainey's Black Bottom,*** which won the New York Drama Critics Circle Award as the best play of the 1984-85 season and, as Frank Rich, chief drama critic for *The New York Times,* wrote, it established Wilson as "a major find for the American theater," a writer of "compassion, raucous humor and penetrating wisdom." (p. 36)

Fences may prove the most accessible of Wilson's plays, faster-moving than ***Ma Rainey*** and less mystical than ***Joe Turner's Come and Gone.*** Several critics have likened this family drama to Arthur Miller's *Death of a Salesman,* centering as it does on a proud, embittered patriarch, Troy Maxson, and his teen-age son, Cory. Their immediate conflict is kindled when Cory is recruited to play college football and Troy, once a baseball star barred from the segregated big leagues, demands he turn down the scholarship because he cannot believe times have truly changed. Behind the narrative looms Wilson's concern with legacy. As Cory Maxson almost grudgingly discovers the value in his father's flawed life, he accepts his part in a continuum that runs from Pittsburgh to the antebellum South and finally to Mother Africa.

For Wilson, at the age of 42, that journey is not only historical, but personal. His father was a white man who all but abandoned him. The playwright dismisses the subject of his parentage in a temperate tone more unsettling than any anger, and one can only speculate how Wilson's origins fueled the pursuit of blackness, his own and his people's. Troy Maxson of *Fences,* then, embodies not only the black stepfather Wilson found in his teens, but something rather more metaphysical.

"I think it was Amiri Baraka who said that when you look in the mirror you should see your God," Wilson says.

> All over the world, nobody has a God who doesn't resemble them. Except black Americans. They can't even see they're worshipping someone else's God, because they want so badly to assimilate, to get the fruits of society. The message of America is 'Leave your Africanness outside the door.' My message is 'Claim what is yours.'

Last April, when *Joe Turner's Come and Gone* was in rehearsal at the Yale Repertory Theater, a Jewish friend invited Wilson to a seder, the ritual Passover meal. *Joe Turner* is the story of Herald Loomis, a black freedman pressed into illegal bondage—decades after the Emancipation Proclamation—by the Tennessee bounty hunter of the play's title. Freed after seven years, he makes his way to Pittsburgh, looking for the wife who had fled north during his enslavement. He is in many ways a crippled man, driven to his knees by visions of slavery, of "bones walking on top of the water," and it takes the powers of an African healer named Bynum to raise him upright again. Set against *Joe Turner,* the seder was a powerful coincidence.

"The first words of the ceremony were, 'We were slaves in Egypt,' " Wilson recalls.

> And these were Yale students, Yale professors, in 1986, in New Haven, talking about something that happened thousands of years ago. Then it struck me that Passover is not just happening in this house in New Haven, it's happening in Jewish houses all over the world. And the concluding line—'Next year in Jerusalem'—they've been saying that for thousands of years. And that is the source of Jewish power and Jewish pride.

> I thought this is something we should do. Blacks in America want to forget about slavery—the stigma, the shame. That's the wrong move. If you can't be who you are, who can you be? How can you know what to do? We have our history. We have our book, which is the blues. And we forget it all.

If Wilson's mission is memory, his method is more artistic than archival. He is one part Dylan Thomas and one part Malcolm X, a lyric poet fired in the kiln of black nationalism. The highly polemical black theater of the 1960's made the play the vehicle for the message, but Wilson encountered literature before ideology, and he still abides by that order. He is a storyteller, and his story is the African diaspora—not because it suits a political agenda but because everything in his life conspired to make it so.

Most of Wilson's plays concern the conflict between those who embrace their African past and those who deny it.

"You don't see me running around in no jungle with no bone between my nose," boasts one character in *Ma Rainey.* Wilson's answer is that Africa remains a pervasive force, a kind of psychic balm available to 20th-century blacks through blues songs, communal dances, tall tales. Wilson the mythologist coexists with Wilson the social realist. There is a broad historical truth to his characters—to Levee, the jazz musician who naïvely sells off his compositions to a white record-company executive; to Troy Maxson, whose job prospects go no further than becoming the first black truck driver in the Pittsburgh Sanitation Department.

Wilson makes these lives ring with dignity. "I do the best I can do," Troy tells his wife, Rose, in *Fences.*

> I come in here every Friday. I carry a sack of potatoes and a bucket of lard. You all line up at the door with your hands out. I give you the lint from my pockets. I give you my sweat and my blood. I ain't got no tears. I done spent them. We go upstairs in that room at night and I fall down on you and try to blast a hole into forever. I get up Monday morning, find my lunch on the table. I go out. Make my way. Find my strength to carry me through to the next Friday.

There is an extraordinary acuity to Wilson's ear, a quality that has a black audience murmuring "That's right" or "Tell it" during his plays, as they might during a Jesse Jackson speech or a B. B. King concert. Wilson's virtuosity with the vernacular can lull an audience into laughter, too. Early in *Fences,* Troy Maxson's best friend needles him about flirting outside his marriage. "It's all right to buy her one drink," he says. "That's what you call being polite. But when you wanna be buying two or three—that's what you call eyeing her."

By evening's end, it is apparent that Troy has done more than eye her, and the kidding has assumed a prophetic power—a prime characteristic of Wilson's work. With one set and a half-dozen major roles, a Wilson play can seem talky and static, but if wordiness is a weakness at times, it is also a masterly way of deceiving the audience into amused complacency. By the end of his first acts, Wilson characteristically begins to detonate his dramatic bombshells, and at the final explosion—a murder, a madman's howl or a self-inflicted stabbing—a shudder ripples through the audience.

Wilson writes of the particulars of black life, elevating his anger to a more universal plane. As a thinker, if not a stylist, Wilson descends less from the Richard Wright tradition of social protest than from the ontological one of Ralph Ellison. Ellison's *The Invisible Man,* like Wilson's characters, confronts blackness not as a function of pigment but as a condition of the soul. The white man in Wilson's plays can be finessed, ignored, intimidated; it is the Almighty against whom his characters rail. After a musician in *Ma Rainey* hears of a white mob forcing a black reverend to dance, he shouts to the rafters, "Where the hell was God when all of this was going on?" (pp. 36, 40)

Wilson received a positive racial identity from his mother, who died in 1983. Living on welfare and, later, on the wages of a janitorial job, Daisy Wilson kept her children healthy, fed and educated. She would stretch eggs with flour to make breakfast go seven ways. She would wait until Christmas Eve for the $1 tree she could afford. She would get second-hand Nancy Drew mysteries and other books for the daily reading she required of her children. Wilson's favorite story about her, and her gifts, involves a radio contest:

> Morton Salt in the 1950's had come out with their slogan, 'When it rains, it pours.' When the announcer said the words, the first caller to identify it as the Morton slogan won a Speed Queen washer. My mother was still doing the wash with a rub board. One night, we're listening to the station and the contest comes on. We didn't have a telephone, so Mommy sends my sister right out with a dime to call in and say, 'Morton Salt.' When they found out she was black, they wanted to give her a certificate to go to the Salvation Army for a used washing machine. And she told them where they could put their certificate. I remember her girlfriends' telling her, 'Daisy, get the used washer.' But she'd rather go on scrubbing.

As a writer, Wilson has honored his mother and imagined the father he might have had. "I know there are not strong black images in literature and film," he says, "so I thought, why not create them? Herald Loomis is responsible. Troy Maxson is responsible. Those images are important. Every black man did not just make a baby and run off."

But unlike the more politicized black writers of the 1960's—or, at the other end of the spectrum, the mass-market creators of television's *Julia* and *The Cosby Show*—Wilson has created fallible humans, not simplistic paragons. Troy Maxson can turn gales of rage on the son who adores him, but he also feeds him, clothes him, teaches him. Troy can sneak around on the wife who loves him, fathering a baby out of wedlock. But when the child is born, Troy brings it home and Rose, however hurt, agrees to raise it as her own.

It is not surprising that Wilson's fictive families form bulwarks against a hostile world, for his own encounters with white Pittsburgh offered the racist commonplaces of America—bricks through the window when the family tried moving into mostly white Hazelwood; "Nigger, go home" notes on his desk at an overwhelmingly white parochial high school; accusations of cheating when a term paper on Napoleon seemed a bit too good to have been done by a black boy. Hounded out of one school, frustrated by another, Wilson dropped out in the ninth grade. At the age of 15, his formal education had come to an end.

He split his days between the street and the library, where he chanced upon a section marked "Negro." There were about 30 books, and he read them all—Arna Bontemps, Ralph Ellison, Richard Wright and Langston Hughes. He remembers especially a sociology text that spoke of "the Negro's power of hard work" because it was the first time anything ever suggested to him that a Negro could have any power in America. "I was just beginning to discover racism, and I think I was looking for something," Wilson recalls. "Those books were a comfort. Just the idea black people would write books. I wanted my book up there, too. I used to dream about being part of the Harlem Renaissance."

Supporting himself as a short-order cook and stock clerk, Wilson began to write: stories, poetry—even a college term paper on Carl Sandburg and Robert Frost for [his sister] Freda. She got an A, he made $20, and it bought a used Royal typewriter, the first he had owned. "The first thing I typed was my name," he would recall years later. "I wanted to see how it looked in print. Then I began to type my poems."

Around the neighborhood, Wilson kept his eyes and ears open: How Miss Sarah sprinkled salt and lined up pennies across her threshhold. He listened to the men talk at Pat's Place, a cigar store and pool room, and if someone said, "Joe Foy's funeral's today," he would find out who Joe Foy was. Most of all, Wilson saw in the Hill a pageant of violence. One night, he watched a black man walk into a bar with a white woman. Another black man, passing the first, said to him, "Say, Phil, I see you got your white whore." Phil drew his knife and began slashing the man across the chest, slashing to the cadence of his cry, "That's my wife! That's my wife! That's my wife!" His rage spent, he got into his car with his wife and drove off.

One part of Wilson understood the futility of the violence, the self-destruction, and he summons it in his plays as the ultimate, diabolical triumph of white bigotry: turning blacks against themselves. *Ma Rainey's Black Bottom,* for instance, ends with Levee stabbing not the white man who has appropriated his music but the bandmate who accidentally steps on his shoe. *Fences* brings Cory to the brink of attacking Troy with a baseball bat, symbol of the father's manhood.

Yet another part of Wilson admired the Hill's criminals. His own family lived near the bottom of the Hill's social scale, which roughly conformed to its topography, and he grew up with a hot hate for the affluent blacks up in Sugar Top, the doctors and lawyers who would send their children to a Saturday movie downtown with the admonition "Don't show your color." In Wilson's plays, the black middle-class exists only as an object of contempt; if he had written *A Raisin in the Sun,* the Younger family would not have moved to the suburbs, it would have joined either the Blackstone Rangers street gang or the Nation of Islam. Wilson's characters are almost all the kind of street blacks for whom his longtime friend Rob Penny invented the term "stomp-down bloods."

"For a long time, I thought the most valuable blacks were those in the penitentiary," Wilson says, recalling his teens and 20's.

> They were the people with the warrior spirit. How they chose to battle may have been wrong, but you need people who will battle. You need someone who says, 'I won't shine shoes for $40 a week. I have a woman and two kids, and I will put a gun in my hand and *take,* and my kids will have Christmas presents.' Just like there were people who didn't accept slavery. There were Nat Turners. And that's the spirit that Levee has, and Troy has, and Herald Loomis has.

In 1969, when Wilson was 24, his stepfather, David Bedford, died. The two had not been close for almost a decade, since Wilson quit his high school football team against Bedford's wishes, and the late 1960's was a time when young black men like Wilson often disparaged their fathers as a generation of compromisers. Then Wilson heard a story about Bedford that changed his life.

Bedford, it turned out, had been a high school football star in the 1930's, and had hoped a sports scholarship would lead to a career in medicine. But no Pittsburgh college would give a black player a grant and Bedford was too poor to pay his own way. To get the money, he decided to rob a store, and during the theft he killed a man. For the 23 years before he met Wilson's mother, Bedford had been in prison. By the time he was free, only a job in the city Sewer Department beckoned.

"I found myself trying to figure out the intent of these lives around me," Wilson says. "Trying to uncover the nobility and the dignity that I might not have seen. I was ignorant of their contributions. Part of the reason I wrote *Fences* was to illuminate that generation, which shielded its children from all of the indignities they went through."

Wilson's personal discoveries coincided with the rise of the black nationalist movement, which was based in large part on venerating the Afro-American past. Wilson and Rob Penny, a playwright and professor, founded a theater called the Black Horizon on the Hill, and it produced Wilson's earliest plays. Poetry readings, jazz concerts and art galleries all flourished. Wilson and Penny also belonged to a group of Pittsburgh's black artists and intellectuals who studied and discussed the writings of Ed Bullins, Richard Wesley, Ron Milner, Ishmael Reed, Maulana Karenga and, most importantly, Amiri Baraka and Malcolm X.

In some ways, though, Wilson didn't quite fit in. His sympathies resided with black nationalism, but as a writer he could not produce convincing agitprop. Nor had he yet found the true dramatic voice of the Hill. His development as a writer shared less with black American authors than with black Africans like novelist Chinua Achebe, who fell under the sway of white writers while studying abroad and only later returned home to adapt those influences to their indigenous oral tradition and tribal lore.

The self-educated Wilson counts among his strongest early influences Dylan Thomas, for the theatricality of his verse, and John Berryman, for the process of condensing language that the poet called "psychic shorthand." Wilson also admired the jazzy rhythms and street sensibility of Baraka's poetry and plays. . . . (pp. 40, 49)

Between performance and publication royalties and grants—including Guggenheim and Rockfeller fellowships—Wilson has been able since 1982 to devote himself wholly to writing. Now, the posters, awards, programs and reviews from Wilson's first six shows line the long hallway of his St. Paul apartment. But, the playwright adds, there is plenty of wall space left to cover.

"You have to be willing to open yourself up," Wilson says of his approach to writing. "It's like walking down the road. It's the landscape of the self, and you have to be willing to confront whatever you find there." (p. 70)

> Samuel G. Freedman, "A Voice from the Streets," in The New York Times Magazine, June 10, 1987, pp. 36, 40, 49, 70.

Clive Barnes

A man searching for wholeness, a man digging for the

roots of his existence, a man reaching into his past to move into his future—this man, disturbed, battered, embittered, is the hero of August Wilson's play *Joe Turner's Come and Gone.* . . .

With it, Wilson moves another step into his grand dramatic design of providing a panoramic view of the American black experience since the days of Lincoln.

This is the third play in the series to reach Broadway, and, like its predecessors, *Ma Rainey's Black Bottom* and the still-running Tony Award-winning *Fences,* it stands completely on its own, while still opening yet another window on Wilson's overall theme, and revealing yet another aspect of his compelling theatrical genius.

Joe Turner is set in a Pittsburgh boarding house in 1911. The scene is peaceful, domestic. A sunny morning. A woman getting breakfast. A man, her husband and master of the house, just home from work.

Into this scene—which seems fugitively like a genre painting, an interior with figures—people, life, and themes gradually intrude. Black people, black life, black themes. This is an America that, in this time slot, few artists have explored. Few have even noticed.

Wilson starts his play with the leisureliness of a Eugene O'Neill slowly pinpointing this family—a boarding house in industrial America, filled with transients. These are Wilson's dispossessed—refugees both from the Africa they were wrested from, and the American South from which they have emigrated.

The mood, however, is funny, odd, eccentric . . . very cozy, very O'Neill himself in blackface, but this is certainly not an amused rendition of *Ah, Wilderness!* played on the black notes of nostalgia's piano.

Joe Turner is a blues lament on a cold street—the memory of a loss. Yet also—for Wilson is an irrepressible, even if often depressed, optimist—the prescription for a future, a hope for a mending.

Into this respectable Pittsburgh boarding house there erupts a huge, straggling man, with staring eyes, a shabby coat, a big battered hat, holding onto a daughter as if his life depended on it. The name is Herald Loomis, and his pain is as formidable as his person.

He is looking for his wife, whom he has not seen in nine years. Where he comes from, what he is doing, why he is searching, these are questions that at first hang unanswered in the play like mist in the air.

Other people walk in and out of the play, in and out of the boarding house—there is a Sunday chicken dinner which ends in the joy of a singing-dancing-chanting *Juba,* an impromptu celebration of the spirit.

Into this joy Loomis suddenly rushes in. He tells of visions, of a sea of skeletons. He has a kind of fit—epileptic perhaps, or some terrible seizure of the soul.

He is both encouraged and quieted down by Bynum Walker, the house's senior resident and an old man with wisdom and the gift of "mending." African society might have called him a conjur-man or a witch-doctor.

In Pennsylvania 1911, Bynum is simply an eccentric who

has seen strange things, knows about herbs and blood, and may have occult power. Bynum believes that every man has a song to sing—the soulsong of his inner journey—and must find it, keep it, sing it.

And Loomis? What is the mystery of his search? Why must he find his wife?

And, for that matter, who was Joe Turner, whom Bynum sings the blues about?

That last much I'll tell you, and leave the rest to Wilson. Joe Turner—now still oddly memorialized in a famous blues by the pappy of New Orleans, W. C. Handy—was at the turn of the century the brother of a Tennessee governor.

His little trick was to lure blacks into an illegal crap game, arrest them, shove them into a chain gang, and sell them off as indentured workers for seven years. It was the last wicked flick of the slave traders' whip.

But Wilson's play is not about slavery. It is about the results of slavery; it is about separation. Separation from roots, separation from kith and kin, separation within one's own psychic self.

He is writing about blacks in 1911, but his apocalyptic vision is so clear—okay, it's a clear look at a muddy vessel—that what he has to say about the atavistic demands of everyone's tribal pasts (we are all tribes of the same monkey-god) and the need to mend ourselves into communal wholeness, must strike a universal note.

But the play is black. The idiom is the black theater, as is the language and the form. In many ways its verbal riffs and emotional cadenzas resemble jazz, so don't go expecting the Grieg-like music and manicured form of Ibsen. . . .

[*Joe Turner*] is a lovely, moving play that carries you with it like a matchbox on a flood.

> Clive Barnes, "O'Neill in Blackface," in New York Post, March 28, 1988.

Frank Rich

August Wilson continues to rewrite the history of the American theater by bringing the history of black America—and with it the history of white America—to the stage. In *Joe Turner's Come and Gone,* Mr. Wilson's third play to reach New York, that history unfolds with the same panoramic sweep that marked *Ma Rainey's Black Bottom* and *Fences.* As the new play's characters hang out in the kitchen and parlor of a black boardinghouse in the Pittsburgh of 1911, they retrace their long hard roads of migration from the sharecropping South to the industrialized North, and those tales again hum with the spellbinding verbal poetry of the blues. Whether a lost young woman is remembering how her mother died laboring in the peach orchards or a bitter man named Herald Loomis is recounting his seven years of illegal bondage to the . . . [Southern] bounty hunter Joe Turner, Mr. Wilson gives haunting voice to the souls of the American dispossessed.

But to understand just why . . . [this] play may be Mr. Wilson's most profound and theatrically adventurous telling of his story to date, it is essential to grasp what the characters do not say—to decipher the history that is dramatized in images and actions beyond the reach of logical narrative. In *Joe Turner,* there are moments when otherwise voluble men reach a complete impasse with language, finding themselves struck dumb by traumatizing thoughts and memories that they simply "ain't got the words to tell." And there are times when the play's events also leap wildly off the track of identifiable reality. Late in Act 1, Herald Loomis becomes so possessed by a fantastic vision—of bones walking across an ocean—that he collapses to the ground in a cyclonic paroxysm of spiritual torment and, to the horror of his fellow boarders, scuttles epileptically across the floor on his back, unable to recover his footing and stand up.

These are occasions of true mystery and high drama, and they take Mr. Wilson's characters and writing to a dizzying place they haven't been before. That place is both literally and figuratively Africa. Though on its surface a familiar American tale about new arrivals in the big city searching for jobs, lost relatives, adventure and love, *Joe Turner's Come and Gone* is most of all about a search for identity into a dark and distant past. That search leads the black characters back across the ocean where so many of their ancestors died in passage to slavery—and it sends Mr. Wilson's own writing in search of its cultural roots. As the occupants of the Pittsburgh boardinghouse are partly assimilated into white America and partly in thrall to a collective African unconscious, so Mr. Wilson's play is a mixture of the well-made naturalistic boarding house drama and the mystical, non-Western theater of ritual and metaphor. In *Joe Turner,* the clash between the American and the African shakes white and black theatergoers as violently as it has shaken the history we've all shared.

To achieve his sophisticated end, Mr. Wilson has constructed an irresistible premise. *Joe Turner* begins when the bizarre Loomis, imposing and intense in Mr. Lindo's riveting performance, comes knocking fiercely at the boardinghouse door with his delicate 11-year-old daughter incongruously in tow. With his years of servitude to Joe Turner at last behind him, Loomis is searching for the wife who deserted him at the start of his captivity a decade earlier. But Loomis is a "wild-eyed, mean-looking" man who looks as if he "killed somebody gambling over a quarter"; he's so pitch-black in mood and dress that there must be more to his story. Bynum Walker, an eccentric fellow boarder with a penchant for clairvoyance and other forms of old-country voodoo, becomes obsessed with the strange intruder, intent on linking Loomis somehow to the supernatural "shining man" who haunts his own search for the "secret of life."

Yet the metaphysical cat-and-mouse game played by Bynum and Loomis is only the spine of *Joe Turner.* Everyone in the boardinghouse is looking, each according to his own experience, for either a lost relative or a secret of life, or both. The proprietor, the son of a free man, seeks salvation by becoming a typical American entrepreneur; he has no sympathy for a new young tenant who arrives in Pittsburgh with rustic cotton-picking manners and crazy dreams of escaping menial labor with his guitar music. The women of the house also range across a wide spectrum—from a worldly cynic to a naïve romantic searching for a man to the good-hearted proprietress who believes that laughter is the best way "to know you're alive."

By throwing such varied individuals together, Mr. Wilson creates a kaleidoscopic pattern of emotional relationships, including some tender, funny and sexy courtships sparked by the endearingly boisterous [Jeremy Furlow]. But each character also has a distinct relationship to the black past, just as each has a different perspective on the white urban present. It's only when all the boardinghouse residents spontaneously break into an African *juba,* singing and dancing at a Sunday fried-chicken dinner, that the extended family of *Joe Turner* finds a degree of unity and peace. As Bynum says to anyone who will listen, each man must find his own song if he is to be free. Loomis, the sole character who fails to join in the *juba,* must find his song if he is to reconnect to life and overthrow the psychic burden of his years of slavery. Only then will Joe Turner—the play's symbol of white oppression as well as the subject of the W. C. Handy blues song that gave it its title—be truly gone.

As usual with Mr. Wilson, the play overstates its thematic exposition in an overlong first act. There are some other infelicities, too, most notably the thin characterization of a pair of children. While one wishes that the director . . . had addressed these flaws with more tough-mindedness during the two years of refinement that followed the play's premiere at the Yale Repertory Theater, the production is in every other way a tribute to its extended development process in resident theaters around the country. . . .

The oblique, symbiotic relationship between . . . [Bynum and Loomis] is particularly impressive. The two men's subliminal, often unspoken connection emerges like a magnetic force whenever they are onstage together. Loomis, we're told, was in happier days the deacon of the "Abundant Light" church. Under . . . [Bynum's] subtle psychological prodding and healing, . . . [Loomis] gradually metamorphoses from a man whose opaque, defeated blackness signals the extinction of that light into a truly luminous "shining man," bathing the entire theater in the abundant ecstasy of his liberation. The sight is indescribably moving. An American writer in the deepest sense, August Wilson has once again shown us how in another man's freedom we find our own.

Frank Rich, "Panoramic History of Blacks in America in Wilson's 'Joe Turner'," in The New York Times, *March 28, 1988, p. C15.*

John Beaufort

Joe Turner's Come and Gone is the most searching of the growing cycle of August Wilson dramas about the black American experience. It was preceded on Broadway by *Ma Rainey's Black Bottom* (the 1920s) and the current *Fences* (the 1950s), winner of the Pulitzer Prize and other awards. The transcendent new work further explores the personal sufferings and struggles born of a diaspora that began with slavery and continued with the post-emancipation migration of blacks to the industrial North.

In the present work, the struggle is as much for self-identity and self-realization as for lost kinfolk. *Joe Turner* is set in Pittsburgh in 1911. Swinging in mood from the richly comic to the poignantly tragic, the play constitutes what Mr. Wilson has described as "a boardinghouse play." Its inspiration comes from a painting by the late Romare Bearden and its title from a W. C. Handy blues ballad about the actual Joe Turner.

The action occurs in the simple but hospitable boarding house operated by Seth Holly, a hardworking factory hand and part-time tinsmith, and his good-hearted wife, Bertha. The $2-a-week rate covers room and two meals a day. The boarders include Bynum Walker, an amateur "voodoo" man with claims to mystic healing and "binding" powers; Jeremy Furlow, a newcomer from the South with a guitar under his arm and an eye for the girls; Mattie Campbell, a pretty woman in search of the husband who deserted her after the death of their two children; and humorous, worldly-wise Molly Cunningham.

The cheerful, occasionally explosive course of events takes a darker turn with the arrival of Herald Loomis and his 11-year-old daughter Zonia. Loomis, a one-time church deacon, has been a victim of the notorious Joe Turner, a bounty hunter who kidnapped blacks and sold them into plantation servitude. After completing his term, Loomis has taken to the road in search of the wife from whom circumstances separated him.

Seth's suspicions of the black-clad, seemingly sinister Loomis explode into hostility when a *juba* celebration leaves the stranger writhing and out of control. Although the benign Bynum proves his healing gift, it requires an even more violent eruption to bring the complex, multifaceted play to its affirmingly mystical resolution.

While Wilson's dialogue abounds in folk-flavored vernacular, his lyric flights . . . give *Joe Turner* its extra dimension of poetic drama. The author also proves once more that he has moved far beyond the conventional "race play." The crimes of Joe Turner are presented as merely part of the pattern of subjugation that black Americans have historically endured. No great stir is caused among the boarders when Rutherford Selig, a white traveling tin salesman who earns a little on the side for tracking down lost loved ones, tells how his father used to apprehend runaway slaves for their masters.

John Beaufort, "New Chapter in Wilson Saga of Black Life," in The Christian Science Monitor, *March 30, 1988, p. 21.*

Robert L. King

In *The Piano Lesson,* August Wilson writes speeches of exposition and hangs out symbols as if he were a neophyte rather than a prize-winning dramatist whose first three plays have gone from Yale to runs on Broadway. In this, his fourth play, a brother and sister clash over whether to sell a piano with legs carved into family totems by their great-grandfather. Berneice tells her brother, "You can't sell your soul for money," but to Boy Willie, the piano is "just a piece of wood" that could give him the means to work a farm of his own on land that saw the exploitation of his black forebears. In their most direct confrontation, Berneice forces our attention and her brother's with a direct gesture to match the explicit language, "Look at this piano," and she elaborates its significance with remarks like "Momma polished this piano for seventeen years." In some of the many expository speeches, we learn that the piano is the key link in a chain of events including the death (perhaps murder) of the white landowner, Sutter, and the brutal murder of several blacks in a boxcar, with the father of Berneice and Boy Willie among them. Sutter's ghost, foreshadowed by a wind-blown curtain at the play's opening, lurks in the Pittsburgh house where *The Piano Lesson* is set; Berneice's uncle and daughter claim to have seen it. One scene ends with heavy melodramatic touches: the billowing curtain lit by a shaft of light, piano music on an empty stage, and an ominous, spectral laugh. Wilson seems to be manipulating a limited past of his own making only to gain sensational effects. He employs standard images of black culture like flashy clothing and one real watermelon from an offstage truckload.

As he builds to his conclusion, however, Wilson brings a gun on stage, announces its presence and purpose, but does not fire it. We see its shape against Berneice's thigh; only its butt protrudes. Boy Willie's friend warns him that he will be shot if he tries to take the piano. All the stuff needed for a stock resolution is here—a clearly labelled symbol in the piano, a family conflict, a gun, a realistic set. At Berneice's invitation, Avery with Bible in one hand and a sprinkler in the other begins to exorcise the house; ever the literal-minded reductionist, Boy Willie grabs a kettle from the stove and mocks him, splashing water on him and the piano while shouting, "Get your ass out of here, Sutter." As Boy Willie takes over the action, a noise builds, one that overwhelms our attention; a wind assaults the upstairs curtain, and Boy Willie moves to the stairs as he has done before to show his courage and command. But intense light from above and the encircling sound of a train freeze the action, and in a radical, Brechtian departure from the expectations created by the realistic set, the melodramatic gun and the explicit speeches, oversized portraits of Sutter and the murdered blacks appear on the wall above the stairs. The boxcar door slams shut and the play ends in abrupt stillness.

All the speeches about the past, Boy Willie's plans for the future and the dispute over the piano are reinformed by the sounds and sights of the final dramatic image. If the past is simply story, it can be retold and shaped to personal ends, as each character does in turn, sometimes to our distraction. If, however, it represents a legacy, its pieces cannot be labelled or isolated one from the other without impoverishing it. No one can trade off it because it is alive, inescapable and immeasureable. It is neither for the literal-minded Boy Willie nor for his sister, whose faith would exorcise it. Both characters are rendered motionless by its complex presence. Wilson sees the images of the past as layered truth; to peel away or to penetrate is to distort, yet as playwright he has challenged himself to explore the black American heritage, a heritage of conflicting, sometimes self-serving voices greater than the sum of its narratives or historical facts. *The Piano Lesson* illuminates how the past means; it is both a dramatic and cultural achievement. (pp. 90-2)

> *Robert L. King, "Recent Drama," in* The Massachusetts Review, *Vol. XXIX, No. 1, Spring, 1988, pp. 87-97.*

Edith Oliver

August Wilson's *Joe Turner's Come and Gone,* was, the playwright has told numerous interviewers, inspired by a painting by Romare Bearden called *Mill Hand's Lunch Bucket,* a collage whose subject is a boardinghouse. The play is the third we have seen here in a series that is exploring the black experience in America in the twentieth century decade by decade. *Ma Rainey's Black Bottom* took place in the nineteen-twenties, *Fences* in the fifties. *Joe Turner's Come and Gone* is set in 1911, in a boardinghouse in a Pittsburgh slum, and it is itself a collage of episodes and characters, but with a strong narrative strain. At the opening, Seth and Bertha Holly, the proprietors, are looking out the kitchen window watching a boarder named Bynum picking leaves and plants from the yard to use for magic spells and such. This voodoo makes Seth and Bertha a bit edgy, but not edgy enough to impair their affection and respect for Bynum. Soon a tall man in a long black coat and black hat enters, leading a little girl. He is Herald Loomis, and he is almost rigid with exhaustion and anguish. Eleven years before, he was captured by one Joe Turner, a white plantation owner from Tennessee who impressed former slaves and black workingmen into service in work gangs and often held them for years. Loomis, a clergyman and farmer, went back home after his release to find that his wife had gone North, leaving their daughter with her grandmother. For the past four years, he and the child have been walking one road after another, Loomis feeling empty and incomplete; he knows that only when he finds his wife will he be able to start living again.

Somewhere near the beginning, Seth says, "Ever since slavery, nothing but crazy-acting niggers keep on coming, carrying their Bibles, niggers coming up here looking for freedom." His boardinghouse is a kind of way station. There is a white man who goes from town to town looking for missing persons and mostly finding them. There is a footloose young man who expects to wander North and earn his living with his guitar. There are two young women—one unlucky in love and dependent, the other a tough free spirit, confident that she can get along on her own.

Joe Turner is the most mystical, most remote and dispersed of all Mr. Wilson's plays; if any work of fiction can be said to be about an abstract noun, this one can be considered a play about dispersal, about a people dispossessed by history. The past, strange and dreamlike, keeps encroaching on the present. There is a passage about bones walking on water, for example, that refers to the slave ships; slavery, still in the memories of many black people, is the underpinning of everything here. I must say quickly that Mr. Wilson's humor is as natural as breathing, and that there are many funny lines and bursts of gaiety, most notably one in which all present sing and dance a clapping song called a *juba*.

> *Edith Oliver, "Boarding-House Blues," in* The New Yorker, *Vol. LXIV, No. 8, April 11, 1988, p. 107.*

Jack Kroll

With the resounding arrival of *Joe Turner's Come and Gone,* and the continuing run of *Fences,* last year's Pulitzer Prize winner, August Wilson, 42, now has two plays running on Broadway, an unprecedented feat for a black playwright. And these two plays, along with the earlier *Ma Rainey's Black Bottom,* make up a sustained and developing synthesis of black history and sensibility.

Joe Turner is Wilson's best play to date and a profoundly American one. Like all of his plays it resonates far beyond its explicit details. Wilson takes the homeliest of locales, a black boardinghouse in 1911 Pittsburgh, and makes it a way station for the destiny of blacks still marked by the trauma of slavery and the haunting presence of their African heritage. The house, run by Seth Holly and his wife, Bertha, is a repository of dreams deferred. The simplest dream is Seth's: a craftsman, he'd like to have his own little shop where he could turn out his pots and pans. The most mystical dream is that of the chief boarder, Bynum Walker, a voodoo conjurer who's looking for the "shiny man" that he once encountered in a vision of transcendence. In the stream of men and women who come to the house on various quests a disturbing force enters in the black-clad Herald Loomis with his 11-year-old daughter, Zonia. Loomis, a storm cloud of a man, is searching for the wife who had left him in Tennessee while he was held in forced labor by the notorious plantation owner Joe Turner.

The dreams, quests, hopes and fears of all the characters interweave in a web of black fatality. It's the mysterious Loomis who finally rips the web apart, leaving everyone freer to pursue their personal variations on the theme of freedom. That freedom becomes visible in a shared *juba* dance, a signal that these blacks will never be free until they accept and build on their African heritage. Wilson is a generous artist; he provides 11 compelling characters, an irresistible story and a power of language that lends a vivid music to a myriad of emotions. Rare for a male playwright, he even includes four strongly imagined women: the earthy, common-sensical Bertha; Mattie Campbell, whose dream is simply to find a man who won't disappear; the cynical Molly Cunningham, who understands on which side her biscuit is buttered, and Martha Pentecost, Loomis's wife, who is the final strand in the play's web of destiny. . . .

Wilson's gift of verbal music reflects his love of the blues. He got his basic idea while listening to a recording of W. C. Handy singing about Joe Turner, who enslaved black workers and got away with it because he was the brother of the governor of Tennessee. Wilson's sense of history tempers his own anger about racism. At Central Catholic High School in Pittsburgh he was the only black:. "Every day I'd find a note on my desk saying, 'Go home, nigger'."

His father was white, a German baker who "came and went." But culturally and psychologically, Wilson's self-definition is entirely black. After more racist incidents he dropped out of school at 15. "I spent the next five years in the library," he says. "It was actually liberating." At 20, he got a job, saved some money and left his mother's house. In the Hill district, Pittsburgh's black ghetto, he met a group of writers and artists, "the people who shaped my life and ultimately provided it with its meaning." Wilson was writing poetry and short stories but he had not seen any theater. Then the *Tulane Drama Review* published an issue on the black theater movement and Wilson promptly sat down to write a play.

But, he found, "I couldn't make the people talk." He asked his friend writer-teacher Rob Penny, "How do you make them talk?" Penny replied: "You don't. You listen to them." "I wasn't sure what he meant," says Wilson. It

wasn't until he had moved to St. Paul, Minn., that it hit him. "Being removed was what enabled me to hear. All those black voices came back in a rush. I sat down to write a play called *Jitney* and the characters just talked to me. In fact they were talking so fast that I couldn't get it all down."

He sent *Jitney* to the Eugene O'Neill Theater Center in Waterford, Conn., which rejected it. After five rejections, they accepted *Ma Rainey's Black Bottom,* his play about jazz musicians in the '20s. It was the beginning of the unique collaboration between Wilson and the O'Neill's director, Lloyd Richards, who has introduced all of Wilson's plays at his Yale Repertory Theatre. Wilson is working on the next in his cycle of plays about the black experience, this one set in the '60s. . . . For Wilson the voices are stronger than ever. When he was writing the climactic scene in *Joe Turner,* in which Loomis slashes himself across the chest, "I had no idea where it was going. When Loomis cut himself it was a surprise to me. I looked down at the page and said, 'Where did that come from?' I was drained. I was limp. But I felt good. I knew I had something." So has the American theater.

Jack Kroll, "August Wilson's Come to Stay," in Newsweek, *Vol. CXI, No. 15, April 11, 1988, p. 82.*

William A. Henry III

The piano in Doaker Charles' living room is a family heirloom, and like most heirlooms it is prized more than used, its value measured less in money than in memories. For this piano, the Charles family was torn asunder in slavery times: to acquire it, the white man who owned them traded away Doaker's grandmother and father, then a nine-year-old. On this piano, Doaker's grieving grandfather, the plantation carpenter, carved portrait sculptures in African style of the wife and son he had lost. To Doaker's hothead older brother, born under the second slavery of Jim Crow, the carvings on the piano made it the rightful property of his kin, and he lost his life in a successful conspiracy to steal it.

Now, in 1936, it sits admired but mostly untouched in Doaker's house in Pittsburgh, and it threatens to tear the family apart again. Boy Willie Charles, son of the man who stole the piano, wants to sell it and use the proceeds to buy and farm the very land where his ancestors were slaves. Boy Willie's sister Berniece denounces as sacrilege the idea of selling away a legacy her father died to obtain.

That is the premise of *The Piano Lesson.* The lesson of the title—an instruction in morality rather than scales or fingering—makes the work the richest yet of dramatist August Wilson, whose first three Broadway efforts, *Ma Rainey's Black Bottom, Fences* and *Joe Turner's Come and Gone,* each won the New York Drama Critics Circle prize as best play of the year. The fact that producers are not shoving each other in haste to bring *Piano Lesson* to Broadway, especially in a season when the Tony Awards are likely to be given to mediocrities by default, underscores the all but defunct place of serious drama in our commercial theater.

Piano Lesson debuted more than a year ago at the Yale Repertory Theater, where Wilson has launched all his plays. In that production, the work seemed an intriguing but unpolished amalgam of kitchen-sink realism (there is literally one onstage) and window-rattling, curtain-swirling supernaturalism. Not much of the actual text has changed. . . . [The] play confidently shuttles spectators between the everyday present and the ghostly remnants of the past, until ultimately the two worlds collide. The first glimpse of the spookily poetic comes before a word is spoken, when a shaft of white light illumines the piano, which by itself plays an eerily cheerful rag. . . .

[Already] the musical instrument of the title is the most potent symbol in American drama since Laura Wingfield's glass menagerie.

> William A. Henry III, "A Ghostly Past, in
> Ragtime," in Time, New York, Vol. 133, No.
> 5, January 30, 1989, p. 69.

Clive Barnes

August Wilson's wonderful Pulitzer-prize winner, **The Piano Lesson . . .** is a play of magnificent confrontations.

The fourth, best and most immediate in the series of plays exploring the Afro-American experience during this century . . . , **The Piano Lesson** is first a confrontation of the heritage of the past and the promise of the future.

But as Wilson well knows, that is the stuff of political speeches rather than living drama, and it is his gift for the seat-edgingly theatrical and thrillingly, mysteriously dramatic that has made him the most acclaimed playwright of his time.

Wilson's plays thrive on danger—the danger of one character squaring up to another, usually each of equal moral and certainly both of equal dramatic worth, with each threatening to destroy the other's world. Wilson never quite takes sides, and as an audience you swing poised between one right and another, wondering which right is really wrong.

The Piano Lesson is a play about a piano, or perhaps about the moral lesson the piano can provide. It is no ordinary piano. We are in Pittsburgh in 1936. It is the house of a railway worker, Doaker Charles, where he lives with his widowed niece, Berniece, and her 9-year-old daughter, Maretha.

And the piano—strange, carved and ghostly—stands in the living room; it is a living symbol of the family's past—its slavery and its escape, its blood and its tears. Two of the family ancestors, a wife and her 9-year-old son, were sold by a white slave-owner for that piano—and the carvings were placed there by the bereft and grieving father in memory of his loss.

And it was his grandson, Boy Charles, born out of slavery but still enslaved, who lost his life in retrieving the piano from the whore masters. But the piano is now with the Charles family—an heirloom of tragic memory and meaning.

On the death of Boy Charles, the piano passed to his two children, Boy Willie, who still lives in the South, and Berniece, who has brought it with her to Pittsburgh. Now the once slave-owning white family, the Sutters, has died out, old man Sutter, the last of his line, mysteriously falling down his own well. And now his land is to be partitioned and sold, and Boy Willie has the chance to buy a prime piece of it. But he needs money.

With his friend Lymon, Boy Willie comes to Pittsburgh with a truck-load of watermelons to sell. With the profits from this, his savings, and half the proceeds from the sale of the now very valuable piano, he will have enough to stake his personal claim in God's land.

But Berniece—hanging onto the past and the memory of what it meant—is adamant in her refusal to sell. Nor, it seems, is she the only claimant to the piano: For possibly the house is being visited by Sutter's ghost, who it seems has his own feeling for the piano.

Just to state the theme does it no justice—it would be possible to make it sound like *Raisin in the Sun* meets *The Exorcist*—and Wilson, and through him his audience, thrive on complexity.

But yes, the ghost is real. Yes, the moral conundrum—this terrible choice between the needs of the present and the demands of the past—is solved. And, yes, those chilling confrontations between man and man, and man and spirit, rush fast and furious through the play.

Yet this iron-firm and fascinating dramatic framework, the skillful architectonics of the play, does not for one moment completely explain Wilson's power and charm. . . .

[The] playwright has a gift for people—he fills his plays with characters you could have known, characters who live and breathe, characters who shiver with life.

How, you might ask, can I, a white writer from a totally different background from that of a black family of sharecroppers in the '30s, offer an opinion on their reality? The same way I can with Shakespeare—by intuition and a feel for human nature. The comparison with Shakespeare is, in at least one sense, very apt, because both playwrights find humor and pain cheek by jowl in the human condition.

Despite the violent drama of **The Piano Lesson,** it is also extraordinarily funny. A dissolute blues-singing uncle called Wining Boy adds to the merriment, as does a solemn yet mildly comic preacher, Avery, who is a suitor for Berniece's hand. And most of all there is the humor of the hero Boy Willie—a clown of iron, a man who boisterously determines to have his own way, and then laughingly has it. . . .

This is a play in which to lose yourself—to give yourself up as hostage for three hours to August Wilson's thoughts, humors and thrills, all caught in a microcosm largely remote for many of us from our own little worlds, yet always talking the same language of humanity.

This is a wonderful play that lights up man. See it, wonder at it, and recognize it.

> Clive Barnes, " 'Piano Lesson' Hits All the
> Right Keys," in New York Post, April 17,
> 1990.

Frank Rich

The piano is the first thing the audience hears in *The Piano Lesson.* Three hours later, it seems as if the music, by turns bubbling and thunderous, has never stopped.

Though Mr. Wilson won a Pulitzer Prize last week for this work, no one need worry that he is marching to an establishment beat. *The Piano Lesson* is joyously an African-American play: it has its own spacious poetry, its own sharp angle on a nation's history, its own metaphorical idea of drama and its own palpable ghosts that roar right through the upstairs window of the household where the action unfolds. Like other Wilson plays, *The Piano Lesson* seems to sing even when it is talking. But it isn't all of America that is singing. The central fact of black American life—the long shadow of slavery—transposes the voices of Mr. Wilson's characters, and of the indelible actors who inhabit them, to a key that rattles history and shakes the audience on both sides of the racial divide.

Set in the Pittsburgh of 1936, just midway in time between *Joe Turner's Come and Gone* and *Fences,* Mr. Wilson's new play echoes his others by reaching back toward Africa and looking ahead to modern urban America even as it remains focused on the intimate domestic canvas of a precise bygone year. Though *The Piano Lesson* is about a fight over the meaning of a long span of history, its concerns are dramatized within a simple battle between a sister and a brother over the possession of a musical instrument. The keeper of the piano, a family heirloom, is a young widow named Berniece, who lets it languish unused in the parlor of the house she shares with her uncle and daughter. Her brother, Boy Willie, barges in unannounced from Mississippi, intending to sell the antique to buy a farm on the land his family worked as slaves and sharecroppers.

One need only look at the majestic upright piano itself to feel its power as a symbolic repository of a people's soul. Sculptured into its rich wood are totemic human figures whose knifedrawn features suggest both the pride of African culture and the grotesque scars of slavery. As it happens, both the pride and scars run deep in the genealogy of the siblings at center stage. Their great-grandfather, who carved the images, lost his wife and young son when they were traded away for the piano. Years later, Berniece and Boy Willie's father was killed after he took the heirloom from a new generation of white owners.

In *The Piano Lesson,* the disposition of the piano becomes synonymous with the use to which the characters put their ancestral legacy. For Berniece, the instrument must remain a somber shrine to a tragic past. For Boy Willie, the piano is a stake to the freedom his father wanted him to have. To Mr. Wilson, both characters are right—and wrong. Just as Berniece is too enslaved by history to get on with her life, so Boy Willie is too cavalier about his family's heritage to realize that money alone cannot buy him independence and equality in a white man's world. Like all Wilson protagonists, both the brother and sister must take a journey, at times a supernatural one, to the past if they are to seize the future. They cannot be reconciled with each other until they have had a reconciliation with the identity that is etched in their family tree, as in the piano, with blood. . . .

Although the second act contains its dead ends, repetitions and excessive authorial announcements—an O'Neill-like excess in most of this writer's plays—Mr. Wilson prevents the central conflict in *The Piano Lesson* from becoming too nakedly didactic by enclosing it within an extended household of memorable characters. The ebb and flow of diurnal activity in Berniece's home thickens the main theme while offering a naturalistic picture of a transitional black America in an era when movies, skyscrapers and airplanes were fresh wonders of the world. A Wilson play feels truly lived in—so much so in . . . [this] supple production that activities like the cooking of eggs, the washing of dishes, and the comings and goings from an audibly flushed toilet never seem like stage events, but become subliminal beats in the rhythm of a self-contained universe.

Still, the play's real music is in the language, all of which is gloriously served by the ensemble company that [this director] has assembled and honed during the more than two years that *The Piano Lesson* has traveled to New York by way of the country's resident theaters. . . .

While there are no white characters in *The Piano Lesson* the presence of white America is felt throughout—and not just by dint of past history. Boy Willie repeatedly and pointedly announces that he will sell the piano to a white man who he's heard is roaming through black neighborhoods "looking to buy musical instruments." Whatever happens to the piano, however, the playwright makes it clear that the music in *The Piano Lesson* is not up for sale. That haunting music belongs to the people who have lived it, and it has once again found miraculous voice in a play that August Wilson has given to the American stage.

> *Frank Rich, "A Family Confronts Its History in August Wilson's 'Piano Lesson',"* in The New York Times, *April 17, 1990, p. C13.*

John Simon

[*The Piano Lesson* takes place in] 1936 in Pittsburgh, where the widowed Berniece lives at her uncle Doaker's with her daughter, Maretha, eleven, and that precious eponymous piano, into which a slave ancestor carved much of the family history. Berniece's brother, Boy Willie, who owns half of the piano, has just driven up from down South with his friend Lymon to sell a truckful of watermelons and the piano; the money, added to his savings, will enable him to buy some of the land his forebears worked as slaves and sharecroppers.

Most of the play concerns the debate between Berniece, who toils as a domestic but will not sell that tradition-steeped piano, and Boy Willie, the agrarian worker to whom land, *that* land, is dearer than any piano, no matter who wept and bled for it. Observing this battle of wills are Doaker, a railroad man, essentially neutral but more sympathetic to Berniece; Lymon, wanted back home by the police, and eager to settle in Pittsburgh and start chasing after its women; and Wining Boy, another uncle, a musician turned gambler, footloose and irresponsible, and thinking of heading south with Boy Willie.

Someone else, too, is hovering over the piano: the ghost of James Sutter, whose ancestor bought the piano from another white man for one and a half slaves—Boy Willie and Berniece's great-grandmother Berniece and her nine-year-old son. It was that first Berniece's husband who carved his lost family into the master's piano. James Sutter has recently drowned in his own well, pushed in, it is believed, by the ghosts of the *Yellow Dog,* the train on which Boy Willie and Berniece's father, who stole the piano back from the Sutters, was fleeing a lynch mob that eventually burned the railroad car with him and three hoboes in it. They became the Yellow Dog Ghosts, drowning guilty parties in their wells, it seems.

Various members of Berniece's family have seen and been scared by James Sutter's ghost, which sometimes even plays the piano. Aside from this ghost subplot, there is also another about Berniece, whose husband was killed stealing wood with Boy Willie and Lymon three years ago, and her suitor Avery, an elevator operator who got the call in a dream and is about to start his own church; he wants the reluctant Berniece to marry him and play the piano for his future choir. Berniece, who keeps putting him off, has a near-fling with Lymon—an episode I don't believe at all. And this still doesn't account for Wining Boy, the ne'er-do-well uncle, who comically gets in the way of Berniece as, in a tense scene, she threatens to shoot Boy Willie, who is trying to make off with the piano. The farce and drama mix poorly.

And there is yet another subplot about a swinging young woman, Grace, with whom both Boy Willie and Lymon try to get involved, but whose husband . . . oh, well, that's enough plot to confuse you, just as it does most of us in the audience. Wilson's play won the Pulitzer Prize even before it opened in New York; myself, I see *The Piano Lesson* as desperately in need of soft-pedaling. It is sincere but overcrowded, overzealous, and, without quite knowing where it is headed, repeats everything three or four times.

It is, in fact, three plays: first, a drama about the conflict between the brother who wants to sell the past for the future, even if farm work may itself be a thing of the past, and the sister to whom the family past is sacred, even though she hates its symbol so much that she won't play it, and lets her daughter do so only at the cost of keeping the piano's tragic history hidden from her. But this battle of ideas is too limited, too repetitious. It does not fan out enough, does not sufficiently involve the others in it, does not provide the audience with surprises and complexity.

Second, it is a play of the supernatural, in which Berniece and Boy Willie, each in his own way, must battle Sutter's ghost. But although it provides the otherwise divided siblings with a common enemy, this aspect of the play remains underdeveloped and serves mostly as a splashy first- and second-act curtain. And not only is the ghost stuff tacked on and uncompelling, it is also contradictorily presented. Whereas the characters see the ghost clearly, the audience gets only a light effect, a wind effect, and piano keys playing by themselves. This is too much for an imaginary ghost and too little for a real one; and why, in this day and age, bring in ghosts at all?

Third, it is a Broadway entertainment with situation comedy, musical interludes (singing, piano playing), halfhearted melodrama (Berniece's gun, promptly dropped), mostly detracting from the real drama. And even that element, the best, is often mishandled. If the piano represents a bitter past that must be remembered and honored, why

would Berniece conceal it from Maretha rather than reverently instruct her in it? (pp. 82-3)

Perhaps the play's long gestation, including two years of testing and rewriting at five leading university and commercial theaters, was a mixed blessing. Though it afforded Wilson and . . . [his director] opportunities unavailable, I believe, to less favored, nonminority practitioners, it also makes the play come across as a palimpsest, with earlier versions distractingly discernible underneath. The most disturbing ghosts in *The Piano Lesson* are those of its former selves. (p. 83)

> John Simon, "A Lesson from Pianos," in New York *Magazine, Vol. 23, No. 18, May 7, 1990, pp. 82-3.*

Robert Brustein

There are reasons why I didn't review the three previous August Wilson productions that moved from the Yale Repertory to Broadway. Lloyd Richards, who directed them all and guided their passage through a variety of resident theaters to New York, succeeded me as Yale's dean and artistic director eleven years ago, and protocol required that I hold my tongue about the progress of my successor. I broke my resolve in an article for *The New York Times* about the role of Yale and other resident theaters in what I viewed as the homogenization of the nonprofit stage. I called this process "McTheater"—the use of sequential non-profit institutions as launching pads and tryout franchises for the development of Broadway products and the enrichment of artistic personnel. Since the universally acclaimed Broadway production of *The Piano Lesson* brings this process to some kind of crazy culmination—and raises so many troubling cultural questions—I'm going to break my silence once again.

First, let's take a look at the Wilson phenomenon. *The Piano Lesson* is an overwritten exercise in a conventional style—to my mind, the most poorly composed of Wilson's four produced works. None of the previous plays was major, but they each had occasional firepower, even some poetry lying dormant under the surface of their kitchen-sink productions. I don't find much power or poetry at all in *The Piano Lesson,* though the play has earned Wilson his second Pulitzer Prize and inspired comparisons with O'Neill. (One critic likened him to Shakespeare!) In one sense, the comparison is apt. Like O'Neill, Wilson has epic ambitions, handicapped by repetitiousness, crude plotting, and clumsy structure. But where O'Neill wrote about the human experience in forms that were daring and exploratory, Wilson has thus far limited himself to the black experience in a relatively literalistic style.

Before his death, O'Neill determined to compose a nine-play cycle about the progressive degeneration of the American spirit. (Only *A Touch of the Poet* was completed to his satisfaction.) Wilson's four plays also have a historical plan: each attempts to demonstrate how the acid of racism has eaten away at black aspirations in the various decades of the twentieth century. *Ma Rainey's Black Bottom,* set in the 1920s, shows how black musicians were prevented from entering the mainstream of the American recording industry. *Fences,* set in the 1950s, shows how black athletes were prevented from participating in major league baseball. *Joe Turner's Come and Gone,* set in 1911, shows how blacks were reduced to poverty and desperation by the chain-gang system. And *The Piano Lesson,* set in the 1930s, shows how black ideals were corroded by slavery. Presumably Wilson is preparing to cover at least five more theatrical decades of white culpability and black martyrdom. This single-minded documentation of American racism is a worthy if familiar social agenda, and no enlightened person would deny its premise, but as an ongoing artistic program it is monotonous, limited, locked in a perception of victimization.

In comparison with the raging polemics of Ed Bullins or Amiri Baraka, Wilson's indictments are relatively mild. His characters usually sit on the edge of the middle class, wearing good suits, inhabiting clean homes. Securely shuttered behind realism's fourth wall, they never come on like menacing street people screaming obscenities or bombarding the audience with such phrases as "black power's gonna get your mama"—which may further explain Wilson's astounding reception. It is comforting to find a black playwright working the mainstream American realist tradition of Clifford Odets, Lillian Hellman, and the early Arthur Miller, a dignified protest writer capable of discussing the black experience without intimidating the readers of the Home section. Still, enough radical vapor floats over the bourgeois bolsters and upholstered couches to stimulate the guilt glands of liberal white audiences. Unable to reform the past, we sometimes pay for the sins of history and our society through artistic reparations in a cultural equivalent of affirmative action.

On its three-year road to Broadway, *The Piano Lesson* could have benefited from some more honest criticism; in its present form, it represents a step backward. A family drama, like *Fences,* it lacks the interior tension of that work . . . , and at three hours it's about an hour and a half too long for its subject matter. Buried inside much tedious exposition is a single conflict between Boy Willie and his sister, Berniece, over a carved piano. Boy Willie wants to sell the piano and buy some farmland down South. Berniece wants to keep it as a token of the family heritage (their mother polished it every day for seventeen years). A repetitive series of confrontations between the two adds little about the conflict but a lot more about the symbolic history of the piano. It belonged to Sutter, a slaver owner, who sold members of their family in order to buy the piano for his wife as an anniversary present. Eventually, their father stole it back from Sutter and was later killed in a boxcar fire, while Sutter fell, or was pushed, down a well.

Wilson pounds this symbolic piano a little heavy-handedly. Like Chekhov's cherry orchard, it is intended to reflect the contrasting values of its characters—Berniece finds it a symbol of the past while Boy Willie sees only its material value. But Chekhov's people are a lot more complicated than their attitudes; and because Wilson's images fail to resonate, the play seems like much ado about a piano, extended by superfluous filler from peripheral characters. Frying real food on a real stove, turning on real faucets with real hot-and-cold running water, ironing real shirts on real ironing boards, and flushing real toilets . . . , these amiable supernumeraries natter incessantly on a variety of irrelevant subjects, occasionally breaking into song and dance. These superfluous riffs are partly intended as comic relief, and *The Piano Lesson* has been praised for its humor. But the domesticated jokes, most of them about watermelons, are about at the level of *The Jeffersons*—even the audience's laughter seemed canned. As for Wilson's highly lauded dialogue, his language here lacks music (except for one potentially strong speech by Boy Willie about his Daddy's hands), usually alternating between the prosaic and the proverbial: "God don' ask what you done. God asks what you gonna do."

What ultimately makes this piano unplayable, however, is the ending, which tacks a supernatural resolution onto an essentially naturalistic anecdote. Sutter's ghost is (inexplicably) a resident in this house, his presence signified from time to time by a lighting special on the stairs. In the final scene, Boy Willie, after numerous efforts to remove the piano (after three hours I was prepared to run on stage and give him a hand), is blown off his feet by a tumultuous blast. He rushes upstairs to do battle with the ghost, now represented through a scrim by flowing, glowing window curtains. Returning, Boy Willie renounces his desire to take the piano from the house, while the supernumeraries laugh and cry, and Berniece praises the Lord. Willie adds: "If you and Maretha don't keep playin' on that piano, me and Sutter both likely to be back." Curtain.

This ending is considerably more forced, though arguably less ludicrous, than the version I saw three years ago at one of the play's numerous station stops. There Willie rushed upstairs as the curtain fell on the illuminated portraits of his slave ancestors in the attic. Either way, the supernatural element is a contrived intrusion. When ghosts begin resolving realistic plots, you can be sure the playwright has failed to master his material. . . . (pp. 28-9)

August Wilson is still a relatively young man with a genuine, if not yet fully developed, talent. O'Neill's early plays were just as highly praised, though he wrote nothing truly great until the end of his life. Premature acclaim was actually one of the obstacles to his development; only by facing the demons in his heart at the end of his days, a sick, lonely man in a shuttered room, was he able to write with total honesty about his true subject. To judge from *The Piano Lesson,* Wilson is reaching a dead end in his examination of American racism, though another play on the subject (appropriately titled *Two Trains Running*) is now gathering steam at Yale on its way through the regional railroad depots to its final Broadway destination. It will probably be greeted with the same hallelujah chorus as all his other work. But if Wilson wishes to be a truly major playwright, he would be wise to move on from safe, popular sociology and develop the radical poetic strain that now lies dormant in his art. It is not easy to forsake the rewards of society for the rewards of posterity, but the genuine artist accepts no standards lower than the exacting ones he applies to himself. (pp. 29-30)

Robert Brustein, "The Lesson of 'The Piano Lesson', in The New Republic, *Vol. 202, No. 21, May 21, 1990, pp. 28-30.*

FURTHER READING

Brown, Chip. "The Light in August." *Esquire* III, No. 4 (April 1989): 116, 118, 120, 122-27.
    Detailed article tracing Wilson's career through events in his personal life.

Davies, Hilary. "August Wilson—A New Voice for Black American Theater." *Christian Science Monitor* 76, No. 226 (16 October 1984): 29-30.
    Interview conducted after Wilson's success with *Ma Rainey's Black Bottom* in which Davies explores the origins of Wilson's plays and his strong involvement with black history.

Poinsett, Alex. "August Wilson: Hottest New Playwright." *Ebony* XLIII, No. 1 (November 1987): 68, 70, 72, 74.
    Biographical article focusing primarily on Wilson's career and the significant effect of cultural heritage on his writing.

Staples, Brent. "August Wilson." *Essence* 18, No. 4 (August 1987): 51, 111, 113.
    Examines the impact of blues music and oral tradition in Wilson's plays.

□ Contemporary
Literary Criticism
Indexes

Literary Criticism Series
    Cumulative Author Index
Cumulative Nationality Index
Title Index, Volume 63

This Index Includes References to Entries in These Gale Series

Contemporary Literary Criticism

Presents excerpts of criticism on the works of novelists, poets, dramatists, short story writers, scriptwriters, and other creative writers who are now living or who have died since 1960.

Twentieth-Century Literary Criticism

Contains critical excerpts by the most significant commentators on poets, novelists, short story writers, dramatists, and philosophers who died between 1900 and 1960.

Nineteenth-Century Literature Criticism

Offers significant passages from criticism on authors who died between 1800 and 1899.

Literature Criticism from 1400 to 1800

Compiles significant passages from the most noteworthy criticism on authors of the fifteenth through eighteenth centuries.

Classical and Medieval Literature Criticism

Offers excerpts of criticism on the works of world authors from classical antiquity through the fourteenth century.

Short Story Criticism

Compiles excerpts of criticism on short fiction by writers of all eras and nationalities.

Poetry Criticism

Presents excerpts of criticism on the works of poets from all eras, movements, and nationalities.

Children's Literature Review

Includes excerpts from reviews, criticism, and commentary on works of authors and illustrators who create books for children.

Contemporary Authors Series

Contemporary Authors provides biographical and bibliographical information on more than 95,000 writers of fiction. *Contemporary Authors New Revision Series* provides completely updated information on active authors covered in *CA*. *Contemporary Authors Permanent Series* consists of listings for deceased and inactive authors. *Contemporary Authors Autobiography Series* presents specially commissioned autobiographies by leading contemporary writers. *Contemporary Authors Bibliographical Series* contains primary and secondary bibliographies as well as analytical bibliographical essays by authorities on major modern authors.

Dictionary of Literary Biography

Encompasses three related series. *Dictionary of Literary Biography* furnishes illustrated overviews of authors' lives and works. *Dictionary of Literary Biography Documentary Series* illuminates the careers of major figures through a selection of literary documents, including letters, interviews, and photographs. *Dictionary of Literary Biography Yearbook* summarizes the past year's literary activity and includes updated entries on individual authors. A cumulative index to authors and articles is included in each new volume.

Something about the Author Series

Something about the Author contains well-illustrated biographical sketches on juvenile and young adult authors and illustrators from all eras. *Something about the Author Autobiography Series* presents specially commissioned autobiographies by prominent authors and illustrators of books for children and young adults. *Authors & Artists for Young Adults* provides high school and junior high school students with profiles of their favorite creative artists.

Yesterday's Authors of Books for Children

Contains heavily illustrated entries on children's writers who died before 1961. Complete in two volumes.

Literary Criticism Series
Cumulative Author Index

This index lists all author entries in the Gale Literary Criticism Series and includes cross-references to other Gale sources. References in the index are identified as follows:

AAYA: *Authors & Artists for Young Adults,* Volumes 1-3
CAAS: *Contemporary Authors Autobiography Series,* Volumes 1-11
CA: *Contemporary Authors* (original series), Volumes 1-131
CABS: *Contemporary Authors Bibliographical Series,* Volumes 1-3
CANR: *Contemporary Authors New Revision Series,* Volumes 1-29
CAP: *Contemporary Authors Permanent Series,* Volumes 1-2
CA-R: *Contemporary Authors* (revised editions), Volumes 1-44
CDALB: *Concise Dictionary of American Literary Biography,* Volumes 1-6
CLC: *Contemporary Literary Criticism,* Volumes 1-63
CLR: *Children's Literature Review,* Volumes 1-22
CMLC: *Classical and Medieval Literature Criticism,* Volumes 1-6
DC: *Drama Criticism,* Volume 1
DLB: *Dictionary of Literary Biography,* Volumes 1-101
DLB-DS: *Dictionary of Literary Biography Documentary Series,* Volumes 1-7
DLB-Y: *Dictionary of Literary Biography Yearbook,* Volumes 1980-1988
LC: *Literature Criticism from 1400 to 1800,* Volumes 1-14
NCLC: *Nineteenth-Century Literature Criticism,* Volumes 1-29
PC: *Poetry Criticism,* Volume 1
SAAS: *Something about the Author Autobiography Series,* Volumes 1-11
SATA: *Something about the Author,* Volumes 1-62
SSC: *Short Story Criticism,* Volumes 1-6
TCLC: *Twentieth-Century Literary Criticism,* Volumes 1-39
YABC: *Yesterday's Authors of Books for Children,* Volumes 1-2

A. E. 1867-1935 . . . . TCLC 3, 10
See also Russell, George William
See also DLB 19

Abbey, Edward 1927-1989 . . . . . . CLC 36, 59
See also CANR 2; CA 45-48;
  obituary CA 128

Abbott, Lee K., Jr. 19??- . . . . CLC 48

Abe, Kobo 1924- . . . . CLC 8, 22, 53
See also CANR 24; CA 65-68

Abell, Kjeld 1901-1961 . . . . CLC 15
See also obituary CA 111

Abish, Walter 1931- . . . . CLC 22
See also CA 101

Abrahams, Peter (Henry) 1919- . . . . . CLC 4
See also CA 57-60

Abrams, M(eyer) H(oward) 1912- . . . CLC 24
See also CANR 13; CA 57-60; DLB 67

Abse, Dannie 1923- . . . . CLC 7, 29
See also CAAS 1; CANR 4; CA 53-56;
  DLB 27

Achebe, (Albert) Chinua(lumogu)
  1930- . . . . CLC 1, 3, 5, 7, 11, 26, 51
See also CLR 20; CANR 6, 26; CA 1-4R;
  SATA 38, 40

Acker, Kathy 1948- . . . . CLC 45
See also CA 117, 122

Ackroyd, Peter 1949- . . . . CLC 34, 52
See also CA 123, 127

Acorn, Milton 1923- . . . . CLC 15
See also CA 103; DLB 53

Adamov, Arthur 1908-1970 . . . . . CLC 4, 25
See also CAP 2; CA 17-18;
  obituary CA 25-28R

Adams, Alice (Boyd) 1926- . . . CLC 6, 13, 46
See also CANR 26; CA 81-84; DLB-Y 86

Adams, Douglas (Noel) 1952- . . . CLC 27, 60
See also CA 106; DLB-Y 83

Adams, Henry (Brooks)
  1838-1918 . . . . TCLC 4
See also CA 104; DLB 12, 47

Adams, Richard (George)
  1920- . . . . CLC 4, 5, 18
See also CLR 20; CANR 3; CA 49-52;
  SATA 7

Adamson, Joy(-Friederike Victoria)
  1910-1980 . . . . CLC 17
See also CANR 22; CA 69-72;
  obituary CA 93-96; SATA 11;
  obituary SATA 22

Adcock, (Kareen) Fleur 1934- . . . . . . CLC 41
See also CANR 11; CA 25-28R; DLB 40

Addams, Charles (Samuel)
  1912-1988 . . . . CLC 30
See also CANR 12; CA 61-64;
  obituary CA 126

Adler, C(arole) S(chwerdtfeger)
  1932- . . . . CLC 35
See also CANR 19; CA 89-92; SATA 26

Adler, Renata 1938- . . . . CLC 8, 31
See also CANR 5, 22; CA 49-52

Ady, Endre 1877-1919 . . . . TCLC 11
See also CA 107

Agee, James 1909-1955 . . . . TCLC 1, 19
See also CA 108; DLB 2, 26;
  CDALB 1941-1968

Agnon, S(hmuel) Y(osef Halevi)
  1888-1970 . . . . CLC 4, 8, 14
See also CAP 2; CA 17-18;
  obituary CA 25-28R

Ai 1947- . . . . CLC 4, 14
See also CA 85-88

Aickman, Robert (Fordyce)
  1914-1981 . . . . CLC 57
See also CANR 3; CA 7-8R

Author Index

Author Index

Author Index

CLC Cumulative Nationality Index

Nationality Index

Nationality Index

CLC-63 Title Index